ISBN 978-0-266-14994-1
PIBN 10926680

1 MONTH OF
FREE
READING

at
www.ForgottenBooks.com

By purchasing this book you are
eligible for one month membership to
ForgottenBooks.com, giving you
unlimited access to our entire
collection of over 1,000,000 titles via
our web site and mobile apps.

To claim your free month visit:
www.forgottenbooks.com/free926680

English
Français
Deutsche
Italiano
Español
Português

www.forgottenbooks.com

Mythology Photography **Fiction**
Fishing Christianity **Art** Cooking
Essays Buddhism Freemasonry
Medicine **Biology** Music **Ancient
Egypt** Evolution Carpentry Physics
Dance Geology **Mathematics** Fitness
Shakespeare **Folklore** Yoga Marketing
Confidence Immortality Biographies
Poetry **Psychology** Witchcraft
Electronics Chemistry History **Law**
Accounting **Philosophy** Anthropology
Alchemy Drama Quantum Mechanics
Atheism Sexual Health **Ancient History**
Entrepreneurship Languages Sport
Paleontology Needlework Islam
Metaphysics Investment Archaeology
Parenting Statistics Criminology
Motivational

COMMITTEE ON WAYS AND MEANS.

HOUSE OF REPRESENTATIVES.

SERENO E. PAYNE, *Chairman.*

JOHN DALZELL.
SAMUEL W. McCALL.
EBENEZER J. HILL.
HENRY S. BOUTELL.
JAMES C. NEEDHAM.
WILLIAM A. CALDERHEAD.
JOSEPH W. FORDNEY.
JOSEPH H. GAINES.
ROBERT W. BONYNGE.

NICHOLAS LONGWORTH.
EDGAR D. CRUMPACKER.
CHAMP CLARK.
WILLIAM BOURKE COCKRAN.
OSCAR W. UNDERWOOD.
D. L. D. GRANGER.
JAMES M. GRIGGS.
EDGAR W. POU.
CHOICE B. RANDELL.

WILLIAM K. PAYNE, *Clerk.*

II

PREFACE.

Tariff hearings were begun on November 10, 1908, pursuant to the following notice:

The Committee on Ways and Means will hold hearings on tariff revision, at Washington, D. C., commencing on the following dates:

Tuesday, November 10, 1908, on Schedule A—Chemicals, oils, and paints.

Thursday, November 12, 1908, on Schedule H—Spirits, wines, and other beverages.

Friday, November 13, 1908, on Schedule F—Tobacco, and manufactures of.

Monday, November 16, 1908, on Schedule E—Sugar, molasses, and manufactures of.

Wednesday, November 18, 1908, on Schedule G—Agricultural products and provisions.

Friday, November 20, 1908, on Schedule D—Wood, and manufactures of.

Saturday, November, 21, 1908, on Schedule M—Pulp, papers, and books.

Monday, November 23, 1908, on Schedule B—Earths, earthenware, and glassware.

Wednesday, November 25, 1908, on Schedule C—Metals, and manufactures of.

Saturday, November 28, 1908, on Schedule N—Sundries.

Monday, November 30, 1908, on Schedule J—Flax, hemp, and jute, and manufactures of.

Tuesday, December 1, 1908, on Schedule I—Cotton manufactures, and on Schedule L—Silks and silk goods.

Wednesday, December 2, 1908, on Schedule K—Wool, and manufactures of.

Friday, December 4, 1908, on Sections 3–34, and miscellaneous matters.

Hearings on articles now on free list will be held on the above dates in connection with the above subjects to which they most nearly relate.

The hearings will be held in the rooms of the committee, third floor, House of Representatives Office Building.

Sessions will begin at 9.30 a. m. and 2 p. m., unless otherwise ordered.

Persons desiring to be heard should apply to the clerk of the committee previous to the day set for the hearing, to be assigned a place on the programme for that day. A person making such application should state:

1. His name.
2. His permanent address.
3. His temporary address in Washington.
4. Whom he represents.
5. Concerning what paragraphs he desires to be heard.
6. Briefly, what position he expects to advocate.
7. How much time he wishes to occupy.

He should also inclose a copy of his brief and of any documents he desires filed with the committee.

All briefs and other papers filed with the committee should have indorsed on them the name and address of the person submitting them, and the numbers of the paragraphs of the present law (act of July 24, 1897) to which they relate.

WILLIAM K. PAYNE,
Clerk, Committee on Ways and Means.

The committee subsequently extended the time for hearings to December 24, 1908.

SCHEDULE C.

METALS, AND MANUFACTURES OF.

SCHEDULE C—METALS AND MANUFACTURES OF.

IRON ORE.

[Paragraph 121.]

J. LEE SMITH & CO., NEW YORK CITY, SUGGEST A NEW CLASSIFICATION FOR ORES OF IRON.

NEW YORK CITY, *November 17, 1908.*

Hon. SERENO E. PAYNE,
Chairman Committee on Ways and Means,
Washington, D. C.

SIR: We beg to suggest to your honorable committee when considering Schedule C—metals, and manufacturers of—a change in paragraph 121, to read as follows:

Suggested paragraph 121.

" Iron ore, unwrought or unmanufactured, chiefly used for smelting, including manganiferous iron ore and the dross or residuum from burnt pyrites, and not otherwise specially provided for in this act, 40 cents per ton, provided that in levying and collecting duty on iron ore no deduction shall be made from the weight of the ore on account of moisture which may be chemically or physically combined therewith; basic slag, ground or unground, $1 per ton."

The reason for the desired change in paragraph 121 is that during the past six years many importations of high-grade and expensive hematites and iron ores, used exclusively for the manufacture of paint, have been entered at 40 cents per ton as iron ore. The Board of United States General Appraisers has uniformly classified such importations as crude colors or pigments, under paragraph 58. Under such decisions suits have been brought by the importers, claiming that as iron ore was specially mentioned, whereas iron paints were not specially mentioned, that the goods should pay duty at 40 cents per ton rather than 30 per cent ad valorem as an unenumerated paint, and the court held that such was the case. And Judge Townsend, in his opinion, filed November 10, 1902, in part said:

" The merchandise is, in fact, crude hematite ore or iron ore. In its present state it can not be used as a pigment or color, and even if it be assumed that it is, in fact, a color or pigment, then it is a color, specially provided for as iron ore in paragraph 121. Congress having seen fit to levy a duty of 40 cents per ton on iron ore without classification as to its use, and without limitation, not specially provided for, such designation must stand."

In accordance with the principles laid down in Judge Townsend's decision, we suggest changing the paragraph as above, so that iron ore and hematites of high grade, suitable and actually used entirely for paint, shall pay the duty provided for paint, and unless the ore imported is for use chiefly for smelting purposes it shall not be admitted at 40 cents per ton duty.

There has been no end of contention over this clause, and at the present time there are a great many appeals and protests from various ports of entry, claiming practically that all oxides of iron, whether natural or artificial, whether crude or powdered ready for use as paint, shall come in as iron ore at 40 cents per ton. We refer you to a few decisions upon this question, showing how it has been agitated since 1902: (T. D. 24189, G. A. 5267) January 26, 1903; (T. D. 24816) December 8, 1903; (T. D. 26248, G. A. 5695) March 30, 1905; (T. D. 26356, G. A. 6391) May 3, 1905; (T. D. 26806, G. A. 9048) November 16, 1905; (T. D. 26895) December 11, 1905; (T. D. 28856) February 14, 1908.

Congress undoubtedly intended to admit iron ore for smelting purposes at 40 cents per ton, many foreign ores being very suitable and beneficial for mixing with low-grade southern ores, and also, no doubt, intended that high-grade ores, used chiefly or entirely as crude paints, by simply grinding or pulverizing them, should pay the duty of 30 per cent ad valorem, as provided for in paragraph 58.

In order to make the classification complete and to avoid confusion in the assessment of duties, we also suggest a change in paragraph 58, Schedule A, to read as follows:

Suggested paragraph 58.

All paints, colors, pigments, lakes, crayons, smalts and frostings, colcothar, and Venetian red, including oxide of iron, hematites, and iron ore, used as paint or polishing powder, whether crude or dry or mixed or ground with water or oil or with solutions other than oil, not otherwise specially provided for in this act, thirty per centum ad valorem; all paints, colors, and pigments, commonly known as artists' paints or colors, whether in tubes, pans, cakes, or other forms, thirty per centum ad valorem.

As manufacturers and importers of dry paints and pigments, we suggest the above changes in paragraphs 121 and 58, and are confident that such change will have the indorsement of—

First. The customs division of the United States Treasury Department, by avoiding much contention and loss of revenue.

Second. The mine owners of the United States, many of whose ores are suitable for and used as paints, and come into competition with the foreign iron ore that is also used entirely or chiefly as paint.

Third. The manufacturers (with possibly one exception) of metallic paint, oxides of iron, Venetian red, etc., used for the same purposes as the ground foreign iron ore.

In conclusion, we may say that the alterations, if made in the above paragraphs, will correct the injustice to the class of paints made from burnt copperas, waste iron liquors, and domestic hematites, of having similar goods used for identically the same purposes admitted in competition at 40 cents per ton (par. 121) instead of 30 per cent ad valorem, as in paragraph 58.

As to rate of duty in paragraph 58, we are satisfied to have it remain at 30 per cent, or to have it reduced to 25 per cent, as may be for the best interests of all concerned.

We remain,

Very respectfully, yours, J. LEE SMITH & Co.

———

HON. JAS. S. SHERMAN, M. C., SUBMITS LETTER OF D. DE W. SMITH, UTICA, N. Y., RELATIVE TO IRON ORE.

UTICA, N. Y., *November 20, 1908.*

Hon. JAS. S. SHERMAN, M. C.,
 Utica, N. Y.

DEAR SIR: Referring again to the matter of tariff, concerning which I wrote you some days since, I beg to say that I now learn that the matter of iron-ore schedule is to be considered November 25, under the general subject of metals and manufactures thereof. Here, as I understand it, under schedule 121 the question of iron ores will be treated.

The Clinton Metallic Paint Company is probably as much interested in this particular schedule as it is in any of the schedules under the paint line. At present writing, we enjoy a duty of 40 cents a ton on iron ores, which would certainly seem relatively moderate, the element of wages being considered.

    *   *   *   *   *   ι

Thanking you in advance for your courtesy, I am,

Very truly, yours,

D. DE W. SMITH.

———

STATEMENT OF FRANK S. WITHERBEE, OF PORT HENRY, N. Y., REPRESENTING IRON-ORE PRODUCERS OF THE EAST.

WEDNESDAY, *November 25, 1908.*

Mr. WITHERBEE. I am here to represent the iron-ore producers of the East. It is fair for me to say to you that I have only returned from Europe on Saturday, and I have had no opportunity of talking this matter over with my associates in business, nor have I had any time to group together some facts and figures which may be of interest to you all; but if it meets with your wishes, I will be very glad to give you some figures, showing the cost data of ore produced in the eastern part of this country, and, so far as it lies in my power, to give you the corresponding cost in Europe. I visited a great many of the iron-ore centers of Europe and became acquainted with the cost of their labor, and so forth, and anything I have in my knowledge you are quite welcome to. I feel certain that there is a widespread demand for tariff revision, and there is reason for it. Undoubtedly there are a great many articles which can properly be reduced, there are other articles that can not be reduced, and I think there are a few articles that perhaps ought to be increased.

But confining myself more to the iron-ore industry, with which I am more familiar, I would say that in any revision you might make of the present schedule I think due consideration should be given to these facts: In the first place, the labor that the iron-ore manufacturer has to compete with is almost the cheapest in the world—that of Spain and Lapland and Cuba—whereas the ordinary manufacturer of iron and steel has to compete with the labor of France and Germany and Great Britain, which is much better paid. There is also another fact, that while a great many branches of the iron trade have but little competition in the way of imports, iron ore has always had a very great competition. There have at all times been large amounts of iron ore brought into this country from Europe, and I think that should be given some consideration also. At times it does not affect the domestic iron-ore producers as much as it has; for instance, during this past season, when for a period of quite a number of months, so far as my own company goes, we simply were not able to make any sales whatever of certain grades of ore as against foreign ores that were being landed in this country.

Another thing is, you should lend encouragement to the mines in the eastern part of our country. There are several large mining districts that are about to be developed, and to develop an iron mine of any size costs from $500,000 to two or three million dollars. The investment at best is an uncertain one. One may open up on a vein that seems large in a year or two years, but the quality is likely to vary, and the amount one has before one is always uncertain, and therefore you can not, as you would in the investment in an ordinary business, look upon a small return in interest as fair. You have got to have a return on your capital which will correspond to the amount of your principal that you are absorbing and disposing of from time to time, and also to give due regard to the uncertainties of the trade. I do not know that there is anything else that I am prepared to say to you to-day. I am sorry that I have not had more time to study this matter, but if hereafter there is anything else I can give you in the way of information I will be glad to do it. Or if to-day there are any questions you wish to ask me I will do my best to answer them. I am afraid it must be in a very general way, however. I could not carry in my mind all the details of the cost.

Mr. CLARK. What is it you suggest?

Mr. WITHERBEE. In what way?

Mr. CLARK. As to the tariff. That is the subject under discussion here.

Mr. WITHERBEE. In general, or as to the proposition I am speaking of?

Mr. CLARK. Do you want it increased, or held as it is, or cut down?

Mr. WITHERBEE. I think if there is going to be a general revision of the tariff, iron ore should stand its share.

Mr. COCKRAN. Should stand its share of reduction?

Mr. WITHERBEE. Should stand its share of reduction. There are times like this summer when the competition would probably stop the production of many grades of domestic ore. In other years they could stand competition.

Mr. CLARK. This year is not a fair illustration?

Mr. WITHERBEE. No; but I think probably three years out of ten would be as bad for the domestic ore producers as this year.

Mr. CLARK. As a matter of fact up here in these Minnesota iron beds iron can be mined cheaper than anywhere else on the habitable globe, can it not?

Mr. WITHERBEE. No, sir; I doubt that. I think the Minette ore of Germany is much more cheaply mined.

Mr. CLARK. Why, they scoop this up with a shovel, do they not?

Mr. WITHERBEE. Yes; but it lies in beds, whereas in this Minette district in Germany and France it covers acres, you migth say miles, in extent.

Mr. CLARK. You do not know any device by which it is cheaper to handle that sort of material than a steam shovel, do you?

Mr. WITHERBEE. No, sir; but that is true abroad also as it is in Minnesota.

Mr. CLARK. Then there are those fields of iron ore in the United States that can be used in competition with them, are there not?

Mr. WITHERBEE. I am not very familiar with the Lake Superior conditions. I am just giving you my personal opinion. I do not think the Mesaba ore region is as cheap a producer as it was ten years ago, and the production must increase in cost very materially. After they get to a certain depth they have a soft body of ore which can not be held up by pillars of rock, but must be held up by timbers, and their costs will increase. If you will investigate, I think you will find that the costs of the Mesaba region are higher than they were eight or ten years ago.

Mr. CLARK. Everybody knows that it costs more to get ore out of the ground than it does to scoop it off of the top.

Mr. WITHERBEE. They can not do that in many mines.

Mr. CLARK. I say it is true if they have scooped it all off of the top.

Mr. WITHERBEE. They have in many mines.

Mr. CLARK. They have the cheapest transportation rates on earth, too, have they not?

Mr. WITHERBEE. No, sir; they do not compare to the rates on the foreign ores to points of consumption.

Mr. CLARK. I say that the steel trust, which owns the Mesaba range, has the lowest freight rates to the centers of manufacture of any mines in the United States, have they not?

Mr. WITHERBEE. No, sir; I do not agree with you. In the first place, there is Alabama.

Mr. CLARK. Where is there one cheaper?

Mr. WITHERBEE. Alabama; Alabama is much cheaper, because the average rate from Lake Superior mines to the points of consumption is, I think, somewhere from $2 to $2.50. The average rate of transportation of iron ore from the Alabama and Tennessee fields to the points of consumption will vary anywhere from 25 to 60 cents. Now, I will go a step further and I will say that in the East we can get to points of consumption cheaper than in the West.

Mr. CLARK. Do you mean to say they can ship ore from the Alabama points to St. Louis, Pittsburg, Chicago, Minneapolis, and New York cheaper than they can ship it from the Mesaba Range to Pittsburg?

Mr. WITHERBEE. No, sir; but I understood your question to be, to iron centers. I consider Birmingham and Chattanooga iron centers.

Mr. CLARK. Certainly. Birmingham will be the biggest iron center on earth, eventually.

Mr. WITHERBEE. My idea was, the rate to reach points of consumption; that they could be reached for less money.

Mr. CLARK. They do not consume any large quantity of that down in Alabama. I understand their market is in New York, Philadelphia, Baltimore, and all these other big places.

Mr. WITHERBEE. The market for Alabama, do you mean?

Mr. CLARK. Yes.

Mr. WITHERBEE. Alabama's market for iron is chiefly in the West and Southwest. I know this, for I was an official at one time of the Tennessee Coal and Iron Company.

Mr. CLARK. Do you think Alabama can put its products—I am asking you for information—into St. Louis and Kansas City cheaper than Pittsburg can?

Mr. WITHERBEE. I should say on general principles, yes, sir. I think more iron is taken from Alabama to St. Louis and that vicinity than there is from Pittsburg.

Mr. CLARK. You say the price of getting out this ore in the Mesaba Range has increased. Do you live at Pittsburg?

Mr. WITHERBEE. No; I live in New York.

Mr. CLARK. Do you not know that they are fixing to get their ore at Pittsburg a great deal cheaper than they ever have gotten it heretofore, that is so far as the freight rates are concerned, by means of a canal from Pittsburg to Lake Erie? [Laughter.]

Mr. WITHERBEE. I have heard so.

Mr. CLARK. Mr. Dalzell stated when he was getting that thing through that it was going to work.

Mr. DALZELL. We have not got the money yet.

Mr. CLARK. I supposed you had already got it.

Mr. DALZELL. If you will furnish the money we will get the ore very soon.

Mr. CLARK. Yes; but I understood you had the money to dig the canal.

Mr. WITHERBEE. I think that any great saving in iron ore freights from Lake Erie to Pittsburg, if that canal should be built, is questionable, for I served on the Roosevelt New York State Canal Commission and we thoroughly investigated the cost of moving raw material over the canal systems of this country and Europe, and also went very thoroughly into the cost of handling the same over our railroad systems, and we found iron ore was being hauled from Conneaut Harbor on Lake Erie to the Pittsburg district at the lowest cost of any rail cost in this country.

Mr. DALZELL. You mean over the Bessemer road?

Mr. WITHERBEE. Over the Bessemer road. And even should it now be put into Pittsburg that would not very materially decrease the rate.

Mr. CLARK. If that is so, what did Mr. Dalzell want with a bill to build that canal?

Mr. WITHERBEE. I do not think there is any question that it would be cheaper, but not materially cheaper.

Mr. CLARK. Where do you produce your ores?

Mr. WITHERBEE. Lake Champlain.

Mr. Clark. How much of a cut do you think you could stand on iron ore and still live and flourish?

Mr. Witherbee. We have not flourished, nor lived very much, this year.

Mr. Clark. To start right now?

Mr. Witherbee. On the average of ten years—I would rather not state that definitely, unless you press me.

Mr. Clark. That is exactly what I am up to.

Mr. Witherbee. I might be stating an opinion that others would not share. I can only give you my personal opinion.

Mr. Clark. That is what I want.

Mr. Witherbee. In the long run, a reduction of possibly 15 or 20 per cent.

Mr. Dalzell. A reduction of 15 or 20 per cent?

Mr. Witherbee. I am only speaking for myself.

The Chairman. You are standing a reduction of 20 per cent on Cuban ores?

Mr. Witherbee. I was not thinking of that.

The Chairman. And the importations have not increased from Cuba under that cut?

Mr. Witherbee. Yes.

The Chairman. They have been a little over a million tons a year. They were a little over a million tons in 1903 and 1904, and about a million tons a year since, half of which comes from Cuba.

Mr. Dalzell. It was only half a million tons last year.

The Chairman. From Cuba?

Mr. Dalzell. Yes.

Mr. Witherbee. Cuba is going to export very much more than in the past. There are fields there that are being developed now that are going to ship ore into this country at a much lower rate than it has ever been delivered for from Cuba.

The Chairman. Mr. Witherbee, it is more expensive to mine ore in your mines than in any other part of the United States, is it not?

Mr. Witherbee. No, sir; it is not.

The Chairman. What is that?

Mr. Witherbee. No, sir; I do not think so.

The Chairman. You do not think it is?

Mr. Witherbee. No, sir. Our cost is not the cheapest, by any means, but at the same time I think that it is not the highest.

The Chairman. Are they not above the average cost?

Mr. Witherbee. No; I should think they were about the average cost. Of course when you say "cheap mining" you have to take into consideration the point of consumption to which the product goes. We reach the point of consumption at a lower freight rate than western mines.

The Chairman. By the point of consumption you mean where it is turned into pig iron?

Mr. Witherbee. Yes.

The Chairman. That is what you meant in regard to Alabama?

Mr. Witherbee. Yes; it is the same way in the eastern field.

The Chairman. Where do you make your pig iron?

Mr. Witherbee. We do not make any, practically; we ship our ore.

The Chairman. Where does it go?

Mr. Witherbee. Into eastern Pennsylvania and New Jersey.

The CHAIRMAN. They use it to mix with foreign ore?

Mr. WITHERBEE. They use it with foreign ore and Lake ore.

The CHAIRMAN. For the purpose of making a better iron?

Mr. WITHERBEE. Yes; all pig iron is mixed with other ores.

Mr. DALZELL. That is where the Cuban ore goes, is it not?

Mr. WITHERBEE. That is where the Cuban ore goes; yes, sir.

Mr. BOUTELL. I would like to ask you about the amount of reduction that could be sustained by the trade under paragraph 121 of the Dingley law. The tariff to-day is 40 cents a ton?

Mr. WITHERBEE. Yes.

Mr. BOUTELL. That is the same duty that was imposed under the last preceding, or Wilson, tariff bill?

Mr. WITHERBEE. Yes; I think it was 60 cents in the Wilson bill, and then it was reduced to 40 cents.

Mr. BOUTELL. It was 75 cents under the McKinley bill and 40 cents under the Wilson bill.

Mr. WITHERBEE. Yes.

Mr. BOUTELL. In other words, the rate of duty was the same under the Wilson bill as it is now under the Dingley bill. In other words, you have had a stable rate of duty on the ore for fourteen years.

Mr. WITHERBEE. Yes; except in the case of Cuba.

Mr. BOUTELL. Which has been mentioned?

Mr. WITHERBEE. Yes.

Mr. BOUTELL. As an expert in the business and from your experience, do you not think that this duty of 40 cents can be very well placed at 25?

Mr. WITHERBEE. No, sir; I do not. I think there might be years when it could, but I think it is only fair to consider that we have periods once in awhile, such as we have been through this year, and as we also went through in 1896, 1897, and 1898, when our mines were practically closed. This year, for a period up to the 1st of August, we made not a single sale from last November of certain grades of ore competing with foreign ore. The price at which we could afford to sell our ore in the East—and I think the Lake Superior mines were in the same condition—were such that we could not meet the competition of the foreign ores dumped into this country. They used us as a dumping ground.

Mr. BOUTELL. Can you state the amount of ore in Cuba now?

Mr. WITHERBEE. I do not think anybody can do it. It is something phenomenal. I think that the development that the Cambria people have and that the Bethlehem Steel Company people have will show up—well, I may be exaggerating, but I think it will approach the quantity on Lake Superior, not possibly in actual units of iron, but practically of tonnage. There are enormous deposits of iron ore in Cuba, and also in South America, and also in Newfoundland.

Mr. DALZELL. Are they as cheaply mined as our ore?

Mr. WITHERBEE. The Newfoundland ore is. The Newfoundland ore is so cheaply mined that we have had to stand aside and see every pound of Newfoundland ore disposed of before we could sell a pound of ours.

Mr. DALZELL. Are Cuban ores used for blending purposes?

Mr. WITHERBEE. Yes; all ores are used that way.

Mr. DALZELL. Cuban ore is more valuable for blending purposes than other ores?

Mr. WITHERBEE. Yes.

Mr. DALZELL. What does it come into competition with for that purpose here?

Mr. WITHERBEE. Lake Superior ore and Lake Champlain ore.

Mr. DALZELL. They are the only ones?

Mr. WITHERBEE. No, sir; they are the principal ones.

Mr. DALZELL. Is the Cuban ore the same as the manganese iron ore in Colorado; that is, manganese, or, rather, ferro-manganese, and ought to pay a higher rate of duty?

Mr. WITHERBEE. No, sir; there is some manganese ore in Cuba, but it is principally found in Russia, Greece, and India.

Mr. DALZELL. It comes in free as manganese ore?

Mr. WITHERBEE. Yes, sir.

Mr. DALZELL. Manganese ore and manganiferous ore are entirely different things?

Mr. WITHERBEE. Yes; most of our manganese ore comes from Russia and should carry about 45 per cent of manganese, while manganiferous carry about 5 to 20 per cent of manganese, and there are many deposits of that character in this country.

Mr. DALZELL. The Cuban ore is manganiferous ore?

Mr. WITHERBEE. Some of it is, but not all of it.

Mr. DALZELL. Who owns the Cuban ore?

Mr. WITHERBEE. It is owned largely by Americans, although I believe some large concessions are owned by Spaniards. It may be of interest to the committee to know that probably the largest deposits of iron ore in the world are located in Lapland, about 1,000 miles north of Stockholm. I have seen there one deposit which is said to contain almost as much ore as there is in the Lake Superior field. These ores have not yet come into competition with our ores, for the Swedish Government has in the past limited the amount that can be exported to about 1,500,000 tons per annum, their theory being to conserve it until the other large deposits of the world are depleted, when they think it will have a much higher value; but many believe the reason for its restrictions is that the state wishes to acquire the deposits. Bearing on this supposition, I have heard recently that the interests controlling these deposits have ceded to the state a one-quarter interest in them and they are now allowed to export 3,000,000 tons annually, and that later on, as the Government is ceded a larger interest, the exports will be proportionately increased, and that eventually all restrictions as to the amount of ore that can be exported will be removed. When that time comes, we are going to feel very keenly the competition of this ore, for it is the richest in the world and very cheaply mined.

Mr. BOUTELL. The continuity of our interrogatories was suspended by some interruptions.

Mr. WITHERBEE. Yes.

Mr. BOUTELL. I had asked in reference to your opinion as a business man and an expert in the business in reference to the exact amount of reduction that could be sustained without any injustice, and you made reply in reference to my query, about 25 cents a ton, as I understood it; that it might be sufficient in some years but not in others?

Mr. WITHERBEE. Yes.

Mr. BOUTELL. And what I was about to question you about when the interruption came was this: We can not regard either a revenue tariff or a protective tariff, of course, as an insurance policy.

Mr. WITHERBEE. I do not know, sir, about that. My theory of protection is that we can—that is, the aim of a protective tariff is to protect and foster in a legitimate way with reasonable duty against foreign labor, and give protection to the capital invested. My idea of a protective tariff is that it is not for revenue purposes, but to foster and stimulate the growth of industries in that way, but not to the extent that they shall become in any way monopolies.

Mr. BOUTELL. You misapprehended my question.

Mr. WITHERBEE. I beg your pardon.

Mr. BOUTELL. But even at that you would not suppose that any tariff could be framed by the wisdom of man which could produce industrial depression?

Mr. WITHERBEE. Oh, no. I understand you now.

Mr. BOUTELL. You understand?

Mr. WITHERBEE. Yes.

Mr. BOUTELL. What I am trying to get at is the principal question, whether, with the steady and stable and uniform duty of 40 cents a ton in the past fourteen years, and with the experience gained thereunder, you do not think that for the next ten years, or for the next ten years so far as you can see in your business, 25 cents a ton would be the amount of protection that would put the American producer in fair competition with any foreign producer of ore?

Mr. WITHERBEE. No, sir. I think there are too many fields that are about to be developed, and too many cheap fields in Cuba, to say that. Of course I would be very glad, personally, not to see any reduction, because even with the tariff at 40 cents a ton there has never been a year but what there has been 500,000 to 1,000,000 tons of ore brought into this country, and, as I said, there were times when the sale of foreign ores has stopped the sale of domestic ores, so that you can see the danger in it, and I would not say that 25 cents a ton was a safe duty to put on it.

Mr. BOUTELL. When you said it might stand a reduction of 10 or 15 per cent——

Mr. WITHERBEE. That was on the 40 per cent.

Mr. BOUTELL. You meant a reduction of 10 or 15 per cent of that 40 per cent?

Mr. WITHERBEE. Yes.

Mr. BOUTELL. I see; that would be 4 or 6 cents a ton?

Mr. WITHERBEE. Yes.

Mr. BOUTELL. Which would reduce it to 36 or 34 cents a ton?

Mr. WITHERBEE. Yes.

Mr. BOUTELL. But let me call your attention to the fact that while the iron and steel duties in the Dingley law have been substantially the same as those of the Wilson bill, with at least three notable exceptions of decrease in the Dingley law below the Wilson bill, still there has never been a time in the history of the world when there has been any such development or prosperity as there has been in the iron and steel business in this country during those ten years.

Mr. WITHERBEE. That is true.

Mr. BOUTELL. And one of those notable reductions is the reduction in paragraph 125 of one-tenth of a cent a pound in the Dingley bill below the Wilson bill on beams and girders and structural steel, where there has been, perhaps, the largest profit.

Mr. WITHERBEE. Are you putting an inquiry to me? I beg your pardon.

Mr. BOUTELL. I was just hesitating a moment to see if you would make an observation.

Mr. WITHERBEE. I do not consider myself well posted on it.

Mr. BONYNGE. The continuity of the interrogatory was interrupted. [Laughter.]

Mr. BOUTELL. If you have no observation to make, I will ask a question.

Mr. WITHERBEE. Very well.

Mr. BOUTELL. Taking the steel industry, structural steel, prosperous as it was before, as it was from 1904 to 1907 with this protection of one-tenth of a cent a pound from the Wilson bill, is it not reasonable to suppose that a reduction of 20 to 45 per cent on the iron ore might be followed by an equal demand and equally great prosperity in that branch of the iron business?

Mr WITHERBEE. I would not be willing to admit that the prosperity which has come to structural steel manufacturing of this country is due to the question of duties. I think it has been due rather to the fact that as our forests are being cut down steel is taking the place of wood for construction purposes. Improved machinery has also had much to do with the improvement in the structural steel business.

Mr. BOUTELL. Be that as it may, the duty on structural steel did not act to depress the business?

Mr. WITHERBEE. No, sir.

Mr. BOUTELL. That is all.

Mr. UNDERWOOD. I believe you stated that you had visited most of the foreign ore mines.

Mr. WITHERBEE. Yes, I have; most of them.

Mr. UNDERWOOD. I would like you to give me some data in reference to that. If you can, please give me the labor cost at the German mines that you know about.

Mr. WITHERBEE. It is the most difficult thing to extract any information from a German. You have got to make up your own figures practically. I have tried every way in the world, from local people and otherwise; but I should imagine that their ore cost on board the cars would be not to exceed 50 cents a ton.

Mr. UNDERWOOD. That is the cost on the cars, 50 cents a ton?

Mr. WITHERBEE. Yes, sir; it is shoveled. It is like so much dirt. It requires no mining.

Mr. UNDERWOOD. Of that cost how much is represented by labor?

Mr. WITHERBEE. I should say almost all of it. We use air drills to take the place of men. Over there this material is in the form of dirt and not rock, so that you might say that practically all of it is labor. It is shoveled up. They have lately got to using some steam shovels.

Mr. UNDERWOOD. It is a question of pumping the mines?

Mr. WITHERBEE. It is almost all surface mining.

Mr. UNDERWOOD. I would like to take up the same proposition in regard to Cuba. What is the cost f. o. b. Cuba?

Mr. WITHERBEE. I can not give you that.

Mr. Underwood. You are more or less familiar w.th the business in Cuba. Can you give us any idea?

Mr. Witherbee. I can not.

Mr. Underwood. Can you give us the same data as to England?

Mr. Witherbee. Yes; I can to a limited extent, for the Middlesbrough district.

Mr. Underwood. I would like to have that. You understand that the question is, give the cost aboard the cars and then differentiate the labor cost, so that I will have both.

Mr. Witherbee. I do not know that I can do that. The English ore is a carbonate ore, 32 per cent, and corresponds more to our red ore in Alabama. It is a soft ore to mine, and I should say probably they could put it on board cars for 75 cents.

Mr. Underwood. How much of that is labor?

Mr. Witherbee. I should say fully 80 to 90 per cent.

Mr. Underwood. Fully 80 to 90 per cent is labor?

Mr. Witherbee. Yes, sir. Mind you, it is a soft ore, which does not require machinery to handle it, as many of our ores do.

Mr. Underwood. In the United States I would like to have you take up three points and give me the same figures. You were with the Tennessee Company in Alabama, were you not, and were familiar with that business?

Mr. Witherbee. Yes, sir.

Mr. Underwood. I would like you to give me the cost, f. o. b. cars in Alabama, and the labor cost; and the same in reference to the Messaba field and the same in reference to the eastern field.

Mr. Witherbee. I have not the figures for Alabama definitely enough in my mind to give them to you. Very likely there is some gentleman here who can give them to you. The same way with the Messaba; I am not as familiar with their costs as I am even with those in Europe. But I know, for instance, in the Lake Superior region, of course, there are different grades of ore—some ores that are very difficult to mine and some very cheap. There are some of the Messaba ores that cost a great deal of money.

Mr. Underwood. I mean the average that they are shipping out of the Messaba Range?

Mr. Witherbee. I would rather not answer that question, because Mr. Mather, who follows me, is very much more thoroughly posted than I am.

Mr. Underwood. Can you give me the cost of your ores at the mines in New York?

Mr. Witherbee. I can give it to you in a rough way. Of course it varies from month to month according to the width and size of the vein. In our mines we have this additional cost that does not exist anywhere else in the world except in Sweden. That is, we concentrate our ore. After it is mined we grind it down and then put it over a magnetic separator, and the particles of ore are attracted by the magnetic separator and fall into one bin, and the rock falls into another bin. That is to save the cost of transportation on the rock and to make the ore richer.

Mr. Underwood. I would like to have the cost of that ore, including, of course, the cost of separating.

Mr. WITHERBEE. That will range anywhere from $2.75 to $3.50 a ton, according to the grade of the ore at our mines. You see we have different mines.

Mr. UNDERWOOD. $2.75 to $3.50?

Mr. WITHERBEE. Yes.

Mr. UNDERWOOD. That is f. o. b. the cars?

Mr. WITHERBEE. That is f. o. b. the cars.

Mr. UNDERWOOD. How much of that is labor?

Mr. WITHERBEE. We always estimate that our labor cost runs from 60 to 75 per cent. I suppose it would be fair to say that it averages somewhere from 60 to 70 per cent. I mean by "labor" simply the labor employed in the mining of ore, not that employed, for instance, in the coal and other material used to mine the ore.

Mr. UNDERWOOD. I understand.

Mr. WITHERBEE. We divide it up into labor and supplies.

Mr. UNDERWOOD. The labor in the coal is something that goes into the labor account and not the furnace account?

Mr. WITHERBEE. Yes, sir.

Mr. UNDERWOOD. Of course the market for the raw ore is the furnace.

Mr. WITHERBEE. Yes.

Mr. UNDERWOOD. I would like to ask what is the cost of transportation of this German ore to the furnace.

Mr. WITHERBEE. About like that in Alabama.

Mr. UNDERWOOD. How much is that?

Mr. WITHERBEE. A great many of the deposits are very close to the furnaces. In fact, the furnaces have been built on the iron ore deposits.

Mr. UNDERWOOD. What do you estimate that to be?

Mr. WITHERBEE. I should say at the outside 25 to 50 cents a ton. They have adopted an entirely different policy in Europe from what they have here. We locate next to the coal and they next to the ore.

Mr. UNDERWOOD. In Cuba what is the cost of transportation to the furnace, from where it is laid on the car or the boat to the furnace, to the place of production?

Mr. WITHERBEE. I can only give you that from hearsay.

Mr. UNDERWOOD. Give what information you have.

Mr. WITHERBEE. I should say that the rate was somewhere from 80 to 90 cents to a dollar a ton, and the inland charge to the coast.

Mr. UNDERWOOD. How much will the inland charge increase it?

Mr. WITHERBEE. I do not know. One of these other gentlemen can tell you that.

Mr. UNDERWOOD. In England what is it?

Mr. WITHERBEE. Very much as in Germany. Furnaces are located largely where the ore is mined.

Mr. UNDERWOOD. What is the cost of transportation; practically what would you fix it at?

Mr. WITHERBEE. I should say 25 to 50 cents a ton, the same as in Germany, because the blast furnaces are located purposely up close to the mines.

Mr. UNDERWOOD. And you make the same statement in regard to the Alabama mines, of course?

Mr. WITHERBEE. Yes.

Mr. UNDERWOOD. What is the cost of transportation from the Messaba mines? I believe the principal points of consumption of the Messaba ores are at or near Chicago, or Gary, and at Pittsburg, are they not?

Mr. WITHERBEE. Gary is not yet started. It will be soon, though. I would rather leave that to Mr. Mather, who follows me, because I am not familar with Lake Superior costs.

Mr. UNDERWOOD. There is one other question that I would like to ask you. As to this foreign ore that you say may possibly come in competition with American ore, coming from Lapland and other countries, what would be the cost of transportation of bringing that into this country?

Mr. WITHERBEE. That varies anywhere from ballast rate up. When there is an enormous amount of grain to go out, it will come almost as ballast. I should say that the rate would run from 5 to 7 shillings, on the average. That would be $1.25 to $1.50.

Mr. UNDERWOOD. The cost of transportation of that foreign ore that may compete with ours would amount to $1.25 to $1.50 a ton, then?

Mr. WITHERBEE. Yes.

Mr. UNDERWOOD. That is all that I wanted to ask.

Mr. HILL. What was the total amount of iron ore mined in 1907, about?

Mr. WITHERBEE. I think it was about 52,000,000 tons.

Mr. HILL. And we imported about 1,000,000 tons?

Mr. WITHERBEE. Rather more than that, I think, in 1907.

The CHAIRMAN. Half from Cuba and half from the rest of the world?

Mr. WITHERBEE. Yes.

Mr. HILL. What I was bringing out when I said 1,000,000 tons was that the eastern iron-ore manufacturers have met that. What proportion of the supply in the United States is controlled by the United States Steel Company?

Mr. WITHERBEE. What proportion?

Mr. HILL. Yes; I mean owned and controlled.

Mr. WITHERBEE. Well, I only know what I see in the papers and have read, and I would have to give you that from recollection.

Mr. HILL. If you do not know, do not attempt to answer.

Mr. WITHERBEE. I would rather not answer.

Mr. HILL. Very well.

Mr. GRIGGS. I understood you to say that you were apprehensive of great developments in iron ore in Cuba?

Mr. WITHERBEE. Yes.

Mr. GRIGGS. That is, for the future?

Mr. WITHERBEE. Yes, sir.

Mr. GRIGGS. Are you in competition with anything in Belgium?

Mr. WITHERBEE. Not directly; only the finished material in Belgium competes with the finished material of America.

Mr. GRIGGS. I ask you that because you are the only man I have seen who is not, directly. Do you not think we had better annex Belgium?

Mr. WITHERBEE. I would be very glad to own the iron and coal deposits as they are located in Belgium. I have visited Belgium often, and I think they produce the cheapest steel there in the world. I do not think there is any part of the world that can compete with Belgium, because if you go through the plants you will see the women and children taking the ore out of the cars, and the coke, and putting it in the hoists to go up to the furnace top, and you will see all kinds of labor used around the plant.

Mr. GRIGGS. Then she even competes with you?

Mr. WITHERBEE. Yes.

Mr. GRIGGS. A pestiferous little cuss, isn't she?

Mr. WITHERBEE. Yes; she is. I have a great respect for Belgium, and I think anybody has, even England.

Mr. RANDELL. You say you would like to have Belgium annexed to this country. Would not that ruin our iron industry?

Mr. WITHERBEE. That might be true, but at the same time I do not like her where she is now, competing with us.

Mr. RANDELL. Yes; but there would be no tariff wall between her and this country if she was in this country. Would it not ruin every industry in the country?

Mr. WITHERBEE. No; I think I ought to retract that. What I had in mind was the resources of Belgium. I said I would like to have its iron and coal, located as they are.

Mr. RANDELL. Do you not need protection?

Mr. WITHERBEE. Against Belgium? Certainly.

Mr. RANDELL. Do you not need protection against the Lake Superior and Minnesota fields more than any others in the world? ·

Mr. WITHERBEE. No, sir; I do not fear Lake Superior competition. The amount of ore they ship to the seaboard is a help rather than a hindrance, for it is needed for mixing with eastern ores. Lake Superior ore prices are always higher than eastern ores, on account of their long transportation.

Mr. RANDELL. Where do you get your principal competition?

Mr. WITHERBEE. From the foreign ore.

Mr. RANDELL. Where, principally?

Mr. WITHERBEE. All through eastern Pennsylvania and New Jersey, wherever our ore is used. Lake Superior ores are used as mixing ores.

Mr. RANDELL. Where is your competition?

Mr. WITHERBEE. In Pennsylvania and New Jersey.

Mr. RANDELL. You have no competition from foreign ores?

Mr. WITHERBEE. No; our competition is with foreign ores. What I understood you to say was where was our competition. I say our competition is from foreign ore that comes into New Jersey and Pennsylvania.

Mr. GAINES. Mr. Randell's question is, Where does the ore come from which competes with you?

Mr. RANDELL. Yes.

Mr. GAINES. Where does it come from?

Mr. WITHERBEE. The ore that competes with us comes from Spain and Newfoundland and Cuba. .

Mr. RANDELL. You get that in competition?

Mr. WITHERBEE. Yes, sir. The rates into Pennsylvania from Cuba and Newfoundland are less than they are from our mines.

Mr. RANDELL. That ore is used for blending?

Mr. WITHERBEE. No; they substitute it for ours.

Mr. RANDELL. The ore from Cuba——

Mr. WITHERBEE. Yes.

Mr. RANDELL (continuing). Is substituted for what?

Mr. WITHERBEE. For our ores; but they do blend it a little, to be perfectly fair.

Mr. RANDELL. Yes; I supposed you wanted to be fair about it.

Mr. WITHERBEE. Yes.

Mr. RANDELL. Suppose Cuba was annexed, would not that ruin the iron industry? There would be no tariff wall then.

Mr. WITHERBEE. I think it would injure the iron-ore trade. I suppose that eventually we would come around to reduced wages, and take less return on our money, and possibly meet the Cuban ore.

Mr. RANDELL. Do you think we would have less industry in the United States if we let Cuban ore in?

Mr. WITHERBEE. I do not think it would affect the industry. There is nothing produced in Cuba but ore.

Mr. RANDELL. Do you not know as a fact that the tariff on iron ore and iron products does affect the price to the consumer of this country in all the products of iron and steel?

Mr. WITHERBEE. I do not know that I understood your question. Would you mind stating that question again?

Mr. RANDELL. Does not the tariff bring up the price to the consumer in iron and steel products?

Mr. WITHERBEE. No, sir; I do not think so; not altogether.

Mr. RANDELL. Then you think that the products would be just as low without the tariff?

Mr. WITHERBEE. I think that it depends entirely on the conditions of the trade. I think last year there was such a condition.

Mr. RANDELL. You think it was higher?

Mr. WITHERBEE. It was higher last year than this year.

Mr. RANDELL. I am not talking about any special month. They do or do not have an effect. Do they have any effect?

Mr. WITHERBEE. Yes, sir.

Mr. RANDELL. We could shorten the time very much if you would just answer my questions, and we will be through in a very few minutes. In that case does it have any effect?

Mr. WITHERBEE. The duty?

Mr. RANDELL. Yes; on the price?

Mr. WITHERBEE. Yes.

Mr. RANDELL. Is that effect up or down?

Mr. WITHERBEE. Up.

Mr. RANDELL. Then it does raise the price?

Mr. WITHERBEE. Yes.

Mr. RANDELL. Now, we have gotten through with that proposition. The industry is a well-established one, is it not?

Mr. WITHERBEE. The iron and steel industry?

Mr. RANDELL. Yes.

Mr. WITHERBEE. Yes.

Mr. RANDELL. Will there ever be a time when, if the tariff should be removed, this industry will be strong enough to walk on its feet and sustain itself and quit levying a higher price on the consumer in order to exist?

Mr. WITHERBEE. Why, yes, sir; the time will come.

Mr. RANDELL. Has not the time already come?

IRON ORE—FRANK S. WITHERBEE.

Mr. WITHERBEE. No, sir; I do not think so.

Mr. RANDELL. If we took the tariff off of iron and steel, the industry would drop?

Mr. WITHERBEE. I can not answer that question by " yes " or " no." I can answer it better by an illustration than in any other way. Pig iron is selling to-day for about $12.50 f. o. b. ship at Middlesbrough, England. It costs $1.50 or possibly $2 to bring it over, making it worth, without duty, say, $14.50, New York Harbor. Now, putting it at cost, I don't believe domestic pig iron can be put in New York Harbor for less than $16.

Mr. RANDELL. Do you not think that the tariff ought to be so arranged that you can get the New York market absolutely, practically without competition? Do you not look at it from that standpoint?

Mr. WITHERBEE. Partly.

Mr. RANDELL. Do you not think you ought to get nine-tenths of the trade in New York City? That is the way you look at it, is it not?

Mr. WITHERBEE. I look at it that the tariff ought to be so arranged that it will compensate for the difference in wages.

Mr. RANDELL. If you will answer that, I will soon be through with you.

Mr. WITHERBEE. I am trying to.

Mr. RANDELL. Do you not think a proper tariff would give you at least nine-tenths of the trade of New York City?

Mr. WITHERBEE. A proper tariff?

Mr. RANDELL. Yes.

Mr. WITHERBEE. A proper tariff; yes, sir.

Mr. RANDELL. Would that not give you a monopoly, practically, over all the rest of the country?

Mr. WITHERBEE. It is hard to differentiate one point from another. New York is hardly a competitive point.

Mr. RANDELL. The foreign article would have to pay the freight to the interior, would it not?

Mr. WITHERBEE. Yes.

Mr. RANDELL. Would it not give the manufacturers in the iron industry practically all over the United States a monopoly? Just answer yes or no.

Mr. WITHERBEE. It would ordinarily, under ordinary conditions. Not this year.

Mr. RANDELL. I am talking about ordinary conditions. Then your answer is that it would give a monopoly?

Mr. WITHERBEE. Yes.

Mr. RANDELL. Do you mean that or not?

Mr. WITHERBEE. I mean, with a tariff framed as it should be, to give a reasonable compensation between the two—that is, the cost of the pig iron abroad and the cost of the labor in producing it in America— that it ought to be so adjusted that it would give the benefit to the American producer.

Mr. RANDELL. I did not ask you that. Here is what I ask you. Let us get through with it.

Mr. WITHERBEE. I want to get through, if I can.

Mr. RANDELL. You said you wanted it so that it would give you nine-tenths of the market of the United States?

Mr. WITHERBEE. Yes. It never has been so.

Mr. RANDELL. Now, you admit that that would give the iron industry a monopoly almost all over the country; you admit that, do you not?

Mr. WITHERBEE. No, sir; I do not.

Mr. RANDELL. Then you take that back?

Mr. WITHERBEE. The cost of making pig iron might be less in the interior.

Mr. RANDELL. You are supposed to know something about it, in the ordinary condition of things?

Mr. WITHERBEE. Yes.

Mr. RANDELL. Would it not give the domestic manufacturer practically a monopoly in the balance of the country? If you control business by the effect of the tariff, you could control nine-tenths of the business in the port of New York?

Mr. WITHERBEE. Practically, except that the one-tenth might influence the other nine-tenths in prices, which it does right along. Five thousand tons of foreign ore might influence the price of the sale of 50,000 tons of our ore.

Mr. RANDELL. If you will deal more in facts and less in speculation, I think we will get more information.

Mr. WITHERBEE. Yes, sir.

Mr. RANDELL. Then do you know of any reason why the foreign producer could compete with the domestic manufacturer in the balance of the United States under the conditions you have just stated, if the tariff would shut him out from nine-tenths of the trade in New York?

Mr. WITHERBEE. That condition has never existed, you know.

Mr. RANDELL. I did not ask you that.

Mr. WITHERBEE. It never has done it in the past and I do not think we are going to raise the tariff to do it now. Foreign ore goes as far west as Pittsburg and all through the Eastern States and is landed at Philadelphia and New York, and frequently delivered at eastern furnaces in the interior at a price that is equal to or less than domestic ores.

Mr. COCKRAN. You have lost sight of your first statement; that is that you thought your industry could stand a reduction. You stated, did you not, I think, that if there is to be a reduction of the tariff your industry can stand its share?

Mr. WITHERBEE. Yes.

Mr. COCKRAN. Could you give us any idea of the reduction which your industry could stand?

Mr. WITHERBEE. I stated, I think, about 15 or 20 per cent.

Mr. COCKRAN. I did not get that part of it.

Mr. WITHERBEE. Fifteen or 20 per cent.

Mr. COCKRAN. You thought a reduction of 15 or 20 per cent?

Mr. WITHERBEE. Yes.

Mr. COCKRAN. Thank you. I beg your pardon for asking you that over again.

Mr. POU. Have you ever examined the steel schedule under the Wilson bill as compared with that under the McKinley bill?

Mr. WITHERBEE. No, sir; I have not. My interest is entirely in iron ore and not in the manufacturer's end.

Mr. POU. That is all.

STATEMENT OF WILLIAM G. MATHER, OF CLEVELAND, OHIO, REPRESENTING LAKE SUPERIOR IRON-ORE INDUSTRY.

WEDNESDAY, *November 25, 1908.*

Mr. MATHER. I represent the Lake Superior iron-ore industry, Mr. Chairman; that is, I have interests in Lake Superior iron ore, and I have come down to appear before the committee with reference to that industry. What Mr. Witherbee has said practically echoes my own sentiments in reference to the general situation with regard to iron ore. We do not ask for any increase in duty; but I think Mr. Witherbee is fair, and I think perhaps the Lake Superior iron-ore men outside of myself would be willing to subscribe to his opinion that the iron-ore industry could stand a reduction of 15 to 20 per cent on the present rate of duty, which would make it 8 cents. A reduction of 20 per cent would make it 8 cents off.

The Lake Superior iron-ore industry has developed to a very large proportion, as of course you all know. Something like 42,000,000 tons were shipped from there last year, and in the development of that industry, which has come up under the revenue laws which prevail, of course the conditions have grown consistently with that. The costs of labor are high. The conditions of the laboring population are correspondingly good. We have had practically very few labor troubles or strikes in connection with the industry for a great many years. It is difficult to say what would happen under certain conditions of reduction of tariff, but I should say that such a reduction as Mr. Witherbee stated would not affect, materially at any rate, the conditions of the mining industry up there. But if you should attempt to reduce it further, or take it off entirely, naturally the tendency would be to disarrange those conditions under which the mining industry has grown and make the operators try to bring about lower costs. Therefore, I should say that it would be unwise for the industry as a whole to make any further reduction in the tariff on iron ore than that which has been suggested by Mr. Witherbee. I have no brief, Mr. Chairman. I am coming down here somewhat unexpectedly for several reasons. I shall be quite ready and willing to make a brief before your committee at the time that you should suggest. I shall be glad to answer questions to the best of my ability which may come to you.

Mr. HILL. May I renew my question which the other gentlemen did not answer or could not answer at the time? Do you know about what proportion of the iron ore supplies of the United States are under one control?

Mr. MATHER. No, sir; I do not.

Mr. HILL. That is, in the control of the United States Steel Company?

Mr. MATHER. I do not think anybody could answer that question.

Mr. HILL. I mean what per cent, one-half, three-quarters, or 10 per cent?

Mr. MATHER. I say I do not think anybody could answer that question intelligently, because we do not know just how much iron ore there is in the country. It is rather difficult to answer.

Mr. HILL. My question was as to the supply of the United States?

Mr. MATHER. The supply of the United States?

Mr. HILL. Yes.

Mr. MATHER. Of course I am not speaking of our own.

Mr. HILL. Yes; how much?

Mr. MATHER. I should say 40 or 50 per cent.

Mr. HILL. Under one control?

Mr. MATHER. Yes.

Mr. HILL. Under one control. How much of that 50 per cent is subject to an annually increasing cost charge, a lease charge?

Mr. MATHER. A lease charge?

Mr. HILL. Yes.

Mr. MATHER. A royalty charge?

Mr. HILL. A royalty charge, annually increasing. Is it a large proportion?

Mr. MATHER. I do not know, sir.

Mr. HILL. It is a large proportion; is it not?

Mr. MATHER. I do not know, I would not be able to answer that.

Mr. HILL. The result of that situation is that it is bound to result in a constantly increasing cost of iron in this country; is it not? If half of the entire production is under one control, and that half is subject to a continually annual increasing charge, is it not bound to result in a constantly increasing cost of iron—practically the same situation that the lumber industry is in to-day, with a constantly increasing cost of the product?

Mr. MATHER. Of the iron ore?

Mr. HILL. Yes.

Mr. MATHER. From the mines that are now being operated, the cost is gradually increasing. In the case of the present known supply. the cost is increasing on account of the greater depth of the ore.

Mr. HILL. And it looks to a constantly increasing cost of iron and steel; does it not?

Mr. MATHER. If we find new deposits, sir, that would keep the price down.

Mr. HILL. I am speaking about the known supply.

Mr. MATHER. The known deposits?

Mr. HILL. Yes.

Mr. MATHER. There would be a slight gradual increase in the cost, on account of, perhaps, greater depth of the mines.

Mr. HILL. Do you not think that it is somewhat the duty of the United States to conserve that product, and look out for the future as well as for the immediate present?

Mr. MATHER. Oh, that product is not, of course, fixed at all. I should think it would be wise for the United States to increase its output and product of iron ore, and encourage the development of iron-ore bodies.

Mr. HILL. Do you not think it would be more for the interest of the United States to conserve its own product and draw ore at cheaper prices from other countries?

Mr. MATHER. If we knew just how much we have, yes; but we have no idea how much we have. I think we have infinitely more that we can now see, and I think it is bound to increase.

Mr. NEEDHAM. There is no danger of the immediate exhaustion of the supply?

Mr. MATHER. No, sir; I do not think so.

Mr. CLARK. Is it not true that the trust, and perhaps other large manufacturers of iron, are buying up low-grade ore fields, now that they do not expect to work for twenty-five, thirty, forty, or fifty years, just to have it in stock?

Mr. MATHER. That I do not know, sir.

Mr. CLARK. And so that nobody else can get it in the meantime?

Mr. MATHER. I do not know whether they are or not. That would not be, however, an unnatural investment for persons to make who are operating in iron ore.

Mr. CLARK. I know; but it would be a very unpleasant thing for the mills that have to use iron ore.

The CHAIRMAN. Mr. Mather, have you noticed any more competition in the sale of your ores for the last five years on account of the foreign import? Have you had to reduce the price at all on account of foreign importation for the last five years, up to, of course, the 1st of October a year ago?

Mr. MATHER. It has not been, Mr. Payne, what I should call an appreciable factor. It has had an influence, but I should not say it was a marked influence.

The CHAIRMAN. How much did it lower the price of the ores from 1905 up to the 1st of January, 1908?

Mr. MATHER. What was the price?

The CHAIRMAN. How much lower was it? How much lower did you make the price of the ores from 1905 up to January 1, 1908?

Mr. MATHER. The prices have fluctuated. I should say that in 1908 they were lower than they were in 1907; in 1907 they were somewhat higher than they were in 1906.

The CHAIRMAN. There has been no appreciable lowering of prices, then?

Mr. MATHER. From 1905 to 1908?

The CHAIRMAN. Yes.

Mr. MATHER. I should say not, sir.

The CHAIRMAN. During all of that time?

Mr. MATHER. Not on the average.

The CHAIRMAN. There has been no appreciable lowering of the price for the five years previous to 1905 compared with the three years after 1905?

Mr. MATHER. That would be 1900 to 1905?

The CHAIRMAN. Yes. The price did not go down any?

Mr. MATHER. The price fluctuated, Mr. Payne; but I would not be able to say that it was lower in 1905.

The CHAIRMAN. But would the average price from year to year decrease?

Mr. MATHER. I think it has been about the same.

The CHAIRMAN. So that half a million tons of the Cuban ore coming in here at 32 cents you have not felt at all in the market?

Mr. MATHER. Not appreciably. The Lake Superior people have not felt it appreciably; no, sir.

The CHAIRMAN. That is all.

Mr. UNDERWOOD. I should like to ask the witness a few questions. Mr. Mather, what corporation do you represent?

Mr. MATHER. The Cleveland Cliffs Iron Company.

Mr. UNDERWOOD. Are you familiar with the cost of production of the ore fields of the world?

Mr. MATHER. No, sir.

Mr. UNDERWOOD. Do you know anything about the cost abroad and in Germany and in Cuba in comparison with the cost here?

Mr. MATHER. Not on the average, sir; no.

Mr. UNDERWOOD. I notice from the reports that I have before me that the importations of ore in 1907 were about a little over 1,000,000 tons. The consumption in the United States was about 35,000,000 tons. Has that average kept up for the last four or five years?

Mr. MATHER. That average of importation?

Mr. UNDERWOOD. That average of importations as compared to consumption.

Mr. MATHER. The importations in the past have been higher than that, sir. I have not the figures before me, but I should say that in some years they have been a million and a half tons at a time when there was a less production of Lake Superior iron ore.

Mr. UNDERWOOD. Was the consumption of 35,000,000 a fair estimate?

Mr. DALZELL. It was 55,000,000, was it not?

Mr. MATHER. When?

Mr. DALZELL. Last year.

Mr. MATHER. No, sir.

Mr. HILL. That figure of 35,000,000 was in 1902, Mr. Underwood.

Mr. MATHER. The production of Lake Superior iron ore in 1907 was about 42,000,000 tons.

Mr. HILL. But the total production in the United States?

Mr. MATHER. In the United States? I do not know, sir.

Mr. UNDERWOOD. The total amount of iron ore in 1902 was 35,000,000 tons.

Mr. DALZELL. Yes.

Mr. UNDERWOOD. You can not state what the total amount of iron ore was that was produced in the United States?

Mr. MATHER. In 1902?

Mr. UNDERWOOD. In 1907.

Mr. MATHER. I do not know, sir; no.

Mr. UNDERWOOD. Mr. Witherbee stated, I think, that you could give us the cost of production f. o. b. the steamer or the car of the Mesaba ore.

Mr. MATHER. That varies, sir, from those mills which are surface mines, which are operated partly with the steam shovel, and those which are strictly underground mines. I should say that that would average, on board the cars, from 50 to 60 cents a ton.

Mr. UNDERWOOD. That is the cost of production?

Mr. MATHER. Yes.

Mr. UNDERWOOD. What is the labor cost? How much labor cost is involved, as distinguished from capital investment?

Mr. MATHER. The labor cost on the average of those ores is about 70 per cent.

Mr. UNDERWOOD. Seventy per cent. The point of assembling that ore at the furnace is either Pittsburg or, in the future, would be Gary, would it not—probably those two points?

Mr. MATHER. Some of it will go to Gary; yes, of course.

Mr. UNDERWOOD. What would be the cost of assembling that ore at the Pittsburg furnaces?

Mr. MATHER. That ore would cost, at Lake Erie, about——

Mr. UNDERWOOD. I want to get the assembling cost; not the cost of the ore. You have given me that. I want to get the shipping cost.

Mr. MATHER. Oh, outside of the mining? *

Mr. UNDERWOOD. You gave me the cost of the ore f. o. b. the boat at 50 cents.

Mr. MATHER. No; f. o. b. the cars at the mines.

Mr. UNDERWOOD. At the mines, which has to be shipped to the boat?

Mr. MATHER. Yes; f. o. b. the boat at Duluth, it would cost 80 cents more.

Mr. UNDERWOOD. Yes. Now, excluding the cost of the ore at the mine, I want to get the cost of shipment to Pittsburg from the Mesaba Range—the freight rates, in other words.

Mr. MATHER. Yes. The freight rate would be——

Mr. DALZELL. Do you mean from Lake Erie ports to Pittsburg?

Mr. UNDERWOOD. Yes; the freight rates from the mines to the furnaces.

Mr. MATHER. The freight rates from the mines to Pittsburg—the rail rate to Duluth from the mine is 80 cents. The lake rate last year was 75 cents. This year it was 65. I should say that 75 would be a fairer rate. That would be $1.55. The rate from Lake Erie to Pittsburg is from 95 cents to $1. I am not certain; I think it is $1, sir.

Mr. UNDERWOOD. That would be $2.55?

Mr. MATHER. Yes.

Mr. UNDERWOOD. Will you give me the same figures to Gary?

Mr. MATHER. The freight rate to Gary would be the same as to Lake Erie. You would deduct the freight; it would be $1.55.

Mr. UNDERWOOD. Do you know the cost of Cuban ore?

Mr. MATHER. No; I do not.

Mr. UNDERWOOD. Do you know the cost of transportation from Cuba?

Mr. MATHER. I do not. I have had no experience with that.

Mr. UNDERWOOD. That is all I desire to ask.

Mr. DALZELL. Do we get ore from Canada?

Mr. MATHER. Do we get ore from Canada?

Mr. DALZELL. Yes.

Mr. MATHER. A li .e: very little.

Mr. DALZELL. About how much?

Mr. MATHER. That would have to be a guess, Mr. Dalzell. I should say that it would be less than 250,000 tons.

Mr. DALZELL. That would be an average yearly, would it?

Mr. MATHER. I do not know how much ore has come from Newfoundland, but I was thinking of the mines up north of Lake Superior. I should think that 250,000 tons would be the maximum. I doubt if, from that part, they have ever reached quite that amount.

Mr. DALZELL. And where do they come in?

Mr. MATHER. They would come into the lake port at Sault Ste. Marie.

Mr. COCKRAN. You represent what is known as " the Mesaba Range interest? "

Mr. MATHER. No, sir.

Mr. COCKRAN. Where is the Mesaba Range?

Mr. MATHER. The Mesaba Range is in Minnesota, west of Lake Superior.

Mr. Cockran. Then these interests that you represent are entirely different?

Mr. Mather. I represent one mine there, but it is only a small mine.

Mr. Cockran. In the Mesaba Range?

Mr. Mather. Our interests are in Michigan.

Mr. Cockran. Did you hear Mr. Witherbee's statement as to the comparative cost of production in the Mesaba Range and in Germany?

Mr. Mather. No; I did not.

Mr. Cockran. How does that matter strike you? Is the product of the Mesaba Range as cheap, as easily produced, as the product of the German mines? Is it as cheaply produced? Can it be produced as cheaply as the product of the German mines?

Mr. Mather. I would not want to answer that. I have not any sufficient knowledge about that, Mr. Cockran. As to the Mesaba mines, it occurs to me that perhaps there is a slight misapprehension in the minds of some people with respect to them, on account of their being operated by a steam shovel, but they are only operated by a steam shovel after a very large amount of surface has been taken off. Sometimes that has amounted to as high as the thickness of 100 feet. That is a very large development cost, which, of course, has to be added to the ore.

Mr. Cockran. Oh, yes.

Mr. Mather. And that, in its way, you understand, is similar in its application to the cost of development of an underground mine.

Mr. Cockran. Certainly. It is part of the capital outlay.

Mr. Mather. It is part of either the capital outlay or the operating cost.

Mr. Cockran. Yes. Making allowance for that, do you know of any place in the world where iron ore can be produced as cheaply as there in the Mesaba Range?

Mr. Mather. Yes; they can produce it in the northern part of Sweden as cheaply. I happen to know that.

Mr. Cockran. That is practically not in competition with the American mines yet?

Mr. Mather. That is the only place I know about.

Mr. Cockran. That is an apprehension rather than a fact?

Mr. Mather. At present that does not come into our country.

Mr. Cockran. So that at this moment you can produce your ore as cheaply as it can be produced anywhere in the world?

Mr. Mather. The Mesaba ore?

Mr. Cockran. Yes.

Mr. Mather. The Mesaba ore, I should say, could be produced as cheaply as any ore in the world that comes into the United States. I think that is what you are asking.

Mr. Cockran. That is all we are concerned about.

Mr. Mather. Yes.

Mr. Cockran. Now, about your own ore, which you describe as the Lake Superior ore——

Mr. Mather. The Michigan mines.

Mr. Cockran. Is that more expensive—more costly to produce— than the Mesaba product?

Mr. Mather. Yes.

Mr. Cockran. How much more?

Mr. MATHER. Probably twice as much.

Mr. COCKRAN. How are you able to get a market at all in competition with the Mesaba product, then?

Mr. MATHER. We are nearer the lake, and have a less lake-rail freight.

Mr. COCKRAN. And that balances the cost?

Mr. MATHER. That balances the cost.

Mr. COCKRAN. If that be so, how could any foreign product, which has to cross the sea, come into competition with yours, in view of the fact that it must pay the cost of transportation, and you are close to the place of final disposition?

Mr. MATHER. You mean how can it come in competition with us?

Mr. COCKRAN. Yes.

Mr. MATHER. Why, it costs us more to get down to the eastern furnaces than it would cost ore from Cuba.

Mr. COCKRAN. But you go to Gary, do you not?

Mr. MATHER. No; we do not.

Mr. COCKRAN. I understood you to say that you did. Was I wrong?

Mr. MATHER. There is ore that goes to Gary, but we do not necessarily go to Gary.

Mr. COCKRAN. But that is where you practically dispose of your product, is it not?

Mr. MATHER. Oh, no; there has not been any disposed of there yet.

Mr. COCKRAN. I understand that; but under the arrangement that is now being made for manufacturing in the future, it is reasonably certain that that is where you will deliver your product, is it not?

Mr. MATHER. We might deliver part of it there. That is only one port of consumption.

Mr. COCKRAN. Will you not deliver practically all of it there?

Mr. MATHER. No, sir.

Mr. COCKRAN. Where else will you send it?

Mr. MATHER. It will go to all the ports of Lake Erie. They will consume much more than Gary will.

Mr. COCKRAN. It will be all around the ports of Lake Erie?

Mr. MATHER. Yes.

Mr. COCKRAN. Would you not have as much advantage over foreign competitors there as you have over the Mesaba product now?

Mr. MATHER. At Lake Erie?

Mr. COCKRAN. Yes.

Mr. MATHER. We get to Lake Erie at about the same cost as the Mesaba ore.

Mr. COCKRAN. I understood you to say that you were able to maintain your competition with the Mesaba ore, though it cost twice as much to produce, because you were nearer to the Lake Erie ports.

Mr. MATHER. Precisely; but that makes our cost at the lake ports the same.

Mr. COCKRAN. Exactly. Then would you not have a still greater advantage as against any foreign competitor?

Mr. MATHER. Why should we? We are just the same as the Mesaba ore. You are talking about us in competition with the Mesaba ore, are you not?

Mr. COCKRAN. No; I am talking about your company with reference to the foreign producer--the producer in Spain, Cuba, etc.

Mr. MATHER. Yes.

Mr. COCKRAN. You would have a still greater advantage over foreign competition in the way of proximity to the place of manufacture than you have over the Mesaba producer?

Mr. MATHER. Not in the eastern market; no, sir. They can get there cheaper than we can.

Mr. COCKRAN. I am speaking now about all the Lake Erie ports.

Mr. MATHER. At the Lake Erie ports we have an advantage over the foreign ore.

Mr. COCKRAN. And you could defy competition there?

Mr. MATHER. I think we could defy competition at Lake Erie ports.

Mr. COCKRAN. What proportion of your product goes to the eastern factories?

Mr. MATHER: That varies. It has been from 2,000,000 to 3,000,000 tons.

Mr. COCKRAN. And that is about a little less than a tenth of your entire product?

Mr. MATHER. About a tenth.

Mr. COCKRAN. About a tenth. So that for nine-tenths of your product you are practically beyond the reach of competition with the foreigner?

Mr. MATHER. At the present rate of duty; yes.

Mr. COCKRAN. No, no; I mean without any rate of duty whatever. I mean under absolutely free-trade conditions, you have the cheapest ore?

Mr. MATHER. You must bear in mind, sir, that our ore is not all consumed at Lake Erie; it is consumed at Pittsburg.

Mr. COCKRAN. My dear sir, you have explained that to me very thoroughly, and your answers are all very luminous. There is no room for doubt about it.

Mr. MATHER. I beg your pardon.

Mr. COCKRAN. I understand that about 90 per cent of your product either goes to Lake Erie ports, or will go there when the Gary furnaces are opened, and about 10 per cent of your product goes to eastern factories?

Mr. MATHER. It does not stay at Lake Erie, 90 per cent of it. The bulk of it goes down to interior points by rail from Lake Erie.

Mr. COCKRAN. Let us get back to that, then, at the risk of wearisome repetition. The advantage that you have over the Mesaba product in the Lake Erie transportation is sufficient to balance the difference in cost of production. Am I correct about that?

Mr. MATHER. Yes; we get to Lake Erie at about the same price as the cost at Mesaba.

Mr. COCKRAN. You have that advantage against every other producer in the world. You have that equal advantage over any other producer in the way of access to Pittsburg or any of these places where the article is manufactured in this country?

Mr. MATHER. I should think that Cuban ore could get to Pittsburg as cheaply as we could, as far as transportation cost is concerned.

Mr. COCKRAN. Does all this mean that Cuban ore can come into competition with your product at Pittsburg?

Mr. MATHER. I should think it might. I am not definite in regard to that.

Mr. COCKRAN. You see, when it comes to fixing the revenue laws of a country, one has to be certain about one's facts.

Mr. MATHER. Precisely. I shall be glad to put in a brief on that point.

Mr. COCKRAN. So you would not want to speak of that affirmatively now—positively?

Mr. MATHER. Not definitely one way or the other; no, sir.

Mr. COCKRAN. Frankly, is there any place in the world where iron ore can be produced more cheaply than in America?

Mr. MATHER. Than where?

Mr. COCKRAN. Than in your place and in the Mesaba Range?

Mr. MATHER. Why, certainly.

Mr. COCKRAN. Where?

Mr. MATHER. I have already said particularly, I know, in Sweden.

Mr. COCKRAN. I know; but that is not produced.

Mr. MATHER. You asked me if it were produced.

Mr. COCKRAN. No, no; I mean actual production, where mines are actually in operation. I am not speaking of a potential production in Sweden.

Mr. MATHER. It is produced there.

Mr. COCKRAN. I am speaking of an actual production there.

Mr. MATHER. It is produced there, sir.

Mr. COCKRAN. For export?

Mr. MATHER. It is exported—not to the United States, but to other parts of Europe.

Mr. COCKRAN. I am speaking of what comes into this country.

Mr. MATHER. Ah; I did not know that.

Mr. COCKRAN. I am speaking of the product of foreign mines coming into this country. Is there any that, west of the Alleghenies, could compete with you?

Mr. MATHER. Yes; I think the mines of Spain and the mines of Cuba can mine the ore cheaper than we can.

Mr. COCKRAN. If we grant that, still they have a much longer transportation, an added cost of transportation.

Mr. MATHER. No; I think not—not very much. Of course water transportation is not as costly as rail transportation.

Mr. COCKRAN. The most of the Spanish product comes from Vigo, does it not?

Mr. MATHER. Bilbao, I believe; and some of it from the Mediterranean ports.

Mr. COCKRAN. It comes from Vigo principally?

Mr. MATHER. I would not have said so. I thought it came from Bilbao—which is practically the same thing, however.

Mr. COCKRAN. Yes; I think that is so. You are right. That has to be landed at New York, has it not?

Mr. MATHER. At our Atlantic ports; yes.

Mr. COCKRAN. And then it has got to be transshipped and transported across the Alleghenies to Pittsburg. Do we understand you to say that the freight on a ton of that ore from Bilbao to Pittsburg is less than the freight on a ton of ore from your mine to Pittsburg?

Mr. MATHER. No; I did not say that. I said it would not be far away from that; I thought we would meet them very close to Pittsburg.

Mr. COCKRAN. Very well, then; you could meet them very close to Pittsburg. There would not be any decisive advantage over you at Pittsburg?

Mr. MATHER. No.

Mr. COCKRAN. You would have the advantage over them at the Lake Erie ports?

Mr. MATHER. Yes.

Mr. COCKRAN. Do you think there is any great necessity for a protective tariff under those conditions?

Mr. MATHER. A protective tariff on iron ore?

Mr. COCKRAN. Yes.

Mr. MATHER. Yes; I do. I think there ought to be some protective tariff under the conditions under which we have developed this industry. It should not be taken off at this time.

Mr. COCKRAN. You consider that you ought to have a protection rather by way of reward for what you have done than to meet any actual necessity that you now experience?

Mr. MATHER. No; I would not say that—to keep up the conditions under which we are now operating.

Mr. COCKRAN. What conditions?

Mr. MATHER. Conditions of cost—labor cost.

Mr. COCKRAN. But at the present cost, I understood you to say— perhaps I am wrong about it; let me repeat it again—that at Pittsburg you would meet them in close and deadly earnest, with little advantage on either side; that at all the Lake Erie ports you would have a decided advantage over them.

Mr. MATHER. Yes.

Mr. COCKRAN. Under those circumstances, can you explain what necessity you find for protection?

Mr. MATHER. If they could come into Pittsburg that would cut off the market which we now occupy to a certain extent.

Mr. COCKRAN. But you say you have a rather good fighting chance against them at Pittsburg even under existing conditions.

Mr. MATHER. Precisely. We might have to lower our prices to meet them, might we not?

Mr. COCKRAN. Yes; that is quite possible. But by lowering your price you might enormously increase your output, might you not?

Mr. MATHER. Not necessarily.

Mr. COCKRAN. I said "might;" I did not say "necessarily."

Mr. MATHER. I would not think so, under the circumstances that you mention, if it were only to meet Cuban ore.

Mr. COCKRAN. But wherever there is a reduction of price it always stimulates consumption, does it not?

Mr. MATHER. Not necessarily; no.

The CHAIRMAN. How long is this argument going to be prolonged?

Mr. COCKRAN. Just until I get an answer, Mr. Chairman, if I can. You can stop it if you want to.

The CHAIRMAN. It did not seem to me that you were asking him any questions.

Mr. COCKRAN. I have been trying to find out from this witness a reason for any protective tariff.

The CHAIRMAN. Why do you not ask him, then?

Mr. COCKRAN. Unfortunately, I am afraid, Mr. Chairman, that you can not hear me.

Mr. DALZELL. Are you not interrogating him as to competition with another home producer?

Mr. COCKRAN. No; I am asking him with reference to the product of Bilbao, in Spain.

The CHAIRMAN. If you will agree to stay with us until midnight to-night, I will not object.

Mr. COCKRAN. I will stay with you, Mr. Chairman, whenever I get a chance, with the utmost possible pleasure. I always part from you with regret.

Now, I come back to the question which was pending. Will you give us any definite reason why it is necessary to retain a protective tariff here in competition with these products from Bilbao, in view of your testimony that you can meet them practically on equal terms at Pittsburg, and with an advantage at the Lake Erie ports?

Mr. MATHER. Yes; because it would restrict our market. It would take away our market in the East, and it would restrict us at Pittsburg.

Mr. COCKRAN. Conceding that reason, a very small protective tariff would be sufficient to give you an advantage, would it not?

Mr. MATHER. I think, as I said, that 30 to 32 cents would be a fair thing.

Mr. COCKRAN. But if you have got them on practically equal terms at Pittsburg, and at an advantage on Lake Erie, surely you do not want the tariff taxation as high as 32 cents for protection? You do for advantage, but not for actual protection?

Mr. MATHER. Well, we do not want to have to reduce our industry.

The CHAIRMAN. This gentleman has stated that he can not see any appreciable difference in the competition on ore coming in here from Cuba at a Cuban ad valorem of 10 per cent. It seems to me that that has gotten down to a pretty small——

Mr. COCKRAN. I did not understand him to say that.

The CHAIRMAN. Oh, yes; he said he did not see any appreciable difference in the last five years.

Mr. COCKRAN. If that is his testimony, that there is not any appreciable difference between the two, I am perfectly willing to let the testimony rest on that and to express my acknowledgments for having had so much light on the question.

Mr. CLARK. How much pig iron will a ton of iron ore make?

Mr. MATHER. About half a ton.

Mr. CLARK. Why do you not make it into pig iron up there, and ship it to the ends of the earth in that shape? Is there any difference in the rate on iron ore and pig iron for a given distance?

Mr. MATHER. Oh, yes. Pig iron, as a general thing, as a commodity, costs more.

Mr. CLARK. Not much more, does it—not double?

Mr. MATHER. I do not know, sir, about that. It costs more.

Mr. CLARK. Is that the reason you do not make it into pig iron up there?

Mr. MATHER. It costs too much to get the fuel up there.

Mr. CLARK. Does it cost any more to get the fuel up there than it does to get the ore down to the fuel?

Mr. MATHER. Yes; per ton of iron, it does.

Mr. CLARK. That is all.

Mr. DALZELL. You have not got the coal or the limestone?

Mr. MATHER. No, sir.

Mr. BOUTELL. Is not the upshot of this whole discussion with reference to the duty, that 25 cents a ton duty would give you a distinct advantage over all foreign competitors in the United States?

Mr. MATHER. I would not want to say that, sir.

Mr. BOUTELL. I know you would not want to say it, but won't you say it?

Mr. MATHER. No; I won't. [Laughter.]

Mr. BOUTELL. Of course I can not compel you to; but our sources of information, of course, are not limited to the witnesses that appear before us.

Mr. MATHER. No.

Mr. POU. Mr. Chairman, I do not think I have taken up my full share of the time. I should like to be permitted to ask just one question.

The CHAIRMAN. I hope the gentleman will not fail to occupy it.

Mr. POU. Just one question: I have frequently seen it stated that the average rate of duty under the steel schedules of the Wilson bill was higher than under the same schedules of the McKinley bill. Do you know whether that is true or not?

Mr. MATHER. I can not answer that, sir, because my interests are almost entirely confined to iron ore.

Mr. POU. That is all.

Mr. GRIGGS. You are not afraid of Belgium?

Mr. MATHER. Not on iron ore; no.

ANDREW J. ENNIS, OF ENNIS & CO., PHILADELPHIA, PA., RECOMMENDS REPEAL OF DUTY ON IRON ORE.

PHILADELPHIA, PA., *December 2, 1908.*

Hon. SERENO E. PAYNE, M. C.,
Washington, D. C.

DEAR SIR: As I am in the business of importing and assembling foreign iron ores for pig-iron and steel-making purposes probably anything I may say favoring the repeal of present duty on iron ore will be received with suspicion of self-interest, but that this view would be unfair to me I trust will develop ere the close of this letter. I have been in the foreign ore business for half a lifetime and am, I think, very conversant with such sources of supply and probable quantities available to this country. With the exception of Cuba, and to some extent Newfoundland, I believe that unless new deposits are discovered and operated the repeal of the entire duty of 40 cents per ton would not in itself add much tonnage to our iron-ore imports. I say this for two prime reasons: (1) As soon as the repeal became effective foreign miners would demand part of the duty in higher prices. (2) Any increased demand for transports would advance freights, and that portion of the duty not obtained by the miner would be taken by the shipowner. But while the eastern smelter would not benefit by putting the actual duty in his pocket, he would greatly benefit by insurance, to the extent of the duty, against increased cost through miners' higher demands and of increased cost of transportation. It is said that the United States Steel Corporation owns or controls some 60 per cent of the Lake Superior iron-ore production, and enjoys sufficient influence over the remaining 40 per cent to shape its policy; hence at any day a lake ore combination may increase the ore cost to independents to a point where operation would be impossible. The really poor end of the steel business is the end that creates its prime necessity—pig iron—while the high prices made possible for steel have conferred great benefit on steel itself—benefit that the manufacturer of pig iron has not been able to share in anything like due proportion. I know furnace men with their worldly goods invested in pig-iron plants who are as poor to-day as ten years ago—the spread in the selling price between pig iron and steel having all along been unfair to pig iron. In conclusion, I have every hope that your wide investigations will uncover the truth— truth that the American ore producer will not be disadvantaged one iota through the repeal of iron-ore duty, and that the pig-iron producer by reason of its repeal will be able to carry on his avocation with less menace to his business welfare. In fact, increased importations of the foreign low phosphorous ores free of all duty would stimulate development of domestic mining (and consequent increased employment of domestic labor), especially in Eastern States, where iron-ore properties remain unworked because phosphorus in the ore is too high to make merchantable iron without admixture of ores low in phosphorus which are best available from foreign sources free of duty. On the other hand, if, in order to be consistent, repeal of ore duty would mean the encouragement of repeal or a lowering of the present duty on pig iron, then it were better to leave the duty on ore where it is, for, be assured, that pig iron can stand no reduction from present duty. One has only to glance at foreign free-on-board pig-iron prices, and add the ocean freight rate, insurance, and charges, to realize the blow to our eastern makers by any lowering of the tariff on pig iron. Whether the duty on iron ore stands or is repealed will make no difference to the writer, as he sees it. He speaks unselfishly for a great interest (pig iron) in the eastern portion of this country that stands in urgent need of your wise conclusions.

Respectfully,

ANDREW J. ENNIS.

THE U. S. GEOLOGICAL SURVEY FURNISHES INFORMATION RELATIVE TO PERCENTAGES OF IRON IN ORES.

WASHINGTON, *January 6, 1909.*

Hon. SERENO E. PAYNE,
  Chairman Committee on Ways and Means,
    House of Representatives, Washington, D. C.

SIR: In accordance with your request of December 31 regarding the percentage of iron in the ores of various districts in the United States and in those imported from Newfoundland, Spain, and Cuba, I have collected the following data:

Percentage of iron in Lake Superior ores, 1905, 59.6 per cent; 1906, 53 to 65 per cent, average about 59; 1907, 52 to 64 per cent, average about 58.

Average analysis for 1905.

Iron	59. 600
Silica	7. 500
Phosphorus	. 067
Sulphur	. 019

Average analyses of the Clinton ores of Alabama, showing the gradation from "hard" to "soft" ores.

	1.	2.	3.	4.
Iron	37.00	45.70	50.44	54.70
Silica	7.14	12.76	12.10	13.70
Lime	19.20	8.70	4.65	.50
Phosphorus	.30	.49	.46	.10
Sulphur	.08	.08	.07	.08

By far the larger part of the Clinton ores mined in Alabama are hard ores and have an average percentage of iron somewhat below 37.

Average analyses of magnetite ores of the Adirondacks.

CRUDE ORE.

	Per cent.
Bessemer:	
Iron	40.000 to 67.00
Phosphorus	.002 to .05
Non-Bessemer:	
Iron	40.000 to 67.00
Phosphorus	.500 to 1.30

CONCENTRATED.

	Per cent.
Iron	64 to 68

Analyses of brown ores of Moa, Mayari, and Cubitas fields in northern Cuba.

	1.	2.	3.
Iron	46.03	52.00	54.69
Phosphorus	.015	.037	.019
Silica	5.50	2.62	2.51

Analysis No. 1 shows the average of a large number of samples collected in the Mayari field, while analyses 2 and 3 show the composition of selected samples taken from the other fields.

Analyses showing the composition of iron ores imported from Spain as given by Whitwell, of the Iron and Steel Institute.

	Per cent.
Brown hematite	48 to 50
Red hematite	54 to 56
Spathic iron ore or iron carbonate:	
Before roasting	40 to 45
After roasting	55 to 60

Average analysis of iron ores from Belle Isle, Newfoundland.

	Per cent.
Iron	52.00 to 54.00
Silica	13.00 to 9.00
Phosphorus	.85 to .74
Sulphur	.03 to .05

This analysis shows the composition of the oxidized ores which have now been nearly exhausted, so that the present ores would probably not average more than 40 or 45 per cent iron.

I trust that these analyses will be satisfactory.

Very respectfully,

GEO. OTIS SMITH,
Director United States Geological Survey.

F. S. WITHERBEE, OF WITHERBEE, SHERMAN & CO., NEW YORK CITY, FILES A SUPPLEMENTAL STATEMENT RELATIVE TO IRON ORE DEPOSITS.

UNITED STATES EXPRESS BUILDING, 2 RECTOR STREET,
New York, January 6, 1909.

Hon. SERENO E. PAYNE,
Chairman Committee on Ways and Means,
Washington, D. C.

DEAR SIR: Yours of the 31st ultimo is at hand, and in reply I would say that we mine two grades of iron ore, known as our "new bed" and "old bed" deposits.

The "new bed" deposit averages about 50 per cent in metallic iron as it is mined, but when crushed and separated it has a yield of about 65 per cent metallic iron. The purpose of concentrating this ore is to eliminate the rock and other gangue connected with it, so that it will bear transportation to distant points of consumption, which it would not do if shipped in its crude state.

The "old bed" deposit, when mined, runs about 60 per cent metallic iron, and after being concentrated runs up to 66 per cent metallic iron. The object of crushing and concentrating this grade is to remove the phosphorus from the same, which in its crude state amounts to 1½ to 2 per cent, and when concentrated is reduced to about one-half of 1 per cent, and therefore its consumption is greatly augmented, as the amount of phosphorus in pig iron is limited, and if our "old bed" ore were sold only in its crude form its sale would be that much curtailed.

I might say in this connection that this separating process requires considerable additional labor and increases materially the cost of the ore; but, as I have said above, this is somewhat offset by the fact that our customers have to pay for less freight on our ore, as a ton of it contains higher units of iron than when in its crude form.

I am preparing a short brief, which I will hope to get off to you in the near future, somewhat amplifying my testimony before your committee on November 25. This brief will go in to you at the same time that the iron and steel people present theirs on the other schedules.

Yours, truly,   F. S. WITHERBEE,
President Witherbee, Sherman & Co.,
Iron Ore, Pig Iron, and Phosphates.

F. S. WITHERBEE, NEW YORK CITY, FILES ADDITIONAL STATEMENT RELATIVE TO DUTIES ON IRON ORE.

2 RECTOR STREET,
New York City, January 13, 1909.

COMMITTEE ON WAYS AND MEANS,
Washington, D. C.

GENTLEMEN: In accordance with the promise made your committee when I appeared before it on November 25, 1908, I herewith submit a short brief, amplifying somewhat my testimony on the iron-ore schedule.

The principal iron-ore districts in the East are located in the States of Pennsylvania, New Jersey, and New York, and to show the effect foreign ore importations have upon the iron ore produced, I will submit to your committee the production of these States separately, and then compare with their total production the amount of foreign ore imported in the corresponding years.

Year.	Pennsylvania.	New York.	New Jersey.	Total.	Importations.
1897	723,742	335,725	254,285	1,313,702	489,970
1898	773,082	179,951	275,438	1,228,471	187,2L8
1899	1,009,327	443,7E0	256,185	1,709,302	674,082
1900	877,684	441,4*5	344,247	1,663,416	897,831
1901	1,040,684	420,218	401,989	1,862,891	966,950
1902	822,932	555,321	441,879	1,820,132	1,165,470
1903	644,599	510,460	484,796	1,669,855	980,440
1904	397,107	842,308	499,949	1,739,359	487,613
1905	808,717	1,139,937	526,271	2,474,925	845,651
1906	949,429	1,041,992	542,518	2,533,939	1,060,390
1907	837,287	1,375,020	549,760	2,762,067	1,229,168

I make this comparison to show to what extent foreign ores compete with the domestic ore mined in the East.

In fixing a duty on iron ore I think three important points should be considered.

First. The present duty of 40 cents a ton is practically the equivalent of an ad valorem duty of about 10 per cent. This is lower than almost any other duty in the iron and steel schedule, and is really a duty based on the principle of "a tariff for revenue only" rather than of one designed to protect "home industry."

Secondly. Due allowance should be made for the fact that nearly all the deposits of Spain, Cuba, and Newfoundland—the principal sources from which foreign ore is exported—are located practically on the seaboard, and they possess, therefore, unusual facilities for reaching this country at very low freight rates. I understand that freights from Spain vary from ballast rates up to, say, very rarely $2.50 per ton, while from Newfoundland and Cuba steady rates can be obtained under $1 per ton. As the bulk of foreign ore comes from these last two countries, through rates can be obtained from the mines to points of consumption in the East at an average of not over $1.50 per ton, while the average rate from the Lake Champlain ore district—which is the largest in the East—to the same points of consumption is at least $1.90 per ton.

The third point which you should take into consideration is that the miner has to compete largely with the very cheap labor of Spain and Cuba. As bearing on that point, I would say that my own company—and, I believe, all Eastern mining corporations are paying about the same wages—have paid the following average wages:

Year:
1905 _____ per day__ $1.94
1906 _____ do____ 2.00
1907 _____ do____ 2.13
1908 (to December 1) _____ do____ 2.02

This average is made up by averaging the different classes of those employed in actually mining our ore and does not include any of our salaried officials.

I have no actual data to show what wages are being paid for a similar class of labor in foreign ore-producing countries, but from what I know personally of their mining conditions, I am confident the average will be considerably below $1.25 if not below $1.

As to costs, I must again confine myself largely to what my own company is doing, but our Lake Champlain deposits are so much more extensive than those of New Jersey, I can safely venture to say that in giving you our costs I am understating those of nearly all other eastern mines, with the possible exception of the Cornwall (Pa.) district. We have always calculated that the lower freight rates from New Jersey mines to the same points of consumption in eastern Pennsylvania put the delivered price of their ore on about the same basis as our Lake Champlain ores. As a large proportion of eastern ores are separated to eliminate the deleterious or lean gangue, the following costs submitted to you include the cost of separation, viz: For the year 1907, the cost at average points of competition with foreign ores was $4.669 per ton, which is equivalent to about 0.073 cent per unit metallic iron; for the eleven months of 1908 (January to November, inclusive) the cost as above was $4.507 per ton, which is equivalent to about 0.070 cent per unit metallic iron.

In these costs no return is allowed on capital invested or profits.

Owing to the hazards of mining, together with the extinguishment of ore reserves, a fair return on value of ore beds and capital invested is essential.

Labor in mining alone (including separation) is represented by the following percentages: In 1907, 58 per cent of the cost of ore; in 1908, 52 per cent of the cost of ore.

I have not been able to obtain any actual costs of foreign ore, but I know large quantities have been sold during the past year, delivered at competitive points of consumption on the basis of $7\frac{1}{4}$ to 8 cents a unit, which undoubtedly includes a profit to the producer. I also know that in Germany some ores are sold at points of consumption from 75 cents to $2.50 per ton, according to the grade.

In conclusion, I believe that reductions should be made in our present tariff where practicable, but that such reductions should be conservative, not radical in character, and afford adequate protection alike to capital and labor employed in the industries affected.

Respectfully submitted.

F. S. WITHERBEE,
Witherbee, Sherman & Co., Port Henry, N. Y.

PYRITES ORE.

[Paragraph 674.]

THE GENERAL CHEMICAL CO., NEW YORK CITY, THINKS THAT A DUTY ON SULPHURET OF IRON WOULD BE INJURIOUS TO THE CHEMICAL INDUSTRY.

NEW YORK, *November 25, 1908.*

COMMITTEE ON WAYS AND MEANS,
House of Representatives, Washington, D. C.

GENTLEMEN: The General Chemical Company would regard the enactment of any duty on pyrites ore, or sulphuret of iron, as injurions to the chemical industry, and to all industries dependent thereon.

The following are some of the reasons:

This article is the principal raw material of the whole chemical industry. It is the raw material from which sulphuric acid is well and cheaply made, and sulphuric acid is an article of manufacture which is essential to almost all other chemical operations. The United States is relatively poor in deposits of pyrites. The domestic production of pyrites in 1907 amounted to 262,000 tons, while importations amounted to 656,000 tons.

Twenty years ago most of the sulphuric acid was made from brimstone imported from Sicily. In 1887 sulphuric acid of 50° Baumé, known as chamber acid, which is the acid used in making fertilizers, sold at about $12 a ton on the average. At the present time it sells for only about $6 per ton. This enormous reduction in price has been due in large measure to the substitution of cheap pyrites ore, or sulphuret or iron, for Sicily brimstone as the raw material.

Outside of the chemical trade sulphuric acid is directly essential to the prosecution of many industries. Its greatest use is in the manufacture of fertilizers for farming operations. It is equally essential in the refining of oil, in the making of smokeless powder and of dynamite. It is consequently almost directly essential to all forms of mining operations and railroad construction work. The tin-plate industry is dependent upon it, as is that of steel and wire, and so is it with the textile industries. Analysis will show that there are few articles of manufacture in the production of which sulphuric acid has not entered directly or indirectly at some stage of the operation. So great an authority as Humboldt has said that the best measure of the degree of civilization of any country is the extent of its use of sulphuric acid. The present development of the chemical industry is regarded by those who should know as but the beginning of the capabilities of that industry. New products of chemical manufacture are developing continually; the possibilities of such in the future are limited only by human ingenuity and the cost of producing. A country which at this stage of the world's progress should be placed at a disadvantage as regards other countries in the production of sulphuric acid would have no chance whatever in the struggle for industrial supremacy.

For the reasons stated, it would seem that pyrites is more nearly related to the chemical schedule than to the schedule regarding metals now under discussion.

Pyrites is absolutely essential to the cheap production of chemicals; it has almost an infinitesimal bearing upon metals. The total iron contents of all the pyrites ore imported hardly amounts to 1 per cent of the iron ore mined in this country. On the other hand, the sulphur contents of the pyrites so imported constitutes more than 70 per cent of this country's entire consumption of pyrites ore. The United States is incapable at the present time of supplying this raw material from its own resources.

The success and the continued development of the chemical industry are dependent upon having this principal raw material free.

Free raw materials are the more necessary to the chemical industry because of the small measure of protection afforded to its products by the present tariff. A glance at the present tariff will show that about 2,148 articles are treated therein. Of these some 1,692 are protected by duties, while some 456 is the total number on the free list. The chemical schedule is composed of about 288 articles, of which about 138 are on the free list. Thus the chemical schedule, furnishing but 13½ per cent of the total number of articles treated, furnishes to the free list nearly 30 per cent of its subject-matter. In other words, there are proportionately more than twice as many chemical articles on the free list as there are of articles from the other schedules. To the extent that this great discrimination against the chemical industry has tended to injure that industry, the injury has been partly offset in the past by the placing on the free list of several of its important raw materials, more particularly the article here in question. If sulphuret of iron is now to be placed upon the dutiable list, the whole subject of the chemical schedules will have to be revised from that point of view, and in order to do justice a very considerable duty will have to be placed upon almost every article now free. Not only so, but the duties of the dutiable list will have to be raised, for the degree of protection accorded to the chemical articles that are protected is much inferior to that given as the average of the other schedules. Such a course would inevitably enhance the price of sulphuric acid and of all other chemicals made by the undersigned and other chemical manufacturers. It would increase the cost of all articles in which sulphuric acid enters largely. It would in particular raise the price of fertilizers and the cost of farming operations. It would tend to check the expansion of the chemical industry.

The artificial encouragement by means of a protective tariff of the mining of pyrites in this country would mean a step backward in the policy of conserving the national resources.

It would tend to cause our own meager supplies of pyrites to be exhausted long before their time. It is doubtless good policy to encourage the use of our own natural resources where these are of vast extent, but it can not be wise, in the interest of the nation as a whole, to stimulate such consumption to a premature exhaustion where the natural supplies are meager. The General Chemical Company is able to look at this question in a disinterested way, since it not only imports but mines large quantities of the ores in question. We do not believe that it is good policy for us to exhaust rapidly our reserve supplies of these ores when we can get a large part of such supplies at reasonable prices from foreign countries. We submit that what is a wise policy for the conservation of natural resources for us in our smaller affairs would be an equally wise policy for the nation in its larger affairs.

The business of the General Chemical Company is more particularly that of heavy chemicals, such as sulphuric acid in its various forms, muriatic acid, nitric acid, acetic acid, sulphate of soda, alums, sulphate of alumina, phosphate of soda, and the like—articles of great bulk and selling at low prices, from a fraction of a cent to a few cents a pound, and all entering as constituents into the manufacture of other articles. The company has a list of several thousand customers on its books. Its principal interest in the contemplated revision of the tariff is that such a revision may be had as will conduce to the prosperity of these customers; and whether their prosperity shall require a higher or a lower tariff in particular cases, the General Chemical Company knows that it can not conduce to the prosperity of manufacturers if sellers of acid should be compelled to raise the price of sulphuric .acid by reason of a duty imposed on pyrites or other raw material.

SCHEDULE A.—*Production, imports, and consumption of pyrites in the United States.*

[In tons of 2,240 pounds.]

	Production.	Imports.	Consumption.
1903	199,387	425,989	625,376
1904	173,221	413,333	586,806
1905	224,980	515,722	740,702
1906	225,043	597,347	822,302
1907	261,871	656,477	918,348

NOTE.—The foregoing is an extract from " The Mineral Industry during 1907," Volume 16, edited by W. R. Ingalls, page 840.

SCHEDULE B.

The data given in the foregoing statement as to the relative number of articles on the free list and the dutiable list, comparing the tariff schedule generally with the chemical schedule alone, have been taken from a compilation of the Department of Commerce and Labor, Bureau of Statistics, known as ' Schedule E, Classification of Merchandise, with Rates of Duty, etc."

GENERAL CHEMICAL COMPANY,
E. H. RISING, *President.*

——

THE PENNSYLVANIA SALT MANUFACTURING COMPANY., PHILADELPHIA, PA., OBJECTS TO THE PLACING OF A DUTY ON PYRITES ORE OR SULPHURET OF IRON.

PHILADELPHIA, *November 11, 1908.*

Hon. JOHN DALZELL, *Washington, D. C.*

DEAR SIR: There is a report that the domestic producers of pyrites (used for making sulphuric acid) intend asking Congress to impose a duty upon foreign pyrites. Under the Dingley tariff and tariffs prior to 1897 pyrites is on the free list.

It would be an unfortunate occurrence to the sulphuric-acid manufacturers of the United States, and others, if this article should be made dutiable. We beg to submit the following facts showing why it should be continued on the free list.

The present annual production of sulphuric acid in the United States is about 3,500,000 tons. It is produced from pyrites, sulphur, zinc ore, and copper ore—from the two latter, because of the quantity of sulphur contained therein injuring farms nearby, it resolved itself into a question of stopping the smelting of ores or erecting acid works to utilize the escaping gases.

The quantity of foreign pyrites imported in the United States in 1907 was 700,000 short tons, averaging over 50 per cent sulphur. The quantity of domestic pyrites produced was 247,000 tons, averaging about 43 per cent sulphur.

The quantity of sulphuric acid, 50° Beaumé, produced from the above pyrites was about 2,150,000 short tons, the balance amounting to 1,350,000 tons, being made mostly from the sulphur in zinc and copper ores, the quantity of acid made from sulphur, pure, being comparatively small. The value of the acid produced is about $18,000,000 at factory.

The quality of foreign pyrites, particularly the Spanish, is much superior to any domestic pyrites thus far discovered. The market price is about $6 per ton for material containing 50 per cent sulphur, whereas the price of the domestic article is only $4.50 per ton for material containing 43 per cent sulphur.

The mines in the United States are meager, and from what we know it would be a physical impossibility for them to supply the .needs of all the acid makers in the country. If they could supply more than stated above, viz, 247,000 out of a total consumption of 947,000 tons, they would have sufficient margin between $4.50 per ton for domestic ore and $6 for foreign, to pay handsomely.

The low price now ruling for sulphuric acid in the United States is due principally to the use of the fine quality of Spanish ore, which unquestionably is without a rival. To put a duty upon it would mean a corresponding increase in the price of acid, which would affect pretty much everything in the arts, since sulphuric acid is such an important factor in the majority of other manufactures. It enters into the composition or is used in almost every textile and metallic article made, besides being directly the base of the paper, glass, soap, and fertilizer trade.

Trusting, sir, that pyrites containing sulphur, suitable for the manufacture of sulphuric acid, will remain on the free list, and asking your attention to the exhaustive discussions on the subject before the Ways and Means Committee during the consideration of the Dingley tariff, and prior thereto, we remain,

Yours, very truly,

PENNSYLVANIA SALT MANUFACTURING COMPANY,
THEODORE ARMSTRONG, *President.*

STATEMENT OF CHARLES W. LEFLER IN ADVOCACY OF THE RETENTION OF PYRITES ORE ON THE FREE LIST.

FRIDAY, *November 27, 1908.*

Mr. GRIGGS. Are you a manufacturer?

Mr. LEFLER. No; I represent importers. It may be a work of supererogation anyway for me to say anything, because pyrites is now on the free list. We simply want it to remain there. The principal product of pyrites is sulphuric acid, and it is used as a basis for fertilizers. It constitutes the basis of all artificial fertilizers. It is therefore of importance to the farmers, who are a principal element in the country.

The CHAIRMAN. Have you a brief there?

Mr. LEFLER. No; I have not.

The CHAIRMAN. That comes in with chemicals used for the purpose of fertilizers, and it is free, is it not?

Mr. LEFLER. Yes.

The CHAIRMAN. Nobody is asking for a duty on it. No one has appeared before the committee for that purpose.

Mr. CLARK. Yes; they did. There was a man here from Missouri the first two days of the hearings on that.

Mr. BONYNGE. What paragraph do you come under?

Mr. LEFLER. This is now on the free list.

Mr. CLARK. What is this stuff you are talking about?

Mr. LEFLER. Pyrites.

Mr. CLARK. What is it?

Mr. LEFLER. The common name is " fool's gold."

The CHAIRMAN. It is sulphur ore, is it not?

Mr. LEFLER. Yes; it is commonly called " fool's gold." It looks like gold. It is this stuff that you see in your coal.

The CHAIRMAN. Nobody is asking for a duty on it.

Mr. LEFLER. I understood there had been or might be.

The CHAIRMAN. I will tell you what we will do. If anybody appears or files a brief on that, we will send you a copy and give you time to reply.

Mr. LEFLER. How much time will I have to reply?

The CHAIRMAN. We will give you plenty of time to reply to it.

Mr. LEFLER. Very well. Thank you.

THE GRASSELLI CHEMICAL COMPANY, CLEVELAND, OHIO, URGES THAT PYRITES ORE BE LEFT ON FREE LIST.

CLEVELAND, OHIO, *December 1, 1908.*

Hon. SERENO E. PAYNE, M. C.,
Chairman of the Ways and Means Committee,
House of Representatives, Washington, D. C.

DEAR SIR: Prior to the passage of the act of 1890 sulphur ore as pyrites or sulphuret of iron in its natural state, was dutiable at 75 cents per ton. In 1890 the McKinley Act placed this raw material on the free list after full consideration.

We are a corporation under the laws of the State of Ohio, and have manufacturing plants consuming large quantities of iron pyrites, to which this question is probably of as much importance as to any other single concern in the United States.

There is no existing available supply of sulphur ore as pyrites or sulphuret of iron in this country to supply the demand of the consumers. We have endeavored to secure in this country the needs of our business and have failed.

The only existing available deposits are limited in quantity and comparatively poor in quality. The extent of the deposits will not supply the needs of the sulphuric acid manufacturers of the United States. It is impossible for the manufacturers of sulphuric acid, including those who manufacture it exclusively for fertilizers, to secure in this country what is necessary to supply the aggregate needs, to say nothing of the future growth of the trade.

We respectfully refer you to volume 16 of the Metal Industry, 1907, page 840, in which it is shown that the domestic production and the consumption have made it necessary in 1907 to import the large amount of 656,477 tons to enable the domestic consumer to supply the demand.

Production, imports, and consumption of pyrite in the United States.[a]

[In tons of 2,240 pounds.]

Year.	Production.	Imports.	Consumption.
1897	133,368	259,546	392,914
1898	191,160	171,879	363,039
1899	178,408	310,008	488,416
1900	201,317	322,484	523,801
1901	234,825	403,706	638,531
1902	228,198	440,363	668,561
1903	199,387	425,989	625,376
1904	173,221	413,585	586,806
1905	224,980	515,722	740,702
1906	225,045	597,347	822,392
1907	261,871	656,477	918,348

[a] These statistics do not include the auriferous pyrite used for the manufacture of sulphuric acid in Colorado.

We therefore protest earnestly against any change in the position of sulphur ore as pyrites, or sulphuret of iron in its natural state. There is not known to the trade to-day any supply of ore in this country of this class adequate to the needs of the trade, and the limited deposits of the domestic mines are so uncertain in extent and quality that the business interests using this ore could not predicate thereon with any certainty their supply for even a brief period.

The many industries in this country which have to depend upon sulphuric acid for the success of their operations would be made to suffer unnecessary hardships in the nature of tribute which they would have to pay to take care of the imposed duty which the manufacturer of sulphuric acid can not absorb on account of the small margin of profit which now exists. A brief review of the industries affected include practically all the great and many small interests of the country. The agricultural interests would be vitally affected on account of a heavier tax for the fertilizer which it must use. The development of scientific fertilization, which has as its main theme the greater and freer use of fertilizer, would receive a setback on account of the farmers' inability to buy the higher-priced product, which will prevent the freer use of these commodities which are so necessary to the prosperity of the farmer.

It is hardly necessary to call the attention of your committee to the great importance of fertilizer to the farmer, but as a matter of information, fertilizers used have as their basis acid phosphate, of which 50 per cent is sulphuric acid.

The steel business is dependent for its successful operation largely upon sulphuric acid to perform the important details of the various processes in the manufacture of tin plate, wire, nails, tacks, tubing, sheet iron, etc.

The steel entering into all of the above products must first be properly cleansed and treated with sulphuric acid to fit it for the later operations in the process.

Sulphuric acid enters as an important factor in the refining of oils for various purposes; also in the manufacture of dynamite and nitroglycerin, which have such an important bearing upon the development of the various industries of our country, particularly mining, and directly and indirectly upon the tanning of leather, the manufacture of wall paper, soaps, glass, sugar, and glucose, and almost every textile article.

It has been well said that from the shoes of one's feet to the hat on his head sulphuric acid, directly or indirectly, contributes to the manufacture of every article of clothing worn. Furthermore, sulphuric acid is the basic acid from which nearly all other acids are produced.

It therefore seems clear to us that the committee and Congress should leave sulphur ore as pyrites, or sulphuret of iron, where the McKinley Act of 1890 and the Wilson Act of 1894 and the Dingley Act of 1897 placed it—on the free list.

Respectfully submitted.

THE GRASSELLI CHEMICAL COMPANY,
By C. A. GRASSELLI, *President.*

JOSEPH B. CARPER, WEST MILAN, N. H., THINKS A PROTECTIVE DUTY SHOULD BE PLACED ON PYRITES ORE.

WEST MILAN, N. H., *December 1, 1908.*

We ask 25 per cent ad valorem duty to be placed on imported pyrites ore, for the following reasons:

First. The pyrites mines in the eastern part of the United States can not possibly compete with Rio-Tinto Spanish ore, which is delivered on board cars at any eastern seaport at 8 cents per unit.

Second. The imported pyrites is of poorer quality than domestic United States pyrites—that it contains a larger percentage of arsenic dust, etc.

Third. Labor: The miners in the eastern United States pyrites mines get $3.25 to $3.50 per diem. In Rio-Tinto Spain, $1.50 to $2 per diem.

Fourth. If the pyrites mines now in operation had to rely solely upon the pyrites contents of their ores for revenue they would have to go out of business (as dozens of other pyrites mines have done, due to foreign competition cutting the price from 16–18 cents per unit down to 8 cents).

Fifth. There are enough pyrites deposits in the country to fill all the demand now usurped by the imported pyrites, and easily, fostered by a duty which means immense revenue to the Government on Rio-Tinto pyrites which are all pure profit to the importers, as they are waste-dump products accumulated during thirty-five to forty years' operations of the Rio-Tinto mines as a copper property.

JOSEPH B. CARPER, B. S. E. M.

THE DAVIS SULPHUR ORE COMPANY, NEW YORK CITY, OBJECTS TO THE PLACING OF DUTY ON PYRITES ORE.

NEW YORK CITY, *December 31, 1908.*

Hon. SERENO E. PAYNE,
Chairman Committee on Ways and Means,
Washington, D. C.

DEAR SIR: Our attention has been called to a letter sent to your honorable committee asking you to impose a duty upon sulphuret of iron or pyrites ore. This letter contains so many misleading statements that we wish to correct them. We maintain that there are several very cogent reasons why no duty should be imposed upon this ore, the most important being that it is in the interest of the public. There is no duty upon it now, and we assert very forcibly that there should be none.

While it is in the interest of every person in the country, either directly or indirectly, that pyrites remain upon the free list, the number of persons who would profit by the imposition of a duty could almost be counted on the fingers of one hand. The statement contained in this letter that "there are enough pyrites deposits in the country to fill all the demand now usurped by the imported pyrites" can not be sustained by proof. In truth, it is absolutely impossible for the demand of this country to be supplied by the domestic mines. There has been diligent prospecting in the United States for the last twenty-five years, and the result has been the development of only three or four mines of any consequence; such mines can be operated without tariff protection. We have been profitably operating pyrites mines in Massachusetts for the last twenty-seven years, and have no need of tariff protection. While we believe in the protective tariff, we maintain that it is almost a self-evident truth that an industry that must be artificially supported under those circumstances, and that, too, at the expense of almost all of the people of this country, is unworthy of encouragement and support by tariff protection. The domestic output at the present time is worth from $500,000 to $600,000 at the mines, while the imported product is worth from three and one-half million to four million dollars, and substantially all of this comes from Spain. A very small production comes from Canada. Although, therefore, the "revenue to the Government" might be "immense," as the letter states, yet it would be so simply because it would be a heavy tax on the great body of the people for the benefit of the few mentioned. It would be a work of supererogation to occupy space in explaining to the members of your honorable committee that the additional cost due to the imposition of a duty would inevitably be shifted to the ultimate consumer.

We shall now explain why it is of such universal interest that no tax be imposed. Pyrites is used for the production of sulphuric acid, which, together with phosphate rock, each composing three-tenths, form a mixture which is used as a basis for all artificial fertilizers. The great and increasing value of and necessity for fertilizers by that most important element of the community, the farmer, is too manifest to require demonstration. From 60 to 70 p cent of all sulphuric acid produced is used in the manufacture of fertilizers and the remainder of all sulphuric acid made is used in the manufacture of other articles of commerce consumed by the people at large.

Moreover, all of the pyrites ore imported is treated and converted into sulphuric acid in this country, and this gives employment to American labor. Even as to the wages paid for mining the ore, the letter referred to does not correctly state the facts. Miners of pyrites in the United States receive from $1.75 to $2.25 per diem instead of from $3.25 to $3.50 per diem.

As to the market price for domestic ore, the writer of the letter quoted from above is also in error, for the usual market price in the United States for years past has been and now is 9 to 11 cents per unit at mines instead of 16 cents to 18 cents per unit. It has been sold only in exceptional instances at higher prices. And as to the price of imported fine ore, the writer is again mistaken. The market price is 9 cents per unit and not 8 cents, and that, too, for only about 10 per cent of the quantity imported; 90 per cent of the imported product is lump ore and is sold at from 12½ cents to 13 cents per unit, ex ship. Moreover, it is not true, as asserted in the same letter, that the foreign pyrites is inferior to that of the United States. Indeed, the imported article is superior to the domestic in that it contains more sulphur than the latter, and sulphur is the valuable constituent.

Another unfair effect of the imposition of a duty would be to the importers. We are importers from Spain as well as domestic producers, although we have larger investments in the pyrites business in the United States than we have in Spain. The importers would not only have the volume of their business diminished, but would also suffer heavy losses because of their having many contracts to supply imported pyrites, which do not expire until from three to five years hence. These contracts, of course, were entered into upon the basis of no tax.

It must therefore be evident that any duty imposed would be in the interest solely of an insignificant few and at the expense of the great mass of American people.

Respectfully submitted.

DAVIS SULPHUR ORE COMPANY,
By CHARLES B. STRANAHAN,
President.

IRON ORE AND PIG IRON.

[Paragraphs 121 and 122.]

THE EMPIRE STEEL AND IRON COMPANY, CATASAUQUA, PA., WRITES RELATIVE TO IRON ORE AND PIG IRON.

CATASAUQUA, PA., *December 19, 1908.*
COMMITTEE ON WAYS AND MEANS,
Washington, D. C.

GENTLEMEN: Understanding that my friend, Mr. Joseph G. Butler, jr., of Youngstown, Ohio, was to represent the makers of pig iron, both East and West, before your committee, I have up to this time refrained from approaching you direct, although I had the pleasure of being present at the hearing in Washington on the 27th ultimo, when Mr. Butler informed you that he proposed to present a brief for your consideration, embodying the facts as seen from the standpoint of the pig-iron producer relative to the duty on pig iron and iron ore at this time.

I have not as yet had an opportunity of reviewing the brief, which will doubtless clearly outline to your good selves our position in the premises, but can not allow the recent communications on this subject you have received from other sources to pass by without comment on my part, for the statements made, if the reports shown by the trade papers are correct, are so misleading, from our way of thinking, that I feel compelled to encroach on your good nature by giving you my views in answer thereto.

First of all, I wish to touch on the statement made by Messrs. Colne & Co., of New York, who claim that the present duty of $4 per ton should be either considerably lowered or entirely abrogated on what they are pleased to call " silicon iron," claiming that it is practically unprocurable in this country, the product being confined principally in the hands of one house, and that with the duty out of the way a supply sufficient for their needs. could readily be secured from England at a lower price than the American quality, even after the addition of freight charges.

Whilst the latter fact is admitted, I am obliged to disagree with their statement as to the manufacture of the product in America, for the metal is nothing more than ordinary iron, known in the trade as " low phosphorus pig iron," and does not differ in any respect from iron used in our open-hearth acid furnaces excepting in the matter of silicon, which is an element that is controlled entirely in the blast furnace, and can be made high or low to meet the requirements of the trade.

The average requirements in silicon are from 1 per cent to 2 per cent, but we have contracts on our books now calling for the same iron running from 2 per cent to 3 per cent in silicon, which percentage is sufficiently high for the so-called " tropenas converter," a system of melting used by Colne & Co., and which I understand requires iron with silicon from 2.25 per cent upward.

As to one house controlling this low phosphorous iron, I have positive knowledge of 10 concerns having made it for many years past, and the company I represent has made a specialty of this metal since 1885; but although we own and operate 8 blast furnaces, not more than 1 of them has been continuously in operation on this particular metal, because of the failure of the trade to require a sufficient amount to warrant our increasing the output.

If the present duty of $4 is to be reduced more than a maximum of 25 per cent the industry will be killed, and not only does this statement apply to the so-called " silicon iron," but in spite of what others have said on the subject, it will put out of business practically every eastern furnace, for English iron could very profitably be brought in here practically all the time were it not for the duty, although, as I have already stated, a moderate reduction can be made without damaging effect on the American producer.

In a letter to Mr. Butler, under date of November 28, I stated that in order to carry out the party's pledges a revision of the Dingley tariff was surely necessary, and that I saw no reason for cutting out the products of iron and steel and iron ores, if each commodity throughout the entire line was to be fairly dealt with regardless of selfish or personal interests, nor could I, on the other hand, see why iron ore should be placed on the free list, as suggested by some of my colleagues.

As to pig iron, I felt in the beginning that a 25 per cent reduction could be made without any harm to the producer, either East or West, but after going considerably deeper into the question I now think 25 per cent would perhaps be more than the industry as a whole could stand at this time, and therefore recommend not over 10 per cent, or, say, 40 cents a ton, thereby fixing the new schedule at $3.60.

For iron ore, 2 tons of which are required for a ton of pig, I suggest 10 cents per ton, or 30 cents, instead of 40 cents, as provided in the Dingley tariff.

It is of course easy to see why some of my near-by competitors, whose investments in iron-ore properties are altogether in Cuba, whilst urging the retention of the duty on finished products of iron and steel, favor free ore, but having during the last three or four years spent a half a million dollars in the development of iron ore properties in the State of New Jersey, thereby aiding American labor to a greater extent than would have been the case had we resorted to Cuba for our needs, I hardly think it would be fair to make ore free at one stroke, preferring a gradual reduction in all these products over a series of years, otherwise labor will be severely dealt with before our business can be made to compete with the foreign situation.

The next quotations I refer to are those of Mr. Frank Samuel and Major Ennis, of Philadelphia, neither of them producers, but both importers, and apparently looking entirely at the mercantile end, for their branch of the industry would certainly be benefited by anything that you can do to enable them to import foreign material at a price that will undersell the American manufacture at home.

These remarks are certainly not intended to reflect any selfish interest or throw discredit anywhere, but they are made by one who has spent the last fifteen years of his life in attempting to build up a business in such a way as to warrant a fair return to the investor, but which, since the formation of the company (the Empire Company) some ten years ago, has not enabled me to pay more than an average of, say, 6 per cent to those who put in their money at the start, and in making this statement I feel that only the closest attention to the business has enabled us to make any returns, and that a reduction of over $1 on pig iron at this time would force us to close down every plant we control before the end of the year.

In conclusion, you will please understand that our business is purely that of the mining of iron ore and manufacture of pig iron, our maximum capacity of pig being approximately 26,000 tons monthly, all of which is sold in the open market before going through any further stages of refinement.

This is the situation as seen from our standpoint, and apologizing for having encroached on your time to any such degree, I am,

Yours, respectfully,

LEONARD PECKITT, *President.*

IRON ORE, PIG IRON, AND INGOTS.

[Paragraphs 121, 122, and 135.]

FRANK SAMUEL, PHILADELPHIA, CLAIMS THAT MANUFACTURERS OF IRON AND STEEL PRODUCTS NEED NO PROTECTION.

PHILADELPHIA, PA., *November 19, 1908.*

Hon. SERENO E. PAYNE,
Chairman Committee on Ways and Means,
Washington, D. C.

DEAR SIR: The undersigned respectfully submits to your committee the following brief. Being impossible to treat such an extensive subject as the metal schedule of the Dingley tariff bill at such short notice, he will confine himself entirely to presenting to your committee the subjects as covered by clauses No. 121, iron ore and manganiferous iron ore, etc.; No. 122, iron in pigs, iron kentledge, spiegeleisen, ferromanganese, ferrosilicon, wrought and cast scrap iron, and scrap steel, etc.; No. 135, steel ingots, cogged ingots, blooms, slabs, etc. The articles in clauses named are used as a basis of cost for all iron and steel manufactured products.

The importation of iron ore to the United States, paying a duty of 40 cents per ton for the year 1906, was 1,060,390 tons, and for 1907 1,229,168 tons. Of the tonnage specified 639,362 tons were shipped from Cuba in 1906 and 657,133 tons in 1907. The production of iron ore during the same period in America was 47,749,728 tons in 1906 and 51,720,619 tons in 1907. The greater part of ore imported was for special purposes, for which the American ore could not be used, and a further tonnage of the ore was again exported in finished material, for which the manufacturer received in return the 99 per cent duty. The revenue derived by the United States for the importation of ore is, consequently, a small factor. The prices of American lake ores, which regulated the prices of other ores in the United States, were as follows:

Standard Bessemer ore f. o. b. lake ports: Average price for six years 1894–1899, $2.48; price 1900, $4.50; average price for six years 1901–1906, $3.51; price 1907, $4.75; price 1908, $4.75:

It will be seen that due to various causes the price of American ore has almost doubled in the last ten years. It is a well-established fact that the cost of labor per ton on lake ores in the past ten years has been most materially decreased, due to the improved methods of mining, and the increase in cost has been entirely due to increased capitalization and the increased royalties paid to the ore properties and increased cost of rail transportation. Consequently, 40 cents per ton to-day, charged to the ore user, is merely a tax in the making of pig iron to such furnaces as find it necessary to buy this mineral, due to their special requirements. Labor is not benefited or the revenue of the country materially increased.

Manganese ore.—According to the schedule, manganese ore is on the free list at the present time.

Schedule No. 122.—Iron in pigs, iron kentledge, spiegeleisen, ferromanganese, ferrosilicon, wrought and cast scrap iron, and steel scrap, $4 per ton duty. This duty has been in effect since 1894.

during which time the price of pig iron has made wide fluctuations. Taking the ordinary making of pig iron, it requires 2 tons of ore to 1 ton of pig, or where foreign ore is used, the difference in the blast furnace in using foreign ore would be in the neighborhood of 80 cents per ton. The present duty on pig iron is $4 per ton. If all foreign ore was used in making a ton of pig iron, the duty would be 80 cents. The maker is, therefore, protected against the importation of foreign pig to the extent of $3.20. One dollar and fifty cents per ton for labor more than covers the cost taken by blast furnaces; consequently the duty on pig iron is excessive, even on the basis of the present duty on ore. If your committee would consider favorably the appeal for a reduction of $2 per ton on the duty of pig iron, it would not only give the blast furnaces ample protection for their labor, but would materially aid the users of pig iron, and not only prevent exorbitant profits being made by the makers of iron, but would prevent the wide fluctuations that have at times taken place, due to unnecessary protection given to the manufacturers by an unnecessary duty. Scrap iron and steel scrap, under clause No. 122, takes a duty of $4 per ton. There can be no argument given either as to the labor on scrap iron or the revenue derived from the maintenance of this tariff or for the continuance of same.

Ferromanganese.—While this is included in the schedule, taking duty of $4 per ton, manganese ore, from which it is produced, is on the free list, due to the fact that there is an insufficient supply of manganese ore found in this country, and while manganese ore was originally placed on the free list with the purpose of inducing manufacturers to enter into the production of ferromanganese, there is at present practically but one maker of ferromanganese in this country, and there has been practically no increase in the tonnage produced for some time past. The importation of ferromanganese for the year 1906 was 84,359 tons, and for the year 1907, 87,400 tons, and, inasmuch as every maker of steel is compelled to use a percentage of ferromanganese, there is every indication that the importations of this material will increase materially in the coming years. Inasmuch as the giving of free ore has not induced the manufacture of this material here, and inasmuch as every steel works is using same, there would not appear to be any further necessity for the duty on this material. There would not only be the direct benefit to every steel manufacturer, but no injury done to any material interest in this country by giving the users free ferromanganese.

Clause No. 135.—Steel ingots, cog ingots, blooms, etc. As the duties covering the articles under this heading are most complex, and inasmuch as the framers of the Dingley tariff found the necessity of making the duty specific as well as ad valorem, according to the character and price of the material to be imported, and inasmuch as every article in finished steel, excepting cast steel, is at one time or another in the shape of a billet or ingot, the duty to be charged on same must be considered from the objects manufactured from the dutiable article. As a general principle, however, free ore and free pig iron, or $2 per ton duty on pig iron, would be a material aid to the manufacturer of steel, and a corresponding reduction of the duty should be made on billet to conform to the reduction of duty above stated. The base duty at present existing being three-ths of 1 cent per pound, or $6.72 per gross ton, and inasmuch as the loss in the use of pig iron in the open-hearth furnace is only about 5 per cent, the present duty on billets is excessive and should hardly be more than the duty on pig iron. The actual cost of labor per ton on billets in this country, due to our improved machinery and methods, would not exceed the average cost of labor per ton in the English mills. Evidence of this fact can be produced before your committee if you so desire.

The importation of billets in 1906 was 21,300 tons, and in 1907, 19,334 tons. Our export of billets during the same period was, in 1906, 192,618 tons, and 79,931 tons in 1907. In other words, for the actual protection of the manufacturers no duty at all would be required. The billets, however, that were imported to this country were probably of special quality not produced here, no billets being imported of the quality exported. The export of billets in itself, even with the duties of pig iron and ore, is evidence that, as far as the protection of manufacturers is concerned, or labor interests, there is no need of the duty in question. On the other hand, with the materials asked for the exportation of the articles named would be further aided.

Additional evidence that manufacturers of iron and steel products need no further protection to enable them to give their labor the highest and best returns is in the fact that in publishing reports of the largest maker in this country—and, in fact, in the world—of pig iron and billets is that during the period of the existence of this corporation they have made an average profit over a period of five years of $14 per gross ton, and in their published report of the last three months' operations, where they produced on an average of 60 per cent of their capacity, their averaged profits were in the neighborhood of $12 per ton.

FRANK SAMUEL,
Philadelphia.

IRON ORE, PIG IRON, AND COKE.

[Paragraphs 121, 122, and 415.]

THE UNITED METAL TRADES ASSOCIATION, PORTLAND, OREG., WANTS THESE ARTICLES DUTY FREE.

319 PIONEER BUILDING,
Portland, Oreg., January 5, 1909.

WAYS AND MEANS COMMITTEE,
Washington, D. C.

GENTLEMEN: We have wired you as follows:

Entire Pacific coast interests want duty on pig iron, iron ore, and coke removed. Letter follows.

UNITED METAL TRADES ASSOCIATION OF OREGON.

If there is to be a revision of tariff, the above articles surely should be considered with a great deal of care, and we, representing the manufacturing industries of the State of Oregon, recommend that the duty be taken off of the above.

Would say that pig iron is to the manufacturing industries of this country what wheat is to the people—an actual necessity. No subjects of your revision need more attention. One of the reasons other than those as suggested in the resolutions forwarded you is that under the present duty when business is prosperous the producer raises his price to any named market value he so desires. The foreign market has no influence on him until he gets to a certain very high price. Then it is possible to land foreign iron here which can be sold here.

Germany quotes pig iron as follows: Best hematite, $14.25.

Birmingham, England, quotes pig iron: Best English and Scotch, $12.01.

Same quality is being sold in New York at from $17.25 to $17.75. You have testimony there that pig iron can be produced in this country as cheap as anywhere in the world. Is it not plain the injustice the manufacturer bears under the present duty regulation? Let in the foreign iron and keep the price where it should be, a reasonable profit to the furnace man, that the manufacturing industries can reproduce the pig iron into a manufactured article that can be sold and compete in foreign trade, where at the present time this is impossible.

We shall await, with a great deal of anxiety, your action on this subject.

Yours, very truly,

UNITED METAL TRADES ASSOCIATION OF OREGON,
By O. E. HEINTZ, *Chairman.*

PORTLAND, OREG., *January 2, 1900.*

To the CHAMBER OF COMMERCE,
Portland, Oreg.

GENTLEMEN: Mr. A. S. Patullo, secretary of the Oregon Iron and Steel Company, this city, has handed this office your correspondence regarding the above subject.

Consistent with your suggestion we are herewith submitting resolutions accepted and adopted by the Oregon district membership of the United Metal Trades Association.

Might say that this association consists of about 100 concerns using directly in furnaces or indirectly by machining or structural about 50,000 tons of pig iron annually. This does not include an even larger tonnage of scrap iron, which amount would be decreased and more pig iron used if it could be purchased at a reasonable figure.

The coast States being so far away from the supply of the domestic pig iron, iron ore, and coke, the high freight rates make the use of it prohibitive, much to our chagrin. We are thus obliged to depend upon foreign pig iron and coke for our use here.

We are requesting your honorable board to assist, encourage, and in every way possible to further the interests contained in the resolutions which follow:

Be it resolved, That we [Chamber of Commerce], representing manufacturers of materials produced from pig iron and coke, would urge upon the Ways and Means Committee, now sitting at Washington, to report to Congress recommending the removal of the present tariff on pig iron, iron ore, and coke.

Resolved, That it is our belief if the duties on these articles were taken off, the Pacific coast States could and would produce thousands of tons of iron and steel materials for domestic use which now have to be produced at the cost of high freight rates from other parts of this country and the world; also that the Pacific coast States would ship large quantities of these materials to South America, Africa, Australia, China, Japan, and other oriental countries which are at present supplied by Germany, France, and Great Britain.

Resolved, That if said duties were taken off it is a foregone conclusion that many large eastern manufacturing concerns doing business on the Pacific coast would put in factories on the coast, in this way saving the present high freight rate from the East and enabling them to compete in the foreign trade with the countries bordering on the Pacific Ocean, with which they are now not able to compete successfully.

Resolved, That the importance of this production is far-reaching and would have its effect upon other industries in this country. At the present time many ships are chartered abroad, with no cargo destined here, to come to this country to get wheat, hay, oats, barley, and other agricultural products, lumber, and manufactured articles. Many of these vessels come to the Pacific coast in ballast with sand, and the ship is to the expense of unloading same, which is of no monetary value, only to be used to increase our dockage space. Should this duty be removed, a ballast of pig iron, iron ore, or coke could be brought here, decreasing the charter price of the vessel to our foreign purchaser and raising the price of our farm, lumber, and manufactured products of the American producer.

Be it further resolved, That copies of this communication be forwarded to each Congressman and Senator from the coast States, and thus urging upon them the great necessity for immediate and energetic action to further our request,

Beg to remain,

Yours, very truly,   UNITED METAL TRADES ASSOCIATION,
Oregon District.

THE FOUNDERS AND EMPLOYERS' ASSOCIATION, LOS ANGELES, CAL., WANT FREE PIG IRON, ORE, AND COKE.

233 BRYSON BUILDING,
Los Angeles, Cal., January 6, 1909.

The WAYS AND MEANS COMMITTEE,
Washington, D. C.

GENTLEMEN: The Founders and Employers' Association of Los Angeles, Cal., held their annual meeting last evening, when the following was unanimously voted, viz:

Resolved, That it is our belief that if the duties were taken off of iron ore, pig iron, and coke, the Pacific Coast States could and would produce thousands of tons of iron and steel materials for domestic use which now have to be procured at the cost of high freight rates from other parts of this country and the world; also, that the Pacific Coast States would ship large quantities of these materials to South America, Africa, Australia, China, Japan, and other oriental countries, which are at present supplied by Germany, France, and Great Britain.

Resolved, That if said duties were taken off it is a foregone conclusion that many large eastern manufacturing concerns doing business on the Pacific coast would put in factories on the coast, in this way saving the present high freight rates from the East and enabling them to compete in the foreign trade with the countries bordering on the Pacific Ocean, with which they are now not able to compete successfully.

Resolved, That the importance of this reduction is far-reaching and would have its effect upon other industries in this countries. At the present time many ships are chartered abroad, with no cargo destined here, to come to this country and get our wheat, hay, oats, cotton, and other agricultural products, lumber, and manufactured articles.

Many of these vessels come to the Pacific coast in ballast with sand, and the ship is to the expense of unloading same, which is of no monetary value, only to be used to increase our dockage space. Should this duty be removed a ballast of pig iron, iron ore, or coke could be brought here, thus decreasing the charter price of the ve to our foreign purchaser and raising the price of our farm, lumber, and manufactured products to the American producer.

We trust that your honorable body will see the importance of this matter and endeavor to give this coast the necessary relief.

Yours, very respectfully,

THE FOUNDERS AND EMPLOYERS' ASSOCIATION,
Per WM. B. HOSWELL, *Secretary*,

IRON ORE, LUMBER, AND COAL.

[Paragraphs 121, 194, 195, and 415.]

JOHN W. GATES, NEW YORK CITY, THINKS THE DUTY ON STEEL PRODUCTS CAN BE CUT IN HALF.

Port Arthur, Tex., December 26, 1908.
NEW YORK OFFICE, TRINITY BUILDING.

Hon. Jos. G. CANNON,
Speaker House of Representatives,
Washington, D. C.

SIR: I notice a great deal of evidence is being taken on tariff matters in Washington.

It seems to me there are three articles that ought to be put on the free list—iron ore, coal, and lumber.

I have a large portion of my fortune in steel business, but I say this to you conscientiously and candidly. A cut of 50 per cent in the schedule would not hurt the manufacturers of iron and steel a particle.

Yours, truly,

J. W. GATES.

THE NATIONAL GRANGE FILES RESOLUTIONS RELATIVE TO FREE IRON ORE, LUMBER, AND COAL.

WASHINGTON, D. C., *November 20, 1908.*

Hon. SERENO. E. PAYNE,
Chairman Ways and Means Committee, Washington, D. C.

MY DEAR SIR: I have the honor to present to you the position of the National Grange on the revision of the tariff, and request that it be read before your committee and placed on record.

I am, yours, truly,

C. M. FREEMAN,
Secretary of the National Grange P. of H.

WASHINGTON, D. C., *November 18, 1908.*

Whereas the incoming National Government administration is pledged to a revision of tariff schedules; and

Whereas the position of the Grange upon tariff regulations has been and now is, that whatever the policy of existing Government may be, the farmers of the United States demand that so far as possible such measure of direct benefit therefrom as is given to manufacturers or any other of the important industries of the country shall also be accorded to agriculture; and

Whereas, that in line with the recommendation of the master of the National Grange, at a so-called trust conference held in Chicago, in October, 1907, a special commission has been appointed by Congress and is now in the city of Washington, D. C., and is giving hearings to the various industrial interests; and

Whereas the National Grange is looked to by all members of the order and farmers throughout the whole country to be at all times alert in the interests of agriculture: Therefore

Resolved, That it now becomes the duty of the National Grange to follow up its policies and declarations, and to now give its best thought and efforts to this most vital question before the nation.

Further resolved, That, as a present declaration upon the tariff and some of its hearings upon agriculture, we affirm the following:

First. That from the natural conditions many agricultural products are produced in surplus quantities and are not benefited in price to the extent of import duties placed upon them as manufactured products are benefited. We believe it to be the duty of the Government to protect agriculture from such unjust burdens as are placed upon it by the exactions of combinations and so-called "trusts," made possible by the double advantage given them by excessive duties and rebates of duties paid on raw material used in manufactured articles exported.

Second. We believe the duty upon any article should be, and never exceed, the difference in cost of labor in this country and in foreign countries in the production of such articles.

Third. We believe that the product of the forest, coal, and iron ore should be placed in the undutiable list. We believe this would give great relief to agriculture and be an aid in conserving the natural resources of our country. Such conservation is and will be of immense benefit to the entire country.

We hereby request and instruct the legislative committee of the National Grange to present and urge upon the special tariff commission now in session in the city of Washington, D. C., the position of this widespread farmers' organization on the tariff, and also to cause a copy thereof to be placed on the desk of every Member of Congress and use all honorable means to have agriculture receive equal advantage with other industrial interests in the revised tariff legislation promised by the incoming administration.

PIG IRON.

[Paragraph 122.]

STATEMENT OF J. N. M. SHIMER, REPRESENTING THE DUNBAR FURNACE COMPANY, OF PHILADELPHIA, PA.

WEDNESDAY, *November 25, 1908.*

Mr. SHIMER. Mr. Chairman and gentlemen of the committee, I represent the oldest furnace and the first furnace to make pig iron in the United States west of the Allegheny Mountains.

Mr. DALZELL. Where is that?

Mr. SHIMER. At Dunbar, Pa. At the time of the last change in the tariff under the Dingley Act I represented the Eastern Pig Iron Association. I said at that time, with regard to the duty of $4 a ton that was imposed under great opposition by the pig-iron people under the Wilson bill, that we ought to have more protection at that time, because really $4 a ton protection does less under the Dingley Act than it did under the Wilson Act, and that is the case only to a greater extent to-day than it was then. In other words, $4 is less protection to the trade to-day than it was when the Dingley Act was passed for the reason that all ores or practically all ores that came to the furnace for the past fourteen years have been gradually receding in metallic contents, and if you want to protect it, $4 a ton on pig iron, with an ore worth 40 cents a ton duty with less metallic contents than it was before, you would be giving less protection to the manufacturer, and what I wish and what I claim is that we still should have the protection of $4 on pig iron. If parties in Philadelphia, New York, Boston, or Baltimore want to take advantage of the export it is all free to them, excepting the cost of weighing the iron—1 per cent—just as free as it could be if there was no duty on it. Such concerns as R. D. Wood & Co. and the Maryland Steel Company and others situated on the seaboard pay no duty on the iron they manufacture into finished products if they want to ship abroad, and if they do pay it they only pay it temporarily, and they get 99 per cent of it back. If the German Rhine iron, costing to-day or costing last year in the neighborhood of $13.36 per ton f. o. b. on the upper Rhine, and with a German subsidy on the Mercantile Marine which is said to exist of something like a dollar and a half a ton to New York or Philadelphia, making $13.36 plus $1.50, or about $16 plus the duty, put it onto the wharves at Philadelphia—that is, a No. 2 iron—why should we in eastern Pennsylvania be compelled to worry about the importation of pig iron when that is the case? We ought not to be worried with it. We do not make much money on the pig iron that is made—that is, very little profit. It is very soldom that you can make much profit. To-day you can not make a cent. Last year you could not run at a profit; you could run, but you did not know whether you were going to get a profit or not.

Now, I represent about a thousand men. We have been trying to keep them busy all this year by running, and I ask for a retention of the $4 per ton duty on pig iron.

The CHAIRMAN. Do you desire to file a brief?

Mr. SHIMER. I would like——

Mr. CLARK. What is it you want?

Mr. SHIMER. Four dollars a ton retention for pig iron.

Mr. CLARK. I thought you said $44?

Mr. SHIMER. No, sir; I would like to, but I refrain.

Mr. BOUTELL. If we should repeal the duty on iron ore, would that make any difference in the duty?

Mr. SHIMER. It would not change the duty on pig iron. The benefits that have accrued on iron ore and on the iron here have been by the sale of the material out of this country, and we do not want to repeal it if it is used here.

Mr. CLARK. Why do you want the tariff retained on iron ore. I thought you said it ought to be taken off the iron ore?

Mr. SHIMER. Simply because if it starts with iron ore it would affect the pig iron.

Mr. CLARK. Why would it affect the pig iron, or your profits in pig iron?

Mr. SHIMER. I have to buy my ore.

Mr. CLARK. If you buy your ore cheaper you could afford to make pig iron cheaper, could you not?

Mr. SHIMER. No, sir; we would sell it at the same price. We would have to sell it that much cheaper.

Mr. CLARK. Is that not exactly what I asked you, that if you bought your ore cheaper——

Mr. SHIMER. And make the same amount of money, we could sell the iron cheaper.

Mr. CLARK. You mean that you could make your iron cheaper?

Mr. SHIMER. Yes, sir.

Mr. CLARK. And sell it cheaper?

Mr. SHIMER. Yes, sir.

Mr. CLARK. Then what do you want the tariff retained on iron ore for?

Mr. SHIMER. Simply for the benefit of the trade in general it should be retained.

Mr. CLARK. Do you not think you would have plenty to do to look out for your own particular phase of the trade?

Mr. SHIMER. The Pennsylvania iron ores we used up until the discovery of the ore up in the Lakes. We have some 8,000 acres of ore land carrying ore underlaid, 33, 34, and 35 per cent iron that it is impossible to-day to smelt because the cost would be above the German price.

Mr. CLARK. Now, really, when Mr. Boutell asked you if we should take the duty off of iron ore if it would not help you to manufacture the pig iron, you harked back then in your mind to the fact that you also own iron lands?

Mr. SHIMER. Not available at the present time.

Mr. CLARK. I know; but you ought to make them available.

Mr. SHIMER. No, sir; they would not be available with a dollar a ton duty on them.

Mr. CLARK. Then, why do you want the tariff on iron ore kept on, then?

Mr. SHIMER. Because they would be less available if it was taken off.

Mr. CLARK. If they are not available now they could not be less available, could they?

Mr. SHIMER. Yes, sir; by reason of the lowering in percentage of metallic contents quality of the Lake iron and by reason of the point of delivery, Pennsylvania, as against the Lake ores, they may become more available.

Mr. CLARK. Do you not know that the United States Steel Trust is buying up low-grade ores all over the country as reserve stock to be held 20 or 30 or 50 years?

Mr. SHIMER. I do.

Mr. CLARK. Why do they not take your ores then? It is because you will not sell them, is it not?

Mr. Shimer. They are not large enough for them. They want to buy 50,000 acres.

Mr. Clark. You are not arguing for the tariff to be cut down on the steel product or iron ore, are you?

Mr. Shimer. Not the slightest. I do not want anything cut off.

Mr. Clark. How much have you got invested in this business, if I may inquire?

Mr. Shimer. Something like $4,000,000.

Mr. Clark. How long have you been at it?

Mr. Shimer. Something like 35 years.

Mr. Clark. Did you make $4,000,000 out of the iron business?

Mr. Shimer. No, sir.

Mr. Clark. Did you inherit it?

Mr. Shimer. No, sir.

Mr. Clark. Where did you get it?

Mr. Shimer. I made part of it out of farming.

Mr. Clark. I will withdraw that question. Do you know anybody who is farming, who is worth $4,000,000?

Mr. Shimer. No, sir. I am not worth $4,000,000 either.

Mr. Clark. I asked you how much you were worth?

Mr. Shimer. No, sir; I did not so understand you. You asked me how much I had invested; you did not ask me how much I was worth.

Mr. Clark. As a matter of fact do you not know that there is only one farmer in the United States who is worth a million dollars?

Mr. Shimer. One farmer?

Mr. Clark. I say a general farmer worth a million dollars, and he lives in Missouri.

Mr. Shimer. It does not make any difference; I am worth a part of a million dollars, and I have farmed and have made part of a million out of farms.

Mr. Clark. Now how long has it been since you have had $4,000,000 invested?

Mr. Shimer. I think since about in 1872, around there, or 1875.

Mr. Clark. How much profit did it make in 1907?

Mr. Shimer. Something like $150,000.

Mr. Clark. What did you make in 1906?

Mr. Shimer. About the same amount.

Mr. Clark. That was 2½ or 3 per cent, was it not?

Mr. Shimer. About that; it has never paid any dividends.

Mr. Clark. What did you do with the profits that you got out of it?

Mr. Shimer. We bought coal lands.

Mr. Clark. You got coal lands?

Mr. Shimer. Yes, sir.

Mr. Clark. Now, how much profit in a year did you make out of it?

Mr. Shimer. About $150,000 net.

Mr. Clark. That represents the entire profit?

Mr. Shimer. Net profit.

Mr. Clark. On $4,000,000?

Mr. Shimer. On four millions of value.

Mr. Clark. That would be about 3½ per cent, would it not?

Mr. Shimer. Something like that.

Mr. Clark. That is all the iron business pays, is it?

Mr. SHIMER. That is all the independent iron business pays at the present time. When you buy your Lake ore and make your coke it takes every solitary cent that you can possibly save to pay the current present rate of labor and keep running.

Mr. CLARK. And yet you can take money and lend it on first rate real estate security and get 6 per cent?

Mr. SHIMER. Well, you know that interest would go down to 1 per cent if everybody should lend it on first-class security.

Mr. CLARK. I ask you if that is not the case, that you can lend money on first-class real estate security at 6 per cent interest?

Mr. SHIMER. In Oklahoma we can get 8 and 10 per cent.

Mr. CLARK. You can get it in Missouri, and the money is just as safe as if you had it locked up in a vault. Of course I know there is some shylocking in Oklahoma. You can lend it at 12 per cent if you were down there with personal security.

Mr. SHIMER. No, sir; I mean real estate, checks, and tax certificates, and anything that you want money on.

Mr. CLARK. Now, the reason that you do not make any more money in the Pig Iron Trust is because the Steel Trust squeezed you; did it not?

Mr. SHIMER. No, sir; we can make pig iron in a general way nearly as cheap as they can.

Mr. CLARK. It is astonishing that no one makes anything out of this business, or any other business that has been suggested here.

Mr. BOUTELL. Except tin plate.

Mr. COCKRAN. And yet nobody speaks in figures of millions.

Mr. SHIMER. You have to renew your plant every three years. The thing gets ahead of you.

Mr. CLARK. I understand that. I would be glad to have somebody tell me how there happened to be so many millionaires and multi-millionaires, and so many rich men in the iron and steel business when some of them make over 6 per cent interest?

Mr. SHIMER. I do not make 6; that is the trouble with me.

Mr. CLARK. How do they all get rich?

Mr. SHIMER. I do not know.

Mr. CLARK. How much do they pay the president of your company?

Mr. SHIMER. I think he gets something like a hundred dollars a month.

Mr. CLARK. Are all the stockholders of the company officers?

Mr. SHIMER. No, sir.

Mr. CLARK. Now, did you say that you paid the president of your company $100 a month?

Mr. SHIMER. Yes, sir.

Mr. CLARK. Is that all you pay him?

Mr. SHIMER. That is all that is paid him. We pay the manager a little more than that.

Mr. CLARK. How much do you pay the manager?

Mr. SHIMER. Six thousand dollars a year.

Mr. CLARK. Is that the highest-priced officer in the company?

Mr. SHIMER. That is the highest-price officer in the bunch.

Mr. CLARK. Now, these steel men expect people to believe statements that none of them are making over 3 or 4 or 5 per cent?

Mr. SHIMER. I think you ought to believe what they say.

Mr. CLARK. But there is such a thing as appearances, and the reputed fortunes that they have and the acknowledged fortunes that they have do not correspond.

Mr. SHIMER. But it is largely on paper.

Mr. CLARK. Andrew Carnegie could not have made $500,000,000 if he had lived until he was as old as Methuselah?

Mr. SHIMER. Unless he had sold out. [Laughter.]

Mr. CLARK. He did not have to sell out to have two or three millions?

Mr. SHIMER. I do not know whether he did or not; I can not tell you about that; but unless he had sold out he would never had made anything in the steel or iron business. You can never make anything in the iron business until you sell out.

Mr. CLARK. How did Frick make his money; did he sell out?

Mr. SHIMER. Yes, sir.

Mr. CLARK. How did Carnegie happen to get a million dollars in salary?

Mr. SHIMER. They gave it to him.

Mr. CLARK. And Schwab?

Mr. SHIMER. That is another matter.

Mr. CLARK. If they can afford to pay such salaries they are making money?

Mr. SHIMER. Undoubtedly they are.

Mr. CLARK. You can not afford to pay it out of dividends of 3 or 4 per cent?

Mr. SHIMER. No, sir; but they can buy ore lands, which is a sort of unearned increment.

The CHAIRMAN. That is the way you get at it?

Mr. SHIMER. Yes, sir.

The CHAIRMAN. And that is the way you got the $4,000,000 invested?

Mr. SHIMER. Yes, sir.

The CHAIRMAN. And the money you invested in the business brought it up to $4,000,000, did it not?

Mr. SHIMER. Yes. sir.

The CHAIRMAN. And you were paying three and three-quarters per cent on that?

Mr. SHIMER. Yes, sir.

———

STATEMENT OF JOSEPH G. BUTLER, JR., OF YOUNGSTOWN, OHIO, REPRESENTING A LARGE PERCENTAGE OF THE MERCHANT BLAST FURNACES OF THE UNITED STATES.

WEDNESDAY, *November 25, 1908.*

Mr. BUTLER. Mr. Chairman and gentlemen of the committee, I represent a large percentage of the merchant blast furnaces of the United States. The product of these furnaces is used in the malleable works, foundries, cast-iron pipe works, and the independent steel works in the form of basic iron. I get my authority for this representation, first, by letters that I have from, perhaps, 30 or more of the independent furnaces; and, second, as the result of a meeting which was held in Cleveland on last Wednesday, which was largely attended; and at that meeting a committee was appointed to meet with the eastern producers in New York on Monday. We met with them on Monday and again on Tuesday, and the matter was then placed in my hands. I may say that I think perhaps there are one or two others that may want to be heard on this question.

The CHAIRMAN. What are their names? Have we got them?

Mr. BUTLER. The only one that I know of positively is Mr. Schirmer—Mr. Samuel M. Schirmer. He is an eastern man.

I want to say that this matter was placed practically in my hands yesterday, and I am not prepared to give you the information that it seems to me you should have. I judge from the questions that have been asked here this morning that what you want is information, and not opinions.

I intend to go home and prepare and file as quickly as I can get it ready a brief showing the cost of making iron in the different localities, showing the labor, and showing the transportation rates; and I intend, further, to get some information from abroad with reference to the same matter. I have already sent off two long cable messages, and when I get through I intend to do it conscientiously and fairly, and I will file my brief with the committee.

At the third meeting, which was held in New York on Tuesday (yesterday), there was official action taken which I will read; and I want to file this as a preliminary paper:

At a meeting of the pig-iron producers, held in New York on November 24, the following resolution was unanimously adopted:

"We recommend that ferro-manganese be placed on the free list, but that no change be made in the balance of the pig-iron schedule, believing that any reduction will be to the detriment of the manufacturing interests, the transportation companies, and the labor employed in the production of pig iron, coke, and iron ore."

Mr. GAINES. You want to file a brief, you say?

Mr. BUTLER. I am going to file a brief; and, as I have said, I am going to make it complete, and I am going to try to give you the information that it seems to me you ought to have in order to formulate this bill.

The CHAIRMAN. Does any gentleman wish to inquire about this resolution any further?

Mr. UNDERWOOD. I would like to ask you who you represent—what companies?

Mr. BUTLER. My particular company is the Brier Hill Iron and Coal Company, of Youngstown.

Mr. UNDERWOOD. And you say you have not the information to answer the questions we desire to ask you now?

Mr. BUTLER. I do not think I could answer them satisfactorily. I think I know pretty nearly what you ought to have, and I am going to try to get it for you.

Mr. CLARK. I think if you will get a copy of these hearings on this iron-ore business as they have been reported here, you can find out every phase of it, possibly, that you want to.

Mr. BUTLER. There are a lot of things that you already have in the way of statistics.

Mr. CLARK. I know; but they are not very definite, most of them.

Mr. BUTLER. I will try to make definite what I send you.

Mr. CLARK. I wish you would.

Mr. BUTLER. And I will be glad to come before you again if I am wanted.

Mr. COCKRAN. We shall be very glad to see you. Let me ask you this question: Suppose there was a reduction in the duty on iron ore to, say, 25 cents, as suggested by Mr. Boutell: Would that have any influence upon the rate that should be exacted for pig iron?

Mr. BUTLER. Very likely it might, Mr. Cockran; but I think that if there was very much of a reduction made on iron ore, it would increase the demand for it in the East, and it would perhaps raise the price of the iron ore.

Mr. COCKRAN. That would be a pretty good protection in itself; would it not?

Mr. BUTLER. That would help some.

Mr. GRIGGS. Then you would be willing to see a reduction in the duty on pig iron?

Mr. BUTLER. I think not.

Mr. GRIGGS. All right; I just wanted to know.

Mr. POU. Have you the information that I have been asking for here from one or two witnesses, as to the difference in the steel schedules under the Wilson bill and under the McKinley bill?

Mr. BUTLER. No; I have not, sir.

Mr. POU. Could you get that information?

Mr. BUTLER. I can get it for you.

Mr. POU. Will you kindly incorporate that in your brief?

Mr. BUTLER. I shall be very glad to do so, sir.

(Several members of the committee suggested that the information desired would be found in the statutes.)

Mr. BOUTELL. Do I understand that you want to know the ones that are higher under the Wilson bill than under the Dingley bill?

Mr. POU. I want to know the amount of the importations under the two bills. That is what I mean.

The CHAIRMAN. That is right here in this book—all the importations.

Mr. GRIGGS. Is your company afraid of Belgium?

Mr. BUTLER. In a certain sense we are not afraid of anything.

STATEMENT OF NELSON LYON, OF TARRYTOWN, N. Y., RELATIVE TO THE DUTY PLACED ON PIG IRON.

FRIDAY, *November 27, 1908.*

Mr. LYON. I am secretary and treasurer of the Holt-Lyon Company, of Tarrytown, N. Y.

Mr. GRIGGS. Are you making any money?

Mr. LYON. Some; very little.

The CHAIRMAN. Proceed.

Mr. LYON. Mr. Chairman and gentlemen of the committee, we have been taught that the tariff was made to develop industries, cheapen the cost of production, and thereby benefit the consumer. The tariff has certainly built up the iron industry and cheapened the production, but we do protest that the present tariff is not in the interest of small manufacturers or consumers.

I might explain that this article of my own is on pig iron, which is only one step from the raw material which we use. We use castings and wire, and our prices are drawn up, giving pig iron as the base upon which our prices are to continue.

Mr. DALZELL. Do you manufacture pig iron as well as wire rope?

Mr. LYON. No, sir; we do not manufacture pig iron, but we are users of wire and castings.

Mr. DALZELL. Do you manufacture wire?

Mr. LYON. No, sir; we do not.

Mr. DALZELL. What is it you manufacture?

Mr. LYON. We manufacture wire carpet heaters and wire egg beaters.

The CHAIRMAN. Proceed.

Mr. LYON. It is not in the interest of small manufacturers or consumers, for just as soon as there is demand sufficient to consume all the American production the tariff enables the manufacturer to, and the manufacturer does, immediately, or has in the last ten years, advanced the price to the European price plus the tariff and the ocean freights; and when he reaches that point he stops. During these times the furnace men's profits have increased to 50 and sometimes 100 per cent. We do protest that the consumer is not deriving any benefits from the tariff on pig iron. Really it is a very great detriment to all the small manufacturers; also to the consumers of iron of every description. It has brought the great depressions in many kinds of business; and the great panic, which we hope is just passing by, was brought on by excessive tariff duties, which brought the great prosperity which President-elect Taft has told the country produced the present depression and recession in business. Then follows the first thing desired by small manufacturers—a steady price for raw materials throughout the year and from year to year. This they are not able to obtain under the Dingley law. Steady employment is also the great desire of labor. Of all kinds of raw material entering into the manufacture of American products there has been none so unstable and unreliable in price as pig iron in the last ten years. There was no raw material more stable and reliable in price for the five years previous to 1898 than pig iron. Since 1898, a year after the Dingley law was passed, and before the steel trust was formed, the average price for five years previous did not vary 10 per cent. The following prices are for No. 2 southern pig iron at Cincinnati. That seems to be the place where we get our prices, and our base and everything seems to be taken from them. From February 1, 1897, to December 31, 1898, a period of twenty-two months, the price of No. 2 southern pig iron at Cincinnati averaged about $9.50 per ton, and no month's price averaged as high as $10 a ton. Very soon after the American Steel and Wire Company was organized the price of iron began to advance and reached $16 in June, 1899, and $20.75 in October following. This was the European price plus the tariff and ocean freights, and when they reached that point, and they advanced to that point almost immediately—within two or three months—they stopped, and it remained at this price until April, 1900, a period of six months, at $20. Then it receded to $19.75 in May and $12.87 in October, 1900. This showed an advance of 120 per cent in nine months, and one year later the price fell over 40 per cent. From October, 1900, to April, 1902, a period of eighteen months, it did not vary $2 per ton, prices ranging from $12.87 to $14 per ton. In June, only two months later, the price advanced to $20, and in October of the same year to $25.60. This was an advance of 150 per cent from the prices in 1899.

The CHAIRMAN. I suppose there had been a corresponding advance abroad, had there not?

· Mr. LYON. There had not.

The CHAIRMAN. How did they get in? Was the tariff $4 a ton?

Mr. LYON. Four dollars a ton.

The CHAIRMAN. Only $4 a ton. If it did not cost but $10, how did they get $25 for it here? Was there not any advance abroad?

Mr. LYON. The price of $25 was temporary. The manufacturer of iron and steel in this country has his peculiar iron that he uses, and he can not turn around and buy iron of this man and that man. It does not work in his manufactory.

The CHAIRMAN. All right.

Mr. LYON. He is not in position to buy at once from the foreign manufacturer, and he has to wait.

The CHAIRMAN. Proceed.

Mr. LYON. Wire nails sold at $1.27 per hundred pounds in December, 1898. You understand, December, 1898, was after the Dingley law was passed, and was the first calendar year under the Dingley law, and nails should have advanced to a fair price. They were advanced to $2.30 in the June following, and to $3.20 in January, February and March—over 150 per cent advance.

Mr. COCKRAN. June of what year?

Mr. LYON. Of the same year; that is, 1898.

Mr. COCKRAN. June, 1898, you say?

Mr. LYON. Yes, sir; I think the American Steel and Wire Company was formed about that same time. Not in 1898, but this was 1900.

Mr. COCKRAN. You are speaking now of 1900 or 1898?

Mr. LYON. I will just repeat this so that you will get it clear.

Mr. COCKRAN. Yes.

Mr. LYON. Wire nails sold at $1.27 per hundred pounds in December, 1898——

Mr. COCKRAN. December, 1898?

Mr. LYON. December, 1898. That was the price after the Dingley law had been in effect for a year.

Mr. COCKRAN. One dollar and twenty-seven cents?

Mr. LYON. One dollar and twenty-seven cents. They were advanced to $2.30 in the following June, and to $3.20 in January, 1900.

Mr. COCKRAN. June, 1899?

Mr. LYON. June, 1899.

Mr. COCKRAN. How much?

Mr. LYON. Two dollars and thirty cents.

Mr. COCKRAN. Proceed with your statement.

Mr. LYON. They were $3.20 in January, 1900. This was an advance of over 150 per cent.

Mr. HILL. Meanwhile there had been no change in the tariff, had there?

Mr. LYON. No, sir.

Mr. HILL. How do you account for the advance?

The CHAIRMAN. He just said that they had combined; that the American Wire and Steel Company had been formed.

Mr. LYON. They had combined. I might say now, what I have not in my minutes here, that during that time the American wholesale dealers purchased their wire nails in Germany, brought them into this country, paid the freight across the ocean and the Dingley tariff, and undersold the trust in their own market. Of course those things could not be carried on so extensively, but nearly a year later they took $1 per hundred pounds off at one solitary stroke. I have the prices of nails for nine years, every month of every year, and the price of pig iron, and I can give you those facts and leave them with you, and also I have the prices of wire nails every month from that down to 1907. The price before the Dingley traiff was made was $1.27 a hundred, and from that day to this, after they reduced the price and took off $1 a hundred, the nails have been advanced to 50 or 70 per cent above the regular price previous to the passage of the Dingley law.

Mr. DALZELL. For instance, what was the price of wire nails in 1906?

Mr. LYON. I have not got it in the year 1906.

Mr. DALZELL. I thought you said you had it for all those years?

Mr. LYON. That is one year before, brother.

Mr. DALZELL. What was the price in 1895.

Mr. LYON. I do not go back to 1895.

Mr. COCKRAN. I thought you went back to 1898.

Mr. LYON. What?

Mr. COCKRAN. Did you not say you did not go back to 1905?

Mr. LYON. Well, I have the sheet right here.

Mr. DALZELL. You have got the prices for 1899 and 1900, and you say you have the prices for seven or eight years. I would like to know the prices for 1901, 1902, 1903, 1904, 1905, and 1906, or any one of those years you can take.

Mr. LYON. Here are the figures which I have. I have the prices from 1897 down to and including 1905, any month that you like.

Mr. COCKRAN. Just let us have each year.

Mr. LYON. On wire nails?

Mr. COCKRAN. Yes.

Mr. LYON. Shall I take the first month in each year and give you that?

Mr. COCKRAN. That will be for what year?

Mr. LYON. First, Jannary, 1897.

The CHAIRMAN. Can you not give the average price, the Jannary price?

Mr. DALZELL. Take the average price.

Mr. LYON. I will take the January price for each year.

Mr. COCKRAN. Have you the prices for each year averaged?

Mr. LYON. No, sir; we have not got that, but the January prices will not vary, scarcely.

Mr. COCKRAN. Give us the January price, and put it in the record.

Mr. LYON. For 1897 it was $1.39, for 1898 it was $1.42.

Mr. COCKRAN. What are you giving us now?

Mr. LYON. I am giving you the price at Pittsburg.

Mr. COCKRAN. The selling price?

Mr. LYON. Yes.

Mr. COCKRAN. All right. Now let us start at that.

Mr. LYON. The 1898 price, the price for January, 1898, was $1.42. In 1899 I will have to give you February. It was $1.57. January is blotted. In 1900 it was $3.20; in 1901, $2.22; in 1902, $1.99; in January, 1903, $1.89; in January, 1904, $1.89; in January, 1905, $1.75; and January, 1908, $2.05.

Mr. DALZELL. You skipped 1906.

Mr. COCKRAN. And you skipped 1907, too. You did not give us 1906 or 1907.

Mr. LYON. Well, I do not have those on this list—1905. This list is from the Iron Age of January 11, 1906. I had very little time to prepare these figures.

The CHAIRMAN. If you can not give us 1906 and 1907, you can supply that information afterwards. Please go on with your statement.

Mr. LYON. Yes; I will give you that later.

The CHAIRMAN. What year was it that you said there was this large importation?

Mr. LYON. That was in 1898 or 1900, about. Now, the total production of pig iron in the United States in the year 1907——

The CHAIRMAN. I thought you were speaking of wire nails?

Mr. LYON. I have finished with wire nails.

The. CHAIRMAN. Did you not give us a large importation of wire nails in 1900, I believe it was?

Mr. LYON. That was during the high prices here.

The CHAIRMAN. How much was imported?

Mr. LYON. I do not know; but I know there were great quantities of them.

The CHAIRMAN. You would be surprised to learn that the greatest quantity about that time, in 1900, was 36,000 pounds?

Mr. LYON. When did you say?

The CHAIRMAN. In 1900; 36,000 pounds; nearly 37,000 pounds.

Mr. LYON. Thirty-seven thousand pounds?

The CHAIRMAN. That was the largest importation of any of these years.

Mr. LYON. Did you get that from the government figures?

The CHAIRMAN. These are the government figures. The next year the importation amounted to about 1,200 pounds.

Mr. LYON. In 1900 the price was $3.20 in January, February, and March. In the month of April they took off $1 per hundred at one swoop.

The CHAIRMAN. You are giving us the importations?

Mr. LYON. I am not giving you the importations.

The CHAIRMAN. You did a few moments ago, and said they were large for those years.

Mr. LYON. I said they were what?

The CHAIRMAN. You said they were large for one or two particular years.

Mr. LYON. I have been told that they were very large.

The CHAIRMAN. That is presumably a mistake, according to the report. You can go on with your statement.

Mr. LYON. Yes, sir. The prices would admit of it at least. They were large, apparently; and I know $1 a hundred was taken off at one swoop. When I was in Scotland—I presume I will reach that again in my argument—when I was in Aberdeen, Scotland, they were selling nails from German manufacturers at $1.60 a hundred, delivered; and that party said he was receiving nails from the National Steel Company, delivered in Scotland, at $1.70 to $1.75. United States Steel Company prices were £7 5s. per ton=$1.74. German prices were £6 12s. 6d. per ton=$1.60.

The CHAIRMAN. We would like to have those figures; file them with your brief.

Mr. LYON. Yes; I will. He said that the only reason that the price was any different between the German and the American importations was that they were ordered several months earlier from the United States than from Germany.

The CHAIRMAN. We will be very glad to have those statements.

Mr. LYON. Very well. Now I revert to pig iron. The total production of pig iron in the United States in 1907, as quoted in the Iron Age for January, 1908, was 25,781,361 tons. The total production in the year 1904 was 16,276,641 tons. This year, 1904, was the year when the production was nearly doubled between January and December. Now, I contend if prices had not been sufficient to afford a good margin of profit the steel trust would not have increased their production in 1904, for it is the policy of that corporation never to produce unless they can produce at a profit. The average price in 1907 was $23.08; the average price in 1904 was $12.75. This shows the price in 1907 to be $10.33 per ton above the average price in 1904, and the market price of the product of 1907 to be $266,321,597 greater than the market price for the same quantity would have been at the price of 1904. That is quite an amount to be extracted from the American people unjustly. Now, remember, the productions of both these years were under nearly the complete control of the trust.

Mr. HILL. You find absolutely no change in the tariff during any of these years?

Mr. LYON. There has been no change in the tariff since the Dingley law went into effect.

Mr. HILL. Of the basic material or any one element of the manufacture?

Mr. LYON. I did not know that there had been any change in the tariff since the Dingley law. The tariff does not make any difference in the price of pig iron, except when they advance it until they reach the English and German price plus the tariff and the freight across the ocean, and then it stops, and it never stops when it advances until it reaches that price.

The CHAIRMAN. Do you know whether the foreign price did not fluctuate about the same way?

Mr. LYON. It does not.

The CHAIRMAN. It fluctuates a good deal, according to the government reports during those years. There are great fluctuations of the price during those years in the imported nails?

Mr. LYON. Oh, on imported nails?

The CHAIRMAN. Yes.

Mr. LYON. But the price of pig iron can not fluctuate but very little.

Mr. COCKRAN. Why?

Mr. LYON. In the foreign market.

Mr. COCKRAN. Why?

Mr. Lyon. Because prices do not go up and down there and advance, as they do here. The Englishman makes his price so that it does not vary scarcely from year to year.

Mr. Dalzell. Would you give us the price of pig iron in the foreign market for the years for which you have given us the American price?

Mr. Lyon. I will obtain those figures and file them in the record.

Mr. Dalzell. If you please.

Mr. Gaines. Do you know the price of iron ore for the same years?

Mr. Lyon. I do not.

Mr. Gaines. I mean the price of iron here in this country during the years you have compared.

Mr. Lyon. No; the price of iron ore has varied very much. During the high prices during the past two or three years they have advanced it very much, but the trusts are the owners of the mines and have advanced it just to suit themselves.

Mr. Griggs. I understood you to be objecting to the violent fluctuation in prices?

Mr. Lyon. I do; yes, sir.

Mr. Griggs. Will you give us a remedy?

Mr. Lyon. I will show before I get through here that even if you took the whole of the tariff off from pig iron the price last year was still $150,000,000 more than it should have been, and more than it was in 1904, and I will give you those figures before I finish.

Mr. Hill. The figures on the importation of iron in pigs imported into the United States show that there is a greater fluctuation in the importation of the foreign ore than your figures show in the domestic ore, dropping from $24.22 in 1901 to $13.68 in 1902, about 80 per cent difference in value.

Mr. Lyon. Yes.

Mr. Hill. That is on page 491. Then it starts in to advance again and gets up to $15.99 in 1907.

Mr. Lyon. Yes.

Mr. Hill. So that there does seem to be a similar fluctuation abroad?

Mr. Lyon. It is a fluctuation in the importations.

Mr. Hill. No; this is the unit value.

Mr. Lyon. I beg your pardon; yes.

The Chairman. The value per ton.

Mr. Hill. I would like to have you, before you get through, give the explanation of those changes.

Mr. Griggs. Right on that point of fluctuation, suppose you should know that cotton fluctuates from 7½ cents to 12 cents, we will say, in three months.

Mr. Lyon. Yes.

Mr. Griggs. Would you say that was from the same cause?

Mr. Lyon. No, sir. We derive cotton in a very different manner. That depends upon the growth of the product that is raised in America from year to year. Some years we have a good year and some years we do not. With iron ore and coal there is no variation. It is in the mine and there is very little difference in the price of coal and in the price of labor to dig it out.

Now, had the tariff been entirely removed, the European competition would have kept the price down at least $4 per ton less than the average last year, and still the price of last year's product, if the price had been $4 lower, would have been $153,197,000 greater than the price that it sold for in 1904, and that price we have heretofore shown was amply remunerative, or they would not have increased the production from January to December nearly 100 per cent. That is evidence enough that there was plenty of profit on it in 1904. This $4 per ton would have been a saving to the small manufacturers. It would not have been so much of a saving to the large manufacturers, because they make their contracts from year to year, but we small manufacturers are not in position to make our contracts for the year. That is, the $4 per ton on the production of 1907 would have been $103,125,444.

The CHAIRMAN. How much would $4 a ton on pig iron save on your production?

Mr. LYON. I am not discussing that here. I am here in the interests of the people.

The CHAIRMAN. Sir?

Mr. LYON. I am here in the interests of the people.

The CHAIRMAN. I asked you how much less you could manufacture your articles for if you got the pig iron at $4 less a ton; how much less a dozen or a hundred, however you sell your articles?

Mr. LYON. We are a small concern. It would have saved us about $600 last year.

The CHAIRMAN. On how much of an output?

Mr. LYON. That is on the use of about 140 or 150 tons.

The CHAIRMAN. It would have saved you $600. What is the output of your factory?

Mr. LYON. Our output is about $40,000.

The CHAIRMAN. It would have saved you $600 on $40,000, would it?

Mr. LYON. Yes; but it is not so much my interest as it is in the interest of others.

The CHAIRMAN. I understand that. If we reduce the tariff on pig iron, we want to know how much we would reduce the cost of your production.

Mr. LYON. It would have reduced ours about $500 or $600.

Mr. CLARK. Following that up with the question that ought to follow it, if you save $600 on that proposition do you sell any cheaper to the trade or the consumers, or not?

Mr. LYON. I did vary my price immediately, when I got cheaper pig iron this year.

Mr. CLARK. Well, do you do it?

Mr. LYON. I told you I did, and it has not advanced. When I got the low price of pig iron this year—that is, when I got my castings low—I immediately took off such a percentage on my own, which equaled almost one-half of my profit in the year 1907.

Mr. DALZELL. What are you advocating? Are you advocating an abolition of the duty on pig iron?

Mr. LYON. Let me explain: I told you if the w' ole tariff was taken off of pig iron, still they would make $153,000,000 more than they would have made at the price in 1899, the first calendar year of the Dingley tariff.

Mr. LONGWORTH. Who made that?

Mr. LYON. The manufacturers of pig iron.

Mr. HILL. And you take the difference between the price of the American iron and the foreign iron to draw that conclusion?

Mr. LYON. I draw it from the prices at which Americans made iron in 1899, and those which they charged us in 1907.

Mr. HILL. Let me ask you this question: Would this in any way cause you to reconsider your argument? In 1900 the price of foreign iron was $24.22, and we imported 11,000 tons. The very next year the price dropped to $13.68, and we imported 85,000 tons. The next year it was $15.05, and we imported 749,000 tons. Now, I can not see where you get your $153,000,000 unless you follow down each year and show the difference.

Mr. LYON. I am taking it on the production of last year. Last year they advanced the price 50 per cent.

Mr. HILL. And they dropped it in 1902 100 per cent abroad, according to the official statistics of the Government. It was down then to $13.68; and it seems to me that wholly destroys your argument.

Mr. LYON. Well.

Mr. COCKRAN. In other words, if you are going to hold the tariff responsible for all the increases, Mr. Hill thinks you ought to give it credit for all the decreases.

Mr. HILL. Yes.

Mr. COCKRAN. That is a proposition which logically appeals to me as a free trader very strongly.

The CHAIRMAN. Do you accept the amendment?

Mr. HILL. I accept the amendment. If we take the increases, we have got to take the decreases.

Mr. CLARK. Do you want the tariff taken off from pig iron or not?

Mr. LYON. Off from pig iron?

Mr. CLARK. Yes.

Mr. LYON. There would have been no question but what it might have been all taken off last year and still the European people would not have been able to sell any in this country.

Mr. CLARK. You know we can not put it up this year and put it down the next year.

Mr. LYON. Yes.

Mr. CLARK. What I want to know is, whether you want the tariff taken off on pig iron or not?

Mr. LYON. I do not think there is any question but what it should be taken off.

Mr. CLARK. All right; that is a square answer.

Mr. LYON. Yes; you will get a square answer from me every time.

Mr. DALZELL. The duty on your product, do you want that taken off the finished material you make out of the pig iron? If we take the $4 off of pig iron, do you want the tariff taken off of your product?

Mr. LYON. I do. I can go over and sell in the foreign market. I have been over there. I shipped 23 tons of egg beaters into England in six months four years ago and I shipped over 12 tons there this year, and I got more price in England than I did here.

Mr. DALZELL. More there than you did here?

Mr. LYON. Yes.

The CHAIRMAN. Are you sure about that?

Mr. LYON. I know just what I am talking about.

The CHAIRMAN. I supposed you did.

Mr. LYON. I will give you the figures.

The CHAIRMAN. I want our friends to take notice of that.

Mr. CLARK. That is satisfactory information. You are perfectly willing that the tariff should be taken off your product if you get the tariff taken off of pig iron?

Mr. LYON. Yes.

Mr. CLARK. That is a valuable proposition.

Mr. BOUTELL. As a result of that, how much cheaper will we get our egg beaters?

Mr. COCKRAN. Without an egg beater, you see, no family is complete. [Laughter.]

Mr. LYON. The price of those is very low.

Mr. POU. I move that the gentleman be allowed to complete his statement.

The CHAIRMAN. Without objection, that motion will be considered carried.

Mr. LYON. I am very much pleased to have questions asked me.

Mr. POU. I do not think you ought to be embarrassed.

Mr. LYON. It is not a bit embarrassing to me. I would rather you raised your objections as I pass along.

Mr. GAINES. I would like to ask another question.

The CHAIRMAN. Why not let him finish his statement?

Mr. GAINES. Very well; I will wait.

Mr. LYON. To keep these facts plainly in your minds I would say President McKinley was elected in 1896 and inaugurated in 1897, and the Dingley law was passed in 1897, and the first calendar year under the Dingley law was 1898. The price of pig iron in January, 1897, was $10, and this was under the Wilson bill, and it did not bring this price again until January 2, 1899, two years later. The average price for these two years, 1897 and 1898, was $9.50 per ton. This was before the American Steel and Wire Company was incorporated and the United States Steel Corporation formed. The average price in 1897 and 1898 was $9.50 per ton. This was under the Dingley law. The average price for 1904 was $12.75 and the average price for 1907 was $23.08. This shows an advance on purely raw material of nearly 150 per cent.

Now, if we multiply the production of 1907 by $13.68 we have the fabulous amount of $350,110,862. The total amount paid to the employees of the United States Steel Corporation in 1907, and this includes the officers and every workman, from the digging of the ore and coal from the ground until the product is marketed, was $160,-825,822. So you can plainly see that this amount of $350,110,862 is greater than the total amount paid by all the iron-producing companies similar to and including the United States Steel Company, in digging the ore from the ground and transporting it to the furnaces and in the production of the merchandise such as is made and sold by the United States Steel Corporation. The advance that they got last year over what the price was in 1898, you see, is greater than the total amount paid by corporations in the manufacturing of steel and iron, and the taking of it from the ground and putting it into merchandise, including what was paid to the officers besides. This amount paid amounts to a tax of $4 on every man, woman, and child in the United States, and $20 on every family of five.

I wish you to compare the prices of 1904, which was the year succeeding the depression that began in July, 1903. This year, 1908, succeeded the panic of 1907, which was very much greater than the depression of 1903, and the prices should have gone lower.

Here is another thing. Before the United States Steel and Iron Company was permitted to absorb the Tennessee Coal and Iron Company, I want to state to you the difference of prices under depression. July 21, 1904, the Iron Age quotes the price in Birmingham in almost every instance to have been $9 per ton. These prices were made only four years ago. In September they say there is no doubt that plenty of southern can be purchased at $9.25 basis.

Now, here is July, 1908, after the great panic, the greatest panic we had had since 1894, and after the steel trust absorbed the Tennessee Coal and Iron Company, its chief competitor, the Iron Age says, "A schedule of $12.50 at Birmingham has been adopted by practically all the producers."

July 25 this year they say, " One of the largest interests is practically out of the market, refusing to depart from the schedule of $12.50. The announcement that the output is not to be increased to the extent recently arranged for is significant." Now, here you are treated to this spectacle before the steel trust absorbed the Tennessee Coal and Iron Company; during the depression of 1904 they reduced the price to $9 and $9.25 per ton. After the Tennessee Coal and Iron Company was absorbed by the steel trust, its chief rival, the combination price of $12.50 was strictly adhered to, which is a price over 33 per cent higher. The policy of the oil trust was said to be to strangle its competitors. The policy of the steel trust is to purchase their competitors, no matter at what cost, and the great consuming public pays the price. The manner which other manufacturers pursued previous to the time the trust absorbed the business of the country was this: In times of depression the manufacturers would reduce the price of their product and encourage trade. If this was not sufficient for their purpose, they would decrease the price paid to their employees, or further reduce hours of employment.

The CHAIRMAN. Mr. Lyon, after you have finished your statement we may want to ask you a question or two.

Mr. LYON. During the height of the panic last fall our great and good President, Theodore Roosevelt, who rules our land in righteousness, allowed the steel trust to throw 147,126 people out to starve, or on the cold charity of the world. They reduced their output 72 per cent, and according to their own statement now (the last statement they made) only 60 per cent of their plants are in operation—147,126 were thrown out to starve, or on the cold charity of the world, leaving only 63,054 employed, out of an army of 210,180.

Now, the President, by his own admission, encouraged this trust to absorb its chief competitor, the Tennessee Coal and Iron Company, that it might allay the panic, which promised ruin, and which was brought on, as President-elect Taft said, by overprosperity; and this overprosperity was induced by high tariff. We are told also that President Roosevelt promises this trust immunity from prosecution, and since that time the steel trust and their combinations came out boldly every month during the early part of the year and told us plainly that they would not reduce the price of their production; that it would not encourage trade, and also that they had kept their prices from going high, and that they were strong enough to prevent them from going low.

Mr. GRIGGS. Pardon me. Have you noticed in the papers recently the case of the man who was suffering from nerve prosperity?

Mr. LYON. That has probably escaped my notice.

Mr. GRIGGS. Well, it is a fact.

Mr. LYON. Yes. Why our great President is following the Standard Oil Company to prevent them from shipping their oil a few cents a hundred pounds less than their competitors, but is allowing this great steel trust to go scot-free while it is stealing from the public through the robber tariff from one hundred to two hundred million dollars annually, is beyond my conception.

Now, I have some very important figures here. This is only a very short statement. I take new ground regarding foreign sales. I have never seen it advocated before. I presume it is only because others have not accumulated the commercial evidences that I have been accumulating in my scrapbooks for the past thirty years. I advocate that it is no longer of any more importance to sell a million dollars' worth of goods in a foreign market than it is to increase sales at home by that amount and that the time has now arrived when our tariff laws should be adjusted to compel manufacturers to make prices for home consumption, that our own people will consume the greatest amount possible.

To prove my position, I have gone back over our imports and exports for over one hundred years, and present them as follows:

Our imports eighty-seven years previous to 1876 were $14,546,-994,000, while our exports were $12,309,653,384, which left an unfavorable balance of $2,237,340,616; while for twenty-three years since 1875, down to 1896, our exports were $18,662,344,445 and our imports were $15,770,903,493, leaving a favorable balance of $2,891,440,952. From this we deduct $2,237,340,616, which leaves a favorable balance of $654,100,336. That brings us down to 1896.

The CHAIRMAN. We have all those figures, and I hardly think you need take up the time to read them.

Mr. LYON. I have only a half page more.

The CHAIRMAN. Are they all figures?

Mr. LYON. No.

The CHAIRMAN. We have all the statistics.

Mr. LYON. I will not take two minutes more, brother.

The CHAIRMAN. Go ahead.

Mr. LYON. Now, since 1895, down to and including 1907, the favorable balance was $5,450,977,321. This added to our favorable balance previous to 1896 makes a favorable balance previous to 1908 of $6,105,077,657. This is the balance to our credit on the other side, save some other things which, you know, enter into it. Now for the conclusion: All excesses of exports over imports must be settled either in gold, merchandise, stocks, or bonds. This favorable balance can not be paid in gold, because all the gold money in the world does not very much exceed $6,000,000,000, and a large proportion of that is owned by the United States. We can not go on gaining this large favorable balance of trade but a few years more. We can not draw on the European gold reserves, as they need all they mine to keep pace with their improvements in manufacturing and business. There is less than $400,000,000 of gold mined annually, and over one-quarter of that is produced in the United States. Now, if Europe is to continue to buy largerly of us, we must accept more merchandise and less stocks and bonds in return for the same, on which we can draw only our annual dividends.   Therefore I conclude that it is time our tariff was adjusted so that our people will consume the greatest amount possible.   This must be done by manufacturing at a less profit and by making lower prices to consumers, whether users of raw material or purchasers of merchandise.

By manufacturing on a lower basis of profit there must be some reduction in wages of certain kinds of labor, but employment would be steady, and a reduction of living expenses would follow, which is now acknowledged to be over 40 per cent greater than a few years ago.   The workingman certainly would be benefited thereby, as living expenses would be greatly reduced.   This increased living expense of everyone has been brought on since the Dingley tariff went into effect, and the workingman has very little benefit from the lower cost of production of the necessities of life, some of which should be obtained from foreign countries.

Should the tariff be adjusted to the advanced price of labor at the present time, and if the Dingley law was not too high when made, we would now have to add largely to the present tariff law, which no sane man would advocate, instead of making a deduction from the same.

The CHAIRMAN. The gentleman from West Virginia was interrupted a while ago when he wanted to ask a question. You have completed your statement, have you, Mr. Lyon?

Mr. LYON. I have completed the statement, brother.

The CHAIRMAN. Ask your question now.

Mr. GAINES. I want to ask you whether the articles you manufacture are patented articles?

Mr. LYON. They are. We make the best in the world and get the highest prices of anybody.

Mr. GAINES. They are protected by patent?

Mr. LYON. They are.

Mr. GAINES. That is all.

The CHAIRMAN. Are there any others made that are not protected by patent?

Mr. LYON. The patents have run out on the whole of them.   I have to sell in competition with them.

The CHAIRMAN. So that if you could get the duty you ask for you would have a monopoly of the market on account of your patents?

Mr. LYON. No, sir.   I am here in the interest of the great consuming public, just as much as I am in my own interest.

The CHAIRMAN. Certainly; but you are protected by patent and your competitors are not.

Mr. LYON. They have been protected, and they have made their money.   They have retired, or they are manufacturing and selling their goods in the markets of the world.

Mr. GRIGGS. Can you compete with Belgium in the manufacture of these articles?

Mr. LYON. I do not have to compete with anybody.   We make the best goods on the market and get the highest prices.   We do not ask what our competitors sell at.

The CHAIRMAN. I do not see what difference it makes about the price of pig iron.

Mr. LYON. It makes a difference to me. Let me tell you about that. Every time pig iron has gone up to $20 or $24 a ton it has brought on great depression all over our country. Every one of our manufacturing, retailing, and laboring men has suffered by reason of it. There is not one single instance where pig iron has gone to $20 a ton but what they have suffered——

Mr. DALZELL. Did it reduce the demand for egg beaters?

Mr. LYON. It reduced the demand for everything.

Mr. HILL. Have you foreign patents?

Mr. LYON. I did have patents in England, France, and Germany.

Mr. HILL. When the price of pig iron fell 100 per cent between 1901 and 1902 in Europe, did you reduce the price to the export trade?

Mr. LYON. We did not have any export trade then. We are young in that business.

Mr. CLARK. Did you say just at the close of your remarks that anybody who wanted the tariff raised was insane?

Mr. LYON. Well, on that great product. I do not mean that to apply to everything. It is on the general principle of advancing the tariff on everything, because the present price of labor is higher than it was when the Dingley law was passed. That is why I speak——

Mr. CLARK. If they are all insane then we have had a good many lunatics around here in the last two or three weeks.

Mr. LYON. I have no doubt about that. They may be another class of men than lunatics.

Mr. BOUTELL. How much longer have your American patents to run?

Mr. LYON. About eight years.

Mr. BOUTELL. In how many foreign countries have you still patents?

Mr. LYON. We forfeited them in all the foreign countries, even England this year.

Mr. HILL. You had to under the law, did you not?

Mr. LYON. Yes; under the law of England, that we have to manufacture there or give up the patents.

Mr. HILL. Why did you not go there and manufacture?

Mr. LYON. Because England never manufactures small things like egg beaters. She is looking for bigger fish.

Mr. HILL. Then you have no competition?

Mr. LYON. No competition in England.

Mr. GRIGGS. You think no home is happy without this egg beater?

Mr. LYON. If they had one once they would not do without it for twice the price. [Laughter.]

The CHAIRMAN. It is useful in every household?

Mr. LYON. It is.

Mr. POU. What is your price for them per dozen?

Mr. LYON. Seventy-five cents and upward. Seventy-two cents is the cheapest one. They sell for 10 cents apiece. Others sell all the way from 15 to 25 cents. Really, 8 cents is the lowest possible price when we sell to the retail dealer—8¼ cents to the department stores.

Mr. BOUTELL. Is there any suggestion in your sales to jobbers as to the price they should charge the retailers?

Mr. LYON. There is none.

Mr. BOUTELL. Or what the retailers should charge?

Mr. Lyon. There is none. We leave them to sell just as they will.

Mr. Boutell. Do you know for what they do sell?

Mr. Lyon. They sell them for from 10 cents up, and when the market price of the raw material advances all that loss comes between the retailer and us. We have to stand all that. We can not advance our prices.

Mr. Boutell. When the price of the raw material goes down, where is the gain going to be?

Mr. Lyon. The gain comes between the manufacturer, the jobber, and the retailer. They all get a better profit. That is——

Mr. Boutell. And the poor ultimate consumer keeps on paying the same price?

Mr. Lyon. There are so many things on which they cut the price——

Mr. Boutell. This is as good an illustration to ask this question on as any other. Carpet beaters and egg beaters are used in the household?

Mr. Lyon. They are.

Mr. Boutell. They are paid for by the housewife?

Mr. Lyon. Yes.

Mr. Boutell. And if we should give free iron ore and repeal the duty on pig iron, can you hold out any hope (without treating this question as ridiculous, although those are humble articles) that the housewife will get these things, in connection with other things, at any cheaper price?

Mr. Lyon. That would not make so much difference. That depends on the price that the department store would make. They are the great consumers, and they make their prices. I can say that R. H. Macy & Co., of New York, make a price of 8 cents. All others make a price of 10 cents.

Mr. Boutell. But take the majority of the small towns, where there are no department stores.

Mr. Lyon. There they pay a price of 10 cents, and in the small country towns they pay 15 cents.

Mr. Boutell. What is the carpet beater? What is the price of that?

Mr. Lyon. From 10 cents up to 50 cents. We give them the value of their money in everything we give them—full value.

Mr. Longworth. Would you reduce that price?

Mr. Lyon. I would reduce my price just as quick as I would otherwise. I sell to the wholesale men almost exclusively.

Mr. Longworth. If the duty were taken off altogether, I mean, would you sell at a lower price than you do now?

Mr. Lyon. If I got a lower duty I would, but it has not mattered in the past year what the duty was. We have to pay a very advanced price for our raw material.

The Chairman. Does the steel trust make egg beaters and carpet beaters?

Mr. Lyon. I do not think they do. But they produce the raw material for us to make them.

Mr. Griggs. If we take this tariff off of pig iron you would reduce the price of the egg beaters at least $4 a ton, would you not?

Mr. Lyon. I think we would be able to do more than that. [Laughter.]

Mr. RANDELL. You said just now that you would give some figures to the public, and you were interrupted and did not give the figures. What was it you started to give?

Mr. LYON. I will give them to you now. I have purchased the wire entering into our carpet beaters from the Trenton Iron Company, which is now, I am told by the steel trust themselves, owned by it. I did not know it before. They charged me $4.75 a hundred for the very best spring-steel wire. I made my purchases from the Roeblings for $4 per hundred, for a better class of goods. I got the figures the day before I came away from the agents of the steel trust, the men of whom I purchased for three years. They were selling 75 cents or 80 cents a hundred higher than the independent manufacturers.

Mr. CLARK. Are you through with that particular statement now?

Mr. LYON. Yes, sir.

Mr. CLARK. We have been trying for two weeks here to get at who it is who absorbs all of the profits between the manufacturer and the man who ultimately buys the stuff—not your egg beaters especially, but everything.

Mr. LYON. Yes, sir.

Mr. CLARK. Now, you sell these egg beaters, and it is just as good an example as anything I know of. You sell these egg beaters to the wholesaler at 72 cents a dozen?

Mr. LYON. To the retailer, you might call him.

Mr. CLARK. That is 6 cents apiece?

Mr. LYON. Yes; not the retailer, but the wholesaler.

Mr. CLARK. But the retailer sells for 10 cents?

Mr. LYON. Ten cents.

Mr. CLARK. Four is about 75 per cent of 6; so in that instance it is the retailer that gets the exorbitant profit.

Mr. LYON. Many times it is; yes, sir.

Mr. CLARK. Well, this is the day of pennies. Why do they not scale their prices down some so that if we do remodel this tariff the consumer of the article will get some of the benefit of it?

Mr. LYON. The consumer, very frequently.

Mr. CLARK. Not if it remains at 10 cents, they do not.

Mr. LYON. But it does not remain at 10 cents. The department stores to-day have bargain days when they cut them right down to a point, almost, where it is not above cost.

Mr. CLARK. But there are no department stores, as Mr. Boutell suggested, in the innumerable multitude of small towns in this country.

Mr. LYON. Yes.

Mr. CLARK. Of course, in Washington and Philadelphia and New York and all these big towns they have department stores where they make a run on those things.

Mr. LYON. Yes, sir.

Mr. CLARK. But what I am trying to get at is how is the consumer ever to get any benefit out of the reduction or the raising of the tariff if somebody gobbles it all between the manufacturer and the consumer?

Mr. LYON. As I tell you, there is plenty of opposition in this country and one is underselling the other. They are cutting the price.

Mr. CLARK. I would like to discover a community where that actually takes place, and locate there. [Laughter.]

Mr. LYON. I will tell you. You inquire of Sears, Roebuck & Co., of Chicago——

Mr. CLARK. I know; that gang is busting up all the retail merchants of the country.

Mr. LYON. They are compelling the retail merchants of the country to cut down their price to a proper price.

Mr. BOUTELL. Right along that line, I would like to ask this: You spoke of having extracts running back over thirty years?

Mr. LYON. Imports and exports. I will file all this with the committee.

Mr. BOUTELL. But you spoke of having a scrapbook.

Mr. LYON. Oh!

Mr. HILL. You spoke of that——

Mr. LYON. Yes, sir.

Mr. BOUTELL. And also said that you had been in business for a great many years. Now, along the line of what Mr. Clark was saying, could you tell us whether you know what system is adopted by certain manufacturers for regulating the retail prices to the final consumer? I can think right offhand, for instance, of a certain kind of shoe that is advertised in the street cars, and I have seen it from Belfast, Me., to Portland, Ore.—all selling at the same price.

Mr. LYON. Yes.

Mr. BOUTELL. And another quality of crackers or biscuit, done up at the same price, all over the country?

Mr. LYON. Yes.

Mr. BOUTELL. And this Gillette razor that has been mentioned, advertised at one price. And a great many of those prices are apparently put on not to dictate a large price, but to dictate a small price, because it says on some of these packages the purchaser will kindly report to the factory or to somebody whether they have ever been charged higher than such a price.

Mr. LYON. Yes, sir.

Mr. BOUTELL. Do you know what system it is that can carry a retail price down to the consumer?

Mr. LYON. That is an agreement between the manufacturer and the seller. Years ago, in the seventies, I had a little article that went into almost every home in the United States, and the very first thing, when I withdrew my agreement with the jobbers to sell them, one man went right out and advertised to all the trade that he would sell a single gross at the absolute price for 10 gross or 100 gross. No jobber was interested in my goods, and I was compelled absolutely to go to the jobbers—and the biggest ones in the market—and sign their contracts in black and white.

Mr. BOUTELL. How does the jobber carry it on to the retailer?

Mr. LYON. He was compelled to sell to the retailer at a certain price. That was so in the seventies.

Mr. BOUTELL. What is it that compels the retailer to sell to the customer at that price?

Mr. LYON. There is nothing that compels him, except his competitors.

Mr. BOUTELL. As to these articles that I refer to—take, for instance, a certain shoe. You see it advertised in the papers and in the windows for $3.50 from one end of the country to the other, with no change in the price of the shoe.

Mr. Lyon. There is a watch [exhibiting watch] made by the Elgin Watch Company, of Illinois. I bought it in London for $12.50 American money. The wholesale dealer referred to a list, and he says: "There is number so-and-so. I will sell that watch just as low as they will allow me to sell it to you." And that was $12.50. I referred it to my jeweler at home—I bought it this summer—and he said the Elgin Watch Company would not allow him to sell it for less than $18 here. They have a price clear through—to the very retailer.

Mr. Boutell. You have got my question just reversed. [Laughter.]

Mr. Lyon. I beg your pardon, then. I meant to answer you correctly.

Mr. Boutell. On this little article that you sold in the seventies, and on these articles that are sold to-day and advertised in the newspapers and in the store windows at a given price all over the country, is that a contract that comes from the manufacturer and governs the retailer?

Mr. Lyon. I do not think it is, frequently. It is in some cases, but only where they have an absolute and complete control in some way.

Mr. Boutell. That must be the case, then, in this kind of shoe that is advertised all over the country at a certain price.

Mr. Lyon. Yes. They will bind their retailer to get such a price, and if they do not get it they will not furnish them.

Mr. Boutell. What I am trying to get at from you is whether there is any legitimate way in which, when you get lower raw material, you can see to it that the ultimate consumer gets the benefit of it.

Mr. Lyon. Yes. I can go no further than the one I sell to. I do sell to certain classes of department stores or retailers, and then I sell to the wholesaler, and do not limit him in any way as to what he sells for. He is at liberty to sell to the retailer at any price he chooses, and the retailer is at liberty to sell to the consumer at any price he chooses. There are a very few things, of course, that are limited all the way down.

In conclusion, let me say it is constantly asserted, and generally believed, that the object of the tariff is to protect the American workingman against the lower-paid workman of other countries. The facts herein stated are positive proof that the great object of the present American tariff is not so much to protect the workingman as it is to compel Americans to pay much higher prices than Europeans pay for the same goods.

The steel trust have told us they were earning 7 per cent on $360,281,000 preferred stock, and 5 per cent on $563,993,873 of bonds, and 2 per cent on $508,302,500 common stock, generally supposed to be "water." The dividends have all been paid from earnings during the panic, with lower prices for production and an average of less than half of their plants in operation.

Were they running full they could more than double the above dividends, or sell for much lower prices than they are now making, and really need no tariff protection.

NELSON LYON, OF TARRYTOWN, N. Y., FILES SUPPLEMENTAL BRIEF RELATIVE TO FREE PIG IRON.

TARRYTOWN, N. Y., *December 16, 1908.*

COMMITTEE ON WAYS AND MEANS,
        Washington, D. C.

GENTLEMEN: My supplemental brief with statements, productions, prices, and arguments apply to pig iron and their associate industries. I ask for free pig iron. I also ask for free raw material in the coarser products of iron and wire. I thank you for the courtesies extended to me in my former hearing before your honorable committee, and was greatly pleased at your desire to get at the real facts necessary for an equitable revision of our tariff.

In reply to your requests I herewith file various memorandums of the productions of pig iron; extending back to 1890 down to date; also the average yearly prices for earlier years; and for many of the later years I have obtained monthly productions and monthly prices. I have also been able through the courtesy of the Iron Age, to corresponds with our No. 2 southern coke. American and Scotch prices are filed side by side with each other. The Scotch prices are for every other month from 1896 down to and including 1907. These prices are f. o. b. Glasgow. To compete with American prices, $2 per ton for transportation will have to be added to make the price f. o. b. New York. By comparing them with prices here, you will see at a glance they would not prevent our producers getting a " fair profit " on their production.

Have also filed prices of Lake Superior iron ore for years of 1904, 1905, 1906, 1907, and 1908; also Lake ore shipments for 1906, 1907, and 1908.

You will find the prices of Lake ore shipments average 75 per cent higher in 1908, during the depression, than during the depression in 1904. The grip of the trust is again disclosed in the ore prices.

I have also filed prices of pig iron during the years of depression 1904 and 1908, and wish you to compare them closely. In the year 1904 the Tennessee Coal and Iron Company were in open competition in pig iron. During 1908, after the United States Steel Corporation absorbed the Tennessee Coal and Iron Company, prices were 33 per cent higher during the depression. This shows just how they rob the people, and will continue to do it as long as there is a tariff to protect them in it.

I also file production and prices of wire nails since 1896 down to 1908.

The first calendar year under the Dingley tariff was 1898, and the price of wire nails at Pittsburg in February, 1898, was $1.45, and they did not sell again for that price during the year, and closed the year at $1.27 per 100 pounds.

The American Steel and Wire Company and their combinations, the largest trust previous to the National Steel Company, was formed the latter part of 1898. They were powerful enough to control the output of wire rods, wire nails, wire, steel beams, and rails.

During the year 1899 they advanced the price of wire from $1.27 in December, 1898, to $2.95 in December, 1899, and to $3.20 in January, 1900, an advance of over 135 per cent. This advance was all clear profit.

I also present statistics showing imports and exports of iron and steel, commencing with 1893, when the imports and exports were about even, $30,000,000 each. From that day onward the exports increased and imports decreased, until the year 1900, when there were—

Exports _____ $129, 633, 480
Imports _____ 20, 443, 911

In 1904 there were—

Exports _____ $128, 553, 000
Imports _____ 21, 621, 000

In 1907 there were—

Exports _____ $197, 066, 000
Imports _____ 38, 789, 000

Showing an excess of exports _____ 158, 276, 000

The highest prices for labor in America in a great many years was reached, and our cost of production must have been as high as it ever was; our exports were $197,066,781; imports only increased to $38,-789,861. This shows we are able to make iron and steel at the very highest possible cost that they have ever reached and still increase our sales in European market nearly 20 per cent in 1907 over 1906, a very prosperous year.

These figures absolutely refute Mr. Schwab's statement that we export more in dull times than we do in good times; the higher the American production the higher are our foreign sales. It will be seen by comparing last year's exports with this year's that they will be less this year than they were last, when Mr. Schwab would give your committee to understand that they would equal 20 per cent this year or about three times what they were last.

December reports for ten months show exports to be as follows:

Ten months in—
1907_____ $1, 099, 652
1908_____ 815, 315

Deficiency in exports in 1908 compared with 1907_____ 284, 337

I again here repeat, if the tariff is to be in the interests of the workingman and consumer, when the American manufacturer can produce his goods here and sell freely in foreign market, the tariff should be entirely removed.

The above figures are conclusive proof that Europe can not compete with them, notwithstanding we pay freight for delivery in Europe, which amounts to nearly $2 per ton.

Again, I wish to refer to the cost of producing pig iron; Mr. Schwab tells use that the average cost of pig iron is about $14 per ton to-day, and he has known furnaces which have shut down because they could not make and sell pig iron at $14 and make money.

The average price of No. 2 pig iron at Cincinnati in 1904 was $12.73 per ton, and manufacturers had doubled their output between January 1 and December 31. Here is another absolute proof of the falsity of Mr. Schwab's statement that we are selling more iron and steel this year than last.

By referring to the United States Steel Corporation's report of December 31, 1904, their gross sales and earnings were $444,405,430, with a balance of $90,778,000, from which they paid, general expenses, $14,785,366, and all interest charges and dividends on capitalization, as reported in their December 31, 1903, statement, of $1,583,845,000.

Anyone who knows the conditions of the iron industry to-day knows that with one-half of their employees idle they could produce pig iron to-day just as cheap as they did produce it in 1904. Their employees would prefer to work for less wages than to have half of them idle, and they could and should have reduced their labor cost at that time, which would have lessened the cost of production, therefore should have reduced the selling price of the product.

The facts are they have maintained until very recently the high prices of last year on nearly their total production, and in the face of this they dare not reduce the price of labor of their employees.

According to the rule of law "false in one, false in all," Mr. Schwab should again appear before your committee under oath, and he would not affirm his statement of December 15.

Treatment of labor by steel trusts during the panic and recession in business since October 1 is the worst it could possibly be. When business slackens they close their furnaces and rolling mills. They tell the country they would not be so inhuman as to reduce the price of labor after having three prosperous years; they also tell us they will not reduce the price of their product.

They closed furnace after furnace until only 28 per cent were in operation. Their policy is and has been to only produce to supply the immediate demand. When the raw material is not produced, the rolling mills must close; also all other productions must reduce their output.

During their slackest time this year, 28 per cent only of their workingmen were employed. Their total employees were 210,180; 70 per cent of same being out of work would number 147,126. Nearly eight months passed before they were working to 50 per cent of their capacity. This would leave idle eight months after the panic commenced 105,000. Their latest reports published showed only 60 per cent of their capacity employed. On the basis of these figures they would have idle 84,000.

Was there ever a more inhuman treatment of labor? The trusts themselves are not deserving of any consideration, as far as a protective tariff is concerned.

The prices of finished products have not been advanced as great as raw material, but their finished products have been much too high. Raw material (pig iron) prices have been advanced so that the market price has been over 100 per cent above the cost of production. It was these extreme high prices of 1906 and 1907 that brought the great recession in business, as acknowledged by our honest President, W. H. Taft, recently elected, and they will continue to come as long as we have a high tariff.

The following is the price for No. 2 southern pig iron at Cincinnati: From February, 1897, to December 31, 1898, a period of twenty-two months, the price of No. 2 pig iron at Cincinnati averaged about $9.50 per ton, and in no month did the price average over $10 per ton.

Very soon after the American Steel and Wire Company was organized the price of iron began to advance and reached—

In June, 1899_____ $16.00
In October, 1899_____ 20.75

PRICE OF SCOTCH IRON.

The Scotch price of £3 8s. 8d_ $16.50
Add—
    Tariff_____ $4.00
    Freight_____ 2.00
                            6.00

        Total_____ 22.50

and remained at this price until April, 1900; in May, 1900, receded to $19.75; October, 1900, to $12.87. This showed an advance of nearly 120 per cent in price in nine months.

From October, 1900, to April, 1902, a period of eighteen months, it did not vary $2 per ton, prices ranging from $12.87 to $14.

In June, 1902, price advanced to $20; October, 1902, to $25.60.

Wire nails were sold at $1.27 per 100 pounds in December, 1898; in June were advanced to $2.30 per 100 pounds; January, 1900, to $3.20 per 100 pounds. From that day to this the price of nails has held the advance of 50 to 70 per cent above the regular price at which they were sold before the trusts were formed.

The following are prices of Scotch pig iron, Cleveland No. 3 f. o. b. Glasgow; also No. 2 foundry, at Cincinnati, Ohio, commencing 1896 down to 1908, every other month, which will be a fair average. Two dollars per ton must be added to make price Scotch pig iron f. o. b. New York:

	Scotch pig iron, Cleveland No. 3.		No. 2 foundry, Cincinnati.	Total production of America.
	Price.	United States currency.		
1896.	£ s. d.			*Tons.*
January	1 17 3	$8.94	....	
March	1 18 7	9.26	....	
May	1 17 4	8.96	....	
July	1 16 11	8.86	....	8,623,127
September	1 17 11	8.10	....	
November	2 0 5	9.70	....	
December	2 0 5	9.70	....	
1897.				
January	2 1 2	9.86	$10.00	
March	2 0 5	9.70	9.69	
May	1 19 7	9.50	8.75	
July	1 19 6	9.48	8.95	9,652,680
September	2 1 7	9.98	9.35	
November	2 1 5	9.94	9.50	
December	2 0 4	9.68	9.50	
1898.				
January	2 0 9	9.78	9.50	
March	2 0 6	9.72	9.25	
May	2 0 7	9.74	9.37	
July	2 0 4	9.68	9.25	11,773,934
September	2 3 0	10.32	9.55	
November	2 9 1	11.78	9.75	
December	2 4 3	10.66	9.90	
1899.				
January	2 6 .10	11.24	10.31	
March	2 7 9	11.46	13 75	
May	2 15 11	13.42	14.56	
July	3 11 6	17.16	17.56	13,620,703
September	3 17 7	18 62	19.94	
November	3 10 0	16.80	20.75	
December	3 6 9	16.02	20.75	

	Scotch pig iron, Cleveland No. 3.		United States currency.	No. 2 foundry, Cincinnati.	Total production of America.
	Price.				
1900.	£	s.	d.			*Tons.*
January	3	7	10	$16.28	$20.69	
March	3	13	10	17.72	23.50	
May	3	14	2	17.80	19.75	
July	3	9	3	16.62	16.81	13,789,942
September	3	10	9	16.98	13.62	
November	3	3	6	15.24	12.95	
December	2	13	6	12.84	13.75	
1901.						
January	2	8	0	11.52	13.45	
March	2	5	8	10.96	14.00	
May	2	5	10	11.00	13.85	
July	2	4	6	10.78	13.00	15,878,334
September	2	5	3	10.86	13.06	
November	2	3	6	10.44	14.00	
December	2	3	1	10.32	14.25	
1902.						
January	2	3	11	10.54	14.55	
March	2	6	9	11.22	14.75	
May	2	8	10	11.72	13.35	
July	2	10	9	12.18	20.75	
September	2	13	6	12.84	25.00	17,821,307
June price					25.65	
November	2	10	9	12.18	23.62	
December	2	7	11	11.50	22.44	
1903.						
January	2	7	8	11.84	21.65	
March	2	11	10	12.44	21.37	
May	2	6	1	11.06	18.87	
July	2	6	7	11.18	16.15	18,009,252
September	2	5	7	10.94	14.75	
November	2	2	10	10.28	12.00	
December	2	1	11	10.96	12.05	
1904.						
January	2	2	8	10.14	12.87	
March	2	3	3	10.88	12.10	
May	2	6	1	11.06	12.25	
July	2	6	7	11.18	11.81	16,497,033
September	2	5	7	10.94	12.00	
November	2	2	10	10.28	15.19	
December	.2	1	11	10.06	15.85	
1905.						
January	2	8	11	11.74	16.25	
March	2	9	6	11.88	16.25	
May	2	11	5	12.34	15.81	
July	2	5	9	10.98	13.94	22,992,380
September	2	8	8	11.68	14.37	
November	2	12	9	12.66	16.60	
December	2	13	3	12.78	16.75	
1906.						
January	2	13	9	12.90	....	....
March	2	8	1	11.54		
May	1	10	2	12.04		
July	2	10	6	12.12		
September	2	14	6	13.09		
November	2	18	6	14.04		
December	3	2	4	14.96		
1907.						
January	2	19	7	.14.30	....	....
March	2	14	3	13.02		
May	3	0	10	14.60		
July	2	17	2	13.72		
September	2	15	1	13.22		
November	2	10	.2	12.04		
December	2	9	3	11.82		

Pig-iron production by steel companies.

	Amount.	Price per ton.
1906.	*Tons.*	
January	1,358,015	$16.75
February	1,226,760	16.75
March	1,400,395	16.65
April	1,333,591	16.63
May	1,372,428	16.75
June	1,293,437	16.44
July	1,323,391	16.06
August	1,237,485	17.30
September	1,264,380	18.69
October	1,452,200	20.00
November	1,411,350	23.38
December	1,463,035	25.00
1907.		
January	1,406,397	26.00
February	1,317,923	26.00
March	1,424,827	26.00
April	1,446,788	25.06
May	1,470,080	24.25
June	1,457,230	24.10
July	1,452,557	23.85
August	1,445,685	23.00
September	1,417,153	21.50
October	1,514,521	20.95
November	1,084,114	19.50
December	659,459	17.00

Total production, 1906, 25,307,191 tons.
Total production, 1907, 25,781,361 tons.

The total productions noted above are for all producers. The production by steel companies shows how quickly the trust corporations close furnaces when they have over $90,000,000 in the bank subject to check.

If the tariff on pig iron was removed, they would have kept their workingmen employed similar to Merchant furnace.

You will also see how close our furnace men kept to Scotch prices plus $4 tariff and $2 freight.

We have also given you the Scotch prices from 1896 down to 1908. To make a parallel you will have to add for freight from Cincinnati price to equal New York price, $2 per ton; you will also have to add freight to Scotch prices to be f. o. b. New York, $2 per ton.

You will notice the price of pig iron advanced from $13 per ton in May, 1901, to $25.65 in June, 1902, without any apparent change in cost of production.

Prices receded again in November, 1903, to $12, and remained at nearly this price until it commenced to advance again in October, 1904, advancing in October, 1906, to $20; in December, 1906, to $25; in January, February, and March, 1907, to $26; in August, 1907, receded to $23; in December, 1907, receded to $17.

The total productions noted above are for all producers.

The above figures show that furnace men will get not only Scotch prices, $4 for tariff, $2 for freight, but from $2 to $4 besides.

There is no way to prevent it except by the reduction of the tariff and give them an open competition with Europe.

The following tables are prices of No. 2 coke foundry pig iron at Cincinnati, Ohio, steel beams at Philadelphia, and wire nails at

Pittsburg, for the following years, 1897, the last fiscal year under the Wilson bill, and 1898, the first calendar year under the Dingley law, and also the prices for the years 1899 and 1900. The two latter years show the great advance and recession in prices of foundry iron, steel beams, and wire nails, also pig iron.

	1897.			1898.		
	Southern No. 2 foundry, Cincinnati.	Steel beams, Philadelphia.	Wire nails, Pittsburg.	Southern No. 2 foundry, Cincinnati.	Steel beams, Philadelphia.	Wire nails, Pittsburg.
January	$10.00	$1.70	$1.39	$9.50	$1.30	$1.42
February	9.75	1.70	1.35	9.25	1.30	1.45
March	9.69	1.70	1.46	9.25	1.30	1.43
April	9.25	1.70	1.40	9.25	1.30	1.31
May	8.75	1.49	1.35	9.37	1.30	1.31
June	8.75	1.25	1.31	9.30	1.30	1.35
July	8.95	1.15	1.31	9.25	1.30	1.31
August	9.00	1.15	1.25	9.37	1.37	1.26
September	9.35	1.15	1.41	9.55	1.40	1.32
October	9.50	1.20	1.49	9.75	1.38	1.33
November	9.50	1.20	1.41	9.75	1.35	1.28
December	9.50	1.20	1.39	9.90	1.35	1.27

	1899.			1900.		
	Southern No. 2 foundry, Cincinnati.	Steel beams, Philadelphia.	Wire nails, Pittsburg.	Southern No. 2 foundry, Cincinnati.	Steel beams, Philadelphia.	Wire nails, Pittsburg.
January	$10.31	$1.40	$1.43	$20.69	$2.40	$3.20
February	11.69	1.42	1.57	20.50	2.40	3.20
March	13.75	1.55	1.94	20.30	2.40	3.20
April	14.50	1.64	2.05	20.19	2.40	2.95
May	14.56	1.63	2.10	19.75	2.40	2.20
June	16.00	1.82	2.30	18.75	2.22	2.20
July	17.56	2.08	2.42	16.81	2.05	2.20
August	18.35	2.20	2.50	14.25	1.89	2.20
September	19.94	2.40	2.76	13.62	1.65	2.20
October	20.75	2.40	2.87	12.87	1.65	2.20
November	20.75	2.40	2.95	12.95	1.65	2.20
December	20.75	2.40	2.95	13.75	1.65	2.20

	1901.			1902.		
	Southern No. 2 foundry, Cincinnati.	Steel beams, Philadelphia.	Wire nails, Pittsburg.	Southern No. 2 foundry, Cincinnati.	Steel beams, Philadelphia.	Wire nails, Pittsburg.
January	$18.45	$1.65	$2.22	$14.55	$1.75	$1.99
February	18.12	1.63	2.30	14.75	1.75	2.05
March	14.00	1.66	2.30	14.75	1.85	2.05
April	14.50	1.75	2.30	16.87	1.90	2.05
May	18.85	1.75	2.30	18.35	1.99	2.05
June	18.87	1.75	2.30	20.19	2.11	2.05
July	18.00	1.75	2.30	20.75	2.27	2.05
August	18.00	1.75	2.30	23.06	2.21	2.05
September	18.06	1.75	2.30	25.00	2.10	2.03
October	18.75	1.75	2.28	25.65	2.09	1.89
November	14.00	1.75	2.17	23.62	2.00	1.85
December	14.25	1.75	1.99	22.44	1.97	1.85

	1903.			1904.		
	Southern No. 2 foundry, Cincinnati.	Steel beams, Philadelphia.	Wire nails, Pittsburg.	Southern No. 2 foundry, Cincinnati.	Steel beams, Philadelphia.	Wire nails, Pittsburg.
January	$21.65	$1.78	$1.89	$12.37	$1.74	$1.89
February	21.50	1.75	1.92	12.12	1.74	1.90
March	21.37	1.75	2.00	12.10	1.74	1.91
April	20.15	1.74	2.00	12.50	1.74	1.90
May	18.87	1.73	2.00	12.25	1.74	1.90
June	17.75	1.73	2.00	11.80	1.74	1.89
July	16.15	1.73	2.00	11.81	1.74	1.71
August	15.19	1.73	2.00	12.00	1.74	1.60
September	14.75	1.73	2.00	12.00	1.58	1.60
October	13.50	1.73	2.00	12.81	1.54	1.62
November	12.00	1.73	1.97	15.19	1.54	1.73
December	12.05	1.73	1.87	15.85	1.58	1.73

	1905.			1906.		
	Southern No. 2 foundry, Cincinnati.	Steel beams, Philadelphia.	Wire nails, Pittsburg.	Southern No. 2 foundry, Cincinnati.	Steel beams, Philadelphia.	Wire nails, Pittsburg.
January	$16.25	$1.64	$1.75	$16.75	$1.83	$1.85
February	16.25	1.67	1.80	16.75	1.83	1.85
March	16.25	1.74	1.80	16.65	1.83	1.85
April	16.25	1.74	1.80	16.63	1.83	1.85
May	15.81	1.74	1.74	16.75	1.83	1.85
June	14.65	1.74	1.74	16.44	1.83	1.85
July	13.94	1.74	1.70	16.06	1.83	1.84
August	14.40	1.77	1.70	17.30	1.83	1.82
September	14.37	1.89	1.74	18.69	1.83	1.86
October	15.31	1.88	1.80	20.00	1.83	1.85
November	16.60	1.84	1.80	23.38	1.83	1.88
December	16.75	1.84	1.80	25.00	1.83	2.00

	1907.					1908.	
	Southern No. 2 foundry, Cincinnati.	Steel beams, Philadelphia.	Wire nails, Pittsburg.			Southern No. 2 foundry, Cincinnati.	Wire nails, Pittsburg.
January	$26.00	$1.83	$2.00	January		$16.00	$2.05
February	26.00	1.83	2.00	February 6		15.75	2.05
March	26.00	1.83	2.00	February 19		15.75	2.05
April	25.06	1.83	2.00	March 12		15.75	2.05
May	24.25	1.83	2.00	March 26		15.25	2.05
June	24.10	1.84	2.00	April 8		15.25	2.05
July	23.85	1.85	2.00	April 16		15.25	2.05
August	23.00	1.85	2.00	May 7		14.75	2.05
September	21.50	1.85	2.05	May 14		14.75	2.05
October	20.95	1.85	2.05	May 21		14.75	2.05
November	19.50	1.85	2.05	May 28		14.75	2.05
December	17.00	1.85	2.05	June 4		15.25	2.05

Table showing the production of pig iron in United States, gross tons, from 1890 down to and including 1901; also the total capacity per week for the years 1900 and 1901.

Production in United States, 1890-1901.		Prices for No. 2 southern pig at Chicago.	Total capacity per week and prices at Cincinnati.				
				1900.		1901.	
	Tons.			*Tons.*		*Tons.*	
1890	9,202,703	....	Jan	294,186	$20.69	250,851	$13.45
1891	8,279,870	....	Feb	298,014	20.50	278,258	13.12
1892	9,157,000	....	Mar	292,648	20.30	292,899	14.00
1893	7,124,502	....	Apr	289,482	20.19	296,676	14.50
1894	6,654,388	$10.75	May	293,850	19.75	301,125	13.85
1895	9,446,308	11.75	June	296,376	18.75	315,505	13.37
1896	8,623,127	11.40	July	283,413	16.81	310,950	13.00
1897	9,652,680	10.25	Aug	244,426	14.25	303,847	13.00
1898	11,773,934	10.45	Sept	231,778	13.62	299,861	13.06
1899	13,620,703	17.75	Oct	223,169	12.87	307,982	13.75
1900	13,789,242	18.35	Nov	215,304	12.95	320,824	14.00
1901	15,878,354	14.60	Dec	228,846	13.75	324,761	14.25

Monthly pig iron production.

	Tons.	Price per ton.
1902.		
January	....	$14.55
February	....	14.75
March	....	14.75
April	....	16.87
May	....	18.85
June	....	20.19
July	1,441,858	20.75
August	1,468,165	23.06
September	1,418,600	25.00
October	1,480,941	25.65
November	1,432,879	23.62
December	1,587,247	22.44
1903.		
January	1,472,788	21.65
February	1,392,081	21.50
March	1,590,470	21.37
April	1,608,431	20.15
May	1,716,174	18.87
June	1,673,228	17.75
July	1,550,840	16.15
August	1,573,648	15.19
September	1,556,717	14.75
October	1,425,282	13.50
November	1,039,622	12.00
December	852,575	12.05
1904.		
January	922,746	12.37
February	1,205,449	12.12
March	1,465,507	12.10
April	1,558,350	12.50
May	1,292,080	12.25
June	1,553,850	11.80
July	1,082,784	11.81
August	1,169,407	12.00
September	1,352,677	12.00
October	1,448,973	12.81
November	1,480,602	15.19
December	1,614,846	15.85

Production of pig iron by steel companies.

[Iron Age, December 10, p. 1734.]

	1906.	1907.	1908.
January	1,358,015	1,406,397	664,415
February	1,226,760	1,317,923	745,802
March	1,400,395	1,424,827	841,502
April	1,333,591	1,446,788	725,548
May	1,372,423	1,470,080	759,674
June	1,293,437	1,457,280	717,689
July	1,328,391	1,452,557	798,039
August	1,237,485	1,445,685	897,052
September	1,264,380	1,417,153	933,154
October	1,452,200	1,514,521	996,481
November	1,411,850	1,084,114	981,167
		15,487,275	9,061,123
December	1,445,528	659,459	....

Lake ore shipments, returns from Lake Superior docks, show the following:

[Iron Age. December 10.]

	1908.	1907.	1906.
Escanaba	3,354,952	5,761,988	5,851,095
Marquette	1,487,487	3,013,826	2,791,033
Ashland	2,513,670	3,437,672	3,388,111
Two Harbors	5,702,237	8,188,905	8,180,128
Superior	3,564,030	7,440,386	6,083,057
Duluth	8,808,168	13,445,977	11,220,218
Total shipments by boat	25,430,544	41,288,755	37,513,642

Prices of Lake Superior iron ore, per gross ton.

[Iron Trade, p. 29.]

Grades.	1904.	1905.	1906.	1907.	1908.
Old Range Bessemer	$3.00–$3.25	$3.75	$4.25	$5.00	$4.50
Old Range non-Bessemer	2.60– 2.80	3.20	3.70	4.20	3.70
Mesabi Bessemer	2.75– 3.00	3.50	4.00	4.75	4.25
Mesabi non-Bessemer	2.35– 2.50	3.00	3.50	4.00	3.50

The above figures show production of pig iron by steel companies during the years 1906, 1907, and 1908, showing just the reduction in this year's business, which has been reduced to the lowest possible minimum in dull times.

I call special attention to prices of Lake Superior ore during depression of 1904; also 1908:

Average ore prices during 1904 depression ____ $2.80
Average ore prices during 1908 depression ____ 4.00

Showing an advance per ton of ____ 1.80

Comment is unnecessary. If the steel companies are permitted to continue under the present tariff, soon they will own or control absolutely the whole output and furnace.

The tariff on iron ore certainly should be removed; after corporations have exhausted their mines and made fortunes out of them they will want the tariff increased.

With a balance of $6,100,000,000 to our credit in exports, nearly all gained since 1895, shown in my former statement, it is time the people were considered.

It is now no longer of any more importance to sell $1,000,000 worth of goods in a foreign market than it is to increase our home sales that amount.

Our high tariff should be reduced so our home people will consume the greatest amount possible.

Imports and exports of iron and steel from the year 1893 down to and including 1907.

	Imports.	Exports.		Imports.	Exports.
1893	$29,656,539	$30,159,363	1901	$20,395,015	$102,534,575
1894	20,853,576	29,943,729	1902	41,468,826	97,892,036
1895	25,772,136	35,071,563	1903	41,255,864	99,035,865
1896	19,506,587	48,670,218	1904	21,621,970	128,553,613
1897	13,835,950	62,737,250	1905	26,401,283	142,930,513
1898	12,474,572	82,771,550	1906	34,8.7,132	172,555,588
1899	15,800,579	105,690,047	1907	38,789,851	197,066,781
1900	20,443,911	129,633,480			

The above imports and exports of iron and steel, beginning in 1893, were nearly equal; from that year our exports increased, down to 1900.

Exports in 1900 _____ $129,633,480
Imports decreased to _____ 20,443,901

    Showing excess of exports _____ 109,189,579

Exports, 1907 _____ 197,066,781
Imports, 1907 _____ 38,789,851

    Showing excess of exports _____ 158,276,930

The above figures tell their own story. Our exports of all kinds of iron and steel show what we are making successfully with American labor during a year when prices have been the highest in years. We pay the ocean freights, which must be $2 per ton and upward, and are underselling Europe in their own market; also underselling Germany, which is proof that no tariff is needed and serves only to compel Americans to pay higher prices than our manufacturers sell for in Europe.

Our tariff laws are asserted to be in the interests of labor and consumers. These figures show that they are solely in the interests of the trusts and their combinations in the iron and steel productions.

The exports of 1907 show exports nearly equal to one-third of the steel trust's total output, and can not be said it is simply to dump surplus.

The exports of 1907, the year with the highest priced production we ever had, we increased our exports of iron and steel over $25,000,-000. There can be no stronger proof that no tariff is needed in the United States, as we can manufacture much more cheaply this year than last.

It has been constantly asserted and generally believed that the tariff is to protect the American workingman against the lower-paid workman of other countries. The facts herewith presented are positive proof that the greater object of the present Dingley tariff is not so much to protect the workingman as it is to compel the American consumer to pay much higher prices than Europeans pay for the same goods, and when the American prices advance to the European price, plus the tariff and ocean freights, that the workman does not share in that advanced price, but really has to pay this advance on much of the goods he consumes here.

If the tariff is to be in the interests of the workingmen and consumers, when the American manufacturer can manufacture his goods here and sell freely in the foreign market the tariff should be entirely removed.

The Dingley tariff enables the manufacturers to, and the manufacturers do, often advance the market price so they get unreasonable profits, and the prices have been advanced so great that they unsettle the whole business of the country and produce panics and recessions in business. The workingmen and consumers do not get the benefit of the advance in prices, and the workingmen are frequently thrown out of employment, waiting for confidence to be restored.

If the tariff was entirely removed on pig iron and the coarser makes of wire for manufacturing and wire for farm uses, the prices and production would be far more normal; labor would be constantly employed at fair wages.

Since the large combinations have been formed, like the American Steel and Wire Company, and later the United States Steel trust, they absolutely control production and the prices of what they produce. They meet together monthly, when the situation is extreme, and tell us what a great blessing they have been to the country in maintaining high prices. Such a meeting was very recently held.

As Haaman built the gallows on which he afterwards was hung, so the steel trust have supplied us certified statements of assets, production, and sales to show themselves to be the greatest robbers under our tariff of any corporation that exists in the United States that has come into the limelight. They are a public leech on nearly every industry in the land.

The greatest of American industries, the railroads, shipbuilding, stove and foundry trades, agricultural works, building trades, and hundreds of others all pay tribute. Scarcely one of these great industries dare appear before your committee and ask for free pig iron or a reduction of tariff on wires for fear of offending this giant corporation, and fear it will interfere with future dealings; they can not go outside and supply their wants.

Mr. Collier, president of the National Manufacturing Company, of Worcester, Mass., who also represented three others in the same city who use about 4,500 tons of wire in house-furnishing articles, appeared before your committee to ask for 50 p   cent increased duty on strainers in addition to a greatly increased specific duty. When I asked him why he did not ask for free or freer raw material he would not reply. Many other large manufacturers have told me they could not get supplied outside of the trust and dare not offend them, and told me I could give the facts, but must not give their names; and some said if they could have a prohibitive duty on the goods they make they would use tariff-protected raw material. This might in some cases answer for the manufacturers, but where do the great public come in?

From their own statement, the United States Steel Corporation show an apparent overcapitalization of $1,000,000,000.

Their first annual statement, December 31, 1902, with which they were to commence doing business January 1, 1903, showed assets of	$1,546,544,234
Their fifth annual statement, December 31, 1906, upon which they would do 1907 business, was	1,681,309,769
Showing an apparent increase of assets of	134,765,535
Gross sales and earnings for year to December 31, 1907, were	757,014,767
Gross sales and earnings for year to December 31, 1902, were	560,510,479
Increase sales in 1907 over 1902	196,504,288
Increase in assets in 1906 over 1902	134,765,535
Increased sales of 1906 over 1902	196,504,288

If the steel trust have made a correct statement of assets, as above quoted, and they produced $196,504,288 worth of goods in 1907, with additional assets of $134,765,767, they should produce their output of 1907, $757,014,767, with capital assets of $518,555,000.

Assets of December 31, 1907, were	$1,681,309,769
Amount of capital required to produce output of 1907 would be only	518,555,000
Showing an apparent overcapitalization of	1,162,654,769

American Iron and Steel Association.

[Kegs of 100 pounds.]

	Cut nails.	Wire nails.	Total.		Cut nails.	Wire nails.	Total.
1896	1,615,870	4,719,860	6,335,730	1902	1,633,762	10,982,246	12,616,008
1897	2,106,799	8,997,245	11,104,044	1903	1,435,898	9,631,661	11,067,554
1898	1,572,221	7,418,475	8,990,696	1904	1,283,362	11,926,661	13,210,023
1899	1,904,340	7,618,130	9,522,470	1905	1,857,549	10,854,892	12,212,441
1900	1,573,494	7,233,979	8,807,473	1906	1,189,289	11,486,647	12,675,886
1901	1,642,240	9,803,822	11,346,062	1907	11,109,138	11,731,044	12,840,182

By referring to prices of wire and cut nails you will see that soon after the American Iron and Steel Wire Company absorbed that industry in 1898 they at once advanced the price from $1.27 in December, 1898, to $2.30 in June, 1898, and $3.20 in January, 1900, on a greatly decreased product, which dropped from 11,104,044 kegs of 100 pounds each in 1897 to 8,807,473 kegs of 100 pounds each in 1900, and have not been below $2 per keg but a few times since, and prices were reduced $1 per keg at one stroke, nearly 33 per cent, in May, 1900. This should be sufficient proof that corporations have no souls. If they are going to heaven I do not want to be there. Kindly see that the production of 1907 does not exceed the production of 1897 only about 15 per cent.

Seven per cent is a fair profit.

I am very glad to be able to call your attention to a very important contract made by Mark A. Hanna & Co., of Cleveland, Ohio, with the Pittsburg Steel Company.

M. A. Hanna & Co. contracted to sell to the Pittsburg Steel Company 6,000 tons of pig iron per month on a sliding scale.

When the cost was $14 per ton the consumer is to pay 7 per cent above the cost, and for every advance of 50 cents per ton in the cost of making up to $17 the payment to be 1 per cent more, but the maximum to be 12 per cent above actual cost. The contract is to run two and a half years, with the privilege of a renewal for two years longer.

This seems to be a very equitable contract. I have always claimed 10 per cent to be an excellent profit on cost of goods by a large concern that can market their product with traveling salesmen.

The United States Steel Company on manufacturing and producing cost and operating expenses make a profit of 36 per cent. In 1903 on year's business their profit was 31 per cent; in 1904, 25 per cent; in 1905, 33 per cent; in 1906, 34 per cent; in 1907, 35 per cent; and they increased their assets from $1,325,267,583 in 1902 to $1,758,113,013 at the end of December, 1907.

Theirs is a class higher product and should make over 7 per cent profit. Our tariff laws should not allow them to increase their assets and working capital to this extent. I see that Mr. Schwab is a standpatter and does not think them overcapitalized and their profits none too large. They will take all the law allows them.

As per statement of United States Steel Corporation December 31, 1903, they show assets of $1,583,845,298 with which they were to commence doing business January 1, 1904. Their statement of December 31, 1904, shows their gross sales and earnings $444,405,430, and their manufacturing and producing cost and operating expenses were only $353,627,315, showing a balance of $90,778,115.

Will anyone who knows anything about manufacturing believe that their real actual assets were as above stated and only produced that amount of goods? By the above statement we show you, copied from their own certified statement, that with $134,000,000 of real added capital they did produce $196,504,000 additional goods. We think, beyond question, that any corporation that is not overcapitalized should produce manufactured goods equal to their capitalization.

Our own corporation, the Holt-Lyon Company, was incorporated for $20,000 capital nearly eight years ago; over one-half was supposed to be water or future profits capitalized. The president's and my salary is limited to $1,000 per year; we have added some to our assets, but have never been able to pay a dividend, because we have been robbed on our raw material to the amount of over $1,000 per year; our total assets, not including patents, to-day will not inventory over $12,000, and yet we produce over $36,000 worth of goods per annum, three times our working capital.

The Maxwell-Briscoe Motor Company, who manufacture automobiles in my home town, Tarrytown, N. Y., are capitalized for $1,500,000, and their production to-day exceeds $3,000,000 per annum, or fully twice their capital.

They believe in the seasons, the seed time and the harvest, and that the rose will bloom again, and also in the Maxwell motor. The season for selling automobiles is over, yet they are running to their fullest capacity making up parts to assemble next spring. They use up their surplus capital, go to their bankers and borrow hundreds of thousands of dollars, and pile up stock and are fully ready for the harvest in the spring.

Gentlemen of the committee, sweep from under the steel trust the tariff no longer necessary.

Put pig iron and iron ore on the free list, reduce the high tariff to the lowest minimum, and make competition close between this country and Europe, and the United States Steel Corporation will treat their employees right. You will hear no more about 150,000 employees being thrown out of work because of dull times after three years of unprecedented prosperity. They will not be trying to sell their production in times of depression. At panic times they will reduce the cost of production and selling price to manufacturers and consumers, who with reasonable concessions will absorb their surplus production, and will use up their cash surplus of $94,730,490 reported December 31, 1907, in keeping labor employed producing goods which are a sure sale, instead of closing furnaces and rolling mil s.

What is true of the steel trust is nearly equally true with every other monopolized industry that combines all American producers and dictates the selling price.

Gentlemen, the remedy rests with you and Congress soon to assemble. In your bill to be prepared and recommended to Congress take thoroughly into your consideration the great mass of consumers and small manufacturers, the 90 out of the 100; the 10 are able to take care of themselves. With an equitable tariff bill passed, in the preparation of which there are other things to be considered besides just the difference in the price of labor, which the great American consumption can keep, as Mr. Carnegie says rolling mills are, constantly employed without changes; so it will be with every other American industry; then confidence will be restored; prices will no longer go skyrocket high, which recessions in business can only restore. Labor will be constantly employed, and we will have the millennium in business which everyone desires. All of the foregoing of which is

Respectfully submitted.

NELSON LYON,
Secretary and Treasurer Holt Lyon Co.,
Rug, Carpet, and Egg Beaters.

HENRY G. McHARG, OF THE VIRGINIA IRON, COAL, AND COKE COMPANY, NEW YORK CITY, ASKS RETENTION OF PRESENT DUTY ON PIG IRON.

NEW YORK, N. Y., *November 30, 1908.*

Hon. SERENO E. PAYNE,
Chairman, Washington, D. C.

MY DEAR SIR: In the published reports of the newspapers of the proceedings before your committee it has seemed to me steel and iron as affected by the existing duties have for the most part been considered as one subject, whereas, to my mind, the latter is upon a very different basis from the former, and it will be my endeavor in as concise a manner as possible to give you, knowing full well your laborious duties, the reason why from my standpoint the present duty on pig iron should not be changed, and I would be glad to appear before your committee at any time after this week and to verify any statements made herein, or to answer any further questions the committee may desire.

This company owns nine blast furnaces—seven in the State of Virginia and two at Middlesboro, Ky. It owns and leases a large acreage of iron ore lands, mostly in the State of Virginia, but some few of the properties are in Tennessee, Kentucky, and Georgia. It also owns approximately 950 coke ovens situated at Inman and Toms Creek, Va., and some 30,000 acres of coal lands in Virginia, and 80,000 or 90,000 acres of coal lands in Kentucky, these latter being mostly at long distances from the railroad, and all being undeveloped. We practically sell no coke, it being made and used in our furnaces in producing pig iron.

On February 6, 1901, I was appointed one of the receivers of the company by the United States court at Harrisonburg, Va. On January 1, 1903, all debts having been paid, the property was restored to the stockholders and I became president. The company has never paid any cash dividend to its stockholders. When our furnaces, ore mines, coke ovens, and coal mines are in active operation, we employ from five to six thousand men, and, figured on the basis of four persons to a laborer, furnish food, clothing, and a living for from 20,000 to 25,000 people. From July, 1906, to July, 1907, this company made 202,453 tons of pig iron, 394,791 tons of coke, and mined 1,166,445 tons of coal, and during this year—I have not the official figures at hand—believe it to be very conservative when I make the statement that we paid out for labor alone between $2,000,000 and $3,000,000.

We use no foreign ores, and practically our entire consumption is furnished by mines in three States—Virginia, Tennessee, and Georgia—in the past, probably 95 per cent Virginia alone. With few exceptions our ores are washed; in some cases it takes 20 cars of material in its natural state to produce one car of iron ore that will assay 45 to 50 per cent metallic iron, and our cost for making pig iron for the period named from July 1, 1906, to July 1, 1907, was $14.11.

At Roanoke, where we have two furnaces, is our nearest point to tide water and to points in New England, where 40 to 50 per cent of our iron finds a market. Our average railroad rate to New England points is $4 per ton; from Radford and Pulaski, which are 60 to 75 miles farther west on the Norfolk and Western road, our rate is 25 cents additional, and from Max Meadows and Bristol, which are, respectively, about 100 to 125 miles farther west from Roanoke, the rate is 50 cents additional. At each of these places we have one furnace, and considering the additional distance and additional haul, the above rates are fully justified; in fact, although our all-rail rate to New England, in which way 95 per cent of our shipments are made, averages about $4 per ton, it is practically a haul of 800 miles, which gives the railroad but 5 mills per ton per mile, and is as low as the business can be expected to be handled.

Let us look now to the foreign market for iron. The New York papers give the quotation as 49s. 6d.; this is practically $12. It is well known that it is a habit for vessels bound to the West from

England, Belgium, Germany, and France, bound for Boston, New York, Philadelphia, and Baltimore to come largely in ballast. The rate by Cunard Line being lately quoted $1.22 per ton from Liverpool to New York. They will take iron or any other heavy commodity as freight for whatever rate they can obtain, for outside of the handling whatever sum they receive is all gain. They can, therefore, put English iron down at our ocean ports, irrespective of the $4 duty, at about $14 a ton, a price less than our cost prices for the year referred to at our furnaces in Virginia. This is the basis of my argument: That it is unfair, under conditions which prevail, owing to subsidies given by some foreign nations to their mercantile marine, and the known bulky nature of our exports to England, Belgium, Germany, and France, creating as it does a large proportion of empty cargo room in vessels bound to the States, from above countries, and that therefore the rate on freight shipments bound West bears no proportion to the actual cost of carrying the same, but simply results in an unfair competition, which in the case of pig iron needs fully the present duty of $4 per ton to place our manufacturers on an equal footing.

Our company has from $10,000,000 to $15,000,000 invested in furnaces, ore mines, coke ovens, and coal lands; we give a living to 20,000 or 25,000 people when our plants are in active operation, and have from the different agitations lost money in the past eighteen months in common with the majority of our fellow-citizens. After the presidential election, we enjoyed for two weeks the best market for iron since April, 1907, since which time these hearings began and newspapers reported the same, sales have stopped and a relapse is once more in full force. It is hardly necessary to remind your committee that the wages paid in our furnaces are double those of England, Belgium, Germany, and France for common labor. That our maritime laws, very justly, reserve to American bottoms the coastwise trade, which precludes our shipment by water north from Norfolk, except at rates as measured by distances six or seven times greater than English or Norwegian tramp ships will bring it from foreign ports. There can never be a combination of pig-iron producers, they are too many in number, and their location and condition surrounding them are so widely different, and because iron is the basis of steel. Should the interest of those that have their money invested in the production of the former be punished for the sins of the latter, which in some lines of production are controlled by a few companies and individuals of large means.

As long as present hard times and depression exist in England, Belgium, and Germany, and prices of iron remain there as at present, I believe any reduction of duty on pig iron will compel us to close our entire operations, with the exception of our coal mines, throwing necessarily a large number of worthy American workingmen out of employment.

After Mr. McKinley's election in 1896, the ten years following gave this country, its business men, its farmers, and its laborers, such prosperity and wages as the most optimistic would hardly have conceived. Let well enough alone. Certainly any lowering of duty on pig iron will be an unjust discrimination against those citizens who have their money invested in furnaces and ore lands in

our own country, and who employ a large force of employees mining
and manufacturing the same.

Very truly, yours, HENRY K. McHARG.

P. S.—Since the above I have received from a large importing
firm the following statement:

In 1906 and 1907 we chartered nine steamers with pig iron from Middlesboro, England,
and to New York, Philadelphia, and Baltimore, and the highest rate paid was 6 shillings
and 9 pence—the lowest 6 shillings. Ocean freights are lower now than they were
then.

———

THE OREGON IRON AND STEEL COMPANY, PORTLAND, OREG., ADVOCATES REDUCTION OF DUTY ON PIG IRON.

PORTLAND, OREG., *December 8, 1908.*

WAYS AND MEANS COMMITTEE,
  House of Representatives, Washington, D. C.

GENTLEMEN: We beg respectfully to call to your attention some
particulars regarding the tariff on pig iron.

We are manufacturers of cast-iron pipe in our foundry at Oswego,
close to Portland, Oreg., and by reason of the high tariff of $4 per
ton on pig iron from abroad we have to close down our foundry
from time to time. For example, we have not operated our pipe
foundry since November, 1907, and are not operating it now.

We believe that were the tariff on pig iron cut in two that a very
large development would take place on this Pacific coast. It seems
more logical for the best interests of this country that the tariff on
what may be called the " raw material " should be cut down rather
than cut the tariff on the manufactured material, such as steel beams,
etc. Were the tariff on the raw material cut in two, this coast would
be enabled to purchase pig iron from Europe and China, from which
latter source we are now beginning to receive some, so that large
manufacturing establishments could be operated and employment
given to American workmen in same. But if a cut is made on steel
beams and other manufactured goods and no cut made on the tariff
on pig iron, it simply means, as far as this coast is concerned, that
the manufacturer of iron and steel commodities will be placed at a
greater disadvantage than ever when competing with foreign manufactured goods; and not only with foreign manufactured articles,
but with domestic eastern manufactured articles also.

We trust that you may see your way to help us in this respect.

We shall be glad to give you any further information that you
may desire.

Yours, respectfully, OREGON IRON AND STEEL CO.,
  . A. S. PATTULLO, *Secretary.*

61318—SCHED C—09——7

EDGAR S. COOK, PRESIDENT WARWICK IRON AND STEEL COMPANY, POTTSTOWN, PA., SUBMITS BRIEF RELATIVE TO PIG IRON AND DUTY THEREON.

POTTSTOWN, PA., *December 30, 1908.*

COMMITTEE ON WAYS AND MEANS,
Washington, D. C.

GENTLEMEN: The Warwick furnaces are typical merchant blast furnaces.

They are not connected with any steel works, nor with any works wherein pig iron is fabricated into finished forms.

All the iron made is sold at competitive prices.

Different grades and qualities of pig iron are made by the same furnaces, to suit the varying requirements and specifications of the consuming public.

The eastern merchant blast furnaces are located in Pennsylvania, New Jersey, and New York, east of the Allegheny Mountains.

The sale of their pig iron is confined to a narrow strip of territory along the Atlantic coast.

Their iron can not go south of Baltimore, in view of the competition of Virginia and Alabama furnaces, nor west of Altoona, where it meets western iron. The consumptive requirements of northern New York and Pennsylvania are met by furnaces located at Buffalo, and the Beech Creek district of Pennsylvania.

While eastern pig iron can not invade the districts named, the territory naturally contributory to the eastern merchant blast furnace is easily reached by Virginia and southern irons, as well as Buffalo irons. Large tonnages of western iron are also sold and delivered to eastern consumers, especially when the industrial conditions are not favorable.

It can thus be easily seen that the eastern merchant blast furnaces are peculiarly sensitive to any change in tariff duties that would add to the competition for the sale of their product.

Ocean freight rates from England or Germany to Atlantic ports of entry offer no protection, as the inland railroad rates of transportation from the furnaces to many of the points of consumption are in excess of the ocean rates.

The profits of the eastern merchant blast furnaces do not bear any comparison to the profits of other branches of the iron and steel trade.

While there has been a growth of capacity in the last ten years, it has been brought about largely through the necessity of reducing costs of production by increasing the capacity of the furnace and equipping it with the very best of modern machinery and labor-saving appliances in order to protect the investment already made and maintain the competition with other districts.

A large tonnage multiplied by a small profit per ton of iron fairly represents the average conditions of the past ten years.

The continued existence of the eastern merchant blast furnace is of importance to the eastern consumer as a comparative near-by source of supply for his raw material. Preference is therefore likely to be given to the local iron, other things being equal.

This preference would not be likely to extend, however, to paying more per ton for eastern pig iron than English or German pig would cost delivered at the works of the consumer.

There are a few small eastern furnaces so located with respect to ore supplies owned by themselves that they can run under any and all conditions. The product, however, is small, and under ordinary conditions they are an unimportant factor.

The Warwick furnaces, located at Pottstown, Pa., may be taken to illustrate the class of eastern merchant blast furnaces that buy in the open market all of the ore, fuel, etc., required to supply their furnaces.

While the bulk of the pig iron made is consumed within a radius of 100 miles, with railroad transportation rates varying from 25 to 90 cents per ton of iron, yet a large tonnage is shipped to and consumed at points in New England, where the railroad freight is $2.10 per ton.

The ownership of the Warwick furnaces is widely scattered, being distributed among 600 stockholders. The capital stock is $1,500,000. Many of the stockholders are women. No single holding amounts to over $100,000 at par value of the stock. The capitalization, including bonds issued, does not exceed $6 per ton of iron capacity.

The aim of the management has been to keep the plant up to date in every particular, so as to secure the most effective instrument to produce pig iron at the lowest possible cost of converting the raw materials into a salable product.

The tariff duty of $4 per ton of pig iron came into effect at a time when raw material was low enough to permit of the production of pig iron at such a cost that the duty of $4 per ton, as compared with $6.72, was not productive of any serious consequences, so far as foreign competition was concerned.

Experience has shown that the duty of $4 was sufficient to protect when such protection was most needed, and at the same time not too high to become a source of considerable government revenue when foreign iron was needed to make up any deficit in the domestic supply to meet unexpected large increase in the consumptive requirements of our country.

It has served its purpose so well that it would scarcely be wise to run the risk of disturbing the balance apparently so satisfactory to maker and consumer.

Pig iron is a true barometer of trade from the fact that its production is so widely scattered and that it is all sold without any concert of action, the competition being unrestricted.

Prices are determined by the consumptive demand, the production and the competition of the makers.

The net earnings of the makers have not been sufficient to build new furnaces. The new furnace of the Warwick Company was built from the proceeds of the new stock sold to old and new stockholders. The earnings over a period of ten years, 1898 to 1907, inclusive, have not been sufficient to more than keep the furnace in a good state of repair and pay very moderate dividends to stockholders.

These statements are proven by figures taken direct from the books of the Warwick Company. (See Exhibit A.)

Calculated upon the tons of iron made, the "bad debts" written off 1897 to 1907 were insignificant.

During the years 1897 and 1898 the cost of production, based upon low price of ores, coke, railroad freight rates, labor, etc., was so low that we were almost in a position to export iron. In fact, Alabama and Virginia furnaces did make some shipments to England.

We sold several lots to New York exporters for shipment to Havana, Panama, and Chile.

Only about 33 per cent of the eastern merchant blast furnaces were able to run during the years 1897 and 1898. Since 1877 the Warwick furnace has always been in the race, except for a few months at intervals of three to five years, when necessary repairs were being made.

Accompanying increased demand for iron and the starting of additional furnaces raw materials rapidly advance in price.

Railroad freight rates on raw material and pig iron are also sensitive to improved conditions, but are slow to respond to adverse trade conditions.

During the active demand for iron the first half of 1907 many thousand tons of English and German iron were brought into this country to make good the deficit in the American product, thus giving to the Government no little revenue, but without affecting injuriously the eastern merchant blast furnaces.

English iron was delivered to points in eastern Pennsylvania, after paying 80 cents railroad freight per ton from ocean port to works, at a lower price per ton than our cost of manufacture.

Following the financial crisis of 1907, orders for English iron ceased, but shipments upon contracts continued to arrive, causing no little embarrassment to local makers.

With the decreased consumption of pig iron for 1908, consequent upon partial industrial paralysis, fully 75 per cent of the capacity of the eastern merchant blast furnaces was forced to temporarily discontinue operations

Prices for iron fell below cost of production, due to the competition of American furnaces in the eastern territory.

The trade of England and Germany was depressed 'at the same time. Without the tariff duty of $4 per ton on pig iron, our eastern markets would have been invaded by foreign iron at prices several dollars per ton below our cost of manufacture.

Such importations would doubtless have added to the revenue of the Government, but at a time when the eastern merchant blast furnaces would have been crushed, with the attendant suffering to the employees and their families.

Any reduction whatever in the duty of $4 per ton might have made the bad conditions worse.

Under the conditions of 1908 any inducement to encourage importations of foreign iron into our eastern markets would scarcely be looked upon as wise, even from the standpoint of a tariff reformer, to say nothing of the point of view of a protectionist.

Running under conditions of greatly reduced production compared with capacity, the fixed expenses increase rapidly per ton of iron produced. Our sales of iron from April to September, 1908, inclusive. averaged $14.94, the cost being $14.88, showing estimated profit of 6 cents per ton. The failure of a rolling mill company owing us $2,700 just about wiped out our profit on the iron made during the same period.

Upon the basis of $14.88 cost f. o. b. cars Pottstown, Pa., plus $2.10 freight to Boston and 25 cents commission for selling, the price should have been not less than $17.23 delivered, to cover actual cost.

English iron, Cleveland brand, at $12 Middlesboro, plus $2 freight and charges, could be delivered Boston at $14.

English iron could be placed at Philadelphia for $14.

Freight and charges, Pottstown to Philadelphia, 80 cents, would make a total cost of $15.68.

The duty of $4 per ton prevented English iron from invading the eastern coast, thus preventing the further curtailment of the output of the eastern merchant blast furnaces.

We argue, therefore, whatever sentimental reason seemingly may exist for any change in duty on pig iron, it is not justified by the facts as presented.

American competition has been sufficient to keep the selling price of iron down to cost.

Steady and continuous running is essential to the blast furnace, and especially to keep organizations intact. A loyal, capable organization, with teamwork developed by practice, is considered to be worth 25 per cent of the cost of the plant.

The great difference in cost between 1898 and 1908 can readily be seen as follows:

Year.	Ore cost per ton of iron.	Fuel cost per ton of iron.
1898	$4.54	$3.02
1908	8.11	4.00

The actual cost of conversion for 1908, as compared with 1898—that is, labor, salaries, fixed expenses, etc., with two furnaces in operation—is as low as in 1898, notwithstanding that the wages paid labor are considerably higher than during 1898. The increased wages paid employees have been neutralized by the benefits derived by expenditures on capital account. (See Exhibit B.)

While cost of fuel for 1908 per ton of iron shows $4 as compared with $3.02 for 1898, the consumption of fuel per ton for 1908 was fully 300 pounds less per ton of iron than for 1898.

Attention is called to these items in order to show the practical value of expenditures on capital account, to improve the efficiency of the furnaces, and to lower the cost of conversion, and thus helping us to pay the higher wages.

The increased cost per ton of ore delivered to furnace, and of coke, is due to higher prices paid f. o. b. cars at shipping points for these raw materials, and also to the higher rates of transportation paid to railroad companies, 1908 as compared with 1898. The railroad freights paid on incoming materials entering into the cost of a ton of iron constitute from 35 to 40 per cent of the total cost of pig iron.

There are exceptions, as related to certain small furnaces working local material, but the statement is true of the Warwick furnaces and other furnaces of the East working under like conditions.

As to what percentage of the increased cost of ore and coke is due to higher wages paid miners, higher prices for supplies, etc., I am unable to specify.

All indications, however, would seem to show that the low prices of 1898 are not likely to be repeated except as the result of some dire calamity in the industrial and financial world.

Those who conducted business enterprises through the period from 1893 to 1898, inclusive, would scarcely welcome such a return, from whatever cause, and the community àt large would doubtless prefer a prohibitory tariff scheme rather than endure again the era of low prices of 1893 to 1898.

Following upon an increased consumption of pig iron and a larger production, the cost of ore per ton of iron will increase through an increased demand.

Many of the eastern ore mines sold their ore during 1908 at little or no profit, and in some cases at a loss, in order to keep the mines in operation.

The question of a foreign ore supply is surrounded with many uncertainties so far as the eastern merchant blast furnaces are concerned.

We feel certain that even a small reduction in the duty on pig iron under certain conditions would seriously embarrass the eastern merchant blast furnaces, while it might have little or no effect upon the western blast furnaces, protected by a long-distance railroad haul from the coast to the interior.

Acting, then, upon such an assumption, any reduction in the duty on pig iron based upon a reduction of duty on iron ore, or even the placing of ore on the free list, would be risking a certain loss in the hope of gaining an advantage that might not be realized, based upon the known sources of foreign ore supply.

The present chief sources of supply of foreign ore are Newfoundland, Sweden, Spain, and Cuba. Scattering lots come from Russia, the islands of the Mediterranean, and Algeria.

The supply from Newfoundland is limited. A large portion of the product of the mines is marketed in Germany. The high phosphorus content makes it a desirable mixture for the German furnaces, producing a high phosphorus iron for their basic Bessemer steel converters. This process for making steel is not used in the United States, so that only a small percentage of the Newfoundland ore is desirable in the ore mixture of merchant furnaces, called upon to furnish pig iron comparatively low in phosphorus content.

Sweden. Experience has shown that the demand for Swedish ores abroad, especially Germany, is such that they are only offered to the American furnaces at prohibitory prices. Even if duty was removed, Swedish ores would not help the production of low-cost iron.

Spain. The three largest producing mines of best grade of ore in Spain, I am informed, are owned and controlled by English, German, and French capital. The product of these mines is used by the owners.

The tonnage of good grades of Spanish ore available for the American market is limited.

Inferior grades, not acceptable to foreign furnaces, are in more abundant supply. These ores, however, are just as undesirable for the American furnace as for the English, German, and French.

Any considerable demand from American sources would not only enhance the Spanish owners' ideas of value, but would bring about a revolution in ocean freight rates, as bearing upon the cost of transportation.

In such an event the ore itself would have to pay sufficient revenue to the shipowner to afford him a profit on the carriage. This would mean a greater advance in ocean freight rates than the present duty on iron ore.

The present low ocean freight rates are based upon the ore being sought after by the vessel as ballast cargo, because of the dangerous passage over the Atlantic for vessels not well loaded. This applies to the winter months especially.

The American user of foreign ore to the exclusion of the domestic product would run extra risks in having his ore supply at such a great distance and subject to conditions adding to cost bearing no relation to the conditions of the iron trade in the United States.

Cuba. The known iron-ore resources of Cuba are largely owned by the Pennsylvania Steel Company and the Bethlehem Steel Company.

As a rule they are not offered for sale. Several small operations, with limited tonnages, are now, or soon will be, prepared to sell their ore in the American market. This tonnage, however, is not likely to be large for several years yet to come.

If the iron-ore interests of the United States are satisfied to have the duty of 40 cents per ton cut in half, or removed altogether, there will be no objection on the part of the eastern merchant blast furnace companies. At the same time, if a reduction in whole or in part should be considered a convincing argument in favor of a reduction in the $4 duty on pig iron, it would be exchanging at the best a small benefit (and even then a doubtful one) for an existence at the mercy of our European competitors.

Respectfully submitted.

EDGAR S. COOK,
President Warwick Iron and Steel Co.

EXHIBIT A.

	Selling price f.o.b. Pottstown.	Cost.	Profit per ton.	Production.
				Tons.
1894	$10.59	$10.48	$0.11	511,163½
1895	10.74	10.36	.38	53,932
1896	11.29	10.88	.41	37,107
1897	10.41	10.10	.31	63,137
1898	9.79	9.52	.27	64,816
1899	13.36	11.01	2.35	62,608
1900	17.78	15.11	2.67	53,787
1901 a				
1902	16.02	15.83	.19	146,363½
1903	17.60	16.75	.85	173,096
1904	13.72	13.45	.27	125,933
1905	15.18	14.65	.53	205,789
1906	16.86	15.53	1.33	219,781
1907	20.18	18.79	1.39	256,750

a Furnaces out of blast or building.

EXHIBIT B.

	Labor.	Wages, fillers.	Keepers.	C. H. helpers.	Engineers.
1894, No. 1	$0.90	$1.15	$1.65	$1.25	$1.45
1895, No. 1	.90	1.15	1.65	1.30	1.45
1896, No. 1	1.00	1.25	1.75	1.35	1.55
1897, No. 1	1.00	1.25	1.75	1.35	1.55
1898, No. 1	.90	1.25	1.65	1.05	1.45
1899, No. 1	1.25	1.45	2.05	1.45	1.85
1900, No. 1	1.25	1.55	2.05	1.85	1.85
1901, No. 1	1.25	1.55	2.05	1.85	1.85
1902 No. 1	1.30	1.65	2.15	1.95	1.95
1902 No. 2	1.30	1.65	2.15	1.95	1.95
1903 No. 1	1.40	1.75	2.25	2.05	2.05
1903 No. 2	1.40	1.75	2.25	2.05	2.20
1904 No. 1	1.25	1.60	2.05	1.85	1.90
1904 No. 2	1.25	1.60	2.10	1.90	2.05
1905 No. 1	1.35	1.70	2.15	1.95	2.00
1905 No. 2	1.35	1.70	2.25	1.90	2.15
1906 No. 1	1.50	1.75	2.30	2.10	2.15
1906 No. 2	1.50	1.75	2.40	2.05	2.30
1907 No. 1	1.50	1.75	2.30	2.10	2.15
1907 No. 2	1.50	1.75	2.40	2.05	2.30
1908 No. 1	1.25	1.50	1.90	1.70	1.85
1908 No. 2	1.25	1.50	1.95	1.70	1.90

EXHIBIT C.

Cost of ore, coke, and labor per ton of iron.

	Labor per ton of iron.	Ore cost per ton of iron.	Yield of ore.	Cost of fuel.
			Per cent.	
1894	$0.80	$5.06	63.4	$3.20
1895	.81	4.93	61.5	3.15
1896	.92	5.04	62.4	3.51
1897	.75	5.10	61.3	3.07
1898	.74	4.58	61.2	3.02
1899	1.01	4.67	62.5	3.59
1900	1.22	6.76	61.2	5.08
1901	1.23	6.28	63.0	4.86
1902	1.21	6.56	53.0	5.52
1903	1.03	6.69	53.2	6.52
1904	.78	6.01	54.4	4.54
1905	.75	7.11	53.1	4.75
1906	.76	7.56	53.8	4.82
1907	1.07	8.39	56.0	5.82

EXHIBIT D.

Ore supply.

	Lake.	Foreign.	Local and eastern.
	Per cent.	*Per cent.*	*Per cent.*
1894	17.2	....	82.8
1895	50.5	....	49.5
1896	50.5	....	49.5
1897	61.5	....	38.5
1898	59.7	....	40.3
1899	61.4	....	38.6
1900	53.9	12.5	33.6
1901	59.0	10.0	31.0
1902	58.0	10.0	32.0
1903	45.0	10.0	45.0
1904	47.0	9.6	43.4
1905	57.0	12.0	31.0
1906	61.0	12.0	27.0
1907	43.0	20.0	37.0

EXHIBIT E.

Authentic yearly average of English iron, Cleveland brand, furnished by London Iron House, 1893 to 1907, inclusive.

	s.	d.		s.	d.
1893	34	10	1901	45	3
1894	35	9	1902	49	3
1895	36	3	1903	46	4
1896	38	3	1904	43	11
1897	40	7	1905	49	6
1898	42	2	1906	53	0
1899	60	1	1907	56	2
1900	68	9			

EXHIBIT F.

Railroad freights on coke and iron ore, 1896 to 1908.

Year.	Rate on ore, Buffalo to Pottstown.	Rate on coke, Latrobe district to Pottstown.
1896	$1.38	$1.50
1897	1.20	1.50
1898	1.25	1.30
1899	1.10	1.60
1900	1.35	1.95
1901	1.35	1.65
1902	1.35	1.65
1903	1.35	1.75
1904	1.35	1.75
1905	1.35	1.75
1906	1.35	1.75
1907	1.45	1.85
1908	1.45	1.85

EXHIBIT G.

Eastern Pig Iron Association, December, 1908.

	Orders.	Stocks.	In.	Out.
	Tons.			
January	176,760	69,500	....	....
February	176,920	81,710	12	22
March	179,200	88,350	15	24
April	178,000	107,950	15	29
May	159,010	114,320	14	29
June	234,254	106,756	16	27
July	235,870	92,810	16	27
August	285,440	80,140	19	25
September	329,950	63,340	20	24
October	333,820	55,035	21	23
November	355,470	45,970	22	22
December	427,528	32,961	23	21

At the regular monthly meeting of the Eastern Pig Iron Association at Philadelphia, December 16, 1908, the chairman made a report of the meetings held in New York with regard to the discussion respecting the tariff.

He submitted a statement prepared by him, together with costs, prices, etc., of the Warwick Furnaces, of which company he is the president. This statement, etc., was taken to represent the average merchant blast furnace operating in the East.

On motion it was resolved that the Eastern Pig Iron Association accepts this statement as expressing the views of its members, and approves the action of President Cook in preparing and forwarding it to the tariff commission.

Exhibit H.

ESTIMATED COST OF PRODUCING PIG IRON, MERCHANT FURNACES IN EASTERN PENNSYLVANIA, DURING THE FIRST HALF OF THE YEAR 1909, BY EDGAR S. COOK, PRESIDENT WARWICK IRON & STEEL COMPANY, MANUFACTURERS OF PIG IRON, POTTSTOWN, PA.

POTTSTOWN, PA., *January 16, 1909.*

Following upon the starting up of additional furnaces to meet the increased demand of pig iron, local ore mines have responded in the way of higher prices for their product. Certain by-products of the steel mills and rolling mills, known as scale and cinder and used by the blast furnaces to reconvert into pig iron, have also advanced. The selling price of coke is considerably higher than during the month of April to September.

A fair estimate of the cost of making pig iron for the next six months, based upon 1908 prices for Lake Superior ores and a varying percentage of local and foreign ores, is as follows:

Based on product of 22,000 tons per month.

Ore: Cost per ton of pig iron		$9.00
Coke:		
At ovens, per ton (2,000 pounds)	$2.00	
Freight per ton (2,000 pounds)	1.85	
2,000 pounds delivered	3.85	
2,200 pounds coke per ton of iron at $3.85 (per 2,000 pounds)	4.23	
Limestone: 950 pounds per ton of iron at $1 per 2,240 pounds	.42	
Cost of material		$13.65
Salaries	.21	
Wages	.73	
Sundry supplies	.45	
Relining	.25	
Total		1.64
Manufacturing cost at furnace		15.29
Interest on bonds, taxes, insurance, commission on sales	.30	
Depreciation, to cover necessary replacements not otherwise provided for, and improvement	.30	
		.60
Total		15.89

The ore cost per ton of pig iron in the above estimate is based on the use of 30 per cent old range ore, 30 per cent Mesaba ore, 20 per cent Magasaka ore, and 20 per cent foreign ore, all taken at the price paid for same, including freight delivered at the furnace. It was also estimated that the metalloids will balance loss in furnace.

EDGAR S. COOK,
President Warwick Iron and Steel Company.

I, Edgar S. Cook, president Warwick Iron and Steel Company, Pottstown, Pa., having knowledge of the facts, do solemnly, sincerely, and truly declare that the foregoing statements are correct and true to the best of my knowledge and belief.

EDGAR S. COOK, President.

Sworn to and subscribed before me at Pottstown this 18th day of January, 1909.

[SEAL.]

SAMUEL H. FRIDY,
Notary Public.

Commission expires January 19, 1911.

JOSEPH G. BUTLER, JR., YOUNGSTOWN, OHIO, FILES SUPPLEMENTAL BRIEF RELATIVE TO PIG IRON.

YOUNGSTOWN, OHIO,
January 20, 1909.

Hon. SERENO E. PAYNE,
    Chairman, Ways and Means Committee,
        Washington, D. C.

SIR: On November 25, 1908, I had the honor of appearing before your committee as the representative of a large percentage of the merchant blast furnaces of the United States.

All of these furnaces are independent producing concerns. They buy their ore, coal, coke, limestone, and all necessary raw materials in the open market, and their finished product is pig iron, which is sold by them in the open market in open competition with each other and the foreign producers.

In pursuance of the promise made at the hearing on November 25, I herewith present my brief relative to the tariff on items covered by paragraph 122 of the Dingley Act.

STEEL AND IRON SCRAP.

Maintenance of the present tariff on steel and iron scrap is of the greatest importance to those whom I represent, as this material is used principally as a substitute for pig iron, and generally at a much less average cost.

A reduction in the tariff on steel and iron scrap would result in great disturbing injury, especially at the present time, to railway companies, farm machinery manufacturers, and others, who are its principal sellers.

PIG IRON.

Among the largest customers of the railroads are the merchant pig-iron furnaces. These furnaces are enormous consumers of large tonnages of iron ores, coke, limestone, fire brick, sand, clay, etc., and the furnace companies pay out millions of dollars yearly, which is practically all absorbed for labor in mining, transportation, etc.

The merchant furnaces pay freight on about 4 tons of materials assembled to produce each ton of pig iron, besides the freight on the outgoing product, hence the production of pig iron swells into an enormous indirect value, outside of that to its makers and users.

The fact that all iron in pigs must be cast in sand or iron chilled molds restricts the size and capacity of the merchant blast furnaces, and thus increases their tonnage cost. The capacity of these furnaces is approximately one-half that of the large furnaces making pig iron, which is taken direct to the steel works in molten state, thus omitting the casting process. The costs of materials entering into the cost of manufacturers vary greatly, owing to local variations in freights, cost of coke, and cost of labor.

There are many times when the present duty does not protect, and when the selling price of pig iron is less than it would be by adding the tariff to its cost.

The duty should be protective under the most adverse circumstances, such as the practice of dumping of foreign pig iron here, the payment of export bonuses, special through freights to seaboard and interior domestic points, this product being frequently carried as ballast.

There never has been a general combination as to selling prices by the merchant furnace companies of America, hence selling prices have been regulated by supply and demand; consumers as a rule make the prices, which have been at several periods below cost.

During the most of last year prices were profitable, but during the most of this year are unprofitable, owing to high costs, small production, and low prices through excessive competition, the production this year being but little over half that for corresponding months of 1907.

In the last analysis practically all the cost of the materials for making pig iron—ore, flux stone, coke, coal, sand, etc.—is for labor, exclusive of mining royalties or interest, and taxes.

To sum up this part of the brief, without protection iron in pigs can not be made and sold at a profit in this country.

DOMESTIC COSTS.

I have obtained from various manufacturers costs of making pig iron in the principal producing districts of the United States. These costs cover operations during the year 1907. The details are submitted and attached hereto as Exhibits A to Q, inclusive. For convenience these costs are summarized together with foreign costs so far as ascertainable in the following table:

Furnace costs—Pig iron.

	Exhibit No.	Cost per gross ton.
Eastern Pennsylvania	1	$18.79
Buffalo	2	16.45
Southern Ohio	3, 4, 5	16.44–16.19
Mahoning and Shenango valleys	6, 7	16.50–17.79
Middle West	8	16.10
Virginia	9, 10, 11	14.21–14.17 -14.43
Alabama and Tennessee	12, 13	12.98–11.00
Germany	14	8.71–10.16
England	14	9.48

The following tables are also attached and submitted as part of my brief:

Exhibit No. 15.—Comparative blast furnace wages in the United States and England.

Exhibit No. 16.—Comparative costs of foreign and domestic pig iron at principal seacoast points in the United States.

Exhibit No. 17.—Pig-iron freight rates from producing centers to points of consumption in the United States.

Exhibit A.

Exhibit A in brief dated December 30, 1908, of Edgar S. Cook, president Warwick Iron and Steel Company, Pottstown, Pa.

	Selling price f.o.b. Pottstown.	Cost.	Profit per ton.	Production.
				Tons.
1894	$10.59	$10.48	$0.11	511,163¼
1895	10.74	10.36	.38	58,932
1896	11.29	10.88	.41	37,107
1897	10.41	10.10	.31	68,137
1898	9.79	9.52	.27	64,816
1899	13.36	11.01	2.35	62,608
1900	17.78	15.11	2.67	58,787
1901	(a)	(a)	(a)	(a)
1902	16.02	15.83	.19	146,363¼
1903	17.60	16.75	.85	173,096
1904	13.72	13.45	.27	125,033
1905	15.18	14.65	.53	205,789
1906	16.86	15.53	1.33	219,781
1907	20.18	18.79	1.39	256,750

a Furnaces out of blast or building.

Exhibit B.

Furnaces located at Buffalo, N. Y.

2.10 tons iron ore	$8.53
1.25 tons coke	4.87
0.65 tons limestone	.55
All other manufacturing costs except interest	2.50
Cost per ton of pig iron f. o. b. cars at the furnace	16.45

Freight rate, Buffalo to New England, is $2.45 per ton, making cost delivered in New England $18.90.

The above does not include interest, which most companies have to pay to a more or less extent, nor insurance, nor any return on the capital employed.

The effect of the tariff reduction would be more severely felt by the eastern furnaces, which are unable to manufacture as cheaply as plants located on the lakes.

Exhibit C.

Total cost f. o. b. cars of a furnace located in southern Ohio.

[Detailed cost of 69,806 tons of foundry and malleable iron, 1907.]

	Tons.	Cost per ton.	Total.	Cost per ton, iron.
Ore	132,816	$4.78	$632,390.08	$9.06
Scale	264	3.93	1,039.63	.01½
Coke	79,526	3.74	295,108.79	4.23
Limestone	38,049	.93	35,691.64	.51
Material				13.81½
Labor			121,611.68	1.74
Salaries			9,366.00	.13
Supplies			10,688.47	.15
Expense (water, legal, etc.)			4,246.86	.06
Repairs			10,645.03	.15
Tools			489.24	.01
Insurance			1,253.90	.02
Taxes			6,156.25	.09
Sand and clay			4,004.27	.06
Laboratory			3,342.10	.05
Steam coal			11,034.15	.16
Office supplies			367.57	.00½
Total			1,147,485.66	16.44

Exhibit D.

The following letter, giving the costs and selling price and the net gain or loss for a series of years, is valuable and is reproduced in full:

Yours November 27th received. Below is given the information regarding price, cost of production, etc., covering ten years, which we think is what you want. Selling expenses, losses, improvements and repairs, depreciation, discount and interest, etc., are closely deducted always.

Year.	Made tons.	Cost per ton.	Net selling price.	Gain per ton.
1907	69,806	$16.44	$17.70	$1.26
1906	64,938	15.65	16.06	.41
1905	72,446	14.78	15.70	.92
1904	44,556	12.67	13.40	.72
1903	37,292	16.13	15.68	a.45
1902	60,572	14.92	18.07	3.15
1901	53,588	12.99	14.66	1.47
1900	40,508	15.32	16.50	1.18
1899	53,049	11.08	15.37	4.2
1898	48,603	8.43	9.60	1.17

a Loss per ton.

We give the above in confidence for what it may be worth to you in making up your brief. We can still make iron at the 1898 cost if labor at the ore and coal mines, on the railroad, and at the furnace is put back on the basis of $1 per day for common laborers, or 50 per cent reduction on everything, from present costs. Only sentimentalists and theorists want such conditions.

Exhibit E.

Letter below is from a southern Ohio furnace and is reproduced in full, as it shows the cost and selling price:

Our fiscal year ends on March 31, and we have statistics here for two years, beginning April 1, 1906, and ending March 31, 1908, which shows that the average cost for that period of our iron was $16.19, and the average price of iron shipped during the same period was $17.82.

We think that the average of the two years named is as fair a comparison as can be made.

Exhibit F.

Detailed cost of 119,081 tons of basic and Bessemer manufactured during year 1907.

	Tons.	Cost per ton.	Amount.	Number.	Cost per ton iron.
Material:					
Ore	228,001	$4.86	$1,108,478.65	4,289	$9.3086
Converted slag	712	.75	534.00	13	.0045
	228,713	4.85	1,109,012.65	4,302	9.3131
Sand	3,363	.90	3,026.79	56	.0254
Coke	140,073	3.98	557,120.05	2,353	4.6785
Limestone	57,941	1.10	63,748.90	1,089	.5853
			1,732,908.39		14.5523
Operating, labor:					
Office and laboratory			19,114.59		.1605
Engine and boilers			14,693.00		.1234
Furnace labor			80,945.85		.6797
Yard labor			1,212.55		.0102
Unloading stock			16,161.95		.1357
Metal yard			4,214.45		.0354
Casting machine			14,572.15		.1224
			150,914.54		1.2673
Running expenses:					
Office and laboratory			5,717.53		.0480
Coal to boilers			1,624.65		.0137
Light			580.55		.0049
Tools			987.45		.0083
Supplies			10,403.91		.0873
			19,314.09		.1622
Casting machine:					
Coal to boilers			1,270.53		.0107
Supplies			771.43		.0065
Tools			16.42		.0001
Ladles			442.02		.0035
Lime for molds			404.40		.0034
			2,884.80		.0242
Running repairs:					
Supplies			100.12		.0008
Casting machine			1,523.15		.0128
Labor					
			1,623.27		.0136
Taxes and insurance			10,237.16		.0860
Relining and depreciation			59,540.50		.5000
Book cost for year 1907			1,977,422.75		16.6056

Material	$14.5523 per ton of iron.
Labor, expenses, etc	2.0533 per ton of iron.
	16.6056
Yield	52.07 per cent.

Exhibit G.

Average yearly cost per ton manufacturing standard Bessemer and basic pig iron furnace plant, Mahoning and Shenango valleys, 1903–1907, inclusive, two to four furnaces in operation.

	1903.	1904.	1905.	1906.	1907.
Metallic mixture	$7.014	$7.142	$7.474	$8.764	$9.338
Coke	5.172	3.243	3.978	4.786	5.582
Flux	.623	.461	.521	.679	.822
Labor	1.745	1.190	1.205	1.259	1.368
Supplies	1.392	.782	.660	.628	.686
	15.946	12.818	13.838	16.116	17.796

Average yearly selling price per ton, standard basic and Bessemer pig iron, f. o. b. cars, same furnace plant:

1903	$17. 61	1906	$18. 38
1904	12. 71	1907	21. 23
1905	15. 33		

Exhibit H.

Plant in the Middle West. Detailed cost of 140,359 tons of pig iron produced in 1907—basic malleable foundry.

	Tons.	Cost per ton.	Amount.	Number.	Cost per ton iron.
Material:					
Ore	231,511	$4.50	$1,042,150.74	3,695	$7.4249
Cinder	28,707	2.49	71,342.66	458	.5083
Coke	169,494	4.17	707,425.34	2,415	5.0401
Limestone	84,303	.70	59,691.24	1,201	.4252
Sand	5,966	.80	4,772.59	85	.0340
			1,885,382.57		13.4325
Operating, labor:					
Management and account			8,925.03		.0636
Wages			197,208.49		1.4050
Laboratory wages			2,220.00		.0158
			208,353.52		1.4844
Running expenses:					
Coal			8,231.55		.0587
Salaries			13,400.00		.0955
Office expenses			2,412.73		.0172
General expenses			22,678.63		.1616
			46,722.91		.3330
Running repairs:					
Chills, supplies			4,622.12		.0329
Repairs and labor			44,951.28		.3203
			49,573.40		.3532
Relining and renewals			70,251.18		.5002
Taxes and insurance			4,757.06		.0339
Company insurance			1,328.66		.0094
			2,266,369.30		16.1466
Credit					
Interest and discount			5,701.03		.0406
			2,260,668.27		16.1060

Material per ton of iron	$13.4325
Labor, expenses	2.6735
	16.1060

Exhibit I.

The following is from a furnace that produces its own ores and coke, and is located south of Mason and Dixon's line:

Your circular letter of the 27th ultimo relative to the hearing before the Ways and Means Committee in Washington was received some days since, but it has been impossible, owing to absence, for us to reply earlier.

For the year 1907 our net sales of pig iron.f. o. b. cars at furnace averaged $19.43. The average was rather high, owing to our having been fortunate in contracting well ahead at high figures. The cost of producing iron was $14.21.

Our net selling price f. o. b. cars at furnace for the years given below were as follows:

1899	$12. 64	1904	12. 20
1900	14. 33	1905	13. 89
1901	11. 87	1906	15. 83
1902	16. 05	1907	19. 43
1903	15. 08		

Making the average for the nine years of $14.59.

For the year 1908 to the 1st instant our average net sales were $14.51.

About 50 per cent of our product is shipped to eastern Pennsylvania and New England tide-water points. Our freight to such Pennsylvania points is $3.25, and to New England $4.25 per gross ton.

Exhibit J.

The following letter is from E. C. Means, general manager of the Low Moor Iron Company, and is reproduced by permission:

Replying to your letter of the 27th instant, the average cost of making pig iron in Virginia for the five years 1903 to 1907, inclusive, where furnaces owned and operated their own ore mines, coal mines, limestone quarries, and coke ovens, approximately was as follows:

Wages in all departments	$9.42
Supplies and renewals of equipment	.80
Horses, mules, etc.	.49
Assembling freights	2.10
Taxes	.18
Royalties on coal, ore, and limestone	.70
Depreciation of plants to keep modern	.20
Selling commissions	.28
Total	14.17

$14.17 total costs, exclusive of freight on pig iron to customers. Freight to New York, $2.80, by rail and water (the lowest rate) make total delivered price in New York $16.97. Adding $1 for reasonable profit for investment makes fair selling price New York $17.97 per ton.

During the five years above named, common labor in Virginia was paid a daily wage varying from $1.75 per day of ten hours; average daily wage during that period was about $1.50. This, however, includes only common day labor at furnaces, ore mines, and limestone quarries. In West Virginia at the coal mines wages averaged $1.75 per day of nine hours.

The writer's opinion of the revision of the tariff is that present tariff of $4 per ton should apply when No. 2X iron silicon 2.25 to 2.75 per cent sulphur under 0.05 is selling at $18 f. o. b. New York Harbor; that for each $1 advance in the price of iron, tariff should be reduced 50 cents per ton; that is to say, when 2X iron is selling at $19 New York Harbor, tariff should be $3.50 per ton; when it is selling at $20, the tariff should be $3 per ton. The tariff should not, however, be less than $2 per ton, otherwise the revenue derived from the tax on iron would be less than if maintained at $2.

The Virginia situation is as outlined in William W. Hearne's letter to you under date of December 1, copy of which I have, except that Mr. Hearne's letter does not go into costs as closely as this letter.

Referring to that portion of your letter asking for the cost of pig iron during the year 1907 and the tonnage, would state that during 1907, on account of the high prices for iron, we used a considerable portion of lake ore and thereby increased our cost of production, so that for the year 1907 we show higher costs than was the average in Virginia.

Referring to selling price during a series of years, say five or ten years, I do not believe that statistics as to the average selling price would fairly represent the market price. During part of that period, by selling so far in advance, our average returns were lower than the market price, while on the other hand, by refusing to sell during the latter part of 1906 we reaped nearly the full benefit of the advance of 1907.

There is also some question in my mind as to whether the average selling price of the past five or ten years would govern the future selling prices. It seems more essential that costs based upon rates of wages should determine whether the Virginia furnace interests are entitled to protection through the tariff, and with daily wages of $1.50 for common labor under a tariff of $4 per ton, there is only a fair profit to the Virginia manufacturer.

Pig iron made in Virginia is sold to the general trade. None of the companies have finishing plants. Two-thirds of the Virginia pig iron production is sold in the eastern or seaboard States.

EXHIBIT K.

I have the following letter from John B. Newton, vice-president Virginia Iron, Coal and Coke Company, reproduced by permission:

In line with my letter to you of yesterday on the subject of proposed revision of the tariff on pig iron, I am to-day inclosing herewith tabulated statement showing the amount of pig iron produced by this company, the cost of same per ton, and an analysis of that cost for three years—the year ended June 30, 1906, the year ended June 30, 1907, and the year ended June 30, 1908. An examination of this statement will show that practically 50 per cent of the cost of our pig iron is labor, consequently any reduction that we might be forced to make on account of foreign competition would have to be made principally in labor. Our freights on raw materials are very low, and the item of " other expenses " is as low as we could ever reasonably hope to get it.

An examination of the statement will show further that for three years the cost of producing pig iron has steadily and rapidly increased, the total increase in cost during the three years being $1.90 per ton, of which increase labor received the benefit of $1.07 per ton.

As noted on the inclosed statement, the item of " Other expenses " included tools and supplies, royalties, general expenses, repair fund, and depreciation of improvements, but does not include insurance and taxes, bond interest, development, and dead rents. In the item of " Supplies," which is principally coal consumed under boilers, there is quite a percentage of labor which might properly have been included under the labor cost, but was not. The greater portion of the item of " General expenses " being salaries and clerk hire, might, I think, properly have been included under labor cost also, but was not.

Our principal market for pig iron is in the Eastern States—a large portion of our product going to New York, Philadelphia, Boston, and Providence. Our average freight rates from furnace to those ports being $3.25 per ton, our product for the year ended June 30, 1906, would have cost us laid down at these ports $16.37 per ton; for the year ended June 30, 1907, $17.68 per ton, and for the year ended June 30, 1908, $18.28 per ton, whereas English iron can be laid down in New York, duty paid, to-day with profit to foreign manufacturers added, at $18 per ton. The inclosed statement shows only operating cost, and all reference up to this point made in this letter as to cost has reference to operating cost only. While I do not contend that the amount paid for taxes, insurance, bond interest, development, and dead rents should be properly charged to the cost of producing a ton of pig iron, yet it is certainly fair to consider the fact that with our company these items in 1906 amounted to $1.70 per ton of pig iron produced; in 1907 to $1.85 per ton, and in 1908 $2.85 per ton. It will be seen, therefore, by adding these amounts to the costs as set forth in the inclosed statement, our selling price in 1906 would necessarily have been in excess of $14.82 f. o. b. furnaces; in 1907, $16.31, and in 1908, $17.88 before any net profit at all could have been earned. By adding the average freight rate on a ton of pig iron from our furnaces to our eastern ports to the above figures, it will be seen at a glance that the maintenance of the present tariff on pig iron is a matter of very grave importance to us. Our company is the largest producer of pig iron in this section of the country, and in fact is the largest employer of labor in the State of Virginia, common carriers excepted. We employ, when running to full capacity, between 5,000 and 6,000 men, and contribute to the support of probably 25,000 people. There are numerous other manufacturers of pig iron in this State, the pig-iron industry being one of the State's principal industries. It is hard to imagine anything that could happen to the working people of this State that would so seriously affect so large a number of men, as such tariff legislation as would make it impossible for our pig-iron manufacturers to compete with foreign iron. In the light of the facts as they exist to-day, we feel that a radical reduction of the tariff on pig iron would be disastrous to the iron industry in this section, and any reduction whatever would be very harmful to it.

All of Virginia pig iron is marketed, none of it is converted into steel or any other finished product by the manufacturers of it. Our company owns and mines its own coal and iron ore and manufactures its own coke, and on account of the coal mines being in one section of the State, the ore mines in another, and the limestone in another, the transportation charge on raw materials is of necessity an important item of our cost, but, as stated before, transportation rates on raw materials are already low, and we can not hope for any material reduction in them.

VIRGINIA IRON, COAL, AND COKE COMPANY STATEMENT.

Number of tons and cost of pig iron produced during the year ended June 30, 1906: Tons produced, 237,113.5; total cost, $3,111,-029.83; cost per ton, $13.1204.

Analysis of the cost to produce a ton of pig iron for the year ended June 30, 1906.

	Ore.	Coke.	Stone.	Furnace.	Total.
Labor	$2.0873	$2.1904	$0.2896	$1.6569	$6.2242
Transportation	1.4831	1.6632	.2955	....	3.4418
Other expenses	1.5492	.5521	.0927	1.2904	3.4544
Total cost	5.1196	4.8757	.6778	2.9473	13.1204
Labor	....	....	....	....	6.2242
Transportation on raw materials	....	....	....	....	3.4418
Other expenses	....	....	....	....	3.4544
Total cost	....	....	....	....	13.1204

Number of tons and cost of pig iron produced during the year ended June 30, 1907: Tons produced, 202,453; total cost, $2,921,-557.40; cost per ton, $14.4308.

Analysis of the cost to produce a ton of pig iron for the year ended June 30, 1907.

	Ore.	Coke.	Stone.	Furnace.	Total.
Labor	$2.2299	$2.4091	$0.4384	$2.0091	$7.0865
Transportation	1.1934	1.6429	.2735	....	3.1098
Other expenses	1.7784	.6127	.1699	1.6735	4.2345
Total cost	5.2017	4.6647	.8818	3.6826	14.4308
Labor	....	....	....	....	7.0865
Transportation on raw materials	....	....	....	....	3.1098
Other expenses	....	....	....	....	4.2345
Total cost	....	....	....	....	14.4308

Analysis of the cost to produce a ton of pig iron for the year ended June 30, 1908.

	Ore.	Coke.	Stone.	Furnace.	Total.
Labor	$2.0507	$2.6173	$0.4538	$2.1738	$7.2956
Transportation	1.3763	1.3828	.1369	....	2.8960
Other expenses	2.0474	.6262	.2824	1.8781	4.8342
Total cost	5.4744	4.6253	.8731	4.0519	15.0258

Number of tons and cost of pig iron produced for the year ended June 30, 1908: Tons produced, 133,927; total cost, $2,012,361.32; cost per ton, $15.0258; labor, $7.2956; transportation of raw materials, $2.8960; other expenses, $4.8342; total cost, $15.0258.

Other expenses mentioned in the statement includes tools and supplies, royalties, general expenses, repair fund, and depreciation of improvements, but does not include bond interest, taxes, insurance development, and dead rents.

EXHIBIT L.

The following letter from Capt. H. S. Chamberlain, one of the representative manufacturers of merchant pig iron in the South, is all very interesting, and I have his permission to reproduce the letter over his own signature:

As representing the merchant pig iron manufacturers, would be glad to have you say to the Ways and Means Committee at Washington, in connection with the tariff hearings that from our experience of many years in the manufacture of pig iron in Tennessee, I consider the present rate of duty an absolute necessity, in order to successfully meet foreign competition in the seaboard market.

Our freight rate to New York is $4.14, and Boston, $4.49 (which is the shipping point for New England business); say it is $4.31 per ton from Tennessee and $4.42 from the Birmingham district, this is nearly if not quite twice the rate from Liverpool or German ports, and as these are large and important markets it is vital that they be retained for American producers.

Our cost for the manufacturing of pig iron in 1907 was $12.93 per ton, leaving out interest on investment, and this cost was made up entirely of labor, with the exception of 85 cents per ton charged on pig iron as royalty on ore, coal, and limestone entering into the manufacture. Add to this a freight rate of $4.31 per ton and (with low labor cost and low ocean freights for the foreign make) without the tariff the eastern, our natural market, is lost to southern manufacturers.

Our average selling price for the past five years was $12.82 per ton, yet cost for a portion of the time was less than in 1907, owing to lower wages, which varies greatly in the different years.

The consumption of pig iron in the South is comparatively small, so producers are compelled to seek northern markets. As a great deal of capital has been invested in the past twenty years in the iron and coal industry in the South and large developments have been made (an important factor in the material welfare of the section), it would not seem the part of wisdom to so change the tariff rates as to jeopardize present investments and retard further progress.

There is also submitted an original affidavit by Captain Chamberlain covering the cost of producing pig iron by his company during the year 1907 as follows:

STATE OF TENNESSEE,
  Hamilton County:

Personally appeared before me, O. L. Hurlbut, a notary public in and for said State and county, H. S. Chamberlain, of Chattanooga, Tenn., with whom I am personally acquainted, who, being duly sworn, deposes as follows: That he is president of the Roane Iron Company and has been connected with that company for the past thirty-eight years; that they make pig iron exclusively at Rockwood, Roane County, Tenn., and that they have two furnaces of the most modern type. He further deposes that for the year 1907, the last annual report of their operations shows that the actual cost of manufacture of pig iron per ton at said furnaces was $12.93, and that embraced in this cost is an item of only 83 cents, which covers all royalties on ore, coal, and limestone, the balance of the $12.93 being made up entirely of labor, current repairs, etc. He further says that the freight to New York is $4.14 per ton, and to Boston, an important shipping point for the New England market, $4.49 per ton, and that he firmly believes that a reduction of the tariff on pig iron from present rates would have the effect of depriving this company of the eastern market for its product.

(Signed)   H. S. CHAMBERLAIN.

Subscribed and sworn to before me this 12th day of Jannary, 1909.

[SEAL.]   (Signed)   O. L. HURLBUT,
Notary Public.

EXHIBIT M.

The Central Iron and Coal Company of Alabama writes me as follows, under date of December 9:

Replying to your circular letter of November 27, addressed to this company at New York, will state that we commenced producing pig iron in August, 1903. For the next four years our average cost and selling price was approximately $11 furnace. The company made absolutely nothing on the $1,000,000 invested. We made some money during the remainder of 1907, on account of the high price of pig iron. Have just about been holding our own on present market.

EXHIBIT N.

The committee will remember I stated I had cabled abroad for information, and I beg herewith to copy the following cablegrams which are given as received here from an absolutely reliable source:

Translation of Cablegram received December 3, 1908.

Average German cost.	Marks per 1,000 kilos.	U. S. gold per 1,000 kilos.	U. S. gold per ton of 2,240 pounds.
Coke	13.00	$3.094	$3.14
Ore, Lorraine District	2.00	.476	.48
Ore, foreign	10.00	2.38	2.42
Other German	4.00 to 5.00	.0962 to 1.19	.97 to 1.2
Pig iron, Lorraine District	36.00	8.568	8.71
Pig iron, other	42.00	9.996	10.16

Steel Making Pig Iron Middlesboro District.

1 ton Spanish ore	$2.53
1¼ tons Cleveland ore at $1.25	1.56
	$4.09
1⁷⁄₁₀ tons coke at $3.77	4.14
⅓ ton stone	.25
Other items	1.00
Total	9.48

OCEAN FREIGHT FROM EUROPEAN SEAPORTS TO BOSTON, NEW YORK, PHILADELPHIA, AND BALTIMORE.

Iron ore and pig iron.   6/6 (say $1.60) per gross ton.

The export price of pig iron in Germany is nominally the same as the domestic price. In periods of depression the export price is frequently reduced to cost or lower, in order to enable the syndicate controlling this commodity to dump the surplus into England and other foreign countries.

TRANSLATION OF CABLEGRAM RECEIVED DECEMBER 9, 1908.

Pig iron costs are present and include economy effected by and revenue from by-products, use of gas engines, modern appliances. Works: Luxembourg, Lorraine, Sarr District (Germany), Moselle (France), Liege, Middlesboro. Information as to lowest costs given is from principal works above districts which represent our principal competition but numerically as to general average does not represent cost of less favorably situated works, geographically or otherwise, which varies equivalent to £0.4.0 ($1.00 to £0.6.0 ($1.50) per ton. Position is similar to that in the United States in this respect.

TRANSLATION OF CABLEGRAM RECEIVED DECEMBER 10, 1908.

Pig iron costs include taxes, depreciation, interest, labor, insurance. Subdivision of these charges is not obtainable at the moment. Information given you is very reliable.

EXHIBIT O.

Table showing comparative blast-furnace wages in the United States, and England.

	United States.	England.
Furnace keeper	$2.90	$1.82
Top fillers	2.55	1.27
Cindermen	2.30	1.21
Bottom fillers	2.30	1.12
Laborers	1.65	.91
Blast enginemen	2.90	1.37

EXHIBIT P.

Comparative costs of foreign and domestic pig iron at principal seacoast points in the United States.

Point of production.	Seaboard point.				
	Philadelphia.	Boston.	Mobile.	New Orleans.	San Francisco.
Eastern Pennsylvania:					
Cost	$18.79	$18.79	$18.79	$18.79	$18.79
Freight	.60	2.10	6.72	6.72	14.00
	19.39	20.89	25.51	25.51	32.79
Buffalo:					
Cost	16.45	16.45	....	....	16.45
Freight	2.45	2.65	....	....	14.00
	18.90	19.10	....	....	30.45
Southern Ohio:					
Cost	16.19	16.19	16.19	16.19	16.19
Freight	2.65	3.25	6.72	6.72	14.00
	18.84	19.44	22.91	22.91	30.19

Comparative costs of foreign and domestic pig iron at principal seacoast points in the United States—Continued.

Point of production.	Seaboard point.				
	Philadel-phia.	Boston.	Mobile.	New Or-leans.	San Fran-cisco.
Mahoning and Shenango Valley:					
Cost	$16.50	$16.50	$16.50	$16.50	$16.50
Freight	2.65	3.25	6.72	6.72	14.00
	19.15	19.75	23.22	23.22	30.50
Middle West:					
Cost	16.10	16.10	16.10	16.10	16.10
Freight	2.65	3.25	6.72	6.72	14.00
	18.75	19.35	22.82	23.82	30.10
Virginia:					
Cost	14.17	14.17	14.17	14.17	14.17
Freight	2.80	3.17	6.72	6.72	14.00
	16.97	17.34	20.89	20.89	28.17
Alabama:					
Cost	11.00	11.00	11.00	11.00	11.00
Freight	4.00	4.60	2.75	3.00	13.20
	15.00	15.60	13.75	14.00	24.20
Tennessee:					
Cost	12.93	12.93	12.93	12.93	12.93
Freight	4.00	4.60	2.75	3.00	13.20
	16.93	17.53	15.68	15.93	26.13
Germany:					
Cost	8.71	8.71	8.71	8.71	8.71
Freight	2.50	2.50	3.35	3.35	7.50
Duty	4.00	4.00	4.00	4.00	4.00
	15.21	15.21	16.06	16.06	20.21
England:					
Cost	9.48	9.48	9.48	9.48	9.48
Freight	2.50	2.50	3.35	3.35	7.50
Duty	4.00	4.00	4.00	4.00	4.00
	15.98	15.98	16.83	16.83	20.98

EXHIBIT Q.

Pig-iron freight rates from producing centers to points of consumption in the United States.

[Rail and water rates are given in all cases where available, as they are the cheapest and most generally used.]

From—	To Bos-ton.	To Phila-delphia.	To Balti-more.
Birmingham, Ala.	$4.60	$4.00	$3.85
Virginia furnaces	3.17½	2.80	2.65
Mahoning and Shenango Valley	3.25	2.65	2.55
Pittsburg	2.85	2.25	2.15
Buffalo	2.65	2.45	2.45
Erie	2.85	2.25	2.15
Emporium	2.55	1.80	1.80
Bellefonte	2.55	1.45	1.50
Harrisburg	2.10	.85	.85
Reading	2.10	.60	1.25
Temple	2.10	.65	1.25
Emaus	2.10	.75	1.40
Swedeland	2.10	.40	1.15
Other Eastern furnaces (about the same as Reading)	2.10	.60	1.25

In conclusion, I beg to say that in view of the enormous amount of capital invested in merchant blast furnaces of the United States, the very large number of men employed, and the narrow margin of profit, it would seem to me that no change should be made in the pig-iron schedule.

Respectfully submitted.

JOSEPH G. BUTLER, Jr.

PIG IRON AND CAST SCRAP.

[Paragraph 122.]

ABENDROTH BROTHERS, PORT CHESTER, N. Y., ASK REMOVAL OF DUTIES FROM PIG IRON AND CAST SCRAP IRON.

PORT CHESTER, N. Y., *December 8, 1908.*
COMMITTEE ON WAYS AND MEANS,
Washington, D. C.

GENTLEMEN: Being large consumers of pig iron and cast scrap, to the extent of 16,000 to 18,000 tons per year, we wish to enter a plea for the duty to be taken off both pig iron and cast scrap, for the reason we think that this would have a tendency to steady the market and not fluctuate as it has in the past. For instance, during June and July, 1905, the price was between $14 and $15 per ton; June and July, 1906, $17 and $18 per ton; June and July, 1907, $23 to $25 per ton. These prices were f. o. b. New York.

In the last-mentioned period there was no reason for an advance of from 30 per cent to 40 per cent on this commodity, as labor and material had not advanced to this extent, and we think if pig iron and cast scrap were duty free it would be a great benefit to the consumers, as the pig-iron interests at the present time are controlled to a great extent.

We trust you will do everything within your power to see that the duty is reduced or entirely abolished.

Thanking you in advance for any attention shown this subject, we remain,

Yours, respectfully,   ABENDROTH BROTHERS,
                              J. F. MILLS.

STEEL-HARDENING METALS.

[Paragraph 122.]

BRIEF SUBMITTED BY WALTER M. STEIN, PRESIDENT OF THE PRIMOS CHEMICAL COMPANY, PRIMOS, PA., RELATIVE TO VARIOUS FERRO ALLOYS.

PRIMOS, PA., *November 17, 1908.*

On behalf of the industry of manufacturing ferrotungsten, tungsten metal, tungstic acid, tungstate of soda, tungstate of ammonia, ferromolybdenum, molybdenum metal, molybdic acid, molybdate of ammonia, ferrovanadium, and similar metals and alloys.

The industry of mining tungsten ore, molybdenum ore, vanadium ore, and the industry of manufacturing high-grade steel and steel alloys by the use of said metals.

That it is essential to the growth and very existence of these industries in the United States that they be protected by fair and reasonable tariff legislation against the ruinous competition of the cheaper products, cheaper power, and cheaper labor of foreign lands, and that with such just protection they can thrive and develop without hardship or injustice to the consumers of such of their products, the following facts will show:

In the act of 1897 and former tariff acts, tungsten, molybdenum, and vanadium have not been provided for by name, but by departmental construction have been placed in Paragraph 183 of Schedule C:

Metallic mineral substances in a crude state, and metals unwrought, not specially provided for in this act, 20 per cent ad valorem.

On several occasions in the past, importers of these valuable products have tried to have them classed " by similarity " with ferromanganese, under paragraph 122, which provides that:

Iron in pigs, iron kentledge, spiegeleisen, ferromanganese, ferrosilicon, wrought and cast scrap iron, and scrap steel $4 per ton; but nothing shall be deemed scrap iron or scrap steel except waste or refuse iron or steel fit only to be remanufactured.

During such periods the American manufacturers have been compelled practically to shut down their works, as they could not continue to exist under such conditions. Even the 20 per cent ad valorem duty on " metals unwrought " does not allow a fair or just margin of profit.

It is manifest that the classification, even the possibility or fear of classification, of products such as these under such vastly different rates of tariff can only serve to unsettle and ruin the industries of mining and manufacturing them. These industries not only need a reasonable protection against cheap foreign competition, but they have a right to expect certainty and stability in the classification of their products for duty. This can be best accomplished by naming them in the act and clearly defining what duty they shall pay.

The ferromanganese and spiegeleisen upon which a duty of $4 a ton is placed by paragraph 122, have nothing in common with the valuable metals referred to above.

Ferromanganese and spiegeleisen are cheap products, made in large quantities, like pig iron (named in the same sentence), ferromanganese being made direct from the ore in the blast furnace, the same as pig iron, and from an ore that is abundant, found in masses and cheaply mined, at a cost of from $6 to $8 per ton. The market price of ferromanganese is from $42 to $60 per ton. The market price of tungsten, however, is from $1,200 to $2,000 per ton, depending on the prices of ore.

The manufacture of tungsten and molybdenum metals, and of ferrotungsten, ferromolybdenum, and ferrovanadium entails a great deal of care and requires a combined chemical metallurgical plant, as the finished products must be in such shape that they can be used by the steel works in the finest grades of steels, and the cost of the chemicals used and the large amount of manual, as well as trained, scientific, labor involved makes the cost of manufacture high, as the ore as received from the mines requires very complicated treatment before it can be reduced to a metal or alloy.

As stated above, the market price of tungsten is from $1,200 to $2,000 per ton, depending on ore prices.

Tungsten, molybdenum, and vanadium are principally used in high-grade and high-class steels, as, for instance, high-speed tool steels, magnet steel, etc. The business of manufacturing such steels was practically unknown at the time of the last tariff legislation, and the industry has therefore not received sufficient protection against foreign competition, and the manufacturers of high-grade steels are at a great disadvantage against European competition. The present tariff has provided only for steel worth 16 cents per pound, on which the duty is 4.7 cents per pound, and there the schedule stopped, whereas the special steels, in which the above-named metals and alloys are used, cost from 16 cents to $1 per pound and have no further protection than the 4.7 cents per pound. About 6,000 tons of these expensive steels are made in the United States, while about 12,000 tons are imported (principally from England), showing plainly the lack of protection. If these steels were made entirely in this country, as they should be, the manufacture of tungsten, molybdenum, etc., would treble in the United States, as would also the manufacture of alloy steels.

About $6,000,000 is invested in the United States in the manufacture of tungsten, molybdenum, vanadium, and the metals and alloys mentioned herein, and about $5,000,000 in tungsten mining property in the United States. The cost of production of tungsten ore in this country amounts to $8 minimum per unit of tungstic acid, W O_3, per ton of ore, 2,000 pounds. Ore sold on a basis of 60 per cent at $8 per unit would cost $480 per ton.

Mining of the necessary rare ores has not been profitable, notwithstanding the large amount of money invested therein in the United States, on account of foreign ore usually coming in at a lower price, and whenever business is poor in Europe the foreign ore is shipped to this country at a price much below the cost of production, and on this account the American mines are forced to shut down at such periods. The ore conditions are similar all over the world, and the cost of production depends entirely on the cost of labor at the mines—i, e., wages.

About $2\frac{1}{2}$ tons of tungsten ore are required to make 1 ton of tungsten metal or 1 ton of tungsten contained in the ferro.

In connection with the foregoing, the following facts are submitted:

MANUFACTURERS OF FERRO-TUNGSTEN METAL, TUNGSTIC ACID, TUNGSTATE OF SODA, TUNGSTATE OF AMMONIA, FERRO-MOLYBDENUM, MOLYBDENUM METAL, MOLYBDIC ACID, MOLYBDATE OF AMMONIA, FERRO-VANADIUM.

United States.—Six. Investment about $6,000,000.

Great Britain.—Three.

France.—Two making ferro-tungsten, ferro-molybdenum, ferro-chrome, ferro-vanadium, and ferro-titanium. The two French companies have works located in southern France, Savoie, where they have the additional advantage of cheap water power. They also have additional works in Switzerland and in Norway.

Germany.—Fifteen. Germany is the principal seat for the manufacture of tungsten and molybdenum metals and their products. Two works are located at Berlin; one of these has the tungsten and molybdenum manufactory near the Saxon border, in the southeastern part of the province of Brandenburg. Saxony, four manufacturers—one at Altherzberg, one at Rosswein, one near Dresden, and one at Zwikau. Near Hanover, two manufacturers—one at Annaberg, in Thuringia. Barmen one manufacturer. Siegen one; Hamburg two manufacturers—one near Koln, one near Brunswick.

The chief advantages which the manufacturers in Europe have over the manufacturers in the United States are, first, cheap chemicals used in the reduction of ores; second, low cost of labor; third, cheaper ores; fourth, cheaper electric and water power.

The principal chemicals used are muriatic acid, the cost of which is 25 cents per 100 pounds in Europe, against $1.35 per 100 pounds in the United States. About 5 pounds of this is used to every pound of tungsten metal produced, showing at a glance the advantage in this one chemical alone. Nitric acid is also one of the acids used, and is proportionately much cheaper in Europe than in this country. Ammonia is used largely in the manufacture of molybdenum products, and also for some tungsten products, and this is considerably cheaper in Europe.

The wages paid to labor employed in the manufacture of alloys at the various points in Germany vary from 45 cents per day for youthful labor, under 21 years old, to 70 cents per day for good adult day laborers. For the same class of labor we have to pay $1.25 to $2 per day at our manufacturing centers. The difference in skilled labor is still greater. The proportionately large number of chemists required in the manufacture of these metals and alloys is also an important item, as an equally good chemist can be had in Europe for one-half the salary paid in this country. Labor in France, 70 to 80 cents per day.

About 85 per cent of the cost of tungsten, molybdenum, and vanadium is represented by labor. Ore mining, 60 to 65 per cent; chemicals, 15 per cent; fuel and supplies, 5 per cent; converting cost at chemical works, 20 per cent.

Wages in principal tungsten ore-producing districts.

Europe:
    Portugal—
        Miners, 44 to 56 cents per day.
        Ordinary workmen, 30.4 to 36 cents per day.
        Women and boys, 16 to 19.2 cents per day.
    Spain—
        One mine 110 workmen average 40 cents per day.
        Other mines, 50 to 60 cents per day.
        Boys and women, 20 to 25 cents per day.
    Bohemia—
        Laborers, 35 to 45 cents per day of ten hours.
        Miners, 75 cents per day.
South America:
    Argentina—
        Laborers, 20 to 25 cents per day.
        Miners, 75 cents per day, United States money.

United States:
  California—
    Laborers, $2 to $2.50.
    Miners, $3 to $4 per day.
  Colorado—
    Laborers, $2 to $2.50.
    Miners, $3 to $4 per day.
  Arizona—
    Laborers, $2.
    Miners, $3 to $4.50 per day.
  South Dakota—
    Laborers, $2.
    Miners, $3 to $4.50 per day.

Mechanics, United States ore-mining centers, $5 per day.
About $5,000,000 is invested in tungsten mining property in the United States.

Vanadium-ore production.

Spain, South America (Peru and Argentina): Wages same as for tungsten ore.
United States (Colorado and Arizona): Wages same as above shown in the United States.

Molybdenum ore.

Spain: Same as on the other ores.
Norway: 50 to 75 cents per day for general laborers.   Miners, $1 to $1.25.
United States (State of Washington, Arizona, and Maine): Wages as under tungsten ore.

We would respectfully ask you to consider, in providing new tariff provisions, a duty on ferro-tungsten, ferro-molybdenum, ferro-vanadium, tungsten metal, molybdenum metal and their salts, a just duty, which should be not less than 35 per cent ad valorem.

Tungsten ores.—On account of the difference in the cost of labor in the United States and in foreign countries, it would be but fair and reasonable to place a duty of 20 per cent ad valorem on tungsten ore, which is now on the free list.

Molybdenum and vanadium ores could also be produced in large quantities in the United States if they were protected by a duty of 10 to 20 per cent to induce their production in the United States.

Alloy steels.—As the manufacture of high-grade steels is so closely dependent upon the alloys and metals in question, they should also be considered, and either an ad valorem duty provided for steels valued at above 16 cents per pound or such other provision made as would protect this new industry.

The consumer of the finished product will not be prejudiced by the placing of a reasonable duty on the chemical-metallurgical products for which we ask a duty, nor by a duty upon the ore or an increased duty on the high-grade steels as are used for such high-class work that an increase of a few cents in the cost will be no hardship to anyone.

In presenting this paper we have considered all interests, and have shown briefly where these manufactures can be greatly developed in the United States, and their output more than trebled, and the industries given the leading position they should hold in the markets of the world—and which they can and will hold with proper tariff protection.

All of which is respectfully submitted for the consideration of the committee.

WALTER M. STEIN,
President Primos Chemical Co.

H. C. HARRISON, REPRESENTING SUSQUEHANNA SMELTING CO., LOCKPORT, N. Y., WRITES RELATIVE TO FERROSILICON.

LOCKPORT, N. Y., *November 17, 1908.*

The COMMITTEE ON WAYS AND MEANS,
House of Representatives, Washington, D. C.

GENTLEMEN: In presenting our application to you for amendment to paragraphs 122 and 183 of the act of July 24, 1897, we wish to briefly outline the history of the manufacture of ferrosilicon, upon which commodity we ask, in place of the present tariff of $4 per ton, adequate protection to enable a manufacturer in this country to compete upon fair terms with the foreign imported material.

Ferrosilicon is a ferro alloy (an alloy of silicon and iron made in an electric furnace) upon which the tariff has been expressly fixed by Congress, act July 24, 1897, paragraph 122, together with ferromanganese, at $4 per ton, whereas every other ferro alloy, such as ferrochromium, is at present appraised in the class of "metals unwrought," act July 24, 1897, paragraph 183, carrying a 20 per cent ad valorem duty.

The use of both of these alloys by the steel makers is now large and increasing. We are not ourselves interested in the question of the duty upon ferromanganese and wish to submit no data for arguments upon this commodity. In the case of ferrosilicon, however, we wish to point out that the present conditions are essentially different to those that existed at the time that Congress passed the act of July 24, 1897. At that time it was represented that this commodity was a necessity to the steel makers, and there being no domestic industry involved, no injustice was done to a domestic industry by admitting this commodity practically untaxed. Since the fixing of this nominal tariff upon ferrosilicon, up to a comparative recent date, nearly all of the ferrosilicon consumed in this country has been imported from abroad, a fact that is clearly shown by the customs returns. During this period no serious attempt was made in this country to supply the domestic needs. Within the last two years, however, several manufacturers have turned their attention to the establishing of a domestic industry with a view to supplying the demand for ferrosilicon in this country, and in addition to this, some works have been erected on the Canadian side, using Niagara power, in order to save the freight and transportation charges from Europe and be in close touch with American market.

The points we wish to put before you relevant to Canadian competition are that our principal raw materials, namely, iron and charcoal, enjoy, respectively, a protection of $4 per ton and approximately $2 per ton, which means that to make 1 ton of finished product of ferrosilicon indirectly we pay $3 duty on our raw materials and enjoy ourselves only $4 per ton protection. To realize what this means it must be remembered that our chief competitor in Canada buys charcoal at two-thirds the price at which we can obtain it, and, using government bounty-fed power, obtains power, the principal item of cost in the manufacture, actually from the same company who supply us, at a price fully 25 per cent cheaper than we, with a most advantageous power contract, can buy it in this country.

The additional points we wish to put before you relevant to competition from Europe are as follows:

It is well known that Norway, Sweden, and the Austrian Tyrol are all abundantly supplied with potential water-power developments, which, owing to the local conditions, are capable of extremely cheap development. It is claimed that in Norway and Sweden together there is easily 30,000,000 to 40,000,000 horsepower which can be cheaply developed if required, and already some very big factories have been erected in both of these countries, where the cost of power is so low that processes can be carried on there commercially which it would be difficult to carry on even with Niagara power. It is claimed that horsepower in these two countries can be bought at $6 to $7 per h. p. y., and there seems nothing unreasonable in this assertion.

With reference to the Austrian Tyrol, from which district principally the ferrosilicon which has been imported into this country has come, we submit the following information in greater detail. In this district, without pretending to compile a complete list, we instance seven separate water-power companies, as below, of which the total horsepower capacity is in the neighborhood of 33,000 horsepower.

	Horsepower.
Innspruch	6,500–13,000
Landecher Carbide	6,000
Brennerwerke Matrei	6,000
Rienzuerk de Brixen	2,700
Das werk bei Kardaum zwol malgreim	2,000
Etschwerke, Bozen, and Meran	6,000
Trient	1,000

In these works we have definite information that the cost of horsepower to the customer is between $7 and $8 per h. p. y., and that the customer pays for this power by contract upon terms which are more beneficial to him than the terms of power contracts common in this country. In addition to these concerns actually noted there is some 36,000 horsepower generated in the Austrian Tyrol by plants of $1,000 horsepower and over. In Bosnia, too, one large works employs great quantities of power, probably as much as 20,000 horsepower. All of this power is available for the manufacture of electric-furnace products, and will, when steel trade is busy, be largely employed upon the manufacture of ferrosilicon.

It is obvious that the European market will not absorb all the material so made, and the necessary result follows that in times of prosperity in this country the foreigner will dump his surplus make into this country, which to all intents and purposes, so far as this commodity goes, is an open market. It is well known that the surplus production of any industry tends to be dumped at an artificially low price in any free-trade center of industry, and it is this unfair competition against which we ask adequate protection.

In addition to the extremely cheap power which these continental countries enjoy, it must be remembered that the material so made is made by labor which is paid approximately upon less than one-third the scale of wages existing in similar industries in America. For instance, common labor in the Tyrol is paid at the rate of 5 cents per hour, superior labor at approximately 6 cents per hour, furnace men working on the furnace at 7 cents per hour, and competent foremen in charge at 10 cents per hour, whereas the scale of wages for

men conducting similar operations in this country will be, respectively,
17¼ cents, 20 cents, 25 cents, and 30 cents. This is a direct consequence of the principle of protection, the benefits of which we do not
ourselves yet enjoy.

To put the matter in a nutshell, it is certain from these two considerations alone that the foreigner is able to produce fully 25 per
cent cheaper than a manufacturer in this country.

We suggest that this is a case where a new American industry is
in grave danger of being killed by foreign competition, and unfair
competition at that, and it seems hard that American capital should
be lost in an honest endeavor to establish an American industry to
manufacture a product the use of which is now large and increasing,
and which is closely connected with one of the great industries of the
country.

> Yours, very truly,
> SUSQUEHANNA SMELTING CO.,
> HERBERT C. HARRISON,
> *Vice-President.*

HON. GEORGE F. HUFF, M. C., SUBMITS LETTER OF THE PAGE WOVEN WIRE FENCE CO., MONESSEN, PA., RELATIVE TO DUTIES ON FERRO ALLOYS.

MONESSEN, PA., *November 25, 1908.*

Hon. GEORGE F. HUFF, M. C.,
> *Greensburg, Pa.*

DEAR SIR: Information reaches us that the Ways and Means Committee have revised paragraph 183 for the purpose of establishing new
rates of duty on ferro alloys. Now, as these are raw materials instead
of finished products, and being used for obtaining certain definite results in the production of steel and iron, we firmly believe that any
increase in duty over that under which these have been admitted
would tend to increase costs of production for American manufacturers of iron and steel. While the production of these alloys progresses
to a certain extent in the United States, yet the American production
of these materials does not appear in due proportion to the demand
or use of them, nor does it appear probable that home manufacturers
could meet the demand if a prohibitive or greatly increased duty were
to be levied thereon; hence we believe the greater interests are better
protected by maintaining lower duty rate than by advancing these
port entrance charges; hence this letter to you, with special request
that you urge putting the alloys in question under their proper classification of $4 per gross ton.

In connection with the above, we understand that the Ways and
Means Committee are meeting to-day for the consideration of this
subject-matter and we thought perhaps you would be interested in advancing our interests in the matter, which are only similar to others
of the other manufacturers, and that possibly other parties might be
taking up the same issue with you and the various Congressmen, Senators, and committee, and that the necessary opposition would be
such as to protect us accordingly.

Thanking you for giving this proposition such consideration as it
deserves, and with best regards, we are,

> Yours, very respectfully,
> PAGE WOVEN WIRE FENCE CO.,
> E. C. SATTLEY, *Manager.*

STATEMENT OF EVERIT BROWN, OF NEW YORK CITY, RELATIVE TO VARIOUS FERRO ALLOYS AND DUTIES.

WEDNESDAY, *November 25, 1908.*

Mr. BROWN. May it please the committee, I had not supposed that I should be called upon at this stage under the steel schedule, but——

The CHAIRMAN. Do you want to wait?

Mr. BROWN. I am quite ready to say the things my client would like to have me say here.

The CHAIRMAN. Go ahead, then.

Mr. BROWN. Let me premise by saying that I am not a merchant nor a manufacturer, but only an attorney. I represent here the Electro-Metallurgical Company.

Mr. GRIGGS. Did you say you were nothing but a lawyer?

Mr. BROWN. Nothing but a lawyer, sir.

Mr. BOUTELL. That is enough.

Mr. BROWN. I trust the members of the committee will hear me, for the reasons which I am about to state.

Mr. GRIGGS. I am nothing but a lawyer.

The CHAIRMAN. I hope they will hear you and not interrupt you any more. Proceed.

Mr. BROWN. I do not mind, sir.

The Electro-Metallurgical Company, whom I represent here, have interests in common with other manufacturers in the United States, and I am empowered to say that their interests jump together in this matter. The subjects which they wish to discuss are ferrosilicon, which is enumerated in paragraph 122 of the tariff act, and several other ferro alloys, some of which have rather curious names to the ordinary individual, such as ferromolybdenum, ferrotitanium, and ferrovanadium, and some of which have names that perhaps have become a little more current by reason of their being seen in the newspapers, such as ferrochromium and ferrotungsten.

In the present tariff act ferrosilicon is the only one of these which is enumerated by name, and it bears a duty of $4 a ton. At the time the present act was passed, in 1897, almost all, if not quite all, of the ferrosilicon was produced by what is called the blast-furnace process. Since that time there has been a remarkable development, as I have no doubt the committee knows, in the production of alloys by an electrical process in electrical furnaces, which are exemplified in the works at Niagara especially. By these electric furnaces, an enormous degree of heat is obtained, that results in producing certain articles in a purer state than could be procured under the old-fashion blast-furnace processes.

The chief element of value in all of these ferros about which I speak particularly is not the ferro, which is the iron, but several other elements, named secondly but of primary importance, such as the chromium, the tungsten, the silicon, etc. The value of these alloys varies with the contained amount of that secondary element. A ferrosilicon which contains only 10 or 12 per cent of silicon is naturally worth very much less than a ferrosilicon which contains 60, 80, or 95 per cent of silicon. The kind of ferrosilicon which contains 10, 12, or 15 per cent is the kind which was produced by the blast furnace, and the possibilities of that furnace were exhausted in producing ferrosilicon of about that percentage of silicon; whereas the electrical processes, and also other nonelectrical but chemical processes, have resulted in producing ferrosilicon that has as high a degree of silicon as 95 per cent; and of course the price varies accordingly. The same is true of these other ferros—ferrochromium, ferrotungsten, etc.

As these other ferros (other than ferrosilicon and ferromanganese, which are enumerated in paragraph 122) were not being imported into this country, there was no place for them in the tariff act by name. They had to seek such classification as they could under general language. It was claimed, on behalf of the Government and the Treasury Department, that the logical place for them was in paragraph 183, which provided for "metals unwrought;" and it seemed to the Government that that clearly covered them, and that a duty of 20 per cent ad valorem should be put upon them accordingly. The importers, however, claimed that the expression, "metals unwrought," did not cover these articles; that therefore there was no niche for them in the tariff act, and that consequently they became nonenumerated articles, and in so becoming nonenumerated articles they became subject to what is called the "similitude clause." That is section 7 of the present tariff act, which provides that when an article is not enumerated in the tariff act it shall be classified for duty at the rate of the article which it most resembles in material, quality, texture, or use. They claimed that while these articles were not enumerated they did assimilate to articles which were enumerated, to wit, ferrosilicon and ferromanganese, in paragraph 122, and that therefore they took a duty of $4 per ton.

It happens that some of these ferros are extremely valuable. Ferrovanadium, for instance, runs as high as over $4,000 per ton in foreign value; and a duty of $4 a ton, it was thought in many circles, was an infinitesimal duty, and one which was not in accordance with any intention which anybody in Congress might have had.

The case went into court in New York, and it was there held by the circuit court of appeals for the second circuit that the expression "metals unwrought" covered only metals capable of being wrought, and that before a metal could be called "capable of being wrought" it must be such a metal as could be made, in and by itself, into utensils or definite, particular objects; and that the use of a metal to melt up with other things to make a compound, to perfect a compound, or for some similar purpose, was not such a purpose as would entitle an article to be called a "metal unwrought."

That decision was temporarily accepted by the Treasury Department, and all these ferro alloys came in at a rate of duty of $4 a ton, which was practically nothing on many of them. But subsequently the circuit court of appeals in Philadelphia, in the third circuit, in another class of goods somewhat similar, to wit, bronze hardener (not ferro-tungsten, but an alloy of metals), held differently on the proposition of what the term "metals unwrought" meant; and the Treasury Department determined to try a new case on the subject to secure what they thought was a reasonable rate of duty. In the trial of that case they sought special counsel, and it is because of my connection with the case that these people have asked me to appear here for them to make this explanation to the committee.

Mr. BONYNGE. What was your connection?

Mr. Brown. I was special counsel for the Government there to endeavor to secure the assessment of the duty which they thought proper, of 20 per cent; on the theory that "metals unwrought" did cover articles of this character. That case went before the Board of General Appraisers, and was there decided in favor of the Government, and it has been appealed to court and is now pending in Philadelphia.

The Chairman. The second and third circuits have decided this question in directly opposite ways, have they not?

Mr. Brown. On the question of "metals unwrought;" yes, sir.

The Chairman. Yes; on the question of "metals unwrought."

Mr. Brown. Yes, sir; they have. And it is with the hope that the committee will make it clear beyond peradventure that I am here.

The Chairman. Have you any suggestions to make as to changes in the language?

Mr. Brown. Yes, sir. The gentleman whom I represent would suggest that—I do not suppose you would want me to give the language offhand?

The Chairman. Will you reduce it to writing?

Mr. Brown. It will be reduced to writing, sir, and we will file a brief. Some of the interested parties have already filed a brief.

The Chairman. Suppose you make your suggestion in writing as to the change.

Mr. Brown. I think that would be better, perhaps. But in general I may say that "metals and alloys, crude or unwrought, whether capable of being wrought or not," would perhaps answer the purpose.

The Chairman. It is simply with reference to the classifications that you appear, and not at all with regard to the duty?

Mr. Brown. I may say a word or two in regard to that, if the committee will pardon me; although of course I can not go into the exact figures, which can be supplied by the other gentlemen who are here.

The Chairman. Very well.

Mr. Gaines. Your recommendation, then, would be in line with the one made in our suggestions here from the Treasury Department, to wit, to transfer it from paragraph 122 to paragraph 183?

Mr. Brown. And to make paragraph 183 so clear that there can be no longer any dispute about it.

Mr. Gaines. Will you furnish, in writing, suggestions as to what you deem to be a proper classification of these several articles?

Mr. Brown. Yes, sir; I will take pleasure in doing so, but I thought it better to wait until after the discussion before the committee to do that.

Mr. Gaines. I understand that the making, for instance, of ferro-silicon of a high percentage of silicon is a comparatively new process; is it not?

Mr. Brown. It is, sir; and it competes with the blast-furnace process, the old process, to such an extent that some of the people who are interested in this proposition have lost practically all the business of their blast furnaces. A few years ago in the Hocking Valley there were 8 or 10 of those blast furnaces making silicon irons. There is just one there to-day. On the other hand, the electro-metallurgical people are unable to compete on some of these ferros with foreign countries, and are unable to make them practically and keep up their works; and there is a point there which is of great value from a little different standpoint from what is usually brought before this committee. I should say that these ferros are used in the making of what are called special steels—steels of peculiar characteristics, either of great hardness or of great toughness or great strength, either tensile or otherwise. Some of them are what are called high-speed steels, having the peculiar property of not getting soft when red-hot, and so on; and they are becoming of great use in the steel industry. Several of them, particularly ferrochromium and ferrotungsten, are articles which are used in the manufacture of armor plate, and particularly projectiles; and unless the industry of making those things in this country is developed, the country will some time, very probably, in case of war, find itself at a great disadvantage. That is not a revenue proposition, nor is it a protectionist proposition in the ordinary sense; but it is a proposition which will appeal not only to the patriotism but to the national spirit of everyone.

During the Russo-Japanese war, for instance, Japan wanted ferrochromium, and could not get it, and was scouring the world for it; and it was practically only at that time, when her emissaries were scouring this country as well as other countries, that our people made some little money from ferro-chromium.

Mr. CLARK. Mr. Witness, if you took the tariff off entirely, would you stop making it? If it was put on the free list, would it have anything to do with your going on and making it?

Mr. BROWN. Yes, sir; some of them are not capable of being made now because there is not the proper tariff upon them.

Mr. CLARK. You are only getting a protection of $4 a ton, are you not?

Mr. BROWN. No, sir; we are getting now protection to the extent of 20 per cent. But that is by executive order, and not by law.

Mr. CLARK. Who had a right to make any such executive order?

Mr. BROWN. The Secretary of the Treasury made it. It was an order that pending the decision of the court they should pay the higher duty.

Mr. CLARK. An order changing the law?

Mr. BROWN. No; it was an order construing it and changing the classification.

Mr. CLARK. Following the construction of one of the courts in case of a divergence between the two courts.

Mr. BROWN. Yes.

Mr. CLARK. Does any appeal lie from that court to the Supreme Court?

Mr. BROWN. The case is now pending, on appeal, in the circuit court in Pennsylvania.

Mr. CLARK. Does an appeal lie from the circuit court of appeals to the Supreme Court?

Mr. BROWN. No.

Mr. CLARK. Why does it not lie to the Supreme Court?

Mr. BROWN. I beg your pardon.

Mr. CLARK. Why do they not have it certified to the Supreme Court and get through with it?

Mr. BROWN. They can not get through with it until the circuit court of appeals decides the case, and then, not as a matter of right, but only by application to the Supreme Court, when it could, if it chose, issue the writ of certiorari.

Mr. GAINES. Do I understand that the two circuit courts have decided differently, and that the case is now before the circuit court of appeals and has not been acted upon by it?

Mr. BROWN. It is before the circuit court in Pennsylvania. The circuit court of appeals in Philadelphia has decided the principle of the case. It has decided the case of alloy, but not the cases of ferrochromium, ferromolybdenum, and ferrotitanium, involved in the question. So that, while 20 per cent of protection is now accorded, it is not certain how the court will decide the question, and the gentlemen here who are interested, and who can not manufacture without that or greater protection, are desirous of having the thing fixed by law. There is another point to which I would like to call attention; and that it this: A large part of these things are made by water power. It is an electro-metallurgical proposition. Those water-power plants in this country have not been extremely successful, so far as profits are concerned. The Niagara plant, while it has been very creditable, has never paid. If this kind of business is developed as it ought to be, it will involve the development of those water powers, which will give employment to a great many people, and will give an opening by means of this power to other manufactures which now are not possible. In that way also there will be an incidental saving in the coal supplies of the United States. So it seems to us that all of these reasons go in favor of the proposition we make. I may say also that there will be no practical addition to the price to the consumer in this case, because the amount of ferro that is used is infinitesimal.

Mr. CLARK. What you want is to have the verbiage of the law changed so as to clear up the obscurity?

Mr. BROWN. Yes, sir.

Mr. CLARK. Well, everybody is willing to do that, I think.

Mr. BROWN. And at the same time to have a reasonable duty put on.

Mr. CLARK. Oh! [Laughter.]

The CHAIRMAN. You state in your brief, I suppose, facts showing that it is necessary to have a duty?

Mr. BROWN. Certainly.

The CHAIRMAN. I hope that you also show what advantage you have owing to the cheap water power of Niagara Falls.

Mr. BROWN. We do not have any advantage owing to the cheap water power of Niagara Falls. On the contrary, the cheap water power of Europe has considerable advantage over us, including the Niagara Falls.

The CHAIRMAN. I hope you will show that.

Mr. BROWN. We will.

Mr. COCKRAN. Is there pauper water in Europe as well as pauper labor?

Mr. BROWN. My impression is, from observation, that the water there is often quite poor.

Mr. HILL. You want ferromanganese and these other things transferred to the other section and made dutiable at 20 per cent?

Mr. BROWN. Not ferromanganese. We do not care about that. We are not interested in it. I am speaking of ferrosilicon.

Mr. HILL. What is the principal use of ferrosilicon?

Mr. BROWN. It is used in purifying steel and in deoxidizing it.

Mr. HILL. How much would be used to a ton of steel?

Mr. BROWN. I can not give you that. I am not technically informed as to that. There is some ferrovanadium used, in the proportion of one-tenth of 1 per cent.

Mr. HILL. You are satisfied to leave ferromanganese where it is?

Mr. BROWN. Yes.

Mr. HILL. Why did the gentleman who preceded you want ferromanganese to go on the free list?

Mr. BROWN. I do not know.

Mr. HILL. Why do you suppose he wanted it to go on the free list?

Mr. BROWN. That is rather a difficult question to answer.

Mr. HILL. You do not want it to go on?

Mr. BROWN. I presume it is because he imports it.

Mr. BONYNGE. You are not interested in ferromanganese?

Mr. BROWN. I am not.

Mr. HILL. That is produced in large quantities in this country, is it not?

Mr. BROWN. Yes; but we are not interested in it, and there are a great many other things that are produced that we are not interested in.

Mr. HILL. May I inquire the name of the gentleman who preceded you?

Mr. BROWN. I think his name was Butler, of Youngstown, Ohio.

Mr. HILL. Possibly it was because ferromanganese is used extensively in the manufacture of steel.

Mr. BROWN. I do not know.

Mr. BONYNGE. What is the rate you ask? Twenty per cent ad valorem on ferrosilicon?

Mr. BROWN. We ask a rate of 20 per cent on ferrosilicon and a similar duty on the other ferros which belong to that class.

Mr. BONYNGE. You want them changed from paragraph 122 to paragraph 183?

Mr. BROWN. Yes; with a corresponding change in the verbiage. And incidentally the manufacturers assert that 20 per cent is hardly enough to enable them to develop their industry here. We shall have to leave that to the committee on the facts as we present them.

The CHAIRMAN. Have you any practical men here?

Mr. BROWN. Yes; there are two or three here.

Mr. COCKRAN. As I understand, the court in Philadelphia, by its decision, gives you 20 per cent now. By the decision of the court in Philadelphia you are now actually enjoying a protection of 20 per cent?

Mr. BROWN. Not on the identical goods; but we are enjoying 20 per cent.

Mr. COCKRAN. And all you ask is, practically, to have that decision embodied in the law?

Mr. BROWN. Practically, but if you will consider giving 20 per cent or 30 per cent that will be agreeable to us.

Mr. COCKRAN. I have no doubt you would like it.

Mr. BROWN. Does the committee desire to hear any practical people on this proposition?

SUPPLEMENTAL STATEMENT OF HERBERT C. HARRISON, LOCK-
PORT, N. Y., RELATIVE TO PROTECTION FOR FERRO ALLOY
MANUFACTURING INDUSTRY.

WEDNESDAY, *November 25, 1908.*

Mr. HARRISON. Mr. Chairman and gentlemen, I do not propose to
offer very many arguments to-day, because I have filed a brief with
you, and Mr. Brown has pretty well covered the ground as to all the
arguments I could bring forth. I come before you as a manufacturer,
not as a lawyer, and I can assure you that this industry is in danger
of being absolutely killed. All these electric furnace processes are
dependent upon cheap water power, and this industry is located at
Niagara, where the cheapest water power in the country is obtainable. Labor is cheap, freight rates are cheap, and there is no reason
why that industry could be located anywhere else to better advantage.
I contend that when we are endeavoring to meet foreign competition,
and especially competition from Canada, where water power is
cheaper than we can obtain it in this country, owing to government
bounties which have been given to the power companies, an American
industry has a perfect right to ask you for protection. I realize,
gentlemen, that any manufacturer, or anybody who comes to you and
asks for an increase in tariff, is at a disadvantage; but there are cases
where an increase is just, and I submit that on the facts in my brief
and the facts Mr. Brown presents to you our case is a just one, and
I ask your consideration. I do not wish to offer any further arguments.

———

STATEMENT OF JOHN L. COX, REPRESENTING THE MIDVALE
STEEL COMPANY, OF PHILADELPHIA, PA., RELATIVE TO THE
DUTY ON TUNGSTEN.

WEDNESDAY, *November 25, 1908.*

Mr. GRIGGS. Mr. Cox, I shall have to put the usual question.

Mr. COX. What is the question, sir?

Mr. GRIGGS. Is your company making any money?

Mr. COX. Some; yes, sir.

Mr. GRIGGS. I am very glad to see you.

Mr. COX. We are not asking for any increase of duty, sir.

The CHAIRMAN. Do you want the reporter to take this?

Mr. GRIGGS. Why, certainly. I am very glad to see him.

Mr. COX. The Midvale Steel Company, which I represent here, is
not engaged in the manufacture of what might be called tonnage
steel. That is to say, it does not make large quantities of low-priced
material. Its output is altogether high class, and really in the line
of specialties. To get the special qualities required in its product,
it is necessary that it should use special and elaborate manufacturing
methods, and also employ a large number of the ferro alloys, such as
ferrochromium, ferrotungsten, ferrovanadium, and ferrotitanium, as
well as the ordinary alloys, such as ferromanganese, spiegeleisen,
silico-spiegel, and ferrosilicon. The effect of all these alloys is,
roughly, in the same direction—to increase the toughness or the hardness, or both, of the steel to which they are added, at either normal
temperatures or sensibly elevated temperatures. At the present time
ferrotungsten, which is the thing of which I wish to speak particu-

larly to-day, is not specifically mentioned on the list. Under a decision by the New York circuit court of appeals, applying to section 7 (the " similitude " section) of the present tariff law, ferrotungsten has been held as dutiable under paragraph 122.

Mr. BONYNGE. Did you hear Mr. Brown's statement to-day, in which he went over all of that litigation?

Mr. Cox. Yes.

Mr. BONYNGE. The committee has all of that.

Mr. Cox. Yes; but there are some errors in Mr. Brown's statement that I should like to correct.

Mr. CLARK. Are you talking about the same stuff now that he was talking about?

Mr. Cox. I think we are rather at opposite ends of the same subject.

Mr. CLARK. I know; but are you talking about the same subject?

Mr. Cox. I am talking about ferro-tungsten in its application to steel. He was talking about it as its manufacturer, or, rather, as a lawyer representing its manufacturer.

Mr. CLARK. You want to reduce it, and the other man wants to increase it?

Mr. Cox. Precisely.

Mr. CLARK. He produces it, and you use it?

Mr. Cox. Exactly.

The CHAIRMAN. And are you in accord with his ideas about the duty on wire?

Mr. Cox. The duty on wire? Yes; I heard it——

The CHAIRMAN. Oh, I see; proceed. You are on the opposite side of the case from Mr. Brown?

Mr. Cox. Exactly.

Mr. CLARK. Are you a lawyer or a manufacturer?

Mr. Cox. A manufacturer.

Mr. CLARK. Go on.

Mr. Cox. Under this decision of the New York court, the ferro-tungsten that we employ was imported at a duty of $4 per ton, being held similar to ferro-manganese. On importations which were made for us in 1906 and 1907 the General Board of Appraisers held that ferro-tungsten should be taxed under paragraph 183 as " metals unwrought," holding as controlling a decision made by the Philadelphia court in a case which they held to be analogous, though, as a matter of fact, it did not treat of tungsten nor of ferro-tungsten nor of tungsten metal, but of an alloy of iron, tin, and manganese.

My company holds that this addition (which is at present being collected from us under protest) from $4 a ton, the standard rate, which it has been for years, to 20 per cent ad valorem should not be collected. We hold that the material should be specifically mentioned under paragraph 122, or else admitted entirely free of duty. Our reasons are, roughly, as follows:

In the first place, as Mr. Brown explained, the material in every way resembles ferro-manganese. It is a pure melting stock. It has no practical application as ferro-tungsten, except to steel as a melting stock, and its action on the metal is similar to that of manganese in many respects. Both of them are added to the charge either at the first or in the fluid state. Both of them produce hardness and toughness. Both of them improve the quality.

Secondly, we believe that it is very inadvisable to tax materials entering into the production of what Mr. Brown very properly termed "high-speed steel," which is simply another name for the more modern varieties of tungsten steel; for by doing so it simply increases their cost to the consumer or limits their use. The advantages which have been gained to the machinists of this country by the introduction of these high-speed steels are very great. They have enabled an enormous increase in the amount of work done by a tool, as a lathe, or a planer; and anything that tends to oblige the machinists to lock up more money in their machine equipment is not to their advantage in any way.

Then we think that there is a great disparity between the industry which is either protected or might be protected by anything like this 20 per cent duty and the cost to the general public of that duty. The high price of ferro-tungsten, which varied from 63½ cents a pound in 1903 for ferro-tungsten made in America to $1 a pound in 1907 for ferro-tungsten imported, counting on the pound of ferro-tungsten in the ferro, is not at all due to the cost of manufacture. It is entirely due to the rarity of the ore, and the great and increasing demand for it.

Furthermore, a very large proportion of the tungsten ore at present used is produced in the United States, and an exceedingly small proportion, if any, of the ferro-tungsten is made here.

Mr. BONYNGE. You say a large proportion of the tungsten ore is produced in the United States?

Mr. COX. Yes.

Mr. BONYNGE. One witness here to-night said there was only about one-tenth of it produced here, or something like that.

Mr. COX. I know that; but probably twelve States of the United States are producing tungsten.

Mr. BONYNGE. I thought Colorado and California were the only two.

Mr. COX. Oh, no; Connecticut is another. I have a list over here of the States. There are twelve of them which are to-day producing tungsten ore. It is also produced in California. But he was quite correct in stating that Colorado is much the largest producer, Boulder County being the principal county in Colorado where it is produced. There is one large steel company in the United States which produces all its own ferro-tungsten from its own mines in Colorado.

Mr. CLARK. Do you want the tariff on this material put down or up?

Mr. COX. We want it maintained where it has been before this (as we consider) mistaken decision by the Board of Appraisers, which matter is at present under litigation, or else removed entirely.

Mr. CLARK. You want it cleared up or removed?

Mr. COX. Cleared up or removed.

Mr. CLARK. Which would you rather have?

Mr. COX. We would rather have it removed. We would rather have all the tariff removed. We believe that any increase or any tax placed upon ferro-tungsten is simply a tax upon the American manufacturer, because it obliges him to pay that much more than is paid by his foreign competitor; and to that extent it is a protection of the foreigner and a disadvantage to the American.

Mr. CLARK. Is there any tariff on your finished product?

Mr. COX. There is.

Mr. CLARK. You want to get all of it, then? That is the whole tale, is it not?

Mr. COX. Not at all; not at all.

Mr. BONYNGE. Do you want the tariff reduced on your finished product?

Mr. COX. We would be very glad to have it done. We are quite willing.

Mr. CLARK. On the finished product?

Mr. COX. Yes, sir; we are entirely willing to have it done.

Mr. CLARK. As far as I am concerned, you can have it done. [Laughter.]

Mr. COX. If you take the tariff off of our raw material, we shall be most glad to have it taken off the finished product.

Mr. CLARK. Did you ever study about the meaning of the word "frazzle" that President Roosevelt has lately adopted?

Mr. COX. Yes, sir; I have heard the word used.

Mr. CLARK. That applies to this committee.

Mr. COX. I should think it might, from what I have heard to-day.

Mr. CLARK. We are just "worn to a frazzle." [Laughter.]

Mr. COX. We think that any increase of duties is contrary to the spirit of the times. We think that to add (as has been suggested) to the present duties on bar steel containing tungsten a further duty to represent the duty on the tungsten contained in it, as advocated by Mr. Park, is a retrograde step. We think it is contrary to the spirit of the times, and repugnant to the general sentiment that calls for a reduction of the tariff rather than an increase in it.

Mr. CLARK. The whole protective system is opposed to the spirit of the times, is it not?

Mr. COX. Yes; I think it is. I do not think the time is ready for a complete relaxation of the system; but I think it is certainly ready for a very considerable modification of it.

What has been said with reference to ferro-tungsten applies equally well to ferro-chromium, ferro-titanium, ferro-vanadium, and most of the other ferro alloys. In all these cases the cost is not in the labor required to produce the material, but lies altogether in the initial value of the raw material.

In the case of chromium, almost the entire source of chromium is foreign to this country. I am not positive that there is any chromium ore mined in America. It is almost all Turkish ore. In the case of vanadium, the principal vanadium mines are situated in South America—I believe in Peru. The classification of ferro-tungsten, ferro-vanadium, and ferro-chromium under paragraph 122 has already been held as settled by the New York circuit court of appeals; but we think they should be specifically mentioned, so as to avoid such a condition as we are in to-day, of having a high duty collected from us, and being obliged to sue for the recovery of it.

Mr. BONYNGE. How much is a pound of ferro-vanadium (if that is the correct name of it) worth?

Mr. COX. It varies a little, according to quality, but the usual price to-day is $5 a pound of contained vanadium.

Mr. BONYNGE. Mr. Brown said it went up to $4,000, I believe.

Mr. COX. Four thousand dollars a ton—well, I have never heard of such a price. Many years ago it used to be offered at $10 a pound, but for the last three or four years it has been offered at $5 a pound.

Mr. BONYNGE. Does a pound vary in value according to the amount of iron which it has in it, or the amount of vanadium?

Mr. COX. The vanadium in it. The vanadium is the only thing whose value is counted.

Mr. BONYNGE. Does it greatly vary in value according to the amount of vanadium that is in the pound?

Mr. COX. No. A ferro-vanadium which is richer than about 35 per cent is hardly applicable to the manufacture of steel; so it practically all ranges between 15 and 35 per cent of vanadium, and that vanadium is charged for by the American Vanadium Company usually at $5 per pound.

Mr. BONYNGE. It varies from 15 to 35 per cent?·

Mr. COX. Yes; but they do not charge per pound of ferro-vanadium. They charge per pound of the vanadium contained in the ferro. So if it contained 30 per cent, they would charge $1.50 for it.

Mr. BONYNGE. They charge on the vanadium, and not on the pound?

Mr. COX. They charge on the vanadium alone.

Mr. BONYNGE. Not on the iron and vanadium, but simply on the vanadium?

Mr. COX. They charge on the vanadium. The iron they throw in without any extra price.

Mr. GRIGGS. What do you manufacture?

Mr. COX. We manufacture steel specialties. We manufacture self-hardening steels.

Mr. GRIGGS. Is there a duty on them?

Mr. COX. In some cases; yes.

Mr. GRIGGS. What do you say to taking some of it off?

Mr. COX. We are perfectly willing.

Mr. GRIGGS. Perfectly willing?

Mr. COX. Perfectly willing.

Mr. GRIGGS. Take that down, Mr. Stenographer. [Laughter.]

Mr. COX. We are perfectly willing; but we would like, as far as possible, to have the taking of protection from us coupled with a reduction of the duties that we are obliged to pay.

Mr. CLARK. What is the volume of the business in these articles? How much does it amount to in the course of twelve months?

Mr. COX. Are you referring to our own output, or to the output of the country?

Mr. CLARK. The output of the country.

Mr. COX. I do not know.

Mr. GRIGGS. What is your output?

Mr. COX. Our output is worth about $275,000 a year.

Mr. GRIGGS. You say you are paying a duty under protest on the stuff?

Mr. COX. Yes.

Mr. GRIGGS. And you are suing for it back?

Mr. COX. Yes. We were placed in the anomalous position of paying $4 a ton duty in New York and 20 per cent in Philadelphia; and as at that time· the ferro-tungsten we were importing was costing us about a dollar a pound, we were paying altogether $1.20 a pound. [After making a calculation.] Yes; that is right. We were paying a hundred cents a pound, a dollar a pound, for the tungsten content, and we were paying 20 cents duty. We were paying 20 cents a pound duty in Philadelphia, and paying $4 a ton duty in New York for the same material.

Mr. GRIGGS. Are you putting that on the price of the article to the consumer?

Mr. Cox. The extra duty?

Mr. GRIGGS. Yes.

Mr. Cox. We can not say positively that we are, except that we can not sell as cheaply as we would if we did not have to pay that duty.

Mr. GRIGGS. Yes. I suppose the best reason that you can not be positive that you are putting it on the article is that it would be so hard for you to ascertain how to distribute it back among your customers?

Mr. Cox. The idea is simply that what you have to pay extra on your raw materials means that your cost is that much higher. If you sell at the same price, and your raw materials cost more, you make less profit; or if you make the same profit, you go higher.

Mr. GRIGGS. If you recover, you are going to divide what you recover among your customers, are you?

Mr. Cox. I do not believe that would be possible.

Mr. GRIGGS. You could not ascertain it correctly?

Mr. Cox. No.

Mr. CLARK. If there are two rates, one in Philadelphia and one in New York, why do you not import at the port where it costs you the least?

Mr. Cox. That is what we did, practically; but we did not know anything about it until the imports were in there, and we happened to have quite a large quantity of the material. We have not imported any since.

Mr. CLARK. You can not get that back; but you might provide for the future?

Mr. Cox. That is true.

Mr. CLARK. By importing at the point of least——

Mr. Cox. Of least resistance.

Mr. CLARK. Yes; of least resistance.

Mr. BONYNGE. Where do you get your ferro-tungsten?

Mr. Cox. Wherever it can be purchased most cheaply.

Mr. BONYNGE. What markets can you get it from?

Mr. Cox. Most recently altogether from the importing houses in this country.

Mr. BONYNGE. From what country does it come?

Mr. Cox. I do not know. I know a good deal comes from England, from the firm of R. G. Blackwell & Co., who are large makers of ferro-tungsten; but usually we do not deal with them. We deal with some importing house.

I wish, however, to correct one impression that I think was made by Mr. Brown, and that is as to the very small quantities of these ferroalloys that are used, according to him. There are to-day, I think I might say, four special grades of this self-hardening steel, or these high-speed steels, the content of tungsten in which varies all the way from 6 per cent to 20 per cent; so that there is 20 cents a pound at once on the cost of steel in the shape of tungsten that it contains. The plea that he practically made for the retention of a very high duty on electrically-made ferrochromium—on account of its necessity for war uses—I do not think is a very practical one, because the source of supply of the raw material is not in this country, and unless they had in this country enormous stocks of the raw material it would not be forthcoming in time of war under any circumstances, and would at once be declared contraband of war, just as niter has more than once been declared contraband of war because of its entering into the manufacture of the old forms of black powder.

The amounts of ferrochromium used are even much greater than in the case of ferrotungsten, because to-day practically all armor plate contains a very notable proportion of chromium, and so do most projectiles; and the weights of armor plate and projectiles run into very, very heavy tonnage, considering the high class and the high grade of steel that they are—not into the millions of tons, but still into the thousands of tons.

The CHAIRMAN. Is there anything further?

Mr. Cox. That is all, sir.

ELECTRO-METALLURGICAL CO., NIAGARA FALLS, N. Y., SUBMITS SUPPLEMENTAL BRIEF RELATIVE TO FERRO ALLOYS.

WASHINGTON, D. C., *December 4, 1908.*

COMMITTEE ON WAYS AND MEANS,
Washington, D. C.

GENTLEMEN: We beg to submit our reasons for asking that in the coming revision of the tariff you give special attention to the status of ferro-silicon, ferro-chrome, ferro-tungsten, and the other ferro alloys (except ferro-manganese, which is in a different category, and with which we are not concerned), and of the metals which are the most valuable components of those alloys.

We ask (1) that the rate of duty be made clear and certain; (2) that the duty be equalized on the articles mentioned and be an ad valorem one; (3) that the duty be made a reasonable one on them all.

THE DUTY SHOULD BE MADE CLEAR AND CERTAIN.

It is not so now on the ferros we speak of (except ferro-silicon). They are not mentioned in the law by name, and it has been held in court that they are not "metals unwrought" because they are not capable of being wrought, and that they are therefore dutiable by similitude to ferro-manganese at only $4 a ton, although some of them are worth over $4,000 a ton. (United States *v.* Roessler & Hasslacher Chemical Co., 137 Fed., 770, C. C. A., second circuit, New York.) But later another court held that certain bronze-hardening alloy, not any more capable of being wrought than our ferros, was properly dutiable at 20 per cent ad valorem as "metals unwrought." (Thomas *v.* Wm. Cramp & Sons Ship and Engine Building Co., 142 Fed., 734, C. C. A., third circuit, Philadelphia.)

So, while for a time the foreign ferros were admitted at the trivial duty of $4 a ton, they (except ferrosilicon and ferromanganese) are now being assessed at 20 per cent ad valorem to await the final result of renewed litigation. A new case was made, which was decided by the Board of United States General Appraisers in favor of the 20 per cent assessment, but this is now pending on appeal in the United States circuit court in Philadelphia (Lavino v. United States, Hempstead v. United States, and Hampton v. United States). The result of that litigation will doubtless be favorable, but we submit that the law should be made clear beyond peradventure.

As the foreign ferros have been admitted at one time at only $4 a ton, and possibly may again secure that rate of duty by some court decision, the domestic interests can not go ahead with the development of their expensive plants with the requisite assurance of stability.

THE DUTY SHOULD BE EQUALIZED AND BE MADE AD VALOREM.

The reason which once existed for putting ferrosilicon at $4 a ton duty no longer exists. This rate, the same as that on pig iron, originated when ferrosilicon was made in a blast furnace only, contained only 10 per cent or 12 per cent of silicon, and was worth about $20 a ton, making the duty equivalent to about 20 per cent ad valorem. It may be added that spiegeleisen and ferromanganese have always, even up to date, been made in blast furnaces only.

Ferrosilicon to-day, besides being still produced by the blast furnace, can be and is made by electro-metallurgical processes to contain as high as 75 per cent or more of silicon, and this is worth from four to eight times as much as the lower-grade article. It is not right that these different products should carry the same per ton duty, and an ad valorem rate will give the proper proportion in the duty automatically, because the value varies with the silicon content.

Each one of the other ferros also varies in the content of its valuable material—the chromium, tungsten, etc.—and takes a correspondingly variable price. Here, also, an ad valorem rate is the only feasible one.

And ferrosilicon and the other ferros (except ferromanganese), being made of varying grades and values by blast furnace, or electric furnace, or chemical process, should all be put on a parity in the tariff.

Of course, the duty should be levied on the metals themselves—chromium, tungsten, etc.—at the same rate as on the ferro alloys of them, since otherwise there would be great inducement to evasion of the intended duty. Moreover, our arguments are applicable to both the metals and their alloys.

THE DUTY SHOULD BE A REASONABLE ONE FOR DEVELOPMENT AND PROTECTION.

The present duty of $4 a ton on ferrosilicon has seen the decay of many blast furnaces in the United States which formerly produced the low grade, while, on the other hand, the electric furnaces can not effectively compete in high-grade ferrosilicon with the foreign product on the basis of the present duty.

The duty on all the ferro alloys (except ferromanganese), and the metals from which they derive their chief characteristics, should be put at 30 per cent ad valorem. A less rate than that will not place the industry upon a stable basis and enable it to successfully compete with foreign producers.

There ought to be no dispute of our statements concerning the cost of the ferro alloys. The official record of the cases now pending in

Philadelphia shows that the ones actually involved there had a foreign value of $4,317 per ton for the ferrovanadium, of from $1,032 to $1,991 per ton for the ferrotungsten and of from $98 to $715 per ton for the ferrochromium.

The amount of protection which we ask is, of course, based on the supposition that the ores which are our raw materials remain, as they are now, on the free list. Naturally, if these are made dutiable (as to which we say nothing now) we should need a correspondingly higher rate of duty on the ferro alloys, etc., so as to have the benefit of an appropriate differential.

WHAT ARE FERRO ALLOYS?

In general the term " ferro alloy " signifies an alloy in which iron, constituting the base metal, is alloyed with another and more valuable metallic element, such as chromium, silicon, tungsten, molybdenum, etc. Many elements are commercially obtainable as ferro alloys which are not readily obtainable as separate metals, and such ferro alloys are in better form for use than if they were not alloyed with the base metal iron.

USE OF FERRO ALLOYS.

The principal use of the various ferro alloys is in the manufacture of steel, most of them going into " special steels," or " alloy steels." Generally speaking, each of the alloys imparts a different characteristic to the finished product, as, for instance, chromium imparts toughness; nickel, hardness and toughness and greater tensile strength; vanadium, hardness and greater tensile strength and resistance to strains and shocks; and the use of tungsten produces a steel which retains its temper even when red-hot. The manufacture of alloy steel is of comparatively recent growth, and is capable of still further development, and undoubtedly this development will take place, as such alloy steels are superior in quality to ordinary carbon steels. Silicon, which is usually added to steel in the form of ferrosilicon, is largely used to remove occluded gases and to make steel solid and free from blowholes or other imperfections.

It should be borne in mind that ferro alloys are used in the most minute quantities in the manufacture of steel—usually small fractions of 1 per cent. Therefore they form a very insignificant part of the cost of the finished steel.

HISTORY OF FERRO ALLOYS.

In the early use of ferro alloys in the manufacture of steel some of the alloys of inferior quality, of low grade and low content of the metal alloyed with the base metal iron, were produced in blast furnaces. In general these products were unsatisfactory, and it was only after the wonderful development which has taken place in recent years in electric furnaces that these products could be manufactured satisfactorily and with any degree of economy. For instance, the ferrosilicon, which was specifically mentioned in the tariff act of 1897, was the blast-furnace product which contained only from 10 to 12 per cent of silicon. This product has been largely superseded by high-grade ferrosilicon containing 50 per cent to 75 per cent or more of silicon, and this is the product of the electric furnace. Now the electric-furnace product is, depending upon its silicon content, from four to eight times as valuable as the blast-furnace product, and yet it has received no more protection than the low-grade blast-furnace product, which was specifically enumerated at $4 per ton in the act of 1897. This unfortunate condition has materially retarded the development of the business in the United States.

The following figures of imports of ferrosilicon, taken from government records, show the startling change that has taken place in the last ten years:

Year.	Tons.	Average value per ton.	Rate of duty per ton.	Equivalent ad valorem duty.
				Per cent.
1897	1,324.93	$17.60	$4	22.73
1907	12,653.12	72.26	4	5.54

When the demand arose for better steels and better and more alloys for producing special steels, American inventors, American capital and enterprise, and American research and experiment succeeded in producing a number of these alloys in the electric furnace, many of which were totally unknown previously. This refers especially to higher silicon compounds with iron, and to a number of other alloys which had previously not been known at all. In the course of the development of this industry, which is truly an infant industry, American engineers and metallurgists have seen the results of their efforts rapidly snatched from them by foreign manufacturers, because of the disparity in the conditions under which the manufacturing operations take place in the United States as compared with foreign countries.

GROWTH OF FERRO-ALLOY BUSINESS IN EUROPE.

The foreign manufacturers of ferro alloys have not only had a practical monopoly of supplying the foreign steel manufacturers, but have also largely had the control of the same business in the United States, due to natural conditions in Europe as regards cheaper water power and labor, and to inadequate protection in the United States. As a result they have built up large plants to manufacture various ferro alloys. These plants are located in Norway and Sweden, France, and Austria, and, to a more limited extent, in Switzerland, Italy, and Germany. In the aggregate they use between 100,000 and 150,000 electric horsepower. More recently a similar development has taken place in Canada, and works have been constructed to take advantage of the lower cost of power and other lower elements of cost prevailing in Canada, and yet the principal market is in the United States.

DEVELOPMENT IN THE UNITED STATES.

There has been no corresponding development of the ferro alloy business in the United States, because of inability to compete under the conditions prevailing under the act of 1897, and, by comparison, less than 10,000 horsepower is being used in the United States for this purpose, as against approximately 150,000 horsepower abroad. In the course of the last ten years a number of companies have gone into this line of industry in the United States, but have failed, and have either entirely discontinued their endeavors to manufacture anything or have directed their efforts to the manufacture of something else than ferro alloys.

NECESSITY FOR FURTHER DEVELOPMENT IN THE UNITED STATES.

Entirely aside from the desirability of developing such a manufacturing industry in the United States from the standpoint of increasing the material wealth of the country, utilizing certain natural resources and conserving others, employing American labor, etc., there is the necessity for encouraging the development of the industry here in order to insure to manufacturers of special steels the certainty of their supply, and to render them entirely independent of foreign manufacturers. There have been times when the supplies from abroad have been precarious and expensive, and it has been the custom of foreign manufacturers to form syndicates or trusts to artificially increase prices, after they succeeded in killing off domestic competition.

It should be noted that the production of each of the ferro alloys requires some variation in the process, and, generally speaking, in the plant, so that they should all be protected to secure the home production of all.

THE UNITED STATES GOVERNMENT SHOULD HAVE A SPECIAL INTEREST IN THE HOME DEVELOPMENT OF THIS INDUSTRY.

Many of the ferro alloys are essential in the manufacture of products for the United States Government. For instance, the largest single use of ferrochromium is in the production of armor plate and projectiles. Chromium is absolutely essential for this purpose, and no other element will take its place in imparting proper qualities to armor plate and projectiles. Other ferro alloys, including ferrovanadium, give special properties to armor and projectiles, and are also used. It is certainly for the best interest of the United States to have large responsible manufacturers of these ferro alloys in the United States, thus insuring certainty of supply in case of war with some foreign power. Such a war might be against one of the principal producing countries, in which event the supply necessary for the United States would be interfered with and probably cut off. It is even possible that ferrochromium might be classed as contraband of war, just as other munitions are so classed under such circumstances, and without question a cargo of ferrochromium which should prove to be destined specifically for warlike purposes would be within the category of contraband. During the Russo-Japanese war the representatives of the Japanese Government were scouring the markets of the world for ferrochrome to be used in its ordnance works, and, it may be incidentally remarked, it was only during this period that the United States manufacturers were able to export at a profit. The demand for some of these ferro alloys, as, for instance, ferrochromium, is intermittent, depending upon the requirements of the Government, and this necessitates the keeping of sufficient plant in reserve to take care of sudden requirements, while at other times the plant is idle.

It is no answer to this argument to say that in case of war there would also be a difficulty in obtaining from abroad the ores themselves. Tungsten ore is now produced to some extent in this country, and could be more largely produced if necessary. Chromic ore is not merely useful in the manufacture of ferrochrome, but also is very extensively and constantly used for making the bichromates of potash and soda and for the linings of copper and steel furnaces, so that there is always within our territorial limits a very large quantity of this ore, quite sufficient for the immediate exigencies of the Government in case of war if the proper plants exist for converting it into chromium and ferrochromium.

It will be shown later that the duties we ask will not increase the cost to any appreciable extent, but even if they should, there are sound reasons for imposing them, just as there have been sound reasons of national defense for encouraging the building of shipyards and the production of armor plate, projectiles, and heavy guns in the United States. Even Mr. Carnegie, in his famous article, recognizes such cases and says some of them open "the question whether it is economically best to use the domestic product at greater cost. The reply seems to be: If it involve the loss of a home supply of an article essential for the national safety, yes; if not, no."

EUROPEAN LABOR.

It appears unnecessary to discuss in detail the comparative cost of labor in the United States and in the principal European countries. This is well understood by all students of the subject, and it is assumed to be a premise in the policy of the United States to adequately protect American labor. By way of illustration it may be said, however, that in this particular industry the comparative wage scales are substantially as follows:

	Europe, per day of 12 hours.	United States, per day of 8 hours.
Ordinary unskilled labor	$0.50 to $0.60	$1.75 to $2.00
Semiskilled labor, as furnace attendants	.60 to .80	2.00 to 2.40
Skilled labor	.80 to 1.00	2.50 to 4.00
Foremen and assistant superintendents	1.00 to 1.25	4.00 to 6.00

By way of further illustration, in one electro-metallurgical plant in Austria, on one furnace unit on which 26 men were employed the average rate of pay was 80 cents per day, and on a corresponding unit in the United States the average rate of pay was $2.24 per day. In the European works the men work twelve hours per day, while in the United States in this line of industry the invariable custom is to work eight hours per day. Furthermore, skilled and technical men—as chemists, metallurgists, and engineers—can be employed in Europe on a basis which in the United States would correspond to nothing more than an apprenticeship.

Since the element of labor is one of the chief items of cost, the higher wage paid in the United States constitutes one of the largest items of increased cost and one of the chief reasons for asking adequate tariff protection.

COST OF ELECTRIC POWER USED IN FURNACES.

Another of the large items of cost in the manufacture of all of these ferro alloys is the cost of electric power (and in producing ferrosilicon this is the largest single item of cost), which, on an average, costs more than double in the United States what it costs in Europe. This is due somewhat to the natural conditions in European countries, where most of the waterfalls average higher in head than in the United States, thus (irrespective of labor conditions) making them cheaper to develop per unit of power. In addition it should be borne in mind that the principal item of the cost of developing water power itself is that of labor, this item alone constituting upward of 80 per cent of the total cost of making a water-power development. The difference in natural conditions and the difference in the cost of labor abroad, as compared with the United States, therefore explain the reasons for the increased cost of electric power in the United States. (It should be borne in mind that none of these ferro alloys can be economically manufactured in electric furnaces from power derived from sources other than water power.) Electric power in Europe is sold, according to the technical journals, at from $5 to $8 per horsepower year, whereas the price in the United States is more than double. Taking Niagara Falls, N. Y., as a typical illustration (which is one of the points at which this company buys power), electric power is sold within the limits of $15 and $25 per horsepower year, and averages in the neighborhood of $18 per horsepower year, delivered at points adjacent to the power house. On the other hand, electric power is sold on the Canadian side of Niagara Falls at from $10 to $12 per horsepower year.

THE DEVELOPMENT OF WATER POWERS.

No just criticism can be aimed at those who at great risk and large expenditure have electrically developed some of the water powers in the United States on account of their higher charges for power, because this higher selling price of power is made necessary by the higher initial cost of development. A mistaken idea prevails that the development of water powers in the United States has proven to be very profitable. This pioneer work of development is, undoubtedly, of immense value to the country, aiding its development and adding to its material resources, but as yet no adequate financial return has been earned by these enterprises. As a matter of fact, most of the large electric power plants developed in the United States during the past fifteen years have been failures from a financial standpoint, and most of them have been through receivers' hands and some of them more than once. Among others, the original companies which developed the large water-power plants at Massena, N. Y., at Sault Ste. Marie, Mich., on the Hudson River near Glens Falls, N. Y., and on the Yadkin River in North Carolina have all been in the hands of receivers, and at least three of these companies are still in the hands of receivers, as they are not in a position to earn interest on the capital invested. Even the pioneer company which developed the power at Niagara Falls after the expenditure of many millions of dollars (and which company is probably more favorably located as regards sale of its power than any other large water-power company in the United States) has never paid a dividend on its stock. It has reached its present stage of development only through personal pride of those financially back of the enterprise, and it was probably many years after the inception of the enterprise and the investment of many millions of dollars before it could earn its bond interest.

The successful development of water-power plants, from a commercial and financial standpoint, can only be made possible in the future when they can sell a portion of their power for the manufacture of articles of commerce by new electro-chemical and electro-metallurgical processes. Such development of water powers, however, aids materially in the upbuilding of the community for many miles around, as from such a plant power can be transmitted to advantage for the purposes of lighting, traction, and the lighter lines of manufacturing. However, these avenues for use of power are not alone sufficient, and the market does not come quickly enough to enable a power company to become a commercial success unless some of its power is sold for electro-chemical or electro-metallurgical uses. Therefore, in protecting and building up these industries, including the ferro-alloy industry, in the United States the Government will be indirectly encouraging the development of water powers, and thus utilizing some of the energy of nature which would otherwise be wasted, as well as conserving another great natural resource, viz, coal. All of this gives employment to American labor and adds to the material wealth and progress of the country. In view of the millions of horsepower available for development in the United States, it will be decidedly advantageous to the whole country to encourage in every way possible the development of these water powers.

COMPARATIVE INVESTMENTS.

From the best information obtainable, it is certain that the construction cost of a plant to manufacture ferro alloys in the United States is at least double the investment of the European manufacturer for a corresponding output. Furthermore, plants of this kind are equipped with electric furnaces of special design and machinery peculiarly adapted for this business alone, and in order to build up this industry, substantial encouragement is needed to induce the investment of the necessary capital.

HIGH INTEREST RATES.

Other items which enter into the cost of these products in the United States, in addition to the mere items of labor and material, are the interest and depreciation on the larger investment necessary in this country, and as the interest rates themselves are higher they are necessarily reflected in a higher total cost of manufacture.

LOCATION OF FOREIGN COMPETING PLANTS AND EFFECT ON FREIGHT RATES.

In a general way the large water-power developments in Norway, Sweden, Austria, and Italy, from which the principal competition to us comes, are located either on or very near deep-water ocean ports, whereas the large water-power developments in the United States are located at interior points, the two ferro-alloy plants of this company, for instance, being located, respectively, at Kanawha Falls, W. Va., and Niagara Falls, N. Y. The foreign manufacturers shipping in subsidized vessels, obtain very low freight rates on their products, and hence there is no advantage to American manufacturers on the question of freight rates. Furthermore, many of the alloys sell for high prices compared to ordinary iron products, and hence the amount of the freight is a comparatively small percentage of the selling price. In fact, the through combined ocean and rail import rates from certain foreign ports to interior domestic points where ferro alloys are used are as low as the domestic rail rates.

THE MANUFACTURE OF FERRO ALLOYS IS A NEW INDUSTRY.

The manufacture of ferro alloys is truly a new and infant industry. It needs encouragement and protection as much as steel did many years ago. It is an industry that requires a large technical staff, a high degree of skill, and large expenditure for experimental and research work. Electric furnaces employed utilize complicated electric and chemical processes and require frequent and expensive repairs, owing to the high temperatures necessarily used. Oftentimes these furnaces have to be entirely rebuilt, and owing to the newness of the industry, plants become obsolete frequently and require an entire new and duplicate investment of capital. Many new products are being developed for the benefit of the steel industry, and old products are being discarded. It occasionally happens that one of the products which has been in demand hitherto, and for which an expensive plant has been erected, is superseded by some new product which does the particular work desired either better or cheaper, and it becomes necessary to supply the new product, with the consequent abandonment or change of the appliances for manufacturing the old. This development, not only in the ferro-alloy business itself, but in the manufacture of alloy steels in the United States, entails a risk in this line of manufacturing much larger than the ordinary commercial risks.

RAW MATERIALS.

In manufacturing ferrosilicon we use charcoal, on which the duty is 20 per cent ad valorem; scrap steel, on which the duty is equivalent to 25 per cent or 30 per cent ad valorem; and large quantities of expensive electrodes, on which the duty is 35 per cent ad valorem. We actually use in making 1 ton of 50 per cent ferrosilicon, on which the duty is only $4, materials which enjoy in the aggregate protection amounting to as much as $5.90. Some of the ores which are used in the production of certain of the ferro alloys are comparatively rare, and have to be imported, and generally from remote parts of the world. These ores fluctuate in value, and, in the case of chrome ore, must be imported in shipload quantities, which necessitates tying up a large amount of working capital. Owing to the fluctuating demands for ferrochromium, this investment is oftentimes tied up indefinitely and makes another uncertain item of cost. On account of comparative freights on the raw materials, some of these ores are cheaper in Europe than in the United States, thus giving the foreign manufacturer another point of advantage. For instance, chrome ore is mined largely in Turkey and can be delivered to European works at lower freight rates.

COMPARATIVE COST OF MANUFACTURE.

From the best data obtainable, as indicated above, the cost of producing these ferro alloys abroad ranges from 60 to 65 per cent of the cost in the United States. This difference enables the foreign manufacturers not only to dump their surplus on the United States at practically any price they see fit, but actually enables them to sell and make a profit at less than the goods can be produced for in this country.

CONDITION OF THE TRADE.

The domestic manufacturers during the past ten years have been endeavoring to build up a ferro-alloy business in the United States. Some of these alloys they have manufactured for a time and discontinued on account of the foreign competition. The manufacture of ferrochromium has survived, though the competition has been most severe; but owing to the greater relative importance of both labor and power in the manufacture of ferrosilicon it has been almost impossible to build up the business in this country, though a market of considerable magnitude is available and could be extended. At the present time foreign 50 per cent ferrosilicon is being offered and sold as low as $64 per ton, delivered at interior points in the United States, and therefore this company has found it almost impossible to effect sales, as the cost of manufacture and delivery under conditions prevailing in this country have been found to be about $75 per ton. Many of the other ferro alloys could be manufactured in the United States if adequate protection was given, and the industry as a whole could be made one of considerable proportions and one which would afford employment for a large number of men.

While the foreign manufacturers have been consistently and regularly selling their products in the United States, the American manufacturers have been unable to compete with them on their own ground, and hence these products have been exported from the United States only to an infinitesimal extent and in the most desultory way. For instance, no ferrosilicon whatever is exported, and three-fourths of our domestic consumption is supplied by the foreign product, of which thousands of tons per year are imported. At the present time 50 per cent ferrosilicon and high and low carbon ferrochromium are quoted in England and Germany by foreign makers at less than the cost of production in this country. Not only has it been impossible to build up under the present tariff a large business in the United States devoted to the production of electric-furnace ferrosilicon, but the established manufacturers of the blast-furnace product are suffering and are facing the wiping out of their business, due to the competition of the foreign, practically duty-free, electric-furnace product, which can, to a certain extent, be substituted for the blast-furnace product.

The companies in this country interested in having the duty on ferrosilicon, ferrochromium, etc., made certain and sufficient are found in many States. The following have appeared personally or by brief in this matter, and their works are located as indicated:

Electro-Metallurgical Company, Niagara Falls, N. Y., Kanawha Falls, W. Va.; Primos Chemical Company, Primos, Delaware County, Pa.; Bessie Ferro-Silicon Company, New Straitsville, Ohio; Susquehanna Smelting Company, Lockport, N. Y.; Ashland Iron and Mining Company, Ashland, Ky.; Red River Furnace Company, Louisville, Ky.

DIVIDENDS.

The Willson Aluminum Company was engaged in the development of the ferro-alloy business for more than ten years. It discovered new products, improved old ones, and invented complicated electric-furnace processes therefor, but it has been unable to market its products at a profit. Its work and business have been merged into the Electro-Metallurgical Company. Neither company has ever made profit enough to pay dividends.

FERRONICKEL HAS A REASONABLE PROTECTION; WHY NOT OTHER FERRO ALLOYS?

By paragraph 185 of the tariff nickel alloys and nickel are dutiable at 6 cents per pound, which is $134.40 per ton. A ferronickel containing 50 per cent of nickel is worth abroad about 20 cents per pound, so that it pays a duty of 30 per cent ad valorem. Why should not we have a corresponding protection? Ferronickel and nickel are also used in the manufacture of special steels and enter largely into armor plate, etc., as do various of the other ferro alloys.

INCREASED COST OF SPECIAL STEELS WOULD BE LITTLE OR NOTHING.

The duty at present paid on ferrochromium, ferrotungsten, etc., is 20 per cent ad valorem, so that to make that rate certain in the new tariff by precise language will not increase prices. And to raise that duty to a point where domestic production could commence and continue with a reasonable expectation of success, to wit, 30 per cent, would not make the special steels cost substantially more, because in the manufacture of such steels the ferro alloys are used in extremely small quantities, sometimes as little as one-tenth of 1 per cent.

So far as ferrosilicon is concerned, the grades low in silicon (the product of the blast furnace) now pay a duty of $4 per ton, which is approximately equal to 20 per cent ad valorem, and it is only right that the grades high in silicon, which are proportionately more expensive, should pay a proportionately greater duty. This can only be accomplished by the automatic operation of an ad valorem rate. Such a duty would tell little, if at all, on the price of finished steel.

Moreover, it may be pointed out that if Congress should continue the grading of steel in paragraph 135 to a higher point than the present 16-cent line. so that special steels worth perhaps $1 or $1.50 a pound should pay a proportionate duty, there would be a speedy increase in the domestic production of special steels (which are now more largely imported), with a consequent call on domestic producers of the ferro alloys, and then the increased production and competition would permit a lowering of price.

If the domestic production of ferro alloys is not encouraged, our manufacturers of special steels will be at the mercy of the foreign makers of ferro alloys, because these foreign houses can combine, as they have actually been known to do in the past, to keep prices up beyond all reason. The encouragement of the manufacture of ferro alloys in this country will only result in more competition and prevent the outrageous prices which foreigners have sometimes charged when they had the market to themselves. So the consumer would actually benefit by our protection.

The effect of our proposal on the revenue would be inconsiderable. During the fiscal year ending June 30, 1907, there were imported 12,653.12 tons of ferrosilicon, paying duties (at $4 per ton) of $50,612.16. But since much of this was high in silicon content, and hence more valuable, it was worth an average of $72.26 per ton, or, in total, $914,328, and only paid a duty equivalent to 5.54 per cent ad valorem. If a duty of 30 per cent ad valorem were imposed, with the possible effect of cutting the importation down to one-fifth of the figures just named, the Government would get even a larger revenue, while incidentally the domestic production would be encouraged and placed on a competitive basis with the foreign products.

In regard to the other ferros which we are discussing the government statistics are not very full. It appears that during the period above named there were imported of ferrochrome 161.93 tons, worth $46,463, on which the duty was only $3,533.50, because the bulk of the merchandise, under the divergent court decisions, was admitted at $4 per ton, while the rest of it paid 20 per cent ad valorem. It is evident that a smaller quantity imported, if it paid 30 per cent ad valorem, or even if it all paid 20 per cent ad valorem, would yield a larger revenue to the Government. And doubtless the same is true of the other ferro alloys which are not separately mentioned in the official statistics.

It must be borne in mind, however, that although the imported ferros (other than ferrosilicon) have not been great in amount they have been potent in effect. They have acted as direct and distinct deterrents to the development of the domestic plants and products. We need certainty in the law and a reasonably protective duty before capital and brains can be profitably invested in this industry.

In view of the preceding facts, arguments, and explanations, we request that the following changes be made in the present tariff:
Par. 122. Strike out the word "ferrosilicon."
Par. 183. Insert the following words: "Silicon, chromium or chromium metal, tungsten, molybdenum, titanium, vanadium, tan-

talum, ferrrosilicon, ferrochrome or ferrochromium, ferrotungsten, ferromolybdenum, ferrotitanium, ferrovanadium, ferrotantalum, ferrophosphorus, ferroboron, and all other metals and alloys, all the foregoing crude or unwrought, whether capable of being wrought or not, and not otherwise specially provided for in this act, thirty per centum ad valorem."

All of which is respectfully submitted.

ELECTRO-METALLURGICAL Co.

COLNÉ & CO., NEW YORK CITY, WISH A LOWER DUTY OR REMOVAL OF DUTY ENTIRELY FROM FERROSILICON.

NEW YORK CITY, *November 24, 1908.*

COMMITTEE ON WAYS AND MEANS,
House of Representatives, Washington, D. C.

GENTLEMEN: We wish to place before your committee a few facts concerning the duty upon a certain quality of pig iron upon which, like all other pig iron, an import duty of $4 per ton is imposed.

This pig iron is used in making steel with the surface-blown converter, and analyses as follows: Silicon, 2.25 to 3.50 per cent; manganese, 0.50 to 0.90 per cent; carbon, 3 to 4.50 per cent; sulphur, 0.03 to 0.04 per cent; phosphorus, 0.03 to 0.04 per cent.

This iron is very scarce in the United States, the production small, the price high, and is confined principally into the hands of one house. This quality of iron could be imported from England at a reasonable price, lower than the American quality even with the addition of freight charges.

For the last twelve years we have been engaged in the business of putting up plants for making steel by the converter process, and though we have been able to develop it successfully to a certain degree, yet its wider extension has been very much hindered by the high price of the required pig iron.

We have made efforts with several furnace men to make this so-called silicon iron, but the demand for iron used in the open-hearth process is so great that no one cares to divert from his regular work.

The surface-blown converter has proved its usefulness at the present time. It has been introduced with much success and advantage as an adjunct to cast-iron foundries, malleable-iron works, and open-hearth steel foundries. It fills a field not reached by the open-hearth process for making small and medium perfectly sound castings of high tensile strength, free from blow holes. Steel is rapidly being substituted for cast or malleable iron. There is much demand for good castings from the machinery trade, steam fittings, electrical business, etc. The industries interested in such castings represent a vast amount of money interest, and anything that can be done to promote their success would be quite welcome.

The surface-blown converter being now free, the patent having expired, it is to be presumed that its use will be largely extended, provided the duties now paid on the quality of iron needed will be lowered.

It has always been the policy of our Government to put on a very low duty or to enter free materials used by our manufacturers when they can not be procured at home.

We bespeak, therefore, in the name of the machinery trade, the electrical business, growing so rapidly, the steel-casting interests, and many other allied industries, a consideration at your hands, for lowering or taking away the duty on pig iron of the quality mentioned.

The thriving industry around and about Sheffield, England, is a striking exhibition of what can be done with the proper kind of iron where such is extensively used.

By lowering or suppressing the duty on this high silicon iron you will not hurt any existing furnaces, as they do not make this brand of iron, and you will benefit all the industries mentioned.

The iron could be imported upon analyses made on the other side and certified before our consuls.

Under the circumstances, we believe that our request is in harmony with the policy of the Republican party, with which we have acted in accord for over fifty years.

Very respectfully,   COLNÉ & CO.

DANA & CO., NEW YORK CITY, THINK THAT THE VARIOUS FERRO ALLOYS NEED NO PROTECTIVE DUTY.

NEW YORK, *November 30, 1908.*

Hon. SERENO PAYNE,
   Chairman Tariff Committee,
      House of Representatives, Washington, D. C.

SIR: We trust you will not be misled by the cunningly devised plan to make an entirely new schedule in a new tariff law which shall include ferromanganese, spiegeleisen, ferrosilicon, ferrochrome, and other ferro alloys at an ad valorem rate of duty—we have heard 20 per cent ad valorem was the rate mentioned—which would be an increase of a good deal more than double the present duty on the first three mentioned articles, present rate being $4 per ton.

In the first place, ferromanganese and spiegeleisen is a raw material, like pig iron, and made from the ore in an ordinary smelting furnace, and is absolutely essential to steel making.

There is but one maker in this country of ferromanganese (the Carnegie Steel Company, member of the United States Steel Corporation, who, at times, make ferromanganese and spiegeleisen for their own use, and occasionally offer for sale their surplus).

We represent in America the English maker, the Wigan Coal and Iron Company (Limited), of Wigan, Lancashire, England, for the sale of their ferromanganese only, and it requires about 2½ tons manganese ore, about 3 tons coke, about 16 hundredweight limestone, about 12 shillings sterling labor, and about 11 shillings sterling wear and tear to produce 1 ton 80 per cent ferromanganese under about normal conditions for ore, etc. Ore supply comes from Russian Caucasus mines, India, and Brazil.

If the present rate of duty was reduced just one-half (if not put on the free list), we believe it would meet the approval of everyone interested, and would be a revenue producer at the $2 per ton rate.

Ferrosilicon consists of a cheap article much required for steel making, for the purpose of adding heat, thereby enabling the molten metal to throw off impurities, insuring sound steel, free from blow-holes, hard spots, etc.

The lower grades, such as 10 per cent, 11 per cent, and 12 per cent silicon generally used, is produced in an ordinary furnace, similar to pig iron.

But the high grade, such as 25 per cent, 50 per cent, and 75 per cent silicon, generally used, are produced in an ordinary furnace similar being done by electric pencils. Electric supply is by water power, and cost of production depends upon the cost of the necessary water power. We understand and believe it absolutely requires not less than 3,000 horsepower to produce the higher grades, at a cost of somewhere in the neighborhood of $9 to $10 in Europe, as against about $12 in America.

There are but two makers of moment in the States, and they could not begin to supply the demand.

This material is really nothing but metallic sand and iron. Ferrochrome is also produced largely by the electric furnace from chrome ore, and is used for hardening steel for armor-piercing projectiles, and for armor plate very extensively; for other kinds of steel its use is comparatively small in the metal line, and really but one maker in the States, who could not supply the demand.

The other high-grade ferro alloys, mentioned in the referred-to new schedule, would be a revenue producer if a specific rate of duty, moderately low, is made; otherwise an ad valorem rate of duty would greatly interfere with importations, besides opening the door for dishonest values in invoices.

Mr. Carnegie's view that our manufacturers of steel do not now need protection is entirely correct, as our labor-saving machinery entirely removes the question of the so-called "cheap labor" abroad.

But as a help in this direction to the American steel makers, should not 80 per cent ferromanganese, and 20 per cent spiegeleisen, as well as all ferrosilicons, be either on the free list or a greatly reduced specific rate of duty made?

Respectfully,   DANA & CO.

THE MIDVALE STEEL CO., PHILADELPHIA, SUBMITS SUPPLEMENTAL BRIEF, CLAIMING THAT ALL FERRO ALLOYS SHOULD BE FREE OF DUTY OR CLASSED WITH FERROMANGANESE.

PHILADELPHIA, PA., *December 1, 1908.*

COMMITTEE ON WAYS AND MEANS,
Washington, D. C.

GENTLEMEN: The paragraphs and sections of the present tariff act. to which this brief relates are:

Paragraph 122. Iron in pigs, iron kentledge, spiegeleisen, ferro-manganese, ferro-silicon, wrought and cast scrap iron and scrap steel, four dollars per ton.

Paragraph 183. Metallic mineral substances in a crude state, and metals unwrought, not specially provided for in this act, twenty per centum ad valorem.

Section 7. That each and every imported article not enumerated in this act, which is similar, either in material, quality, texture, or the use to which it may be applied, to any article enumerated in this act as chargeable with duty, shall pay the same rate of duty which is levied on the enumerated article which it most resembles in any of the particulars before mentioned.

The particular articles to be discussed in this brief are: Ferro-tungsten, ferrochromium, ferrotitanium, ferromolybdenum, and ferrovanadium.

The position of the Midvale Steel Company is as follows: (1) The above-named ferro compounds are not specifically mentioned in the present tariff act. (2) They should either be specifically excluded from duty or specifically mentioned in the act under section 122, where the remaining ferro compound, ferromanganese, is mentioned.

The ferro compounds, ferromanganese, ferrotungsten, ferrochromium, ferrovanadium, ferromolybdenum, are added to the steel mixture for the purpose of adding certain qualities to the steel and the formation of special steels.

Thus, ferromanganese, in addition to being a deoxydizer, is added to the steel mixture for the purpose of having in the steel a certain percentage of manganese which, in low percentages up to, say, 2 per cent, produces hardness. Beyond about 2 per cent and up to, say, 7 per cent, the steel becomes brittle. Beyond 7 per cent and up to, say, 20 per cent, the hardness remains and the brittleness is exchanged for toughness.

Chromium in steel, obtained by the addition of ferrochromium to the steel in process of manufacture, causes the steel, as does manganese, to become hard and tough, and it has the added capacity of enabling the steel to harden more energetically.

Tungsten in steel, obtained by the addition of ferrotungsten to the steel in process of manufacture, produces, as does manganese and chromium, hardening and toughening of the steel. It has the quality also of enabling the steel to remain hard (not lose its hardness) when heated to a high temperature, thus enabling cutting tools to work even at incandescence.

All of these ferro compounds, including ferromanganese, are improvers of the steel, and all improve it, as does ferromanganese, by increasing its hardness or toughness, or both. Of course each has its own individuality, else they would not resemble or be similar to each other, but would be the same.

All of these ferros are made in the same manner, by heating the ore with reducing agents and iron or iron oxide. In the case of ferromanganese it is done in a blast furnace. In the case of ferrotungsten, the melting point being so high, the heat of the electric furnace is required.

No one of these ferro compounds now under discussion has been used to make or do anything with except as an addition to steel in process of manufacture. None of these ferro compounds is capable of being made into any useful article. They can only be crushed into a powder.

While the prices of ferrotungsten, ferrovanadium, and some of the other ferros are exceedingly high, this is not caused by the cost of making the ferros, but by the rarity of the ores from which they are made and the great demand compared with the supply.

The United States is especially well fitted to make ferrotungsten, for instance, without protection, for one of the principal sources of the supply of tungsten ore is the State of Colorado. The water power and electric facilities of Niagara Falls and other water powers enable the production of ferrotungsten to be readily and cheaply carried on.

About the year 1900, with respect to the importation of one of these ferro compounds, ferrochromium, an attempt was made to levy duty under a paragraph of the act of 1894 as "manufactured articles not enumerated or provided for," subject to duty at 20 per cent ad valorem, the importer contending that under the similitude clause in the act it should be taxed under the paragraph relating to ferromanganese. The United States circuit court of appeals for the second circuit (New York) sustained the position of the importer. This case, United States v. Dana et al., is reported in 99 Federal Reporter, page 433.

The court said in that case, speaking of the similitude of ferromanganese and ferrochromium:

> It appears that both articles are used in the process of producing extra tough, hard metal, their distinct use being as an admixture with the iron ore which is to be converted into steel.
> It would seem that similitude between two articles is established when the predominant use of both is to effect in a particular art or process the same concrete result.
> The uses of the two articles, though not identical, are affiliated.

In 1905, under the tariff act of 1897, the question was again adjudicated by the United States circuit court of appeals for the second circuit, United States v. Roesseler & Hasslacher Chemical Co. (137 Fed. Rep., 770.)

In that case there was involved, in addition to ferrochromium, ferrotungsten, ferromolybdenum, and ferrovanadium. The contention of the Government was that they should be taxed under paragraph 183, while the contention of the importer was, as in the Dana case, that they should be taxed under paragraph 122. The court of appeals, as in the Dana case, sustained the position of the importer that these ferro compounds should be taxed under paragraph 122 by reason of their similarity to ferromanganese.

The court stated:

> The proper classification of ferrochrome for tariff purposes has been several times passed upon by the courts, and as it is conceded that all of the ferros here in controversy are, in essential particulars, alike, it will simplify the discussion if it be confined to ferrochrome alone.
> Ferrochrome is produced, in its most advantageous form, by reducing chrome iron ore with carbon in an electrical furnace; it contains iron, chromium, and carbon. One of its principal uses is in the manufacture of armor-piercing projectiles and armor plates. It is also used generally to impart hardness and toughness to steel structures and implements where these qualities are particularly needed, such as burglar-proof safes, crushers, cutting tools, and the like. Its principal use is as an alloy for steel. It can not be hammered or rolled or worked into any commercial article, and this is true of all of the ferros in controversy.
> Ferromanganese, like all the others, is produced by smelting the ore containing iron and manganese; it is added to the steel in the process of manufacture. It is used in making steel for the cheaper class of projectiles and for other purposes where hardness, strength, and ductility are necessary.
> A decision that ferrochrome is not a metal unwrought does not necessarily involve a decision that it is a manufactured article; it is enough if the collector's classification be erroneous. The ordinary meaning of "wrought" is worked up, elaborated, worked into shape, labored, manufactured, not rough or crude. "Unwrought" imparts the reverse of these conditions. When one speaks of an unwrought material he means one which has not been worked into shape, one which is unlabored, unelaborated, rough, and crude. But the word also implies a material which is capable of being transformed from its crude material to an improved condition, produced by the labor to which it may be subjected. To be more specific, "unwrought metal" implies a metal

which is capable of being wrought and not a substance which is only fit to be thrown into the crucible to be melted up with other ingredients to produce an entirely different and distinct product.

The question remains, Is ferrochrome similar to ferromanganese? This question has been passed upon by this court in United States v. Dana (99 Fed., 433; 39 C. C. A., 590), and what is there said is applicable to the present case. The counsel for appellant have taken pains to point out numerous instances wherein the two articles differ; but it must be borne in mind that the statute does not require identity; if that were necessary the statute would have no raison d'etre. It is enough if there be a substantial similitude in any one of the particulars mentioned—material, quality, texture, or use. (Arthur v. Fox, 108 U. S., 125; 2 Sup. Ct., 371; 27 L. Ed. 675.)

Ferrochrome and ferromanganese look alike; even the experts are unable to tell them apart, and they are similar in quality and in use, notwithstanding the fact that they produce different results and are not applied at the same stage of the process of making steel. We agree with the expert for the appellee when he says:

"The steel that is made by the use of these other ferros is along the same lines as the steel produced by the use of ferromanganese. There are differences but the qualities imparted are of the same general family."

In 1906 and 1907, the Midvale Steel Company, through importers, purchased ferrotungsten, which was entered through the port of Philadelphia. With respect to these importations, the collector again levied the duty under paragraph 183 of the present tariff act. Upon the hearing of the protest, in the name of the importers, E. J. Lavino & Co., the Board of General Appraisers held that the duty should be levied under paragraph 183, notwithstanding the two previous decisions of the circuit court of appeals for the New York circuit, that ferrotungsten should be taxed under paragraph 122 as resembling ferromanganese. This case is now on appeal in the United States circuit court for the eastern district of Pennsylvania. The general ground on which the Board of General Appraisers based their action was that there was a decision in the circuit court of appeals for the third circuit (142 F. R., 734), containing a ruling contrary to that of the circuit court of appeals for the second circuit, and the importation in question having been brought into this country through the port of Philadelphia, the ruling of the circuit court of appeals of that circuit, and not the ruling of the circuit court of appeals of the second circuit, should prevail.

At the hearing before the Ways and Means Committee of the House of Representatives on November 25, 1908, it was stated by Mr. Brown, counsel appearing and speaking before the committee, that tungsten metal was the subject-matter involved in this decision referred to by the Board of General Appraisers. This is a mistake, and probably will be rectified by Mr. Brown in his brief. As a matter of fact, the subject-matter involved in that suit was a malleable and workable material composed of iron, tin, and manganese, having no tungsten whatever in it.

The situation with respect to these ferro compounds—ferrochromium, ferrotungsten, ferromolybdenum, ferrovanadium, and ferrotitanium—is that they are unenumerated articles in the present tariff; that, notwithstanding the two decisions by the circuit court of appeals in the second circuit, the Government is still, even in the port of New York, continuing to levy duty contrary to such decisions, if the statement by Mr. Brown in his argument be correct.

It is therefore eminently proper in a revision of the tariff that this uncertain condition with respect to these ferro compounds should be eliminated and their status set forth with certainty. As stated before, the position of the Midvale Steel Company is that these ferro compounds should be admitted free of duty because they are essentially raw materials, and if the original ore from which they are obtained exists in the United States, it is of sufficient value itself without protection to compensate for its removal from the mines. The manufacture of the ferro compounds from the ore is by a simple metallurgical method requiring but little labor, the blast furnace being used where the heat produced thereby is sufficient, and an electric furnace being employed where great heat is required to melt, as in the case of tungsten. The United States is in an exceptionally good position without protection to produce these compounds in competition with the world, having the best water power and electrical facilities of all countries in the world. As to the element of labor or facilities, this country needs no protection to enable the compounds to be manufactured in competition with foreign countries.

It is always inadvisable to tax materials which enter into the manufacture of special steels, thus increasing their cost to the buyer, or restricting their use. If a special rate, or any ad valorem rate, be placed on these materials, the price of many of which is now exceedingly high by reason of the rarity of the ores from which they are made, it will add greatly to the price of the finished steel, which has now become essential for use in the tools of modern machine shops and for other purposes. Such added cost will materially add to the cost of the product of such tools.

The industry which would be created by the manufacture of these ferro compounds would be very small, and, with an ad valorem duty, tremendously profitable, as may readily be seen with, let us say, ferrovanadium at $3,000 per ton and a 20 per cent ad valorem duty.

As stated before, the labor necessary to produce ferro compounds from the ore is small, and the United States have as great facilities as any other country to produce them at a low cost.

It was stated at the hearing on November 25, by Mr. Brown, that if, for instance, the manufacture of ferrochromium were not protected, it might seriously jeopardize the United States in case of war, when its supply of ferrochromium might be cut off. Such an argument as this is absolutely fallacious when we recognize the fact that this country contains no, or practically no, ore from which chromium can be obtained, and must rely entirely upon foreign countries for chromium ores. Even if this industry were protected, it would be dependent upon foreign countries for its chromium ore, which could, in times of war, be as equally well cut off as ferrochromium. It would be just as easy to maintain a supply of ferrochromium for the contingency of war as it would be a supply of chromium ore for the same contingency.

It seems clear to the Midvale Steel Company that if there should be any duty put upon the importation of these ferro compounds under discussion, it should correspond to that of ferromanganese, because of the close analogy and similarity between ferromanganese and the other ferros mentioned herein. Such position has been twice sustained by the highest federal court in the second judicial circuit, and it has never been controverted in any decision of any court.

Of course the ferro compounds are not identical with one another, nor are they all in turn identical with ferromanganese. As Judge Cox (who rendered the decision in the case referred to before, and reported in the 137 F. R., p. 770) said, on page 773, that identity was not necessary, and "if that were necessary the statute would have no raison d'etre."

It is absolutely true that all are used as an addition to the mixture in the manufacture of steel for the purpose of improving the steel and forming special steel, and it is the real, practical, and only use of the ferro compounds under consideration.

It has been suggested that it is advisable to increase the tariff rate on special steels to thereby protect those special steels, which would enable a duty to be placed upon the ferro compounds without affecting the profits on the manufacture of the steel. The objections to this suggestion are many. In the first place, increased duties are contrary to the spirit of the times. In the second place, it is simply an attempt to cure one evil by introducing a greater evil, because it increases the cost to the consumer, not only by the increased price of the raw material entering into the manufacture of the steel, but in addition by reason of the protection given to the finished product. This is repugnant to all idea of progress and the general demand for the lowering of the tariff.

It is further contended that if the tariff upon the finished product be maintained at the present rate, the stability and certainty of the price of the raw material, so far as the tariff is concerned, should also be maintained, and maintained at a figure corresponding to that which present conditions require. To accomplish this, these ferro compounds used in the manufacture of steel for a purpose corresponding to that of ferromanganese should be taxed at a rate corresponding to that of ferromanganese, no greater and no less.

MIDVALE STEEL COMPANY.

THE AMERICAN VANADIUM COMPANY, PITTSBURG, PA., FILES A BRIEF RELATIVE TO FERROVANADIUM AND ITS USES.

PITTSBURG, PA., *December 3, 1908.*

Hon. SERENO E. PAYNE,
    Chairman Ways and Means Committee,
        Washington, D. C.

SIR: With reference to the tariff levied on importations of ferro-vanadium, cupro-vanadium, alumino-vanadium, and the various vanadium alloys, on vanadium salts and oxides, and on vanadium ores and vanadiferous ores, and to the statement presented to your honorable committee by the Primos Chemical Company, Primos, Pa., a copy of which is annexed hereto, we beg to present the following facts for your consideration in determining the tariff to be fixed thereon in your recommendations to the Congress of the United States:

First. That the duty now being collected on ferrovanadium importations is 20 per cent ad valorem; the legality of such collection is now up for adjudication before the courts of the United States, owing to ambiguity on this subject in the act of July 24, 1897.

Second. That the works of the American Vanadium Company are located at Bridgeville, Allegheny County, Pa.; that American labor is used in the production of the various vanadium alloys and in the reduction of the vanadium ores and vanadiferous ores; that American capital exclusively is invested in the American Vanadium Company; that the wages and salaries paid by the American Vanadium Company are equal to if not higher than the average wages and salaries paid by other producers of vanadium alloys either in America or abroad.

Third. That the price of commercial ferrovanadium of comparable quality, and of other vanadium alloys, is lower in the United States than it is in any European country or elsewhere, due in large measure to the improved and economical methods of production devised after much scientific research and laboratory experimentation and at considerable expense by the American Vanadium Company.

Fourth. That the business of producing and selling ferrovanadium and other vanadium alloys is profitable.

Fifth. The vanadium ore supply of the American Vanadium Company is derived from the mines owned by them located in Peru, South America; the work of extraction of the ore is directed by officials of the company in Peru, the ore being transported in American-owned steamers from Callao (Peru) to New York, thence shipped by rail to Bridgeville, Pa., for reduction; such ore is in the crude condition when shipped from Peru; the cost of reduction of the ore to ferrovanadium—by skilled labor, the materials used therein being American products—at Bridgeville, Pa., is three times that of the mining and transportation charges on the ore.

Sixth. The vanadium content and the extent of vanadiferous deposits located in the United States of America are of such nature as to preclude the possibility (in so far as such deposits have been discovered) of providing to the steel and iron producers of this country sufficient vanadium alloy to meet the existent demand, or to provide for the growing demands of the future.

Seventh. The imposition of a tariff on vanadium ores or vanadiferous ores would be highly injurious to our business.

Eighth. The American Vanadium Company was instrumental in exploiting vanadium for use in iron and steel, copper, brass, bronze, and aluminum, and its use in these metals is being rapidly extended, which growth will be accentuated if consumers are encouraged to believe there will be either no advance in the present market price for the vanadium alloy or a reduction thereof; prior to the development of our ore deposit and manufacturing process about 90 per cent of the vanadium alloys consumed in the United States were imported from Europe.

Ninth. Ferrovanadium is used in the production of practically all classes of wrought steel and steel castings and in cast iron, and by all processes of steel and cast-iron manufacture, the common purposes for which such vanadium steels and vanadium cast irons are employed being—

(a) In wrought (or worked) steel:
(1) General forging steel, for locomotive piston rods, and piston rods for other purposes, connecting rods, crackshafts, axles, side and main rods, gears, hammer rods, bolts, gun barrels, tires, springs,

high-tensile structural material, etc. The price charged therefor by steel producers varies from 4½ cents per pound to as high as 13 cents per pound for specially finished vanadium crucible steel, on which more or less rough forging work has been done.

(2) Cutter and punch and die steel, for rotary rock cutters, punches and dies, saws, edged tools, etc.; the base price charged by producers ranges from 10 to 13 cents per pound.

(3) High speed tool steel, containing from 15 to 25 per cent tungsten, from 3 to 5 per cent chromium, and about three-tenths of 1 per cent vanadium, used for cutters on lathes, planers, etc. The price charged by producers ranges from 55 cents per pound to 65 cents per pound; parenthetically it may be observed that the use of vanadium in such steel consumes a comparatively unimportant quantity of the ferrovanadium produced.

(4) " Governmental " steel, for use in protective deck plate, armor plate, gun shields, torpedo tubes, projectiles, defense guns, and artillery, in which vanadium—owing to four properties it imparts, namely, scavenging, toughening, strengthening, and prevention of erosion—is either now being used, or will be used in the immediate future, in considerable quantities.

(b) In steel castings, for locomotive frames, transmission bars, drawheads, crossheads, and the multifarious other uses for which steel castings are employed, the price charged by producers is from 2 to 3 cents per pound in excess of that charged by them for steel castings not containing vanadium.

(c) In cast iron for car wheels, piston-rod bushings, cylinder-plow moldboards, water-chilled rolls for steel mills, etc.; as such castings (with exception of the rolls and plow moldboards) are made by the railways and engine builders using same, no figures as to additional price, if any, which would be charged therefor are available.

Tenth. That the addition of vanadium to steel greatly increases the static strength of the steel and imparts the highest attainable resistance to molecular disintegration arising from shock, impact, and fatigue, and as vanadium is likewise efficacious in other metals, the lower the price charged therefor the more rapidly will its use be extended and the more certain will be:

(a) The use of American-made steels, irons, bronzes, etc., by American consumers.

(b) The use of American-made steels, irons, bronzes, etc., by foreign consumers.

In brief, we have a large amount of money invested in the development of this industry, in which we are the largest producers, and believe that the best interests of all would be subserved by retaining crude vanadium ore on the free list and that ample protection would be afforded to American manufacturers by the imposition of a duty of 20 per cent ad valorem, as suggested by the Treasury Department, as such duty would liberally cover the difference in the labor cost in producing this article in this country over the cheaper labor cost obtaining in European countries.

Yours, respectfully,   JAS. J. FLANNERY, *President.*

TITANIUM ALLOY MANUFACTURING CO., NIAGARA FALLS, N. Y., ASKS FOR PROTECTIVE DUTY ON FERROTITANIUM.

NIAGARA FALLS, N. Y., *December 2, 1908.*

COMMITTEE ON WAYS AND MEANS,
Washington, D. C.

GENTLEMEN: In the act of 1897 and previous tariff acts the alloys of titanium have not been provided for by name, but have been placed in paragraph 183 of schedule C, "metallic, mineral substances in a crude state and metals unwrought, not specially provided for in this act, 20 per cent ad valorem." On several occasions importers of these products have tried to have them classed "by similitude" with ferromanganese under paragraph 122, which provides that "iron in pigs, iron kentledge, spiegeleisen, ferromanganese, ferrosilicon, wrought and cast scrap iron, and scrap steel, $4 per ton, but nothing shall be deemed scrap iron or scrap steel except waste or refuse iron or steel fit only to be remanufactured." It is obvious that such an uncertain classification under such widely different rates of tariff can only serve to unsettle and ruin the industry of manufacturing ferrotitanium and its various alloys. Ferromanganese and ferrosilicon, upon which a duty of $4 is placed in paragraph 122, have nothing in common with our alloys. Ferromanganese and ferrosilicon are comparatively cheap and are made in very large quantities. Ferromanganese is made direct from the ore in a blast furnace and sells at a price of from $42 to $60 a ton, and ferrosilicon from $62.50 to $100 a ton. The manufacturer of the various titanium alloys entails great care and an enormous outlay of capital for an electro-metallurgical plant and also a large force of thoroughly trained scientific labor.

In Great Britain there are 3 manufacturers of ferrotitanium, in France 2, in Germany 15, besides some in Switzerland and Sweden.

The advantages of ferrotitanium in various fields has long been known to the steel trade of Europe. Nothing, or comparatively nothing, was known on the subject in this country until we started operation. We have been put to a vast amount of expense and labor in showing the steel makers how to use titanium and also the advantages to be derived therefrom. In the manufacture of the articles we have also spent a vast amount of time and money in satisfactorily developing the various processes. All these things have been known in Europe, and we are compelled in justice to ourselves to ask that titanium be put on a tariff basis of at least 35 per cent ad valorem for the following reasons, to wit:

1. *Cost of labor.*—The wages paid the labor employed in the manufacture of alloys in Germany varies from 45 cents per day for labor under 21 years old to 70 cents per day for adult labor. For the same classes we pay our men from $1.25 to $2. A much greater discrepancy exists in skilled labor.

2. *Cost of electricity.*—Abroad electricity can be purchased in large amounts at from $6 to $8 per horsepower per year. In this country it costs us, even under the most favorable circumstances, from $16 to $20 per horsepower per year, a difference of over 100 per cent in favor of the foreigners. Titanium being the most refractory material known, its reduction from an oxide to metallic state requires an intense heat, which can only be obtained in an electric furnace. We use

a very large quantity of electric current, and any difference in the price of this current, such as the foreigners enjoy over us, materially decreases the cost of the alloys. Electrical power is one of our great costs of production.

3. *Cost of ores and raw materials.*—In foreign countries there being a regular demand for titaniferous iron ores the mines have been opened and we have been offered these ores at $5 per gross ton at a Norwegian port, while in this country these huge masses of titaniferous iron ores being undeveloped it costs us over $8 per ton to get the ore on the railroad car. In addition to the ore costing more in this country than abroad, other of our raw materials are in the same category, namely, our reducing agent, either aluminum or carbon, as well as steel scrap with which we dilute our ores to the required percentage of titanium, are more expensive here than abroad.

4. *Cost of the various electrical contrivances and machinery necessary for all electrical smelting.*—The smelting of various ores by electricity abroad has become an established industry, and the various contrivances necessary for said smelting can be bought at a very much less price than in this country, where the industry is in its infancy and where said contrivances have to be manufactured especially at an exceedingly high cost.

5. *Cost of electrodes.*—The cost of electrodes in this country is exceedingly high. In our furnaces it is necessary that we use electrodes of great size, which up to the present we have been unable to buy here. We have been compelled to purchase them in France and Sweden at large cost, on account of the freight and tariff of 20 per cent.

6. The contention of some importers of alloys that titanium is not produced in this country shows that our concern is a genuine infant industry.

7. Being an entirely new industry, and the demand for the various titanium products having to be created in this country depending entirely on our own efforts, it is but due to us as a genuine infant industry that the Government afford us protection from the cheaper products of the foreign countries, where titanium and its effects are well known and where industries producing the same are on a firm and stable basis. If there be no material tariff imposed on these articles all our efforts and expense of the past few years must necessarily be wasted, and the opportunity for creating a large and prosperous industry irrevocably lost.

Respectfully submitted.

THE TITANIUM ALLOY MFG. CO.
WILLIAM F. MEREDITH, *President.*

————

C. W. LEAVITT & CO., NEW YORK, RECOMMEND THAT FERRO ALLOYS BE MADE DUTIABLE AT FOUR DOLLARS PER TON.

NEW YORK CITY, *November 19, 1908.*

Hon. CHAIRMAN WAYS AND MEANS COMMITTEE,
                    Washington D. C.

DEAR SIR: At the coming meeting of the Ways and Means Committee we understand that a suggestion will be made to revise paragraphs Nos. 122 and 183 of the customs tariff. For instance, we understand that it is the intention to classify chrome metal, chromium metal, manganese metal, molybdenum metal, tungsten metal, and wolfram metal, all of which are high-priced metals, usually sold on the per pound basis, in the same class with the ferro alloys. We believe that this would be working a great hardship on all of the steel works in this country. The ferro alloys are really a crude material required by most of the works in this country in the manufacture of their finished product, and if the ferro alloys are put on an ad valorem basis it will add greatly to the cost of production of the American steel works and place them at a disadvantage in their competition with the European manufacturers of the finished product.

We therefore believe and would recommend that the ferro alloys, viz, ferrochrome, ferromanganese, ferromolybdenum, ferrophosphorus, ferrosilicon, ferrotitanium, ferrotungsten, ferrovanadium, silico manganese, silico spiegel, and spiegeleisen, be classed at the rate of $4 per gross ton, which, apparently, was the intention of the framers of the present Dingley tariff.

Yours, truly,   C. W. LEAVITT & Co.

THE ROESSLER & HASSLACHER CHEMICAL CO., THINKS IN NO CASE SHOULD A RATE EXCEEDING TEN PER CENT BE PLACED ON STEEL-HARDENING METALS.

100 WILLIAM ST., NEW YORK CITY,
November 24, 1908.

Hon. SERENO E. PAYNE,
Chairman of the Committee on Ways and Means,
House of Representatives, Washington, D. C.

SIR: We are engaged in the importation of ferromanganese and ferrosilicon, for which a duty of $4 per ton is provided in paragraph 122 of the tariff act of July 24, 1897, and we also import ferrochrome, ferrotungsten, ferromolybdenum, ferrovanadium, and other goods of a similar nature, which should be dutiable under the provisions of paragraph 122 when taken in connection with the so-called "similitude clause" found in section 7 of the tariff act of 1897.

The rate of duty applicable to the articles just mentioned has been the subject of many decisions of the Treasury Department, Board of General Appraisers, and the federal courts, and the most comprehensive of these decisions is that reported as United States v. Roessler & Hasslacher Chemical Company (137 Fed. Rep., 770). This case was a decision of the circuit court of appeals for the second circuit, dated March 1, 1905, in which it was held that the four ferros not mentioned in paragraph 122 were dutiable at the same rate as the two mentioned in that paragraph, by virtue of the application of the similitude clause, and this case was a most elaborate discussion of the whole subject. In addition to the services of the United States attorney, the Government had the benefit of special counsel of very high standing at the bar, and the witnesses called to testify numbered among them some of the finest experts to be found in the class of those who are well acquainted with these articles. The Treasury Department accepted the conclusions of the court in this case and the matter was presumed to have been a settled issue until a new case on this subject was made, which is reported as General Appraisers' Decision 6755, dated April 16, 1908, wherein it was held that in consequence of some of the testimony offered, and largely on the authority of the case of Thomas v. Cramp (142 Fed. Rep., 734), these ferros were not dutiable under the provision of paragraph 122, but were subject to a duty of 20 per cent ad valorem under the provisions in paragraph 183 of the tariff act of 1897 for " metallic mineral substances in a crude state, and metals unwrought, not specially provided for in this act, 20 per cent ad valorem." From this decision an appeal was taken to the United States circuit court in the third circuit, where the matter now rests, and the Government is now exacting a duty of 20 per cent ad valorem on these articles.

That these ferros are different from the articles intended to be covered by the provisions of paragraph 183 is very evident, because in the opinion of the circuit court of appeals in the Roessler case it was stated that all of the ferros in controversy were in the essential particulars alike, and this view was admitted by the counsel for the Government. When, therefore, Congress made the provision for two of these ferros in paragraph 122, those two at least were not intended to be dutiable under the provisions of paragraph 183, and if they were not dutiable then all of them were not dutiable. Again, the court stated in the Roessler case that the principal expert witness for the United States, Doctor Waldo, gave the metal aluminium in its pig form as an example of an unwrought metal, because it had passed through a complicated preparation of ore refining, solution, melting by electrical heat, and electrolysis itself, and this metal aluminium, of course, is a very different thing from these ferros, which are combinations of the metal and iron, as, for instance, ferrochrome is a combination of chromium metal and iron. Another article can be given as an illustration of an unwrought metal, and that is the tungsten metal, which was so classified by the orders of the Treasury Department in their decision 21217, dated June 3, 1899. It will be seen that both of these articles are entirely different from the ferros with which we are dealing here, because the ferros have as a constituent very large proportions of iron, which are not found in the two articles just mentioned as subject to duty at 20 per cent ad valorem.

The case of Thomas v. Cramp, which was cited in a recent decision of the General Appraisers as an authority for their action, should not be considered as any authority whatever upon the subject of ferros, for in the opinion of the circuit court, which is quoted in the opinion of the court above, it is stated that " the merchandise in question is an alloy of metal, composed of 62 per cent of iron, 32 per cent of tin, and 6 per cent of manganese," but it was held by the circuit court that the General Appraisers were in error in finding that this article was dutiable under the provisions of paragraph 172 of the tariff act for " aluminium and alloys of any kind in which aluminium is the component material of chief value, in crude form, 8 cents per pound," and it was accordingly held that the article was dutiable under the provisions of paragraph 183. From this decision the United States appealed, and it may well be noted that the importer did not appeal from the decision of the circuit court, although the claim was made before the General Appraisers and the circuit court that the article was dutiable by similitude under the provisions for ferromanganese in paragraph 122. The appellate court sustained the circuit court and held that the article was dutiable under the provisions of paragraph 183, but it would seem that it was justified in not holding that the article was dutiable at the same rate as ferromanganese on account of the great difference between its composition and that of ferromanganese and other ferros. The article in the Cramp case contained 32 per cent of tin, while it is stated in the opinion of the Roessler case that " ferromanganese, like all the others, is produced by smelting the ore containing iron and manganese." It would therefore seem that the article in the Cramp case was entirely different from the ferros in the Roessler case, and the Cramp case should not therefore be considered any authority for the propositiou that these ferros are dutiable under the provisions of paragraph 183, and until a court of equal jurisdiction has held to the contrary the ferros should be clearly dutiable where they were placed by the circuit court of appeals in the second circuit—that is to say, under the provisions of paragraph 122.

It has been deemed desirable to refer to these decisions of the courts, the General Appraisers, and the Treasury Department in order that the committee may have before it the present status of these articles, as the provisions in the tariff act of 1897 would be applicable to them.

All of the ferros mentioned by us herein are used as one of the raw materials for the manufacture of steel in this country. Each of them has some particular quality which makes it especially desirable to produce a given purpose. From the elaborate testimony taken in the Roessler case it appears that ferrochrome is used where special hardness and toughness are required, which are not found in the ordinary commercial steel. Ferromanganese is used in the manufacture of steel for its cleansing properties and to rid the steel of certain impurities, and it also imparts toughness to the steel. Ferrotungsten is also used in the manufacture of steel for making a special kind of steel, and ferromolybdenum and ferrovanadium are used for similar purposes. The last mentioned of these ferros is becoming more commonly used than formerly, because the increased production has decreased its cost, and it has been found to have good qualities for producing a steel which is very valuable in the manufacture of such articles as require great tenacity, light weight, and great endurance.

From other sources it may be stated that ferrosilicon is employed as a deoxidizing agent, and, generally speaking, these ferros have the effect of producing a more homogeneous product than could be obtained without their use. Among the uses to which these ferros are applied may be cited the manufacture of the steel used in armor plates uppn the battle ships of this country, the projectiles fired from the great guns of these ships, the steel required in railroad bridges where heavy trains are constantly passing over the road, the connecting rods and axles of the locomotives which draw the heavy express trains on the principal railroads, the connecting rods and axles and some other parts of high-grade automobiles, the walls of burglar-proof safes, the jaws of ore crushers, cutting tools of a very high grade, and many other articles which might be mentioned if not for lack of space. The great improvement in the manufacture of steel in recent years is largely due to the use of these ferros and the immense consumption of these high-grade steels would seem to justify such action on the part of your committee as would tend to increase their use by steel makers.

It may be said further that the more extensive the use of these ferros the more cheaply they can be made. Ferrochrome, which is used in the production of armor plates, projectiles, safes, and similar articles requiring great hardness, was formerly sold as high as $300 per ton, while the present price is about $225 per ton. Ferromanganese was formerly sold at about $100 per ton, and for a short period during the war between Russia and Japan it was sold as high as $150 per ton, the present price being about $43 per ton. Ferrosilicon has sold as high as $125 per ton. Ferrovanadium, which is the most expensive of all these ferros, in 1901 was worth $12.50 per pound for the vanadium contents in the alloy, while a better article can now be supplied for one-third that price. Ferrotungsten is not used much, but the tungsten metal is sometimes used as an imitation of a rapid-cutting steel. Ferromolybdenum, on account of its erratic action, is not used very much. Ferrosilicon, ferromanganese, and ferrochrome are now manufactured to some extent in this country, but the domestic product is not sufficient to supply the requirements of the steel makers. Although we have not all the figures relating to the quantity of these ferros which are used, it may be stated that from official sources it appears that during 1907 57,794 tons of ferromanganese and ferrosilicon were manufactured by the United States Steel Company, while the imports during that year were as follows:

Ferromanganese, 94,543¼ tons, valued at $6,027,240; duty, at $4 per ton, $378,173.11; average value, $63.75 per ton; average rate of duty, 6.27 per cent.

Ferrosilicon, 12,653.12 tons, valued at $914,328; duty, at $4 per ton, $50,612.16; average value, $72.26 per ton; and average rate of duty, 5.54 per cent. It will thus be seen that it was necessary to import about two-thirds of the quantity of these two articles which were needed to supply the want of the steel makers in this country and the duty paid by them was about $428,000 on the imported articles, while at the rate of 20 per cent ad valorem, which it is sought to place on them, the duty which they would have been compelled to pay would have been $1,388,313. These figures will give some idea of the tax on manufacturers of steel which an ad valorem duty of 20 per cent would impose.

It further appears that during 1907 the United States Steel Company produced 130,554 tons of spiegeleisen, and there was imported during the year 82,422.51 tons, valued at $2,486,086, the average value of which was $30.16 per ton, the duty of which, at $4 per ton, was $329,690.03, and the average rate of duty was 13.26 per cent. The prices of these ferros are principally regulated by the supply and demand, and as the demand for them is constantly increasing, it necessarily follows that the price will decrease.

It is presumed that it will be suggested to your committee that an ad valorem duty should be placed on these ferros upon the ground that the specific duty heretofore levied on them is very small from an ad valorem point of view. The answer to that is that this provision in paragraph 122 at the rate of $4 per ton for the three articles mentioned there, which are used as materials for steel makers, namely, spiegeleisen, ferromanganese, and ferrosilicon, was placed there with the idea of furnishing a low rate of duty for materials absolutely essential to the manufacture of high grades of steel. In consequence of this low rate of duty, the use of these ferros has increased enormously since 1897 with the exception that for a while the application of the 20 per cent duty and the possibility that it might become final was sufficient to disorganize the trade in the imported ferros and consequently decrease their use.

It may be well to submit to your committee some particulars as to the origin of the articles which are used to produce these ferros. Manganese ore comes from Russia, Brazil, and India; chrome ore from Asia Minor and New Caledonia; silica is found nearly all over the earth in the shape of quartz; the phosphorus used is largely made in Europe and is a by-product in the manufacture of the phosphorus of commerce; molybdenite, from which molybdenum is made, is found in Scandinavia and also in this country, this article is not much used, because it is very erratic in its action; wolframite, used for making tungsten, is found here, but a better grade comes from Australia to Germany, where it is refined as a metal; vanadinite, for making vanadium, comes largely from Peru, Spain, Mexico, and Argentina. It may also be stated that spiegeleisen, which is mentioned in paragraph 122, is also a ferro, being composed of from 10 to 40 per cent of manganese and the remainder of iron, while the standard quality is about 20 per cent of manganese and 80 per cent of iron.

It appears from the published synopsis of the intentions of your committee that a new paragraph has been suggested for the new tariff to come under the provisions of paragraph 183, and this suggested paragraph requires some attention on our part. The paragraph as provided covers three distinct articles—namely, ores, metals, and ferros—and it is submitted that three such diverse articles ought not to be subject to the same rate of duty and for the following reasons: Molybdenite is a sulphide of molybdenum and is the condition in which the latter is found as an ore, rich pieces of which will sometimes run up to 60 per cent of metal and 40 per cent of sulphur.

In General Appraisers' decision 6673, dated October 24, 1907, in passing on an importation of certain vanadium ore, they held that it was vanadium in the crudest form obtainable and as dug out of the earth, and that this ore was not a metallic mineral substance and dutiable at 20 per cent ad valorem under the provisions of paragraph 183 of the tariff act of 1897, but was exempt from duty as a crude mineral under the provisions of paragraph 614 of the tariff act of 1897. It would therefore seem from this decision of the General Appraisers that the ores from which these metals and ferros are made are very distinct articles from the metals themselves, and ought not, therefore, to be subject to the same rate of duty as metals and ferros.

The metals are chrome, chromium, manganese, molybdenum, and tungsten, or wolfram metal. These metals are highly finished products and nearly 100 per cent in purity. Chromium and manganese are not made in the United States; molybdenum is made here, but in small quantities; tungsten is made here and in large quantities. Chromium, manganese, and tungsten are very largely and almost entirely used in the manufacture of crucible steel, which is an article of very high grade, chiefly used for tool steel, and the production of which, on account of its high price, is limited. The purity of the ferros is very distinct from that of metals, as, for instance, we have a blast-furnace ferrosilicon which comes as low as 10 per cent in purity, while we have an electro-ferrosilicon which is as high as 95 per cent in purity, and the other ferros range as follows: Ferrovanadium, 35 to 40 per cent; ferrochrome, 60 to 70 per cent; ferromanganese, 80 to 85 per cent; ferromolybdenum, 50 to 90 per cent; ferrotungsten, 50 to 90 per cent; ferrophosphorus, 17 to 25 per cent; ferrotitanium, 10 to 50 per cent; and spiegeleisen contains from 10 to 40 per cent of manganese. The distinction between the metals above given and the ferros is that in the latter iron is added to the metal to form the compound article, which is a ferro. This may be a ferro of very high purity, such as ferrosilicon, which is sometimes 95 per cent in purity, the remaining 5 per cent being iron and impurities. A very important point to be remembered in considering the difference between these metals and the ferros derived from them is that a chemical analysis of the articles is not of itself sufficient to determine the difference between the two articles, the processes of manufacture being the most important feature.

In this suggested paragraph now before your committee, ferrophosphate is mentioned, but this alloy should be described as ferrophosphorus, a production containing 25 per cent of phosphorus and 75 per cent of iron.

It is respectfully submitted that a new provision can be made in the tariff act in which all of these ferros and spiegeleisen as well, can be mentioned with the specific rate of duty of $4 per ton, which is now provided for two of the ferros and spiegeleisen under the provisions of paragraph 122 of the tariff act of 1897, and which it was held by the circuit court of appeals for the second circuit in the Roessler & Hasslacher case also applied to other ferros of a similar nature; but if your committee shall desire to place an ad valorem rate on these articles, it is suggested that such should be 5 per cent, which is about the rate now paid on ferromanganese and ferrosilicon, as above shown, or in no event should an ad valorem rate exceeding 10 per cent be applied to any of these articles.

Respectfully submitted.

THE ROESSLER & HASSLACHER CHEMICAL COMPANY,
LOUIS RUHL, *Assistant Secretary.*

WALTER GASTON, ELECTRO METALS (LIMITED), WELLAND, ONTARIO, FILES BRIEF RELATIVE TO FERROSILICON.

WELLAND, ONTARIO, *December 14, 1908.*

COMMITTEE ON WAYS AND MEANS,
House of Representatives, Washington, D. C.

GENTLEMEN: Ordinarily we know it would be very much out of place for us, a foreign corporation, to address the Ways and Means Committee in connection with a tariff schedule covering materials produced by us, and we certainly would not presume to do so now were it not that in a statement made to you by Mr. H. C. Harrison, vice-president of the Susquehanna Smelting Company, of Lockport, N. Y., asking for an increase in the duty on ferrosilicon. He gives as one of the necessities for such an increase the inability of the domestic manufacturer to compete with the Canadian manufacturer of this alloy, and in doing so cites some reasons so wholly at variance with the actual facts that we, as the chief Canadian maker, and the one he refers to, feel it incumbent on ourselves for the enlightenment of the committee and in the interest of the users of ferrosilicon in the States, as well as in justice to ourselves, to correct.

The statement that we purchase Canadian charcoal at two-thirds of the cost to the Susquehanna Smelting Company is incorrect, as we use no Canadian charcoal whatever.

The statement that we profit by "government bounty-fed power" is also incorrect, as the Canadian government pays no bounty for the development of Niagara power; on the contrary, the Canadian power companies pay to the Canadian government a royalty on each electric horsepower developed.

While we do not know just what the Susquehanna Smelting Company pays for electric power, the information we have fully warrants us in saying the statement that we pay 25 per cent less for power than that company, is also incorrect. Should we be paying any less, it must be remembered that Niagara power costs more the farther the consumer is located from the generating plant, and that power at Lockport would therefore, naturally, cost somewhat more than at Niagara Falls and immediate vicinity. Our power cost should be compared with the latter, and in this connection we would say that we have been offered power on the American side for less than we are paying for it on the Canadian side.

We certainly do not consider that, in the cost of producing ferrosilicon, we have any advantage over the producer in the United States, so far as the elements that enter into the production, i. e., labor, raw materials, and power, are concerned.

Our labor is fully as high as in the United States, on the basis of wages actually paid, as the American consul at Niagara Falls, Ontario, will vouch for, and higher on the basis of efficiency.

All our raw materials, excepting silica, come from the United States, the additional freight charges making the cost of these materials greater than to the producers in the United States, to say nothing of very much greater cost of the Canadian silica we use.

Furthermore, there are the additional freight charges of the Canadian railroads on ferrosilicon into the States, a very material addition to the cost.

As a further evidence that ferrosilicon can be produced as cheaply in the United States as by us at Welland is the fact that in the face of the Canadian duty of $2.50 per ton the United States producers have been able to make such low prices in the Canadian market as to either undersell us or force us to sell at most discouraging figures.

As to the statement that we have located our works on the Canadian side, using Niagara power, in order to save freight and transportation charges from Europe: In the first place, this would give the impression that we are a European company, which is not so. So far as incorporation is concerned, ours is a Canadian company, but our stockholders, both in numbers and interests, are principally citizens and business men of the United States. In the second place, if we were a European company, we would not want to work under the less favorable conditions of the manufacture of ferrosilicon existing in European countries, but would aim, as we are now doing, to work under the much more favorable conditions existing in the United States.

When we located in Canada our aim was to make pig iron and some other iron products, as well as some steel products, as will be seen from the following extract from a paper on "The reduction of iron ores in the electric furnace," read by R. Turnbull (vice-president of our company), of St. Catharines, Ontario, at the March (1908) meeting of the Canadian Mining Institute, i. e.:

In the spring of last year Mr. R. H. Wolff, of New York, and I decided to erect a plant in Canada in order to demonstrate that iron ore could be commercially and profitably smelted in the electric furnace.

As the use of the electric furnace commercially, in the production of pig iron, depends largely on the cost of coke, we selected Canada as a favorable location for our plant, because of the high price of this material, and Welland, because of the advantages it offered in rail and water transportation, and in Niagara electric power available for the entire year.

In the beginning we had not the slightest idea of making ferrosilicon, and it was only when the results of certain experiments, then being made, in the making of pig iron in an electric furnace, had demonstrated the necessity of further experimental work before the production of it on a commercial scale could be undertaken that we incidentally turned to ferrosilicon, with the making of which some of our technical men were familiar, as a source of revenue pending the completion of our pig-iron experiments.

Regarding the statements of Mr. Harrison relative to the cost of water power and the cost of making ferrosilicon generally in European countries, they are so misleading that it is but right for us to state what we understand to be the actual facts.

In the first place, it must not be understood that ferrosilicon is being actually made or is likely to be made at all of the water power he names. There are undoubtedly many places in the countries he names where water power has been and can be developed comparatively cheap, but these places, as well as the places he mentions, are chiefly found at points difficult of access—in most cases in the mountains, where, as in Sweden, the French Alps, the Austrian Tyrol, etc., the maximum power is only available for about seven months—October to April—owing to the scarcity of water in the rivers, which are fed by glaciers in the mountains, and from which practically no supply is obtained between the months of October and April. In most cases only one-third of the power is available during the five months—November to March—thereby necessitating the development of three times the power required for these latter months.

Thus in the case of the manufacturer developing and owning his own power, as is quite general in Europe, while in some instances $8 might be taken as the cost, based on the maximum power, as the latter is only available for seven months of the year, the overhead, depreciation, interest, etc., charges which must be made for the entire year, materially increase the power cost, in many cases at least 50 per cent.

Many of the European works produce other products than ferrosilicon, which products must be produced during the entire year, and in such cases to insure a sufficient supply of power for this purpose it is customary to close down the ferrosilicon and other alloy furnaces as soon as the power commences to fail. Here again the charges covering the metallurgical staff (which must be retained during the stoppage), the cost of stopping and starting the furnaces, always considerable, interest charges, etc., materially add to the power cost.

It must not be considered that $8 power, as above, can be had all over Europe. On the contrary, it is very rare; the average charge being from $10 to $20, the low charge of $8 being only made in cases where it would be impossible to produce anything at all unless power is very cheap. A proof of this is that one of the foreign works, using $12 power, shows a much lower cost price in its product than other works using $8 power; the reason for this being mainly the more favorable location of its works and the availability of a larger percentage of its power during the winter. As to cost of power in Sweden, the Swedish producers of ferrosilicon, with whom we are in touch, are paying as much as $20 per horsepower per year.

It is possible to buy power in some parts of Europe at $8 per horsepower; but this is only six or seven months' available power, it being generally what is known as "second-rate" or "surplus" power, to be had from those generating stations having a surplus during the summer months, when the maximum power can be obtained, and when much less power is required for lighting purposes, etc.

Surplus or second-rate power can be had on the American side of the Niagara River at an exceedingly low rate, and is supplied continuously during the year. The only disadvantage in the use of this power is that the power company has the right to stop the supply during from four to six hours of each day. However, as the consumer, by buying a small amount of firm (first-class) power, can keep his furnaces going, and as he can also work by intermittent charges, this second-rate power is more advantageous in the States than the same or six or seven months' power is in Europe.

As to the water powers Mr. Harrison mentions, as capable of development for electric-furnace work, in most cases their locations mean very high freight rates on raw materials into the plants and on the finished product out; and these reasons alone, in the most favored cases, make them expensive locations, and in the majority of them impossible locations for ferrosilicon plants.

Ferrosilicon of the higher percentages, on which the increased duty is asked, can be made as cheaply in the United States as in Europe. Though in the latter case the labor costs are less, the materials really cost more, iron and silica being about the same, the coal, coke, and charcoal costing much more, particularly the coke, which costs from $7 to $8 per ton. As the cost of power determines the location of plants for the making of the higher percentages of ferrosilicon, makers must go to the power, and in France, from whence has been imported the great bulk of the higher percentages of ferrosilicon into this country, the makers have had to locate their plants in the French Alps, at the expense of high costs of freight on materials in and finished products out, the rate to seaboard being from $5 to $6 per ton, to which, if ocean freights to New York, Baltimore, etc., including insurance—say, $2.75—be added, $7.75 to $8.75 per ton must be added to the foreign cost at works, making, with the duty of $4 per ton, a total charge of $11.75 to $12.75 per ton to deliver the product at a port of entry in this country. This certainly should be a very good protection on a product of which the labor costs in the United States should not exceed, say, $7 to $8 per ton on 50 to 60 per cent ferrosilicon, which, of the higher grades, is chiefly used in steel making.

So well satisfied are we that ferrosilicon of the higher percentages can be made cheaper in the United States than in European countries that we have no hesitation in saying that we would be perfectly willing to undertake the production there, in competition with foreign makers, without the aid of any duty whatever and with every confidence of success.

To do this, it would not be necessary to use Niagara power, although we could readily do so at cost to the present producers at Niagara Falls. There are other locations in the States where power can be had at a considerably lower cost than Niagara power, and we venture to say that electrolytic ferrosilicon is now being produced elsewhere in the United States at a considerably less horsepower cost; therefore, even the cost of Niagara power should not be taken, by any means, as the lowest cost of power in the States.

As in European countries, inaccessible and accessible power are to be found in the United States, costing more or less, as the case may be, it being simply a matter of location and barter.

There are two other matters to which we beg to call attention: One is the selling price of ferrosilicon, taking 50 per cent as the grade of the high percentages chiefly used in the making of steel. This, within the last two to three years, has sold as high as $115 per ton of 2,240 pounds, while at present the price has dropped to about $62 to $64, the lowest price at which it was ever sold, and at which the foreign makers are all losing money. Although this low price has been made during the present business depression, it is, by reason of the largely increased manufacture, not likely that the price will ever again, as a rule, range higher than $70. The other is that, unlike ferrochrome, ferrotungsten, ferrovanadium, etc., in which the cost of materials increases with the higher percentage of ores used, the cost of materials entering into the production of the higher percentages of ferrosilicon does not increase as the percentage of silicon increases, but, on the contrary, decreases, the silica, the cheaper material, taking the place of iron, the more expensive material; therefore, the higher prices of the past and the increased percentages of silicon should not be considered as a basis for an advance in duty, as has been urged by some of the domestic manufacturers.

Respectfully submitted.

ELECTRO METALS (LTD.),
WALTER GASTON,
General Manager.

ROBERT GILCHRIST, REPRESENTING THE WESTERN FOUNDRY SUPPLY CO., ASKS THAT THE PRESENT DUTY BE MAINTAINED ON FERROMANGANESE.

TUESDAY, *December 15, 1908.*

The witness was duly sworn by the chairman.

Mr. GILCHRIST. I have asked permission to appear before you in the interest of only one concern, the Western Foundry Supply Company, with the request that you maintain the present duty on ferromanganese, which is $4 a ton, and is covered by Article 122 and Clause C.

The reason I have asked for permission to appear before you is because I have been told that the steel makers, at their meeting in New York, and some steel makers in their talks before you, have advocated the abolition of this duty, and it seems to me that a man that appears before you and asks that the duty should be taken off of everything that enters into his manufactured product and then views with horror any suggestion that the duty should be taken off the manufactured product, is trying to work both ends against the middle.

Mr. COCKRAN. That we agree to.

Mr. GILCHRIST. Now, on the face of it, it is apparently good sense that the duty should be taken off of ferromanganese, because most all of the ferromanganese used in this country is imported from England. There is ferromanganese made in this country by the Carnegie Steel Company very largely, and altogether from imported ores; a little by the Maryland Steel Company; a little by the Illinois Steel Company, and a very little by the Colorado Fuel and Iron Company. But in 1907 there were 100,000 tons imported at a duty of $4 a ton, netting the Government $400,000.

Now, as all this ferromanganese is imported, it would seem right and proper that the duty should be taken off so that the manufacturer in this country should get his raw material free, make his product cheaper, and sell it as cheap as he could. But there is one thing that enters into that that perhaps is not known to many of the steel men. In the first place the reason that ferromanganese is not made very largely in this country is that it has been impossible to find ferromanganese here in sufficient quantities to justify the erection of a blast furnace.

Manganese is found in the Blue Ridge Mountains, but the Blue Ridge Mountains, from Vermont to Georgia, are strewn with manganese wrecks. What I mean by that is the wrecks of plants where people have spent their time and money developing, and then found them useless. No ferromanganese deposits have heretofore been found that justified the erection of a blast furnace for the manufacture of manganese until the Western Foundry Supply Company, which I represent——

Mr. DALZELL. Where is it located?

Mr. GILCHRIST. In St. Louis, Mo.; Elizabeth, N. J., and New York.

They have found in Virginia, and spent $75,000 to find and develop, manganese-ore deposits which justify the erection of a blast furnace, and they are ready to spend a half million dollars more to inaugurate in this country an industry which has never existed, which is the manufacture of 80 per cent of the ferromanganese used in the country.

I would not be foolish enough to appear before you and ask you to protect one person if two persons were going to be injured by protecting one—and when I say injured I mean injured materially. If there were only one other person, then I would think I had as much right to demand consideration as the other one person.

But in order to see what injury will be done by a retention of the duty, you would have to find out how much ferromanganese is used

by the steel manufacturers. Mr. Schwab said you could put down the
cost of ferromanganese used in a ton at 60 cents.

From the letters I have been able to get on the subject and from
the works on the subject which I have been able to examine, I find
that the cost of ferromanganese at the present time, the present market price, is about 30 cents—from 25 to 40 cents. That is, for the
amount needed in a ton. But let us call it 60 cents on a ton of steel.
Ferromanganese to-day is worth $40. I say $40. It is, as a matter
of fact, about $42, but for the sake of easier figuring I prefer to call
it $40.

If the cost of the ferromanganese is $40 a ton, and the amount
required in a ton of steel is 60 cents, and the duty is $4, or one-tenth
the price the steel maker is paying for it, it makes a difference of
6 cents in a ton of steel.

Steel is sold by the pound, 2,240 pounds to the ton. The steel
maker is suffering in order that the Government may have $400,000
a year, and incidentally that the Western Foundry Supply Company may go into existence, they are suffering 6/2240 of a cent, which
is 3/1120 cent per pound. That is what they are suffering.

Now, in spite of that fact, I would not ask you to keep the duty
on if in your estimation, as small as that saving would be, the steel
men would go to the consumers of the United States and say,
" Gentlemen, owing to the abolition of the duty of $4 a ton on ferro-
manganese we can make the steel at 6 cents a ton cheaper, or 3/1120
of a cent per pound cheaper, and we cheerfully hand it over to you."
But if you believe, as I believe, that the steel men will put that
3/1120 in their own pockets, and will simply add that to the profits
that do not need anything added to them, then I think it is eminently right and proper that the Western Foundry Supply Company,
that has one separate entity, should be entitled to go into business
and establish in this country a business that has never heretofore
existed.

If there is anything in a tariff for protection, it seems to me right
and fair that the Western Foundry Supply Company, if they do not
ask for any more protection than has existed in the past, are entitled
in their childhood to as much protection as these overgrown industries. I think they are an industry entitled to as much consideration
as any other industry.

If, on the other hand, there is anything in a tariff for revenue
only, it seems to me that there is no way in which the Government
could get a revenue and work less hardship on the general consuming public than by maintaining the duty on ferromanganese.

There is one other industry in this country that uses ferromanganese that has not asked for the abolition of the duty, so far as I
know, and that is the manufacturer of car wheels.

This knowledge is common property. It is common practice in
the matter of car wheels that ferromanganese is used, but only to
the extent of one-quarter of 1 per cent. The standard car wheel up
to a short time ago was 600 pounds. A quarter of 1 per cent of 600
pounds is a pound and a half. At $40 a ton, a pound of ferroman-
ganese is worth approximately a cent and a half. A pound and a
half would be worth, roughly, 2½ cents.

In other words, the car-wheel maker is suffering a loss by the retention of the duty of 2½ cents on a 600-pound wheel, and with the
duty being $4 a ton.

I did not get that right. The cost of the ferromanganese in a 600-pound wheel is 2⅓ cents, and the cost of the duty to the car-wheel maker is one-fourth of 1 cent. In other words, the cost per pound of car wheels, the car-wheel maker is suffering a loss of $0.0124, and in view of the small losses which are divided, as Mr. Schwab said, among very few people—because the steel manufacturers are very few in number—and divided among people who are eminently able to stand them—it seems to me right and proper that this concern should be permitted to inaugurate its business in this country and establish a new business.

The CHAIRMAN. This is in the same paragraph with pig iron, is it not?

Mr. GILCHRIST. I think so.

The CHAIRMAN. And requires the same duty?

Mr. GILCHRIST. Yes.

The CHAIRMAN. Do you think it should bear the same duty as pig iron?

Mr. GILCHRIST. Well, there is no criterion by which one who hopes to be a manufacturer of ferromanganese can go, because there are no commercial ferromanganese manufacturers. I do not know absolutely what it is going to cost to make ferromanganese in this country. All I can do is to go on estimates, ask as many questions as I can. You can realize that it is impossible for me to go to the Carnegie Company and ask them what it costs them.

The CHAIRMAN. Do you not think that you ought to give some information by which the committee can find out what it costs?

Mr. GILCHRIST. Yes, sir. As far as we can figure, it will cost us $40 a ton.

The CHAIRMAN. What is the price laid down in New York to-day?

Mr. GILCHRIST. About $43; it has been $39; it varies.

The CHAIRMAN. And you can make it for $40?

Mr. GILCHRIST. We can make it for $40. We can not tell what the Englishman makes it for.

The CHAIRMAN. Laid down at $40 before the duty is paid?

Mr. GILCHRIST. That is, with the duty paid. It is common talk in the ferromanganese business that the Englishman gets just about cost for his ferromanganese when he gets £8 for it laid down in this country.

The CHAIRMAN. You only manufacture small quantities?

Mr. GILCHRIST. Yes; we would manufacture about 35,000 tons a year.

The CHAIRMAN. You have manufactured?

Mr. GILCHRIST. We would if we were allowed to go into the business.

The CHAIRMAN. You say it would cost $40 a ton?

Mr. GILCHRIST. As far as we have figured, it would cost us $40 a ton, sir.

Mr. CRUMPACKER. You are not in the manufacturing business?

Mr. GILCHRIST. No, sir.

Mr. CRUMPACKER. You are prospectors?

Mr. GILCHRIST. We have prospected so far that we are ready to go into the business of manufacturing now.

Mr. CRUMPACKER. And you personally have had no experience in manufacturing ferro-manganese?

Mr. GILCHRIST. No, sir. It is not manufactured in this country. I want to go a little further and say that it is impossible to tell you from facts what it costs the Englishman to manufacture it, but it is common talk among the ferro-manganese men that it will cost us $40. If you take the $4 a ton duty off, it is our understanding, it will cost them about $34 to lay it down here, and that would preclude the possibility of our going into business.

Mr. LONGWORTH. Have you put up a plant?

Mr. GILCHRIST. No; not yet. We are ready to put up a plant. We are ready to spend half a million dollars to put up a plant and inaugurate this business in this country if the duty of $4 a ton is maintained.

THE NORTHERN IRON COMPANY, PHILADELPHIA, PA., OBJECTS TO REMOVAL OF DUTY FROM SILICON IRON.

PHILADELPHIA, *December 17, 1908.*

WAYS AND MEANS COMMITTEE,
Washington, D. C.

DEAR SIRS: In the printed reports Colné & Co., New York, say:

We wish to place before your committee a few facts concerning the duty upon a certain quality of pig iron upon which, like all other pig iron, an import duty of $4 per ton is imposed. This pig iron is used in making steel with the surface-blown converter, and analyzes as follows:

	Per cent.
Silicon	2. 25 to 3. 50
Manganese	. 50 to . 90
Carbon	3. 00 to 4. 50
Sulphur	. 03 to . 04
Phosphorus	. 03 to . 04

This iron is very scarce in the United States, the production small, the price high, and is confined principally in the hands of one house. This quality of iron could be imported from England at a reasonable price, lower than the American quality even with the addition of freight charges.

For the past twelve years we have been engaged in the business of putting up plants for making steel by the converter process, and though we may have been able to develop it successfully to a certain degree, yet its wider extension has been very much hindered by the high price of the required pig iron. We have made efforts with several furnace men to make this so-called "silicon iron," but the demand for iron used in the open-hearth process is so great that no one cares to divert from his regular work.

By lowering or suppressing the duty on this high-silicon iron, you will not hurt any existing furnaces, as they do not make this brand of iron, and you will benefit all the industries mentioned.

We respectfully beg to state that these statements are untrue. This so-called "silicon" pig iron is what is known in the trade as "low-phosphorus" pig iron. It does not differ in any respect from pig iron used in the open-hearth acid furnaces, excepting that the silicon is somewhat higher. The open-hearth furnaces use iron usually with silicon from 1 to 2 per cent. The Tropenas converter, represented by Colne & Co., requires iron with silicon from 2.25 to 3.50 per cent. The same furnaces which make the open-hearth iron produce the so-called "silicon" iron. It is not true that only one house is interested in this matter. This iron has been produced during the past few years by the following concerns:

Northern Iron Company, Standish, N. Y.
Empire Steel and Iron Company, Catasauqua, Pa.
Bethlehem Steel Company, Bethlehem, Pa.
Pennsylvania Steel Company, Steelton, Pa.
Carbon Iron and Steel Company, Parryville, Pa.
R. Heckscher & Sons Company, Swedeland, Pa.
Carnegie Steel Company, Pittsburg, Pa.
Cambria Steel Company, Johnstown, Pa.
Stewart Iron Company, Cleveland, Ohio.
Cranberry Furnace Company, Johnson City, Tenn.

There has been no period during the past twenty years when an abundant supply of this iron has not been available from at least three to six of these furnace companies. More of the iron would have been produced had the demand called for it. Any discrimination in duty on this so-called " silicon " iron would be a distinct blow at the capital and labor interested in the manufacture of low-phosphorus pig iron, and would be an injustice to users of low-phosphorus iron by the acid open-hearth process.

Respectfully, yours,   NORTHERN IRON COMPANY,
W. S. PULING, *Treasurer.*

THE BESSIE FERROSILICON COMPANY, NEW STRAITSVILLE, OHIO, ASKS MORE DUTY ON FERROSILICON.

NEW STRAITSVILLE, OHIO, *December 18, 1908.*
Hon. SERENO E. PAYNE,
Chairman Ways and Means Committee, Washington, D. C.

DEAR SIR: We earnestly beg that Congress will give us the protection on ferrosilicon, which was evidently intended but which we are not now receiving. The conditions of the business, and particularly new methods of manufacturing, have altered the situation from what it was in 1897, when the present tariff act was passed, so that a readjustment of the duty is imperatively required. Otherwise an established business in this country, which has already declined, is threatened with extinction. During this last year our furnace has been shut down for almost all the time, owing chiefly to foreign competition.

Ferrosilicon is a combination of silicon and iron and is used in the manufacture of steel to make it sound and to prevent blowholes, etc. It was formerly made only in blast furnaces, and perhaps for that reason was classified in the tariff with pig iron, which is also made in blast furnaces, though, as indicated below, it never really belonged in that class. However that may be, since 1897 an important change in manufacturing has occurred, so that ferrosilicon can be and is now largely made by electro-metallurgical processes.

The value of ferrosilicon depends on the " silicon content "—that is, the amount of silicon present—so that a ferrosilicon of 8 per cent silicon is worth correspondingly less than the ferrosilicon of 50 per cent silicon. The blast-furnace ferrosilicon only runs about as high as 15 per cent silicon, whereas the electrical-furnace product runs from 50 per cent silicon up and has a correspondingly higher value. Yet all these kinds of ferrosilicon are now being admitted for duty, whatever their value, on a basis of $4 per ton.

The official figures of the importations of ferrosilicon show three marked facts as between the year 1897 and the year 1907: First, that the importations have increased from 1,324.93 tons to 12,653.12 tons; second, that the value per ton has increased from $17.60 to $72.26, which, of course, is due to the fact of the increasing importations of the electric-furnace product with its correspondingly higher values; third, that the equivalent percentage of duty on an ad valorem basis has consequently diminished from 22.73 per cent to 5.54 per cent. The figures by years are as follows:

Year.	Duty per ton.	Tonnage.	Value per ton.	Equivalent percentage on ad valorem basis.
1897	$4.00	1,324.93	$17.60	22.73
1898	4.00	679	21.92	18.24
1899	4.00	1,559.26	24.00	16.66
1900	4.00	4,666.25	36.85	10.92
1901	4.00	546.22	30.92	12.94
1902	4.00	3,567.63	20.77	19.26
1903	4.00	23,795.35	24.63	16.24
1904	4.00	6,262.04	33.30	12.01
1905	4.00	6,833.99	48.93	8.18
1906	4.00	10,275.20	60.07	6.66
1907	4.00	12,653.12	72.26	5.54

The only way to secure proper protection on ferrosilicon is to remove it entirely from the class of pig iron and put it with such other ferro alloys as are made by both the blast furnace and the electric processes. Ferrosilicon, whether in the form of pigs or otherwise, never really belonged in the class with pig iron. To make a ton of it by the blast-furnace process costs from two to three times as much for labor cost alone, besides requiring twice as much fuel as to make a ton of ordinary pig iron.

The total labor cost in making ferrosilicon, if we regard the entire cost of the manufacture from mining the ore to the complete ferrosilicon, is doubtless at least 80 per cent to 90 per cent. If we take the actual cost of the blast-furnace process alone, it is, as before stated, from two to three times as great as in making pig iron; and if we compare this blast-furnace part of the manufacture alone with the cost abroad, we have a striking contrast in the wages. paid. From the best information we can obtain, after careful inquiry, we believe that these comparative costs of labor would be as follows:

	Europe.	United States.
Ordinary unskilled labor_____per day..	$0.50 to $0.60	$1.80 to $2.00
Skilled labor_____do____	.80 to 1.00	2.50 to 3.50

We understand that foreign blast-furnace ferrosilicon (of 10 per cent silicon content) is being offered at the present time at New York and at Philadelphia on a basis of $22.50 per ton, duty paid. The average cost of making our 10 per cent grade during the last four years has been about $21.50 per ton at furnace (in the Hocking Valley), which, with freight added, means $25.20 at New York and

$24.80 at Philadelphia, without figuring in any profit whatever. In other words, the foreign manufacturers can pay $4 per ton duty and sell their products here at from $2.70 to $2.30 per ton less than our cost price, without including in such cost any profit whatever for us. The following tabulation shows this clearly:

Our average cost for the last four years for putting down 10 per cent ferrosilicon in Philadelphia, without any allowance whatever for profit _____ $24.80
Foreign value of imported 10 per cent ferrosilicon per ton, say___ $16.75
Expenses for freight, brokerage, etc., about 10 per cent, say_____ 1.75
Duty at $4 per ton_____ 4.00

Selling price of imported ferrosilicon at Philadelphia_____ $22.50

Advantage to foreigners_____ 2.30

To put us on an equal basis in that territory with the foreigner, even without any profit to ourselves, we need a duty of $6.30 on 10 per cent ferrosilicon, which, on the basis of the foreign value, would equal about 37½ per cent. And if we regard territory somewhat nearer our furnace, as, for instance, between Philadelphia and Pittsburg, we need a protection of 30 per cent to 35 per cent.

It is true that there have been times when we have been obliged to make sales at below cost to hold our trade or to get rid of a surplus stock, and about the only times when we can get into the eastern market are those when the foreign supply happens to be short while there is a local demand for immediate delivery. But the situation is summed up when we say that at the present time we have been practically driven out of the eastern market and can not compete profitably in the Pittsburg territory.

We do not ask for the required protection on the ground that ours is an infant industry needing encouragement, but on the ground that it is an old industry threatened with extinction. Only a few years ago there were in the Hocking Valley seven or eight blast furnaces making silicious iron. To-day our company is the only one left, and even we for a long period have been unable to keep our furnace in steady operation, while at the same time the importers have been bringing over and selling the foreign product. Possibly our industry might have been able to maintain itself on the present duty if conditions of manufacture had not changed so tremendously, but as it is now there is no hope for us except in a change of the tariff.

We do not wish to object to the electric-furnace manufacturers receiving proper protection, but we do firmly believe that manufacturers of blast-furnace ferrosilicon should also receive due consideration in the tariff, and we beg that the same may be accorded us.

We therefore ask that you remove ferrosilicon from paragraph 122 in the tariff and put it in paragraph 183 with the other ferro alloys (except ferromanganese, as to which the facts are very different and in which we are not interested). We also ask that you insert in paragraph 183, in order to prevent any doubt of the intention of Congress, some such words as " whether produced in electric furnace, in blast furnace, or by chemical process, or otherwise." As to the rate of duty, as before pointed out, we need a protection of about 37½ per cent ad valorem (on the foreign value) to compete (even without reckoning profit to us) with the foreign product at the seaboard, though possibly 30 per cent or 35 per cent ad valorem would enable us to compete in the Pittsburg territory.

We are authorized to state that we speak also for the Ashland Iron Mining Company, of Ashland, Ky., who also did manufacture ferro-silicon by the blast-furnace process, but who for a long time have been obliged to discontinue such manufacture. We are, sir,

Yours, very respectfully,

BESSIE FERROSILICON CO.

PHILIP BAUER COMPANY, NEW YORK CITY, WRITES RELATIVE TO TUNGSTEN ORES AND CONCENTRATES.

NEW YORK, *December 31, 1908.*

Hon. SERENO E. PAYNE,
Chairman Ways and Means Committee,
House of Representatives, Washington, D. C.

DEAR SIR: Mr. Walter M. Stein, president of the Primos Chemical Company, of Primos, Pa., submitted a brief on November 17, 1908, on steel-hardening metals.

In the first two paragraphs Mr. Stein states that this brief is submitted on behalf of the industry of manufacturing ferrotungsten, etc. He furthermore claims that the brief is submitted on behalf of the industry of mining tungsten ores, etc.

We are in the business of importing tungsten ores and concentrates from foreign countries, and at the same time are working a mining property in Colorado producing wolfram.

We want to state that Mr. Stein's statement that the cost of production of tungsten ore in this country amounts to $8 per unit of tungstic acid and ton of ore of 2,000 pounds or to $480 per ton of concentrates is incorrect.

⊢ In a report made under date of October 14, 1908, by Frederick H. Minard on the property known as the "Clarasdorf Tungsten Mill," a statement was embodied as follows:

PRODUCTION.

From the date on which the mining of tungsten ores began on the Rogers patent up to the time the property was taken over by the Philip Bauer Company the following production was made:

	Pounds.	Per cent WO$_3$.	Pounds concentrates.	Per cent WO$_3$ concentrates.	Value per ton.	Per cent mill saving.	Total value.
Sorted ore:							
Upper tract	2,890,331	12.36	313,772	62.74	$313.70	55.17	$49,216.13
Lower tract	1,453,595	11.65	145,300	53.66	268.30	46.00	20,833.97
Crude ore, lower tract	274,053	10.50			29.21		4,002.52
Total	4,617,979	12.02	459,072				74,052.62

The average price paid for this production was $5 per unit of WO$_3$, the highest and lowest returns having been $6 and $3.25.

The poor mill saving from this production is accounted for from the fact that the ore was milled in six different plants scattered all over the country. None of them was adapted to the concentration of tungsten ores, as they were all old mills erected for the treatment of gold ores and used stamps as crushing machinery, which slimed the wolframite.

A statement of profit and loss in operating under this Stevens lease is as follows:

Paid out in royalties	$18, 513. 13
Operating cost	39, 539. 49
Profit	16, 000. 00
Total	74, 052. 62

From this you will see that on a total value of $74,052.62, there was a profit of $34,503.13, at prices ranging between $6 down to $3.25 per unit and ton of 2,000 pounds, and the fact is not to be overlooked that the mining at that time was done in a very crude way, as was also the milling.

This shows that the statement of Mr. Stein that the cost of production is $8 per unit must be erroneous.

Furthermore, we produced on our property during the months of May, June, and July, 1908, 153,000 pounds of concentrates, averaging 53 per cent, which would be 4,284 units, at a cost of $12,700 for mining, carting, milling, concentrating, etc., or at an average cost of less than $3 per unit and ton of 2,000 pounds.

In regard to Mr. Stein's tabulation of wages in principal tungsten ore-producing districts, we beg to say that his statements are correct, but the countries mentioned by him, viz, Portugal, Spain, Bohemia, and Argentine are only very small producers of wolfram ores and concentrates, and the quantity produced by these countries is hardly in excess of 500 to 750 tons of wolfram, and we doubt very much whether the production of these countries combined reaches anywhere near this quantity.

The principal producing country of wolfram in the world to-day is not the United States, nor is it any of the countries mentioned by Mr. Stein. The principal producing country of wolfram to-day is Australia and the Straits Settlement. This fact is very well known to every man in the tungsten business.

We have no figures on hand at the present time as to the cost of production in Australia and-as to the miners' wages, but this information can be easily obtained from the American consuls in Australia and partly from the Department of Commerce and Labor.

To our best knowledge the wages of miners in Australia are in excess of those paid to miners in the United States. Furthermore, the cost of production in Australia is in excess of the cost of production in the United States.

Australia and the Straits are by far the largest producers of wolfram ores and concentrates, supplying about 2,000 to 3,000 tons annually.

Colorado, and especially Boulder County, can produce wolfram cheaper than any other district in the world.

Furthermore, the amount of tungsten produced in the United States is not sufficient to come anywhere near the demand for tungsten in this country, which statement can be corroborated by the York Metal and Alloy Company, of York, Pa., and the Crucible Steel Company, of Pittsburg, Pa., and other concerns.

To our knowledge, there are four manufacturers of tungsten metal, tungstic acids, etc., in this country. The Primos Chemical Company is one, having their own mine.

There is another concern manufacturing tungsten metal and tungstic acid, also working their mine in Colorado, but these people exclusively use their product in their own manufacture, and do not sell in the market.

There are two manufacturers of tungsten metal and tungstic acid who do not have their own mines, and, therefore, if a duty of 20 per cent should be put on wolfram ores and concentrates, as petitioned by Mr. Walter M. Stein, it would simply mean that these two manufacturing concerns, which are, at the present time almost entirely depending upon imported wolfram ores and concentrates, would have to go out of business, as they would not be in a position to compete with the Primos Chemical Company, and the Primos Chemical Company would control the market of tungsten metal and tungstic acid in the United States and would have no competition whatsoever in this country.

Inasmuch as it is not the intention of this government to restrict business, but to further business and encourage competition, we would respectfully request that no duty be placed on wolfram ores and concentrates, as those manufacturers of tungsten metal and tungstic acid who do not have their own mines would suffer great hardships and practically be driven out of business, and at the same time it would increase the cost of these metals to the steel trade.

Very truly, yours,

PHILIPP BAUER Co.
O. WEHRENBERG,
Vice-President.

YORK (PA.) METAL AND ALLOY CO. SUBMITS STATEMENT RELATIVE TO TUNGSTEN AND MOLYBDENUM PRODUCTS.

YORK, PA., *December 31, 1908.*

Hon. SERENO E. PAYNE,
Chairman Ways and Means Committee,
House of Representatives, Washington, D. C.

SIR: Our attention has been called to the brief submitted on November 17, 1908, to your honorable committee by Mr. Walter M. Stein, president of the Primos Chemical Company, Primos, Delaware County, Pa., on the subject of steel alloys and metals, purporting to be acting in behalf of the whole of that industry in the United States, not only of the metals and alloys, but also of the ores thereof.

We are the principal American competitor of the Primos Chemical Company in tungsten and molybdenum products and are therefore much interested in the brief submitted, and any subsequent action your committee might recommend on the readjustment of tariff schedules.

COST OF ORE PRODUCTION.

While we have not the actual cost figures in hand, the cost of producing tungsten ore quoted by Mr. Stein must be very excessive, as we know it to be a fact that when tungsten ore (wolframite) is selling at $8 per unit and ton of 2,000 pounds (say on basis of 60 per cent ore, $480 per ton) the miners are satisfied that they are getting a good round profit. The cost therefore can not be $8 per unit for production. We believe Messrs. Philipp Bauer Company, 68 Broad street, New York City, can furnish your committee with exact cost of production, as they are the only other considerable producers of tungsten ore (wolframite) in the United States that is sold on the open market.

The Primos Chemical Company is the only manufacturer of tungsten products for the market in this country who own their own mines, and consequently by the impost of duty on tungsten ore, it would mean an absolute and sole monopoly of the business for them, as it would be impossible for us, or any other manufacturer not owning mines, to compete, thus compelling all independent metal and alloy manufacturers to go out of business. From this you will quickly see that it would be a serious hardship not only to the metal and alloy manufacturers, but also to the steel and other industries to impose a duty on tungsten ore.

At the time of writing, it is practically impossible to buy a ton of American wolframite for competitive use, for the following reason: The Primos Chemical Company manufacture their own production and naturally would not sell ore to their competitors. The only other manufacturers owning their own mines manufacture for their own use only, and we are reliably informed that they have not sufficient for their own use. The small independent miners producing low-grade ores, which must be concentrated, sell all their crude ore to the mills for concentration, and that is therefore practically controlled through the above concerns. The present production of the only other considerable producer of wolframite (Bauer Company) is all contracted for. This situation leaves the several independent manufacturers of metals and alloys, who do not own their own mines, entirely dependent on foreign wolframite, domestic production not being nearly enough for their needs.

Mr. Stein's last paragraph therefore, that he has considered all interests, is rather ambiguous and misleading.

We feel that it is not your desire nor intention to recommend legislation creating such a monopoly, which would be the means of destroying all independent competition and placing all the steel and lamp makers at the mercy of one concern.

Our position on molybdenum ore is practically the same as that of tungsten, excepting that, in so far as our knowledge goes, no manufacturer of molybdenum products owns their own mines. In fact there is little, if any, produced in the United States, and therefore any impost of duty on same would mean a relative restriction on this industry, to no apparent purpose.

DUTY ON FINISHED PRODUCTS.

We very heartily indorse Mr. Stein's petition for an increase of tariff on products of tungsten and molybdenum, such as the metals, their alloys, and the salts and acids thereof. These are probably the most costly alloys that there are manufactured, and we may say, from our own experience, that Mr. Stein's statement of wages, cost of manufacturing materials, etc., contained in his brief are substantially correct.

We respectfully submit that the present duty of 20 per cent ad valorem is inadequate protection for this comparatively new industry in the United States. Our own experience leads us to respectfully ask that the tariff on tungsten and molybdenum metals, alloys, and the salts and acids thereof be adjusted to 35 per cent, as this amount would place the industry on about an equal basis of competition with foreign manufacturers, without causing any injustice to the consumers of the products.

It will undoubtedly be of some weight with your honorable committee in its deliberations as to the inadequacy of the duty on tungsten and molybdenum metals, alloys, and their salts and acids, when we inform you that during the recent depression in business in Europe, particularly in Germany, the United States manufacturers had to compete even more than usual with cheap foreign metals and alloys, caused by their home consumers being out of the market, destroying the business of our own domestic industry to such an extent that it has been imposisble to compete during 1908 with said foreign products excepting at a loss. Had the duty been 35 per cent, as respectfully petitioned, it would have at least placed the foreign products on what is practically American cost of manufacture.

It would also be beneficial to the industry to have the duties on tungsten and molybdenum metals, alloys, their salts and acids, specifically named in the schedules. As it is at present classified by decisions of the courts, under heading of metals wrought or unwrought, it leaves the subject continually open to attack by individual interests, and consequent uncertainty and instability.

We also respectfully submit that this being a practically new industry in the United States it should be fostered and protected to those not owning their own mines, as well as those who do, by leaving the ores on the free list, and granting further protection on the finished products.

All of which is respectfully submitted to your honorable committee for its earnest consideration.

YORK METAL AND ALLOY COMPANY,
R. W. EMERTON, *President.*

THE WESTERN FOUNDRY SUPPLY COMPANY, NEW YORK CITY, SUBMITS ADDITIONAL INFORMATION RELATIVE TO FERRO-MANGANESE.

CORTLANDT BUILDING, 30 CHURCH STREET,
New York, December 31, 1908.

Hon. SERENO E. PAYNE,
Chairman Ways and Means Committee, Washington, D. C.

DEAR SIR: On Tuesday, December 15, Robert Gilchrist appeared before you in the interests of the Western Foundry Supply Company and requested the retention of the present duty on ferromanganese.

We take this method of laying before you a few additional facts.

First. We inclose herewith letters from various steel makers and users of ferromanganese which show that a domestic manufacturer of ferromanganese would be heartily welcomed.

Second. The first year we are in business we will make 40 per cent of the amount of ferromanganese at present imported.

Third. Please differentiate in this respect between us and other manufacturers who have appeared before you. They have discussed with you the duty on the product of an established business, while our request for the retention of the present duty on ferromanganese is simply a request for permission to establish in this country a new industry—the manufacture and sale in the open market of 80 per cent ferromanganese.

Fourth. Other manufacturers have a profit assured to them by the duty on their product. This is not the case with us. Our cost will be $40 per ton. The foreigner's cost is $38.80 laid down in this country with the duty paid. The duty simply makes the foreigner's cost approximate ours. If you will protect our cost, we will be glad to fight in the open market for our profit.

Fifth. Expert testimony before you shows that the cost of steel is $21.50 per ton and that the cost of the ferromanganese in a ton of steel is $0.60. Ferromanganese is selling to-day at $40. The duty is one-tenth of this. This makes the duty cost the steel maker $0.06 per ton.

Our cost will be $40 per ton, and if you remove the duty of $4 per ton you will take away from us 10 per cent of our cost and make it impossible for us to go in business, while you help the steel maker only to the extent of the proportion which $0.06 bears to $2.50, which is twenty-eight one-hundreths of 1 per cent. This is not just. Of course any reduction of the duty would hurt us and help the steel maker in the same proportion.

Sixth. We have letters from steel makers, letters from ferromanganese sellers, and practical treatises on the use of ferromanganese in steel making by the most expert metallurgists in this country, which show that the cost of the ferromanganese in a ton of steel is only one-half of that taken as a basis for our figures in this letter and in Mr. Gilchrist's talk before you. In addition, the writer has for twenty years been engaged in the manufacture of iron and steel and selling of pig iron and ferromanganese to steel makers and knows from experience that the above statement is correct. The figures used in our testimony and this letter are taken from Mr. Schwab's testimony before you and are, we think, amply low enough to prove our case, although in fact they should be cut in two.

Finally, no matter how much the present tariff schedule may need revising, we believe that any revision which deprives us of the opportunity to establish a new business in this country is manifestly unjust, providing always that such business will not injure others while benefiting us alone. We are satisfied to leave to your judgment, after analyzing the figures we have given and the letters we inclose, whether or not we are justified in asking you to retain on ferromanganese the present duty of $4 per ton.

Yours, truly,

WESTERN FOUNDRY SUPPLY CO.,
R. GILCHRIST.

PHILADELPHIA, *December 22, 1908.*
WESTERN FOUNDRY SUPPLY COMPANY,
New York City, N. Y.

GENTLEMEN: Your favor of 19th instant received. For a reliable supply of ferromanganese, quality and other things being equal, we should certainly feel like favoring the home production.

Yours, truly,

BRUALL STRECKHOUSE, *President.*

———

PHILADELPHIA, *December 21, 1908.*
WESTERN FOUNDRY SUPPLY COMPANY,
New York, N. Y.

GENTLEMEN: We beg leave to acknowledge receipt of your favor of the 19th instant advising that you are contemplating erecting a blast furnace for the production of 80 per cent ferromanganese.

We certainly believe that such an enterprise would be welcomed by all ferromanganese users. We always prefer to buy domestic rather than imported material when we can get the same quality and price.

We are, very truly, yours,

THE MIDVALE STEEL COMPANY,
H. L. HUMPHREY, *Buyer.*

———

DENVER, COLO., *December 24, 1908.*
WESTERN FOUNDRY SUPPLY COMPANY,
New York City.

GENTLEMEN: Your letter of December 19 in regard to manufacture of ferromanganese in this country. It seems to me it would be a paying venture, inasmuch as the use of the smelted product is very large and on the increase. If you had the right kind of ore, I do not see any reason why ferromanganese can not be made as cheaply in this country as in Europe. We are using several thousand tons per annum and importing all of it from Europe. Of course, everything being equal, would give the preference to material manufactured in this country.

Yours, truly,   S. G. PIERSON.

———

PHILADELPHIA, *December 22, 1908.*
WESTERN FOUNDRY SUPPLY COMPANY,
New York City.

DEAR SIR: Your letter of December 19 has been referred to the writer by the Maryland Steel Company. I have no doubt but what the consumers of ferromanganese would welcome a manufacturer in this country who would dispose of his output. You undoubtedly would have to meet foreign competition and furnish at the same price a metal of a quality as good as the imported. The use, however, of this material is constantly increasing, and the prospects are, with the larger proportion of open-hearth steel which is being manufactured each year, that it will not be long before the consumption in this country will be double.

Before, however, going into the manufacture, it would be well to make certain of an ore supply, as the deposits of manganese ore in this country have been very disappointing. If, however, the furnace where the metal is made is located near tide water, you would have the benefit of using imported ore when domestic ore was not available.

Yours, truly,   FRANK TENNEY,
                                          Assistant to President.

COATESVILLE, PA., *December 22, 1908.*

WESTERN FOUNDRY SUPPLY COMPANY,
          New York, N. Y.

GENTLEMEN: We have your favor of 19th, and carefully note contents. We use from 100 to 125 tons of 80 per cent ferromanganese per month. We always try to keep a goodly stock on hand, as it is an imported article, and we would welcome very much a good source of domestic supply, where we could order in, say, one car per week regularly, so as to avoid having so much money tied up in it. As it is now, we do not feel safe unless we have at least two months' stock on hand, which at the high price of this material ties up considerable capital. We think there are numerous other mills which would welcome a home supply. If you go into the matter, we would be very glad to take the matter up with you later. At present we are supplied for the first half of 1909.

Yours, etc.,

LUKENS IRON AND STEEL COMPANY.

NEW YORK, *December 21, 1908.*

WESTERN FOUNDRY SUPPLY COMPANY,
          New York City.

DEAR SIR: Your communication of December 19 in regard to ferromanganese is before us. We most certainly would purchase our supply of 80 per cent ferromanganese in this country provided we could get as good a price and as good an article as we can from abroad. It would appear to us there is no question whatever but what you could dispose of all the ferromanganese you might make.

Very truly, yours,

GOULD COUPLER COMPANY,
F. A. HUNTLEY,
Vice-President and General Manager.

BUCYRUS, OHIO, *December 28, 1908.*

THE WESTERN FOUNDRY SUPPLY COMPANY,
          New York, N. Y.

GENTLEMEN: Replying to yours of the 19th, beg to advise that we most certainly would prefer domestic ferromanganese to the foreign and if we can, at any time, buy same at an even figure, you may rest assured that we will in every instance specify domestic.

Yours, very truly,

THE BUCYRUS STEEL CASTING COMPANY,
C. F. VOLLMER.

PITTSBURG, PA., *December 22, 1908.*
WESTERN FOUNDRY SUPPLY COMPANY,
New York, N. Y.

GENTLEMEN : We have your valued letter of the 19th, and note that you are contemplating engaging in the manufacture of 80 per cent ferromanganese, and ask our opinion as to whether such an enterprise would be welcomed by domestic consumers.

The purchasing of imported 80 per cent ferro has always seemed to us undesirable, and we would very much prefer purchasing a domestic article at the same price, thus avoiding annoyance and delay. We hope you can see your way clear to go ahead with this enterprise and to produce the material profitably.

Yours, respectfully,

ALLEGHENY STEEL COMPANY.

———

PITTSBURG, PA., *December 21, 1908.*
WESTERN FOUNDRY SUPPLY COMPANY,
New York City, N. Y.

GENTLEMEN : Replying to your favor of the 19th instant, we would be pleased if some one would manufacture 80 per cent ferromanganese in the United States, and if such were the case we would be disposed to favor them, other things being equal.

Yours, respectfully,

UNION STEEL CASTING CO.,
C. C. SMITH, *President.*

———

CHICAGO, ILL., *December 24, 1908.*
THE WESTERN FOUNDRY SUPPLY COMPANY,
New York City.

GENTLEMEN : Replying to yours of December 19, regarding the proposition of manufacturing ferromanganese from Virginia ores, our use of ferromanganese is somewhat limited, so that we are not in good position to advise you whether its production would be profitable; but we buy some quantity of it, and for ourselves would say that it would depend somewhat upon the quality of American ferromanganese as compared with foreign as to whether it would be worth as much money to us. Assuming that the qualities would be the same, we would certainly welcome the opportunity of purchasing domestic ferromanganese on basis competitive with the imported brands.

We trust the above gives you the information desired.

Yours, respectfully,

AMERICAN RADIATOR COMPANY,
J. H. BORDEN, *Purchasing Agent.*

———

GRAND CROSSING, ILL., *December 22, 1908.*
WESTERN FOUNDRY SUPPLY COMPANY,
New York, N. Y.

GENTLEMEN : Referring to yours of the 19th, we should think that a domestic manufacturer of ferromanganese ought to find a ready market for his output, provided, of course, that he can compete as to quality and price with the foreign production.

If you should decide to go into the manufacture of this material we will be pleased to have your name upon our buying ledger.

Hoping to hear from you again, we are,

Yours, very truly,

GRAND CROSSING TACK CO.

———

MAHWAH, N. J., *December 22, 1908.*

Messrs. WESTERN FOUNDRY SUPPLY COMPANY,
New York City.

GENTLEMEN: Referring to your letter of the 19th instant, regarding 80 per cent ferromanganese, we would not object to using the domestic article; in fact, we would prefer it at equal prices to the foreign.

Yours, very truly,

AMERICAN BRAKE SHOE AND FOUNDRY CO.,
H. T. WINGERT, *Purchasing Agent.*

———

PITTSBURG, *December 23, 1908.*

Mr. J. A. ROGERS,
Secretary Western Foundry Supply Company,
New York, N. Y.

DEAR SIR: We have your favor of the 19th instant.

In normal times there is something like 200,000 tons of 80 per cent ferromanganese used in this country, all of which is coming in from abroad, except what is made by the Carnegie Steel Company for their own use from foreign ores. The latter company have spent a great deal of time and money in hunting for manganese ore in this country, and have decided that there are no large bodies of suitable quality.

Before building a furnace in Virginia for the purpose of making ferromanganese, it would be well for you to determine the quantity and quality of your ore. If you have the ore, it seems to us the manufacture of ferromanganese should be a profitable venture.

Yours, truly,

WILLIS L. KING, *Vice-President.*

You should also have a good coke supply. I believe it takes over 3 tons of coke to 1 ton of ferromanganese.

———

PITTSBURG, *December 22, 1908.*

THE WESTERN FOUNDRY SUPPLY COMPANY,
New York City, N. Y.

GENTLEMEN: In reply to your favor of the 19th instant, we are not in the steel business ourselves, our operations only going so far as the mining of iron ore and making pig iron, which we sell to the makers of steel. We also sell iron ore to other blast furnace companies. From the knowledge I have regarding ferromanganese I would think that your proposition was a good one if you have the right kind of ore and have it in sufficient quantities, and I would be very glad to see domestic competition in this line.

Yours, very truly,

UNITED IRON AND STEEL COMPANY,
EDWIN N. OHL, *President.*

———

CLEVELAND, OHIO, *December 21, 1908.*

WESTERN FOUNDRY AND SUPPLY COMPANY,
New York, N. Y.

GENTLEMEN: Acknowledging yours of the 19th instant, we beg to say that there is a large market in this country for 80 per cent ferromanganese, and if you can manufacture it of suitable quality at a price to compete with the imported article it would undoubtedly be a good business.

We are inclined to think, however, that if your deposits are of the right sort you would save a good deal of trouble by selling them to the United States Steel Corporation, who are the only makers in this country, and who would undoubtedly welcome the opportunity of getting a new source of supply, as ores of this description are very scarce.

Yours, very truly,

OTIS STEEL CO. (LTD.),
G. BARTOL, *General Manager.*

———

CLEVELAND, OHIO, *December 21, 1908.*

WESTERN FOUNDRY SUPPLY COMPANY,
New York City.

GENTLEMEN: Your favor of the 19th instant, by your Mr. J. A. Rogers, with regard to building a blast furnace for the production of ferromanganese, received this morning.

In reply we would say, in a general way, that in our judgment there would be no question whatever with regard to the successful sale of this proposed product, provided you could furnish the quality, even at the same price as now paid for the imported commodity.

You doubtless have made calculations to learn what your cost of production will be, so that you can probably determine for yourselves what prices you can afford to name.

Yours, very truly,

THE WELLMAN-SEAVER-MORGAN COMPANY,
HERBERT P. GLIDDEN, *Sales Department.*

———

BUFFALO, N. Y., *December 21, 1908.*

WESTERN FOUNDRY SUPPLY COMPANY,
New York, N. Y.

GENTLEMEN: Yours of the 19th, in reference to the construction of a blast furnace in Virginia for the manufacture of 80 per cent ferromanganese. The only interest we have in the matter is the purchase on this material at the lowest possible price; that is, of course, it makes no difference to us whether it comes from abroad or whether it is purchased in the United States. We simply buy it where we can get it the cheapest and of a grade which we require.

If you have manganese ore enough in Virginia and of a grade suitable for making this alloy, the proposition should not be a bad one. If, however, you are obliged to buy foreign ores, you are absolutely at the mercy of foreign mine owners, and when the selling price of ferro is at a point where good profits can be made, the price of the ore, you will find, has also advanced.

I have always been at a loss to understand why this material has not been produced in this country, as there is an immense tonnage of it consumed, and even the Steel Corporation, who ordinarily manufacture it for their own consumption only, are sometimes buyers of the imported material.

At present prices I should not imagine there would be much of a margin of profit, although, of course, you have the $4 a ton duty in your favor. From the best information I can get the present market prices are fairly above the cost of production to the foreign producers. We always make our purchases through reputable brokers, and shipments are made as specified on our contracts. All the details of the importation of this stuff are handled by these brokers and there is really no inconvenience to us.

Yours, truly,   JNO. N. ALLEN,
General Purchasing Agent.

PITTSBURG, PA., *December 21, 1908.*

Mr. J. A. ROGERS,
 Western Foundry Supply Company,
  New York, N. Y.

DEAR SIR: Replying to your favor of the 19th instant, would say that I would certainly welcome any enterprise looking toward domestic production of 80 per cent ferromanganese, and while we are small users compared to some of our larger steel mills, I believe they will all agree with me that there is a large field open to some one who will take the initial step in this direction.

Yours, very truly,

CARBON STEEL COMPANY,
S. M. WETMORE,
General Superintendent.

COATESVILLE, PA., *December 23, 1908.*
THE WESTERN FOUNDRY SUPPLY COMPANY,
 New York, N. Y.

GENTLEMEN: Acknowledging your esteemed favor of the 19th instant, we note that you have extensive manganese-ore properties in Virginia and are seriously considering the advisability of erecting a blast furnace for the production of 80 per cent ferromanganese and inquiring our opinion of the proposition.

Responding, beg to remark that we think very favorably of it, providing, of course, you have strictly first-class ore from which you can manufacture 80 per cent ferromanganese, equal in quality to the imported article and at sufficiently low figures to compete successfully with the same.

Presume you realize, too, that the prospects are favorable to the present import duty of $4 per ton being removed from ferromanganese. Everything being equal, we would invariably give preference on making our bids to the article of domestic manufacture.

Thanking you for addressing us on the subject, and awaiting with interest your further advices, we remain,

Very truly, yours,   WORTH BROS. CO.,
L. F. NAGLE, *General Sales Agent.*

———

MILWAUKEE, *December 22, 1908.*

WESTERN FOUNDRY SUPPLY COMPANY,
New York.

GENTLEMEN: We have your valued favor of the 19th instant, advising us of your intention to open up extensive manganese properties in Virginia and placing upon the market an 80 per cent ferromanganese, and asking an expression from us as to whether or not we would welcome an enterprise of this kind.

In reply, we venture to say that a domestic blast furnace of this kind should certainly be able to do a lucrative business, providing the material is equal to that imported.

Yours, truly,   E. A. WURSTER,
Secretary and Treasurer.

READING, PA., *December 22, 1908.*

———

WESTERN FOUNDRY SUPPLY COMPANY,
New York, N. Y.

GENTLEMEN: We have your valued favor of the 13th instant, and in reply would say we can hardly advise you as to the wisdom of considering a blast furnace on ferromanganese in this country. We have purchased ferromanganese as low as $37 a ton, and have also paid almost $200 a ton. The market at the present time, or when we last bought, was $42.

We were always of the impression that ferromanganese could not be made in this country at that price. However, we may be wrong. We further understand that there is to be an effort to have the tariff on alloys reduced, which would undoubtedly further lower this price. It seems to me that all these matters should be pretty carefully investigated before any action is taken.

Yours, very truly,   J. TURNER MOORE,
Vice-President and General Manager.

HON. L. P. PADGETT, M. C., SUBMITS LETTER OF ROCKDALE IRON CO., ROCKDALE, TENN., RELATIVE TO FERROPHOSPHORUS.

ROCKDALE, TENN., *January 8, 1909.*

Hon. L. P. PADGETT, M. C.,
    Washington, D. C.

DEAR SIR: I beg to acknowledge receipt of your kind letter of December 28, which has been carefully noted. The main ground, I think, for increasing the duty on ferrophosphorus is that it costs three times as much to make it as it does pig iron. Pig iron comes in on a $4 tariff, and on that ground alone I think the duty on ferrophosphorus should be $12. All I want is a reasonable profit.

As to other people manufacturing ferrophosphorus, I beg to say that I have a patent on manufacturing it in a blast furnace, and am the only one in the world, I believe, who is making it in a blast furnace. They make it abroad, however, in an electrical furnace, like all of the other alloys are made. The material made in an electrical furnace, on account of getting such an intense heat, can be made much higher in phosphorus than it can in a blast furnace, and therefore brings a higher price. The users of ferrophosphorus, which are the steel plants of the United States, would prefer the higher grade; that is, the 25 per cent phosphorus material, and the highest I can make in a blast furnace is about 20 per cent. The foreign material running 25 per cent phosphorus brings from $60 to $75 per ton, whereas my material only brings from $40 to $48 per ton. If there was a tariff of $12 or $15 a ton on this foreign product, it would almost equalize our prices and allow me to compete with this high-grade ferrophosphorus. Anyhow, I think the United States should protect her own industries.

As a matter of fact, about 2,000 tons of ferrophosphorus is all that is used per year in this country, while I can make here at Rockdale, by running the furnace steadily on it about 7,000 tons a year, so you can see that the demand for it is so limited that it really does not amount to very much, and yet I think I should be protected from foreign material coming in here under these conditions, or at least to put up the tariff so they can not run me out of business, as they have threatened to do.

Yours, truly,   J. J. GRAY, Jr.

H. R. CONKLIN, CHICAGO, ILL., WISHES LOW RATE OF DUTY PLACED ON FERROMANGANESE.

145 MICHIGAN BOULEVARD,
    Chicago, Ill., January 11, 1909.

WAYS AND MEANS COMMITTEE,
    Washington, D. C.

GENTLEMEN: I presume you all realize the importance of putting ferromanganese 80 per cent on the lowest possible basis. There is no 80 per cent ferromanganese produced in this country; the highest we can produce with our ore is from 30 to 50 per cent, and very little of it. The 80 per cent ore is found principally in Russia, in the Balkan Mountains. Such ore should be admitted free. The 80 per cent grade is the most used because its the most economical. All **the** steel plants require it, and the thousands of foundries are learning the value of it, and their consumption is increasing rapidly, and they should be able to obtain it as cheaply as possible.

Yours, truly,

H. R. CONKLIN.

MANGANESE STEEL.

TAYLOR IRON AND STEEL CO., HIGH BRIDGE, N. J., SUBMITS BRIEF RELATIVE TO MANGANESE STEEL.

TUESDAY, *December 8, 1908.*

To the COMMITTEE ON WAYS AND MEANS,
House of Representatives.

The Taylor Iron and Steel Company, of High Bridge, N. J., respectfully suggests, in view of the recent development of the manufacture of manganese steel—i. e., steel containing not less than 7 per cent manganese—and the many forms and shapes of useful articles manufactured therefrom, such as safes, vaults, rails, frogs or switches for steam, electrical, or industrial railways, grinding or crushing machinery, or parts thereof; excavating or dredging machinery, or parts thereof, car wheels, etc., that the new act should contain a separate and distinct clause for manganese steel so that all uncertainty as to its classification will be eliminated.

After more mature consideration of the whole subject than could be given in the short time allotted prior to the filing of our brief on the 25th of November [a] ultimo, we conclude as to this article specific duties are preferable to ad valorem, and suggest the following as reasonable and necessary to the continued success of this industry in the United States:

All manganese steel, i. e., steel containing not less than 7 per cent manganese, whether cast, forged, or rolled, valued at 3 cents and not above 6 cents per pound, 2 cents per pound; valued above 6 cents and not above 9 cents per pound, 3 cents per pound; valued above 9 cents and not above 12 cents per pound, $3\frac{1}{2}$ cents per pound; all valued above 12 cents per pound, 4 cents per pound.

This will not afford abnormal profits, but is believed to be the minimum duty that will protect this industry, in which the element of labor is by far the greatest factor.

It may be further said that home competition is rapidly growing and the consumer is assured of reasonable prices from this cause.

The Taylor Iron and Steel Company is preeminently within that class referred to by Mr. Carnegie in his recent article in the December Century, wherein he says:

The Republic has become the home of steel and this is the age of steel. It may probably be found that there exists the small manufacturer of some specialty in steel which still needs a measure of protection. The writer hopes, if such there be, the committee will give patient attention to such cases. It is better to err on the side of giving these too much rather than too little support. Every enterprise of this kind should be fostered. The writer speaks only of the ordinary articles and forms of steel as being able to stand without protection.

Respectfully submitted.

TAYLOR IRON & STEEL CO.
GEORGE H. LARGE.

---

[a] See page 1892.

SCRAP IRON AND STEEL.

[Paragraph 122.]

THE COLLINS COMPANY, COLLINSVILLE, CONN., AND THE AETNA NUT COMPANY, SOUTHINGTON, CONN., ASK FOR REMOVAL OR REDUCTION OF DUTY ON SCRAP IRON AND STEEL.

COLLINSVILLE, CONN., *December 1, 1908.*

Hon. SERENO E. PAYNE,
  Chairman Ways and Means Committee,
      Washington, D. C.

DEAR SIR: We beg to submit the following for consideration of the Ways and Means Committee in framing the new tariff bill:

We are consumers of scrap iron and scrap steel in the manufacture of bar iron and tool steel, which we consume ourselves in the manufacture of edge tools. For this purpose we use per annum about 2,000 tons of scrap iron and 1,000 tons of scrap steel.

The bar iron and tool steel produced form the basis of our whole industry, which employs about 900 men and is the support of this village.

The difficulty of obtaining scrap iron and scrap steel is increasing annually on account of the demand from the West and possibly the decreased production in New England.

Although we are about the only consumers of high carbon steel scrap in New England, it is, at times, impossible to get this scrap within the limit of distance which transportation charges permit. Such scrap is produced to some extent in Canada, but we think is not consumed there. Occasionally we have obtained it there, but usually the duty makes the cost prohibitive. On account of occasional scarcity we are obliged to carry on hand sometimes a year's supply of steel scrap to carry us over periods like the present, when the production is light.

In view of these conditions we ask that the matter of the rate of duty on scrap iron and scrap steel be considered, and, if consistent with protection principles, in which we firmly believe, we suggest that the duty be removed or materially reduced.

We think the continuation of the present duty will tend to encourage steel and iron making in Canada, in order to use this scrap there, and thus take away Canadian markets for tool steel now supplied by United States producers.

We regret that we are unable to give more extensive data on this question, but the limited time makes it impossible.

Yours, truly,

THE COLLINS COMPANY,
  By WILLIAM HILL, *President.*

THE ÆTNA NUT CO., STONINGTON, CONN., WISHES SCRAP IRON AND SCRAP STEEL PLACED ON FREE LIST.

STONINGTON, CONN., *December 1, 1908.*

Hon. SERENO E. PAYNE,
  Chairman Ways and Means Committee, Washington, D. C.

DEAR SIR: We wish to call your attention to the items of scrap iron and steel which enter largely into our manufacture of rolled iron and steel and at the present time are of vital importance to the continuance of our business. The new formula for making open-hearth steel rails and other products of steel has created such a demand for melting scrap that not enough is made in this country to supply the demand and we are unable to supply our mill one-half capacity, and we respectfully ask that you endeavor to place scrap iron and steel on the free list in the coming tariff revision. We do not expect that with scrap material free of duty the supply will be great enough to reduce prices which are now advanced about 50 per cent since July 1, 1908, but we do hope that the supply will be nearer the actual demand.

Below we give actual figures of our purchases ending July 1, 1907, in which year our profits were not to exceed 6 per cent on our investment:

Paid for scrap bought year ending July 1, 1907, $144,661.19; pay roll, year ending July 1, 1907, $124,994.59, making our labor cost nearly equal to the scrap material.

We employ about 200 men and have a plant that we have expended over $250,000 to build and owing to the present scarcity of scrap material we are unable to run, and without relief we must close our mill permanently, and we think the same will occur in practically all eastern rolling mills.

We thank you in advance for any attention you will give this matter.

Respectfully submitted.

THE ÆTNA NUT COMPANY,
J. H. PRATT, *President.*

CLARK BROS. BOLT CO., MILLDALE, CONN., RECOMMENDS REMOVAL OF DUTY FROM SCRAP IRON AND STEEL.

MILLDALE, CONN., *December 2, 1908.*

Hon. SERENO E. PAYNE, M. C.,
Chairman Ways and Means Committee, Washington, D. C.

DEAR SIR: In connection with the consideration of paragraph 122, particularly wrought and cast scrap iron and scrap steel, we believe it would be of benefit to manufacturer, merchant, and consumer if these items were put on free list. We are producers and sellers of iron and steel scrap; nevertheless we would recommend taking off all duty on this "raw material" item. This country needs all the raw material in the way of iron and steel scrap that can be encouraged across our borderland or to our shores. When once American labor and equipment has been applied, then protect it in its remanufactured form.

Very truly, yours,

CLARK BROS. BOLT COMPANY,
CHAS. H. CLARK, *President.*

W. P. WORTH, OF COATESVILLE, PA., RECOMMENDS THAT SCRAP IRON AND STEEL BE PLACED ON THE FREE LIST.

SATURDAY, *December 19, 1908.*

(The witness affirmed.)

Mr. WORTH. We are manufacturers of plates and tubes, and will be within six or eight months manufacturing pig iron. We are, of course, separate entirely from the trust, and you have had a great many of the trust officers here—or, we will say corporation men—during the last few days, and I think you will see from your investigations that it is rather a difficult matter for the independent people to stay in the business, and especially for those of us in the East, who are away from the ore supply, quite distant from the coal and coke supply, and are not in the position that Mr. Carnegie said they were in when he was a manufacturer situated at Pittsburg, that he could flap his wings in both directions and find trade. When we flap to the east, you know we get out into the ocean. We have only the market north and south, and for a short distance, possibly, to the west. Therefore I think that we are in this position to-day, that we want relief in every direction we can possibly secure it in.

About 25 per cent of the charge of an open-hearth furnace is made up of scrap, which has to be bought outside. When the Bessemer plants were in operation they were producing scrap all the time, and the scrap-iron market was more nearly balanced; but, as Mr. Schwab told you the other day, the Bessemer plants are a thing of the past, and there will not be any of them here in five years, and they are rapidly going out now, and as a result their place is being filled by the open hearth, and instead of the Bessemer, producing scrap, we have the open hearth, which is consuming more than it makes. Therefore there is a shortage of scrap. Now, as I understand it, the tariff is to protect capital and labor employed in manufacturing. Nobody manufactures scrap for sale. It is a by-product, you know, or it is the result of wear and tear. Therefore, why protect it?

Mr. UNDERWOOD. I would like to ask you this, which I think is more relevant to that question than the question of protection. Where are you going to get the scrap from if you put it on the free list?

Mr. WORTH. Scrap is made all over the world.

Mr. UNDERWOOD. I understand that; and all the world consumes it. Where are you going to get it?

Mr. WORTH. You know in eastern countries there is not much steel made.

Mr. UNDERWOOD. You could not get it out of any European country. They consume their own scrap.

Mr. WORTH. I think we can get some from Africa and considerable from south of us; but it is not so much, of course, that, except that if we could get free scrap we expect to get quite a considerable amount of it. But what we particularly want with the duty off scrap is to have it help to regulate this market.

Mr. RANDELL. If there is no scrap that can be gotten to be brought in here, what good is it going to do you?

Mr. WORTH. There will be a great deal brought in.

Mr. UNDERWOOD. I am not arguing for the tariff; I am rather inclined to agree with the gentleman about his proposition as to free scrap; but I am interested in knowing where he is going to get it, because, necessarily, scrap is not like rails and pig iron that you can ship and carry cheaply; it is unwieldy.

Mr. WORTH. There is lots of scrap brought from California right around the Horn.

Mr. UNDERWOOD. Yes; I suppose there is some.

Mr. WORTH. You let us have free scrap and we will get some of it in here. Of course we would like to have it free, but if we can not get it free we would rather put 50 cents on it and make a revenue proposition out of it. You can not import it to-day.

If there is one thing that the corporation has done in this country it is to steady things. We have been free from those violent fluctuations which were experienced before, and which a gentleman would have referred to on the stand here to-day if he had been questioned a little further. In 1899 we had a regular skyrocket market, you know, and pig iron was up to $22, $23, or $24; and since the corporation has got hold of things and a large lot of mills have been brought together we have had a steadier market, and there has been less money, probably, lost and made in speculation. I think the scrap position to-day is this: There is such a scarcity of scrap that a lot of speculators get hold of it, and within ten days to two weeks the scrap market has advanced $10. There is no reason for it. There is no advance in finished material; there is no extra amount of orders in finished material; but it is just through speculation. Now, if we could have free scrap you would find that that matter would be nicely regulated and there would be quite a lot of scrap brought in when the market was abnormally high.

Mr. UNDERWOOD. I agree with you if we could get plenty of free scrap it conserves our natural resources and it has a tendency to produce the finished product cheaply; there is no question about that; but I do not believe you are going to get much scrap.

Mr. WORTH. I believe we will get it if we can only get it on the free list.

Mr. UNDERWOOD. Well, argue that with these other gentlemen.

Mr. WORTH. After being here at a number of your sessions, I believed that it was quite the thing for the eastern people to come here and ask for relief that I think you can give them. I think you must have seen as a result of these sessions that without ore and with coal at a great distance, we are at a great disadvantage in manufacturing. Now, we have got a great deal of capital invested, and thousands of men employed in our eastern industries, and they will be very seriously affected if we do not get the relief we are asking for. I would like to see scrap put on the free list, or at least with nothing more than a 50-cent duty on it.

I would like also to see as much of a reduction on ore as the eastern producers of ore can stand. I am not here particularly advocating free ore, because I am a protectionist; I thoroughly believe in it, and I want to see the eastern ore producers protected; but you know there are only about one or two ore interests in the East, and their ores are rather high in phosphorus, and I think it would be to their advantage, really, to admit some blending ore at a pretty low duty so as to bring other ore in.

Mr. UNDERWOOD. What is the difference between free ore and free scrap? Free scrap is more of a competiter with ore in this country than free ore.

Mr. WORTH. Yes; but a duty on scrap does not protect anybody. It is not manufactured.

Mr. UNDERWOOD. I understand that; but theoretically it is more of a competitor with ore in this country than all the free ore in the world you could bring in, if you get the scrap.

Mr. WORTH. No; I beg to differ with you there.

Mr. UNDERWOOD. Scrap is more easily and less expensively converted into pig and into rails than the ore.

Mr. WORTH. No; I beg your pardon. I am talking of wrought scrap for milling purposes. You can use about so much scrap in an open-hearth furnace, and you can not use much more. If you increase the amount of scrap, you will not get a satisfactory result.

Mr. UNDERWOOD. Of course not.

Mr. WORTH. And if you use too little you will not get a successful heat.

Mr. UNDERWOOD. But the scrap produces a great deal more than the ore?

Mr. WORTH. It helps the manufacturers.

Mr. UNDERWOOD. Of course.

Mr. WORTH. And if scrap was manufactured, you understand I would not be here to plead for a lower duty, or a much lower duty, on it; but it is not manufactured.

Mr. RANDELL. Would not a tariff on the ore give an artificial value to scrap?

Mr. WORTH. No; I think not. My idea is to get the tariff down a little on the ore and cut it off scrap, and let the eastern people live.

Mr. DALZELL. You are not now making pig iron?

Mr. WORTH. We have our furnaces very well along.

Mr. DALZELL. You have made your arrangements to go into the making of pig iron?

Mr. WORTH. Yes, sir.

Mr. DALZELL. Under the present tariff bill?

Mr. WORTH. Yes, sir. We felt this way about it, that there was quite considerable fluctuation in pig iron as well, and we simply, for the protection of our other industry there, were obliged to go into pig iron.

Mr. DALZELL. You could stand $4 on scrap?

Mr. WORTH· We would be very glad to see free scrap, but as manufacturers of pig iron, putting money right into as good a plant as can be produced to-day, we are ready to see pig iron reduced 50 cents.

The CHAIRMAN. What is pig iron now?

Mr. WORTH. Four dollars. If you will take half the duty off of ore we are willing for 50 cents on pig iron. If you see fit to admit ore free, we are willing for a duty on pig iron.

The CHAIRMAN. Three dollars instead of $4.

Mr. WORTH. Yes; but we would want free ore.

The CHAIRMAN. Fifty cents on scrap?

Mr. WORTH. We think 50 cents on scrap will be a maximum charge; make it a revenue proposition.

Mr. DALZELL. With ore as it is now you would not reduce the duty on pig iron?

Mr. WORTH. No; we could not. My friend Mr. Lukens used the word "corralled." It is corralled. Some years ago, when our works started, and others in the East, the 35 and 40 per cent ore in Pennsylvania was all right. To-day it is not, you know.

Mr. UNDERWOOD. If you get free ore, where will you get it from?

Mr. WORTH. From Spain and Nova Scotia and Cuba.

Mr. UNDERWOOD. Have you investigated the question of what it will cost you to get it?

Mr. WORTH. Yes, sir.

Mr. UNDERWOOD. What will it cost you, per ton of ore, to bring it from Cuba?

Mr. WORTH. We have not gone into that very thoroughly; but if you give us free ore, or a small duty on ore, there are many places from which we can get it.

Mr. UNDERWOOD. I thought you had the facts.

Mr. WORTH. We have got them, in a general way. We know that ore is being brought in here now from Nova Scotia and Spain, right along, and from Cuba.

Mr. UNDERWOOD. At what cost; at what price?

Mr. WORTH. We have not gone into figures. I can not give you those things; but we know it will help us just to that extent.

Mr. UNDERWOOD. You think it will help you? You do not know the facts? I think it probably will myself.

Mr. WORTH. We know that large quantities of ore are coming in now. Will it not help us that much more?

Mr. UNDERWOOD. I think it will help you, but I do not think you know it, if you do not know the facts.

Mr. WORTH. Yes; I think we do, in a general way, being in the iron business as we are. There is one other point that I would like to bring out, and that is about the duty on Swedish blooms—$12.

The CHAIRMAN. That is what I want to hear about. We heard about that yesterday. What is the use of keeping that $12 duty on there?

Mr. WORTH. There is no use in it.

Mr. DALZELL. What good will it do to take it off?

Mr. WORTH. It will help us wonderfully.

Mr. DALZELL. It will?

Mr. WORTH. I could give you a good deal of history on that matter.

The CHAIRMAN. We do not care so much about the history as we do for the reason for the reduction of the duty.

Mr. WORTH. There is no reason to have it there, and it certainly is a great injury to us in the East. We have got to depend on that iron, you know, and we feel that if you take the duty off it will materially assist us.

The CHAIRMAN. What do you use that iron for?

Mr. WORTH. It goes into the manufacture of skelp, and that skelp is made into high-grade boiler tubes, and they have attempted, you know, to put steel in the place of that work, but steel is of a granular construction.

The CHAIRMAN. It has taken its place in many things.

Mr. WORTH. Yes, but you can not use it for lots of things.

The CHAIRMAN. In carriage hardware, for instance.

Mr. WORTH. Yes, that is heavy material; but I mean, you take a stovepipe or roofing material, and you will find you want to stick to the iron. It will last several times as long. And so of a tube which is only one-eighth of an inch thick; and under heat and gases and severe treatment, of course iron will last much longer.

Mr. DALZELL. There is not much of it comes in?

Mr. WORTH. No, sir. I think we have about 3,000 tons under contract to come along.

Mr. UNDERWOOD. Where moisture comes in direct contact with iron or steel the iron has the greatest life?

Mr. WORTH. That is the point exactly.

The CHAIRMAN. What duty would you suggest on Swedish blooms?

Mr. WORTH. I would like to see the duty taken off. If you want to make a revenue measure of it a dollar is all right. I would like to see it all off, and let us increase the use of it.

The CHAIRMAN. You have the virtue of being more liberal in taking off duties on the things that you consume than on the things you make.

Mr. WORTH. Do you think, after listening to the testimony you have had here the last few days, that you could conscientiously ask me to reduce the duty on finished material when you see what we are up against in the East? Now, I am talking for the eastern people.

The CHAIRMAN. I am not making the tariff bill to-day.

Mr. WORTH. No; but you see we have no advantages here at all. We were placed there because our forefathers planted us there years ago, and we have gone along and held our own, but it has been against great odds. Those people in the West, with their ore at their door, have a great advantage over us. Judge Gary told you yesterday he would have nothing but a water rate, and, of course, a small inland rate up from Lake Superior, up to the lake port, and the water rate down to Gary; and you see they are going to have great advantages.

Mr. UNDERWOOD. They have a $4 freight rate to go into your country.

Mr. WORTH. Four dollars?

Mr. UNDERWOOD. Yes.

Mr. WORTH. No; less than that. They go over there for about that, yes; about 20 cents from Gary; I imagine it will be.

Mr. UNDERWOOD. And that is all to your advantage as manufacturers.

Mr. WORTH. Yes; but you take the duty off finished material and we are the first affected. There is the trouble again.

The CHAIRMAN. A reduction from $12 to $1 a ton is a pretty good reduction on Swedish iron.

Mr. WORTH. We would like to have it taken off entirely.

———

THE PORTLAND IRON AND STEEL COMPANY, BOSTON, WRITES RELATIVE TO SCRAP IRON AND STEEL BILLETS.

BOSTON, MASS., *December 14, 1908.*

Hon. SAMUEL W. MCCALL, M. C.,
  Washington, D. C.

MY DEAR SIR: As a New England member of the Ways and Means Committee on the revision of the tariff, we write you in the interest of an industry which we are operating at Portland, Me.

We have a rolling mill there which employs about 300 men, turning out a product of merchant bar iron which we distribute to the railroads and jobbers in the New England States.

The raw material which we use is entirely wrought scrap iron. There is a present import duty of $4 per ton on this material coming into the States. Canada is close to us, with the Grand Trunk Railroad running into the city of Portland. We have a dock at our mill, with tide water, where we can discharge our coal vessels from Philadelphia on low rates of freight.

We feel that the duty on scrap iron should be taken off to enable us to buy this material from Canada and other foreign countries.

Large quantities of this material are shipped into Pennsylvania which are used by the mills making the same product that we do, and the quantity produced during the last year has been less than heretofore on account of the depression in business; and we find that market advancing now so that the profit on our manufactured product is seriously affected. If we had another source of supply where we could import scrap, we would be better off than we are to-day.

One other product, which we advocate a radical reduction on, is steel billets. Situated as we are on tide water with our mills, we feel that lower duty on billets, or none at all, would give our industry in New England a great advantage over what it now has. We are obliged to pay the makers of open-hearth billets in Pennsylvania almost the price of the finished product of steel bars, which prohibits our using steel billets to reroll into soft steel bars for our trade in New England. We are well equipped to roll this material and feel that this industry should be supported and prospered.

We have an up-to-date, well-equipped plant, equal to any first-class Pennsylvania mill turning out the same product, and all we ask is an equal chance with Pennsylvania mills to make the same product and sell it in New England.

From your past record in supporting and fostering industries in New England, we believe you will take this matter up and bring it before the proper parties for consideration.

Very truly, yours,

PORTLAND IRON AND STEEL Co.,
R. M. BOUTNELL, *Treasurer.*

HON. JOHN W. WEEKS, M. C., WRITES RELATIVE TO CANADIAN AND AMERICAN DUTIES ON SCRAP IRON AND STEEL.

WASHINGTON, D. C., *January 4, 1909.*

Hon. SERENO E. PAYNE,
  Chairman Ways and Means Committee,
    House of Representatives.

MY DEAR SIR: A constituent of mine calls my attention to the duty on scrap iron and steel and thinks it a place where a change may properly be made. I might add that the writer of the letter is a high-tariff man, so that he has no prejudices in this case. His statement is to this effect: That there is now a duty of $4 a ton on scrap iron and steel, while the Canadian duty from the United States is $1 a ton, and that rolling mills in this country near the

Canadian line are at a disadvantage on that account. He adds, what is evidently a fact, that it is a waste product pure and simple, does not represent any labor, or at least comes as near being a raw material as any product which we have to consider. I therefore trust that the advisability of reducing the duty to the rate imposed by Canada be taken into consideration by the Ways and Means Committee when that schedule is reached.

Yours, very truly,　　　　　　　　　　JOHN W. WEEKS.

SUPPLEMENTAL STATEMENT SUBMITTED BY THE PORTLAND IRON AND STEEL COMPANY, BOSTON, MASS., RELATIVE TO THE DUTY ON SCRAP IRON.

1009 AND 1010 BOARD OF TRADE BUILDING,
Boston, Mass., January 6, 1909.

Hon. S. E. PAYNE,
　Chairman Ways and Means Committee,
　　　　　Washington, D. C.

DEAR SIR: Under date of December 14, 1908, we submitted to the Committee on Ways and Means, through Representative McCall, a brief statement relative to the removal or reduction of duties on scrap iron. Since then we have had the opportunity of reading the testimony given before your committee relative to the tariff on iron and steel production in the United States, and we find that there has been but very little testimony offered regarding the duty on scrap iron.

As stated in our former communication, the raw material which we make use of is largely wrought scrap iron, upon which the present import duty is $4 per ton. This duty is sufficiently high to almost absolutely prevent the importation of scrap iron into this country. That is, the difference between the cost of domestic scrap iron and imported scrap iron of the same quality, upon which duty is paid, prohibits the importation of that material. The supply of scrap iron in this country is not adequate to meet the demand of the manufacturers. During the present year scrap iron has been purchased in different parts of New England by Pennsylvania manufacturers and shipped to the rolling mills of Pennsylvania and elsewhere. We have experienced great difficulty in obtaining a supply sufficient for our mill, and what is true of us is undoubtedly true of manufacturers in other parts of New England and in other parts of the country. We are informed that the duty upon the importation of scrap iron into Canada is only 50 cents a ton. This enables the Canadian manufacturer to obtain this material from abroad at a price less than what we are now paying, and gives to the Canadian manufacturer a decided advantage over the manufacturers of this country. If the present duty of $4 per ton were reduced to $1 per ton—that is, a reduction of 75 per cent—scrap iron then could be purchased in Europe and imported into this country at a price a trifle below the present price at which scrap iron is selling in New England. It would not, however, be so low as to seriously depress the present price of that material in this country, but would enable the New England manufacturer to obtain scrap iron from abroad, and at the same time would give to the United States a considerable revenue from the importation of that material.

From the information which we have at hand we believe that all the manufacturers of iron and steel in New England favor this reduction of duty, and believe that such a reduction would be of great benefit to the manufacturing interests here and could not possibly work any serious harm to any interest.

The New England manufacturer of finished products in iron and steel, if located upon tide water, is not at a serious disadvantage with the manufacturer in Pennsylvania and other parts of the country, except in the matter of the price of the iron and steel which he makes use of in manufacture. Those of us located upon tide water are able to purchase coal at a reasonable price, as our freight rates are low. The prices paid for skilled labor in rolling mills in New England are substantially the same as those paid in the rolling mills in Pennsylvania and elsewhere, and the labor is equally efficient. Wrought-iron scrap, which is purchased largely from railroads, is sold in New England at a price substantially the same as in other parts of the country. It can be readily seen that a rolling mill located at tide water and making use of wrought-iron scrap is not at any disadvantage with the rolling mills located in Pennsylvania and other parts of the country in the manufacture of finished product from that material. The difficulty we labor under is that we can not obtain a sufficient supply of the material which we so largely make use of.

Your committee can readily understand the advantages which must come from the location of rolling mills in this section of the country. It enables the people of New England to obtain the finished product at a price quite as low as they can obtain it from Pittsburg, by reason of the larger freight charges from that point to New England, and also affords our people the advantage of having their orders filled with far less delay.

We have always favored the policy of protection, and do not desire to advocate any method of revision that is not founded upon the protective principle. We do not, however, believe that the suggestion which we make for the reduction of the duty upon scrap iron is in violation of that principle, or that its reduction could work serious harm to any industry in this country.

Respectfully submitted.

ROSWELL M. BOUTWELL,
Treasurer Portland Iron and Steel Company.

W. W. LUKENS, PHILADELPHIA, PA., FILES BRIEF RELATIVE TO DUTIES ON SCRAP IRON AND STEEL.

519 ARCH STREET,
Philadelphia, Pa., January 19, 1909.

COMMITTEE ON WAYS AND MEANS,
House of Representatives, Washington, D. C.

GENTLEMEN: In connection with the proposed revision of the Dingley tariff, your attention has already been called both by individual statements and by briefs to the matter of scrap iron and scrap steel. The subscriber to this brief, representing many millions of invested capital and many thousands of workingmen, again bring to your notice the opportunity offered by this commodity to meet the popular demand for tariff revision and to provide an increased revenue for the Federal Government, with great benefit to all manufacturers of open hearth steel, and the labor employed by them, and without injury to anyone.

If it be your desire to so legislate as to provide additional revenue for the Government, we recommend a duty not exceeding 50 cents per ton. We believe that such a duty would allow of large imports from Cuba and the West Indies, from South America, and at times from England, Germany, and Belgium, and would result in greatly increased revenue; while under the present tariff imports have been so small that the revenue therefrom has been only nominal.

Paragraphs 492, 505, 533, 637, and 690 of the Dingley tariff provide for the free admission of the scrap of other metals for remanufacturing, notably copper and brass. We believe that the same reasoning that placed these articles on the free list should govern in the case of scrap iron and scrap steel, to at least the extent of a greatly reduced duty. There is no capital invested or labor employed in its manufacture; it is strictly a by-product, the result of waste and wear, so that manufacturer, laborer, dealer, and consumer alike would benefit by increased imports.

There is a shortage in the supply available for use in open-hearth furnaces, brought about largely by the gradual passing of the Bessemer furnace, which produces scrap, and the rise of the open-hearth furnace, which consumes scrap. The following figures speak for themselves:

Production of Bessemer steel in the United States in—

	Tons.
1907	11, 667, 549
1897	5, 475, 315
Increase since 1897	6, 192, 234

Or increase of over 113 per cent.

Production of basic open-hearth steel in the United States in—

1907	10, 279, 315
1897	1, 056, 043
Increase since 1897	9, 223, 272

Or increase of over 873 per cent.

Production of basic pig iron in the United States in—

1907	5, 375, 219
1897	556, 391
Increase since 1897	4, 818, 828

Or increase of over 866 per cent.

You will note:

(a) That in the ten years from 1897 to 1907 the percentage of increase in the production of open-hearth steel was nearly eight times as great as the percentage of increase in the production of Bessemer steel.

(b) That during the same period the percentage of increase in the production of basic pig iron (which forms 50 per cent of the charge in an open-hearth furnace) was almost exactly the same as the percentage of increase in the production of open-hearth steel.

In other words, the production of the chief manufactured ingredient of a ton of open-hearth steel has kept pace with the demand; while on the other hand, with manufacturers abandoning their Bessemer converters, we find ourselves facing a decreased production of scrap and an increased consumption, with a consequently steady decline in the available supply of scrap per furnace per annum.

The result is a highly speculative market, working a hardship on all steel melters and dealers in scrap, and we believe that these evils would be greatly lessened by large importations.

We respectfully urge the serious attention of the Committee on Ways and Means to this matter. We are strong protectionists and believe that tariff revision should be handled only with great care and conservatism, but we believe, also, that an unmanufactured commodity, the supply of which in the United States is unequal to the demand, offers, as stated at the outset, a peculiarly good opportunity to revise the present schedule without harm to any one, and with gennine benefit to all those directly or indirectly interested in its consumption.

Yours, very truly,
ALAN Woon IRON AND STEEL COMPANY,
W. W. LUKENS, *Assistant Secretary.*
WORTH BROS. CO.,
By W. P. WORTH, *Treasurer.*
LUKENS IRON AND STEEL COMPANY,
H. B. SPACKMAN, *Purchasing Agent.*
JOHN A. ROEBLINGS SONS COMPANY,
F. W. ROEBLING, *Secretary and Treasurer.*
SHARON STEEL HOOP COMPANY,
MORRIS BACHMAN, *President.*

BAR IRON.

[Paragraph 123.]

STATEMENT OF JAMES LORD, PRESIDENT OF THE AMERICAN IRON AND STEEL MANUFACTURING CO., LEBANON, PA.

WEDNESDAY, *November 25, 1908.*

Mr. GRIGGS. Before you proceed I will put the usual question to you. Is your company making any money?

Mr. LORD. We are, yes, sir, except this year. We usually do.

Mr. UNDERWOOD. Will you please give us a reference to the paragraph to which you desire to address yourself?

Mr. LORD. It is paragraph 123; bars. The present duty on that is six-tenths of a cent a pound. I was requested to come here by the American Iron and Steel Association and I have discussed the matter with the principal western interests, and with some of the eastern interests, in bar iron and they have authorized me to say that they would be content to have a reduction in bars of one-tenth.

Mr. UNDERWOOD. I did not hear you.

Mr. LORD. I say I was authorized to say for the interests that I have consulted, being the principal western interests and some of the eastern interests, that they are willing to have a reduction in the price of iron bars of one-tenth of a cent. That would make it five-tent1s.

Mr. UNDERWOOD. There is no bar iron being imported into this country at all now, is there?

Mr. LORD. The only bar iron that I know of being imported is a very high grade of Staybolt iron.

Mr. UNDERWOOD. That is not really in competition.

Mr. LORD. That is not competitive.

Mr. UNDERWOOD. How much is the production of this bar iron in the United States at this time?

Mr. LORD. As near as I can ascertain, it is about one million and a quarter tons.

Mr. UNDERWOOD. What is the cost of producing this bar iron in this country?

Mr. LORD. Well, the present profit on bar iron is about $1 a ton; sometimes it is not that.

Mr. UNDERWOOD. What is the selling price?

Mr. LORD. The selling price at the present time is about $28 a net ton.

Mr. UNDERWOOD. Twenty-eight dollars, and the cost is $27?

Mr. LORD. It costs about $27, the ordinary merchant bar iron.

Mr. UNDERWOOD. What is the principal market abroad in which this iron is produced, the principal foreign market, England?

Mr. LORD. England and Germany.

Mr. UNDERWOOD. What is the selling price in the markets of England to-day?

Mr. LORD. I am not acquainted with those prices.

Mr. UNDERWOOD. Can you get those prices and furnish them to the committee?

Mr. LORD. They are in the trade papers, and I could get them.

Mr. UNDERWOOD. It may save us some trouble. In other words, we have access to that information ourselves, and we will probably look it up, but we may come to a different conclusion from yourself as to foreign iron, and it will be well for you to file your conclusions as to what is the price of the foreign market and the freight rates of this country. I suggest that you give us your view as to what is the selling price.

Mr. LORD. I will be very glad to do so. I will file a brief.

Mr. HILL. The reduction of one-tenth of a cent a pound, which you say will be satisfactory, I suppose is based on the same continued duty on ore, etc., beforehand. If the proposed reductions were made, you would not object to a corresponding reduction?

Mr. LORD. That was considered in coming to this conclusion.

Mr. HILL. That was considered in the one-tenth of a cent reduction.

Mr. LORD. Yes, sir.

The CHAIRMAN. Is Mr. Ward here?

Mr. LORD. I was requested to speak for Mr. Ward; I am in the same line of business that he is in.

The CHAIRMAN. You may proceed.

Mr. LORD. I refer now to paragraph No. 145.

Mr. GRIGGS. Just a moment. Is Mr. Ward making any money?

Mr. LORD. I forgot to ask him.

Mr. GRIGGS. When you file your brief will you state whether he is or not?

Mr. LORD. I will try to ascertain that. I wish to speak with reference to paragraph 145, and with respect to that portion of the paragraph that refers to bolts and not to hinges, and also to paragraph 163 and that portion of it which refers to spikes, nuts, and washers, and not to horse or mule shoes; also, with respect to paragraph 167, on the subject of rivets.

On bolts, the present tariff is a cent and a half a pound; on spikes, nuts, and washers, 1 cent a pound; on rivets, 2 cents a pound. I wish to call the attention of the committee to the fact that there is some class of finished case-hardened nuts that sell for 50 cents a pound, while the odrinary hot-pressed nut of standard size sells for 2 cents a pound, and yet the duty is the same—1 cent a pound on both classes. In the Canadian tariff they recognize that feature by making on all of these items that I have mentioned a tariff of 75 cents specific and 25 per cent ad valorem.

The CHAIRMAN. How is that?

Mr. LORD. The Canadian tariff has 75 cents specific and 25 per cent ad valorem.

The CHAIRMAN. Seventy-five cents a pound, or what?

Mr. LORD. Seventy-five cents a hundred pounds.

The CHAIRMAN. And 25 per cent ad valorem?

Mr. LORD. Yes, sir.

Mr. UNDERWOOD. That is in order to cover the different grades of nuts?

Mr. LORD. Yes, sir; the different grades, and the different grades refer also to bolts, but not to the same extent.

Mr. UNDERWOOD. Do you suggest that to the committee as an amendment?

Mr. LORD. I would suggest that as a proper method of applying the tariff.

The CHAIRMAN. It is stated here at 1½ cents a pound, and you propose to change that from 1½ to seventy-five one-hundredths of a cent and 25 per cent ad valorem?

Mr. LORD. I did not make that suggestion; I was stating how the Canadian tariff provided for it. I have consulted with several bolt manufacturers—not by any means with the greatest number of them—and they are willing to have some decline in this duty.

Mr. DALZELL. Something below 1½ cents a pound?

Mr. LORD. Yes, sir; to about one and a quarter.

Mr. HILL. Will you supplement that suggestion with the suggestion that the form of the duty be divided and half be made specific and half ad valorem?

Mr. LORD. I think that would cover the ground very well.

The CHAIRMAN. Well, it is pretty nearly prohibitive on all these brackets, and in some cases it is entirely so.

Mr. LORD. Bolts are not a product that can be imported to any great extent.

The CHAIRMAN. That would be reduced because the present duty is 15 per cent ad valorem.

Mr. LORD. On bolts it is 1½ cents a pound. I refer to paragraph 145.

Mr. DALZELL. There were 287,171 pounds imported last year.

The CHAIRMAN. Now, he wants to make that three-quarters of a cent a pound and 25 per cent ad valorem?

Mr. LORD. That would be satisfactory if it were made in that way.

Mr. HILL. How much a ton would the bolt be with or without thread or nut. You said that some ran up very much higher than others?

Mr. LORD. About $35 or $40 a ton.

Mr. DALZELL. The ad valorem is intended to adjust itself to the various concerns.

Mr. LORD. The higher grade would be from $150 to $200 a ton.

The CHAIRMAN. That would raise that from 1½ to 2.

Mr. LORD. No, sir; it would cut it down.

Mr. HILL. Mr. Lord suggests that the specific rate as it stands be reduced a cent and a quarter with an alternative of three-quarters of a cent and 25 per cent ad valorem; that is, three-quarters of a cent and 25 per cent ad valorem.

The CHAIRMAN. It would be a reduction; including the ad valorem it is 28. It is quite an advance and ought to be reduced. You propose to make it 75 cents a hundred and 25 per cent ad valorem.

Mr. LORD. Twenty-five per cent ad valorem would be satisfactory, I think.

The CHAIRMAN. The ad valorem now is 15 per cent.

Mr. LORD. There is no ad valorem on bolts.

The CHAIRMAN. Yes, it is 15 per cent according to this statement here.

Mr. LORD. I am referring to paragraph 145.

The CHAIRMAN. You are right about that. There is another heading to that.

Mr. LORD. The present tariff, as stated in paragraph 163, spikes, nuts, and washers, is not in proportion to the present tariff on bolts, as stated in paragraph 145. That is 1 cent a pound, and yet some classes of nuts are very much more expensive than the bolts.

The CHAIRMAN. Have you any statement as to the cost of this article manufactured in Mr. Ward's factory at Port Chester, near the city of New York?

Mr. LORD. The cost of these things differs very much on account of the diameters and the sizes; they differ from 2 cents to 50 cents a pound.

Mr. UNDERWOOD. Will you file with the committee, on these three items, the cost of production in this country according to the grades of the bolts and the foreign-market price, and freight and tariff?

Mr. LORD. I can not give you the foreign-market price; I have not access to it.

Mr. UNDERWOOD. Can you not ascertain it?

Mr. LORD. I could not get it in time.

Mr. UNDERWOOD. You have up to the 4th of December to file your brief.

Mr. LORD. I will endeavor to do so, but I doubt if I can get that information.

Mr. BONYNGE. Your suggestion has reference to paragraph 167?

Mr. LORD. Yes, sir; 167; that could stand a reduction of half a cent a pound.

Mr. BONYNGE. That is, rivets of iron or steel, 2 cents a pound.

Mr. LORD. Yes, sir.

STATEMENT OF J. H. NUTT, OF YOUNGSTOWN, OHIO, SECRETARY OF THE WESTERN BAR IRON ASSOCIATION.

FRIDAY, *November 27, 1908.*

Mr. NUTT. Mr. Chairman and gentlemen, I appear here on behalf of the Western Bar Iron Association.

Mr. GRIGGS. Is that an association of manufacturers?

Mr. NUTT. It is an association of manufacturers organized for the sole purpose of negotiating the question of wages. I simply want to distinguish between the workmen and the manufacturers.

Mr. GRIGGS. Are you a manufacturer or a workman?

Mr. NUTT. I presume neither; standing between organized labor in these mills and the employer, a kind of arbitrator on the wage question.

Mr. GRIGGS. If you are neither a workman or a manufacturer, what are you?

Mr. NUTT. Well, I have tried to say, sir, that my position was that of arbitrator between the manufacturers' association and the workers' associations for the purpose of negotiating wages and adjusting disputes.

Mr. COCKRAN. Are you a public official, may I ask?

Mr. NUTT. No, sir; I am paid by the manufacturers to look after the wage question with the different mills that compose this association.

Mr. COCKRAN. What is your occupation outside of that; what is your trade, profession, or calling?

Mr. NUTT. My time is devoted at present, and has been for some years, to that solely. Before that I was employed, from boyhood, in the rolling mills.

I appear in behalf of the bar-iron manufacturers, members of the Western Bar Iron Association. This association is composed of manufacturers of bar iron having plants in the States of Ohio, Indiana, Missouri, and Illinois, and organized for the sole purpose of adjusting wage scales for their employees through the officers of the amalgamated association. They employ a secretary who devotes all of his time to the adjustment of rates of wages and disputes between any member of the association and his employees.

The manufacturers of bar iron have appeared before your committee and suggested a reduction in the tariff of one-tenth per pound, or $2 per ton. And I would respectfully ask that in the adjustment of clause 123 of Schedule C you give due consideration to the difference in wages paid in this country and Europe. Unfortunately, I am only able to obtain the wages paid for similar labor in England, while on the Continent we believe wages to be considerably less. British statistics do not give the price per ton on mill men's wages, but they appear to be based upon the price of puddling, advancing and declining with the same. In the year 1907 the wages paid for puddling in Great Britain was—

	Per ton.
In the Northumberland district	$2. 25
In the west of Scotland district	2. 43
In the Midlands district	2. 31
Average price	2. 33

While during the same year, 1907, the price per ton paid by the members of this association to its employees for the same class of work was from $6.50 to $6.62½ per ton or, in other words, the English puddler received from 35 to 40 per cent of what was paid to the puddlers in the mills of your petitioners; and it is fair to assume that there is substantially the same proportion of difference in all other classes of labor.

Our agreement with the amalgamated association provides that whenever the selling price of bar iron advances $1 per ton above the base rate that the labor shall advance from 1 to 2½ per cent, according to the scale of each particular department. That at the present time is 6 per cent above base rates. So that if by any undue reduction in the tariff rates you should bring about lower prices for bar iron, the labor employed in its manufacture must suffer its proportion of the lower prices.

The mills making iron bars are in no way interested in the manufacture of steel, but as steel bars can in a large number of places be used to take the place of iron bars the price of steel largely influences the selling price of iron bars. The manufacture of steel bars being largely a mechanical proposition, while the manufacture of iron bars must necessarily remain one of skilled manual labor, the cost of producing the same is considerably higher, and at the present time at least $3.50 per ton above the cost of steel bars. Therefore we ask that the same differential be maintained as in the present tariff bill.

The mills making iron bars are scattered all over this country from Maine to California and are, for the most part, what are considered small mills, whose tonnage is not large, but who supply a certain locality with its merchant bars largely made from the scrap made in its own market, which is considered greatly to the advantage of those producing scrap in those sections and should be considered in making up this schedule. For the above reasons we ask that in fixing the tariff on iron bars you give due consideration—

First. To the difference in wages paid to the labor in this country and that paid in other countries engaged in manufacturing the same product.

Second. That on account of the largely-increased cost of producing iron bars over steel that, whatever may be the rate agreed upon, you will maintain a corresponding differential between steel and iron bars as in the present tariff measure.

Third. That on account of the mills making iron bars being scattered through so many localities the people in so many States of this Union are interested in the preservation of this industry.

Mr. UNDERWOOD. You say that the English puddlers receive from 35 to 40 per cent out of what is paid to the puddlers in the mills of this country. Do you mean that there is 60 per cent difference between the cost there and here?

Mr. NUTT. I was saying that simply to show that the puddlers in England receive from 60 to 65 per cent less than the American puddlers receive.

Mr. UNDERWOOD. You ask that the same difference be maintained. Do you mean the same tariff?

Mr. NUTT. No, sir.

Mr. UNDERWOOD. What do you mean—the same adjustment of the schedule?

Mr. NUTT. No; difference in wages. Steel bars come in at three-. tenths while iron bars come in at six-tenths, a differential of three-tenths per pound.

Mr. UNDERWOOD. You say that on account of the mills making iron bars being scattered through so many localities the people in so many States of this Union are interested in the preservation of this industry. Are these mills connected with the steel corporation?

Mr. NUTT. Not in any way whatever.

Mr. UNDERWOOD. Is there a large production of those articles in this country independent of that corporation?

Mr. NUTT. The business of manufacturing iron bars, I believe, is conducted entirely outside of that corporation.

Mr. UNDERWOOD. That corporation does not make any iron bars?

Mr. NUTT. No; not so far as I am aware.

Mr. UNDERWOOD. You are here seeking to have a reduction of the present schedule of the tariff, are you not?

Mr. NUTT. I am not speaking as to any reduction in the tariff other than what the manufacturers have offered to you gentlemen.

Mr. UNDERWOOD. Do you know the cost of making these bars in England?

Mr. NUTT. No, sir.

Mr. UNDERWOOD. You are not familiar with anything except the wage scale?

Mr. NUTT. No, sir.

Mr. UNDERWOOD. Where did you ascertain your information? Did you get your information and these figures from the government reports on the subject? Is it a matter of personal knowledge with you?

Mr. NUTT. They are the British statistics on file in the Department of Labor in this city.

Mr. UNDERWOOD. The Department of Commerce and Labor?

Mr. NUTT. Yes, sir.

Mr. UNDERWOOD. They are the British statistics of their wage scale?

Mr. NUTT. Yes, sir.

————

THE PITTSBURG FORGE AND IRON CO., PITTSBURG, PA., PROTESTS AGAINST REDUCTION OF DUTY ON IRON BARS.

PITTSBURG, *November 30, 1908.*

Hon. JOHN DALZELL, M. C.,
    Washington, D. C.

MY DEAR MR. DALZELL: It has come to our notice through the public prints that some of the manufacturers appearing recently before the Ways and Means Committee have advocated or suggested a change in the differential between the duty on steel and iron bars and a lowering of the present duty on iron bars. We wish to do what we can to counteract any impression that may have been given your committee that any considerable portion of the manufacturers of iron bars are in sympathy with such a change, believing that if such statements were made they were uttered without full and careful consideration of the subject.

Our company is one of a large number of independent manufacturers of iron bars in this country, employing a large amount of labor, and our product in this line is being sold to-day at or below cost. The price of iron bars is largely regulated by the price of steel bars, both commodities being used for practically the same purposes. The manufacturer of iron bars employs almost four times the labor in the production of a ton of iron bars that is employed in the production of a like amount of steel bars; consequently a differential in the protective duty is but fair.

The introduction of improved machinery and methods in the manufacture of steel, which machinery and methods are not applicable to the manufacture of iron, have served to so reduce the selling price of both steel and iron bars as to make it impossible for the iron manufacturer to get any return on his investment except in the most prosperous times, when prices rise to a living basis. We are firmly of the belief that any reduction of the duty on either of these commodities that will make possible the importation of any quantity of either steel or iron bars will so affect our markets that many of the small independent producers of iron bars will be forced out of business or great reductions in labor be made necessary, and thus in either event work great hardships on many thousands of men engaged in the iron industry, many of whom are getting up in years and could not well adapt themselves to any other business.

We earnestly protest against any reduction of the present duty on iron bars, and believe we voice the opinion of a large majority of the iron manufacturers.

We will be glad if you will present our views and protests to the Ways and Means Committee as herein set forth, and oblige,

Very respectfully,

PITTSBURG FORGE & IRON CO.,
F. E. RICHARDSON, *Secretary.*

———

PITTSBURG, *December 1, 1908.*

Hon. JOHN DALZELL, M. C.,
    Washington, D. C.

MY DEAR MR. DALZELL: Supplementing our letter of yesterday on the subject of duty on iron and steel bars, we beg to inclose herewith copy of brief that has been filed with the committee by Mr. James H. Nutt, secretary Western Bar Iron Association, and wish to say that we are in hearty accord with the sentiments contained therein and the requests for the maintenance of the present duties upon these articles.

We are not members of that association, but our interests are identical.

Very respectfully, yours,

PITTSBURG FORGE AND IRON CO.,
F. E. RICHARDSON, *Secretary.*

THE AMERICAN IRON AND STEEL MANUFACTURING COMPANY, OF LEBANON, PA., FILES SUPPLEMENTAL STATEMENT RELATIVE TO BAR IRON.

LEBANON, PA., *December 3, 1908.*

Hon. SERENO E. PAYNE,
Chairman Committee on Ways and Means,
Washington, D. C.

DEAR SIR: On the 25th ultimo I addressed your committee in reference to paragraph 123 of metal schedule of Dingley tariff, which states the duty on bar iron as six-tenths cent per pound.

As the events of the year have clearly indicated that we are to have a new tariff law, revised along lower rates of duty, a meeting of iron and steel manufacturers was held in New York on the 23d ultimo to consider the situation and present their views before your committee.

I was designated by them to speak on the above item. The suggestion of reduction of the tariff on bar iron from six-tenths to five-tenths cent per pound was made after consultation with as many bar-iron interests as the limited time permitted. I have since written to all the manufacturers whose addresses could be procured, except those on the Pacific coast, and have received 30 replies, representing the great majority of the tonnage produced in the United States.

While the preference of an overwhelming number would be to make no change, and thus avoid the disturbance to business consequent upon tariff revision, 25 of the 30 recognize the inevitable by indorsing the suggested reduction as above cited; 5 wish to be counted as greatly opposed to any reduction whatever.

In comparing the duty on iron bars with steel bars, it should be remembered that the former carry a much higher labor cost, as steel bars are rolled with automatic mechanism, which can not be applied to iron; and it should be remembered that during this period of great depression that wages have to a remarkable extent been maintained, and in no case have I heard of any considerable reduction of wages in this industry.

The brief submitted by Mr. James H. Nutt shows that the wages paid for puddling in Great Britain is less than half the American rates.

It is in order to continue the wage of labor at the present remunerative rates that manufacturers are so interested in not reducing the duty below five-tenths. I believe that amount is needed as a tariff on labor.

If bar iron was put on the free list it would still be manufactured in this country, but it would be at the expense of labor, whose wages would necessarily fall to the level of the competing countries—Great Britain, Germany, and Belgium.

The ordinary refined iron of commerce (when partially made from scrap material) is now sold at from $1.35 to $1.50 per 100 pounds, the quality determining the difference between these rates. The average profit to the manufacturer at present is about $1 per ton or less. The labor cost in making iron bars is about one-third of the total cost where scrap is largely used; if all muck bar is used the labor is greatly increased.

The price of refined iron bars in England November 1 was $29.84 per gross ton on cars at the mill, equivalent to 1.33¼ cents per pound.

A number of manufacturers have requested me, in presenting this brief, to advocate much lower duties on iron and steel scrap. I will, however, merely state conditions. The demand for this scrap material has been greater than the visible supply, due in part because it has been largely held by speculative dealers.

Canada puts a practically prohibitive duty on iron and steel bars, but only a nominal duty on scrap. Consequently that country can feed her mills with our scrap, while our mills can not sell them manu.actured bars.

Please consider me at your command if I am needed to throw any further light on this subject.

Very truly, yours,   JAMES LORD, *President.*

STRUCTURAL STEEL.

[Paragraph 125.]

THE KING BRIDGE COMPANY, CLEVELAND, OHIO, ASKS FOR REDUCTION OF DUTY ON STRUCTURAL SHAPES.

CLEVELAND, OHIO, *November 24, 1908.*

CHAIRMAN WAYS AND MEANS COMMITTEE
ON REVISION OF TARIFF,
House of Representatives, Washington, D. C.

DEAR SIR: We are interested with a large number of others in the future of structural steel and kindred lines of business. A revision and lowering of the tariff on rolled shapes, such as I beams, channels, angles, plates, etc., have long seemed to us a necessity.

It is a well-known fact to all in the manufacturing or finished lines of the iron and steel business that outside of the United States Steel Corporation, and perhaps three or four others, there are no makers of the class of materials we use, excepting the item of plates. With but few exceptions all of the makers of this class of raw material do fabricating, i. e., putting it together in the shape of bridges, girders, columns, and what is designated generally as fabricated work, although perhaps their aggregate tonnage in the fabricating line itself would not amount to more than one-third of the total fabricating output of the country. At present, however, with the high prices they are enabled to maintain on the material before it is fabricated, these makers are given undue advantage over those fabricators who are not makers of the material, but to whom they sell, and can make much lower prices on fabricated work, and are doing so to-day and virtually controlling the price on this class of work, the reason being that the tariff, now so excessive, enables them to make a good profit on the material as first rolled into the shapes mentioned above, so that they can afford, if necessary, virtually to throw in the fabricating for little or nothing. This, you will see, works an injustice on a large manufacturing industry that is virtually at the mercy of this combination, who, bolstered up by the tariff, are enabled to meet together at the Waldorf-Astoria or other fashionable places of entertainment in the

East and arrange among themselves agreed prices that these materials, together with rails, etc., shall be sold to their customers throughout the country, and there seems to be no recourse.

So that it would seem that if there is really a desire on the part of your committee to correct an evil that is fast tending to create a monopoly, in comparison with which any others now existing would be mere infants, we would respectfully call your attention to the present bolstering-up effect the tariff has on materials of all kinds entering into the manufacture of iron and steel, as sold to the general trade for its various uses, thereby enabling the producers from the mine to the furnace and rolling mill to maintain regular published price schedules which they are all bound by gentlemen's agreement to maintain and which seems thus far to have escaped the general investigation into such agreements in restraint of trade, notwithstanding that it is really the greatest and most far reaching in existence.

Yours, very truly,

KING BRIDGE COMPANY.

FORGINGS, CAR WHEELS, AND TUBES.

[Paragraphs 127, 152, 171, and 193.]

STATEMENT OF THOMAS PROSSER, REPRESENTING THOMAS PROSSER & SON, OF NEW YORK CITY.

WEDNESDAY, November 25, 1908.

The CHAIRMAN. Mr. Prosser, I understand, wishes to make a very brief statement.

Mr. PROSSER. In favor of reduction.

Mr. DALZELL. What schedule or paragraph do you refer to?

Mr. PROSSER. There are several paragraphs that I should like to refer to.

Mr. GRIGGS. Are you in favor of a reduction on your own product?

Mr. PROSSER. I am not a manufacturer, sir; I am an importer.

Mr. GRIGGS. I see.

Mr. PROSSER. If it is the pleasure of the committee, I should like to read a few figures from the reports of the Government, taken from Census Bureau Bulletin No. 78, 1905, on the subject of iron and steel (reading):

VALUE OF DOMESTIC PRODUCT.

[Census Bureau Bulletin 78. Census of Manufactures, 1905. Iron and Steel. Table 1, p. 12.]

Iron and steel, value of products.

1905	$905, 854, 152
1900	804, 034, 918
1890	478, 687, 519
1880	296, 557, 685
1870	207, 208, 696

Imports, $12,396,045, or 1½ per cent.

METALS, METAL COMPOSITIONS, AND MANUFACTURES OF.

[Bulletins Nos. 3 and 6, Bureau of Statistics.]

Exports and imports of merchandise during the years ending June 30, 1903–1907.

1903—Exports	$91, 740, 475
Imports	17, 789, 453

1904—Exports		$105, 038, 638
Imports		13, 741, 527
1905—Exports		126, 503, 297
Imports		12, 396, 045
1906—Exports		152, 029, 612
Imports		12, 092, 265
1907—Exports		167, 436, 600
Imports		13, 715, 877

1905:

Salaries, officers and clerks, number 16,566	20, 758, 412
Wages, number 242,740	141, 439, 906
Miscellaneous expenses	47, 164, 970
Cost of material used	620, 171, 881
	829, 545, 169
Value of product	905, 854, 152
Cost of production	829, 545, 169
Excess in value over cost of production	76, 308, 983
Capital reported	948, 689, 840

Profit 8 per cent+ on reported invested capital.

I.—Steel forgings are now dutiable under paragraph 127, which reads:

Forgings of iron or steel, or of combined iron and steel, of whatever shape, or whatever degree or stage of manufacture, not specially provided for in this act, 35 per centum ad valorem.

Under the act of 1864, United States Revised Statutes, page 465, the duty on this article was 45 per cent ad valorem.

By the act of 1890, paragraph 139, a specific duty of $2\frac{3}{10}$ cents per pound was made, with the proviso " that no forgings of iron or steel, or forgings of iron and steel combined, by whatever process made, shall pay a less rate of duty than 45 per cent ad valorem."

By the act of 1894 the specific duty thereon was reduced to 1½ cents per pound, with like provision that such duty should not be less " than 35 per cent ad valorem."

The act of 1897, paragraph 127, as quoted above, fixes the duty at 35 per cent ad valorem.

We urge a reduction in this duty to 20 per cent ad valorem.

II. *Steel forgings, machined.*—Steel wire (nickel, alloy) and machinery (grinding and crushing mills) are now dutiable under paragraph 193 of 1897, which reads:

Articles or wares not specifically provided for in this act, composed wholly or in part of iron, steel, lead, copper, nickel, pewter, zinc, gold, silver, platinum, aluminum, or other material, and whether partly or wholly manufactured, 45 per centum ad valorem.

With the exception of the years 1894–1897, under the Wilson Act, this rate of 45 per cent has been in force since 1864. (See U. S. Rev. Stats., p. 465; act of 1890, par. 215; act of 1897, par. 193.) The Wilson tariff act of 1894, par. 177, made the duty 35 per cent ad valorem.

We earnestly urge that the duty be reduced to 30 per cent ad valorem on these articles.

No change is asked in the language or wording of the present tariff act, but only in the rate of duty imposed.

It is important, in our view, that language which has stood in successive tariff acts, and become the subject of departmental and judicial interpretation and decision, should not be so changed. The government officials and all persons interested have come to thoroughly understand the meaning of such classifications and what they cover, and a mere change in language would be sure to bring confusion and much litigation.

The suggestions we submit, upon all the paragraphs on which we desire to be heard, involve only the change of rate, and not change in language for the reasons just stated.

III. *Locomotive and car tires and wheels.*—These are dutiable under paragraph 171 of the act of 1877, which provides:

Wheels for railway purposes, or parts thereof, made of iron or steel, and steel-tired wheels for railway purposes, whether wholly or partly finished, and iron or steel locomotive, car, or other railway tires or parts thereof, wholly or partly manufactured, one and one-half cents per pound * * *.

By the act of 1870 (U. S. Rev. Stats., p. 465) this duty was made 3 cents per pound; by the act of 1890, paragraph 185, 2½ cents per pound; by the act of 1894, paragraph 156, 1¼ cents per pound.

But in 1894 the selling price of tires in this country was 5 cents per pound, and the duty of 1¼ cents was reasonable. Now the price is 2 cents per pound for tires, and under the new process whereby the entire wheel is made in one piece will approximate 2½ cents per pound. With such large reductions in the value and price of the article it is manifest a duty of three-quarters of a cent per pound is most ample. Indeed, under such circumstances the duty should be put for revenue only.

IV. *Boiler and other tubes.*—These are dutiable under paragraph 152 of the act of 1897, which reads:

Lap welded, butt welded, seamed, or jointed iron or steel boiler tubes, pipes, flues, or stays, not thinner than number sixteen wire gauge, two cents per pound; welded cylindrical furnaces, made from plate metal, two and one-half cents per pound; all other iron or steel tubes, finished, not specially provided for in this act, thirty-five per centum ad valorem.

By the tariff act of 1865 (U. S. Rev. Stats., p. 466), the duty was made 3½ cents per pound; by the act of 1890, paragraph 157, 2½ cents per pound; by the act of 1894, paragraph 130, 25 per cent ad valorem.

The lap-welded process is competitive with the new process of seamless tubes. It would seem that no duty, save wholly for revenue, should be required, inasmuch as the American manufacturers are able to compete with the foreign seamless tubes when sold abroad, and the American article is quoted at lower prices. As an instance, tubes were recently sold in Mexico, of American manufacture, at a price less than could be quoted by the European competitors. It is hence obvious that no duty is required here except for purposes of revenue, and hence it is submitted that a reduction to 20 per cent from the present rate of 35 per cent ad valorem is both just and reasonable—for while it could not possibly injure any American manufacturer, it would give opportunity to benefit the public revenue.

V. *Bar steel.*—The act of 1864 (U. S. Rev. Stats., p. 465), imposes upon bar steel valued from 7 cents to 11 cents per pound, a duty of 3 cents per pound; and all above 11 cents per pound in value, a duty of 3½ cents per pound and 10 per cent ad valorem.

The act of 1890 made eleven distinct classifications of bar steel on value bases beginning at 1 cent value and less, with a duty of $\frac{4}{10}$ per cent, and extending thence through successive increases in value up to 16 cents per pound, with a duty of 7 cents per pound.

The act of 1894 maintained the same classifications as to values, but reduced the duty.

The act of 1897 maintained the same classifications (par. 135), and precisely the same duties imposed thereon by the act of 1894, thus recognizing the propriety of reduction of duties on this article in fair relation to the increase and progress of the manufacture. Upon precisely like reasoning, it is hence now plain that further reductions would be both sound and logical. Thus, in the first three classes a reduction of $\frac{1}{10}$ cent per pound; in the next two values, of $\frac{2}{10}$ cent per pound; in respect of bar steel, valued at 3 to 4 cents per pound, a duty of $\frac{8}{10}$ cent per pound; valued at 4 to 7 cents, a duty of $\frac{8}{10}$ cent per pound; valued at 7 to 10 cents per pound, a duty of $1\frac{1}{10}$ cents per pound; valued at 10 to 13 cents per pound, a duty of $1\frac{7}{10}$ cents per pound; valued at 13 to 16 cents per pound, a duty of $2\frac{7}{10}$ cents per pound, and valued at 16 cents and above per pound, a duty of 4 cents per pound.

Bar steel, imported as such, is, of course, brought here to be manufactured into useful articles; it is, in a large sense, raw material, and a duty based upon revenue thereon would, in effect, encourage and not retard domestic manufacture here of countless articles wherein bar steel is the basic element. Indeed, in such view, and in aid of American manufacturers, bar steel could well be placed upon the free list.

Mr. GRIGGS. Do you import all of those things that you read about?

Mr. PROSSER. We import very few now, because they are barred out by the tariff.

Mr. GRIGGS. But do you deal in all of them?

Mr. PROSSER. We have for the last fifty years; yes, sir.

Mr. LONGWORTH. Who are you representing?

Mr. PROSSER. Do you mean what foreign manufacturers?

Mr. LONGWORTH. No; who are you representing here?

Mr. PROSSER. Just my own firm.

Mr. LONGWORTH. Do you represent any foreign manufacturers?

Mr. PROSSER. Yes; we represent Krupp in this country.

Mr. LONGWORTH. Any others?

Mr. PROSSER. No; we confine ourselves to that manufacturer.

ANTIFRICTION BALL FORGINGS.

[Paragraph 127.]

SAMUEL S. EVELAND, OF PHILADELPHIA, PA., ASKS AN INCREASE OF TEN PER CENT IN THE DUTY ON ANTIFRICTION BEARINGS.

FRIDAY, *November 27, 1908.*

Mr. GRIGGS. Mr. Eveland, are you a manufacturer?

Mr. EVELAND. Yes, sir.

Mr. GRIGGS. What do you manufacture?

Mr. EVELAND. We manufacture steel balls, ball bearings, and roller bearings, and use a large amount of raw steel.

Mr. GRIGGS. Are you making any money?

Mr. EVELAND. I did not this last year. Prior to that I made some.

Mr. GRIGGS. But prior to this last year you made money?

Mr. EVELAND. Yes, sir.

Mr. GRIGGS. That is all. Go ahead.

Mr. EVELAND. I did not make enough, though.

Mr. GRIGGS. None of us ever did, you know.

The CHAIRMAN. Proceed, Mr. Eveland. That is not in the nature of a "hold up" at all. [Laughter.]

Mr. UNDERWOOD. What is the number of your paragraph in the schedule?

Mr. EVELAND. I will have to ask the secretary, Mr. Payne. I have forgotten.

Mr. UNDERWOOD. You say you manufacture ball bearings?

Mr. EVELAND. Steel balls, ball bearings, and roller bearings. I am a consumer of steel, and I would like to advocate the retention of the duties on steel, if that is not contrary to your regulations.

Mr. CLARK. That statement has nothing to do with the other statement, has it?

Mr. EVELAND. It only comes in incidentally.

Mr. CLARK. If that is the end of the steel statement, I want to ask you a question or two about it.

The CHAIRMAN. What did he say?

Mr. CLARK. He said that he was a consumer of steel and he wanted the tariff to stay on it. Why do you?

Mr. EVELAND. Because I think that any benefit that the manufacturer or the consumer of steel would receive by reason of a reduction would be more than offset by the injury to the business as a whole. In my case I use about $500,000 worth of steel and about $100,000 worth of pig iron a year, and I do not believe any material benefit would result from the reduction of the duties whatever. It would not be a benefit, and would possibly be an injury to the country as a whole. I am aware of the fact—at least I infer it from what I have heard from steel men—that they are in favor of a reduction, or at least would be willing to have a reduction made.

Mr. CLARK. If you simply buy the steel and work it up, what is the reason you do not want to get the steel as cheaply as you can get it?

Mr. EVELAND. In my case I do not think there would be any benefit in it.

Mr. CLARK. If it was cheaper it would be a benefit to you?

Mr. EVELAND. Yes; it would reduce the first cost of the steel to me, but I think the country as a whole would suffer to such an extent that the consumption of my product as well as the product in many other lines would be reduced. I do not think you can possibly reduce the cost of steel to the consumer here without reducing the wages of the workingman. I base that upon some investigations that I made about six months ago in Europe.

Mr. CLARK. If it can compete with the whole world outside of the United States by way of exports, what is the reason the tariff could not be cut down and it still live and flourish?

Mr. EVELAND. Do you mean if the steel company was——

Mr. CLARK. Yes; the steel trust, and the rest of these steel companies that come in here and testify.

Mr. EVELAND. I do not think they can, Mr. Clark.

Mr. CLARK. The other night one of them stood right where you are standing now and testified that they had sold steel rails abroad for $6 a ton less than to the American consumer, and did it since the tariff.

Mr. EVELAND. I think that is justified under certain conditions.

Mr. CLARK. You think it is?

Mr. EVELAND. Yes, sir; it is justified on the principle that the thing a manufacturer in the United States ought to do is to keep his factory at work. I think there are times when I could run my factory and sell 20 or 30 per cent of my output abroad below what it would sell for in the United States.

Mr. CLARK. Are you interested in manufacturing steel?

Mr. EVELAND. Not directly.

Mr. CLARK. Do you own any stock in a steel company?

Mr. EVELAND. I own a small amount of stock.

Mr. CLARK. Well, that explains it. •

Mr. EVELAND. I do not think so. I have not had any dividends on it at all.

The CHAIRMAN. When you and Mr. Clark have come to an agreement you may go on.

Mr. CLARK. We have come to an agreement. He says he is interested in it and wants it kept up.

The CHAIRMAN. And you agree to that?

Mr. CLARK. I agree with his explanation.

Mr. POU. Do you own any stock in the steel trust?

Mr. EVELAND. None whatever.

The CHAIRMAN. Proceed, Mr. Eveland.

Mr. UNDERWOOD. I would like to find out what paragraph he is interested in.

The CHAIRMAN. It is paragraph 137.

Mr. DALZELL. No; paragraph 127.

The CHAIRMAN. Yes; paragraph 127, "Antifriction ball forgings of iron or steel or of combined iron and steel, 45 per cent ad valorem."

Mr. EVELAND. That is correct.

The CHAIRMAN. It is the next to the last clause in the paragraph.

Mr. EVELAND. I desire to submit the following arguments in favor of an increase in the tariff on steel balls, ball bearings, and roller bearings, for the purpose of protecting the American industries engaged in the manufacture of the products named.

Antifriction bearings are divided into three classes, comprising steel balls, ball bearings, and roller bearings, and each item will be treated separately in the following, but the three classes of products are so closely allied that they are manufactured in this country very largely in the same factories, so that general remarks on the subject apply to all three of the products named.

GENERAL INFORMATION.

There are engaged in the United States, in the manufacture of steel balls, ball bearings, and roller bearings, several thousand employees, which number will be greatly reduced if the tariff is lowered.

Heavy importations are made into the United States from foreign countries of steel balls and ball bearings, which are manufactured in foreign countries by the same classes of machines as are used in the United States, the machine being almost exclusively the product of American inventors and copied by the foreign users, and the use of which it has been found impossible to prevent through our patent laws.

Owing to the very low labor costs in those countries, the cost of manufacture is much below what it costs to manufacture the same article in the United States.

I have made a personal investigation of the matter, visiting England and Germany during the present year, at which time I made a thorough investigation of the subject and found that labor, which is paid from 50 cents to $1.20 per day in those countries, is the same class as is paid from $2.25 to $3.50 per day in the United States. The raw material from which their products are made costs approximately the same as with us, and as the machines used are the same and produce the same amount in a given time, they have a great advantage over the manufacturer in the United States, because of their greatly reduced labor cost.

IMPORTATIONS.

At the present time there is very keen competition in the United States with ball bearings which are being imported into this country from England and Germany. The following list gives the prices at which the bearings are being sold in England and Germany and at which they are being sold in the United States, the article in each case being identically the same shape, size, weight, design, material used, and construction, and alike in every particular:

Foreign and United States selling prices.

England.	Germany.	United States.
$1.44	$1.50	$2.25
1.38	1.44	2.13
1.62	1.68	2.49
2.04	1.96	2.92
3.84	3.84	5.76

Mr. UNDERWOOD. How do you get figures of the kind you quote? The government reports show that the total value of the importations was only $47,000 last year.

Mr. EVELAND. Why, one concern alone sold to the American consumers a little over $1,000,000 worth. I can give the sales and all that.

Mr. COCKRAN. That is important. Give us the name of the person.

Mr. EVELAND. I can give you all the importations without any difficulty. I can get that data ready for you.

Mr. UNDERWOOD. We would like to have that.

Mr. EVELAND. They have sold over $1,000,000 worth.

Mr. COCKRAN. You see what a striking assertion that is, so you can see the importance of giving us the details.

Mr. EVELAND. For what year?

Mr. DALZELL. 1907.

Mr. EVELAND. I tried to get information from the Treasury Department, but they refused to give me any detailed information. I know that the sales amounted to over $1,000,000 by one concern and nearly one and a half million by two concerns during 1907.

Mr. UNDERWOOD. Give the names.

Mr. EVELAND. The Hessbright Company, of Philadelphia——

Mr. UNDERWOOD. How much?

Mr. EVELAND. A little over $1,000,000.

Mr. HILL. Foreign made?

Mr. EVELAND. Made in Germany.

Mr. HILL. According to the government report, the importations for 1907 were $47,818, and for 1906, $1,450.

Mr. EVELAND. Well, that is not correct.

Mr. UNDERWOOD. I would like to have those names.

Mr. EVELAND. The Hessbright Manufacturing Company, of Philadelphia, and the——

The CHAIRMAN. Proceed with the reading of your paper, and let the questions come afterwards.

Mr. EVELAND. The list I have given shows but five sizes, but there are approximately over 100 sizes, all showing the same relative difference. If the tariff is reduced, it will be possible for the foreign manufacturer to send ball bearings into this country to such an extent that it will be unprofitable and impossible to manufacture here in competition with them, and the manufacture of these products in America will be discontinued.

The manufacture of ball bearings, referred to, is a new industry in the United States, having been established only three or four years, during which period a great increase has been made in the output, which, however, will cease entirely, if the foreign bearings are brought into more active competition than at present, as the margin of profit is not sufficient to admit a reduction in their selling price.

STEEL BALLS.

The foreign ball makers are securing some trade in America, which would be greatly enlarged, if the tariff on such products is not increased. The selling price in England, Germany, and the United States, for the same article, consisting of steel balls used on bicycles, sewing machines, etc., is as follows:

Foreign and domestic selling prices.

[Cost per thousand.]

Size.	England.	Germany.	United States.
One-eighth inch	$0.35	$0.35	$0.50
Three-sixteenths inch	.59	.60	.90
One-fourth inch	1.03	1.03	1.35
Five-sixteenths inch	1.89	1.80	2.50
One-half inch	10.08	9.00	15.00

The greater portion of the cost of manufacturing steel balls and antifriction bearings is in the cost of the labor, a very small proportion of it representing the raw material used in the manufacture of the product.

In the ball bearings above referred to the raw material consumed in the manufacture of the product of the five sizes named is, respectively, as follows:

Size.	Cost of material.	United States selling price.
One-eighth inch	each	$0.27	$2.25
Three-sixteenths inch	do	.16	2.13
One-fourth inch	do	.26	2.49
Five-sixteenths inch	do	.29	2.92
One-half inch	do	.71	5.76

For steel balls of the size referred to above the raw material or steel consumed in their manufacture is as follows:

Size.	Cost of material.	United States selling price.
One-eighth inch_____each__	$0.02	$0.50
Three-sixteenths inch_____do____	.06	.90
One-fourth inch_____do____	.15	1.35
Five-sixteenths inch_____do____	.30	2.50
One-half inch_____do____	1.80	15.00

It will be noted from the above lists that an average of less than 8 per cent of the selling price of the ball bearings and steel balls is represented by the cost of the raw material used, the remainder being the labor cost, which is due to the fact that the product is one exceedingly difficult to manufacture, requiring great accuracy, in which highly skilled labor is employed, which results in the greatest portion of the cost of manufacture being for labor.

If the duty on the foreign product is reduced it will be impossible for the American manufacturer to remain in business in competition with the foreign product. The fact that the machinery and methods of making are identically the same in the foreign countries and in America shows conclusively that the higher wages paid the American workman adds so much to the cost that it would be impossible for us to manufacture in competition, if the duty is reduced.

ROLLER BEARINGS.

The same general remarks apply to roller bearings as are made in reference to steel balls and ball bearings. The foreign makers have some slight advantage over those of the United States in the cost of their raw material, but because its value per unit of manufacture is very low, as is shown in the above lists, it is not a sufficiently large item to enable the American manufacturer to produce his product, if the tariff on steel was reduced, to compete with the imported steel balls, ball bearings, and roller bearings, if a reduction was made in the tariff on steel.

If a reduction in the tariff was made, and a corresponding reduction was made in the selling price of the products above enumerated, there would be no corresponding advantage to the individual consumer, while all cost of the change would have to be borne by the American laborer, who would be unable to secure employment at the present existing wages.

The difference to the consumer if the tariff was entirely removed would be exceedingly light. Steel balls, for instance, ⅛-inch size, sell in the United States at 50 cents per thousand, or 5 cents per hundred; the foreign prices are 35 cents and 3½ cents, respectively, or a difference of 15 cents per thousand and 1½ cents per hundred between the foreign and domestic prices. Such balls are used on bicycles, sewing machines, etc., in which from 10 to 25 balls are used in each article. Therefore, if the tariff was removed entirely the difference in the cost of the finished article to the American manufacturer of bicycles and sewing machines would amount to from 2 mills to 3 mills, or less than 1 cent on the finished article.

For ¼-inch balls the difference in price is 33 cents per thousand, or 3$\frac{3}{10}$ cents per hundred, making a difference to the consumer between the foreign and domestic prices of ¾ cent to 1½ cents for each bicycle, sewing machine, etc., on which they are used.

For ball bearings the difference in price for the average size is from 75 cents to $2 each. These bearings are used on automobiles, etc., where the difference in the cost of an automobile to the consumer would be from 75 cents to $8 each if the tariff was entirely removed.

Analysis of the above shows that the saving that would result, even if the duty was entirely removed, is as follows:

On sewing machines, bicycles, etc., according to the size used, 2 mills to 1½ cents each; automobiles, 75 cents to $8 for each automobile.

The same remarks apply to steel balls, ball bearings, and roller bearings, used on various other products, as in no case is the value large of the balls or bearings so used, and a reduction in price, which would result from a reduction in the tariff, would give no material or compensating benefit to the consumer; while, on the contrary, labor now receiving high rates of wages from the American manufacturers, amounting to $1,500,000 to $2,000,000 per annum, in the total wages paid, would be very largely out of employment in this particular business, or would be forced to accept greatly reduced wages in order to permit the American manufacturer to continue manufacturing his product.

FREIGHT RATES.

Freight rates have very little bearing upon the subject, as they amount to but little and do not exceed 5 per cent, and usually less on a majority of products referred to above. Ball-bearing products are very light in weight, and the freight is no considerable item, either in importation or in distributing the products throughout America. In balls, for instance, there are the following in a pound:

	Balls per pound.
$\frac{1}{16}$ inch	28,000
⅛ inch	3,400
¼ inch	430

Ball bearings weigh from one-quarter ounce to 3 or 4 pounds each, for average size, and in no case would the freight rates protect the American manufacturer against foreign importations.

The estimated total sales of steel balls, ball bearings, and roller bearings and allied products in the United States is between $4,000,000 and $5,000,000, of which from $1,500,000 to $2,000,000 represents the amount paid for direct labor on their manufacture.

Foreign makers have imported into the United States several million dollars in value per·annum in these productions, which it has been found impossible to prevent, either through patents upon the product or the machines used in the manufacturing of the product, or in any other manner, and they are selling at such low prices that they undersell the American manufacturer, while if there is any reduction in the tariff it would force the American manufacturer out of business entirely; but if a reasonable increase is made all of the sale now being made of the foreign imported product would cease and the

American manufacturer would be able to supply this material at reasonable prices to the American consumer, thereby employing a larger number of American skilled laborers, which can not be done under existing circumstances and with the tariff as at present.

GENERAL.

As in all other products, the use and consumption of steel balls, ball bearings, and roller bearings is limited, and if the tariff is reduced the foreign product will be imported at no benefit to American industry. On the contrary, the foreign manufacturers will be able to increase their force of employees in order to supply the demand for their products in the United States, and for which they will give no corresponding benefit. It will foster and develop the business of the foreign manufacturer at the expense of the American manufacturer and laborer and enable them to send their product into this country, thereby reducing the number of employees now engaged in the business in the United States, in addition to which it will draw from this country a large sum which will be paid to the foreign manufacturers for their product, covering their cost and their profit, all of which would be expended by the foreign manufacturers in their own countries in the purchase of raw materials and supplies, also the payment for their cheap labor, producing no corresponding advantage to the consumer in the United States.

Respectfully submitted.

SAMUEL S. EVELAND,
President Standard Roller Bearing Company.
PHILADELPHIA, *November 25, 1908.*

Mr. EVELAND. That is all, Mr. Payne. If you wish the other name, the other concern is J. S. Bretz & Co., of New York.

The CHAIRMAN. Have you concluded your statement?

Mr. EVELAND. Yes, sir.

Mr. COCKRAN. How much did you say Bretz & Co. disposed of?

Mr. EVELAND. About $350,000 worth, and the two combined a little over a million and a half dollars.

Mr. COCKRAN. Let me see if I have your statement correctly. You say that there were actually sold in this country during the year 1907 about one million and a half dollars' worth of these articles manufactured abroad?

Mr. EVELAND. That is correct.

Mr. COCKRAN. And you repeat that statement, notwithstanding——

Mr. EVELAND. Notwithstanding what the government records show.

Mr. COCKRAN (continuing). Notwithstanding the assertion of the Treasury that the importations amounted, all together, to about $47,000?

Mr. EVELAND. Then they have been greatly undervalued, that is all; because I can absolutely prove the sales. I know to whom they were sold; I know what the product was and where it was made. I went through the factories abroad. I know what representations were made to me there by the managers of the factories; and I have every reason to believe that the facts I have given you are correct, even if they are contrary to the government reports.

Mr. COCKRAN. You have an undervaluation here of about a million and a half of dollars.

Mr. EVELAND. I can not help that. Those are the facts. I know the sales that were made. I can probably prepare a list——

Mr. COCKRAN. This undervaluation of $1,500,000 was on an importation of $47,000 according to the port figures—a $47,000 product?

Several MEMBERS. There must be some mistake.

Mr. EVELAND. Well, it may be that it is put under some other heading. I do not know anything about that. That is absolutely a fact, however, Mr. Cockran. The material has been bought and sold in this country, and I can give you the facts and figures as to who bought it. You can confirm all the statements. There will not be the least difficulty in doing so.

Mr. RANDELL. Do you know when the importation was made?

Mr. EVELAND. It began in 1906, 1907, and 1908—those three years. Prior to that there was very little.

Mr. GRIGGS. Can you not give it now, so that it will go in the record?

Mr. COCKRAN. He has given it.

Mr. EVELAND. I have given the year that is the most important. This year there was a considerable reduction—that is, since the panic. Those facts are absolute facts, Mr. Cockran. They are not guesswork. I know who bought the stuff. The only thing as to your government records is that it is barely possible that some of it comes under different headings. It should not, I presume, however.

Mr. COCKRAN. But this, you see, would be a scheme of fraud on such a stupendous scale that it staggers the imagination to conceive of its being possible.

Mr. EVELAND. I am very sorry about that, but it is a fact.

Mr. DALZELL. Is there a firm making these goods in Canton, Ohio?

Mr. EVELAND. Yes, sir.

Mr. DALZELL. By the name of Timpkins?

Mr. EVELAND. Yes, sir; they have asked me to represent them, also, in presenting their side of the case. They make roller bearings; and we make steel balls, ball bearings and roller bearings.

Mr. DALZELL. I just wanted to identify the goods.

Mr. EVELAND. That is it exactly. They sell about a million dollars' worth a year.

Mr. COCKRAN. You are not seeking to increase the tariff, are you?

Mr. EVELAND. I think if you could increase the tariff about 10 per cent, you would practically prohibit importation; and if the tariff is left as it is, I do not see how the American manufacturer can continue in business.

Mr. COCKRAN. You are continuing, are you not?

Mr. EVELAND. Yes, sir; but I do not expect to.

Mr. COCKRAN. How long have you been in business?

Mr. EVELAND. I started about six years ago, and there was no money made until about three years ago; and there was one good year prior to the importation of the foreign bearings. But since then there has been practically no money made. I have invested about $4,000,000 in the business; and I do not see how it is possible to continue in business with the foreign products coming in more and more, as has been the case.

Mr. COCKRAN. Your disposition is to prohibit the importation of these goods altogether by an increase of the tariff to 10 per cent?

Mr. EVELAND. I do not think you would absolutely prohibit it, but I think you would cut it down.

Mr. COCKRAN. I understood you to say that that would prohibit it.

Mr. EVELAND. It would very largely prohibit it. I think it would let a portion of the product come in, but a very small amount; and it would enable the present prices to be maintained. There would be no expectation of raising the present prices at all; but at present they are cutting prices very badly, and if the present standard prices are maintained I think all the American manufacturers would be perfectly willing to agree not to increase their prices. We have no desire to do it.

Mr. COCKRAN. You would not hold out any prospect at all for a reduction in prices?

Mr. EVELAND. I think there is no question about that—that as far as the Standard Roller-Bearing Company is concerned they will go out of business.

Mr. COCKRAN. They will go out of business?

Mr. EVELAND. I have no doubt whatever about that. That is our expectation.

Mr. COCKRAN. So that so far as the consumer's prospect is concerned it is rather gloomy as to any improvement?

Mr. EVELAND. I do not think the difference to the consumer will be very great in either case.

Mr. COCKRAN. It would be if there was a substantial reduction, would it not?

Mr. EVELAND. No; because, as I have stated here, for instance, it amounts to 2 mills on the price of a sewing machine. I do not believe anybody will make a reduction in the price of sewing machines to that extent. If you took the duty off altogether that is all the difference it would be.

Mr. COCKRAN. But every person that has come here has shown us that an increase of his particular tariff would not hurt anybody, while it would make him very comfortable. But when you come to add all these various items together—and you have no better claim to tariff favors than your neighbor—the result to the consumer must be serious.

Mr. EVELAND. Well, I do not think——

Mr. COCKRAN. You will admit 2 mills, will you not?

Mr. EVELAND. Yes; without any doubt. It will amount to 75 cents to $8 on an automobile. That is all it would amount to if the tariff were entirely removed, Mr. Cockran.

Mr. BOUTELL. What would it be on an automobile?

Mr. EVELAND. From 75 cents to $8, according to the number used on an automobile. It would be from 2 mills to 8 or 10 mills on a sewing machine, bicycle, or lawn mower.

Mr. GAINES. How much did you say it would amount to on a bicycle? Let me hear that answer.

Mr. COCKRAN. Seventy-five cents on a bicycle.

Mr. EVELAND. No; on an automobile.

Mr. COCKRAN. Seventy-five cents on an automobile?

Mr. DALZELL. Seventy-five cents to $8 on an automobile.

Mr. EVELAND. It is from 2 mills to 1½ cents, according to the number used, on a bicycle, sewing machine, or lawn mower; and on an automobile, 75 cents to $8.

Mr. GRIGGS. Will you explain, now, how an increase in the tariff will reduce these undervaluations?

Mr. EVELAND. I do not say that there is an undervaluation. I merely make the statement that I am quite able to prove that there were over a million dollars' worth of these articles sold here by foreign agents. It must have been put under some other heading. It is actually a fact, easily proven; and I do not know how it is possible to change that by any change in your tariff. I think the tariff is wrong in its method. I think the selling price here would be a better guide than the selling price abroad. Take the case of a ball bearing—it consists of what is called a " cone," and a race, and a set of balls. You can take out the balls and have three parts. Now, it may be that there is some way in which those three parts can be imported separately at a lower rate of duty. I do not know.

Mr. BONYNGE. When you say a million and a half were sold in this country last year, do you refer to the retail price, the wholesale price, or the import price?

Mr. EVELAND. The price at which these concerns, these foreign agents, sold—the amount of money which they received.

Mr. B   GE. The amount of money that the foreign agents received? ONYN

Mr. EVELAND. Yes; the actual amount received.

Mr. DALZELL. Do you know whether the firm in Canton that I referred to has been making money or not?

Mr. EVELAND. I believe they have been fairly successful, though they have not made a very large amount. I do not think anyone in the business has ever made over, possibly, 8 or 9 per cent on the capital invested in any one year, as far as I know.

Mr. UNDERWOOD. I should like to ask you this question: You stated that there is over a million and a half dollars' worth of this article imported into this country, whereas the Treasury figures only show $47,000. There evidently can not be an undervaluation to that extent. If the articles have come here to the extent shown by your figures, they must have been smuggled; and therefore they did not affect the revenue, but came in without paying the duty. In other words, you have been competing with a smuggled free-trade article.

Mr. EVELAND. Well, if you can put a duty on it, so that you can collect it, I will be satisfied.

Mr. UNDERWOOD. As a matter of fact, where the duty is paid we have only gotten $47,000 out of a total consumption of five millions. That is not equal to 1 per cent of the consumption of the product in this country. And bearing in mind that this committee has, besides other questions, to consider the question of raising revenue, do you not think your industry should furnish part of the revenue, or that we should be allowed to secure some part of the revenue through your industry?

Mr. EVELAND. It depends very largely upon how you propose collecting it. If that is a fact, that only $47,000 of importations paid duty, we should be glad if you could collect the balance of it, and I think I would be satisfied. Possibly that would account for the cut prices and the trouble there has been in the trade. But I can assure you that if the duty has been paid properly on the entire amount that I know was imported into this country, I do not think there is anything you can do to save the American industry and the workmen engaged in it except increase the duty.

Mr. UNDERWOOD. But here is a figure that can not be controverted—the returns of the Treasury Department as to the amount of these articles that were imported and the amount of duty raised on them. If they came in, they must have been smuggled.

Mr. EVELAND. I can not make any statement as to that. I can give you almost exactly—that is, I can prepare it and submit it to you—a list of those purchasers, and the purchasers will confirm where they got their material—that it was imported, made in Germany, and so marked. Whether they got it here by smuggling or otherwise, I know nothing about, one way or the other. In fact, I did not know of the existence of those figures until you gave them. I endeavored to get the information from the Treasury Department and failed.

Mr. UNDERWOOD. I hope you will file those figures with the committee.

Mr. EVELAND. I shall be very glad to do so.

Mr. UNDERWOOD. But, as a matter of fact, the amount that did come into this country and paid a duty as a dutiable article is an insignificant amount when compared with the production, is it not?

Mr. EVELAND. It does not amount to anything at all worth considering.

Mr. UNDERWOOD. And if that is the case, there is no reason in the world for an increase of the duty. As a matter of fact, it would warrant a reduction, would it not?

Mr. EVELAND. I can assure you that if there is a reduction you are sure to have several thousand highly-paid American mechanics out of work. This is not a case of "bluff." It is an absolute fact; that is all.

Mr. UNDERWOOD. According to your statement, you have been competing with a free-trade article smuggled in here?

Mr. EVELAND. Yes; but pardon me—the prices have not been upon that basis. The prices that we have been competing with are the prices prevailing abroad, to which 50 per cent has been added—45 per cent duty and about 5 per cent expense of getting the article here. That is what we always supposed we were competing against. On that basis I think this industry is a little different from some that I have heard discussed here.

Mr. UNDERWOOD. Let me ask you this question right there: If the price that the foreign product is maintaining on this market is the foreign price with 50 per cent added, and it is being smuggled in here, of course that indicates that the foreign manufacturer and the foreign importer can not cut the price on you under this duty, does it not?

Mr. EVELAND. You say that he can not? He is cutting it.

Mr. UNDERWOOD. No; because he has 45 per cent of duty there.

Mr. EVELAND. I gave you the selling prices, right here. The bearing that sells in England for $1.44 and in Germany for $1.50 sells here for $2.25. Add 75 cents and that makes exactly 50 per cent. I had no idea that there were any such figures as those available; and I am just as much surprised as you are, because I know positively, without any qualification whatever, that from a million to a million and a half dollars' worth of those bearings were sold the year prior to the panic year—that is, including part of the panic year. How they got them here I do not know.

Mr. UNDERWOOD. But you can readily see that they did not come through the custom-house, because they are not shown here.

Mr. EVELAND. Is there any other classification under which they could have been admitted?

Mr. UNDERWOOD. I do not see how they could come in under any other, because the classification here says: "Antifriction ball forgings." I should think that would cover the proposition.

Mr. EVELAND. That possibly might cover the balls only and not the bearings. The bearing comprises steel balls and steel rings or races or cones, as they are called. Possibly they would come in under some other heading of manufactured products, but I could not get any information whatever from the Treasury Department about them.

Mr. HILL. This is practically a new industry?

Mr. EVELAND. It is practically a new industry.

Mr. HILL. When did it begin, along about 1900?

Mr. EVELAND. Yes; 1901 or 1902.

Mr. HILL. This may give you some information on the subject: In 1900, at the beginning of the industry, the importations were only $11; the next year $2,000. Then it runs three, two, three, one, and forty-seven thousand dollars. So that would indicate that it was the right heading. If that is true, and your argument for a million and a half importations justifies a higher duty, if these statistics are correct, your argument must, on the other hand, justify a lower duty. Must it not?

Mr. EVELAND. I think you will find that in all probability this refers to steel balls exclusively, and has nothing whatever to do with the completed bearing as a finished product, which is an entirely different thing.

The CHAIRMAN. That is the only item mentioned in the report for 1907. I have the original report here. I did not know but that possibly there might have been a printer's error in the book that we have before us. It is precisely the same, and undoubtedly it is all that the Government collects duty on. I wish you would give the clerk, before you go out, a memorandum showing the names and addresses of these parties who, you say, imported these goods and sold them here during the year 1907.

Mr. EVELAND. I shall be very glad to do it, Mr. Payne.

The CHAIRMAN. So that we can find out; and if we do find out, you will agree with us that the duty ought to be lowered instead of increased?

Mr. EVELAND. No; I can not agree with that at all.

Mr. BOUTELL. What proportion in value in a million and a half of dollars of finished product would the balls bear to the balance of the bearings?

Mr. EVELAND. Oh, possibly 10 per cent; not over that.

Mr. BOUTELL. That is, the balls would be 10 per cent?

Mr. EVELAND. Possibly; yes.

Mr. BOUTELL. Ten per cent of the value of the entire bearing?

Mr. EVELAND. Possibly; yes.

Mr. BOUTELL. That, then, is doubtless the explanation.

Mr. EVELAND. I think that is it.

Mr. BOUTELL. This is simply for the balls; and probably the bearings are covered under another item.

Mr. EVELAND. I think probably that is it.

Mr. COCKRAN. Under which other item?

Mr. BOUTELL. Under "steels otherwise imported," or something of that sort.

Mr. EVELAND. It must come in under some other heading, because I know these are being imported. I have imported them myself, in order to see what they cost; and I have had to pay 45 per cent duty on them. There was no difficulty whatever in getting them classified.

Mr. COCKRAN. How were they classified in your case?

Mr. EVELAND. I do not know. I never had occasion to look that matter up. I supposed the records would be very much larger than that under any circumstances.

Mr. CLARK. Mr. Witness, how long have you been engaged in this business?

Mr. EVELAND. For about seven years—six or seven years.

Mr. CLARK. How much money have you put into it?

Mr. EVELAND. Abut $4,000,000 in cash.

Mr. CLARK. And what per cent did you make the first year?

Mr. EVELAND. There was a loss the first two years. The third year there was about 2 or 3 per cent made. Two years ago—that is, our business year closes—July 1—during the year closing July, 1907, there was about $350,000 profit. Last year there was practically no profit at all—about $30,000 or $40,000.

Mr. CLARK. I know; but that is not a fair year to base conclusions on.

Mr. EVELAND. No; it is not a fair comparison, I admit that.

Mr. CLARK. You would estimate your net profits at 9 or 10 per cent in a fairly good year?

Mr. EVELAND. Approximately 10 per cent, if prices are maintained. But prices are not maintained this year at all.

Mr. CLARK. Did you put $4,000,000 into it when you first started?

Mr. EVELAND. No; I put in about fifty or sixty thousand dollars, and gradually increased the investment as the business warranted it. I put in $125,000 the second year; $500,000, I think, the third year, making about $625,000; and about a million and a half dollars two years ago, prior to the panic.

Mr. CLARK. That was when the business flourished?

Mr. EVELAND. Yes.

Mr. CLARK. Was that all put into the mill or the factory, or whatever you please to term it?

Mr. EVELAND. Yes; real estate, buildings, machinery, and equipment.

Mr. CLARK. You have no outside possessions, as we might call them, that you have charged in that?

Mr. EVELAND. Nothing whatever. That is actual cash, subscribed by the subscribers for the stock and invested in the plant.

Mr. CLARK. How much money have you invested in the steel business?

Mr. EVELAND. None whatever; the company does not own a dollar, nor——

Mr. CLARK. I know; but you?

Mr. EVELAND. Not over ten or fifteen thousand dollars.

Mr. CLARK. Not over ten or fifteen thousand dollars?

Mr. EVELAND. No; and that is simply a Wall street speculation.

Mr. CLARK. What you really want Congress to do is this: It would simplify matters very much to gratify your desire if Congress would put a short section in the tariff law absolutely prohibiting the importation of these articles into the United States at all, would it not?

Mr. EVELAND. No; I do not think I want that.

Mr. CLARK. It would remove all difficulty about the custom-house?

Mr. EVELAND. No; I do not ask that, Mr. Clark.

Mr. CLARK. But that is practically what you are after.

Mr. EVELAND. No. What I stated is that this is a product which is manufactured in Germany particularly and on identically the same machines that we have here. The men turn out the same amount of product. You asked that a few moments ago of some one here. They turn out the same amount of product. I went abroad this year, in the early part of the year, to see about that.

Mr. CLARK. Another question: Suppose that we should put this product on the free list—you say you would quit?

Mr. EVELAND. I would have to.

Mr. CLARK. What would you do with the factory, or mill, or whatever it is?

Mr. EVELAND. I could not possibly manufacture ball and roller bearings. I would have to sell the plant; that is all.

Mr. CLARK. Could you change the business that you are conducting in that factory into something else that would pay, if this stuff were put on the free list?

Mr. EVELAND. Why, I could not do that, because we make nothing else. There is probably half a million dollars' worth of machinery in our plant that would be absolutely worthless for any other purpose. We could not make anything with it except steel balls or ball bearings. We could not do anything else with it at all.

Mr. CLARK. I take it, from your appearance, that you are an American citizen?

Mr. EVELAND. I certainly am—and a Republican.

Mr. CLARK. Did you ever consider the proposition that one of the duties of this committee or of Congress is to get an adequate amount of revenue, and that if everybody got his tariff put up to a practically prohibitive point we would not have any revenue?

Mr. EVELAND. I do not ask for a prohibitive tariff.

Mr. CLARK. It is mighty near it, according to your answer to Mr. Cockran's question.

Mr. EVELAND. No; I do not agree with you. I say that here is a case where an industry is unable to get any protection abroad at all. We have, for instance, agreements with parties in Germany that they will not under any circumstances ship into America any steel balls or ball bearings—an ironclad agreement which they entered into when they secured machinery from America. Now, on a technicality, they start importing. I tried to protect myself by a lawsuit against them, and I found that according to the rules and regulations of the courts in Germany, which are very peculiar, I have to put up $20,000 in cash to start with, and the result is that I get no protection there. If the tariff is reduced, my product will be imported here more largely. It has a good hold here to-day, and if the tariff is reduced 5 or 10 per cent you will undoubtedly add to the revenues of the Government—I have not the slightest doubt of that—but if you do it will be at the expense of our workmen. Now, I can continue in business if I cut wages. I do not want to cut wages, but that is the only way I can do it. It would reduce the cost of the raw material if you cut the duty on steel products.

Mr. CLARK. Do these laborers get all the tariff that is on the product now, or do you pocket some of it?

Mr. EVELAND. Well, in Germany——

Mr. CLARK. I am not asking you about Germany. I am asking you this question: Do the American men that work for you get all the tariff that is levied on this article now, or do you pocket some of it yourself?

Mr. EVELAND. The American laborer in my factory is paid from $2.50 to $3 a day.

Mr. CLARK. That is not what I asked you.

Mr. EVELAND. I can not separate it.

Mr. CLARK. I ask you, do you give to the American laborer working for you some of this tariff tax, or do you pocket some of it yourself?

Mr. EVELAND. I am answering you in the only way I can. I do not see how I——

Mr. CLARK. There is a tariff on it now, is there not?

Mr. EVELAND. Precisely.

Mr. CLARK. Who gets the tariff?

The CHAIRMAN. Why, the Government.

Mr. EVELAND. The Government gets all that anybody gets.

Mr. CLARK. It is ultimately added to the man that uses it, is it not?

Mr. EVELAND. I will say this, Mr. Clark: If you will give me an increase of 10 per cent on the tariff on ball bearings and roller bearings, I will do what I did two years ago, when I invested a million and a half dollars in my plant, and $500,000 last year. I will duplicate that; and I will take care of the trade here and the American workman to the extent of a thousand or fifteen hundred more workmen. That will be a total of 4,000.

Mr. CLARK. No; if we gave you what you want, you would mark up the price of these things to whatever suited your convenience.

Mr. EVELAND. No; I would not.

Mr. CLARK. You have already stated that the consumer would simply pay that much higher price for them.

Mr. EVELAND. No; I am willing——

Mr. CLARK. And it does not make any difference whether it is 2½ mills on a sewing machine or a bicycle or what it is, somebody pays it at last.

Mr. POU. If we give you an increased duty, you will agree to put down the price somewhat, will you not?

Mr. EVELAND. An increased duty?

Mr. POU. Yes.

Mr. EVELAND. No; but I will agree to maintain the present price. Instead of increasing the price, I will agree not to increase it; and I will agree to employ a thousand or fifteen hundred more hands.

Mr. POU. Will you not agree to sell somewhat cheaper?

Mr. EVELAND. No; I can not afford to do it.

Mr. POU. Almost every one has offered to do that.

Mr. EVELAND. I can not afford to do it.

Mr. POU. The higher we put the tariff, the cheaper they say they can sell their goods.

Mr. EVELAND. No; I do not agree with you on that proposition. That does not seem reasonable.

Mr. GRIGGS. You say you would not say that?

Mr. EVELAND. Hardly.

Mr. GRIGGS. You say you are going to put a million and a half dollars more into this business if you can get a little increase in this tax?

Mr. EVELAND. Absolutely. I will guarantee to do it in any way that you want me to guarantee it. But if we do not, the only redress we have is to cut the wages of the workmen, which constitute at least, I should say, 80 or 85 per cent of the cost of our product.

Mr. GRIGGS. I think you would get along pretty well without any tariff, myself.

Mr. EVELAND. I can assure you that we will go out of business; that is all.

Mr. GRIGGS. Well, you are able to go out of business.

Mr. COCKRAN. Not if you made 10 per cent; would you?

Mr. EVELAND. Yes; I can not sell—that takes away my profit.

Mr. COCKRAN. Do you mean that if you made a profit of 10 per cent you would go out of business?

Mr. EVELAND. I say if that was cut off there would be nothing left to me.

Mr. COCKRAN. But you made 10 per cent?

Mr. EVELAND. I have made 10 per cent in the best year we have ever had—the largest sales, boom times.

Mr. COCKRAN. You are not losing any money now?

Mr. EVELAND. Yes; I am losing now.

Mr. COCKRAN. How much?

Mr. EVELAND. Well, I will take that back; I am not losing, but I am not making anything.

Mr. COCKRAN. Is there anybody in this country who is really making any money now?

Mr. EVELAND. Yes; I think so.

Mr. COCKRAN. I have not known any. No one has come here and said he was making any money.

Mr. EVELAND. Call a few of the automobile men. They are making plenty of money.

Mr. COCKRAN. That is an exceptional industry.

Mr. EVELAND. It is a mammoth industry, growing at the rate of $120,000,000 a year.

Mr. COCKRAN. As a matter of fact, you know perfectly well that, generally speaking, trade has not been profitable this year.

Mr. EVELAND. Precisely; I know that.

Mr. COCKRAN. And a great many industries have lost money. The worst you can say for your factory is that while you made 10 per cent up until this period of depression, you are now absolutely running even?

Mr. EVELAND. I do not say I made 10 per cent up to this period. I say that we made that during the best year we have ever had, for one year.

Mr. COCKRAN. What year was that?

Mr. EVELAND. The year closing July, 1907.

Mr. COCKRAN. 1907?

Mr. EVELAND. And I say that since then we have not. That is no criterion at all.

Mr. COCKRAN. Nobody has made money since?

Mr. EVELAND. I quite agree with that.

Mr. COCKRAN. Is not this the fact: That up to the panic year of 1907 you were making 10 per cent, and that was a steadily-growing profit on a very young industry. In this year of panic and general loss you, who can claim nothing in the way of hardship or loss except that you are running about even, come down here and ask us, at the expense of the community, to give you the means of making a larger profit?

Mr. EVELAND. It is not at the expense of the community.

Mr. COCKRAN. You admitted that it was to the extent of 2 mills on a sewing machine.

Mr. EVELAND. That is rather a small percentage.

Mr. COCKRAN. Even that, small as it is, the community has to pay. Somebody has to pay it; and you want to get it by taxation. That is the fact, is it not?

Mr. EVELAND. I do not think that is taxation; it is not favoritism.

Mr. COCKRAN. Let us not call it taxation, then; let us call it benevolence.

Mr. EVELAND. That is worse.

Mr. COCKRAN. Will you call it that?

Mr. EVELAND. That is worse.

Mr. COCKRAN. At all events, however, you will admit that you want to get it through the statutes?

Mr. EVELAND. What I am particularly anxious for is not to have any cut made in the tariff. I say that if that is done you will have in the whole industry, some three or four thousand employees that will either have greatly reduced wages or no wages at all. Personally, I should not care to stay in the business; that is all.

Mr. COCKRAN. But if you got your raw material much cheaper, how would it be?

Mr. EVELAND. But it does not amount to anything. I have attempted to explain that here.

Mr. COCKRAN. I thought you said it amounted to $500,000.

Mr. EVELAND. Yes; the steel that we buy does amount to between four and five hundred thousand dollars—steel and iron. But in the case of a ball bearing the steel costs 27 cents on a selling price of $2.25. In the case of a steel bearing selling at 50 cents it amounts to 2 cents.

Mr. COCKRAN. Will you allow me to put the question to you in another way, which, I think, will make it clearer to some of us? You put in $500,000 as the cost of your raw material?

Mr. EVELAND. Yes.

Mr. COCKRAN. What is the cost of your finished product—the total cost; the selling price to you?

Mr. EVELAND. The balance would be the profit.

Mr. COCKRAN. What is the selling price to you of your finished product?

Mr. EVELAND. You would have to get the profit. Do you mean including the profit, or not?

Mr. COCKRAN. Your selling price—your selling price. You know what I mean.

The CHAIRMAN. Do you not know what it is—how much a year?

Mr. EVELAND. It varies. On a basis of $500,000 for raw material, I should say that the selling price would be about two millions and a half.

Mr. COCKRAN. Very good—two millions and a half. That includes your profit?

Mr. EVELAND. That includes the gross sales—yes; and, I should say, 10 per cent profit on the present basis, which is a reasonable profit, I believe.

Mr. COCKRAN. Suppose you had a reduction of this $500,000, so that you got the same material for, say, $400,000. I am assuming, now, that the same amount of material costs you $400,000. Then you would have $100,000 available to carry over either to profit or to reduction in the amount charged the consumer; would you not?

Mr. EVELAND. I think the disadvantage of that would be that you would injure general business to such an extent that you would never sell that two and a half million dollars' worth.

Mr. COCKRAN. That is perfectly understood. Now that we understand that general philosophical reflection, will you answer my specific question? I ask you, on your particular product, if the cost of your raw material, as we have denominated it, were reduced to you $100,000 (that is to say, one-fifth, 20 per cent), would not that $100,000 be available——

Mr. EVELAND. No.

Mr. COCKRAN (continuing). Either to increase your profit or else to reduce the cost?

Mr. EVELAND. It would reduce the selling price to the consumer; competition would bring it down.

Mr. COCKRAN. I am very much obliged to you.

Mr. EVELAND. And on that reduction I would not make any money whatever.

Mr. COCKRAN. Not at all; but the community would be $100,000 richer?

Mr. EVELAND. The community would buy its product of foreign manufacturers, and all the money would go abroad; that is all.

Mr. COCKRAN. I thought you said you would reduce the price of your product.

Mr. EVELAND. I say that would be the natural result; and on that basis I can not stay in business.

Mr. COCKRAN. But how would you suffer any loss in that way?

Mr. EVELAND. You are assuming also, I understand, that the tariff is reduced on our finished product. If you simply reduced the tariff on the steel, possibly——

Mr. COCKRAN. I was confining myself for this moment to the effect of a reduction on the raw material.

Mr. EVELAND. Only?

Mr. COCKRAN. Well, that is the beginning.

Mr. EVELAND. Oh, no; they must go together, as far as I am concerned.

The CHAIRMAN. This has all been taken down. Is it necessary to go all over that again?

Mr. COCKRAN. I think myself that this is enough. I will let it go at that.

Mr. RANDELL. You say that if we increase this tariff 10 per cent you will put a million and a half dollars more in this plant?

Mr. EVELAND. Yes.

Mr. RANDELL. And you will maintain prices as they are at present?

Mr. EVELAND. Yes; I will be very glad to.

Mr. RANDELL. And employ several hundred more men?

Mr. EVELAND. Several thousand—one thousand or fifteen hundred.

Mr. RANDELL. Then you would be working at a good business and getting a handsome profit?

Mr. EVELAND. On a fair 10 per cent manufacturing net profit.

Mr. RANDELL. You say that if this is not done, if the tariff is reduced in any degree, all of that must come out of the labor item?

Mr. EVELAND. That is my feeling at present—that it would have to come from that.

Mr. RANDELL. You would have to fix the price of wages lower in your manufactory?

Mr. EVELAND. I should be obliged to reduce wages to compensate for that.

Mr. RANDELL. And I understood you to say that it would all come out of labor. Is that the effect of this protective system—that the manufacturer can dictate the price of labor, so as to recoup any loss that may be sustained, and cut it out of the price of labor, and that labor must stand every reduction? Would that be the effect of the system, or is that simply peculiar to your line of manufacture?

Mr. EVELAND. I am not qualified to speak for others. That, I say, would be undoubtedly the fact in my own business. I know no other way of continuing in business. There is no other way in which I can reduce the cost.

Mr. RANDELL. You hold the laboring man up as the buffer between you and the lawmaking power, and say: "If you hit me you have got to hit the laboring man first?"

Mr. EVELAND. I say that if you change the tariff, you will hit him first, undoubtedly.

Mr. RANDELL. You hold him up, anyhow, as far as you are concerned?

Mr. EVELAND. That is my opinion. I think that is undoubtedly the case.

Mr. RANDELL. And you say, on the one hand, that if we increase the tariff, you will increase your business, but if we cut the tariff down you will cut down labor?

Mr. EVELAND. We will be forced to do that.

Mr. RANDELL. But you will do that?

Mr. EVELAND. I shall be obliged to do it.

Mr. RANDELL. Why has not labor some voice in that as well as you?

Mr. EVELAND. I do not know just how to answer that question. I know that very few of us remain in business on a losing basis, and that is the position I would be in.

Mr. RANDELL. They will have no work in your factory unless money is invested there, and you can not run the factory unless you have labor?

Mr. EVELAND. No; and I can not run the factory unless I make a profit.

Mr. RANDELL. But my question was, Why should all the reduction come out of labor?

Mr. EVELAND. Because I do not know anything else on which I could make a reduction in our particular product.

Mr. RANDELL. That is the only thing you could cut on?

Mr. EVELAND. That is the only thing. It represents from 80 to 90 per cent, or 80 to 85 per cent, of the cost of the product we manufacture. Therefore it would have to take a portion of it.

Mr. RANDELL. You could not do that without the consent of the laboring men, unless you have them in your power.

Mr. EVELAND. Well, I certainly have not——

Mr. RANDELL. Which is it in your case—that you have their consent or that they are in your power? Which is the reason that you would put all of that cost on them?

Mr. EVELAND. I certainly have not got them in my power, and I do not imagine that they would consent very willingly.

Mr. RANDELL. Have you their consent?

Mr. EVELAND. No; I say I do not think they would consent very willingly.

Mr. RANDELL. It would have to be one way or the other, would it not?

Mr. EVELAND. It would be a case of absolute necessity either for them to consent or to go out of business entirely so far as we are concerned.

Mr. RANDELL. You have assured us that you would cut it all out of labor?

Mr. EVELAND. I say that at least 80 to 85 per cent of it would have to be carried by labor, because that represents the labor cost of the finished article.

Mr. GRIGGS. You say you have half a million dollars' worth of special machinery for making these things?

Mr. EVELAND. Yes.

Mr. GRIGGS. And you will have to quit business if we reduce this tariff?

Mr. EVELAND. Precisely.

Mr. GRIGGS. How can you afford to do it?

Mr. EVELAND. I can certainly afford that better than to run for a year at a loss of from two hundred to three hundred or four hundred thousand dollars, and keep on doing that year in and year out. I do not know of any other method by which the cost of the product can be reduced appreciably.

Mr. GRIGGS. You are not speaking seriously when you say you would go out of business, are you?

Mr. EVELAND. I mean that that is absolutely the fact of the matter. That is absolutely what would be done. There is no " bluff " about that. There is no guesswork about it. I simply could not remain in business; that is all.

Mr. GRIGGS. You said to Mr. Randell a moment ago that in case what you ask is not done you would either have to go out of business or reduce wages.

Mr. EVELAND. That is precisely what I mean—I would either have to do one or the other. It is an alternative.

Mr. GRIGGS. In the beginning you announced voluntarily, without any suggestion from anybody, going clear out of your field of business, that you wanted us to understand that you wanted the tariff to remain on steel and iron.

Mr. EVELAND. Precisely. I repeat it.

Mr. GRIGGS. You prefer, then, to take the fall out of labor rather than out of the steel magnates?

Mr. EVELAND. I believe it will not come from the steel magnates; it will come from their labor, if you reduce it.

Mr. GRIGGS. Do you think so?

Mr. EVELAND. I am reasonably sure of it; and I know quite a little about the steel industry—the cost of manufacture.

Mr. GRIGGS. You are a philanthropist as well as a manufacturer?

Mr. EVELAND. No; but I think it is about time that some of the people who use steel give you their views on the subject, instead of your getting simply the suggestions of the steel makers, and people who, like the gentleman who just preceded me, would cut off the tariff altogether. I do not think it is a fair proposition at all.

Mr. GRIGGS. No steel man has insisted very strenuously here on retaining the tariff.

Mr. EVELAND. I think they are mistaken in not doing it. I think they all want it, but they feel that public opinion rather demands that they should be sacrificed.

Mr. GRIGGS. They have almost all admitted, before they got through, that they thought steel could stand a pretty good reduction.

Mr. EVELAND. Yes; because they all seemed to think that they have got to stand the sacrifice. Somebody has to.

Mr. GRIGGS. Are you not willing, if they are willing, for them to stand it?

Mr. EVELAND. I think possibly they may be able to continue in business. I certainly can not continue in business.

Mr. GRIGGS. Then, as you answered Mr. Cockran a few moments ago, you can not get the benefit of the difference in cost of your material?

Mr. EVELAND. But that is a very small part of what my loss would be. If you cut the cost $100,000, which is the maximum that he referred to—and I do not suppose that any such amount was really anticipated—it would still leave me a very heavy loser, if you made a corresponding reduction in the tariff on my manufactured product.

Mr. BOUTELL. Where is your corporation located, Mr. Eveland?

Mr. EVELAND. In Philadelphia.

Mr. BOUTELL. How many stockholders are there?

Mr. EVELAND. About two hundred or two hundred and twenty-five.

Mr. BOUTELL. How large a proportion of the stock do you hold individually?

Mr. EVELAND. Is it necessary for me to answer that?

Mr. BOUTELL. No.

Mr. EVELAND. I do not own a controlling interest.

Mr. BOUTELL. Nothing is necessary.

Mr. EVELAND. I will be very glad——

Mr. BOUTELL. You have come here voluntarily to give us information, however.

Mr. EVELAND. Well, I have no objection. I own about 12 or 13 per cent, perhaps.

Mr. BOUTELL. Now, would you mind telling what the steel company is from which you buy your raw material?

Mr. EVELAND. Very largely the Crucible Steel Company of America; also some from the Union Drawn Steel Company; and some small lots from the steel corporation, but only when we can not get it from the others.

Mr. BOUTELL. Was the steel stock which you said you owned in any one of those three?

Mr. EVELAND. No.

Mr. BOUTELL. To what extent are the stockholders in your ball-bearing company interested in the steel corporations from which you buy your raw material?

Mr. EVELAND. Do you mean those three concerns?

Mr. BOUTELL. Yes.

Mr. EVELAND. Some individuals in the Crucible Steel Company have a small interest with us; about 3 per cent altogether.

Mr. BOUTELL. That is, 3 per cent——

Mr. EVELAND. Three per cent of the total.

Mr. BOUTELL. Three per cent of the stockholders in your company?

Mr. EVELAND. No; perhaps 3 per cent of the total value.

Mr. BOUTELL. Three per cent of the stock of your company is represented in the companies which manufacture the raw material?

Mr. EVELAND. Yes.

Mr. BOUTELL. So that there is no community of interest, if we may call it that, on the part of the stockholders in your company?

Mr. EVELAND. None whatever.

Mr. BOUTELL. In the way of keeping the tariff on the raw material?

Mr. EVELAND. There is none whatever. We purchase where we please, and there is only one company that we purchase steel from that has the slightest interest in our company, and we do not buy exclusively from them.

Mr. RANDELL. I understood the question to be whether the members of his company had stock in the steel company?

Mr. BOUTELL. That is what I asked.

Mr. RANDELL. He did not answer in that way.

Mr. BOUTELL. I do not want to have any misapprehension about it. The question I asked was whether any of the stockholders in your Ball-Bearing Company owned any stock in the steel company from which the Ball-Bearing Company purchases its raw material?

Mr. EVELAND. I misunderstood your question. None whatever, so far as I know; none whatever.

Mr. LONGWORTH. What is the total capitalization of your concern?

Mr. EVELAND. Five million dollars; and there is some seven or eight hundred thousand dollars in the treasury. There is about $4,200,000 of stock issued.

Mr. LONGWORTH. Has the stock a market value?

Mr. EVELAND. Yes.

Mr. LONGWORTH. Do you mind stating it?

Mr. EVELAND. It has been selling at par. Last year a large amount of that stock, prior to the panic, was sold at 140 by the company, and 120, and placed in the treasury of the company. So it has sold beyond par at one time. The last sales made were at about 98, I think—about that.

Mr. LONGWORTH. And all this represents subscriptions for the stock from outside, and not profits?

Mr. EVELAND. No.

Mr. LONGWORTH. What proportion of that represents profits?

Mr. EVELAND. Do you mean in the total capitalization?

Mr. LONGWORTH. In the total capitalization?

Mr. EVELAND. Practically all of it, with the exception of a small amount in the beginning of the company, perhaps $75,000, some years ago, represents what has been paid in by the stockholders for stock.

Mr. HILL. Mr. Eveland, this process of making these ball bearings requires specially patented machinery, does it not?

Mr. EVELAND. Yes; some of it does at least.

Mr. HILL. And your company owns those patents?

Mr. EVELAND. We own a large number of them.

Mr. HILL. And I understood you to say that you had sold the right to manufacture abroad, with an agreement that there should be no competition here as the result of that sale?

Mr. EVELAND. That is not quite correct.

Mr. HILL. What was the statement you made?

Mr. EVELAND. I made that statement, possibly; but the facts of the case are that the ball and roller bearing businss as a whole has been in very bad condition for a number of years, and during the past five or six years I have purchased seven or eight companies, located in Boston; Springfield, Ohio; Cleveland, and one place or another, and consolidated them all in Philadelphia, paying cash for them—no stock or bonus or anything of that sort being given. One of those companies had an agreement with a German concern by which they sold them their German and English patents on ball-making machinery, and they agreed in return not to ship any of their products into this country. I acquired that by right of purchase from the company that made this agreement. I never made that agreement myself.

Mr. HILL. That agreement was a factor in the purchase price which you paid?

Mr. EVELAND. No; unfortunately I did not know it at the time. I learned it afterwards.

Mr. HILL. Then that was not a direct agreement made by you. You had no expectation that the United States would protect you against competition under those circumstances?

Mr. EVELAND. Not the slightest; no. The situation is that all of these companies were bought by me for from 25 to 75 cents on the dollar on what they actually cost. They were absolute failures and always had been failures; and it has only been because there has gotten to be a fair market for the product, by getting them all together in one plant, that we were able to make anything at all. The second year—not the first year—the second year they managed to make any money the panic following injured the trade, and now the cut prices of the foreign product coming in here in greatly enlarged amounts have seriously interfered with the business.

Mr. HILL. I made the suggestion because I thought perhaps you would like to look over your first statement and correct the report, in the notes, if other people understood it as I understood it—that you had, by your own voluntary act, restricted competition from abroad.

Mr. EVELAND. No; that——

Mr. HILL. And that they had violated the agreement, and now you wanted protection against them.

Mr. EVELAND. I merely made that statement because I have found it increasingly difficult to secure foreign patents. You can not get any satisfaction from them.

Mr. GRIGGS. You stated a moment ago, as I understood you, that you bought in these companies, which were all failures, below par?

Mr. EVELAND. We bought them in at from 25 to 75 cents on the dollar of what they cost.

Mr. GRIGGS. And that you put them in your corporation at——

Mr. EVELAND. Exactly what they cost. There was no stock or bonus. They were all purchased for cash.

Mr. GRIGGS. And that you put them in at cost?

Mr. EVELAND. No; I said for exactly what we paid for them. There were no bonuses.

The CHAIRMAN. This importation of a million and a half in 1907, you said, was at New York and Philadelphia. Was there any other port at which it entered?

Mr. EVELAND. Is Hartford a port of entry?

Mr. HILL. Yes.

Mr. EVELAND. It might have been under Hartford, then—Hartford, Conn.

The CHAIRMAN. Hartford, Conn.?

Mr. EVELAND. I do not know of any other. I think probably I could get some information on that subject for the committee. I do not want you to misunderstand me, Mr. Payne; I know absolutely and positively that those sales were made.

The CHAIRMAN. Do you remember what quantity was imported at Hartford, Conn.?

Mr. EVELAND. What name, you say?

The CHAIRMAN. What amount.

Mr. EVELAND. J. S. Bretz & Co. was the name.

The CHAIRMAN. Do you remember what the amount was?

Mr. EVELAND. No. I say I merely give that as a possibility—that they came at that port.

The CHAIRMAN. There is a possibility of their coming in there?

Mr. EVELAND. Yes. You asked at what places the product came in.

The CHAIRMAN. I have had the Bureau of Statistics look this matter up since you first made this statement. They say that the $47,000 includes all the importations into the United States, with the possible exception that at some small port the product may have been entered under the general basket clause of 45 per cent on material not enumerated. They say that if it was so it would be a very slight percentage of the total forty-seven thousand, if any at all. So it would look as though you were a little mistaken in your statement.

Mr. EVELAND. I am not mistaken, Mr. Payne, about the total amount that was sold.

The CHAIRMAN. We will find out exactly whether you are or not, but it looks so now. The previous four or five years there was only about twelve or fourteen hundred dollars' worth imported.

Mr. EVELAND. Yes; I guess that is undoubtedly correct, because there was very little shipped here.

The CHAIRMAN. During that time you were doing business under this tariff and making money?

Mr. EVELAND. No.

The CHAIRMAN. What is that?

Mr. EVELAND. There was no money made; 1906 and 1907 were the only years in which anybody in this business made any money.

The CHAIRMAN. And how much money did you make then—what percentage on your capital?

Mr. EVELAND. From 9 to 10 per cent on the capital invested.

The CHAIRMAN. Nine or 10 per cent?

Mr. EVELAND. Three hundred and fifty thousand dollars.

The CHAIRMAN. You were doing well under this tariff?

Mr. DALZELL. He has given you all that before.

The CHAIRMAN. I know it; but I was trying to lay a foundation for a question.

Mr. DALZELL. All right; go ahead.

The CHAIRMAN. And I did not hear it when he gave it, and I wanted to be sure about it. If you could have the conditions of 1906 and 1907 restored in this country, you could still do business under this tariff, could you not, and make money?

Mr. EVELAND. I presume I could if I had to.

The CHAIRMAN. The prospect is that you could?

Mr. EVELAND. Yes.

The CHAIRMAN. And the prospect is that those conditions are coming about very rapidly, is it not?

Mr. EVELAND. You mean the general business conditions?

The CHAIRMAN. Yes.

Mr. EVELAND. Undoubtedly; there is no question about that.

The CHAIRMAN. Yes; they are coming about very rapidly. And if those conditions are restored, with an importation starting with only twelve or fifteen hundred dollars and going up to $47,000 a year, is not that an indication that the tariff was plenty high enough?

Mr. EVELAND. Mr. Payne, if I thought that was a correct statement (that there were only $47,000 worth of bearings imported into the United States), I would not waste your time and mine by appearing here and saying anything at all about the duty. But I know it is not the case.

The CHAIRMAN. Unless it was to ask us to reduce it?

Mr. EVELAND. No; I have no interest in reduction at all.

The CHAIRMAN. You would not do that anyway?

Mr. EVELAND. No, sir. [Laughter.]

The CHAIRMAN. You have conscientious scruples against reduction?

Mr. EVELAND. Yes; I am a Republican.

The CHAIRMAN. That is all.

Mr. CLARK. Mr. Witness, it is always claimed by the proponents of the high protective-tariff system that a reduction of the tariff puts down prices. Is not that true?

Mr. EVELAND. I never heard of that.

Mr. CLARK. You never heard a high protective-tariff man claim that cutting down the tariff puts down prices?

Mr. EVELAND. I have only been here two or three days, and I have not heard that.

Mr. CLARK. You surely had heard something before you came here, had you not? [Laughter.] Is not that the theory of the proponents of the high protective tariff—that if the tariff is cut down, it demoralizes business and puts down prices?

Mr. EVELAND. Undoubtedly. I misunderstood your question.

Mr. CLARK. You testified, in answer to the chairman's question just now, that the prospects are for a greatly increased business in the United States.

Mr. EVELAND. Precisely; but what has that to do with prices?

Mr. CLARK. If that is true, you do not believe that Congress or this committee is going to recommend a reduction of the tariff, do you?

Mr. EVELAND. I hope they will not.

Mr. CLARK. I know; but I am not asking you what you hope; I am asking you what you believe.

Mr. EVELAND. I do not think I can answer a question like that.

Mr. CLARK. It is as plain a question as was ever asked since the invention of language. [Laughter.]

Mr. EVELAND. I think you are a better judge of that than I. I do not think I ought to form any opinion on it. If I were sure, Mr. Clark, that you were not going to reduce the tariff, I would not waste your time nor mine by coming here.

Mr. CLARK. I know; but I can not see to save my soul how you can contend that cutting down the tariff cuts prices down and demoralizes business, and then say, in the next breath, that you think business is going to improve, and then refuse to come to the conclusion that you do not believe that Congress is going to reduce the tariff.

Mr. EVELAND. I think the general feeling about the country is that you are not going to make a great reduction.

Mr. CLARK. You came here in the hope that Congress was going to raise the tariff all along the line, did you not?

Mr. EVELAND. Oh, no; not at all.

Mr. CLARK. Especially in your business?

Mr. EVELAND. I hoped you would; yes.

Mr. CLARK. Well, I think you will be very much mistaken. That is my guess about it. [Laughter.]

Mr. GRIGGS. What is the salary of your president?

Mr. EVELAND. Fifteen thousand dollars.

Mr. GRIGGS. Fifteen thousand?

Mr. EVELAND. Yes.

Mr. GRIGGS. Are there any other general officers, such as a vice-president?

Mr. EVELAND. Nobody except working officers who get from three to five or six thousand or seven thousand dollars—the superintendent, etc. The salary list is very small. The directors secure no compensation whatever.

Mr. GRIGGS. You have no general manager?

Mr. EVELAND. No; just a superintendent, who gets $6,000.

Mr. CLARK. Are all the stockholders salaried officers?

Mr. EVELAND. No; there are two who are salaried officers.

Mr. CLARK. Now I will ask you the question I asked before, and if you do not know, do not say anything about it. That is, if one of the tricks of showing small dividends on the part of these great manufacturing concerns is not to make everybody into an officer, and pay him a whacking good salary, whether he does anything or not?

Mr. EVELAND. Not to my personal knowledge; it certainly is not in my company. There is not an officer in the company, with the exception of myself, who receives a salary—not a director.

Mr. CLARK. That is all I want to ask you.

The CHAIRMAN. Mr. Eveland, if the tariff is reduced to a point of protection, if protection still remains, you have not any fear, so far as business is concerned?

Mr. EVELAND. On general products, you mean?

The CHAIRMAN. On any product.

Mr. EVELAND. I think it would make a vast difference.

The CHAIRMAN. If we still left a protective tariff on it, you have not any fears about business?

Mr. EVELAND. I do not think that is quite the correct way to put it. I think that if you reduce the tariff very materially, you are certainly going to injure business very materially; and I think that if there was a general understanding here that you were going to do so, you would find a reduction in business. You will find in the steel business to-day that they are all waiting to see what is going to happen.

The CHAIRMAN. Well, you are a hopeless case. [Laughter.] Is there anything further?

Mr. EVELAND. That is all. I am very much obliged to you.

Mr. GRIGGS. I will yield five minutes of my time to Mr. Gaines, Mr. Chairman, if he wants to ask questions.

The CHAIRMAN. Mr. Gaines will take care of himself.

The CHAIRMAN. Is there any other party here who desires to talk about ball bearings?

Mr. POU. I would suggest to the chairman that there are quite a number of gentlemen who want to leave town to-night who desire to talk about mica.

The CHAIRMAN. There are many others in the same condition, and I think we shall have to follow the regular order.

THE EXCELSIOR STEEL BALL CO., BUFFALO, N. Y., ASKS FOR INCREASE OF DUTY ON ANTIFRICTION BALL FORGINGS.

BUFFALO, N. Y., *December 1, 1908.*

COMMITTEE ON WAYS AND MEANS,
Washington, D. C.

GENTLEMEN: We understand you are going to take up the question of tariff revision in the near future, and we as manufacturers are interested in this matter, especially the tariff on steel and brass balls, ball bearings, and roller bearings, these being the articles which we manufacture.

A great many workmen are employed in the United States making steel and brass balls, ball bearings, and roller bearings for antifriction purposes, and should the tariff be reduced the probabilities are that these men will be out of employment for the reason that American workmen demand more than a bare living. At the present time competition is very keen with European countries, so much so that we have every reason to believe that steel balls are being imported right here in the city of Buffalo for less money than we can produce and make a reasonable profit.

It is a fact that German-made balls are being sold here in Buffalo, and while it is a hard matter to find out just what the invoice price is, we have been told the reason is that they can be bought cheaper; this would show an argument for an increase in the tariff so that home industry would be protected.

We also understand that wages are much lower in other countries (especially in Germany), and as the cost of making balls and ball bearings depends largely on the wages paid to skilled workmen would show another argument why the tariff on these articles should be increased.

The cost of raw material that goes into the make-up of steel and brass balls, ball bearings, and roller bearings is very slight compared with the amount of money paid in wages to skilled workmen. The articles manufactured must positively be extremely accurate, balls being gauged to about one-quarter to one-thousandth of 1 inch.

It is true that machinery enters greatly into the manufacture of balls and ball bearings, but the finishing of same depends more or less on the ability of the skilled workmen, and these skilled workmen demand good wages. We have mentioned the wages paid to workmen several times, for this reason: We wish to show that it is not so much the price of raw material as the amount of money paid in wages that makes the cost in the production of steel balls, brass balls, ball bearings, and roller bearings. If it is possible to hire two or three men in European countries for the cost of one man in the United States, naturally there would be no room for the American manufacturer should the tariff be reduced.

Prices of balls and ball bearings have been forced downward now by foreign competition.

The small cost per ball or bearing that goes into the average machine is so slight that it does not take many cents to equip a sewing machine, a bicycle, or a roller skate with ball bearings throughout, so that there can not possibly be any hardship to the general public by allowing the present tariff on balls and ball bearings to remain as it is, or rather increase same, so that American industries can be better protected.

The ball-bearing industry is comparatively young, and in our judgment should be fostered, because it is only by taking care of anything that results can be obtained. This argument can be applied to anything under the sun, whether it be something of natural or mechanical growth. If a seed is planted, care is given to produce the best results, and results show that care has been taken. So it is with any new industry; care must be taken to produce a natural, healthy growth. It is rather discouraging to call on a customer and offer an article that has had good honest work placed on same, and good money paid for the making, and to be calmly told that the same article can be brought over from Germany for a lower price. The writer has had this actual experience, and we do not think that it is because that any other country has better men or better machinery, but simply that labor can be bought cheaper. It is not as if the present price of balls and ball bearings were prohibitive, because we have endeavored to show that to equip a sewing machine or similar article costs but a few cents. It is the fact of these bearings being so cheap that makers of sewing machines, etc., have adopted the ball bearing, thereby making very easy-running machines and conferring a boon on humanity in general. We are often told that surely the laborer is worthy of his hire, and surely the manufacturer should be protected for the expenditure of his energy and brains when his life is devoted to producing something that will prevent friction.

Respectfully submitted.

EXCELSIOR STEEL BALL CO.,
DAVID ROUGHEAD, *Manager.*

THE TIMKEN ROLLER BEARING AXLE COMPANY, OF CANTON, OHIO, ASKS AN INCREASE OF TWENTY PER CENT DUTY ON ANTIFRICTION BALL FORGINGS.

CANTON, OHIO, *December 2, 1908.*

COMMITTEE ON WAYS AND MEANS,
House of Representatives, Washington, D. C.

GENTLEMEN: The Timken Roller Bearing Axle Company, engaged in the manufacture of roller bearings and axles, respectfully calls the attention of your committee to the proposed revision of the tariff upon articles of its manufacture.

It is our understanding that paragraph 127, covering " antifriction ball forgings," upon which a duty of " 45 per cent ad valorem " is fixed, includes our product.

There are at the present time a number of factories in this country devoted exclusively or to a large extent to the manufacture of antifriction bearings, including ball and roller bearings, as well as the manufacture of steel balls. This industry is comparatively new, having been carried on to any extent only during the past five or six years. The early growth of this industry was very slow, but owing to the large number of automobiles manufactured within the past few years the business of manufacturing roller bearings has considerably increased.

The foreign makers of roller bearings have been engaged in this business for a much longer time than American manufacturers, and but for the protection of this industry afforded by the Dingley bill this industry would not now be in existence, as it would not have been possible to compete with the foreign manufacturer.

By far the greater portion of the expense of manufacturing roller bearings is in the cost of the labor, a very small proportion of the entire cost being represented by the raw material going into this product.

It is the labor put upon the raw material that almost entirely fixes the final cost of producing roller bearings. There is not a great difference in the price paid for the raw material by the foreign manufacturer from the cost of the same article to our manufacturers, there being a slight advantage in favor of the foreign maker.

The writer during the past summer of 1908 visited a number of plants in France, England, and other foreign countries where roller bearings, steel balls, and various parts connected with antifriction devices are manufactured and personally investigated the cost of the production of these articles in the foreign factories. It was at once apparent that the wide difference in the cost of production in favor of the foreign maker was owing to the fact that he paid his labor only a small per cent of the amount that our manufacturers pay for similar work in this country. In one factory employing about 2,000 hands the writer found skilled labor working on machines at an average price of $3.75 per week. On these same machines and for the same work we pay our employees an average of $15 per week.

It can therefore be readily understood that the 45 per cent duty does not nearly compensate for the difference in the wages paid by the American manufacturer to his employees, considering the price of the same labor to the foreign manufacturer. To afford American workmen an opportunity to continue to earn fair wages in this industry there should be an increase rather than a reduction in the tariff.

The American manufacturer of this product already feels keenly the competition arising from the importation into this country of similar foreign goods produced by underpaid labor.

The freight rates on this class of goods from Europe to points in this country are but a trifle in excess of the freight rates from the local manufacturers of antifriction bearings to the users thereof; hence the foreign manufacturer is at little disadvantage in this respect. Our factory has already felt the effect of foreign competition to the disadvantage of our workmen. About two months ago we were approached by one of the largest manufacturers of automobile parts in this country. For more than two years we have been supplying this concern with our roller bearings. This manufacturer advised us that it would be necessary to reduce the price of our bearings to meet lower figures at which the Hess-Bright roller bearings made in Germany were being offered. The Hess-Bright roller bearings being well adapted to the use of the manufacturer, it was necessary for us to meet the price of the German maker or lose the entire business. In order to keep our men employed we thought it best to make a contract at the price fixed by the German maker, although in order to meet this price and not sustain a loss it was necessary for us to c in a measure the wages of our workmen engaged in filling this order.

We know from actual experience that if a reduction in the tariff on roller bearings is made the result will be the destruction of the industry in this country. We have invested about $1,000,000 in the business and have been giving constant employment to about 500 men. A large portion of our investment is represented by special machinery adapted to the peculiar needs of manufacturing roller bearings. This machinery is suitable for no other purpose, and if we are forced to abandon this industry by reason of the loss of adequate protection, the greater part of our investment will be an absolute loss and our force of workmen must seek other means of earning a livelihood.

Our roller bearings are used exclusively on automobiles. An automobile can be built without antifriction bearings, but the purchaser of an automobile is usually a man who can afford to indulge in at least moderate luxuries, and therefore desires antifriction bearings upon his machine since they require less attention and have many advantages. An automobile is strictly a luxury—not a necessity in any sense of the word—since other much less expensive means of transportation have in the past and will in the future meet all the requirements of the great mass of the people.

tariff upon roller bearings would not materially change the cost of automobiles. The foreign-made bearings answer the purpose, and if their price is lower, will be purchased in preference to American bearings by manufacturers having need of such supplies.

The maintenance of at least the present tariff upon roller bearings is not subject to the criticism that the price of an article in common use among the people is thereby maintained above what it should be. These bearings are purchased and used in connection with automobiles by those who can best afford to pay a fair price therefor. The vital question is not whether the manufacturer of roller bearings is permitted longer to carry on this industry so far as his personal advantage is concerned, but rather whether American labor shall be permitted to manufacture roller bearings used in our automobile works rather than by injudicious legislation surrender this new industry to our foreign competitors.

We earnestly insist that in place of a reduction of the tariff upon roller bearings there should be an increase in order that the return therefrom should be sufficient to afford fair remuneration to our workmen employed in this industry.

Feeling the need of a broader market, we have recently concluded an arrangement to manufacture our roller bearings in England, as we had no hope of creating a foreign market for our goods made in this country, due solely to the fact that the existing rate of wages in this country is far in excess of that in England.

The cost of the raw material for our bearings in England is but little less than we pay here, however, owing to the fact that our cost of labor will be so much less in England than in this country we will be enabled from that point to compete with the foreign maker in his own legitimate territory. This situation demonstrates the fact that it is the price of labor that alone renders it impossible for the American manufacturer to compete with others engaged in a like industry in Europe.

We believe that in order to safely maintain the wages that have been paid in the past to employees engaged in this industry there should be an increase of the tariff rate of at least 20 per cent.

We earnestly urge that the above increase be granted, not alone for ourselves, but for our workmen, upon whom eventually must fall the burden of invited foreign competition.

Respectfully, yours,

THE TIMKEN ROLLER BEARING AXLE COMPANY.
W. R. TIMKEN, *Secretary.*

THE STANDARD ROLLER BEARING COMPANY, OF PHILADELPHIA, PA., FURNISHES LIST OF IMPORTERS OF FOREIGN BALL BEARINGS AND STEEL BALLS.

PHILADELPHIA, PA., *December 4, 1908.*

W. K. PAYNE,
    Clerk Ways and Means Committee,
        Washington, D. C.

DEAR SIR: Replying to your letter of the 3d, I inclose herewith a list of the importers of foreign ball bearings, importers of steel balls, automobile manufacturers using annular ball bearings, manufacturer================================ings, and users of steel balls.

The total amount of bearings used by the concerns mentioned is easy to ascertain, and I have positive knowledge that many orders ranging from $50,000 to $150,000 each have been placed during 1907 for the foreign make of bearings.

If you will kindly let me know what other information you desire me to supply to you, I shall be glad to do it. You, of course, understand that it is impossible for me to give you accurate data as to the exact number of bearings purchased by the different concerns, or the exact amount of the purchase. I can, however, supply a list showing the number of automobiles manufactured by the majority of the concerns mentioned, together with the number of bearings which they use on a car, but I think that you would prefer to secure this information from some other sources, so as to have it absolutely accurate.

There are a large number of concerns that have purchased a larger amount in value of foreign ball bearings in one year than the total imports, amounting to $47,000, which was reported as being the full amount shown in the records of the Treasury Department.

In the package of bearings which I left with you, you will find one bearing consisting of two rings with balls between them, which constitutes an annular ball bearing, and which is similar to the bearing shown on the page of our catalogue which we herewith inclose.

This type of bearing could be imported so that the balls would be classified under their proper heading, while the rings, constituting the races and cones, might be imported as steel and duty paid upon them at that rate. If this is the case, it is entirely wrong, as the greater portion of the value of the bearing is in the rings, the balls representing perhaps 10 per cent of the cost of the completed bearing.

If any further information is desired, I shall be pleased to furnish it to you.

Yours, very truly,   S. S. EVELAND, *President.*

Users of foreign annular ball bearings.

Holley Brothers Company, Detroit, Mich.; McCarthy Brothers & Ford, Buffalo, N. Y.; New Process Raw Hide Company, Syracuse, N. Y.; Long Arm System Company, Cleveland, Ohio; A. O. Smith Company, Milwaukee, Wis.; Brown & Lipe Company, Syracuse, N. Y.; Warner Gear Company, Muncie, Ind.; Westinghouse Electric and Manufacturing Company, Pittsburg, Pa.; General Electric Company, Schenectady, N. Y.; General Electric Company, West Lynn, Mass.; Western Electric Company, Chicago, Ill.; Heinze Electric Company, Lowell, Mass.; Continental Motor Manufacturing Company, Muskegon, Mich.; Albert Champion Company, Boston, Mass.; Jeffrey Manufacturing Company, Columbus, Ohio; Lincoln Electric Company, Cleveland, Ohio; J. H. Lehman & Co., New York, N. Y.

Users of foreign steel balls.

The White Company, Cleveland, Ohio; American Ball Bearing Company, Cleveland, Ohio; Stanley Motor Carriage Company, Newton, Mass.; Illinois Sewing Machine Company, Rockford, Ill.; National Sewing Machine Company, Belvidere, Ill.; Sharpless Cream Separator Company, West Chester, Pa.; Chicago Roller Skate Company, Chicago, Ill.; Buick Automobile Company, Flint, Mich.; Olds

Motor Works, Lansing, Mich.; Garford Company, Elyria, Ohio; S. P. Townsend & Co., Orange, N. J.; Sheldon Axle Company, Wilkes-Barre, Pa.

Automobile manufacturers using foreign annular ball bearings.

Acme Motor Car Company, Reading Pa.; Allen-Kingston Motor Car Company, Kingston, N. Y.; American Locomobile Company, Providence, R. I.; American Motor Car Company, Indianapolis, Ind.; Austin Automobile Company, Grand Rapids, Mich.; Belden Motor Car Company, Pittsburg, Pa.; Cadillac Motor Car Company, Detroit, Mich.; Cameron Car Company, Beverly, Mass.; Chadwick Engineering Works, Pottstown, Pa.; Chalmers-Detroit Motor Company, Detroit, Mich.; Cleveland Motor Car Company, New York, N. Y.; Colburn Automobile Company, Denver, Colo.; Columbus Buggy Company, Columbus, Ohio; Corbin Motor Vehicle Corporation, New Britain, Conn.; Daimler Manufacturing Company, Long Island City, N. Y.; Dayton Motor Car Company, Dayton, Ohio; De Luke Motor Car Company, Detroit, Mich.; Electric Vehicle Company, Hartford, Conn.; Elmore Manufacturing Company, Clyde, Ohio; H. H. Franklin Manufacturing Company, Syracuse, N. Y.; Garford Company, Elyria, Ohio; Knox Automobile Company, Springfield, Mass.; Locomobile Company of America, Bridgeport, Conn.; Lorraine Automobile Manufacturing Company, Chicago, Ill.; Lozier Motor Company, New York, N. Y.; Nordyke & Marmon Company, Indianapolis, Ind.; Matheson Motor Car Company, Wilkes-Barre, Pa.; Mitchell Motor Car Company, Racine, Wis.; Mora Motor Car Company, Newark, N. Y.; National Motor Vehicle Company, Indianapolis, Ind.; Olds Motor Works, Lansing, Mich.; Packard Motor Car Company, Detroit, Mich.; Peerless Motor Car Company, Cleveland, Ohio; George N. Pierce Company, Buffalo, N. Y.; Pope Motor Car Company, Toledo, Ohio; Premier Motor Manufacturing Company, Indianapolis, Ind.; York Motor Car Company, York, Pa.; Pungs-Finch Automobile and Gas Engine Company, Detroit, Mich.; Rainier Company, Saginaw, Mich.; Royal Motor Car Company, Cleveland, Ohio; Simplex Automobile Company, New York, N. Y.; F. B. Stearns Company, Cleveland, Ohio; Stevens-Duryea Company, Chicopee Falls, Mass.; Stilson Motor Car Company, Pittsfield, Mass.; Studebaker Automobile Company, Cleveland, Ohio; E. R. Thomas Motor Company, Buffalo, N. Y.; Walter Automobile Company, Trenton, N. J.; Winton Motor Carriage Company, Cleveland, Ohio; Woods Motor Vehicle Company, Chicago, Ill.; Anderson Carriage Company, Detroit, Mich.; Babcock Electric Carriage Company, Buffalo, N. Y.; Baker Motor Vehicle Company, Cleveland, Ohio; Waverly Company, Indianapolis, Ind.; Rauch & Lang Carriage Company, Cleveland, Ohio; Mack Brothers Motor Car Company, Allentown, Pa.; Elwell Parker Electric Company, Cleveland, Ohio.

Importers of foreign ball bearings.

Hess-Bright Manufacturing Company, 2101 Fairmount avenue, Philadelphia, Pa.; J. S. Bretz Company, 410 Times Building, New York, N. Y.; Lavalette & Co., 112 West Forty-second street, New York, N. Y.; Barthel & Daly, 42 Broadway, New York, N. Y.; R. I. V. Company, 1771 Broadway, New York, N. Y.

Importers of steel balls.

Herman Boker & Co., New York, N. Y.; J. S. Bretz & Co., New York, N. Y.; Brandenburg Brothers Company, Chicago, Ill.

———

THE PACKARD MOTOR CAR COMPANY, DETROIT, MICH., ADVOCATES RETENTION OF THE PRESENT DUTY ON ANTIFRICTION BALL BEARINGS.

DETROIT, MICH., *December 19, 1908.*

Hon. SERENO E. PAYNE,
  Chairman Ways and Means Committee,
    Washington, D. C.

DEAR SIR: Relative to duty on ball bearings, I would like to register with the Ways and Means Committee the attitude of this company toward the duty on ball bearings. This company favors the retention of the existing duty, namely, 45 per cent, on ball bearings.

We are now large importers of ball bearings, importing over $100,000 worth from Germany and other European countries each year, on which we pay 45 per cent duty. We do this because there are no ball bearings made in America of the same quality and durability as those which we import. We feel that with the existing tariff the American ball-bearing manufacturers may learn to make better bearings, as good as those in Germany, in the course of time. In this event the American competition would naturally reduce the price. American ball-bearing manufacturers have not yet gotten to a competitive basis. They have all been so busy supplying a new trade that it was more of a question to get the stuff out than it was as to price or quality, but the whole situation is rapidly shaking itself down to a competitive basis.

Yours, very truly,

PACKARD MOTOR CAR CO.,
HENRY J. B. JOY, *President.*

———

STEEL HOOPS, BANDS, AND COTTON TIES.

[Paragraph 128.]

WALLACE H. ROWE, OF PITTSBURG, PA., PROTESTS AGAINST REDUCTION OF DUTIES ON THESE ARTICLES.

PITTSBURG, *December 3, 1908.*

Hon. SERENO E. PAYNE,
  Chairman Ways and Means Committee.

DEAR SIR: As a manufacturer of steel hoops, steel bands, and steel cotton ties, and the authorized representative of other manufacturers of this class of product, I beg to submit to you the following suggestions as to tariff on these commodities:

Our average wages per day for years 1906, 1907, and 1908 were as follows:

	1906.	1907.	1908.
Heaters	$4.85	$4.88	$4.93
Rolling-mill hands	2.99	2.99	3.06
Mechanics	2.82	2.78	2.79
Laborers	1.99	1.99	1.99

Average wages for same work in Germany and Belgium:

Heaters	$1.65–$1.88
Rolling-mill hands	1.88– 2.35
Mechanics	1.16– 1.43
Laborers	.75– .83

The ocean freight from seaports of Germany and Belgium to our Atlantic Ocean and Gulf ports is less than the railroad freight from steel manufacturing centers to the same destinations. Hence, these advantages of the foreign manufacturer can be met, if the tariff is removed, only by such reduction of wages as will enable us to meet that competition at the Atlantic seaboard. Of course, as you recede from the Atlantic seaboard these factors change in our favor, because the railroad freight rates diminish relatively on our products and increase on the foreign products.

It is therefore evident that if the tariff is taken off steel hoops, steel bands, and steel cotton ties, we must reduce or surrender the Atlantic coast and Gulf trade to the foreigners. This will include substantially the entire cotton-tie trade, because all of the cotton is baled at Atlantic and Gulf ports or near-by points. Furthermore, the producers of cotton realize a profit instead of being at an expense in the use of cotton ties in the baling of cotton, for the reason that all cotton is sold at the total gross weight as shown per bale. This includes bagging and ties.

Even at the present tariff of five-tenths of a cent per pound, the imports of cotton ties have been as follows:

For year ending June 30:

	Bundles.
1902	95,760
1903	54,990
1904	46,860
1905	11,449
1906	108,305
1907	15,929

From this it seems that we are now on or near to the point of foreign invasion of steel cotton ties. Hoops are similar products, manufactured of the same materials and in the same mills as cotton ties.

If a reduction is made in the present protective tariff, wages must be reduced proportionately or the trade surrendered. I would consider any reduction of the present tariff as compelling a surrender to the foreign manufacturers of our steel hoop trade in New England and Atlantic seaboard, and of our steel cotton tie market in substantially the entire cotton belt.

Respectfully submitted.

WALLACE H. ROWE.

COTTON TIES AND JUTE BAGGING.

[Paragraphs 129 and 344.]

HON. BOURKE COCKRAN, M. C., SUBMITS MEMORIAL OF THE NEW ORLEANS COTTON EXCHANGE.

NEW ORLEANS, LA., *November 9, 1908.*

Whereas the Ways and Means Committee of the House of Representatives will meet in the near future to hear argument in relation to tariff amendments; and

Whereas the present tariff on jute bagging used for baling cotton and on steel cotton ties amounts to 9 cents or more per bale; and

Whereas this tax is a direct burden on the cotton-raising industry of the South for the benefit of a few manufacturers who are thus enabled to thrive at the expense of the most important class of agriculturists in this country: Therefore be it

Resolved, That the New Orleans Cotton Exchange earnestly urges that all bagging and ties used in the baling of cotton be put on the free list.

Resolved, That our Senators and Representatives in Congress from Louisiana and those from the other cotton States be earnestly urged to present this matter before the Committee on Ways and Means, or any other congressional committee before which it may be considered, in such light as will prove the justice of our request and the urgency for all proper relief in the premises.

A true copy.

H. G. HESTER,
Secretary.

———

THE NATIONAL COTTON ASSOCIATION, ATLANTA, GA., URGES THE SPEEDY REPEAL OF THE PRESENT DUTIES ON COTTON TIES AND JUTE BAGGING FOR COTTON.

ATLANTA, GA., *December 8, 1908.*

COMMITTEE ON WAYS AND MEANS,
Washington, D. C.

GENTLEMEN: As an official representative of the cotton-growing interests of the South I desire to file with your committee an urgent appeal for a speedy repeal by the Federal Government of the present duty on imported iron cotton ties and imported jute bagging used as a covering for cotton. It is quite evident that the American manufacturers of these two articles do not now require the present protective tariff levied as an import duty on these commodities. It should be borne in mind that the purchase of bagging and ties by the cotton growers of the South is a distinct and definite loss to them, as their customers, the spinners, both in this country and Europe, only pay for the actual weight of the lint cotton, tare being always deducted in the price of the original purchase from the growers. This being true, it should be the duty of the Federal Government to see that this very large class of its citizens should be protected against the unnecessary expenditures of their earnings for articles which are protected from outside competition by high and useless import duties.

The large American corporations which are at present engaged in the manufacture of these articles no longer need or require a protective tariff except for the purpose of annually increasing the net earnings or dividends on the capital invested in their plants and to prohibit competition. The very high duty of 22 cents per bundle on cotton ties has practically prohibited their importation. Under the present duty on jute bagging only about 15 per cent of jute bagging is imported annually, notwithstanding that raw jute is entirely grown abroad, and, furthermore, the western farmers get their binding twine duty free. The only real service of the present tariff on cotton ties and jute bagging is to enable a few large corporations in this country to stifle competition and force the growers of American cotton to pay abnormally and unnecessarily high prices to secure these articles.

I beg to call your special attention to this matter and hope to secure your favorable consideration of the appeal hereby entered.

Yours, respectfully,

HARVIE JORDAN,
President National Cotton Association.

HON. JOHN S. WILLIAMS, M. C., WRITES IN ADVOCACY OF THE PLACING OF COTTON TIES AND JUTE BAGGING FOR COVERING COTTON ON THE FREE LIST.

YAZOO CITY, MISS., *November 13, 1908.*

Hon. SERENO E. PAYNE,
    Chairman Ways and Means Committee,
        House of Representatives, Washington, D. C.

MY DEAR SIR: I received some time ago, from your clerk, a circular card saying that the committee was open to hearings from me and other people. In addition to that the card made a requirement that the person asking to be heard give his name, permanent address, temporary address in Washington, and the names of those whom he represents. One part of it I ought to respond to in making the request that I now do. I represent every cotton farmer and laborer, as well as every cotton broker and factor, in the country.

I urge upon the committee the desirability of putting jute bagging and cotton ties upon the free list. Cotton is about the only agricultural product in the United States being produced this year for less than the cost of production, except for skillful farmers. The producers of 12,000,000 or 13,000,000 bales of cotton ought no longer to be burdened with the tax on bagging and ties. If they were situated in the North or the West or the East, I am sure that they would not be burdened with it. I hope it is not necessary for me to appear before the committee and be sworn in order to express this opinion or to have it communicated to the committee.

Very truly, yours,

JOHN SHARP WILLIAMS.

SAWS AND SAW PLATES.

[Paragraphs 128, 135, 141, and 168.]

THE SIMONDS MANUFACTURING COMPANY, FITCHBURG, MASS., MAKERS OF SAWS, RECOMMENDS NEW CLASSIFICATION.

FITCHBURG, MASS., *December 2, 1908.*

Hon. SERENO E. PAYNE,
    Chairman Committee on Ways and Means,
        House of Representatives, Washington, D. C.

DEAR SIR: In the matter of the revision of the Dingley tariff we beg to submit for the consideration of your honorable committee the recommendation that the clause in paragraph 128 which reads "Steel bands or strips untempered, suitable for making band saws, three cents per pound and twenty per centum ad valorem; if tempered or tempered and polished, six cents per pound and twenty per centum ad valorem," should be stricken out, and that in paragraph 135 should be inserted after the clause, "Saw plates, wholly or partially manufactured," the following: "Steel bands or strips untempered, suitable for making band saws;" and that at the end of the paragraph there should be added: "*Provided,* That on steel bands or strips, tempered, or tempered and polished, suitable for making band saws, there shall be paid thirty per centum ad valorem in addition to the rate provided in this act for steel bands or strips untempered, suitable for making band saws."

Paragraph 141. That the clause which reads "and on steel circular saw plates there shall be paid one-half of one cent per pound in addition to the rate provided in this act for steel saw plates" should be stricken out.

The effect of the changes desired would be to make the duties on "steel bands or strips, untempered, suitable for making band saws," and on "steel circular-saw plates" the same as on "saw plates, wholly or partially manufactured," and to preserve approximately the same increase in duty on "steel bands or strips, tempered, or tempered and polished," compared with "steel bands or strips, untempered," as exists in the present tariff.

Our reasons for asking these changes:

First. All crucible steel for whatever form or bars or plates is first produced in the form of ingots and afterwards rolled down to the form and thickness and sheared to the shape adapted to its ultimate use. Steel bands or strips, untempered, suitable for making band saws, steel circular-saw plates, or saw plates may be made from ingots of different money values per pound, but the selling price is regulated by the value of the ingots used plus the labor of rolling and shearing, and the losses due to shearing to specified shapes. Therefore, if the ingot values, labor, or shearing losses in any one of the steel products referred to are more than in others, the result would naturally be that they would be invoiced at a higher price per pound, and thus be required to pay a higher rate of duty, and it seems a decided injustice to place the tariff on steel bands or strips, untempered, suitable for making band saws, and on circular-saw plates of a given value per pound, on a higher plane than the duty on other saw plates of the same value per pound.

Second. It appears from the government statistics of imports of steel bands or strips, untempered, suitable for making band saws, and steel circular-saw plates, and from figures which we have made up covering our purchases of these same articles imported for us, that we consume a majority of the total imports coming under these two headings.

We beg to state in this connection that the printed statistics of imports of steel bands or strips, untempered, suitable for making band saws, for the fiscal years ended June 30, 1903 to 1907, inclusive, are apparently incorrect, for during each of those five years we purchased more imported steel coming under this heading than is shown in the statistics as having been imported. So far as we have knowledge, the statistics of imports for this item for the fiscal year ended June 30, 1908, appear correct, and it is on this last year's figures that we base the statement earlier in this paragraph.

Would further state that we do not import in our own name, but buy from the United States agents of the foreign mills.

Third. The extra duties now levied on these two articles make it necessary for the consumer of saws made from these plates to pay a higher price in order that they can have goods of the quality required for their work.

Fourth. We are forced to buy certain steel plates from foreign producers, as we are unable to obtain from mills in this country such plates and bands of the high quality and continuous uniformity that we require.

Fifth. We are in a neutral position as to any revision of the existing specific duties on saw plates and other steels as now in effect under paragraph 135, and only ask for the changes above outlined in order that the present discriminating duties on steel bands or strips untempered, suitable for making band saws and steel circular saw plates, may be eliminated.

We commend the above to your favorable consideration, and if there is further information that we can furnish we trust you will so advise us.

Very respectfully, yours,

SIMONDS MANUFACTURING CO.,
DANIEL SIMONDS, *President.*

HENRY DISSTON & SONS, PHILADELPHIA, URGE RETENTION OF PRESENT RATES FOR SAWS AND SAW PLATES.

PHILADELPHIA, *December 5, 1908.*

Hon. SERENO E. PAYNE,
    Chairman Committee on Ways and Means,
      House of Representatives, Washington, D. C.

DEAR SIR: We desire to enter with your committee our earnest request that no changes be made in Schedule C, metals and manufactures, particularly with reference to paragraph 128, steel bands for band saws; paragraph 135, saw plates; paragraph 141, circular saw plates; and paragraph 168, saws.

The tariff with reference to these particular items has enabled us to build up a large and important business in this country, by which we are enabled to give employment to about 4,000 persons. Our work people are making good wages, living contentedly and peaceably, and, as evidence of this, we have been free from the disturbing influence and effect of strikes. The tariff protection which is furnished by the paragraphs above referred to is particularly beneficial to the working people, protecting them and enabling us to pay them the wages which they receive.

We do not know that any request has been made or any movement will be started to affect these particular items. If so, we would crave the liberty of being heard in defense and justification thereof.

Yours, respectfully,

HENRY DISSTON & SONS (INCORPORATED),
WM. MILLER, *Secretary.*

E. C. ATKINS & CO., OF INDIANAPOLIS, IND., ASKS THAT THE PRESENT DUTIES ON SAWS BE RETAINED.

INDIANAPOLIS, IND., *November 24, 1908.*

Hon. SERENO E. PAYNE,
Chairman Ways and Means Committee,
Washington, D. C.

MY DEAR SIR: Knowing that the hearings before your committee on tariff revision will reach Schedule C, Metals and the manufactures thereof, on November 25, we take this opportunity of writing you in reference to tariff matters concerning the manufacture and sale of saws of all kinds.

We know full well that your committee is exceedingly busy and pressed for time in this matter, and we do not ask to be heard in person unless it is the desire of your committee to be enlightened as to the general conditions concerning the manufacture and sale of saws. We want to merely say in connection with the tariff proposition as it affects our own business that:

In the first place, English manufacturers are to-day underselling us in export markets, and they will continue to do so, owing to the large difference in the cost of manufacture abroad and in our own country. If the tariff should be revised in our business the foreign manufacturer would then enter our own market, and between the two evils—namely, our inability to compete with them in foreign markets, on the one hand, and their ability to compete with us in our own market, on the other hand—we would much prefer the present state of affairs.

In the second place, there are large saw manufacturers in Canada, and the duty on our goods into Canada is 30 per cent ad valorem on the whole line. If the tariff should be changed, it would allow Canadian manufacturers to come into our markets and undersell us right away. This we would not consider advisable. Such a condition of affairs would mean material reduction in cost of manufacture, which would mean reduction in wages and the earning power of our workingmen.

In the third place, Sweden is now sending in crosscut saws notwithstanding our duty of 6 cents per foot, proving beyond question that our duty on saws is not prohibitive as it now stands.

In the fourth place, we want to call your attention to the difference in the cost of labor here and abroad as it applies to our own business. Saw smiths are earning to-day in the United States from 40 to 50 cents an hour, abroad from 20 to 25 cents, other labor in proportion.

We also want to say that a comparison between the Dingley tariff and the Wilson tariff shows no change in the charges on products of our factory. The Wilson tariff was supposed to be a tariff for revenue and not, in the strictest sense of the word, a protective tariff, and in no respect is the tariff on saws prohibitive.

We do not care to take your time or that of the committee to enlarge upon this subject further than is absolutely necessary, but if there is any disposition to change the tariff in any way, we should want to have an opportunity to be heard before such changes are made.

Very truly, yours,

E. C. ATKINS & Co.,
H. C. ATKINS, *President.*

STEEL RAILS.

[Paragraph 130.]

STATEMENT OF E. C. FELTON, OF HAVERFORD, PA., REPRESENTNG THE STEEL RAIL MANUFACTURERS OF THE UNITED STATES.

WEDNESDAY, *November 25, 1908.*

Mr. FELTON. Mr. Chairman and gentlemen, I was asked to come here in behalf of the steel-rail manufacturers of the United States, to state to the committee that in their opinion the present rates in the Dingley tariff are fair rates and that if any considerable reduction in those rates were made it would be a very considerable hardship to the American manufacturers and would necessitate a saving in our costs by reducing our labor, which is about the only element of cost which we can now change. I might say——

Mr. GRIGGS. Are you a manufacturer?

Mr. FELTON. Yes, sir; I am president of the Pennsylvania Steel Company. I represent that company directly, which has works in central Pennsylvania and also on the Chesapeake Bay, near Baltimore. We are the only large producer of steel located on tide water. Therefore any change in the rates on steel rails and other steel products would affect us to a greater extent than it would any other manufacturer of steel in the United States. Now, I might take up half an hour, but I do not think I could state what I came here to say any more elaborately than that. We feel that the present duty is a proper duty, and we wish to ask that the committee allow the duty on steel rails to remain where it is to-day.

The CHAIRMAN. Is that all?

Mr. FELTON. Yes, sir; that is all we have to say.

The CHAIRMAN. This committee will want a good deal more information than that on this question.

Mr. FELTON. Well, I am here to give it to you, and I will give you detailed information as well as I can.

The CHAIRMAN. In 1907 we exported nearly $8,500,000 worth of steel rails, and we imported $133,000 worth. Nearly all of this came from Germany. We are exporting steel rails all the time.   Mr. Carnegie, in the article which I quoted, says you can make them cheaper here than they can be made anywhere else in the world. Now, we want a very full statement of every element of the cost of steel rails abroad, all stages of it; and every element of the cost in this country.

Mr. FELTON. If you will tell me how I can get a statement of the cost abroad, I would like to have it. It is impossible to get such a statement. As for the cost in this country——

The CHAIRMAN. If you can not get it, we shall get part of it.

Mr. FELTON. I hope you can, and I want to assure you that any information we can give, we are ready to give.

The CHAIRMAN. You can give a very full and complete statement of the cost here.

Mr. FELTON. We can give you an absolute statement of the cost here. I do not know whether the committee know it, but the agents of the Bureau of Commerce and Labor have spent more than a year and a half in going over our books. They have our detailed costs for 1902, 1903, 1904, 1905, and 1906—five years. They have those costs under a pledge of secrecy.

The CHAIRMAN. We want that reduced to the cost per ton of steel rails—the hours of labor, the cost of labor of different kinds, and all that sort of thing. We want to get the cost per ton of the labor and of the materials. Does you firm export any rails?

Mr. FELTON. We have exported rails; yes.

The CHAIRMAN. In 1907 did you export rails?

Mr. FELTON. In 1907 we did; yes, sir.

The CHAIRMAN. Did you export rails at a profit when you exported them?

Mr. FELTON. We exported rails at a profit in 1907, but not in some of the years previous.

The CHAIRMAN. When you exported rails abroad, did you have to pay a duty in the foreign country?

Mr. FELTON. We have not exported rails into any country which levies a duty on steel rails except, possibly, Mexico.

The CHAIRMAN. What countries did you export to?

Mr. FELTON. We have exported to Argentina and to Cuba. There is a duty in Cuba. We have exported to Mexico, and we previously exported to Siberia. We furnished a very large order to the Russian Government for laying the Trans-Siberian Railway. We have exported rails to Japan and to British India.

The CHAIRMAN. Did you export any to Canada?

Mr. FELTON. Not within recent years; no, sir.

The CHAIRMAN. How long ago did you export any to Canada?

Mr. FELTON. We have not exported any since the tariff regulations went in force in Canada.

The CHAIRMAN. Their tariff regulations are the same as ours, are they not?

Mr. FELTON. No; I do not know just what the Canadian tariff is, because we have not been interested in sending anything in there. We were absolutely shut out by the duty.

The CHAIRMAN. As to these rails that you exported, of course you came into direct competition with Germany, England, etc.?

Mr. FELTON. Yes, sir.

The CHAIRMAN. And you were able to meet them and sell the rails, and sell them at a profit?

Mr. FELTON. I did not say that we always sold them at a profit.

The CHAIRMAN. You did in 1907 sell at a profit?

Mr. FELTON. Yes, sir.

The CHAIRMAN. And in 1907 you met the same competition. What prices did you get for them in this country in 1907?

Mr. FELTON. If you will just let me take a little time——

The CHAIRMAN. In 1907 was it not about $28 a ton?

Mr. FELTON. No, sir; not exactly.

The CHAIRMAN. In this country?

Mr. FELTON. In 1907, for the rails which we sold in this country, we obtained $28.08. For the rails which we sold in foreign countries we obtained $27.52.

The CHAIRMAN. Where did you deliver them?

Mr. FELTON. Well, I can obtain that for you, but I can not carry all these things in my mind.

The CHAIRMAN. I say, did you deliver them in New York at that price, or where?

Mr. FELTON. That was our price f. o. b. at the works at Sparrows Point, on the Chesapeake Bay.

The CHAIRMAN. In both cases?

Mr. FELTON. In both cases; yes, sir.

The CHAIRMAN. That was the average price in 1907?

Mr. FELTON. That was the average price obtained by us in 1907 on foreign and domestic rails; yes, sir.

The CHAIRMAN. At that price you were able to meet the competition in the Argentine Republic, and these other countries, of Germany and Great Britain?

Mr. FELTON. You must remember that 1905, 1906, and 1907, but especially 1907, were years when the foreign rail mills were exceedingly busy supplying their own home markets. Therefore the price of rails naturally in their home markets was high, and the price of rails in the foreign markets in which we met them was exceedingly high. That is the reason we were able to obtain that price.

The CHAIRMAN. During the rest of that time how did the price in the foreign market compare with yours—during those years when that situation did not exist?

Mr. FELTON. The price in the foreign producing countries was in every case, I think, higher than our price here. That is, the average price in England was over $28 a ton and the average price in Germany was up to $31 and $32 a ton.

The CHAIRMAN. For what period?

Mr. FELTON. For what period? 1907.

The CHAIRMAN. I was speaking of those two or three years prior to that, when you did not export any.

Mr. FELTON. Oh, we have exported in every year since back in the nineties.

Mr. DALZELL. For the last eighteen years?

Mr. FELTON. Yes, sir.

Mr. DALZELL. You have exported every year since 1890?

Mr. FELTON. There was only one year—1903—when we did not export.

The CHAIRMAN. During those years has the market abroad been lower than your price?

Mr. FELTON. I did not catch that.

The CHAIRMAN. During any of those years has the market price abroad been lower than your price?

Mr. FELTON. The market price in the countries to which we exported has been lower than our price; yes.

The CHAIRMAN. When was it?

Mr. FELTON. In 1899 it was about $1.60 lower. In 1900—and, mind you, these are our average prices; I do not know that these would cover the prices in all countries, but these were the prices we obtained——

Mr. GAINES. What does he say?

The CHAIRMAN. He says the price of steel rails was lower in the countries to which he exported them in 1899 by one dollar and some cents than here.

Mr. FELTON. Yes. In 1900 there was a difference of $3.70. In 1901 there was a difference of $3.40. In 1902 there was a difference of $5.55. In 1903 we did not export any. In 1904 we only exported one order, where we got badly fooled by the wily Turk. We exported some rails to the Hejaz Railway. In that year the price was about $9 less than it was in this country. But that was an accident and a piece of bad management on the part of our agent in Constantinople.

The CHAIRMAN. That was not the regular price abroad, then?

Mr. FELTON. No. That was the price of those particular rails, when we got up against some exceedingly hard German competition, and when our agent there took a contract not knowing the exact terms under which it was to be filled.

The CHAIRMAN. Go on with your statement, then.

Mr. FELTON. It was not a large order. In 1905 the price was $6.80, or something like that.

Mr. COCKRAN. The difference, you mean?

Mr. FELTON. The difference; yes, sir. In 1906 the price was $4.50; and in 1907 (which, as I say, was an exceptional year when the foreign mills were occupied with the demands of their own countries), the price rose in neutral markets so that we were able to obtain there $27—let me see. We were able to obtain there within 50 cents of the home price.

The CHAIRMAN. I wish you would put that statement in the record, the whole statement. In each case, I understand you, the foreign price was lower than the price here?

Mr. FELTON. In each case the foreign price was lower than the price in this country; yes, sir.

The CHAIRMAN. That is all.

Mr. COCKRAN. The foreign price was not lower than the price you obtained for the goods you exported?

Mr. FELTON. I do not understand that question.

Mr. COCKRAN. I understood you to say that the foreign price was lower than the price charged for the same article here.

Mr. FELTON. We obtained for the rails which we delivered in the foreign countries a lower price f. o. b. our mill than we did for the rails which we sold in America.

Mr. COCKRAN. Yes; I understand that. Now——

Mr. FELTON. In the United States, I mean; not in America.

Mr. COCKRAN. Yes; that was your statement, then. When you speak, then, of the lower price abroad you mean the lower price that you obtained for your goods and not the lower general market price?

Mr. FELTON. All that I have to guide me is the price we obtained, and I assume we obtained pretty nearly the market price.

Mr. COCKRAN. Did any of these sales represent a loss to you?

Mr. FELTON. Those sales represented, in some years, a book loss, but not an actual loss, for this reason. I do not want to be too technical in these things, but I want you to understand it.

Mr. COCKRAN. Yes; I would like you to explain it.

Mr. FELTON. We can manufacture rails for export more cheaply than we can manufacture rails for delivery in the United States.

Mr. COCKRAN. Why?

Mr. FELTON. Because we use very largely imported iron ores, on which we obtain a rebate of the duty which we pay when the iron ore comes into this country.

Mr. COCKRAN. I see.

Mr. FELTON. We also use, very largely, imported spiegeleisen, which is dutiable at $4 a ton. We obtain there, also, a rebate amounting to 99 per cent of the duty paid when that comes into the country. So we are able really to produce rails for export more cheaply than we can produce rails for delivery in the United States.

Mr. COCKRAN. Can you say how much more cheaply?

Mr. FELTON. It is a very simple matter; yes.

Mr. COCKRAN. About how much?

Mr. FELTON. I would have to figure it out. All these figures, you understand, which are in the possession of the Bureau of Commerce and Labor go into this matter absolutely in detail. You can get everything there, if you wish to do so, and it seems to me it would be much more satisfactory for you to obtain that information, which has been taken directly from the books of our company, than to have me figure it out roughly here and take up the time to do it.

Mr. COCKRAN. I will not ask you to do that.

Mr. FELTON. In a rough way—let me see—it takes off from $1 to $1.25 a ton.

Mr. COCKRAN. That is the reduction in the cost to you?

Mr. FELTON. Yes, sir.

Mr. COCKRAN. From $1 to $1.25 a ton?

Mr. FELTON. Yes, sir.

Mr. COCKRAN. Now, will you go on and explain how it was that you experienced a book loss with an actual profit?

Mr. FELTON. That accounts for part of it, you understand.

Mr. COCKRAN. Yes, sir.

Mr. FELTON. That we were able to make these rails for export more cheaply than we could make the rails for delivery within the United States. Then we also obtain an advantage by means of these orders—filling up our order books at times when we could not otherwise run steadily. We are enabled then to run our mills continuously, which, in the manufacture of steel rails, is a very considerable advantage. That is, in the manufacture of steel we take our pig iron in the molten state directly from the blast furnace, and it goes into the converting works, and so on through to the finished rail without ever losing its heat. If we slacken up and stop our converting mills, then that pig iron which would otherwise go through continuously in this operation must be piled up cold. Then when we start up again it must be remelted at very considerable expense. That probably adds from 80 to 90 cents a ton to do that. So you can see that, if by acquiring these orders for rails in foreign markets we can run our works continuously, it incidentally means a cheaper cost of production for our whole product.

Mr. COCKRAN. Exactly; but taking all that into consideration, as a matter of fact you have always sold in the foreign market at an actual profit?

Mr. FELTON. No, sir; we have not.

Mr. COCKRAN. I understood you to say that you sold at a profit except in one or two years, when there was a book loss.

Mr. FELTON. I can give you the figures here, sir.

Mr. COCKRAN. Yes; I would like to know. You have given the figures now, from 1899 to 1907. During that time you sent goods abroad as far as Russia, in competition?

Mr. FELTON. No, sir; not to Russia—to eastern Siberia.

Mr. COCKRAN. That is Russia, is it not?

Mr. FELTON. Not as we understand it. It was really in Manchuria. Those rails went to Manchuria.

Mr. COCKRAN. That was the extreme limit. It was for the Trans-Siberian Railway, was it not?

Mr. FELTON. Yes, sir.

Mr. COCKRAN. You delivered those in competition with the producers of the world?

Mr. FELTON. With the producers of the world? I expect so.

Mr. COCKRAN. And you got a profit on them, did you not?

Mr. FELTON. No; I am afraid we did not.

Mr. COCKRAN. I thought it was only the " wily Turk " that got away with you.

Mr. FELTON. I said the average during these years would probably have shown a small profit.

Mr. COCKRAN. I beg your pardon.

Mr. FELTON. I say the average for all these years I have mentioned in exporting would probably show a small profit.

Mr. COCKRAN. Yes.

Mr. FELTON. But a book loss; which I say was probably made up by the cheaper cost to us of the foreign materials, and all these incidental advantages which we gain by running our works regularly.

Mr. COCKRAN. Undoubtedly. Did you enjoy this rebate before the Dingley law?

Mr. FELTON. Before the Dingley law?

Mr. COCKRAN. Yes; was this rebate also enjoyed by you under the prior law?

Mr. FELTON. No; I do not think we manufactured any rails for export before the Dingley law went into effect. It went into effect in 1896, I think.

Mr. COCKRAN. I thought you testified that you had been exporting since 1890?

Mr. FELTON. No; I said since the nineties.

Mr. COCKRAN. Oh, I see. I beg your pardon.

Mr. FELTON. Yes, sir. We began exporting, I think, in 1897.

Mr. COCKRAN. And your first exportation was in 1897?

Mr. FELTON. I am pretty positive it was.

Mr. COCKRAN. You belong to the Maryland Steel Company, do you not?

Mr. FELTON. We own the Maryland Steel Company.

Mr. COCKRAN. You are still exporting steel rails?

Mr. FELTON. We are still exporting steel rails when we get a chance to do it.

Mr. COCKRAN. I mean, you are getting chances to do it?

Mr. FELTON. We have not had very many chances this year. There does not seem to be any demand for rails in foreign markets, or anywhere else.

Mr. COCKRAN. There is no foreign market where you fear competition to-day, is there?

Mr. FELTON. Where we fear competition to-day?

Mr. COCKRAN. I mean, there is no competition that you are afraid of in a neutral market? There is no neutral market in which you fear competition now, is there?

Mr. FELTON. Absolutely.

Mr. COCKRAN. Where, for instance? If you are able to deliver rails in Argentina and in Siberia, that pretty nearly covers the whole extent of the globe.

Mr. FELTON. Those rail deliveries in Siberia were made many years ago, when the cost of steel rails to us was very much less than it is to-day. In the ten years for which I have figures the cost of steel rails to us has risen enormously. It has increased $7 or $8 a ton. That may seem extraordinary to you, but I think it perhaps explains some of the things in Mr. Carnegie's article in the magazine, which I have not seen. Mr. Carnegie was familiar with the steel trade in the United States in the late nineties. I do not think he has had anything to do, directly, with the steel trade of the United States since 1896 or 1897. In making his statement I think he was figuring on the cost of rails at that time. If he knew the increased cost, at least as shown by our cost books, he would not, I am sure, have made the statement he did.

Mr. COCKRAN. The increasing cost is largely due to the increase in the cost of the raw material, is it not?

Mr. FELTON. Raw materials, freight, and labor. If you will let me state it, I will tell you just what those costs are.

Mr. COCKRAN. Certainly.

Mr. FELTON. Iron ores which in 1898 cost us $2.25 a ton at lower lake ports——

Mr. COCKRAN. $2.25?

Mr. FELTON. Yes; [continuing] in 1907 cost us $4.75.

Mr. GAINES. In 1898 it was what?

Mr. FELTON. In 1898 they cost us from $2.15 to $2.25 per ton at lower lake ports. In 1907 they cost us $4.75 for those same ores. The unit price, which, after all, is the thing which determines the cost of ore going into a ton of the pig iron, cost us in 1898 $5.75— that is, the amount of iron ore necessary to make a ton of pig iron cost $5.75, and in 1907 it cost us $11.25.

Mr. DALZELL. What was that last statement?

Mr. FELTON. The iron ore which was necessary to make a ton of pig iron—not the price per ton of the iron ore, but the iron ore necessary to produce a ton of pig iron—cost us at our Maryland works in 1898 $5.75 a ton. In 1907 the same ore cost us $11.25 a ton.

Mr. CLARK. You do not mean to say there was $6 a ton difference in two years?

Mr. FELTON. No, sir; in ten years—from 1898 to 1907.

Mr. CLARK. Oh, eight or nine years.

Mr. FELTON. Ten years, I think—from 1898 to 1907. Then there have been advances in freight rates and on coke, and there have been advances in labor, so that the cost of steel rails has advanced during those years, as I say, some $7.50 a ton, probably.

Mr. COCKRAN. The cost has not advanced any more in this country than in England and Germany, has it?

Mr. FELTON. I wish I knew. I do not know. The only thing we have to guide us as to the cost of rails in foreign countries is their selling price. In Germany, as you know, the Government there places a bounty on export rails. Now, how much that bounty decreases their cost, and whether the price at which they sell in the foreign markets is anything like a legitimate price, I do not know. German rails are selling now f. o. b. Antwerp at something like $23 a ton, I think.

Mr. GRIGGS. Did you say Antwerp?

Mr. FELTON. Yes, sir; that is that " Belgian nightmare." [Laughter.] These are the latest advices I have. These came over to us from London.

Mr. COCKRAN. Surely you can tell us what the price of iron ore is in Germany, can you not?

Mr. FELTON. I have not the slightest idea.

Mr. COCKRAN. You would not undertake to say that the price of iron ore, or pig iron, has advanced in this country in larger proportion than it has in Germany, would you?

Mr. FELTON. I do not know. If I attempted to tell you, I would be drawing on my imagination. I do not want to do that.

Mr. COCKRAN. I understand that perfectly. Therefore, when you undertake to explain the increase in the cost of production here in this country you must see the value of your explanation is very much reduced if it turn out that this increase is not any greater than has occurred in other countries?

Mr. FELTON. I do not know.

Mr. COCKRAN. You would not state the contrary of that?

Mr. FELTON. I would not state the contrary?

Mr. COCKRAN. No.

Mr. FELTON. Well, I should think it extremely likely the contrary was true, because I know, from the price which these rails are selling at now, that the home market has slackened up, and these foreign mills are now pushing their products out into the markets of the world.

Mr. COCKRAN. But notwithstanding all the advantages which the Germans have, you have been able up to this year to maintain competition against them in neutral markets, have you not?

Mr. FELTON. We have, by making great sacrifices.

Mr. COCKRAN. These sacrifices did not involve a positive loss, I understand you to say?

Mr. FELTON. I can tell you about what we can——

Mr. COCKRAN. Would you mind answering that?

Mr. FELTON. I think it would be a great deal better to give you the figures, sir.

Mr. COCKRAN. All right; go ahead.

Mr. FELTON. In the ten years our total export business showed a book loss of $1.49 per ton. Does not that answer your question?

Mr. COCKRAN. I understood you to say that that was not an actual loss, but a profit.

Mr. FELTON. I say that is partly made up by the cheapening of our product, due to the steady operation of our mills.

Mr. COCKRAN. Will you tell me in cash? Take it in cash. Did these sales in foreign markets result in an actual payment by you for the privilege of selling your product or did it result in a profit to you in cash?

Mr. FELTON. I should say that we just about came out even on it.

Mr. COCKRAN. Now, can we rely on that?

Mr. FELTON. I think you can. I have said it.

Mr. COCKRAN. That there was no positive loss. Very good. We can accept that as a definite and final statement that in competition with Germany, where they have this bounty, as you say, and in competition with England, Belgium, and all the rest of the world, in neutral markets, you were able to hold your own, without loss.

Mr. FELTON. I think that is true; yes.

Mr. COCKRAN. You do not think you would have great trouble in holding your own in this country, where all the advantages are in your favor and where you have no freight to pay?

Mr. FELTON. What do you mean?

Mr. COCKRAN. I mean that you would not have any trouble in holding your own in this country against foreign competition.

Mr. FELTON. Of course we would when the demand in these producing countries slackens up. Remember these conditions in the last two or three years have been exceptional. We have all been so busy that we did not know what to do. Those conditions have changed. The Germans, the English, and these Belgians also are now sending their rails out into the markets of the world. They send them out at a much lower price than they are willing to sell for in their own countries. That is especially true of Germany, where, as I say, the export of rails by the Government is encouraged by an indirect bounty.

Mr. COCKRAN. That did not occur in the last ten years, did it, since 1898? You were sending out yourself. You were actually exporting yourself. They were not sending any goods in here, were they?

Mr. FELTON. I do not know just what the imports of rails into this country were. The statistics, I think, would show that.

Mr. COCKRAN. So they would. That is quite true.

Mr. FELTON. I have it here.

Mr. COCKRAN. The statistics we can look up ourselves. What I want is this: According to your own testimony, there would be no fear of competition with foreign countries unless it were under conditions where they could not find a market at home, and where they were prepared to send their rails to this country and sell them at less. That is the only condition under which you could have ruinous competition in this country, is it not?

Mr. FELTON. They would send them in and sell at a loss. We know they won't.

Mr. COCKRAN. That is what I want to get at—that unless they sold their goods at a loss in this country they could not compete with you?

Mr. FELTON. Now, you are making me assume that I know what their costs are. I have stated that I do not know. I can not find out. I wish I could.

Mr. COCKRAN. I understood you to say—perhaps I am entirely wrong—that you were able in perfectly neutral markets, for the last ten years, to meet them and beat them in fair competition. Is not that so?

Mr. FELTON. In neutral markets, I do not know—yes; we sold— of course these mills have made their prices. I do not know what the prices of the German mills are.

Mr. COCKRAN. If you could meet their prices in neutral foreign markets with the additional cost of transportation, do you think you would have any trouble in meeting their competition in your own home market, with no cost of transportation whatever to reach the point of consumption?

Mr. FELTON. These prices that I have given are our prices f. o. b. at our mills. They are not the prices at the point of delivery in other countries.

Mr. COCKRAN. Regardless of that, I ask you this question. I seem to have great difficulty in making myself clear. You have testified that for the last ten years you have met their competition in neutral markets and have overcome it. Now, I ask you what the reason is why you could not meet the same competition in your own market, where your condition is no worse than it is in the foreign markets.

Mr. FELTON. Because if we sold all our rails at cost or less than cost, we could not exist.

Mr. COCKRAN. As a matter of fact, at the prices you have obtained in these markets you have been able to meet their competition?

Mr. FELTON. We have been able to secure some portion of the business.

Mr. COCKRAN. And that you secured in competition with all the world, did you not?

Mr. FELTON. Yes, sir.

Mr. COCKRAN. Now, I ask you, under normal conditions, under the conditions we have had for the last ten years, would you not be able to meet their competition here, without reference to your business during the past year?

Mr. FELTON. I do not believe we would, because our costs have advanced during that year to such an extent that if the German rails were sold in our market and the foreign market at the prices they brought in 1900, 1901, and 1902—our prices in the meantime, our costs have advanced as I have said some $6 or $7 a ton, and we could not meet that competition.

Mr. COCKRAN. You say you do not know whether their price has advanced or not?

Mr. FELTON. I say at the prices which they would make in these quotations which we have here, which only came yesterday, indicate that they are putting their prices down, then, I say, with our increased cost to-day we could not meet that.

Mr. COCKRAN. That is an exceptional condition, the condition of last year and this year?

Mr. FELTON. I think the exceptional conditions were last year, and the conditions this year are normal.

Mr. Cockran. Excluding the adjective "exceptional," and taking the experience of this year, it is different from the experience you have had with the nine years preceding it, is it not?

Mr. Felton. The experience of this year?

Mr. Cockran. Yes; it is different from the experience of the last nine years.

Mr. Felton. You mean——

Mr. Cockran. Will you not answer that question? I mean this year has been one of depression in your business, and the other nine years were years of experience. Am I not right in that?

Mr. Felton. Yes; but during a large portion of the years for which I have figures here our rail costs were very much less than they are to-day. We were therefore able to meet these foreign mills in the markets of the world. If the prices of the German mills come down to what they were in the five years which these figures that I have here cover, and which these figures indicate that they are coming to, then I say with our increased cost we could not meet that competition.

Mr. Cockran. If a hypothetical condition should turn out to be an actual condition, then you say you could not meet the competition?

Mr. Felton. That is not a hypothetical condition, but an actual condition.

Mr. Cockran. You say " if " these rates come down.

Mr. Felton. They have come right down.

Mr. Cockran. Will you get your mind away from this year altogether, and go back to the years preceding this year, from 1899 to 1907. Taking those years, is it not a fact that you defeated that competition?

Mr. Felton. We did, but our costs were very much below what they are to-day or what we conceive they are to be in the future.

Mr. Cockran. We grant all that——

Mr. Felton. That is the important point——

Mr. Cockran. We grant that; but assuming that conditions are equal to-day, you will not have any reason to fear their competition to-day, would you?

Mr. Felton. We certainly would, because our costs to-day are much higher than when we were getting very low rails before.

Mr. Cockran. But assuming that their costs to-day are in proportion to yours——

Mr. Felton. I am not going to assume that.

Mr. Cockran. Well, try to. It seems you are only willing to assume conditions that will justify a protected condition. I want you to assume conditions that are actual, the same as those that have actually occurred.

Mr. Felton. The position I take covers the conditions that actually occur, not the suppositious conditions that you try to put before me.

Mr. Cockran. I am taking the conditions from 1899 to 1906.

Mr. Felton. I understand.

Mr. Cockran. Under those conditions you met their competition, did you not? Do not be ashamed of it; it is very creditable.

Mr. Felton. I told you we had met their competition——

Mr. Cockran. Very good.

Mr. FELTON. But let me go on and explain——

Mr. COCKRAN. I do not think you had better explain that——

Mr. FELTON. We want to get at the truth——

Mr. COCKRAN. I assume that you told the truth.

Mr. FELTON. I am trying to; yes. I say that the competition we met in the early years of those ten years we were able to meet because our costs were very much lower than they are to-day.

Mr. COCKRAN. Yes. I say that to-day we could meet this competition, but you say——

Mr. FELTON. We could not meet their competition with those costs.

Mr. COCKRAN. But you say——

Mr. FELTON. We could not meet their competition.

Mr. COCKRAN. That is, you assume that the cost has not increased to them in the same proportion that it has increased to you?

Mr. FELTON. I say the latest quotation I have for German rails indicates that they are willing to sell on that low basis, on that low price, and that the only way I have of determining their basis of cost is what they are willing to sell them for.

Mr. COCKRAN. You do not know whether their raw material has increased to them in the same proportion as it has to you or not, but u assume that it has not, on account of these quotations. Am I right?

Mr. FELTON. I assume that their cost is in the neighborhood of what it was five or six or seven years ago. I assume that because of the information I have.

Mr. COCKRAN. Let us see what your answer is based on. Your answer, that you need protection in this country of any kind is based on the assumption that the cost of the raw material in Germany did not increase in the same proportion that it has increased in this country; you do not claim to have positive knowledge of that, but you assume it from the rates asked for the foreign product?

Mr. FELTON. What would you assume from it to-day?

Mr. COCKRAN. I would not assume anything. I am simply asking what goes on.

Mr. FELTON. I would like to know what you would assume from it.

Mr. COCKRAN. Am I correct about that?

Mr. FELTON. What was that question?

Mr. COCKRAN. Am I correct in that assumption?

Mr. FELTON. You are trying to get me to say——

Mr. COCKRAN. I am not trying to get you to say anything——

Mr. FELTON (continuing). That I think we could meet German competition at these prices, which are quoted here, in the Antwerp market.

Mr. COCKRAN. I am not trying anything so hopeless as to induce you to say that, but I am trying to find out just what you are basing your present conclusions on.

Mr. FELTON. I have stated that over and over and over again.

Mr. DALZELL. He has stated that half a dozen times.

Mr. COCKRAN. I do not think he has, and he will not state it now. Will the stenographer read the question?

(The stenographer read the question, as follows:)

Mr. COCKRAN. Let us see what your answer is based on. Your answer, that you need protection in this country, of any kind, is based on the assumption that the cost of the raw material in Germany did not increase in the same proportion that it has increased in this country; you do not claim to have positive knowledge of that, but you assume to from the rates asked for the foreign product?

The CHAIRMAN. Which one of those questions do you want answered first?

Mr. COCKRAN. I am stating his testimony as I understand it. Is that a correct statement of your testimony?

Mr. FELTON. That is a correct statement of your question.

Mr. COCKRAN. It is a repetition of my question. I want to know if that is a correct statement of your testimony.

Mr. FELTON. My testimony is—it was asked me whether we could go ahead, as I understand it, and meet the competition of the foreign mills in our own market. I said that we could not do it to-day, because our costs are so much higher than they were when we formerly did meet the prices which they made.

Mr. COCKRAN. Very good. Now——

Mr. FELTON. Could I make anything plainer?

Mr. COCKRAN. Now, if the cost of their raw material advanced in an equal proportion, would you then be able to meet their competition in this country as you did before?

Mr. FELTON. If they charged for rails in the foreign markets of the world, the neutral markets of the world, what they charged last year, then we would be able to meet their competition.

Mr. COCKRAN. That is not exactly an answer to my question, but I will put it this way—perhaps this will cover it: Is the same statement embodied in your answer true of each of the other years from 1898 down to 1905—what you say of 1906, is it equally true of each of the years preceding that up to 1897?

Mr. FELTON. Is that true?

Mr. COCKRAN. The statement you made about conditions under which you could meet competition in 1906?

The CHAIRMAN. If the price was the same as it has been in Germany for the past ten years, up to 1908, could you meet their competition? That is the question.

Mr. FELTON. We could not to-day; no.

The CHAIRMAN. You could at the time, I understood you.

Mr. FELTON. We could back in 1898 and 1899. We could in 1898 and 1899 and 1900, when our costs for producing rails were very considerably below what they are to-day, due to this lesser price we were paying for raw material, freights, and labor.

Mr. COCKRAN. And you do not know whether the cost in Germany has increased in the same degree or not?

Mr. FELTON. I do not know.

Mr. COCKRAN. That is it.

Mr. CLARK. One of these years, I forget which, you sold rails abroad for $6 cheaper than you did in the United States?

Mr. FELTON. I think that is what I stated.

Mr. CLARK. I think so—substantially so. You need not look at your figures in regard to that.

Mr. FELTON. I like to have these things right.

Mr. CLARK. All right; we want to get substantially what is correct.

Mr. FELTON. I am very sorry that it takes so long. In one of those years—that was the year, 1904—when I explained that we had bad conditions——

The CHAIRMAN. You sold them for $9 less, I think, that year.

Mr. FELTON. Yes.

Mr. CLARK. That is when the Turks got us?

Mr. FELTON. Yes; the Turks got us in their claw that year. There is one year here—I think there is one year here—when we sold for $6.80 less.

Mr. CLARK. What year was that?

Mr. FELTON. That was the year 1905.

Mr. CLARK. Did you make money or lose it on that exportation?

Mr. FELTON. We lost money.

Mr. CLARK. How much did you lose? [After a pause.] Oh, if you have to go into your papers for it——

Mr. FELTON. I can not remember, you know, as to the figures in a mass of papers like this. You know that perfectly well.

Mr. CLARK. I thought that would give you such a jolt that you would recollect it.

Mr. FELTON. I have not got the exact amount for that one year, but I happen to have it for all the years figured up, and, as I say, that is one of the years covered by these figures which are in the hands of the Bureau of Commerce and Labor, which you gentlemen are welcome to.

Mr. CLARK. Do you have any idea of telling us how or who can give us this information as to the cost of steel rails abroad?

Mr. FELTON. I do not know how you can get that. We have tried to get it.

Mr. CLARK. I would like very much to find out——

Mr. FELTON. I would, too. It would be a most valuable thing, if we could find out that. I am afraid what I am stating here is now going right out in the press dispatches and being given to the mills of the world—what we can not get from them.

Mr. CLARK. There is no mystery about it, is there?

Mr. FELTON. Why, absolutely.

Mr. CLARK. Here is what seems to me—of course I have not manufactured any steel rails—but it looks to me like the man who is in the business of manufacturing steel rails in the United States would, for his own satisfaction and protection, find out what it costs his competitors to make them. That is simply a statement, but I want to ask you a question now.

Have you any connection with the steel trust?

Mr. FELTON. What do you mean by the steel trust?

Mr. CLARK. The United States Steel Company is the technical name for it, I understand.

Mr. FELTON. Not at all.

Mr. CLARK. You do not own any stock in it?

Mr. FELTON. No, sir.

Mr. CLARK. You have nothing to do with it?

Mr. FELTON. No, sir.

Mr. CLARK. Do they fix prices in the United States or not?

Mr. FELTON. They do not.

Mr. CLARK. You are sure of that? Do you sell at the same price that they sell at?

Mr. FELTON. We sell generally at the same price that they do. Let me explain to you exactly what is done in the rail business of the United States.

The presidents of the rail mills have frequent conferences at which they discuss the question of a fair price to charge for steel rails. After that discussion, we each one act as we think is best for our company. That has resulted largely in a price of $28, the price of steel rails having been quoted in a general way at $28. It does not mean that we sell all our rails at $28. That is perhaps what you want to know, is it?

Mr. CLARK. You fix the jump, but you don't jump together—that is about it, is it not? You do everything, now, at one of these meetings that you can think of to do to try to avoid the law, and at the same time to come to an agreement?

Mr. FELTON. We have nothing in the nature of an agreement at all.

Mr. CLARK. You do all sell at the same price?

Mr. FELTON. I don't know what the other mills sell at. I think they sell at $28.

Mr. CLARK. You never inquire what the other people sell at?

Mr. FELTON. I never inquire; it would not do any good.

Mr. CLARK. You do not care what the other people sell for, I suppose?

Mr. FELTON. I think they sell at that price, because I would find out when I come to quote prices to railroads if that price were cut to any considerable extent; that would develop.

Mr. CLARK. You would be very much surprised, then, to find one of them getting $30 a ton, when you are only getting $28 a ton for your product?

Mr. FELTON. I would be surprised, and I would think that our selling department was very lax if that was the case.

Mr. CLARK. You would be very much surprised and chagrined—not chagrined, but surprised—if you found out that they were selling at $27 a ton and that you were selling for $28 a ton?

Mr. FELTON. I would think in such a case, also, that we ought to find that out.

Mr. CLARK. Are there not natural or artificial advantages that enable one steel mill to make steel a great deal cheaper than another mill?

Mr. FELTON. No doubt there are.

Mr. CLARK. And yet they all sell, by accident, at the same price?

Mr. FELTON. It is not by accident. I told you just exactly what was done in the steel-rail trade.

Mr. CLARK. I want to ask you another question. How long have you been in this steel-rail business?

Mr. FELTON. I have been in the steel-rail business since 1880.

Mr. CLARK. I mean making steel rails.

Mr. FELTON. The company that I went to work for made steel rails in 1880.

Mr. CLARK. When did you get into this company that is making steel rails—the company that you are in now?

Mr. FELTON. I have been in it ever since I have been in business.

Mr. CLARK. How long is that?

Mr. FELTON. Since 1880.

Mr. CLARK. Do they do anything except make steel rails?

Mr. FELTON. They do all sorts of steel work—produce all sorts of steel products.

Mr. CLARK. How much is the company capitalized for? [After a pause.] Now, can you not tell without looking in those papers?

Mr. FELTON. I want to give you accurate information.

Mr. GRIGGS. He wants to get the daily quotation.

Mr. FELTON. No; I do not.

Mr. DALZELL. Just for information, in what capacity did you enter that company?

Mr. FELTON. I went into the chemical laboratory and went up through the mills and have been with them ever since.

Mr. CLARK. How much is the company capitalized for?

Mr. FELTON. The capital invested in works and in the business is just about $50,000,000.

Mr. CLARK. That is the whole capital?

Mr. FELTON. Yes.

Mr. CLARK. How much dividend did you pay in 1907?

Mr. FELTON. In 1907 we paid $1,155,000.

Mr. CLARK. What per cent is that?

Mr. FELTON. Understand, that is not the capital stock of the company; that is the amount of money which is invested in the business.

Mr. CLARK. Actually invested?

Mr. FELTON. Actually invested in the business. There is no water in it.

Mr. CLARK. And you only got a million dollars profit in 1907?

Mr. FELTON. I said we paid that to our stockholders. I did not say that was our profit.

Mr. CLARK. What were your profits?

Mr. FELTON. Our profits in that year—I have taken the two best years we have had in ten years; 1907 was not the best year; it was a poor year for us on account of the high prices for materials. Our income was $5,420,000.

Mr. COCKRAN. How much did you say?

Mr. FELTON. Five million four hundred and twenty thousand dollars. Deducting our bonded interest or interest on bonds, amounting to $748,000, left net earnings of $4,671,000, from which we charged off, depreciation, $1,572,000, leaving our net income $3,099,000. Out of that dividends of $1,155,000 were paid to our stockholders.

Mr. CLARK. In counting up this three and a fraction per cent of profits, how much capital did you say you had?

Mr. FELTON. I have the percentages here.

Mr. CLARK. All right, give them.

Mr. FELTON. The percentage of income on the total capital invested was 10.79 per cent. Our interest on bonds was 1.49 per cent. Our depreciation was 3.13 per cent. The net income out of which dividends were paid was 6.17 per cent.

Mr. CLARK. Was there any increase in value of your property that you have not counted there? Did you add to your holdings?

Mr. FELTON. You mean did we increase our works?

Mr. CLARK. Yes; or did you buy anything else of value that belongs to the company?

Mr. FELTON. No, sir; nothing at all. If anything had been bought here it would have been shown up here—that is, we did not conceal any of our profits. That is what I think you are trying to get at.

Mr. CL   . How much does the president of your company get for salary? ARK

Mr. FELTON. I do not believe I am called on to answer that question.

Mr. CLARK. That is exactly what we want, whether you answer it or not. We want to arrive at how much profit you are making.

Mr. FELTON. How much profit we are making?

Mr. CLARK. Yes.

Mr. FELTON. I have——

Mr. CLARK. Let me ask you another question to lead up to that. Is every stockholder in the company an officer in the company?

Mr. FELTON. Absolutely no.

Mr. CLARK. Are you paying anybody any such price as president as the steel trust is paying Corey, a million dollars a year?

Mr. FELTON. We are not; no.

Mr. CLARK. The only fair way to find out about what the profits are is to find out whether the managers of the company, the top notchers——

Mr. FELTON. I see.

Mr. CLARK. Wait a minute. Whether the salaries paid to those men do not swell up the expenses to such an extent that you make a poor showing as to your profits, when, as a matter of fact, there are a lot of fellows in the company who are becoming millionaires and multimillionaires.

Mr. FELTON. Will you allow me to show you that? [Handing a memorandum on a slip of paper to Mr. Clark.] That is what the president is getting.

Mr. COCKRAN. I would like to see that, too.

Mr. FELTON. Pass it around.

Mr. CLARK (after examination of memorandum). Whew! How many vice-presidents have you got?

Mr. FELTON. We have one vice-president.

Mr. CLARK. Now, you are pulling along with six and some odd per cent dividend.

Mr. LONGWORTH. Can you state what your net profits per ton were for the year 1907?

Mr. FELTON. I have that right here, I think.

Mr. COCKRAN. For what year do you ask them?

Mr. LONGWORTH. For the year 1907.

Mr. FELTON. Remember, I am speaking now simply of rails.

Mr. LONGWORTH. Of what?

Mr. FELTON. Of steel rails. We manufacture a lot of other things——

Mr. LONGWORTH. I would prefer to hear it for the whole product.

Mr. FELTON. I have not got that, because I came here to talk about rails. I will be glad to give it. In fact, these figures which I can give will show that to the smallest detail.

Mr. LONGWORTH. The reason I ask that is that I saw in a copy of the Wall Street Journal for this year that the net earnings of the steel corporation for the year 1907 were $15.50 a ton. Were your earnings approximately the same?

Mr. FELTON. We made a profit on rails. We have this one plant running on rails, you understand, and the percentage of profit on that one work is about the same as the general percentage of profit on all the works, but on rails our profits per net ton, before any depreciation is charged off, was 1.66 per ton. That was in 1907. In 1906 our profits were 3.28 a ton. In 1905 our profit was 3.71 a ton.

You have heard all sorts of talk about the cost of steel rails. It is all based on figures that were made up in the late nineties when we were paying our men 10 cents an hour and they were working nine hours a day, when our rates on the railroad did not scarcely pay the cost, and when everybody that was selling us any supplies—iron ore or anything like that—was not getting back a new dollar for an old one.

On that basis we made the steel awfully cheap. We were then able to make steel a great deal cheaper than anybody else in the world, we think. Since then prices have gone up, as I have tried to show you, until to-day—last year—those were the actual profits per ton which we made on steel rails at our Sparrows Point plant.

Mr. LONGWORTH. If you will permit me, I would like to read a sentence from a letter that I received this morning from a correspondent. After calling attention to this article in the Wall Street Journal, he says:

If we called the value of a ton of steel as $30, you will observe that the net profit in the manufacture of iron is from 40 to 45 per cent. You know what the tariff is that enables this to be maintained. That increased cost goes through everything which is being done in the United States, whether it be house building, manufacture of hardware, or railroad building. In comparison with the profit of 40 to 45 per cent, I may say to you that manufacturers are usually well contented with a 10 per cent net profit.

Mr. FELTON. I do not believe any steel manufacturers have made anything like that.

Mr. GAINES. Is the writer of that article a manufacturer of steel rails?

Mr. LONGWORTH. No; I do not know what he bases his argument on, but on the general steel business, not steel rails.

Mr. FELTON. When you compare the earnings of the United States Steel Company with the earnings of these smaller corporations, you must remember that the United States Steel Company owns all their raw material; you must remember that they own the means of transporting those raw materials to their mills; that they own the steamships and the cars; that they own their supplies of fuel, and everything from the ground up that goes to make a ton of steel. Now, they are entitled to a profit on each one of those things; their money is invested in it and they ought to have a profit on it.

Mr. HILL. Has that caused additional cost to you in your production?

Mr. FELTON. Has it caused——

Mr. HILL. Has the additional cost that you state has occurred since 1898, when the steel trust was organized, been caused by the organization of the steel trust?

Mr. FELTON. I could not—I do not see how it has been caused by it. We all know that everything has gone up in these years. Railroad rates have advanced, and the steel corporation has nothing to do with that. Possibly the price of iron ore in the Lake Superior region has gone up because of the steel corporation.

Mr. HILL. That it has a natural advance and not an arbitrary one, for which they are responsible?

Mr. FELTON. It would seem to me so, because it has been since the steel corporation was formed, and I can not see that because there has been an advance since the steel corporation was organized that it has been because of that organization.

Mr. HILL. That is what I wanted to know. What proportion of the steel-rail production of the country do you produce?

Mr. FELTON. Last year there was about 3,600,000 tons of rail made, I think. Let me give you the exact figures.

. Mr. HILL. I wish you would.

Mr. FELTON. That is what we ought to have in these things. The production of all kinds of rails was 3,663,000 tons made in 1907. That was a little smaller than the year before. The year before the production was 3,977,000 tons. That was the maximum. That is the maximum year; 4,000,000 tons, in round numbers, you might call it. In that year we made about 450,000 tons, I think.

Mr. HILL. As I understood you at the beginning of your remarks, you stated that you came here to represent the entire steel industry?

Mr. FELTON. I was asked to come here by the steel-rail producers to say that they did not feel that under present conditions the duty of $7.84 a ton on steel rails is an excessive one.

Mr. HILL. The United States Steel Company, then, will not appear; is that it?

Mr. FELTON. I do not know. I am pretty sure that they will not, because you know that your committee asked to have special individuals appointed to come here and talk to you on these separate schedules, and meetings were held at the offices of the American Iron and Steel Association, at which all the interests we could get together in the short time were represented.

Mr. HILL. Then, speaking for the whole trade, Mr. Felton, I would ask whether there is any international agreement between England, France, Germany, Belgium, and the United States as to a distribution of the world's territory in the steel-rail trade?

Mr. FELTON. There is nothing that we are a party to.

Mr. HILL. Is there any to your knowledge?

Mr. FELTON. To my belief there is a hard and fast association between the German, English, French, and Belgian mills.

Mr. HILL. Not with the United States?

Mr. FELTON. No, sir.

Mr. HILL. Pardon me if I read you just a sentence. I think it is from the Wall Street Journal of July 14, 1908, if I am not mistaken. [Reading:]

It is understood that some sort of an agreement bearing up exports of steel has existed for several years between the United States and the leading iron-producing countries of Europe. This agreement, it is said, has done a great deal to stimulate the foreign branch of the steel business and has resulted in great benefits to the companies concerned. There is also an understanding regarding the armor-plate trade.

To your knowledge, is there any truth whatever in that statement?

Mr. FELTON. That is, is the Pennsylvania Steel Company a party to it?

Mr. HILL. No; not the Pennsylvania Steel Company. I am asking you as representing now the entire steel-rail trade of the United States——

Mr. FELTON. Understand, I do not know as to what the other steel mills may do.

Mr. Hill. Then you could not say as to the truth of that statement?

Mr. Felton. No; but I do know that that arrangement is in force abroad, and I do know that we would like very much to be put in a position where we could join it.

Mr. Hill. Why?

Mr. Felton. Because it would protect the entire steel-rail market of the world. We would get better prices. We would not cut one another's throats. We would save liabilities which exist now.

You understand there is nothing to prevent the German or the English mills from subsidizing any one of their mills which is well located to simply flood this country with cheap steel rails and make up the difference in cost between them. We can not oppose that sort of thing.

Mr. Hill. Mr. Felton, are you at liberty to make any price you see fit for rails delivered in Germany?

Mr. Felton. Certainly we are.

Mr. Hill. Is the German manufacturer, under the syndicate agreement, permitted to make any price he sees fit for rails delivered in the United States?

Mr. Felton. I don't know.

Mr. Hill. Are not the prices between Germany, England, France, and Belgium and the United States fixed in London, and is not the price of rails in the world controlled——

The Chairman. Let him answer the question you asked——

Mr. Felton. Not as far as I know.

Mr. Hill. Is not the price controlled by international agreement rather than by tariffs?

Mr. Felton. No, sir; not as far as we are concerned.

Mr. Hill. I am asking you for the whole trade.

Mr. Felton. I know it, but I can not answer what I do not know about.

Mr. Gaines. But you represent the whole trade.

Mr. Felton. I am not taken into the secret councils.

Mr. Hill. Will there be anybody before the committee who can answer that question?

Mr. Felton. I don't know.

Mr. Cockran. Probably not.

Mr. Gaines. What do you believe as to whether the prices of rails are fixed by an international agreement made in England?

Mr. Felton. I know that the German, English, and French mills have some sort of an understanding, and I say I think it would be very much to the advantage of the American steel trade if the American mills were allowed to do the same sort of thing.

Mr. Gaines. Now, do you think that those French, German, and English mills have an understanding with any of the American manufacturers of steel rails?

Mr. Felton. I say I do not know.

Mr. Gaines. What do you think about it?

Mr. Felton. I have no reason for making up an opinion.

Mr. Gaines. A lawyer has no right to think against his clients.

Mr. Cockran. Besides which, you would not bring any such thoughts in here anyway.

Mr. Gaines. Another question, if you please, Mr. Felton. You must have some reason, with your intimate knowledge of the steel trade, to have one impression or another. Which impression do you have in reference to the mattter?

Mr. FELTON. Well, I know that steel rails are being sent into this country. That is, I just heard yesterday that the Louisville and Nashville Railroad had placed an order for steel rails delivered at Pensacola or Mobile, for foreign rails to come in here, and I do not believe those rails would have come in here if there had been any ar·rangement among the foreign mills and the American mills as to a price here; I do not see how they could come in in such an event.

Mr. GAINES. That is the circumstance that tends to make you believe that there is no such agreement. Have you observed anything which has induced you to at any time suspect that there was such an agreement?

Mr. FELTON. No; I can not say that there has been.

Mr. GRIGGS. I understood you to say, Mr. Felton, that you would like very much to be in a position to join this combination.

Mr. FELTON. I think it would be for the entire good of the steel trade of the United States.

Mr. GRIGGS. What would prevent you from doing it?

Mr. FELTON. The law.

Mr. GRIGGS. Does the law prohibit it?

Mr. FELTON. I think it does.

Mr. GRIGGS. Joining a foreign combination?

Mr. FELTON. Joining any kind of a combination.

Mr. UNDERWOOD. Have you stated what the cost of production of steel rails is in the United States?

Mr. FELTON. I can only state as to my own article.

Mr. UNDERWOOD. I wish you would state what was the cost in 1907 of the production——

Mr. DALZELL. I think he gave it for every year—for five or six years.

Mr. UNDERWOOD. I want what the cost of a ton of steel rails has been—what it costs to produce a ton of steel rails.

Mr. FELTON. I can tell you that very quickly. As I say, these figures, which you can have, will show you that. You want what it costs us at our Maryland works in 1907 to make a ton of rails?

Mr. UNDERWOOD. Yes.

Mr. FELTON. Before deducting anything for depreciation, it cost us $26.42.

Mr. UNDERWOOD. In 1907?

Mr. FELTON. Yes.

Mr. UNDERWOOD. You sold those rails at $28.08 f. o. b. the mills?

Mr. FELTON. Yes, sir.

Mr. UNDERWOOD. You stated that the cost of the raw material had risen $5.50 a ton. What did you include in that?

Mr. FELTON. Merely the cost of ore. That was only the cost of ore.

Mr. UNDERWOOD. You manufacture your own pig iron?

Mr. FELTON. Yes. We purchase some, but we manufacture most of the pig iron that we use.

Mr. UNDERWOOD. Pig iron has depreciated some $8 per ton since 1907 in the price, has it not?

The CHAIRMAN. Since 1907?

Mr. FELTON. Yes; I think it was stated——

Mr. COCKRAN. Since the panic, I suppose he means, of 1907.

Mr. FELTON. Yes, sir.

Mr. UNDERWOOD. Evidently the items of cost—that would reduce the pig iron that goes into a steel rail to that extent, would it not?

Mr. FELTON. That is not the kind of iron that goes to make up the steel rails. It is iron used in foundries. The iron that is used to make steel rails is a special grade of iron, known as Bessemer iron.

Mr. UNDERWOOD. I must beg to differ with you there, because we claim in our part of the country to be able to make good steel, and we make it from another iron.

Mr. FELTON. Yes; you make it from basic iron?

Mr. UNDERWOOD. Yes.

Mr. FELTON. But the pig iron we use is what we call Bessemer iron. We make all Bessemer rails. We do not make any open-hearth rails.

Mr. UNDERWOOD. But has there not been a decrease in the price of that?

Mr. FELTON. Yes; there has been a decrease in the price of that. That has probably been due to a lowering in the price of coke. There has been a lowering in the price of coke. There has also been a marking off on the book values of ore in the hands of furnace men. That is, they marked that off and accepted a loss on it, and went ahead to try and meet the new prices.

Mr. UNDERWOOD. You stated about the great increase in cost in book value, as you produce everything, from the ore on up, from 1898 to 1907, has not been—not as much decrease, I know, but has there not been a decrease in the cost of production by marking down these figures since 1907 up to the present time?

Mr. FELTON. There has been a lowering in cost in 1908 due to a decrease in the price of raw material, but that has not been sufficient to make up the increased cost due to the very slow running. For instance, we have only been able to run our rail plant about 45 per cent of the time this year.

Mr. UNDERWOOD. What was the amount of the reduction in the cost of the raw material that you just said you had marked down?

Mr. FELTON. Lake ores, I think, were reduced 50 cents a ton over the high prices of these last years.

Mr. UNDERWOOD. What did it amount to in steel rails?

Mr. FELTON. That would amount to, roughly, about——

Mr. UNDERWOOD. Now, will you state, has there been any reduction of wages in your mills?

Mr. FELTON. No; we have tried to hold up wages, with the hope that this thing was going to turn.

Mr. UNDERWOOD. What has been the total reduction of your cost items within the——

Mr. FELTON. Our cost items this year, I am afraid, will be more than they were last year, notwithstanding the fact that we are paying less for our raw materials.

Mr. UNDERWOOD. I understand——

Mr. FELTON. Due to our slow running.

Mr. UNDERWOOD. I understand that, but I am trying to get at what it would be if the market picks up, and you can run every day with the reduced cost of material. What has been the reduction in cost aside from the slow running?

Mr. FELTON. If we could run—that is, you mean if we could run normally?

Mr. UNDERWOOD. Yes.

Mr. FELTON. What would be our probable reduction this year?

Mr. UNDERWOOD. As over 1907; yes.

Mr. FELTON. I should think that would probably be 1.50 or something like that.

Mr. UNDERWOOD. 1.50?

Mr. FELTON. That is a hasty calculation, you know.

Mr. UNDERWOOD. I want to ask you if the present tariff on steel rails is not a prohibitive duty?

Mr. FELTON. Not at all. In the Gulf States and on the Pacific coast we are liable at any time to have rails sent into this country.

Mr. UNDERWOOD. As a matter of fact, do you have them sent in?

Mr. FELTON. We have not had them sent in in the last couple of years, because, as I said, foreign mills were so largely occupied with their home market and the demand that came on them from this great activity all over the world that they did not send in these rails, apparently; but I believe we are right up against it now.

Mr. UNDERWOOD. That is an apprehension and not sustained by——

Mr. FELTON. It has been our experience in the past, and we would have to reason that from what our experience has been——

Mr. UNDERWOOD. I notice here that the production of steel rails in this country amounted to 3,600,000 tons in 1907 and something like 4,000,000 in 1906. That is what you stated, I believe?

Mr. FELTON. Yes, sir; I think that was it.

Mr. UNDERWOOD. That many tons. I want to call your attention to this fact: I notice that in the year 1895—and that was in a very profitable year—there were only 775 tons imported. In the next year there were 958 tons imported. In the next year there were 2,335 tons imported. In 1898 there were 5,530 tons imported. In 1899 there were 298 tons imported. In 1900 there were 2,385 tons imported. In 1901 there were 933 tons imported. In 1902 there were 14,836 tons imported. In 1903 there were 123,000 tons imported. In 1904 there were 49,000 tons imported. In 1905 there were 19,473 tons imported. In 1906 there were 10,037 tons imported, and in 1907 there were 3,911 tons imported.

Now, that is the total importation of steel rails from 1895 to 1907, and in no year did the importation amount to 1 per cent of the consumption of the American market. Now, do you not call that a prohibitive tariff?

Mr. FELTON. I do not consider—if rails can be sent in here, and we know that they can, I do not think the tariff would prohibit their coming here.

Mr. UNDERWOOD. I suppose there are exceptional cases, when they could come in absolutely at a loss, but really want to get at the facts in the case.

Mr. FELTON. I understand. I have tried to give them to you the best I can.

Mr. UNDERWOOD. But I want to have something we can base the facts on as to this tariff, and I want to ask you whether it is not a fair statement of the case that when, in a period of nearly—well, in a period of twelve years—the total importation of rails into the United States amounted to less than one-half of 1 per cent, do you not call that a prohibitive tariff?

Mr. FELTON. Well, I think it is a tariff that has protected the American manufacturer very effectively. A prohibitive tariff is something that would keep rails out of this country absolutely, and I know that it is perfectly possible, under normal conditions, to ship some of these Belgian rails and the other cheap rails to our Pacific coast.

Mr. UNDERWOOD. I want to ask you some questions right there. My idea of this proposition is that when the price is high at home here—and I am asking you simply for information—there is a great demand among the railroads to buy rails, that that is an opportunity when the foreigner comes into our territory; but you say it is not. Now, in the figures I give you, in 1895 and 1896 and 1897, when the market was low and conditions in this country were not so very prosperous—I believe we will agree on that?

Mr. FELTON. In what years?

Mr. UNDERWOOD. In 1895, 1896, and 1897 they were not as prosperous as they were in 1903 and 1904?

Mr. FELTON. Yes, 1895; yes, 1896 and 1897. Those were very dull years.

Mr. UNDERWOOD. Dull years?

Mr. FELTON. Very low prices in those years.

Mr. UNDERWOOD. And dull, too?

Mr. FELTON. Yes, sir.

Mr. UNDERWOOD. The whole markets of the world were dull?

Mr. FELTON. Yes.

Mr. UNDERWOOD. But at that time, with this same duty of $7.84, there was only less than a thousand tons imported in the years 1895 and 1896, and only a little over 2,000 tons imported in 1897, and yet when we got to the prosperous years of 1903 it has increased about 123,000 tons, and in 1904 to 49,000 tons, and in 1905 to 19,000 tons. Now, that does not seem to sustain—of course there was a minimum amount imported in each year, but it does not seem to sustain your proposition that in a bad year the importation will be larger than in good years.

Mr. FELTON. Those were years when our prices here were extremely low, and the steel rails could not come in.

Mr. UNDERWOOD. That does not seem to be the case as shown by these statistics, because the value of the unit——

Mr. FELTON. I think you will find that so.

Mr. UNDERWOOD. That is, the value of the unit was lower in those years than now.

Mr. FELTON. Yes; because the last year I have here—that is, the years these figures were prepared for, the first year was 1898. In that year our price for domestic rails was $19.44.

Mr. UNDERWOOD. But I call your attention to this, that in the year 1907, when you say the price was very low in this country, the value of the imported article was $23, and yet only 2,000 tons came in, and yet in the year 1906 this unit value of rails as given for the imported article was still $23 and 10,000 tons came in. So that does not seem to sustain your idea.

Mr. FELTON. That was a pretty low price for rails in this country, was it not?

Mr. UNDERWOOD. As I understand, that was not the selling price; that was the value on which the duty was assessed. Of course the $7——

Mr. FELTON. Would come off that?

Mr. UNDERWOOD. The $7.84——

Mr. FELTON. Oh, no; I am pretty sure——

Mr. UNDERWOOD. I am giving you now the selling price in 1906, being $23, and you say the selling price in 1906 of steel rails was $28.

Mr. FELTON. In what year?

Mr. UNDERWOOD. 1906.

Mr. FELTON. 1906, yes; but you were talking about 1896.

Mr. UNDERWOOD. I have given you both dates. I am giving you now the value of the article as fixed by the imported rail that came in here without the duty added, as $23.44, for the importation of 10,000 tons of rails in 1906. Now, the price in America, the American rail, was selling, according to your statement, for something like $28.

Mr. FELTON. In eighteen hundred and ninety what?

Mr. UNDERWOOD. 1906.

Mr. FELTON. 1906; yes.

Mr. UNDERWOOD. Therefore the duty was not added to that rail; that was the value of the export price as fixed by the Government— while they fix the price abroad; they fixed the price abroad as $23.44 in 1906.

Mr. FELTON. Then the duty would have been added to that price.

Mr. UNDERWOOD. Of course——

Mr. FELTON. Then those rails would have cost in this country something over $30.

Mr. UNDERWOOD. Yes.

Mr. FELTON. Those rails probably went to the Gulf ports and to the Pacific coast.

Mr. UNDERWOOD. I understand, and that is the reason they were able to come in at that price; but what I wanted to show is that your assertion that because we are going to have dull times would encourage the importation of rails is not shown by the fact that there was only in the year 1897 a little over 2,000 tons of rails imported, the value abroad being fixed by the Government at $23, and in 1906, a very prosperous year, there were 10,000 tons imported, and the value of steel being fixed at $23, with the same values in the prosperous year, the amount of importation had increased. Now, does that not indicate that what you say, that the importations will increase in bad years, is not sustained by this record?

Mr. FELTON. Well, those years were years when the foreign mills were well occupied by the foreign markets.

Mr. UNDERWOOD. Do you mean to say that in 1897——

Mr. FELTON. In 1897? No.

Mr. UNDERWOOD. That is what I say. This is 1897.

Mr. FELTON. I thought you said in 1907.

Mr. UNDERWOOD. In 1897, when there was a low market, and the same value of rails abroad, as compared with rails in 1906, the importations were small, and in 1906 they had increased, which evidently does not sustain your theory that they come in here in bad times, does it?

Mr. FELTON. I am afraid—I am pretty stupid, I guess, but I can not get the point you are trying to make. Of course, in 1906 we were very busy, and the foreign mills were also very busy. There may have been some railroads not able to get the rails in this country, and they imported foreign rails.

Mr. UNDERWOOD. We agree to that; but in 1897 you were not very busy?

Mr. FELTON. No.

Mr. UNDERWOOD. And the foreign mills were not very busy?

Mr. FELTON. No.

Mr. UNDERWOOD. But in that year there was only one-fifth the number of rails brought into this country that were brought in nine years later, in 1906.

Mr. FELTON. Yes.

Mr. UNDERWOOD. And that does not sustain your proposition that a dull market would mean an importation of rails?

Mr. FELTON. Would not that be explained by the low selling price of rails in this country in 1897?

Mr. UNDERWOOD. I was going to say that I do not think the low selling price in this country would be what fixes it, but it would be the low price of rails abroad as to whether they would come in here.

Mr. FELTON. If rails would come in here at $19, the foreign maker would have to meet the price, or approximately meet the price of $19, and pay the duty in that way, so that the low price at which rails are selling here would be almost sure to shut out the foreign rails.

Mr. UNDERWOOD. I think so. That is what I was coming to. Therefore, when we have a poor market—we agree absolutely on that proposition. When we have dull times and a poor market here, and a low price here, the American producer need not fear competition.

Mr. FELTON. Yes; that is true, but we could not get back to those low prices and live unless prices of raw materials, labor, and freights would go back to where they were. That would enable us, of course, to reach these low costs again.

Mr. UNDERWOOD. I would like to call your attention to the fact that we did import into this country in 1907, 4,610 tons, which, of course, was a negligible amount as to the total production——

Mr. FELTON. Yes, sir.

Mr. UNDERWOOD. But we did import 4,610 tons, at a value of $133,000, or a price per ton of rails of $29, just a little more than the American price.

Mr. FELTON. I happen to know about some rails that were imported in that year, and they were special rails; that is, they were rails that were used by street railways. It is a special rail that is made in Germany for going around the curves in street railway tracks, in the streets. I know that some of those rails were imported in that year. Whether those were the rails or not, whether that would explain it, of course I do not know.

Mr. UNDERWOOD. In other words, if they were special rails, they did not come in competition with the American product; but the importation of that small amount of rails seems to have been the basis on which the American market was fixed, and it was just below the price of rails that came in.

Mr. FELTON. I think if you could have that matter investigated you would find out that they were what was known as girder guard rails, for the purpose of these curves. They are specially designed rails, made in Germany.

Mr. UNDERWOOD. This is what I want to ask you: If they came in here at $29—that was their valuation—were those rails sold in this country at $29, or were they sold here at $29, with the duty added?

Mr. FELTON. I do not know.

Mr. UNDERWOOD. Do you know what the importation of rails was at that time, these German guard rails; were they sold at $29?

Mr. FELTON. I do not know. I simply know of the fact of their having come in. I should think the custom-house could tell you what that was. I don't know.

Mr. UNDERWOOD. Do you know or have you any idea of what a European rail can be purchased for in New York, or could have been purchased for in 1907, with the duty and all paid, if any came in?

Mr. FELTON. I do not know; but I could tell you what they could be purchased for now.

Mr. UNDERWOOD. In New York?

Mr. FELTON. Pretty nearly.

Mr. UNDERWOOD. All right; tell us.

Mr. FELTON. I could not tell you exactly. It is something better than $33, but just what I do not know. That is figuring on $3 freight rate, which I think is high.

Mr. UNDERWOOD. About $33?

Mr. FELTON. Something less than $33.

Mr. UNDERWOOD. Very much less? One dollar less?

Mr. FELTON. I do not know; I simply know that rails were sold at Antwerp at less than this figure I have used in computing this price.

Mr. UNDERWOOD. That will give me what I want. What do you say they are sold for at Antwerp?

Mr. FELTON. This is the latest report we have. Rails have been sold at Antwerp at $23.04, or better.

Mr. UNDERWOOD. Twenty-three dollars and four cents?

Mr. FELTON. Or better.

Mr. UNDERWOOD. And to that, how much freight do you add to cover the cost of bringing it to this country?

Mr. FELTON. That, of course, depends upon the foreign freight rate. I figured on $3, but I think they could be brought for a good deal better than $3—perhaps $2.50.

Mr. UNDERWOOD. Could they be brought here for $2?

Mr. FELTON. We have had freight rates on iron ore of between 6 and 7 shillings; that is $1.75. Rails would be more than iron ore. I do not think they could come in for less than $2.

Mr. UNDERWOOD. So there is at least $2, and the duty must be added to those rails to bring them into this country?

Mr. FELTON. Yes.

Mr. UNDERWOOD. Splitting the difference and putting it $2.50 to bring them in here would make the cost of bringing rails in this country $25.70. Now, is there any marine insurance on that?

Mr. FELTON. I think that ought to cover the marine insurance.

Mr. UNDERWOOD. So that the difference between what your cost is and what they can be landed here for from Antwerp amounts to about $1 a ton under the present prices?

Mr. FELTON. Will you kindly repeat that?

Mr. UNDERWOOD. You gave me the cost a while ago at $26.42.

Mr. FELTON. $23.04 at Antwerp.

Mr. UNDERWOOD. No; your cost of production is $26.42?

Mr. FELTON. Yes.

Mr. UNDERWOOD. And you give the selling price at Antwerp as $23 and add $2.50 for freight, which makes $25.50; which makes the difference between your cost and their selling price in New York of 90 cents a ton?

Mr. FELTON. Yes.

Mr. UNDERWOOD. Is that correct?

Mr. FELTON. That would be according to your figures; yes.

Mr. UNDERWOOD. Now, you get a duty of $7.84 a ton to protect a difference in cost of 90 cents.

Mr. FELTON. Well, remember that all our rails are not delivered at New York.

Mr. UNDERWOOD. Of course not.

Mr. FELTON. They are delivered all along the Atlantic coast, and even for delivery in New York we have to pay freight, and the prices I gave you are f. o. b. mill prices. The German mills from Antwerp would probably get a lower rate to the Gulf ports than they would to New York.

Mr. UNDERWOOD. I understand that.

Mr. FELTON. Those vessels go out very light to get cotton and will take almost any rate.

Mr. UNDERWOOD. But as to interior points, the mill located in the interior would have the advantage of that differential in freight, which you do not have.

Mr. FELTON. A mill located in the interior has the natural protection due to the freight from the seaboard always, and I said when I began here that we are the most vulnerable to any lowering of the tariff rate.

Mr. UNDERWOOD. That being the case, there being only 90 cents difference, according to your statement, in the difference of your cost and what the rail can be laid down at from Antwerp, and having nearly $7 clean protection on it above the cost of production, do you not think that for the sake of revenue, with a government deficit of many millions of dollars, the rail interests of this country can concede something?

Mr. FELTON. I have to look back to the profits on our business which we transacted in those years, and I have given you those profits, and I have shown you what we realized out of the business in 1905 and 1906, which were the best years we ever had, and, based on those figures, I do not see how we could do it, and I do not believe you do.

Mr. UNDERWOOD. I am not answering the question. I want to get it from you.

Mr. FELTON. I say I do not think we could. I have given you those figures.

Mr. UNDERWOOD. You have given me the cost of your production.

Mr. FELTON. And I have given our profits per ton.

Mr. UNDERWOOD. And you have given the Antwerp price, with the freight added, and there is only ninety-odd cents difference, and you have $7.80 duty out of which to make profit, and I think that if you were to make a profit of $1 or $2 a ton you would be making a handsome profit. Suppose you made a profit of $2 a ton on the amount of production of steel rails, you would be making a handsome profit, would you not?

Mr. FELTON. Just remember that the steel mill, to keep up, has to renew itself absolutely once in ten years. That is an expense which you have to figure into your cost, because it will come out in the end.

Mr. UNDERWOOD. You included that in the $26.42, I understood you, did you not? Into that amount did you not put all of your cost?

Mr. FELTON. That was before anything was charged off for depreciation.

Mr. UNDERWOOD. How much are you going to charge off on that for depreciation?

Mr. FELTON. I think we charged off something like 50 cents a ton.

Mr. UNDERWOOD. Fifty cents a ton for depreciation?

Mr. FELTON. I think so.

Mr. UNDERWOOD. That makes the total cost of the steel rail, allowing for depreciation, $26.92?

Mr. FELTON. Our average depreciation in this period I find was 55 cents a ton.

Mr. UNDERWOOD. That would make what, then?

Mr. FELTON. But you are figuring on the prices delivered at New York, while we would have to pay, I think, $1.25 freight to New York from our mill.

Mr. UNDERWOOD. Let us fix the cost price first, as I have started to do. That makes the cost of your steel rail $26.97, including everything, depreciation and all, does it not?

Mr. FELTON. I think it is about that. Our cost or our profit?

Mr. UNDERWOOD. No; I am asking for your cost. I am not worrying about the profit. I want to know if you stand on the proposition that your total cost, including depreciation and everything else, is $26.97.

Mr. FELTON. I am sorry it takes me so long to find these things in my papers. I am afraid I have not that here.

Mr. UNDERWOOD. Were not your figures stated a while ago correct?

Mr. FELTON. The profits in 1907——

Mr. UNDERWOOD. I do not want the profits; I want the cost.

Mr. FELTON. Oh, yes. I have that right here. After deducting our general depreciation, $26.15. Our depreciation that year was not as heavy as the average.

Mr. UNDERWOOD. Then $26.15 is what you say it cost you per ton, everything included?

Mr. FELTON. Yes; everything included.

Mr. UNDERWOOD. Twenty-six dollars and fifteen cents?

Mr. FELTON. Yes.

Mr. UNDERWOOD. Now, taking the Antwerp price, adding $2.50 for freight, makes it $25.50, which leaves——

Mr. FELTON. Just wait a minute. I made a mistake. It should be $26.70.

Mr. UNDERWOOD. All right; $26.70. Taking the Antwerp price, and adding $2.50 for freight, and then deducting that, leaves a difference between you at your mill and the foreign product in New York Harbor of $1.20, prepared to reach out into this country for business.

Mr. FELTON. You mean that is the price of foreign rails delivered in New York compared to our f. o. b cost at mill?

Mr. UNDERWOOD. Yes. Now, above that cost is profit, and the duty now being $7.84, you have $6.64 duty out of which to make your profit?

Mr. FELTON. I think that is an extreme case, because we deliver very few rails at New York. Our business, you know, is largely delivered at Savannah and through the Southern States—Pensacola and Galveston, for instance.

Mr. UNDERWOOD. But let me call your attention to this fact: If there were a steel mill located at New York that would compete from New York with you in your business, you would be starting out on an equal basis at that point. The cost price there of that mill's product and your cost price when you start out to go across the continent in competition would be about on an equality. In other words, I put the foreigner into New York. That is the best place for him to land his freight cheaply, because there are more vessels coming there?

Mr. FELTON. I suppose so; yes, sir.

Mr. UNDERWOOD. I have located his industry at the cheapest point he can land on American soil, where he can get in here the cheapest, to put him in competition with you, and under this present tax you have $6.64 the advantage of him. I want to know if the steel-rail business, with $6.64, according to your own figures, advantage of the foreign product landed in the cheapest port of New York does not think it would be fair to concede something to the American Republic in the way of producing revenue?

Mr. FELTON. I think your figures must be wrong somewhere, because when we got $28 at our mill we only made one dollar and——

Mr. UNDERWOOD. If there is anything wrong with those figures, will you call the attention of the committee to it?

Mr. COCKRAN. You stated your figures were wrong.

The CHAIRMAN. Yes; you stated your figures were wrong.

Mr. FELTON. Yes, sir; I did. I said something more than that.

The CHAIRMAN. Did the reporter take it down?

The STENOGRAPHER. Yes, sir; I have it.

The CHAIRMAN. Will the stenographer read that, as far as the witness had gone?

The STENOGRAPHER (reading):

I think your figures must be wrong somewhere, because when we got $28 at our mill we only made one dollar and——

The CHAIRMAN. Now, what were you going to say in addition to that, Mr. Witness?

Mr. FELTON. I was going to add that we only made $1.66. Those are the actual figures shown by the year's business.

Mr. UNDERWOOD. I think the whole reason it is wrong is that you did not use the entire amount of protection afforded you, and your local competition in the American market pulled down your profit.

Mr. GRIGGS. We have been all theorizing over this question for about three hours. Do you know Mr. Andrew Carnegie?

Mr. FELTON. Yes, sir.

Mr. GRIGGS. Pretty rich, is he not?

Mr. FELTON. He is said to be.

Mr. GRIGGS. Do you know Judge Gary?

Mr. FELTON. I do.

Mr. GRIGGS. He is pretty well off, is he not?

Mr. FELTON. I do not know.

Mr. GRIGGS. Do you know Mr. Schwab?

Mr. FELTON. Yes, sir.

Mr. GRIGGS. He is pretty well off?

Mr. FELTON. I do not think he is as well off as he was at one time.

Mr. GRIGGS. Do you know Mr. King, who was here this morning?

Mr. FELTON. Yes, sir.

Mr. GRIGGS. He is pretty well off?

Mr. FELTON. I do not know.

Mr. GRIGGS. Do you know of a poor man in the steel business?

Mr. FELTON. I do.

Mr. GRIGGS. Where is he?

Mr. FELTON. Right here—I am he. [Laughter.]

Mr. GRIGGS. That is why they sent you here. [Laughter.] You are the only one.

Mr. FELTON. I do not think I am the only one.

Mr. GRIGGS. Do you know of any more?

Mr. FELTON. I do not think that has much to do with this question before the committee at this time.

Mr. GRIGGS. Are you the gentleman drawing this modest salary you handed up here to the committee this afternoon?

Mr. FELTON. I handed to Mr. Clark a memorandum of what my salary was.

Mr. GRIGGS. And you began in the chemical office of the steel mills and you went up through the mills to the presidency of this Pennsylvania Steel Company?

Mr. FELTON. I did.

Mr. GRIGGS. You own no stock in it?

Mr. FELTON. I own 550 shares.

Mr. GRIGGS. What is the capitalization of that company?

Mr. FELTON. The capitalization is $16,500,000 of preferred, 7 per cent preferred, and $10,750,000 of common.

Mr. GRIGGS. $27,250,000 altogether?

Mr. FELTON. Yes, sir.

Mr. GRIGGS. What was the original capitalization?

Mr. FELTON. The original capitalization?

Mr. GRIGGS. Yes, sir.

Mr. FELTON. That is the original capitalization of the business when the company was formed, and ever since the company has been formed.

Mr. GRIGGS. Since the company was formed?

Mr. FELTON. Yes, sir.

Mr. GRIGGS. How much actual money was put in?

Mr. FELTON. The full amount of money.

Mr. GRIGGS. Every dollar?

Mr. FELTON. Excepting the common stock does not represent cash paid in.

Mr. GRIGGS. And that is $10,000,000?

Mr. FELTON. Ten million seven hundred and fifty thousand dollars.

Mr. GRIGGS. Have you paid any dividends on that?

Mr. FELTON. Never.

Mr. GRIGGS. Never paid any dividends on that?

Mr. FELTON. No, sir.

Mr. GRIGGS. But you do know that the great fortunes of the United States have been made out of the steel industry, do you not?

Mr. FELTON. That is said to be the fact. There have been great fortunes made in the steel industry, and in the mining industry, and in the oil industry, and all kinds of things where people were smarter than I am.

Mr. GRIGGS. In everything that is protected great fortunes have been made?

Mr. FELTON. I do not think oil is protected.

Mr. GRIGGS. Then I have no further questions to ask you.

The CHAIRMAN. That $10,000,000 of original capital was increased to $50,000,000?

Mr. FELTON. No, sir; that represents the actual money engaged in the business.

The CHAIRMAN. But you started out at $10,000,000?

Mr. FELTON. No, sir; our actual capital stock issued is $16,500,000 of preferred and $10,750,000 of common, and besides that we have some $17,000,000 of bonds.

The CHAIRMAN. You say the $50,000,000 is actual cost?

Mr. FELTON. The $50,000,000 is the actual cash engaged in the business. It is the value of our plant, plus our working capital and all that. There is $50,000,000 of money engaged in doing this business, which I have been trying to describe.

The CHAIRMAN. What I am trying to get at is whether the $50,-000,000 was actually put in?

Mr. FELTON. Yes, sir; the $50,000,000 was actually put in.

The CHAIRMAN. Or did you improve the plant with money that you made out of it—the profits?

Mr. FELTON. That has been growing and increasing ever since 1865, when the company was started.

The CHAIRMAN. From money made out of it?

Mr. FELTON. Yes, sir. I think it started with a capital of perhaps $1,500,000.

The CHAIRMAN. And to cover the amount of money made out of it you issued stock—money that went into the construction that was made out of it?

Mr. FELTON. In 1901 or 1900 there were $10,000,000 of new cash put into it.

The CHAIRMAN. At any other time?

Mr. FELTON. Since then we bought an ore property in Pennsylvania, for which we paid in bonds some $7,000,000, trying to get out supplies of raw material.

The CHAIRMAN. That is $27,000,000.

Mr. FELTON. Then there have been issued $1,250,000 of bonds to pay for some by-product coke ovens.

The CHAIRMAN. That is $28,250,000.

Mr. FELTON. I can go on and tell the whole thing, if you care for it.

Mr. GRIGGS. I deducted $10,000,000 from that, because he said for $10,000,000 common stock no money was paid.

The CHAIRMAN. Is that correct?

Mr. FELTON. Ten million dollars of common stock? I say when the $10,000,000 of new money was put in a bonus of $10,000,000 in common stock was given to the people who subscribed for that stock. No dividends have ever been paid on that.

The CHAIRMAN. Capital stock is how much, preferred?

Mr. FELTON. Sixteen million five hundred thousand dollars.

The CHAIRMAN. How much common?

Mr. FELTON. Ten million seven hundred and fifty thousand dollars.

The CHAIRMAN. That is $27,250,000?

Mr. Felton. We have bonds of something like $17,000,000.

The Chairman. That is $44,000,000?

Mr. Felton. I say there is besides that, in accrued earnings and so on, the present value of the plant, and the working capital employed in the business, amounting to a total of $50,000,000.

The Chairman. The bonds were issued for property you bought, were they?

Mr. Felton. Property and money.

The Chairman. You sold some of the bonds and bought additional property, so that the only water in the $50,000,000 is the $10,000,000 common?

Mr. Felton. That is all.

The Chairman. When you pay dividends of course you pay the interest on the bonds?

Mr. Felton. First, of course.

The Chairman. Then you pay dividends on the preferred?

Mr. Felton. Dividends of 7 per cent.

The Chairman. How long have you been paying 7 per cent on the preferred?

Mr. Felton. Since 1900.

The Chairman. How much do you pay on the common?

Mr. Felton. None at all.

The Chairman. Never paid anything on the common?

Mr. Felton. No, sir.

The Chairman. So that is water yet? You have presented some figures here; did you make them yourself?

Mr. Felton. No; I had our accountant make them up. I had our statistician or chief clerk make them up. They are taken right off of our books. I could not go over our books.

The Chairman. Of course you have bookkeepers and they keep the accounts showing the cost of material and labor for making steel rails, and at the end of each year you have a summary of that, do you not?

Mr. Felton. We have a monthly report of our cost.

The Chairman. Well, at the end of each month you have a report?

Mr. Felton. Yes, sir.

The Chairman. Your monthly report shows the various items of cost per ton of steel rails?

Mr. Felton. Yes, sir.

The Chairman. And from that you get the average cost each year?

Mr. Felton. Yes; and every six months we check them up by taking stock, or taking our inventory, and checking up our actual value as shown by the actual figures as against the book value.

The Chairman. Well, can you not furnish this committee a copy of the summary made each month for the years 1902 and 1907?

Mr. Felton. I do not know whether I can or not. Yes; I can for 1902.

The Chairman. 1902, 1903, or 1901—any one of those years.

Mr. Felton. It would be easier for us to do it for 1902 and 1906, because those years were the first year and the last year during which we prepared figures for the Bureau of Commerce and Labor.

The Chairman. You do not do that now?

Mr. Felton. They have not asked for any figures since 1906.

The CHAIRMAN. Who has not?

Mr. FELTON. The Bureau of Commerce and Labor.

Mr. GRIGGS. Has the Census Bureau?

Mr. FELTON. No, sir. Those figures are in the possession of the Bureau of Commerce and Labor now, being itemized figures for those five years.

The CHAIRMAN. Have you any objection to furnishing to the committee the figures for which I have asked?

Mr. FELTON. If you will say you will not make those figures public, because it is a great damage to us to have our figures known, not only among our American competitors, but if those figures should go out and get into the possession of the foreign mills you would be giving them just that information which you are trying to get from the foreign mills and can not get.

The CHAIRMAN. I do not want to make any such bargain as that. I suppose they were given to the Bureau of Commerce and Labor in the same way?

Mr. FELTON. They were. They promised us they would not be made public.

The CHAIRMAN. Have you any objection, if I should call on the Bureau of Commerce and Labor, to letting them furnish me a summary showing the cost per year of the product of steel rails—the average cost—without disclosing the figures themselves?

Mr. FELTON. I certainly will take pleasure in consenting to that.

Mr. LONGWORTH. How many other corporations make the same product you do, outside of the United States Steel Corporation?

Mr. FELTON. Rails? There are the Colorado Fuel and Iron Company, the Lackawanna Company, the Cambria Steel Company, the Bethlehem Steel Company. Mr. Topping's company also makes rails—what is the name of his company? The Republic Iron and Steel Company, I believe; and our own, of course. All of those make rails. Did you inquire with reference to any other lines of product besides rails?

Mr. LONGWORTH. Generally with whom are you in competition?

Mr. FELTON. In construction steel, with the Lackawanna—that is, the Lackawanna, ourselves, the Cambria Steel Company, the Bethlehem Steel Company, and some mills in Chicago are in competition. There are quite a number of mills in all lines. Jones & Laughlin are the largest manufacturers of structural steel outside of the United States Steel Corporation, and there are others.

Mr. LONGWORTH. In your opinion, does your average yearly profit substantially approximate the average yearly profit of other corporations outside of the United States Steel Corporation?

Mr. FELTON. I think so. The concerns in the Pittsburg district have a great advantage over us in the cost of fuel. They also have advantage over us in the cost of iron ores from the Lakes, but we have the advantage of foreign imported ore, and I do not think they can vary very widely. Of course, they do vary some. The situation has a great deal to do with it.

Mr. LONGWORTH. You think, then, that the United States Steel Company's average profit per ton is greater than that of the independent companies?

Mr. FELTON. As shown by their annual reports it certainly is, but remember that all these figures are due to their owning their ore and transporting ore by water and rail, and the production of coke and limestone, and everything going into the manufacture of steel, on which they get profit all the way up.

Mr. LONGWORTH. Could you state substantially what the average profit per ton is of the independent steel companies?

Mr. FELTON. I could not do it. I do not know.

Mr. LONGWORTH. Is it 20 per cent?

Mr. FELTON. Twenty per cent on their sales?

Mr. LONGWORTH. On the total cost.

Mr. FELTON. I do not know. I do not like to say anything I do not know.

Mr. COCKRAN. The United States Steel Company, by their reports, you say, show a much larger profit? Do you know what their profits were as shown by their reports on the manufacture of steel rails?

Mr. FELTON. They do not show what the profit is on steel rails.

Mr. COCKRAN. Would you be prepared to deny or do you think it doubtful it is $10 a ton?

Mr. FELTON. What do you mean by cost?

Mr. COCKRAN. I mean cost.

Mr. FELTON. Their cost and ours are very different. Do you mean that they figure in as profit the legitimate profit on the iron ore, making a ton of rails, or the legitimate profit in transporting the ore to their mills, the legitimate profit in mining their coal and converting it into coke, and all those things all the way down?

Mr. COCKRAN. I assume all the profits are legitimate. Now, go ahead and add them together and tell us what profits you think you can find in cash.

Mr. FELTON. I do not know.

Mr. COCKRAN. Would you be surprised to find it is $10 a ton?

Mr. FELTON. I should; yes.

Mr. COCKRAN. You think it is not as much as that?

Mr. FELTON. I do not think it can be.

Mr. COCKRAN. Do you think it is $9?

Mr. FELTON. What is the use of guessing at it?

Mr. COCKRAN. You can do nothing but guess?

Mr. FELTON. That is all.

Mr. COCKRAN. You do know it is much larger than yours?

Mr. FELTON. I do.

Mr. COCKRAN. What proportion of the 4,000,000 tons do they produce? You say there are 4,000,000 tons produced altogether?

Mr. FELTON. There were in 1906.

Mr. COCKRAN. You produced 400,000 tons, or about 10 per cent?

Mr. FELTON. Yes.

Mr. COCKRAN. Do you know what proportion the United States Steel Corporation did produce?

Mr. FELTON. It is shown in each one of their annual reports.

Mr. COCKRAN. It is?

Mr. FELTON. Yes.

Mr. COCKRAN. Well, we can get it then from their reports. Now, as I understand this, you stated this company of yours began with a capital of $1,000,000?

Mr. FELTON. I said I thought so. It was long before I became connected with the company. I think they started with a $1,500,000 company. That was the first Bessemer steel company in the United States.

Mr. COCKRAN. And then $10,000,000 cash was put in?

Mr. FELTON. There was cash put in along at different periods all the way along.

Mr. COCKRAN. At what time? When was the stock next increased?

Mr. FELTON. I could not fix the date.

Mr. COCKRAN. When were the $16,500,000 preferred stock issued?

Mr. FELTON. That was in 1901.

Mr. COCKRAN. I want to show the value of the common stock.

Mr. DALZELL. He gave those figures to the chairman.

Mr. COCKRAN. Begging your pardon, he did nothing of the kind. There were $10,000,000 cash put in?

Mr. FELTON. Yes, sir.

Mr. COCKRAN. And for that, $10,000,000 of common stock and $10,000,000 of preferred issued?

Mr. FELTON. Yes, sir.

Mr. COCKRAN. That made $16,500,000 of preferred stock?

Mr. FELTON. Yes, sir; $16,500,000 of preferred stock.

Mr. COCKRAN. And $10,750,000 of common stock?

Mr. FELTON. Yes, sir.

Mr. COCKRAN. There were $17,000,000 of bonds issued. That makes altogether $44,000,000 of capitalization, and you have over $50,000,000 worth of property?

Mr. FELTON. Yes, sir; about $50,000,000.

Mr. COCKRAN. The preferred stock and the bonds represent together $33,500,000, being $17,000,000 of bonds and $16,500,000 of preferred stock. That makes a total of $33,500,000. Now, the difference between $33,500,000 and $50,000,000 of property represents the value of the common stock? Is not that so?

Mr. FELTON. I think so; yes.

Mr. COCKRAN. So your $10,750,000 of common stock represents an actual value of $16,500,000 of property, and would be worth about $160 a share on the basis of breaking up the property to-day?

Mr. FELTON. The property would not sell for that value if broken up.

Mr. COCKRAN. Oh, no; I understand that. You said to Mr. Payne that the common stock was issued as water and remains water. It would not be exaggerating to describe it as at least equal to cream, as "cream" is generally understood? [Laughter.]

Mr. FELTON. I suppose the value of it, of course, is fixed by the return on it, and it has never paid any returns.

The CHAIRMAN. Was the United States Steel Corporation required to file a similar report with the Department of Commerce and Labor?

Mr. FELTON. I think they were. I think Mr. Garfield told me, when he asked for ours, that——

The CHAIRMAN. Will you leave those statistics there with the reporter?

Mr. FELTON. Can you not let me get a report of what has gone on here to-day and make up a brief and put these things in?

The CHAIRMAN. We want to print that to-night, and you will have a chance after it is printed to correct it, but we want it printed with our regular daily edition.

Mr. FELTON. These are on slips of paper, and I am afraid the reporter would get them mixed.

The CHAIRMAN. I notice they are, and the only thing we desire is that they be preserved in our record.

Mr. FELTON. I shall be very glad to leave them here.

The CHAIRMAN. If you will put them in proper shape and hand them in, we will be glad.

Mr. FELTON. I would much rather do it in that way.

The CHAIRMAN. I would much rather you would; so we agree on that proposition.

E. C. FELTON, PRESIDENT OF THE PENNSYLVANIA STEEL COMPANY, PHILADELPHIA, FILES SUPPLEMENTAL BRIEF.

PHILADELPHIA, PA., *December 14, 1908.*

COMMITTEE ON WAYS AND MEANS,
Washington, D. C.

GENTLEMEN: For the manufacturer whose works are located near the seaboard, the present rate of duty is none too high to give the protection necessary to enable him to make a reasonable profit on his investment and at the same time pay his labor such wages as the present scale of living in this country demands. The competition of foreign rail manufacturers reaches him first; works located in the interior having a natural protection because of the freight which must be paid on foreign rails coming into their market, while he not only has no such protection, but because his market is along the seacoast must pay in freights to reach his points of delivery an amount often equal to or in excess of that paid by the foreign manufacturer to reach the same points.

To illustrate: The works of the Maryland Steel Company are located at Sparrow Point, on the Patapsco River, near Baltimore. Their market is along the Atlantic and Gulf seaboard and on the Pacific coast of the United States. To reach a considerable part of the market, notably Gulf of Mexico points, and more especially the Pacific coast, this company must pay in freights an amount equal to or in excess of that paid by the foreign mills shipping to the same points.

The equipment of Maryland Steel Company's plant is modern, and was designed with special regard to the economical manufacture of steel rails. Its location on the seacoast is favorable to its engaging in the export business, and this it has done to a large extent. At the low prices received for exported rails a book loss has been shown, but it is felt that the business as a whole has been advantageous, since the foreign orders taken have allowed of the steady and regular operation of the mills, and so cheapened the entire output of the plant, besides permitting the fixed charges to be distributed over a larger tonnage.

The following table gives for the ten years 1898 to 1907, inclusive, the average prices received per ton, f. o. b. mill, for rails sold in domestic and foreign markets:

	1898.	1899.	1900.	1901.	1902.	1903.	1904.	1905.	1906.	1907.	Average.
Domestic	19.44	22.42	29.78	25.84	27.72	27.92	27.44	27.66	27.93	28.08	27.13
Foreign	17.61	18.64	26.06	22.46	22.17	......	17.98	20.79	23.42	27.52	21.43
Average	18.72	21.04	28.00	25.12	27.46	27.92	22.76	25.96	27.33	28.02	25.89

During the ten years the Maryland Steel Company sold an average of 76.42 per cent of its product in the domestic market and exported 23.58 per cent, the proportion sold abroad varying from nothing to about 50 per cent in different years.

The profit per ton during this same period on this business, after deducting all fixed charges, but without charging off anything for general depreciation, is as follows: 1898, $1.136; 1899, $1.1999; 1900, $1.643; 1901, $2.011; 1902, $2.880; 1903, $1.644; 1904, $1.745; 1905, $3.718; 1906, $3.280; 1907, $1.664; average, ten years, $2.133.

During these years an average of 52.8 cents per ton was charged off to depreciation, leaving the net profits available for dividends and plant additions and extensions, $1.605 per ton of rails. It is impossible to determine with absolute accuracy the comparative costs of rails made for the foreign and domestic markets, since both are often produced concurrently and the cost items can not be separated. A careful estimate has been made, however, by crediting to the costs of foreign rails all rebates received from imported materials, such as iron ore, pig iron, and spiegeleisen used in their manufacture, but not crediting the incidental advantages coming from steady, regular operation, the spreading of fixed charges over a larger output, etc. This estimate shows that for the above period of ten years the exported rails show a book loss of $1.489 per ton and the domestic rails a profit of $3.138, and after deducting the 52.8 cents charged to general depreciation, a loss of $2.017 and a profit of $2.610 per ton, respectively.

The net cost of rails during this same period, before deducting anything for general depreciation, was as follows: 1898, $19.856; 1899, $19.841; 1900, $26.357; 1901, $23.109; 1902, $24.580; 1903, $26.276; 1904, $21.015; 1905, $22.242; 1906, $24.05; 1907, $26.356.

Much has been said in the public prints about the low costs at which rails could be made in the United States. These statements were true in the period between 1895 and 1900. The low costs have, however, permanently disappeared in the last ten years, as is indicated in the above table, which shows an increase of $6.50 in that time. This increased cost has been brought about by higher wages paid to labor, higher freight rates, and higher costs of raw material. The higher wages paid to labor have been largely offset by improved machinery, but the higher freight rates and higher costs of raw material are, it is believed, permanent elements of cost, which must always be considered in the future.

While the prices of raw materials have fluctuated widely in the past, the present level, or higher, will undoubtedly be maintained in the future, as a result of the withdrawal from the open market of many of the most important sources of supply through their acquisition by owners who reserve them for their own purposes.

The following tables indicate some of the important advances which have taken place during the period under view:

Price of lake ores at lower lake ports, 1898 to 1907, inclusive.

	1898.	1899.	1900.	1901.	1902.	1903.	1904.	1905.	1906.	1907.
Bessemer Mesaba ..	$2.15 to 2.25	$2.25 to 2.40	$4.40 to 4.90	$2.75 to 3.00	$3.00 to 3.25	$4.00	$2.75 to 3.60	$3.50	$4.00	$4.75
Non-Bessemer Mesaba	1.90 to 1.85	1.90 to 2.10	4.00 to 4.25	2.35 to 2.65	2.60 to 2.85	3.20	2.35 to 2.50	3.00	3.50	4.00
Old range Bessemer	2.75 to 2 95	2.80 to 3.25	5.50 to 5.75	4.25 to 4.65	4.25 to 4.65	4.50	3.00 to 3.25	3.75	4.25	5.00
Old range non-Bessemer	1.80 to 2.00	2.00 to 2.15	4.15 to 4.25	2.85 to 3.15	3.00 to 3.25	3.60	2.60 to 2.80	3.20	3.70	4.20

A still better idea of the increased cost of iron ore from the Lakes is given in the following table, which shows the cost of lake ores required to produce a ton of pig iron at Sparrows Point:

	1898.	1899.	1900.	1901.	1902.	1903.	1904.	1905.	1906.	1907.
Bessemer Mesaba..	$5.75	$5.85	$10.68	$7.58	$7.68	$9.66	$7.60	$8.65	$9.50	$11.25
Non-Bessemer Mesaba	5.35	5.52	9.68	6.82	7.28	8.46	6.90	8.40	9.25	10.70
Old range Bessemer	7.15	7.35	12.08	10.18	10.18	10.76	8.10	9.10	10.30	11.70
Old range non-Bessemer	5.78	6.05	10.18	8.48	8.88	10.06	7.60	8.70	9.70	11.00

In this same period freight rates on coal and coke have advanced, as follows:

	1898.	1907.	Advance.
Coal per ton, 2,240 pounds	$1.25	$2.15	$0.90
Coke per ton, 2,000 pounds	1.10	1.60	.50

To summarize the foregoing. In the ten years considered the average price obtained for rails at Sparrows Point was $25.89 per ton, showing a profit of $2.13 per ton, or after depreciation had been charged off, of $1.60 per ton. The costs had advanced in this period from $19.85 to $26.35 per ton, or $6.50 per ton.

Let us now consider not the profit per ton, but the return on the capital employed, and let us take not the whole period, but the two most profitable years—1905 and 1906.

The total amount employed in those years in plant and property, materials on hand, and working capital was, approximately, $10,500,000. The average profit per year without depreciation was as follows:

	Amount.	Per cent on $10,500,000 capital employed.
Gross profit	$1,369,602	13.08
Less interest on bonded indebtedness	182,137	1.74
Net income	1,187,465	11.34

From the net income a charge for depreciation averaging $652,799 each year was made, leaving a net profit of 5.09 per cent.

As the Maryland Steel Company, whose figures are those given, is a subsidiary company of the Pennsylvania Steel Company, which owns other companies engaged in similar and related lines of business directly concerned with steel manufacture, a diversion of profits legitimately arising from the operations of the Maryland Steel Company might appear to have been made to those other companies and the true state of affairs concealed. The total amount employed in all the companies owned by the Pennsylvania Steel Company (and these companies are all engaged in the line of business connected directly with steel and iron making, such as ore and coal mining, transportation, and the manufacture of many kinds of steel products besides rails) was approximately $50,000,000.

The average aggregate profits of these companies (including the Maryland Steel Company) for 1905 and 1906 were as follows:

	Amount.	Per cent on $50,000,000 capital employed.
Gross profit	$5,420,117	10.79
Less interest on bonded indebtedness	748,313	1.49
Net income	4,671,804	9.30

From the net income a charge for depreciation, averaging $1,572,787 each year, was made, leaving a net profit of 6.2 per cent.

It will be seen from these figures that the percentage of profit made by the Maryland Steel Company (which is a manufacturing company only) is somewhat in excess of that made by the combined companies, and that no misrepresentation has been made, either knowingly or unintentionally, in the figures presented.

To again summarize: On the capital investment in rail manufacture the Maryland Steel Company has earned yearly in the two best years of the last ten years 11.34 per cent. It is submitted that an average profit during the last ten years of $2.13 per ton on rails and a return of 11.34 per cent before charging off any amount for depreciation, during the two most profitable years of that period, on the capital invested is not unreasonable or excessive.

Any reduction in the present duty will bring about a reduction in the price at which rails sell along the seaboard and will reduce or wipe out the existing margin of profit. The present rate is not higher than necessary to prevent the dumping in this country of surplus by foreign manufacturers, and that it has not resulted in exorbitant profits or unreasonable prices to American railroads is shown by the foregoing statements and by available records of prices in the steel-producing countries of Europe. It is therefore asked that no change be made in the existing duty of $7.84 per ton on rails unless a corresponding reduction is made in the duties on the materials which enter into the manufacture of rails, viz, iron ore, pig iron, spiegeleisen, and ferromanganese.

While the figures presented apply only to the operations of the Maryland Steel Company, they are believed to represent substantially those of other American rail manufacturers.

Respectfully submitted.

E. C. FELTON,
President Pennsylvania Steel Co.

STATEMENT OF JESSE F. ORTON, SECRETARY TARIFF REFORM COMMITTEE, REFORM CLUB, NEW YORK CITY.

FRIDAY, *November 27, 1908.*

Mr. GRIGGS. Is your concern making money?

Mr. ORTON. I do not think so.

Mr. GRIGGS. You do not know?

Mr. ORTON. It is not a money-making concern.

Mr. GRIGGS. You are not one of the objectionable protected manufacturers?

Mr. ORTON. No, sir.

Mr. Chairman and gentlemen of the committee, I appear before you, first, as a producer who is not protected by any tariff duties, and, second, as a consumer of goods paying a portion of the taxes imposed by protective duties, both those which go to the Government and the larger amounts which either go to private interests or are wasted by the forced pursuit of unprofitable industries, but merely as such a producer and consumer I should not be able to be here. As a representative of the tariff-reform committee of the Reform Club of New York City, I came to listen to your proceedings and to report upon them, not expecting to address the committee; but the broad invitation of the chairman, spoken here and published in the press, has led me to ask your attention very briefly.

The committee which I represent directs its efforts toward the reduction of duties in the interest of the great body of consumers and producers of unprotected goods. Some years ago this committee went to the trouble of making extensive investigations into tariff subjects and the publication of the results. Since my connection with the committee, during the last nine months, it has been unable to make very extensive detailed investigations, but has sought to popularize, through the newspapers of the country, such knowledge as might be available. Therefore I can not speak to you with a technical knowledge or with very detailed data upon any particular industry. To do so would require investigations so extensive and expensive that the ordinary citizen could not undertake it, and the organized movement which I represent has been unable with the means at its disposal to prosecute such investigation in addition to the work I have mentioned.

I will speak for a few moments on the iron and steel schedules partly because my attention has been given to that more particularly than to others and partly because those schedules are undoubtedly the most important of all in their effect upon the consumers, and constitute what may be termed a plain case for the relief of the people. My proposition is that the iron and steel industry, at least the basic industries relating to the extracting of the ore and the production of the well-established forms of iron and steel products, including pig iron, rails, bars, ingots, sheets, and the further finished products of nails, wire, cutlery, etc., have no need of any protective duty whatever, according to the protective theory itself, and have not needed any protection for years. Justice to the 80,000,000 of consumers who use iron and steel in thousands of different forms demands not the reduction, but the total abolition of these duties by your committee and by Congress. The protective theory, as laid down in the platform, which is binding on the majority of Congress, and as interpreted by the incoming Executive, justifies the levying of no taxes in favor of any industry except to compensate for its greater cost of production as compared with its foreign competitors, the ordinary and reasonable return to capital being considered as one element of the cost of production. That the making of iron and steel is now, and has for years, been carried on at less cost in this country than in any foreign country is shown, first, by the statements of those qualified to speak for the business itself; second, by the undisputed fact that the iron and steel industries send their products in large quantities into the open markets of the world and compete successfully with their strongest foreign rivals.

Under the first heading we have the statement of Mr. Schwab, formerly president of the United States Steel Corporation, in 1899, to the effect that steel rails were made in this country at that time for less than $12 per ton, while in England they cost $19 per ton. Some years ago the relative cost of iron and steel in this country and in England was the subject of investigation and report by an English commission, which found the Pittsburg cost of a ton of pig iron was $7.90 per ton as compared with an English cost of $12.70 a ton, the labor cost at the furnaces being 2s. in Pittsburg and 3s. at the British works. Within the last few days we have the published statement, with which you are familiar, of Mr. Andrew Carnegie, for many years the master of the iron and steel business and now a heavy owner of its securities. Referring to steel manufacturers, he says:

To-day they need no protection unless, perhaps, in some new specialties unknown to the writer, because steel is now produced cheaper here than anywhere else, notwithstanding the high wages paid per man. Not a ton of steel is produced in the world at as small an outlay for labor as in our country.

Mr. HILL. Have you any facts in your paper to prove that statement?

Mr. ORTON. No, sir.

Mr. DALZELL. Have you any facts in your paper to help us? We do not care for an academic discussion of the tariff.

Mr. ORTON. I stated at the outset that I had no detailed facts.

Mr. DALZELL. That is what I thought. What is the use of reading a paper like that?

Mr. ORTON. I understood from the invitation of the chairman that everyone interested in tariff revision was invited to express their views.

The CHAIRMAN. Proceed to read the paper, but we would like the facts. That is what we are seeking for.

Mr. ORTON. This showing, I think, is not refuted by the representations made before you in regard to the production of steel rails. It would be more satisfactory if a representative appeared from some of the plants having the lowest cost, and not from a plant which appears to be at a disadvantage in that regard. Yet this particular plant has competed on the whole successfully in the foreign rail markets for ten years, and its $10,000,000 of watered stock has paid no dividends only because the profits have been kept in the business. Under the second heading, regarding competition abroad, we have the fact that about 10 per cent of the production of the Steel Corporation was sold abroad in 1907, more than 1,000,000 tons of iron and steel goods. Much of our exports generally of iron and steel manufactures are sent to the homes of our strongest competitors, Great Britain, Germany, and France, as well as to the neutral markets of the world. That protection is no longer needed is also shown by excessive profits, especially of the huge corporation controlling more than one-half of the business. The last annual report shows net profits of $160,000,000. By a certain manipulation of figures these profits are made to appear to be earned upon gross sales and earnings amounting to $757,000,000, which would indicate a profit of about 27 per cent on the cost price. But the percentage of profit was much greater than 27 per cent, probably twice that amount, because the gross sales given in the report are admitted to include sales made between subsidiary companies. The report does not state the amount of genuine gross sales—that is, between the corporation and the outside world—but from common knowledge as to the average market price of its output of about 10,000,000 tons it may be safely estimated that the gross sales were not more than from $460,000,000 to $500,000,000, which would indicate a profit of about 54 per cent, or upward of 50 per cent on the cost price.

As indicating excessive profits, we have the further fact of lower prices being habitually charged for exported goods than for those sold in the United States. A few days ago certain members of this committee inquired of a witness if he personally knew of any case of a lower price for foreign than for domestic consumption. With reference to iron and steel, we have the statement of the steel corporation itself and its officers. In 1901, before the Industrial Commission, President Schwab testified that under normal conditions export prices were always lower than home prices. We have the statement in the corporation's last annual report that the average mill price per ton received for all exported material was 7½ per cent less than the average price received for all domestic shipments. This is another peculiar statement, for it is well known that the exports consist mainly of products much more highly finished and bearing on the average much higher prices than the products sold in the United States. While such products as nails, wire, tin plate, etc., were sold abroad the domestic tonnage consisted mainly of heavy products, like rails, structural steel, etc., so that the actual difference between the export and domestic prices figured on the same class of goods would be much greater than 7½ per cent, and has been estimated at from 15 per cent to 30 per cent for the year 1907, covered by the report, and a higher percentage for the present year.

The steel interests, led by the great corporation, has kept prices up during the industrial depression of the past year, protected by tariff duties, to the embarrassment of thousands of manufacturing concerns dependent upon iron and steel for their materials, keeping steel rails up to the high prices which prevailed before the panic, more than double the cost of production, if we may believe reasonable statements, to the great detriment of the railroad industry. And these interests, without any pretense at secrecy, have met from time to time in New York City to fix the price of the most important material of American industry.

The monopoly prices of iron and steel products, possible only through the tariff duties, are an oppressive tax upon the people who must buy machinery, hardware, and other articles containing iron and steel, and a tax upon every person who rides in a railway car or pays freight on goods transported by rail. If the railways had enjoyed reasonable prices for rails and other iron and steel supplies, they would not find any necessity now for increasing freight rates and placing the burden of millions each year upon the consumers of the country.

The case against the iron and steel duties could be made much longer, but it is not necessary. It is a plain case by the admission of those connected with the industry. The consumers of the country know the essential facts and are waiting to hear whether you and Congress will not only make good the pledges that have been made, but will do justice by relieving them of these taxes now paid to private interests, conservatively estimated at upward of $100,000,000 a year. The reduction of these duties will not suffice. An apparent considerable reduction might give no substantial relief. The people demand not a compromise, but the simple justice to which they know they are abundantly entitled.

Mr. UNDERWOOD. You say what they are entitled to as a matter of justice, but you do not state what that is. What is it that you contend for?

Mr. ORTON. Abolition.

Mr. UNDERWOOD. Absolute abolition?

Mr. ORTON. Yes, sir.

Mr. UNDERWOOD. On all iron and steel articles?

Mr. ORTON. On all basic materials, as I stated.

Mr. CLARK. And if there was a cut of 50 per cent it would still leave the steel people an absolute monopoly of the market?

Mr. ORTON. I think so.

There are other schedules in which the case for the abolition of the duty is a plain one, notably the duties on coal, petroleum and lumber. There are schedules which call loudly for at least a decisive reduction, notably the woolen, sugar, and certain chemical schedules, but the head and front of tariff injustice in this country are the iron and steel schedules. Unless you wipe these out it will be shown that the people can not get justice, as I conceive it, at the hands of their representatives.

I think it can not be doubted that the removal of these duties and most of the other removals and reductions called for would benefit the actual and final consumers. I have been a little surprised by certain discussions on that subject in this place, not that the matter is unimportant, but that it would seem to belong more properly to supplementary legislation with reference to combinations and restraint of trade. The ordinary laws of trade teach that the imposition even of a trifling tax upon a consumable commodity is ordinarily transferred to the consumer, casting upon him the burned not only of the tax itself, but also of the added profit which must be made by the manufacturer and middleman upon the increased capital required on account of the tax. Likewise the removal of such a tax benefits the consumer by more than the amount of the tax, because there is a decrease in the capital required by the manufacturers and dealers, and consequently a decrease in the amount, though not in the percentage of their profits.

The only thing which will prevent the consumer from getting the benefit of such a reduction of taxation is monopoly and restraint of trade. It would seem to be the proper function of a legislative body to devise and apply a remedy for such monopoly and restraint of trade and not to make an abnormal condition, if it exists, the occasion or excuse for failure to remove a burdensome or unjust tax. As some such remedy may be necessary in certain cases in order to insure the consumer the benefit of tariff reduction, I would ask whether it is not time for Congress to consider the advisability of preventing the abnormal lowering of prices in particular sections of the country for the purpose of forcing a rival out of business? This has been a common method of creating a monopoly. Such a law, if provided with suitable penalties to be recovered by the party injured, would be largely self-executing like the laws against theft.

The members of this committee seem to be very alive to the necessity of considering not only the difference in daily wages in comparing labor cost in this and foreign countries, but also the relative efficiency of the labor here and there. The chief trouble, so far as the testimony adduced here is concerned, would seem to be that the information comes through interested sources. I wish to emphasize the necessity of also considering the relative cost of living to which American and foreign workmen are subjected and of remembering that with any fair and just revision of the tariff the cost of living of the American workman will be decidedly reduced and he might then accept a lower scale of daily or money wages without injuring his situation in any respect. In like manner the other costs besides the labor cost of the great body of manufacturers will also be reduced, leaving them free to accept without injury lower prices for their finished products. It is quite misleading to consider each schedule as a separate matter without giving due weight to the benefits that would accrue to workmen and employers through the reduction of other schedules.

The question of tariff revision is unfortunately involved with questions of revenue. We protest against the retention for revenue purposes of any of these duties which are now used for the purpose of plunder rather than protection. If the revenue of the Government must continue to be drawn from import duties, let other objects be chosen than the necessities of the people on which they have paid tribute to monopoly for a great many years; but we would earnestly inquire whether it is not time for Congress to find other means of obtaining revenue besides taxing the people upon their consumption of goods. A tax upon men in proportion to their expenditures, especially their expenditures for the necessities of life rather than upon their income or property or the privileges which they enjoy under the Government, is indefensible according to any just principle of taxation. Under such a system, if taxes were strictly in proportion to the expenditures of different individuals, either collective or on particular objects, those of small and moderate means would pay an excessive tax as compared with those of greater wealth. But as indirect taxes are actually levied, the poor man pays at a much higher rate even on his actual expenditures, and the system becomes nothing less than a travesty upon fairness and equality. If desired, I could point your committee to many instances in the Dingley tariff in which the cheaper grades of an article consumed by people of moderate means pay three or four times the rate of duty paid on the more expensive grades of the same article purchased by the rich and well-to-do. On account of the inherent injustice of customs duties as a means of taxation, even when arranged as best they can be according to the wisdom of man, we urge you to take steps toward the collection of at least a portion of the Government's revenue by less objectionable methods.

That closes my paper.

Mr. HILL. Will you kindly give me your name and whom you represent, if anybody besides yourself?

Mr. ORTON. My name is Jesse F. Orton, of New York City. Besides representing myself as a citizen I also represent the tariff reform committee of the Reform Club of New York City.

Mr. BOUTELL. Who are the officers of that club?

Mr. ORTON. I have a list of the 13 members of the committee, if you desire to know them.

Mr. HILL. I am very glad to see the Reform Club represented here. You stated a moment ago that the only information which we seemed to have was from interested parties. Who would we expect to hear from except interested parties? I speak of the people of the whole United States.

Mr. ORTON. In that sense. That is a broader sense than I used the word.

Mr. HILL. What was the meaning?

Mr. ORTON. I said so far as these hearings were concerned. I admit that the committee may be getting information on its own account, but so far as these hearings are concerned those who have given information on the foreign cost have been chiefly those interested in manufacturing in this country.

Mr. HILL. You are not included in that class?

Mr. ORTON. I am not engaged in manufacturing.

Mr. HILL. Then I suppose you are here to give us information as a disinterested party?

Mr. ORTON. I said that we had not been able to make investigations of that sort as to their costs.

Mr. HILL. It is not information from abroad that I personally desire. I sat here all day Wednesday and so far as I recall no member of the steel corporation appeared before the committee. Can you give us any information in regard to that organization and its work?

Mr. ORTON. I have pointed to certain information which is contained in its reports. We have no inside information.

Mr. HILL. You have no facts in regard to the matter?

Mr. ORTON. We have known facts.

Mr. HILL. I asked one of the witnesses here whether or not the price of steel rails was fixed in London and whether the area of the earth's surface was distributed in parts where the different companies supplied the demand?

Mr. ORTON. We have not been able to get that information.

Mr. HILL. Can you give any information in regard to the tin-plate business, whether the prices are fixed by international agreement?

Mr. ORTON. We have not been able to get that information.

Mr. HILL. Can you give me any information as to whether there is any agreement that the United States manufacturers shall only export tin to a certain amount in consideration of the sale of back plates to foreign tin-plate makers?

Mr. ORTON. Those questions relate to matters which are. the most difficult in the world for parties outside of the companies to obtain.

Mr. HILL. Can you give me any information as to whether there is an international agreement fixing the price of wire nails and the distribution of the product?

Mr. ORTON. We are not in the confidence of the companies.

Mr. HILL. Can you give me any information as to whether or not there is any international agreement in regard to fixing the price of steel in any form or shape or method of distribution?

Mr. ORTON. I have pointed to the statement of the steel corporation.

Mr. HILL. As to the cost of production, the unit cost?

Mr. ORTON. I have referred to that.

Mr. HILL. All the criticism you make is based purely on hearsay and not upon actual facts?

Mr. ORTON. I think not. It is based on the published reports of the steel corporation and the published statements of its officials.

Mr. HILL. I am earnestly seeking for information, not for criticism. I am not asking these questions with any idea of criticising your paper. You stated that our information came from interested sources. You appear as a disinterested party. I would like to have the information for my own personal knowledge. If you say absolutely that you are unable to give us any direct and practical facts in regard to these matters, of course it is useless to ask further questions. If you have any such information I, for one, would be glad to have it.

Mr. ORTON. I do not know whether you were present at the beginning of my paper, but I stated distinctly that the organization which I represent has no means of making detailed. investigations on any particular schedule.

Mr. HILL. In the three or four weeks which we have for securing detailed information it seems it is necessary for us to get the facts from somebody rather than general criticism.

Mr. ORTON. We would have been more than delighted to have been able to furnish that information; but I will state, as I stated in my paper, that the gathering of the information would cost thousands of dollars, where the committee has had only hundreds or tens of dollars to spend.

Mr. HILL. Your committee or this committee?

Mr. ORTON. No; our committee.

Mr. HILL. Then you have failed to secure the actual practical facts to put before the committee in connection with your paper?

Mr. ORTON. We endeavored during the last summer to obtain actual quotation of the export and home prices, such as this same committee did obtain about four years ago and submitted in a pamphlet, but we were unable to do so.

Mr. HILL. Will you inform me how your committee could arrive at a correct conclusion without the facts that you say you have not been able to obtain?

Mr. ORTON. We had certain facts which are admitted in the published reports of the steel corporation and the published statements of their present and ex-officials.

Mr. HILL. And yet you say that the committee ought not to rely upon such interested information?

Mr. ORTON. There is an old principle of law that an admission "against interest" party can be relied upon.

The CHAIRMAN. Will you please give us the reference to that report where the steel makers state the unit of cost of their articles? I understood you to say in your paper that you stated the unit of cost from the published report of some steel corporation. I would like to have the date, etc. Of course, we can look it up, but if you have the date we can turn readily to that report and get it before the committee.

Mr. ORTON. I do not know that there is any official report of the steel corporation referring to exactly that point.

The CHAIRMAN. But whatever report there is on that point I would like to have a reference to it so that the committee can get it.

Mr. ORTON. I have a reference in one of the publications of our club to a letter said to have been written by Mr. Schwab in 1899, stating that the cost of steel rails was less than $12 a ton. I can not refer you more definitely at this time, but I will try to do so.

Mr. HILL. I have that in my pocket, so it will not be necessary; I can hand it to the chairman.

The CHAIRMAN. I wanted to learn whether there was any other published report in which the unit of cost was given?

Mr. ORTON. I do not think the steel corporation in its annual reports, although they contain a great deal of information, go into the subject of the unit of cost.

The CHAIRMAN. That was my information that the annual reports contain a great deal of information, but they do not contain this specific fact which you mention. That is the reason I wanted to get at the information to which you have access.

Mr. ORTON. I do not know.

Mr. CLARK. The steel men came here and stated with perfectly straight faces that they only make from $3\frac{1}{2}$ to $4\frac{1}{2}$ and 5 per cent, and in extreme cases 8 per cent profit, and yet everybody knows that the whole crowd has gotten rich. It is extremely difficult to break them down when you ask them questions on cross-examination, because they go back and repeat the same story over. Individually, I do not believe a word of it, and for that reason I am going to try to put all the steel and everything of that sort on the free list. If they would be frank and tell their profits it would be illuminating. Now, if you know of any way to get the truth out of those people I would like to have you suggest it.

Mr. ORTON. The committee has a number of experienced attorneys among its membership whom I do not believe I could attempt to teach in the art of cross-examination.

Mr. CLARK. I know, but they just simply go back and repeat the very same statement, that their profits are $3\frac{1}{2}$ per cent and $4\frac{1}{2}$ per cent, and up to 8 per cent, which I believe is the highest that any steel or iron man has testified here he has made, and yet, judging from outside appearances and reports and all that, they have made more money than any other people in America, and they could not make it off 3½ and 4½ per cent dividends. There is some trick about the evidence or some trick about the way they keep the books. If you can shed any light on it, either to-day or at any other time, I will be very much obliged to you.

Mr. ORTON. I would like to make a suggestion in that regard. I notice that you have had before you from the steel-rail industry, which includes broader lines, only one representative from one plant. Now, whenever the tariff duties or other causes give a large monopoly to an industry there are certain unit plants which do not make large profits, unless the owners, the controlling force of the industry, ruthlessly shut out all competition, which I do not believe they have tried to do or it is to their interest to do.

Mr. CLARK. Do you know of anybody who does know the inside of the iron and steel business who is willing to come here and tell the truth about it?

Mr. ORTON. I do not know of anyone except those on the inside of the corporations who would know or could well know the inside truth.

Mr. CLARK. I have been practicing law ever since I was a grown man, and I have tried all sorts of criminal cases on both sides—as prosecuting attorney and as defending counsel—and I have never run across a crowd of witnesses in any criminal procedure on earth that stuck to the same story on cross-examination with such absolute and unvarying fidelity as these people do. That may be a very plain and blunt statement, but that is my statement, and I am responsible for it.

Mr. ORTON. I may say that I think you are right.

Mr. BOUTELL. I think it would give weight to your argument if you would kindly give the officers of your league right in this connection.

Mr. ORTON. Yes, sir; I was interrupted. The president of the Reform Club itself is Mr. Calvin Tomkins, of New York. The secretary is Mr. Bert Hanson. Mr. Tomkins, I might say, is interested in various business enterprises, but I do not know just what they all are—building materials and other things. Mr. Hanson is a lawyer and also deputy police commissioner of the city of New York. The members of the tariff reform committee of the Reform Club are Byron W. Holt, chairman, Everett V. Abbot, John G. Agar, Henry de Forest Baldwin, Henry George, jr., Bert Hanson, Wallace Macfarlane, Robert Grier Monroe, Albert Plaut, Calvin Tomkins, Frank L. Underwood, John De Witt Warner, and Louis Windmuller.

Mr. BOUTELL. Does that include the board of directors?

Mr. ORTON. I have not a list of the board of directors, but several of those men are members of the board.

Mr. BOUTELL. On about the next page to the last of your remarks you used this expression, as I recall it, without qualification the schedules that are designed for protection and those that are designed for plunder?

Mr. ORTON. Yes, sir.

Mr. BOUTELL. You represent, of course, the opinion of the officers whose names you have given, and I take it the members of the organization as a whole?

Mr. ORTON. I think so.

Mr. BOUTELL. Will you give us now the list of the schedules that, in the opinion of your organization, are designed for plunder?

Mr. ORTON. I can give you a partial list, but I can not give you a complete list. I am guided in that by the principle of protection, not any opinion that some of us may hold against protection itself, the principle of protection which requires no duty unless the cost of production here is greater than it is abroad, and in that list I would include the duties on iron and steel, as I have said, at least the well-established forms of the industry; the duty on petroleum, which is exported in its crude form and its products to almost every civilized country on the face of the earth; the duty on lumber, which, as brought out in the testimony here, has benefited no one except the owners of timber lands in the United States; the duty on varnish, as brought out in the testimony here, the representative of that industry stating that they compete with the whole world and that he simply wanted a tariff duty because he might have trouble in the future; the duty on borax, which bears about double the price in this country that it does in foreign countries simply because of the tariff. I think that the duty, though I am not so familiar with that myself, on most of the raw mineral products like lead and copper would also be included in that list, and the duty on a great many heavy products like salt which defy competition in the interior, but whose manufacturers claim the right to furnish to every person in the United States even clear to the Atlantic seaboard. My memory does not serve me to mention others at this time.

Mr. BOUTELL. Those that you have mentioned are the ones that you referred to as "designed for plunder?"

Mr. ORTON. They represent that class.

Mr. BOUTELL. And among those you put steel?

Mr. ORTON. Yes, sir.

Mr. BOUTELL. You must be aware, or you would not undertake to discuss this question, that the steel schedule, which you put as the most plunderous of all, was designed and inserted in the Wilson bill in 1894?

Mr. ORTON. I am.

Mr. BOUTELL. So that plunder began at that time?

Mr. ORTON. I beg pardon. Do I understand you to say that this schedule originated in the Wilson bill?

Mr. BOUTELL. That is what I asked you. Whether you were aware that the present steel schedule was designed in the Wilson bill and adopted in the present bill with one or two schedules made considerably lower?

Mr. ORTON. I have understood that the iron and steel industry was well protected before that.

Mr. BOUTELL. Yes, sir; but these were the schedules fixed in 1894.

Mr. ORTON. They may be; I am not sure of that.

Mr. BOUTELL. You speak of the classes of consumers also without any qualification. Now, there have been a number of witnesses before our committee who have advocated a reduction in certain duties for the benefit of the consumer, but when I came to analyze their testimony I found that they meant a different person by "consumer" from what I did. I would like to see this tariff benefit the "ultimate consumer," the man who buys and uses the thing. Most of the wit-

nesses who have appeared here have used the word " consumer " as
referring to a class of people who buy what you might call the crude
material, or the material in its first form, and who pass it on through
three or four other agencies before it reaches the ultimate consumer.
That is, the man who uses lumber for making boards spoke of himself as the consumer, whereas he passes it on to the box manufacturer,
and the box manufacturer passes it on to the user of the boxes, and
the user of the boxes to the man who buys the contents of the boxes;
and so, I think, almost invariably the word " consumer " has been
used in these hearings by the man who expected to benefit by a reduction on his raw material—that is, what was raw to him, but which he
passes on to the next consumer. You use the word " consumer "
without qualification. Do you use that word in speaking of the raw
steel to the makers of cutlery and so on, or do you speak of what I
mean by the " ultimate consumer ? "

Mr. ORTON. I speak of what you mean, but the benefit can be given
to him only through the mediation of these various dealers who pass
the goods on to him.

Mr. BOUTELL. Do you think that we can make a reduction in the
steel schedule by abolishing all the duties on the raw material which
will be passed on and reach the ultimate consumer of the product?

Mr. ORTON. I think there is no question of it, and my memory
serves me to recall a number of instances in these hearings where witnesses have given the information that the benefit would be passed
on to the ultimate consumer, although in most cases they have been
what we might call intermediate consumers.

Mr. BOUTELL. But rather the trend of the testimony has been that
the profits were being sought by what you might call the inter-
mediary consumer?

Mr. ORTON. It would naturally be so, because those who have appeared before you who were not manufacturers have been almost
exclusively importers and wholesalers.

Mr. BOUTELL. Is your organization in favor of continuing to raise
substantially the present proportion of national income from taxes on
foreign imports or are we to understand from your paper that your
organization favors abolishing all duties on foreign imports, and
providing that proportion of our revenue now raised from the tariff
from some other source?

Mr. ORTON. Speaking for myself and for most of the organization,
though that has not been officially decided that I know of, they prefer
any just direct tax to the indirect tax on imports, and perhaps, while
not expected at the present time, they would welcome any change in
that direction.

Mr. BOUTELL. I understand. We can not reverse our entire revenue system at this session of Congress to raise $300,000,000, and raise
half of that revenue from some other source. Is that your object,
the substitution of a direct tax for the tariff?

Mr. ORTON. That is the object, as far as I am personally concerned,
and I know of certain others, but I do not think it has been officially
decided.

Mr. BOUTELL. The abolition of all duties on imported goods?

Mr. ORTON. Yes, sir.

Mr. CLARK. I think that this committee wants information, I know
that I do, and I do not think I am any better than the rest. How

much would it cost to employ an expert—just taking this steel schedule and nothing else—to go to Belgium, which seems to be the real seat of all the devilment that takes place on the tariff question, and find out what it costs to make steel and steel products? Do you have any idea what it would cost to send that expert over there, assuming that we are not getting the information here that we ought to get?

Mr. ORTON. I do not know that I have any better idea than you would have, but I imagine it would cost several thousand dollars at least, and considerable time.

Mr. CLARK. There will be more than three and one-half months' time, practically four months, before the extra session of Congress will be called. That is, the extra session can not be called in less than three months and the chances are it will be about the middle of March. I have not very much money, but I am willing to contribute $100 to send some expert over there and find out whether the information given here in regard to steel is correct or whether it is not correct. If there is any way of getting money enough to send an expert over there I am in it.

Mr. ORTON. I will be glad to contribute to that fund myself.

The CHAIRMAN. Perhaps I ought to say that we have had government experts at work now for about six months, not particularly in regard to steel, but all the schedules.

Mr. CLARK. When are we going to get the results?

The CHAIRMAN. We have secured some results now, but they are not entirely satisfactory, I am sorry to say. They will be placed before the committee in due time.

Mr. UNDERWOOD. This question of the tariff is one that has been before the country for a long time, and always will be in some form of taxation. The dominant party in control of the Government at the present time stands for a protective tariff. The Democratic party has declared in its platform for a revenue tariff. Do I understand that your association stands in opposition to both those propositions?

Mr. ORTON. I do not know that I can say officially that the committee which I represent stands against a revenue tariff. I know the opinion of some of its members is that way, and I know my own opinion is.

Mr. UNDERWOOD. Against a revenue tariff?

Mr. ORTON. Against any tariff. I might say that they very much prefer a revenue tariff to a protective tariff.

Mr. UNDERWOOD. Of course that is a step in your direction.

Mr. ORTON. Yes, sir.

Mr. UNDERWOOD. You do not stand for the declaration of the Democratic party?

Mr. ORTON. We recognize that taxation by indirection according to consumption is not a just principle of taxation.

Mr. DALZELL. What form of direct taxation would you prefer?

Mr. ORTON. In the first place, I believe it is one of the most unfortunate things that our Constitution prevents the levying of direct taxes upon the States without being in proportion to the population. It has prevented practically the levying of any of the direct taxes, except we include income taxes in that category, which were used in our early history. It has prevented of late years the application of the income tax. I can not speak for the organization on this point, but personally I believe that an income tax would be preferable for a part of our revenues to the tax on imports, and if the constitutional limitation were removed, a tax upon States in proportion to their ability to pay; that is, their property instead of their population, would be a much more just form of taxation.

Mr. DALZELL. Under the existing condition, the Constitution being as it is and the construction of the court as it is, what form of direct taxation do you suggest?

Mr. ORTON. I suggest that the President elect has said that an income tax can be framed which would meet with the approval of the court, and I would respectfully suggest that Congress meet that suggestion by framing an income tax along the lines recommended by the President elect and at the same time submit to the States of this nation a constitutional amendment which will take away any supposed constitutional prohibition.

Mr. DALZELL. So you confine yourself to an income tax as a direct tax?

Mr. ORTON. That would make a step in the desired direction. I think the National Government has heretofore availed itself of other taxes during the civil war, the inheritance tax and possibly others, which might be also employed.

Mr. GRIGGS. Do you intend to go so far as to tax land?

Mr. ORTON. If I had my own way I would.

Mr. UNDERWOOD. You would have the Federal Government levy its taxes on the lands of the country?

Mr. ORTON. I do not see any reason why they should not bear their share of the cost of the Federal Government as well as the state and local governments.

Mr. BOUTELL. Then you would abolish the excise taxes as well as the tariff?

Mr. ORTON. Personally—I speak personally only—I would, unless they were thought to be desired for the purpose of preventing the consumption of liquors and tobacco—as police measures rather than revenue measures.

Mr. BOUTELL. Past experience will show that they have not prevented their use?

Mr. ORTON. Possibly that is so.

Mr. GRIGGS. You would not favor the abolition of the tax on whiskey?

Mr. ORTON. What I said was that I would not, purely as a taxation measure, retain it, but as a police measure I might wish to retain it.

Mr. UNDERWOOD. You would be willing to retain it for its power of suppression?

Mr. ORTON. Yes, sir.

Mr. UNDERWOOD. As a matter of theory I understand that you are opposed, as I am, to using the taxing power for the purpose of building up a man's business. In theory can you reconcile that to the proposition of using the taxing power to destroy a man's business?

Mr. ORTON. It would not be for the purpose of destroying a man's business, but for the purpose of destroying a noxious custom among the inhabitants, as a police measure.

Mr. UNDERWOOD. In other words, instead of using the power of the courts you would use the power of taxation to punish a man without giving him a trial in the courts?

Mr. ORTON. I do not see it in that way.

Mr. UNDERWOOD. That is what the result would be.

Mr. ORTON. I do not know that I made myself plain on that subject. The only reason that I can see for the taxing of any commodities, more especially with reference to liquors and tobacco, would be that it was wise as a public policy to discourage their use, not, perhaps, necessarily to prevent their use.

Mr. GRIGGS. Then you are in favor of them?

Mr. ORTON. Personally, I would not take the tax off of whisky at the present time.

Mr. COCKRAN. What do you understand by a revenue tax, and what do you understand by a revenue tariff?

Mr. ORTON. As I understand, a revenue tax is levied for the purpose of obtaining government revenue and not for the purpose of protecting native industries.

Mr. COCKRAN. You would not object to such a tariff as that even if you were a free trader, as I am?

Mr. ORTON. Personally, I go further and object to the taxation of citizens in proportion to their consumption of commodities in any way.

Mr. COCKRAN. But apart from all that, as a mere matter of procuring revenue, is it not a fact from the experience of the only country that has tried it, that confining the tariff tax to a few articles of general consumption results not in decreasing but in increasing the revenue?

Mr. ORTON. I think that is very true.

Mr. COCKRAN. In England after the tariff-tax changes of 1846–1848, which resulted in abolishing the tariff tax on 1,200 articles and confining it, I think, to five, the result was an enormous increase in the revenue?

Mr. ORTON. Undoubtedly.

Mr. COCHRAN. Leroy-Beaulieu has discerned a deficit in the French national revenues. You know of him as an author of great distinction on economics. Is it not a fact that he recommended as the only way of curing the deficit in the French national revenues the confining of tariff taxation to about five or six articles?

Mr. ORTON. I think very likely that is the case.

Mr. COCKRAN. Mr. Dalzell has stated that a change in the system of taxation would of course affect the revenues. Is it not a fact that by confining tariff taxation to a few articles it might be that the revenues would be very largely increased instead of diminished?

Mr. ORTON. I think there is no doubt whatever about that.

Mr. DALZELL. You do not believe in raising taxes by tariff at all?

Mr. ORTON. Personally, I do not.

Mr. DALZELL. Do you advocate what is known as the "Henry George theory" of taxation?

Mr. ORTON. What do you understand by that theory?

Mr. DALZELL. Taxes on land.

Mr. COCKRAN. Taxes on land values.

Mr. DALZELL. Single taxes.

Mr. ORTON. I can not say that I advocate his views without reservation. I think there is some virtue in them.

Mr. LONGWORTH. What do you mean by an income tax?

Mr. ORTON. A tax such as was originally included in the Wilson bill of 1894 was an income tax.

Mr. LONGWORTH. Upon your theory of an income tax, how should the income be ascertained—by voluntary statement or by inquisition?

Mr. ORTON. That is a matter of detail.

Mr. LONGWORTH. No; I do not think so.

Mr. ORTON. It has been done in different ways in different income-tax measures. I believe that both methods might be relied upon with advantage.

Mr. LONGWORTH. Have you made any estimate what an income tax such as you propose would produce annually?

Mr. ORTON. I have not made any detailed estimate.

Mr. HILL. I am not half as much interested in these theories as I am in practical facts right now for the information of the committee. It is common rumor that the price of steel rails throughout the world is fixed by what is known as the "International Steel Rail Association," with its headquarters in London. Have you any information whatever in regard to that?

Mr. ORTON. I have no knowledge except the rumor you refer to.

Mr. HILL. Would you base your action on such rumors if you were in the position of this committee?

Mr. ORTON. I do not think it is necessary to rely on those rumors with reference to the international agreement. I think we have sufficient facts without that.

Mr. HILL. Assuming it is true that such an association exists and that it fixes the price in England precisely the same as it does in other countries?

Mr. ORTON. Yes, sir.

Mr. HILL. Would any change in the duty, raising or lowering it, tend to minimize the power of such an association if it was worldwide?

Mr. ORTON. I think a change or the abolition of the duties would be of benefit.

Mr. HILL. Why is it not so in England where there is no duty?

Mr. ORTON. I am not informed of any oppressive monopoly in the steel business in England.

Mr. HILL. You understand from rumor that there is such an association?

Mr. ORTON. I do not know whether there is or not.

Mr. HILL. Why would not that be true in the matter of rubber, on which there is no duty into the United States, and on all articles where the raw materials are imported, if such an international agreement exists?

Mr. ORTON. I may say that I think that can be done. I am free to admit I can conceive of a situation, that with all tariffs removed, where there would be a world's trust controlling any or all of these articles of raw material, they would dictate the price the world over the same as a national trust may dictate the price now.

Mr. HILL. You must admit that the question is not governed by the tariff.

Mr. ORTON. I think under present conditions it is very largely governed by the tariff.

Mr. HILL. The fact is against you if there is an international agreement controlling the price.

Mr. ORTON. I am not informed whether there is an international agreement on this material or any other material.

Mr. HILL. But you believe there is on the question of steel rails?

Mr. ORTON. I know of nothing but rumors.

Mr. HILL. And yet you can give us no information on that subject?

Mr. ORTON. I am not in the confidence of the steel corporation.

Mr. HILL. But you appear here as a disinterested party and criticise the general course of procedure on the ground that information is being received from interested parties?

Mr. ORTON. Perhaps I was misunderstood on that point. I did not mean to criticise the committee for hearing the statements of those individuals in any way whatever. I only meant to suggest that it would be desirable to secure, as Mr. Clark has suggested, information from other sources.

Mr. HILL. The committee is doing that, and is supplementing that with such information as you seem to be wholly unable to give. I want to make my own position clear. I am just as earnest and just as enthusiastic in getting this information as you are in giving it.

Mr. ORTON. I have no doubt of it.

Mr. HILL. And yet I do not pride myself on having one whit of advantage over the other members of the committee in seeking information and not considering theories to be applied a hundred years from now.

Mr. COCKRAN. Mr. Orton, while the tariff may not be the sole cause or necessary condition giving rise to these trusts, yet anything that tends to restrict the free competition of the world necessarily, in your judgment, I suppose, tends to create a trust in any one article?

Mr. ORTON. It certainly does, because it is much easier to create a local trust in a particular country than to create a world trust.

Mr. COCKRAN. In other words, whatever diminishes the supply or access to the world's supply necessarily facilitates the formation of these combinations, and accordingly, so far as the tariff operates to restrict the supply, it must necessarily facilitate the raising of prices?

Mr. ORTON. Certainly.

Mr. COCKRAN. There is another question I want to ask you, and that is concerning the consumer, the ultimate consumer. We have had a great deal of discussion about that, and Mr. Boutell's questions, put to the witnesses, have been singularly penetrating, and the answers given tended to illumine the subject a great deal. The consumer, as Mr. Dalzell pointed out, is somewhat of an elusive person when you come to identify him. Sometimes he is a middleman and sometimes an original purchaser and sometimes, as Mr. Boutell pursues the quest with vigor, he proves to be the man who uses the article in daily life. When you say the consumer pays the tax, I do not suppose you mean that he pays it all? There is a tendency to distribute it in every direction. The consumer pays some and the manufacturer who uses the raw material pays some. All through the community it is distributed, although the tendency everywhere is to push it off to the last person who uses the article taxed?

Mr. ORTON. Yes; I think that is the tendency, and in some cases it is all pushed off.

Mr. COCKRAN. And the consumer is the one who gets it, as Mr. Clark says, " in the neck? "

Mr. ORTON. Yes. [Laughter.]

The CHAIRMAN. If this joint discussion is now over, we will go on. If not, I suppose it must continue.

Mr. RANDELL. I would like to ask the witness some questions. These different theories you have been questioned about, as I understand, are not the object of your visit here; but you appear before the committee realizing the fact that we are going to pass a protective-tariff bill, or a revenue-tariff bill, and you personally favor, and your organization favors, a bill for a revenue tariff?

Mr. ORTON. We certainly do, in preference to a protective tariff.

Mr. RANDELL. I understand you also to take the position—I wish to see if I am correct about it—that the steel trust, as it is commonly called, not having appeared before the committee and sending simply a representative from one of the plants that has the most competition and the least profit, and the monopoly of their business being apparent and the revenue from it exceedingly small, that they ought to be put on the free list; that the revenue loss would be very little and the consumer would be benefited and the company itself, not caring to testify about the matter, would have no cause to complain. Is that your position?

Mr. ORTON. That is substantially my position.

Mr. RANDELL. I agree with you very fully.

STATEMENT OF CHARLES M. SCHWAB, OF SOUTH BETHLEHEM, PA., PRESIDENT OF THE BETHLEHEM STEEL CO.

TUESDAY, *December 15, 1908.*

The witness was duly sworn by the chairman.

The CHAIRMAN. Mr. Schwab, the committee desires to know a number of things that they think you know with reference to the iron and steel schedule. Would you like first to make a statement?

Mr. SCHWAB. No; I have nothing to ask, or nothing to state, Mr. Chairman; but I would be very glad to answer any questions that you have.

The CHAIRMAN. Well, we will see if we can not find something to ask you. You are connected with the Bethlehem Steel Company?

Mr. SCHWAB. I am.

The CHAIRMAN. In what capacity?

Mr. SCHWAB. I am an unfortunate stockholder, as well as president.

The CHAIRMAN. Stockholder and president?

Mr. SCHWAB. Yes.

The CHAIRMAN. Is that one of the branches of the United States Steel Corporation?

Mr. SCHWAB. No connection whatever.

The CHAIRMAN. No affiliation with it?

Mr. SCHWAB. None whatever.

The CHAIRMAN. And you were formerly connected with the United States Steel Association?

Mr. SCHWAB. I am not now, excepting as a stockholder.

The CHAIRMAN. But you were formerly an official there, were you not?

Mr. SCHWAB. I was.

The CHAIRMAN. During what year?

Mr. SCHWAB. About from 1900, I think, to 1905. I am not very sure about the dates.

The CHAIRMAN. A letter has been quoted as having been written by you to Mr. Frick in 1899, stating the cost of the production of steel rails at that time.

Mr. SCHWAB. I think that is correct.

The CHAIRMAN. Is that an authentic letter?

Mr. SCHWAB. It is.

The CHAIRMAN. What did you state was the cost of steel rails in that year?

Mr. SCHWAB. I have not a copy of the letter and——

Mr. HILL. Had we not better have the letter read?

Mr. SCHWAB. If you will, because I haven't a copy of the letter; but I know that I wrote the letter, and I have no doubt that the publication that you have is correct.

The CHAIRMAN (reading):

PITTSBURG, PA., *May 15, 1899.*

MY DEAR MR. FRICK: You asked me to give my views as to the probable future earnings of the Carnegie interests and as to the proposed reorganization on a basis of $100,000,000 bonds—$250,000,000 preferred stock and $275,000,000 common stock.

Permit me to say that, commencing in 1879 as engineer constructing the works, ten years as general superintendent of our principal works, and over two years as president, I feel that I know the properties and their possibilities as well, or better, than anyone in or out of the concern.

While we have been highly successful in the past, as everyone knows, I believe we are only now getting in shape to be truly successful and truly profitable. Our April profit-and-loss sheet shows earnings slightly over $1,500,000, with rails netting us only $17.50 and billets $16. Lowest prices we ever had, on an average, were $16.50 for rails and $14.50 for billets; so, you see, we have reaped very little of the advantages of increased prices. With prices anywhere near to-day's selling prices we could easily make over $3,000,000 per month, and then our new works to be started in two months will, I estimate on present prices, bring us an additional profit of $600,000 per month, or a total of $3,600,000 per month.

As to the future, even on low prices, I am most sanguine. I know positively that England can not produce pig iron at actual cost for less than $11.50 per ton, even allowing no profit on raw materials, and can not put pig iron into rails, with their most efficient works, for less than $7.50 per ton. This would make rails a net cost to them of $19. We can sell at this price and ship abroad so as to net us $16 at works for foreign business, nearly as good as home business has been. What is true of rails is equally true of other steel products. As a result of this, we are going to control the steel business of the world.

You know we can make rails for less than $12 per ton, leaving a nice margin on foreign business. Besides this, foreign costs are going to increase year by year, because they have not the raw materials, while ours is going to decrease. The result of all this is that we will be able to sell our surplus abroad, run our works full all the time, and get the best practice and costs in this way.

Very truly, yours,

C. M. SCHWAB, *President.*

The CHAIRMAN. Was that the letter?

Mr. SCHWAB. To the best of my knowledge that is the letter.

The CHAIRMAN. Were those facts stated in that letter true at the time?

Mr. SCHWAB. Yes.

Mr. CLARK. I hope the chairman will publish the letter.

The CHAIRMAN. Certainly; I will hand it to the reporter and it may be published.

Mr. COCKRAN. It is dated in 1899, you say, Mr. Chairman?

The CHAIRMAN. May 15, 1899. You say it was true at that time, Mr. Schwab?

Mr. SCHWAB. It was.

The CHAIRMAN. That you could produce steel rails at $12?

Mr. SCHWAB. We did. May I make an explanation, for you are asking questions?

The CHAIRMAN. One moment. I wish to ask you a few questions, and you will have a full opportunity to explain.

Mr. SCHWAB. Very well, go ahead.

The CHAIRMAN. You stated there that you knew positively that England could not produce pig iron at actual cost for less than $11.50 per ton, allowing no profit on raw materials. Was that true?

Mr. SCHWAB. At that time it was.

The CHAIRMAN. And could not put pig iron into rails, with their most efficient works, for less than $7.50 per ton?

Mr. SCHWAB. Quite right.

The CHAIRMAN. Which would make a net cost to them of $19?

Mr. SCHWAB. Quite right.

The CHAIRMAN. While you could make them for less than $12?

Mr. SCHWAB. Yes, sir.

The CHAIRMAN. So that the relative cost of making steel rails at that time in this country and England was $7 less here than there?

Mr. SCHWAB. That is not quite right, but very nearly so.

The CHAIRMAN. But substantially so?

Mr. SCHWAB. Substantially; yes.

The CHAIRMAN. Now, Mr. Schwab, we will hear your explanation.

Mr. SCHWAB. First of all, I want to say that that letter was written as an enthusiastic and optimistic young man seeking preferment in a great company.

The CHAIRMAN. Well, what was your age at that time?

Mr. SCHWAB. Well, we will let the worthy chairman guess at that.

The CHAIRMAN. You have no conscientious scruples against stating your age, have you?

Mr. COCKRAN. Better let us know your age, so that we can measure the enthusiasm for truth.

Mr. SCHWAB. Mr. Cockran can be assured that the truth is it was written in an optimistic vein.

Mr. COCKRAN. It is entirely true?

Mr. SCHWAB. Yes, sir; it is. That letter was written from the point of view of a manufacturer's department; in other words, while president of the company, I was particularly in charge of operation and was anxious to make the best showing possible in that department. That $12 per ton was actual mill cost, and it included none of the general charges which would be incident to any great business.

The CHAIRMAN. What did it include?

Mr. SCHWAB. I am going to tell you. The actual cost of making steel rail, other than interest charges, depreciation, and similar charges, which were always made by the auditing department in making up the yearly report.

The CHAIRMAN. Including the office force?

Mr. SCHWAB. Including the office force at the works but none of the general charges of selling or administration. The English cost did include it; and I will give you this cost in detail, if I may.

The CHAIRMAN. We would be very glad to have the costs right now.

Mr. SCHWAB. I should be glad to do that. Secondly, I want to explain the motive of that letter. The letter was written at Mr. Frick's solicitation. It was at a time when he was anxious to dispose of the Carnegie Company; and it was also written in an optimistic vein for a like reason. If you will bear that in mind in reading that letter, you will probably understand it better.

Now, I will go to the cost—as to how I arrived at a cost of $12 at that time for making rails, which was quite true then. We were leasing our ores at that time in the Northwest. We were not large owners of ores. We started out to buy them. But we were purchasing and leasing ores, as people familiar with the trade will recollect, at 10 cents and 15 cents a ton. The cost of mining in the Mesaba, because that was about the time the Mesaba ores were being made entirely on the surface and there was no depth mining at all, that was being done at a cost of 15 to 25 cents a ton, so that our cost of ore at the mines at that time was about from 35 to 40 cents a ton. Now, we transported those ores to the lakes for from 60 to 70 cents a ton. We transported them on the lakes for 60 cents a ton, and we transported them from the lakes to Pittsburg for 70 cents a ton more.

Mr. UNDERWOOD. That makes $2.40.

Mr. SCHWAB. I think that is right—in Pittsburg for these ores. Now, if you will divide by 58 per cent, which was then the average amount of iron in the ore, you will get the cost of the ore to make a ton of pig iron.

The CHAIRMAN. About $2, is it not?

Mr. SCHWAB. It is more than $2. If you will divide by 58 you will get the exact figure. Fifty-eight per cent was the contained iron in the ores in that year. It makes quite a difference between 50 per cent and 58 per cent. I will divide it if you like, but I see several members of the committee making the calculation, and I am sure it will be correct.

Mr. DALZELL. Mr. Hill makes it $4.31.

Mr. SCHWAB. $4.31. Now you must allow something for loss in that, because you do not get entirely all the iron; some passes over in dust, but it will be approximately $4.50. In that year it was from $4.50 to $5 a ton—$4.50 nearly—for the amount of ore to make a ton of pig iron.

The CHAIRMAN. About $4.50?

Mr. SCHWAB. Yes, ore to make a ton of pig iron. Now, the coke was the next thing. It cost us about $1 a ton to make our coke at the ovens in that year, and we had the coke carried to our furnaces for 75 cents, so that you will have to add $1.75 for fuel to make a ton of pig iron.

The CHAIRMAN. That is the total coke to make a ton of pig iron?

Mr. SCHWAB. It takes 1 ton of coke to make a ton of pig iron with 58 per cent ore.

Now, I will go on. Then you take the limestone. The limestone in the Pittsburg pig was carried 14 miles at 10 cents a ton. Our cost of limestone was about 35 cents for each ton of pig iron. If you will add to that about $1.65—it will cover all the expenses outside of material for making a ton of pig iron—you will have the approximate cost of a ton of pig iron that year.

The CHAIRMAN. What were those expenses, labor?

Mr. SCHWAB. Labor expense, and small things about the works.

The CHAIRMAN. Steam?

Mr. SCHWAB. Well, there was no steam in making pig iron—there was some at that time, but very little. Now, that was the cost of making pig iron in that year. If you will recollect, in that same year Pittsburg made a great many conversion contracts for making billets, the cost of which is not widely different from the cost of making rails, at $5 per ton above the cost of pig iron. That $5 a ton included our profit in those years, and I am not stating anything that is not generally known. If you will add, therefore, about $3.75 more a ton to that you will have the cost of making rails in Pittsburg in that year—that is, the mill cost, absolutely. It was about $12. Now, that would vary from month to month——

Mr. COCKRAN. Do you mean allowing for depreciation and things of that kind?

Mr. SCHWAB. I do not; I mean absolutely the cost at the mill. I stated that at first. My estimate was made up from the mill.

Mr. BONYNGE. You have given each of the items that make that up?

Mr. SCHWAB. I have, but I have not included depreciation, interest, or similar charges.

Mr. BONYNGE. It simply includes those items that you have mentioned, giving the amount of each item?

Mr. SCHWAB. Certainly.

Mr. COCKRAN. That would be $5 for conversion?

Mr. SCHWAB. I can give you that in detail if you would like.

Mr. COCKRAN. But that $5 included the profit?

Mr. SCHWAB. We had about a dollar to a dollar and a quarter.

The CHAIRMAN. How much is the total cost of converting pig iron into rails?

Mr. SCHWAB. From $3.75 to $4 a ton, that year.

Now, I want to tell you something else about that year. We have taken that part of the cost. We paid common labor that year a dollar a day. The lowest salary I ever received myself up to that time was in that year. There never was a time when we had everything connected with the steel industry on such a low basis as in that year. Men were most anxious for work, and you could get lots of men at from a dollar to a dollar and a quarter a day who would do the work of two men of to-day. The number of men employed in the mills was only one-half what it is under similar conditions to-day. I only speak of some of the things that go to make up the rail rates in that year. If you will read Mr. Carnegie's article on rebates you will see that we had rates in many instances one-third of what they are to-day.

Mr. HILL. Do the same conditions exist in Great Britain in regard to labor with which you made comparison at that time?

Mr. SCHWAB. Quite true; excepting this: At that time, in Great Britain, they had no mechanical appliances such as we had. Our great advantage in cost was because of our ability to mechanically produce things that they did manually.

Mr. HILL. Does that special advantage exist now?

Mr. SCHWAB. No, sir; it does not, for the reason that they have been able to adopt the things that we developed.

Mr. HILL. There is less necessity for a difference in the tariff now than there was then?

Mr. SCHWAB. I will come to that later, if I may go on, because I want to be very frank about the whole situation. I want to point out to you an apparent inconsistency which is not so inconsistent when you come to analyze it; in other words, let me put the question: "If I were writing that letter to-day, at what would I put the cost of steel rails?"

Mr. DALZELL. I was going to suggest that you tell us, in the same detail, what it would cost to-day.

Mr. SCHWAB. I would be very glad to do so. First of all, some seven or eight years ago—no, probably in 1901 or 1902, I am not sure—I testified before one of your committees in Washington that I placed a value on the ores of the United States Steel Corporation of a dollar a ton in the ground.

Mr. RANDELL. In order that I may understand you, are you going to talk in an optimistic vein or a pessimistic vein?

Mr. SCHWAB. I will let you be the judge of that; you may be the judge of that, sir. As I say, I then testified that the ore was worth a dollar a ton. It was then thought to be an optimistic estimate. I would call attention to the fact that since that time ores have not only been sold at a loss at a dollar a ton, but the lowest grade we have. I then spoke of 58 per cent ores, the same kind we have been using. The steel corporation are leasing to-day from the Great Northern Railroad—Mr. Hill—ores, the minimum of which are 89 cents, and in three years will be above a dollar a ton. So I want you to appreciate——

Mr. UNDERWOOD. Is that royalty alone?

Mr. SCHWAB. Yes; without any cost of taking it out of the mines. Now, I can not say accurately—the steel corporation can testify to this—but I think from one-fifth to one-fourth of all the ores that they take out this year will probably come from the properties on which they pay from 85 cents to $1 a ton royalty. That is first. Secondly, these mines that were formerly shoveling it—I have read in the newspapers some expert testimony on the cost of shoveling out Mesaba ores—but those ores were shoveled out at a cost of from 5 to 10 cents a ton. These mines are much deeper to-day, and much more costly to operate, and I do not believe that the Mesaba ores on an average can be produced to-day, mined to-day, anywhere below 50 cents a ton, and I think the cost is between 50 and 60 cents. You can not buy Mesaba ores to make steel, you must use old ores, or hard ores, and the cost is nearly double that, varying from 75 cents to $1 a ton.

Mr. COCKRAN. In what proportion?

Mr. SCHWAB. The best proportion is half and half. Please put these figures down, Mr. Hill. You have the cost of the ore in the ground at $1 per ton, as against our 10 and 15 cents I spoke of. If you will put the cost of mining now at 50 cents per ton; if you will put the cost of getting it to the lakes at 85 cents (I am giving you actual charges now); if you will put the cost of carrying it on the lakes at 70 cents, the cost of unloading and taking it to Pittsburg at $1, you will have the cost of the ores in Pittsburg.

Mr. Hill. Has the freight rate from the mines to the lakes increased in these ten years?

Mr. Schwab. It has.

Mr. Hill. How much?

Mr. Schwab. My best recollection is—I have not the exact figures—that it has increased from 60 to 85 cents. And it has increased on the lakes not so much, but from 60 to 70 cents.

Mr. Hill. Then there is an increase of about $1 in the transportation?

Mr. Schwab. Yes.

Mr. Hill. And the United States Steel Company owns and controls the transportation?

Mr. Schwab. I can not speak about that. You must ask them about that. Now, if you will divide that by 49, which is the average percentage of iron in the ore brought down last year, you will have the cost of the ore to make a ton of pig iron during these past several years.

Mr. Calderhead. Instead of 58?

Mr. Schwab. Instead of 58. We rejected ore up to that time that ran below 58, but now we take all of it that runs as high as 48. The other is not procurable, you can not get it.

The Chairman. Go on, Mr. Schwab.

Mr. Schwab. I would like to have these figures.

The Chairman. You had better make your own figures.

Mr. Hill. I make it 8.26.

Mr. Schwab. Well, I believe in labor saving.

Mr. Dalzell. 8.26, Mr. Hill says.

Mr. Schwab. If you will add what I did in the previous instance, the usual loss.

Mr. Underwood. I have worked it out and make it 8.20.

Mr. Schwab. Now, if you will add the usual losses in there you will find that that will be another 50 cents a ton. I allowed a lesser amount before——

Mr. Underwood. Your figures, then, show the cost of ore at the Pittsburg furnace, to make a ton of pig iron, amounts to $8.50.

Mr. Longworth. And it was $4.50 in 1889?

Mr. Schwab. Yes, sir; I will give you further details if you desire it.

Mr. Gaines. You are talking about different figures. Mr. Underwood said $8.50——

Mr. Schwab. Well, I added 50 cents a ton. $8.76 is right.

Mr. Hill. That is right?

Mr. Schwab. That is about right.

Now, if you will come to the cost of coking coal, you will find that in those years coking coal in the Connellsville region—I am calling on my memory for this; Mr. Dalzell will probably know better than I—was about $600 an acre, and to-day it is worth $3,000 an acre, the same coal. The cost of coke, therefore, made from Connellsville coal is proportionately greater. These are approximate figures, because it is hard to fix a definite value on those two things. Therefore, I know that coke may not be produced in the ovens to-day under $1.50 a ton;

and—I am not quite sure of this—but I think the freight rate to Pittsburg is 85 cents, again, on coke. It is within 10 cents.

Mr. HILL. You mean to make a ton of iron?

Mr. SCHWAB. No, I mean that is for a ton of coke. Now, this is a thing I would also call your attention to. In the year I wrote that letter 1 ton of coke made 1 ton of pig iron, because the ores contained 58 per cent of iron. Last year it took 1¼ tons of coke to make 1 ton of pig iron, because the ore only contained 39 per cent of iron. Therefore, you must add one-fourth to the value——

Mr. HILL. That is 52½, which would make $2.62 for the coke.

Mr. SCHWAB. If you will add that to the $8.50 you have $11.10, or something like that.

Mr. HILL. Then there is another item, there is labor.

Mr. SCHWAB. There is limestone. It costs 30 cents to mine limestone and $1.20 to take it to Pittsburg—$1.50. And you use about one-half a ton of lime to pig, making 75 cents for your lime for each ton of pig iron. The reason that more lime is used now than in that year is because the ores are leaner now. There is more waste material to flux away. I want to make this——

Mr. HILL. That makes $12.13 for your cost, eliminating your office force?

Mr. SCHWAB. No; there is another item to go in there yet; you have your labor and your conversion cost, which you can put now at about $1.25 or $1.30.

Mr. CRUMPACKER. What is the last item?

Mr. SCHWAB. The labor and charges other than material.

Mr. HILL. How much—$1.30?

Mr. SCHWAB. About $1.30. That is about the cost of making pig iron in Pittsburg to-day. And if you will add the general charges the cost is about $14. I mean to make a ton of pig iron in Pittsburg.

Mr. CALDERHEAD. What do you include in general charges?

Mr. SCHWAB. General administrative expenses and similar items.

Mr. HILL. The taxes and insurance?

Mr. SCHWAB. No; the works' taxes have been included in the other.

Now, I would like to make one explanation. There are works and works. Some works can do a little better than other works. But what I have given you is the nearest average of one of the good works of Pittsburg. My assertion can well be borne out. If you have examined the papers recently you know that nearly all the furnaces in the valley and about Pittsburg have been shut down this year because, as many of the operators told me, they could not afford to sell pig iron at $14 a ton. If you have noted, that has been about the market for pig. The pig will cost, for converting it into rails— I do not believe we can convert it from pig iron into rails, in our mill, for less than $7.50 a ton to-day.

The CHAIRMAN. Making a total cost of $21.50?

Mr. SCHWAB. About that; yes, sir.

The CHAIRMAN. Fourteen dollars and $7.50——

Mr. HILL. One moment.

Mr. UNDERWOOD. $7.50?

Mr. DALZELL. You have made the pig iron cost $14 up to this time, adding the different items given.

Mr. SCHWAB. Yes, sir; and $7.50 for converting that into rails.

Mr. DALZELL. That would be $21.50?

Mr. SCHWAB. Yes; that is about the cost.

Mr. HILL. You gave us the cost of conversion nine years ago as being $3.75.

Mr. SCHWAB. Quite right; but I am telling you why it is so much more to-day.

Mr. COCKRAN. Let us have that, if you please.

Mr. SCHWAB. Yes. Let us take the question of loss first.

Mr. HILL. Your letter said your cost was going to decrease.

The CHAIRMAN. You said then that your cost was going to be less.

Mr. SCHWAB. Yes; my letter was very optimistic, and one sees things very different sometimes from what the realization is. Let me take the item of loss, Mr. Chairman. I can not give you the exact losses from memory, but they are approximately 10 per cent. Now, 10 per cent on $8 is 80 cents loss; I mean when you convert iron into steel. You lose the silica and the carbon, which go into the air. Eighty cents loss on that. Now, there is nothing that enters into that that has not increased almost proportionately. The freights on everything you use to convert your pig iron into steel—like ganisters, like refractories, like coke for melting—has gone up two-thirds in many instances.

Mr. COCKRAN. Did you say the freights?

Mr. SCHWAB. Yes; on all the materials for converting pig iron into steel. Labor has increased more than anything else.

Mr. HILL. In your statement just now, in making a ton of pig iron you have made a reduction of 38 cents in the cost for labor.

Mr. SCHWAB. Quite so. Now, I shall tell you why. The labor in making a ton of pig iron is not skilled labor at all. It is common labor. It has not changed, or at least changed very little; and, secondly, the appliances in making pig iron have changed very radically in that period of time, while the appliances for making rails have not changed materially.

The CHAIRMAN. What do you put down as the cost of labor in converting pig iron into steel?

Mr. SCHWAB. There are several methods, so I would have to give you the cost by each method.

Mr. UNDERWOOD. Will you give the cost by the Bessemer method first, and then follow that with the cost by the open-hearth method?

Mr. SCHWAB. I will, if you like; but I would prefer not to. I will tell you the cost of one.

Mr. COCKRAN. If you will give us the figures for both, we will make the comparison.

Mr. SCHWAB. I would prefer not to give you the figures for both.

Mr. DALZELL. How do you make your steel?

Mr. SCHWAB. By the open-hearth method.

Mr. DALZELL. Will you give us the figures for that, then?

Mr. SCHWAB. Yes. The labor cost in the open-hearth part of the process is about 85 cents a ton. In the blooming mill the cost is 40 or 50 cents, and the cost of the rails proper is from $1 to $1.25, depending on the section, drilling, and kind of rail. That is the actual labor at the mill. Of course, there is this to be borne in mind in analyzing the cost of a ton of rails—that there is nothing that enters into the cost of a ton of rails in its finality but raw material and labor.

Mr. CALDERHEAD. What do you mean by the expression " the kind of rail? "

Mr. SCHWAB. There are different sections and weights of rails. If a rail is 50 pounds to the yard it costs more than a rail that runs 100 pounds to the yard.

Mr. HILL. You are speaking of the standard rail?

Mr. SCHWAB. Yes. Then, there are different kinds of specifications.

Mr. CALDERHEAD. Please make that a little plainer.

Mr. SCHWAB. I thought I had made that plain. When I say different kinds of rail I mean different specifications and different patterns and different weights.

Mr. FORDNEY. It costs you more per ton to make rails that run 35 pounds to the yard than to make rails that run 90 pounds?

Mr. SCHWAB. Yes.

Mr. CALDERHEAD. That is what I want.

Mr. SCHWAB. Yes. And then there are other things that also vary the cost.

The CHAIRMAN. Proceed with the remaining items of cost to make up this $7.50.

Mr. SCHWAB. Against that cost you will have to go through the same calculation as before.

Mr. UNDERWOOD. You have labor at 85 and other items here, which I figure out make a total of $3.65 for labor and losses.

Mr. SCHWAB. I will have to go further. The open hearth, put that at 80. It takes 100 tons of open-hearth ingots to make 80 tons of rails. So to arrive at the $7.50 we have to go through a long calculation of percentages that I think you will find pretty difficult.

Mr. UNDERWOOD. You have to add one-fifth of this labor cost, then.

Mr. SCHWAB. Quite so.

Mr. UNDERWOOD. The labor cost would be——

Mr. SCHWAB. You will have to do the same thing with every item that enters into it.

Mr. UNDERWOOD. We have to add 45 cents there.

Mr. SCHWAB. No; 16 cents on labor.

Mr. UNDERWOOD. You said you add one-fifth.

Mr. SCHWAB. One-fifth to 80 cents.

Mr. UNDERWOOD. Oh, that would make $3.81.

Mr. SCHWAB. Now, the other costs are made up of an infinite number of things. There is the refractories, there is manganese, there is fluxes, there is coal for cokes.

Mr. HILL. But a ton of iron does not make a ton of rails——

Mr. SCHWAB. That is an item of loss.

The CHAIRMAN. What is the manganese?

Mr. SCHWAB. The ferromanganese? That question depends on the specification of the rail. You can put it at 65 cents to 85 cents for manganese.

I do not want to give you these figures offhand and then have you add them up and find that they do not add up exactly $7.50, but you will find that they will approximate that.

Mr. HILL. Does this include the profit of $5 a ton?

Mr. SCHWAB. No.

Mr. HILL. As in the previous statement?

Mr. SCHWAB. No.

Mr. HILL. You say you will file with the committee an itemized statement of that cost of the open-hearth steel rail?

Mr. SCHWAB. Yes.

Mr. UNDERWOOD. I would like to have you do that.

Mr. SCHWAB. I will do that.

Mr. UNDERWOOD. If any bill that this Congress may pass goes out to the country and meets with the approval of the country, it has to have facts behind it.

Mr. SCHWAB. I propose to give you the facts. You can do with the tariff, of course, as you see fit.

The CHAIRMAN. I wish you would give us the items—the cost of pig iron, what you allow for waste, the cost of labor, the cost of manganese, the cost of fuel, the cost for steel, the cost for ore——

Mr. SCHWAB. Do you want me to give them to you as you read them off?

The CHAIRMAN. No.

Mr. SCHWAB. I can give them now; I can give every item of cost that enters into it.

The CHAIRMAN. And repairs and maintenance and supplies and tools, miscellaneous and general expenses; the general expenses of the factory, and depreciation.

Mr. SCHWAB. You will have to give me that list.

The CHAIRMAN. I will give it to you.

Mr. SCHWAB. Now, I would like to state this: There has probably not been two months in the last two years in any two mills when rails have cost the same each month. So I will give you a good average cost, not the low cost or the high cost, but a good average cost.

Mr. DALZELL. I think it would be well to give us a statement as to the same things when you wrote that letter in 1899, giving us the items as applying to that time.

Mr. SCHWAB. You mean in writing?

Mr. DALZELL. Yes.

Mr. SCHWAB. I should be very glad to do so.

The CHAIRMAN. Then I would like the details of making pig iron.

Mr. SCHWAB. I have given those.

Mr. CRUMPACKER. Do you know about the cost of manufacturing pig iron and rails in detail in England and other foreign countries?

Mr. SCHWAB. Not as much in detail as I do about the cost in this country.

Mr. CRUMPACKER. Do you know any of the elements of difference in cost and their significance?

Mr. SCHWAB. I am afraid you will have to be a little more specific.

Mr. CRUMPACKER. Well, do you know the comparative cost, as a general proposition, of making pig iron and rails in this country and in foreign countries?

Mr. SCHWAB. To-day?

Mr. CRUMPACKER. Including these years.

Mr. CALDERHEAD. Let him come to that later.

Mr. SCHWAB. I am quite familiar with the other.

Mr. CRUMPACKER. I suggest he put that in his statement.

Mr. SCHWAB. I will offer what I have already said as an explanation of that letter.

The CHAIRMAN. Now, you put the total cost of steel rails—have you got the figures there?

Mr. HILL. $20.93, I make it now.

Mr. SCHWAB. It ought to be in the neighborhood of $21.50. It will approximate $21.50.

The CHAIRMAN. Now, Mr. Schwab, how near is that to the average cost from 1902 down to the present time?

Mr. SCHWAB. I don't know; I would have to go through that. I couldn't give you that from memory. Suffice to say this, Mr. Chairman—let me say this: That in every year since 1900 up to date, in every year the average earnings of the employees of the steel corporation, while I was president, that the average earnings of my own employees have increased each year; there has never been one year that the average has not increased. I have not given the figures for this year——

The CHAIRMAN. Do you mean to say that the cost is higher for this year than for the average of the preceding years?

Mr. SCHWAB. I say I have not the figures for this year; this year has not ended yet. But up to this year the earnings of the employees in the steel works——

The CHAIRMAN. What year do you refer to when you speak of the cost as about $22?

Mr. SCHWAB. This year; the present time.

The CHAIRMAN. What I was trying to get you to do was to compare the present year with the six or eight years preceding this year.

Mr. SCHWAB. The real cost of making rails this year is the highest in ten years, because we have had so few rails to make. In my opinion rail makers will not have made any money on rails this year. That is the reason it is difficult to make a comparison in a year like the present.

The CHAIRMAN. This will answer the q   . Do you mean to say that the average cost has not exceeded $21.50 for the eight years preceding this year?

Mr. SCHWAB. For the eight years, I think it was less than that in 1900. I think the cost has gradually increased.

The CHAIRMAN. Each year?

Mr. SCHWAB. Each year.

Mr. CALDERHEAD. Why is that?

Mr. SCHWAB. Because everything that enters into the cost of rails has gradually increased in that time, and as I stated to you before, the average earnings of the workmen have increased every year since 1900. And so it is with freight.

The CHAIRMAN. Now, can you tell us the average price you have obtained——

Mr. SCHWAB. It has been $28, always.

The CHAIRMAN. That has been the uniform price?

Mr. SCHWAB. Yes, sir.

The CHAIRMAN. For how long?

Mr. SCHWAB. I can not recall.

The CHAIRMAN. For five or six years?

Mr. SCHWAB. More than that.

The CHAIRMAN. Ever since the organization of the United States Steel Corporation?

Mr. SCHWAB. No. And before.

The CHAIRMAN. Before?

Mr. SCHWAB. Yes; I can not tell you the exact year, but I should say——

The CHAIRMAN. That has been the uniform price?

Mr. SCHWAB. Yes, sir.

The CHAIRMAN. Twenty-eight dollars a ton?

Mr. SCHWAB. Yes, sir.

Mr. CALDERHEAD. Notwithstanding the increase in wages.

Mr. SCHWAB. Notwithstanding that.

Mr. LONGWORTH. What was the price in 1899?

Mr. SCHWAB. I can not recall, but I think $28.

Mr. HILL. You do not mean to say that the price of rails was $28 before the organization of the United States Steel Corporation?

Mr. SCHWAB. I do.

Mr. HILL. How long?

Mr. SCHWAB. I don't know.

Mr. HILL. Well, a year?

Mr. SCHWAB. Yes.

Mr. HILL. A year before?

Mr. SCHWAB. Have you the figures?

Mr. HILL. Yes. [Reading: "In 1897, $18.75; in 1898, $17.62; in 1899, $28.12."]

Mr. SCHWAB. That is right. But let me ask you to go back of that

Mr. HILL. In 1896 the price was $28.

Mr. SCHWAB. That is the point I want to make. I will tell you the reason for that. In the year we made rails so cheaply we had, as you well know, a very great steel-rail war between all the manufacturers, and prices went the lowest in history.

Mr. COCKRAN. They were not sold at a loss during those years?

Mr. SCHWAB. I think they were by most manufacturers.

Mr. HILL. They would not be sold at a loss according to your figures.

Mr. SCHWAB. They were not sold at a loss to my companies; I stated that in my letter to Mr. Frick.

Mr. COCKRAN. So those figures read by Mr. Hill showed a profit to your concern?

Mr. SCHWAB. A very small profit. When I say $12 cost, that was mill cost.

Mr. COCKRAN. That was in 1899?

Mr. SCHWAB. Yes, sir. Oh, we made a profit. I said we made a profit.

Mr. COCKRAN. You say a very small profit. Now, you sold them at how much—$18, was it, Mr. Hill, in 1899?

Mr. HILL. That was the generally quoted price. In 1899 they were $28.12. In 1898 they were $17.62.

Mr. COCKRAN. Seventeen dollars and sixty-two cents?

Mr. HILL. In 1897 they were $18.75.

Mr. COCKRAN. You charged $28, then, at the time they cost you $12, and you are charging $28 now, and now they cost you $21?

Mr. SCHWAB. That is right. That is absolutely correct. Now, I want to say something about that cost that Mr. Hill has of $17.62. It is probably the average selling price of rails that year. You want to know why we made a small profit. I said we; I mean the Carnegie Company. The most of the rails we sold that year were sold delivered at Chicago at $17.12, and we had to pay the freight to Chicago and didn't have much profit.

Mr. Cockran. But some?

Mr. Schwab. Yes; I said some profit.

Mr. Cockran. You got $17 and then you go to $28 without any corresponding increase at all in the cost of production. How do you account for that extraordinary rise?

Mr. Schwab. Well, it was time we were making some money.

Mr. Cockran. You had been making some before?

Mr. Schwab. Any manufacturing concern that goes into business and does not expect to make from 20 to 25 per cent had better not put their money in manufacturing.

Mr. Cockran. But here was over 100 per cent.

Mr. Schwab. In that special year——

Mr. Cockran. I am speaking of that.

Mr. Schwab. Yes; quite right.

Mr. Cockran. What I want to get at is this: Whether the relation between the law of supply and demand was what fixed your price, or whether you fixed the price at just what you were able to get?

Mr. Schwab. That year?

Mr. Cockran. I am speaking generally. Take that year. According to your figures, it actually cost about $12.50 to produce steel?

Mr. Schwab. Yes.

Mr. Cockran. And you charged $28 for it?

Mr. Schwab. Right.

Mr. Cockran. Now, that particular year there had been a combination of some steel manufacturers, had there not?

Mr. Schwab. Quite right.

Mr. Cockran. There was the Federal Steel Company incorporated, I think.

Mr. Schwab. There was.

Mr. Cockran. And there was an American Steel and Wire Company incorporated?

Mr. Schwab. Yes, sir.

Mr. Cockran. And that was the first year when there had been a consolidation of steel manufacturers?

Mr. Schwab. There had been no consolidation of steel-rail manufacturers at that time.

Mr. Cockran. Did not the Federal Steel Company produce steel rails?

Mr. Schwab. Yes, sir.

Mr. Cockran. But they were themselves a combination of other companies. What I want to get at is this, and I will ask you to correct me if I am wrong. This jump in prices—I do not want to use any expression that is too strong——

Mr. Dalzell. Rise.

Mr. Cockran. Well, it was a little more than a rise, a rise in price, gradual ascent; this was at least a little more than gradual; we will call it a jump. This jump from $17 to $28 a ton followed a consolidation of several minor companies into some larger companies, did it not?

Mr. Schwab. May I correct you?

Mr. Cockran. Certainly, if I am wrong.

Mr. Schwab. If you will look back several years before that I think you will find the price was $28 a ton.

Mr. COCKRAN. That was not my question.

Mr. SCHWAB. But you said it took place at that time. It did not take place at that time.

Mr. COCKRAN. I will have to repeat my question. Between the charge of $17 by the producers, or thereabouts, and $28, was there not a consolidation or had there not been several consolidations of minor companies into larger companies, of several minor companies into a few larger ones?

Mr. SCHWAB. I can not give you that from memory.

Mr. COCKRAN. About that time?

Mr. SCHWAB. You are probably——

Mr. COCKRAN. Just to refresh your memory——

Mr. SCHWAB. I will tell you very frankly, without all those questions, that we had the steel war in the years already mentioned, and it was ruinous, and the manufacturers got together and agreed to restore the price of rails to their old basis.

Mr. COCKRAN. To end competition that was ruinous would be one thing, but to take advantage of that combination to increase their profit to 100 per cent, or such a matter, would be another thing. I take it that from the small profit that you say you were making under these prices of $17 and $18, you then made 100 per cent?

Mr. SCHWAB. That is probably true.

Mr. COCKRAN. Then, to get back to my question: This jump, this leap, from a moderate profit to 100 per cent was coincident with a consolidation of several minor companies into some larger companies?

Mr. SCHWAB. Your conclusions are right, but your premises are wrong.

Mr. COCKRAN. Why are my premises wrong?

Mr. SCHWAB. Because the price of $28 was established some years before there was any consolidation such as you speak of.

Mr. COCKRAN. Mr. Schwab, I can go back to a time when they were selling at $60 or $70, I think.

Mr. SCHWAB. That is true.

Mr. COCKRAN. But I am not——

Mr. SCHWAB. Your conclusions are entirely correct.

Mr. COCKRAN. I am entirely correct as to that?

Mr. SCHWAB. Entirely correct.

Mr. McCALL. When was the United States Steel Company formed?

Mr. COCKRAN. I am coming to that. After this combination of several minor companies into the few larger companies, another war, I think, was threatened, about 1901 or 1902, by the purchase of some land at a place called Conneaut, and an announcement of the Carnegie company that they were going into the tubing business.

Mr. SCHWAB. You are conversant with that?

Mr. COCKRAN. Perhaps somewhat so, but I want to get it accurately from you.

Mr. SCHWAB. The consolidation, as you term it, of the steel corporations in about the year 1901 came about in this way.

Mr. Morgan asked me if Mr. Carnegie wanted to sell his interests in iron and steel; that he then had large interests in the Federal and other companies. I approached Mr. Carnegie, and Mr. Carnegie said he would sell, and we sold our company to Mr. Morgan under conditions with which you are all familiar. We knew the properties

Mr. Morgan controlled and upon which he was to give us a mortgage bond, and that is all there was to it.

Mr. COCKRAN. All there was to it, perhaps, so far as you were concerned, but a little more, I think, so far as the public was concerned. I said, Mr. Schwab, at least I asked you if there had not been an announcement by the Carnegie company that it was going into the making of tubes?

Mr. SCHWAB. It was published in the newspapers that it was going into the making of tubes, because we were.

Mr. COCKRAN. That is a fact?

Mr. SCHWAB. Yes.

Mr. COCKRAN. And you purchased the property at Conneaut for that purpose?

Mr. SCHWAB. It may have been so published.

Mr. COCKRAN. Following that, as I understand it, there was a consolidation of the Federal company and the American Steel and Wire Company——

Mr. SCHWAB. All these companies; yes.

Mr. COCKRAN. And your company?

Mr. SCHWAB. Yes.

Mr. COCKRAN. Now, could you tell us about what the stocks of these companies were—what the value of their property was, for instance?

Mr. SCHWAB. I could not give it offhand.

Mr. COCKRAN. Well, about.

Mr. SCHWAB. I placed at that time the actual value of all these companies at approximately somewhat more than their total capitalization.

Mr. COCKRAN. Yes; that was the value of the property after consolidation.

Mr. SCHWAB. Yes.

Mr. COCKRAN. But you would not contend that these properties were worth as much when they were either actually or potentially competitors?

Mr. SCHWAB. I contend that the actual value of those properties to-day——

Mr. COCKRAN. I am not asking that.

Mr. SCHWAB. But at that time, was quite equal to the capitalization of that time, and is worth very much more to-day than its capitalization.

Mr. COCKRAN. I am afraid you still have not answered.

Mr. HILL. What do you mean by capitalization—common and preferred stock both?

Mr. SCHWAB. And bonds, and all that.

Mr. COCKRAN. Yes; there is no doubt he believed that after the consolidation.

Mr. SCHWAB. I believed it before.

Mr. COCKRAN. Wait a minute. Before this consolidation these various companies owned all the property that the consolidated company owns now, or owned after the consolidation?

Mr. SCHWAB. Quite true.

Mr. COCKRAN. Take, for instance, your own company, you remember that?

Mr. SCHWAB. Yes, sir.

Mr. COCKRAN. That company was capitalized at how much?

Mr. SCHWAB. We were capitalized at that time, shortly before that, at $320,000,000.

Mr. COCKRAN. Three hundred and twenty million dollars?

Mr. SCHWAB. Yes.

Mr. COCKRAN. When was that capitalization made?

Mr. SCHWAB. I will have to speak from memory. I should say probably two years before the organization of the Steel Corporation.

Mr. COCKRAN. It was capitalized at $320,000,000?

Mr. SCHWAB. One hundred and sixty million dollars in bonds and $160,000,000 of stock.

Mr. COCKRAN. Do you remember at what rate that was put into the steel trust?

Mr. SCHWAB. I can tell you approximately.

Mr. COCKRAN. How many bonds?

Mr. SCHWAB. The bonds were exchanged for bonds at par, bonds for bonds.

Mr. COCKRAN. Yes——

Mr. SCHWAB. The par value of the stock was $1,000 a share. It was not $100 certificates, but $1,000 certificates; and the stock was bought at $1,500 a share.

Mr. COCKRAN. The stock was bought then at $150?

Mr. SCHWAB. At $1,500.

Mr. COCKRAN. That is $1,500 for $1,000 certificate, but that would be $150?

Mr. SCHWAB. Yes, sir.

Mr. COCKRAN. But putting it in the company, it was put in then at an increase of $150 for the stock, which would mean about $75,000,000?

Mr. SCHWAB. Quite so.

Mr. COCKRAN. Now, Mr. Schwab, how much money capital had actually been put into that company which was capitalized at the rate of $150,000,000?

Mr. SCHWAB. I could not tell you from memory; I don't know.

Mr. COCKRAN. About?

Mr. SCHWAB. I don't know.

Mr. COCKRAN. Was there ever $100,000,000 put into it?

Mr. SCHWAB. Oh, yes. I can not give you those figures offhand. I will tell you why I can not. I do not know that any of us know. The Carnegie company was a partnership; it was not a stock company——   .

Mr. COCKRAN. I understand, but that would make it easier——

Mr. SCHWAB. And when you ask how much real money was put in the Carnegie company I can only say that the earnings of the company were put in; none of us had any money to put in.

Mr. COCKRAN. That is it, then; now, we have got it.

Mr. SCHWAB. We developed the company——

Mr. COCKRAN. Exactly. So that whatever capital, whatever property, was owned by this company was the result of profits made in the company.

Mr. SCHWAB. Profit and increase in value of their properties.

Mr. COCKRAN. But that was profit?

Mr. SCHWAB. Certainly; certainly.

Mr. COCKRAN. So that practically the whole of that property was the result—I repeat it again—of profit made in the company over and above the dividends that had been drawn out?

Mr. SCHWAB. Well, they were very small.

Mr. COCKRAN. I do not think Mr. Carnegie ever suffered for the need of anything during that time.

Mr. SCHWAB. Some of the rest of us, perhaps, did.

Mr. COCKRAN. He lived in comfort, and I hope you did also. Now, Mr. Schwab, this entire property at that rate was, as you say, the result of the profits made in the business. Do you remember anything about the organization of the Federal Steel Company?

Mr. SCHWAB. Very little; but I may point out something else to you.

Mr. COCKRAN. I would be delighted, Mr. Schwab.

Mr. SCHWAB. At the time we began leasing and acquiring ore properties, many years before the consolidation of the company, we acquired those ore properties at 10 cents a ton.

Mr. COCKRAN. Yes, sir.

Mr. SCHWAB. They gradually increased, and very rapidly increased each year, so that the four hundred or five hundred or six hundred million tons of ore we had represented a very large profit as any other mining industry will that turns out well and for which there is a large demand. Do not forget that in reckoning the profits.

Mr. COCKRAN. Not at all. Let me see if this is a correct statement of the history of the industry at that time: The rails and the products which had been selling at $17 or $18 a ton at a profit, after the consolidation of these several minor companies into the few larger companies about 1899—I think it was in the year 1899—was followed by a jump in price to $28 a ton?

Mr. SCHWAB. A return in price, if you will permit me to correct you.

Mr. COCKRAN. I beg your pardon.

Mr. SCHWAB. A return in price; was followed by a return in price.

Mr. COCKRAN. Yes; you could say with equal truth a return to a price of $60 or $70 a ton, if such a price had been fixed by the combination.

Mr. SCHWAB. That is right.

Mr. COCKRAN. So, if you do not mind, I will choose the word——

Mr. SCHWAB. I do mind very much.

Mr. COCKRAN. Let us compromise and put it both ways.

The CHAIRMAN. Let us get the facts.

Mr. COCKRAN. It has remained at $28 a ton since the formation of the United States Steel Corporation all the time, regardless of the cost of production. Am I right about that?

Mr. SCHWAB. Quite correct.

Mr. COCKRAN. And in 1901, when there was an announcement or threat that there would be some competition through Mr. Carnegie's going into the tubing business, the Carnegie company going into it, there was another consolidation in which they were all merged in one company, and the price continued the same?

Mr. SCHWAB. Quite correct.

Mr. COCKRAN. Then I understand that in these processes of consolidation your stock was taken in at $150. Now, since the orginization of the steel trust, or the steel company—I beg your pardon, the

United States Steel Corporation—with which you are identified, stocks and bonds were issued, were they not, for all this stock and the bonds of your company?

Mr. SCHWAB. And stock of our company.

Mr. COCKRAN. Yes, that was by preferred stock and bonds both?

Mr. SCHWAB. No, sir.

Mr. COCKRAN. Correct me, then.

Mr. SCHWAB. How?

Mr. COCKRAN. How were you paid for your stock?

Mr. SCHWAB. Mr. Carnegie and most of the partners were paid in bonds for both their bonds and stock. Some of the partners were paid in part bonds and part stock.

Mr. COCKRAN. Which stock?

Mr. SCHWAB. Preferred and common.

Mr. COCKRAN. Well, there was an issue of some $550,000,000 in stock, was there not?

Mr. SCHWAB. Yes, sir.

Mr. COCKRAN. Will you tell me how much of that——

Mr. SCHWAB. I can not tell you from memory.

Mr. COCKRAN. I have not finished.

Mr. SCHWAB. I know what you are going to say.

Mr. COCKRAN. If you do, let us state it. I was going to ask how much of that was issued for property and how much represented—well, shall we say, confidence in the future?

Mr. SCHWAB. Of which?

Mr. COCKRAN. The common stock of the United States Steel Company; how much of the common stock was actually issued for property?

Mr. SCHWAB. It was all issued for property.

Mr. COCKRAN. All of it?

Mr. SCHWAB. Yes, that is my recollection of it. It was issued in exchange for other stock which represented property. That is a technical question that you can probably best explain.

Mr. COCKRAN. What is that?

Mr. SCHWAB. You can probably best explain that, the technical part of it. The broad statement I made at that time, and I make it now. Technically I do not know how you interpret it, but the broad statement I make is that the physical value of the steel corporation's properties at the time of its organization was equal to its capital stock. I can not make it any plainer than that.

Mr. COCKRAN. But the mere consolidation of these companies resulted in a very great increase in the total amount——

Mr. SCHWAB. Total amount of capital stock.

Mr. COCKRAN. And securities issued against it.

Mr. SCHWAB. And so with every company that has been in the steel business.

Mr. COCKRAN. Now, now, that is the point I want to reach. The mere fact of consolidation, then, in itself, is represented by some portion, and a considerable portion, of the stock that was issued; in other words, you have capitalized the mere fact of consolidation?

Mr. SCHWAB. You say that. I do not think so.

Mr. COCKRAN. I ask you.

Mr. SCHWAB. I don't think so.

Mr. COCKRAN. You say there was a very large increase of the capital on the mere consolidation.

Mr. SCHWAB. You must appreciate that the Carnegie company, with $160,000,000 of stock at the time of the organization of the steel company, was worth a great deal more than $160,000,000, and that is why the stock was increased.

Mr. CALDERHEAD. You mean you capitalized the actual property?

Mr. SCHWAB. When we capitalized the Carnegie Steel Company we did; we were a partnership before that.

Mr. COCKRAN. When you issued the stock of the Carnegie company, two years before this consolidation, you capitalized it then for all it was worth, did you not?

Mr. SCHWAB. We did.

Mr. COCKRAN. And then sold it within two years at an advance of 50 per cent?

Mr. SCHWAB. Oh, no; we did not. We sold the stock at an advance of 50. That would be an advance of 25 per cent on the whole——

Mr. COCKRAN. But 50 per cent on the stock?

Mr. SCHWAB. But you asked me how much advance there was on the property?

Mr. COCKRAN. No; I did not.

Mr. SCHWAB. I misunderstood you, then.

Mr. COCKRAN. What I wanted to get at was how much additional securities were issued against the mere fact of consolidation. Now, as far as you are concerned, your stock was increased 50 per cent?

Mr. SCHWAB. No; it was not.

Mr. COCKRAN. You said so——

Mr. SCHWAB. The stock, but not the value.

Mr. FORDNEY. May I interrupt for a moment? Will the witness be heard again after we adjourn at 12 o'clock?

Mr. SCHWAB. I hope not. Can you let me off, Mr. Chairman?

Mr. FORDNEY. I wanted to ask a few questions, and the gentleman had gone pretty thoroughly into it.

The CHAIRMAN. There are a number of things that are material that we want to ask before we get through.

Mr. COCKRAN. Mr. Schwab, I ask you this again, now. You were given 50 per cent more stock than you had issued yourselves; that is to say, you took in payment the steel stock and bonds?

Mr. SCHWAB. Quite right.

Mr. COCKRAN. At 50 per cent more than the stocks you put in. How much common stock was given for all that—how much common stock was there in that?

Mr. SCHWAB. I can not give you that for the reason—it is a matter of record.

Mr. COCKRAN. It is a matter of record?

Mr. SCHWAB. I think so.

Mr. COCKRAN. If it is, it will save time.

Mr. SCHWAB. I think each of the partners in the Carnegie Company had the option to take these different things, but I can not tell you from memory which things they took.

Mr. COCKRAN. Tell us what the option was; what was the option each partner got?

Mr. SCHWAB. The option of each partner was that he could accept his pay all in bonds or half bonds and half stock.

Mr. COCKRAN. You mean to say that each partner had the choice of that?

Mr. SCHWAB. Yes, sir.

Mr. COCKRAN. And do you mean to say that some took common stock——

Mr. SCHWAB. No; I will not say each partner—the minority partners, up to a given amount.

Mr. COCKRAN. Would you have this committee understand that partners who were given choice between taking bonds and common stock took common stock?

Mr. SCHWAB. No; I misstated that.

Mr. COCKRAN. Yes.

Mr. SCHWAB. Let me put this clearly. Mr. Carnegie would accept nothing but bonds——

Mr. COCKRAN. How much bonds did he get?

Mr. SCHWAB. You will have to ask him that; I don't know.

Mr. COCKRAN. What did you take for your stock?

Mr. SCHWAB. I took a certain number of bonds. I took bonds for my bonds, and my recollection is—I am not sure—that I took part bonds and part stock for my stock.

Mr. COCKRAN. Which stock?

Mr. SCHWAB. Some preferred and some common.

Mr. COCKRAN. I want to get the proportion.

Mr. SCHWAB. I don't remember it.

Mr. COCKRAN. You can not state that?

Mr. SCHWAB. I can not state it.

Mr. COCKRAN. You could, I suppose——

Mr. SCHWAB. If I looked it up I have no doubt I could.

Mr. DALZELL. Is that very important?

Mr. COCKRAN. I will state what the purport of it is. I think it is very important in this inquiry. I want to show, if I may, I want to ask this witness whether the mere fact of this consolidation and the right practically to be able to charge $28 a ton was valued in the incorporation at $550,000,000.

Mr. SCHWAB. It was not valued at anything.

Mr. DALZELL. That is a conclusion, and he has given you the fact.

Mr. SCHWAB. I have given you all I know.

The CHAIRMAN. We will have to take a recess now, and we will ask you to come back here at 2 o'clock.

Mr. SCHWAB. Could you not excuse me?

The CHAIRMAN. We will adjourn until 2 o'clock.

AFTER RECESS.

The CHAIRMAN. Mr. Schwab, I want to ask you if you can tell us the price of the production of steel abroad?

Mr. SCHWAB. Merely in a general way, Mr. Chairman; only in a general way.

The CHAIRMAN. You seemed to have a pretty clear idea about it in 1890.

Mr. SCHWAB. I try to have to-day, also.

The CHAIRMAN. What information or knowledge have you now on the subject?

Mr. SCHWAB. I could not give you the same detail that I did of iron manufacture. I can give you a good general estimate of the cost abroad. For example, I know that pig iron can be produced in different parts of Germany at from $9.50 to $12 a ton to-day, depending upon the location and character of the pig.

The CHAIRMAN. Against $14 here?

Mr. SCHWAB. About $14 to $14.50 here. I think the freight is about $2.50 on an average.

Mr. DALZELL. You mean from Germany?

Mr. SCHWAB. Yes; that is, the German pig iron.

Mr. DALZELL. You mean the freight from Germany is $2.50?

Mr. SCHWAB. Yes, sir; not much more than that.

The CHAIRMAN. The cost of converting into steel?

Mr. SCHWAB. The cost of converting that into rails in Germany is about the same as it is here.

The CHAIRMAN. So the difference in cost is the difference in the cost of the pig iron?

Mr. SCHWAB. The difference in cost is to-day about the difference in the cost of the pig iron.

The CHAIRMAN. That is in Germany. How about England?

Mr. SCHWAB. England is probably just a little cheaper, although it is not widely different. If they get their ore from Spain, they make it probably about the same as Germany. If they have local ores, perhaps they make it a little cheaper.

The CHAIRMAN. What is the main reason for the additional cost of the pig iron here?

Mr. SCHWAB. Raw materials and freights being higher.

The CHAIRMAN. Their iron is nearer their coal mines?

Mr. SCHWAB. Yes. They assemble it cheaper than we do. They assemble their materials cheaper than we do.

The CHAIRMAN. I do not suppose they do it any cheaper than we can at Birmingham?

Mr. SCHWAB. No; we do it cheaper at Birmingham than they do in England.

The CHAIRMAN. You think the cost of pig iron in Birmingham would be less than the cost in England?

Mr. SCHWAB. I know it would be.

The CHAIRMAN. The cost of converting the steel is about the same?

Mr. SCHWAB. In Birmingham it is about the same.

The CHAIRMAN. Can you give us any information on other branches of the steel industry?

Mr. SCHWAB. What one, for example?

The CHAIRMAN. Well, any.

Mr. SCHWAB. Yes; I shall be glad to answer you. I am here for that purpose. I shall be very glad to give you any information you desire.

The CHAIRMAN. What do you say about billets?

Mr. SCHWAB. Billets and rails are nearly in the same class. It costs about $1 a ton more to make rails than to make billets; otherwise there is no difference.

The CHAIRMAN. How about structural steel?

Mr. SCHWAB. Structural steel costs about $3 a ton more to make—$3 to $4 more than rails. Steel plates likewise are in about the same class.

The CHAIRMAN. Tin plates, for instance?

Mr. SCHWAB. I could not give any information about them.

The CHAIRMAN. We have pretty full information about those. What else do you manufacture?

Mr. SCHWAB. In steel lines?

The CHAIRMAN. Yes.

Mr. SCHWAB. You have covered the field pretty well, unless you go into specialties. I mean by specialties tools, forgings, axles, wheels, and minor branches of the steel industry. Other than that you have covered the field pretty well. I can not give much information about wire. I have been out of touch with that for some years.

The CHAIRMAN. Do you make wire rods?

Mr. SCHWAB. I do not.

The CHAIRMAN. Any other information you can give us with reference to the steel industry we shall be glad to have.

Mr. SCHWAB. If there is anything specific you want to know—any specific question you will ask me, I will do the best I can to answer you.

Mr. HILL. I would like to ask a few questions. You were president of the United States Steel Company from 1901 to 1905?

Mr. SCHWAB. Yes, sir.

Mr. HILL. I want to ask you this question: With other things remaining equal, would the removal, in part or in whole, of the duty on steel rails affect the price?

Mr. SCHWAB. I want to answer that question, because it is a very important one—a question to which I have given a great deal of thought and is the gist of this whole thing. This is my opinion only. With every condition equal, a steel rail can be made as cheaply in the United States as in any part of the world. The cost of making a steel rail depends entirely on two things, and only two things. The first is raw material and the second is labor, and nothing else enters into it. Give us the same conditions with reference to raw material and labor as in other parts of the world, and rails will cost us the same, and we will not need any tariff; but if you want to keep the transportation cost up, if you want to keep supplies up, the refractories and the numerous things that go into steel, the main cost of which is labor; and you want to conserve your raw materials, which has been a much agitated subject recently, you will have to protect us with a tariff or put us in the same situation they are abroad.

Mr. HILL. I want to ask you, simply as a business proposition—I asked you that question simply as a leader to another question—is the price of steel rails fixed for the world in the United States?

Mr. SCHWAB. Not that I know of.

Mr. HILL. Is it not fixed by the International Rail Syndicate in London?

Mr. SCHWAB. If it is, I know nothing of it, and I know I manufacture rails and I am not a part of it. I mean I have never heard of it.

Mr. HILL. I know that, but I want to read a statement from our consular report, and I would like your opinion or your knowledge in regard to it. It is an official report of the United States consul, who is quoting from a book by Mr. J. Stephen James on the steel industry, and he says finally:

The United States Steel Corporation, the German Steel Syndicate, and the International Rail Syndicate, which last has its headquarters in London, controls the output of some 4,000,000 tons of rails annually in the United States, Germany, and the United Kingdom.

Have you any knowledge concerning that?

Mr. SCHWAB. I have heard of the two syndicates, the German Steel Syndicate and the International Rail Syndicate. They are well known all over Europe. As to the alliance between those two syndicates and the Steel Corporation I know nothing, nor have I heard of anything.

Mr. HILL. In 1905, when you were president of the United States Steel Company, there were shipments of steel rails made from Baltimore as low as $18.60 a ton.

Mr. SCHWAB. Quite right.

Mr. HILL. Was there any profit to the company on that shipment?

Mr. SCHWAB. I can not say, except that I know this, that in 1901, when I was president of the Steel Corporation, the conditions, as they existed in 1901, as I think I said before the Industrial Commission, the removal of the entire tariff would not hurt us. I want to point out distinctly and clearly as I did in the explanation of my cost this morning, that the conditions between that time and the present time have very materially changed. If we want to go back to those conditions and put our raw materials in at those low figures and reduce our labor and other expenses as we did at that time, personally I would not care whether there was a tariff or not.

Mr. HILL. Since 1901 the uniform price of steel rails in the United States has, without any variableness or shadow of turning, been $28?

Mr. SCHWAB. Quite right. It was fixed, I think, along about—I can not be sure about this—1895 or 1896 originally, but about that time the price of $28 per ton for steel rails was fixed by agreement of all the rail manufacturers in this country, or most of them. It went along until this great break came in 1897 or 1898—I am not sure of that year—and that continued for a couple of years. The price of rails was again fixed at $28 at that time, and it has never changed.

Mr. HILL. And all parties are selling at that price?

Mr. SCHWAB. Absolutely, so far as I know.

Mr. HILL. How does it come about that steel rails have for the last five years remained at $28 without any collusion with anybody else?

Mr. SCHWAB. I will tell you. Take the present times as the best illustration. There is not a manufacturer of rails in the United States to-day—I, for example, as a rail manufacturer, feel that if I were to vary that price of $28 for rails, which seems to have been recognized by all rail manufacturers as a fair price, and giving a fair profit—if I were to vary that 10 cents a ton to-day I would precipitate a steel war, to use such a word or expression, that would result in running my works without any profit. Everybody, by tacit and mutual understanding, feel the same thing about that. I would not vary the price of my rails under any circumstances, not if I knew it was to get 100,000 tons in orders, for the reason that my competitor next door would put the price down to $1 a ton, or half a dollar a ton even, and we would be in a position where we would be running without any profit at all.

Mr. HILL. You think absolute uniformity for the last few years in price of steel rails at $28 is without agreement?

Mr. SCHWAB. Absolutely.

Mr. HILL. Without collusion between the parties?

Mr. SCHWAB. Yes.· I will say——

Mr. HILL (interrupting). Now, in 1901, when you were president of the United States Steel Corporation, shiploads of rails were sent to Vladivostok and to the East for construction of the Trans-Siberian Railroad.

Mr. SCHWAB. Quite so.

Mr. HILL. Have you any objection to stating what the price was?

Mr. SCHWAB. No. If I knew, I would very gladly state. I can probably get the information. My recollection is——

Mr. HILL. I want to say, frankly, the prices in Baltimore were on the left-over end of an Argentine contract from some previous years, an unfinished contract.

Mr. SCHWAB. I think the price was about $21 at Baltimore, was it not?

Mr. HILL. There were two shipments, one at $21.80 and one at $18.60.

Mr. SCHWAB. My best recollection was it was about $21. For years I have exported great quantities of rails, and similar things during that·period, at low prices, without profit, or, at least, with very little profit, because it enabled me to make my home product just that much cheaper. That is an old argument, and I do not need to go into that, but it is a true one.

Mr. HILL. While you were president of the United States Steel Company, was there any agreement made with the United States Steel Company that it would not ship abroad tin plate in excess of·the amount of the previous years if a certain amount of black plate were bought from them by the Welsh manufacturers?

Mr. SCHWAB. That is not true.

Mr. HILL. You have heard that statement before, have you not?

Mr. SCHWAB. I never have.

Mr. HILL. There was no agreement between the United States Steel Company and any foreign concern during your term?

Mr. SCHWAB. No, sir.

Mr. HILL. Was there any international agreement with reference to wire nails?

Mr. SCHWAB. No agreement with reference to any manufactured article of the steel corporation while I was its president.

Mr. HILL. I am very glad you know that.

Mr. UNDERWOOD. Mr. Schwab, the cost of making pig iron in Germany is considerably higher than it is in England, is it not?

Mr. SCHWAB. There is not so much difference.

Mr. UNDERWOOD. Is not the transportation charge to the furnace for ore and coke much higher than it is in England?

Mr. SCHWAB. In Germany?

Mr. UNDERWOOD.. Yes.

Mr. SCHWAB. No, sir.

Mr. UNDERWOOD. I thought the mines were not located so conveniently for manufacture.

Mr. SCHWAB. Those with which I am familiar, in Lorraine and in Luxemburg, have their coal and coke very close together. They make about the cheapest pig iron in that part of Germany of any. The materials to make pig iron are not widely separated in Germany.

Mr. UNDERWOOD. In England it is necessary for a good many of the plants there to bring their ore from Spain, is it not?

Mr. SCHWAB. It is.

Mr. UNDERWOOD. Is that cost of transportation high?

Mr. SCHWAB. Not so high. Of course, the greater part of it is so transported. Large manufacturers at Cardiff and through that part of Wales bring their ore there cheaper.

Mr. UNDERWOOD. The price you gave us this morning of the cost of making pig iron and steel rails was the cost without any profit to the manufacturer?

Mr. SCHWAB. It was. I want to make one correction about that, that I think I neglected to state this morning, and that is that the cost which I gave you was the Bessemer steel rail.

Mr. UNDERWOOD. It was?

Mr. SCHWAB. Yes, sir; the Bessemer steel rail.

Mr. UNDERWOOD. Instead of the open-hearth?

Mr. SCHWAB. Yes, sir.

Mr. UNDERWOOD. You stated this morning you did not want to make a comparison of the two, and I do not want you to do so unless you can; but if you can do so, will you state whether the Bessemer rail costs more or less?

Mr. SCHWAB. The open-hearth rail costs about $2 a ton more than the Bessemer rail costs.

Mr. UNDERWOOD. Would you mind describing to the committee the difference in the process of manufacture?

Mr. SCHWAB. You mean technically describing it?

Mr. UNDERWOOD. In as few words as you can.

Mr. SCHWAB. Raw pig iron contains about 3 to 4 per cent of carbon and 1 to 2 per cent of silicon. Steel contains only a trace of these two elements. In order to make steel, it becomes necessary to remove the carbon and silicon. In the Bessemer converter they are removed by the introduction of air, which combines with the carbon and silicon in the pig iron and burns them out, producing steel. In the open-hearth process the carbon and silicon in the pig iron are removed by contact with oxygen in iron ore; that is, liquid iron ore is brought into contact with liquid pig iron, and the oxygen combines with the carbon and silicon and produces steel. Those are the two processes, briefly described.

Mr. UNDERWOOD. In making the Bessemer steel, you put the molten iron into the converter and blow the air into it?

Mr. SCHWAB. Yes, sir.

Mr. UNDERWOOD. That process takes how long?

Mr. SCHWAB. For a single heat?

Mr. UNDERWOOD. Yes.

Mr. SCHWAB. Ten minutes.

Mr. UNDERWOOD. For a single heat in the open-hearth process you put it into a converter——

Mr. SCHWAB (interrupting). No; in a furnace. Then you boil it. You boil it in contact with oxygen in some form.

Mr. UNDERWOOD. How long does that process take?

Mr. SCHWAB. Ten to twelve hours.

Mr. UNDERWOOD. Now, the duplex process?

Mr. SCHWAB. That is a combination of the two. They remove part of the silicon in the Bessemer converter and part of it in the open-hearth. That is the practice in Alabama.

Mr. UNDERWOOD. The duplex process would be more costly than the Bessemer and less costly than the open-hearth?

Mr. SCHWAB. Yes, sir.

Mr. UNDERWOOD. How long would it take to boil it out in the duplex process?

Mr. SCHWAB. About half the time it would take in the open-hearth process.

Mr. UNDERWOOD. So it is the length of time your furnaces are engaged in operating these different processes that makes the difference in cost?

Mr. SCHWAB. Not entirely. The cost of making pig iron in the Bessemer converter is more expensive than the cost of making pig iron for the basic. Pig for Bessemer must contain phosphorus, while pig iron for the basic may——

Mr. UNDERWOOD (interrupting). That is due to a difference in the cost of your ore?

Mr. SCHWAB. Yes, sir.

Mr. UNDERWOOD. The cheaper ores can be used for the basic process and the more costly ores must be used for the Bessemer?

Mr. SCHWAB. That is quite true.

Mr. UNDERWOOD. Then the price that you gave of making pig iron in Germany and in England was the actual cost without counting in anything for the profit of the manufacturer?

Mr. SCHWAB. It was.

Mr. UNDERWOOD. You gave the freight rates from Germany to this country on pig iron at $2.50.

Mr. SCHWAB. That is approximate. It varies very much.

Mr. UNDERWOOD. Yes; I understand that. Approximately, what is it from England?

Mr. SCHWAB. I think it is about the same—$2, probably.

Mr. UNDERWOOD. On steel rails, what would it be?

Mr. SCHWAB. Very nearly the same—from $2 to $3. I have seen it much higher and have seen it much less, but that is probably an average price.

Mr. UNDERWOOD. In regard to competition at present in steel rails or pig iron—I mean material competition—by the foreign manufacturers with this country, is there any?

Mr. SCHWAB. No; for this reason: As a rule the buyers of rails in this country want to get their rails from the people who patronize their railroads. A railroad in this country would naturally rather pay a dollar more for its rails from a man who manufactures on its line of railroad, and therefore there is not much competition in rails in this country. The competition in rails is in countries where we have a mutual field of competition—South American, Siberia, or similar countries.

Mr. UNDERWOOD. Under ordinary circumstances that same condition is true as to pig iron, is it not?

Mr. SCHWAB. There is not much consumption of pig iron there.

Mr. UNDERWOOD. In figuring the pig iron in this estimate which you made, you figured on the molten pig iron carried to the steel plant.

Mr. SCHWAB. The difference in cost is very little. It is not over 10 cents a ton. It costs about 10 cents a ton—from 10 to 15 cents a ton—to cast molten pig iron into cold pig.

Mr. UNDERWOOD. Does that include removing it from the stock house?

Mr. SCHWAB. From the furnace to the casting. It is all done by machinery, and the loading of it in the cars after cast will be covered by the 10 or 15 cents a ton.

Mr. UNDERWOOD. In the manufacture of iron bars, as compared with steel bars, is it cheaper or more expensive to produce steel bars than iron bars?

Mr. SCHWAB. If you were to produce iron bars from pig iron it would cost more than steel bars would cost; but iron bars are not produced in that way. Iron bars are produced to-day by the purchase of old iron scrap that has accumulated over many years of iron manufacture, that has no real use for market, and so they are able to produce iron bars somewhat cheaper to-day than they can produce steel bars.

Mr. UNDERWOOD. There is another question I want to ask you. I notice that in the world's production of pig iron the production in Germany has developed very much more rapidly than it has in Great Britain.

Mr. SCHWAB. Yes, sir.

Mr. UNDERWOOD. I believe the world's production for 1907 was about 61,000,000 tons. Great Britain produced about 11,000,000 tons and Germany about 13,000,000 tons, whereas in 1900 Great Britain produced 8,000,000 tons and Germany 8,000,000 tons. Is the cost of production in German any greater than in Great Britain, so that the cost has brought about the development of the German production so much in excess of the British production?

Mr. SCHWAB. That is a difficult question to answer, but I will give you my view on it very generally. The Germans have made the greatest advance in economic metallurgy of any nation in this world during the last five years. They have utilized their by-products to a greater extent than any other manufacturing nation. Not only that, but they have developed their mechanical appliances with reference to manufacturing to an extent that no other nation has, and they have developed their quality to a greater extent than any other nation during these past five years. In other words, manufacturing in Germany five years ago seems to have had a complete renaissance, and they have advanced very much more rapidly than any other nation for the reasons I have given. For two reasons, the first, the very excellent technical education of their metallurgical engineers in Germany; the second and most important, the labor conditions in Germany as compared with the conditions in England. I think the labor conditions in England are the worst of any of the great manufacturing countries of the world.

Mr. COCKRAN. Worse in what way?

Mr. SCHWAB. That is a delicate subject to talk about. I would rather say nothing about it. I mean for the manufacturer, making cost higher, difficulty of getting production per man, and the difficulty of introducing modern machinery.

Mr. UNDERWOOD. I want to ask you if during the last decade the German Government has not given to manufacturers of iron and steel products a bounty?

Mr. SCHWAB. I can not speak of that. But I do know that no government in the world has given its manufacturers in iron and steel the same encouragement and advantages that Germany has given.

Mr. UNDERWOOD. You are not familiar with that bounty?

Mr. SCHWAB. I can not speak of the bounty. I am not sufficiently familiar to know what it is.

Mr. HILL. You know there is a bounty?

Mr. SCHWAB. Yes, sir.

Mr. HILL. But you do not know the amount?

Mr. SCHWAB. No; I can not tell.

Mr. UNDERWOOD. The reason I asked the question was to find out if the large exportation that has come from Germany and gone into competition with England was not to a large extent due to the bounty given by the German Government.

Mr. SCHWAB. The advance in German steel manufacture in the past few years has been on account of the untiring effort of the German Government in every way, in its diplomatic and consular service throughout the world, to push and promote German manufactures. Wherever you go, to South America or any part of the world, you will find the whole country and its consular service, and every part of it, devoted to the sale of German steel goods and interesting themselves in it.

Mr. UNDERWOOD. If we were to write a minimum and maximum tariff here, and do not give the minimum rate to any country that gave a bounty for the development of their products, would not that relieve us to a great extent from German competition?

Mr. SCHWAB. I do not know about that. I would have to think about that.

Mr. UNDERWOOD. If you come to a conclusion about it, I will be glad to have it.

Mr. SCHWAB. That is a new thought, and I have not considered it at all.

Mr. UNDERWOOD. I will be glad if you will consider that question, because I think it is a material one.

Mr. SCHWAB. It is, indeed.

Mr. UNDERWOOD. Now, I want to ask you about the sale of your steel rails abroad. You sold a large amount abroad?

Mr. SCHWAB. Not very large, no. I can not give you the figures offhand. You no doubt have the figures here. They are a matter of record, but it is not a very large quantity. When I say abroad, I mean all countries other than the United States.

Mr. UNDERWOOD. Have you gone into the European countries with rails?

Mr. SCHWAB. No; very few, at least.

Mr. UNDERWOOD. It has been in the Orient?

Mr. SCHWAB. Countries open to competition; yes. The tariff of Germany and France and Austria is so high we can not ship the products in there.

Mr. UNDERWOOD. The reason you can not get into French markets is that France applies her maximum rate against American iron and steel products?

Mr. SCHWAB. Yes, sir.

Mr. UNDERWOOD. And she gives Belgium and England her minimum rate?

Mr. SCHWAB. Yes; that may be.

Mr. UNDERWOOD. If we had a maximum and minimum tariff bill, by which we could get the French minimum rate, would not there be an opportunity——

Mr. SCHWAB (interrupting). There might be. That is a new thought for me, I must confess, and I have not considered it at all.

Mr. UNDERWOOD. I would like to have your opinion about that.

Mr. SCHWAB. I shall be very glad to think about it, sir.

Mr. UNDERWOOD. Your company does not make any pig iron for sale at all?

Mr. SCHWAB. The Bethlehem Steel Company?

Mr. UNDERWOOD. Yes.

Mr. SCHWAB. Yes, sir; we do.

Mr. UNDERWOOD. Do you export any?

Mr. SCHWAB. None whatever.

Mr. UNDERWOOD. Do you know anything about the exportation of pig iron in recent years?

Mr. SCHWAB. I do not.

Mr. UNDERWOOD. There is one other question I desire to ask. In answer to the chairman, you stated there were some other products of iron and steel which you made besides steel rails. Will you enumerate those and give the cost of the manufacture of those?

Mr. SCHWAB. One of the most important is steel plates. Another very important item——

Mr. UNDERWOOD (interrupting). Give the cost as you go.

Mr. SCHWAB. The cost of plates and the cost of all steel structural shapes—that is, rolled products—in round figures, is about $3 a ton above the cost of rails. There is a great variety of specifications and qualifications with reference to these special grades of steel that make their cost very considerable, but I am taking the common standard shapes. I mean by that, columns for buildings, girders for buildings, or plates for ships, or any similar line, and you can reckon that as a general thing the cost is about $3 to $4 a ton above that of rails.

Mr. UNDERWOOD. You also make car wheels?

Mr. SCHWAB. Yes, sir.

Mr. UNDERWOOD. What is the cost of those?

Mr. SCHWAB. That is a great variety of cost. Common cast-iron wheels are made at very low cost, while the steel-rolled wheels are three times the cost of cast-iron wheels. If you will specify a specific kind, I can give you the cost.

Mr. UNDERWOOD. What is the difference between this country and your foreign competitors, the English manufacturers, on those items?

Mr. SCHWAB. I can not give it; I do not know.

Mr. UNDERWOOD. You are not familiar with that?

Mr. SCHWAB. No, sir; I am not sufficiently familiar with that. The important factors are those I have given you—structural shapes of all sorts, bars, and rails. Steel wire I am not now sufficiently familiar with to give any data.

Mr. UNDERWOOD. Could this committee, if it sees proper to reduce the duty on steel rails and pig iron, taking the figures you have given to base their reductions on, safely make a similar reduction on the other products?

Mr. SCHWAB. Yes, sir. My view of that is this; you can take the tariff off altogether if you want to, and we will be able to compete anywhere, but we have to put the conditions in a similar form. We have to put labor on a similar basis. If you will go into the detailed amount of labor entering into the cost of making steel you will find it is practically everything but the cost of the raw material in the ground. Reduce those labor items along the line—I mean the labor of all the people who furnish fire bricks and refractories and supplies and waste and oil and coal, and everything that goes into the steel, and you will be able to put us on a basis with our natural resources, putting them in at the same price as anybody else's, to compete with the world free, and it will make a very radical and decided change in everything pertaining to the manufacture in America.

Mr. HILL. Right on that very point, is the tariff fairly balanced between pig iron and steel rails? With $4 a ton on pig iron, is not the remaining $3.84 an excessive tariff on the transferring of that into rails?

Mr. SCHWAB. I could not answer that offhand. I would have to figure that a little.

Mr. HILL. Will you kindly look over the iron and steel schedule and point out to the committee in writing any unbalanced items, in your judgment?

Mr. SCHWAB. The only ones with which I am familiar are the ones I have mentioned, and those are the important items which I have mentioned—structural items, rails, and so forth. I think the differential there is all right.

Mr. HILL. That is the duty on pig iron of $4 is fairly adjusted on bars at $3.10?

Mr. SCHWAB. No; I am speaking of the difference between rails and structural steel plates and similar things.

Mr. HILL. You think it is fairly balanced?

Mr. SCHWAB. I do think it is fairly balanced between these two things, considering the cost of making them.

Mr. UNDERWOOD. Let me call your attention to the question of balancing these two duties. As you stated a while ago, almost this entire proposition is dependent on the labor cost, except the cost of the raw material?

Mr. SCHWAB. Yes, sir.

Mr. UNDERWOOD. This morning you stated the cost of pig iron was $13.43?

Mr. SCHWAB. Yes; under present conditions.

Mr. UNDERWOOD. Added to that is $7.70 for converting into steel rails, amounting to about $21.50?

Mr. SCHWAB. Quite right.

Mr. UNDERWOOD. Now, the duty on pig iron is $4?

Mr. SCHWAB. Yes.

Mr. UNDERWOOD. Four dollars stands as a protective tariff to protect $13.43 worth of cost of product of the pig iron. The duty on steel rails is $7.84, or nearly double the protective duty on pig iron, and yet the labor cost or the cost of manufacturing the steel above the pig iron is only $7.50, or almost half as much.

Mr. SCHWAB. But the cost from the pig iron to the rails is all labor.

Mr. UNDERWOOD. So it is from the ore.

Mr. SCHWAB. No; the cost of making pig iron is made up very largely of the raw materials in the ground. If you will remember it, I put ore at $1 a ton, and inasmuch as it takes three tons of ore to make one ton of steel rails, that cuts a very material figure in the cost of rails.

Mr. UNDERWOOD. That is true.

Mr. SCHWAB. Yes.

Mr. UNDERWOOD. It would then make the labor cost of pig iron stand in the relative proportion of two to one.

Mr. SCHWAB. I would have to figure that. This I do know, however, that the cost of putting pig iron into rails is practically all labor in one form or another. That is, you may say I charge so much here for material, for repairs, and so forth, but analyzing the materials or repairs back to their finality, you will find it is all labor, and so every item that enters into the cost of the rails is nothing but labor after you get the raw material.

Mr. UNDERWOOD. There is another proposition you have left out of your statement. If a man has his money invested in any concern he should sell his product at a reasonable profit.

Mr. SCHWAB. Yes, sir.

Mr. UNDERWOOD. What do you think is a fair proposition to add to the cost of pig iron and steel rails for a fair profit to the manufacturer, considering the amount of his investment?

Mr. SCHWAB. I will tell you. I believe that in the manufacture of steel unless a man can see a profit of 20 or 25 per cent a year he had better keep out, for the reason that changes in the methods have necessitated such frequent and radical changes in plants that the charge-off each year for changes and depreciation are very much greater than people not in the business possibly dream of. I could state to you many illustrations of that. During my superintendence of the Braddock Works in five years I rebuilt the converting department three times. Therefore the ordinary charge of 5 per cent for depreciation will not nearly cover the investment. I think that in any manufacturing you ought to have at least 25 per cent. I think where you consider steel from the ore down, where you mine the ore and manufacture the coke, and do all those things incidental to the manufacture of steel, 25 per cent is not a sufficient profit.

Mr. UNDERWOOD. Twenty-five per cent there would include the profit on the mining of the ore, the production of the coke, and making it into pig iron, and the production of steel?

Mr. SCHWAB. I mean if I bought my ores to start to make steel I ought to have 25 per cent profit on it, but I do not think manufacturing will pay that, and I think you will find it will be the experience of people long in the art that it should not pay much less than that.

Mr. UNDERWOOD. I think you are right, but in adjusting the profits we have to consider other people in the ore business who are entitled to a profit, and we have to consider those profits in fixing the rate.

Mr. SCHWAB. I understand that.

Mr. UNDERWOOD. But 25 per cent—I do not know what the steel plant would cost.

Mr. SCHWAB. They grow more costly each year.

Mr. UNDERWOOD. But if you can give the committee a statement of your plant——

Mr. SCHWAB (interrupting). I shall be very glad to do that.

Mr. UNDERWOOD. If you can say what it would cost to erect a plant to make steel rails at a profit, and then tell us how much a ton should be added for profit, we would like to have it.

Mr. SCHWAB. I will give you an illustration of that. The latest plant built in the United States I have just built at Bethlehem. We produce only 500 tons of rails a day and about 1,000 tons of structural steel in this plant. That is a total production of 1,500 tons of steel a day. The cost of the bare plant—that is, not the blast furnace, but from the pig iron to the finished product—was about $15,500,000. That included no working capital. We have spent on that plant, in working capital and plant, approximately $21,000,000—$20,000,000 to $21,000,000.

Mr. UNDERWOOD. Now, with reference to that plant, which is a modern plant and up to date, I want you to state, if you can, how much should be added to a ton of steel to give you a 25 per cent profit on the whole process.

Mr. SCHWAB. I would have to figure that. Shall I do it now?

Mr. UNDERWOOD. I shall be obliged if you can do it.

Mr. SCHWAB. Let us take the cost of that plant at 21 million dollars. These are facts with which I am familiar. Twenty-five per cent of the cost of that plant is approximately 4 million dollars. If you divide that by about one-half a million tons a year of steel output, which is about the output of that plant in rails and structural steel, it amounts to $8 a ton. Taking 4 million dollars of profit, that ought to be earned on a 21-million-dollar plant, and divide that by the tons it will produce annually, and it amounts to just $8 a ton.

I would like to call attention to one thing more. This is hardly a fair computation, inasmuch as it was a hasty one. I took no profit on the blast furnace for this plant, which we already had.

Mr. UNDERWOOD. Take a similar case and put in your mind, if you can, a modern, up-to-date blast furnace, fairly situated in the country to do business, and estimate the cost of building and construction of that blast furnace, and then see what should be added to a ton of pig iron to produce the amount of profit necessary.

Mr. SCHWAB. The situation is somewhat different in pig iron for this reason, that the frequent renewals or changing of plant is not so necessary as it is in the making of steel, because blast furnaces have not changed a great deal, as you well know. I will do the best I can. [The witness here made computations.] I should say $2 a ton, in round figures.

Mr. UNDERWOOD. Two dollars a ton?

Mr. SCHWAB. That is the way I have it figured, and you will pardon me if I have made a mistake. A modern blast furnace costs about one and one-half million dollars. That furnace will produce about 140,000 tons in a year. Twenty-five per cent on the cost of that furnace would be $300,000 a year. Three hundred thousand dollars divided by 140 is something over $2. That is probably low, for the reason that you can not isolate a blast furnace. It is not fair to take a single item like a blast furnace to tell what the cost of that individual output ought to be.

Mr. UNDERWOOD. The reason you said the profit ought to be 25 per cent on the finished product was because you recognized that the man who mined the ore was entitled to a profit, the man who mined the coal was entitled to a profit, and the man who was producing the coke was entitled to a profit, and therefore——

Mr. SCHWAB (interrupting). If you will take my cost as given this morning I think you will find there is some profit allowed in that in this particular. I put ore at $1 a ton.

Mr. UNDERWOOD. That is what you claim to be a royalty?

Mr. SCHWAB. I said for people who own ore it was worth $1 a ton to mine it. It amounts to the same thing. If you buy coke at a certain price, that includes the cost of the coal at the mine.

Mr. UNDERWOOD. There was no profit in your statement outside of the cost of the raw material?

Mr. SCHWAB. No.

Mr. UNDERWOOD. Mr. Cockran has called my attention to the fact that he did not understand whether you said the steel mill you figured on produced 500 tons a day of steel rails and a thousand tons of structural steel in addition.

Mr. SCHWAB. Yes; in addition.

Mr. UNDERWOOD. You figured that in your estimate?

Mr. SCHWAB. Yes, sir; I did. That is one-half million tons a year, Mr. Cockran.

Mr. UNDERWOOD. Did you estimate, or will you estimate, if you can, the difference in the labor cost in a ton of pig iron as between the production in this country and England and Germany?

Mr. SCHWAB. There is not a great deal of difference in the labor cost in the two countries, but our investment in a plant and machinery to make a ton is very much greater than theirs.

Mr. UNDERWOOD. I see that.

Mr. SCHWAB. But the actual difference in labor between the two countries is not very marked. The difference in the actual cost per ton to-day is not very marked.

Mr. UNDERWOOD. The American manufacturer has not lost anything by the increase in the cost of his plant? He has a more modern plant?

Mr. SCHWAB. No; the manufacturer gets cheaper labor. He pays higher to-day for his labor, but does with less men by reason of the increased cost of plant. That is the difference. We operate a furnace with probably one-half the number of men, but pay them twice as much.

Mr. UNDERWOOD. You have a blast furnace that will produce 500 tons a day——

Mr. SCHWAB. That is a good modern furnace.

Mr. UNDERWOOD. What would be the difference in cost in building or construction of that plant here and in England?

Mr. SCHWAB. I would have to guess at that. I can tell what it is in this country.

Mr. UNDERWOOD. About what is the difference?

Mr. SCHWAB. Our cost is about one and one-half millions, and I should say theirs is about one-half million dollars.

Mr. U DE W D. They build their plant for one-third what you do? N R OO

Mr. SCHWAB. Yes, sir.

Mr. UNDERWOOD. What is the difference in Germany, relatively?

Mr. SCHWAB. Germany is rapidly adopting the same methods and blast-furnace practices that we are, with reference to economies in handling the materials, but they have gone much further than we have in the introduction of the use of their waste gases. Germany was the first country to use their waste gases for the development of power, which makes a very large saving in the cost of pig iron. We are rapidly adopting it, but to tell the truth, we are following Germany in that respect.

Mr. CLARK. In your travels, Mr. Schwab, have you ever been to Spain?

Mr. SCHWAB. I have.

Mr. CLARK. Is it true or not true that Spanish iron mines are situated right on the sea?

Mr. SCHWAB. Not exactly on the sea. They have to transport their iron by rail to the water.

Mr. CLARK. The reason I ask that is there was one man here who testified they were right jam up against the sea.

Mr. SCHWAB. In Spain?

Mr. CLARK. Yes.

Mr. SCHWAB. That is not exactly correct. There may be some mines on the sea that I do not know of.

Mr. CLARK. You are still selling steel rails at home at $28 a ton?

Mr. SCHWAB. We are selling at $30. Ours are open-hearth rails.

Mr. CLARK. They cost you $21 and something?

Mr. SCHWAB. No; Bessemer rails cost $21.

Mr. CLARK. How much do these cost?

Mr. SCHWAB. Well, say $23.50.

Mr. CLARK. How much do you sell them for abroad?

Mr. SCHWAB. We do not sell any abroad. We have sold a few, yes; I sold some to Panama and some to Mexico, I think, but very few.

Mr. CLARK. How much are American Bessemer rails selling for here at home?

Mr. SCHWAB. Twenty-eight dollars.

Mr. CLARK. How much do they sell for abroad?

Mr. SCHWAB. I can not tell you exactly. I do not know. I can tell you about what they are selling for. I should suppose they are selling abroad for between $26.50 and $27.

Mr. CLARK. Do you know what the difference was in home consumption and foreign consumption last year?

Mr. SCHWAB. You mean this year or the year before?

Mr. CLARK. I mean this year and last year—in 1907—what was the difference between the home price of Bessemer rails and the export price?

Mr. SCHWAB. I do not know. I think the price last year was about the same as it is this year.

Mr. CLARK. Do you know of your own knowledge what is the greatest discrepancy there ever was between the home price of steel rails and the foreign price?

Mr. SCHWAB. The greatest discrepancy?

Mr. CLARK. Yes.

Mr. Schwab. You mean how high in this country and how low in Europe?

Mr. Clark. How much lower did American manufactured steel rails sell for abroad as compared with what they sold for at home?

Mr. Schwab. I should say probably $10; I am not sure of that, however; that is merely a guess.

Mr. Clark. It is a habitual process to sell them cheaper abroad, is it not?

Mr. Schwab. Yes, sir; and a very wise process.

Mr. Clark. I am not asking whether it is wise or unwise. I am asking for a fact.

Mr. Schwab. I beg your pardon; I offered that information gratuitously.

Mr. Clark. I do not want to go into the realms of speculation. I want to stick to facts. The reason I asked that last question was that an independent manufacturer here testified that one year his recollection was that the difference was $6.80, I think. When you say you ought to have 25 per cent profit, do you mean that the gross profit ought to be 25 per cent?

Mr. Schwab. Certainly. It depends on what you mean as between gross and net profits, however.

Mr. Clark. By net profit I mean your profit after you have subtracted from the amount of money that you get for the article every element of cost, interest, depreciation, and everything counted off.

Mr. Schwab. Then I do not mean that.

Mr. Clark. You do not mean net profit?

Mr. Schwab. No, sir; I do not. I mean we should have 25 per cent manufacturing profit to enable us to charge off 5 or 6 or 8 per cent a year for plant, and so forth.

Mr. Clark. There has been a great deal of talk, first and last, about reasonable profits.

Mr. Schwab. Yes.

Mr. Clark. Take it on a net profit, after all sorts of costs and expenses and everything else that enters into the cost are taken out, what profit do you think you ought to get?

Mr. Schwab. Fifteen to 20 per cent.

Mr. Clark. Net profit?

Mr. Schwab. Yes, sir; I certainly do. I do not think you would succeed in manufacturing unless you do.

Mr. Clark. I am talking about net profit.

Mr. Schwab. I am, too.

Mr. Clark. Clear, clean velvet, as the boys say.

Mr. Schwab. There is an unfortunate thing about the steel business, that although we get a good deal of profit, we do not get much "velvet."

Mr. Clark. If you put a dollar's worth of stuff back into the plant, you are just as well off as if you put it in your pocket?

Mr. Schwab. No; I would make a very liberal reduction for cash. If you want to buy my plant, I will make you a very liberal discount for cash.

Mr. Clark. I do not think I will tackle that to-day. What I am trying to get at is, what this means as a reasonable profit. You say 15 or 20 per cent?

Mr. Schwab. That is my view of it.

Mr. CLARK. Just from your general information—I suppose you have a good deal of it one way or another, from your very clear statements in your testimony——

Mr. SCHWAB (interrupting). Thank you, sir.

Mr. CLARK. Do you not think that is three or four times as much as the average business in the nation, outside of the steel business?

Mr. SCHWAB. In manufacturing?

Mr. CLARK. I am talking about the whole business of the United States—manufacturing and everything else.

Mr. SCHWAB. Banking and manufacturing are two very different things. If you will say manufacturing, it is my opinion that in the general manufacturing business that is not an exorbitant profit.

Mr. CLARK. I will ask you another question in connection with that. Is it your opinion from your general and large observation that the average manufacturer in the United States is making 15 to 20 per cent net?

Mr. SCHWAB. To-day he is not making anything.

Mr. CLARK. I am not talking about this year; this is a Republican year. [Laughter.] Take the last eleven years as a business period, since the revival of business—that is a fair phrase to use—what would you say about the average profit of manufacturing in this country, not counting 1908 as a specialty, but taking that in connection with 1897, and every year down to the present time? How much have they made, would you say?

Mr. SCHWAB. What would be the average net profits of all manufacturers?

Mr. CLARK. Yes.

Mr. SCHWAB. I should say from 10 to 15 per cent.

Mr. CLARK. I am glad to hear that. Nearly everyone has come in here and sworn—not testified under oath, because we only began to swear them here a day or two ago—but solemnly asserted that none of them have made over 3 or 4 per cent, although we did finally persuade one man to testify or state that he made 15 per cent on gypsum.

Mr. SCHWAB. I do not think we ought to take the average manufacturer as the criterion of what this country can do and what the profits ought to be. If we want to compete with foreign manufacturers in foreign countries, we must do so not with the average manufacturers, but with our best manufacturers.

Mr. CLARK. But if the average manufacturer makes 15 or 20 per cent, with all the slovenliness and things of that kind that are attached to some people's manufacturing business——

Mr. SCHWAB. You do not quote me correctly, quite. I said from 10 to 15 per cent.

Mr. CLARK. Well, take 10 to 15 per cent. If the average manufacturers, with all the drawbacks of a large number of people being mixed up, incapables, and all, have made from 10 to 15 per cent, then an expert business man——

Mr. SCHWAB. He ought to make 25 per cent or more.

Mr. CLARK. He would make it?

Mr. SCHWAB. He ought to.

Mr. CLARK. He would make it?

Mr. SCHWAB. He ought to make 25—20 to 25.

Mr. CLARK. I think so, too.

Mr. SCHWAB. And he ought to.

Mr. GAINES. Did I understand you to say you could retain the American market without any duty, but in order to do so you would have to reduce the basis of the cost?

Mr. SCHWAB. Put it in the same condition they have it abroad.

Mr. GAINES. If you reduce the cost of production here, what item other than labor enters largely into the cost of production?

Mr. SCHWAB. Raw material only.

Mr. GAINES. What I would like to ask you is, does not labor enter more largely into the cost of production than anything else?

Mr. SCHWAB. Of course. When you take out the cost of your raw materials, there is no other cost left but the labor.

Mr. GAINES. So if the duty were removed from your product in order for you to retain the American market and compete with foreign manufacturers the cost of production must be reduced?

Mr. SCHWAB. Absolutely. There is nothing else to it.

Mr. GAINES. Labor being the largest item of cost, it would be the first thing to be considered?

Mr. SCHWAB. Yes, sir. It does not mean labor in the steel works only. It means the railroads must reduce their freight, and cousequently their labor. Every man who furnished the steel works any supplies, whether he be a brickmaker or anything else, must be reduced also. You must get all your supplies cheaper, and every man who furnishes you those supplies must get his labor cheaper.

Mr. McCALL. You mean we are to have an exact reproduction of the situation existing abroad?

Mr. SCHWAB. To compete with them, we must have similar conditions.

Mr. GAINES. The gentleman from Missouri referred to this year as being a Republican year. Can you remember ever having a Democratic year?

Mr. SCHWAB. The gentleman has been so courteous and kind, I think I will refrain from taking any part in that argument.

Mr. COCKRAN. I do not know whether you can or not, Mr. Schwab, but I can not.

Mr. CLARK. What is the exact technical name of this " United Steel trust," as we usually call it?

Mr. SCHWAB. United States Steel Corporation.

Mr. CLARK. When was that organized?

Mr. SCHWAB. 1901.

Mr. COCKRAN. I had a few questions pending when the recess occurred at noon. I would like to put them to you now. The prices of steel rails and of all steel products in this country are practically uniform, are they not?

Mr. SCHWAB. The price of steel rails is uniform.

Mr. COCKRAN. How is that fixed?

Mr. SCHWAB. I explained that a little while ago at great length.

Mr. COCKRAN. Where?

Mr. SCHWAB. Right here, a little while ago.

Mr. DALZELL. Since the noon recess he has explained it to the committee.

Mr. COCKRAN. You have explained all that?

Mr. SCHWAB. I did.

Mr. COCKRAN. Very well, I will get that from the record then.

Mr. Schwab. Yes; it has been given here this afternoon.

Mr. Cockran. This much you stated before lunch, that a steady price was very essential to the prosperous conditions of your industry?

Mr. Schwab. It is.

Mr. Cockran. And it was for that reason that you have maintained the price at $28, regardless of what it cost to produce?

Mr. Schwab. You are speaking of rails now?

Mr. Cockran. Yes.

Mr. Schwab. Quite so.

Mr. Cockran. Does the same apply to all other products?

Mr. Schwab. No; it does not.

Mr. Cockran. In other products of steel the price is governed to some extent by the cost of production? It varies from year to year?

Mr. Schwab. I can not say that is true, and yet it is true to some extent.

Mr. Cockran. What you mean to tell me is to some extent it is true——

Mr. Schwab (interrupting). Pig iron, for example, varies. The price has always varied.

Mr. Cockran. I am speaking of steel products.

Mr. Schwab. I think there are a number. Billets vary with the cost of production.

Mr. Cockran. Which of your products vary from year to year?

Mr. Schwab. I have given a sample—billets. The largest single production of any one line of steel we have is steel wires. That varies with the cost of production.

Mr. Cockran. Has it varied much during the last few years?

Mr. Schwab. Very considerably.

Mr. Cockran. Give us the extreme range.

Mr. Schwab. I have sold steel bars at $1.85, and recently at $1.25.

Mr. Cockran. Was that peculiar to this year, 1908, since the panic?

Mr. Schwab. No; steel products were very high the first part of last year.

Mr. Cockran. For the nine years previous to that were those steel products at about the same price, a steady price?

Mr. Schwab. Do not think I am trying to evade you——

Mr. Cockran. I do not think so for a moment.

Mr. Schwab. If you will ask me a direct question I will give you a direct answer. The steel products that have not varied are steel rails and structural steel. They have been nearly uniform. Steel rails are the only thing that has been strictly uniform since 1900. Structural steel, which is the next largest product, has varied some. It is now $2 a ton lower than it was six months ago, and it has varied from year to year.

Mr. Cockran. Everything is a good deal lower now, is it not, with the exception of steel rails?

Mr. Schwab. Not a good deal lower; no.

Mr. Cockran. Somewhat lower?

Mr. Schwab. Yes; somewhat lower.

Mr. Cockran. You said that free steel would make a very great change in conditions?

Mr. Schwab. It would.

Mr. COCKRAN. You spoke of a reduction in wages as being the first essential.

Mr. SCHWAB. Yes.

Mr. COCKRAN. I understood you to say in answer to Mr. Underwood that wages are about the same as in England?

Mr. SCHWAB. No; I did not say that at all. I said the labor cost.

Mr. COCKRAN. That is the same thing.

Mr. SCHWAB. No; it is not the same at all; not by any means.

Mr. COCKRAN. Oh, I understand that, of course. The labor cost per ton is the same to you as it is in England?

Mr. SCHWAB. About.

Mr. COCKRAN. Why should there be any necessity for reducing the rate of wages when the labor cost is the same in order to compete with England—why should there be any necessity for reducing the laborer's wages?

Mr. SCHWAB. Labor is not the only thing in it. It is the chief thing.

Mr. COCKRAN. The labor cost of every commodity is practically all it costs except just what is in the ground?

Mr. SCHWAB. Quite true.

Mr. COCKRAN. If that is so, and your labor cost is the same as in England——

Mr. SCHWAB (interrupting). But, my dear friend, you are taking the labor cost in the making of steel alone, while I am taking the labor cost of everything that enters into the cost of making steel.

Mr. COCKRAN. I see the distinction you make.

Mr. SCHWAB. There is a distinction between the cost of labor in the steel maker's works and the total cost of labor which may mean ten times the number of men you employ at your works.

Mr. COCKRAN. So far as your labor cost is concerned, there is no necessity for a protective tariff to equalize labor conditions, because they are practically the same?

Mr. SCHWAB. Because we have to charge more for interest or some other item.

Mr. COCKRAN. But the labor cost is about the same?

Mr. SCHWAB. Quite true.

Mr. COCKRAN. Concerning this question of reasonable profit, you have fixed that in your answer to Mr. Clark at between 15 and 20 per cent, as the amount a steel company should be allowed to earn, saying that is a reasonable profit?

Mr. SCHWAB. Yes, sir.

Mr. COCKRAN. That means 15 or 20 per cent available for distribution to the stockholders. You do not include in that the salaries and expenses that are paid to officers and managers? You mean 15 or 20 per cent net after all expenses are paid?

Mr. SCHWAB. Fifteen or twenty per cent net profit.

Mr. COCKRAN. So if a man is successful, as you yourself have been——

Mr. SCHWAB (interrupting). I doubt it.

Mr. COCKRAN. You have been finally, in your line, a success. If a man can prove himself worth to a company $400,000 or $500,000 a year, or even a million dollars a year, on your basis of computation that would be taken out as a charge?

Mr. SCHWAB. No, I put that in as a cost.

Mr. COCKRAN. That is a charge against the cost?

Mr. SCHWAB. Yes, sir.

Mr. COCKRAN. You put that in as a practical cost?

Mr. SCHWAB. Yes, sir.

Mr. COCKRAN. Fifteen or twenty per cent would be aside for profits outside that?

Mr. SCHWAB. Quite so.

Mr. COCKRAN. When you discuss the question of profits for the company you mean profits over and above all that can be paid by way of compensation or reward to any individual who contributes to the success of the company?

Mr. SCHWAB. That is part of the cost, certainly.

Mr. COCKRAN. I do not ask anything as to what those amounts are, because I suppose that is a matter of confidential information.

Mr. SCHWAB. I do not know to what you refer.

Mr. COCKRAN. I mean the amount paid for instance by the United States Steel Corporation to its officers.

Mr. SCHWAB. I do not know.

Mr. COCKRAN. You said that they are selling abroad cheaper than here?

Mr. SCHWAB. Yes, sir.

Mr. COCKRAN. You said that it is a very wise process?

Mr. SCHWAB. Quite.

Mr. COCKRAN. Could you explain the wisdom of it to the victims of it as well as to the beneficiaries of it? From the point of view of the American consumer, where does the wisdom of it come in?

Mr. SCHWAB. I am not thinking of the consumer. I am thinking of the manufacturer. [Laughter.] I presume there is no argument there.

Mr. COCKRAN. There is no argument there. The more you get the merrier.

Mr. SCHWAB. I have said it was a wise provision for the manufacturer. You can not let a steel plant stand idle. The fires in your furnaces and the heat costs go on whether you are making steel or not.

Mr. COCKRAN. You said as a matter of fact that there are different rates charged for your products abroad, and you charge less abroad than you charge at home?

Mr. SCHWAB. We usually charge abroad what we can get.

Mr. COCKRAN. You do that at home, do you not?

Mr. SCHWAB. Yes; of course.

Mr. COCKRAN. You can not, of course, put a pistol to a man's head and take all he has.

Mr. SCHWAB. You can in some instances; yes.

Mr. COCKRAN. I mean to say you sell abroad for all that you can get. As a matter of fact, you do sell abroad for less than you obtain here?

Mr. SCHWAB. As a rule, that is true.

Mr. BONYNGE. What percentage of steel rails produced in the United States are sold abroad?

Mr. SCHWAB. In years gone by it was a very small percentage; I should say from 5 to 7 per cent. This year I think it will be larger, because our home consumption has been very small.

Mr. BONYNGE. About how much?

Mr. SCHWAB. I should not be surprised if it ran as high as 20 per cent this year. The reason for that is because we have no market at home and we have been driven abroad to get something to do.

Mr. COCKRAN. Where and in what parts of the world are those sales made this year?

Mr. SCHWAB. Wherever there is a competitive field where we all pay equal tariffs or no tariffs at all, like South America, for example, or Japan or China.

Mr. COCKRAN. Have you ever gotten into Canada, where there is a differential tariff in favor of England?

Mr. SCHWAB. There have been no rails sold in Canada since that differential tariff—none that I know of.

Mr. COCKRAN. Do you not think that the consumers of this country would be entitled to the most favored treatment?

Mr. SCHWAB. I will tell you something about that. We have made a point about the price of steel rails. I have always said to the railroads, "We will make the price of steel rails anything you say if you will proportionately reduce your freight rates to us." In other words, the cost to the steel manufacturer for manufacturing his rails and other steel products that he pays in freight is very nearly 30 per cent of his total cost.

Mr. COCKRAN. I understand that.

Mr. SCHWAB. While the cost to the railroad of their steel rails is a very small percentage of their cost, a reduction in the price of steel rails to a railroad would be a very trivial amount compared to a similar reduction in their rates to us. The consequence is, so far as I know, railroads do not want the price of steel rails reduced.

Mr. COCKRAN. The railroads do not?

Mr. SCHWAB. No, sir; they do not. The same is true of all kinds of other articles of steel to the consumer. Let me say something about structural steel, in which there is a uniform price throughout the United States and has been for some years. The buyers of structural steel, whether they be large or small, whether they have great advantages by reason of shop or otherwise, have no advantage to-day in the purchase of structural steel, and the small consumers want to see that price maintained steadily all the time. For example, I had within a few months a call from seven of the largest users of structural steel in America, and they all asked that I use my influence to keep the price unchanged. One of the great advantages of a steel corporation during the great period of prosperity and the fact that this steel business was in the hands of comparatively few people, is the fact that although they could have had ten or fifteen or twenty dollars more for their steel than they got, they did not raise the price, nor have they lowered it during this depression. The result is that whether they be railroads or whether they be small consumers of structural steel, they feel better satisfied and like the present conditions much better than when we had violent fluctuations in the market.

Mr. COCKRAN. There is no question at all that a steady price would be better than uneven prices; but surely it does not follow that consumers also want prices not only steady, but high?

Mr. SCHWAB. No; but I do not think that the prices of steel are unreasonable.

Mr. COCKRAN. You would not be expected to think that.

Mr. SCHWAB. No; I do not think they are high enough, personally.

Mr. COCKRAN. Oh, no; I understand that.

Mr. SCHWAB. I mean by reason of advances that have been made in everything entering into the cost of steel—railroad freights have gone up, and everything has gone up. Wages have advanced steadily every year since 1900, but steel has not advanced.

Mr. COCKRAN. But you started in in 1899 with a profit of 100 per cent, on your showing?

Mr. SCHWAB. That was about right.

Mr. COCKRAN. Yes; that was about right; I understand that perfectly. We have your view of what is right. You have said that the steel companies could have obtained easily $10 or $20 additional.

Mr. SCHWAB. No; I said $5 or $10 or $20, dependent on the market.

Mr. COCKRAN. Surely, you did not mean that if they undertook to exact such a price they would not have discouraged the use of steel?

Mr. SCHWAB. They probably would, but other and independent manufacturers did get it.

Mr. COCKRAN. You say other independent manufacturers?

Mr. SCHWAB. Yes. I was an independent manufacturer at that time, and I always got more for my steel than the Steel Corporation did.

Mr. COCKRAN. Independence has many virtues, has it not?

Mr. SCHWAB. And some disadvantages.

Mr. CLARK. You say that the railroads do not object to your charging this high price—I will call it that for my own satisfaction—for steel rails?

Mr. SCHWAB. No.

Mr. CLARK. They just simply load the cost of the steel rails off onto their patrons, do they not?

Mr. SCHWAB. Quite true.

Mr. CLARK. So that the bottom fellow pays the whole business at last?

Mr. SCHWAB. That is going pretty far down the line.

Mr. CLARK. I will ask another question simply for information. You have stated about rebuilding these furnaces up at Braddock three times in five years.

Mr. SCHWAB. It was a converting mill.

Mr. CLARK. What I want to ask is, if this has been going on in the last five years more than ever before—these changes in processes that necessitate this rebuilding of plants?

Mr. SCHWAB. I will give you an illustration of that. I make this prediction, that in five years from now there will not be a single Bessemer converting works for making steel in the United States. That means that every man who has his money invested in Bessemer works for making steel rails will have to throw it away as useless and of no value before five years. The change is rapidly taking place now. If you will look at statistics you will see all the steel rails are getting to be the open hearth. Bessemer will be of no use. The result is all these changes will have to be made at tremendous cost. The same is true of structural steel. The new mills which I have built at Bethlehem have made a radical change in the character of structural steel, so that most of the structural-steel plants of the United States will have to be changed within the next five years, and that has been the history of the steel business since I have been connected with it.

Mr. CLARK. Now, two questions——

Mr. SCHWAB. Not at one time?

Mr. CLARK. No. I do not know nearly so much about this steel question as Mr. Underwood does. I want to ask a question for my own information. I take it from what you said in a portion of your evidence here to-day that this open-hearth steel is superior to the Bessemer steel?

Mr. SCHWAB. For certain purposes.

Mr. CLARK. The question I wanted to ask a while ago, and will ask now, though your answer a while ago possibly does away with it, is whether, in your judgment, the time has come when these rapid changes in the very expensive business of building these plants have reached their limit, or whether there is a prospect of improvements being constantly made that will later wipe out that process and cause the throwing away of these big plants and building new ones?

Mr. SCHWAB. I think that the latter is true. The open-hearth process has been developing during these past ten years. It was not believed it would make any material change in the plants except for special things. The demand for quality has made it of such a character that practically all steel must be made by the open-hearth process. We have taken another step in advance, which has been developed by the Germans, and that is the electric method of producing steel, which is an advance again over the open hearth, that I am certain that in the next ten years, or probably quicker, depending upon the rapidity of the development, changes will probably make all open hearths practically useless.

Mr. CLARK. Well, you are able to get your product out cheaper on account of these?

Mr. SCHWAB. No; we are not.

Mr. CLARK. It seems you have to lose a great deal in rebuilding?

Mr. SCHWAB. We do. You do not get it cheaper. These processes have not been for the purpose of cheapening the product, but of bettering the quality. Each betterment of quality has added to the cost.

Mr. CLARK. In the end that is to the advantage of the public, who consume it, provided they get it at the same price?

Mr. SCHWAB. The advance is about equal to the cost.

Mr. CLARK. Do you know what the proportion of the output of steel made by all of the independent concerns in the United States is as compared to the total output of the United States? How much does the United States Steel Corporation make and how much do the rest of them make?

Mr. SCHWAB. That is a matter of record, but I think it is about 40 per cent.

Mr. COCKRAN. Which is 40 per cent?

Mr. SCHWAB. The steel corporation makes between 40 and 45 per cent.

Mr. CLARK. The steel corporation?

Mr. SCHWAB. Yes, sir.

Mr. CLARK. Does that include the Tennessee company?

Mr. SCHWAB. No; I did not include that.

Mr. CLARK. If you include with the United States Steel Corporation output the output of this Tennessee concern, which they bought with the consent of the President of the United States [laughter], how much would the proportion be?

Mr. SCHWAB. Probably 44 or 45 per cent.

Mr. CLARK. You do not think they make a majority?

Mr. SCHWAB. No, I do not think so.

The CHAIRMAN. You are not swearing the President did consent to its purchase?

Mr. SCHWAB. No; I know nothing about it.

Mr. CLARK. I am not, either, but it was a matter of common notoriety that before they dared to buy that concern Morgan or someone representing him went to the President and got his permission to do it.

The CHAIRMAN. That was before the election.

Mr. COCKRAN. You would bet on it with your money, although you might not attest it with your oath?

Mr. SCHWAB. I do not know anything about it.

Mr. UNDERWOOD. The percentage of production of the United States Steel Company was estimated a short time ago at 47 per cent of the total production for the United States.

Mr. SCHWAB. Yes, that is probably nearly right.

Mr. BONYNGE. What other steel products are sold abroad for less than the same steel products are sold in the United States, besides steel rails?

Mr. SCHWAB. The principal lines of steel of which I have spoken—structural steel in all its forms—plates, girders, and similar things, and steel rails.

Mr. BONYNGE. All sold for less than in the United States?

Mr. SCHWAB. I can not say that always, but as a rule, that is true.

Mr. BONYNGE. What is the percentage of steel products produced in the United States of all kinds that is sold abroad?

Mr. SCHWAB. I could not tell offhand. I could make a guess. I think it is about the same as rails—from 5 to 7 per cent. That is my judgment. I think it is higher this year. I am guessing at that, but I should not be surprised if it is 20 per cent this year.

Mr. BONYNGE. If those sales had not been made at the reduced prices abroad, would it have had any effect on the prices charged to the home consumer?

Mr. SCHWAB. Under existing conditions I think not, although it made a difference in the profit. Their profits would have been much higher on the home product if they had not sold abroad in this way.

Mr. BONYNGE. The selling price would have been the same?

Mr. SCHWAB. I think probably it would. I am sure it would in the matter of rails, and I think in most of the other lines.

Mr. CLARK. Suppose you put the market price of rails and steel products down to the home consumer to the same basis you did to the foreign consumer, do you not think the home consumption would have swelled to the extent of this foreign export?

Mr. SCHWAB. I do not think it would have increased a ton.

Mr. CLARK. I believe, then, there is no hope of getting a lower price.

Mr. SCHWAB. No; I am afraid not. [Laughter.]

Mr. HILL. You have been very frank in your answers from the manufacturer's standpoint.

Mr. SCHWAB. Thank you, sir.

Mr. HILL. I want to ask this question: Taking the general welfare of this country, the foreign trade, and your industry in consideration, what change, if any, would you suggest with reference to the iron and steel tariffs?

Mr. SCHWAB. My personal view is that I would not make any change. I do not mind saying a moderate change is not going to seriously hurt. I think a radical change will make a very great difference. I am a manufacturer, and this is a manufacturer's point of view, and I would not make any changes.

Mr. LONGWORTH. You are familiar with the iron ores production of Cuba?

Mr. SCHWAB. Yes, sir.

Mr. LONGWORTH. Can you state what amount of ore is in sight there now?

Mr. SCHWAB. There is a very large tonnage in sight. There is a peculiar condition that, to my mind, is going to make a radical change in the iron-ore situation. There has been discovered in Cuba within the last few years a very large deposit of ore; indeed, some engineers estimate it quite as large as the Mesabi Range. It is of a different character, however, in that it is wet and needs drying before it can be transported. It has some problems in connection with it to be worked out, but very important deposits as to tonnage.

Mr. LONGWORTH. How would it compare with the ore in the Mesabi Range in quantity?

Mr. SCHWAB. I say that some engineers I have had on the property estimate it to be about as much as the Mesabi Range.

Mr. LONGWORTH. And in quality?

Mr. SCHWAB. The quality is a totally different proposition. In some respects very much better, in that the ore contains nickel, and steel made from that ore will contain from 1 to 3 per cent nickel, and that, of course, adds much to its value for certain purposes.

Mr. LONGWORTH. At what figure can that ore be landed in Pittsburg to-day?

Mr. SCHWAB. About the same as lake ore.

Mr. LONGWORTH. About the same?

Mr. SCHWAB. Yes. It can be landed at the eastern furnaces at much less, but the cost of getting the coke to the eastern furnaces is an item of serious consideration. When I say the same in Pittsburg, I am assuming the same expenditure in appliances for shipping, etc., as are made for Pittsburg. The cost to the eastern furnaces is much less for ore, but, on the other hand, the cost of fuel to the eastern furnaces is much greater, so that the total cost of producing pig iron in the East as compared with Pittsburg is slightly in favor of Pittsburg.

Mr. CRUMPACKER. Who are the owners of the principal deposits in the Mesabi Range?

Mr. SCHWAB. You mean the owners or the lessees?

Mr. CRUMPACKER. The lessees; yes.

Mr. SCHWAB. Most of the ore was acquired by lease from many people who owned the original property.

Mr. CRUMPACKER. Who are the lessees in the main?

Mr. SCHWAB. All the large manufacturers in the West, in the United States, the Steel Corporation being the largest.

Mr. CRUMPACKER. Has your company a lease?

Mr. SCHWAB. In the Mesabi Range?

Mr. CRUMPACKER. Yes.

Mr. SCHWAB. We do not use any lake ores.

Mr. CRUMPACKER. Where do you get your ores?

Mr. Schwab. Cuba.

Mr. Crumpacker. If the duty were removed from iron ore, you would be able to get your ore at how much less per ton?

Mr. Schwab. Thirty-two cents a ton less.

Mr. Crumpacker. That would be quite an item?

Mr. Schwab. It would be. In the event of a lower tariff, the chief sufferer in the steel industry will be the East, because the West is protected by the freight to the West, as you can easily see. Therefore, if there is a reduction in the tariff—I did not intend saying this, because it is pertinent to my own business—if there is a reduction in the tariff generally, the ores coming to the eastern manufacturers ought to be brought in much lower, too.

Mr. Crumpacker. If the duty were taken off the ore altogether, it would not affect the value of the Mesabi ores, would it?

Mr. Schwab. Not at all. If the duty were taken off the ores from Cuba, it would in no way affect the value of the Mesabi ores.

Mr. Crumpacker. It would enable such manufacturers as your establishment to produce iron and steel considerably cheaper?

Mr. Schwab. It would amount to about 50 cents a ton cheaper.

Mr. Crumpacker. Fifty cents a ton cheaper?

Mr. Schwab. Yes. One important thing for the eastern people in that respect is the Cuban situation, whether any change is made there, because a large part of our ore comes from there. It would have to be done, inasmuch as their people buy their ores from other countries.

Mr. Crumpacker. The Mesabi deposits are almost owned entirely now by the large manufacturers?

Mr. Schwab. They are.

Mr. Crumpacker. The small, independent manufacturer has to buy his pig iron or his ore from competitors?

Mr. Schwab. That is true.

Mr. Crumpacker. The Mesabi deposits are the chief source of iron ore for the northern producers?

Mr. Schwab. Not Mesabi alone, but the Northwest.

Mr. Crumpacker. Lake Superior?

Mr. Schwab. The Lake Superior district is the chief source of supply.

Mr. Crumpacker. The price has gone up from 10 cents to $1 a ton?

Mr. Schwab. That is a royalty. That is for the right of taking the ores out themselves.

Mr. Crumpacker. The cost of mining and transportation has correspondingly increased?

Mr. Schwab. Exactly.

Mr. Longworth. Are these Cuban deposits on the north coast?

Mr. Schwab. Yes; on the north coast.

Mr. Longworth. The old deposits were nearer Santiago?

Mr. Schwab. Yes, sir; and this is directly north of Santiago.

Mr. Longworth. This is north of there?

Mr. Schwab. Yes, sir.

Mr. Randell. Mr. Schwab, you say that if the tariff were taken off it would be harder on the people in the East than it would on those in the West?

Mr. Schwab. Yes.

Mr. RANDELL. You mean by the people in the East, the manufacturers in the East?

Mr. SCHWAB. Certainly.

Mr. RANDELL. Therefore it would not affect the manufacturer in the West as it would the one in the East?

Mr. SCHWAB. Just the difference in the freight.

Mr. RANDELL. On the same basis, the consumer in the West has less hope of being delivered from his present burden than the consumer in the East?

Mr. SCHWAB. From present burdens?

Mr. RANDELL. Yes.

Mr. SCHWAB. I do not see that they have any burdens.

Mr. RANDELL. You do not see their burdens on account of the profit between you and the consumer?

Mr. SCHWAB. No; I do not. I think they get everything they are entitled to. I make the prediction——

Mr. RANDELL (interrupting). You understand my question, do you not?

Mr. SCHWAB. I do.

Mr. RANDELL. Then give me a candid answer, for which you have been given some credit here.

Mr. SCHWAB. I thought I answered your question.

Mr. RANDELL. You said you did not think the western man was under any burden.

Mr. SCHWAB. You did not ask me whether he had a burden. I volunteered that information.

Mr. RANDELL. Mr. Schwab, if it was a fact that the manufacturers in the East could take off the tariff, that would mean it would have a tendency to reduce the price of their product?

Mr. SCHWAB. Quite so.

Mr. RANDELL. Then it would be to the interest of the consumer in the East?

Mr. SCHWAB. Quite so.

Mr. RANDELL. In the West it would not have that tendency on account of the freight rates, and the manufacturer could still keep up his price? Is that what you meant?

Mr. SCHWAB. That is right.

Mr. RANDELL. Do you not understand, then, that I said, therefore there was less hope for the consumer in the West to be relieved of his burden?

Mr. SCHWAB. Yes, sir.

Mr. RANDELL. That is, for his products to be reduced in price?

Mr. SCHWAB. Yes.

Mr. RANDELL. You understood that?

Mr. SCHWAB. Quite, but I did not understand what you meant by "burden."

Mr. RANDELL. The burden of the higher prices he has to pay by reason of the tariff.

Mr. SCHWAB. Well, we will not quibble about that. You are quite correct.

Mr. RANDELL. You say, I believe, that the cost of labor entering into this matter is all the cost, except the price of the material in the ground?

Mr. SCHWAB. Raw materials.

Mr. RANDELL. And this cost, 30 per cent of it, if I understood you correctly, goes to railroads for transportation?

Mr. SCHWAB. Right.

Mr. RANDELL. That is according to my recollection.

Mr. SCHWAB. Yes.

Mr. RANDELL. Then you were figuring the rails at $28 a ton at your factory?

Mr. SCHWAB. Yes.

Mr. RANDELL. So at that time the railroads had already gotten 30 per cent of the cost to produce those rails, excepting, I mean, leaving out the cost of material in the ground?

Mr. SCHWAB. Quite so.

Mr. RANDELL. There was a charge, you say, of royalty, of about $1 a ton?

Mr. SCHWAB. Yes.

Mr. RANDELL. Twelve years ago the ordinary price of royalties for iron ore was about 25 cents a ton, was it not?

Mr. SCHWAB. I have leased it as low as 10 cents a ton.

Mr. RANDELL. The iron mines are scattered in various parts of the country, are they not?

Mr. SCHWAB. Most of them are in the Northwest, in the lake district.

Mr. RANDELL. And twelve years ago they were owned by a great many people?

Mr. SCHWAB. Yes.

Mr. RANDELL. Since then they have been bought up and are now owned by a few corporations?

Mr. SCHWAB. Quite true.

Mr. RANDELL. About what percentage of the visible or known deposits in the country are owned by the steel trust—the steel corporation?

Mr. SCHWAB. I could not say.

Mr. RANDELL. The corporation that you say makes 45 per cent of the output.

Mr. SCHWAB. I could not answer; I don't know.

Mr. RANDELL. Have you any idea about how much?

Mr. SCHWAB. I should say 45 per cent, about proportionate to the production.

Mr. RANDELL. And the other deposits are owned by other corporations, other steel companies?

Mr. SCHWAB. The other steel companies.

Mr. RANDELL. And all these steel companies, by common consent, as distinguished from by agreement, sell their product of rails and structural steel at the same price?

Mr. SCHWAB. They do.

Mr. RANDELL. That is not by accident, but is considered as a business proposition, the best course to pursue for the interests of the manufacturers?

Mr. SCHWAB. I do not want to evade that at all, and I want——

Mr. RANDELL. I did not insinuate that you would evade it——

Mr. SCHWAB. But the question I rather thought put me in that light.

Mr. RANDELL. I understood it was not by positive agreement, but by——.

Mr. SCHWAB. No; I said this——

Mr. RANDELL. Is it by positive agreement?

The CHAIRMAN. We have been all over that question once, and it is hardly fair to go over it again.

Mr. RANDELL. I have not been absent——

The CHAIRMAN. That has all been covered.

Mr. RANDELL. I am not taking up very much time. My question was this, Mr. Chairman. I asked him another question and he said he had not testified to that.

The CHAIRMAN. Your question was whether there was any agreement about the price of $28 a ton——

Mr. SCHWAB. There is not.

The CHAIRMAN. Or any understanding.

Mr. SCHWAB. I have explained to you exactly——

Mr. RANDELL. My question before that was this: That as he had, I understood, testified that it was not by agreement, but by mutual consent, as distinguished from agreement, that they had fixed the prices; then I asked him if that was considered by him a business proposition or mere accident.

The CHAIRMAN. Let us get through with this.

Mr. RANDELL. I am very sorry that I am taking up the time of the committee, but I have not taken up very much time——

The CHAIRMAN. We want to get through.

Mr. RANDELL. I understand; but my people have to pay the tariff on this; there are a great many consumers of this article.

Mr. SCHWAB. As I explained before, we had an agreement to maintain the price of rails along in 1896 and 1897, and then came the steel war, the great break in prices, and after that was all over—this was before the time of the steel corporation—the steel manufacturers got together and agreed to restore the price of steel rails.

Mr. RANDELL. You need not go over that——

Mr. SCHWAB. But this is an answer.

Mr. RANDELL. I know, but I am asking you with reference to present conditions. I do not care how you came by it.

Mr. SCHWAB. Gentlemen, I came here to give you this information freely, and I will do it in my own way or not at all.

Mr. RANDELL. If you will answer my questions——

Mr. SCHWAB. You must permit me to answer them in my own way. I can not answer the direct question yes or no without an implied understanding that is wrong.

Mr. DALZELL. Go ahead.

The CHAIRMAN. Of course, answer it as far as you please.

Mr. SCHWAB. I am going to give you the exact reasons. Then we got together as manufacturers and restored the price of rails to $28.

Now, there has been no manufacturer selling rails that would dare to change that price for fear of another steel-rail war. That is true of every line of which I spoke, that we had the same arrangements about.

Mr. RANDELL. Practically all lines of steel products?

Mr. SCHWAB. No; all lines of which I spoke. Structural steel and steel products.

Mr. RANDELL. Of course, then that applies to foreign sales? You said something about foreign sales.

Mr. SCHWAB. No; I did not say it was the same with foreign sales. That varies very much.

Mr. RANDELL. The record will show that. I thought you did.

Mr. SCHWAB. If I did I wish to correct it.

Mr. RANDELL. What I wish to ask you is this. That present condition, whether you call it by mutual agreement of fear of change, or what, that condition is a matter that is absolutely in the control of the present steel corporations, is it not, that makes these prices?

Mr. SCHWAB. It is by the mutual—I can not say consent. I do not know the word to use that will not be misconstrued, or misunderstood.

Mr. RANDELL. It is a matter in their control, that is the question?

Mr. SCHWAB. But the manufacturers of various products of steel in the United States——

Mr. RANDELL. The question is, Is it not a matter in their control?

Mr. SCHWAB. I suppose it might be.

Mr. RANDELL. It is.

Mr. SCHWAB. I do not say it is, but it could be.

Mr. RANDELL. They not only have the control of the market at present, but they have the control of all the ore deposits in the United States, as you stated?

Mr. SCHWAB. I did not state anything of the sort.

Mr. RANDELL. Then I misunderstood your question.

Mr. SCHWAB. I said that the steel manufacturers of the United States, as a rule, control most of the iron deposits, but not all. Every great steel works must have its own ore.

Mr. RANDELL. I understood you to say that the steel company owned about 45 per cent, which was about the same proportion of the ore as its proportion of the business.

Mr. SCHWAB. I said 45 per cent of the Lake ores. I did not say of the iron deposits of the country. Mr. Longworth was asking me about the lake ores, and I said that the Steel Corporation controlled about 45 per cent. That is vastly different from 45 per cent of the ores of the country.

Mr. RANDELL. Then I asked you if the balance of the ore in the country was not controlled by the other steel corporations——

Mr. SCHWAB. And I said yes.

Mr. RANDELL. And are there any deposits not owned or controlled by the steel corporations of the country?

Mr. SCHWAB. Other than the lake ores, many.

Mr. RANDELL. Where are they located?

Mr. SCHWAB. All over the United States; in Virginia, Alabama, Cuba, New Jersey, Pennsylvania, and, indeed, there is scarcely a State in the Union that does not have some iron ore.

Mr. RANDELL. You say, as I understand it, as a reason, or perhaps it might be so construed at least, for the increase in royalty, is that the land is worth more?

Mr. SCHWAB. Oh, no; I did not. I said ore lands. When I say ore lands, I mean ore deposits.

Mr. RANDELL. Well, that is by the acre. You said that there were some acres that were worth $3,000.

Mr. Schwab. I was speaking of coal then.

Mr. Randell. That was in reference to coal?

Mr. Schwab. Yes.

Mr. Randell. Now, then——

Mr. Dalzell. That was in reference to the Connellsville coal?

Mr. Schwab. Yes.

Mr. Randell. That increased the price of coke?

Mr. Schwab. Yes.

Mr. Randell. On account of the increase in the price of the coal?

Mr. Schwab. Yes; which is measured by the acre.

Mr. Randell. Now, then, the iron deposits, paying royalties to them, you have gotten them for from 10 cents to $1 a ton. in round figures.

Mr. Schwab. In round figures; yes.

Mr. Randell. That is, it has increased in value, say, from 400 to 900 per cent in price. Now, as to these deposits where you pay these royalties, is that royalty paid to any steel corporation?

Mr. Schwab. No; to individuals or companies owning it.

Mr. Randell. That is what I was going to ask about. Now, are most of those deposits owned by the companies engaged in the steel business, or by men or other persons having an interest in the companies producing steel?

Mr. Schwab. Not at all. To give you an illustration, the Great Northern Railroad owns great deposits of iron ores. It leases its iron-ore lands to companies at so much a ton.

Mr. Randell. The railroad company, you say, is interested in the business?

Mr. Schwab. How?

Mr. Randell. It ships the freight.

Mr. Schwab. It ships the ore over its road, certainly, but I cite that only as an illustration.

Mr. Randell. I am coming to that very point that you were speaking of a while ago in the illustration you gave. The railroad company has the iron-ore deposit and charges a higher profit for that than used to be charged, a higher royalty; is that right?

Mr. Schwab. Yes.

Mr. Randell. And the railroad, you say, does not want a reduction in the price of the rails, and yet they use them to make their road.

Mr. Schwab. I was unfortunate in my illustration.

Mr. Randell. I think so, but is that not a fact, and is not the reason of it that the interests of the steel companies and of the railroads——

Mr. Schwab. Let me give you an illustration.

Mr. Randell. Let me finish my question.

And the great corporations are so blended and dovetailed and interwoven together to-day that they, pursuing their various functions, controlling their various interests, combine and plunder the common people? When I say plunder, I mean by charging a higher price than they could without such combination.

(Several members: "Answer yes or no.")

Mr. Randell. Yes or no. You would have to say yes to that, would you not?

Mr. Schwab. I give up. I do not even understand the question.

Mr. RANDELL. Well, I think I can make the question very plain. Is it not a fact, in accordance with your observation and your idea, that the reason that the railroad companies do not want a reduction in the price of steel rails is because the various interests that own the coal companies and the steel companies and the railroad companies are blended in such a way as that it is to the interest of all of them to put up the price of the product and each get his price, so levying upon the consumer this tribute? I hope you understand that question.

Mr. SCHWAB. I must confess I do not.

Mr. LONGWORTH. Can you tell me how much a blast furnace has to pay per ton for its ore if it has no supply of its own?

Mr. SCHWAB. It depends on its location.

Mr. LONGWORTH. There is no quoted market price for ore?

Mr. SCHWAB. I think there is a market price for lake ores at lake ports.

Mr. LONGWORTH. About what is the price?

Mr. SCHWAB. I don't know; I do not buy it. I think it is about $4 a ton, or something like that, but I am not sure. I do not buy ores. And so, the same thing is true in the East; there is a different price in different locations, dependent upon the cost of producing right at that point.

STATEMENT OF ELBERT H. GARY, OF NEW YORK, REPRESENTING THE UNITED STATES STEEL CORPORATION.

FRIDAY, *December 18, 1908.*

(The witness was duly sworn by the chairman.)

Mr. GARY. Mr. Chairman, I brought some figures with me, thinking that possibly we might be called upon for them.

The CHAIRMAN. Judge, you are president of the United States Steel Corporation?

Mr. GARY. No, sir; the chairman of the board of directors, and the chairman of the finance committee, of the United States Steel Corporation.

The CHAIRMAN. And have been for how long?

Mr. GARY. I have been chairman of the board of directors for about five years, and chairman of the finance committee about two years; and before that I was chairman of the executive committee (which at that time was pretty nearly the same), since the organization of the corporation.

The CHAIRMAN. You have been connected actively with the management and operation of the corporation since its organization?

Mr. GARY. Yes, sir.

The CHAIRMAN. If you would prefer, Judge, to go on and make a statement, you can do so, and then answer questions afterwards. You will, of course, have opportunity to do that.

Mr. GARY. No; I prefer to answer questions.

The CHAIRMAN. What do you manufacture?

Mr. GARY. The United States Steel Corporation is the owner of the shares of stock of various manufacturing corporations, and those corporations manufacture iron and a great many different lines of steel; also mine ore, mine coal, manufacture coke; and also these corporations own the shares of various transportation companies, including several railroads and a steamship line on the Lakes.

The CHAIRMAN. Now, won't you state the principal lines of manufactures in iron and steel which your company is engaged in?

Mr. GARY. Our corporations manufacture ten or eleven million tons of pig iron per annum; about twelve or thirteen million tons of finished steel (not quite so much as that of finished steel, but about ten or eleven million tons of finished steel at the present time; a larger tonnage of semifinished steel), including rails, structural steel, wire and steel-wire products.

The CHAIRMAN. Wire nails?

Mr. GARY. Wire nails.

The CHAIRMAN. Wire fence?

Mr. GARY. Wire fence, woven wire fence; a great many different kinds of wire, as small as piano wire, and so forth; tubes, tin plates——

The CHAIRMAN. If you have a paper there, you can refresh your recollection by referring to it.

Mr. GARY. The finished products include steel rails, blooms, billets, slabs, sheet and tin plate, bars and plates, heavy structural shapes, merchant steel, skelp, hoops, bands and cotton ties, tubing and pipe, rods, wire and products of wire, sheets, block and galvanized steel plates, spikes, bolts, nuts and rivets, axles, car wheels, and sundry and various other items that would be connected with or kindred to these various things; spelter, sulphite of iron, cement.

The CHAIRMAN. Cement, you say?

Mr. GARY. Yes. We have a very large cement business.

The CHAIRMAN. Now, commencing back with ore, you control extensive fields of iron mines?

Mr. GARY. Yes; we do.

The CHAIRMAN. Where are they situated?

Mr. GARY. In the Lake Superior region, the Menominee, Gogebic, Marquette, and Tennessee and Alabama fields.

Mr. COCKRAN. Did you say Mesaba?

Mr. GARY. Mesaba is in the Lake Superior region. The Lake Superior fields are divided between the Vermillion and Mesaba ranges.

The CHAIRMAN. Will you give us the cost of mining ore in the Lake Superior region?

Mr. GARY. Yes; I can give that accurately. Seventy-three cents is the average mining cost.

The CHAIRMAN. Per ton?

Mr. GARY. Yes; per ton.

The CHAIRMAN. That does not include any royalty?

Mr. GARY. No; nor depreciation. One dollar and forty-three cents includes the mining expense, the depreciation, and the royalty.

Mr. UNDERWOOD. Will you state, Judge, right there, what you mean by "depreciation," so that the committee can understand?

The CHAIRMAN. That is just what I was going to ask him.

Mr. GARY. A sufficient sum to keep the properties in condition and to take care of the exhaustion. We calculate it at 40 cents.

The CHAIRMAN. Is that, Judge, calculated on the basis of acquiring additional mines to take the place of the exhausted mines?

Mr. GARY. Yes; it is calculated to restore depleted capital.

The CHAIRMAN. Calculated how—on the basis of new mines?

Mr. GARY. No, sir; it is not. Mines could not be purchased. Yes; if they were for sale and if they could be purchased at the same price.

The CHAIRMAN. You have recently acquired mines, according to public rumor, from the Northern Pacific. Is that correct?

Mr. GARY. Yes; we buy good iron-ore properties whenever we have opportunity.

The CHAIRMAN. Is that true as to the Northern Pacific?

Mr. GARY. Yes; it is true. The Great Northern you refer to particularly?

The CHAIRMAN. Yes. Judge, the $1.43 included the cost of mining, as I understood, and the replacing of exhausted mines of ore by the acquirement of new mines. Did it include anything else?

Mr. GARY. The royalties which we pay.

The CHAIRMAN. You do pay a royalty, then?

Mr. GARY. Yes.

The CHAIRMAN. Anything else?

Mr. GARY. Of course that 40 cents would not take care of the fund for replacing the property, if we would have to do it on the basis of what we would have to pay at the present time. For instance, in our Great Northern deal, we pay them on the basis of 85 cents a ton for iron ore running as high in iron as fifty-nine. Our iron ores, are many of them, very much higher than that. Now, if properties such as we own up there could be had, if they were on the market for sale, situated as they are, accessible, and as easy of mining, and with as good analysis, we would have to pay very much higher than that, and the 40 cents, of course, would not take care of that; but we allow 40 cents for depreciation on the basis—it is more or less an arbitrary basis—on the basis of what those properties originally cost, and so forth.

The CHAIRMAN. On the basis of the exhaustion of the ore?

Mr. GARY. Yes.

The CHAIRMAN. Now, take the next item, transportation.

Mr. GARY. Yes. Well, the transportation by rail and lake, $1.45; 73 cents for rail transportation and 72 cents for the lake.

The CHAIRMAN. Is that taking it to the Pittsburg district?

Mr. GARY. No, sir; to the lower lake ports.

The CHAIRMAN. What is your principal lower lake port?

Mr. GARY. Chicago is one, of course; Cleveland, Lorain, Ashtabula, Conneaut, and Fairport.

The CHAIRMAN. In Chicago it goes to the Illinois Steel Works, one of your corporations?

Mr. GARY. Yes.

The CHAIRMAN. And from the Lake Erie ports—one or more of them—from there it is transported to Pittsburg over your own railroad?

Mr. GARY. Part of it.

The CHAIRMAN. What is it from Chicago to the steel works in Illinois? What is the freight cost of transportation?

Mr. GARY. From the docks at Chicago?

The CHAIRMAN. Yes.

Mr. GARY. Of course we take the ore at Chicago right into our furnaces and mills. There is no rail transportation at Chicago.

The CHAIRMAN. You land at your furnace there?

Mr. GARY. Yes; land at the furnace.

The CHAIRMAN. Now, Judge, what does it cost to produce a ton of ore in the Tennessee region?

Mr. GARY. You mean what is the cost of assembling the ore at the furnace?

The CHAIRMAN. Producing it there at the mine—the royalty on the value of the ore, the royalty on the ore and the cost of working the mines? What is that?

Mr. GARY. I have not those figures, Mr. Chairman. The cost of pig iron at Birmingham is not far from the cost of pig iron at South Chicago. It is very little different.

The CHAIRMAN. How close to it is it?

Mr. GARY. I am not certain which is lower, but the cost at Chicago, the manufacturer's cost, is probably $14.75 to $15. That is the manufacturer's cost. Of course that does not give credit for any profit to the United States Steel Corporation which it derives by reason of its investment in mines or railroads or ships.

Mr. COCKRAN. $14.50, did you say?

Mr. GARY. $14.75 to $15, manufacturer's cost.

Mr. CLARK. $14.75.

The CHAIRMAN. Can the Bethlehem Steel Company produce it cheaper than you can?

Mr. GARY. I do not think it can.

The CHAIRMAN. We have a statement from them at $14.

Mr. GARY. I think that is pretty low, allowing for depreciation and administration charges.

The CHAIRMAN. Does it cost more to-day than it did on the average in 1906?

Mr. GAINES. Do you mean 1906 or 1896?

The CHAIRMAN. I mean 1906.

Mr. COCKRAN. Two years ago.

Mr. GARY. A little more.

The CHAIRMAN. How much more?

Mr. GARY. Fifteen cents, maybe, besides extra cost of raw materials. Wages have been increased a little.

The CHAIRMAN. Fifteen cents?

Mr. GARY. Yes, sir.

The CHAIRMAN. Then it cost $14.60 in 1906. What in 1905?

Mr. GARY. I can not answer that. It is not much different from 1906.

The CHAIRMAN. Would you be surprised to know that the cost in the United States from 1902 to 1906, both inclusive, averaged $14.01 on over 90 per cent of the entire production of pig iron?

Mr. GARY. That depends a little on the basis of cost or the way of getting at it.

Mr. COCKRAN. You mean the basis of computation?

Mr. GARY. Yes, sir; the basis of computation.

The CHAIRMAN. Let us see what you take into consideration as the basis of cost.

Mr. DALZELL. As to this $14.75 that you gave us, Judge, do you count in that depreciation?

Mr. GARY. Yes, sir; I count depreciation.

The CHAIRMAN. I understood he did not.

Mr. GARY. You misunderstood me.

Mr. DALZELL. The figures that Mr. Schwab gave us did not take that into account.

Mr. GARY. This includes administration charges and overhead cost and all those things. I do not think Mr. Schwab's figures took those into account, Mr. Chairman.

Mr. DALZELL. They did not.

Mr. CLARK. It took in everything except the overhead charges——

Mr. GARY. And the depreciation.

Mr. GAINES. He took in the administration charges at the mills, but not the corporate costs,

Mr. BONYNGE. He gave the mill charges, as I understand.

The CHAIRMAN. How much do you allow in your estimate? What are the figures there?

Mr. GARY. Forty cents a ton on the blast furnace.

Mr. CLARK. Judge, do you mean that the blast furnace depreciates 40 cents for every ton of iron that is made?

Mr. GARY. Yes; I think that is very moderate, Mr. Clark.

Mr. CLARK. I just wanted to understand. That is all.

Mr. GARY. Furnaces wear out very fast.

Mr. CLARK. How long does one of those things last?

Mr. GARY. I can not answer that definitely.

Mr. CLARK. Never mind, then. Go on.

Mr. GARY. Our depreciation charges and everything are regularly and carefully made, and intended only to be the actual depreciation. Of course we do intend to keep up the properties. We do intend to make it large enough to keep up the properties, but not for the sake of burying any money that is received. And I may add there, Mr. Chairman, that as a rule, in my judgment, the manufacturers of this country have not taken enough depreciation charges to keep up their properties.

The CHAIRMAN. Now, I wish you would give me, if you have them figured out there, the elements of cost to make pig iron at $14.75 a ton. What do you charge, Judge, for the metallic mixture, the iron basis per ton of pig iron?

Mr. GARY. The average for all of our pig iron was: For the iron ore, $4.70 for the ore delivered at the furnace; $8.62 in the iron. Cinder and scale——

Mr. COCKRAN. Will you go a little more slowly, may I ask?

Mr. GARY. Yes.

Mr. COCKRAN. You say the iron ore is $4.70 delivered at the furnace?

Mr. GARY. Yes, sir; per ton of ore.

Mr. COCKRAN. What is the next item?

Mr. GARY. That would be $8.62 in the iron.

The CHAIRMAN. Now I will ask you about coke.

Mr. GARY. I will give you all the items; the coke next, if you wish. Coke, $3.93 per gross ton of coke at the furnace, which would be $4.15 in the iron.

The CHAIRMAN. Now limestone.

Mr. GARY. Limestone, $1.06 per gross ton. That is 49 cents in the iron, 49 cents per ton of iron. Scrap, 16 cents per ton in the iron. Cinder and scale, 11 cents.

Mr. COCKRAN. Cinder?

Mr. GARY. Cinder and scale, 11 cents per ton of iron. The cost of labor, material, and expense in operating, $1.37 per ton of iron.

Mr. COCKRAN. $1.07?

Mr. GARY. One dollar and thirty-seven cents, and the depreciation, 40 cents. That makes a total of $15.30. That is the average of all our furnaces. Of course it is less than that at some points. It is less at South Chicago and higher in other places.

Mr. COCKRAN. That makes $15 and what?

Mr. GARY. Fifteen dollars and thirty cents, Mr. Cockran.

The CHAIRMAN. Now, Judge, was $7.30 per ton of pig iron a fair average price from 1902 to 1906, both inclusive, for the iron ore going into the pig iron?

Mr. GARY. What year?

The CHAIRMAN. From 1902 to 1906.

Mr. GARY. Seven dollars and thirty cents. It was lower then. The ore was a little lower at that time. You understand, Mr. Chairman, that the ores on the average are becoming a little less in quality, a little poorer in quality, a little less iron per ton of ore; and as the quantity of iron in the ore decreases, the cost of the iron in the furnace, of course, increases, because it costs just as much to handle a ton of ore with 40 per cent iron as a ton of ore with 60 per cent iron. And the same is true in the transportation; and then, when you get to the furnace, the cost of smelting is increased. It costs more to extract the iron per ton of ore.

The CHAIRMAN. What has that loss been since 1906?

Mr. GARY. It might account for that difference.

The CHAIRMAN. What has it been since 1906?

Mr. GARY. I can not answer that, Mr. Chairman.

The CHAIRMAN. You can not state that?

Mr. GARY. No, sir; I can not state that.

The CHAIRMAN. Has the cost of iron ore increased since 1906?

Mr. GARY. Yes, sir; I think it has.

Mr. DALZELL. Have you got there the percentage of iron in the ore that went to make pig iron at $15.30 a ton?

Mr. GARY. No, sir; I have not got that.

Mr. UNDERWOOD. He figures a ton of ore at $8.70.

Mr. GARY. Now, what year did you desire?

The CHAIRMAN. 1906 and 1908.

Mr. GARY. In 1906 and 1908 the base prices were substantially the same. The price was higher in 1907.

The CHAIRMAN. Now, Judge, are you able to say what the percentage of iron in the ore was in 1906 and again in 1908, on the average?

Mr. GARY. No; I can not. I certainly can not give it on the average. I might possibly give it with reference to some one ore.

The CHAIRMAN. Give what you can. I do not insist on a categorical answer. I only ask for information. I only want information.

Mr. COCKRAN. Is there any difference in the relative richness of the ores?

Mr. GARY. Yes; there is. The ores are decreasing in richness.

Mr. COCKRAN. Can you tell in what proportion?

Mr. GARY. Take what we call our Hull-Rust district. In 1906 the Pillsbury ore contained 64.33 per cent in iron.

Mr. COCKRAN. In 1906?

Mr. GARY. In 1906. In 1907 the same mine produced ore containing 63.63 per cent in iron.

The CHAIRMAN. Now, the Superior district.

Mr. GARY. The Aragon mine, on the Menominee Range, the Grenada ore in 1906 contained 59.16 per cent of iron, and in 1907, 58.82 per cent in iron.

The CHAIRMAN. That was the average for that mine?

Mr. GARY. For that mine; yes.

The CHAIRMAN. Have you the figures there for 1902?

Mr. GARY. No, sir; we have not. We have not back of 1906.

The CHAIRMAN. Have you the figures for the price of pig iron— the cost of pig iron in 1902 per ton?

Mr. GARY. No, sir; we have not.

The CHAIRMAN. You do not go back so far as that?

Mr. GARY. Of course I have it in the office at home, but not here.

The CHAIRMAN. I mean here. I asked with reference to what you had here.

Now the item of coke; has that increased in price since 1906 as compared with 1908?

Mr. GARY. It has increased somewhat.

The CHAIRMAN. How much?

Mr. GARY. That I can not answer. The cost at the oven last year was $1.75 a net ton. We have slightly increased the wages there. In fact, we have slightly increased all our wages since we were organized.

The CHAIRMAN. You gave the cost of that as how much—the cost of coke?

Mr. GARY. At $4.15 per gross ton of iron.

The CHAIRMAN. Had it increased as much as to justify the statement of an increase of 46 cents in the cost of the coke that goes to make that ton of pig iron?

Mr. GARY. All of that, I would think, as compared with 1906.

The CHAIRMAN. But you have not the figures there?

Mr. GARY. No, sir.

The CHAIRMAN. Now, you did not give the limestone as a separate item, did you?

Mr. GARY. Yes; at 49 cents per ton of iron.

Mr. COCKRAN. Judge, you say now the cost of coke is $1.75 a ton?

Mr. GARY. The cost of the coke at the ovens was $1.75 a net ton, but the figure I gave you before was the cost to the manufacturer of coke per ton of iron in the iron. The coke cost to produce it at the coke oven in the coal fields was $1.75.

Mr. COCKRAN. Yes.

Mr. GARY. Now, that same coke, with the transportation, etc., added, brought to our furnace and put in the iron, cost per ton of iron $4.15.

Mr. COCKRAN. How many tons of coke to the ton of iron?

Mr. GARY. The cost of coke would be $3.93 per gross ton and in the iron $4.15. It would be about 1½ tons of coke for 1 ton of iror

The CHAIRMAN. I have a statement here showing that when coke costs $3.37 a ton the amount or value of coke in a ton of pig iron was $3.89.

Mr. GARY. $3.37 and $3.89?

The CHAIRMAN. $3.37 in a ton of coke, and $3.89 for the price of coke that went to make up the pig iron.

Mr. GARY. That is about it. Ours is exact.

The CHAIRMAN. Now the limestone. By the way, do you give credit for the by-products in the production of a ton of coke when you say the cost is so much?

Mr. GARY. Of course we would to the extent that we make it. We do; but we have not very many by-product coke ovens.

The CHAIRMAN. You have not got to that point of competition where you have to take care of little things like a by-product?

Mr. GARY. We are putting them in now.

The CHAIRMAN. How much do you estimate you would save by saving the by-products?

Mr. GARY. That is more or less problematical. There will be some saving, a little saving, enough to justify us in putting them in, although we have had very grave doubts about it and have delayed putting them in for that reason.

The CHAIRMAN. Other companies have put them in in the making of coke.

Mr. GARY. There have been different reasons. For instance, the Cambria put them in some years ago. They had their coal rather of poor quality, a poor quality of coal, and it needed a different character of oven to utilize that coal. They were obliged to do it. In foreign countries, perhaps, in some places the by-product ovens were put in because of the peculiarity of the coal. But with our coking coal, which, I suppose, is recognized as the best, the Connellsville coal, the by-products would not probably be of utility or benefit.

The CHAIRMAN. But it has been so successful that you are changing over some of your works and putting in your ovens so as to save the by-products?

Mr. GARY. There are two reasons for that. Connellsville coke is getting more or less scarce, and we will use in the by-product ovens a mixture of Pocahontas coal and the Pennsylvania coal outside of that of the Connellsville district; but if we had enough Connellsville coal I doubt if we would put in the by-product ovens.

The CHAIRMAN. You will make a saving by that?

Mr. GARY. There will be some saving.

Mr. GAINES. It is not proposed to do away with the regular coke ovens?

Mr. GARY. No, sir.

The CHAIRMAN. You will have to put in new coke ovens?

Mr. GARY. Yes.

The CHAIRMAN. You are throwing away the old and putting in new?

Mr. GARY. No; this is not for the old. We are putting in new ovens at Gary, Ind. We shall use a mixture of the Pocahontas and Pennsylvania coal outside of the Connellsville district and get the coke, which will be a little cheaper than the Connellsville coke, saving the by-products.

Mr. Cockran. These ovens would be available even if the by-products would be profitless? They would be available for both purposes?

Mr. Gary. Yes, sir.

The Chairman. Now, we will get on to limestone. How much did you estimate for the limestone?

Mr. Gary. Forty-nine cents per ton of iron.

The Chairman. Does that cost any more than it did in 1906?

Mr. Gary. Not much more; possibly a little more, but not any appreciable amount, I would say; not very much more; very little, if any. I will put it that way.

The Chairman. What makes it cost more?

Mr. Gary. Labor costs generally a little bit higher.

The Chairman. Then material and maintenance, what do you estimate for that—materials and repairs in maintenance? Did you estimate that separately?

Mr. Gary. No, sir. The cost of material and expense in operating in all is $1.37.

The Chairman. Does that include steam and power?

Mr. Gary. Yes.

The Chairman. What else do you put in besides depreciation? That is 40 cents, separately?

Mr. Gary. Depreciation is 40 cents; yes.

The Chairman. Did you put in any other items in your statement?

Mr. Gary. Forty cents is not included in the last item of $1.37.

The Chairman. You stated that was what it was.

Mr. Gary. I may be mixed.

The Chairman. You stated it was 39 cents in 1906. That is a pretty close figure. That is the reason I asked that question; so that you make the total cost of pig iron $15.30 to-day, produced in your works?

Mr. Gary. Yes; on the average.

The Chairman. On the average of all your works?

Mr. Gary. All our furnaces; yes, sir.

The Chairman. State whether you can produce it cheaper than your rivals in business?

Mr. Gary. Yes; I think we can. We certainly can at a large number of our furnaces. I think there is no doubt that we can produce iron and steel materially cheaper than most of our competitors.

The Chairman. "Materially?" How much? Take pig iron, for instance.

Mr. Gary. On the same basis of calculation—that is, on the basis of their having due regard for depreciation, and so forth, as we do——

The Chairman. Forty cents depreciation?

Mr. Gary. I think on the average. Of course anyone hesitates to speak about a competitor; but I would not hesitate to say, in my opinion, at least $1 a ton, certainly from the standpoint of the Steel Corporation.

The Chairman. Cheaper than your competitors?

Mr. Gary. Yes, sir.

Mr. Bonynge. On what items do you make the difference? Is it in the cost of iron ore, or coke, or what, that makes the difference between you and your competitor? The labor is the same, I suppose?

Mr. GARY. Yes.

Mr. BONYNGE. What items make that difference?

Mr. GARY. In methods, in equipment; the character of our equipment, largely, I would say.

Mr. BONYNGE. Do you get your iron ore cheaper than they do, owning the iron fields, as you do?

Mr. GARY. My figures are based on the price they would have to pay for iron ore at the lower lakes or at the furnace.

The CHAIRMAN. How much of that dollar did you allow for the difference in iron ore, the cost of it?

Mr. GARY. I did not itemize it, but not any.

The CHAIRMAN. Not any?

Mr. GARY. No, sir.

The CHAIRMAN. How about coke? Is there any difference in the cost of coke between you and your rival companies?

Mr. GARY. I think there is.

The CHAIRMAN. How much difference is there in the coke to make a ton of iron?

Mr. GARY. I can not answer that.

The CHAIRMAN. When you say you think it is as much as a dollar, you believe it is more than that?

Mr. GARY. I do, Mr. Chairman.

Mr. COCKRAN. How much do you really believe it is? That is not binding. Let us get your best opinion.

Mr. GARY. Of course, you see, Mr. Cockran, that would put me in the position, to some extent at least, of guessing. The figures I have given you are intended to be exact, and it seems to me our competitors ought to give their figures exact.

Mr. COCKRAN. We try to get them. When you say a dollar, it is a guess. The other might be a little better guess. We understand it to be a guess.

Mr. GARY. If you carried that to a logical sequence I might do our competitors an injustice.

Mr. COCKRAN. We understand you are only guessing.

The CHAIRMAN. Give us your best judgment, Judge. You say not less than a dollar?

Mr. GARY. I would rather not guess any further than that.

The CHAIRMAN. Would it be safe to say $2?

Mr. GARY. Not on the basis of manufacturing cost, I think. Of course, I am not speaking from the standpoint of the corporation, Mr. Chairman—from the standpoint of the corporation, which has a decided advantage in the quantity and quality of its ores and in owning its transportation companies to carry the ores to the Lakes, and its transportation facilities on the Lakes, and all that sort of thing. The advantage to the corporation is very much more, very much more than that.

The CHAIRMAN. Very much more than a dollar?

Mr. GARY. Oh, yes; very much more.

The CHAIRMAN. Is the entire difference more than $2?

Mr. GARY. Take an item of rails, for instance——

The CHAIRMAN. No; let us keep to pig iron.

Mr. GARY. All right. I think it is possibly more than $2, Mr. Chairman.

The CHAIRMAN. You think it is more than $2?

Mr. GARY. Yes; I think it is. I think there is no doubt it is more than that.

The CHAIRMAN. You think there is no doubt it is more than $2?

Mr. GARY. Yes.

The CHAIRMAN. That answers that question. Can you give me the cost of producing pig iron by your corporation in 1906?

Mr. GAINES. Before you go to that, you gave the cost of coke as $1.05.

Mr. GARY. That is the cost of producing at the coke ovens.

Mr. GAINES. That is the cost of producing coke to you. That is not the cost to your competitor?

Mr. GARY. There are times when he pays very much more than that.

Mr. GAINES. Sometimes it seemed to me your statements were dealing with what your competitor would have to pay for the article, and sometimes it seemed you were giving what the article that entered into a ton of pig iron costs you to produce, not what it would cost to purchase in the open market. As to the coke that entered into the pig iron, you seemed to be giving not the cost to anyone in the open market, but at the actual cost to you at the mines at Gary and in my State. Was there that confusion in the figures?

Mr. GARY. I understand your question very well. The difference is, perhaps, because of the fact that we have no transportation companies from our coke works to our furnaces. Therefore the cost of the coke in the iron would be the same to our competitor that it would be to ourselves, except the difference in the cost of coke to us, who produce it, and to our competitors, who have to buy it.

Mr. GAINES. Exactly.

Mr. GARY. That would be included in my conservative guess of $1.

The CHAIRMAN. Gentlemen, we will have to suspend here and take a recess until 2 o'clock; and, Judge Gary, I shall ask you, immediately after the recess, the cost of pig iron each year from 1902 to 1906, inclusive.

Mr. GARY. I am afraid I have not those figures here, Mr. Chairman; but if I have, I will submit them.

Mr. DALZELL. If you have not got them here you can furnish them later?

Mr. GARY. Oh, yes; certainly. I will furnish you with any figures that you ask for.

The CHAIRMAN. I would be very glad to have you file them; and also, in that connection, a statement of the cost of steel rails and the cost of iron ore.

Mr. GARY. What is meant by the cost of iron ore?

The CHAIRMAN. The same cost you have given to-day; the cost of labor at the mines and the same items you have given to-day on that cost.

Mr. GARY. Yes.

The CHAIRMAN. Pig iron, rails, and structural steel.

Mr. GARY. Yes.

The CHAIRMAN. Now, you do not import any iron ore, I suppose?

Mr. GARY. No.

The CHAIRMAN. There is some imported from Cuba and Spain, I believe?

Mr. GARY. Yes.

The CHAIRMAN. Do you know what the import price is on the Cuban ore, laid down in New York?

Mr. GARY. No; I do not.

The CHAIRMAN. You have no idea what it is?

Mr. GARY. No.

The CHAIRMAN. Are you at all acquainted with the quality of that ore—ore from Spain?

Mr. GARY. The Spanish ores are very good.

The CHAIRMAN. Is it of a character similar to the Superior ores, or similar to the ores you get in the East that are mixed with the Superior ores?

Mr. GARY. Similar to our old-range ores, as we call them, coming from the Marquette, Vermilion, and Menominee ranges; not so much like Mesabi.

The CHAIRMAN. It is not a Bessemer ore, is it?

Mr. GARY. Yes.

The CHAIRMAN. It is a Bessemer ore?

Mr. GARY. Yes.

The CHAIRMAN. How about the ore from Spain?

Mr. GARY. I was referring to the ore from Spain. That was your question, I think. The ore from Cuba I do not know so much about. I think, though, there is a good deal of Bessemer ore that comes from Cuba.

The CHAIRMAN. Do you know anything about the extent of the deposits of ore in Cuba?

Mr. GARY. No; I do not think those are ascertained definitely. I think the ores which have been mined have come from the southern coast, in the vicinity of Santiago; but they have lately discovered a large body of ore on the northern coast.

The CHAIRMAN. Does your corporation buy any pig iron?

Mr. GARY. Yes; we do buy pig iron.

The CHAIRMAN. I supposed you did.

Mr. GARY. Yes; we do.

The CHAIRMAN. What is the price at which they are producing it at the present time?

Mr. GARY. We are not buying any at the present time.

The CHAIRMAN. When did you last buy any?

Mr. GARY. In any quantities, a year and three months, I think.

The CHAIRMAN. At what price?

Mr. GARY. Well, at about $18.75, I think.

The CHAIRMAN. Where was that delivered?

Mr. GARY. It was delivered at Pittsburg.

The CHAIRMAN. From whom did you buy it?

Mr. GARY. Largely from the Mahoning Valley furnaces.

The CHAIRMAN. From what point did they ship it? I do not know where they are located. At Youngstown, are they?

Mr. GARY. I can not give you the name of the places, but it came from the Mahoning and Shenango valleys.

The CHAIRMAN. An Ohio concern?

Mr. GARY. Yes, sir.

The CHAIRMAN. Do you know the amount of freight from the point at which it was shipped?

Mr. DALZELL. That would include Sharon, would it not?

Mr. GARY. Yes; it would include Sharon. Eighteen dollars and seventy-five cents would be the delivered price.

The CHAIRMAN. Delivered to you?

Mr. GARY. Yes.

The CHAIRMAN. You do not know the amount of freight they paid?

Mr. GARY. No, sir.

The CHAIRMAN. Mr. Underwood desires to ask you some questions in regard to pig iron before we pass to some other subject.

Mr. UNDERWOOD. Yes; I would like to ask Judge Gary a few questions about pig iron, because they come in at this time. Judge, this morning in making your estimate of the cost of pig iron at $15.30, you made the cost at Chicago of the ore in a ton of pig iron $8.62, whereas in giving the items of cost you said that the cost of mining the Lake Superior ore was 73 cents and that the royalties and other charges made the ore cost $1.43, total cost at the mine; that the transportation to the lake was 73 cents, and by water on the lake 72 cents, making the total cost of transportation $1.45, making a total cost of $2.88 a ton. Now, estimating at the same average that gave the total cost of a ton of ore at Chicago, at your works, at $2.88, whereas you make your estimate in estimating the cost of ore, $4.70 a ton. I wish you would explain to the committee wherein the difference comes.

Mr. GARY. The difference is due to the fact that the figures you quote are based on actual mining and transportation cost to lower lake ports (which figures of cost would apply only to ore smelted in furnaces located on the lake shore), while the costs I furnished were the average for ore used at all our furnaces, inland as well as on the lakes; and also to the fact that the figure of $4.70 includes the profit to the ore mining companies. You have a total of what?

Mr. UNDERWOOD. I have $2.88.

Mr. GARY. It should be $4.70.

Mr. UNDERWOOD. The other was $4.70?

Mr. GARY. Yes, sir.

Mr. UNDERWOOD. The difference between $4.70 and $2.88 is profit?

Mr. GARY. Yes, sir; profit to the mining company and transportation from lakes to inland furnaces.

Mr. UNDERWOOD. That would make a total difference in the cost of ore in a ton of pig iron $6.58?

Mr. GARY. I have given you a figure of $2.88, which represents the average cost to the mining interests for all ore delivered at lower lake ports. The figure of $4.70 represents the average price at which all ore was charged to all furnaces. The difference between these two figures is made up of profits to the mining interests plus the freight paid for transportation from lower lake ports to furnaces on such ore as was moved inland.

Mr. UNDERWOOD. Now, on the coke. In estimating the cost of coke this morning at $3.93, was that estimate made of the cost of coke at Chicago?

Mr. GARY. No; that is the average of all the coke delivered at all our furnaces in all the districts.

Mr. UNDERWOOD. That is the average cost of the production of coke at all the furnaces of the United States Steel Company?

Mr. GARY. It is the average cost to the manufacturer at the furnace of coke consumed.

Mr. UNDERWOOD. Does that include the profit to the mining company?

Mr. GARY. Yes; 54 cents per gross ton.

Mr. UNDERWOOD. The profit on that is 54 cents?

Mr. GARY. Yes; per gross ton.

Mr. UNDERWOOD. Fifty-four cents per ton?

Mr. GARY. Per gross ton.

Mr. GAINES. Per ton of which—coke?

Mr. GARY. Coke.

Mr. UNDERWOOD. Then you figure that the cost of coke to a ton of pig iron is $4.15. Will you eliminate the profit from that item, please, and give us what it would be without the profit—the actual cost?

Mr. GARY. Of the coke?

Mr. UNDERWOOD. Yes; at the furnace. It would be a little over 54 cents?

Mr. GARY. It would be about 60 cents less per ton; not quite. It would be $4.15 less 60 cents.

Mr. UNDERWOOD. That would make it about $3.55?

Mr. GARY. That is about it, $3.55 to $3.60, as the average for all furnaces.

Mr. UNDERWOOD. Now, as to the lime rock. You estimated the cost of lime rock at 49 cents. Is that the cost of lime rock at the Chicago furnaces, or is that the average at all your works?

Mr. GARY. The average.

Mr. UNDERWOOD. What is the profit you included in that?

Mr. GARY. It is not in it.

Mr. UNDERWOOD. No profit?

Mr. GARY. No, sir.

Mr. UNDERWOOD. The item of 16 cents for scrap. Is it the usual practice of your furnace business to include scrap in the manufacture?

Mr. GARY. Yes, sir.

Mr. UNDERWOOD. Is there any profit in that, or is that cost?

Mr. GARY. That is cost.

Mr. UNDERWOOD. Labor and operation. Is that the average cost of all your works?

Mr. GARY. Yes.

Mr. UNDERWOOD. I suppose that the cost at the various works differs materially, though, as to labor and operation?

Mr. GARY. Oh, yes.

Mr. UNDERWOOD. I suppose the most improved furnaces are at Gary and Pittsburg, are they not?

Mr. GARY. Pittsburg, South Chicago, Youngstown, Lorain, and Cleveland. We have some good furnaces at various points.

Mr. UNDERWOOD. Is there much difference in the cost of operation between your plants?

Mr. GARY. The new furnaces at Gary are not yet in operation. There are furnaces at South Chicago, Lorain, Cleveland, Pittsburg, and Youngstown whose cost is very nearly the same, but, of course, I am speaking now of the most modern and latest furnaces. Their cost of production is considerably less than a great many other furnaces which we operate.

Mr. UNDERWOOD. Judge, I figure that the difference in cost between the statement this morning that it included the profits on coke and ore and what it is with that eliminated amounts to $2.65. Is there any other difference in those figures that stands for profits? Taking that $2.65 out, does that eliminate all the profit there was?

Mr. GARY. Profit to the corporation?

Mr. UNDERWOOD. Yes.

Mr. GARY. It does not. There is some profit on transportation. Of course, United States Steel is the owner of subsidiary corporations, which corporations own, as an independent investment, various railroads; two important railroads in Minnesota; the Bessemer Railroad, running from the Lakes to Pittsburg, and the steamship line, consisting of, say, 110 steel boats on the Lakes; and those transportation lines are given a profit amounting to the difference of the actual cost to the companies and the price which they receive, and they receive the same prices that other railroads or other boats doing similar business would receive. In other words, they are treated as an independent investment and get the ordinary profits.

Mr. UNDERWOOD. Of course, that is very proper and very necessary; but can you say, in estimating your profits to the transportation companies, you only estimate a profit which would be equal to that which a person shipping the same freight by an independent company would have to pay?

Mr. GARY. Exactly.

Mr. UNDERWOOD. Then the actual cost, not eliminating the profits of transportation cost that any furnace would have to pay, of your producing a ton of pig iron at Chicago would be $12.75, about— eliminating the profits on the coke and the ore?

Mr. GARY. It is not that much, is it? I think your figures must be wrong.

Mr. UNDERWOOD. I subtracted $2.05 for ore and 60 cents for coke. That would be $2.65, which, deducted from $15.30, according to my figures, leaves $12.75.

Mr. DALZELL. $12.65.

Mr. UNDERWOOD. That is right; $12.65 instead of $12.75.

Mr. GARY. Yes; that is about right for the average for all furnaces; at Chicago the cost would probably be a little less, about $12.

Mr. UNDERWOOD. Now, where do you bring your coke from? Do you coke your coal at the Chicago furnace?

Mr. GARY. No.

Mr. UNDERWOOD. You bring your coke to it?

Mr. GARY. Yes.

Mr. UNDERWOOD. Where do you bring that coke from?

Mr. GARY. From Pocahontas, and some from the Connellsville region.

Mr. UNDERWOOD. Now, what is the transportation charge? I think you have given that, though. You have given the transportation charge on the coke to the furnace?

Mr. GARY. At Chicago?

Mr. UNDERWOOD. At Chicago.

Mr. GARY. Two dollars and thirty-five cents from Pittsburg to Chicago; the same from Pocahontas to Chicago.

Mr. UNDERWOOD. Is that a ton or for the amount of coke that goes into the pig iron?

Mr. GARY. That is a net ton.

Mr. UNDERWOOD. That $2.35 is a ton of coke?

Mr. GARY. Yes.

Mr. UNDERWOOD. How much would it be to a ton of pig iron?

Mr. GARY. You would have to add the same percentage. I have forgotten just what the percentage of increase is, but if the percentages are kept up would be in the neighborhood of $2.80, would it not?

Mr. UNDERWOOD. I think that is about right. And that being the cost, $4.15, you estimated this morning for the coke? You estimated this morning that the coke cost you $4.15?

Mr. GARY. Yes; $4.15 is the average for all furnaces.

Mr. UNDERWOOD. The transportation charges were $2.80. That leaves $1.35 for the coke?

Mr. GARY. No; $4.15 is the average cost of coke in pig iron at all furnaces. At Chicago the cost for coke in a ton of iron in 1907 was more, about $5.50, or $2.80 for transportation and $2.70 for the coke.

Mr. UNDERWOOD. I would like to have you make the same estimate as to your Pittsburg furnaces, so we can get that estimate. How much more does it cost you to carry your ore, per ton of ore and per ton of pig iron, to the Pittsburg plant?

Mr. GARY. Well, you add the freight rate from Conneaut, say, to Pittsburg, which would be $1.18. The rate is the same on the independent railroads.

Mr. UNDERWOOD. That would be $1.18 per ton of ore. If you will kindly figure what that means per ton of pig iron, I will be obliged.

Mr. GARY. It is $2.16. That is, figuring on the basis that iron would be 183 per cent.

Mr. UNDERWOOD. So that it would cost you $2.16 more to land that ore to make a ton of pig iron at Pittsburg than it would at Chicago?

Mr. GARY. Yes.

Mr. UNDERWOOD. I would like to get the same figures on coke.

Mr. GARY. Transportation of coke would be at the rate of 70 cents.

Mr. UNDERWOOD. It would cost 70 cents?

Mr. GARY. Seventy cents per net ton.

Mr. UNDERWOOD. Seventy cents a ton for the transportation of coke?

Mr. GARY. Yes.

Mr. UNDERWOOD. And in a ton of iron that would amount to how much?

Mr. GARY. About 85 cents.

Mr. UNDERWOOD. About 85 cents for coke?

Mr. GARY. Yes.

Mr. UNDERWOOD. Then on pig iron at Pittsburg it would cost you $2.16 more to get your ore there, and it would cost you $1.95 less to get your coke?

Mr. GARY. You are getting into our secrets fast.

Mr. UNDERWOOD. I do not intend to do that, Judge, but the committee wants to balance these things, because the freight rate will depend on where you are shipping from.

Mr. GARY. Yes. Of course, in locating our new furnaces, in extending our works, the cost of assembly is one of the important elements to be considered, as you know by experience.

Mr. UNDERWOOD. Yes. So that we can practically estimate, then, that either at Pittsburg or at Chicago the cost of a ton of pig iron, excluding all profits except transportation profits, is about $12.65.

Mr. GARY. $12.65 is about the average for all furnaces, but at those furnaces located at Chicago and at Pittsburg, the cost referred to is about $12.

Mr. UNDERWOOD. Can you give us the cost of labor in the coal mines where you operate?

Mr. GARY. The ore mines, you mean?

Mr. UNDERWOOD. I want the cost of labor both in the ore mines and the coal mines.

Mr. GARY. The rate of wages?

Mr. UNDERWOOD. Yes.

Mr. GARY. Yes; I have that.

Mr. UNDERWOOD. You haven't it figured in tons, have you?

Mr. GARY. No; I haven't it figured in tons. I can give you the rate per day.

Mr. UNDERWOOD. I will ask you this, Judge. Are the wages for ore mining in the Mesaba Range and in Pennsylvania and in Alabama anything like equal, or is there a difference in the cost?

Mr. GARY. I have no statistics in regard to Tennessee, but we hope to get down to a good basis there. I don't hesitate to say we can not manufacture there as cheaply as the Woodward Company.

Mr. UNDERWOOD. That is quite a compliment to the Woodward Company.

Mr. GARY. The average earnings per man per day, outside of administrative positions, in manufacturing companies in 1907 was $2.43; in coal and coke companies, $2.39; in ore-mining companies, $2.46; in transportation companies, $2.44; in other sundry companies, $1.92; a total average of $2.42, as against $2.26 in 1902. Of course with your knowledge of the Birmingham district, you personally know something about the advantage we have there, but I can not give you those figures. I did not bring them.

Mr. UNDERWOOD. You have not the figures that would give us the data for the Birmingham district?

Mr. GARY. No, sir.

Mr. DALZELL. What are those figures you have just given?

Mr. UNDERWOOD. He was giving the general cost of their labor.

Mr. GARY. Outside of the Birmingham district.

Mr. DALZELL. At the mines?

Mr. UNDERWOOD. At the mines.

Mr. GARY. Manufacturing companies, coal and coke companies, ore-mining companies, and transportation companies, respectively.

Mr. UNDERWOOD. Judge, I would like to ask you where is the place where you dispose of your product from your pig-iron furnaces. Do you convert it into finished product?

Mr. GARY. So far as possible, and to a large extent—it is not true of every locality—but ever since we were organized we have been more and more concentrating, with the idea of making each plant complete in itself.

Mr. UNDERWOOD. Where is the radius of sale of your finished product from your Chicago furnaces? What is the zone in which you dispose of that product?

Mr. GARY. West, northwest, and southeast.

Mr. UNDERWOOD. In that zone you will have a differential in your favor on freight rates over any imported iron or steel, will you not?

Mr. GARY. Yes.

Mr. UNDERWOOD. Now, as to your southern properties, the Birmingham property, where is the zone in which you dispose of those products?

Mr. GARY. Well, south and southwest from that point, mostly. We could not go to the eastern seaboard.

The CHAIRMAN. What was that statement?

Mr. UNDERWOOD. None of that product goes into competition on the eastern seaboard.

Mr. GARY. No; it could not.

Mr. UNDERWOOD. I asked him if any of the product of the Birmingham district went into competition on the eastern seaboard. He said it did not. It goes westward, toward California.

Mr. GARY. Yes, sir.

Mr. UNDERWOOD. And northwestward into somewhat the same territory as the product of the Chicago furnaces?

Mr. GARY. Yes.

Mr. UNDERWOOD. In that zone, Judge, the differential in the freight rate would be in their favor as against a foreign competitor, would it not?

Mr. GARY. Yes.

Mr. UNDERWOOD. Now, as to your eastern plants, where is the zone in which they would dispose of their products?

Mr. GARY. Well, from the shores of the Atlantic to the Chicago district, or about that, I should think.

Mr. UNDERWOOD. Leaving out the territory in that zone, where do you dispose of your eastern product, taking the point of competition in this country as New York or the Atlantic seaboard, and your point to reach the market at Pittsburg, which I suppose is a central point for most of your finished products in the eastern market?

Mr. GARY. Yes; for the majority of the tonnage.

Mr. UNDERWOOD. I want to know in whose favor—leaving out for the time being the ocean freight—in whose favor is the differential on the freight rates to reach that territory?

Mr. GARY. I did not hear the first part of the question.

Mr. UNDERWOOD. The zone in which the Pittsburg plants operate lies between Chicago and the Atlantic ocean?

Mr. GARY. Yes, sir.

Mr. UNDERWOOD. Now, assuming that the foreign manufacturer had his plant in New York City, or along the seaboard line where the principal boats land, that his plant was located there, and he was competing with you, I want to know in that territory in whose favor would be the differential on freight rates; that is, domestic freight rates, not foreign freight rates.

Mr. GARY. The rate from Germany, for instance, would be, on rails, $1.60, and from Pittsburg to the same point, $2.50; so that it would be in favor of the foreigner 90 cents a ton.

Mr. UNDERWOOD. What point are you figuring on?

Mr. GARY. The Atlantic seaboard.

Mr. UNDERWOOD. The export freight rate from Germany would be to New York City $1.60?

Mr. GARY. Yes.

Mr. UNDERWOOD. And from Pittsburg to New York City, how much?

Mr. GARY. $2.50.

Mr. UNDERWOOD. But I was figuring on the entire territory.

Mr. GARY. The average of the district?

Mr. UNDERWOOD. Yes; because, you see, the foreign competitor has got to go in there.

Mr. GARY. Yes. I can not give you the point where they would come together. Of course it would depend upon the product. If it was billets delivered to a finishing mill situated inland, your suggestion would apply. It would not apply to rails, because rails would be delivered to the railroad at its eastern terminus.

Mr. UNDERWOOD. On pig iron from Germany to this country, of course, I know the rate varies very greatly, from practically nothing to a good high freight rate.

Mr. GARY. Yes; it is carried as ballast, sometimes.

Mr. UNDERWOOD. Depending on the needs of the vessel for ballast?

Mr. GARY. Yes.

Mr. UNDERWOOD. But is not $1.60 a rather low freight rate from Germany for rails or pig iron? I mean an average.

Mr. GARY. No; I think that is the rate. That is the regular rate, I think, from the seaboard.

Mr. UNDERWOOD. In Germany?

Mr. GARY. In Germany, to the seaboard in America.

Mr. UNDERWOOD. What is the freight rate from the English coast?

Mr. GARY. Just the same.

Mr. UNDERWOOD. It would be just the same?

Mr. GARY. Yes.

Mr. UNDERWOOD. Please state the freight rates on your finished products, including steel rails, pig iron, billets, etc., from Chicago, Pittsburg, and Birmingham to New York, Buffalo, Mobile, New Orleans, and San Francisco; that is, I want the rates to the principal Atlantic, Pacific, and Gulf ports and the Canadian frontier.

Mr. GARY. The following is a memorandum of the domestic freight rates between the points mentioned:

	Rails (per gross ton).	Pig iron (per gross ton).	Billets (per gross ton).	Finished products (per 100 lbs.).
From Chicago to—				
New York	$4.70	$4.62	$4.95	$0.30
Buffalo	2.80	2.80	3.00	.18
Mobile	4.00	6.272	6.272	.28
New Orleans	4.00	6.272	6.272	28
San Francisco	11.00	*.50	*.60	.80
From Pittsburg to—				
New York	2.60	2.45	2.60	.16
Buffalo	1.65	1.75	1.80	.11
Mobile	4.44	6.72	6.72	.29
New Orleans	4.44	6.72	6.72	.29
San Francisco	18.50	14.00	16.44	.85
From Birmingham to—				
New York	....	5.95	5.95	.29
Buffalo	....	4.90	4.90	....
Mobile	2.50	2.75	2.75	.12
New Orleans	3.00	3.00	3.00	.18
San Francisco	11.75	13.20	13.20	.75

Per 100 pounds.

Mr. UNDERWOOD. Please state the railroad and steamship freight rates on the leading iron and steel products from the mills, factories, and furnaces in Germany and England to the principal United States points of consumption of those products.

Mr. GARY. The inland freight rates from the mills, factories, and furnaces in Germany and England to the principal ports, including Montreal, Canada, are as follows:

	Rails (per gross ton).	Pig iron (per gross ton).	Bil ets (per gross ton).	Finished products (per gross ton).
From foreign mills to—				
New York	$2.85	$2.85	$2.85	$3.00
Mobile	3.35	3.35	3.35	3.50
New Orleans	3.35	3.35	3.35	3.50
San Francisco	7.50	7.50	7.50	8.75
Montreal	2.75	2.75	2.75	2.90

Mr. UNDERWOOD. Judge, can you give us some information, if you have it, of the cost of production of pig iron in Germany and in Great Britain?

Mr. GARY. Yes. I can not give you the cost at all the places, but we have had a pretty careful inquiry made in regard to it, and I would say that for the production of large quantities of pig iron the lowest cost is in the Lorraine or Luxemburg district, where they produce at about $8.50 per ton.

Mr. UNDERWOOD. That is in Lorraine?

Mr. GARY. Yes; there are some furnaces which produce at $7.75, but I would not think in large enough quantities to make it a very important question, when considered in comparison with our own.

Mr. DALZELL. Where is your $7.75?

Mr. GARY. I have the name of the particular furnace. It is spelled Ilsede-hutte.

Mr. DALZELL. Where is that?

Mr. GARY. That is east of Dusseldorf, midway between there and Berlin.

Mr. UNDERWOOD. Judge, I have been laboring under the impression that on account of the material in the German iron and steel districts being farther apart, it costs considerably more to assemble the raw material there than it does in the English districts.

Mr. GARY. There is a great deal of iron there and a great deal of coal. Take, for instance, the works at Neunkirchen as an illustration. The coal is in the immediate vicinity of the furnaces and mills and the ore is within 25 or 30 miles.

Mr. UNDERWOOD. Would that be an average throughout the German district?

Mr. GARY. No; I think perhaps it would be more distant than that, but it is low. Their costs are low all through that district. Of course their labor is very low, as you know.

Mr. UNDERWOOD. What would you estimate as the cost of the production of a ton of pig iron, if you know, in England?

Mr. GARY. That is about $10; $8.50 is the best cost in the Lorraine-Luxemburg district.

The CHAIRMAN. But not in all Germany?

Mr. GARY. Not in all Germany. I think it is about $11. That is my impression. In the Luxemburg-Lorraine district the average is about $9.50.

Mr. CLARK. The Lorraine and Luxemburg district is the place where the materials are the closest together of any place in Europe; are they not?

Mr. GARY. I think that is probably so, not including England. In England the native ores and the coal are very close together. England makes cheap iron. I have the figures somewhere. I think it is about $10.25. The pig iron made from Cleveland ore is $9, in my figures.

Mr. UNDERWOOD. Have you the average of the English furnaces there?

Mr. GARY. No; I have not the average. They are higher than that, though—the average of all English furnaces.

Mr. COCKRAN. Higher than $11?

Mr. GARY. Of course it is the low man we have to contend with; but that is a matter of argument. That is not a question.

Mr. UNDERWOOD. But you have not the average of the English production?

Mr. GARY. No.

Mr. UNDERWOOD. You say it would be about $9, as the low price?

Mr. GARY. Yes, sir. They have immense tonnages of ore in Germany; not so much in England, but they have at least a billion tons left in England, I think.

Mr. UNDERWOOD. In your estimate of cost at the furnace for labor and operation, you included the overhead charges, did you? I mean the office charges, and so on.

Mr. GARY. No; the administration charges all go to the finished product.

Mr. UNDERWOOD. Mr. Schwab, when he was on the stand a day or two ago, made this statement, and I will ask you whether you agree with him or not. He stated that the cost of the labor in a ton of pig iron in this country and in England was about the same, but it was due to the increased efficiency of American labor in this country over that of the English labor, which was due to the improved methods of production and improved plants in this country over those in Great Britain and Germany.

Mr. GARY. I think that is probably correct, as applied to pig iron. It is not true as applied to some steel products, by a good deal.

Mr. UNDERWOOD. By reason of that increased efficiency or methods here, in your judgment, does that increase the cost of the plants here over those in England to any extent?

Mr. GARY. It certainly does.

Mr. UNDERWOOD. Can you give us an estimate?

Mr. GARY. No; it would be substantially——

Mr. UNDERWOOD. A substantial increase; but you can not give it?

Mr. GARY. No.

Mr. UNDERWOOD. I think that is all I desire to ask on this special point.

Mr. COCKRAN. I would like to ask one question, Judge. Do you say you do not include, in this deduction you make, the profit which your company makes on transportation?

Mr. GARY. No; I do not give credit for that.

Mr. COCKRAN. Could you give us some statement of about how much that would be? Let me see if I understand you correctly. I understood you to say that your cost of transportation by rail to the lower lake ports—Chicago, Cleveland, Lorain, and Ashtabula—is $1.45 for the ore. Am I correct in that?

Mr. GARY. I think so.

Mr. COCKRAN. What proportion of that is profit?

Mr. GARY. You mean profit to the carrying companies?

Mr. COCKRAN. Yes; which I understood you to say the steel company owns.

Mr. GARY. I can give you those figures if you think they are important. I have them. That is, if it is important in considering this question to know what the profit to the carrying companies is, of course, I will give it.

Mr. COCKRAN. No; I am asking for the purpose of ascertaining the cost of the raw material to you.

Mr. GARY. You see, when you say the cost to me——

Mr. COCKRAN. I mean the United States Steel Company.

Mr. GARY. That is susceptible of two constructions.

Mr. COCKRAN. I understand that. I want to get the information from whatever point of view you look at it.

Mr. GARY. From the standpoint of the United States Steel Corporation, the cost of pig iron is the manufacturing cost, which I have given you, less any credits the corporation gets by reason of its outside investments which are connected with that particular industry or that branch.

Mr. COCKRAN. I understand that, Judge, but to get at the actual status of the industry of the country it seems to me we will have to get information as to the returns that come back to the company by reason of that very condition you have described—not by any means with an idea of criticising it.

Mr. GARY. I understand.

Mr. COCKRAN. But simply to get the facts.

Mr. GARY. If you think it material to this inquiry I will give it.

Mr. COCKRAN. From the deductions you make by reason of the profits upon ore and coke it seems to me your ownership of the transportation companies is just as complete as your ownership of the coke and ore, and we might as well have it.

Mr. DALZELL. The transportation is common to all the companies.

Mr. COCKRAN. But they control the transportation companies.

Mr. GARY. It would not strike me in the same way, Mr. Cockran, for this reason: The United States Steel Corporation, owning control of the railroads, so far as the cost of the manufacture of iron and steel is concerned, is no different than what it would be if you owned that railroad. That is the point.

Mr. COCKRAN. That might be.

Mr. GARY. Don't understand I want to withhold anything that you think is proper.

Mr. COCKRAN. I understand all that, but I think it is also important, or at least valuable, that the methods by which your economies are accomplished should be thoroughly understood. It is just as important to you as to the committee. If there is any objection to it I do not insist upon it, but for the completeness of the inquiry I do not see any reason why we should not get before us to what extent the company profits by its control of transportation lines.

Mr. GARY. Taking into account all of the ore which we use, the profit to the transportation companies by land and by water averages, on the whole of it, 55½ cents per ton. That is the net profit.

Mr. COCKRAN. That would be the profit upon the coke and upon the ore, would it?

Mr. GARY. No; we do not own transportation companies to carry the coke.

Mr. COCKRAN. I understand that. That is very important.

Mr. GARY. This is ore.

Mr. COCKRAN. The United States Steel Company controls the transportation agencies by which it obtains the ore and transports it from the mine to the furnace.

Mr. GARY. Yes; the most of them; a large portion of them.

Mr. COCKRAN. When it comes to coke, it has to go in and get such rates as it can from the railroads?

Mr. GARY. Exactly.

Mr. COCKRAN. In the transportation of this ore, do those companies serve other producers?

Mr. GARY. Yes; they do.

Mr. COCKRAN. So that you have to carry the ore for your competitors as well as for yourselves?

Mr. GARY. Yes.

Mr. BONYNGE. Judge Gary, you actually pay for the transportation of this ore, do you? You actually make a real payment for it?

Mr. GARY. Oh, yes; certainly.

Mr. BONYNGE. And if you did not own the transportation company you would pay the same amount or a different amount?

Mr. GARY. Just the same amount.

Mr. COCKRAN. That is perfectly clear.

Mr. GARY. Mr. Cockran, you asked a question this morning that I would like to give you information in regard to. I think you had an impression that 40 cents a ton was pretty large for depreciation of the furnaces, and therefore it is only right to tell you the basis for that. Our modern furnaces produce about 140,000 tons a year, which, at 40 cents a ton, would be $56,000 per furnace. We think the life of the furnace is about twenty years. That would be $1,120,000 in twenty years. That represents just about the cost of the furnace. In other words, we intend to have those figures accurate.

Mr. COCKRAN. It was not I who made the suggestion.

Mr. CLARK. I was the one who made it.

Mr. COCKRAN. I think it is very valuable.

Mr. CLARK. I want to ask a question or two. Mr. Chairman Payne asked you this morning about the cost of ore. There was one item mixed up in the cost of ore that I could not understand. I guess it was because I was stupid. You pay 85 cents royalty on the ore, as I understand?

Mr. GARY. Oh, no; when I speak of the 85 cents, I refer to the recent acquisition of the Great Northern ores, so called, for which we pay——

Mr. CLARK. You bought the ore?

Mr. GARY. We bought the ore and agreed to pay 85 cents a ton for that ore, they paying the royalties. We also agreed to allow their railroad companies to transport it to the Lakes at the regular rate, which is the same rate we charge.

Mr. CLARK. How much did you figure it at that the ore cost when you were answering the chairman this morning?

Mr. GARY. At the lower lake ports?

Mr. CLARK. Yes. I did not want to bother you and make you go over the figures again.

Mr. GARY. No; that is all right.

Mr. CLARK. There is one item I want to ask you about. You need not hunt that up.

Mr. GARY. It is $2.88, including transportation.

Mr. CLARK. You included in that somewhere, somehow, as I understood it, some kind of a charge for depreciation.

Mr. GARY. Yes.

Mr. CLARK. Depreciation of what? That was it.

Mr. GARY. That depreciation of 40 cents——

Mr. CLARK. That is on the other product?

Mr. GARY. No; it is not the same. It happens to be the same in amount. That takes care of the depreciation of the equipment, which at every plant is very large in cost, and also an arbitrary price to buy new ore, if you please, to take the place of that we use.

Mr. CLARK. That is on the plant?

Mr. GARY. No; on the ore.

Mr. CLARK. I know; but if you take out enough to make up for the ore that you dig out of the ground, that ought not to be charged in as a part of the expense of making the pig iron, ought it? If you hold out enough now in this calculation to recoup you on the ore that you actually take out of the ground, that is so much profit, and ought to be charged up on the other side, too, ought it not, as well as on the debit side?

Mr. GARY. I do not see it that way.

Mr. CLARK. Well, if you do not see it that way, then you have always got as much on hand as you started with, theoretically, and you never diminish the amount of ore, and yet you charge 40 per cent off for the depreciation of the ores. That is what I could not understand about it. If there is such a thing as using up an acre of land, for instance, and you charge off enough depreciation to pay for the acre of land, then you are just exactly where you started, are you not?

Mr. GARY. But we have not got the land.

Mr. CLARK. But you have got the stuff to buy the land with?

Mr. GARY. That is our capital, which we must keep intact.

Mr. UNDERWOOD. When you sell your ore, you mean, you depreciate your   stock and make an attempt to reimburse that capital stock ?capital

Mr. GARY. Certainly; we take it right out of the capital, 40 cents, and thus hold cash to represent the capital stock instead of fixed property. As a matter of fact, as I said this morning, Mr. Clark, it would not be possible to buy this quality of ore at any such price.

Mr. CLARK. That is admitted.

Mr. GARY. We charge that 40 cents in order to keep our capital intact. That is the object of it.

Mr. CLARK. You make pig iron cheaper at Chicago than you do anywhere else, do you not?

Mr. GARY. No; I have said the cost is not very far apart between the best furnace at Chicago and the best furnace at Pittsburg, Lorain, Cleveland, or Youngstown.

Mr. CLARK. Will not the Missouri coal make coke as good as the Connellsville coal?

Mr. GARY. No; it is not practicable up to date.

Mr. CLARK. They do make good coke out there. Is not this coke business now a sort of fashion, and do you not prefer that because it does come from Connellsville?

Mr. GARY. No; if you could discover a way of practically satisfying us to that effect, you would be a rich man very suddenly.

Mr. CLARK. I wish I could.

Mr. GARY. No; that is not so, Mr. Clark. The best Illinois coal is cokeable, but in the first place it is very high in sulphur, which could be eliminated at a certain cost; but worse than that, the physical structure is such that it is not practicable. It will not carry the burden in the furnace. Oh, no; we have a great deal—I say a great deal; we own quite a substantial acreage of Illinois coal, and would be very glad to utilize it for coke. We could buy a great deal more at a very low price, and we have other contracts whereby we get that coal for steam purposes, and it would be an immense saving if that coal was cokeable.

Mr. CLARK. Do you make any considerable amount of charcoal products?

Mr. GARY. No, sir.

Mr. CLARK. You do not make any?

Mr. GARY. No.

Mr. COCKRAN. Judge, I find here in my notes one suggestion, which I think needs further explanation. You answered Mr. Underwood that with products coming in from abroad, if they were billets, there would be a charge against the foreign producer of transportation from the seaboard to the neighborhood where they would be manufactured, and that as to structural steel you expected a majority of it would probably be disposed of along the Atlantic seaboard, if any came. Did I understand you to say that?

Mr. GARY. No; I did not say that.

Mr. COCKRAN. Well, you said something about rails?

Mr. GARY. Yes, sir; the railroads would take their rails at the seaboard, because their lines reach the seaboard.

Mr. COCKRAN. Now, is not the majority of the railway construction some distance away from the terminus? For instance, take Buffalo and Chicago.

Mr. GARY. Yes; but that does not affect the question very much.

Mr. COCKRAN. The rails would be delivered, then, at the point in the West where the construction was in progress?

Mr. GARY. Yes; but the railroad companies do that. They would do it at a very small cost to themselves.

Mr. COCKRAN. But so far as the railway freight upon steel rails cuts any figure in your calculations, there would be a good charge against the foreigner delivering rails, would there not?

Mr. GARY. Not very much as to rails.

Mr. COCKRAN. How would it affect structural steel?

Mr. GARY. As to structural steel, of course the suggestion which was made by Mr. Underwood would apply; that is, you would have to get the point where the costs come together.

Mr. COCKRAN. Now, there is another thing Mr. Underwood suggested to me here which I think it would be well to spread upon the record, that in discussing the cost of depreciation, fixing it at 40 cents——

Mr. GARY. On the furnace or the ore?

Mr. COCKRAN. On the ore; 40 cents per ton for the ore, there is a constant necessity for relining the furnace?

Mr. GARY. Yes.

Mr. COCKRAN. That is included in the 40 cents?

Mr. GARY. No; it is not.

Mr. COCKRAN. Where do you include that in your calculations?

Mr. GARY. That is included in the $1.37.

Mr. COCKRAN. I see. I just wanted to get that clear.

Mr. GARY. That goes to the cost of operating.

Mr. RANDELL. Judge Gary, may I ask you a few questions?

Mr. GARY. Yes, sir.

Mr. RANDELL. In giving the rates you gave only the rate across the ocean and not the rate in Germany?

Mr. GARY. That is right.

Mr. RANDELL. Of transportation?

Mr. GARY. Yes.

Mr. RANDELL. What is the rate in Germany?

Mr. GARY. That depends on circumstances. The German Government takes care of German manufacturers, and when it comes to exporting products the Government, owning the railroads, will make almost any rate; and then they have other ways of reducing those rates.

Mr. RANDELL. Somebody will have to carry the product at somebody's cost. It would be an expense?

Mr. GARY. Yes.

Mr. RANDELL. And whether the Government pays it or the railroad pays it——

Mr. GARY. Yes; but of course we have to meet it just the same.

Mr. RANDELL. The question was as to what that was. Do you know?

Mr. GARY. That depends upon the point.

Mr. RANDELL. Do you know what the rate is?

Mr. GARY. The rate from where?

Mr. RANDELL. Anywhere. What would be the rate from any of the principal manufactories or mills there to the seaboard? Would it compete with you, if such a thing were possible in this country?

Mr. GARY. The rate, I think, from the Lorraine district, perhaps, would be about $1.25. The rate from the mill—that is what you want.

Mr. RANDELL. To New York.

Mr. GARY. To New York would be about $3. That is the open rate.

Mr. RANDELL. Then that is greater than your rate?

Mr. GARY. What is it?

Mr. RANDELL. That is greater than your rate?

Mr. GARY. It is from Pittsburg to that same point.

Mr. RANDELL. On the face of it, it sounded as though you had to pay a higher rate, and you really pay a less rate, to a considerable amount. Am I not correct about that? because I want to understand you.

Mr. GARY. You are correct in assuming that the rate from the mills in Germany to New York, on the average, would be higher than the rate from Pittsburg to New York.

Mr. RANDELL. The way I understood your statement a while ago was that you had to pay a higher rate. That was because you only gave the ocean rate and not the inland rate in Germany?

Mr. GARY. I think you are right, as you figure it.

Mr. RANDELL. That is, it was calculated to deceive parties who do not understand it like you do, and I did not understand it. That is the reason I asked you about it. Now, you have the advantage by over a dollar a ton now, even in New York, which is the great entrance port into this country.

Mr. GARY. Let me see if I can make that plain, in a word.

Mr. RANDELL. If you will answer my question first and then explain, I would rather you would do so. Is it not a fact that you have the advantage of about a dollar a ton, according to that statement, at New York?

Mr. GARY. It is $2.85 against $2.50.

Mr. RANDELL. That would be 65 cents?

Mr. GARY. The difference between $2.85 and $2.50.

Mr. RANDELL. I thought you said $3.50. I misunderstood you.

Mr. GARY. No; $2.50.

Mr. RANDELL. That is the entrance port. If any of these products were really to compete with you, they would have to be sold in New York City, or they would have to pay an additional freight to the point of consumption?

Mr. GARY. Yes.

Mr. RANDELL. Whether that was a railroad rail or any other product, the same thing would apply, would it not?

Mr. GARY. Yes.

Mr. RANDELL. Because either the importer would have to ship the rails to the point of consumption, or the railroad would have to carry it. It would have to be transported. That is a fact, is it not?

Mr. GARY. Yes; I think it is only fair, as that is an argumentative question, it seems to me, to let me give you what are facts.

Mr. RANDELL. Certainly.

Mr. GARY. Not that our company is so much interested in it, perhaps, but assuming you could make pig iron in the Lorraine district at $8.50, as I think you can, the cost of conversion there into billets would be about $5 a ton. That would be $13.50.

Mr. RANDELL. I thought you had been over that in your testimony.

Mr. GARY. No; I have not, at all. You add the freight charges, say $3, and it would be $16.50 for the billets in New York. Now, the cost of conversion at the eastern furnaces and mills is not less than $5, and, including all legitimate charges, I do not believe they can make pig iron for less than $15. Fifteen dollars and $5 would be $20. In other words, the German billets would be laid down in New York at $16.50, whereas the eastern mills at their mills would have to pay $20 for the same thing. That would be their cost, or, laid down in New York, the cost of transportation added. Of course I admit that is argumentative, and I only give you the facts and make the point to make the facts clear. As I say, it applies to these eastern furnaces and eastern mills.

Mr. RANDELL. Then the fact of the matter is—I am asking the question if it is not a fact—that without any tariff on any of these products the iron manufacturer in this country can control the American market as against the foreigner.

Mr. GARY. Did you say " can " or " can not? "

Mr. RANDELL. Can he not do it?

Mr. GARY. My figures do not seem to show that.

Mr. RANDELL. I ask you for an answer to that question. Then, of course, I would not have to go through the figures to get the conclusions.

Mr. GARY. No; I think not.

Mr. RANDELL. He can not control it? ·

Mr. GARY. No; that is true of various other products.

Mr. RANDELL. Then, under present conditions—it is immaterial to me what your answer is. I want to get at the facts.

Mr. GARY. That is all you will get, of course.

Mr. RANDELL. That is what I am after.

Mr. GARY. It is very material to me what I answer.

Mr. RANDELL. The American manufacturers, you say, can not control the American market?

Mr. GARY. I do not say that controlling the market——

Mr. RANDELL. That is a very plain question.

Mr. GARY. It is a very unfortunate question. Nobody can control any market.

Mr. RANDELL. Some people can control some markets, and do.

Mr. GARY. For how long a time?

Mr. RANDELL. It is according to how long——

Mr. GARY. The man who attempts to control any market, up or down, is soon in the poorhouse.

Mr. RANDELL. Some people take a very circuitous route and go through diamond mines before they get to the poorhouse; but whether that is true or not, I only want to get an answer to the question I propound, so that I may understand, from my standpoint, what the conditions are.

Mr. GARY. You say you ask for conclusions?

Mr. RANDELL. No matter what may be the cost, the conditions in this country are such that, in your opinion, the iron manufacturers can not control the American market without the help of the tariff. Is that your opinion?

Mr. GARY. Yes; it is. You are speaking of the manufacturers generally?

Mr. RANDELL. Of the iron producers.

Mr. GARY. I have made no answer in regard to the United States Steel Corporation. I don't know. I think, with reductions in the tariff, the United States Steel Corporation would endeavor to take care of itself; but I think many, if not most, of our competitors would soon be out of business, and we would have the field.

Mr. RANDELL. Then, from a selfish standpoint, it would be to the interest of the United States Steel Company to take the tariff off?

Mr. GARY. You might think so, but I do not think so. I think it would be the worst thing that could happen to United States Steel, because the people would not stand it. We do not want those conditions, and instead of trying to bring about such conditions as that, we have done what we could, fairly and justly, to prevent it and to assist our competitors.

Mr. RANDELL. Judge, I am not making any charges against anybody. All I want to get are the facts. You say they can not control it. Now, let us see as to the reason, in as short order as possible, without argument. Please answer my questions yes or no, as far as you can, and then explain them if need be. The iron in this country is of as good quality as any in the world, is it not—iron in the mines?

Mr. GARY. Of course, our ores, on the average, would not be as good as the Spanish ores.

Mr. RANDELL. As the Spanish ores?

Mr. GARY. No.

Mr. RANDELL. There is no trouble about competition with the Spanish ores, is there? You are not troubled about competition with the Spanish ores, are you?

Mr. GARY. I do not think so, at present. That may be true of the Swedish ores, too.

Mr. RANDELL. Is not the United States peculiarly rich in the possession of iron ore?

Mr. GARY. Yes.

Mr. RANDELL. Is it not a fact that it is easily accessible, in comparison with other ores, for the markets of the world, so far as access to it is concerned? I am not talking about the cost, but about the access to it.

Mr. GARY. Yes.

Mr. RANDELL. Is it not remarkably well situated for access?

Mr. GARY. I think so.

Mr. RANDELL. Now, is not the United States rich in coal?

Mr. GARY. Yes.

Mr. RANDELL. And that wealth is in bituminous coal and practically a monopoly of anthracite coal, is it not?

Mr. GARY. I presume so, but anthracite coal has nothing to do with our business.

Mr. RANDELL. That is a very proper statement. You do not use the anthracite in your business?

Mr. GARY. No.

Mr. RANDELL. You use bituminous coal?

Mr. GARY. We use good bituminous coals.

Mr. RANDELL. Is it not a fact that the iron and coal are well situated in reference to each other in the United States in comparison to other countries?

Mr. GARY. So far as the Birmingham district is concerned, yes; but not so far as the other districts are concerned. They are remote one from another, as compared with England and Germany.

Mr. RANDELL. You have the coal in Pennsylvania. You have an immense amount of coal in Pennsylvania and West Virginia, have you not?

Mr. GARY. Yes; we haul that coal to Chicago at a cost of $2.35; that coke from the Connellsville region to Chicago at $2.35; also from Pocahontas at the same rate; to Pittsburg from the Connellsville region at 70 cents a ton, and the transportation of the ore to the point of assembly——

Mr. RANDELL. You have given those figures before, have you not?

Mr. GARY. Yes; I have.

Mr. RANDELL. You can refer to them in that way. They are in the record.

Mr. GARY. The ores are away North. The coal is South.

Mr. GAINES. I do not think Judge Gary has given those figures— the distance the coal is from the furnaces and the ore is from the furnaces and the lime is from the furnaces.

The CHAIRMAN. He has given the locations. I think the committee can come pretty near to it.

Mr. GAINES. I should think so.

Mr. RANDELL. There is a transportation rate on the railroads?

Mr. GARY. Limestone is another principal thing.

Mr. RANDELL. Have you not limestone, coal, and coke together in the United States outside of Alabama?

Mr. GARY. Limestone, coal, and coke?

Mr. RANDELL. Yes.

Mr. GARY. No; we have no coke at our furnaces. Neither have we any limestone at our furnaces.

Mr. RANDELL. And no iron ores?

Mr. GARY. And no iron ores.

Mr. RANDELL. You have your furnaces where there is neither coke, coal, nor iron ore?

Mr. GARY. That is right.

Mr. RANDELL. Everything has to be hauled to you?

Mr. GARY. I am not speaking of the Birmingham district.

Mr. RANDELL. You are talking about Pittsburg, the Pennsylvania region.

Mr. GARY. No; they are situated far apart. We select the points where the cost of assembling all these is the lowest. That is our aim.

Mr. RANDELL. That depends, does it not, on the place where you have put your former manufactory? You have to consider the fact that you have already an investment there, have you not?

Mr. GARY. It was originally located with that in view.

Mr. RANDELL. But when conditions change you still hold it there because you have your investment there?

Mr. GARY. We hold it or abandon it, as we have done in a great many cases, and build elsewhere.

Mr. RANDELL. Is it not a fact that a very large part of the expense of the manufacture of iron in this country is brought about by railroad charges in carrying the raw material and in carrying the finished product to the place of consumption? Is not a large part of it railroad charges?

Mr. GARY. Yes.

Mr. RANDELL. Do you not believe it is a fact, as I think Mr. Schwab said—I think he was the witness who testified to it—that while you charge the railroads $28 a ton for steel rails they make no complaint about that, that they are perfectly willing to pay a high price for steel rails, and are not asking any reduction? Is not that a fact?

Mr. GARY. It is not a fact that they pay a high price.

Mr. RANDELL. Is it not a fact that they make no complaint and have not made any about the rise in the price of steel rails, but pay it cheerfully and willingly?

Mr. GARY. No; that is not a fact. On the contrary——

The CHAIRMAN. Mr. Randell, I suggest you exhaust the witness on the ore business and the pig iron, and then we will take up the steel rails regularly and go through this matter connectedly. We have not had anything on that, and I do not like to have it drawn out piecemeal.

Mr. RANDELL. Very well, sir. The point I was getting at is a matter not specially connected with the price of steel rails at all, but it is a condition I am talking about.

The CHAIRMAN. I only make the suggestion.

Mr. RANDELL. I will follow the chairman's suggestion, but the chairman misunderstood me. I am not going into the question of steel rails, but a condition. Now, is it not a fact that the men who own and control the iron interests also to a large extent own and control the railroad interests and transportation facilities?

Mr. GARY. Well, just to how large an extent I can't say, but not to an extent that I think influences the question of prices in the slightest.

Mr. RANDELL. I did not ask you that, because that is a conclusion. You might think one thing and somebody else another. I was getting at the fact. Is it not a fact that the interests are largely controlled by the same men and the same interests?

Mr. GARY. I don't think so.

Mr. RANDELL. Then the railroad stocks are owned by entirely different men from the men who own the steel stock?

Mr. GARY. Well. entirely is one word. You used one word in one question and another word in another question. There are some men who have interests in steel manufactures and in railroading, both.

Mr. RANDELL. They are men of large interests in both, as a rule, are they not?

Mr. GARY. No: I don't think so.

Mr. RANDELL. The men who have the largest interests in the steel business have large interests and a certain amount of controlling and directing interest in railroads. Is not that a fact?

Mr. GARY. No: I don't think so.

Mr. RANDELL. Then, according to your opinion, the interests that operate the iron and steel industries have no power or control in reference to the regulation of railroads?

Mr. GARY. Yes; that is my opinion. I have been up against the question too many times to agree with you.

Mr. RANDELL. You have never been trying to get low rates, have you?

Mr. GARY. Yes. indeed: and I have had a great many discussions in regard to the price of rails with these people. That does not contradict what Mr. Schwab said, as applied to certain railroads and certain manufacturing companies. For instance, if a certain railroad is receiving large amounts of freight from a manufacturing company located on its lines, then the business between those two proceeds without any friction; but we sell rails to large numbers of railroads who have no business of that kind.

Mr. RANDELL. I did not mean to ask you if the people who own the steel industry own the largest per cent of all the railroads in the United States, but the railroads that they need to use. They have interests in them, have they not?

Mr. GARY. To some extent. It is not a question of the interests. It is a question of freights, a question of the interchange of business, not a question of interest in the securities of one company or the other.

Mr. RANDELL. Take it that they consider their interests are the same. Then is not this the practical situation, that the steel industry and the railroad transportation business, having a community of interests, that the high freight rates are tolerated by the steel companies and the high prices of steel are tolerated by the railroad companies, and it all comes out finally to the consumer, and the steel company, being a producer, and the railroad company, being the carrier, which is also a producer, simply pool issues and get the benefit of a higher price, which is protected by a tariff on the steel product?

Mr. GARY. I know of no case where that is a fact; where your premises are justified by the facts.

Mr. RANDELL. When, in your opinion, will the steel industry get strong enough so that it can maintain itself just as an independent industry, without having to tax the balance of the country to support it, if you ever thought about that proposition?

Mr. GARY. You might as well ask me how long a string is as to ask me in regard to the future.

Mr. RANDELL. I might as well ask you how long the Government will last, or something like that.

Mr. GARY. Yes.

Mr. RANDELL. In other words, the proposition is to keep it everlastingly.

Mr. GARY. But in reference to that question, outside of the net profits realized by the corporation and the value of its raw products, everything is paid to labor, goes to labor.

Mr. RANDELL. I am glad you mentioned that subject. I want to ask you about that. My understanding is that all this tariff and everything is for the benefit of labor.

Mr. GARY. No; you don't understand that from me.

Mr. RANDELL. I have understood it from most people who have been here, and it has always been the cry in every tariff bill. It is the cry of the Republican party. We will not discuss those things. I want to get at the facts. I wanted you to tell me the fact, if it is— and I take it to be the fact, because it has been testified to by various witnesses here who are not antagonistic to your interests—that in reference to food products, the cheapest food, the most uninviting kinds of food, are imported and brought to the different parts of the country here and consumed among the mill towns and among the laboring people; that the most uninviting, unwholesome, and the commonest food is the kind that is sold to these people. Do you know where that is?

Mr. GARY. I doubt the statement of fact, to begin with.

Mr. RANDELL. Then you could not give an opinion on it?

Mr. GARY. Therefore I could not; no.

Mr. RANDELL. Now, in reference to clothes. People have been here before this committee, and everything that wants a tariff seems to think they must keep out the coarser clothing. We find further testimony that the commonest, meanest, most undesirable clothing is the kind that is bought by the laboring people who are in the manufacturing business. Can you explain where that is, if they are going to get any benefit from this tariff?

Mr. DALZELL. I suggest, Mr. Chairman, that we have wandered a long way from the point at issue here.

Mr. RANDELL. With all due respect to the gentleman from Pennsylvania, it seems to me we have not wandered as far as, perhaps, the investigation did yesterday on the peanut question, when it came to tariff matters.

The CHAIRMAN. Of course the important inquiry here is the difference of cost of foreign ore and pig iron and ore and pig iron in this country. If you will tell me that, I will not have much trouble adjusting the rate of duty. That is what I want to get at.

Mr. RANDELL. Mr. Chairman, my idea was that it might be well that the tariff he is asking for in reference to this commodity be done away with in the interest of the laboring man, and my questions were directed in reference to that matter.

The CHAIRMAN. I did not hear your question, Mr. Randell.

Mr. RANDELL. I was through with the witness, and I will not take up the time of the committee further.

The CHAIRMAN. If you think the question is material, go ahead.

Mr. RANDELL. I did think so, but I have an answer to it. Your answer was that you did not know why that was, was it?

Mr. GARY. I did not answer the last question.

Mr. RANDELL. I would like to have an answer to it.

Mr. CRUMPACKER. If this were a court of justice, a valid objection would be that it assumes a fact that has not been proven.

Mr. RANDELL. I assume the testimony that is before this committee is to that effect, or at least in that direction. If I am not correct about that, a perusal——

Mr. CRUMPACKER. No; I think it is based on an assumption that the record does not justify, Mr. Randell. That is my point.

Mr. RANDELL. I am sorry the gentleman's memory is not the same as mine; and still——

The CHAIRMAN. The record will show, gentlemen. There is no use debating about that.

Mr. RANDELL. Yes; the record will show. If that is the case, and the testimony is in that direction, can you explain why that is so?

Mr. GARY. You ask me why the workingmen use the cheapest kind of goods for clothing?

Mr. RANDELL. Why the commonest clothing, not merely for the laborer, but for the community, for his family—the cheapest and most undesirable clothing is sent to those sections where they have manufacturing establishments?

Mr. GARY. Of course the obvious answer is that the workingman is influenced a good deal like other people, and that if he is disposed to be economical and saving he will buy and wear the goods which he can get at the lowest price.

Mr. RANDELL. If your idea is that it is on account of his being saving, then I will ask if it is not a fact that it has taken all his wages, and he has saved practically nothing, but that, on the contrary, he is coming and asking a continuation and in some cases an increase of the tariff in order to permit him to work more than half time, in order to give him a chance to work more than half time?

Mr. FORDNEY. Before you answer that question, Judge, let me ask you this: Do you know whether the men who work for you wear any different clothes than the average laboring man elsewhere?

Mr. GARY. No; I do not. I think they are fully as well dressed. I should like to have you see a picture that was taken a short time ago at our Vandergrift mill, in Pennsylvania, showing drawn up in front of the public park about 20 automobiles, owned by our own employees and operated by them.

Mr. RANDELL. They were the high-priced men.

Mr. GARY. Well, they were the rollers in the mills. They get good wages compared to the foreign wages. I could give you, if I were talking tariff, some facts concerning our workingmen as compared with workingmen abroad that I believe would astonish you.

Mr. RANDELL. Have you any pictures of any of the soup houses?

Mr. GARY. Soup houses?

Mr. RANDELL. Yes.

Mr. GARY. Well, we used all sorts of houses during the last year, taking care of our men temporarily who were out of employment. I don't think that is any crime.

Mr. RANDELL. Let me ask you this question. It is not a question of tariff; it is a question of humanity for the country.

Mr. GARY. The tariff question is a question of business, I think.

Mr. RANDELL. It is a question of humanity, from my standpoint; it may be a question of business with you. What is the trouble in your industry that makes it so frequently the case that there are too many men for the work, so that you can only give them about half time each, and you have to work some a while and others a while, so as to support all, and you are unable to give them a full day's work?

Mr. GARY. That is, what produces panics, do you mean?

Mr. RANDELL. No; what produces that condition?

Mr. GARY. When there is no panic?

Mr. RANDELL. Yes.

Mr. GARY. There are various things. One thing would be, for instance, large quantities of foreign products brought into this country at a price our people could not compete with, reducing our production at some of our mills, and to that extent throwing our people out of employment. That is one reason.

Mr. RANDELL. You mean to say, then, that the foreign production, even with the present tariff, has made all that calamity for the laboring man in this country?

Mr. GARY. What calamity do you refer to?

Mr. RANDELL. The time you are talking about. You said it occurred when there was not a panic, or between panics.

Mr. GARY. I have not fixed any time nor spoken of any calamity.

Mr. GAINES. Judge Gary, you have not stated, have you, that there is any such condition prevailing in your business now?

Mr. GARY. No.

Mr. GAINES. Or that there has been in the last few years?

Mr. GARY. There has not.

Mr. RANDELL. Do you mean to say such a condition has not existed?

Mr. GARY. I mean to say during the last year the volume of business has not been as great as it was before that time. At the present time it is pretty good.

The CHAIRMAN. It is hardly fair to ask the witness to prophesy about what would happen.

Mr. RANDELL. I am not asking him to be a prophet or a patriarch, either.

The CHAIRMAN. It comes pretty close to it.

Mr. RANDELL. The chairman evidently did not understand my question. I was not asking this gentleman to prophesy. I would not take him for a prophet.

The CHAIRMAN. You were asking him whether if such and such conditions existed they would not be employed for the full time.

Mr. RANDELL. I asked him what was the cause, more as a philosopher and historian than as a prophet.

The CHAIRMAN. Proceed, Mr. Randell. We will stay with you. I want to say to the gentlemen who are here upon other matters that the committee will probably sit until 7 o'clock, and take a recess for an hour for dinner, and continue until we get through.

Mr. RANDELL. As the chairman is restless with reference to time, I will ask this question and quit. I have taken up too much time.

The CHAIRMAN. Certainly not; but there are a number of gentlemen here and I do not want them to go away.

Mr. RANDELL. I would hate to discommode them in any way. Can you explain to me why it is that under your present system there are so many men that are employed, who have no other business except to work in your manufactories, and still can not get an average of more than about half time to work?

Mr. GARY. Unless you refer to times of panic, I think your assumption is wrong. I do not believe the conditions you refer to ever applied. On the contrary, we have had difficulty——

Mr. RANDELL. Is the assumption wrong in reference to the amount of time they are out of employment?

Mr. GARY. Yes.

Mr. RANDELL. How much, then?

Mr. GARY. Or their being out of employment.

Mr. RANDELL. You mean to say, then, that there are no more men than you could keep employed all the while if your mills were running full time?

Mr. GARY. This will answer your question, I think. In 1905, 1906, and 1907, at our mills, labor was so scarce that a good deal of the time we had difficulty in getting as many men as we needed. During the last year the conditions have been different, but since the election conditions have been improving.

Mr. RANDELL. You have not answered my question as to whether or not there is a percentage of men commonly unable to get work because you have more men there who depend upon that industry and upon it alone for work than you can give employment to?

Mr. GARY. I don't think that is true.

Mr. RANDELL. Then, you have no percentage of that kind?

Mr. GARY. I would not say that.

Mr. RANDELL. That is what I am asking you about. Then you do not know?

Mr. GARY. I think I know pretty well, but when you say any percentage, one man would be a percentage.

Mr. RANDELL. I mean any appreciable percentage.

Mr. GARY. You will have to give me figures.

Mr. RANDELL. I was asking you to give me figures.

Mr. GARY. If I give you the general rule, give you the average, give you substantially the situation, it seems to me that does answer your question fully.

Mr. RANDELL. What I was getting at was whether or not you have a surplus of labor.

Mr. GARY. As a rule?

Mr. RANDELL. As a rule, you have a surplus of labor?

Mr. GARY. Ever, at any time? I confess I don't know what you mean.

Mr. RANDELL. Do you ordinarily, on the average, have a surplus of labor?

Mr. GARY. At our mills?

Mr. RANDELL. About your mills, depending upon your mills for labor.

Mr. GARY. And exclusive of times of panic?

Mr. RANDELL. Yes.

Mr. GARY. We do not.

Mr. RANDELL. Then you have full employment for all the men in your business?

Mr. GARY. As a rule, yes; we do. That is the rule.

Mr. RANDELL. And yet with full employment their condition, whatever it is, is chargeable to the wages that they get and the opportunities that they have and the expenses they are put to under the system in which they live?

Mr. GARY. Yes; the conditions which I speak of are the result of wages paid in this country as compared with wages paid in other countries.

Mr. RANDELL. And to make a long matter short, if you will excuse the expression, the condition that the laboring man is under, whether it is good or bad, is by your admission the result of the environment about him, by reason of the institutions and the laws that control your business there?

Mr. GARY. Of course I don't state that or admit that, because during the last year this country has been passing through a panic, not resulting from any question concerning which you have been talking, the tariff or this investigation, and that has brought about certain conditions with reference to the laboring men.

Mr. RANDELL. Then previous to the panic he was the natural result of his environment there. Is that right?

Mr. GARY. The conditions of our mills and furnaces as I have stated them; yes.

Mr. RANDELL. Whether that is good or bad? That is all.

The CHAIRMAN. That seems to be all. Judge, I want to ask you one or two questions about this same subject: What is the cost at which ore can be laid down in New York from Germany before the duty is paid—at what price?

Mr. GARY. I do not find it, but the freight rate is about $1.50 a ton; not perhaps actually that.

The CHAIRMAN. It can be laid down in New York for $1.50 a ton?

Mr. GARY. I think so.

The CHAIRMAN. German and English ore both?

Mr. GARY. That is, the freight rate?

The CHAIRMAN. No; I mean the total cost.

Mr. GARY. Oh, the total cost; iron laid down?

Mr. BONYNGE. Iron ore.

Mr. GARY. No; I can not answer that, because I have not the separate mining costs and the royalties and things of that sort. I have no figures on that. I know about the cost of iron or billets, but the ore, I could not give it.

The CHAIRMAN. You think the freight on the ore is about $1.50 a ton?

Mr. GARY. I think so.

The CHAIRMAN. You did give the figures to Mr. Underwood—the cost of the ore?

Mr. UNDERWOOD. No; I asked him about pig iron.

Mr. GARY. I could give you pig iron and billets.

The CHAIRMAN. I would like to have you put that in later, and then I would like to have you show the relative richness in iron of the American ore and the English ore and the German ore. You have said that all American ore had a certain per cent of iron in it.

Mr. GARY. I can not give you that exactly; but I think it requires about 3 tons of German ore to 2 tons of our ore.

The CHAIRMAN. Three tons of German to two of ours?

Mr. GARY. Yes; and I would not be surprised if English ore was about the same. Their processes are somewhat different. They make basic iron in Germany, largely; they import some ore from Sweden, some from Spain, more from Sweden; and Belgium, I think, for instance, imports all its ore. That is why their tariff on ore is different from our tariff on ore. That accounts for the difference, because they have to bring it in.

The CHAIRMAN. For mixture, I suppose?

Mr. GARY. Yes; exactly.

The CHAIRMAN. But, generally speaking, 2 tons of our ore goes as far as 3 tons of theirs?

Mr. GARY. That is my recollection.

The CHAIRMAN. Can you tell me what it would cost to lay down a ton of pig iron in New York, including the total cost of the iron, from Germany and also from Great Britain?

Mr. GARY. I think about $11.50 from Germany to $12 from England.

The CHAIRMAN. Laid down in New York?

Mr. GARY. Yes. Steel is still more favorable to Germany.

The CHAIRMAN. Why, then, does not Germany drive you out of the market? Seven dollars and fifty cents and $4 added would make $11.50 against your $15.50 cost.

Mr. GARY. Eight dollars and fifty cents and $3 would be $11.50, and the tariff, $4, $15.50. If they had a surplus of iron at any time, of course it would come in here; it does come in here, lots of it.

The CHAIRMAN. Then there is nothing but their need for it for their own manufacturing purposes that keeps it out?

Mr. GARY. That is exactly right. Selling pig iron, German pig iron, would not pay them very well, and they can do very much better by converting it into steel of all kinds.

The CHAIRMAN. Would the same rule apply if the $4 were taken off the duty?

Mr. GARY. That I can not answer; I do not know. We are not much interested in the question of iron; we buy pig iron.

The CHAIRMAN. You think that is in the range of prophecy again, do you?

Mr. GARY. Yes.

The CHAIRMAN. I do not think I can take any exception to that.

Mr. GARY. I am better acquainted with the facts, so far as they apply, relating to our business.

The CHAIRMAN. England has no surplus of iron ore?

Mr. GARY. No.

The CHAIRMAN. She uses all in manufacturing what she mines and imports?

Mr. GARY. She has no surplus of pig iron, I should say.

The CHAIRMAN. She does not export pig iron?

Mr. GARY. No. It pays better to convert it. They do a very large export business of the finished steel.

The CHAIRMAN. Certainly; but I mean either as ore or pig iron she does not export to any extent?

Mr. GARY. No. My impression would be that she would not do it—that she will not do it; but as you have suggested, I can not answer.

Mr. CLARK. Do you believe it would make any difference with the steel business if the tariff was taken off pig iron and ore?

Mr. GARY. I can not answer that question. It would be an opinion.

The CHAIRMAN. We will go up to pig iron if you have not anything further to say there.

Mr. GARY. Mr. Chairman, the importations of pig iron in 1907 to this country were 489,440 tons, as I have it.

The CHAIRMAN. How much do you say?

Mr. GARY. Four hundred and eighty-nine thousand four hundred and forty tons.

The CHAIRMAN. That would include manganese and spiegeleisen?

Mr. GARY. No; that is just pig iron. It does not cover scrap iron or bar iron or bars or spiegeleisen or manganese.

Mr. UNDERWOOD. Here are the exact figures for 1907 as given by the statistics we have before us. Eliminating spiegeleisen and ferromanganese and ferrosilicon and tungsten, coming down strictly to pig iron, these statistics give 366,706 tons, valued at $5,862,930, paying a duty of $1,466,825; and the value of a unit, the average value of each ton that was imported, which does not include the duty, was $15.99.

Mr. GARY. Are those government statistics?

Mr. UNDERWOOD. The statistics that were prepared for the committee.

The CHAIRMAN. That is taken from the government statistics.

Mr. GARY. My figures are supposed to be from the government statistics, and accurate.

Mr. DALZELL. What are your figures?

Mr. GARY. Four hundred and eighty-nine thousand four hundred and forty tons.

Mr. BONYNGE. What do you take, the calendar year or the fiscal year?

Mr. GARY. The calendar year.

Mr. BONYNGE. You have the fiscal year, Mr. Underwood.

The CHAIRMAN. Is it the calendar year or the fiscal year?

Mr. GARY. The calendar year.

The CHAIRMAN. This is the fiscal year.

Mr. COCKRAN. Is this the fiscal year?

Mr. UNDERWOOD. Yes; ending June 30.

Mr. BONYNGE. We have the fiscal year and he has the calendar year.

Mr. GARY. That accounts for it.

The CHAIRMAN. Do you think that is a fair valuation, $16 a ton landed at the port of New York?

Mr. GARY. I can not answer that; I do not know.

The CHAIRMAN. For the last five years, including 1907, the average valuation was $15.33 a ton.

Mr. GARY. At that price that was iron from certain localities.

The CHAIRMAN. I suppose that it was the importation that actually squeezed into this country—a very small amount—from Cuba and from Spain, but none was coming from Great Britain or Germany.

Mr. COCKRAN. Right there, will you ask the witness to explain the great difference in importations between 1907, 1906, and 1905?

The CHAIRMAN. Certainly, I will call his attention to that. In 1906, 110,000; 1905, 54,000; and we have found, Judge, that generally the importations were abnormally large in 1907 on steel or anything else. It runs all through the schedules.

Mr. GARY. For 1906 I have 379,828.

Mr. COCKRAN. When is that?

Mr. GARY. Nineteen hundred and six—the calendar year 1906.

The CHAIRMAN. I do not know where you got your figures.

Mr. BONYNGE. He has the calendar year every time.

The CHAIRMAN. Even with the calendar year you can not have it three times as much right along. There seems to be some discrepancy in his figures or ours.

Mr. UNDERWOOD. If you will let me suggest, his calendar year overlaps the fiscal year, and the dumping from Europe had commenced in his calendar year, whereas it does not show until our fiscal year.

The CHAIRMAN. What was it the year before?

Mr. GARY. Nineteen hundred and five, pig iron, 212,466.

The CHAIRMAN. There is something out of joint between your figures and ours.

Mr. COCKRAN. The figures are out of joint.

The CHAIRMAN. There can not be any doubt but what yours are much higher than ours.

Mr. UNDERWOOD. Judge, suppose you take this book and have our figures before you.

Mr. GARY. I suppose these are taken from the government statistics, but I do not understand what the mistake is, unless they have included something here that is not included there.

The CHAIRMAN. These were prepared for the use of the committee with a good deal of care, and we have not found any mistakes in them.

Mr. COCKRAN. Mr. Chairman, would it be explained by the fact that he may have the various forms of iron?

The CHAIRMAN. No; I do not think so, because that would not come in in pig.

Mr. COCKRAN. It says, "iron in pigs."

The CHAIRMAN. There is speigeleisen comes in, 2,000 tons.

Mr. COCKRAN. And ferromanganese.

The CHAIRMAN. Ferromanganese, $94 a ton. That may account for it.

Mr. GARY. You see, I have no separate item for speigeleisen or ferromanganese.

The CHAIRMAN. That probably accounts for the difference.

Mr. DALZELL. Your figures include all of these?

Mr. GARY. Yes; I presume that explains it.

Mr. CLARK. If the Europeans could lay this pig iron down in New York at the figures that have been agreed on here, and do not import any more than they do, how can you explain the fact that they do not come in and get more of your trade than they do?

Mr. GARY. Business has been very good abroad during the last two years, up to a comparatively recent period; at least most of the time. That would account for it in a large measure. Then, when business is dull over there, they would dump here, if they could, just as all countries do.

Mr. CLARK. It could not be possible that you estimated the cost of the American pig too high and the cost of this foreign pig a little too low, could it?

Mr. GARY. No; not intentionally.

Mr. CLARK. I did not say intentionally.

Mr. GARY. I think our figures are accurate during this last summer.

The CHAIRMAN. Where do you get your foreign figures?

Mr. GARY. We had two men travel through the country this year visiting the furnaces and mills and going into that question very carefully, getting well acquainted with the local people, and while they may have been deceived at any place, I think not. In 1899—that is a long time ago—I was at the furnaces and mills at Neunkirchen, where I found the lowest cost of manufacture, and I do not believe I was mistaken there. If not, they were making basic iron at that point at that time for $6.50.

Mr. COCKRAN. Was that the time Mr. Schwab testified that things were so cheap in this country? Mr. Schwab fixed 1898 and 1899.

Mr. GARY. Not in 1899; it was before that, I think. Still, I do not know.

Mr. CLARK. It was about 75 cents or a dollar a ton difference in this European price laid down in New York and your price, was it not? That is, they get in here 75 cents or a dollar cheaper than you do?

Mr. GARY. Very much cheaper; more than that difference.

Mr. CLARK. We have it over and over here before this committee that if you give the foreigner the slightest profit imaginable he will send all the stuff he has got over here.

Mr. GARY. Of course, I do not like to characterize any other person's testimony, but that would seem to be an exaggeration, if it covers the whole period.

Mr. CLARK. That is what I thought.

Mr. GARY. At times that is true, but it is not true all the time. Every man gets the most he can for his product at particular times.

Mr. CLARK. Certainly.

Mr. GARY. When business is dull, they do in Germany what we do here—to keep their mills running and the men employed, they dump the surplus.

Mr. CLARK. I am glad you confirm my opinion about the correctness of this other theory that has been broached here so often.

Mr. GARY. I am only giving you facts as I understand them.

The CHAIRMAN. For a period of five years some of the manufacturers of iron and steel threw their books open to the Bureau of Corporations for examination by experts, allowing them to look at their balance sheets, and so forth, regarded by the companies as confidential, so far as each individual company was concerned, whatever figures they gave. Do you care to say whether your company did that or not?

Mr. GARY. Gave the figures to whom?

The CHAIRMAN. To the Bureau of Corporations.

Mr. GARY. We did; we were the leaders.

The CHAIRMAN. What is that?

Mr. GARY. We were the first to do it.

Mr. CLARK. You do not know if the same experts examined into the steel question who examined into the beef-packing business and came back here and reported that they only made 98 cents on a steer?

Mr. GARY. I know they were not the same.

Mr. CLARK. I hope they were not. [Laughter.]

Mr. GARY. Mr. Clark, the examination in our case occupied a period of, I think, two years.

The CHAIRMAN. Five years.

Mr. GARY. Nearly three years, and we furnished all the assistance we could. I think it was thoroughly done.

The CHAIRMAN. You were allowed to go over the work with the department men and test it, I suppose, to see whether their work was correct or not?

Mr. GARY. No; we have not been allowed that; probably we will be allowed that.

The CHAIRMAN. I understood that the steel expert would go over the work with the clerks from the Bureau of Corporations, and that they had access to the books, the balance sheets, and the cost of these individual items?

Mr. GARY. That is true.

Mr. CLARK. Not any reflection on you or your company, but I was just wondering what kind of arithmeticians they had up there in that Bureau of Corporations when they got to the steer question, because I do know something about that.

The CHAIRMAN. Let us keep out of that steer question.

Mr. CLARK. Very well.

Mr. GARY. They have very competent men. I do not know any more than you do what the conclusion is.

The CHAIRMAN. You have stated without any reservation that your company was examined with the others. I want to say to you that the total aggregate of the output of pig iron of the companies—there were certain companies examined, including yours—was 93 per cent of the total output in this country, and that the average cost of pig iron for the five years, including 1902 and 1906, was $14.01 a ton. The report gives the items in detail from beginning to end.

Mr. GARY. Including depreciation? Does it include depreciation and overhead charges and administration charges?

The CHAIRMAN. I will read you the items it does include: "Net total metallic mixture, coke, limestone, labor, steam, materials in repairs and maintenance, supplies and tools, miscellaneous and general works expenses, general expense, relining and renewals, depreciation, 39 cents," which is within a cent of what you put it; so I suppose you confirm the depreciation.

Mr. UNDERWOOD. What was the total?

The CHAIRMAN. $14.01.

Mr. GARY. Of course, the basis is different, evidently. The cost last year, which I have given, must be considerably less than the cost this year, because when the mills are running full the cost is less, as one can see. In those figures they certainly could not have allowed any profit to the mining-company, to any of the mining companies.

The CHAIRMAN. I should infer they did, p   s; I am not disputing you. Of course, you are testifying, I cannot; but I should infer that they did allow the profits on the coke and on the iron ore.

Mr. GARY. Have you got, for instance, the cost of the ore in the furnace?

The CHAIRMAN. Yes.

Mr. GARY. What is the cost of the ore?

The CHAIRMAN. Net total metallic mixture, $3.97; total, $7.30; coke, $3.37; total, $3.89.

Mr. GARY. That is for 1902 to 1906, inclusive; that is the average for the whole time?

The CHAIRMAN. Yes.

Mr. GARY. The cost of ore has been materially increasing right along, Mr. Chairman, very materially increasing, largely because of the reduction in metallic ore, the percentage of metallic ore in the ton of iron mined.

The CHAIRMAN. I know you stated that and said it was very slight.

Mr. GARY. For that particular year.

The CHAIRMAN. It is not large according to your figures, as I understood them this morning. Of course I could not repeat the figures given this morning, but I noticed at the time; I thought the percentage was very small.

Mr. GARY. It is very much larger now than it was in 1902.

The CHAIRMAN. It says here:

The item of labor does not include, for much of the tonnage, the labor in unloading raw materials and in producing steam, which some companies include in the cost of raw materials and in the item steam.

The tonnage covers 93 per cent of the Bessemer pig iron made in the United States during the period.

The item of labor is put down at 77 cents, and, of course, when steam is put down at 12 cents, I understand that includes the cost of labor in making the steam, and so on with the other items, the cost of labor in the making of coke and producing iron ore and all the way through. Taking that into consideration, in connection with your statement this morning that the cost to your company was $2 less per ton for pig iron than that of the other companies—by the way, what percentage of the pig iron did your company turn out during those five years?

Mr. GARY. I can not give it for five years, but I can give it for some period. Our percentage last year was 41.7 per cent of the whole.

The CHAIRMAN. How does that compare with 1902, for instance; did it increase it?

Mr. GARY. No; our percentage has been decreasing a little.

The CHAIRMAN. Decreasing?

Mr. GARY. Yes.

The CHAIRMAN. Then it was greater during this period of five years?

STEEL RAILS—ELBERT H. GARY.

Mr. GARY. Yes.

The CHAIRMAN. Do you think it would average 50 per cent?

Mr. GARY. No; 45, I presume. About 45.

The CHAIRMAN. Then the other companies were producing 48 per cent, so that you were producing not quite half of what the other companies were. Your company, with the other six, produced 93 per cent of the entire output?

Mr. GARY. Yes.

The CHAIRMAN. If you produced 45, of course the others produced 48, or a little more than you produced in the aggregate, and of course it would be fair to deduct from this general average about $1 per ton, because of the advantage which you had, showing that your total cost of production of pig iron during this period would be $13, or very close to that. Are you able to say whether that is correct?

Mr. GARY. No; I am not. The figures I have given here for last year are accurate, on the basis which I have given them.

The CHAIRMAN. I want to ask you this question in that connection: You stated that the cost per ton of pig iron was larger this year because of the smaller production, and of course that is quite obvious, and there has been quite an addition to the cost per ton during this last year over a period of high production like 1907. You have not the figures here to show the cost per ton before 1907?

Mr. GARY. No; I have not, prior to that.

The CHAIRMAN. The committee desires that you go back to 1906 as a normal year, 1907 being a boom year and a year of large importation of everything, because the people could not get enough of what they wanted and were willing to pay the foreign prices for the article and we had such large importations, abnormal importations; 1906, we calculate, was a normal year, and of course figures on that would be more acceptable. I blame myself somewhat for not writing you to that effect, although you are here under subpoena, but it would be, perhaps, more to the point if you had the figures for 1906, and still we are not entirely without them, because this statement from the Bureau of Corporations includes the year 1906. We do not regard the present conditions, under the present conditions of the industries of the country, as the determining factor in fixing the amount of the tariff.

Mr. GARY. That is right; I think that is right. But we will be glad to give you, Mr. Chairman, the figures for any year, all these years, and also give you the bases, so that you can determine how they are made up.

The CHAIRMAN. Have one of your assistants make up a statement for the year 1906, attach his affidavit to it and send it on, with regard to these matters, and we will go over it.

Mr. BOUTELL. Do you want the calendar year or the fiscal year?

The CHAIRMAN. The calendar year.

Mr. BONYNGE. The figures that you gave this morning were for 1907?

Mr. GARY. Yes.

Mr. BONYNGE. Not the present time, but for 1907?

Mr. GARY. They were 1907; all 1907.

Mr. BONYNGE. But not for the present time?

Mr. GARY. No.

The CHAIRMAN. Everything was higher in the steel business, even, than it is now?

Mr. GARY. Yes.

The CHAIRMAN. Now, Judge, coming down to the making of steel rails, or up to it, how much pig iron does it take to make a ton of rail? What does the iron cost necessary to make a ton of steel rails, including the waste?

Mr. GARY. The manufacturing cost is on that basis which I gave with reference to the pig iron.

The CHAIRMAN. For 1907?

Mr. GARY. 1907; the cost of pig iron and scrap used, exclusive of depreciation, was $15.06 per ton of iron.

The CHAIRMAN. $15.06?

Mr. GARY. Yes.

The CHAIRMAN. And the waste is how much?

Mr. GARY. I can not answer that.

Mr. UNDERWOOD. You have excluded your waste in the cost that you give?

Mr. GARY. Yes; I think so. The waste is in the conversion.

The CHAIRMAN. Will you not repeat that last answer? Mr. Dalzell did not get it, and I did not understand it.

Mr. GARY. The cost of pig iron and scraps, the manufacturing cost of pig iron and scraps used, exclusive of depreciation, was $15.06 per ton of iron. I think you mean to ask me what the cost of the iron is in a ton of rails.

The CHAIRMAN. Yes; the total cost of pig iron in a ton of rails.

Mr. GARY. I have not any such figures, Mr. Chairman; I have made up the cost of rails.

The CHAIRMAN. Then give us the items of the cost as you have made it up.

Mr. DALZELL. The cost of rails made by what process, Bessemer?

Mr. GARY. Bessemer. This is the way our cost of rails is made up, Mr. Chairman: We start with the cost of pig iron and scrap used, exclusive of depreciation, $15.06; the conversion cost, pig iron to ingots, $2.88; ingots to rails, conversion cost, $3.22; depreciation, 84 cents.

The CHAIRMAN. Eighty-four cents?

Mr. GARY. That includes the iron and the steel both, the whole depreciation, you see; I did not include the depreciation in the iron cost.

The CHAIRMAN. The depreciation in this item is 16 cents, but by depreciation of the iron you speak of what is called "waste" here?

Mr. GARY. No; the depreciation covers the plant used in manufacturing both the rails and the iron.

Mr. UNDERWOOD. You mean the amount of iron that is burned up in the process?

Mr. GARY. No; wear and tear.

Mr. COCKRAN. Wear and tear of machinery and plant?

Mr. GARY. Yes; furnaces and converters and mills. Then the administration and taxes, 81 cents.

The CHAIRMAN. What do you make the total?

Mr. GARY. Twenty-two dollars and eighty-one cents.

The CHAIRMAN. The average cost was $22.23 for this factory during that period of which I spoke, including 1907.

Mr. GARY. The basis, of course, is different; it must be.

The CHAIRMAN. I think that you have included the item of taxation, which is not included in this estimate; I can not set it out from any of these items.

Mr. GARY. I think there is a difference, too, in the profit to the mining companies; there must be.

The CHAIRMAN. I suppose the same rule holds good, that your company produces at least $2 a ton cheaper than your competitors?

Mr. GARY. Of course it does hold true that we can manufacture cheaper than our competitors.

The CHAIRMAN. The difference is as much as $2?

Mr. GARY. Yes.

The CHAIRMAN. So that your lower price was included in this table made up by the Bureau of Corporations?

Mr. GARY. Apparently.

The CHAIRMAN. The lowest cost reported of any company for any year was 1905, $19.33; the average cost for 1905 was $21.30. That difference would be $1.97. That would be within 3 cents of your two-dollar business.

Mr. GARY. That must be giving credit to the manufacturer to some things that do not belong to him.

Mr. COCKRAN. What might they be, for instance?

The CHAIRMAN. I am told that the experts were detailed to make these examinations and that they spent more than a year and had a sufficient corps of clerks and had expert steel men to help them in the accounts. But coming to your last answer, will you tell me what you think might be excluded?

Mr. GARY. The profit of the mining companies, for instance.

The CHAIRMAN. You do not think for an instant that your corporation omitted that from your books, do you?

Mr. GARY. No.

The CHAIRMAN. But this was taken from your books, so that it would look as though it were excluded?

Mr. GARY. It might not be made up in the same way, Mr. Chairman.

The CHAIRMAN. The other factories might not have done that.

Mr. GARY. The figures which you give, in my judgment, represent the cost to our corporation; that is, it excludes all these items of cost, and if those are our figures, that is the basis.

Mr. DALZELL. These are the average figures of seven companies.

The CHAIRMAN. What percentage of the steel rails did you produce during the five years from 1902 to 1906, inclusive?

Mr. GARY. I think I have those figures somewhere—about 50 per cent.

The CHAIRMAN. This statement includes seven companies which produced more than 93 per cent, so that in that you would have more than 50 per cent as the average; but while you should only be a dollar under the general average, if your steel costs $2 less a ton, it would seem you would be $2 below.

Mr. GARY. I do not think our rails cost $2 less than the others, from the manufacturers' standpoint, probably.

The CHAIRMAN. It would look as though, from the statement from your books, that it costs a good deal more than $2 less from this comparative statement that is made.

Mr. GARY. I have not seen the figures.

The CHAIRMAN. Have you any objection to the Bureau of Corporations giving over to us what was submitted to them originally as confidential, the results which they obtained?

Mr. GARY. Do you mean for use by this committee?

The CHAIRMAN. I will be perfectly fair with you. I will not undertake to keep the secrets of any such thing from the public. I do not know; there are a good many men who think the public ought to know anything that this committee does, and it is very hard work to keep a secret within the committee. Of course, I refer generally to the enterprising newspaper men. It is a part of their business; I am not complaining of them, but I can not promise you that they will not ever get into print.

Mr. GARY. I will answer that in the negative. We have no objection.

The CHAIRMAN. You have no objection. All right; that is sufficient. We can get that information, then, from the Bureau of Corporations, and after it is printed in the record, if you desire to make any correction in the statement, or any comment upon it, it will be entirely fair that you should do so. Of course you will have an opportunity to do that.

Mr. GARY. I do not know what that may lead to as affecting our business relations with one another, but during the last year we have been pretty frank with one another anyhow, but we have got to stand, and that will be my position; we have to stand on the merits of the proposition, whatever the merits may be, based on actual figures.

The CHAIRMAN. I am in hopes that it will lead the other companies to give up the same information to the committee. I would judge from what Mr. Felton, the president of the Pennsylvania Steel Company, said in his hearing before the committee that possibly he would not be adverse to it. I think perhaps it may open up the whole subject, and the committee want to get all the information they can, Judge, from first hand; that is our object in pursuing these inquiries.

Mr. GARY. Of course the business man can see there is some objection to a manufacturer making public the costs relating to his production, because that not only extends to this country but to every other country, and while we have that with reference to some of the products abroad, we have not got it with reference to a good many, and we are doing business at neutral ports with foreign countries. Still your question is such that I do not see how we can very well answer except to allow it.

The CHAIRMAN. I am obliged to you for the concession, and I want to say to you that I can see how, from your standpoint, your company of all others might well afford to give up the secrets to the committee and give us the information which we desire.

Mr. GARY. I am very certain it will be found on a careful examination of our figures, which any member of the committee is at liberty to make at any time and place he desires, that on the basis which we have determined as right our figures are strictly accurate. If not, it is because of mistake.

The CHAIRMAN. Have you figured on all the products of the steel company—tin plate, and so forth?

Mr. GARY. The leading ones, anyhow.

The CHAIRMAN. Tin plate?

Mr. GARY. Yes, sir.

The CHAIRMAN. And you make cast-iron pipe, do you not?

Mr. GARY. No; we do not. We make steel pipe. We do not make any cast-iron pipe.

The CHAIRMAN. You do make steel pipe?

Mr. GARY. Yes.

The CHAIRMAN. Have you the figures in such shape that you can file them with the committee so that they can examine them, and if later they want further information, we can either ask you or some man familiar with the figures to come over here and give us such information on the figures as we desire?

Mr. GARY. Yes.

The CHAIRMAN. I think, so far as I am concerned, I do not want to ask you any more questions at this time, except one. I have a final inquiry with reference to the royalty on the ore in the bed. As I understand it, you pay 85 cents a ton to the railroad company, and that includes royalty, the whole price that you pay for the ore?

Mr. GARY. Yes; the Great Northern, except, Mr. Chairman, interest is added to that every year at the rate of 4 per cent so as to make it on the basis of paying that in cash now.

The CHAIRMAN. What do I understand, that you do not actually take the ore now?

Mr. GARY. No; it may extend over a very long period of years, a very large quantity of ore.

The CHAIRMAN. You are required to take so much a year?

Mr. GARY. Yes.

The CHAIRMAN. Not less than so much?

Mr. GARY. Yes; or pay the royalty.

The CHAIRMAN. Not less than a specified amount a year?

Mr. GARY. We must take out a minimum or pay on that basis.

The CHAIRMAN. You have to pay for the minimum amount, the royalty each year, and when you do pay, you own it; that is, your own iron ore in the ground?

Mr. GARY. That is right.

The CHAIRMAN. I do not see how the matter of detail of interest comes in very well.

Mr. GARY. It comes in in this way, that if we only had to pay 85 cents per ton when we took it out, if we did not take it out for twenty years it would make very cheap ore.

The CHAIRMAN. If it is made upon the ratio you indicate in your contract, I do not think you are losing much of that 4 per cent interest.

Mr. GARY. That is what we hope.

The CHAIRMAN. It looks a good deal that way to a disinterested outsider.

Mr. GARY. That is right.

The CHAIRMAN. Of course, you are not charging anything for what the lead-ore miners call amortization? You are not charging that on this 85-cent ore, not adding 40 cents for that, are you?

Mr. GARY. No.

The CHAIRMAN. That did not enter into your figures—I thought your assistant was telling you.

Mr. GARY. No, my assistant is suggesting that we are spending large sums of money developing these mines, and of course we have to charge to take care of that.

The CHAIRMAN. Is that 40 cents a ton?

Mr. GARY. Oh, no.

The CHAIRMAN. That is not the amortization charge?

Mr. GARY. No.

The CHAIRMAN. You do charge that on your other ore, ore you did own, as a part of the cost of the ore at the rate of 40 cents a ton?

Mr. GARY. Yes.

The CHAIRMAN. Have you any knowledge of whether that charge goes into the cost of the German or the English ore you have been speaking of?

Mr. GARY. It does, as I understand it.

The CHAIRMAN. At the same rates?

Mr. GARY. I do not know about that; I can not answer.

The CHAIRMAN. That is all.

Mr. CLARK. Do you have any information who imported that word " amortization " into our vocabulary?

Mr. GARY. No.

Mr. CLARK. I would like to find out. To get back to the steel question, how much do you say steel rails cost you?

Mr. GARY. Twenty-two dollars and eighty-one cents, made up in the way I have stated.

Mr. CLARK. Your whole price for American consumers of rails is $28 a ton. That is true, is it not?

Mr. GARY. Yes; that has been the price for the last six or seven years.

Mr. CLARK. Now, is it true that the United States Steel Corporation absolutely fixes the price of steel rails and of other steel products of the United States?

Mr. GARY. Certainly not.

Mr. CLARK. How did it happen that they all got on to this $28 price?

Mr. GARY. The $28 price started, I think in 1899. That was the result of conferences and discussions between the steel makers as to what would be a fair price, and perhaps more or less talk with the railroad companies. Since that time the steel manufacturers have adhered to that price as a fair price. The manufacturers have no regular meetings, have no agreements, and have no way of fixing that price, but I doubt if any one of them would change the price without telling the others he was going to change it. The price has seemed to all concerned to be fair and reasonable, and the adherence to that price, in my judgment, is the result of knowledge and information on the part of all in regard to the business of each. In other words, publicity of each one's business.

Mr. CLARK. Publicity to each other or to all of them?

Mr. GARY. All of them.

Mr. CLARK. To all of us, everybody; do you mean the publicity to the men engaged in manufacturing or do you mean publicity to everybody, the public in general?

Mr. GARY. Publicity in regard to prices, of course, is to everybody.

Mr. CLARK. Certainly.

Mr. GARY. But as to the individual business, to each other and to the railroads. As an illustration, you know there was great agitation concerning the quality of steel rails during the last year or two, and so much had been said by way of criticism in the newspapers and magazines that some of the rail users, some of the railroad presidents, were asking us to improve the conditions, to make a better rail, and they were making some complaints. In fact, some complaints of Mr. Harriman and others were published, whereupon we called a meeting of all the rail manufacturers and the presidents of all the leading railroads. They met in my office, and we there went over the whole subject-matter of the manufacture of rails, the cost of rails, the analysis, the treatment; that is, the process in the mills; and since that time have had frequent conferences with them in regard to these, and as a result have produced a somewhat improved rail; and the cost of some of the railroad companies, who are specifying a special analysis or test, will be larger than the $28, and I think I can not state it any more accurately than to say that the adherence to this price is the result of this knowledge by those interested in the subject in regard to the business.

Mr. CLARK. If you want to; that is, if the United States Steel Corporation wants to fix the price of steel rails in this country at a given figure, have you not such a hold on these independent operators that not a single solitary one of them would dare to mark under your price?

Mr. GARY. I think, as applied to steel rails, that is probably true. That is, I believe if our people should say to the independents, " We are going to make a lower price," I believe the others would follow suit. Mr. Clark, that is a fair and a frank answer, and the reason I say that is that at times, when the demand has been very great, the other manufacturers have frequently said to us that they wanted to increase the price, they could just as well get more, and we have said, " We will not change our price," and as a result they have adhered to theirs. I think it works both ways.

Mr. CLARK. You are all making over $5 a ton on steel rail sold to American railroads?

Mr. GAINES. Would you not insist upon an answer? I do not think Judge Gary did answer your question, which was whether they did not have such a hold on all the other companies producing steel rails that none of them would dare to mark their prices under the price fixed by the steel corporation.

Mr. CLARK. I thought he did answer that.

Mr. GARY. No; I do not think I did answer that question at all. We have no hold whatever upon them, and they would dare do anything they pleased. Of course, that is dealing technically in language, but I suppose you meant to ask me whether or not our influence with the trade was not so great as to give us the power to fix the prices.

Mr. CLARK. I did.

Mr. GARY. I think there is quite a difference. They are under no obligations to us whatever, directly or indirectly.

Mr. CLARK. I understand they are under no obligation to you except the obligation of fear.

Mr. GARY. Of course, if we make 50 per cent of the business and we should reduce our price to $26, or any other amount, they would not expect to get any business at a higher price, at least what they would consider their fair proportion at a higher price, until our mills were filled. That is true of all industries.

Mr. CLARK. Now, you are all making over $5 a ton on steel rails, as I understand it?

Mr. GARY. It is not that.

Mr. CLARK. It is the difference between $22 and something and $28, is it not?

Mr. GARY. While the price is $28, that is reduced by the seconds; that is, if the first-class rails and the seconds fell at a little less the price, say, is $27.50, not to be accurate as to figures, and $22.80; you see, that does not leave $5. That is for the risk of business and the interest on our capital invested.

Mr. CLARK. The reason I asked that question was to lay the foundation for another. Suppose you take it into your heads—that is, the United States Steel Corporation—to mark steel rails up to $30 a ton. These independents and you and the rest are all making over $4. Do you think there is an independent maker of steel rails in the United States who would dare to undertake to keep his product below $30 a ton if you marked yours up to $30?

Mr. GARY. Of course I would have to guess at that answer. I am inclined to think they would mark theirs up if we marked ours up first; I believe so; I may be mistaken.

Mr. CLARK. One other question. I do not want to be impertinent——

Mr. GARY. Not at all; it is proper.

Mr. CLARK. Suppose this case; suppose you did conclude, for any reason, no difference what, to mark yours up to $30, and one of these independent concerns thought it had a good opportunity to make money, and it held its at $28 or marked them down to $27, have you not such a hold on the American market that you could immediately mark yours down to $20 or $25 long enough to put that fellow clear out of business, and then mark yours up again to where you wanted it?

Mr. GARY. Quite likely; that may be true. I will not say that is not true. I will not say that in the competition we could not drive a good many of our competitors out of business.

Mr. CLARK. Now, another thing.

Mr. GARY. It is not because of our hold on the market.

Mr. CLARK. What is it, then?

Mr. GARY. It is because of our ability to produce cheaper, and because of our ownership in the independent concerns, such as the railroads, the steamship lines, and so forth, which gives a large credit from the United States Steel Corporation's standpoint.

Mr. CLARK. That amounts to the same thing in the end, exactly, does it not?

Mr. GARY. Well——

Mr. CLARK. Now, with regard to the first question—that is, that you absolutely dominate the steel market in the United States.

Mr. GARY. Oh, no; that is very much out of the way. During the last year, when business was dull, a great many people, not the majority, but a great many of the smaller producers, have sold at prices less than our prices, less than the prices of the majority, and have taken business that belonged to the others in the sense of being old customers, and so forth. It is the man with the small price who can pretty nearly dictate.

Mr. CLARK. He can dictate if he has money enough.

Mr. GARY. He can dictate so long as he lasts; so long as he keeps within his cost or a little above his cost. Of course, if we were in competition in defense, and that is the only competition I believe in—speaking for myself—that is, destructive competition—if we were in destructive competition in self-defense, of course we would mark down to pretty nearly our cost, and the result would be that the competitor who could not manufacture as low as we could would go out of business in the course of time.

Mr. CLARK. Now, if he was obnoxious enough to you, you could mark down temporarily with perfect impunity below your cost to get rid of him, could you not?

Mr. GARY. No; I do not think we could. I do not think we are as poor business men as that. We might do it in some particular instance or as to some particular commodity for some time, but that is the theory, so far as we are concerned. During the last year we have been tempted to put some prices pretty low to meet certain competition, but of course the effect upon our workmen and the effect upon business conditions generally would have been such, in our opinion—in my opinion, at least—that we lost some business we ought to have had.

Mr. CLARK. You do not want any steel war, of course, if that is what that amounts to?

Mr. GARY. We do not want any war that would affect trade conditions generally, Mr. Clark. I consider that as more important during the last year. I consider the action of the steel people more important to be considered, in connection with general business conditions, than the condition of the steel trade.

Mr. CLARK. When the government statistics show that in 1902 the average price of steel rails was $27.65, and in 1903 $28.07, the little variation is due to these seconds, and so forth, as you call them.

Mr. GARY. Yes; I think so. I think the basis of price was the same for those years.

The CHAIRMAN. That is, the freight; that might be a variation in freight?

Mr. GARY. Yes; that might be.

The CHAIRMAN. That is taken out of the cost of delivery?

Mr. GARY. Yes.

Mr. CLARK. Now, all the large steel products of your mills pay about the same profit as steel rails, such as plates, and all that?

Mr. GARY. Some pay more.

Mr. CLARK. Do any of them pay less?

Mr. GARY. Yes; I think so; certainly at times. The prices of no other commodity have been uniform like steel rails, as I remember.

Mr. CLARK. Your selling price for the United States is $28 a ton. What is your selling price abroad?

Mr. GARY. For 1907, the last figures made up, the price of export rails was, on the average, about 22 cents per ton higher than the domestic price.

Mr. COCKRAN. How much higher?

Mr. GARY. Twenty-two cents per ton.

Mr. COCKRAN. Higher?

Mr. GARY. Yes.

Mr. UNDERWOOD. Is that at the factory?

Mr. GARY. Yes; at the factory.

Mr. CLARK. What was it in 1906; how did it run?

Mr. GARY. In 1906 it was $24.08.

Mr. CLARK. Higher?

Mr. GARY. No; that would be lower, you see—$24.08 at the mill.

Mr. CLARK. That was $3.92?

Mr. GARY. The average of the domestic was $27.52; therefore that would be $3.44 lower on the export.

Mr. CLARK. In 1905?

Mr. GARY. In 1905 there was a still greater difference. The export price was $20.98, or a difference of——

Mr. COCKRAN. Seven dollars and two cents.

Mr. GARY. No; $20.98 deducted from $27.37.

Mr. COCKRAN. That would be $6.39, would it not?

Mr. GARY. I presume so.

Mr. CLARK. In 1904?

Mr. GARY. I have not gone back that far.

Mr. CLARK. Was there generally more difference or less difference, do you think, back for ten years?

Mr. GARY. Ten years?

Mr. CLARK. Beginning in 1897; we have got into the habit of beginning there.

Mr. GARY. I should think fully as much as the figures I gave you.

Mr. CLARK. You sell all of your steel products abroad, as a rule, cheaper than you do at home?

Mr. GARY. Sometimes we do. I think maybe I can give you the figures on the average for 1907.

Mr. CLARK. We would be glad to have them.

Mr. GARY. The average mill price per ton received for exported materials was $7\frac{1}{2}$ per cent less than the average price for domestic shipments.

Mr. CLARK. Now, you sell this stuff that you ship abroad at a profit, do you not?

Mr. GARY. We do; yes; our company, some of the companies we own, have, at times, shipped at less than profit, I think, taking into account depreciation and administration charges, and all that sort of thing. But it is a fact that manufacturers at times export at prices down to or below cost.

Mr. CLARK. Why do they not reduce the price for the domestic consumer so as to use up this surplus?

Mr. GARY. That probably would not be the result.

Mr. CLARK. There would not be any result?

Mr. GARY. I say that probably would not have the result of increasing the domestic sales. As a rule, the consumers supply their demands at the best price they can get.

Mr. CLARK. Certainly.

Mr. GARY. Then, reducing the price would not increase the quantity, and therefore you would have the same surplus.

Mr. CLARK. There might be somebody around who wanted to use steel who was prohibited from using it by the higher price.

Mr. GARY. There might be, but I think that would be exceptional.

Mr. CLARK. A good many railroads in the United States, at one place or another, at places out West that we call jerk-water places, or something of that kind, are still using iron rails, that would be glad to use steel rails if they could get rails at the prices they are able to pay for them.

Mr. GARY. How much are they able to pay?

Mr. CLARK. I do not know. They might be able to pay $20 or $22 or $24, or $25 per ton.

Mr. GARY. I think not.

Mr. CLARK. If they could get them as cheap as these foreigners get them, it would make a good deal of difference.

Mr. GARY. I do not think any railroad company able to pay $22 or $25 for rails has gone without rails because the price was $28.

Mr. CLARK. Of course that is a case where there are only practically a few consumers, but you take the price of steel generally, structural steel and all these other steel products, and do you not think the difference that you have stated there would make a good deal of difference in the amount consumed in the United States?

Mr. GARY. I do not think so, Mr. Clark; of course, I may be mistaken.

Mr. CLARK. I know.

Mr. GARY. I think the question should be approached from the other standpoint, as a matter of opinion; that is, I do not think a manufacturer ought to be allowed, on account of tariff laws or anything else, to charge or receive more than a fair return on the value of his property and the amount of business done. I think that is where you ought to start. Now, if he does not charge more than that price, then he should not be compelled to sell at less than that price, that is, the fair price, and in that case, if he can keep that price down to a fair basis by exporting the surplus, by dumping the surplus, it seems to me that is good business, and works to the benefit of the domestic user, because it reduces the total cost of production on the part of the mill which runs full, keeps the men employed, and as a total result is beneficial. I think it is the same argument that every man in every kind of business uses in disposing of his surplus. So I think this tariff question—I speak to you because of your peculiar position, and I am not making any tariff speech—but I think in some way the manufacturer ought to be restricted to fair dealings with the public on the basis I have suggested, without the introduction of tariff laws or anything else that might be very harmful to some of the industries and to the working people. That is my theory. I am speaking as an individual, Mr. Clark.

Mr. CLARK. Have you any idea how that thing could be accomplished?

Mr. GARY. Personally, yes; I have.

Mr. CLARK. I would like very much to hear it.

Mr. GARY. Now, I am binding myself only.

Mr. CLARK. I understand.

Mr. GARY. Publicity and government control.

Mr. CLARK. What is that?

Mr. GARY. Publicity and government control.

Mr. CLARK. Government control of the railroads and other industries?

Mr. GARY. Yes; government control as distinguished from government management. I am not talking about that; I think that would be a failure. But I believe in thorough publicity on the part of corporations, railroads, and manufacturing concerns, and I believe in the Government having some way of controlling the manufacturer within reasonable bounds. I think this tariff question should be determined at the point where real protection leaves off and opportunity to oppress begins. Our theories must be alike, it seems to me.

Mr. CLARK. Just exactly.

Mr. GARY. Therefore it is only a question of figures.

Mr. CLARK. I agree with you thoroughly in that statement you have made. Now, I want to ask you right on that. You make over $4 a ton on a ton of steel rails that costs $22 a ton?

Mr. GARY. Yes, sir.

Mr. CLARK. In round figures; I am not counting the cents. That is a dividend of 20 to 30 per cent now?

Mr. GARY. No; you have left out the investment; the cost of the investment is very large.

Mr. CLARK. I know, but my understanding has been all the time that you have been talking here to-day on the basis of counting in every item of expense.

Mr. GARY. Not interest on our investment.

Mr. CLARK. Why did you not start out with that as one of your basic facts?

Mr. GARY. We could not get that; we are not getting that, in my judgment, Mr. Clark, on the fair basis of the value of our total investment; we are not getting an adequate return, it seems to me. And I think our figures will show that. I believe we shall do it.

Mr. CLARK. Not getting an adequate return now?

Mr. GARY. No.

Mr. CLARK. Do you know how much profit you are making?

Mr. GARY. On the value of the property?

Mr. CLARK. Yes; the real value of the property.

Mr. GARY. Of course there is involved the question of real value. I would have to give you my opinion, my figures, and, if you please, the reason for my figures.

Mr. CLARK. All right; we would be delighted to hear them.

Mr. GARY. Did you happen to read the article published in the June number of Munsey's Magazine on our corporation?

Mr. CLARK. No; I was too busy doing other things in June and July. [Laughter.]

Mr. COCKRAN. Who is the author?

Mr. GARY. Mr. Munsey.

Mr. COCKRAN. Munsey wrote it himself?

Mr. GARY. Munsey wrote it himself.

Mr. CLARK. What number is it? I will get it myself, unless you put it in the record.

Mr. GARY. I will put it in the record.

Mr. COCKRAN. That is the best way.

Mr. GARY. I am perfectly willing to put it in the record.

The CHAIRMAN. You are sure it is not copyrighted?

Mr. CLARK. If you give him credit for it, he will be glad to have it in the record.

Mr. COCKRAN. It can be put in subject to any copyright.

Mr. GARY. This is the result of an independent examination by Mr. Munsey concerning the values of our properties. He gives the properties in detail, and his valuations, and if anything I would say that it is a little high, but not very much too high, and certainly properties could not be reproduced for anything like that; in fact, it would be impossible to reproduce them at any price, perhaps, some of them.

Mr. COCKRAN. Could you tell us the amount at which he values the property—that is, the whole value?

Mr. GARY. $1,782,187,383.

Mr. COCKRAN. Does he include in that good will of any kind, or is it naked property?

Mr. GARY. No; naked property. He gives the details here, itemized.

Mr. CLARK. Does he state there anywhere how much that property cost you?

Mr. GARY. No; he does not.

Mr. CLARK. He did not know?

Mr. GARY. Of course he did not know. I do not know.

Mr. CLARK. You do not know?

Mr. GARY. I do not know. I know, so far as the mills and railroads and all the physical properties are concerned, what it would cost to reproduce them, of course.

Mr. CLARK. Yes; and what other cost is there, besides the mines?

Mr. GARY. The raw products are a very important item. We have an immense tonnage of raw products to make of the very best kind.

Mr. CLARK. Of course.

Mr. GARY. They could not be reproduced at any price, but they have a value based on the cost to us of some properties in cases where we have had opportunities to buy.

Mr. CLARK. Now, unless Mr. Munsey or Mr. Anybody knew what your properties cost you, simply knowing what the properties are worth now, his conclusions about how much profit you have made since the United States Steel Corporation was affected would have very little value, would they not?

Mr. GARY. I do not know whether I quite understand.

Mr. CLARK. Here is what I say. In order to ascertain fairly how much money the United States Steel Corporation has made, you would want to know three things. In the first place——

Mr. GARY. He does not go into the question of how much we have made. That is only a valuation of our properties; nothing else.

Mr. CLARK. That would be practically worthless, that fact standing out by itself. If you or I or anybody else knew how much the properties cost you, and we knew how much profits you had distributed, in one way or another, and then knew how much your properties were worth, we could come to a rational conclusion as to what you really had made during the life of this United States Steel Corporation.

Mr. GARY. I have all those figures. I can give you all those figures.

Mr. CLARK. I will be very glad to have them.

Mr. GARY. There is no dispute about that.

Mr. CLARK. Well, how much are you making?

Mr. GARY. Coming back to your original inquiry——

Mr. CLARK. Yes.

Mr. GARY. If this represented the value of our properties; assuming that it does for the sake of the question——

Mr. CLARK. Yes.

Mr. GARY. Then I say the profits we have realized from year to year have not been adequate and have not been a fair return on the investment. Now, our ore products, the raw products, perhaps, ore and coal and so forth, did not originally cost anything like their valuation, but they are really worth that at the present time; and in my answer, therefore, I assume that we are entitled to the same return which you would be entitled to if you purchased a piece of real estate to-day for a million dollars and held it five years and were able to sell it for $2,000,000; you would be entitled to the return on the $2,000,000, regardless of what it cost you originally.

Mr. CLARK. I would have made a million dollars, though, in the transaction, and that is what I am trying to get at with you. How much are you making? You say you are not getting an adequate return. How much profit are you making?

Mr. GARY. The increase in value you would charge as a part of the profits?

Mr. CLARK. I undoubtedly would if I were estimating how much you are worth when you organized and how much you are worth now, so as to get at what you have made.

Mr. GARY. But what becomes of a man's risk in investment?

Mr. CLARK. Every man takes a risk.

Mr. GARY. If you buy a piece of property you are entitled to, say, 4 or 5 per cent annually on that property. Now, if it increases in value year by year, it seems to me you are entitled to that increase in value in addition, as against the risk you take in buying that property. It might have gone the other way.

Mr. CLARK. Why, certainly; that is all true.

Mr. GARY. That is all I am saying.

Mr. CLARK. But coming back to your own proposition; now, that I thoroughly agree with you about, that if it was possible—and I hope somebody will have ingenuity enough to work it out—to restrain people from making undue profits, then you have got to count in what you make.

Mr. GARY. That is, increases in value?

Mr. CLARK. Why, certainly. Suppose a case, now. Suppose a corporation organizes with a million dollars capital, and that it takes $500,000 of its profits and invests them in outside property which increases in value; then, is it not fair to count the increase of that property in with your total profits?

Mr. GARY. If it is property outside of your business, and you have realized on it, perhaps—well, I would say no, in answering the question; I do not think that would be a part of your manufacturing profit at all. The profit you would get I think is the return for the risk of your investment, which risk every man takes.

Mr. CLARK. Take your own case. You get hold of these lands up there from the Great Northern at practically a royalty of 85 cents. Suppose circumstances worked out so that the iron you pay 85 cents for in the ground turns out to be worth $10—I do not suppose it will, but suppose it might?

Mr. GARY. Yes.

Mr. CLARK. Do you not think that the difference between $10 and 85 cents ought to be counted in in the profits you are making?

Mr. GARY. Manufacturing profits?

Mr. CLARK. Yes; the profits of the United States Steel Corporation.

Mr. GARY. Certainly not; certainly not.

Mr. CLARK. Of course I would charge against the corporation a loss if it made a poor investment. I think that is what ought to be.

Now, is not this possible, under your theory, then, that a corporation that starts in with a million dollars might reinvest its profits on the side and get to be worth a billion, and still declare small dividends to the stockholders all the time?

Mr. GARY. Certainly; certainly. If the corporation acts within the domain of its power, and acts fairly and openly with its stockholders and takes the risk of making an investment, I think it is entitled to the benefit of that, if there is a benefit, independently of its manufacturing profit. I think it is exactly the same as your investment in real estate. If you buy a piece of ground in the city and put a building on that ground that costs you a million dollars, you are entitled to 4 per cent return on that, annually, on your investment; and if values of property in that neighborhood increase from year to year, and as a consequence new investments like that bring a higher yield, a larger percentage, you are entitled to a rental which will pay 4 per cent on the actual value of your property, or on the amount which you could realize if you sold. Otherwise, it seems to me, it would be a good idea for you to sell it and invest in something else, if you have got to the point where the increase has ceased.

Mr. CLARK. That is what I would do, if I could.

Mr. GARY. Certainly. That is outside of manufacturing returns, it seems to me.

Mr. CLARK. Now, can you tell how much profit you are making?

Mr. GARY. You mean in what way?

Mr. CLARK. I mean this United States Steel Corporation. I do not care a straw how it makes it—that is, for the purposes of this inquiry.

Mr. GARY. I do not figure increases in value.

Mr. CLARK. Will you please state how much you are making, without figuring the increases in value?

Mr. GARY. Yes; I can give you those figures, and I can tell you how much this valuation is that is given, in the manner I have stated, over and above the estimate we put of the value, the value we estimated these properties to have at the time the United States Steel Corporation was organized.

Mr. CLARK. Very well.

Mr. GARY. I can give you that. That is represented by its capital stock and bonds.

Mr. CLARK. Well, how much is it?

Mr. GARY. I think these figures will cover it. Since we were organized, in the beginning of 1901, we have paid out in interest; that is, from our earnings we have paid out in interest $180.711,000. We have paid out in dividends $262,354,600. We have carried to surplus $97,645,000, and we have paid out for construction $163,694,000. That has returned to our properties through expenditures for extensions and improvements of 1.7 per cent on our capitalization annually, and on account of interest on debt and dividends 4.6 per cent, and added to surplus 1 per cent, making a total on our capitalization per annum of 7.3 per cent.

Mr. COCKRAN. On your total capitalization?

Mr. GARY. Yes.

Mr. CLARK. That accounts for all you have got. When you started this capitalization were you connected with the corporation yourself?

Mr. GARY. Yes; that is, I assisted in the organization. I was connected with the organization of the United States Steel Corporation, and before that I was president of the Federal Steel Company.

Mr. CLARK. These properties that were put in to make up the United States Steel Corporation, were they put in at a fictitious value, or were they put in at the real value?

Mr. GARY. They were put in at what we believed was the real value.

Mr. CLARK. How much is it capitalized for?

Mr. GARY. The preferred stock is $360,281,100, par value. The common stock is $508,302.500. That is the capital stock.

Mr. CLARK. How much dividend is guaranteed on the preferred stock?

Mr. GARY. No dividends are guaranteed, but the stock is 7 per cent cumulative; that is, the 7 per cent must be paid before anything is paid on the common stock, annually.

Mr. CLARK. Did not the preferred stock represent really the valuation of that property?

Mr. GARY. No; it did not.

Mr. CLARK. Is the common stock paying anything?

Mr. GARY. It is paying 2 per cent.

Mr. CLARK. As a matter of fact, did not the preferred stock represent the value of the property and the common stock represent what in popular parlance is called " water? "

Mr. GARY. No; it did not.

Mr. CLARK. And you have only made 3½ per cent?

Mr. GARY. What?

Mr. CLARK. You have only made 3½ per cent profit?

Mr. GARY. Oh, no. No; we have earned on all the capital, including bonds, 7.3 per cent.

Mr. CLARK. I know; that is the preferred.

Mr. GARY. I mean we have earned that on all the capital stock and bonds. We have paid 7 per cent on the preferred. We paid 4 per cent on the common stock for three years and then suspended for two years, and since then for two years have paid 2 per cent.

Mr. UNDERWOOD. What interest are you paying on your bonds?

Mr. GARY. The bonds of the United States Steel Corporation are $480,199,000, and the rate of interest is 5 per cent.

Mr. COCKRAN. Will you include both classes of bonds?

Mr. GARY. Yes. The capitalization would be $480,199,000 of bonds of all classes, $360,381,100 of preferred stock, and $508,302,500 of common stock.

Mr. COCKRAN. I see.

Mr. GARY. And then the subsidiary companies have bonded indebtedness.

Mr. COCKRAN. How much would there be of the subsidiary bonded indebtedness?

Mr. GARY. $125,346,000.

Mr. COCKRAN. That is $1,475,000,000?

Mr. GARY. $1,474,028,000.

Mr. COCKRAN. Practically a billion and a half?

Mr. GARY. Yes.

Mr. CLARK. Do these subsidiary corporations make more profit than the parent corporation?

Mr. GARY. The parent corporation is not an operating corporation at all. It gets its income from dividends declared by the subsidiary company, except it gets interest on money loaned and things of that sort.

Mr. CLARK. Suppose you were to subtract from this estimate of Munsey's—if that estimate of Munsey's is anywhere near right—the real value of your property when you put it in, and then were to convert the difference, whatever it is, into profits and distribute it, how much do you suppose that would increase this 3 per cent and an odd fraction of a per cent profit?

Mr. GARY. What do you mean by 3 per cent?

Mr. CLARK. I may have been mistaken, but I understood you to say that you were making a little over 3 per cent profit.

Mr. GARY. No; it is 7.3 per cent annually.

Mr. CLARK. Seven and three-tenths per cent?

Mr. GARY. Seven and three-tenths per cent annually.

Mr. CLARK. Suppose that to the 7.3 per cent you were to add whatever the difference was between your property when you acquired it and what Munsey estimates it at—if Munsey is anywhere near correct—that is, convert that into a per cent and add it to the 7.3 per cent, where would you come out?

Mr. GARY. I have not any figures on that. Of course figures speak for themselves.

Mr. CLARK. Yes.

Mr. GARY. As a matter of fact, we have put large sums of money into new properties, some of which have increased in value over and above the values of our properties when we took them over, and the other portion of which has been necessary to take care of old properties which have become obsolete. Of course that is the trouble with manufacturing business. We have abandoned, dismantled, scrapped a great deal of property. Manufacturing property wears out very rapidly. And then the methods change. We are now, as you know, going into the open-hearth process very largely. We are obliged to do it for certain reasons; first, because the demands of trade require it, it being supposed that for some things, at least, the open-hearth steel is better, and for another reason, and more particularly, because of the changes in the quality of our ores, which are becoming poorer from year to year, lower in iron and, perhaps, higher in phosphorus. We are making over our properties, so to speak, and abandoning the Bessemer process and increasing the open-hearth process, in order to keep parallel with the changed and changing conditions of the iron ores, so that when we take the ore out of the mine from time to time, instead of separating it at large cost and setting the Bessemer ore aside and abandoning the poorer ore for the present, we can use it all as it comes out. Now, that involves very large expenditures, and therefore a great deal of this money has been made necessary.

Mr. CLARK. The money that is put in you have first taken out, have you not? You do not borrow it? The moneys you put into these new properties were not made out of an original investment?

Mr. GARY. Yes, that is true; but are counted as profit in my figures to you. That is included in the 7.3 per cent.

Mr. CLARK. Has it been the general experience that a mine gradually peters out the deeper you get, in quality? Of course that is a common colloquial expression, but a very expressive one.

Mr. GARY. It depends upon the range and the location of the ore. Some is irregular and some is in pockets; but it is not entirely uniform. You take a large mine; suppose, for instance, we uncover, as we have done in places, a great many acres, stripping the earth, as we call it, from the ore, so that we can shovel the ore from the mine to the car. Now, we have exposed a very large area of iron ore. That is, perhaps, more or less in streaks.

Mr. CLARK. Yes; of course it is.

Mr. GARY. Under our old practice, when the ore was cheap and seemed to be plentiful, it seemed the most reasonable thing for the miner and manufacturer to do was to select the best and leave the other, and in that way we could get all the Bessemer ore we needed. But as the business of the country has grown, there has not been enough of that, and we have been obliged to use the other, and a great deal of that other can be utilized only by taking very great pains. We want to use it up.

Mr. CLARK. If you were to run across a deposit equal to the Iron Mountain you would get right at this business now.

Mr. GARY. There are no more of those. We have searched pretty thoroughly.

Mr. CLARK. I know; you never did find anything like it.

Mr. GARY. No.

Mr. CLARK. I understood you to say, and I know that Mr. Schwab said—of course I am not trying to play one against the other—that the railroads did not object to paying this price of $28 a ton.

Mr. GARY. That is true of him, or it is probably true of him, because he sells his rails to the railroad companies whose tracks go by his mills, and who get large sums of money from him in the way of freight.

Mr. CLARK. What would the railroads out in that part of the country say to that proposition, do you suppose, in Missouri? Do they really want to pay $28 a ton?

Mr. GARY. This is what they would say: "If $28 is a fair price, taking everything into account, we will pay it, and, if not, we will do better if we can."

Mr. CLARK. But they can not.

Mr. GARY. They can if they can satisfy us that $28 is too much on them. They can, as far as our company is concerned.

Mr. CLARK. It would take a good deal of argumentation to do that, would it not?

Mr. GARY. Well, yes. Of course, I have expressed my opinion.

Mr. CLARK. Yes.

Mr. GARY. And I believe, taking our investments into account, the risks of the business, and so forth, that is a fair price; but I think it is enough, and we have stood against any increase in it at times when we could just as well have gotten a higher price, as you know, probably.

Mr. CLARK. I take it for granted, now, to tell you the truth, that you can get what you want.

Mr. GARY. Well——

Mr. CLARK. But the secret of the railroads not objecting to this price of $28 a ton is that they simply shove that $28 a ton off onto the shoulders of the people who patronize the railroads. Is not that true?

Mr. GARY. Oh, no; no.

Mr. CLARK. They have recouped on us? That is a practical proposition.

Mr. GARY. No. Do you think the railroads are charging the passengers too high rates?

Mr. CLARK. I do; and I think the Pullman Palace Car Company is charging them twice as much as they ought to. I never had a pass on a Pullman car in my life, and I pay for what I get, and I think that the railroads would be better off universally if they charged 2 cents a mile instead of charging 3 and holding the rates up.

Mr. GARY. I do not think so, but you may be right.

Mr. CLARK. You may be, too, now. Suppose this committee-and Congress were to cut down the rate on steel one-half, would it affect your business a particle?

Mr. GARY. The United States Steel Corporation?

Mr. CLARK. Yes, sir.

Mr. GARY. I can not answer that. I do not know.

Mr. CLARK. You do not want to volunteer or, rather, I will say, venture, an opinion here?

Mr. GARY. Intentionally I would not want to say anything that would hurt any of our competitors who are entitled to be in business. I think, Mr. Clark, that the manufacturer of this country who is justified in continuing in business should be protected against the foreign manufacturer who can manufacture at a less cost. I think that is only fair. I think that is for the best interests of this country, and I think that condition, and that condition only, is what has made the prosperity of this country. If that condition should be changed I think you would be back to the times and conditions when the laboring man's wages were very materially reduced, when strikes all over the country were in existence; and I believe that Germany and some of the other foreign countries which are thoroughly protected, and will be thoroughly protected, will get a decided advantage. That is my opinion, so far as that question is concerned.

Mr. RANDELL. What is the time you are referring to?

Mr. GARY. The period following the passage of the " Wilson bill," so called.

Mr. CLARK. They had the worst strike that ever was had under the McKinley bill, did they not?

Mr. GARY. When was that?

Mr. CLARK. The Homestead riots, when Pinkerton had his army down there and they killed people. It was in the summer of 1892.

Mr. RANDELL. My purpose in asking the question was to get the actual time.

Mr. GARY. They had a pretty bad strike there. I remember that; but I am not familiar with it, and can not answer your question. I speak of general conditions. I think there is no doubt about wages being very much lower and therefore strikes much more frequent during the period when the Wilson bill was in force. The wages for common labor at South Chicago during that period were about 90 cents per day, as I remember it, and at the present time they are $1.60 per day.

Mr. CLARK. I will ask you another question. Do you not think that the facilities which American citizens have had for going out and getting hold of a piece of land and being independent, taken in connection with the labor unions, has had a great deal more to do with putting up the price of labor in the United States than all the tariffs that have been passed since the flood?

Mr. GARY. I do not think so. I think to the contrary. We have, as a rule, no union labor, as you perhaps know. We are at peace with our men generally. Large numbers of them are holders of our shares. They are prosperous and contented, as a rule. When the panic occurred a year ago, and the question of reducing wages came up, when it seemed to a great many to be inevitable, following the precedents of the past, that wages should be reduced, we stood out pretty strongly against any reduction, and said we would not consent to it unless we were driven to it.

Mr. CLARK. I think you are to be congratulated on that. But you have not answered my question, and that is whether if this tariff were cut in two you would not still be able to bar these foreigners out and control the American steel market, or, rather, dominate it? I would rather use the word " dominate " than the word " control."

Mr. GARY. I tried to answer that by saying there might be one answer as applied to the United States Steel Corporation——

Mr. CLARK. That is the one I want.

Mr. GARY. And another as applied to outsiders. If there should be such a horizontal cut as that, I think it would certainly be very damaging.

Mr. CLARK. How would it strike you?

Mr. GARY. The United States Steel Corporation is pretty strong and could stand reduction, I have no doubt, and still prosper.

Mr. CLARK. It is really stronger than the Federal Government, is it not?

Mr. GARY. No; we are so weak in comparison with it that, so far as I am concerned at least, I would not do anything disapproved by the Federal Government.

Mr. CLARK. You are in better financial fix than the Federal Government. You have no deficiencies in your revenues, have you?

Mr. GARY. No.

Mr. CLARK. And the Government, as I understand it, is running behind about $10,000,000 a month.

Mr. GARY. It has been more extravagant in its expenditures, made necessary by a great many political exigencies not necessary for me to refer to.

Mr. CLARK. I wish you would refer to them.

The CHAIRMAN. Especially the Spanish-American war, of which my friend was one of the chief promoters.

Mr. CLARK. And that is one of the things I am willing to answer for until the day of judgment.

Mr. GARY. There are times and circumstances when the Federal Government should not hesitate to expend money, even if it has to borrow it. All patriots believe that.

Mr. CLARK. Suppose that Congress should wipe out these duties entirely, the United States Steel Corporation would still survive, would it not?

Mr. GARY. I do not know that I would like to answer that question. In the first place I do not know, and therefore can not answer it with certainty; but I have an impression that if we did we would have a monopoly of the business in this country.

Mr. COCKRAN. That is about what you have now.

Mr. GARY. No, sir; far from it. If you should hear some of these people talk, you would not think so.

Mr. CLARK. What I want to get at is this: Whether the United States Steel Corporation, through natural advantages and acquired properties is not in a condition to dominate the American steel market against the world, tariff or no tariff?

Mr. GARY. No, Mr. Clark; I do not think it is. That is, I do not think we could make any fair or reasonable profit on our investment, or on the value of our property, on such a basis.

Mr. CLARK. Suppose we take the tariff off from ores and pig iron.

Mr. GARY. You should not ask me that question. We are not interested particularly in them, it seems to me. I think you should call on men who are interested in that question, and who are better capable of speaking about it than I am. I submit that you should not ask me any question that could be interpreted to have the effect of injuring any of our competitors, even if it does not injure us at the same time.

Mr. CLARK. But when we had your competitors here we had to operate on them with a corkscrew because they seemed to be so afraid of giving any information which might injure you. To tell you the truth about it, Mr. Schwab and yourself are the two men who have come before this committee who have been willing to answer the questions that were asked them.

Mr. GARY. It was not because they feared to injure us.

Mr. CLARK. But because they were afraid you would injure them?

Mr. GARY. No; it was because they were afraid of injuring themselves, perhaps. I do not know about that. I am not familiar with their testimony; but there is no doubt that many of the independents labor under a disadvantage.

Mr. CLARK. Certainly they do.

Mr. GARY. Is not this merely a question of figures, if you can ascertain accurately what the figures are? I will start out with the proposition on which the questioner and the witness agree, as I understand it; that is, that protection means protection, and does not mean any more than what is necessary for protection. It does not mean the fostering of any particular industries to enable them to get an unreasonable price. Is not the whole question, after all, determined by figures?

Mr. CLARK. Certainly it is.

Mr. GARY. That is, when you find out the cost abroad, the cost here, the facilities for supplying the markets, taking into consideration the disposition of the foreigners to protect their own countries thoroughly, so as to keep us out of there, and the disposition to dump their surplus here, is it not a mere question of figures? Germany is exporting four or five million tons annually at the present time. She has a big surplus. You know the disposition of Germany, for instance, to sell abroad at prices very much less than she sells at home. If our costs are such that she can sell in this country at less than the producing cost here—that is, if she will sell at such a cost—does not that determine whether the industry here needs protection? I would like to give you one or two figures with reference to one or two items merely by way of illustration. During the last four years a substantial tonnage of rails has been sold at different times on the western coast of this country at $31.50, or about that, duty paid, and on the Gulf of Mexico at $30.50, or about that. Now, the freight rate from our nearest mill to the western coast is $15 a ton, and to the Gulf of Mexico and New Orleans about $7 a ton. To meet those sales our people must sell at less than cost and at considerably less than cost. That applies more or less to some other commodities, depending upon the state of trade abroad.

Mr. CLARK. I can not understand, to save my life, why, if you can ship this stuff to Europe, Asia, Africa, and the islands of the seas and sell in open competition with all mankind in a free-trade market, you could not hold this market, tariff or no tariff, against all comers.

Mr. GARY. Does it follow that because a grocer sells his brown sugar below cost, or because a dry goods man in the spring cleans his counters at less than cost, that he ought to sell his whole product at the same price?

Mr. CLARK. No.

Mr. GARY. It is the same thing. This is the surplus.

Mr. CLARK. No; it is not the same thing. These people are handling perishable stuff, and they get rid of it and have got to get rid of it.

Mr. RANDELL. They sell it to their home people.

Mr. CLARK. Yes; they sell it to their home people. I want to state for myself that I do not believe there is a single man on this committee or in the House of Representatives or in the United States Senate who has the slightest desire to injure any American industry.

Mr. GARY. I believe that.

Mr. CLARK. I know that is my feeling about it, and I think I reflect the feelings of my fellows.

Mr. GARY. I believe that is right. I sincerely believe it.

Mr. CLARK. This committee has to revise this tariff, and wants to work out the exorbitant features of it. I want to get it down to a revenue basis, and if I could discover the revenue basis for steel, I would vote for it; but I know, as every man who has any common sense knows, that whenever he votes for a given revenue tariff, whether he wants it to work out that way or not, pro tanto it is a protective tariff.

Mr. GAINES. You have told us about the difference between the domestic price and——

Mr. GARY. May I interrupt you one moment, because a thought is in my mind, and I desire to give one fact in regard to a commodity which is important and in line with this other inquiry. It relates to tin plate and sheets. At the present time they are produced in Wales and England at about $5.32, less than the cost to us, and that represents the difference in wages paid to the men, the labor element being large as to those commodities. So that if we should make our costs as low as their costs, we could only do it by cutting the wages of our men about these mills in half—that is, making them one-half as large as they are at the present time.   I think I am perfectly accurate in those figures.   I mean to be.

Mr. COCKRAN. You do not think you could cut the wages of your labor in half?   You would get no men to work for you at all, would you?

Mr. GARY. No; if it applied to only one commodity.

Mr. COCKRAN. That is what I am speaking of.

Mr. GARY. No; I do not think so.   They would work for some one else.

Mr. COCKRAN. You have to keep the wages up to get them to work at all?

Mr. GARY. We would go out of that business then, perhaps.

Mr. GAINES. You have told us about the difference between the domestic price of steel rails and the export price of steel rails in this country for the years 1907, 1906, and 1905.   Can you tell the difference between the export and domestic price in other countries for the same years?

Mr. GARY. I can for the present time.   I have not got it for other years.

Mr. GAINES. I would like to have it for the present, and then, if you will be kind enough to furnish it, I would like to have you send the figures for the other years.

Mr. GARY. On German rails the domestic price is $29.02 and the export price is $22.20.   In Great Britain the domestic price is $27.98 and the export price $23.61.   In France the domestic price is $33.33 and the export price $25.69.   In Belgium the domestic price is $27.45 and the export price $22.50.

Mr. GAINES. When you furnish the figures for the other years, I would be glad if they extended back for a period of ten years, if possible.

Mr. GARY. It would be very difficult to get it as to the foreign prices.   I will give it as far as I can get it; but it has been very difficult to get that information.   That which I have has been obtained with difficulty.

Mr. GAINES. In connection with that, may I ask you whether it is true that the German Government, through the ownership of railroads, aids its manufacturers in the matter of exporting more cheaply to other countries than they sell at home?

Mr. GARY. It does, very much.

Mr. GAINES. Have you any facts or any foreign publications which would throw light on the question of foreign governments favoring the practice of selling abroad cheaper than they do at home?

Mr. GARY. I am not certain whether I can get anything or not; but I will try to do so.

Mr. GAINES. It has seemed to me rather remarkable, in view of the extent to which we are told foreign manufacturers do ship out of their own country and sell cheaper than they sell at home, that we seem not to have access to any foreign government publications which bring out the fact just as a similar practice in this country is being brought out now.

The CHAIRMAN. Have you asked him to give the costs abroad?

Mr. GAINES. No.

The CHAIRMAN. He may have some figures as to the cost of rails abroad.

Mr. GARY. I did give the cost of iron and cost of conversion; and the percentages just about keep up.

Mr. GAINES. I understood that you were to furnish these matters of cost with reference to the several stages of manufacture.

Mr. GARY. I want to say to you what you probably already know, that it is quite difficult to get any information abroad in regard to these matters. I believe some of the government officials have been trying to get information relating to costs during the last year, and have not succeeded very well; but I may be mistaken. If the Government has succeeded, of course we would all be delighted. We would like very much to know in detail about their costs. We do know by experience, in meeting them in competition at various times and places, that the German Government does a great deal to assist its own manufacturers in every way. It encourages all sorts of combinations, syndicates, etc., as they are called.

Mr. DALZELL. Does the German Government pay a bounty to the steel industry?

Mr. GARY. It does not at the present time, except in the way of low freights.

Mr. DALZELL. Bounties are paid to the steel industry in Canada?

Mr. GARY. Yes.

Mr. DALZELL. Do you know what those bounties are?

Mr. GARY. I have not the figures before me. There is one thing which I think is important for tariff makers. You know Canada has a countervailing tax, or a dumping tax, which is really a great thing. If Germany, for instance, is proposing to dump its products in this country at any time because business is dull, there ought to be such a tax as would prevent them selling here more than 5 per cent below the price they get in their own country. In that case, you see, you would protect this country against dumping.

Mr. CRUMPACKER. Then you would not need so high a rate of duty.

Mr. GARY. No; in that case you would not.

Mr. UNDERWOOD. Do you not think that, under the trade conditions of the world, it is advisable for us to write a minimum and maximum tariff by which we can force concessions from other countries?

Mr. GARY. Amongst manufacturers there is some difference of opinion about that, but personally I would favor it. I may not be well enough posted to be competent to speak on the subject, but I have thought favorably on that subject. Some people think we would be in trouble all the time; that it would be so indefinite and so subject to changes in the conduct of business that it would make it impracticable. You gentlemen can answer that question very much better than I can, because you have studied it and you are experts, while I am not. My opinion, however, is favorable to a maximum and a minimum tariff.

Mr. COCKRAN. With relation to the profits of your company, concerning which Mr. Clark questioned you, let me call your attention to what Mr. Schwab said in an answer to me during the giving of his testimony. I was inquiring into the original capital of the Carnegie Company, which, as you know, is one of the chief elements in your combination.

Mr. GARY. Yes.

Mr. COCKRAN. I asked him how much money was put into the Carnegie Company, and he said: " I can not give you those figures offhand. I will tell you why I can not. I do not know that any of us know. The Carnegie Company was a partnership; it was not a stock company."

Then I broke in on him, and he continued: "And when you ask how much real money was put in the Carnegie Company I can only say that the earnings of the company were put in; none of us had any money to put in."

Then the report reads as follows:

Mr. COCKRAN. That is it, then; now we have got it.
Mr. SCHWAB. We developed the company.
Mr. COCKRAN. So that whatever capital, whatever property was owned by this company was the result of profits paid in the company.
Mr. SCHWAB. Profit and increase in the value of property.

Now, is that true of all the property taken over by your company?

Mr. GARY. Certainly not; and I do not think it is true as to that company. I think it is a mistake to say so.

Mr. COCKRAN. We will come to that in a minute. So far as these stupendous figures of $1,782,187,383 are concerned, are you in a position to inform this committee how much of that represents capitalized profits as distinguished from the original investment of capital?

Mr. GARY. No; I can not. When the United States Steel Corporation was formed, the original board took testimony in relation to the values of all the property taken over, and those valuations were made up in various ways—upon the possibility or probability of earnings, the cost of reproducing the mills, furnaces, and other properties which would have the capacities and facilities those companies had, the values of the raw products based on what they were being sold at, and so forth.

Mr. COCKRAN. Of this whole sum of $1,782,000,000, was not $1,000,-000,000, at least, capitalized profits as distinguished from original investment?

Mr. GARY. I should have to guess at that; but I should guess yes, including increases in value.

Mr. COCKRAN. So that when you speak of the profits which this industry has yielded, you do not mean to be understood as confining your statement of profits to what have been entered or actually distributed as earnings, but it should also include this vast sum which has been added to the capital?

Mr. GARY. I have done that. I have included that, as I have given you the figures.

Mr. COCKRAN. What I want to call your attention to is this, that when you are speaking of profits the impression naturally made would be that it meant a profit on investment. What I want to ascertain, if I can, is the amount of cash investment and the amount of accumulated profits that have entered into the capitalization.

Mr. GARY. In considering the value of the United States Steel properties, I start out with the assumption that those properties are of a certain value. In determining the profits since the company was organized I take the amount paid as interest on bonds, the amount paid as dividends on stock and the amount expended for new property, and the amount carried forward to surplus. .

Mr. COCKRAN. That company itself was a combination of several other companies?

Mr. GARY. That company acquired, by purchase, properties belonging to these other corporations at a certain price, namely, the amount of their bonds and stocks.

Mr. COCKRAN. And those companies which it purchased were themselves consolidations of several other companies, were they not?

Mr. GARY. Some of them were, at least.

Mr. COCKRAN. The Federal Steel Company was?

Mr. GARY. Yes.

Mr. COCKRAN. The American Bridge Company was?

Mr. GARY. Yes.

Mr. COCKRAN. And the Steel and Wire Company?

Mr. GARY. Yes.

Mr. COCKRAN. And the American Tube Company?

Mr. GARY. The National Tube Company; yes.

Mr. COCKRAN. And the Tin Plate Company was?

Mr. GARY. Yes; the Tin Plate Company was.

Mr. COCKRAN. Let us take up one of them—the Federal Steel Company. You assisted in the organization of that, did you not?

Mr. GARY. Yes.

Mr. COCKRAN. What companies were combined in that, if you remember?

Mr. GARY. The Illinois Steel Company was one.

Mr. COCKRAN. Do you remember what the capitalization of that company was?

Mr. GARY. No; I do not remember now. I have forgotten. It seems to me the stock and bonds were about $32,000,000.

Mr. COCKRAN. What other companies do you remember that were combined into that company?

Mr. GARY. The Lorain Steel Company.

Mr. COCKRAN. Do you remember what that was capitalized for?

Mr. GARY. No; I do not. I think it was $10,600,000.

Mr. COCKRAN. Were there any other companies in it?

Mr. GARY. Yes; the Minnesota Iron Company.

Mr. COCKRAN. How much was that capitalized for?

Mr. GARY. I don't remember that.

Mr. COCKRAN. At about how much were the constituent companies which were taken into the Federal Steel Company capitalized?

Mr. GARY. I should think the capital stock and bonds of those companies exceeded considerably the amount of stock issued by the Federal Steel Company, which was about $100,000,000.

Mr. COCKRAN. Then the capitalization of the Federal Steel Company was a reduction of the total capital?

Mr. GARY. Yes; I think it was. Its capital stock was $200,000,000, but we only issued about $100,000,000. . I would be glad to give those figures. I may be mistaken, but I believe I am right.

Mr. COCKRAN. If what you say is correct, and of course it is because you speak from knowledge, it tends to explode a very general idea that the formation of each of those companies was accompanied by a large inflation of stock, and that then the inflated stock of these various organizations was brought together in the United States Steel Company and still further increased.

Mr. GARY. You call it inflation.

Mr. Cockran. I will call it increase, so as not to use any adjective in regard to it.

Mr. Gary. All large corporations are issuing additional stock all the time for improvements and extensions.

Mr. Cockran. I will come to that.

Mr. Gary. I understand your point. I think you are right as to that company.

Mr. Cockran. You will give us the information as to just what that amounts to?

Mr. Gary. Certainly.

Mr. Cockran. When you finally came to form the United States Steel Company I understand that you capitalized it at $1,475,000,000, and that there is, according to your figures now, a profit already of about $307,000,000—that is to say, its property has increased in value from $1,475,000,000 to $1,782,000,000, and that increase, as I understand you, represents the investment of earnings in new buildings, in the expansion of your plant, and the increase in the value of your ore properties and real estate.

Mr. Gary. Yes.

Mr. Cockran. Assuming that valuation to be a fair and reasonable one, the amount over and above your original capitalization is represented by increase in value and additional cash put into the property out of the earnings, amounting to $166,000,000?

Mr. Gary. I gave the figures.

Mr. Cockran. You put it at $163,694,000 in new buildings and $97,000,000 in surplus.

Mr. Gary. Yes.

Mr. Cockran. The balance of the increase is the increased value of the property?

Mr. Gary. Yes.

Mr. Cockran. And not due to anything that you have done, but to the general increase in values all around.

Mr. Gary. It is not hardly fair to us to say it is not due to anything we have done.

Mr. Cockran. I say it so as to accept your own view in the most liberal sense, because I am willing to concede that if you have a building here in Washington and are doing business in it and the value of that building doubles, just as it would have doubled if you were not in the steel business at all, such an increase is not properly chargeable to the profits of the steel business. That is your position, and I agree with you. But the money you put back into new enterprises are undoubtedly profits of the steel business. That is what I want to separate and distinguish from the increase in values.

Mr. Gary. I separated them in my figures—that is, I included one and excluded the other.

Mr. Cockran. I agree with your classification of it. I understood you to say, in answer to Mr. Clark, that you are able to face any competition that may possibly arise in this country so far as you are concerned, but if the tariff on steel be abolished that you are apprehensive of the effect upon your competitors.

Mr. Gary. I have not said that, Mr. Cockran. I have not answered that question. I do not know, and I prefer not to answer it.

Mr. Cockran. Just conceive for a moment the position of the committee and your position. We are here discussing the amount of protection—that is to say, of tax that ought to be levied on the community for the protection of this industry—and if the chief factor in that industry is not able to say how much is necessary, it would be difficult for us to decide that it is necessary at all, for surely you would not have us impose a tax on mere suspicion.

Mr. GARY. As a fair-minded citizen I would have you impose a tax which would protect our competitors, even if we did not need it.

Mr. COCKRAN. I have no doubt whatever about your sensitiveness and concern for your competitors. I am not addressing my question to your sensitiveness, but to your knowledge and to your business. I want to know whether your steel company would continue to do business without any protection, merely and entirely as a matter of business.

Mr. GARY. Of course I can not say certainly.

Mr. COCKRAN. You would not say you could not?

Mr. GARY. No; I would not.

Mr. COCKRAN. Therefore, so far as you are concerned, you are not prepared to state on your own responsibility as a citizen and under your oath as a witness that any protection whatever is necessary.

Mr. GARY. For the United States Steel Corporation?

Mr. COCKRAN. Yes; so far as the United States Steel Corporation is concerned.

Mr. GARY. No.

Mr. COCKRAN. Now, that is clear. There is just one thing more I want to question you about.

Mr. GARY. Of course I would have to go through the list carefully, Mr. Cockran, before I could answer your question accurately. That might be true of some commodities and not true as to others; that is, it might drive us out of business so far as some commodities are concerned.

Mr. COCKRAN. You are not prepared to name one now?

Mr. GARY. No; the only way that could be determined is to look up the figures of cost.

Mr. COCKRAN. About that, unfortunately, there is a great deal of doubt, because the figures given here in the government returns seem to be so much at variance with the expert figures.

Mr. GARY. This occurs to me: I do not see how we could survive in the sheet and tin-plate business if the tariff is removed. I think we would be driven out of that business.

Mr. COCKRAN. As to that, what tariff is essential to keep you afloat in that business? Do you need the present rate, or would one-half of that rate be sufficient?

Mr. GARY. What is the present rate?

Mr. DALZELL. The tariff is 1.5 cents a pound, which would be equal to 1.2 cents a pound under the Wilson bill.

Mr. GARY. My impression is that the amount which was fixed under the Wilson bill, which was 1.2, would protect us. I think it would.

Mr. COCKRAN. Could you get along with any less?

Mr. GARY. I would not like to say, because I don't know.

Mr. COCKRAN. I suppose you would be willing to admit that this is a fair principle on which to frame a tariff, that in the absence of very satisfactory evidence of necessity for the imposition of a tax, the tax ought not to be imposed. I am speaking now from a pro-

tective point of view, to which I do not agree at all, but which I am
willing to concede is the policy that will govern the framing of this
bill.

Mr. GARY. Yes; but I think the responsibility of getting that evidence and of being certain is just as great or greater with the Congressmen than it is with the manufacturers. That is what I think.

Mr. COCKRAN. The fact that we are sitting here and probably will
sit all through the Christmas holidays, and have given you the trouble
of coming here, shows you how anxious we are to obtain it.

Mr. GARY. It is our duty to give you all the information we can;
and I am trying to do that.

Mr. COCKRAN. Could we go to a more responsible source for information than to the manufacturers themselves?

Mr. GARY. Yes; but have not I covered the question from the
standpoint of my duty, when I say that it does not seem to me it
would be safe to make it lower than 1.2?

Mr. COCKRAN. That is to say, you suspect or apprehend that any
change below that might hurt you?

Mr. GARY. No; I think that is the consensus of opinion of those
who have studied the question very carefully. That seems to be the
common belief.

Mr. COCKRAN. You, as the head of this company, can tell whether
you could go on making tin plates if we reduced this tariff to 60
cents, which would about cut it in two?

Mr. DALZELL. It is 1.5 now; it was 1.2 under the Wilson bill.

Mr. COCKRAN. Say we cut it down to 75 cents?

Mr. GARY. No; I must confess I can not answer that question.

The CHAIRMAN. Some of the manufacturers came in here and recommended a reduction of 20 per cent. They said that was a sufficient
protection for tin plate.

Mr. GARY. I did not know that.

Mr. COCKRAN. That is what these independent manufacturers think,
and you say their necessity for protection is very much greater than
yours. I would like to get your testimony as to how much protection
you would need, regardless of what these weaker competitors might
need.

Mr. GARY. Well, I may be mistaken; but I certainly believe we
could stand 10 per cent less than our competitors.

Mr. DALZELL. I do not recall now who made that statement; but it
seems to me it was one of your constituent members.

The CHAIRMAN. I think not.

Mr. GARY. There has not been any one of our people here.

Mr. COCKRAN. I think it was one of the Follansbee Brothers.

Mr. GARY. He is a well-posted man. I may be mistaken, and I may
do him an injustice; but I believe if he could stand 1.20 we could take
10 per cent off from that and make a fair profit.

Mr. COCKRAN. So that if we regulate this protective duty to the
necessities of Follansbee, we would be affording you a luxurious margin?

Mr. DALZELL. And if you regulate it by the United States Steel
Company, what will you do to Follansbee?

Mr. GARY. That is right. If you protect our competitors, you leave
us more than protection. I say that the United States Steel Corporation ought to take the position of not only making public the con-

duct of its affairs and business, but of submitting to government control. Now, that is a radical view, and you understand that I am not speaking for the corporation when I say that.

Mr. COCKRAN. I understand that.

Mr. GARY. We have got to come to that, in my opinion.

Mr. COCKRAN. I am questioning you now solely with reference to the effect of the tariff on your industry.

Mr. GARY. Yes; I understand that.

Mr. COCKRAN. I am one of those who believe that you can not make dollars for yourself without making hundreds for the community, provided you make it without any aid from the Government. I would rather see you make it than not, if you make it solely by your own efforts and not by assistance from or discrimination by the Government. If you receive no favors from the Government I do not think the Government has any right whatever to interfere with you, because you are not in the position of a corporation exercising a public franchise. Personally I do not think there is any foreign manufacturer in the world who can compete with you, even in a neutral market, much less in this one. That is what I am seeking to find out now. I do not want you to think that when I am questioning you as to profits I am in the slightest degree critical of any profits that can be made by any man through the exercise of his labor and genius, provided it is made without any aid from the Government, because he can not enrich himself without enriching the community more.

Mr. GARY. That seems to me to be a pretty fair statement.

Mr. COCKRAN. I mean to say that you can not make steel cheaper without increasing the welfare of every man in this country. Now, the particular question I put to you is with that object in view. I hope to see hundreds of millions of dollars made by the industry without any assistance. Now, Judge, in answer to Mr. Clark, you said you did not dominate the market. Is it not a fact that if you have competitors to-day it is because you tolerate them? Are you not in a position, if you wish, to compel——

Mr. GARY (interrupting). That is a pretty strong statement.

Mr. COCKRAN. I know it is a strong statement.

Mr. GARY. It is a fact, however, that we have been friendly and of benefit to our competitors, not simply because we are so much better than anybody else, but as a matter of policy. It is good business policy for us to pay heed to the interests of others, including our competitors and our customers, the Government, and the public generally. It is good business policy.

Your question, if I really understand it, answers itself, provided my facts are right—that is, if, in any particular line, by reason of our opportunities, our wealth, our organization, and our ownership of the best raw products, we can manufacture cheaper than our competitors, then with reference to that line we could drive them out of business.

Mr. COCKRAN. You can get your pig iron $2 a ton cheaper than your competitors and you can produce your rails at least $2 cheaper, and therefore you could sell them, say, at 5 per cent profit, while your competitor would be selling at an actual loss and would be hastening toward bankruptcy; so if you have competition it is because of your liberality. Is not that so?

Mr. GARY. Yes; with reference to any line and on the basis of fact which I have given.

Mr. COCKRAN. Take the question of rails. I understood that your explanation——

Mr. GARY. Of course that is true of every line of business.

Mr. COCKRAN. No; it would not be true of any line of business.

Mr. GARY. Take it in the line of business in which there is an element of strength, where some are superior by comparison with others, and, of course, the inferior ones would be driven out.

Mr. COCKRAN. I do not think that would be true of several industries that could be mentioned where no such policy of forbearance as you have described is pursued and yet where several independent producers are found apparently in active competition. There is no chance in the case of the meat industry, for instance, for any one producer to hold all others at his mercy. There are a number of meat men competing, but no one of them could drive the others out; but in this industry of yours, the steel industry, I understand you to say that all competitors are practically at your mercy for their existence on this account; you control the raw products and you control the means of transportation, and then you have also, I am free to admit, very efficient organization. With those three elements of advantage there is no person or combination of persons that can compete with you if you choose to drive them out. That is true, is it not?

Mr. GARY. Of course your whole question characterizes—and I do not like to do that. You put it so broadly that if I could and should answer it in the affirmative, it would almost seem like boasting. We have competitors, you know, who are just as able to take care of themselves as we are, perhaps, particularly in some lines, but I do believe large numbers would be driven out of business if we were willing to drive them out, either because we thought it was right to do so or good policy to do so.

Mr. COCKRAN. To be perfectly frank about it, there is nobody who could compete with you if you made up your mind to take this market and exercise all your powers to control it?

Mr. GARY. Would you not think it looked like boasting for me to say so, if I believe it? I do not know.

Mr. COCKRAN. No; I do not think so. I do not think so, because your position in the trade is so preemiment that you can afford to be candid without exposing yourself to the reproach of boasting. I think you can speak the truth about that.

Mr. GARY. I think we have a commanding position in the trade, and I believe we recognize our responsibility to all on account of that position.

Mr. COCKRAN. I think you do. If by any chance the management of this stupendous organization should pass from hands as wise and as prudent and as just as yours into the hands of somebody more reckless and more avaricious and with less foresight, and he should undertake to exercise this power to its limit, there is little doubt that for a while, at least, he would have a monopoly of the entire trade and be without practical competition. That is one of the conditions that we are confronting.

Mr. GARY. You are asking for an opinion. Your opinion is just as good as mine.

Mr. Cockran. I think it is, on your statement. Now, among the conditions that contribute to that situation, an important element is your ownership and control of the ore supply?

Mr. Gary. Yes; of course it is.

Mr. Cockran. You practically do control the ore supply of the country?

Mr. Gary. No; not now; not for the immediate future.

Mr. Cockran. Well, the ultimate supply?

Mr. Gary. Yes; I think so—that is, pretty nearly. It is not absolute control.

Mr. Cockran. Sufficient to make the competitor——

Mr. Gary (interrupting). For instance, take the Woodward Company, just as an illustration—excuse me for being personal—with the amount of capital in their business they have a very large supply of ore, and it will be a long time before they get out of the business, no matter what comes. They can manufacture——

Mr. Cockran (interrupting). That is a small company?

Mr. Gary. Yes; in comparison with ours.

Mr. Cockran. These ore properties of yours do not constitute the only supply of the world by any means, do they?

Mr. Gary. Oh, no.

Mr. Cockran. So if the supply of the world were open to these competitors, and with the advantage of cheap transportation by water, which you described a short time ago, they might be able to make a stand for life and liberty even against the United States Steel Corporation in the hands of some successor of yours who might undertake to crush competition?

Mr. Gary. If you remove the duty from ore alone, and it remains so, no doubt that would protect the people here, who will in the future have to buy their ore, against a possible oppression on the part of our corporation. That is your question, only in my words.

Mr. Cockran. That is a perfectly frank answer. It states the situation admirably. Then, so far as the transportation is concerned, you really have not any advantage over your competitor, so long as you discharge faithfully your duty as a common carrier in the matter?

Mr. Gary. You are speaking of our manufacturing companies?

Mr. Cockran. Yes.

Mr. Gary. No; they have none.

Mr. Cockran. You have no advantage whatever in transportation, unless you should abuse your duty as a common carrier?

Mr. Gary. No.

Mr. Cockran. Of course you could give yourself an advantage?

Mr. Gary. Not under the present régime.

Mr. Cockran. I am mighty glad to hear that. That is the first adequate testimony I have heard as to the efficiency of the present inspection.

Mr. Gary. The Interstate Commerce Commission and the railroad commissioners of the various States—take Minnesota, for instance—are very strict in regard to the matter. There would not be much chance for us to discriminate against our neighbors in the matter of transportation.

Mr. Cockran. If I may return for one moment to the capitalization of the steel company, for the purpose of fixing these profits, I want to direct your attention to the common stock. For what was that issued?

Mr. GARY. It was issued for the properties which we received—or perhaps I do not understand your question.

Mr. COCKRAN. The total capitalization of the companies that you acquired was not nearly equal to the bonds and preferred stock of the new company?

Mr. GARY. No. The total capitalization of the companies acquired was in excess of the bonds and preferred stock issued by the new company. We issued our common stock, I think, in exchange, in some cases at least, for the common stocks of other corporations, and on a basis agreed upon.

Mr. COCKRAN. It was not by any means computed by those receiving it that that stock was worth par or anything of that kind?

Mr. GARY. Yes; it was.

Mr. COCKRAN. How did you manage to give some more and some less? There were $508,302,000. Mr. Schwab said, I think, that Mr. Carnegie declined to take anything but bonds. There were others that took bonds and preferred stock.

Mr. GARY. I do not think anything else was offered to Mr. Carnegie.

Mr. COCKRAN. You paid him a tribute in advance?

Mr. GARY. No; I think the basis of the negotiation was that he should receive bonds and nothing else, and neither side ever considered anything else; and I do not know that either side would have considered anything else at that time. You remember, Mr. Cockran, perhaps better than some of the others, some of the circumstances leading up to the acquisition of the Carnegie property.

Mr. COCKRAN. I was just going to ask to see if Mr. Schwab's recollection and yours agreed. As I recall it, that comes back to the price of steel rails, and you have always made it a policy to keep the prices reasonable?

Mr. GARY. Yes.

Mr. COCKRAN. But you are getting very much less profit at $28 a ton now than you did when that rate was fixed?

Mr. GARY. Yes; we are.

Mr. COCKRAN. Mr. Schwab testified that when the rate of $28 a ton was fixed the rails were costing actually less than $14, so the original profit was 100 per cent.

Mr. GARY. That was Mr. Schwab's statement?

Mr. COCKRAN. Yes.

Mr. GARY. He has made his own explanation. They are not my figures, and I have no explanation to make, and I do not know anything about his figures.

Mr. COCKRAN. Quite so.

Mr. GARY. He is a very competent man.

Mr. COCKRAN. His statement was, as I recall it, to see if you agree that the price of $28 was fixed when the cost of the article was $14 a ton, and it was fixed by an agreement with a number of producers, among others, your company, the Federal Steel, and the Carnegie Company, and some others.

Mr. GARY. If he made that statement he overstated it.

Mr. COCKRAN. You mean he overstated the amount of profit?

Mr. GARY. No; he overstated the whole thing.

Mr. COCKRAN. Was not there an understanding or agreement——

Mr. GARY. In this way. I will be very frank with you——

Mr. COCKRAN. We are giving you credit for that all through. You have not shown the slightest disposition to evade any question.

Mr. GARY. When the steel manufacturers fixed a price for their rails which was uniform, or practically uniform, it was done because two or three individuals said they would recommend to their companies so and so.

Mr. COCKRAN. What do you mean by " so and so?" Recommend what?

Mr. GARY. That whenever they changed their prices of rails they would notify the others and give every other person the same chance; that they would not act independently; that they would come into consultation from time to time whenever it was necessary.

Mr. COCKRAN. Was that after the formation of the Federal Steel Company?

Mr. GARY. Yes, sir.

Mr. COCKRAN. And the steel and wire company?

Mr. GARY. Yes, sir.

Mr. COCKRAN. After these several consolidations that occurred in 1898 and 1899?

Mr. GARY. Yes; and that was the understanding, if you may call it such, amongst a very few individuals, and was not communicated to the companies themselves or the officers or the boards of directors of the different companies or anything of that kind.

Mr. COCKRAN. It was a gentlemen's agreement?

Mr. GARY. It hardly amounted to an agreement, but it resulted about the same, and it ran along for a year or two, and there was a question in my mind whether even that was not a breach of the law, or so close to it that it should not exist; and therefore the meetings were abandoned and they did not meet at all, and those connected with it stated positively they would not regularly be bound by anything, and everyone would have to take his chance, except they said they would furnish information at any time to anybody concerning what they were doing.

Mr. COCKRAN. The net result was $28 a ton as a price?

Mr. GARY. That has been the result.

Mr. COCKRAN. That continued uninterruptedly down to 1901?

Mr. GARY. The price was not $28 then—yes; it was, too.

Mr. COCKRAN. Twenty-eight dollars, Mr. Schwab said.

Mr. GARY. Yes.

Mr. COCKRAN. Now, in 1901——

Mr. GARY. Well, the price of $28 was established by the different ones for themselves in the latter part of 1902. I have the prices of rails from 1896 for every year down to date.

Mr. COCKRAN. But what I want to direct your attention to is this: In 1901 was there not a fear of a steel war coming from Mr. Carnegie's announcement that he was going into the tubing business?

Mr. GARY. Yes; and that he was going to build a railroad from Pittsburg to New York, and so forth.

Mr. COCKRAN. One result apprehended from that was a cutting of prices of rails, among other things, was it not?

Mr. GARY. No.

Mr. COCKRAN. Was not that one of the things apprehended?

Mr. GARY. No; I do not think the price of rails changed.

Mr. COCKRAN. Was not there a fear of a general steel war?

Mr. GARY. Yes; there was a fear, but there was no change in the prices.

Mr. COCKRAN. I do not say there was a change made, but a change apprehended?

Mr. GARY. I misunderstood your question.

Mr. COCKRAN. I understand there has been no breach in the price of rails, but I asked this question: Was there not in——

Mr. GARY (interrupting). There was apprehension of trouble.

Mr. COCKRAN. And it was to quiet that apprehension and remove the doubt that the steel corporation was formed?

Mr. GARY. That was one of the governing motives, I think, on the part of Mr. Morgan. It was not mine, Mr. Cockran; not at all.

Mr. COCKRAN. I understand that. I am speaking of the men who formed it.

Mr. GARY. I think I had something to do with forming it.

Mr. COCKRAN. From that time down to this the price has never been disturbed, and, as you testified to Mr. Clark, if anybody should undertake to disturb it now, you are in a position to make it unpleasant for him if you want to.

Mr. GARY. Yes; of course.

Mr. COCKRAN. Now, Judge Gary, this common stock which was issued for property was issued at a very much lower valuation than the preferred stock and bonds—I mean nobody estimated it was worth par?

Mr. GARY. The market did not estimate it so.

Mr. COCKRAN. The concensus of opinion of the men who took it under this distribution did not value it any higher than the market, which was about 10 cents on the dollar?

Mr. GARY. Everyone will have to answer for himself on that.

Mr. COCKRAN. I would like to get the theory of it.

Mr. GARY. This was dominant in my mind, Mr. Cockran, and I was one of the participants, that shares of stock of the old companies, even though selling on the market at a price less than par, as applied to common stock at least, when they were put together, as they would be put together after acquired, would be worth at least par—at least the capital stock which was delivered in exchange for those old shares on the basis of par.

Mr. COCKRAN. You mean the combination itself added to the value of each element that entered into it?

Mr. GARY. Yes; I thought so. I believed that then, and I was just as certain of it as I am now as a result.

Mr. COCKRAN. I believe in that implicitly. I think events have shown it. The United States Steel Company itself added nothing to the property of these various companies?

Mr. GARY. No; except $25,000,000 cash.

Mr. COCKRAN. That was a kind of a guaranty that nobody would be hurt, was it not?

Mr. GARY. No; the syndicate raised that and paid it in cash and turned it over to the treasury of the United States Steel.

Mr. COCKRAN. But they took stock?

Mr. GARY. They took stock; yes, sir.

Mr. COCKRAN. Outside of that, there was not a single building or even a wheelbarrow contributed to the net property of the constituent companies?

Mr. GARY. No, sir.

Mr. COCKRAN. It held exactly the same property as before?

Mr. GARY. Yes, sir.

Mr. COCKRAN. It secured the additional value by the fact of the combination and the additional strength which the combination gave it?

Mr. GARY. Yes, sir.

Mr. COCKRAN. The common stock to a certain extent was issued against this future value which the company would have by reason of the combination?

Mr. GARY. It was all a part of the same transaction.

Mr. COCKRAN. I suppose it was also a capitalization to some extent of the skill with which the company would be managed, its business management and ability?

Mr. GARY. Really, the increase in the total capitalization to which you refer applies to the securities of the old companies on the basis of their being put together under one management. Then the new stock of the United States Steel was issued against those old securities, and that increased the valuation.

Mr. COCKRAN. Could you give us about what the property of all the constituent companies was valued at? Judging even by the market values—it was about $400,000,000, was it not—that is to say before they went into the new company——

Mr. GARY (interrupting). That is, you mean to say——

Mr. COCKRAN (interrupting). I mean to say these companies before they went into the combination were worth, as a matter of fact, $400,000,000?

Mr. GARY. I should say very much more than that. I presume the selling value of the old securities was $400,000,000 less than the total amount of all the new securities—stock and bonds. I presume that is so.

Mr. COCKRAN. I think it was a good deal more than that on paper value, but I mean what was the actual value? Could you give us about what it was? Think what the stock of the new company sold at immediately after organization, and what the aggregate of the constituent companies' stock sold at, not immediately before, because they appreciated very much under the prospect of consolidation, but before the prospect of forming the new company started.

Mr. GARY. I can not answer that, because there was included in these properties the Carnegie property, which did not have any common stock.

Mr. COCKRAN. Oh, yes; they did.

Mr. GARY. They had bonds and stock, but there was no market value for them. They were not on the market at all. They were worth, intrinsically, at that time very much more than the par value, I think.

Mr. COCKRAN. Do you not remember that about that time there was published an option which Mr. Carnegie had given on that property at that time, which was even less than par?

Mr. GARY. And which he took the first opportunity to back out of.

Mr. COCKRAN. Yes; but I mean taking the valuation of the property according to the option which Mr. Carnegie himself gave, that stock was not worth par, was it?

Mr. GARY. I think so.

Mr. DALZELL. This is all very interesting, but how it contributes to the question of determining the proper duty on steel or whether there should be any I do not understand.

Mr. COCKRAN. I am just showing the value of this company.

Mr. DALZELL. You have all the figures there and you are asking for his simple conclusions.

The CHAIRMAN. What difference does it make about his capital as compared with that of other people?

Mr. COCKRAN. It makes a great deal of difference.

Mr. DALZELL. Let him go, Mr. Chairman; perhaps he will get through after a while.

Mr. GARY. Immediately after it was known the United States Steel——

The CHAIRMAN (interrupting). He was almost through when you interrupted him. Let him go; do not interrupt him any further. [Laughter.]

Mr. COCKRAN. O gentlemen, you should not show so much sensitiveness about this little matter. [Laughter.]

Mr. GARY. It may be my fault, but I intend to answer your questions to the best of my ability.

Mr. COCKRAN. I understand that, and I appreciate it. What I want to ask is this, in brief, and I merely mention the option that Mr. Carnegie gave for the purpose of refreshing your memory:

Are you able to state and will you state just what the value of all these constituent stocks was before the beginning of the negotiations for the consolidation of the steel companies into the United States Steel Corporation, and the market price of the new company's securities at the time of consolidation?

Mr. GARY. I could tell you that so far as the companies whose stocks were on the market, but I could not tell you that as to Mr. Carnegie's and, of course, Rockefeller's—very large quantities of ores and the ships and the railroads up there represented great values, and those stocks were not on the market at all. That price which Mr. Carnegie gave is no test, I think, whatever. He gave it at too low a figure, and discovered it, and he seized the first opportunity to get out of it; and his only source of annoyance now is that he did not make the United States Steel Company pay very much more than it did pay; and Mr. Rockefeller probably the same—because those two believed the intrinsic value of these properties and these securities would be materially increased by reason of the combination, and now believe that the results have demonstrated their original belief. I do not know whether I have answered your question very clearly or not.

Mr. COCKRAN. I think it is perfectly clear. Now, Judge Gary, suppose steel were put on the free list, do you think it would have any serious effect on the value of these securities?

Mr. GARY. Our securities?

Mr. COCKRAN. Yes.

Mr. GARY. Of course that is another way of asking the same old question.

Mr. COCKRAN. Yes; it is.
Mr. GARY. I do not know.
Mr. COCKRAN. All right. I thank you.

———

EXHIBIT A.

[By Frank A. Munsey, in Munsey's Magazine for June, 1908.]

THE UNITED STATES STEEL CORPORATION.

AN INVENTORY OF THE PROPERTIES OF THE UNITED STATES STEEL CORPO-
RATION, JUST COMPLETED FOR MUNSEY'S MAGAZINE, REACHES THE
AMAZING FIGURES OF ONE BILLION SEVEN HUNDRED AND EIGHTY-TWO
MILLIONS OF DOLLARS—A STATEMENT SHOWING OVER THREE HUNDRED
MILLIONS IN EXCESS OF THE TOTAL CAPITALIZATION OF THE STEEL COR-
PORATION IN STOCKS AND BONDS AT PAR VALUE—AND FIGURED AT THE
PRICE AT WHICH THE SECURITIES OF THE CORPORATION ARE NOW
SELLING, THIS INVENTORY SHOWS OVER SIX HUNDRED MILLIONS IN
EXCESS OF THE TOTAL CAPITALIZATION.

There are to-day well-nigh 100,000 individual investors in the
securities of the United States Steel Corporation, and it is safe to
say that few, if any, of this great army, scattered all over the civilized
world, have any well-defined notion of its properties and their vast
aggregate value at the present time.

A stockholder in any concern ought to know pretty accurately about
the assets of the concern—know what they consist of and what they
are worth—what they are worth prospectively, strategically, and
actually. I wanted this information about the Steel Corporation for
myself. I wanted it for these hundred thousand investors, and I
wanted it for Munsey's Magazine.

But there was no such information obtainable. No inventory of
the kind had ever been published, and none was in existence. Even
the Steel Corporation itself had no compilation showing present
values—no tabulated and itemized record that would give me the
facts for an article on the properties of the company—no record that
would give the investor the facts that he ought to have at his fingers'
tips before purchasing the securities of the corporation.

The American investor has been false to his own interests. He has
not made a wise and comprehensive study of the properties into
which he has put his money. He has not known them as he would
know about his own farm. And he should know them as he would
know about a piece of real estate that he owns, or small manufacturing
business in which he is engaged. The quarterly, semiannual, and
annual reports of a corporation are not comprehensive enough. They
do not tell all that an investor should know. They are not inventories, and give no well-defined idea of the physical condition of its
properties.

It has not been the policy of corporations and railroads to make
public the facts and figures that purchasers of securities should have.
These periodical reports of earnings and of business transacted furnish the information on which the buying and selling of securities are
done, on which the price of securities is made. I repeat that this is not
enough. It does not get down to the bottom of the matter. It serves
for our American slap-dash, take-a-chance way of doing things, but

to invest wisely in securities one must know what he is doing—must know, and not depend on the rumors of the minute, on " tips " on the market, on the advice of incompetent and characterless brokers, or on their irresponsible representatives, talking knowingly about finance, of which they understand nothing.

The followers of such inane methods are certain to lose their money. The man who is successful in investing in securities is the type of man who is successful anywhere—the man who puts brains into his work and knows what he is doing—knows by mastering the problem from top to bottom.

Of course the Steel Corporation knows what properties it owns, but the facts had not been tabulated, and had not been assembled in one comprehensive record with up-to-date valuations placed on the various classifications. And values have been changing so fast in the last half-dozen years that the estimates placed on the various properties at the time the corporation was formed mean little to-day. An enormous amount of money has been put into new mills, new transportation facilities, ore lands, and into the general reconstruction and upbuilding of the concern.

What I wanted to know was how many tons of ore the corporation owns, and what it is worth a ton. I wanted to know about its coal and coke properties, its natural-gas and limestone properties, about its railroads, its ships, and its docks, about its mills and its coke ovens. And so I scheduled an article on these lines, and we began work on it at that time. That was three or four months ago. Without realizing how big a job we had on our hands, I announced the article for the forthcoming issue of this magazine. We have had to postpone it several times, but at last we have the facts and figures, which make a showing worth waiting for.

It has been a very difficult task to cover the many classes of these immense possessions, and to get a fair estimate of their value. The work could not be hurried; hurried work of this kind would be worthless. And we should not have the article ready even now but for the courtesy and assistance of the Steel Corporation. Indeed, without this courtesy it would not have been possible to get the facts and figures in this compilation—to get facts and figures worth while—a compilation which shows $1,782,000,000 worth of property. The following is the inventory:

Ore and mining timber properties:

Unmined ores located in the Lake Superior districts on the Marquette, Menominee, Gogebic, Vermillion and Mesabe iron ranges, and in the Baraboo district, Wisconsin, in all an estimated tonnage of 1,182,815,200 tons of all grades, exclusive of the Great Northern ores, at 60 cents per ton_____ $709, 689, 120

Mining plants, improvements, and development work at active mines, including mine and stripping equipment, tracks, etc., and cost of removing overburden from ore not yet mined, mine dwellings, etc_____ 23, 432, 886

Timber property—808,868,000 feet of standing mining and saw-log stock, 1,461,000 cords of lagging, pulp wood and cord wood; 191,837 acres of land—all located on above-named iron ranges_____ 5, 744, 011
                                                           ——————————
                                                           $738, 866, 017

Coal and coke properties:
    Unmined coking coal in the Connellsville
        region, Pennsylvania—60,003 acres owned
        (coal only, not including surface), 1,515
        acres leased on royalty basis; also, 21,100
        acres of surface land (of which 750 acres
        are river-front) owned in connection with
        foregoing_____ $93, 656, 200
    Unmined coking coal in the Pocahontas
        region, West Virginia—65,497 acres leased—
        Valuation in equity above royalties_____   3, 274, 850
    Unmined steam and gas coal in the Pittsburg
        district in Pennsylvania, in Ohio, Indiana,
        and Illinois—30,252 acres owned (coal only,
        not including surface), 3,548 acres leased on
        royalty basis; also, 998 acres of surface land
        owned in connection with foregoing_____   8, 898, 828
    Coking plants, comprising 20,225 ovens in the
        Connellsville region and 2,151 ovens in the
        Pocahontas region, including mine openings,
        shafts, slopes, tipples, power plants, mine
        and over tracks, and all machinery and
        equipment in connection with the mining
        and coking of coal at the above plants;
        also, complement of tenement houses for
        employees_____   29, 875, 150
    Coal-mining and shipping plants at mines in the
        Connellsville and Pittsburg districts, not
        constructed in connection with coking plants.   2, 741, 412
    Miscellaneous, including standard-gauge rail-
        road equipment (6 locomotives, 700 steel cars,
        and 1,964 wooden cars) operated in connection
        with the foregoing properties: Water-pump-
        ing stations, pipe lines, and reservoirs; shops,
        office buildings, stores, telephone lines, live
        stock, etc_____   4, 393, 339
                                                                    $142, 839, 779
Limestone and natural gas:
    Unquarried limestone located at various places
        in Pennsylvania, West Virginia, Ohio, Illinois,
        Wisconsin, and Michigan, at an estimated
        valuation of about 3 cents per ton, including
        quarry equipment _____   2, 619, 529
    Gas territory in Pennsylvania and West Vir-
        ginia (leased), in all 208,985 acres, on which
        there are 376 gas wells and 5 oil wells, with
        about 600 miles of pipe lines, 12 pumping
        stations, telephone lines, field equipment, etc.   10, 360. 940
                                                                    12, 980, 469
Transportation properties:
    Standard gauge railroad lines, including the
        Bessemer and Lake Erie, 233 miles; Chicago,
        Lake Shore and Eastern, 282 miles; Duluth
        and Iron Range, 229 miles; Duluth, Missabe
        and Northern, 274 miles; Elgin, Joliet and
        Eastern, 230 miles; and other lines, 107 miles
        —in all, 1,355 miles of main lines and branch
        lines, with 298 miles of second tracks and 659
        miles of sidings and yard tracks, but exclu-
        sive of docks and equipment_____   91, 517, 750
    Railroad equipment—692 locomotives and
        37,902 cars of various classes_____   42, 348, 825
    8 forwarding ore docks on Lake Superior and
        two receiving ore docks on Lake Erie, in-
        cluding equipment_____   7, 396, 700

Transportation properties—Continued.
  76 ore and freight carrying steamers and 29
    barges, plying on the Great Lakes, with a
    total carrying capacity of 635,250 tons of
    iron ore_____ $21, 440, 700
                                                              —————————
                                                              $162, 703, 975

Manufacturing properties (exclusive of Gary, Ind.) :
  Furnaces, mills. and factories, numbering in all 145 separate
    plants, including the sites (a total area of 8,089 acres),
    and all equipment and appurtenances other than manufac-
    turing supplies and product on hand_____   382, 248, 897

NOTE—The following table shows the principal items in the manufacturing plants of the various subsidiary companies:

	Number of works.	Blast furnaces.	Open-hearth furnaces.	Bessemer converters.	Rail mills.	Structural shape mills.	Bridge plants.	Nail and wire factories.	Plate mills.	Puddling furnaces.	Rod mills.	Foundries.
American Bridge Company	20		11			2	20					6
American Sheet and Tin Plate Company	36		12							4		2
American Steel and Wire Company	28	12	17	4				23	3		17	6
Carnegie Steel Company	24	47	86	18	4	9	2		9			3
Clairton Steel Company	1	3	12			1						
Illinois Steel Company	5	21	24	6	2	2	1		3		3	2
Lorain Steel Company	1											2
National Tube Company	19	12		7	1					96		7
(And other tube companies.)												
Tennessee Coal, Iron, and Railroad Company	5	16	8	2	1				1			2
Union Steel Company	2	5	24					4	1		4	
Universal Portland Cement Company	4											
Total	145	116	194	37	8	14	23	27	17	100	24	30

Gary, Ind., plant, actual expenditure to January 1,
  1908, for the real estate, about 9,000 acres; for
  construction work on the new steel plant, for development and construction work in the city of
  Gary, and for connecting railroad work_____   _____ $24, 063, 388
Sundry real estate situated contiguous to manu-
  facturing plants, and improvements thereon
  (principally dwellings for employees) ; also, un-
  improved tracts of land owned, available for
  manufacturing sites and for terminal railroad
  and dock facilities, etc. :
    Value of real estate exclusive of improvements. $4, 975, 900
    Improvements thereon_____   1, 719. 073
                                                          —————————
                                                                        6, 694, 973
Tennessee Coal and Iron Company, including ore,
  coal, manufacturing plants, and general equip-
  ments of a complete and independent steel manufacturing concern_____   _____   50, 000, 000
Net liquid assets, December 31, 1907 (includes cash,
  accounts, and receivables, inventories and investments, in excess of current liabilities)_____   _____   261, 789, 885
                                                                        —————————
    Total _____   _____   1, 782, 187, 383

The Tennessee Coal and Iron Company is entered as a separate item in this inventory. Its ore and coal and mills and furnaces and other properties are not included in the other classifications. This company is put in at an estimated value of $50,000,000, which is somewhat more than the Steel Corporation paid for it, but probably a much smaller sum than it is worth to the Steel Corporation. Its chief value lies in its coal and ore properties. Its ore is estimated at 700,000,000 tons. It is not as high grade as the Northern ores, but assuming that it is worth 15 cents per ton, it alone would amount to $105,000,000. Its coal is estimated at about a billion tons, which at 10 cents a ton would be $100,000,000.

From the fact that the known supply of ore in the country is limited, it may well be worth two or three times this price. There is no way of telling just what it is worth. But as a guide to the value of ores, we may take the price fixed upon for the Great Northern ores between James J. Hill and the Steel Corporation. The Great Northern Railroad and the Northern Pacific had vast holdings of iron ore in the Messabe Range, and after many months of negotiation the Steel Corporation entered into a contract a year ago to take all this ore at a certain price per ton, the price to be advanced each year over the preceding year, 3.4 cents.

The first year's price, which covered the year 1907, was 85 cents a ton. This year it is 88.4 cents a ton. On this basis the price will soon be over $1 a ton, and the average cost for the entire supply will be considerably in excess of that figure.

And this ore is supposed to be of a lower grade, as a whole, than the ore owned by the United States Steel Corporation, which in this inventory has been conservatively, ultraconservatively, figured at 60 cents a ton. If the Hill ore is worth over $1 a ton, the ore of the Steel Corporation is worth quite as much, and even more, as it is of better grade. And these prices of this Northern Pacific ore have an important bearing on the ore properties of the Tennessee Coal and Iron Company.

I should think that Mr. Charles M. Schwab is as good an authority as there is in the world on the value of iron ore. He said to me two or three days ago that the ore holdings of the Steel Corporation were easily worth $1 a ton, and, in fact, might safely and conservatively be regarded as worth still more, for the reason that they can not be duplicated.

You will observe that the contract for the Great Northern ores has not been listed as an asset in this inventory. No account has been taken of it, though it is of immense value to the Steel Corporation. It is not only an insurance against competition, but it makes certain a longer period of easily obtained ore. One of the directors of the Steel Corporation, who is a very big man in the financial world, said to me yesterday that he thought this contract worth $500,000,000 to the Steel Corporation, and that if an offer of that kind were made for it he should vote against the sale. Whether this estimate of its value is excessive, is problematical. His judgment, however, is usually very sound.

If there are items in this inventory that have been overvalued, there are other items that have been undervalued, greatly undervalued. Our purpose has been to keep under actual values, rather than to exceed them, and in the case of the ore lands and coal lands our figures are probably very much under actual values to-day. Indeed, if a less conservative policy had been pursued in this compilation the total property of the Steel Corporation could easily be figured up to 2 billions of dollars.

In the preparation of an article of this kind I have, as a matter of course, had to rely mainly upon others—men who possess technical knowledge—for facts, figures, and valuations. The whole thing is so enormous, so overwhelmingly enormous, that it looks like fiction, but there is no fiction in it.

The publication of this article is not for the purpose of telling what a wonderful concern the United States Steel Corporation is. It is to give the readers of Munsey's Magazine a rationally correct inventory of its properties, based on present valuations.

If other big corporations and important railroads will show us a similar courtesy, and give us a similar amount of help in working up an inventory of their properties, we shall follow this article with other articles of a like nature. Nothing can be of greater service to the investor in securities than accurate information of this kind about the great railroads and great corporations whose stocks and bonds occupy so big a place in the financial interests of America, and in fact, the financial interests of the whole world.

Assuming that this inventory of the Steel Corporation is reasonably accurate, it makes a wonderful showing for the company—a showing of more than $300,000,000 in assets in excess of the total capitalization of the concern in both stocks and bonds at par value. And figured at the price at which these stocks and bonds are now selling, the assets exceed the total capitalization by over $600,000,000.

Total assets of the United States Steel Corporation on January 1, 1908, as per the foregoing inventory		$1,782,187,383
Outstanding securities of the corporation at the same date:		
Bonds	$602,320,511	
Preferred stock	360,281,100	
Common stock	508,302,500	
		1,470,904,111
Excess of assets		311,283,272

STATEMENT OF COSTS, PRICES, AND PROFITS OF STANDARD STEEL RAILS FOR SERIES OF YEARS, FURNISHED BY BUREAU OF CORPORATIONS.

DEPARTMENT OF COMMERCE AND LABOR,
BUREAU OF CORPORATIONS,
Washington, December 14, 1908.

Hon. S. E. PAYNE, M. C.,
Chairman Committee on Ways and Means,
Washington, D. C.

MY DEAR CONGRESSMAN: In reply to the letter of November 25 of the clerk to your committee and in accordance with our conversation of the 11th instant, I inclose herewith a statement as to the costs, prices, and profits of standard rails for the years 1902 to 1906, inclusive, which I showed you on that day. I have made one or two slight modifications, but nothing of importance, in that statement.

I desire to call your attention to one or two points of explanation which are perhaps referred to somewhat too briefly in the statement itself.

(1) The figures on the upper part of page 1 are taken from the profit and loss accounts of the various companies examined by the

bureau. You will note that they give an average cost per ton for the five years, of all the companies examined, of $22.39.

The figures in the lower part of page 1 under the heading of cost items are obtained in a different way, to wit, directly from the cost sheets of the companies themselves and give an average cost of $22.23, a difference of 16 cents in costs on every ton, as obtained by these two methods. This difference, which is very slight, is due to the different sources used in compiling the figures, i. e., accounting as against cost-keeping work in a given company. The same company gets at the same result in two ways and uses often different tonnages in doing so, thus getting a slight variation; and their approximation by the small sum of 16 cents is about as excellent a confirmation as could be desired of the accuracy of the results.

(2) You will note that under "cost items," on page 1, we start with Bessemer pig iron, $14.52." On page 3 we go a step farther back and bring it up to the Bessemer pig iron, starting with the ore. We show here the cost of Bessemer pig iron to be $14.01, a difference of 51 cents between the cost as shown here and the cost of Bessemer pig iron as set forth in the second half of page 1. The difference between these two figures is due to the fact that the Bessemer pig iron figure on page 3 includes all the iron of this sort for all districts, while the figure used on page 1, $14.52, is simply the Bessemer pig used for steel rails. In regard to this particular division of Bessemer pig, there were some variations due to excess tonnage and the higher freight costs on this class of iron, and to the fact that some of the iron was purchased.

(3) There is, of course, a certain amount of labor included in the items on page 3 for raw material, such as limestone and coke, as there necessarily must be in the cost of any raw material. So far as the steel companies are concerned, the only labor that they have put into these raw materials is substantially that of unloading.

(4) I have set forth on page 2 certain extremes of cost and profit which I think may be of interest to your committee. You will note that I have stated that the highest cost for any company in any year was $31.27 for one company in 1903. It should be noted, however, that this is not a normal case, as the company was a new one. I have therefore inserted what was the next highest cost, to wit, $30.29, for another company for the same year. This company presented a normal condition. I felt also that possibly the figures for 1906 would be of especial interest, so I have inserted the lowest profit of any company during that year, to wit, 99 cents. The average profit for all companies during that year was $4.85. All of these figures, of course, are per ton.

These results appear simple and are stated in comparatively small space, but they cover companies which have produced more than 93 per cent of all rails produced in the United States during that period. This means an enormous volume of tonnage and an enormous mass of transactions. To get these figures required the work of a considerable force of men in this office for over a year in an examination of thousands of accounts under the direction of an expert steel man. I think it is safe to say that no such complete or accurate figures have been compiled in this country, and that while they necessarily involve some variations, these are small in amount, and nothing approaching this statement in reliability can be obtained from any other source.

I will endeavor to furnish you as quickly as possible such other information as I have available.

Very respectfully,

HERBERT KNOX SMITH,
Commissioner.

Standard rails.

	Cost of rails sold and used.			Sold.		
	Tons.	Cost per ton.	Amount.	Tons.	Price.	Profit per ton.
1902	2,594,338	$22.32	$57,910,323.72	2,594,961	$27.65	$5.34
1903	2,641,857	23.78	62,820,909.08	2,615,754	28.07	4.32
1904	1,934,682	21.57	41,735,625.60	1,898,057	25.70	4.17
1905	2,974,926	21.30	63,361,006.09	2,883,671	27.13	5.88
1906	3,491,649	22.77	79,512,433.50	3,396,381	27.61	4.85
Five years	13,637,452	22.39	305,340,298.59	13,388,824	27.34	4.97

Cost items of rails produced for five years, 1902–1906.

Tons produced _____ 14,020,303

COST ITEMS.

Bessemer pig iron	a$14.52
Waste	1.95
Cost pig iron in rails	16.47
Labor	1.98
Manganese, etc	.99
Fuel	.85
Steam	b.62
Molds	.15
Rolls	.17
Materials in repairs and maintenance	.42
Supplies and tools	.27
Miscellaneous and general works expense	.51
General expense	.14
Depreciation	.16
Total cost	c22.23

Cost of conversion from pig iron, $7.71.

	Any company for any year.	Any company, average for 5 years.
Lowest cost	$19.83 (1905)	$20.74
Highest cost	31.27 (1903)	26.61
Next highest cost	30.29 (1903)	
Lowest profit for any company in 1906	$0.99	
Average profit for all companies in 1906	4.85	

This statement includes the production of seven companies, and covers more than 93 per cent of all rails produced in the United States during the period.

---

a The difference of 51 cents between the average cost of Bessemer pig iron and of pig iron used for rails is due to variation in the cost of the excess tonnage and to freight on some of the iron. (See p. 3.)

b The item of labor does not include, for much of the tonnage, the labor in producing steam, which some companies include in the item "Steam."

c The difference of 16 cents between the cost of rails sold from sales statements and rails produced from cost sheets is due to difference in tonnage and in inventories.

DECEMBER 10, 1908.

Cost of Bessemer pig iron, all districts, 1902–1906.

[Tons produced, 51,902,699.]

Cost items.	Price.	Cost per ton pig iron.
Net total metallic mixture	$3.97	$7.30
Coke	3.37	3.89
Limestone		.43
Labor		.77
Steam		.12
Materials in repairs and maintenance		.16
Supplies and tools		.13
Miscellaneous and general works expense		.28
General expense		.36
Relining and renewals		.18
Depreciation		.39
Total		14.01

The item of labor does not include, for much of the tonnage, the labor in unloading raw materials and in producing steam, which some companies include in the cost of raw materials and in the item " steam."

The tonnage covers 93 per cent of the Bessemer pig iron made in the United States during the period.

" MY EXPERIENCE WITH, AND VIEWS UPON, THE TARIFF," BY ANDREW CARNEGIE.

In 1870 the writer was not of sufficient importance as an iron and steel manufacturer to be called into counsel with his older friends in the business, the directors of the Iron and Steel Association, then led by Mr. Swank, who still keeps watch and ward as secretary. He attended to tariff legislation as of vital importance to the iron and steel industry, then in its infancy.

Our Edgar Thomson Steel Rail Works were not started until after the tariff of that year was passed. The duty on rails was then fixed at $28 per ton, the cost of foreign rails being about $100; so that the duty was, say, 28 per cent ad valorem, which was not then excessive.

Upon repeated visits to England I anxiously watched the progress of the Bessemer process, and saw it emerge from the experimental stage to undoubted success. Several pioneers in America began too soon.

Ward, at Detroit, was the first, followed by Griswold, of Troy; then came the Pennsylvania Steel, the Freedom, followed by the Cleveland, Chicago, the Cambria, the Joliet, and the Bethlehem works, the latter under the Nestor of steel superintendents, John Fritz, still with us, and known to all as " Uncle John."

All of these had their manufacturing troubles, as pioneers usually have who attempt the task of introducing new processes in countries

with conditions necessarily differing from those under which success
has been attained. Not one of these concerns escaped financial embarrassment. Several were reorganized, and two were sold by the
sheriff. .

The bold men who ventured upon the manufacture of steel, often
denounced as "robbers under the tariff," are entitled to great credit
for having served their country well. Few of them lived to receive
proper return for their enterprise.

When I saw with my own eyes the Bessemer process fairly
launched, and became acquainted with Bessemer himself and the leading steel manufacturers of Britain in 1875, I was ready to take the
plunge into steel. But none of my partners in the business was
then willing to take the risk. But soon after our success they agreed
to amalgamate the two branches. Even when we ventured into steel
manufacture it required some faith in our star. It was not a task for
timid men.

The Edgar Thomson Works beat the record in one particular; it
certainly was the first Bessemer steel concern to make a profit during
the first month's run. We figured $11,000 to the good in the starting
month—a bright omen for the future. We owed this to one of the
most original characters the steel industry has revealed, Capt. Bill
Jones. He refused partnership, which entailed financial responsibility, but would have made him a millionaire, declaring that he was
no business man and had troubles enough managing the works.
"Just give me a thundering salary," was his decision.

Our competitors in steel-rail manufacture regarded our temerity
with something bordering on contempt, knowing the long and serious
trials through which they had passed before their works produced
marketable product. They decided to ignore us.

Steel rails were made only in small amounts and by a few mills.
All had enough to do; there was no competition. Railroads, the
only customers, amicably agreed with makers upon fixed prices, as
they do still. Boycotted by the established makers, there was nothing
for us but quietly to find distant customers in various parts of the
country who were willing to try our rails at certain, or rather very
"uncertain," prices. We sold what was then considered by our competitors an enormous quantity. My recollection is that the Cambria
Works boasted of 4,000 tons in one month; to-day 50,000, all from
one set of rolls, is not unusual.

When our appearance as a seller came to the notice of the regular
makers, we were invited to a conference, and thereafter graciously
recognized. They were grievously shocked when they found that we
had already booked for that year more tonnage than all of them
combined. In all important conferences the Edgar Thomson Works
thereafter had a representative, and in this way I became acquainted
with the tariff question.

My views upon this important subject, which I still hold as firmly
as ever and have never changed, had been formed by Adam Smith,
who was not the bigoted "free trader" he is generally supposed to
have been, and by John Stuart Mill's celebrated paragraph, which

sums up the matter.[a]   Mention of that recalls an incident.   When dining in Birmingham with a few friends in the early seventies, John Bright being one, he asked me if I would explain to the company how any educated man in America could favor a tariff.   This was rather embarrassing for a young and, I may truly add, then a most modest man; but I did my best, winding up with Mill's paragraph, which is to the effect that it is best to buy in the cheapest and sell in the dearest market, but until the resources of a new, undeveloped country be tested, it can not be known which will be the cheapest producer, and a protective duty for a time to encourage capital and skill to test this was permissible.   Bright immediately said that the harm done by Mill by that paragraph was greater than all the good done by what he had ever written.

The prices for steel rails charged Americans by foreign manufacturers before rails were produced at home were $166 per ton in 1867, $158 in 1868, $132 in 1869.   For two years they fell to $107 and $102, but in 1873 and 1874 they rose again to $112 and $120.

When Mr. Blaine was with us in London in 1888 he attended a dinner at which Mr. Chamberlain was present and the tariff question naturally came up.   Mr. Chamberlain remarked that " Carnegie was a good fellow, and we all liked him, but still he didn't see why the United States should present him with $28 per ton protection upon his steel rails."   This brought laughter and applause.   When quiet was restored, Mr. Blaine replied: " We don't look at it in quite that way.   I am interested in railroads, and before we put on that tariff we had to pay you $100 per ton for steel rails.   Just before we sailed our board bought a large amount from Carnegie, and he charged us only $30.   I guess if we had not put on that tariff you would still be charging us $100."

After the laughter subsided, Sir Charles Tennant, president of the Scotland Steel Company, exclaimed: " Yes; $100 per ton; we all held to that price, and could have got it to-day if Carnegie and others hadn't interfered."

Mr. Blaine said, " Mr. Chamberlain, I don't think you have made much by this frank confession."

---

[a] In Principles of Political Economy (Vol. II, pages 487–488), John Stuart Mill says: " The only case in which, on mere principles of political economy, protecting duties can be defensible is when they are imposed temporarily (especially in a young and rising nation) in hopes of naturalizing a foreign industry, in itself perfectly suitable to the circumstances of the country.   The superiority of one country over another in a branch of production often arises only from having begun it sooner.   There may be no inherent advantage on one part or disadvantage on the other, but only a present superiority of acquired skill and experience.   A country which has this skill and experience yet to acquire may in other respects be better adapted to the production than those which were earlier in the field; and, besides, it is a just remark that nothing has a greater tendency to promote improvements in any branch of production than its trial under a new set of conditions.   But it can not be expected that individuals should, at their own risk, or rather to their certain loss, introduce a new manufacture and bear the burden of carrying it on until the producers have been educated up to the level of those with whom the processes are traditional.   A protecting duty, continued for a reasonable time, will sometimes be the least inconvenient mode in which the nation can tax itself for the support of such an experiment.   But the protection should be confined to cases in which there is good ground of assurance that the industry which it fosters will after a time be able to dispense with it.   Nor should the domestic producers ever be allowed to expect that it will be continued to them beyond the time strictly necessary for a fair trial of what they are capable of accomplishing."

" No," replied Mr. Chamberlain; " how could I, with Sir Charles
sitting there giving me away?"

Our tariff policy previous to the war was the football of parties
and far too uncertain to induce prudent men to invest capital in new
enterprises, especially in those requiring so much experimental work
as new branches of manufacturing. The civil war put an end to all
this. Our experience in that contest convinced not only the members
of the Republican party, but also, fortunately for our country, a large
number of potent Democrats, that we could no longer depend upon
Europe for our supplies of iron and steel.

When the war broke out, the demand for these indispensable articles
was imperious. We had instantly to get large supplies of both. The
Baldwin Locomotive Works and others promptly sent agents abroad
to buy up all that could be had, and through this wise policy disaster
was averted. The escape of the *Alabama* and other privateers
brought home to reasonable men the fact that we must have a home
supply of all material needed for our national safety. Hence the
leading steel and iron people were called to Washington, a satisfactory protective policy promptly agreed upon, and the " Schenck "
tariff passed. The same Congress (in July, 1870) also repealed the
income tax.

This action committed the Republican party to the policy of protection, and the tariff remained in force undisturbed for thirteen
years, but an almost equally important point gained was that many
leading Democrats also favored it. Thus the protective tariff now
became for the first time a national policy, and this gave capitalists
the assurance of continuity.

The steel-rail industry, thus assured of a period of protection,
developed rapidly. In 1882, twelve years after the tariff began, it
reached an output of 1,187,770 tons. Repeated attempts to repeal or
reduce duties were made, notably in 1876, 1878, and 1883, the Democrats having control of the House in these years. That the protective
policy was no longer a party question was conclusively proved, since
all of these attempts were defeated by the aid of Democratic votes,
one being that of Mr. Randall, Democratic Speaker of the House.

In the effort of 1883, to defeat a proposal that the duty upon steel
rails be reduced at one step from $28 to $10 per ton, I visited Washington, not to oppose a reduction of the duty, but to urge that it
should be made more gradually. The Hon. Abram S. Hewitt, then
in Congress and a power in the Democratic party, as well as an iron
and steel manufacturer, counseled moderation, and there was little
opposition to the smaller yet important reduction which we proposed,
namely, from $28 to $17 per ton, equal to 39 per cent reduction. In
1884 the Democrats attempted to pass another reduction bill, but
were defeated by their own members, no fewer than 40 Democrats
in the House voting against the measure.

The protective policy had full swing until 1890, when the McKinley bill was passed. People generally think of this bill as highly
protective; on the contrary, it reduced the duty on steel rails, beams,
and all structural shapes, nails, forgings, etc., from 20 to 30 per
cent, which I strongly advocated; but for the first time it also gave
adequate protection to the tin-plate industry, which previously had
no existence in America, one experiment having failed through pressure of foreign competition. Now it is firmly established. Another

feature of the McKinley bill was novel. It provided that 99 per cent of the duty should be refunded upon foreign iron and steel used in manufacturing articles for export. This gave American manufacturers all the benefits of free trade in their contests with foreign manufacturers through the world, and should be a feature in all future tariffs. All things considered, the McKinley bill was the wisest tariff reform measure ever framed.

All this proves that President McKinley belonged to our school of protectionists, strong when protection is needed, but equally strong in abolishing unnecessary duties. If alive to-day, I am certain he would approve the policy recommended in these pages. We labored long together to develop and guard our own resources, and now the time has come when most of these can and should stand upon their own feet and conquer.

Upon Mr. Cleveland's second election, in 1892, Democratic rule came in again, followed by distrust regarding the tariff. In 1894 the Wilson bill was introduced. As expected, it proved to be of the most drastic character and alarmed conservative reformers like myself. It became necessary to modify the measure in many respects if several of the manufacturing interests of the country were not to be sacrificed. I visited Washington and did what I could to obtain a measure which, while lowering duties generally and decidedly, would nevertheless enable manufacturers in all classes to continue work.

To two Democrats belong the chief credit of defeating the revolutionary features of the Wilson bill—Senator Gorman, Democratic leader of the Senate, and Governor Flower, of New York, an influential leader in the House. With these two gentlemen my relations had long been intimate. Few men have enjoyed for as many years as Senator Gorman did the confidence of his party as its leader and of the Senate as a whole. Wise, moderate, honest, he led his party with consummate address. When we met in Washington upon this serious business I found him quite satisfied that the proposed bill would injure some of our industries. After several conferences, he finally said to me: " I can afford to oppose this bill and beat the President, but I can not afford to oppose and be beaten by him. Now, if the Republican party will stand firm for a measure that carries great reductions of duties—remember, great reductions we must have, especially upon iron and steel—I can carry a reasonable bill. Our people have little confidence in the representatives of manufacturing interests. All of these clamor against any measure that touches their pockets; but if you will make out a schedule of reductions in duties which you assure us can be made without injury to American industries—for I don't want to injure one of these any more than you do— I can carry enough of our people with me who are good Americans and feel as I do." He kindly added that in testifying before committees I had gained their confidence, and as I had always been reasonable and had agreed to reductions in the past, his people would accept my is. " But, remember," he said, " there must he heavy reductions."

Then I met Governor Flower, and he was emphatic. " I am as sound a protectionist as you are," he said, " and would not vote for a reduction of duty that would injure one American industry; and I believe this Wilson bill would do so."

These men represented a sufficient number of Democratic Members who, combined with Republicans, insured the adoption of a less revolutionary measure. I made and submitted a list reducing the duties about one-third upon articles of iron and steel. This was accepted as thorough but judicious, and became a law. Meeting Senator Gorman afterwards, he laughingly explained: "I carried every one of your figures but one. I had to submit to free cotton ties to secure two Senators whom I did not wish to lose."

In this struggle that wise, practical Senator, the Hon. Stephen B. Elkins, was a power, supported as he was by his father-in-law, Senator Davis, a leading Democrat. Both Senator Elkins and I were lectured severely by the extreme protectionists, as also by the editor of one of the greatest of protection organs, for yielding and agreeing to reduce duties so much, but we survived. Our party, however, did not enthusiastically approve some of the large reductions made. At all events, the election of President McKinley in 1896 resulted in a special session, called two days after his inauguration (March 4, 1897), which resulted in our present Dingley tariff, restoring part of the reductions. After eleven years this is now to be superseded by another.

Much water has run under the bridges since then. Many changes have occurred, and hence many changes can be judiciously made in the tariff. There is no doubt about this; but on the other hand I have been led to the conclusion that conditions have changed so greatly in the interval that the tariff should now be viewed from a new standpoint.

The writer assumes that a decided majority of our voters are agreed—

First. That it is advisable for new countries to encourage capital by protective duties when seen to be necessary to develop new industries.

Second. That after full and exhaustive trials, if success be not finally attained, such protection should cease, except as noted hereunder.

Third. That should the experiment succeed, protection becomes unnecessary, and should steadily but gradually be abolished, provided that the home supply of any article absolutely necessary for the national safety shall not thereby be endangered.

So much for the doctrine of protection. That there is a cult who regard that doctrine as sacrosanct and everlasting, none knows better than the writer; but its members are few and not likely to increase, since our country has admittedly developed and gained and is to continue gaining manufacturing supremacy in one department after another until it reaches a position where free trade in manufactures would be desirable for it, all the markets of the world open to her, and hers to the world. Our difficulty will then be to get other nations to agree to free trade.

There will remain importations of foreign luxuries, which should be still heavily taxed for revenue, not protection; the aim being to levy the tax that would produce the greatest revenue from luxuries. This would not seriously affect the producer since the buyer pays all duties, and demand would not be greatly affected by the higher price, since only the rich use them.

SCHEDULE C—METALS AND MANUFACTURES OF.

We have already become by far the greatest of all manufacturing nations. Our "infant industries" of the past have reached maturity, and, speaking generally, are now quite able to protect themselves. The puling infant in the nurse's arms that Congress in 1871 nursed so tenderly will appear next year before its guardian as the stalwart champion who has conquered competitors in many fields, thus proving himself worthy of the protection bestowed upon him in his youth, and fully vindicating the protective policy pursued.

While the tariff, as a whole, even to-day has ceased to be primarily beneficial as a measure of protection, it has become of vast importance from the standpoint of revenue, and it is to this feature I bespeak the special attention of readers of all parties, for duties upon imports, not for protection, but for needed revenue, should not become a party question. Reasonable men of all parties may be expected to approve this plan of obtaining revenue.

That the huge industrial combinations of our time tend to enlarge the unfair inequalities which existed even before their day in the distribution of wealth will not be questioned; that it is desirable the contrast between the new cult of multimillionaires and the laborers should be lessened by every available means will also be generally accepted. The tariff is to-day a potent engine for this purpose, and it can be made even more so.

The following should be carefully considered by intelligent men of all parties. The amount of revenue from our imports in 1906 was $292,000,000; the last fiscal year (1907) it increased 14 per cent, to $332,000,000, exactly one-half of the total national revenue, $663,000,000.

Among the duties collected in 1906 (the details for 1907 have not yet been published) were the following:

Duties collected upon—

Cotton manufactures	$33,340,000
Leather manufactures	5,073,000
Silk manufactures	17,351,000
Wood manufactures	4,143,000
Wool manufactures	6,700,000
Stone and china ware	7,542,000
Fibers	18,900,000
Fruits and nuts	6,550,000
Glass	3,837,000
Furs	1,780,000
Jewelry	3,523,000
Malt liquors	1,507,000
Spirits, distilled	6,555,000
Oils	1,622,000
Wines	5,464,000
Toys, dolls, etc	2,065,000
Tobacco	23,927,000
Raw wool, camel and goat hair, alpaca, etc	39,068,000
	188,956,000

adding 14 per cent increase for 1907, a total of, say, $216,000,000.

Here we have $216,000,000 out of a total of $332,000,000 collected upon the luxuries of the rich, who alone use foreign articles to any extent.

This general statement may, and probably will, be disputed by agents of foreign manufacturers, claiming that the poor do use several of the articles named to some extent. Some of the wool imported, for instance, may go into inferior cloth used by the poor; so with other articles. But, notwithstanding all that can justly be urged of this nature, the indisputable fact will remain that with trifling, if any, exceptions, these imported articles are used almost exclusively by the rich or well-to-do.

Two articles of domestic production yielded all except $2,000,000 of the internal taxes, which were in 1907, $269,000,000.

Liquors (wines, whisky, and beer)	$215, 000, 000
Tobacco	52, 000, 000
	267, 000, 000

The workman who neither drinks nor smokes is thus virtually free from national taxation either through tariff or internal revenue, except upon sugar, which is the only important imported taxed article of general consumption by rich and poor alike. In 1901 this tax yielded $52,500,000. It is protective, with a view to securing a home supply from the beet root, and the Secretary of Agriculture recently informed the writer that he hopes to succeed. Last year we manufactured 500,000 tons, one-fifth of our consumption, and the growth of beets is increasing yearly. A few years should determine the success or failure of this experiment.

The difference between the United States on the one hand and France and Germany on the other is that the former supplies its own food products and taxes chiefly imported luxuries used by the rich (sugar excepted), while the latter must import food products which are consumed by both rich and poor; hence in France and Germany tariff duties imposed upon food to protect their own agriculturists reach the masses and must be paid by them. For instance, in 1905 Germany imported articles for consumption valued at no less than $512,000,000. In 1905 France imported food products valued at $156,000,000.

In 1905 customs duties yielded	$89, 000, 000
Internal taxes, sugar	28, 000, 000
Internal taxes, tobacco monopoly	90, 000, 000
Internal taxes, matches	10, 000, 000
	217, 000, 000

All classes consumed these articles, hence the duties upon them tax the poor.

Britain does not levy duties upon imported grain products, but taxes other articles, as follows:

In 1906:	
Tobacco	$65, 000, 000
Tea	34, 000, 000
Sugar	31, 000, 000
Coffee, cocoa, etc	3, 500, 000
Excise (internal) taxes upon whisky and beer	147, 000, 000
Total	280, 500, 000

These articles are consumed by rich and poor; but what we have said in regard to our tariff applies in great part to the British—those who neither smoke nor drink pay little taxation. The tax upon sugar has been reduced one-half this year, and Britain does well to tax liquor heavily, for intemperance is her greatest evil; it would be better if the excise taxes were increased; the tobacco tax is already very high. So also with America, if higher taxes can be collected without leading to illicit distillation. It is believed that we can now safely increase the tax upon domestic liquors and tobacco. By all means let the experiment be made, for these are articles hurtful to the people.

Thus does the American tariff, in happy contrast to others, almost exempt the poor and heavily tax the rich, just as it should, for it is they who have the ability to pay as required by the highest economic authority.

We have shown a revenue of $216,000,000 collected yearly upon the luxuries of the rich, without being seriously felt.

The excited free trader is often found declaiming against these heavy duties and others of the same class. To his appeals Congress should turn a deaf ear and rather increase than reduce them, not as a protective but as a revenue measure. That they could be advanced in most cases without materially reducing consumption is highly probable, since the rich will have what is desirable or fashionable regardless of a small increase in cost. The experiment should be made and on no account should the Representative, having the interests of the masses at heart, agree to one iota of reduction upon any of these or other luxuries, for in no other way can the wealthy classes so surely be made to pay so great a sum toward the support of the Government.

This is sound and fair policy, for the man who has no more income than sufficient to meet the physical wants of himself and those dependent upon him should be considered as not having ability to pay any taxation whatever, just as the humble homestead is exempt from sale under a mortgage or the small income is exempt under taxes upon incomes in countries laboring under that burden. Adam Smith's dictum is in these memorable words: " The subjects of every state ought to contribute toward the support of the government, as nearly as possible, in proportion to their respective abilities; that is, in proportion to the revenue which they respectively enjoy under the protection of the state." Every legislator should bear these words in mind. This is the feature of the tariff in which the great mass of our working people is most deeply interested.

Virtually, as we have seen, the working classes of America who neither drink nor smoke are exempt from national taxation, sugar excepted. So are the British, who, however, are still taxed upon tea, coffee, and chocolate. They are vastly better off in this respect than the German working classes, who, in addition, have a tax upon imported food, which also raises the prices of the home-grown food supply.

The next Congress dealing with the tariff will probably be inclined at first to reduce duties all round and perhaps to abolish some, but its first care should be to maintain present duties, and even in some cases to increase them, upon all articles used almost exclusively by the rich, and this not for protection but for revenue, not drawn from the workers but from the rich. That is the first and prime duty of Congress. We should not forget that government expenditures have increased enormously in recent years and that additional revenue is required.

Its second duty is to reduce duties greatly upon manufactured articles and to abolish entirely those no longer needed.

The writer has cooperated in making several reductions as steel manufacturers became able to bear reductions. To-day they need no protection, unless perhaps in some new specialties unknown to the writer, because steel is now produced cheaper here than anywhere else, notwithstanding the higher wages paid per man. Not a ton of steel is produced in the world at as small an outlay for labor as in our own country. Our coke, coal, and iron ores are much cheaper, because more easily obtained and transported, and our output per man is so much greater, owing chiefly to the large standardized orders obtainable only upon our continent; the specialized rolling mills; machinery kept weeks upon uniform shapes without change of rolls, and several other advantages. Britain and Germany are the only important steel manufacturing nations other than ourselves. I am assured by one who has recently examined the matter that he found even in Germany to-day that the cost per ton for labor was greater than with us, unusually high as our wages are at present. Were there free trade in iron and steel between America and Europe, a few orders might go abroad at times when American mills were fully occupied and high prices prevailed, and this would be advantageous to our country; but if these shipments amounted to much, prices would rise in Europe and prevent further exports to our market. The United States made last year more steel (over 23,000,000 tons) than Germany, Britain, France, and Belgium combined. New steel works are under construction which will produce enough to enable her to make more than the whole world besides. This she will do within five years, probably within three. The day has passed when any foreign country can seriously affect our steel manufactures, tariff or no tariff. The Republic has become the home of steel, and this is the age of steel. It may probably be found that there exists the small manufacturer of some specialty in steel which still needs a measure of protection. The writer hopes, if such there be, the committee will give patient attention to such cases. It is better to err on the side of giving these too much, rather than too little, support. Every enterprise of this kind should be fostered. The writer speaks only of the ordinary articles and forms of steel as being able to stand without protection. He hopes there are to-day pioneers in several new lines requiring protection which will be generously given temporarily. The committee should welcome such special cases.

There are several features in our tariff affecting the masses of our people which should be carefully looked into, since they subject these to the increased cost of some of the necessaries of life. I notice three charges often made against our present tariff.

The first in importance relates to illuminating oils. It is charged that Congress refused to place a duty upon these, but by some means a bill was passed which provided that upon oil from any country that taxed American oils a corresponding tax would be collected in America upon oils imported from such country. Russia then taxed American oils, and our oil producers enjoy protection from Russian oils, and the ludicrous spectacle is seen of each country protecting itself from importations of oil from the other. If all this be true this is clearly not a case of genuine protection. It gives to each interest a monopoly of oil in its own country.

It is said, but how truly the writer does not know, that although the Russian and American companies had agreed between themselves not to invade each other's country, nevertheless oils found their way in through sales made by these companies to other parties, and that existing legislation was therefore secured by the oil companies in Russia and America. It is such and other kindred charges published throughout the country that make the tariff the object of attack as a vehicle of corruption. No duty is more imperative upon the part of the honest upholders of the principle of protection when needed than to purge the next tariff of every trace of other than open and honest legislation, clearly intended to shield the masses from unfair taxation and thus promote national prosperity. The oil producers, like the steel producers of our country, need no protection from the products of other lands, and the retaliatory act should be promptly repealed.

The second charge often presented relates to the thread industry. The leading producers in Britain and America have consolidated, and it is said virtually fix prices. The present duty enables the home producer to maintain higher prices here, while its abolition would enable the continental manufacturers to export their product to America in competition with the consolidation, which has now a monopoly, except that there is one cotton-thread producer still in our country ostensibly outside of the combination. When international combinations like this appear, or when any of our manufacturers enter into international agreements, it may be found necessary in the future to provide that the Interstate Commission should have control. It is clear there must be some control or the consumer will be seriously affected. The labor in the mills of America is higher paid, and thread actually costs more per spool, I am told, than in Scotland, differing in this respect from steel rails. On the other hand, home manufacturers have cheaper cotton. The thread combination needs careful scrutiny. No doubt the congressional committee will give this due attention and listen to the " other side " of the question, for there are always two sides.

Foreign cutlery is the third and last subject, often in evidence. The duties upon this class of articles are complained of as being far too high, but I take it that imported cutlery is used exclusively by the rich. The tariff committee should maintain present high duties upon the extra fine and costly ware, but fix much lower duties upon the ordinary grades used by the masses, just as the present tariff admits sewing and darning needles free, although other kinds are taxed. There seems no reason, however, why steel for cutlery should not be purchased cheaper in our country than abroad, nor why our home manufacturers should not supply our home demands for cutlery.

The Republican party has nursed home industries, supported, however, as we have seen, by an element in the Democratic party which we sober protectionists may be excused for considering the wiser element of that party. Hence the tariff has become a national, not a party, issue.

That the value of our manufactures in 1905, $16,866,706,985 (£3,373,000,000), exceeds those of our closest competitor, Britain, three times over, and that our exports of these in 1906 were $686,-000,000 and of crude materials for use in manufacturing $510,000,000, is ample vindication of the protective policy of the past.

In our day a different duty devolves upon our party and its democratic protectionist allies. The infant we have nursed approaches
the day when he should be weaned from tariff milk and fed upon
the stronger food of free competition. It needs little, if any, more
nursing, but the change should not be made abruptly. It is better
to err upon the safe side, if we err at all; but he is the best of protectionists who corrects all faults as they are revealed and positively
declines to subject the nation to protection in any branch where it is
not clearly needed, affording protection always with the resolve that
it shall be temporary. A class of excellent citizens has arisen who
really see in the tariff one of the chief causes of national demoraliza-
tion; not a few consider it should be the leading issue in a presidential campaign. The writer has personal friends on both sides—those
who see in it the chief source of political evil and those who think it
the country's salvation. For neither view is there sound foundation
to-day, for protection is no longer the vital issue it was; but the first
class will have something to rest their contentions upon, however, if
there be continued upon the statute books duties and provisions manifestly out of date. All such and everything of a dubious character
in our tariff legislation, our party, in the forthcoming revision as the
legitimate protection of the true protective policy, should boldly
sweep away.

In conclusion, a "tariff for protection," which was the issue forty
years ago, should now give place to a "tariff for revenue," and therefore the strict maintenance of the present duties upon foreign luxuries paid by the rich. The present tariff rightfully exempts the masses
of the people from almost all national taxation, because they have not
"the ability to pay," as required by Adam Smith, the greatest economic authority.

The writer, having often been classed with the "robber tariff
barons," may probably be proclaimed as a convert to new views since
he retired from manufacturing, but his associates know better, and
many a foreign manufacturer could tell of the prophecy with which
he has so often startled them; namely, that in a short time America
would become the leading manufacturer and foremost apostle of free
trade, while their own countries would be discussing whether or not
to put up the barriers. Britain to-day is seriously considering this
very question.

The writer has not changed one iota since he first formed a clear
and definite view in regard to protection. For new countries possessed of natural but undeveloped resources it is the only policy available, hence we see Canada, Australia, and New Zealand all adopting
it, even against their motherland, to whom they are indebted for protection from enemies, a seemingly most ungrateful return, could they
not plead that it is indispensable for the development of their own
resources.

The question assumes another form when old and fully developed
countries like Britain, after having fully tested their capacity to produce any article in competition with other lands, are considering
whether to handicap outside competition. This is not a case of temporary protection through duties upon competing imports, but one
which opens the question whether it is economically best to use the
domestic product even at greater cost. The reply seems to be: If it
involve the loss of a home supply of an article essential for the

national safety, yes; if not, no. This is also true Adam Smith doctrine. Each case must be judged on its merits from that point of view.

There is no occasion for haste or for any revolutionary step in coming tariff legislation. It is better to go a little too slow than a little too fast. In the writer's opinion, the revision of the tariff could to-day safely and advantageously be made a radical one upon the lines suggested; but if Congress, in deference to the timid manufacturer, "whom we have always with us," thinks it prudent not to disturb his dreams unduly, and only halves present duties upon some articles and abolishes them entirely upon others—always provided it guards zealously the present duties upon the luxuries of the rich for revenue—the writer will be thankful and philosophic as usual, because one step in the right direction will have been taken, and he knows the final step must come before long; the sooner the better.

Just as the Republic has won supremacy in steel, and can to-day, even during this temporary world-wide depression, send it profitably to every free market in the world in successful competition with all other manufacturers, so is she to win this proud position in one field of industry after another, her enormous standardized home market being one of the chief elements of her conquering power. Many foreign luxuries will still be imported, but these should yield revenue paid by the rich consumer.

The writer is confident that this prophecy will soon be fulfilled, for nothing can keep the Republic from speedily dwarfing all other nations industrially, if she only frowns upon great navies and increased armies and continues to tread the paths of peace, following the truly American policy of the fathers.

ALFRED O. CROZIER, WILMINGTON, DEL., REPLIES TO TARIFF ARTICLE OF ANDREW CARNEGIE, PUBLISHED IN THE CENTURY MAGAZINE.

WILMINGTON, DEL., *November 24, 1908.*

Hon. SERENO E. PAYNE,
    Chairman Ways and Means Committee,
                Washington, D. C.

DEAR SIR: Andrew Carnegie's declaration in favor of complete abolition of the protective policy, so far as iron and steel are concerned, substituting a mere revenue tariff, is a thrust at the heart of the entire protection system; for if his position is true as to iron and steel, it is true respecting many other great industries. It raises the most dangerous and difficult situation in the history of tariff legislation. It seems to put Mr. Carnegie on the side of the people and against the trusts, while those who oppose his proposition may be accused of favoring trusts at the expense of the people. But this is a superficial view. Whether so intended by Mr. Carnegie or not, no more clever plan could be devised to permanently intrench the steel trust in absolute mastery and monopoly of the entire iron and steel business of the United States. Incidentally, every one of its nearly 200,000 employees and the 1,000,000 wives and children dependent upon them would forever and constantly be at the mercy of the Wall street managers of that trust. They would be obliged to submit to any terms as to wages and hours imposed by the corporation. with no possible way of escape.

Trusts are all overcapitalized. They must charge high prices to pay dividends on such excessive capitalization. The one menace to a trust's supremacy is establishment of new competitive industries. It is well known that, other things being equal, a corporation with actual capital equal to one-third the total of the stocks and bonds of the United States Steel Corporation could easily handle the same volume of business done by that trust. When the trust maintains high prices that will yield a profit on its enormous total of securities, capital is constantly tempted to start independent plants. This can be done over and over, forcing the trust to buy them out, and at high prices, except when, as with the Tennessee Coal and Iron Company, Providence or Wall-street controlled agencies sends a panic to aid the trusts in their process of benevolent assimilation of competitors, for it is wholly impracticable for a big trust to cut prices on its entire output to crush an independent plant with a comparatively small output.

The rigid enforcement of stringent laws against rebates and special transportation advantages and combinations in restraint of trade ultimately will largely settle the trust problem, chiefly because trusts are so excessively capitalized. It may be necessary also to so regulate banking as to insure that small producers can borrow money at the same rates paid by trusts, and to limit the monopoly of raw materials.

The trust problem will be worked out gradually and satisfactorily to the people and to such trusts as are satisfied with reasonable profits, unless Mr. Carnegie's plan to abolish the protective tariff is adopted. If his plan is put in force the trusts, in their most offensive and oppressive form will be fastened upon the people forever, for they no longer would be endangered by the starting of independent plants. The constant menace of competition of products made abroad by cheap foreign labor would scare independent capital from embarking in an enterprise that would be threatened on one side by an aggressive trust and on the other by unrestricted foreign importations. The danger of new competing plants being thus removed by act of Congress, the trust would be left free to both lower wages and increase prices of its products with impunity, for there is no means known to the law to force them to maintain wages or reduce prices. In case of a strike the international trust would produce in its mills abroad and ship here, closing its American plants until labor is starved into submission. To protect itself against foreign importations, the trust has only to internationalize itself. This could be done easily by offering foreign producers the temptation of greater gains, aided by the spur of threatened retaliation and competition abroad by the American trust, and by reenactment here of the high tariff. In the long run it is safe to assume that producers the world over will unite for greater profits. In fact, wages here could then be reduced so goods can be produced much cheaper and used abroad to whip foreign producers into a general combination to plunder, with excessive prices, the consumers of the world. It is a dazzling scheme, such as the genius of modern finance is capable of conceiving

and executing, and it is wholly practicable. There is some inducement to them in the fact that the international trust would largely
be beyond the reach of our antitrust and other laws.

Four years ago, in an address, and recently in The Magnet, I
pointed out the probability and danger of international trusts and
abolition of the protection policy as a means of further trust aggran-
dizement and for tightening upon the people the screw of trust
monopoly and attendant financial and political domination. Since
then the iron and steel men of the United States and those of Europe
have held meetings abroad which seem clearly to foreshadow the
ultimate creation of a gigantic international trust to control the iron
and steel business of the entire world. Whether Mr. Carnegie was
chosen to inaugurate as a benificent philanthropy the one thing needed
to make the international trust practicable or possible, or whether
Providence moved him to so speak on his own account in all inno-
cence as to the ultimate ruinous effect upon American workingmen
and producers generally, I do not know. Doubtless it was the latter,
for Mr. Carnegie is an excellent gentleman, who has done many
patriotic acts. But it is time for the American people to "Look,
stop, listen!" before taking a step of such possible danger to their
welfare.

Tariff reduction and readjustment is due and right. It should be
thorough, honest, unselfish. How to do it and avoid these perils is a
problem that will tax the wisdom and patriotism of Congress to the
utmost. Whether it would be practicable and legal to maintain the
high tariff to guard against these dangers, and then, in lieu of tariff
reduction and in return for this protection, impose upon products of
American manufacturers engaged in interstate commerce a special internal tax equal to a fair proportion of the general tariff, I am not
yet prepared to say. It may be worth considering. It is made
merely as a suggestion. In this way all the people would share in
such excessive profits as might be realized because of the high tariff
maintained by the people's laws for the common good. Consumers
would not so object to high prices if a fair proportion of the excessive
profits were contributed to the general welfare.

A billion dollars is needed by the Government for the improvement
or construction of natural and artificial waterways. And other billions will be needed as time goes on. Such a tax on interstate commerce would yield it without appreciable harm either to producers
or consumers. And the public improvements it would enable, and the
general progress and prosperity such improvements would cause, certainly would offset any such burden. If this plan should be considered wiser than to let down the bars to all the evils mentioned, and to
the uncertain menace of the products of 15 cents a day Asiatic labor,
some practicable and legal plan doubtless can be devised by Congress
for putting it into effect, for the people have not by their Constitution permanently tied their own hands in a way to prevent what may
be for the general welfare. Surely American workmen and producers that are not such trusts as are seeking by international action to
rid themselves of all responsibility and accountability to the people's
laws, while they enjoy the country's rich markets, will prefer such
interstate-commerce tax to the uncertainty and dangers incident to a
destruction of the protective-tariff policy, and our home markets
would be saved to our industries. The American manufacturers and

workmen have come to look upon the protective doctrine the same as the people of South America revere the Monroe doctrine. Congress surely will not enforce the latter, even at the risk of war, for the benefit of alien peoples, and then expose our own citizens to unrestricted commercial and industrial exploitation by foreign nations.

Very respectfully, yours,

ALFRED O. CROZIER.

STATEMENT OF ANDREW CARNEGIE, OF NEW YORK CITY, RELATIVE TO DUTIES ON STEEL PRODUCTS.

MONDAY, *December 21, 1908.*

(The witness was duly sworn by the chairman.)

The CHAIRMAN. Mr. Carnegie, the committee desired you to come before us because, first, there was an article published by you a short time since with reference to the tariff, and the committee would like to have such a statement from you in the first place as you desire to make in regard to the matter contained in that article, and especially showing the reasons why the article mentioned by you is no longer in need of a protective duty.

Mr. CARNEGIE. Mr. Chairman, I presume it would be more informal for me to sit—more like a conference. I do not want to appear as an orator.

Mr. Chairman, I am delighted to give you all the information in my power—the truth, the whole truth, and nothing but the truth. I am a reluctant witness, as you know. I thought that, not being an iron manufacturer, perhaps you would excuse me from appearing. You have judged otherwise; and now, as a citizen, it is my duty to tell you everything I know, and I shall do so.

Most fortunate, Mr. Chairman, am I, in the postponement of my appearance which has taken place. Events have traveled fast since I wrote that article early this year as a reminiscent article, a companion to an article giving my experience upon rates and rebates. I do not appear this morning as the sole announcer of the fact that the steel industry no longer needs protection. I am flanked on the right by the head of the greatest corporation that the world has ever known, who told you that we could get along without a tariff; and on the left by the harvester—what is his name?

Mr. GAINES. Mr. Metcalf.

Mr. CARNEGIE. Mr. Metcalf, yes. On the left by the head of the greatest agricultural manufacturing concern that the world has ever seen; and from the mouths of these two my statement is justified. But it was no news to me that Judge Gary would make that statement. He has never hesitated to make it. Long before I wrote my article the officials of the Government knew that these were his views; not only his, but others in the steel business. It was a matter of common acquiescence, if men talked steel, that they were quite independent of the tariff. I did not think it necessary for me to go into any details to justify my statement. I produce these two witnesses that have been before you.

The CHAIRMAN. Mr. Carnegie, the president of the Pennsylvania Steel Company appeared before the committee and gave us items of cost of steel rails in his mill. He made the cost considerably higher than that of the United States Steel Corporation, and Judge Gary said in his statement that the cost of the United States Steel Company was at least $2 per ton less than some or all of their rivals in business. One aspect of his testimony—one view of it—looked as though it might be more than $2 per ton less; and the committee desires to get at the facts that will tend to show whether the taking off of the entire duty upon steel rails, for instance, would cripple the independent concerns, what few there are outside of the United States Steel Corporation, and perhaps stop their business—if we should remove the whole duty or a part of it—I think that is what Mr. Felton, the president of the Pennsylvania Steel Company, said.

Mr. CARNEGIE. Well, Mr. Chairman, there are more ways of figuring cost than there are ways of killing a cat. It is a simple matter of bookkeeping. You have a statement from Mr. Schwab that we made steel rails at $15 a ton—$12 a ton shop cost, and $3 a ton, I believe, for general expenses. Now, if the mode of keeping accounts of cost that we adopted and also held to were held to now, I do not think that the cost of steel rails to any concern in this country would be as great as either Judge Gary or the other witnesses have testified. I made a statement that a ton of steel is now made cheaper in America than any foreign countries, and if that were tested to-day at the works at Pittsburg, which made the $15 rate, and a commission should make the foreign manufacturer adopt the same mode of telling cost, then I do not believe the result would be that Pittsburg would lose the trophy or the honor of being to-day the cheapest producer of steel in the world.

Mr. DALZELL. Mr. Carnegie, the statement that Mr. Schwab made, whereby he showed the mill cost of rails at $12 a ton, related to a period some ten years or more ago. And he also gave us the present figures, based upon the same method of bookkeeping and covering the same detail of items, to show the present cost of steel rails at his mill to be $21.50 a ton mill cost.

Mr. CARNEGIE. You are quite mistaken, Mr. Dalzell. Mr. Schwab did not give you—I have not read the testimony, nor I have not read Judge Gary's testimony. I wish to be questioned, and to give you my own impressions, and tell the truth as I see it; but Mr. Schwab told me that he was not speaking for any steel mill; that he got his information from a private producer of ore in Pittsburg.

Mr. DALZELL. Well, Mr. Schwab gave us the cost of his $12 rails by items, beginning with the ore, the coke, and all that sort of thing; and he also gave us the cost of rails at the present time, commencing with the same figures, the same method of bookkeeping, and going on and following precisely the same details as in the previous case.

Mr. CARNEGIE. Mr. Chairman, upon the ore the United States Steel Company is smelting to-day, to make a ton of rails in Pittsburg they pay royalties in perpetuity of 20 cents a ton.

The CHAIRMAN. Mr. Gary testified that they paid 85 cents a ton for all they bought of Mr. Hill, of the Northern Pacific.

Mr. CARNEGIE. Quite true; but Mr. Gary has not smelted a ton of ore from Mr. Hill's mines; they are not open yet. Gentlemen, here is the proposition——

STEEL RAILS—ANDREW CARNEGIE.

The CHAIRMAN. He stated that he made a contract to take ore during the present year, a large quantity—I do not know as he stated the quantity—at 85 cents a ton, and that they are bound by that contract to pay 4½ per cent upon the value at 85 cents of the ore they were to take out this year, and so on from year to year, the price increasing annually; the 4½ per cent is paid as a deferred payment.

Mr. CARNEGIE. Certainly; and they have a right to cancel that contract after ten years. It is a speculation in ore. My statement was that if you take the things to-day to make a ton of steel, you will make it as cheap as the party abroad can do it, and therefore that no tariff is needed, because nature has placed a tariff in favor of the home producer which not even Congress can remove. Take into consideration the cost of transporting rails from the English mill, if you please, to the seaboard, to be shipped across the Atlantic 3,000 miles to land at a seaport here, when four-fifths of that steel that they would import would be needed, on the average, at the center of population, which would be near Chicago, and therefore they would have to pay freight out there again; it is impossible that foreign manufacturers can compete seriously to the injury of our home manufacturers; otherwise, how could Judge Gary say he could do it without the tariff?

The CHAIRMAN. What do you say as to the Pennsylvania Steel Company's mill located at Harrisburg, where freights are substantially the same as Chicago or New York?

Mr. CARNEGIE. Quite true; but they do not have to pay the ocean freight.

The CHAIRMAN. That is correct.

Mr. CARNEGIE. Now, Mr. Chairman, Judge Gary is the ablest man I know in the steel business, and he tells you that their great concern does not need a duty; but the solicitude of the Judge for his competitors, or those who should be his competitors, is sublime. [Laughter.]

Mr. COCKRAN. Competitors by his own commission; perhaps you will concede that?

Mr. CARNEGIE. Allow me to continue this strain. It is sublime. It reminds one of one of Æsop's fables, where the monkey wanted to rake the chestnuts out of the fire, but put that duty upon the cats. And that is what Judge Gary is trying to do here. When he told you that his vast company could do without a tariff, that was the Judge who spoke. But when he introduced the smaller concerns, that was the lawyer, and he is equally eminent in both.

The CHAIRMAN. What do you say of the president of the Pennsylvania Steel Company?

Mr. CARNEGIE. I say, Mr. Chairman, that if he is making rails at $26.50 cost and selling rails to Canada at a loss, his stock would not be above par to-day. And the Pennsylvania Railroad Company, who own and control that work, would, I think, very soon put it under a different management. Let him produce statement for five years and see the result. His statement embraces no dates. A short period of small output might show $26.50 and yet mean nothing.

Now, let me tell you about these dear, weak competitors that Judge Gary has introduced. We will take the case of the Cambria Company, because it is the oldest. The Cambria Steel Company now is a tremendous institution. It has departments connected with its works in the manufacture of wire and other things, and it has been very successful. It can compete with the United States Steel Company within a dollar or a dollar and a half a ton, for the reason that it has everything which I know the United States Steel Company has, except that the steel company has railroads, one that I built to Pittsburg and the other that it got with the North Chicago Works. Now, the profit on transportation of their ore is the only advantage that I know that the steel company has over the Cambria, and if ever they were to compete, that profit of a dollar or a dollar and a half, whatever it is, on the transportation—it would be a cold day for the United States Steel Company—a dollar or two a ton profit on their product. It would not pay interest on their bonds. Why, Mr. Chairman, the thought is stifling; it would make me doubt about the security of my bonds, and I have not the slightest.

Now, we will take the Lackawanna Company—Mr. Chairman, I would like to hear that remark that you just made to my friend Mr. Dalzell. [Great laughter.] That is not fair. Now, just tell us what you told him.

The CHAIRMAN. I did not make a remark. I said " We are getting a little more fun than information."

Mr. CARNEGIE. I am sorry. I will step out if I am not giving information.

Mr. COCKRAN. That is his personal view. I do not think that represents the view of the committee.

Mr. CARNEGIE. Mr. Chairman, I can quite understand how you have fun, because the chairman is as full of information as I am; but I am here to tell the truth, I am bound to do it, I have sworn to tell the whole truth, and come what may I am going to do it.

The CHAIRMAN. Of course I did not mean that as a reflection on you.

Mr. CARNEGIE. I have no suspicion that you did. On the contrary, I think you whispered to Dalzell: " The jig is up." [Great laughter.]

Mr. COCKRAN. I think perhaps it was that " The jig is down."

Mr. CARNEGIE. Well, " Where was I at?" I had spoken of the Cambria Iron Company. I will now speak of the Lackawanna Company. That is another of " Lawyer " Gary's competitors that he expects to use to rake the chestnuts out of the fire. He has no cause for himself, mark you, not the slightest; therefore he must find some weak and struggling people whom a reduction of the tariff would injure. Is that not true?

The CHAIRMAN. The Lackawanna Company has an ideal location, has it not, at Buffalo?

Mr. CARNEGIE. Certainly; it is a good location. What are business men for?

The CHAIRMAN. Sometimes I wonder, when I see some of them locate, what they are for.

Mr. CARNEGIE. Perhaps, because you do not know the steel business as well as those who locate it.

The CHAIRMAN. I agree with you on that.

Mr. CARNEGIE. Now, let me speak of the Lackawanna. It was a good location, but I am sorry to say, corporation like, it placed its works upon the sand, and there has been a continuous struggle ever since to make these works run; so that it has no advantages in that respect. The Lackawanna Company has its own coal, coke, iron, stone—I place it with the Cambria in regard to United States Steel. We come, then, to the Pennsylvania Steel Company. Now, the Pennsylvania Steel Company has great works at Harrisburg and great works at Baltimore. When the Judge talks about little ones—little manufacturers—there is not one of these that is not bigger than anything I know of in Europe excepting Krupps. and that is not a manufacturer of ordinary things; its principal business is in armor. The Pennsylvania Steel Company has a mine of wealth in its ore in Cuba I am delighted to say, because the question of ore threatens to be a serious one; and they are going—they expect and I believe they are going—to make a quality of steel rails so far superior to any made now, at a cost which no other can reach except that enterprising young man, Schwab, of the Bethlehem Company, for he has a mine in Cuba, too. They are going to make a great fortune in their ore.

Now, I have said he can not figure cost, anyway. That is the same gentleman who told you he had no agreement with other steel companies; that he could sell where he pleased, to whom he pleased, and as much as he pleased. Well, Mr. Chairman, if you had asked him if he had not a sort of understanding, which had the same result as the agreement, he would have had to tell you that he had; and I do not like witnesses to talk in a double sense. We have not only to tell the truth, but we have to tell the whole truth, and I tell it.

The Pennsylvania Steel Company and the Cambria Iron Company and the Lackawanna Company were making steel before the Carnegie Steel Company began to build steel works, and if either of these companies is unable to compete with the world in making steel, it is quite time for the Government to cease to give them artificial protection in order to enable them to do it. That is my opinion. What is best for the country? Remember, I am one who believes that the total abolition of the duties on steel they make will not affect one of these companies to any serious extent. There may be a few shiploads of steel landed in San Francisco, or in Galveston, that would not otherwise have arrived, but if you are going to take the money of the people to injure the Pacific coast and the Galveston coast, I think it is an unjust use of money. The Pacific coast is benefited by having ships coming there for their exports to get a little lading, because it reduces the price of transportation for their products to the competing market; and to rob the Pacific coast of its natural advantages, and Galveston of its natural advantages, in order simply that the manufacturer of the East, 3,000 miles away, should not pay $15 a ton freight upon the 2,000 tons of rails that reach the Pacific coast—there is no great amount of rails needed there—would, I believe, be an unfair policy to the people.

Now, I want to make just one remark here. There is not one of these companies that was not in the business before the Carnegie Steel Company was, and it is not the policy of any government to coddle and nurse inefficient management. These companies have had opportunities to get into a position to compete with anything, and if the Government is going to bolster up the inefficient, then it is a bad outlook for the position of America in the steel business.

The CHAIRMAN. California can be supplied from the Alabama, the Birmingham Works, can it not?

Mr. CARNEGIE. Thank you, sir, for pressing that very cogent reason for not bolstering these works in the East.

The CHAIRMAN. Mr. Carnegie, the Bureau of Corporations of the Department of Commerce and Labor have inquired into the cost of making pig iron, steel rails, and structural steel for a period of five years from 1902 to 1906, both inclusive. They had access to the books of seven great companies, making 93 per cent of the total output of each of those articles. They have tabulated the cost ascertained from the books of those companies by an efficient corps of clerks, and with a steel expert to help them. We have the results of that tabulation, which show the average cost of steel for those five years to be $22.39 per ton. It was $22.32 for 1902, $22.78 for 1903, $21.57 for 1904, $21.30 for 1905, and $22.77 for 1906. Now, they make up a table of the items of cost of steel rails as prepared from the books, and they put the cost of Bessemer pig iron at $14.52, and for other pig iron not Bessemer, they make the cost $14.01. They say: " The difference of 51 cents between the average cost of Bessemer pig iron and of pig iron used for rails is due to the variation in the cost of the excess tonnage and to freight on some of the iron." They add that 51 cents to the cost of pig iron which they have ascertained from the same source to be $14.01 on the average for five years, and then they allow for waste $1.95, making a total cost for pig iron in a ton of rails $16.47. They make a cost of labor $1.98; manganese, and so forth, 99 cents; fuel, 35 cents; steam, 62 cents—of course labor is included in that item; molds, 15 cents; rolls, 17 cents; materials in repairs and maintenance, 42 cents; supplies and tools, 27 cents, miscellaneous and general works' expense, 51 cents; general expense, 14 cents; depreciation, 16 cents; making a total, on the average, of $22.23 for the five years.

Now, they further show that the lowest cost of steel rails by any one company for one year in their investigation was $19.33 for the year 1905, while the highest cost was $31.27 in 1903, but that, they explain, was in the starting of new works. The next highest cost was $30.29 in 1903 under normal conditions of work. And, then, they have also compiled the prices obtained for these steel rails, which were $28 a ton less freight, allowed in certain instances to certain points, which made it something over $27. I can give you about what the prices were: 1902, $27.65; 1903, $28.07; 1904, $25.70; 1905, $27.13; 1906, $27.61. And that shows a profit per ton in 1902 of $5.34; 1903, $4.32; 1904, $4.17; 1905, $5.88; 1906, $4.85, with an average of $4.97.

That is the result of this investigation made by the Department of Commerce and Labor. Of course those figures are as close as we can get at it with our information, such as we have, and they are confirmed by the testimony of Mr. Gary, who did not know that we had the figures when he came before the committee; and also by the president of the Pennsylvania Steel Company, although they spoke of 1907, when there was a boom on, and prices were a little higher—and I think they also spoke of 1906. But if those prices are correct, do you say that the removal of the whole duty on pig iron and steel rails would not cripple any steel corporation or any pig-iron producing corporation in the United States by competition coming from abroad?

Mr. CARNEGIE. Mr. Chairman, I will answer that question by asking you another.

The CHAIRMAN. Oh, do not ask me——

Mr. CARNEGIE. But " turn about is fair play; " I have answered a great many of your questions, and now answer one for me. If those figures were correct—and remember the celebrated adage of the man who said "As for figures, I know they lie "—but I ask you, as a man of sense and judgment, if those figures be anything like the real truth, how can Judge Gary stand up before you on oath, and declare that he does not need protection?

The CHAIRMAN. If he tells the truth in other respects, that he can produce steel rails at least $2 a ton cheaper than anyone else; and if his product goes into this percentage, as it must, his being 50 per cent of the whole output, then it may be that Judge Gary is not so far out of the way.

Mr. CARNEGIE.. Judge Gary is the ablest man in that business. If I had followed the advice which parties gave me, to gain control of the United States Steel Company when its prices were at $8 or $9 a share, which I could easily have done, I should immediately have said to Judge Gary: " Judge, I want you to remain with me; you are the ablest manager I know; " and I would have doubled his salary, or, better still, I would have followed my practice and made him a partner. The judge spoke the truth, just as Schwab spoke the truth when he told you the cost of our steel rails, which was $15, against your $22; but it was the " judge " who spoke, as I said before, but when he pities the other people, it is the " lawyer; " and the judge is equally eminent in both. I can describe him best by a Scotch term that comes to me, and if there was a Scotchman here I would speak it, but it is not translatable, because I can not find a synonym. The Judge is what the Scotch call a " pawkee chiel." [Laughter.]

Now, there is another question that I want to ask you. If steel rails of the Pennsylvania Company cost $26.50, why is its stock, even in the depressed times, above par?

The CHAIRMAN. Oh, well, when you get into that realm, I will have to say that I do not know why stocks are above par.

Mr. CARNEGIE. Gentlemen of the committee, allow me to address you in one word: Figures will do nothing but mislead you, if you do not apply your brains to such questions as these upon which I address you. Why do these people not require a tariff? And I would advise you to take Judge Gary's word for that.

The CHAIRMAN. Mr. Carnegie, how much profit should a manufacturer receive on steel rails in order to pay a reasonable interest on the investment, and to renew his plant, if necessary?

Mr. CARNEGIE. Gentlemen, that depends on what steel company it is and what the management of it is. When we made rails at $15— I have sold them at $16 in competition, but that is not a fair profit. But I refrain from naming what is a fair profit, because I think if you have competition and a free market it is for the interests of this country that the most enterprising manufacturer should make the greatest profit. If you want to keep this country ahead in steel, you can not depend upon great combinations. In the nature of the case they become conservative. Now, as an illustration: We are the foremost nation in the manufacture of steel, admittedly so, and we should be to-day. We make 23 million tons of steel; Britain only makes 5. We have suffered ourselves to fall behind in adopting improvements, except in the case of the Bethlehem Steel Company. I think Mr. Schwab deserves a vote of thanks by Congress for two things he has done. He visited Germany, and he found in one mill the practice of rolling girders of scientific form. There is not a girder made in America that does not charge the consumer for 15 per cent of steel in that beam which is useless. The form is not scientifically right. Mr. Schwab is a genius. I have never met his equal, and when he had me as a partner we were a great team. [Great laughter.]

The CHAIRMAN. That is quite evident.

Mr. CARNEGIE. He had genius and I had a little saving, common sense, and I could boss Schwab because I brought him up as a boy; and genius is, of all things, most difficult to control. And that one fellow, not in the combination, and struggling against them, beset by financial difficulties that would have almost overwhelmed any other man, nevertheless resolved that his mill should have a beam mill equal to any in the world, and he has improved upon the German and is making beams to-day scientifically correct. And he has all the orders he can take. He made 20,000 tons in one month, while we used to think when we began that beams at 2,000 a month was good work. He has carried forward America. And not only that; he saw a mill in Germany where there was not a pound of coal used. They utilize the gases over there in their blast furnaces. He adopted the same thing at Bethlehem. I tell you I am in earnest, and I hope, Mr. Chairman, and you members of the committee, that you will give Mr. Schwab the unique honor of having retrieved for America its rightful position as foremost in steel. And Mr. Schwab is rolling rails to-day that he gets $51 a ton for, because the rails we have been making are inferior, and the railroad companies are willing to pay any price for better rails. He will make those rails, and so will the Pennsylvania Steel Company next year, and sell them for $28 a ton at a good profit, because to-day he has to buy the needed nickel, but in the mines they have in Cuba there is the nickel in its natural state.

Now, I will imagine, from my own experience, what happens in a board of directors of a corporation such as that of the United States Steel Company, for instance, or the Pennsylvania Steel Company, or the Cambria Company, or any of them that is not under individual management, and where there is not strong competition to spur them on to adopt every improvement and keep our country ahead. When I started into steel, not one of my partners in Pittsburg would join me; I was so rash. They thought—and fortunately for me, gentlemen, people in the steel business have differed with me so much and so often. They did not see things as I saw them or I would be working to-day for a competence to keep my family. Now, the meeting of the board was called—mind you, this is all imaginary, but from my own experience and just what I went through. A druggist or a merchant sits over there. I had to take him because he had money and I had not. A banker sits there who owns stock——

Mr. COCKRAN. A stockbroker?

Mr. CARNEGIE. I want to say that I had no stock gambling, and I have never in my life associated with stock gamblers; but there were others just as ignorant as the speculator. I think that a stock gambler is one of the worst citizens that a country can have. They are parasites feeding upon values, creating none. It is gambling.

Now, Judge Gary has just read his annual report to his directors, and he shows one hundred and fifty-eight millions of profit, averaging $15.50 on every ton of steel he sold, and what do they think of that?

The CHAIRMAN. Is that on the steel rails or on the whole business?

Mr. CARNEGIE. On the whole business. It does not matter much what it is upon, but the treasury has that $150,000,000, and it is all in the steel business.

The CHAIRMAN. It would be more satisfactory if I knew what it was upon the steel-rail business.

Mr. CARNEGIE. Excuse me, but I do not think any corporation could keep its cost on steel rails separate from its general work. It would have to be estimated. But it is not steel rails that we are concerned with here; it is all articles of steel that the company make, and I am only talking about the published reports. It is impossible for me to give you detailed statements, but here are the published reports. The Judge says that he made in one year $158,000,000 on 10,-000,000 tons of rails. Everything he sold averaged $15.50. Now, this is public property, and probably you have all had the reports; they are published. And it is a great credit to the United States Steel Company that they do publish these reports.

Now, at a subsequent meeting—and this is all imaginary, but it is my own experience—at a subsequent meeting the president may suggest that his beam mills are not up to date, and that the American people are paying for 15 per cent of steel that is useless; and he proposes an appropriation of so many millions of dollars to place his company in its rightful position, to roll beams such as Schwab is now rolling. Now, one member who has to go in a hurry to his legitimate business will say : "Well, gentlemen, I vote against that resolution; we are doing well enough now, and we can not create any competition, because we have an understanding with all of the manufacturers;" and Mr. President has to let well enough alone, and the proposition is voted down.

Such was my experience with the directors that I had in the steel company. Fortunately, I bought them out and got rid of it, and then I got men like Schwab and others around me; and we went on and produced the cheapest steel that has ever been made in the world; and if you will contrast the two costs to-day, on the same basis as we make profits, and if every susidiary department is placed at cost, and the total profit credited to the steel company on the proper cost, you will find what I tell you to be true, that what we make at the mill at Pittsburg will show that it is the cheapest mill in the world to-day.

The CHAIRMAN. Can you tell us where we can get that proper cost; that is what we are after ? You have been at the steel business a number of years, since 1899 ?

Mr. CARNEGIE. Yes; but, Mr. Chairman, when you put the price of rails in that year—please show me now how far you go back?

The CHAIRMAN. Well, 1899. Mr. Schwab wrote his letter in 1899, and placed it at $12 a ton. That is the lowest price I have ever heard stated by anybody, and I did not know but that you might make it lower.

Mr. CARNEGIE. Never, never. As I have told you, that is the banner mill, and America beats the world.

The CHAIRMAN. It was rather intimated the other day that the letter was written for other purposes and did not place the cost accurately.

Mr. CARNEGIE. My dear sir, allow me to tell you just what happened about that. I purposely refrained from reading the statements of interested parties. They are incapable of judging justly. No judge should be permitted to sit in a cause in which he is interested; and you make the greatest mistake in your life if you attach importance to an interested witness. You would not do it in a court of justice, would you? If the judge was interested in a cause, would you respect his decision? [No response.] Silence in the court. [Great laughter.]

Mr. COCKRAN. The chairman was never so eloquent.

The CHAIRMAN. I want to say to you very frankly that I always weigh the witness's silence as well as his words.

Mr. CARNEGIE. Listen. Will you read me again what your expert told you, based upon information he derived from interested parties? What was the average cost of making steel rails in America the year that we were making them at $15.50?

The CHAIRMAN. We have not got that. These are only from the year 1902 to 1906, both inclusive.

Mr. CARNEGIE. Well, 1902; that is a long time ago.

The CHAIRMAN. But 1906 is more recent, while 1902 is only five years ago. They give the average cost for each year. It happens to be the only year that the Bureau of Corporations have gone after the steel business in order to get this information, so that what we have is all that is available.

Mr. CARNEGIE. Well, Mr. Chairman, does it stand to reason that a works that makes rails at $15 a ton and cover everything, in the year that Schwab said it did, and then in those years that you mention that the average cost of rails should be so much greater?

Mr. DALZELL. But isn't that the fact, Mr. Carnegie? What do you say as to the relative cost of making steel rails in 1899, and in 1906 or 1907?

Mr. CARNEGIE. Well, gentlemen, I have told you over and over again that I do not judge by figures given by interested parties. I put it to you, Mr. Dalzell. If steel rails cost $26.50 at Harrisburg and they have to sell them at $28, why is their stock above par? Why does not the Pennsylvania Company change its management?

The CHAIRMAN. To an ordinary man that looks like a pretty good profit on a ton of steel rails.

Mr. CARNEGIE. Oh, no; oh, no.

The CHAIRMAN. I am trying to get you to say how large a profit a man ought to have.

Mr. CARNEGIE. Well, Mr. Chairman, I do not want to limit a man's profit. I would let the steel manufacturers strive to compete and manage their own business; and a man who was clever enough to make $3 or $4 more than another who was lazy, and with inert corporation management, I would be glad to have him do it in the interest of my country. It is the enterprising man that needs to go ahead.

The CHAIRMAN. What I want to know is whether, in your judgment, $5 a ton is too large or too small a profit?

Mr. CARNEGIE. Well, I say again that one man might deserve $5 a ton profit, and it would be for the good of the country if another man should make eight.

The CHAIRMAN. But I want your judgment on it as a man of sense and an expert in the steel business, as to whether $5 a ton is too great or too small a profit upon steel rails?

Mr. CARNEGIE. That is a question that I will not answer, because I do not believe it is the fair gauge of what a man ought to get. I think if a man goes in like Schwab has done in the adoption of that new experiment from Germany, for it was, mind you, an experiment, because conditions in this country might have been very different, and it is a chance that nobody else took, then I should like to see Schwab make $10 on steel rails when the slow coaches are making five; and that is for the interest of our country.

Mr. Chairman, do you know what philanthrophy can do if it gives its alms to undeserving people? It encourages those people; and if you want to do the most harm with money, give it away to those who will not struggle for themselves. And so it is in the steel concern, and with all other enterprises.

Mr. UNDERWOOD. The proposition, however, is this: In a well-organized, well-equipped, well-managed mill would $5 a ton on steel rails be an excessive profit?

Mr. CARNEGIE. I do not think it would in the best managed mill with every improvement; no, I should think not. And yet I say this, without study, as I have never—I do not attach importance to the question—but you have nothing to do with reasonable profits, as the President-elect has shown by the Republican platform, excepting in this way, and here is one of the soundest deliveries that I have heard a public man make for many a long day. Our platform is somewhat obscure and ambiguous. It can be twisted a little when you add a cost and " reasonable profit." What did the President-elect say? He said two things. First, he says that we are to allow a duty comparing costs abroad with costs here; and we are to add a reasonable profit to both parties alike. That is the platform. Now, he also says there is no doubt but a tariff makes it much easier for people to combine and exact excessive profits, and therefore we should have as little " of it as possible." Now, the leading steel manufacturer of the world has declared he does not need protective duties any longer. A protective duty in its nature and in its object means that the consumer has to pay a higher price than he otherwise would for the articles protected. In my opinion—and I am a protectionist like the President-elect is, and a strong one—I have studied, and I labored many years with President McKinley on the tariff; and I have never appeared before Congress without urging reduction in iron and steel, as the records will show. And I have been abused by the foremost advocate of protection in this country, the New York Tribune, for doing so. But now the Tribune itself—you have read it, I suppose—in its editorial, accepts President Taft's construction of our tariff plank, which the President-elect says we are duty bound to conform to. I would give you the Tribune article—I have a copy here—approving of that, and also Mr. Taft's stereotyped words from the report.

The CHAIRMAN. Well, of course, the Tribune is entitled to opinions, as all other newspapers are, but what we are most anxious to get at are facts upon the question. It becomes our duty to report a tariff bill, and in doing so we must have due regard for several things. In the first place, not to make the tariff unnecessarily high where we can get the required information. On the other hand, not to withdraw protection from an industry so as to force a decrease in the price of wages. And another thing that we must bear in mind, that laterally, through large combinations of capital, there is more or less stifling of competition, and we do not want to destroy competition, Mr. Carnegie. Hence, the responsibility is up to us. It is easy for a newspaper editor or a newspaper writer to go on and talk generally about the tariff and about reducing it, scaling it down or putting it up—that is comparatively easy. They can publish something else the next day. But we are to perform a work which has to stand, and which is to have its effect one way or the other upon the industries of the country for some time to come. And what we want are facts.

Mr. CARNEGIE. Mr. Chairman, would you set yourself up, even when you are armed with all the information you can get, in opposition to Judge Gary as a judge whether the steel industry needs a tariff or not?

The CHAIRMAN. But what I want of Judge Gary is the facts. I do not want his judgment; he is not the judge in this case at all.

Mr. DALZELL. Mr. Carnegie, I think Judge Gary did not make any such broad statement as you seem to understand him to have made.

Mr. CARNEGIE. I see it announced in the newspapers.

Mr. DALZELL. But he did not. For instance, he was asked about the duty on tin plate. The duty on tin plate is a cent and a half now, and he said, when we told him that, that tin plate was manufactured at a loss, that he thought they could stand a reduction to 1.2 cents. We asked him whether or not the United States Steel Company could stand any further reduction, and he said he thought they could to the extent of 10 per cent, but not any more. So that Judge Gary is not on record at all in the way in which you put him, by saying that the United States Steel Company does not need any duty on steel. You are mistaken about it.

The CHAIRMAN. He said further in that connection that the United States Steel Company could go on and do business if steel rails were put on the free list, but that they would have to cut down wages of employees. He made that statement.

Mr. DALZELL. The newspaper report of Judge Gary's testimony, to which you referred, is evidently wrong.

Mr. COCKRAN. He said, in answer to a question of mine, page 5512 of the hearings—my question is:

> Mr. COCKRAN. Therefore, so far as you are concerned, you are not prepared to state on your own responsibility as a citizen and under your oath as a witness that any protection whatever is necessary?
> Mr. GARY. For the United States Steel Corporation?
> Mr. COCKRAN. Yes, so far as the United States Steel Corporation is concerned.
> Mr. GARY. No.

And then he goes on and makes an exception of certain things.

Mr. DALZELL. It is just as I have said.

Mr. COCKRAN. He said as to production generally; but, so far as the steel corporation was concerned, that no protection was necessary. But as to the tin plate he did not speak of his own knowledge.

Mr. DALZELL. Oh, yes; he spoke of his own knowledge.

Mr. COCKRAN. I think you will find on that same page that he declined to state.

Mr. PAYNE. Allow me to read following what you read:

> Mr. COCKRAN. Now, that is clear. There is just one thing more I want to question you about.
> Mr. GARY. Of course I would have to go through the list carefully, Mr. Cockran, before I could answer your question accurately. That might be true of

some commodities and not true as to others; that is, it might drive us out of business so far as some commodities are concerned.

But he also stated in another place——

Mr. COCKRAN. And, to go further, the record shows:

> Mr. COCKRAN. You are not prepared to name one now?
> Mr. GARY. No. The only way that could be determined is to look up the figures of cost.

The CHAIRMAN. Then he says a little farther down, in the very next clause:

> Mr. GARY. This occurs to me: I do not see how we could survive in the sheet and tin-plate business if the tariff is removed. I think we would be driven out of that business.

Mr. COCKRAN. Now, if you will look back, Mr. Chairman, on page 5511, you will see a reference there to this point. [Reads:]

> Mr. COCKRAN. Just conceive for a moment the position of the committee and your position. We are here discussing the amount of protection—that is to say, of tax ought to be levied on the community for the protection of this industry—and if the chief factor in that protection is not able to say how much is necessary it would be difficult for us to decide that it is necessary at all, for you would not have us impose a tax on suspicion.

And the answer of Judge Gary was:

> Mr. GARY. As a fair-minded citizen I would have you impose a tax which would protect our competitors, even if we did not need it.

The question was whether he could say that there was a single item on which protection was necessary.

Mr. DALZELL. And he mentioned tin plate. ·

The CHAIRMAN. Mr. Gary said: " My impression is that the amount which was fixed under the Wilson bill, which was 1.2, would protect us." That is, tin plate.

But we are here to get at the facts. Mr. Gary did state explicitly in another case that if we removed the entire duty, while the steel companies would still make steel rails, they would be obliged to reduce the price of wages. He said that, but whether it is true or false I do not know.

Mr. COCKRAN. I do not think he said that.

Mr. CARNEGIE. Well, Mr. Chairman, Mr. Gary only thought so. Mr. Gary has not had any experience in running under free trade. In my opinion it will make only the slightest possible difference to the American manufacturer.

The CHAIRMAN. Have not any of us had experience with the steel schedule?

Mr. CARNEGIE. Mr. Chairman, I would like to call your attention to this discussion, about what President Gary said, and the costs of this thing and that thing—you can not agree among yourselves as to what the real purport of his answer is; and the further you depend upon figures given you by interested parties—mind you, I do not think that they want to misrepresent, but naturally you would not tolerate an interested judge for a moment that sat in a cause in which you are interested, and you should not place much value upon the testimony of interested parties.

The CHAIRMAN. But your criticism is entirely unjust about our not agreeing among ourselves. We have not had any opportunity of going over the evidence since it was printed. Of course, before making a just tariff bill, we would go very carefully over what Judge Gary said and what you have said on the subject.

Mr. HILL. You stated, Mr. Carnegie, that Mr. Schwab's statement made when he was with you, and set forth in his letter of 1899, that $12 a ton as the cost of rails was correct?

Mr. CARNEGIE. Yes, sir; and I wish to say that I did not know the letter had been written. I was abroad at the time. I took no part in the negotiations for the sale of our property. I only told my young partners that if they wished to change I was delighted; I would retire from business. But I do well remember that that was our cost; and when Mr. Schwab came to me, the first words I said to him were: " Schwab, your follies and not your sins are accountable for much of your experience." He told the truth there, and you have said, Mr. Chairman, that it seemed to weaken and it did weaken his statement when he began to explain that he was " looking for preferment in a great company," and that it was written at the suggestion of Mr. Frick. If there ever was a more foolish or gratuitous statement than that, and there was no cause for it— the man told the absolute truth.

The CHAIRMAN. As it was?

Mr. CARNEGIE. As it was.

The CHAIRMAN. He said he did.

Mr. CARNEGIE. He said he might have put in some other items that he mentioned. I do not know how he could, Mr. Chairman, because when we sold rails for $16 I did it because we knew we were not losing money.

Mr. HILL. We asked him then to give the items of cost—that is, the chairman did—and to compare those items, item by item, with the cost now. I took down his figures making up the $12 cost, and I then took down his figures making up, as I had it, on the paper, $20.93.

Now, I took down his figures making up the $12 cost; and I then took down his figures making it, as I had it on the paper, $20.93. Now, is that last item of $20.93 as correct as the figure of $19 given by Mr. Schwab?

Mr. CARNEGIE. No, sir. It is based on entirely different terms.

Mr. HILL. I would like to give you the items of cost and have you tell us in what way they are wrong.

Mr. CARNEGIE. I could not tell you about the division of costs between different departments. You can make them anything you please.

The CHAIRMAN. You mean you could not do that and tell the truth?

Mr. CARNEGIE. Yes; the truth—in a fashion, if you can say so. [Laughter.]

Mr. COCKRAN. A kind of a truth?

Mr. CARNEGIE. Yes. Now, Mr. President, I will tell you the difference in Mr. Felton's statement, that he was free and could sell anything and do anything that he chose and he had no agreement; and the truth was he had no agreement but " an understanding." Now, that is a distinction without a difference, and it is the whole truth that you have to tell, and Mr. Schwab told you, and this is what he told me—I did not read his testimony—but he told me expressly they were not based upon any figures of his manufacture, as I understood him.

Mr. HILL. Mr. Schwab started with ore, and said that at that time, when he made those figures, you were paying a royalty of 10 to 15 cents a ton, and that now the ore costs a dollar.

Mr. CARNEGIE. Excuse me, Mr. Hill. Mr. Schwab told the commission the cost of ore to a private miner of ore in Pittsburg. The royalties on the steel ore we have sold—and there were hundreds of millions of tons—and it was 20 cents a ton, and that is the cost to-day to the United States Steel Company on that ore, and it is in perpetuity. Now, he takes the value of ore to-day. Certainly there have been purchases recently of ore at higher prices. The same thing is going on in Europe. England is in far worse position as to ore than we are, or even than Germany is. Her ore supply has been derived from Spain, and these mines are now failing, and where Britain is to manufacture a ton of steel cheaply in a few years from now I confess I do not see. They are in far worse condition that we are.

Then, gentlemen, my statement was to compare the English or German cost at this time and take the two to-day. From all I know—and I have talked to steel men generally on the other side, and I have many friends there among the steel men in Britain; much of my fortune was made by learning of them and seeing their failures, and I still know them well and they visit me at Skibo and we talk over matters—and that is their complaint as well as ours, so that the relative cost of making the foreign article is rising like ours.

We are exporting steel to all the countries of the world to-day, and unless you take these broad facts into account and give them their proper bearing upon divisions of cost, arbitrary divisions of cost, you will become befogged, and the difficulty is you have had various testimony, which is an evidence of it. We must use our brains. [Laughter.]

Mr. HILL. We must have something to work on with our brains.

Mr. CARNEGIE. I say that because you have plenty of them to use, and really it was a superfluous remark to make. [Laughter.]

Mr. HILL. Mr. Schwab said it was 58 per cent ore then, and it is now 49 per cent ore. He figured the ore on the basis of 10 to 15 cents per ton royalty delivered in Pittsburg at $4.31 per ton of rails, and made an allowance, calling it, in round figures, $4.50 for the ore in a ton of rails. He says now that that royalty on ore costs a dollar. In his statement he figures the freight to the lake, the lake freight, and the rail freight to Pittsburg on 49 per cent ore. He says now that that costs $8.26. Which is correct, or are both correct?

Mr. CARNEGIE. Probably, if you purchased the ore; but I am not talking about people who buy ore and sell ore. The question is whether the steel interests of America can do without protection, as Judge Gary says they can, or whether they can not. I agree with Judge Gary. What your commission should do would be to let them go to European works and see what their costs are, and you will see what the condition of affairs is.

Mr. HILL. The question of whether they can do without it or not depends on the cost of the articles to-day, does it not? And this is the evidence of Mr. Schwab.

Mr. CARNEGIE. Let me say again these are not the manufacturer's costs that Mr. Schwab gave you. He told me he did not appear for the steel companies at all.

Mr. DALZELL. He told us they were the actual costs.

Mr. CARNEGIE. There you are again, gentlemen; you are on figures. If you are going to assume that you gentlemen, who know nothing about steel, can in a cursory examination of the case get at the facts of the case, you are deluding yourselves.

Mr. DALZELL. We want you to give the facts.

Mr. CARNEGIE. I tell you expressly that I have no details to give, but I look at the broad fact that we are exporting to all the world, and we make $15.50 a ton on everything we sell.

The CHAIRMAN. How do you know that fact, that you are making something on everything they sell? Do you know?

Mr. CARNEGIE. I read the last report of the United States Steel Company, and in that year it made that.

Mr. DALZELL. Won't you give us information how you make that $15 profit on every ton of steel rails, out of the United States Steel Company's report? Tell us how you make that out.

Mr. CARNEGIE. Mr. Dalzell, I have already stated. Have you not read that report?

Mr. DALZELL. Yes.

Mr. CARNEGIE. Did you not find that they sold 10,000,000 tons of steel?

Mr. DALZELL. I have read the figures. Tell us how you work the problem out.

Mr. CARNEGIE. I did so once before. The steel company in their last report stated that they made something over 10,000,000 tons of steel of various forms, and their profits were $160,000,000. Now, it does not take much figuring to show that that is $15.50 profit for every ton they have sold, or they would not have made $160,000,000 on 10,000,000 tons of steel.

Mr. DALZELL. Is that the way you would arrive at that result? You would divide the $160,000,000 profit by 10,000,000 tons of steel?

Mr. CARNEGIE. Sold; yes.

Mr. DALZELL. Yes; and the result you arrive at by that process, without any other figures, is a profit of $15.50 a ton on all the steel sold?

Mr. CARNEGIE. Certainly. Can you arrive at any other conclusion? I want to ask you a question: Can you arrive at any other conclusion? There is silence in the court again. [Laughter.]

Mr. HILL. Mr. Schwab said that the royalty nine years ago was from 10 to 15 cents and now it is $1, and that the cost of the ore nine years ago per ton of steel was $2.40 and now costs $4.50. Then he said that the coke cost $1.05 a ton of steel nine years and that it costs $2.05 a ton of steel now.

Mr. CARNEGIE. I have no judgment on that except that Mr. Schwab stated to you distinctly that he was not giving manufacturing costs.

Mr. HILL. Mr. Schwab said that the labor nine years ago on a ton of steel was $1.65, and then, to my great surprise, he said it was only $1.30 now. He said that the cost of conversion of iron, including the profit, nine years ago was $3.75 and that now it is $7.50, or just twice as much.

Mr. CARNEGIE. Conversion of steel?

Mr. HILL. Conversion of iron into steel. Now, that makes a dif‹ ference of $3.84 in the price of rails.

Mr. COCKRAN. How much did you say he said the cost of conversion of steel was?

Mr. HILL. Nine years ago $3.75, including profit, and $7.50 now.

Mr. CARNEGIE. Did he explain how that extraordinary increase was made?

Mr. HILL. It was a strange thing that he did not, to me, because his letter, the letter that has been referred to, said that all costs would be reduced, while the European cost would be continually advancing; and yet here is his own statement, with his own figures, showing a double cost now. Now, I want to know whether—whether the rest of the committee do or not—this latter statement is correct— just as correct as the first one?

Mr. CARNEGIE. You are asking the wrong person.

Mr. HILL. I ask your judgment.

Mr. CARNEGIE. Oh, my judgment. I decline to give my judgment against a positive statement. I believe there is a mistake there, a misunderstanding. But that is another evidence that if you gentlemen—professional gentlemen, public men—imagine that you can get at a basis of legislation while ignoring the great facts before you— that we are exporters of steel and do not import steel—and, above all things, are attempting to gainsay the evidence of a witness who is truthful because he testified, as it were, against his own company—I put the word of Judge Gary beyond all figures, and I would take the word of Judge Gary in this matter beyond all the figures—if I were, as you are, a nonmanufacturer, I would take that evidence of Judge Gary rather than the judgment which I could form, if ignorant of the steel business, from the figures you could lay before me. Your proceedings this morning show that you have different ideas and different constructions on all the figures.

The CHAIRMAN. Mr. Carnegie, these figures are almost uniform, drawn from different sources.

Mr. CARNEGIE. They are all uniform in this, that they are the work of interested parties who are incapable of rising, as we would be ourselves if we were interested—of rising to the broad facts of the case.

The CHAIRMAN. Now, you oppose to these figures no knowledge as to their correctness except these two propositions: One is that they are selling steel rails abroad; they claim that they are selling them at a loss; so have the Pennsylvania Steel Company, who testified about that. I do not know whether it is true or not, but that was the statement and explanation, and thereby it was stated that he kept his mill running the year round.

Mr. COCKRAN. I think you are mistaken in stating that Mr. Felton said he was selling at a loss.

The CHAIRMAN. I do not think so. Now, Mr. Carnegie, you base the profits of the United States Steel Company on all their manufactures. You say there are so many thousand tons of steel rails and structural steel produced, as I understand it, and you divide their profits by that and come to the conclusion that they are making $15 a ton. You take into account all their other business. It is enormous, is it not?

Mr. CARNEGIE. Mr. Chairman, you have misapprehended me entirely. I took the statement covering all steel, and you are dealing here—this commission—with the duties on all steel.

The CHAIRMAN. Do they cover tin plate, for instance?

Mr. CARNEGIE. Surely. How could they exclude tin plate? Their statement is a summary of all the business of the year. I do not think they made more than $158,000,000. That was the extreme,-and necessarily included everything.

The CHAIRMAN. The 10,000,000 tons, then, included the tin plate, did it?

Mr. CARNEGIE. I leave you to imagine that the total profits would have included that.

The CHAIRMAN. I do not want to imagine. I want to get out of you the fact of it, if you will give it.

Mr. CARNEGIE. You can not get that fact out of me. There is Judge Gary's published report.

The CHAIRMAN. Then, it comes down to this, that we must rely on Judge Gary for the facts. Is that true?

Mr. CARNEGIE. Judge Gary has already summarized the facts for you and told you you could do without it. I would rely upon that, if I were a member of this committee, as quite sufficient.

The CHAIRMAN. You consider Judge Gary a truthful man?

Mr. CARNEGIE. I do; Judge Gary.

The CHAIRMAN. He has testified here as to what we believe to be the facts.

Mr. CARNEGIE. They are the facts as he understands them. As I told you before, the question of costs of a thing depends entirely upon your bookkeeping.

Now, Mr. Chairman, I would like to ask you a question: If the cost of steel rails abroad—no; steel abroad, because we are not talking about steel rails particularly—if the cost of steel abroad has risen as the cost of steel here, then you would find that according to the interpretation of our tariff plank Judge Gary's statement was quite true, that he could still stand free trade in steel, because the cost abroad had risen as it has risen here.

The CHAIRMAN. He says the cost has risen abroad, and that the price there is $28 up to $31 or $32; $31, I think, was the highest. He put it at $31 and some odd figure. That is the selling price.

Mr. CARNEGIE. Is not that confirming just what I told you, that you have nothing to dread from free trade in steel?

The CHAIRMAN. In so far as that is concerned, yes; if they were all sold at $31, but some of them sell them at $25 and $26.

Mr. CARNEGIE. Do you know any business in the world where every dealer sells alike at a like price?

The CHAIRMAN. Yes; steel seems to now. For the last two years in this country it sells for the same price, $28, but abroad it has been selling all the way from $20 to $31, according to the demand and supply.

Mr. CARNEGIE. Yes; and very often a manufacturer would very often sell at a low price in order to keep his workmen employed. If he is a wise man, he would never cease to keep his men working, even at a loss.

The CHAIRMAN. Mr. Felton comes in here and gives the figures from his books, and he gives instances where he has sold it, and all that sort of thing, and he says he has sold at a loss of $1 a ton on steel sold abroad. He says that was a big loss, as the gentleman says, but it was a good thing for the steel company, because it enables him to keep his plant running.

Mr. CARNEGIE. I venture a suggestion that you should send for Mr. Felton again and ask him if he agrees with Judge Gary.

The CHAIRMAN. If he what?

Mr. CARNEGIE. If he agrees with Judge Gary. The details of this thing you are not interested in. It is the broad general question, Is it allowable any longer to tax the consumer and make him pay a higher price than he would otherwise have to pay? Because that is the only result of protection.

The CHAIRMAN. It is not justifiable to tax the consumer if you can show that they can compete and get, as you say, a reasonable profit here and a reasonable profit there. It is not justifiable to tax the consumer under such conditions. I agree with you on that. But what we want to know is whether you can do it.

Mr. CARNEGIE. You have Judge Gary's testimony.

The CHAIRMAN. That is the reason we have you here. We have Judge Gary's testimony, and it would seem to show that we could not place steel rails on the free list without injury to American industry.

Mr. CARNEGIE. Excuse me. About half of the American industries would not be injured, he said. He can stand it on half the product of American industry.

The CHAIRMAN. He says he could not stand it unless he reduced the price to his workmen. He made that plain statement.

Mr. COCKRAN. I do not recall that.

Mr. CARNEGIE. The lawyer, Gary, is equally adroit in calling in the workmen. But he did not make that remark in reference to steel, but to tin plate, and I agree with him as to that. [Laughter.]

The CHAIRMAN. Now you refer to Judge Gary, whom you referred to a moment ago as being a truthful witness, as being a lawyer. My experience has been that lawyers are as truthful as other men. Now you are taking a fling at lawyers.

Mr. CARNEGIE. No. I take it that a lawyer in defending his own cause makes the best statement he can for it.

The CHAIRMAN. He was sworn to tell the truth, and the whole truth, and nothing but the truth, and you say he is a truthful man?

Mr. CARNEGIE. Yes, sir.

The CHAIRMAN. Now, the question of his being a lawyer or a manufacturer does not enter into that question at all.

Mr. CARNEGIE. No; it does not; but if you are speaking for your own cause I think a man is justified in making the best statement he can, especially since it is a matter of judgment for him to have.

The CHAIRMAN. Even if it conflicts with the truth?

Mr. CARNEGIE. No, sir. I do not say that his judgment was for the future, what would be in the future. My judgment is entirely the reverse.

Mr. DALZELL. You would tell us, Mr. Carnegie, that we can not get truthful figures as to the manufacture of steel from steel manufacturers. Can you tell us where we can get those figures?

Mr. CARNEGIE. I do not believe you can get those figures that you can rely upon, because there are different costs in different works, and because there are different ways of making up costs.

The CHAIRMAN. Can you get them?

Mr. CARNEGIE. No, sir. I could not pretend to get them.

The CHAIRMAN. Then how could you go to work and say what a tariff should be if you can not get the figures as to what the cost would be?

Mr. CARNEGIE. Because I should judge of my general knowledge of the steel business and what the people in the steel business admit. Judge Gary did not make that statement for the first time. He made that statement long before I wrote my article, and there are others that I have conversed with, and it has passed as a matter of general acceptance.

Mr. DALZELL. According to you, Judge Gary is not reliable. He is an interested man.

Mr. CARNEGIE. He is reliable; he is an interested man. He is not reliable, nor is any man who is interested, for estimating future effects; and he only estimated generally and gave you his judgment of future effects as to free trade, that it might injure.

Mr. COCKRAN. Mr. Carnegie, in talking about the difficulty of obtaining figures, you apply, as I understand it, your own experience in the steel trade to these reports that have been published by the steel company, and upon these two premises you base your conclusions as to the power of this industry to get along without protection?

Mr. CARNEGIE. Well, partly so; but, really, I must say, more upon Judge Gary's statement than these figures.

Mr. COCKRAN. You mean Judge Gary's statement here under oath? You are referring to that?

Mr. CARNEGIE. Yes, sir.

Mr. COCKRAN. Now, Mr. Carnegie, with reference to the difficulty of obtaining reliable figures, you mentioned once or twice the capacity of bookkeepers to distribute expenses into various channels and by the multiplication of them magnify costs before the raw material reaches the mill. Now, with reference to ore especially, I think you said that Mr. Schwab, in estimating the increased cost of ore, took its value in the market and not its cost to the United States Steel Corporation.

Mr. CARNEGIE. That is what I believe. He does not take the cost of ore as the United States Steel Company could mine it from the same mines that we mined it when we made the cheap steel.

Mr. COCKRAN. That is to say, in estimating the cost of ore, Mr. Schwab, in your judgment—and this would account for the large difference in various statements of what the ore costs the company—he took the value of the ore in the open markets to-day?

Mr. CARNEGIE. Mr. Schwab states that to you frankly. He does not misrepresent.

Mr. COCKRAN. Now, the advance in the value of ore, as distinguished from its cost to the company, is what?

Mr. CARNEGIE. I can not tell you that.

Mr. COCKRAN. It has advanced enormously?

Mr. CARNEGIE. Yes; the recent purchases of ore have advanced enormously; and also abroad, gentlemen, you neglect half the case if you neglect this.

Mr. COCKRAN. I spent a good deal of time trying to find out from Mr. Felton that very fact when he spoke of the advance in the cost of his material. I tried to find out whether there was a corresponding advance in the cost of materials to the foreign producers, and I must say I made but little headway. Are you able to enlighten us upon that?

Mr. CARNEGIE. Not as to the exact figures, but as to the general facts.

Mr. COCKRAN. Approximately?

Mr. CARNEGIE. Yes, because I was going to repeat that I do not know what Britain is going to do for ore in a few years from now.

Mr. COCKRAN. Now, judging from the general conditions of supply—and we were told there was no particular difference in the labor conditions—the cost, in the nature of things, must have advanced proportionately abroad as it has advanced here?

Mr. CARNEGIE. That is my opinion, that the costs have advanced, from all that I hear.

Mr. COCKRAN. And therefore, so far as protection is concerned, there is no justification for a protective tax based on the cost of materials out of which steel is manufactured?

Mr. CARNEGIE. Not according to the definition of the Republican tariff plank.

Mr. COCKRAN. I am not as familiar with that document as some of the other gentlemen present. [Laughter.] I was asking as to the particular lines of policy you indicated a moment ago.

Mr. CARNEGIE. Yes; you must take the difference in cost on both sides. I do not know whether I stated that I was quite sure that if a commission were appointed to stay at the mills for a month on the other side, the first mill in Britain and the first mill in America would be the one at Pittsburg, if a disinterested expert who knows the steel business was sworn to give you the exact cost and the United States Steel Company put only in what it costs to-day and gives credit to its subsidiary companies—its coke works, its ore works, its railways, and everything that it has subsidiary—the result would be that the cost of a ton of steel abroad would be slightly greater than it is here. That leaves naturally the tariff in favor of the home producer, because they have to transport the steel here.

Mr. COCKRAN. Now, Mr. Schwab, or Mr. Carnegie—excuse me—when you were asked a question about the letter that Mr. Schwab wrote in 1898 or 1899, you said you would like to state the circumstances under which that letter was written, Mr. Schwab having stated that it was written under circumstances that induced him to minimize the cost so far as he could, consistent with the truth. Would you mind stating those circumstances?

Mr. CARNEGIE. Certainly not, Mr. McCormack. I was abroad when that letter was written, and I never saw it until my eyes inadvertently fell upon it the other day, and I read it, and I knew he told the exact truth. Mr. Schwab afterwards called to see me on a matter of business, or friendship, or both combined, and I just told him, " Why did you gratuitously say that that was written under conditions that implied that you were under pressure and were not a free agent?" And he said, " That was a piece of folly, and I am sorry that I did it." That is quite true, gentlemen. Mr. Schwab has told you the truth.

Mr. COCKRAN. You said you would like to state the circumstances under which it was written. You have stated now what Mr. Schwab said about it. Are there any circumstances that you care to speak about?

Mr. CARNEGIE. He said it was written to parties who were talking about buying the steel works.

Mr. COCKRAN. Now, Mr. Carnegie, I understood you to say that in your judgment the only effect of protection to this industry now is to encourage the producers to rely upon the tariff for their profits, instead of upon improvements in the trade and in the methods of production?

Mr. CARNEGIE. That is the tendency in all combinations, in my opinion.

Mr. COCKRAN. That is undoubtedly true?

Mr. CARNEGIE. Undoubtedly true.

Mr. COCKRAN. And what you contend for now in this testimony is that a condition has been reached in the production of this commodity where the producers should be put to the development of their skill and capacity for profits, and not to trust at all to legislation?

Mr. CARNEGIE. I believe that would be best for the American public; for our country.

Mr. COCKRAN. It would be better for our country in the way of increasing the volume and value of the product?

Mr. CARNEGIE. Yes, sir.

Mr. COCKRAN. And to increase the volume of the product would necessitate the employment of more human hands?

Mr. CARNEGIE. Certainly.

Mr. COCKRAN. And therefore it would operate to stimulate the rate of wages?

Mr. CARNEGIE. Certainly.

Mr. COCKRAN. Several gentlemen here, when discussing the matter of decreasing the cost to the consumer, expressed doubt whether that would stimulate consumption. In your experience of the trade have you not found that every reduction in the cost stimulates the demand for consumption?

Mr. CARNEGIE. That is a truism.

Mr. COCKRAN. I had always supposed so, but it seems to have been questioned here, under oath, by several witnesses, whether the decrease in the cost of the commodity would stimulate the production.

Mr. CARNEGIE. I can not imagine an intelligent man doubting that.

Mr. COCKRAN. I have asked you to testify as to that in the industry you have been connected with for many years.

Mr. CARNEGIE. That has been a grave objection to the policy that has been pursued in not reducing prices in the recent panic. Now, I am one political economist who has followed the other plan. I wanted to keep all our men employed. I think the greatest loss an employer can make is to part with his good men. We had such an organization of men in our works that I think never has been equaled upon the face of the earth. We wanted not only the best workmen, but we wanted the best American citizens. We had very strict rules. One man on duty the worse for liquor was suspended for sixty days. For a second offense he was suspended three months. On a third offense we shook him by the hand and said "Good-by."

Mr. COCKRAN. You may be said to have shaken him altogether. [Laughter.]

Mr. CARNEGIE. Yes. Now, I was going to say this: When the recent panic came the policy of the Carnegie Steel Company would have been to reduce prices enormously, and it would have stimulated the capitalist, who is the shrewd man and the valuable man in the country. The man who has money during a panic is the wise and valuable citizen——

Mr. COCKRAN. Such as we see before us now——

Mr. CARNEGIE. Thank you; the same to you. [Laughter.] And the result would have been that if a man wished to build a skyscraper on his property in New York he would have said, " Here is a chance for me. Here is a bargain. I will build now." And that would have employed labor. And the same thing would have been the result in every city in the United States, and we would have run our works—I judge from the past—and kept our men employed.

Mr. COCKRAN. I want you to testify from the past, from your own experience, as distinguished from speculations. Any man may indulge in speculations on an economic proposition. Did you ever find yourself, during your experience as a steel producer, confronted with a situation where there was a depression of industry, and met it by reducing the price? And if so, what was the result?

Mr. CARNEGIE. We did.

Mr. COCKRAN. Insert that on the record.

Mr. CARNEGIE. If I was in business to-day again, I would not change that policy for anything, so satisfactory has been its results.

Mr. COCKRAN. If you were in business to-day as a steel producer, when the demand for steel slackened, would you stimulate it by reducing the price?

Mr. CARNEGIE. I would.

Mr. COCKRAN. And, judging by the experience of the past, that would inevitably result in increasing the demand?

Mr. CARNEGIE. It would.

Mr. COCKRAN. Judge Gary, among other subjects that he enlightened us upon, discussed his relations with the other corporations, and in answer to my question as to whether there was a general agreement among them, he stated that there was no specific agreement in the sense of a treaty or bargain or even understanding reduced to words, expressed or implied; but, by some process which he failed to describe, before he got into the business a figure was fixed, and that figure has remained fixed ever since; that it was threatened at one time after 1899 by yourself; you announced a purpose to build some new works, and that purpose on your part led to apprehensions that the price of $28 a ton might be reduced, and the desire to avert that possibility was the moving cause in the bringing about of the steel combination known as the " United States Steel Corporation." He testified to that, and so stated to the committee.

Mr. HILL. I do not think so. I think you are entirely mistaken, Mr. Cockran. The increase was not made until after the United States Steel Corporation was formed.

Mr. COCKRAN. You are mistaken, Mr. Hill. The price of $28 was fixed in 1899.

Mr. HILL. When was the steel corporation formed?

Mr. COCKRAN. In 1898. Now, Mr. Carnegie, Mr. Schwab testified that they jumped in one year from $14 to $28.

Mr. DALZELL. Oh, no. Look at your figures. You will find no such figures.

Mr. RANDELL. I think you will find in 1898 the price was $20, but in competition they went down to $17 or $18, and then they got tired of that fight and went back to $28 a ton.

Mr. DALZELL. You have got your figures reversed.

Mr. RANDELL. They went back to $28 before the steel trust was formed.

Mr. DALZELL. In 1897 it was $20; in 1898 it was $12.

Mr. RANDELL. Competition brought it down, and they went back to that before the steel company was organized.

Mr. DALZELL. That is right.

Mr. COCKRAN. My statement agrees with your recollection, does it not, Mr. Carnegie?

Mr. CARNEGIE. Well, gentlemen, you are in figures again. [Laughter.]

Mr. COCKRAN. I know I am, undoubtedly.

Mr. CARNEGIE. And look how befogged you get. [Laughter.] These men are trying to tell you the truth, but they talk in languages which you do not understand. [Laughter.]

Mr. COCKRAN. That is quite true.

Mr. CARNEGIE. Mr. Chairman, I wish you would listen to that suggestion or remark from me. [Laughter.]

Mr. COCKRAN. Mr. Carnegie, Judge Gary stated that the various companies sold at that price. He described them as competitors, and in answer to my question whether these men were his competitors because he tolerated them as such, he said that was so; that he could drive them out of business if they went into competition that he considered unfair or objectionable.

Mr. CARNEGIE. That is a question of judgment on the part of Judge Gary. It is a speculation.

Mr. COCKRAN. Does your judgment agree with it?

Mr. CARNEGIE. No, sir; very far from it.

Mr. COCKRAN. If they are combined to agree upon the price, it is your judgment that that combination is the result of independent minds getting together, and not the result of any coercion on the part of the steel company?

Mr. CARNEGIE. You are speaking now of steel rails?

Mr. COCKRAN. I am speaking of steel production generally.

Mr. CARNEGIE. Yes, generally; here is the judgment again. It is not a matter of fact. My judgment is that the Pennsylvania Steel Company, the Cambria Iron Company, and the Lackawanna Company could approach so nearly to the cost of the United States Steel Company that I would begin to fear for the value of my bonds. I have stated that once.

Mr. COCKRAN. Yes; that is another thing I would like to call your attention to. You speak of Judge Gary and other persons being interested. You yourself are an interested party in the solvency of the steel company, are you not—deeply interested?

Mr. CARNEGIE. Well, sir, I consider the steel bonds of the United States Steel Company so much more secure than any other bonds I could get, short of the United States, that I have provided for those dependent upon me by these bonds. I can not answer any more particularly than that.

Mr. COCKRAN. You believe these securities would not be in the slightest degree imperiled if steel were put on the free list?

Mr. CARNEGIE. Not the slightest. On the contrary, I believe it would be better in the long run for the steel company, and especially for the position our country would occupy as a steel manufacturer.

Mr. COCKRAN. Now, I asked Judge Gary also in his testimony where he stated that in his judgment his company could drive his competitors out of business—I asked him if his power to do that rested upon their control of the ore supply, and he said it did; and I asked him, in addition, if the markets of the world, the supply of ore throughout the world, were open to his competitors, if they would not then be in a position to maintain competition, no matter what the steel company did, and he answered that they would. Do you agree with him in that?

Mr. CARNEGIE. I agree in the latter part of the statement.

Mr. COCKRAN. He said immediately they had enough to go on, but that the ultimate supply of ore in the country was in the hands of the United States Steel Company.

Mr. CARNEGIE. We purchased a great deal of ore. I saw this coming, and——

Mr. COCKRAN. I will read his exact language, Mr. Carnegie. I asked him about the effect of this control of the ore supply, whether by reason of it his company could not drive others out of competition if they wanted to. He said, " Yes; " and then I said, " You practically do control the ore supply of the country?" Mr. Gary replied, " No; not now; not for the immediate future." Then I asked him, " Well, the ultimate supply?" and he answered, " Yes; I think so— that is, pretty nearly. It is not absolute control." Then I asked him whether it was sufficient to put the competitor somewhat at his mercy, and he agreed with me. Then I put this question——

This is not the only supply of the world, by any means, is it?

Mr. GARY. Oh, no.

Mr. COCKRAN. So if the supply of the world were open to these competitors, and with the advantage of cheap transportation by water, which you described a short time ago, they might be able to make a stand for life and liberty?

Mr. GARY. If you remove the duty from ore alone, and it remains so, no doubt that you would protect the people here who will in the future have to buy their ore against a possible oppression on the part of our corporation. That is your question, only in my words.

Do you agree with that?

Mr. CARNEGIE. No, sir; I do not. On the contrary, I believe the Pennsylvania Steel Company may have ore when the United States Steel Company may be short of it.

But let me again point out, What have we to do with the future? Is not this commission appointed to legislate under the conditions of to-day? Judge Gary may be wrong or he may be right. You may to-morrow get a telegram that a lode of ore has been found in the Northwest exceeding any that we have now. This country has not been explored. I know several parties now with men searching everywhere for ore. I met one the other day. He told me that he had discovered three pockets of ore. The one was sure for 6,000,000, and he thought the other would be enormously greater. I myself lent a professional man money—he was a great geologist—I lent him money, and he is exploring for ore. If you are going to leave the present and legislate for the future, why, you are liable to mislead the country.

Mr. COCKRAN. Now, Mr. Carnegie——

Mr. CARNEGIE. One moment more. If our steel industry is ever imperiled, how easy for Congress to put on the duty again.

Mr. COCKRAN. Judging by the past, nothing would be easier, Mr. Carnegie. The easiest thing in this country seems to be to get a duty imposed. Now, let me put this question to you: It is a fact, is it not, Mr. Carnegie, that you believe it would wonderfully improve the condition of the steel industry if ore and all other elements were admitted duty free?

Mr. CARNEGIE. I do, in the long run.

Mr. COCKRAN. You believe it would not hurt any industry to-day?

Mr. CARNEGIE. No.

Mr. COCKRAN. You believe it would cheapen the cost of the article and stimulate consumption?

Mr. CARNEGIE. I do not believe it would lessen the cost of the article much.

Mr. COCKRAN. To put it on the free list?

Mr. CARNEGIE. Yes; because I assure you that it is impossible for Europe to compete successfully with the home producer of steel. That is my deliberate opinion.

Mr. COCKRAN. Suppose the tariff be removed now, because, after all, the effect on the consumer is the thing we are interested in here. Do you mean to say if the tariff was reduced or this article put on the free list it would not reduce the cost to the consumer?

Mr. CARNEGIE. Mr. McCormack, no. Once more let me say——

Mr. BONYNGE. Such is fame. [Laughter.]

Mr. CARNEGIE. I wish I could join in the laugh. What was the laugh?

Mr. COCKRAN. The laugh was that you had promoted me to a Mack. That was the laugh. You promoted me to McCormack. I am entitled rather to an O than to a Mack. [Laughter.]

Mr. CARNEGIE. You may be Scotch and Irish.

Mr. COCKRAN. No; I am Irish only. [Laughter.]

Mr. CARNEGIE. There is the same reason for claiming you as a Scotchman as there was for the Scotchman to claim Shakespeare. An Englishman who was visiting a Scotchman said to him: "You have claimed everybody who is great from Chaucer down. You will be claiming Shakespeare for a Scotchman next." The Scotchman said, "There is a prima facie case for that; ye'll allow he had intellect enough." [Laughter.]

Mr. DALZELL. I thought you called him Micawber. [Laughter.]

Mr. COCKRAN. Because something has at last turned up. [Laughter.]

Mr. CARNEGIE. I have not known Mr. Cockran all my life, but I have known him almost as long as I have known you, Mr. Dalzell. There is intellect enough there. [Laughter.] You have derived a mistaken impression of my views if you thought that under free trade the foreign producer could compete with the American in the home market.

Mr. COCKRAN. My question was whether the American would not reduce the price of steel and allow the consumer to get a cheaper article, and therefore the industry would be stimulated.

Mr. CARNEGIE. The steel combination could not raise its prices so high to the consumer if we had free trade with the world. Now, that is all that I can say.

Mr. COCKRAN. And the net result of your testimony is that by placing this article on the free list the cost of it would be reduced to the consumer, the amount of the production would be largely increased, and therefore the number of human hands employed in the industry would be increased also. That is what you would expect from the reduction of this duty?

Mr. CARNEGIE. No, sir; not quite, Mr. Cockran. I must tell you that my opinion is this: That if there were free trade to-morrow between the world and America in steel, it would affect the home steel manufacturer very slightly, indeed. It is not possible for the world to compete with the home producer. But I agree with the President-elect that the effect of a tariff is to render easier combinations raising their prices to an excessive degree, beyond what they could do under free trade.

Mr. COCKRAN. That is an abstraction, Mr. Carnegie. What I want to get at is—if you will excuse me for pressing the question—your view of the reduction or abolition of tariff duties on this particular article, judging by your experience. Do you feel that if the article was put on the free list, it would lessen the price to the consumer, thus increasing the use of it and widening the demand for wages?

Mr. BOUTELL. I was going to suggest that you answer the first part of the question first. He has asked you in another question whether the reduction of the tariff on steel would reduce the price to the consumer.

Mr. CARNEGIE. I have already answered that. It is impossible to answer it. The steel combination might conclude it is best policy to continue the low price on rails, or to make a low price on rails; but what the law would effectually guard against is their raising the price of rails as high as with a tariff they could evidently raise it.

Mr. COCKRAN. They are evidently doing it now. According to your judgment, they must be doing that now. If the cost of producing steel rails is as low as you believe it to be, then the price of $28 a ton is an excessive price.

Mr. CARNEGIE. No; I can not agree with you there. If you will allow me to explain, to get all the truth——

Mr. COCKRAN. Yes; I want to get that.

Mr. CARNEGIE. Well, gentlemen, that agreement between the railroad companies and the producer is in every respect admirable.

Mr. COCKRAN. The railway companies and the producer?

Mr. CARNEGIE. Yes, sir; in every respect admirable. Now, I said in a letter in regard to combinations and interstate commerce—I insist on that as being an exception—the railroad companies in this country have mills upon their own lines, and they wish to distribute the rail orders fairly among the various makers, and they have agreed with the steel people that $28 a ton was a fair price. They get a great deal of traffic from the manufacturers. They make a great deal of money out of them, and they have given them a fair price, you might say a liberal price; but I do not really think it is not a fair price for both parties. Now, the manufacturers accept from the railroad companies the portions which they think proper to give to each of them. Therefore there is no competition; and it is an arrangement which I pronounce admirable in every respect, fair to the consumer and fair to the producer.

Mr. COCKRAN. If your theory is to be believed as to the cost of steel rails, since it varies so widely from Mr. Schwab's conception of it, it is plain that $28 a ton would yield to both of you a different rate of profit. You assume that steel rails could be made at the outside at $18. Is not that what you figure it would cost?

Mr. CARNEGIE. Mr. Cockran, I have never made a statement in regard to that, so far as I know.

Mr. COCKRAN. No; but you said this, and it must mean something, that the cost of $22 or $21 was too high, and you said that in such a way as indicated the belief that it was very much too high.

Mr. DALZELL. I did not hear Mr. Carnegie express any opinion as to the cost of steel rails at all.

Mr. COCKRAN. I think Mr. Carnegie smiled at least, audibly, at our acceptance of Mr. Schwab's figure.

Mr. CARNEGIE. Mr. Cockran, please do not interpret my smile. I am a born laugher, and I have laughed all through my life, and confronted all the troubles of life with laughter. I have escaped a great many troubles by laughing, and I would not lose that little faculty for anything.

Mr. DALZELL. Besides that, the stenographer can not get your smile down. [Laughter.]

Mr. COCKRAN. Would you mind telling us whether you would consider $22 too much?

Mr. CARNEGIE. I do not say anything about it. I told you over and over and over again that I would not sit and figure on these costs and hear the testimony for anything in the world.

Mr. COCKRAN. Do I understand you, Mr. Carnegie, that when you expressed doubt, as I understood, of these costs and figures—the cost of conversion for instance—that $7.50 is too high? Did you not state that?

Mr. CARNEGIE. I did question that, and thought it was a mistake.

Mr. COCKRAN. If it was a mistake——

Mr. CARNEGIE. I am not prepared to say it is a mistake. It is surprising to me; it is surprising that that should be so much.

Mr. COCKRAN. I see. So, then, you do not undertake to say that in your judgment this cost of steel rails, as stated by the chairman, is too high?

Mr. CARNEGIE. I would investigate that subject before forming an opinion; before entering a judgment I would investigate it.

Mr. COCKRAN. So that in point of fact all this testimony that you give before us is nothing but an adjuration to this committee to look to their figures?

Mr. CARNEGIE. If I have succeeded in doing that, I am glad.

Mr. COCKRAN. You have succeeded in doing that.

Mr. CARNEGIE. I do not know as to that.

Mr. UNDERWOOD. I notice in the reports that in the last decade, although the production of iron and steel in this country has nearly doubled, the production of Germany has increased from a third to a quarter, and the production in England has practically stood still. Can you give us the reasons for that condition in the English market?

Mr. CARNEGIE. Here is another opinion that I have to express upon this subject: You see, I may be right or I may be wrong——

Mr. UNDERWOOD. You just stated that at Skibo you talked with English producers. I would like to have you explain that.

Mr. CARNEGIE. I believe I can explain that. I believe I have told you that in my opinion Great Britain has reached the apex of its manufactures; that its coal is dearer as it is getting deeper, and its supply of ore is getting low to a degree; and that accounts for Britain not manufacturing more steel, and it accounts for Germany manufacturing more. Germany has had a great increase of population. She is developing her manufactures. She has 60,000,000 of people, as against Great Britain's 40,000,000, and she has increased her steel production.

Mr. UNDERWOOD. Is any large percentage of British ore brought from Spain at this time to be used in manufactures?

Mr. CARNEGIE. Yes, sir; there is. I am now telling what I hear. I have not personally investigated it, and yet I believe that the impressions I have received are correct. The ore is getting of less value and with less iron in it, and the mines, I am told, are failing in their supply.

Mr. UNDERWOOD. Do you know what the cost to the British manufacturer is to bring the Spanish ore to the furnace?

Mr. CARNEGIE. No, sir; I do not.

Mr. UNDERWOOD. Do you know, Mr. Carnegie, anything about the development of Norwegian ores?

Mr. CARNEGIE. Yes, sir. In an article written for the Nineteenth Century and After, I think I have said that it is a matter of the gravest importance that these Norwegian ores should be found as expected. I should say this, that I have read a recent report of the company called the Blundenberg Company, and I find it most disappointing. It is to be reconstructed and recapitalized, and so far it has not been a success.

Mr. UNDERWOOD. Are these Norwegian ores far from the coast, or are they on the coast line?

Mr. CARNEGIE. I think some of them are some distance from the coast—eighty-odd miles. I think some are that are now worked for Germany—for Germany, even, is compelled to go to those sources of supply and to put on boats for that purpose.

Mr. UNDERWOOD. Do you think it is possible, when the English ore mines play out, for them to obtain or ship a supply of ore from the Norwegian banks?

Mr. CARNEGIE. From what I have told you, you will yourself see that it is wholly problematical. The prospects are not as good as they were.

Mr. UNDERWOOD. In your judgment, then, we are not threatened with cheaper Norwegian ores in English furnaces?

Mr. CARNEGIE. No; on the contrary——

Mr. UNDERWOOD. Now, as to the relation of ore and coal supplies in Germany; from your investigation of these matters is the coal and ore supply near the furnaces, or do they have a long distance to haul?

Mr. CARNEGIE. I must be excused from speaking of Germany. I have not been able to give it the study that I made elsewhere.

Mr. UNDERWOOD. Inasmuch as you have traveled there, I thought perhaps you had made an investigation.

Mr. CARNEGIE. No, sir. I had the pleasure of visiting the Emperor at Kiel and of having a talk with him. He is also a laughing man. But I did not go into the ore question.

Mr. UNDERWOOD. Mr. Schwab made a very important statement here the other day to the effect that he did not think the labor cost on the iron or steel or pig iron was greater here than in England, but that the difference that existed was due to the fact that the American laborer could produce a larger amount; the greater productive capacity was due to improved machinery in the plants and in the furnaces. Do you agree with him in that?

Mr. CARNEGIE. Decidedly. I agree with him fully.

Mr. UNDERWOOD. He also said that the cost of making a pig-iron or steel plant in England was more than double, at least, that of producing the same plant in this country. I believe he said it cost a third in England as compared with the cost of building a modern furnace or steel plant in this country.

Mr. CARNEGIE. You mean that the cost of the furnace abroad was one-third of the cost of it here?

Mr. UNDERWOOD. Yes; that is what he said. What is your information in reference to that?

Mr. CARNEGIE. I have none; but I think, when you speak of furnaces, you are getting into another trouble about costs. You can buy a horse for $100, and another you can not buy for $1,000. You can build a furnace for one or two hundred thousand dollars, and it would be a much dearer furnace, perhaps, than the one you paid half a million dollars for.

Mr. UNDERWOOD. I understand; but I want to know whether, under the conditions, our steel plants require more capital and investment to produce the same tonnage than they do in an English furnace.

Mr. CARNEGIE. I should say that was highly probable; yes.

Mr. UNDERWOOD. Can you give us the difference?

Mr. CARNEGIE. No, sir; I can not. Our furnaces in America— every year or two we build them bigger and bigger and make a cheaper product in consequence.

Mr. UNDERWOOD. That accounts for the additional cost?

Mr. CARNEGIE. Large y. Now, good-by, Mr. Cockran, and good-by, Mr. Underwood. [Laughter.]

Mr. DALZELL. Mr. Carnegie, you expressed some opinion in answer to the question of Mr. Cockran about our future supply of ore. What was your opinion on that subject?

Mr. CARNEGIE. Whose ore?

Mr. DALZELL. Mr. Cockran asked you something about our future supply of iron ore. I do not recall what your answer was.

Mr. CARNEGIE. My answer is, that any man who can see into the future I should like to get him to tell me.

Mr. DALZELL. You are not anticipating any early exhaustion of our ore supply?

Mr. CARNEGIE. Oh, no.

Mr. DALZELL. I think you said before the conservation congress that seventy years from now we would have no ores.

Mr. CARNEGIE. Oh, I beg your pardon; I said first-class ores. That is a very different proposition.

Mr. DALZELL. I am not informed. I was asking for information.

Mr. CARNEGIE. I said, Mr. Dalzell, that would be the case if our rate of increase continued as it had been doing, which is at the extraordinary speed of doubling every ten years. You see, if we used 100,000,000 tons in 1900, we would use 200,000,000 tons in 1910; we would use 400,000,000 tons in 1920, and we would use 800,000,000 tons in 1930; that is, at the rate at which we are going; and in my opinion it would be grossly misleading.

Mr. DALZELL. If you think we are going at that rate that you now describe, in seventy years from now we would have exhausted our high-grade ores?

Mr. CARNEGIE. That is the statement. On the other hand, seventeen years from now England, Britain, will be just where we would be in seventy years, with this difference: Britain will have no ores whatever.

Mr. COCKRAN. You are speaking of seventy years, not seventeen years, as Mr. Underwood understands, I believe?

Mr. CARNEGIE. I think that needs revision. Seven or eight years ago I made an estimate that, in my judgment, there were only two firms making steel in Britain who would have ore in twenty years—that is, thirteen years from now—who would have ore lasting to that time.

Mr. DALZELL. I have just been informed that I did not state your conservation congress opinion correctly. You stated forty years instead of seventy years.

Mr. CARNEGIE. As you said that I said seventy years, I naturally thought that you were correct. I can not pretend to remember. I took your own figures.

Mr. DALZELL. I want to correct my own figures, because they were wrong.

Mr. CARNEGIE. What is it?

Mr. DALZELL. I was informed that you stated at the conservation congress that seventy years from now our ore would be exhausted. I am now informed that you stated forty years from now, instead of seventy years, so I did not put my question correctly in the first instance.

Mr. CARNEGIE. Whatever I stated there was the result of the best expert information at my command. Remember that is first-class ores.

Mr. DALZELL. I just wanted the fact, that is all.

Mr. CARNEGIE. Yes, sir.

Mr. FORDNEY. Mr. Carnegie, this committee is called upon to get information, the most reliable possible or obtainable, and to prepare a tariff bill to present to Congress, and the committee is aiming to obtain the very best possible information, not only on steel and iron, but on each and every article in every paragraph in the bill. I do not believe there is a man on the committee to-day who is interested in the production and manufacture of steel. Therefore we must rely upon the information obtained here from witnesses. The committee called Mr. Schwab. He came here and readily gave information. I am frank to say that I have never met a man who had such a world of information as Mr. Schwab.

Mr. CARNEGIE. He is a genius.

Mr. FORDNEY. I do not think I have ever met a man more thoroughly posted in the business in which he is engaged and who could give such detailed statement of the cost from the raw ore in the ground to the finished steel as Mr. Schwab. We took his testimony and are weighing it for what it is worth. Mr. Gary came here and gave testimony. I believe him to be a thoroughly honest man in the statement which he made. He gave his testimony to the best of his knowledge. You have referred to him as a very competent and a very-well posted man, and if I interpreted your Scotch story correctly, you intended to mean that he was a very " slick article? "

Mr. CARNEGIE. No, no. [Laughter.]

Mr. FORDNEY. Then, I stand corrected. I do not speak Scotch, but some man whispered in my ear that that meant in English " a very slick article."

Mr. CARNEGIE. Not the slightest. On the contrary, it means one of the most lovable and friendly natures. I can not explain exactly what it does mean. It means he is shrewd; it means that he is deeply interested and does not neglect number one, and yet it means that he has such a delightful and sweet nature, yet very shrewd. You have to examine closely what he says. [Laughter.] Now, that does not quite give it to you. But he is not an expert in steel; he has to get his figures from others; then comes in his powers of generalization, which tells him he needs no tariff on steel. Judge Gary had no intention of misrepresenting the conditions——

Mr. FORDNEY. No; I do not believe he did.

Mr. CARNEGIE (continuing). But I think it was the cleverest dodge I have heard of in pushing his weak brethren forward to invoke your sympathy for them and not on his account, not for the world, to forbear abolishing the duties on steel. He can stand it, but his poor brethren [laughter]; for their sake forbear. I have stated my honest opinion. Judge Gary makes the mistake of his life if he thinks that he can compete with his poor brothers without ruining his own company. The difference can not be more—and I put it at the extreme—I do not believe that he can have $2 a ton profit on the few miles of railroad transportation, and beyond that he has nothing.

Mr. FORDNEY. I accept your explanation of what you meant by the Scotch story.

Mr. DALZELL. In your description of Mr. Schwab you forgot the very sweet smile which he always has.

Mr. CARNEGIE. He learned that from me. [Laughter.]

Mr. FORDNEY. After hearing Mr. Schwab and Judge Gary, and after hearing the other men in the steel industry, and now hearing you, and believing that each and every witness, including yourself, testifying aims to tell the whole truth and nothing but the truth, if this committee should form an opinion different from the one they would form if they heard your testimony only, would you criticise it?

Mr. CARNEGIE. Not the slightest; but you must remember that if you form an opinion different from what I have given you, that Judge Gary and myself are together; that Judge Gary expresses an opinion, but when he comes and you ask the question, " Can you do without a tariff on steel," he tells you, " Yes," and the President-elect says that tariffs no doubt enable a combination to exact excessive profits, and therefore we should have as little only as needed. Therefore, as a good Republican, on the Republican platform, I hold it to be your duty to accept Judge Gary's statement.

Mr. FORDNEY. Do you think it only possible to form a combination on account of the tariff?

Mr. CARNEGIE. Why, certainly. On account of the tariff, yes; and raise the price of everything up to the point where the cost to the producer and the freights coming here, plus the tariff, $7, enables them to raise the price. I think the President-elect is entirely right about that.

Mr. HILL. Is there not a steel-rail combination existing to-day in Great Britain, the United States, and Germany, fixing the price, where there is no tariff? I have asked that question of every man who has been on the stand, and I would like to ask you.

Mr. CARNEGIE. I must say to you that I am not conversant with international arrangements. I heard it stated by a witness who was before you—Mr. Miles—but the proper party to ask that question of is the party that you think is in the combination. He could tell you.

Mr. HILL. I have asked that question, but get no satisfaction. I will repeat this question: The official report of our consul in Great Britain says that the three greatest trusts or combinations in the iron trade to-day are the United States Steel Corporation, the German Steel Syndicate, and the International Rail Syndicate, which has its headquarters in London, controlling an output of some 4,000,000 tons of rails annually in the United States, Germany, and the United Kingdom. That was in 1905, if I am not mistaken. Do you know anything about such a combination controlling 4,000,000 tons or any other amount of steel rails in the United States, Germany, and Great Britain and fixing the price?

Mr. CARNEGIE. Mr. Hill, that is a question that you should ask of parties interested in it, if there be such a combination.

Mr. HILL. I was not here when Mr. Gary testified. I have asked that question of everybody else, and my recollection is that they all stated that they did not know of such a combination as our consul reported. Now I am asking you if you know?

Mr. CARNEGIE. I do not know. I have heard it stated. You have the evidence of Mr. Miles that there is an international organization, but I think it highly probable——

Mr. HILL. But——

Mr. CARNEGIE (interrupting). Wait a moment. I do not think, Mr. Chairman, that that is a proper question to ask me, is it? I am not in it.

The CHAIRMAN. If you do not know, of course you can say so; but if you do know, you can give the information.

Mr. CARNEGIE. Well, I would not be telling the whole truth if I said I did not believe there was such a thing.

Mr. HILL. Whether it exists or whether it does not exist, if it exists would changing the tariff here have any effect on the price of steel rails to the consumer if that price was fixed in London?

Mr. CARNEGIE. If that price was fixed in London and it was made permanent and the companies were bound by enormous penalties if they broke it, I would consider, as long as that existed, that it would of course prevent competition here.

Mr. HILL. I would like to supplement that question in regard to steel rails with the same question that I have asked of everybody except Mr. Gary, and I was not present when he was on the stand : Do you know of any combination that exists by which the price of tin plate is fixed internationally?

Mr. CARNEGIE. I do not.

Mr. HILL. Do you know of any combination by which the price of wire nails is fixed internationally?

Mr. CARNEGIE. I do not.

Mr. HILL. You do not answer with as much positiveness in regard to steel rails?

Mr. CARNEGIE. Because I have heard so much. I read Mr. Miles's testimony. Has Mr. Miles's statement been contradicted?

Mr. FORDNEY. He contradicted himself all the time.

Mr. DALZELL. It was not necessary to do that.

Mr. CARNEGIE. Please remember that I do not pose as an authority; that I speak absolutely without knowledge of any combination of that kind, and yet I would not tell you the whole truth if I did not say that I had heard it spoken of.

Mr. HILL. Then I will shape the question in this form: If the official statement of our consul is correct, and 4,000,000 tons of rails are controlled in the United States, Germany, and the United Kingdom by an international arrangement, would any change in the tariff affect the price here?

Mr. CARNEGIE. As long as they continued such an agreement as you specify, why, tariff or no tariff has no bearing upon it. But why do you ask me a question so obvious as that?

Mr. HILL. Because it does control, evidently, in Great Britain, where there is no tariff, just the same as it controls here, where there is a tariff of $7.80 a ton.

Mr. CARNEGIE. Great Britain is the great exporting country of steel. It does not consume the steel that it makes. It has relations all over the world.

Mr. HILL. Let me supplement that by this: You retired in 1901 from the steel business. The price of steel rails then was $28 a ton, as it is now. Was there any international agreement then, when you were in business?

Mr. CARNEGIE. Not that I remember of. Oh, I never heard of such a thing.

Mr. CALDERHEAD. If this tariff was removed, would it not be easier to form an international agreement or combination to maintain prices?

Mr. CARNEGIE. I do not think it affects the formation one iota. The American producer would get more favorable terms if he had a tariff than he would get if he had none; but the formation of a trust, Mr. Chairman, I do not know of anything that can prevent it if it be lawful.

Mr. FORDNEY. If I understood you correctly, you stated that you had read or heard of Mr. Miles's statement here, and you gave some credence to what he said?

Mr. CARNEGIE. I did. It is not likely that he would invent it.

Mr. FORDNEY. I am not criticising you for that.

Mr. CARNEGIE. I hope not.

Mr. FORDNEY. I do not believe that I ever heard a man deal more in theory and hearsay, lest it be one man, in my life.

Mr. Cockran. He stated some facts very clearly. He wanted his own article on the free list.

Mr. Fordney. You can question the witness as you choose, but I think I am right in my premises.

Mr. Carnegie, if we are entitled to give credence and to believe what we hear from people who appear before this committee, hearing so many men on this subject, we are entitled to give credence, then, to the statements made by Mr. Schwab and Mr. Gary, who are thoroughly posted in the business that they are engaged in, are they not? Let me supplement that a little further. When Mr. Hill asked you a question about a combination, you stated, " You must ask a man who is engaged in it. I do not know anything about it. I am not in it," and you suggested that he ask a man in the business to get reliable information. If that is true in the case Mr. Hill asked you about, is it not also true in getting information from Mr. Schwab and Mr. Gary and you?

Mr. Carnegie. The case is different. Whether there is or is not a combination is a single question of fact. If you wish details then you need an expert. From partial statements of cost from interested parties none but experts are capable of drawing the right conclusion. [Laughter.]

Mr. Fordney. I may be far more incapable than I look. [Laughter.]

Mr. Carnegie. You can get honest men to take different views of questions. Now, one man will tell you that it will be very serious for the steel business if you reduce the tariff, and Judge Gary will tell you that it will not be. They deal so much with opinions that neither of them knows exactly what the future will be, and so with the cost; one concern will estimate cost in one way and some in another. The steel business is a business by itself, and the cost to one man means a very different thing from the cost to another.

Mr. Fordney. If we can not get reliable information as we are now aiming to get, how can we get it; can you tell us?

Mr. Carnegie. You ought to cease trying to get it. You have gone wrong in trying to get it. When a gentleman of Judge Gary's character comes to you and tells you that he does not need a tariff, you ought to believe him.

Mr. Longworth. The Republican platform, which you have spoken of with admiration on this subject, says that we must revise the tariff on the basis of the difference between the cost abroad and the cost at home. If there is no way of ascertaining that cost approximately, is not that a rather bare statement in the platform?

Mr. Carnegie. Yes, sir; and it requires a man practiced in the art, interested in neither, to estimate the cost upon the same systems, and, as I have stated, from the best judgment I can form, if a commission were appointed and spent a month in the mill that now holds the record for the cheapest steel made in the world, and that is ours, the Carnegie Steel Company, and a month in the foremost works of England or Germany, you would find that the difference in cost, estimated in the same form, every company credited only with the outlay required, including transportation of the ore, mines, and everything there is, and the same to the foreign manufacturers, you will find that the foreign manufacturer's cost of steel at his works exceeds slightly—I should say, will be the same. You can not do this offhand; it needs time; for during the month one mill might be running finely, and at the other mill there may be some trouble, and vice versa, or the one running full, the other only turning out half its usual amount. The cost at the foreign mill is equal to the best mill in this country, and that leaves a natural tariff between the two, the transportation here, and the many disadvatages under which a foreign manufacturer labors in selling a foreign product to a patriotic American. Therefore, I have stated to Mr. Cockran, perhaps to his great disappointment, that my judgment is that we could start with free trade to-morrow and it would not seriously affect the price, but it would give the combination here the power to raise the price to the consumer to the amount of the duty imposed.

Mr. BONYNGE. If we put steel products on the free list, the present price   the consumer would practically be maintained, in your judgment ‰o

Mr. CARNEGIE. No; I think that the tendency of combination is to raise prices and to exact from the consumer what they safely can.

Mr. BONYNGE. But as to steel rails, I understood you to say, in answer to Mr. Cockran, that you believed the price of $28 would be maintained; if steel rails were put on the free list, that the price would be maintained.

Mr. CARNEGIE. Excuse me; I did not say that the price would be maintained, but I do say that the present arrangement is a fair one, in my judgment, between the consumer and the producer. Let me show you the difference. If there is no tariff, the combination comes together and fixes a price, and it will fix a price lower than if there is a tariff. I think you will agree with me that the tendency of human nature is to get a good profit.

Mr. BONYNGE. Certainly.

Mr. CARNEGIE. And that the tariff would enable them to raise the price to the extent of the duty.

Mr. BONYNGE. But you do not think that the price of steel rails has been raised above what it should be at the present time, $28 a ton?

Mr. CARNEGIE. Steel rails—I say, I think that the railways are not paying too much for steel rails, and I think that the steel-rail mills are making a fair profit.

Mr. BONYNGE. How about other steel products besides steel rails; what about the other present prices; are they above what they should be—structural steel and other steel—do you know?

Mr. CARNEGIE. I do not. I have not a word to say about the price of anything. That is not my province. I came to give you my views of what the effect would be of taking off the duty.

Mr. FORDNEY. When Judge Gary stated, as you put it—I will tell you my recollection of what he said when we get through—when Judge Gary said they could get along without protection on steel, we could believe him?

Mr. CARNEGIE. Yes, sir.

Mr. FORDNEY. Judge Gary in making up his figures of cost showed a profit on steel rails, Bessemer and open hearth rails. the difference in cost—that is to say, the difference in price—showed a profit to his company of $4.69 a ton. Would you have us believe him?

Mr. CARNEGIE. I would have asked him to explain that statement.

Mr. FORDNEY. He did, in the most detailed manner.

Mr. CARNEGIE. Very well.

Mr. FORDNEY. Do you regard one statement as inconsistent with the other?

Mr. CARNEGIE. I do. I thought he was interested, and I thought he gave, so to speak, an opinion.

Mr. FORDNEY. Then do you believe——

Mr. CARNEGIE (interrupting). I thought you said "consistent." You have a capacity for belief that I wish my friends had.

Mr. FORDNEY. You would have us believe what you say under oath?

Mr. CARNEGIE. Yes, sir.

Mr. FORDNEY. Judge Gary was under oath. I have no good reason to doubt the truthfulness or correctness of his statement, and I do not believe that he would testify falsely under oath. I want to believe every man under oath, at least until I find out to the contrary.

Mr. CARNEGIE. Judge Gary was honest, I say.

Mr. FORDNEY. I believe he was honest in both statements. Now, if he was correct in both statements, then what have you to say?

Mr. CARNEGIE. I simply say that I can not understand how with a profit of $4.29——

Mr. FORDNEY (interrupting). $4.69.

Mr. CARNEGIE. $4.69 on rails, how he could stand if the tariff was reduced $7.80.

Mr. FORDNEY. He did not say that he could do that. He said that his company could survive by reducing the cost of the product, and to do that, labor being the largest item that enters into the cost of the product, it would be compelled to reduce labor and the other costs all along the line. That is what Judge Gary said.

Mr. CARNEGIE. Yes, sir. Judge Gary never said that, as far as I have read. It was upon tin plate he said that labor would have to be reduced, and that is not steel at all; and I agree with the Judge in this.

Mr. FORDNEY. And that is what Mr. Schwab said.

Mr. CARNEGIE. Now, that is a matter of judgment.

Mr. FORDNEY. He is in the business and knows what it costs to-day to produce it, and he stated that not for the past ten years had there been a single year that the cost of their labor did not increase each year over the last year, and that this increase in the cost of labor amounted to an increased cost of production from the time that the ore was taken from the ground until it was put into the finished product, and that that accounted for his difference in cost.

Mr. CARNEGIE. I think I heard this morning that Mr. Schwab had referred to a decrease in labor.

Mr. HILL. Yes; 35 cents a ton.

Mr. COCKRAN. The labor cost, not the rate of wages.

Mr. CARNEGIE. Wages per man would have nothing to do with it.

Mr. FORDNEY. Mr. Schwab did say that the amount paid for labor had increased each year, one over the other, for the past ten years.

Mr. COCKRAN. And yet that his total cost of labor had decreased.

Mr. FORDNEY. On account of efficiency.

Mr. HILL. In one item.

Mr. CARNEGIE. There is no reconciling the statements.

Mr. FORDNEY. Without any intention to embarrass or to criticise you, but to get an honest, candid opinion from one who is most deeply interested, one of the most important questions for this committee in rearranging this tariff law is to leave a sufficient revenue to this Government. To-day our revenues are not sufficient to meet the expenditures of the Government. If by a reduction of duty we reduce the revenues to the Government—and it will unless imports are increased, and that is very undesirable from a Republican point of view—would you recommend an income tax to make up that deficit?

Mr. CARNEGIE. I believe, with Mr. Gladstone, who had more experience with income taxes than any man of his day, that an income tax makes a nation of liars. That is what he said, that of all the demoralizing taxes a nation can place upon the people the income tax is the most demoralizing.

Mr. FORDNEY. You and I, who are at the age when we look to something else besides to make the almighty dollar, would not lie?

Mr. CARNEGIE. It is not a question of lying.

The CHAIRMAN. You agree with Mr. Gladstone on that?

Mr. CARNEGIE. Yes, sir.

The CHAIRMAN. So do I.

Mr. COCKRAN. I agree with you, I believe.

Mr. DALZELL. You are getting on common ground.

Mr. CARNEGIE. I would like to interrupt there. When President Roosevelt wrote his article in favor of progressive taxation you may remember that I sent him my Gospel of Wealth, written seventeen years before. His reply was: "I am struck with the fact that seventeen years ago you had it all." Now, I believe the distribution of wealth is unfair. I believe that we should legislate to make a fairer distribution, and I stated in that article that I was in favor of progressive taxation at the death of a man. I would not disturb the honey bee making honey during its life. I do not think that anybody else could make fortunes so well as the man engaged in that business, but wealth is largely the product of the community. I instanced five brothers in that article. One starts at Pittsburg and one in New York, but otherwise they got farms of equal value. One happened to be in the center of business and the other several miles away. One became a millionaire. He did nothing to produce that wealth. It was the community settling there that made that wealth. I shall be glad to send each member of the committee a copy of that article. [Laughter.] You need not read it, but just have your secretary thank me. [Laughter.]

Mr. FORDNEY. I thank you for that.

What was the duty on steel rails when you began the production of steel rails in the United States, do you remember?

Mr. CARNEGIE. I can not tell you that from memory. I never paid much attention to the duty on steel rails. Why, that is not very much of an advantage to the manufacturer when there is competition; but if you permit combination, remember, gentlemen, that is the great question before this country to-day, that is the most serious.

Mr. FORDNEY. But there was no way by law to prevent you from selling your plant to the combination, was there?

Mr. CARNEGIE. None at all.

Mr. FORDNEY. There is no fault to find with any man selling his plant to a combination or corporation engaged in the same business that produces more?

Mr. CARNEGIE. Certainly not. What did I ever say that would make you infer that?

Mr. FORDNEY. You sold your property to a combination?

Mr. CARNEGIE. Certainly.

Mr. FORDNEY. You helped to make that combination? I do not criticise you for it.

Mr. CARNEGIE. Excuse me, there was no combination made when I sold.

Mr. FORDNEY. The United States Steel Corporation is a very great concern and it is a combination of many?

Mr. CARNEGIE. I sold to J. P. Morgan & Co.

Mr. FORDNEY. I am not criticising that.

Mr. CARNEGIE. I am quite willing to be criticised for that, but that is not the point. If any branch of manufacture is in the hands of a monopoly, it stands to reason that they will get more profit than if there is healthy competition. What are monopolies for?

Mr. FORDNEY. Mr. Carnegie, from information given here by the men engaged in the production of steel, it is evident to me—I do not know about the other members of the committee—that the only way that the present manufacturers of all kinds of steel can meet the foreign competition is to reduce the price of cost, and in doing that labor must certainly stand a very great share in that reduction. That, I believe, would be disastrous to the American people or undesirable, and therefore I do not believe that we can remove all the duties on those articles and do justice to American labor. What do you think about that? That is my opinion.

Mr. CARNEGIE. I say that you are entitled to hold it. [Laughter.] This is a free country, and I think for a man with the knowledge you have of the steel business that opinion does not do you great discredit. [Laughter.]

Mr. FORDNEY. In my line of production I think I know just as much about my business as you know about the production of steel.

Mr. CARNEGIE. Undoubtedly; yes, sir.

Mr. FORDNEY (continuing). Which you have been engaged in your whole life. Therefore as to the amount of knowledge I have, are you competent to judge what I know about the production in which I am engaged?

Mr. CARNEGIE. I thought it was steel only we were considering.

Mr. FORDNEY. No; you were criticising me as a manufacturer.

Mr. CARNEGIE. I thought you were asking me about steel.

Mr. FORDNEY. I was; but you did not answer me in reference to steel alone.

Mr. CARNEGIE. I meant steel.

Mr. FORDNEY. That is different.

Mr. CARNEGIE. I bow to you as an authority on manufacture in any branch in which you are engaged, I am sure. I have not attempted to give my views about any manufacture but that of steel, and I do this at the summons of this committee, which I consider my duty as a citizen. I do not volunteer it.

Mr. FORDNEY. Your answer as you gave it caused laughter. It sought to discredit me as to having any reliable knowledge as to my own business.

Mr. CARNEGIE. My dear sir, nothing could be further from my thought.

Mr. FORDNEY. I do not discredit you. I admire you for the fortune you have made by your brains and your efforts in this country. Your efforts have caused a reduction in the price of steel rails in my time from $100 down to the present price of $28, and when

Mr. Gary and the statistics show that American steel to-day is selling cheaper at the mills than English steel is being sold at its place of production, there is no danger of competition between English and American rails in the United States.

Mr. CARNEGIE. Then, what is the necessity for a tariff? There is none.

Mr. FORDNEY. Where do you get your cost of production? You have not given any.

Mr. CARNEGIE. You have information enough. You should cease your labors. You should accept Judge Gary's statement and the statement you have given—I do not know who gave it—but, assuming that the statement is true, then, of course, there can be no competition. That is what I have been trying to tell you gentlemen. When Mr. Cockran asked me if I thought the abolition of the tariff duty would lessen the cost of steel, I said my opinion—remember, my opinion—was, judging from all I know, that it would not.

Mr. FORDNEY. If that statement is true, that the price of steel rails is higher to-day in England than the price of steel rails at the American steel mills, the tariff has absolutely nothing to do with fixing the price in this country, has it?

Mr. CARNEGIE. That is what I am trying to tell you gentlemen, that the tariff has little bearing.

Mr. FORDNEY. It does not in any way enable the manufacturer in this country to put the price up and get more than he otherwise could?

Mr. CARNEGIE. There you are wrong. Assuming that they are selling at $22 in Great Britain——

Mr. FORDNEY (interrupting). They are selling higher there than here.

Mr. CARNEGIE. That is true. If they are selling higher there than they are here, and you add the cost to the foreign producer of bringing his rails here and selling them here in the interior, as he would, most of them, then the parties here can raise the price still higher than $28 a ton, can they not?

Mr. FORDNEY. They can, but they are not. That is the point, they are not.

Mr. CARNEGIE. But, my dear friend, if you are legislating for a country you are not going to legislate to leave a party the power at any moment to raise it, are you?

Mr. FORDNEY. That is not the question.

Mr. CARNEGIE. But that is the question I would like to ask you.

Mr. FORDNEY. I am not the witness.

Mr. CARNEGIE. Oh; I wish I were the cross-examiner.

Mr. FORDNEY. I will go on the witness stand as to the business in which I am engaged and let you or any other man cross-examine me.

The point is this: You have stated that the duty on an article helps to form a combine and put up the price?

Mr. CARNEGIE. I said that it gave the combiners the power to do so.

Mr. FORDNEY. They are not exercising that power in the steel business?

Mr. CARNEGIE. In the steel-rail business—I told you that that had been taken out of competition and stands in a class by itself—by an arrangement with all the consumers of steel rails—the railways and themselves—and it is mutually satisfactory. Now, I would be a very impracticable man if I did not realize that that was a just and a fair and a salutary arrangement; but, as the President-elect tells you, a tariff places in the combination the power to raise the rates higher than they could raise them if there were no tariff. Then I consider it would be your duty to guard against that power.

Mr. FORDNEY. If the tariff would permit the manufacturer in this country to raise the price on an article above what it is selling for in competition with the same article made abroad, is it not a good law if it protects labor and furnishes it a greater income for the labor given?

Mr. CARNEGIE. I do not think I quite understood that question.

Mr. FORDNEY. I will repeat it: If the tariff will permit the manufacturer to put an advanced price on his manufactured product——

Mr. CARNEGIE (interrupting). Here at home?

Mr. FORDNEY. Yes, sir; here at home; so as to compete with the foreign imported article, and by so doing benefits the labor that produces it, is not that a good law?

Mr. CARNEGIE. No; decidedly no. Allow me to explain that. The only justification for a government raising the price to the consumer of any article, because that is what a tariff does—if a tariff did not raise the price it would be of no use—that is only justifiable when you can induce a body of capitalists to risk capital in the experiment of introducing the new industry into the country, which is in its nature temporary. If the experiment be successful, as it has been in steel, it, in my opinion, vindicates the protective policy which we have pursued; but permanent protection, I think, is an injustice to the consumer, and if, after forty years of trial, the American steel industry, contrary to Judge Gary's opinion, does not need a tariff, then I think we should lessen it. The President-elect tells us that a tariff without doubt—he says that there is no doubt but that the tariff puts into the hands of a combination the power to raise the price higher than if that tariff against foreign competition did not exist. In my opinion—and here I think I differ from you—I agree with the President-elect.

Mr. FORDNEY. Then you believe that protection should be granted to every industry that needs it in order to compete with foreign competition?

Mr. CARNEGIE. I do not.

Mr. FORDNEY. You had it when you first went into the business, and you could not have engaged in the production of steel rails without protection?

Mr. CARNEGIE. It is true, and I did not start to make steel rails until I saw that both parties in this country—that is to say, a large proportion of the Democrats—supported that policy. I would never have gone into the manufacture if the tariff was to be the football of the parties, but when I saw that the American people were resolved to make their own steel—the war had demonstrated the necessity for that; we sent an agent abroad to buy all the steel he could find in Great Britain when the war broke out. The man was Philip S. Justice. There were the Baldwin Locomotive Works and others, and we needed all the steel we could get because we were not making steel, and the nation resolved that thereafter it would not be without that invaluable article. Why, so hazardous was the entrance into steel in those days that not one of my partners in iron would touch it, and I went in alone, and I went to the dry-goods merchants and bankers and got the money.

All my life I have been a protectionist, as the President-elect says he is, but after we do not need protection in an industry what gross injustice is put upon the consumer. If taken off to-morrow, the steel business would not be seriously affected, to my mind; it is the combination which permits it to be completed.

Now, I am not appearing here against this movement; it is one to which I keep an open mind. It seems inevitable that we are to give a trial to abolish competition and to depend upon governments to fix the prices, because that is inevitable—the most momentous departure that the world has ever seen. I am a protectionist if I can introduce a new industry into this country. Mark this: I prefer to obtain a cheaper and more regular supply than we could get from abroad, and if, after forty years' experience, we can not develop steel to that condition—fortunately, you have the highest testimony in the world that it is in that position—but if we had failed our protective policy in that instance would be a great failure instead of a triumphant success, which it has become, and the vindication of the protective policy is in the fact that we can agree with Judge Gary and say, " Take back your protection, you paternal government that first nursed this industry. We are now men and we can beat the world in the manufacture of steel, and we shall make half of all the world's product in three years from now." What is the use of continuing that protection when the leading man in the steel business, representing 45 per cent of the total production of steel—and 45 per cent is greater than any other nation in the world makes, even greater than Germany—and therefore I say that its total abolition will leave the steel business of America in a better position for the country's sake than if you coddle it by protection and insist that we " let well enough alone." You want a vigorous, progressive steel industry.

Mr. FORDNEY. You had protection when you went into the business and had it all your life?

Mr. CARNEGIE. I never appeared before a committee without urging a reduction in the tariff on iron and steel. When the McKinley bill was under consideration I labored long with President McKinley. He was a protectionist after my own heart. The McKinley bill reduced the duty on iron and steel 25 to 35 per cent, partly upon my advice, and I am consistent in believing that now the removal of the present duties would not affect injuriously any person engaged in the manufacture of steel.

Mr. FORDNEY. Yet, when you engaged in the business you did not engage until you became satisfied that both the Republican and Democratic parties were for protection?

Mr. CARNEGIE. That is the reason I am a protectionist for any new industry that needs it. Show me anything that needs protection to introduce it into this country and I will go the farthest in claiming it; but in the leading industry of steel I think it no longer needs it.

Mr. LONGWORTH. Whether it needs it or not, it is the difference in cost abroad and home?

Mr. CARNEGIE. Yes, sir.

Mr. LONGWORTH. And your proposition now, reduced to its last analysis, so to speak, is the difference between the cost of producing steel abroad and at home?

Mr. CARNEGIE. I believe to-day, as I have stated before, that the cost at the mill which has the record of the lowest cost, compared with the best mills abroad, in England and Germany—I believe that there would not be much difference in the cost—that the difference of transportation for 3,000 miles on the sea and the difference in inland transportation here renders any serious competition with the steel industry of this country, in my opinion, impossible.

The CHAIRMAN. We will take a recess until 2 o'clock.

Mr. CARNEGIE. Am I through?

The CHAIRMAN. No, sir.

Mr. CARNEGIE. Oh.

AFTER RECESS.

The CHAIRMAN. Mr. Carnegie, I have before me the report of the United States Steel Corporation to which you alluded, dated March 17, 1908, which, I suppose, is the last report. I find that the net earnings for the year 1907 were $133,244,929. The rolled and other finished products for sale were 10,376,000 tons, which would make an average of about $13 a ton, and I find that the 10,376,000 tons were divided up as follows: In the first place, of steel rails there were 1,733,814 tons, or about 17 per cent; blooms, billets, slabs, sheet and tin-plate bars, 758,699; plates, 877,682; heavy structural shapes, 587,954; merchant steel, skelp, hoops, bands, and cotton ties, 1,316,-387; tubing and pipe, 1,174,629; rods, 126,095; wire, and products of wire, 1,481,226; sheets, black, galvanized, and tin plate, 1,070,752; finished structural work, 719,887; angle and splice bars and joints, 195,157; spikes, bolts, nuts, and rivets, 67,991; axles, 189,000; sundry iron and steel products, 77,463. Those products that were rolled, according to this report, were of a higher grade of manufacture than steel rails, except steel rails and billets.

Mr. CARNEGIE. Mr. Chairman, I have spent some time explaining to you that steel rails are an entirely different article from any other.

The CHAIRMAN. I suppose they are. The principal question I want to ask in regard to that, Mr. Carnegie, without taking too much time, is this, that all of those articles, other than steel rails, bring a higher price than steel rails, do they not, per ton?

Mr. CARNEGIE. I think, generally speaking, they do. My judgment is that they probably would bring a higher price than steel rails.

The CHAIRMAN. Of course tin plate would, a much higher price?

Mr. CARNEGIE. Certainly.

The CHAIRMAN. Several times as high; about how much a ton?

Mr. CARNEGIE. I could not tell you about tin plate.

The CHAIRMAN. And billets, nuts, and so forth, would bring a high price per ton compared to steel rails?

Mr. CARNEGIE. Certainly.

The CHAIRMAN. And the same way with wire?

Mr. CARNEGIE. Yes; with wire.

The CHAIRMAN. And wire products?

Mr. CARNEGIE. Yes, sir.

The CHAIRMAN. And so on all through; structural steel brings a pretty high price per ton, does it not, in comparison?

Mr. CARNEGIE. Certainly.

The CHAIRMAN. So that it would not be fair to average the profits on all those articles by the ton, would it?

Mr. CARNEGIE. Surely not.

The CHAIRMAN. The same percentage of profits on each of the others would make a much higher profit per ton than on steel rails?

Mr. CARNEGIE. Certainly.

The CHAIRMAN. That was the question I wanted to ask. I am much obliged to you for calling the attention of the committee to this report.

Mr. CARNEGIE. What report is that, what year?

The CHAIRMAN. This is for 1907. The report is dated March 17, 1908, but it is for the calendar year 1907.

Mr. CARNEGIE. That is probably the report to which I referred, and the difference between the three and the five might lead it to be quoted elsewhere at one fifty-eight. I have made a memorandum from the statement that I have seen, one fifty-eight, but that makes very little difference—yes, it makes considerable difference.

Mr. COCKRAN. It makes a difference of twenty-five millions?

Mr. CARNEGIE. Yes.

Mr. COCKRAN. The difference between one hundred and thirty-three million and one hundred and fifty-eight. You said, Mr. Chairman, that the report shows there were one hundred and thirty-three million; Mr. Carnegie states one hundred and fifty-eight million.

Mr. DALZELL. A difference of $2 a ton?

Mr. CARNEGIE. Yes. I assure you that the figures I have sometimes seen printed were one fifty-eight, and I am delighted that that error is pointed out.

The CHAIRMAN. I did not call your attention to it to point out any error.

Mr. CARNEGIE. It would have been your duty to do that, I should think.

The CHAIRMAN. Not at all; I did not call attention even to that.

Mr. CARNEGIE. I made it in good faith, but I wonder if it is the report before that; I took it from another document, 158.

The CHAIRMAN. That may be, and still, Mr. Carnegie, there was a higher amount of manufacture for the year 1907 in all the articles produced in the United States than in any other year?

Mr. CARNEGIE. Yes.

The CHAIRMAN. According to all our reports; also a greater importation?

Mr. CARNEGIE. I am inclined to think that that is the report from which this statement I made was taken; I haven't a memorandum.

The CHAIRMAN. You only spoke of it from recollection.

Mr. CARNEGIE. Of course.

The CHAIRMAN. It is not material if you did make a mistake.

Mr. CARNEGIE. No; but I have a good head for figures, and I remember them; and I am pretty sure it was printed 158.

The CHAIRMAN. And the profits that year were generally higher in all the lines than in any year previous, were they not?

Mr. CARNEGIE. I think the product was greater; it was a busy year.

The CHAIRMAN. Yes, and the profits were higher?

Mr. CARNEGIE. Well, I have not seen the other reports.

The CHAIRMAN. That would be in accordance with the general experience, that the profits were higher during that year than any year previous?

Mr. CARNEGIE. I do not know about the profits per ton being higher, but I think more tons were made in that year. My impression is that prices were not advanced; that is my impression, but it would affect the gross amount.

The CHAIRMAN. That could be easily determined, of course, by looking at the reports. Mr. Gary testified that in Germany, as to German rails, the domestic price is $29.02, and the export price $22.20; in Great Britain the domestic price is $27.98, and the export price $23.61; in France the domestic price is $33.33, and the export price $25.69; in Belgium the domestic price is $27.45, and the export price $22.50; or, in other words, that the export price in each of those countries is but a trifle, if any, higher than what he testified was the cost price at the mill in the United States. Now, if that is correct, would it not look a little as though he had some grounds for fear if we had free trade in steel rails?

Mr. CARNEGIE. Well, Mr. Chairman, he has told you that he has not.

The CHAIRMAN. No, he did not tell us that; you are mistaken about that. He said that his company could go on and do business, but they would have to cut down wages.

Mr. COCKRAN. I do not think he said that, Mr. Chairman.

Mr. CRUMPACKER. I do not recollect that he said they would have to cut down wages.

Mr. CALDERHEAD. That is his statement.

The CHAIRMAN. That is what I understood.

Mr. CALDERHEAD. I read that yesterday.

The CHAIRMAN. Mr. Calderhead says he read it in his statement yesterday.

Mr. COCKRAN. Could you give us the page?

Mr. CALDERHEAD. I did not bring it with me because I did not think it would be questioned.

The CHAIRMAN. That was my recollection of it, so that it is not quite fair to say that he said they did not need the duty, or anything of that kind. Now, if he does need the duty, in order to keep up the present wages, to meet competition from abroad; if he is right about that and also right about the proposition that the other companies, his competitors, have a cost of $2 more per ton than his, and over, it would look a little as though they needed some protection, would it not?

Mr. CARNEGIE. I do not think that they do, because if ever Judge Gary, with his capital, undertakes to fight his competitors, of whom he has only $2 a ton advantage, as I said before, I would consider my bonds not a good security. Two dollars a ton profit on the earnings of the United States Steel Company would not pay interest upon their bonds.

The CHAIRMAN. Are your bonds a lien on this ore property of theirs?

Mr. CARNEGIE. Yes, and everything they purchase.

The CHAIRMAN. I do not wonder that even if their business were wiped out but what your bonds would be amply good.

Mr. CARNEGIE. But I might have to go, in case of default, and prove them to be good, and that would be very objectionable.

The CHAIRMAN. I do not know; you could put Schwab in charge, and I think you would get out of it.

Mr. CARNEGIE. The trouble is, when I put Schwab in charge, that I would like to be pretty close to him all the time. [Laughter.]

The CHAIRMAN. If the ores of the world are to play out as soon as some people imagine, the ore bed, even without any mill or any prospects of running one for a long time, would be pretty good security for an ordinary business man for even the amount of your bonds which you hold.

Mr. CARNEGIE. I do not like things that are only a pretty good security. [Laughter.]

The CHAIRMAN. Evidently you do not; I agree with you on that, if you think that these ore beds would not be security enough for your bonds.

Mr. CARNEGIE. Now, Judge Gary there again uses his judgment, that it would be necessary to do so and so. I can not say anything about that except that my judgment is that it would not be necessary to do any such thing.

The CHAIRMAN. As to reducing wages, I again call your attention to the fact that it was in reference to tin plate, not to steel, he spoke of reducing labor. I started in at that point to ask Mr. Gary what it cost to produce steel rails abroad, or suggested to a member of the committee who was interrogating him at that time to ask him, but I do not find that that was done, so that we are without his estimate of the cost of steel except in one instance. He said that the cost of pig iron in the Lorraine district in Germany was $7.50 a ton and the cost of converting it, I think, about $7 a ton—$6 or $7—so that they could produce steel rails there at $14 or $15, somewhere near that rate, in that district. He said that was lower than the price generally in Germany. He also stated that as a factor in the competition between Germany and this country the German Government, owning the railroads, in order to give a bounty to the steel business or to any other export business, for that matter, were accustomed to make a rebate in the freights, and while they carry goods to the seashore for export to cut the freights.

Mr. CARNEGIE. Mr. Chairman, if the German maker can make a ton of steel rails at $15 and can send them here at a cost of $6, why does he not send them here and get $28?

The CHAIRMAN. That would be $21 and $7.80, which would make it $28.80. Simply because he could not get his money back.

Mr. CARNEGIE. That is the answer.

The CHAIRMAN. In that case, if he was exporting them at $22 a ton and can find a market at that rate for the surplus which he wishes to dump on the markets of the world, that would be another good answer why he should not send them here, if that is the export price of Germany, $22 a ton. I am not saying this to indicate how I would stand on this question; I am only trying to get at the facts.

Mr. CARNEGIE. Yes; but you are pursuing the wrong policy.

The CHAIRMAN. What is that?

Mr. CARNEGIE. You are on the wrong track altogether. [Laughter.]

The CHAIRMAN. I may be. My only endeavor is to find out the truth, to get it from you. I hope you will not discourage me in saying that I am on the wrong track in that.

Mr. CARNEGIE. Listen to me a minute. Does any foreign country send rails here?

The CHAIRMAN. Not to any extent, I think.

Mr. CARNEGIE. No.

The CHAIRMAN. There is a small importation, I think, every year, a very small importation; nothing to count at all. It is prohibitive now, so to speak.

Mr. CARNEGIE. Very well.

The CHAIRMAN. That satisfies you on that, does it not?

Mr. CARNEGIE. Certainly.

The CHAIRMAN. But we have a pretty big duty now.

Mr. CARNEGIE. You have $7 a ton.

The CHAIRMAN. Seven dollars and eighty-four cents.

Mr. CARNEGIE. That is a gross ton.

The CHAIRMAN. Yes.

Mr. CARNEGIE. Seven dollars a ton is the duty. We go by net tons. I do not care how you fix it.

The CHAIRMAN. I suppose they bring in a gross ton here when they bring them in. But there is no dispute about the duty; that undoubtedly is a strong factor that keeps them down. Our people, when they sell abroad, sometimes run up against about the same duty, and sometimes they pay a duty to get their steel rails into that country, but the bulk of it goes where there is open competition with Great Britain and Germany. That is the fact.

Mr. CARNEGIE. The very year you speak of there we shipped abroad 345,000 tons to different countries, and we met German competition and English competition.

The CHAIRMAN. But the German competition got away with more of the market than our people did.

Mr. CARNEGIE. Because our people had a good home market. We consumed 22,500,000 tons of steel in our country, leaving about 500,000 tons to be exported.

The CHAIRMAN. And if Mr. Felton is right, they had to sell it at less than the cost in order to get it there.

Mr. CARNEGIE. Yes.

The CHAIRMAN. Mr. Felton is a high-toned man, is he not?

Mr. CARNEGIE. I think he must be very high toned; yes. [Laughter.]

The CHAIRMAN. You are speaking of it in a joking way.

Mr. COCKRAN. He is emphasizing the adjective.

The CHAIRMAN. Mr. Felton made a very good appearance before the committee. I never had the honor of his acquaintance before that.

Mr. CARNEGIE. Mr. Chairman, if the Pennsylvania Steel Company——

The CHAIRMAN. He is the president of the Pennsylvania Steel Company?

Mr. CARNEGIE. Yes. That was in business before the Carnegie Steel Company.

The CHAIRMAN. What is that?

Mr. CARNEGIE. It was in business making steel before the Carnegie Steel Company started. It shows the grossest mismanagement if his cost is $26.50 per ton average, but his statement may be based upon a short period of production during dull times—products probably not ·one-half the average. This would bring cost very high. Let him show you his book cost for five years past. His statement without period may mislead you.

The CHAIRMAN. I understand his concern is a very old concern. I do not know how long they made steel.

Mr. DALZELL. He says it was in business before his concern.

The CHAIRMAN. You say it was? I thought you asked me if it was.

Mr. CARNEGIE. I will try to be plain. The Pennsylvania Steel Company was in business before the Carnegie Steel Company was built, and if at this day it can not make steel as cheap as its competitors, whose fault is it?

The CHAIRMAN. Well, at first blush, I should say it was the fault of the management of the company. I might not be right about that; that would be a surface view. If I examined into it more, I might find out that there were some other difficulties, like location. It seems to me they have to carry their iron and coal, and I do not know but their limestone, quite a distance to get it to their works.

Mr. CARNEGIE. Assuming that they made a wrong location, do you think that the Government of the United States is compelled to take hold of every corporation that has made a mistake?

The CHAIRMAN. I made a proposition similar to that the other night about tannin extracts, and I did not know but I should be mobbed by the gentlemen who were presenting the question—whether they had not a bad location.

Mr. CARNEGIE. I have asked you a question. [Laughter.]

The CHAIRMAN. I have answered that question as freely as I know how.

Mr. CARNEGIE. I refer it to the court if he answered my question. Shall I repeat it? [Laughter.]

The CHAIRMAN. Now, Mr. Schwab says that the freight rates in 1899 were about one-third of what they are to-day, and he referred to Mr. Carnegie's article on rebates for proof.

Mr. CARNEGIE. I am delighted he referred to so high an authority. [Laughter.] I do not remember; I do not understand what bearing this has.

The CHAIRMAN. But if the article bears him out, of course there could not be any doubt about the truthfulness of the statement?

Mr. CARNEGIE. What is the statement? I do not grasp your meaning.

The CHAIRMAN. I say, if the article bears out his statement, there would not be any chance for dispute as to its truth.

Mr. CARNEGIE. Well, sir, Mr. Schwab may have quoted a sentence or a paragraph, omitting facts and what it was dealing with, and he would give you a very false impression.

The CHAIRMAN. Certainly. I said if the article bore him out. I did not say if a sentence in it could be twisted.

Mr. CARNEGIE. That is such a large subject, I would like to read the article and see really what bearing it has. If I wrote it, I am disposed to believe it was a very sound article. [Laughter.]

The CHAIRMAN. Mr. Schwab said that Mr. Gary's company was taking out about one-fourth of the ore on the property that they bought from Mr. Hill.

Mr. CARNEGIE. I think you must have misunderstood him there. From my knowledge, what I hear, they have not shipped one load of ore.

The CHAIRMAN. He understood it the other way; he did not claim to have personal knowledge of it.

Mr. CARNEGIE. I think if you want to test Mr. Schwab's statement and mine, it would be very well to get somebody to ascertain what is correct about it.

The CHAIRMAN. He was stating what he believed and you are stating what you believe, and one statement seems to offset the other. I think it is up to the committee to get a little more evidence on the subject to find out about it.

Mr. CARNEGIE. Yes, sir.

The CHAIRMAN. I agree with you on that. I did not know but you would confirm what he said. He said that the cost of coal land was $600 per acre in 1899 and $3,000 per acre now.

Mr. CARNEGIE. Yes, sir. Now, let me answer that. That is coke land. There are 9,000 tons of coke in an acre, and that means that it has increased to 30 cents. What did he say it was, $600 then and now it is $3,000?

The CHAIRMAN. Yes.

Mr. CARNEGIE. That is five times the amount.

The CHAIRMAN. He said that that was in the Connellsville district.

Mr. CARNEGIE. Yes, sir; five times the amount. Five times the amount of $600 is $3,000. That means that the coke in the hill is now worth only 30 cents a ton, and then, in the olden times, when we bought coke property, it was 15 cents a ton. I think I am right—no, $600 for 9,000 tons.

The CHAIRMAN. He said that the coke costs $1.50 a ton.

Mr. CARNEGIE. I do not know what coke is costing to-day.

The CHAIRMAN. And that the freight rate to Pittsburg is 85 cents. He qualified that and said he might be 10 cents out of the way on that, 75 or 85 cents a ton.

Mr. CARNEGIE. Then, if he is 10 cents out of the way, the coke rate used to be 65 cents a ton, and it has been raised 10 cents a ton, and coke has been raised 30 cents a ton, that is 40 cents, and so, on the amount needed to make a ton of pig iron, you see, gentlemen, what figures you get. You take the conclusion that because the coal in the hill costs five times more; coke costs five times more.

The CHAIRMAN. Mr. Schwab ought to know what coke costs.

Mr. CARNEGIE. No, Mr. Chairman. You gentlemen, if you consider that you can possibly understand these figures, it is your fault as much as Schwab's. You read into his statement there of cost five times the ton of coke and begin to figure. What he told you was five times the cost in the hill, and that made a difference of 30 cents a ton.

The CHAIRMAN. Well, he said $1.50 a ton. I do not know how we could construe that into anything else.

Mr. CARNEGIE. That is when the coke is manufactured?

The CHAIRMAN. Certainly.

Mr. CARNEGIE. That is a very different thing.

The CHAIRMAN. Cost of coke, $1.50; not for coal in the mine; I said for the coke.

Mr. CARNEGIE. Mr. Chairman, if a ton of coke costs only $1.50 to-day, and that is five times more than it did cost, then coke only cost 30 cents a ton. It is ridiculous.

The CHAIRMAN. I did not say anything about that.

Mr. FORDNEY. He did not say that.

Mr. CARNEGIE. That is what the chairman read here.

The CHAIRMAN. He said coal lands, $3,000 an acre. I did not imagine you would carry that to the coke. Mr. Schwab said coke cost $1.50 a ton.

Mr. CARNEGIE. Then, there is not much expense there.

The CHAIRMAN. Then, you do not see anything on the face of that that would show it was not true?

Mr. CARNEGIE. No; although I have heard of coke lands selling at $2,000 an acre.

The CHAIRMAN. Coal land in the Connellsville district, $2,000 an acre.

Mr. CARNEGIE. Gentlemen, if you were in the business, experts talking——

The CHAIRMAN. Even I would know enough to know that you did not mean $3,000 an acre for coke.

Mr. RANDELL. He means coke coal.

Mr. CARNEGIE. Mr. Schwab is talking as a Pittsburg manufacturer. Coal is one thing; coke is another.

The CHAIRMAN. So I am aware.

Mr. CARNEGIE. And the coal lands, increasing to $3,000 an acre from $600, would make a rise in the price of coke to 30 cents a ton.

Mr. DALZELL. I think the misunderstanding is here, Mr. Carnegie. Mr. Schwab gave us the cost of coke at the time that he made his original estimate of $12 steel. Then he gave us the cost of coke at the present time; and then, to explain the reason why the cost of coke had risen in the meantime, he said that lands have gone up from $600 to $3,000 an acre, but he is $1,000 out, because I know coal lands in the Connellsville district are selling now at $4,000 an acre.

Mr. CARNEGIE. Then that would raise the price of coke to 30 cents.

Mr. DALZELL. He did not base the exact figure of rise on the different prices.

The CHAIRMAN. He did not say it would cost five times as much; he said it was one element in the rise of coke.

Mr. CARNEGIE. Gentlemen, when you analyze that and get its true basis it would account for an increase of 30 cents per ton in coke. Now, let me show you. What has that to do with a concern that has thousands of acres of coke that it bought at $200 and $300 an acre?

The CHAIRMAN. It has this to do; we are trying to arrive at the cost in American factories of steel rails. That is one of the elements that goes into it; and trying to show why those rails—he was, not we; we are simply taking the facts—trying to show why those rails cost $22 now against $12, as he stated, in 1899.

Mr. CARNEGIE. Yes, Mr. Chairman; but suppose that the United States Steel Company has 40,000 acres of coke land?

The CHAIRMAN. We are talking about the Bethlehem Company; is that part of the United States Steel?

Mr. CARNEGIE. Certainly.

Mr. DALZELL. Not a part of the United States Steel Company?

The CHAIRMAN. That is not a part of the United States Steel Company, is it?

Mr. CARNEGIE. Oh, no.

The CHAIRMAN. It is an independent company, as I understand it.

Mr. CARNEGIE. Yes.

The CHAIRMAN. We are talking about Mr. Schwab's production; we have left Mr. Gary.

Mr. CARNEGIE. Very well. Mr. Schwab's coke costs him more than it did if he purchases his coke from a producer.

The CHAIRMAN. He does not own coal lands?

Mr. CARNEGIE. The Bethlehem does not.

The CHAIRMAN. So they have to buy their coal?

Mr. CARNEGIE. Certainly.

The CHAIRMAN. Then he ought to know what it costs him, ought he not?

Mr. CARNEGIE. What he buys it at; yes, sir.

The CHAIRMAN. We will go a step further. He says that in 1899 a ton of coke would make a ton of pig iron, but since the iron in the ore has gone down from 58 per cent to 49 per cent on account of the other foreign material in the ore, it requires a ton and a quarter of coke to produce a ton of ore instead of a ton of coke. Do you know anything about that?

Mr. CARNEGIE. I should think that is quite understandable, but did Mr. Schwab tell you that in utilizing the gases of his furnaces, which he did not do before, he makes a great saving?

Mr. CALDERHEAD. I do not think he did.

Mr. CARNEGIE. You know, gentlemen, the steel business has not stood still. Great improvements, cheapening the process, have resulted. Another instance occurs to me. The United States Steel Company is now utilizing the slag from making a ton of pig iron that we used to throw over the bank, and it cost us money to haul it away; but now that is a very valuable business, very profitable.

The CHAIRMAN. How much slag is produced in making a ton of pig iron?

Mr. CARNEGIE. I could not tell you that.

The CHAIRMAN. Can you give us any account of the value?

Mr. CARNEGIE. Of the slag? It was an expense. We threw it over the bank before.

The CHAIRMAN. You say now it is valuable?

Mr. CARNEGIE. Yes; it is.

The CHAIRMAN. But you can not say how valuable it is?

Mr. CARNEGIE. I would be afraid to tell you what I heard the president of the subsidiary company estimate it at.

The CHAIRMAN. I wish you would tell me. I will go after the president and find out, not whether he told you, but the statement of fact on his part.

Mr. CARNEGIE. I think he is too sanguine, and that it could not possibly be as valuable as he said. Cement is coming in as a substitute for steel and it is a remarkable advance.

The CHAIRMAN. Give us the name and address of that gentleman, and we will send for him.

Mr. CARNEGIE. I can not give you either the name or the address.

The CHAIRMAN. We will get it, then. Limestone is used. He says it costs 30 cents a ton to mine limestone and $1.20 to take it to Pittsburg, $1.50, and he uses about one-half a ton in making pig, 75 cents. He says that more lime is now used than in the year 1899, because ores are leaner now. There is more waste material to flux away. What is your judgment about that?

Mr. CARNEGIE. That may be true. I think it is, slightly. Did he tell you how much more?

The CHAIRMAN. No; he did not put it in here. He had formerly told us, but I can not turn back this moment to that. He formerly put in what they allowed for the lime in 1899, but I haven't it here now in conjunction with this. I can not tell you offhand without stopping to look it up, but he said now it costs 75 cents to make a ton of pig iron, and then he said that the labor conversion cost was $1.25 to $1.30 a ton.

Mr. CARNEGIE. I thought you said conversion was $7.50 a ton?

The CHAIRMAN. No; Mr. Schwab makes a very interesting statement about the labor.

Mr. DALZELL. Speaking of labor only.

The CHAIRMAN. Well, in effect, he says that he never knew labor so cheap as it was in 1899, the year in which he wrote that letter; that the common laborer earned from a dollar to a dollar and fifty cents a day; that the laborer was very efficient, men were begging for jobs. He said that his own salary was lower that year than it had been in the years before, and that one man working in the big iron foundry would do as much that year in a day as two men to-day at a higher price per day for the labor. That is what he said about the labor. And he made out a large increase—$1.30 a ton—for labor. Do you remember about labor in 1899?

Mr. CARNEGIE. No; I have no recollection of the details. How could I?

The CHAIRMAN. Mr. Schwab seemed to have a very definite recollection on that subject.

Mr. CARNEGIE. He did not have a recollection; he went back and got his data somewhere.

The CHAIRMAN. What was that?

Mr. CARNEGIE. He did not recollect all these things. Perhaps he did, but more likely he went back to the books and figures.

The CHAIRMAN. The fact that his salary was so low that year might have impressed it on his mind.

Mr. CARNEGIE. I do not remember of ever reducing the salaries, but it is possible. I can not remember of a case, but I do know there are many departments in which fewer men are needed than we needed, and it tends to make the labor cost of steel less than it was with us.

The CHAIRMAN. Putting all those items together he made the cost of producing pig iron $14, including the materials, at present, against $7 and $8 in 1899. Then he said that the cost of converting into a ton of steel rails the necessary quantity of pig iron cost $7.50, and that it cost his company $21.50 to make a ton of steel rails.

Mr. CARNEGIE. Yes, sir.

The CHAIRMAN. That was his statement as to the items, and what I was struck with about it was this, that it came pretty near bearing out the statement that these seven companies had made to the Bureau of Corporations, that they made the average price during the five years from 1902 to 1906, both inclusive, twenty-two dollars and about thirty cents a ton, or 80 cents more than Mr. Schwab. Schwab has a good mill, I suppose; he has an up-to-date plant, has he not?

Mr. CARNEGIE. He is the man whom the Congress of the United States should thank, as I told you this morning, for the improved appliances that he has introduced.

The CHAIRMAN. Do you know whether he has an up-to-date plant?

Mr. CARNEGIE. Yes.

The CHAIRMAN. You brought him up, did you not, in the business.

Mr. CARNEGIE. I did.

The CHAIRMAN. There is no excuse for his not having an up-to-date plant?

Mr. CARNEGIE. There is this excuse for him, that I have not been with him for seven years. [Laughter.]

The CHAIRMAN. And still you would advise him if an opportunity offered?

Mr. CARNEGIE. Mr. Chairman and gentlemen, you have got into a maze of figures, and you will never arrive at results in that way. You have got a statement from Mr. Gary that he could do without a tariff. Now, you are in the position of the Irishman who was arrested for stealing a pig, and he was sentenced on the testimony of one man. He told the judge, when he was asked why sentence should not be passed, that he thought it was an injustice to a citizen to convict him on the testimony of one man, who said he saw him steal the pig, when he could bring one hundred men to prove that they had never seen any such thing. [Laughter.]

The CHAIRMAN. That is all very well, but if we sought to make that an excuse, the judges might ask us, Mr. Carnegie, they being the dear people, if we did not have not only the testimony of Mr. Gary, but the testimony of Mr. Schwab, and that after that we had the benefit of the article of Mr. Andrew Carnegie in the magazine, in which he stated with a good deal of emphasis that the duty might all be taken off; although, when we called him before us and asked him to give us the facts and figures, he answered us with a story about an Irishman; or, in other words, indicating that he was one of the men who did not know.

Mr. CARNEGIE. No, Mr. Chairman; I am sorry that you say you did not hear me this morning. I stated that Judge Gary said that the tariff on steel was not important for him, and that long before I made that statement that others made the same statement, and that the judge's solicitude for the weaker brethren was sublime, but it was quite unnecessary; that these weaker brethren will not find their business injured by the tariff being taken off. You can not arrive at a correct judgment until you know what the prices of production are abroad, as far as the tariff is concerned, because you have combinations among these people at home, and they are working together.

Now, the statement of the consul there was very important on the cost abroad, but if you are not willing to act on the fact that we have no foreign importations of steel to-day and that we are sending steel all over the world, then until you know what the absolute costs are in Europe you can not judge whether the cost and interest and the cost of transportation and a reasonable profit for the producer, comparing the same items here with the home producer, as the President-elect requires, I say, you can not judge whether or no they can do without a tariff.

The CHAIRMAN. We expect to get the cost abroad furnished by Judge Gary, but we were led to expect from your article that, in order to make up your mind that these things should be put upon the free list, you had that information, both as to the cost abroad and the cost here, because we believed, as you say you believe now, that the only fair thing to do was to find out the difference in cost between two things; the fact that there is no importation would go to show that the duty was higher, but just how much too high it is impossible to say, unless you can get the cost abroad and here. We expect to get the figures from Judge Gary, whom you certify as a very honorable witness, if he is a lawyer, although he may be somewhat interested. We thought we might get it from a disinterested party in you.

Mr. CARNEGIE. I have a general knowledge of costs abroad.

The CHAIRMAN. Why do you not give them to us?

Mr. CARNEGIE. Because it would not be fair.

The CHAIRMAN. It seems to be fair enough for you to publish a magazine article and base it on them, but not fair enough to tell us.

Mr. CARNEGIE. That statement in my magazine has not been refuted.

Mr. DALZELL. What statement is that?

Mr. CARNEGIE. That the cost of a ton of steel in Britain to-day or in Germany to-day is as dear, or a shade dearer, than the cost is here, taking the cost under similar conditions. That is the statement that I made. I did not make that without general knowledge of the business, and if it is proved untrue, then my reputation for knowledge of the business would be seriously imperiled.

Mr. DALZELL. You see, Mr. Carnegie, that general statement would cover every article of iron and steel without regard. You make the general statement that the cost there is about the cost here, and that covers everything.

Mr. CARNEGIE. Yes, sir.

Mr. DALZELL. Now, for instance, here is what Mr. Gary says with respect to one particular article. You continue to be misled by your newspaper reports of what Judge Gary said here. He never said what you attribute to him. Let me read you just a paragraph:

Mr. GARY. May I interrupt you one moment, because a thought is in my mind, and I desire to give one fact in regard to a commodity, which is important and in line with this other inquiry. It relates to tin plate and sheets. At the present time they are produced in Wales and London at about $5.32, which is less than the cost to us, and that represents the difference in wages paid to the men, the labor element being large as to those commodities. So that if we should make our costs as low as their costs we could only do it by cutting the wages of our men about these mills in half—that is, making them one-half as large as they are at the present time. I think I am perfectly accurate in those figures.

Mr. CARNEGIE. He has not given you figures?

Mr. DALZELL. Yes, he has given the cost abroad, and we also have the cost of making tin plate at home, and you see that does not bear out the position that you assign to Judge Gary.

Mr. CARNEGIE. Now, my friend, when you talk about steel, you do not talk about tin plate.

Mr. DALZELL. Ninety-nine per cent of tin plates are steel; they are steel sheets.

Mr. CARNEGIE. That is quite true, but no man—no steel man—but would differentiate between steel and tin plate.

Mr. DALZELL. Well, they are steel sheets first before they are tin plates.

Mr. CARNEGIE. They are; they are composed of tin. If the harvester man talks of harvesters those are composed of steel, too. But I wish you to know that the expert, the steel man, talks in the language which it is impossible for you to understand.

Mr. DALZELL. I have heard a good deal of it all my life.

Mr. CARNEGIE. Well, John [laughter], you were always considered by us a more experienced lawyer than you were a steel manufacturer. [Laughter.]

Mr. DALZELL. I should be sorry if I was not.

Mr. CARNEGIE. Let me put myself right there, because I am determined that you shall have from me no half truths. There are statements that can be made that do not cover the whole circle of truth, and a witness is not always compelled—he may not think of the other things, and he answers you one question. Now, in regard to tin plate, tin plate has been made for one hundred years in Wales, and girls have been trained to it, and it is the one article where, I think, the British people in Wales could make a ton of tin plate, probably, a shade cheaper than we make here. But if you add the cost of bringing tin plate here, I doubt whether they could import it here to any great extent.

Mr. HILL. If it was free?

Mr. CARNEGIE. Yes, sir. That is my honest opinion about it; so you see, gentlemen, it will not do for you to assume that tin plate was included in the statement of steel. I do not want to hurt any American manufacturer. I do not want to injure the steel trade of this country. As long as I thought we needed a tariff I supported it, but now I have arrived at the conclusion that we do not, as Judge Gary said, for steel. There again, you see, Judge Gary is probably right about tin plate, but he did not embrace steel. I would not say that tin plate should go on the free list.

Mr. LONGWORTH. I was asking you just before adjournment on this general question of costs. You said that you thought the cost was perhaps a little greater in Great Britain in manufacturing steel generally, than it is here?

Mr. CARNEGIE. Yes, sir.

Mr. LONGWORTH. You suggested earlier in your testimony the practical difficulty that confronts this committee of finding out facts, none of us being practical men, but, at the same time, having within our jurisdiction, so to speak, almost every authority except that of practical experience. Now, I think our desire is just as yours is, an absolutely patriotic desire to revise this tariff in steel, as in all other schedules, for the best interests of the community at large.

Mr. CARNEGIE. Yes, sir.

Mr. LONGWORTH. You would not advocate the taking off of the duty on any American article without justification for it. I, personally, admitting that I know very little about the costs of steel, am inclined to think that we can substantially reduce the tariff on steel without injury to the American industry, and yet before I vote for it, if I should vote for it, I want to feel that I am justified in so doing. I do not know of any other way that I can personally feel justified, unless I know or have some opportunity of finding out something about the difference between the cost abroad and the cost at home. Is there any way that you can suggest to me—as a member of this committee, with practically every facility, the right to summon all witnesses, the facilities that this Government has, without the practical experience, and without the means of getting it, because we must act as promptly as possible—of finding out those things?

Mr. CARNEGIE. In reply, Mr. Longworth, I know of only one way that this committee can arrive at anything approaching the real truth of the difference in cost, and that is to have men belonging to the steel industry, men familiar with it, who are not interested in either the foreign or the American works, experts of the highest character and ability, to be charged with visiting the works of Europe, selecting in each country the best works, because you will be greatly misled if you select works that are not properly managed. You can easily, obtain the list of the best works, and these men should go there and study the question. They will be received by the foreign manufacturer with open arms, because they will see in this a probability of the tariff being reduced.

Mr. LONGWORTH. Mr. Carnegie, the trouble is that it is a condition and not a theory that confronts this committee now. The Republican members of this committee are bound, as you have stated, by the Republican platform, which states that the tariff shall be revised as soon as possible. The President-elect, it is understood, proposes to call an extra session of this Congress to do that, and this committee wants to prepare a bill which can be submitted as soon as possible after the inauguration of the President-elect. It is utterly impossible for us to send experts abroad. What authority have we so far which would justify us in wiping off entirely the duty on steel, except your personal opinion—that of a man of great experience—and that of Judge Gary, who I do not think went as far as you do in that respect? Have we any other authority, in other words, Mr. Carnegie, which would justify us in removing absolutely the tariff on steel, except those two statements?

Mr. CARNEGIE. I do not know what other statements you have had here, Mr. Longworth.

Mr. LONGWORTH. They have not been to that effect, Mr. Carnegie.

Mr. CARNEGIE. Very well; then you have two; and I think, again, that if you can not fix the tariff duty on the evidence of two such credible witnesses, because there are hundreds that have not told you so, that is a matter for the judgment of the committee.

Mr. LONGWORTH. I give the greatest weight, Mr. Carnegie, to the statements of those witnesses. At the same time other witnesses have, I think, made quite contrary statements. Suppose that it is true that the tariff is too high; that other countries are not exporting here—

admitting that to be the fact, does that jusify us in immediately wiping it out altogether?

Mr. CARNEGIE. No. Other parties are not exporting here because they have an international arrangement. That is what your consul told you. Why, Mr. Longworth, you know—you are a very clever man and a very nice fellow——

Mr. LONGWORTH. Thank you. [Laughter.]

Mr. CARNEGIE. But you are grappling with problems which really you can not be expected to understand.

Mr. LONGWORTH. Most assuredly, Mr. Carnegie; I realize that; and when I have a source of information such as you are, I desire to find out all I can.

Mr. CARNEGIE. Well, Mr. Longworth, I want to ask you a question.

Mr. LONGWORTH. I will not promise to answer it if it is a technical one, Mr. Carnegie.

Mr. CARNEGIE. You are an intelligent man.

Mr. COCKRAN. He admits that.

Mr. LONGWORTH. Yes; I admit that. [Laughter.]

Mr. CARNEGIE. Have you talked tariff with anybody connected with steel?

Mr. LONGWORTH. Only with those gentlemen who have appeared before us.

Mr. CARNEGIE. You have never heard anything outside from gentlemen talking about the tariff?

Mr. LONGWORTH. Oh, frequently in conversation; but I have never had any steel business.

Mr. CARNEGIE. Did you ever hear any of them say that the tariff was a "back number," so far as steel was concerned?

Mr. LONGWORTH. Only two men.

Mr. CARNEGIE. Here are two witnesses; that makes four.

Mr. LONGWORTH. But they are the same two, Mr. Carnegie. [Laughter.]

Mr. COCKRAN. The two men are equal to four, Mr. Carnegie. [Laughter.]

Mr. CARNEGIE. Well, I am willing to stand with Judge Gary. I have no hesitation in expressing my opinion, to tell you the whole truth. I have dear friends in Britain. I was the only American, or the only foreign citizen, that ever was made president of the Iron and Steel Institute. I have lived with these men; and I profited by their mistakes. I saw where the Bessemer process was a success, and then went into it; and I am deeply indebted to the British manufacturers. In return, when they came to our works, I showed them everything. My old friends (one or two of them dead now), the most eminent men in the business, took them all through our works and showed them everything—all of our new improvements. We never shut our works to anybody. And I have gone, in turn, through all their works and heard all their costs. I have followed the English manufacture with deep interest, and I have studied it; and, without presumption, I would say that there is no American that has had the opportunities that I have had to judge.

Mr. LONGWORTH. Quite so; and do not understand me, Mr. Carnegie, as saying anything in criticism of the authority. In fact, I feel now that I am leaning your way. And yet I am simply asking the question whether, under the circumstances, I have any other authority and justification for voting to wipe out absolutely the tariff on steel, except your statement (which I regard as the highest authority, perhaps, that I could find), and Judge Gary's statement (which I do not think, after listening to the testimony, goes as far by any means as yours does).

Mr. CARNEGIE. That is good.

Mr. LONGWORTH. Is there any other justification that I have at this moment for voting to take off entirely the tariff on iron and steel?

Mr. CARNEGIE. Well, Mr. Longworth, that is a matter for you and your own conscience to settle. You ask me how you could arrive at the difference in cost. There are great evidences. They do not import steel here. That, however, you might well say, was because they had an arrangement to that effect. But knowing the difficulties of British manufacturers, and the trouble about ores, and the cost of coke and coal, I have not the slightest doubt that you will find that the cost of a ton of steel there does not exceed ours, to say the least; that leaves the American manufacturer with the advantage of the cost of bringing the foreign product here, which, upon the average, to the point of delivery, I should place at not less than the present tariff duty. Further than that I can not go.

Mr. HILL. Mr. Carnegie, I was very much interested in the remark you made a moment ago to the effect that they were not allowed to ship here. May I ask what the explanation of that is?

Mr. CARNEGIE. I assume that it was by the arrangement that you spoke of this morning.

Mr. HILL. Then there is an international agreement?

Mr. CARNEGIE. Why, was not that what your man said?

Mr. HILL. That is what the consul said. I wanted to know whether he was right or not.

Mr. CARNEGIE. Well, gentlemen, I rest that on the word of the American consul. Have I a right to do so, or am I justified in doing so, or not?

Mr. HILL. I should like to ask another question.

Mr. GAINES. That is the very question—whether the American consul is correct or not.

Mr. CARNEGIE. But how can I tell you whether the American consul is right or not?

Mr. GAINES. The question was whether you knew the fact yourself about which he made the statement.

Mr. CARNEGIE. I do not know the fact, except as a matter——

Mr. GAINES. It is not as to his accuracy, but as to your knowledge of the same matter.

Mr. CARNEGIE. There is a half-truth again. It has been reported. It is " in the air." I have heard of it. But how do I know? I have seen no documents.

Mr. HILL. Did you know it enough to justify your statement a moment ago that the reason there was not more competition from abroad was that they were not allowed to ship here?

Mr. CARNEGIE. I based that on your——

Mr. HILL. You based it on what I read, and not on what you knew?

Mr. CARNEGIE. Yes; but——

Mr. HILL. All right.

Mr. CARNEGIE. But that is all that I had heard. Now, please—Mr. Longworth, particularly——

Mr. LONGWORTH. Yes, sir.

Mr. CARNEGIE. All that I had heard about it—I can not close my ears. I know so many steel men. I can not meet an old friend without the remark being made: "How is the business?" and all that sort of thing. To the best of my belief—I can not say knowledge—it seems that the statement of our accredited official would not have been made unless he had knowledge on the subject; and it accounts for there being no importations here. But there is another reason, independent of that: The cost to the British manufacturer is so great that in my opinion he would not send rails here even if the duty were taken off.

Mr. HILL. Mr. Carnegie, let me ask you this question: Have you ever heard of an agreement made by the United States Steel Company with the tin-plate manufacturers of Wales that the exports of manufactured tin plate from the United States should not exceed a certain quantity, based on a counter agreement on their part that they would not take a certain amount of black plates from the United States?

Mr. CARNEGIE. Well, Mr. Hill, I have heard all kinds of reports.

Mr. HILL. You have heard that report?

Mr. CARNEGIE. I think I have.

Mr. HILL. Yes.

Mr. CARNEGIE. I would not be so positive. It seems to me as if it is no matter of news to me; but I am——

Mr. HILL. Now, I am reading from the New York Tribune in July. You were in Scotland, were you not, at that time?

Mr. CARNEGIE. Yes, sir.

Mr. HILL. "An agreement was reached in December last year among the tube makers of the United States, Germany, Great Britain, and other countries for a working arrangement, the purpose of which was to put an end to the serious losses resulting from international competition." Do you know anything about that agreement?

Mr. CARNEGIE. I do not. I take the Tribune.

Mr. HILL. I think this is the Tribune I am quoting from.

Mr. CARNEGIE. But I never saw that statement; and that statement is news to me.

Mr. HILL. Then this statement:

LONDON, *July 1.*

According to the Iron and Steel Trades Journal, the English and Scotch steel manufacturers have decided not to join the proposed international combination, and to ally themselves with the national amalgamation that is being formed to fight the international trust. This amalgamation, the paper says, will soon be established. It will consist of the principal American, German, Russian, and French steel companies, and fierce competition, both here and elsewhere, with a slump in prices, may be expected.

Do you know anything about the facts in regard to that?

Mr. CARNEGIE. Not the slightest.

Mr. HILL. It occurred while you were abroad.

Mr. CARNEGIE. I never heard of it before.

Mr. HILL. A combination to fight the "international trust?"

Mr. CARNEGIE. I never heard of it.

Mr. HILL. You made one other statement this morning, to the effect that you thought that the present price of steel rails at $28 was justified by the agreement between the railroad companies and the steel manufacturers.

Mr. CARNEGIE. Yes, sir.

Mr. HILL. And one of the other witnesses before us last week made a similar statement—that it was a mutual agreement, the price of $28 being based on an agreed price of freight rates on the materials used by the steel manufacturers; so that, the steel manufacturers and the railroads being satisfied, where did the general consuming public come in in that higher price of steel, these rates being charged on all steel that is made as well as rails?

Mr. COCKRAN. It is not satisfied.

Mr. HILL. The rates of freight are not only charged on the materials going into the steel rails, but they go on all materials used in all steel production, do they not?

Mr. CARNEGIE. I do not know that the railroads raised these rates.

Mr. HILL. Well, you built the road from the lake to Pittsburg, did you not? Do you remember what the rate was that you charged up your steel production cost for transportation on that road from the lake to Pittsburg? It was a very small rate, was it not?

Mr. CARNEGIE. I could not give you that from memory.

Mr. HILL. Was it not along about 23 cents a ton?

Mr. CARNEGIE. Oh, no; no.

Mr. HILL. From the lake to Pittsburg?

Mr. CARNEGIE. That was the cost of moving it.

Mr. HILL. Yes.

Mr. CARNEGIE. It cost us 22 cents a ton to bring loaded cars—no; it cost us 12 cents a ton to move cars down from the lake to Pittsburg, and 11 cents to take the empty cars back. I remember those figures.

Mr. HILL. Yes.

Mr. CARNEGIE. But that did not include cost——

Mr. HILL. Mr. Schwab testified the other day that in making up his charge for the cost of steel he figured a dollar a ton for bringing the ore from the lake down to Pittsburg. That is a very, very heavy increase over what you charged up in the cost and what he figured in the cost.

Mr. CARNEGIE. Well, gentlemen, I can not tell you what Mr. Schwab did. If we charged it at only 23 cents, we were very foolish, because there are the repairs of a railroad and the maintenance, and there is interest on the capital.

Mr. HILL. Briefly, do you think the general consuming public, in the consumption of steel outside of steel rails should be obliged to stand and make good such an agreement between the railroad companies and the steel companies?

Mr. CARNEGIE. I have no opinion to express upon that. That is a matter between the railroads and the public. It does not touch the question of the comparative price of steel.

Mr. HILL. If the price of steel is to be reduced, it is not to be reduced by revising the tariff, Mr. Carnegie, according to the testimony that is before us. The increase which Mr. Schwab has shown in the cost of steel is in all of these increases of freight rates all the way through. If those are controlled by a combination of the steel manufacturers and a combination of the railroads, acting in harmony, how is the tariff going to affect it?

Mr. CARNEGIE. My dear friend, if we are going into authorizing combinations, the result is this: We shall have a supreme court of industry, and that court will have to fix the prices of everything if the consumer is to be protected.

Mr. HILL. But, Mr. Carnegie, if this committee is to fix the tariff, is it not its duty to find out whether the increased cost is the result of the tariff or the result of something else? I am asking you that question.

Mr. CARNEGIE. That is your duty; but I am unable to give you any opinion about the railroads.

Mr. HILL. But you say that the rate of $28 is a justifiable price, and that it is caused by the agreement between the railroads and the steel manufacturers, both as to freights and the price of steel.

Mr. CARNEGIE. No; excuse me. I have never mentioned freights.

Mr. HILL. If you did not, some of the other witnesses have.

Mr. CARNEGIE. Ah! Well, gentlemen, I have enough sins of my own to answer for. [Laughter.] I do not propose to speak here upon any subject but that question I am called to speak upon, and that is the main question, at last: Has protection done its office? Has it enabled the manufacturers of steel of America (not the inefficient, but the efficient, well-managed manufacturing concerns of America) to do without further support, protection, which should never be given except temporarily; to determine the question whether we can, in our country, produce a home supply of the article temporarily protected, better, more conveniently, more steadily than it was before coming from abroad? If the manufacturers of America, after forty years' nursing, can not to-day do without the crutch of protection, then our policy has been a failure.

Mr. GAINES. Did I not understand Mr. Carnegie to say that there was an agreement between the railroads and the steel concerns as to the prices that were to be paid for freight on the products of the steel concerns?

Mr. CARNEGIE. I did not know that feature, if there were; I never heard it before. I do not know the details of the agreement. I do not know the details of the agreement.

Mr. GAINES. That was my question. I thought that you had said so.

Mr. CARNEGIE. And I never heard that there was an agreement except as to the price of rails.

Mr. GAINES. Then I was mistaken in the fact.

Mr. CALDERHEAD. Aside from that, the issue between Mr. Carnegie and us, it seems to me, is whether we are pursuing the right method to ascertain a reason for reducing the tariff or not; or, if the tariff is taken off of steel, do you think the prices of steel to the people will be less than they are now?

Mr. CARNEGIE. The immediate advantage, in my opinion, which the people of America will have will be that you will have taken from the combination the power to raise their prices above the cost at which the foreigner could enter, and the cost will necessarily be lower to the foreigner if you take the tariff off his products.

Mr. CALDERHEAD. Just a moment. What combination do you refer to?

Mr. CARNEGIE. I refer to the combination of which Judge Gary is the head; for they all meet together. There is no secret about that now; you have read his speeches.

Mr. CALDERHEAD. But if it costs as much in England and in Germany and in France to make the steel as it does in the United States, and the tariff should be taken off in our country, what possible benefit can it be to our people? What combination could be made amongst our own manufacturers?

Mr. CARNEGIE. I have stated the benefit that it would be.

Mr. CALDERHEAD. It would be that there could not be a combination to maintain prices above the price that the foreign man was willing to sell at?

Mr. CARNEGIE. That is it.

Mr. CALDERHEAD. That is all?

Mr. CARNEGIE. That is a great deal—that is a great deal. Now, just one moment.

Mr. CALDERHEAD. Just a moment there: Will there be any probability of a combination with the foreign manufacturers?

Mr. CARNEGIE. I think if combinations are allowed there will be a very great probability.

Mr. CALDERHEAD. A great probability?

Mr. CARNEGIE. Yes, sir.

Mr. CALDERHEAD. You said a while ago, I think, that if it was lawful at all there certainly would be?

Mr. CANEGIE. I would not say certainly; I judge of human nature.

Mr. CALDERHEAD. Yes.

Mr. CARNEGIE. I think it is a dangerous——

Mr. CALDERHEAD. If the tariff is taken off, will the profits of making steel in this country be less than they are now?

Mr. CARNEGIE. In my opinion—I have repeated this several times to-day—nothing that the foreign manufacturer can do toward obtaining business here will affect injuriously any steel manufacturer in this country who deserves to succeed in his business and has the necessary facilities.

Mr. CALDERHEAD. I understand that, and the reason is that the cost of making steel in foreign countries is about the same as it is here now?

Mr. CARNEGIE. I think it is. Well, yes; you can say it so if you like. My best judgment is that——

Mr. CALDERHEAD. That it is substantially the same?

Mr. CARNEGIE. Well, yes; I think we made it a shade cheaper at the works that made the cheapest steel. I believe so.

Mr. CALDERHEAD. It is generally admitted that the wages of laborers in the steel mills, in all branches of labor that contribute to the making of steel, producing ore, making pig iron, etc., are much lower in England and Germany than in the United States. If it costs as much to produce steel in England and Germany as it does in the United States, and the wages of labor are so much less, what effect will it have on the wages of labor in this country if steel is to be sold at the same price there and here?

Mr. CARNEGIE. If the steel of Britain is as dear to make in Britain as it is here, it does not follow that their labor cost is not as great as ours; because they use many more men than we do, having smaller markets and not having the continuous rolling of steel that we have. The costs being the same, there is a natural tariff which even Congress can not surmount. The foreign manufacturer has to pay the freights of bringing his steel here.

Mr. CALDERHEAD. Yes; I am familiar with that, and I have heard it a number of times to-day. But it is evident, if the wages are so much less in those countries than they are in this country, that the cost of steel must be in something else. You say, then, that it is in the increased price of ore, or the approaching scarcity or value of it?

Mr. CARNEGIE. Well, no. There is a very large element in this: That with our machinery, and making such enormous outputs, you must not take the cost of labor which they give you here. The cost of labor per man is much higher here; but if it requires two Englishmen, with their appliances and mills, and so forth (in which it would be folly for them to imitate us), to produce the amount of steel that one man can produce here, then there would not be the labor-cost difference which you assume. You must not take it per man.

You must give credit to the United States Steel Company and the works at Gary. This is what I hear from men who are chiefly interested in the problem of steel; and they are rejoicing. There is a new mill building at Gary. Remember, I was just told this, and I have heard them talk about it.

There is a new mill building at Gary that is much to the credit of the United States Steel Company. I am told that it will make 40,000 tons of rails a month, and that there will only be four men at the rolls; and if they ran them three turns, eight hours apiece, there would be only twelve men employed. Gentlemen, there is no such mill that could be built in any other part of the world, judiciously; because they have not the great market that we have for rails, that allows the mill to go for weeks and weeks on one form of rails without changing rolls. The Englishman is glad if he gets an order for 500 tons of rails of the same pattern. He has to make them, and then he has to change the rolls; and that is a day lost for his mill. Then he has to put in another, and the size is different of the rail that has to be rolled next week. His men have to have time to get accustomed to the lighter or the heavier sections; and it takes a day or two for them to get into it. In the case of this rail mill at Gary, the labor cost there will not be half what it is in England, notwithstanding the cheaper cost of labor per man.

There is another case where the cost of labor——

Mr. CALDERHEAD. Just a moment, before you go to another case. If the tariff is taken off, will the English mill not have just as large a market as we have, and just the same price, barring the natural tariff of the ocean and the railway mileage?

Mr. CARNEGIE. Mr. Calderhead, just one moment. Consider this subject: Do you think that an American would buy a ton of foreign rails if he could get the rails of his own countrymen?

Mr. BONYNGE. Suppose he could get them cheaper abroad?

Mr. CALDERHEAD. Simply from self-interest, I should think he would buy where he could buy the cheapest.

Mr. CARNEGIE. But wait a moment. No, no; other elements come in there. The railroads get the traffic of our manufacturers. They are deeply concerned in keeping them at work, and while they pay $28 a ton for rails, they may have $5 a ton profit on these very rails through the transportation of materials.

Mr. BONYNGE. Mr. Carnegie, that would not apply to structural steel that might be landed on the Atlantic coast.

Mr. CARNEGIE. Thank you for mentioning structural steel. I would have forgotten that illustration. I wish the chairman could hear me. I will try to make him. Do you all hear me?

Several MEMBERS. Oh, yes.

Mr. CARNEGIE. Because I want every man to hear what I am about to say. [Addressing Mr. Calderhead.] You——

Mr. CALDERHEAD. Yes, sir.

Mr. CARNEGIE. I do like to meet with a gentleman that makes such a statement as you have made, or asks such a question as you have asked. Imagine yourself about to build a skyscraper, a big building. That requires structural steel, and it goes principally into that class of construction, bridges, etc. You have got $2,000,000 to invest in a skyscraper that you are going to build in Washington. Your architect comes to you with pages showing every bar, every beam, every angle of steel that goes into that structure; and it is formidable. He says to you—well, no architect would say this to you, because maybe they have had experience. But a seller of steel comes to you and says: "Don't buy this American steel that Schwab is making. I will give it to you at $2 a ton cheaper, or $3 a ton cheaper, or $5 a ton cheaper."

If you have never built a building before, you might accept that offer. What would be the result? Your order takes ten days to reach the maker, 3,000 miles away. He promises to deliver it to you in six months or three months, or whatever it is. He is a little late in deliveries. He ships the second story before he ships the first. You lose a few bars in transportation. You go on with your building, and he delays you. You go on with your building, and two or three bars are lost in transportation; there are so many transfers. I am speaking now practically. You can not get on without those two or three bars, and your building can not be put up. Then there is a blunder made; the man has shipped some steel that belongs to another thing altogether, from the wrong pile.

If you take the American steel, your rolling mill is right here; it is run by your neighbor, probably, a gentleman that you know well. You tell him: "Why, there is a mistake here," and it is remedied in a moment, in a day. He has plenty of structural steel on hand, and he remedies the defect. You get along faster than you thought you would. You want the third story before the architect figured that it would be needed. "Certainly;" the changes are made, and he gives you that.

If ever you tried to send an order 3,000 miles away to build a bridge or a structure, you may do it once when you begin, but you will never do it again. It is impracticable. There are so many contingencies in the one case which you avoid in the other. I do not care if structural steel for a great building were offered in New York or in Pittsburg or in Chicago or anywhere else at $5 a ton less. From my experience I would not consider having my steel made 3,000 miles away.

The CHAIRMAN. Do not people make such blunders as that when they ship bridges all over the earth?

Mr. CARNEGIE. Yes, sir; they do make such blunders as that; but it is a different thing to prepare a finished bridge that has to be put together. If you were shipping a bridge to India, remember, you would not run the risk. In some cases they are so careful that they put the bridge together before it leaves the works; and that is good policy. And so with a steel building. You think a steel building is a very simple thing. It is not.

Mr. BONYNGE. Mr. Carnegie, we are sending structural steel over the world, are we not?

Mr. CARNEGIE. Yes, sir.

Mr. BONYNGE. Notwithstanding these disadvantages that you say would prevent the foreign manufacturer from sending structural steel here?

Mr. CARNEGIE. No; excuse me. I do not think we are selling much structural steel abroad.

Mr. BONYNGE. For bridges and matters of that kind, are we not?

Mr. CARNEGIE. Simply because it is impossbile for the man to whom you sell a bridge to get it any nearer than this country, and of course he has to do the best he can. But I am putting the case where he can order our steel at hand, and get the manufacturer to prevent delays and mistakes. As I have told you, engineers require the bridge to be put together when time is an element, or when they want a "dead sure" thing. That gives the home manufacturer of structural steel practical control of his market, even if the foreign steel were to be delivered to him or promised to be delivered to him at some dollars less per ton.

I thank you for mentioning structural steel. There is another illustration. If that had not been removed you would have taken the books as to the cost of structural steel in America, and you would have based action upon them.

Mr. COCKRAN. Can we not induce you to stay with us a little longer, Mr. Carnegie, so that, as various difficulties arise, we could refer to this practical experience which has shed such a flood of light on this transaction?

Mr. CARNEGIE. Well, gentlemen, I am at your service, if you will give me a telegraph blank. I have an engagement in New York.

Mr. COCKRAN. Are you through, Mr. Calderhead?

Mr. CARNEGIE. I will stay here. It is my duty to stay here for a week. It is my duty as a citizen of America.

Mr. CALDERHEAD. Just one question and I will be through.

Mr. CARNEGIE. I should like to ask you whether that explanation of mine impresses you? [Laughter.]

Mr. CALDERHEAD. Yes; I am very well satisfied with it. You ascribe the question to me, however; it was Mr. Bonynge's question.

Mr. CARNEGIE. No; it was Mr. Longworth that asked that.

Mr. CALDERHEAD. Mr. Bonynge.

Mr. CARNEGIE. Oh, I beg your pardon.

Mr. BONYNGE. Yes; it impresses me, Mr. Carnegie, but it does not altogether satisfy me.

Mr. CARNEGIE. I am sorry.

Mr. BONYNGE. Because I think we are sending structural steel abroad and meeting those difficulties.

Mr. CARNEGIE. Why, certainly.

Mr. BONYNGE. These difficulties will to a certain extent prohibit our people from sending abroad even to get a reduced price; but if the reduction was sufficient I do not think it would absolutely prevent them from sending abroad for their structural steel.

Mr. CARNEGIE. Well, that is a very great " if "—a very great " if."

Mr. BONYNGE. Of course the " ifs " are in the whole transaction, because we have not revised the tariff yet.

Mr. CARNEGIE. I thought you asked the question. Allow me to make one remark. The more experience you got in trying to build your structure out of steel made 3,000 miles away the bigger the " if " would need to be. You would never do it twice—at least, that is my experience.

Mr. CALDERHEAD. There is just one other question I wanted to ask.

The CHAIRMAN. Let him write his dispatch.

Mr. CALDERHEAD. Yes; I will wait until you write your dispatch.

Mr. CARNEGIE. No; I will not telegraph until later, because I can do it as well then.

Mr. CALDERHEAD. The question that I intended to ask you next was, If we have free trade and free competition with the other countries of the world in steel, will we have an international scale of wages for workingmen?

Mr. CARNEGIE. That seems to me about equivalent to asking, "If the sky would fall, would we catch larks?" How can I tell what we would have?

Mr. CALDERHEAD. But that is a serious question with this tariff.

Mr. CARNEGIE. There is nobody that could tell you what would happen. Let me again impress you with the fact that under the law of combination resulting in a monopoly in business, anything may happen.

Mr. CALDERHEAD. Then, Mr. Carnegie, since you first began the manufacture of steel rails, when the price of steel rails in England delivered here was about $140 a ton in gold, and the tariff insignificant in comparison with that, what benefit was the tariff to you?

Mr. CARNEGIE. I do not quite catch that.

Mr. CALDERHEAD. When you began the manufacture of steel rails, if my recollection is right, steel rails from England were sold in America at $140 a ton in gold, or $100.

Mr. CARNEGIE. Oh, my recollection is different. I think when we first commenced the manufacture of steel our competitors did not believe that we would be ready to make steel for a year after we did make it, and we went out to the various railroads and persuaded them to give us orders at $65 a ton, I think. I speak from memory, and I am not sure; but I think I remember well that we went and sold rails freely at $65 a ton. That may have been $5 a ton lower than our competitors were charging; and we sold a great many, because I knew that we were going to avoid the errors of previous builders.

Mr. CALDERHEAD. I was trusting to my memory about the time. I remember very well when English steel rails were sold for the first work on the Union Pacific Railroad at $140 a ton in gold, delivered at Omaha or Kansas City, and I think that in 1869 you tendered the same kind of rails at from $60 to $70 a ton, or they did.

Mr. CARNEGIE. What is this?

Mr. CALDERHEAD. In 1869 or 1870 they tendered rails at $65 or $70 a ton.

Mr. CARNEGIE. That is what I am saying—that our price was $65 or $70 a ton.

Mr. CALDERHEAD. The tariff was insignificant compared with that high price. What benefit was the tariff to you?

Mr. CARNEGIE. The tariff was this benefit—that if the tariff had not been imposed, and not alone by the Republican party——

Mr. CALDERHEAD. Well, by Americans?

Mr. CARNEGIE. I am going to tell you—but by patriotic Democrats that voted for it, also—if that had not been the declared policy of my country, the national policy, acquiesced in by enough of both parties, I would never have ventured upon the making of steel. None of us knew what a ton of steel rails would cost then. It was largely an experiment. But I am very sure that the cost was about as I tell you—$65 or $70.

Mr. CALDERHEAD. Yes.

Mr. CARNEGIE. We did not expect to make a great profit on that. The manufacture was in its infancy, and we sold, as I tell you, a great many steel rails—I think the enormous quantity, then, of 70,000 tons. The Cambria Iron Company boasted of having made 4,000 tons in a month. Do not imagine that you can adopt a new process in a country and go right off from the start.

Mr. CALDERHEAD. I understand that; but what I am trying to get at is just what benefit was the tariff to you?

Mr. CARNEGIE. The tariff benefit was this: Whatever it was, we felt sure (I took the risk of this) that whatever Britain could do, I would try to see whether we could not make rails with duty added. The first tariff put on steel rails was not insignificant. The first tariff put on steel rails was 30 per cent duty on the hundred, $28 a ton.

Mr. CALDERHEAD. Yes, sir.

Mr. CARNEGIE. Well, of course I need not talk further. I did not understand. Now, let me tell you——

Mr. CALDERHEAD. And at the time the price of rails was from $100 to $140 a ton?

Mr. CARNEGIE. I do not agree with you there. I think we made the first rails when it was $65 or $70. No; I am sure you are mistaken.

Mr. COCKRAN. Mr. Carnegie—are you through, Mr. Calderhead?

Mr. CALDERHEAD. Yes; let him finish his explanation, however.

Mr. CARNEGIE. Now, listen. Let me assure you again that if it had not been for a tariff of $28 a ton voted by both parties, and therefore national, not party, action which gave me confidence in its continuance, we never would have touched steel.

Mr. CALDERHEAD. Why not?

Mr. CARNEGIE. I will tell you. I had very enterprising partners in the iron business. I told you this morning that not one of them would put a dollar in the enterprise. I was looked upon as the most sanguine of men. My own partners would not allow the steel business to be incorporated with the iron business; and I tell you that no man that went into the steel business in this country was successful personally— not one of them reaped the recompense he deserved. Almost every steel concern failed or had to be reconstructed. The Cambria Iron Company was in the hands of a sheriff and was transferred into a new company. The Pennsylvania Steel Company, before its mills ran a ton, was only saved from bankruptcy by the Pennsylvania Railroad Company under the greatest president it ever had, John

Edgar Thomson, advancing the then enormous sum of $600,000 and taking the risk of the Pennsylvania Steel Company succeeding. The Bethlehem Company was mortgaged. The Joliet works were sold out. Ward, of Detroit, the first one, failed. Griswold, of Troy—his plant was a failure. It is all very well for you to sit here and know now that the production of a steel rail is so easy. You should have been in at the beginning.

Mr. CALDERHEAD. But the reason for my questions is this: There is a real relation between the tariff and the manufacturer and also between the tariff and the wages of the men who work for him. The tariff is an insurance to the manufacturer that his capital invested will be protected at least to that amount. It is an insurance to him that he can pay the wages necessary to procure the labor.

Mr. CARNEGIE. I do not agree with you at all.

Mr. CALDERHEAD. Then I think there must be quite a difference between us.

Mr. CARNEGIE. There certainly is. When I went into steel I thought that the tariff protected me. I soon found that we did not need $28. You have got to pay men in this country the wages you can get the best men for. Labor is a commodity like anything else.

Mr. CALDERHEAD. Yes, sir.

Mr. CARNEGIE. It pays to get the best men and pay the highest wages for labor.

Mr. CALDERHEAD. Yes, sir.

Mr. CARNEGIE. Fewer men do your work, and you are getting honest, respectable, sober men. Mr. Schwab—no; who was it that spoke about labor this morning? Let me remember. There is a very important thing that was said this morning about labor. Yes; that the men did two men's work then for one that they would do when there is a boom. When labor is plentiful, men do a great deal more work; at least 30 per cent more would be my estimate. When wages are high and men scarce, they do not do the work. The reason is this (I am not blaming the men for it; it is human nature): When labor is plentiful, a man is zealous to keep his job. When labor is very scarce, and you can not get other men, the man will be a great deal less attentive to his duties. That is my experience, and it is that of every employer of labor, I think.

Mr. CALDERHEAD. Admitting all that, then, it still does not explain just what benefit the tariff was to you in starting the manufacture of steel rails.

Mr. CARNEGIE. Did I not explain that? I explained that I would not have started at all without the considerable advantage of the tariff.

Mr. CALDERHEAD. I understand that; but when I asked you why not, you entered into a discourse about the difficulty of procuring friends to invest capital and risk capital, and all that.

Mr. CARNEGIE. Certainly; and they would not have gone in without the tariff.

Mr. CALDERHEAD. Well, just why? What good did the tariff do?

Mr. CARNEGIE. Britain made steel rails long before we did.

Mr. CALDERHEAD. Yes.

Mr. CARNEGIE. And British appliances were such for export trade that they could have deluged us.

Mr. CALDERHEAD. Yes, sir.

Mr. CARNEGIE. I was willing to take the risk of any American beating me; but it comes to a different thing when an old-established works could export its surplus upon us.

Mr. CALDERHEAD. Then the tariff was an insurance?

Mr. CARNEGIE. I have just told you that it was the only insurance. I would not have gone in without it.

Mr. CALDERHEAD. That, then, was the relation of the tariff to capital. What was its relation to wages?

Mr. CARNEGIE. Gentlemen, the interest of capital and the interest of the workman are mutual.

Mr. CALDERHEAD. I understand that myself. You could not induce men to come to that employment in your mills for the same wages that they would have received in England?

Mr. CARNEGIE. That is quite true. But such are the advantages of the American market, the home market, the standardized market, as I have tried to explain to you, that we can beat the English manufacturer all the time, owing to the difficulties he labors under.

Mr. CALDERHEAD. And we no longer need that protection?

Mr. CARNEGIE. We no longer need that protection on steel manufactured in our immense mills, in my opinion. I have repeated that twenty times.

Mr. CALDERHEAD. I understand that. Do you think that if the protection is continued the manufacturer will go to sleep?

Mr. CARNEGIE. There is that tendency in human nature—do you not think so?—that when you are doing well you will let well enough alone and are content.

Mr. CALDERHEAD. I see a good deal of that. I am glad you agree with me.

Mr. BONYNGE. Well, Mr. Carnegie, it has not altogether had that effect, because Mr. Schwab has introduced these new improvements that you gave him very high credit for this morning.

Mr. CARNEGIE. Certainly.

Mr. BONYNGE. So that it has not altogether had that effect.

Mr. CARNEGIE. There are exceptions to every rule, are there not?

Mr. BONYNGE. Certainly; that is one exception.

Mr. CARNEGIE. No; but I wish to explain about Schwab. Mr. Schwab was alone, you might say, in the Bethlehem works. He owns it. He was not financially very strong when he started; and he was most enterprising. If Mr. Schwab, after running awhile, was making the great profits that we hear of, and everything was going well, the influence even upon him might be sedative.

Mr. BONYNGE. Yes; and then do you not imagine that somebody else would arise that would introduce some new improvements and wake Mr. Schwab up or put him out of business?

Mr. CARNEGIE. If there were no combinations that would be the effect; and the policy of trying to bolster the inefficient that may need a tariff to-day, when others say they do not, would be the most unfortunate policy, in my opinion, for the Government to pursue.

Mr. CALDERHEAD. The policy would be unfortunate if the Government was to attempt to fix the prices; but as long as prices will be fixed by the output of the efficient organizations I do not feel as if I have much interest in the inefficient organizations.

Mr. CARNEGIE. How would it be if they all got together and agreed upon a common price that would make the inefficient organization profitable?

Mr. CALDERHEAD. Would legislation either way on the part of the Government prevent their getting together?

Mr. CARNEGIE. Yes; if combinations are unlawful.

Mr. CALDERHEAD. Oh, that would be a criminal statute; but could legislation, either for tariff or for free trade, prevent it?

Mr. CARNEGIE. No; I say again that in our present situation it would not make a rap of difference, in my opinion, to the steel industry of this country if the tariff were now removed; because, to the best of my knowledge and belief, it is impossible for the foreigner seriously to affect the great market we have for steel.

Mr. GAINES. In connection with what you were just saying, Mr. Carnegie, I understand that you question our ability to find out the cost here and abroad, owing to the difficulty of the subject-matter and our lack of the technical capacity to understand the information. which we get; and that you advise us to make up our minds with reference to the steel schedules from two facts: First, the statement of Judge Gary (about which, however, there is some dispute); and then the other known fact, that the United States Steel Corporation exports a considerable amount of steel. In coming to a determination as to whether the steel company makes such a profit that it can be independent of foreign competition, you divide the number of tons of its output by its net profit, and that is somewhere from thirteen to fifteen dollars a ton. The steel company, however, owns its own ore, and has in that profit an ore seller's profit. It owns transportation on the lakes, and in that is included a lake transportation profit. It owns railroad interests, and in that is included railroad profits. It owns coal mines and makes its own coke, and in that is included the profits of the seller of coke. What would be the effect, in your opinion, of a reduction? (It also owns limestone and a number of other raw materials. I do not undertake to name them all.)

Mr. CARNEGIE. No, no; I understand. Say " and all the materials."

Mr. GAINES. Yes. What about the maker of pig iron or steel billets or any other form, at any other stage of the manufacture you choose, who does not own these primary processes of manufacture? What would be the effect on him?

Mr. CARNEGIE. He would make less profit per ton than the man who owned all of these, necessarily.

Mr. GAINES. Oh, yes; he makes much less profit per ton now on any one or two or three items of manufacture or processes of manufacture than the man who has a larger number of them. My question was, Would not the tariff wipe out that small competitor? Take the man who has to buy his ore and his coke, and who has no transportation profits, but must buy transportation from some one else. Have you considered the effect on him of this reduction?

Mr. CARNEGIE. No; I have not. I have considered the effect of the tariff upon men who run their business and make all these things; and then I do not know any small concern that makes just one item of steel, that buys everything and makes steel. I would not regard him, because I consider that he has not managed his business well, and he should not be considered a steel manufacturer at all.

Mr. GAINES. That brings us right up to the point. You have stated that in your opinion it is not the business of the Government, by the use of the tariff or by any other device, to aid the incompetent or the sluggish?

Mr. CARNEGIE. Yes, sir.

Mr. GAINES. I agree entirely with that; but is that intended to include all men who are not in the " aristocracy," as you might call it, of steel production? Everybody can not have your success, Mr. Carnegie, nor that of Judge Gary, nor that of Mr. Schwab; and yet there are men of, I think, very considerable capacity, perhaps, who are not so large. How is any man to start? You were small one day in the iron production, were you not, and in the production of steel?

Mr. CARNEGIE. No; we started with Bessemer works and everything. When I went into steel we had everything.

Mr. GAINES. But you did not start at the top of the steel production, did you? Perhaps you did, but there are other very capable men who did not.

Mr. CARNEGIE. The point you make is this, that you are not considering people abroad.

Mr. GAINES. Oh, no; not except as they affect our own people.

Mr. CARNEGIE. Then, if you are going to protect every manufacturer—small concerns, as you say, who make only one thing—if it is a specialty, you will find he gets a high price for it. There are numerous small manufacturers who make a specialty of a thing, but such a man certainly can not compete with the United States Steel Company in making rails or structural steel or plates or any of these things. The time has gone past for that.

Mr. GAINES. I think you are right on the very question: Has the time for the small independent man gone by? We can not legislate, Mr. Carnegie, for the steel company, or ought not to; and we ought not to legislate at it, but for the general condition of the country. Now, let me ask you this question, based upon that assertion. It may be correct or not, but it is my opinion. Is there not danger, if we take the tariff entirely off of steel products, that we may be aiding the steel company still further to create a monopoly of the business by destroying its remaining competition in this country, or tending to destroy that remaining competition?

Mr. CARNEGIE. Why, these small makers do not compete.

Mr. GAINES. Some of them sell billets, do they not?

Mr. CARNEGIE. I do not know of any concern that makes only billets.

Mr. GAINES. Are there not small makers of pig iron in the country?

Mr. CARNEGIE. If there are small makers of pig iron in the country they may do just as well as the large ones. If you have a furnace plant capable of turning out a few hundred tons a day of pig iron, I do not think the man that has 10 furnaces can make pig very much cheaper—pig iron by itself. And there are many small manufacturers who make specialties for which they get large prices. There will always be room for the able, enterprising man to devote himself to one specialty and make a profit on it. His specialty, probably, would not be imported. But a man who, under present conditions, wishes to go into the general steel business, except on a large scale, is a man whom you need not bother yourselves about. He has not the judgment necessary; and if the Government undertakes to nurse failures in business——

Mr. GAINES. No; I am not talking about nursing the failures. I am talking about a condition under which there is an opportunity for other people to start in a business than those who have already achieved the most pronounced success in the business.

Mr. CARNEGIE. You can not conduct a great steel business, and make rails and plates and girders and all that; the man is destitute of judgment who would attempt it.

Mr. COCKRAN. You mean without large capital?

Mr. CARNEGIE. Well, but one who attempts it is a small man.

Mr. COCKRAN. But I say your answer would indicate that any man who started in the steel business was destitute of judgment.

Mr. GAINES. It was your answer to my remark, Mr. Carnegie.

Mr. CARNEGIE. What is that?

Mr. GAINES. Mr. Cockran was interpreting your answer and not my remark.

Mr. COCKRAN. Yes; I am merely suggesting that you add to your answer " without capital," so as to make it clear.

Mr. CARNEGIE. Oh, but wait. He would still be a bigger fool if he had capital and did not build big works.

Mr. COCKRAN. Well, of course. [Laughter.] In other words, unless he employed it?

Mr. CARNEGIE. The time has gone past when in this great country the things that are used by the hundreds of thousands of tons, of steel, can be economically produced on a small scale.

Mr. GAINES. Then your opinion is that the time for the small manufacturer in steel has gone by, and we are to recognize the day of the large man and legislate solely with reference to him?

Mr. CARNEGIE. I think that that is quite true; but mind you, there will always be specialties which can be made in small quantities by the able man—always.

Mr. GAINES. Oh, yes; a razor or a special sort of high-speed steel or something like that?

Mr. CARNEGIE. Oh, a thousand little things.

Mr. GAINES. But in the general steel business, not the specialties—as you said about tin plate, when we speak of " steel," it has a sort of meaning in a general way to all of us.

Mr. CARNEGIE. Yes.

Mr. GAINES. The day for the small man in the business, in your opinion, has gone by; and in making up this tariff bill we should recognize that there is no longer any hope for him?

Mr. CARNEGIE. That is what I believe. Do you differ with that?

Mr. GAINES. Yes, Mr. Carnegie. I am very reluctant indeed to believe that the day of opportunity for the man of fairly modest means and the man who is not even a great genius has gone by, and that he must simply operate under the shadow of the protective wing and care of the big man. That is a thing that I hate to come to.

Mr. CARNEGIE. My dear sir, the enterprising man under the shadow of what you call the big man, the big establishment, has far more opportunity of rising to fortune than he ever had of conducting a small business.

Mr. GAINES. I am inclined to think so.

Mr. CARNEGIE. And I am sure of it.

Mr. GAINES. But, at the same time, he should have an independent chance, I think. Still, that is a mere question of giving my opinion now, when yours are of much greater interest.

Mr. CARNEGIE. Yes; but hold on a little, now. Let us just get your judgment on this point: You agree with me in the statement that the opportunities for clever men never were so great as since these great aggregations of capital and works have taken place. Why, imagine—take my own experience: I had 43 partners. There is not one of them but one that put a dollar in the business, and they were millionaires when we sold out. There never was such a chance.

Mr. GAINES. That was good work.

Mr. CARNEGIE. There never was such a chance for able men to make a fortune as these immense establishments have given. You have a wrong conception altogether about the small manufacturer.

Mr. GAINES. Yes; but——

Mr. CARNEGIE. Wait a moment. The man that had half of 1 per cent of interest with us—we promoted 42 of them, young fellows; no relatives. There was only one that was a cousin of some partner, and he got in on his merits. No; there were two, but they got in in spite of that. It was ability; and these young fellows—Schwab was one of them—I found Schwab on the Allegheny Mountains. He had a taste for music then, and played a little. He was a bright boy. He wanted a situation. I sent him down to the works. He was a draftsman. He is an awfully clever fellow, Schwab is. He attracted attention, and he got an interest in the firm; and he had—I need not tell the money he had when he left. He was no small man. [Laughter.]

Mr. GAINES. That I can readily believe.

Mr. CARNEGIE. Imagine what chance there would have been for Schwab when men were small manufacturers, pegging away at a hundred small establishments. That genius would never have had a chance to develop; because, besides being a great mechanic, he is the best manager of men I ever knew.

Mr. GAINES. But do you think, Mr. Carnegie, that the fact that there are opportunities under such men as yourselves is any reason for depriving people of opportunity elsewhere—those who want to start on their own account?

Mr. CARNEGIE. Those who want to start on their own account without capital betray a lack of judgment that will prevent them from ever being successful men.

Mr. GAINES. A strange state of affairs is about to develop. The agitation for the reduction of the tariff on steel, and perhaps for revision of the tariff, seemed to start mainly in the country because of the sale of steel rails abroad cheaper than at home. Now you aid the movement for the reduction of tariff, while defending the chief cause of complaint.

Let me ask you this question, Mr. Carnegie: When you were in business, did you sell abroad cheaper than at home?

Mr. CARNEGIE. I never had the glorious opportunity of exporting in my early days, as far as I remember.

Mr. GAINES. You did not export? What is your impression as to the practice of selling abroad cheaper than at home? What is your opinion of that practice?

Mr. CARNEGIE. I think it is good for all parties concerned.

Mr. Gaines. Will you analyze that?

Mr. Carnegie. Yes; with pleasure. You make everything cheaper if you keep your men at work; and if orders are slack at home, and there is the alternative of idle men with families to support, and the other alternative is that you are to run at a loss, or without profit, I know what my practice was. I ran the mills, and I sold everywhere I could sell. I think that the man who disturbs such an organization as we had, instead of maintaining it at a loss every month, is a poor manager.

Mr. Cockran. Why could you not sell at home cheaper?

Mr. Carnegie. Because there is a certain demand at home that is supplied. We never sold abroad if we could sell at home.

Mr. Cockran. I understood you to say that you pursued the policy of reducing prices at home whenever there was a slackening in the demand, so as to stimulate it.

Mr. Carnegie. Oh, the same policy here?

Mr. Cockran. Yes.

Mr. Carnegie. Oh, yes; but he is asking me a different question there.

Mr. Cockran. But why should you sell abroad cheaper than at home? Why not sell just as cheaply at home?

Mr. Carnegie. Because if I sold every rail at a loss, I would soon shut up, and the rails would be dearer than ever.

Mr. Cockran. But would not the loss be just as great in the foreign markets?

Mr. Carnegie. No.

Mr. Cockran. Why?

Mr. Carnegie. Because you only sell the amount needed to keep your works running.

Mr. Cockran. Why not do that at home?

Mr. Carnegie. Because the demands were not here. They were satisfied. You can not force rail sales.

Mr. Cockran. Yes; but I understood that you could create a new demand by a reduction of price.

Mr. Carnegie. I have never found that so with rails.

Mr. Cockran. I questioned you about it this morning, Mr. Carnegie. Perhaps you have forgotten.

Mr. Carnegie. Well, wait a moment; wait one moment. There are two policies—whether the steel company's policy was right in holding up prices, or whether the consumer would benefit if we reduced prices. Now, I have an open mind; the other has not been tested, you remember——

Mr. Cockran. Which other?

Mr. Carnegie. The policy of keeping up prices; it has not been tested yet. But if we had a depression we would rather reduce our prices if we thought it would stimulate orders, which has that effect, but not, sometimes, to a great extent. In regard to steel rails, a railroad company will buy so many steel rails. In depressed times there are no new railroads building, and I do not think that a reduction of prices there would give us 1 ton more orders. No; no railroad would buy a rail that it did not need in depressed times. You come now to general merchandise, and there we reduced prices at home as well as abroad, because you can stimulate demand in this field—not in rails in America, but cheap prices abroad might bring orders.

Mr. COCKRAN. Why, do you mean to say that the cost of rails would not have itself an effect upon a railway if it was contemplating relaying a track or extending its trackage?

Mr. CARNEGIE. Yes.

Mr. COCKRAN. Would it not have some effect?

Mr. CARNEGIE. Yes; some slight effect.

Mr. COCKRAN. Well, that is all. Railroads buy their supplies at the beginning of each year.

Mr. CARNEGIE. No, no! In times of depression railroads are not often contemplating extensions.

Mr. COCKRAN. That would depend upon what they cost; and if the reductions were extensive enough, do you not think that would be a factor in stimulating consumption?

Mr. CARNEGIE. But you do not extend any work on a railroad solely because of the cost of steel rails. A great many other things must be purchased.

Mr. COCKRAN. I understand that; but that is one factor, is it not?

Mr. CARNEGIE. And the tendency is that low prices stimulate production. There is no doubt about that.

Mr. COCKRAN. When a manufacturer decides that he has a surplus (which of course comes from failure of demand), might not that demand be stimulated with good results at home as well as abroad by offering the steel product, whatever it is, at a lower rate?

Mr. CARNEGIE. I really do not believe that the lower cost of rails alone would stimulate railroad companies to buy much more—any reduction that you could make—although, of course, political economy does teach that low prices increase consumption, as a rule.

Mr. COCKRAN. It certainly applies to structural steel; a diminution in prices results in very greatly increased consumption.

Mr. CARNEGIE. It applies to everything in degree, more or less.

Mr. COCKRAN. Yes; I suppose what you mean is that in the case of steel rails the consumption is confined to a single customer—that is, the railroad—whereas, in the case of structural steel, the consumption is extensive?

Mr. CARNEGIE. Yes; I think you might tempt a millionaire who wished to build a skyscraper with a great bargain, a fall of prices, if he were a bold man. A fall of prices would lead him to go on with his work again.

Mr. COCKRAN. Mr. Carnegie, you made a very significant remark——

The CHAIRMAN. Mr. Carnegie, you seem to feel quite weary, and I do not know whether it would be your pleasure to come to-morrow morning at half past 9 and finish up your conversation here.

Mr. CARNEGIE. Well, gentlemen, if you are not weary, I would rather finish now.

The CHAIRMAN. All right; I just wanted to know.

Mr. COCKRAN. Mr. Carnegie, you said to Mr. Gaines that of the 43 partners with whom you started——

Mr. CARNEGIE. I did not start with forty-three; I ended with forty-three.

Mr. COCKRAN. Well, of the 43 you had, only 1 of them ever put in any money?

Mr. CARNEGIE. Yes, sir; that is true. Well, allow me—I think there was another one that went in who had a small interest in some of our other works. There may have been two.

Mr. COCKRAN. For the purpose of fixing what the profits of that industry were, would you mind telling us what capital was put into the Carnegie Company to begin with? With what capital did you start?

Mr. CARNEGIE. I could not tell you. It was in the millions; but really, I would have to refer——

Mr. COCKRAN. Mr. Schwab testified that there was no capital at all; that practically all the capital that ever was in the business had been made out of its profits. Was that a misapprehension on his part?

Mr. CARNEGIE. Oh, I think it was a misapprehension upon your part.

Mr. COCKRAN. I will read you his testimony.

Mr. CARNEGIE. Made out of the business?

Mr. COCKRAN. Yes.

Mr. CARNEGIE. Oh; that is a different thing. We were in iron for many years, and we made money that we put into steel. He is quite right about that.

Mr. COCKRAN. I want to get back to the beginning. Would you mind telling me, then, with what capital you did start?

Mr. CARNEGIE. I could not without refreshing my memory.

Mr. COCKRAN. Would you mind coming within a million or so of it? [Laughter.]

Mr. CARNEGIE. Do you mean when I first started in iron?

Mr. COCKRAN. Yes; we will begin with that.

Mr. CARNEGIE. Oh, well, we started in a small iron mill. You must not take this as correct; I will give it to you as I remember it. It was a small amount, the first interest I took in iron. It seems to me—I can tell you where my start was. Now I remember: My first start for manufacturing was in bridges. I saw that wooden bridges were not things for railroads, and we built a small bridge of cast-iron, and I saw that the time for iron bridges was coming, and I started there with $1,500 which I borrowed from the bank as my share. I got five other partners with me, practical men, and they each put in $1,500; and we made a small start on building bridges. They were just the men who would have delighted Mr. Gaines, and I wasn't too big myself then to be ruled out.

Mr. COCKRAN. So you started with $9,000?

Mr. CARNEGIE. I think that that is about the amount.

Mr. COCKRAN. There were six of you who put in $1,500 apiece?

Mr. CARNEGIE. Five of us. Five of us, I think.

Mr. COCKRAN. You said there were five others besides yourself. That was six altogether?

Mr. CARNEGIE. It was five with me.

Mr. COCKRAN. Yes; five with yourself.

Mr. DALZELL. "Five of us," he said.

Mr. CARNEGIE. I think so; I think so.

Mr. COCKRAN. Then you started with $7,500?

Mr. CARNEGIE. Yes.

Mr. Cockran. Was there any other capital put in after that, or did you go along——

Mr. Carnegie. Oh, of course as we made money we put it into the business.

Mr. Cockran. I mean there was no outside capital put in after that; was there?

Mr. Carnegie. I do not remember of any outside. Of course I made a good deal of money. I went abroad and sold bonds for the Pennsylvania Railroad Company, and I made a good deal of money; and that went into the business.

Mr. Cockran. Could you tell us about how much?

Mr. Carnegie. No.

Mr. Cockran. I mean to say; what I want to get at is——

Mr. Carnegie. At various times we put in capital; but it was not in the millions.

Mr. Cockran. Was it in the hundreds of thousands?

Mr. Carnegie. Oh, yes; I should think it was.

Mr. Cockran. Could you say how many?

Mr. Carnegie. I can not.

Mr. Cockran. Was there altogether $500,000 put in?

Mr. Carnegie. I hardly think so. I do not think there was that much.

Mr. Cockran. Would you say $400,000?

Mr. Carnegie. Oh, now, this is a question that I have not thought over for forty years. I can not recall these things; but I will be delighted to tell you.

Mr. Cockran. We might start, then, I suppose, with the assumption that the capital that you started with was not over $500,000, all told, of every kind?

Mr. Carnegie. Oh, what we started with was not anything like that.

Mr. Cockran. But I mean that you put in at any time from outside sources?

Mr. Carnegie. Do you mean during all of my career?

Mr. Cockran. I mean while you were in the iron business. Well, I will go through all your career; yes. Perhaps that will shorten it. At any time in all your career, while you were in the iron or the steel business, how much capital in the way of cash subscriptions did you put into your business?

Mr. Carnegie. Oh, I could not tell you that; but it was a small amount. I should think half a million dollars would cover it.

Mr. Cockran. That would cover it all?

Mr. Carnegie. Up to a certain time.

Mr. Cockran. Up to what time, Mr. Carnegie?

Mr. Carnegie. Oh, well, now, here again I will give you an estimate, if you like, to the best of my knowledge.

Mr. Cockran. I will take that if you can not give me anything better. I will take the best you can give me.

Mr. Carnegie. I put at various times into the business—first we started to build bridges; then we went into the iron business.

Mr. Cockran. You had $500,000 at some time or other put in. About what time was that? What time could you fix as about the time when your total subscriptions of capital to your enterprise amounted to $500,000?

Mr. CARNEGIE. Oh, I really could not trust my memory as to that.

Mr. COCKRAN. About when?

Mr. CARNEGIE. Oh, but " about." "About". is——

Mr. COCKRAN. Did you ever put any more in? I mean, now, of outside capital; or did you ever get any more capital into your business than $500,000 at any time?

Mr. CARNEGIE. Do you mean when we organized the steel company?

Mr. COCKRAN. I will take any time that you like, Mr. Carnegie, when your memory gets at it. Just take that point.

Mr. CARNEGIE. You would have to give me time to go over all the documents. I am most anxious to give you all these things, but can you go back forty years and tell everything about how much money you had?

Mr. COCKRAN. Yes; I can tell every penny I had forty years ago, and it would not take me very long. [Laughter.]

Mr. CARNEGIE. Well, I can not; I truly can not.

Mr. COCKRAN. I could even tell which pocket I carried it in. [Laughter.]

Mr. CARNEGIE. I am totally unable to do it.

Mr. COCKRAN. Can you not tell us in round numbers——

Mr. CARNEGIE. No; I can not.

Mr. COCKRAN. You have not let me finish my question yet.

Mr. CARNEGIE. Oh, I could not tell you.

Mr. COCKRAN. Could you tell me within a million or so of how much capital you ever had subscribed to your business?

Mr. CARNEGIE. We went on making money.

Mr. COCKRAN. Yes; I understand that.

Mr. CARNEGIE. Let me show you how it was, and then you will see how impossible it is for me now to recall these things. We went on with bridges. Then we went into iron. Then we concluded to build a blast furnace. That was a time when it was very difficult, because blast furnaces are ticklish things. Then we went on to build more and built up an iron business. Then the bridge works grew out of the profits—I can tell you this—principally out of the profits; chiefly out of the profits.

Mr. COCKRAN. Mr. Schwab said all the capital was made out of the profits. If there be any misapprehension about this, I want to get the misapprehension removed.

Mr. CARNEGIE. Oh, Mr. Schwab was not with me then.

Mr. COCKRAN. That is the reason I want you now to supplement Mr. Schwab's misapprehension by your own information.

Mr. CARNEGIE. But I do not know what Mr. Schwab said.

Mr. COCKRAN. Regardless of that, you got $7,500 to start with. Then, we have various contributions from sales of bonds and other sources?

Mr. CARNEGIE. Money put in.

Mr. COCKRAN. Put into the steel business.

Mr. CARNEGIE. Mr. Cockran, I was the capitalist of the concern.

Mr. COCKRAN. I understand that.

Mr. CARNEGIE. I made some money and put it in. We began in a very small way. I wish I could just take a book and show you. I do not want to make blunders.

Mr. COCKRAN. Could you fix the maximum amount beyond which you did not put in money?

Mr. CARNEGIE. No; let me tell you. I will give you the process, and it was in very small amounts. I have told you that we began——

Mr. COCKRAN. Yes; you began.

Mr. CARNEGIE. Then we went into the next venture we made in iron. We kept on in iron and bridges. We put our money back. All the partners were economical. Our finances were always pretty ticklish, and all the money that we made in the business we kept in. We were all very economical. Then it came to the time when I saw that the Bessemer process was a success.

Mr. COCKRAN. What time was that, Mr. Carnegie?

Mr. CARNEGIE. That I can not tell.

Mr. COCKRAN. I mean near it?

Mr. CARNEGIE. I have no more idea what that year was, or about the time, than I have——

Mr. COCKRAN. Was it in the sixties or seventies or what?

Mr. CARNEGIE. Oh, I can not tell. I would have to think it out.

Mr. COCKRAN. Could you tell whether it was in the fifties or the seventies?

Mr. CARNEGIE. No. [Laughter.] Really, there is nothing I wish to conceal. I would with pleasure get my young partners——

The CHAIRMAN. Mr. Cockran, are you not satisfied that you can not get that?

Mr. COCKRAN. I am going to get as much as I can, Mr. Chairman.

The CHAIRMAN. It occurs to me that you have. [Laughter.]

Mr. COCKRAN. Oh, no; Mr. Carnegie will tell me more in detail.

Mr. CARNEGIE. I will tell you all I can.

Mr. COCKRAN. Of course you will, Mr. Carnegie.

Mr. CARNEGIE. We went into the business, into the steel works. That was a great venture. I got a large number of people to go in.

Mr. COCKRAN. About what time was that when you got a large number of people to come in?

Mr. CARNEGIE. Do you know when the steel company was started? I do not remember the year. I suppose that does not make any difference.

Mr. UNDERWOOD. 1891.

Mr. COCKRAN. Oh, no. He means his steel company.

Mr. CARNEGIE. Do you know? I do not. I can not remember what year we started the steel works in; but we started them.

Mr. COCKRAN. Was it in the seventies or the eighties or the nineties? Could you tell us that—or the sixties?

Mr. CARNEGIE. I could tell by the fact that steel rails were $75 a ton.

Mr. DALZELL. Are you talking now about the building of the Edgar Thomson Steel Works?

Mr. CARNEGIE. Yes.

Mr. DALZELL. Is that the beginning?

Mr. CARNEGIE. Yes.

Mr. DALZELL. That was about 1870.

Mr. CARNEGIE. Yes—well, Mr. Dalzell says it was about 1870.

Mr. COCKRAN. The Edgar Thomson Steel Works were your steel works, practically?

Mr. CARNEGIE. Yes, sir.

Mr. COCKRAN. With which you were identified?

Mr. CARNEGIE. Yes, sir.

Mr. COCKRAN. Were they built from the profits earned in the iron company or were they built by the subscription of fresh capital?

Mr. CARNEGIE. Oh, I got a great many partners to go in there.

Mr. COCKRAN. Well, at this time——

Mr. CARNEGIE. John Edgar Thomson, of the Pennsylvania Railroad, was a partner; James A. Scott was a partner; Mr. David McCandliss, and Mr. John Scott, oh——

Mr. COCKRAN. Can you remember what the capital of that was, how much actual cash was put into that enterprise?

Mr. CARNEGIE. No; upon my word, I can not. But we did not build those works. I should think the blast furnace—I should think two or three million dollars.

Mr. COCKRAN. Two or three million dollars?

Mr. CARNEGIE. Now, I may be altogether wrong——

Mr. COCKRAN. They did not exceed $5,000,000, did they?

Mr. CARNEGIE. I will not say; I can not.

Mr. COCKRAN. Your best impression is two or three million dollars?

Mr. CARNEGIE. I think so.

Mr. COCKRAN. The Edgar Thomson Steel Company started at that capital. Was there any additional capital put into it, or did it expand itself by its own earnings, by the reinvestment of its earnings?

Mr. CARNEGIE. I think the Edgar Thomson Works did. There may have been five or six hundred thousand dollars or something of that kind put in.

Mr. COCKRAN. But they were highly successful?

Mr. CARNEGIE. They were successful.

Mr. COCKRAN. And as the money was earned, after the partners took out what was necessary for their support, the surplus was reinvested and the work expanded?

Mr. CARNEGIE. Religiously. The partners were not then millionaires; they had an interest in the firm, but they hoped for it——

Mr. COCKRAN. But they lacked for nothing, and they were putting back their surplus earnings into the company?

Mr. CARNEGIE. Yes, sir.

Mr. COCKRAN. After the Edgar Thomson Works started the Carnegie Iron or Steel Works were started?

Mr. CARNEGIE. The Edgar Thomson started, and none of my partners would go into it.

Mr. COCKRAN. None of your partners would go into it?

Mr. CARNEGIE. No, sir.

Mr. COCKRAN. That is, none of your old partners in the iron business?

Mr. CARNEGIE. That is what we are talking about.

Mr. COCKRAN. Then these other gentlemen, whose names you have mentioned, were not partners?

Mr. CARNEGIE. What is that?

Mr. COCKRAN. Were they partners?

Mr. CARNEGIE. Oh, yes.

Mr. COCKRAN. Those are the gentlemen I speak of, and I understood you to say that they were not partners.

Mr. CARNEGIE. Oh, I never said that.

Mr. COCKRAN. Your old partners in the steel company——

Mr. CARNEGIE. The steel company was not a partnership.

Mr. COCKRAN. The Edgar Thomson Company?

Mr. CARNEGIE. That was a corporation.

Mr. COCKRAN. Yes. It grew under your management and waxed fat, and then you started another one. What form did the extension take?

Mr. CARNEGIE. We built more blast furnaces.

Mr. COCKRAN. Still under the name of the Edgar Thomson Company?

Mr. CARNEGIE. All was under the name of the Edgar Thomson Company, I think. The Union Iron Mills also had blast furnaces.

Mr. COCKRAN. Were they part of the Edgar Thomson Company?

Mr. CARNEGIE. Not until the consolidation.

Mr. COCKRAN. And were the Union Iron Mills—who started the Union Iron Mills?

Mr. CARNEGIE. Those were our iron mills.

Mr. COCKRAN. Those were iron mills in existence before the Edgar Thomson Company——

Mr. CARNEGIE. They were the mills we started to make iron. And then we went into blast furnaces and made pig iron.

Mr. COCKRAN. You say " we." Whom do you mean by " we," the Edgar Thomson Company or the Union Iron Mills?

Mr. CARNEGIE. The Edgar Thomson Company was a later development. We went into making steel as a final plunge.

Mr. COCKRAN. The Union Iron Mills?

Mr. CARNEGIE. My partners would not go in for a time. Finally they were willing to go in, when they saw the success, and then we made the firm of Carnegie Brothers & Co., and that included the steel works and iron works and bridge works—no; not the bridge works; the bridge works was a separate corporation.

Mr. COCKRAN. This was the old corporation, as I understand it, that started originally with $7,500, that became the Union Iron Mills and expanded into the manufacture of steel and everything else.

Mr. CARNEGIE. They were consolidated.

Mr. COCKRAN. They were consolidated with whom?

Mr. CARNEGIE. The Edgar Thomson Steel Works, becoming the Carnegie Brothers & Co.

Mr. COCKRAN. I say they consolidated with whom?

Mr. CARNEGIE. The whole of them; the iron and steel were consolidated.

Mr. COCKRAN. Was there any increase of cash capital in this or any cash capital contributed by anybody during the progress of this consolidation?

Mr. CARNEGIE. No. Of course the first capital was in the Edgar Thomson Company.

Mr. COCKRAN. I understand.

Mr. CARNEGIE. And then we consolidated it. Most of these gentlemen died or sold out or were disappointed, and then we bought them out, and we consolidated the iron department—everything we had in iron except the Keystone Bridge Works, which was separate. Then we consolidated the iron with the steel, and when my partners got over their fright and saw that the rash partner was going to be successful they consolidated.

Mr. COCKRAN. When they discovered who was the real wise partner they were eager to consolidate?

Mr. CARNEGIE. Yes.

Mr. COCKRAN. And then we find the Edgar Thomson Steel Company and the Union Iron Mills merged into the Carnegie Brothers' Company?

Mr. CARNEGIE. Yes, sir.

Mr. COCKRAN. You spoke of the Homestead Bridge Company?

Mr. CARNEGIE. No; the Homestead works. It was the Keystone Bridge Company.

Mr. COCKRAN. The Keystone Bridge Company?

Mr. CARNEGIE. Yes. Will you tell me what you want to get at, and I will tell you.

Mr. COCKRAN. I will tell you frankly, I want to get what the actual profits of your company were—the company which was a great monument to your success. For that purpose I want to find out what cash capital was put into the company and how that has grown.

Mr. CARNEGIE. Why didn't you tell me that? [Laughter.] Do you know, when you have not thought of a subject for thirty years, you can not remember everything. I could lie down in my bed and think for a while and study it up. Practically, Mr. Cockran, one enterprise gave us the capital, of course in a small degree, for another enterprise; one was merged into another, and so on, and so on.

Mr. COCKRAN. Exactly.

Mr. CARNEGIE. I wish you had asked me that.

Mr. COCKRAN. So that practically, Mr. Carnegie, when you sold out your interest—well, when you withdrew, at the time of the formation or prior to the formation of the United States Steel Company, this vast property which had been created by your partners and yourself represented almost entirely profits earned?

Mr. CARNEGIE. Why didn't you ask me that question?

Mr. COCKRAN. I started by citing what Mr. Schwab had said, and you said you thought that was a misapprehension, and you came along finally to this same conclusion——

Mr. CARNEGIE. But Mr. Schwab was wrong.

Mr. COCKRAN. Yes; Mr. Schwab was wrong, then, to the extent of two or three millions of dollars?

Mr. CARNEGIE. Certainly.

Mr. COCKRAN. What do you remember was the amount paid you for this enterprise when you sold it?

Mr. CARNEGIE. My position there was—now, I can tell you exactly—that is, recent.

Mr. COCKRAN. Yes, Mr. Carnegie; thank you very much.

Mr. CARNEGIE. My partners, young partners, received an offer for the mills, to convert them into this great new company, consolidate with the others, and I sent my cousin out to Pittsburg, who was a partner himself, to ask the young men if they were all in favor of making this change; that if they were, I would acquiesce, because I had made up my mind when I was younger that I would never spend my old age grabbing for more dollars. There is a phrase that you know, Mr. Cockran, very well, when an old man says he retires for " the making of his soul." Well, I made up my mind that I would retire early, and then I said to these young men, " I will do whatever you wish," and they all wished to sell out. Now, I had nothing whatever to do with the negotiations. They made their bargain and came to me and asked what I would sell for, and I said I would sell for the same amount of bonds as they were to receive, 7 per cent preferred stock. You see they were continuing in the business and they took 7 per cent stock and I took 5 per cent bonds. Then they got $1,500 a share more of common stock, and I declined to take any common stock because I thought it was then water.

Mr. COCKRAN. It has turned out to be wine, has it? [Laughter.]

Mr. CARNEGIE. Yes. I didn't take any.

Mr. COCKRAN. You regarded water as not a thing financially to be used as a beverage?

Mr. CARNEGIE. Well, I was satisfied with the bonds.

Mr. COCKRAN. You took yours in bonds because you did not like common stock; is that it?

Mr. CARNEGIE. No; I could have gotten the common stock in addition.

Mr. COCKRAN. Oh, you could?

Mr. CARNEGIE. I have no doubt of it.

Mr. COCKRAN. Then, you did not take the common stock because you regarded it as water, and you did not want to carry water even on one shoulder?

Mr. CARNEGIE. But, remember, I do not consider it water now.

Mr. COCKRAN. Of course, I understand that. Nobody could think that who looks at a list of stock quotations.

Mr. CARNEGIE. I think, perhaps, you are inquiring into private matters.

Mr. COCKRAN. The moment I touch that I want you to tell me, because my only object is this: We have been talking a great deal about the profits of the company. You, for instance, have been testifying about the profits in the last year, and you have asked the committee to be careful about going after specific facts on which to fix their tariff legislation, and I thought it important, for the purpose of getting the exact facts in considering possible tariff legislation, to show how this company has grown from a very small beginning to the stupendous amount of $1,780,000,000, as the value fixed by Mr. Gary.

Mr. CARNEGIE. Which great company?

Mr. COCKRAN. The Steel Company itself. First of all, I wanted to find out how much your company was paying, how much it was sold for, to get the growth of that, and then I was in hopes I could find the corresponding growth of the other companies and thus get an idea of what the total profits on manufactured steel might be.

Mr. CARNEGIE. If that is your object, I do not think I am justified in revealing their private matters.

Mr. COCKRAN. Then I haven't the slightest disposition to ask a question which you consider touches private matters.

Mr. CARNEGIE. I would not object for a moment to tell you, and I have told you just what I got.

Mr. COCKRAN. You told us you got bonds, but you did not tell the amount, and I have no right to press you on that against your objection.

Mr. CARNEGIE. No, sir.

Mr. COCKRAN. But I understood you to say to-day that one of the sources of information you considered absolutely reliable as to the cost of producing steel was the report of the company for the last year, and I must say I agree with you as to a company that earned $160,000,000, less $27,000,000 deducted for sinking funds on bonds of subsidiary companies, depreciation and extinguishment funds, replacement funds, and so forth, leaving the amount at $133,000,000, quoted by Mr. Payne, and expenses, the difference between your estimate and Mr. Payne's. Now, if that be a reliable source of information as to whether the industry dominated by this company should have a tariff or not, would it not be equally proper for us to look back and see what the earnings were when you were the chief factor in producing steel?

Mr. CARNEGIE. I do not think the tariff question was an issue then.

Mr. COCKRAN. I do not think it was an issue. I think it was a factor, though.

Mr. CARNEGIE. Certainly.

Mr. COCKRAN. Yes.

The CHAIRMAN. Is not that the amount that is deducted from the interest on those bonds?

Mr. COCKRAN. No; that is deducted from the other amount of $133,000,000. The interest on bonds of subsidiary companies only was taken from this amount of $160,000,000. From $133,000,000 they have deducted the interest on bonds and the preferred stock and the dividends on the common stock of the United States Steel Corporation. That is not net earnings.

The CHAIRMAN. No; they are not net earnings.

Mr. COCKRAN. Oh, no; the $133,000,000 is not their net earnings.

Mr. CARNEGIE. If you want the United States Steel Company to tell you the cost of everything, go to them and get it.

Mr. COCKRAN. The only trouble is that we have the same difficulty with everyone that we have with you. The moment it touches information exclusively within your own control you do not care to give it, and the committee has that difficulty all the time.

Mr. CARNEGIE. Because I am no longer in steel. I have retired.

Mr. COCKRAN. But you have knowledge and information of most important character as to the growth of this industry, and its development under the influence of this tariff, while the tariff was fixed at varying amounts. I think if we take these net earnings for the last year as a source of information in dealing with the cost of producing steel now, we should also be free to take its earnings during that long period when you were the chief factor in production, to ascertain the cost of wrought iron; and I am free to say that the thing that has puzzled me is why steel has been an article on which such extraordinary profits have been made—profits above every other industry in the world. I will ask you the question I asked Judge Gary.

Mr. CARNEGIE. Let me say this to you, that I have no interest in the United States Steel Company, because that is what you are getting at. I have not a dollar in it except bonds.

Mr. COCKRAN. I understand that.

Mr. CARNEGIE. And I have never bought a share of the stock; and I have never bought a share of stock on the New York Stock Exchange in my life, nor sold a share of stock on the New York Stock Exchange.

Mr. COCKRAN. I understand that. I am not getting at the stock value of this company; I do not care what its stock may be quoted at; that is only one indication of its value, but I do want to get at what the actual profits have been.

Mr. CARNEGIE. I am very sorry you told me what your idea was. I would have referred you to the United States Steel Company. I am out of business now, and they have everything right there——

Mr. COCKRAN. But Judge Gary's position, it seems to me, in that respect is absolutely clear. Whatever it may have cost the Carnegie Steel Company in the way of cash investment to acquire the property it possessed at the time of consolidation, he, on behalf of the United States Steel Corporation, had to pay a good round sum for it when he got it. The United States Steel Company started with an investment, and a very large investment, in the Carnegie Steel Company. What I want to do is to go back and see what the Carnegie property came from; whether it did not come almost entirely from the results of profits made in the business. That, I am frank to say, I consider a very important factor in determining the result of the tariff, and I would have pursued that tone of inquiry, and I tried to find out how many fortunes besides those you have referred to as having been taken out of this business have been taken out and are now invested in bricks and mortar. I think that information would have been valuable; don't you think so?

Mr. CARNEGIE. No; I do not think that is for the committee at all. I do not see that that has any bearing on the subject. What bearing has it on the tariff question—what values parties are willing to buy property for?

Mr. COCKRAN. It shows the value of the property; and if the property itself is the result of tariff taxation, it becomes of value in the inquiry. I will ask you another question, because it is——

Mr. CARNEGIE. I must refer you to the United States Steel Company.

Mr. COCKRAN. You will not give us any information yourself on that?

Mr. CARNEGIE. No; I will not go into that.

Mr. COCKRAN. All right. I want to ask you one more question. You have said a good deal here to-day as to the importance of this committee's regarding the interest of the person testifying, and I thought that was proper. I assume that you have no interest in any steel company of any kind except the bonds which you hold of the United States Steel Company?

Mr. CARNEGIE. That is quite true. I never was interested in anything but our own works.

Mr. COCKRAN. Now, passing from that question of profits, you stated this morning, I understood, that there has been a steady decrease in the cost of steel rails and all steel, due to the improved methods since the steel business was organized in this country and to the scientific knowledge that the men have gained. Now, that steady decrease in the price of steel has been accompanied by an equally steady rise in the rate of wages, has it not?

Mr. CARNEGIE. What is that?

Mr. COCKRAN. The decrease in the price of steel as a commodity has been accompanied by an equally steady increase in the rate of wages, has it not?

Mr. CARNEGIE. I hardly think so. I would not be prepared to indorse that.

Mr. COCKRAN. Did you not say that the rate of wages, on the whole, has risen steadily since the steel business has been begun; that the men are getting more than ever now?

Mr. CARNEGIE. Certain specialists are getting more, as they prove themselves to be skillful, but I doubt whether the cost of labor has risen much.

Mr. COCKRAN. I do not mean the cost of labor as measured by its production, but I mean the daily rate of wages; has not that increased steadily? I think we have had almost a consensus of opinion on that.

Mr. CARNEGIE. Well, I think that wages are high now, the rate of wages; but I think we have had periods of depression. Wages have gone up and down.

Mr. COCKRAN. But I mean the general average. While the price of steel has been falling, the general average rate of wages has been increasing, has it not?

Mr. CARNEGIE. My opinion is that it has varied as business was brisk or dull. We have had a great boom in steel in the last five years, and there has been an increase in labor; but my recollection, as far as my recollection goes, we have had a depression, and I think labor did not advance.

Mr. COCKRAN. Then you do not think labor has advanced on the whole in the steel business during the last twenty years?

Mr. CARNEGIE. Well, it has as to experts.

Mr. COCKRAN. Oh, no; I mean the average rate of wages.

Mr. CARNEGIE. In day labor?

Mr. COCKRAN. Yes.

Mr. CARNEGIE. I do not think it has advanced much.

Mr. COCKRAN. You think it is just about the same?

Mr. CARNEGIE. There are periods when it has been so low, and there are periods when it has been higher. Now, we have had a great boom in steel——

Mr. COCKRAN. Take the last ten years; has the rate of wages increased?

Mr. CARNEGIE. In the last five or six years labor has advanced.

Mr. COCKRAN. And during that time the price of steel also has been about stationary, has it not?

Mr. CARNEGIE. Do you mean in the general business?

Mr. COCKRAN. Yes.

Mr. CARNEGIE. But we have ups and downs in prices.

Mr. COCKRAN. I understood Mr. Schwab to testify that wages had risen steadily; that the cost of wages, I think he said, increased from year to year. That is not your belief?

Mr. CARNEGIE. Well, Mr. Schwab is a better authority on labor than I am. I was not watching that and certainly he ought to be better authority, and I would not put my judgment there against his. That is in his department.

Mr. COCKRAN. Mr. Fordney asked you to-day that even if competition could be maintained with the foreigner in this country, whether you would object to maintaining a tariff to make higher prices if labor got the benefit of these higher prices. Do you think it possible for labor to get the benefit of artificial high prices?

Mr. CARNEGIE. No, sir.

Mr. COCKRAN. The effect of it is to reduce consumption?

Mr. CARNEGIE. I think employers would pay the price that they could get competent men for, and I think if business was dull they would not need new men, that some would be idle, and the cost of labor would fall.

Mr. DALZELL. Why should we go into all this academic discussion——

Mr. COCKRAN. I think Mr. Carnegie is able to answer these questions.

Mr. DALZELL. I think he is abundantly able to answer these academic questions——

Mr. CARNEGIE. If you will excuse me, you will make much better progress if you will tell me what you want to know.

Mr. COCKRAN. What I want to know——

Mr. CARNEGIE. You put a man here who has not been in business for seven years, and, naturally, his memory is not so good. Do you imagine that his memory can go back and fix dates? Dates are obliterated in my mind——

Mr. COCKRAN. I was not asking you about dates at all now. After I found your difficulty in remembering dates, I abandoned that.

Mr. CARNEGIE. Because you really must remember I have retired for seven years, and to call upon me unexpectedly to go back thirty or forty years, I am unable to do that.

Mr. COCKRAN. We have had our excursion into the past, and we have come back, with such information as we got.

Mr. CARNEGIE. Tell me what you want.

Mr. COCKRAN. I will ask you one more question, notwithstanding the objection to academic discussion. I understand you have given us as your opinion that putting steel on the free list would not in itself bring around much of a reduction in the cost to the consumer?

Mr. CARNEGIE. Yes; that is quite true.

Mr. COCKRAN. I think you said that of almost all steel products?

Mr. CARNEGIE. Yes, sir; yes.

Mr. COCKRAN. Your belief that they should be put on the free list is to prevent possibilities of exactions in the future?

Mr. CARNEGIE. Yes, sir.

Mr. COCKRAN. And also, I suppose, to make sure that if the cost of production be reduced hereby that the consumer will get the benefit?

Mr. CARNEGIE. I do not understand that.

Mr. COCKRAN. I say. if the product is on the free list, and there should be a reduction in the cost of production both here and abroad, then the native consumer would get the benefit of economies anywhere in the world, would he not?

Mr. CARNEGIE. Certainly, as I understand your question. If there is any reduction——

Mr. COCKRAN. With steel on the free list——

Mr. CARNEGIE. Well——

Mr. COCKRAN. We would not only be protected against any arbitrary advance in this country, but against any arbitrary exaction——

Mr. CARNEGIE. I am glad you asked that.

Mr. COCKRAN. I want that clear.

Mr. CARNEGIE. My opinion is, and I have stated it over and over again, that if I did not think this was true I would not be prepared to favor no tariff taking it all off at once. My opinion is that the American steel industry is on such a foundation that even if the tariff were taken off I do not believe that any foreign steel rails or steel of any kind would come in here to any extent, gentlemen, now.

Mr. COCKRAN. I understand that. Your idea is that we can defeat competition all over the world upon our own shores. That is your belief?

Mr. CARNEGIE. Yes; my belief is that the steel makers of America who are properly equipped and manage their business well need not fear anything that producers abroad can do to affect their home market.

Mr. COCKRAN. So, with this product on the free list, the native producer can hold his market if he improves his skill in production as much as his competitors—if he marshals his skill on as high a standard as the foreigner?

Mr. CARNEGIE. Yes.

Mr. COCKRAN. In other words, you put the American manufacturer to the improvement and development of his skill to maintain his market?

Mr. CARNEGIE. Yes; he would be more alert to improve than he would be if he could make a great profit under the tariff. That is human nature.

Mr. COCKRAN. That is all.

Mr. HILL. Just one subject I would like to clear up in my own mind.

So long as you were in business there was always free and open and keen competition, not only in rails, but in all other forms of steel products, was there not?

Mr. CARNEGIE. No.

Mr. HILL. Open competition in the market?

Mr. CARNEGIE. No; I could not say that. Wars would break out, and we would compete with each other, and then sometimes they would meet and agree to be at peace. Then trouble would break out again.

Mr. HILL. But there was no financial combination in any way that controlled it. If there was an agreement, it was simply an agreement such as men in the same industry often have now?

Mr. CARNEGIE. Yes, sir.

Mr. HILL. So far as financial combination, it was always free and open competition?

Mr. CARNEGIE. Yes, sir; each manufacturer stood upon his own basis.

Mr. HILL. Yes. Do you remember the price of steel rails the year you sold out, the year you sold your company out?

Mr. CARNEGIE. I am sorry to say I do not.

Mr. HILL. There has been a uniform price of $28 per ton for steel rails ever since, has there not?

Mr. CARNEGIE. Oh, you mean steel rails?

Mr. HILL. Yes. Do you not remember the price that year, before you sold out; you do not remember the price you were selling steel rails for then?

Mr. CARNEGIE. I do not remember whether the uniform price did not prevail then or not.

Mr. HILL. No; I think not.

Mr. CARNEGIE. I could not answer that.

Mr. HILL. The price has been uniform ever since. I wanted to know whether you knew that this agreement between the railroad companies and the combination was a prerequisite to the formation of the combination.

Mr. CARNEGIE. I do not think it had the slightest influence.

Mr. HILL. You do not think it had?

Mr. CARNEGIE. Not the slightest bearing.

Mr. HILL. And you sold out and took the bonds of the combination with the expectation that there was to be no uniform fixed price?

Mr. CARNEGIE. I knew nothing, as far as my memory serves me; that never entered into my thoughts. The combination on rails would not be an important factor with any man selling out or not selling out; it is only one form of steel.

Mr. HILL. Yes; but you will admit that the fixing of freight rates and the corresponding fixing of the price of rails would be a very important factor with reference to all other steel products, would it not, because the rates would apply just the same?

Mr. CARNEGIE. Oh, I see your point. I wish to say that I knew nothing about that arrangement between the railroads——

Mr. HILL. And the steel companies?

Mr. CARNEGIE. Yes, sir.

Mr. HILL. And do not know when it was made, of course, if you know nothing about it?

Mr. CARNEGIE. I knew nothing about it. Let me show you: We were western people at Pittsburg; and the Pennsylvania Steel Company and the Cambria Company, with offices at Philadelphia, were the people that mostly conferred with the Pennsylvania Railroad Company, and we of the West heard of that agreement—the price fixed. Mr. Hill, I wish to assure you that I never heard it intimated that it was based on rates in any way.

Mr. HILL. I think that was stated by a previous witness, but not by you.

Mr. CARNEGIE. I was no party to that agreement personally; I did not conduct it, but I did think it was a fair price. It did not strike me as unfair.

Mr. DALZELL. I want to ask you a question to see whether or not I understand your testimony.

Your opinion that steel can be put on the free list is not based on any figured cost, but on broad, general principles, taking into account that we do not import much steel, and we do export some steel, and taking into account also the great resources of the country and the business energy of our people. As I understand you, that is your position. Do I state it correctly?

Mr. CARNEGIE. Yes; that is true. There has been a general consensus of opinion among steel men that the tariff was a back number; I have heard the remark——

Mr. DALZELL. I thought I understood you, and I am glad to have you confirm my understanding.

The CHAIRMAN. I want to correct a false impression that my colleague, Mr. Cockran, got from a cursory examination of this report, the report made by Judge Gary. He spoke of the $160,964,000 of the gross earnings, and then he read provisions for the following purposes:

"Sinking funds on bonds of subsidiary companies, $1,977,761.03, and so forth, leaving $133,244,929.28."

Now, if he had turned to page 7 of this report, he would have found out what those earnings were [reading from sixth annual report of the United States Steel Corporation for the fiscal year ended December 31, 1907]:

Earnings	$160,964,673.72
Less appropriations for the following purposes, viz:	
Sinking funds on bonds of subsidiary companies	1,977,761.03
Depreciation and extinguishment funds (regular provisions for the year)	6,681,746.03
Extraordinary replacement funds (regular provisions for the year)	15,560,237.38
Special replacement and improvement funds	3,500,000.00
Total (net earnings in the year the amount deducted)	27,719,744.44
That makes net earnings in the year	133,244,929.28
Deduct interest on United States Steel Corporation bonds outstanding	22,860,352.82
Sinking funds on United States Steel Corporation bonds, viz:	
Installments	4,050,000.00
Interest on bonds and sinking funds	1,037,497.18
Leaving a balance of	105,247,079.28
Less charged off for various accounts and adjustments	631,515.52
Leaving a balance of	104,565,563.76

Which would seem to be the net profits for the year.

Now, on page 9 you find this memorandum: "The expenditures made by all companies during the year 1907 for maintenance and renewals, including the relining of blast furnaces and for extraordinary replacements, equaled the total sum of $55,828,253.12, an increase in comparison with the expenditures for the same purposes during the preceding year of $7,495,163.75, or 15.5 per cent. The expenditures in the year 1907 were the largest of any year in the organization's history. The annual expenditures since 1902 have been as follows:"

I will not stop to read those figures. "The entire amount of the foregoing expenditures was charged to current operating expenses and to replacement funds reserved from earnings. A statement showing the principal items of replacement and betterment comprehended in the total expenditures for extraordinary replacements is included in the statistical tables printed in this report."

So that the total replacement for that year amounted to $55,000,000. Instead of charging all over, they charged over $27,000,000, and the other they carried along to a future replacement account, it would seem, from that.

Now, the following table shows the amount of the expenditures made during the year for the above purposes by the respective groups of operating properties:

Expenditures for ordinary maintenance and repairs, including blast furnace relining, expended on manufacturing properties, the total, except blast furnace relining	$23,265,791.26
Blast furnace relining	1,481,975.08

Coal and coke properties	$1,527,545.74
Iron ore properties	438,110.56
Transportation properties:	
Railroads	7,863,446.76
Steamships and docks	740,458.53
Miscellaneous properties	195,340.39
Total expended in 1907	35,503,668.32

I want to get that in the record, and I want to show by you, Mr. Carnegie, if you will pay attention, that this was a proper charge against the income for the year and should be deducted before you get the profits per ton of the proceeds of the business.

Now, in the next column are shown extraordinary replacements. These expenditures were paid from funds provided from earnings to cover requirements of the character included in this report, and it says—see page 10—this same list of items foots up $20,324,584.80.

I want to get that in the record, so it can be seen just what the net profits of this corporation were, which will show that there was a profit of $10 a ton on the 10,000,000 tons of steel output instead of $15, as stated originally. That is all I desire at this time. I want to get at the exact truth in this case.

Mr. CARNEGIE. That is right.

[NOTE.—In revising this proof, Mr. Carnegie has referred again to the report of the United States Steel Corporation for 1907 to verify his statement of profit disputed by the chairman. He finds the following:

The total earnings of all properties, after deducting all expenses incident to operations, including those for ordinary repairs and maintenance (approximately $35,000,000), employees' bonus and pension funds, and also interest on bonds and the fixed charges of the subsidiary companies, amounted to $160,964,-673.72.

This is the true profit. What follows is the distribution of part of these profits among the various accounts, amounting to $27,719,744.44. This sum was not expended; it is in the treasury, and part of the enormous surplus which the steel company already has—$122,600,000.

Sinking-fund bonds to the extent of $2,000,000 have been paid out of the profits. This lessened their debt that amount.

Depreciation and extinguishment funds out of profits, $6,700,000.

Extraordinary replacement funds, $15,500,000.

Special replacement and improvement funds, $3,500,000.

Steel mills and furnaces do not depreciate. They can not be allowed to do so. They must be kept up to the highest standard, and improvements introduced when repairs are needed. The statement above shows that ordinary repairs and maintenance were deducted before profits of $160,000,000 were declared. The mills in the future, properly maintained, as they must be, in order to run safely and well, will be more valuable than they are to-day.

The company could have paid every dollar of their profits into their surplus account or various contingent accounts. This is a mere matter of bookkeeping. It has nothing to do with the profits.

Here is the explanation:

The surplus in 1906 was only $97,000,000, in 1907 it is increased to $122,000,000, $25,000,000 difference. If to this we add $2,000,000 paid in 1907 for sinking-fund bonds, which reduced the company debt that amount, we have $27,000,000, the exact sum which was taken from the profits of 1907 to add to the surplus.]

Mr. RANDELL. It is developed, it developed this morning that some of the witnesses have testified that on the sales made abroad, the steel contracts, there was a loss; but on probing the matter they found it was a book loss, but an actual profit. Can you give us any enlightenment on what that means, where they have testified that there was a book loss, but an actual profit, in reference to foreign sales?

Mr. CARNEGIE. I can only imagine that they mean that it enabled them to run their mill. I do not know how many times they sent abroad at a loss. Was it a great number?

Mr. RANDELL. I do not know the amount, but would it mean that it was a book loss because they sold at a less price than they valued at here, but at the same time it was an actual profit because they got more than it cost them?

Mr. CARNEGIE. You had better ask a member of the steel company; I am unable to explain that.

Mr. RANDELL. Then, in reference to the export expenses that they claim they were put to now, special stress was laid upon one item especially, that the price of coal in the ground was so much more, a difference between $600 an acre and $3,000 an acre, making, as you calculate it, a difference of 30 cents in a ton of coke. That would be an extra cost in the manufacture of steel, would it not?

Mr. CARNEGIE. Yes.

Mr. RANDELL. I wanted to get your opinion on this matter. Is that extra expense, and all other extra expenses that you know anything of equal to the savings that have been made, such as utilization of gases, which they did not use before, and the using of slag, something which cost them something to remove before, and other matters of that kind, such as improved machinery; what relation would the cheapening of the product by these things have to the enhancing of its cost by the higher price of coal in the ground?

Mr. CARNEGIE. I should be happy to answer your question if I could. Now, let me say once more, the chairman has just read a report of figures, and a very long report. Can any human being listening to him get an idea of its import? It is impossible. Now, I must say this: To go into the details of a report and try to explain t₁g , just on that statement, really I must be excused; I can not do it.s

Mr. RANDELL. I will excuse you from anything of that kind. I did not mean to ask you that. I want to ask your idea on this proposition, simply, if you can give it, and that is, do these factors that operate to decrease the cost equal, in your opinion, or more than equal the factors that have tended to increase the cost of the production of steel in this country?

Mr. CARNEGIE. I am not prepared to give you an opinion on that.

Mr. RANDELL. Well——

Mr. CARNEGIE. All these improvements have reduced the price, have reduced the cost, but I wish again to call attention to this fact. You can not arrive at a just conclusion upon figures in a report. I have told you over and over that the costs are largely what the system of bookkeeping makes them.

The CHAIRMAN. You brought the figures in in this report, did you not, this morning? You alluded to them?

Mr. CARNEGIE. I alluded to the report, but I do not think I stated any figures, except I remembered the gross earnings were so much.

Mr. RANDELL. You have been questioned a long time, and I will not weary you with many questions, but I want a little information on just one or two matters. I want to get your opinion as to whether or not you think it important in this country to conserve and economize our natural supply of iron?

Mr. CARNEGIE. I have made a report on that to the Government, as to our iron resources.

Mr. RANDELL. Well, do you think it is a matter of importance that we should do so?

Mr. CARNEGIE. Certainly, but see what you mean exactly—to preserve them, you said?

Mr. RANDELL. To conserve and economize them.

Mr. CARNEGIE. Well, I do not think you can economize if you make more steel. Do you mean——

Mr. RANDELL. We should prevent waste at least.

Mr. CARNEGIE. Well, that goes without saying.

Mr. RANDELL. To be candid with you, the idea in my mind was to get your opinion as to the matter of economizing our natural resources, so important to this country at present.

Mr. CARNEGIE. Do you mean for to-day?

Mr. RANDELL. Well, with a proper idea of the future. We owe duties to the future as well as to the present?

Mr. CARNEGIE. Then my answer would depend upon your view of the future.

Mr. RANDELL. Looking forward to the next generation, say. Iron does not grow again I do not suppose. It will sometime give out.

Mr. CARNEGIE. That is the trouble. I think that the wants of this country should be met now, because there is a possibility that we shall find other fields of iron.

Mr. RANDELL. Yet you do not think there is any special necessity for economizing at present?

Mr. CARNEGIE. Economizing is such a vague word. I do not think it is right to waste a pound of anything.

Mr. RANDELL. Then you think the supply in this country such, and its location is such that the producers of steel in the United States have a natural advantage over the producers of steel in other countries, do you not?

Mr. CARNEGIE. Certainly I do.

Mr. RANDELL. They have a natural advantage?

Mr. CARNEGIE. Certainly, for the American market.

Mr. RANDELL. Of course they would not have an advantage in the markets of Germany against German producers?

Mr. CARNEGIE. No, sir.

Mr. RANDELL. They would have an advantage in the rest of the world where the steel was not produced, as I understand it.

Mr. CARNEGIE. I think so. Wait a moment—one moment. When you go to Europe with steel, the German and the Briton would have an advantage over us in the transportation to the eastern world, would they not? They are nearer than we are.

Mr. RANDELL. In other words, unless the other producers are nearer to the market the American producer would have the advantage?

Mr. CARNEGIE. Unless what?

Mr. RANDELL. Unless the other producers are nearer to the market—have an advantage geographically—the American producer would have the advantage?

Mr. CARNEGIE. Yes, but I do not think that the cost of a ton of steel rails or a ton of steel is much less with us than it is in Europe. I think they will be found very close together now.

Mr. RANDELL. For the American market we have a great advantage?

Mr. CARNEGIE. Yes, sir.

Mr. RANDELL. And for the Western Hemisphere, in fact, we have an advantage, do we not?

Mr. CARNEGIE. Yes, sir.

Mr. RANDELL. And we have an advantage as far as South America is concerned?

Mr. CARNEGIE. I think the cost of freight from Europe to South America might possibly be about as cheap as our rate of freight.

Mr. RANDELL. But is not that owing to the fact of artificial arrangements in reference to transportation and not any natural reason for it?

Mr. CARNEGIE. Well, the traffic between Europe and South America is much greater than ours, and a ship would want to load fully, and I think—I am not prepared to say that the manufacturer of Britain would not reach South America cheaper than we would.

Mr. RANDELL. Let me ask you in reference to armor plate. Do you think that the abolition of the tariff would have any effect on that?

Mr. CARNEGIE. Have we a tariff on armor plate?

Mr. RANDELL. My understanding is that it is about the same as steel rails, is it not, Mr. Chairman?

Mr. DALZELL. Armor plate is not specifically named; it comes in under the basket clause, 45 per cent ad valorem.

Mr. RANDELL. It is a higher per cent, then, than steel rails?

Mr. CARNEGIE. Oh, armor plate is between $300 and $400 a ton, and there is less money made on armor plate than there is on the same capital invested in pig iron. I decline to go into armor plate. You know you keep a plate six days in a heating furnace——

Mr. RANDELL. Do you know whether there is any combination that affects the production of armor plate in this country?

Mr. CARNEGIE. No; I do not.

Mr. RANDELL. In reference to one matter I want to make my examination as short as I can, because I suppose you are weary——

Mr. CARNEGIE. Oh, no——

Mr. RANDELL. You said you thought it was fair that the company should receive $28 for steel rails because the railroads are willing for that, and it is an agreement between the consumer and the manufacturer. By the consumer I suppose you mean the railroad companies?

Mr. CARNEGIE. They are the only consumers of steel rails.

Mr. RANDELL. But, Mr. Carnegie, in your opinion, would not an arrangement between transportation companies and the manufacturers of steel rails and the general classes and kinds of steel that are used in structural works, and in the general business of the country, affecting the prices of the product necessary to be used by railroads, and in reference to prices of transportation—such an agreement as that between the transportation companies and the manufacturers would have a great effect upon the mass of consumers in this country, the general public, that have to use the transportation and have their goods carried over the rails of the transportation companies?

Mr. CARNEGIE. That is a very long question.

Mr. RANDELL. I know; but the gist of it is this: Would not a combination between the transportation companies and the manufacturers, no matter how satisfied they might be in reference to prices and rates, yet the public might be robbed by them in combination that way better than it could be if they were not in combination?

Mr. CARNEGIE. In other words, your question means that if the railroad companies and the steel manufacturers mutually agreed upon prices for rails and rates?

Mr. RANDELL. Yes.

Mr. CARNEGIE. Yes, they might if rates were included.

Mr. RANDELL. Suppose they put the rails at $50 a ton, that would make it that much more expensive to build a railroad. Suppose the other arrangements between them, however, were satisfactory, so that the railroad company was able to pay $50 a ton for the steel rails that they now get for $28 a ton; that they had advantages in reference to rates that applied directly or indirectly to all rates, and therefore that the manufacturer would get a higher price by the consent of the carrier, and the carrier would get a higher price by consent of the steel companies, but the general consuming public would get the worst of it, is not that a fact?

Mr. CARNEGIE. I have stated that from everything I have heard and know, I think that arrangement with the railroad companies about steel rails is a very fair arrangement. I never heard that it was based upon any concessions in the rates.

Mr. RANDELL. I will ask you, then, do you not think it a dangerous situation when the steel manufacturers and the railroad companies can make such arrangements and no one has the power to undo them?

Mr. CARNEGIE. The railroad companies and the steel companies are in the relation of a manufacturer and a seller, the railroad companies are buyers.

Mr. RANDELL. Do you not think the general public is interested in that; because they must pay to the railroad companies, they must pay, in the way of rates that they give to the railroads, more money than is invested in the railroads, and the railroads charge up to the public the cost as a part of their investment?

Mr. CARNEGIE. Well, the varying of that is so slight, if it exists, the rails that a railroad company buys are not a very great thing. When the Pennsylvania Railroad buys for its whole system, of course that is a great thing, but I must say that I see no objection whatever, no connection between the general consumer of steel and any agreement made, mutual agreement, between the railroads and the steel company if rates be not included.

Mr. RANDELL. I am speaking of the effect it would have upon the general business of the country. Suppose they just doubled the price of rails; suppose they doubled the price of other things to correspond. It suits the producer of steel and iron. It suits the carrier of goods, and then each one is getting a higher price by mutual agreement?

Mr. CARNEGIE. Yes.

Mr. RANDELL. But somebody has to pay it. Now, is it not a fact that the general public has to pay that?

Mr. CARNEGIE. In reply to that, I wish to state again that it occurs to me—I have been interested in the matter—that when I heard of that I thought it was not an excessive price for steel rails—the price of $28 a ton.

Mr. RANDELL. But you spoke of it, that we ought to guard against the danger of these companies in the future, at some time, perhaps, using the tariff to levy a higher rate on the people than they otherwise could levy. Now, on that same line, do you not think it is not very dangerous to the public for the steel companies and the railroad companies to combine and agree in reference to the price of steel and the price of transportation?

Mr. CARNEGIE. Do you call that a combination, when the seller and buyer agree as to their price for rails?

Mr. RANDELL. I think so, when it affects the general public, the public which has to pay the bills.

Mr. CARNEGIE. I can not agree with you. That is what takes place in every sale and purchase. I can not agree as far as I see that.

Mr. RANDELL. I wanted to get your idea.

Mr. CARNEGIE. I can not class that as a combination.

Mr. RANDELL. That is all, then, I think, Mr. Carnegie.

Mr. UNDERWOOD. We thank you for your presence here.

Mr. CARNEGIE. And I want to express my thanks to you.

The CHAIRMAN. We will now hear Mr. Alfred O. Crozier.

Mr. CROZIER. Mr. Chairman, as I am going to comment upon Mr. Carnegie's testimony, I will be glad to have him remain.

Mr. CARNEGIE. Certainly.

STATEMENT OF ALFRED OWEN CROZIER, OF WILMINGTON, DEL., WHO REPLIES TO ANDREW CARNEGIE.

MONDAY, *December 21, 1908.*

(The witness was sworn by the chairman.)

Mr. CROZIER. Mr. Chairman, a portion of my statement, of course, will be my opinion and will be accepted as such.

I must say that I have been highly entertained to-day, but I have been very much reminded of a definition which I heard, and you have undoubtedly heard, that speech is the instrument with which men conceal their thoughts. However, during the testimony to-day I have been very much surprised as to a point of view industrially that I did not suppose existed in the mind of the gentleman who has enlightened us upon the subject.

As his testimony is public, and as his recent article in a magazine was a public article, I assume that he has no objection to the plainest possible criticism of that article.

Mr. CARNEGIE. Not at all.

Mr. UNDERWOOD. Before you go on with your statement, will you state what business you are engaged in. Are you a manufacturer?

Mr. CROZIER. No, sir. With all due apologies, I would say that I am the author of The Magnet, a recent economic novel, and I am a lawyer and some other foolish things. I have no interest in any schedule or anything of that kind.   It is purely a public matter with me.

Mr. CARNEGIE. I have been here all day long, and when the gentleman makes his speech I suppose it will be printed?

The CHAIRMAN. It will be printed.

Mr. CARNEGIE. And I will have the pleasure of reading it.

Mr. CROZIER. If it will be a pleasure——

The CHAIRMAN. The clerk will send you a copy of it, Mr. Carnegie.

Mr. CROZIER. I thought perhaps you would desire to correct some of my statements if you thought they were improper.

Mr. CARNEGIE. No; I will beg to be excused.

The CHAIRMAN. The clerk will send you a copy of Mr. Crozier's speech and you can reply in writing if you desire it, and send to the clerk what you have to say, and it will not be necessary for you to stay if you do not desire to.

Mr. CARNEGIE. I have been here all day and I am somewhat tired and I will read your criticism later, and then I will say, maybe, if it is against me, "What a pity that man does not know better," and if it is in favor of me I will say "What a wise young fellow that was." [Laughter.]

Mr. CROZIER. Mr. Carnegie, I have no doubt that you will say the former, that it is a pity that I am not better informed.

Mr. CARNEGIE. I do not want to have the pain of saying that to such a nice fellow, and it is well that he should remain for several days in the delusion that he is quite well up on the tariff question.

Mr. CROZIER. Possibly the delusion will be mutual.   Anyway, I am glad to excuse you if you prefer to go.

Mr. CARNEGIE. Yes; because I can not reply to-night.   I have been here all day.   I did not want to treat anybody with discourtesy.   I have tried the best I could to give you my opinions on this subject.   I may be wrong, I may be right.

Mr. CROZIER. We will be friends anyway.

Mr. Chairman, I will try to get to the point and not detain you over twenty or thirty minutes at the most.

In a recent magazine article Andrew Carnegie dealt a severe blow to the entire protective tariff system.   He has moved public opinion appreciably.   He has kindled wide doubt as to the wisdom, necessity, and value of protection.   His experience and knowledge of the subject and claim that he is a protectionist enabled him to do this.   But he is no longer a protectionist in the American sense, for he says: "A tariff for protection, which was the issue forty years ago, should now give place to a tariff for revenue."   He says the infant should be weaned from tariff milk and fed upon free competition.

Unfortunately, his article has created another impression among many.   Mr. Carnegie invoked and obtained the Government's protective arm to hold back foreign competition during the whole time he was, with his genius, building up his industry from nothing to where he sold it for some $300,000,000.   He took his pay largely in first mortgage bonds of the United States Steel Corporation.   He is said to be the largest owner of that trust, deriving therefrom some $15,000,000 annually.   Many believe now he is again invoking the Government's strong arm for his financial benefit or security.   That he wants it to now tear down the tariff wall and admit foreign competition to help his trust ruin and destroy its weaker competitors and to frighten capital so that it will not start new industries to compete with the trust. This would leave his corporation forever in undisputed possession of the American field. This may not be his intention or desire, but it would be the effect. His proposition doubtless was innocent and philanthropic, but many think it looks thrifty.

It would seem that he used the Federal Government to wet nurse his weakling infant until it has become the greatest of all industrial giants, and instead of weaning it from the Government he now asks for a law that would kill off all of the other infants, big and little, so that his giant may have all the profit milk the monopolistic leech can suck, both from the producers and consumers of America. He would encourage race suicide, for his plan would automatically suffocate all industrial infants of the iron and steel variety as soon as they are born.

Judge Gary told you frankly and on oath that free trade would not injure the steel trust; that it could take care of itself. Its splendid organization, huge size, vast power, due to railroad, financial, and political alliances, make its position impregnable against every foe but one. Only by an endless-chain absorption or by enormous loss of profits through fierce competition and cutting of prices can it protect itself against the constant menace of new industries that are induced to spring up by the attraction of rich profits from the high range of prices the trust must maintain to pay dividends on its vast capitalization. This is so, unless Mr. Carnegie's plan of destroying the tariff can be used to frighten capital and prevent the starting of such plants, for no one would risk his money if he had to fight a big trust and also the duty-free products of cheap foreign labor.

If foreign competition became annoying, the trust could effectively retaliate abroad and ultimately bring about an international trust that could evade regulating and restraining laws and combine, for mutual defense and profit, the iron and steel producers of the world. It would then be practicable and possible for the daring genius of high finance to reach its final goal—a universal monopoly of a human necessity that could, with high prices, extort excessive profits continuously and automatically from all mankind for the sole benefit of the few and gradually draining and weakening all peoples to a state tending toward final and helpless servitude. Wise statesmanship diverts at their source such evil currents.

Are antitrust laws justifiable? Is competition, such as contemplated by the common law for hundreds of years, wise? Is private monopoly abhorrent? Is it against public welfare to have control of all industry pass into the hands of a few men and ultimately come under the mastery of one human individual, crushing out all independent operators and forcing the entire citizenship into the hired service of one incorporated, soulless power? We are not drifting that way, but madly galloping.

If this be true, then there never was a time when the establishment of infant industries was more imperatively needed for the common good—not to develop the country, but to compete with the trusts, keep their prices down, and ward off the evil day of the annihilation of all competition, the establishment of complete monopoly, and perhaps a revolution started by the people in some desperate effort to free themselves from the powerful, concentrating, strangling incorporated clutch.

It is as important to the young man of to-day just starting in business life with courage, but without wealth, to have his little infant industry protected as it was for Mr. Carnegie when he was similarly situated. More so, for Mr. Carnegie was menaced only by the danger from abroad, as there were then no powerful trusts to fight him in the market here at home with all the effective means at their command, such as cheaper raw materials, better transportation accommodations and rates, lower interest charges, indirect duress upon purchasers, and the like.

Only the protective tariff can give him any chance and insure the starting of new plants to compete with the trusts and retain in the hands of the Government any effective power of regulation or control of combinations in restraint of trade. Destroy protection and thereafter our economic policies will not be controlled by our Government or its citizens, but largely by conditions abroad, over which we can have no effective control.

Perhaps I should have explained that I have no hostility toward corporations or wealth, no interest in any trust, no personal concern over any tariff schedule. My interest in this matter is only as an humble member of that large body of citizens who desire a good government that will perpetuate itself in the confidence and affections of all the people by adopting and executing policies that will insure to all, rich and poor alike, impartial equality before the law, industrial opportunity, and enjoyment of life, liberty, and the pursuit of happiness.

The tariff should be revised honestly, thoroughly, fearlessly, unselfishly. The people were promised and expect it. But they do not expect you to dump them out of the frying pan into the fire. They want readjustment with due regard to all the ultimate consequences to the welfare of the nation as a whole. It is a difficult task, but the people have confidence in your wisdom, caution, independence, impartiality, and patriotism.

Mr. Carnegie's enumeration of the objects of protection strangely omits the one great purpose of the policy, in fact, the one object which justified its adoption and won the popular support necessary to its continuance, namely, the welfare of American labor and agriculture.

If the protective tariff is abolished and the steel trust, for instance, becomes an international trust, its workmen will be at its mercy absolutely and always. And there is no certainty that its management will always be as wise respecting labor as it now is. If its employees here strike to prevent wage reduction or longer hours, the mills can be closed and the American market supplied from its mills abroad until its American workmen, their wives, and children are starved into submission. It will be comparatively easy to form kindred industries in different countries into international trusts, for capital and investment readily migrate anywhere in the world to the point of greatest profits consistent with safety. But it is not practicable to organize labor internationally.

The ultimate tendency of the policy of internationally consolidating industry, which removal of the tariff would hasten, will be to bring the wages paid to labor in all countries approximately to one common level. With the power of labor to protect itself by effective organization gone, and with human nature as it is, American wages would go down to the foreign level instead of foreign wages being advanced to the American standard. The trust would install American superintendents and improved machinery in its foreign mills. It doubtless would produce abroad with its cheaper labor exclusively if it could do so more cheaply, for the freight rate by water from Europe to the United States is less than it is by rail from Pittsburg to the seaboard. Inevitably wages here would ultimately be lowered or American mills closed altogether.

Marquis Ito, the distinguished Japanese economist, says the Chinese coolies can quickly be trained into the most docile and effective of skilled workmen in almost any kind of industry. There are tens of millions of these coolies ready to work for 10 cents a day. Capital is alive to its opportunity always, and China and Japan in time will rival this country in the number and size of its industries, largely owned by capitalists of this and other countries. There are hundreds of thousands of skilled workmen in Japan anxious to work for 30 cents a day. What is the use of laws excluding Asiatics for the protection of our labor if the tariff is to be removed and our trusts allowed to build great factories in Asia, managed by Americans, but employing cheap oriental labor, the products being shipped here duty free and sold at prices that will force American factories to close or reduce wages?

Already trusts producing oil, steel and iron, powder, tobacco, thread, and other products have taken steps looking toward world-wide control of prices—the first step toward the inevitable international trust.

It has been said that the protective tariff is the mother of trusts. Many good men believe this, but it is not true. However, it is the mother of industry, of that huge family of prosperous and growing industries that employ millions of American workmen, our citizens, at the highest average wages of all human history; and we are proud of her for that reason. But she did not give birth to the great monopolistic monstrosities called trusts. She has mothered agriculture also, and helped create the best home market in all the world.

Excessive and ruinous competition during the years following the panic of 1893 supplied the incentive and industrial bargains that led to the formation of most American trusts. But the real mother of trusts was Wall street. Few would have ever been formed but for its machinations and exigencies. Clever promoters, who since the success of their schemes are called great financiers and bankers, obtained options on different plants in a given industry. Then they formed a huge corporation with almost an endless amount of stock, but relatively no money. They caused the board of dummy directors, consisting of their office boys and irresponsible clerks, to "buy" such options, paying therefor the entire capital stock of the company. All this was valueless unless they could find some way to sell it for real money.

First, they tried, and usually succeeded, to pay for the plants under option by issuing to the original owners a comparatively small portion of the stock of the new company. This was genius, of its kind; the promoters thereby acquiring control and management and a good portion of the title to a lot of going concerns. All this for nothing, by simply promising the owners that Wall street, with its canny powers and machinery for public deception, would hypnotize the public into believing that the plants were worth several times more than the original owners ever dreamed of, so the people would take their savings from the banks and buy the stocks of the new trust to an extent that would enable the original owners and the promoters to unload at fictitious prices and make a clean-up. The scheme worked, thanks to the wizard ways of Wall street. The stock exchange was the wholesale agency and the screen that hid the perpetrators from the despoiled people. This was the way the overnight multimillionaires were made. This was the way trusts were born. The tariff had nothing to do with it.

If it is true, as reported, that Mr. Carnegie was willing to sell for one hundred millions what he afterwards sold to the trust for about $300,000,000, he can not be blamed for driving a good bargain with the promoters even if the people must now pay for it. But it serves to illustrate the basis on which cost of production is now figured, and gives a glimpse inside at the vastness of the volume of trust securities on which the public are expected to supply the money to pay dividends by paying high prices for trust products. The trusts must maintain these high prices or default on interest or dividends. To do this they must have a substantial monopoly. This can be had only by buying up competing plants as fast as they get troublesome, or by crushing them with competition, unless the plan to abolish the tariff can be made to destroy their weaker competitors for them.

One of the prime objects of the promoters of the trusts is said to have been the furnishing of several billions of securities that could be listed and artificially manipulated daily by the insiders as chips on Wall street's great gaming table, where by means that would not be used by the most hardened of professional gamblers the people of the entire country are enticed and daily fleeced out of their earnings and their properties. The legislature refused to act, so Governor Hughes has appointed a private committee to investigate Wall street. Their work will be more thorough and successful if the entire wronged country will promptly rise up and demand the abolition of margin gambling and usurious rates on call loans, the former exceeding in volume the value of all farm and manufactured products, the latter, with rates that often go up to 200 per cent, being the great magnet with which the money of the entire country is enticed away from legitimate business and into gambling uses.

In two years prices of stocks have fluctuated 40 to 150 per cent. An average drop of but 10 per cent on the entire market means a loss equal to all the money in circulation. Yet this is done continuously and artificially by the pools comprised of the same few men who have seized control of the big banks, insurance companies, railroads, trusts, and public currency, who create conditions that ruin the country with panics while they gamble away the prosperity of the nation. This situation is more important than the tariff question. It is dangerous to the public welfare. There is to be a finish fight between the masters of Wall street and the Government and the people of the United States.

Mr. UNDERWOOD. You understand that the jurisdiction of this committee is limited to revision of the tariff and the preparation of a tariff bill?

Mr. CROZIER. Yes.

Mr. UNDERWOOD. And that there are other committees of Congress that have the jurisdiction over those matters?

Mr. CROZIER. That is true, sir; but I want to show you that the organization and the watering of these trusts was to obtain a volume of securities which now amounts—the listed securities—to $25,000,-000,000 that they could list, and by artificial means make the prices fluctuate up and down for their profit and the public's loss. We have seen stocks change in price during the last two years from 40 to 150 per cent—good railroad stocks.

Mr. BONYNGE. We have to confine our examination to the tariff question.

Mr. CROZIER. Perhaps I ought not to go off into that. I see the whole thing together, because the same men are doing that kind of business, and all they have to do is to change the market 10 per cent to cause somebody to lose an amount equal to all the money in the country. I see in this proposition a scheme to tear down the tariff wall for the purpose, by those same men, of destroying the independent producers in this country, and then forming international trusts to protect the trusts here against importations from abroad, and then they will have the workingmen of the world at their mercy, and they will have the consumers of the world at their mercy; and it is for that reason that I have alluded to the fact that all these lines run into the same office in the city of New York, in Wall street, and that is the power that I believe is behind this movement to destroy the tariff upon steel rails and steel products, and it is for that reason that I am here to oppose it.

IRON AND STEEL.

BRIEF OF AMERICAN IRON AND STEEL ASSOCIATION RELATIVE TO TARIFF REVISION, WITH ESPECIAL REFERENCE TO A MAXIMUM AND MINIMUM TARIFF.

PHILADELPHIA, PA., *November 25, 1905.*

COMMITTEE ON WAYS AND MEANS,
Washington, D. C.

GENTLEMEN: The platform adopted by the Republican national convention at Chicago in June, 1908, after declaring " unequivocally for the revision of the tariff by a special session of Congress immediately following the inauguration of the next President," adds that " we favor the establishment of maximum and minimum rates to be administered by the President under limitations fixed in the law, the maximum to be available to meet discriminations by foreign countries against American goods entering their markets and the minimum to represent the normal measure of protection at home."

In accepting the Republican nomination for Congress at Auburn, N. Y., on August 31, Hon. Sereno E. Payne, the chairman of the

Ways and Means Committee and leader of the House, said: "Our rivals in trade, Germany and France, have adopted a maximum and a minimum tariff, and under our existing law we are unable to obtain their minimum rate without too great a sacrifice to American industry. We can only meet them on their own ground with a maximum and minimum tariff." Mr. Payne had previously declared in the House, on February 5, his belief in the wisdom of this kind of a tariff, adding that, "if we have a maximum and a minimum tariff, and the Republican party passes it, that minimum will be a protective tariff to every American industry and to every American laborer in the United States. The maximum will be higher, and in doing this we can be successfully accused of purloining some of the idea from Germany and France and Russia, each of which countries has the same kind of a maximum and minimum tariff."

Other public men who are prominent in the leadership of the Republican party have strongly approved and commended the scheme of a maximum and minimum tariff. On February 26 Hon. John Dalzell said in the House: "I believe with the chairman of the Committee on Ways and Means that we need a maximum and minimum tariff in order to meet the conditions created by foreign nations which have such systems. The minimum tariff must be protective; the maximum tariff will be in excess of that. The two will be so adjusted as to compel our entrance into foreign markets on as favorable terms as are given any other nations."

The Washington correspondent of the Iron Age for October 8 quotes a member of the subcommittee of the Senate Committee on Finance as expressing the following opinion: "I think that the most laborious task that will be encountered in connection with the coming revision will be the rearrangement of the tariff on a maximum and minimum basis, if, as now seems probable, that plan is finally adopted. I assume that the Dingley rates, with a few modifications, will be adopted as the minimum tariff and that the maximum will be fixed by adding certain percentages thereto."

Here, then, is the programme of the Republican leaders. There is, first, to be tariff revision, and, second, the new tariff is to be a maximum and minimum tariff. Indeed, the alleged necessity of counteracting the discrimination of maximum tariff rates against our commerce by some European countries is the sole reason assigned by Mr. Payne for tariff revision at all. Now, let us see if we can what sort of a maximum and minimum tariff the Republican leaders are likely to propose for adoption by the Congress which comes into power on the 4th of March next.

The plank in the Republican platform from which we have quoted at the beginning of this article says that the proposed minimum tariff is "to represent the normal measure of protection at home." What is this "normal measure?" Evidently it embraces duties which have been found necessary in the past to build up and maintain American industries. We are living to-day under duties which have operated so well for the protection of our home industries that the Republican Campaign Text-Book for 1908 says on page 100: "Since 1897 to the present time the Dingley law has been in operation, and under it the United States has shown a progress and prosperity never before known in the history of civilization." Obviously a tariff which has produced such marvelous results not only represents "the normal

measure of protection " for our industries but it should be continued
as our minimum tariff.

Mr. Taft said in his campaign speech at Bath, Me., on September 5, 1906, which was his bid for the Presidency, that " those schedules of the tariff which have inequalities and are excessive will be
readjusted," and in his speech at Milwaukee on September 24 of the
present year he said that " there are many schedules of the tariff in
which the rates are excessive," adding that " it is my judgment that
a revision of the tariff in accordance with the pledge of the Republican platform will be on the whole a substantial revision downward."
Mr. Taft, therefore, says in effect to Mr. Payne, Mr. Dalzell, and
other Republican leaders in Congress: " Your minimum tariff can not
be the Dingley tariff, or embody any rates of duty which approach it
for protective purposes, because I have already decided that the
maximum tariff must be a revision of the Dingley tariff downward."
If some of the Dingley rates are too high and must be reduced how
can these rates be incorporated in a minimum tariff? And if the
maximum rates of the new tariff are to be lower than the Dingley
rates what measure of protection against English, German, and other
European manufacturers will the minimum rates embody? Just
none at all. Is it possible that protectionists can not see the trap
into which free traders are trying to lead them?

We object to a maximum and minimum tariff, because its substitutes for our present tariff policy of uniform treatment of other countries a huckstering policy that will give some countries advantages in
our markets over others, and that is sure to increase our imports of
manufactured products to the serious injury of our own people. As
a reason for the adoption of a maximum and minimum tariff the ad-
vocates of that policy say that the exports of some of our products
will be increased. In making this plea they completely ignore the
fact that our exports have steadily and enormously increased under
the Dingley tariff, and they also ignore the further fact that under
any tariff system we may adopt foreign countries will buy from us
only those products that they can not get at home, like our bread-
stuffs, provisions, petroleum, and cotton.

We emphasize the fact that the free traders in the Republican party
want to increase our imports of foreign commodities. That is what
Mr. Oscar S. Straus, himself an importer, and other New York importers, Democrats and Republicans, are aiming at. That is what
Mr. Roosevelt has already accomplished with his German agreement,
one result of which is that right here in Philadelphia the workmen
in at least one textile factory are walking the streets without work.

By our present tariff system all countries are treated alike and we
maintain friendly relations with all. By a maximum and minimum
tariff policy we would derange our customs service, imposing one set
of duties upon the imports from one country and another set upon
the imports from another country, and opening the door much wider
than it is now to frauds upon the revenue. It would greatly
reduce the revenue of the Government through the lower duties
that would be imposed. That our imports of manufactured goods
would greatly increase there can be no doubt whatever. It will
be noticed that Mr. Payne specifically names " our rivals in trade,"
Germany and France, as countries to which it would be desirable to
apply maximum and minimum tariff rates. These are great manufacturing countries. They would not under any circumstances send

us beef, or pork, or flour, but they are hungering to send us more and more of the products of their factories, which they operate with low-priced labor. And, then, there is Great Britain, also a great manufacturing country. As the British tariff does not discriminate against the products of our country we could not avoid conceding to it the same minimum rates of duty that we would grant to Germany and France. How long would this country be able to maintain anything approximating the activity of the last few years with German, French, and British goods flooding our markets?

Whatever may be the fate of the Dingley tariff at the hands of the Sixty-first Congress a maximum and minimum tariff should be an impossibility. It should be condemned and beaten at the start by the good sense and the courage of all sincere believers in our time-honored protective policy.

THE COST OF PRODUCTION A DELUSION.

The Republican platform which was adopted at Chicago in June last contained this declaration: "In all tariff legislation the true principle of protection is best maintained by the imposition of such duties as will equal the difference between the cost of production at home and abroad." In Mr. Taft's speech of acceptance he approved this declaration in the following words: "The tariff in a number of the schedules exceeds the difference between the cost of production of such articles abroad and at home, including a reasonable profit to the American producer. The excess over that difference serves no useful purpose, but offers a temptation to those who would monopolize the production and the sale of such articles in this country to profit by the excessive rate." Mr. Taft's indorsement of the cost of production policy is couched in language which clearly shows that he considers tariff duties that are in excess of the difference in cost of production at home and abroad as taxes which can be added to the home cost and which afford ready opportunity for the creation of monopolies. These are genuine free-trade pleas, the truth of which has never been established, as we have no tariff-made monopolies; but they need not be dwelt upon, as we desire to call attention to other phases of this question.

One objection to the declaration in the Chicago platform above quoted is that the cost of production either at home or abroad is never a fixed quantity, but always a shifting quantity. The cost of production of any manufactured product varies in all manufacturing countries from year to year and often from month to month, as everybody knows. Shall we have a sliding-scale tariff adapted to these varying costs? If not, what becomes of the Chicago plan which Mr. Taft has approved? Then, again, the cost of production in one foreign country differs from that in another country, as, for instance, in Great Britain and Germany. Which country is to serve as a guide in the construction of the new tariff? And, again, who is to ascertain the cost of production, either at home or abroad? Will the foreigners tell? Will the cost statistics obtained by Mr. Roosevelt's "experts," upon which they have been at work all summer, be worth the paper they are written on six months hence?

Another and an equally fatal objection to the Chicago plan of framing tariff schedules is that various devices are resorted to in some foreign countries to effect sales of their products abroad at prices below the cost of production. It is well known that special railroad freight rates are made by the German Government on State railroads to facilitate the sales abroad of German products, and that syndicates exist in that country which also stimulate these sales by sharing the losses entailed in selling abroad at lower than home prices. Are the framers of our new tariff to take account of these helps to the foreign trade of Germany, or of similar helps to the foreign trade of other countries? What is to be the measure of protection against the dumping on our markets of foreign products so sold, or of any foreign products that may be sent to this country to be sold at prices below the cost of production to get rid of a surplus or to meet a financial necessity? The Chicago platform is silent on these questions.

IRON AND STEEL PRICES TO FOREIGN BUYERS.

With regard to the prices at which our iron and steel products have been sold abroad, it can be said with entire frankness that, while there have been sales made at lower prices than have been charged to domestic consumers, the large majority of the sales have been made at the same prices as have been obtained at home, or at even higher prices. When lower prices have been charged, the inducement to do this has been (1) to dispose of a surplus, as during the years of depression following the panic of 1893 or during the reactionary year 1900, or (2) to secure entrance into a desirable foreign market, or (3) to retain a foothold in a foreign market that has already yielded profitable returns. These reasons for the occasional cutting of prices require no defense. They are akin to the reasons which govern the sales of manufactured and all other products in domestic markets and at the "bargain counters" of our department stores.

Even in years of prosperity it sometimes happens that a rolling mill or steel works, when running to its full capacity, produces a surplus of its products beyond the immediate wants of its customers or of the general market. If this surplus can be sold abroad, even at prices below current quotations, it is better to do this than to reduce production by stopping the rolling mill or steel works for a few days, or even for one day. The workmen would not only lose their wages during the stoppage, but the manufacturers would lose in many ways. As one incident of the stoppage, the home consumers of their products could not be supplied so cheaply as when the plants are running full. A moment's reflection will convince any candid man that the manufacturing establishment that is not kept constantly employed, whether it produces iron, or steel, or cotton goods, or woolen goods, or pottery, or glassware, or any other articles, can not be operated so economically for its owners or so beneficially for its customers as the establishment that is kept running six days in the week and every week in the year.

It should also be remembered that our tariff legislation for more than a generation has encouraged our manufacturers to seek foreign markets by remitting nearly all the duties levied on imported raw materials when these raw materials enter into the manufacture of exported finished products. Under the operation of this drawback system our iron and steel manufacturers have been able to manufacture their products intended for foreign markets at a lower cost than they could supply similar products to home consumers. Pig iron, iron ore, spiegeleisen, and ferromanganese enter into the composition of steel rails, for instance, and when imported are dutiable, but 99 per cent of the duty paid on any of these products is remitted when they are used in the manufacture of rails for export. So with the pig iron that is imported to be manufactured into cast-iron pipe, and which is dutiable at $4 per gross ton. The remission of $3.96 of the duty on a ton of imported pig iron may enable our cast-iron pipe manufacturers to buy cheap foreign pig iron and to sell their pipe in foreign markets. The London Engineering for January 17, 1902, said of this drawback system: "A certain amount of trade is brought into the country that would otherwise be missed and no one loses anything."

Finally it may be said that nearly all the money that is paid by foreigners for American steel rails or for other steel products of American manufacture, no matter at what prices they may be sold, and irrespective of the sources of supply of raw materials, is paid to American labor that is engaged in their manufacture and that fully the half of this money finds its way into the pockets of American farmers. Both the workingman and the farmer should be thankful that our protective tariff policy, through its cheapening influence on the cost of production, by guaranteeing to capital the possession of the home markets and stimulating competition has enabled our manufacturers to sell a part of their products in foreign markets, even if they sometimes sell at a loss. If manufacturers lose, that is their misfortune; the workingmen receive their wages all the same and the farmers get their full share of these wages.

Other countries recognize the economic necessity of keeping their manufacturing establishments fully employed, and habitually sell their surplus products in foreign markets at cut prices. Great Britain and Germany are conspicuous examples of the truth of this statement. American free traders do not complain of the methods adopted by other countries to sell their surplus products, made by cheap labor, in our markets. Their criticism is reserved for the manufacturers of our own country who employ American labor and pay it good wages.

An English writer in Cassier's Magazine for July, 1908, complaining of German competition in English steel markets, says: "The chief factor in the promotion of Germany's foreign trade these last ten years has been the policy of granting cooperative bounties on steel goods for export."

PRICES OF STEEL RAILS IN FREE-TRADE ENGLAND.

The following table, for which we are indebted to Mr. J. S. Jeans, late secretary of the British Iron Trade Association, gives the average annual prices of steel rails at Middlesborough, England, per gross ton, from 1895 to 1905, in American currency, with which we compare the average prices of steel rails in the United States for the same years. We have ourselves reduced the English prices to American equivalents:

	England.	United States.
1895	$21.89	$24.33
1896	21.69	28.00
1897	23.35	18.75
1898	23.49	17.62
1899	26.80	28.12
1900	36.01	32.29
1901	29.45	27.33
1902	27.37	28.00
1903	27.97	28.00
1904	22.48	28.00
1905	26.05	28.00
Average for 11 years.	26.05	26.22

The prices of steel rails in England in 1906 and 1907 are given in the following extract from a letter we have received from a trustworthy English correspondent: "I have made inquiries with reference to the prices of steel rails in 1906 and in 1907. In 1906 they ranged from £5 10s. ($26.76) to £6 ($29.20). Early in 1907 they went up to about £7 ($34.06) until about the middle of the year, and then they gradually declined to £6 5s. ($30.41) in November and December. These prices were given me by a London firm, but they tell me that the prices were the same in Middlesborough, as the prices are controlled by the British Rail Syndicate."

Below will be found a table giving the average monthly prices of British and American Bessemer steel rails from January 1, 1906, to August 31, 1908. The British prices, which we have reduced to American equivalents, are for rails free on board at Middlesborough, and the American prices are for rails at mills in Pennsylvania. The British prices are compiled from quotations in the Iron and Coal Trades Review, the leading iron-trade paper published in the United Kingdom. In 1906 and 1907 the maximum price for British steel rails was reached in August, 1907, the price during the whole month ranging $5.45 per ton above the American price. The average yearly price for English steel rails in 1906 was $30.73 per ton; in 1907 it was $32.59, and in the eight months of 1908 it was $28.97. The uniform price of American steel rails from 1902 to 1908 has been $28.

Months.	British prices and American equivalents.	Prices of American steel rails.	British prices over American.
1906.	£ s. d.		
January	6 0 7 = $29.35	$28.00	$1.35
February	6 3 1 = 29.95	28.00	1.95
March	6 5 0 = 30.41	28.00	2.41
April	6 5 0 = 30.41	28.00	2.41
May	6 7 0 = 30.89	28.00	2.89
June	6 7 6 = 31.02	28.00	3.02
July	6 7 6 = 31.02	28.00	3.02
August	6 7 6 = 31.02	28.00	3.02
September	6 7 6 = 31.02	28.00	3.02
October	6 7 6 = 31.02	28.00	3.02
November	6 7 6 = 31.02	28.00	3.02
December	6 10 0 = 31.63	28.00	3.63
1907.			
January	6 12 6 = 32.23	28.00	4.23
February	6 15 0 = 32.84	28.00	4.84
March	6 15 0 = 32.84	28.00	4.84
April	6 15 0 = 32.84	28.00	4.84
May	6 15 0 = 32.84	28.00	4.84
June	6 15 0 = 32.84	28.00	4.84

Months.	British prices and American equivalents.			Prices of American steel rails.	British prices over American.
1907.	£	s.	d.		
July	6	15	0 = 32.84	$28.00	$4.84
August	6	17	6 = 33.45	28.00	5.45
September	6	15	0 = 32.84	28.00	4.84
October	6	15	0 = 32.84	28.00	4.84
November	6	10	0 = 31.63	28.00	3.63
December	6	7	6 = 31.02	28.00	3.02
1908.					
January	6	2	6 = 29.80	28.00	1.80
February	6	2	6 = 29.80	28.00	1.80
March	6	0	7 = 29.35	28.00	1.35
April	5	18	6 = 28.82	28.00	.82
May	5	17	6 = 28.58	28.00	.58
June	5	17	6 = 28.58	28.00	.58
July	5	17	6 = 28.58	28.00	.58
August	5	16	3 = 28.28	28.00	.28

The above prices for 1906 and 1907 do not exactly correspond with others which have been given to us by our English correspondent, but they do agree in giving English prices in these two years at much higher figures than the uniform price that prevailed in our own country. If American railroad companies had been compelled to purchase British rails during the period covered by the above table at the prices prevailing in England the additional cost to them would have been at least $27,000,000.

We reproduce the above tables and the supplementary statements because they are a complete answer to those free traders of all political parties who are constantly alleging that American railroad companies are charged extortionate prices for steel rails as a result of the protective duty on rails. The duty on steel rails is $7.84 per ton. Where in the figures we have given can the free trader find this duty or any part of it added to the English price?

It may be asked, If steel rails are made in this country and sold at lower prices than in free-trade England, why is any duty on steel rails needed? Because England does not make all the rails that might be sold in our markets; Germany and Belgium are large producers; and because duties on foreign products should be placed high enough to prevent them from being unloaded upon our markets in periods of great depression abroad and great industrial activity at home, when foreign prices fall so low that we could not possibly compete with them. A protective duty on steel rails is also needed to protect our steel-rail makers, and the producers of the raw materials which enter into their manufacture, from the competition which is made possible by continental syndicates and export bounties.

NO MONOPOLY IN THE IRON TRADE.

To refute a common free-trade charge, we republish from our annual report for 1907 the following table, which gives the percentages of production of all leading iron and steel products by the United States Steel Corporation and by independent companies in the year 1907. It also gives for the same year the percentages of shipments of iron ore by the corporation and also by the independent companies from the Lake Superior region, and the percentages of the total production of iron ore and also of coke in the whole country by the corporation and by the independent companies. The statistics of the total shipments of iron ore from the Lake Superior region and of the production of iron and steel we obtain from the Annual Report of the American Iron and Steel Association for 1907, and the statistics of the country's total production of iron ore and coke we have obtained from the publications of the division of mining and mineral resources of the United States Geological Survey, the corporation reporting to us its share of these shipments and production.

Statement of the products of the United States Steel Corporation and of independent companies in 1907 by percentages.

	1907.	
	Corporation.	Independents
Shipments of Lake Superior iron ore	51.7	45.3
Total production of iron ore	43.3	55.7
Production of coke	30.3	69.7
Spiegeleisen and ferromanganese	54.9	45.1
All other pig iron, ferrosilicon, etc	41.7	58.3
Total pig iron, including spiegeleisen, etc	41.9	58.1
Bessemer steel ingots and castings	64.7	35.3
Open-hearth steel ingots and castings	47.9	52.1
Total of above ingots and castings	56.4	43.6
Bessemer steel rails	51.6	48.4
Structural shapes	54.9	45.1
Plates and sheets, excluding nail plate	55.8	44.2
Wire rods	71.5	28.5
Bars, open-hearth and iron rails, skelp, nail plate, etc	33.9	66.1
Total of all finished rolled products	47.5	52.5
Wire nails	66.4	33.6
Tin plates and terne plates	72.6	22.4

This table completely disproves the statement so often made that the United States Steel Corporation is a monopoly which controls the iron and steel industries of the country, and that it stifles all competition in these lines of industrial development. Indeed, there is one branch of the steel industry in which it is not engaged at all—the manufacture of crucible steel.

JAMES M. SWANK,
General Manager American Iron and Steel Association.

IRON AND STEEL PRODUCTS.

CHARLES EUGENE CLARK, COVINGTON, KY., ASKS NECESSARY PROTECTION FOR THE SMALLER PRODUCER.

CHICAGO, *December 18, 1908.*

COMMITTEE ON WAYS AND MEANS,
Washington, D. C.

DEAR SIRS: Having been formerly engaged in the iron-foundry business in Covington, Ky., where I now reside, I desire to state such facts as have come to my knowledge from my connection with the iron industry.

In my brief experience I always found that the small manufacturer and producer paid more for labor and got smaller results from his business and its investment than the larger producer.

The percentage and average cost of production of an article of the iron and steel industries is smaller to the large operator than to the small operator, who is always at a disadvantage.

The average ironworker, "employee," always feels that he should receive a larger price per ton for his work than an employee doing similar work in a plant of greater capacity, because the output, or tonnage, in the large mill far exceeds in a given number of hours, or heats, that of a smaller plant.

The larger plants are always equipped with the latest machinery, are most ably managed, and larger and better results accrue to both employer and employee in same than will accrue to the owner and employee of the smaller mill, or manufactory, because it is absolutely physically impossible for the smaller mill to produce the weight of metal in the same given hours as the larger mill. Consequently the ironworker is dissatisfied in the smaller plant, wants a better scale, and the better or more skillful workmen naturally drift to the big mills, where they can produce the bigger tonnage in a given time and secure a greater recompense for their labor.

So you see that the smaller producer always labors under a great disadvantage.

If protection is of advantage to the iron and steel industry, then surely the small producer stands in sore need of it. The larger producers, such as the United States Steel Company, The Republic Iron and Steel Company, and the Sloss-Sheffield Company, with their immense plants, great coal and iron fields, could produce steel and iron under a modified tariff profitably, perhaps, when the smaller producer would under the same reduction be compelled to run at an inadequate profit, or driven to bankruptcy.

In my humble judgment, it is necessary to adequately protect the iron and steel industries in order that the smaller producers shall not be driven out of business and wiped off of the map.

He who bores with a big auger produces large results, while he who bores with a smaller one produces less results, but all are necessary factors in fulfilling the wants of the nation and adding to its wealth and prosperity.

Very sincerely, yours,   CHAS. EUGENE CLARK.

————

HON. W. BOURKE COCKRAN, M. C., FILES LETTER OF J. E. YOUNG, OF CHICAGO, ILL., RELATIVE TO PRICES OF RAILS.

71 PARK AVENUE,
Chicago, December 25, 1908.

Hon. BOURKE COCKRAN, M. C.

DEAR SIR: In the report of the examination of Mr. Carnegie before your tariff committee, as made by yourself, it appeared to me that your aim was to get at the real merits of the case and not to bolster up any particular theory. There is one item having a bearing on Mr. Carnegie's management as contrasted with the trust, to which I wish to draw your attention. For several years before Mr. Carnegie sold to the trust his plant, he sold his rails at $18 a ton. This was his price up to the date of the transfer and had been for several years, but within thirty days of the transfer to the trust, the latter put the price of rails to $28 a ton. Carnegie made his money at the price named, and the trust pays the interest on the watered stock out of the extra $10 charged.

Very respectfully,

J. E. YOUNG.

MANGANESE STEEL RAILS.

STATEMENT OF GEORGE H. LARGE, FLEMINGTON, N. J., REPRE- SENTING TAYLOR IRON AND STEEL COMPANY.

WEDNESDAY, *November 25, 1908.*

Mr. GRIGGS. You have heard my first question, have you not?

Mr. LARGE. I do not think I have.

Mr. GRIGGS. Is your company making any money?

Mr. LARGE. I hope we are. Now, I appear before the committee not as a practical iron man. Our secretary, Mr. Budlong, is here, and if there are any particular questions to be asked I will have to call upon him to answer them. I have here a very crude, short brief on a point or two which we desire to make, and I have a copy here for each member of the committee. This concern, for which I wish to say but a word or two, is an absolutely independent iron manufacturer, and they are located in the village of High Bridge, in central New Jersey, and it is a concern which for the past ten or eleven years has been engaged more specifically in the manufacture of new articles in which this element of manganese is the principal factor, creating products which are especially hard, and many of which have been in use but a comparatively few years. This is a list of many of these things in a leaflet which is added to this short brief. I will read just a few of them. They are the wearing parts of all kinds of machines used for crushing and grinding ores, rock, coal, coke, matte, slag, and so forth; screens and grates for sizing such material before and after crushing; sprocket wheels, detachable link belting, and so on; a whole lot of things; for instance, the teeth on a steam shovel bucket, things on which the wear is very great, and which require a very hard substance. Our company thought that in contemplation of this revision of the tariff the language of the act of 1897 was so crude and so imperfect, not meeting the requirements of these new products, that is was incumbent upon them to call the attention of the committee especially to that fact, and ask that in their recommendation to Congress they give the products which we produce due consideration. There are two or three of these points. In the first place, paragraph 130 reads:

130. Railway bars, made of iron or steel, and railway bars made in part of steel, T rails, and punched iron or steel flat rails, seven-twentieths of 1 cent per pound; railway fish-plates or splice-bars, made of iron or steel, four-tenths of 1 cent per pound.

Of course that section did not contemplate these manganese steel rails, and therefore we suggest that that section, if that same classification is to be maintained, be amended so as to read as follows:

Railway bars made of iron or steel and railway bars made in part of steel, T rails, punched iron or steel flat rails and girder rails, frogs, switches and parts thereof which when completed shall contain at least 7 per cent of manganese, 30 per cent ad valorem.

That is what they conceive a fair and equitable duty to be placed upon those manganese steel rails.

In the second place, as to castings, under paragraph 135, they would ask that that section should be amended as to all descriptions and shapes of dry sand, loam, or iron-molded steel castings; sheets and plates and steel in all forms and shapes not specially provided for in this act which shall contain at least 7 per cent of manganese, and that the duty on that should be an ad valorem duty of 30 per cent. That, as I take it, leaves it practically as it is now, because that section says at its close, " valued above 16 cents per pound, 4.7 cents per pound." That would be equivalent—that 4.7 cents would be equivalent—to 30 per cent ad valorem; so that if that section contains that which I have read, that would be satisfactory to them.

Now, they are in grave doubt as to just where they stand, because of the inadequacy of this act of 1897. They do not know just what duties are to be imposed upon the various products which they have made, none of which were in existence at the time of the passage of that act, and there has not been any experience upon it whereby they may know just where they stand as to the duties.

Mr. GRIGGS. Is not this a patented article?

Mr. LARGE. There are patents, a number of them, but the patents are not effective, in fact. They do not materialize.

The CHAIRMAN. Did you ever try to enforce them?

Mr. LARGE. No, sir; that is the difficulty.

The CHAIRMAN. You never tried to enforce them?

Mr. LARGE. No, sir.

The CHAIRMAN. A patent will not enforce itself unless it has a man behind it.

Mr. LARGE. That is true, but everyone familiar with patent law knows that it is a very uncertain proposition.

The CHAIRMAN. Are you having any competition from abroad now?

Mr. LARGE. It has just commenced. It has not developed yet to any serious extent. They do not know whether these articles which they are making come under that article 193, which reads:

193. Articles or wares not specially provided for in this act, composed wholly or in part of iron, steel, lead, copper, nickel, pewter, zinc, gold, silver, platinum, aluminum, or other metal, and whether partly or wholly manufactured, 45 per cent ad valorem.

If that general dragnet clause applies, that makes a greater duty than they think they could stand under. In other words, they would be perfectly content, if these various articles come in under that section 193, when they do come in in any considerable volume, that an ad valorem duty of 30 per cent instead of 45 per cent should be imposed, as it is in that section.

Mr. UNDERWOOD. You are willing to have a reduction, but you want the language changed?

Mr. LARGE. Yes, and we want these articles specifically enumerated in any provision that may be recommended. And as I say, we have some of them named here in this leaflet annexed to the brief, and I propose with the consent of this committee to get up a little more elaborate brief than this, enumerating the list of articles which we think should be enumerated.

The CHAIRMAN. We will not be able to print that railroad article in the brief, with illustrations, in our printed hearings. Under the law we can not do it unless the chairman makes a certificate which he can not make.

Mr. LARGE. My proposition is now to submit to this committee a more complete brief.

The CHAIRMAN. You want to revise your brief and send it in?

Mr. LARGE. Yes.

The CHAIRMAN. All right.

Mr. LARGE. That is what we want to do.

The CHAIRMAN. Very well.

Mr. GRIGGS. This printed circular says:

Mr. Hadfield's first patents covered the alloy with the percentage of manganese stated, and the rights for making the alloy in the United States were secured by the Taylor Iron and Steel Company, High Bridge, N. J. William Wharton, jr., & Co., of Philadelphia, first made use of manganese steel in frog and switch work in this country.

You say that patent is no good?

Mr. LARGE. No; I do not say that, but the Hadfield patent, as I understand, has expired. Am I right in that?

Mr. BUDLONG. The basic patent expired.

Mr. GRIGGS. The basic patent has expired?

Mr. LARGE. Yes, sir.

Mr. GRIGGS. You have had twenty years of it, have you not?

Mr. LARGE. No, sir; because they have not been using it that length of time.

Mr. CLARK. You say the Dingley bill was not drawn properly?

Mr. LARGE. No; I did not say that. I said that the act of 1897 did not provide for these articles that these people make, because at the time of the passage of that act they were not in the process of manufacture. They have educated the people of the country up to the use of the things which they are now making.

Mr. CLARK. I understood you to say three or four times that the Dingley bill was inadequately drawn.

Mr. LARGE. To meet their particular products.

Mr. CLARK. Yet the Dingley bill has been held up in the United States for eleven years as the very perfection of human ingenuity.

Mr. LARGE. The things which our company manufacture and produce were not in evidence at the time of the passage of that bill, and hence they could not provide for them.

Mr. CLARK. They were in embryo?

Mr. LARGE. In embryo; that is it exactly.

The CHAIRMAN. Were you manufacturing these things when the Dingley bill was enacted?

Mr. LARGE. Some of them.

The CHAIRMAN. Did you bring the matter before the committee?

Mr. LARGE. No, sir.

The CHAIRMAN. It is strange that the Dingley committee did not know all about that.

Mr. CLARK. You will get yourself in contempt for lese majeste if you talk that way around here.

Mr. LARGE. I do not think that these things were presented at that time.

Mr. CLARK. How much are you getting now?

Mr. LARGE. That is one of the difficulties; we do not know where we are at.

Mr. CLARK. How much do you want? You know that?

Mr. LARGE. I stated that.

Mr. CLARK. Yes; but you stated it so that no one could tell what——

Mr. LARGE. We want steel rails that contain at least 7 per cent of this manganese (and by the way we pay $4 a ton on that ferro-manganese that is imported into this country. We are handicapped on that at the outset in that way) to pay at least 30 per cent ad valorem.

Mr. CLARK. Handicapped how?

Mr. LARGE. As against the foreign manufacturer, by the payment of that duty.

Mr. CLARK. Did you not know that Colonel Cook, of Colorado, has a bill pending before this committee now to increase the duties on manganese ores?

Mr. LARGE. Manganese ores now are free.

Mr. CLARK. Yes, I know; but he wants to put a duty on them. How would that strike you?

Mr. LARGE. What we use is the ferro-manganese.

Mr. BONYNGE. That is different from the manganese ore?

Mr. LARGE. Yes, sir; manganese ore is on the free list to-day. The ferro-manganese which we use, as I say, 60 per cent of that is a Russian product. Eighty per cent of all that is used in this country is imported, and the remaining 20 per cent is produced by a few concerns, which is a part of what they use.

Mr. CLARK. That is the ferro-manganese?

Mr. LARGE. That is the ferro-manganese.

Mr. CLARK. What is ferro-manganese?

Mr. LARGE. It is a product of manganese ore, as I understand. Hold on; I stated in the outset that when you come to such questions as that I do not pretend to be qualified to answer.

Mr. CLARK. Are you a manufacturer?

Mr. LARGE. I am a lawyer, and interested in this concern.

Mr. CLARK. You do not know much about it, yourself?

Mr. LARGE. No, sir; I do not pretend to.

Mr. CLARK. What I am trying to get at is, suppose this committee were to conclude that they would report Colonel Cook's bill favorably and get it passed; how would that affect you?

Mr. LARGE. That is, to put a duty on manganese ore?

The CHAIRMAN. Of 40 cents a ton; that is what he wants.

Mr. LARGE. Anything which would increase the cost of the ferro-manganese which we have to buy would, of course, require a greater duty to help us out.

Mr. CLARK. It is like the house that Jack built.

Mr. LARGE. But if you take the duty off ferro-manganese, of course we could produce it for that much less.

Mr. GRIGGS. The minute you put manganese in iron to the amount of 20 per cent, and not over 20 per cent, you have a patent, and you are protected from the whole world.

Mr. LARGE. We have not patents that will protect us.

Mr. GRIGGS. How much does the product of this concern amount to?

Mr. LARGE. Annually?

Mr. GRIGGS. Yes.

Mr. LARGE. I should say something over a million.

The CHAIRMAN. Is it increasing?

Mr. LARGE. Yes, sir; it is increasing, because the use of these articles is coming more and more into vogue every day.

The CHAIRMAN. Are you making a profit out of it now?

Mr. LARGE. We are making a scant living.

The CHAIRMAN. What duty do you pay—45 per cent?

Mr. LARGE. It depends on what the various articles are that we make.

The CHAIRMAN. What duty does the Government collect now, this day?

Mr. LARGE. On what particular articles?

The CHAIRMAN. On the particular article that you are talking about?

Mr. LARGE. We have a great variety of them. This is in a great variety of things.

The CHAIRMAN. These rails you are talking about?

Mr. LARGE. I can not answer as to them.

The CHAIRMAN. Can you answer as to any part of it?

Mr. LARGE. No, sir.

The CHAIRMAN. All right. If you find that out some day, just send us a brief.

Mr. LARGE. We have made some effort to ascertain just what the duty on these manganese rails is.

The CHAIRMAN. It must be because there are none imported if you can not find it out.

Mr. LARGE. There are very few.

The CHAIRMAN. If there are none imported, I do not see what you want with the duty.

Mr. HILL. You understand Mr. Butler, speaking for the iron manufacturers, recommends the abolition of the duty on ferro-manganese of $4 a ton?

Mr. LARGE. Yes; I understand that.

Mr. HILL. Would that be any benefit to you if it were done?

Mr. LARGE. Yes, sir; pro tanto. Yet because the great element in the cost with us is the labor—finishing the articles up.

Mr. HILL. That would be good as far as it went?

Mr. LARGE. Yes, sir. I think that is all.

STEEL COST.

ENGLISH AUTHORITIES DENY THAT STEEL CAN BE MADE AS CHEAP IN AMERICA AS IN ENGLAND.

520–522 ELLICOTT STREET,
Buffalo, N. Y., January 12, 1909.

Hon. SERENO PAYNE,
Washington, D. C.

DEAR SIR: Your committee may be conversant with the statements in inclosed article. If not, it may interest you to know what our English friends (?) have to say.

Yours, truly,   CHARLES ROHLFS.

[From Journal of the Royal Society of Arts, London, England, January 1, 1909.]

THE COST OF STEEL PRODUCTION.

Mr. Carnegie's recent assertion that steel can be made at less cost in the United States than in this country is not supported by figures or accepted by authorities here. There is no good reason why steel should be made more cheaply in Pittsburg than Sheffield. On the contrary, we have coal, iron, furnaces, and harbors all within easy distance, whereas the enormous distances which separate the iron-ore deposits and the coal fields and the manufacturing plants from the seaboard in America severely handicap the American steel trade. In cheap and convenient supplies of minerals, in geographical situation, in sound capitalization, and in skillful labor the United Kingdom holds a combination of advantages enjoyed by no other country. It may be, says a Sheffield correspondent of the Manchester Guardian, that if the comparison is between the prime cost of a ton of American rails rolled from "piped" ingots insufficiently "cropped"—rails of which about one in every four is defective and the quality of which is deliberately sacrificed to tonnage manufacture—and British rails rolled out of the solid only, Mr. Carnegie's statement may be correct. But taking quality for quality it may well be challenged. Between 1900 and 1907 the price of pig iron was on the average about 17 shillings per ton higher in the United States than in this country. That "price" is not "cost," but there is nothing to show that the American iron smelter, with his high price, has made any greater profit per ton than the British smelter, with his much lower price. With pig iron ranging from about 6 shillings to 29 shillings per ton higher in America than here it would be strange indeed if it were the fact that the cheapest steel in the world is produced in the United States. Mr. J. S. Jeans, a very high authority on the subject, has said that iron and steel profits are somewhat less, generally, in America than in Great Britain, and Mr. Gary, the chairman of the Steel trust, recently declared that pig iron can be made at $3.65 per ton less in England than in America. In 1906-7 pig iron was about $5 a ton dearer in the United States than in England, and the prices of most other products correspondingly high, yet several of the large American iron and steel concerns were not able to make anything like a stand when financial depression overtook them. Threatened industries, like threatened men, sometimes live long, and American predictions about British iron goods have been completely falsified. Excessive capital charges hang like a millstone round the neck of American industry; the cost of construction, repairs, and removals per ton of output is extravagant in America as compared with this country, and the capital charges of the independent iron and steel concerns of the United States are roughly three times those of British works, while the capital charges of the United States Steel Corporation are about equal to $100 per ton of productive capacity. It may well be doubted whether the British steel industry has in the immediate future as much to fear from the competition of the United States in the world's markets as from that of Germany, nor has it anything to fear from Germany, if only it fully utilizes its advantages and capabilities.

STEEL AND NICKEL.

[Paragraphs 132, 135, 141, and 185.]

STATEMENT OF J. B. WILKINSON, ATTORNEY FOR CERTAIN NEW YORK IMPORTERS OF STEEL PRODUCTS.

WEDNESDAY, *November 25, 1908.*

I appear before your honorable committee on behalf of George Nash Company, J. Wilckes Company, and Hermann Boker & Co., all of them New York importers of steel.

My clients are practical business men. They are not requesting that the duty be taken off steel, and they are not clamoring for much lower duties, but they do ask that what business they have left be not killed by higher duties, levied either directly or indirectly.

The tariff on steel, as has been shown, is in most cases prohibitive. Out of $332,000,000 of tariff revenue for the year 1907 only $12,000,000 or 3.7 per cent came from iron, steel, and manufactures thereof. The importation of bars, railway iron, or steel was only $133,936, against $8,600,000 exported; hoop, band, or scroll iron $129,100, as against $267,939; sheets, plates, and taggers, iron or steel, $315,000, as against $6,630,000; wire, $1,000,000 imported, $8,000,000 exported; and structural shapes, $328,000 imported, $6,900,000 exported. In 1905 the domestic production of structural shapes was over $90,000,000. In 1906 pig iron produced amounted to $505,000,000, and that imported to $7,000,000. All of these figures are taken from the last United States Statistical Abstract. Comparisons made to-day would be even more striking.

It does not seem unreasonable, therefore, to ask for importers the preservation of some remnants of the metal schedule and to call attention to the efforts that may be made to make the schedule absolutely prohibitive. I shall confine myself strictly to the paragraphs in regard to which I am commissioned to appear.

The most important of these is paragraph 135, one of the few paragraphs not prohibitive. The material covered by this paragraph is iron and steel to be manufactured in this country into products ready for consumption. The rate of duty ranges, except on the cheaper grades, from about 25 per cent to 30 per cent. On the grade imported for tool steel, for instance, valued between 3 and 4 cents a pound, the duty is over 40 per cent. An effort was made by the Treasury Department some years ago to levy 45 per cent on some of the steel covered by this paragraph. The matter was fought out in the courts for over ten years, and it was finally judicially determined that this steel should come in at the specific rates under that paragraph. Of course, a new attempt will be made to bring it in at the 45 per cent rate. Various provisions of the paragraph have been fought out through the courts, and the phraseology, therefore, has a well-settled meaning. Rather than to have further controversies, the importers are prepared to accept this paragraph as it now stands, except on grades valued at less than 4 cents, which should be assessed on a plane with grades valued at more than 4 cents. Steel valued at more than 4 cents, up to 16 cents, ranges now from 25 to 40 per cent duty.

Paragraph 141. In the phraseology of the tentative draft made by the committee there is " a nigger in the wood pile." It was the purpose of this paragraph to levy an additional duty upon all strips, plates, or sheets that had received a further process to give a temper or a blued, brightened, or polished surface finish. The process of tempering, bluing, brightening, and polishing is an additional process, and the importers admit the correctness of adding a corresponding additional duty.

But the new text would exact the additional duty on cold rolled material. Much of the steel covered by paragraph 135 is cold rolled and the more it is rolled the higher its value and the greater the duty under said paragraph. The thinner the gauge required the oftener the steel has to pass through the rolls. Going through the rolls gives it a certain brightness, but this brightness is simply incidental, adds no value, and is not a surface finish because it is entirely destroyed in the further course of manufacture. In being tempered or otherwise treated in the factories of this country it becomes blackened and is subsequently brightened if a surface finish is required.

There would be no justice in exacting this additional duty, which would range as high as 40 per cent on an incidental and valueless brightness which is destroyed as soon as the steel reaches this country. The words " cold rolled, cold drawn " should be omitted from the paragraph, because as it is now drawn it puts a double duty on most of the steel under paragraph 135.

It is also proposed in this text to make a new paragraph for ' steel strips, strip steel, or steel in strips twenty-five one-thousandths of an inch thick or thinner," and a comparison is made with the rate for flat steel wire.

These strips are now dutiable under paragraph 135 and the thinner they are the more duty they pay. They are not drawn as wire is, but are rolled, and making them dutiable as wire would stop their importation. That matter was fought out through the courts during the last ten years. I am informed that no corset steel is imported since its inclusion in the wire paragraph.

Regarding paragraph 132, I am informed that no iron or steel sheets or wire plated with copper or nickel are produced in this country, and that none is likely to be, as the quantity required is too small. The present 45 per cent duty is prohibitive and forces the use of substitutes, just as the high duty on matting forces the use of domestic rugs. A duty of 20 per cent is all that the article will stand.

As to paragraph 185, the following is suggested:

Nickel, nickel oxide, alloy of any kind in which nickel is component material of chief value, in pigs, ingots, bars, rods, plates, sheets, and strips, 6 cents per pound; all other forms 30 per cent ad valorem.

There is practically no crude nickel imported. The world seems divided between a European combination and a combination composed of Americans and Canadians. The Europeans will not sell here and the Americans do sell in Europe.

The irrepressible conflict that has been so long waged between domestic manufacturer and importer is rapidly drawing to a close. The importer has got the worst of it. But the Government will probably need revenue from duties for some time to come, and our gigantic iron and steel industries are likely to be slightly affected by the trifling competition they have to meet under the paragraphs I have enumerated. That is all I wish to submit.

TIN PLATE.

[Paragraph 134.]

STATEMENT OF WILLIAM U. FOLLANSBEE, OF FOLLANSBEE BROTHERS COMPANY, PITTSBURG, PA., RELATIVE TO TIN PLATE AND KINDRED PRODUCTS.

WEDNESDAY, *November 25, 1908.*

Mr. FOLLANSBEE. Mr. Chairman and gentlemen of the committee, I am to speak on paragraph 134, tin plate, and incidentally 131 and 132 as being a kindred product made by the same plant.

I am glad, in speaking of the tin-plate proposition, we can say it is not now an infant industry. It is, however, the youngest of all the iron or steel products. It is also important to bear in mind that tin plate is an item that has by far the largest labor cost. 'I am here to-day representing 12 independent tin-plate plants that are located in several different States, widely scattered. I believe I am entirely justified in saying these independent plants, while they are making tin plate, are also making money.

Mr. FORDNEY. Good.

Mr. FOLLANSBEE. We are capitalized in an aggregate of $10,000,000.

Mr. GRIGGS. Did you say they are making money?

Mr. FOLLANSBEE. They surely are, sir.

Mr. GRIGGS. I am very glad to hear it.

Mr. FOLLANSBEE. These tin plants have an aggregate of about 103 mills.

Mr. GRIGGS. Permit me to say again that I am glad to find one man who is making money.

Mr. FOLLANSBEE. I would be ashamed to be here if I were not making money.

These tin plants have a capacity of about 300,000 tons, which is equivalent to about 6,000,000 base boxes. They employ in the aggregate about 7,000 hands. Their annual pay roll is about $5,000,000. Taking the tin-plate industry in an entirety, the entire production in this country is about 600,000 tons, equivalent to 12,000,000 base boxes of coated product.

These same mills turn out a large tonnage of the same material which, however, is not coated.

The industry of itself, tin-plate manufacturing, employs about 20,000 hands and pays annually in wages about $13,000,000.

In speaking of the tin-plate industry itself, it is only proper to remind you of the fact that tin plate has been the football of the tariff. The act of 1871 undoubtedly was intended to be highly protective. In that act was written a duty of $2\frac{1}{2}$ cents per pound. Under it two mills started the manufacture of tin plate. After the establishment of those two mills and after they became operative, the foreign manufacturers, through the New York importers, very greatly reduced the prices. The competition was very severe, and in some way which I can hardly understand a decision or interpretation or construction of the law was rendered by Secretary Fessenden whereby he inserted in the act a comma which did not belong there. The act read, " Tin plate, and iron galvanized shall pay $2\frac{1}{2}$ cents per pound duty." The comma was inserted there by Secretary Fessenden, which made it read in effect, " Tin plate galvanized, or iron galvanized." On the face of it was an absurdity. It was ridiculous, putting two coatings on one black sheet. Nevertheless, under that ruling, instead of 2¼ cents per pound, it was assessed at 15 per cent ad valorem, with the result that one of these mills that was in operation went into bankruptcy and the other struggled along for a few years and eventually turned to another line of business.

The act of 1883 called for a revenue tariff of 1 cent a pound, under which no tin plate was made in this country, except that one of the plants which I mentioned made a desperate effort for a short time, but had to give it up as entirely unsuccessful.

The McKinley tariff in 1891 called for a duty of 2.2 cents per pound. That was sufficiently protective to justify capital entering into the business and learning. The industry was getting on its feet when the Wilson bill came along in 1894, with a duty of 1.2 cents and knocked the industry to its knees. The result was that the mills closed for a considerable period and a most bitter labor conflict ensued. That lasted for a period of about six months, and finally, to get work and start the mills, the laboring men took a very severe reduction. That condition existed practically until 1897, when the Dingley bill put on a new tariff of 1½ cents a pound. That was sufficient at the time. The mills which started following the passage of the McKinley law had received lower wages. They had gained in experience. Some of them, true, had failed and had been purchased at sacrifice prices by others, but nevertheless the industry continued satisfactorily up to the present time under the Dingley tariff of 1½ cents per pound.

When the McKinley bill was passed, Wales was sending to this country, in round numbers, 300,000 tons of tin plate. The industry to-day, as I have already said, totals about 600,000 tons, having doubled. To this can be added fully an additional 100,000 tons of black product, made by the same mills. To produce the 600,000 tons of coated products, the following is necessary: One million four hundred thousand tons of ore, 850,000 tons of coke, 400,000 tons of limestone, 750,000 tons of pig iron, 700,000 tons of steel, paying to American wage-earners approximately $20,500,000 in wages. Of this very large sum is directly paid in the tin-plate line, which is protected, $13,000,000, in round numbers—I figure it at $12,800,000—out of the $20,500,000.

I am glad, so far as the tin-plate industry at least is concerned, that the tariff does not advance the price. The average prices of tin plate under the 15 per cent ad valorem duty of the act of 1871, from the years 1872 to 1878, in United States currency, was $6.35 f. o. b. Swansea, Wales. Irrespective of the freight and other small charges, add simply the 15 per cent ad valorem duty, and that means for the seven years from 1872 to 1878 America was paying an average of $7.30 for its tin plate.

During the period of 1879 to 1891, before the McKinley bill became effective, when we had a revenue duty of 1 cent per pound, the average price f. o. b. Swansea, Wales, in United States currency, was $3.81 plus the duty, making a total of $4.81, which America was paying for its tin plate during that period.

For the last five years the average price in this country has been $3.48, showing conclusively that the home competition has tremendously reduced the cost to the American consumer.

As regards the present duty and prospective duty, the American tin-plate manufacturer is only 17 years old. He is the youngest in all the iron or steel industries. The price to-day of Welsh plates is 12 shillings per box f. o. b. Swansea, Wales. That is an open quotation, but I believe I can buy them for less; but we will use that for an illustration. At the rate of $4.86 per pound, that is equivalent to $2.92, from which there is a discount given by the Welsh manufacturer of 4 per cent, making the price to-day of the Welsh plate $2.80 f. o. b. Swansea, Wales.

Without going into details, you can easily see that a freight of 9 shillings 6 pence, or 10 shillings per gross ton, plus a commission for selling, $2.80, f. o. b. Swansea, Wales, will very readily place the plate at the American seaboard at a cost of $3 without duty.

A peculiarity of the tin-plate business is the fact that fully two-thirds of it is consumed at the seaboard—New York, Philadelphia, Baltimore, New Orleans, and San Francisco. As regards the consumption in San Francisco or on the coast—not limited entirely to San Francisco, but the other coast cities—the consumption is seasonable. It is not regular throughout the year. It is easy enough for the consumers to anticipate by months their requirements. The American manufacturer must sell his goods delivered at the seaboard. From the mills in the Pittsburg district a freight rate of 18 cents and a shipping weight of 106 pounds exist, the railroads exacting a tariff on the package as well as the contents, making the cost to deliver in New York City 19 cents per box, or per hundred pounds. To deliver it to New Orleans costs 34 cents. To deliver it to San Francisco costs 70 cents, so far as the American manufacturer is concerned. The facts are, as regards the Welsh manufacturer, selling even to the more distant point of San Francisco for seasonable trade, his plates can be loaded at Swansea, Wales, and carried as ballast, and be delivered at practically as low cost as in New York City. We accordingly have the proposition that the Welsh manufacturer, exclusive of duty, can lay his plates down at the seaboard at $3 per box. If we deduct our 70 cents freight to the coast, the American manufacturer, exclusive of duty, would be compelled to sell his plates f. o. b. the mills at $2.30 per box of 100 pounds.

The market quotation to-day for this character of tin plate is $3.65, or a difference of $1.35. The duty is $1.50. It protects.

The independent tin-plate manufacturers, in considering this question of tariff, felt if any were justified in standing pat, they would be. They have, however, endeavored to look at this in rather a broader light and have recognized a sentiment in the country toward tariff revision downward; and in giving this most earnest consideration, the tin-plate manufacturers are willing to say to you gentlemen of the committee that we will struggle along, and we believe we will continue to make some money if the tariff is revised by reducing it 20 per cent, which will take it from 1.50 to 1.20. It will then be identical with the Wilson bill of 1894; and the only difficulty about the Wilson bill was that it was fourteen years ahead of time. That is the recommendation we are prepared to make, and I think we will put that in our brief, which we will give to you at some later date.

I had no intention of speaking on sheets paragraph 131, but the tin-mill products are influenced. The tariff on sheets reads as follows: " Sheets of iron and steel, common or black, of whatever dimensions."

Tin plate is steel sheets coated with tin. Tin mills make sheets of many dimensions. It was not intended I should look this matter up and I have not gone into the statistics as I have for the coated products, but I can say this, that as regards the lighter gauges the tin-plate manufacturer will accept and, I believe, will continue to run his mill by taking the same number of tenths reduced duty. I think, however, to make a very decided distinction, the matter of heavy gauges should be looked into. I have not looked into heavy gauges, and it may be possible that would not be applicable there.

I shall be very glad to file a brief and show you the difference between Welsh wages and American wages, among other things.

Mr. COCKRAN. Did you say the price of the article at Swansea, Wales, f. o. b., was 12 shillings?

Mr. FOLLANSBEE. Yes, sir.

Mr. COCKRAN. Twelve shillings even?

Mr. FOLLANSBEE. That is the market quotation. I believe I can buy cheaper than that. I believe you can buy cheaper than that if you buy a sufficient quantity and know how to go about it.

Mr. CLARK. Your only competitor in the business is Wales, is it not?

Mr. FOLLANSBEE. Practically so. Germany makes a few tin plates, but not very many. We really do not know them in the industry.

Mr. CLARK. I think the committee would be willing to meet you in a spirit of comity, and I want to ask just a few questions, not to bother you, but solely for information. What are these black sheets you talk about? You must take it for granted, of course, that we do not know all the technicalities of this business.

Mr. FOLLANSBEE. They are steel sheets rolled in tin mills or rolling mills.

Mr. CLARK. Is that a by-product of the tin business, or is it a separate branch of the industry?

Mr. FOLLANSBEE. No; it is the principal part of the business.

Mr. CLARK. You make your own steel sheets to make tin out of, do you, or do you buy the sheets?

Mr. FOLLANSBEE. We make the sheets.

Mr. CLARK. Do you represent all of the tin factories in the United States?

Mr. FOLLANSBEE. I am representing to-day the twelve independents. We call ourselves independents because we are not members of the United States Steel Corporation.

Mr. CLARK. Oh. this is a branch of the United States Steel Corporation?

Mr. FOLLANSBEE. No, sir; we are separate from them.

Mr. CLARK. But those you do not represent, or whatever of the tin industry you do not represent, as I understand it, compose a part of the United States Steel Corporation?

Mr. FOLLANSBEE. Yes; outside of our twelve independents, the manufacture in this country is conducted by the United States Steel Corporation.

Mr. CLARK. That is what I wanted to get at. There is no use asking any questions about the United States Steel Corporation?

Mr. FOLLANSBEE. I do not know.

Mr. CLARK. Nobody else does, so it seems. What I want to know is this: On this $10,000,000 of capital, which I understand you to say you have, what per cent of profit did you make in 1907, for instance?

Mr. FOLLANSBEE. I would rather speak of a period of three or four years. Will that be satisfactory?

Mr. CLARK. Yes. What I did not want you to do was to take 1908 as the basis of any conversation we may have.

Mr. FOLLANSBEE. I have made it my business, as chairman of this committee that was given this matter in charge, to be a little inquisitorial, anticipating the question which you have asked.

Mr. CLARK. I am glad to hear that.

Mr. FOLLANSBEE. I can say that I believe the independent tin-plate plants of this country during the last three and four years have been making profits running from about 8 to 12 per cent.

Mr. CLARK. Now, you think if it is cut down to the basis of the Wilson bill you can still work and live and flourish?

Mr. FOLLANSBEE. I am saying so.

Mr. CLARK. Suppose we cut it down to 1 cent, in the exigencies of having to get some more money to run the Government, do you suppose you could still make a profit?

Mr. FOLLANSBEE. Under certain circumstances. Do you want me to tell you how?

Mr. CLARK. Yes.

Mr. FOLLANSBEE. Reducing labor.

Mr. CLARK. That is the only way, is it?

Mr. FOLLANSBEE. Provided other conditions remain as they are. You know that was exactly the situation when the Wilson bill passed.

Mr. CLARK. I do not know anything about it.

Mr. FOLLANSBEE. I said so.

Mr. CLARK. Of course I take it you know what you are talking about. You seem to.

Mr. FOLLANSBEE. It is a question of history. Mr. Dalzell knows that.

Mr. CLARK. Mr. Dalzell was very largely engaged in making the Wilson bill, and I was not. [Laughter.] He was one of the architects of that bill, and I was not.

Mr. FOLLANSBEE. It was only fourteen years ahead of time, as I told you.

Mr. CLARK. That is the way with most good things. If the price of steel should go down, that of course would help you?

Mr. FOLLANSBEE. Naturally.

Mr. CLARK. Do we make as good tin in the United States as they make in Wales?

Mr. FOLLANSBEE. I do.

Mr. CLARK. I am glad to hear it, because it is frequently stated and currently believed that the American tin is not as good as the foreign tin. Of course I do not pretend to know a thing about it, but if it is as good I am really glad to hear it.

Mr. FOLLANSBEE. You can tell them now you know better.

Mr. CLARK. I will. Where do you live?

Mr. FOLLANSBEE. Pittsburg.

Mr. CLARK. Thank you very much.

The CHAIRMAN. We make better tin plate than they do abroad, do we not?

Mr. FOLLANSBEE. It is natural for each manufacturer to speak for himself. I say I do.

The CHAIRMAN. You do not speak for all of them?

Mr. FOLLANSBEE. I represent myself on that proposition.

The CHAIRMAN. And you say you make better tin plate than they make abroad?

Mr. FOLLANSBEE. If you want a tin roof, and if you will pardon me——

The CHAIRMAN. That is what I have heard—that you do.

Mr. FOLLANSBEE. I have heard it so often, just as Mr. Clark stated, that I want to state here before all the gentlemen of this committee that if any of you want to put on a tin roof, Follansbee Brothers Company will sell that plate and will back it by their capital of $1,000,000 and guarantee it on your house for fifteen years. Did you ever know a Welshman to do that?

Mr. CLARK. I do not know anything about it. My understanding was, and that was one reason for asking Mr. Follansbee that question, that the chairman said the other day, in some interlocutory performance, that foreign tin had twice as much value or strength or lasting quality, or something of the sort, as the American tin. I had heard it so often I did not charge my memory with it especially.

The CHAIRMAN. I have always understood differently.

Mr. CLARK. I am delighted to hear it. I am very glad to know American tin is as good as or better than Welsh tin or anybody's else tin.

Mr. COCKRAN. You admit you make the best quality in the world?

Mr. FOLLANSBEE. Undoubtedly.

Mr. CALDERHEAD. Does the United States Steel Corporation dip tin plate?

Mr. FOLLANSBEE. They coat it; yes. It is sometimes called dipping and sometimes called coating. The words are synonymous.

Mr. DALZELL. They make the same kind the others make?

Mr. FOLLANSBEE. Not quite as good as the independents make, of course.

STATEMENT OF JOHN WILLIAMS, OF PITTSBURG, PA., REPRESENTING THE AMALGAMATED ASSOCIATION OF IRON, STEEL, AND TIN WORKERS OF NORTH AMERICA.

FRIDAY, *November 27, 1908.*

Mr. GRIGGS. Do you represent the manufacturers?

Mr. WILLIAMS. No, sir. I represent the Amalgamated Association of Iron, Steel, and Tin Workers of North America.

Mr. DALZELL. A labor organization.

Mr. WILLIAMS. Yes, sir.

Mr. CLARK. Mr. Williams, I would like to inquire what outfit it is you represent, or whom do you represent? I did not hear it.

Mr. WILLIAMS. I represent the Amalgamated Association of Iron, Steel, and Tin Workers, which is a labor organization.

The CHAIRMAN. A labor union.

Mr. CLARK. I just wanted to find out.

Mr. WILLIAMS. I desire, Mr. Chairman, to speak on paragraph 134, which relates to imports of tin plates, and specifically to touch on the drawback provision of the Dingley tariff law. And I desire, Mr. Chairman and gentlemen, to present a statement which I have prepared, as it pertains to the American tin-plate manufacturers and the employees of American tin mills.

The first statement that I have is one showing the drawback paid on tin and terne plates by the United States Treasury Department for each fiscal year from 1902 to 1907, inclusive; also the estimated number of boxes of imported tin plate used in the manufacture of exported articles, together with the estimated amount which American laborers would have received had this tonnage been manufactured in the United States. [Reads:]

Drawback payments.

Year.	Amount.
1902	$1, 860, 104
1903	1, 826, 966
1904	1, 658, 139
1905	2, 252, 382
1906	1, 788, 762
1907	1, 525, 282
Total	10, 911, 635

Based on the above payments approximately 7,347,902 base boxes of imported tin plate were used in the manufacture of cans or other articles exported. For each box of tin plate manufactured in the United States American laborers receive from $1.50 to $1.75 in wages. Based on $1.50 per box American laborers would have received in wages during the period of six years covered by the above statement $11,021,853.

The amount of wages included in the above that would have been paid to hot-mill workers, based on 30-gauge rates, is $3,430,853. The amount contributed in the past five years ending December 31, 1907, by the Amalgamated Association of Iron, Steel, and Tin Workers in wages to assist American tin-plate manufacturers to compete with imported tin plate was $282,560.36.

Now, Mr. Chairman, if, on account of the fact that I intend when submitting my brief to place in it the contract which we entered into on this export plate with manufacturers, it is your desire that I should do so, I am ready to enter upon an explanation of what that agreement means, or if it is so desired, I can wait until I am through with my statement.

The CHAIRMAN. You can file the contract and have it printed in the hearings. You need not read it now, but if the committee desire to ask any questions about it they can do that when you finish your statement.

Mr. WILLIAMS. The only possible justification for continuing the application of the drawback clause to tin plate is that the concession enables American packers and can manufacturers to obtain foreign trade that otherwise they would lose. The present difference between the market value of imported tin plate and domestic tin plate, exclusive of duty, would amount to less than 2 cents on a 5-gallon oil can, and would amount to approximately one-fifth of a cent on a 1-pound salmon or fruit can. In many lines like canned salmon and canned fruit this difference would amount to less than 2 per cent of the valuation. In some other lines it might amount to as much as 4 per cent, and in extreme cases to 5 per cent of the total valuation. It is a natural inference that so small a difference would not appreciably affect our export trade in cans or canned goods.

The largest beneficiaries of the drawback provisions of the Dingley tariff, as applied to imported tin plate, are the following industries: Oil refineries; tobacco manufacturers; exporters of cottolene, lard, and canned meats; fruit and vegetable packers; salmon and other fish canneries, and can and tinware manufacturers doing an export trade.

An examination of reports published by the United States Treasury Department will show that during the past six years a greater amount has been paid by the Government for drawback on imported tin plate used in the manufacture of exported articles than on any other one item.

Now, I will give a statement of what the securing of the export business in tin plate will mean to the tin-plate workers and manufacturers of the United States. The amount of tin plate annually imported into the United States is from 1,000,000 to 1,500,000 boxes. Using 1,000,000 boxes as a basis for calculations, we have the following: 1,000,000 boxes of 100-pound plate equals 50,000 tons; hot-mill products per week, 40; hot-mill products per month, 160 tons; hot-mill products for ten months, 1,600 tons. Fifty thousand tons divided by 1,600 equals 31¼. In other words, it will take 31 mills running full time for ten months to make the 1,000,000 boxes.

Mr. CLARK. Why don't you count it for twelve months? What makes you take only ten months instead of twelve months?

Mr. WILLIAMS. The idea, Mr. Clark, in using ten months as the basis is the fact that iron workers do not as a rule work more than ten months in the year.

The CHAIRMAN. Why not?

Mr. WILLIAMS. Because of the fact that they have repairs to make and breakages to contend with, and so far as tin-plate works are concerned, they have not had sufficient business in recent years to run the entire volume of time.

Mr. CLARK. If they had the business, they would run only ten months, even barring these accidents and breakages, etc.?

Mr. WILLIAMS. Yes. But you must take into consideration the fact that in tin-plate work they can only work on one turn six days and another turn five days. The day turn works six days, and the turn that follows in the afternoon works five days, and the turn that comes on in the evening works five days.

The CHAIRMAN. Do not all the factories suspend during the summer for a certain time?

Mr. WILLIAMS. Yes; according to the amount of repairs they have to make.

The CHAIRMAN. How much time?

Mr. WILLIAMS. Three or four weeks, or four or five weeks.

The CHAIRMAN. That is part of the two months?

Mr. WILLIAMS. Yes, sir.

Mr. COCKRAN. What do you mean by "turn?"

Mr. WILLIAMS. The tin-plate workers, Mr. Cockran, work twenty-four hours. They work in consecutive shifts. One comes out at 6 o'clock in the morning and works until 2 in the afternoon. That constitutes a turn. The next comes on at 2 o'clock in the afternoon and works up to 10 o'clock at night. That constitutes the second turn, and the next comes on at 10 o'clock at night and works until 6 the next morning. That is the third turn.

Mr. CLARK. You mean a detachment?

Mr. WILLIAMS. Yes. Three 8-hour shifts.

Mr. CLARK. " Turn " and " shift " and " tour " have all been used here interchangeably.

Mr. WILLIAMS. They all mean the same thing, practically.

Mr. RANDELL. The reason you have five days instead of six is the fact that they do not go to work on Sunday?

Mr. WILLIAMS. The first turn on Saturday morning completes the week's work.

The CHAIRMAN. Proceed now.

Mr. WILLIAMS. The hot-mill rate on 100-pound plate is $9.76 per ton, or $488,000 on 50,000 tons. The hot-mill workmen, however, are not the only beneficiaries, as it will give an ordinary sheet-bar mill twenty-three weeks' work at six days per week.

I want to say here, Mr. Chairman, that I have been in attendance upon this committee and I have heard manufacturers make the statement that the ore is worth $1 per ton at the mine, but I base the following calculation on ore at 50 cents per ton. It will require from 55,000 to 57,500 tons of pig iron, or six months' work of a 400-ton blast furnace. To follow the 1,000,000 boxes from the ore mine, where the ore is worth about 50 cents per ton, or $50,000, to the finished product, it would be worth for export purposes about $3 per box, or $3,000,000, a difference of $2,950,000, about $2,200,000 of which, after allowing for the pig tin, will go to the American workmen, manufacturers, railroads, and vessel companies, but all of which at present is absorbed by the foreign competitors. One million five hundred thousand boxes will keep 220 mills in full operation for a period of seven and one-half weeks or 35 mills in constant operation for a period of forty-seven weeks.

In view of the fact that the tin-plate mills of the United States have not operated during the past year more than 70 per cent of their total capacity, for want of business, we petition your honorable body to recommend the abrogation of the drawback agreement and the maintenance of a duty sufficient to enable American manufacturers and workmen not only to make the plate for domestic purposes, but that used for reexport purposes also. It is our opinion that a lowering of the duty would demoralize the tin-plate industry in the United States, which is apparent by a comparison of the wages paid in the United States with the amount paid by our largest foreign competitor.

I have endeavored, Mr. Chairman, to gather together some statistics on the wages paid by our greatest competitor, which is Wales, compared with the amount that the American workmen receive in the tin-plate mills in the United States. I do not know whether it is necessary, Mr. Chairman, to read these or to just give the total.

Mr. UNDERWOOD. I would like to have them read.

Mr. WILLIAMS. Very well. This is a comparative statement, showing the rates and earnings of tin-plate workers in the United States and Wales. It covers a statement both of tonnage and day rates in Wales compared with the tonnage and day rates prevailing in the United States.

In the United States the roller receives $2.25 per gross ton and in Wales $1.38, or in other words there is a differential in favor of the United States of 87 cents.

Mr. UNDERWOOD. You mean the workman in this country gets 87 cents more?

Mr. WILLIAMS. Yes, sir; 87 cents per ton more than they get in Wales. The doubler receives $1.44 in the United States and in Wales he receives $1.11, or a difference of 33 cents.

Mr. GAINES. Have you worked out what that would be per day?

The CHAIRMAN. Let us get these statistics first.

Mr. WILLIAMS. These are simply the tonnage rates, and I expect in the next statement that I will make to show the differences prevailing between the men who work by the day.

The CHAIRMAN. He has it all there.

Mr. CLARK. I want to find out first, Mr. Chairman, exactly what Mr. Williams is stating, the same as Mr. Gaines is asking. You are stating the difference in the daily wage?

Mr. WILLIAMS. No, sir. This is the difference compared with the tonnage of the men.

Mr. GRIGGS. What is the name of this last branch of workmen?

Mr. WILLIAMS. The doubler. Now the heater receives $1.47 in the United States, and in Wales he receives $1.04.

Mr. GRIGGS. What does he get here?

Mr. WILLIAMS. One dollar and forty-seven cents, and in Wales $1.04. The catcher receives in the United States——

Mr. COCKRAN. What is that?

Mr. WILLIAMS. The catcher.

Mr. GRIGGS. You did not give the difference on heaters.

Mr. WILLIAMS. It is 43 cents in favor of the United States. The catcher receives $1.10 in the United States, and in Wales he receives 51 cents. The shear man in the United States receives 40 cents, and in Wales he receives 44 cents.

Mr. COCKRAN. Give me that again—40 cents here, and 44 cents in Wales. He gets more in Wales than here?

Mr. WILLIAMS. Yes.

Mr. CLARK. That is a miracle. [Laughter.]

Mr. WILLIAMS. Total received in the United States, $5.28 per ton more than in Wales on tonnage rates.

Mr. GRIGGS. That is not one man?

Mr. GAINES. That is 1 ton.

The CHAIRMAN. The wages are $5.28 a ton more in the United States than in Wales?

Mr. WILLIAMS. Yes, sir.

Mr. COCKRAN. I understood you to say there is a difference of $5.26 per ton.

Mr. WILLIAMS. It is $5.28.

Mr. COCKRAN. You do not mind my interrupting you to explain those figures?

Mr. WILLIAMS. No, sir. If the committee has no objection, I would be glad to hand you this statement.

Mr. GRIGGS. It only makes $2.60.

Mr. COCKRAN. Here is a difference of 87 and 33 and 43 and 59 one way and a difference the other way of 4 cents.

Mr. UNDERWOOD. Have you given the entire wage scale?

Mr. WILLIAMS. No, sir.

Mr. UNDERWOOD. There is more to go on?

Mr. WILLIAMS. Yes.

The CHAIRMAN. Have you taken out that 4 cents in favor of Wales?

Mr. WILLIAMS. Yes, sir. In the United States we have one more man employed around the rolls, which we call a rougher. He receives 97 cents per ton in the United States. They do not employ a rougher in the mills in Wales.

Mr. CLARK. What is the reason they do not?

Mr. WILLIAMS. Because of the fact that it has been the custom there, ever since the tin plate has had its inception there, that the roller does that work himself.

Mr. CLARK. In the American mill there is a special workman to do the work that is required of these others to do for themselves?

Mr. WILLIAMS. Exactly so.

Mr. CLARK. I can understand why that would happen. He works cheaper than the other man.

Mr. GRIGGS. What do you call this last crowd?

Mr. WILLIAMS. Roughers; r-o-u-g-h-e-r-s.

Mr. GRIGGS. All right.

Mr. WILLIAMS. Now, we have a doubler's helper that we do not have in Wales. He receives 68 cents per ton.

The CHAIRMAN. State what kind of a man does that in Wales.

Mr. WILLIAMS. They do not have them in Wales.

Mr. GRIGGS. What is this helper?

Mr. WILLIAMS. Sixty-eight cents. Now, we have another helper, the heater's helper, who in the United States receives 73 cents.

Mr. GRIGGS. What do you call him?

Mr. WILLIAMS. He is a heater's helper.

Mr. COCKRAN. He gets how much?

Mr. WILLIAMS. Seventy-three cents per ton.

Mr. CLARK. And they do not have him in Wales?

Mr. WILLIAMS. No, sir.

Mr. DALZELL. The heater does the work there?

Mr. WILLIAMS. Yes, sir.

Mr. CLARK. The explanation of having these two extra men is that they are not skilled workmen, and it is an economy to employ them to do this work which in Wales the skilled man himself is required to do?

Mr. WILLIAMS. Yes; the heater's helper and the doubler's helper and the rougher are all practically skilled men. You know we turn out a larger output in this country than in Wales, even when you count the extra number of men we have in the plants.

Now we have another extra man whom we call the screwboy——

Mr. COCKRAN. A schoolboy? [Laughter.]

The CHAIRMAN. I think you will have to spell that for the information of the committee.

Mr. COCKRAN. What does he get to keep him from playing hookey? [Laughter.]

Mr. WILLIAMS. They are really men, but the term was occupied by men that came here from Wales.

Mr. GRIGGS. What does he get?

Mr. WILLIAMS. Seventy-two cents per ton.

Mr. UNDERWOOD. Is that same man used in the Wales mills?

Mr. WILLIAMS. No, sir; he is not employed there at all.

Mr. RANDELL. He has been banished from Wales?

Mr. WILLIAMS. They never used them there.

Mr. GRIGGS. They never have used them in Wales?

Mr. WILLIAMS. Not to my knowledge, sir.

Mr. GRIGGS. Then why or how did the term get here from Wales?

Mr. WILLIAMS. The original tin workers came from Wales and they brought the term with them. It originated with them, I suppose.

(Following is the table used by Mr. Williams:)

Comparative statement showing rates and earnings of tin-plate workers in the United States and Wales.

[Rate per gross ton.]

Occupation.	United States.	Wales.	Differential.	
			United States.	Wales.
Roller	$2.25	$1.38	$0.87	
Rougher	.97		.97	
Doubler	1.44	1.11	.33	
Helper	.68		.68	
Heater	1.47	1.04	.43	
Helper	.73		.73	
Catcher	1.10	.51	.59	
Shearman	.40	.44		$0.04
Screw boy	.72		.72	
Total	9.76	4.48	5.32	.04

Total differential in favor of United States, $5.28 per ton.

The CHAIRMAN. Proceed.

Mr. WILLIAMS. In the next statement I have the headings here: "Occupation," "United States" and "Wales," the "Differential in the United States" and the "Differential in Wales," giving the rates per day. The first is cutting and delivering bars in the United States——

Mr. GRIGGS. Can you not just give us the differential and the figures, too? This is cutting bars?

Mr. WILLIAMS. Yes; cutting and delivering. In the United States they receive, per day, $1.86. In Wales they receive 73 cents. The differential in favor of the United States is $1.13. The openers in the United States receive $2.82. In Wales they receive $1.33, or a differential in favor of the United States of $1.49. The scrap boy—they haven't any in Wales, but they have one in the American mills, and he receives 28 cents.

Mr. GRIGGS. Scrap boy? Did that term develop over there, too, or in transit? [Laughter.]

Mr. WILLIAMS. Pickling foreman——

Mr. GRIGGS. Pickling? [Laughter.]

Mr. WILLIAMS. Yes, sir.

Mr. GRIGGS. Is that from Wales?

Mr. WILLIAMS. No, sir; that is American. In the United States he receives $3.10, in Wales $1.19, a differential in favor of the United States of $1.91. Pickling assistant, in the United States——

Mr. GRIGGS. What?

Mr. WILLIAMS. Pickling assistant. He receives $2.29 in the United States; in Wales he receives 36 cents, or a differential of $1.93. Swilling——

Mr. COCKRAN. Swilling? [Laughter.]

Mr. WILLIAMS. Yes; swilling; s-w-i-l-l-i-n-g.

Mr. GRIGGS. That is, feeding the hogs, is it not? [Laughter.]

Mr. WILLIAMS. In Wales they receive 36 cents a day. We haven't any swillers in the United States, Mr. Chairman. [Laughter.]

Mr. GRIGGS. I am glad you have not.

Mr. WILLIAMS. Annealer——

Mr. COCKRAN. Which?

Mr. WILLIAMS. Annealer; in the United States he receives $4.23; in Wales, $1.61, or a differential of $2.62 in favor of the United States. Helpers in the United States, $1.73; in Wales, $1.02, or a difference of 71 cents. Cold roll foreman——

Mr. GRIGGS. What is that?

Mr. WILLIAMS. Cold roll foreman.

Mr. GRIGGS. Cold roll foreman?

Mr. WILLIAMS. Yes, sir.

Mr. GRIGGS. That is all right. I have no objection to it. [Laughter.]

Mr. WILLIAMS. In the United States he receives $3.37; in Wales, 97 cents, a difference of $2.40.

Mr. UNDERWOOD. In Wales how much?

Mr. WILLIAMS. Ninety-seven cents. Boy rollers, United States, $2.67; in Wales, 36 cents.

Mr. GRIGGS. Boy rollers—they roll the boys? [Laughter.]

Mr. WILLIAMS. No, sir.

Mr. COCKRAN. Are they boys who roll, or boys who are rolled? [Laughter.]

Mr. WILLIAMS. It is in the tin-plate department, where they come in to get the gloss on them.

Mr. COCKRAN. Do they get $2.67 a day?

Mr. WILLIAMS. Yes.

Mr. UNDERWOOD. Are they boys, or men?

Mr. WILLIAMS. They are practically men, but the term is "boy rollers." It does not necessarily mean that boys do the work.

The CHAIRMAN. How old are they on the average?

Mr. WILLIAMS. Around 18 and 21; but there are men 40 and 50 years of age doing the work.

Mr. UNDERWOOD. Repeat that item as to boy rollers in the United States and Wales.

Mr. WILLIAMS. In the United States, $2.67; in Wales, 36 cents, or a differential of $2.31. Catchers, United States, $2.41; Wales, 32 cents, making a differential of $2.09.

Mr. COCKRAN. In Wales how much?

Mr. WILLIAMS. Thirty-two cents.

Mr. COCKRAN. And $2.41 in the United States?

Mr. WILLIAMS. Yes, sir. Greasers, $1.50 in the United States; in Wales, 32 cents, or a differential of $1.18. White plate weigher—we haven't any white plate weigher in the United States, but they have them in Wales, and they pay them 77 cents a day.

In the tinning department the following wages prevail: Tinners in the United States receive $2.78; in Wales, $1.68, or a differential of

$1.10. Risers—and we know them as wash men in the United States—the risers are wash men. In the United States they receive $1.82; in Wales, $1.68, a differential of 14 cents. Grease boys in Wales receive 56 cents.

Mr. GRIGGS. Give the United States first.

Mr. WILLIAMS. They have not any in the United States.

Mr. GRIGGS. What do they get?

Mr. WILLIAMS. They get 56 cents in Wales. Bran—what is meant by that term is the person who puts the bran on the plate to make the polish——

Mr. GRIGGS. How is that?

Mr. WILLIAMS. B-r-a-n.

Mr. GRIGGS. What about him?

Mr. WILLIAMS. In the United States he receives $1.86; in Wales, 30 cents, a differential of $1.56. Laborer, in the United States, $1.55; in Wales, 73 cents, a differential of 82 cents. Fireman, United States, $2.10; in Wales, 73 cents, a differential of $1.37. Sorters, United States, $1.18; Wales, $1.45, a differential in favor of Wales of 27 cents. Reckoners, in the United States, $1.90; in Wales, 36 cents, a differential of $1.54. Boxers, in the United States, $2.23; in Wales, 81 cents, a differential of $1.42.

That covers the tinning department. Now, we have the general positions in the tin-plate mill.

Mr. GRIGGS. The what?

Mr. WILLIAMS. The general positions. Roll turner, United States, $3.70; Wales, $2.42; a differential of $1.28. Tin-house foreman, $4.81 in the United States, $2.02 in Wales; a differential of $2.79. Engineers, $2.64 in the United States, $1.19 in Wales, or a differential of $1.45.

Mr. GRIGGS. What is it in Wales?

Mr. WILLIAMS. One dollar and nineteen cents. Fireman, $1.87 in the United States; in Wales, 81 cents, or a differential of $1.06. Blacksmith, $2.75 in the United States and $1.19 in Wales, or a differential of $1.56. Helper, $1.70 in the United States; in Wales, 73 cents, or a differential of 97 cents. Bricklayers, $4.05 in the United States, $1.19 in Wales.

Mr. COCKRAN. How much did you say in the United States?

Mr. WILLIAMS. Four dollars and five cents.

Mr. COCKRAN. And how much in Wales?

Mr. WILLIAMS. One dollar and nineteen cents, or a differential of $2.86. Helpers, $1.50 in the United States, 73 cents in Wales; a differential of 77 cents.

Now, they have an engine driver in Wales that drives one of these small engines, what we term "dinkey engines," around the works. He is charged up. He receives 60 cents a day.

Mr. COCKRAN. You have the engine, don't you?

Mr. WILLIAMS. The railroad companies usually do all the switching.

Mr. COCKRAN. This is an engine for putting the product out on the tracks?

Mr. WILLIAMS. Yes, sir. The engine driver I have just given you. The next is millwright——

Mr. COCKRAN. What is that?

Mr. WILLIAMS. Millwright. In the United States he receives $2.13; in Wales, $2.02, a differential of 11 cents. Carpenter, in the United

States, $2.16; in Wales, 97 cents, or a differential of $1.19. Laborers, $1.50 in the United States; in Wales, 73 cents, or a differential of 77 cents. Superintendent, in the United States he receives $14.42 and in Wales he receives $4.04, or a differential of $10.38.

Mr. COCKRAN. Fourteen dollars and forty-two cents per week, I suppose?

Mr. WILLIAMS. No, sir; $14.42 per day.

Mr. COCHRAN. Do you mean the superintendent gets $14.42?

Mr. WILLIAMS. Yes, sir. These figures are taken from the actual wages paid to the superintendents in a 20-mill plant. Bookkeeper, in the United States, receives $5.76; in Wales, $1.62, a differential of $4.14. General clerk, $3.27 in the United States, $1.34 in Wales, making a differential in favor of the United States of $1.93. Timekeeper, United States, $1.54; Wales, 81 cents, or a total differential of 73 cents.

That concludes that statement.

(Following is the statement in full:)

Rate per day.

Occupation.	United States.	Wales.	Differential.	
			United States.	Wales.
Cutting and del bars	$1.86	$0.73	$1.13	
Openers	2.82	1.33	1.49	
Scrap boy			.28	$0.28
Pickling foreman	3.10	1.19	1.91	
Pickling assistant	2.29	.36	1.93	
Swilling		.36		.36
Annealer	4.23	1.61	2.62	
Helpers	1.73	1.02	.71	
Cold roll foreman	3.37	.97	2.40	
Boy rollers	2.67	.36	2.31	
Catchers	2.41	.32	2.09	
Greasers	1.50	.32	1.18	
White plate weigher		.77		.77
Tinning:				
Tinners	2.78	1.68	1.10	
Risers	1.82	1.68	.14	
Grease boys		.56		.56
Bran	1.86	.30	1.56	
Laborer	1.55	.73	.82	
Fireman	2.10	.73	1.37	
Sorters	1.18	1.45		.27
Reckoners	1.90	.36	1.54	
Boxers	2.23	.81	1.42	
General:				
Roll turner	3.70	2.42	1.28	
Tin house foreman	4.81	2.02	2.79	
Engineers	2.64	1.19	1.45	
Fireman	1.87	.81	1.06	
Blacksmith	2.75	1.19	1.56	
Helper	1.70	.73	.97	
Bricklayers	4.05	1.19	2.86	
Helpers	1.50	.73	.77	
Engineer		.60		.60
Driver				
Millwright	2.13	2.02	.11	
Carpenter	2.16	.97	1.19	
Laborers	1.50	.73	.77	
Superintendent	14.42	4.04	10.38	
Bookkeeper	5.76	1.62	4.14	
General clerk	3.27	1.34	1.93	
Timekeeper	1.54	.81	.73	
Total	95.20	40.33	57.71	2.84

Net differential on day rates in favor of United States, $54.87.

The CHAIRMAN. Right there I want to ask you a question: Have you anything showing how much the output of each one of these different classes of men is, per day, in tons or pounds?

Mr. WILLIAMS. Yes, sir. I can give you that later on.

The CHAIRMAN. You have that stated in your statistics?

Mr. WILLIAMS. Yes, sir. I expect, Mr. Chairman, to file a brief with this committee in which all that information will be fully gone into and given to this committee in detail.

The CHAIRMAN. And can you give it in the gross, stating the output of the mill per day in finished plate, and stating the number of workmen employed on the per diem basis?

Mr. WILLIAMS. We will endeavor to give that and as much other information as we possibly can.

Mr. DALZELL. Where did you get these figures from as to foreign cost?

Mr. WILLIAMS. We obtained these figures from a statement which was issued in the year 1892 through one of the consuls of the United States who was located on the other side of the water, in Wales, I think.

The CHAIRMAN. Have you anything later than that?

Mr. WILLIAMS. The scale that they worked on at that time, Mr. Chairman, is practically the same scale as they are working on to-day; or, in other words, it is known as the 1874 list.

The CHAIRMAN. What evidence have you of that?

Mr. WILLIAMS. The evidence is I have the scale here in my pocket of the wages paid on the other side.

The CHAIRMAN. What date is that?

Mr. WILLIAMS. One of the scales which I have here is the scale that ends on June 30 of next year, 1909.

The CHAIRMAN. Fixed by what authority?

Mr. WILLIAMS. Between representatives of labor organizations and the manufacturers.

The CHAIRMAN. In Wales?

Mr. WILLIAMS. Yes, sir; in Wales.

The CHAIRMAN. I wish you would file a copy of that with the clerk.

Mr. WILLIAMS. Yes, sir. I will be glad to do that.

Mr. CLARK. Do you say that scale that you have given was the scale of 1874?

Mr. WILLIAMS. It is known as that, Mr. Clark.

Mr. CLARK. Is it still in force?

Mr. WILLIAMS. Yes, sir.

Mr. CLARK. How do you know that?

Mr. WILLIAMS. Because I have the scale of prices right here.

Mr. CLARK. I know, but that is the American scale of prices.

Mr. WILLIAMS. The scale of prices paid in Wales now is known as the 1874 list.

Mr. CLARK. You seem to be trying very intelligently to give us information. How does it happen, when you strike one of those workmen over there where we have none similar here, that his wage is a pretty high wage; that is, it is much higher than somebody else over there where we have got something equal to the same man over here? Now, the greaser, for instance, gets a good deal more pay, I think, in Wales, than several of the other men you mentioned, but we do not happen to have a greaser here. [Laughter.]

Mr. WILLIAMS. It all depends on the method of operation.

Mr. CLARK. I do not understand how it happens that when we do not happen to have a man who corresponds to the particular workman in Wales, he gets a very fair wage, and when we have a corresponding one here, that workman gets a lower wage.

Mr. WILLIAMS. I have endeavored so far as I could to give you the correct data, as near as I could possibly get it.

Mr. CLARK. I am not disputing that at all.

Mr. WILLIAMS. And this data was taken from the consular report that was given in one of the trade papers in 1892. The scale that prevailed in Wales then is practically the scale they are working on to-day.

The CHAIRMAN. Who does the work of a greaser here?

Mr. WILLIAMS. We do not have a greaser here. One of the other jobs does the work. The work is distributed differently.

Mr. COCKRAN. It is a different distribution of the work?

Mr. WILLIAMS. Yes.

The CHAIRMAN. I was trying to get at what class of workmen here did the work of greasers there.

Mr. WILLIAMS. The method is different, and this work is divided up among some of the jobs already enumerated.

The CHAIRMAN. They are different methods of making tin plate?

Mr. WILLIAMS. Yes, sir.

The CHAIRMAN. Have they copied our methods since 1892 at any time?

Mr. WILLIAMS. It is my opinion, Mr. Chairman, that they are adopting American ways in making tin plate now.

The CHAIRMAN. So that they can dispense with the greaser?

Mr. WILLIAMS. Yes.

Mr. CLARK. I am not casting any reflections on your testimony. I think you are very luminous about it, but the peculiar discrepancy that struck my mind was that when there was a particular person over there under a particular name doing a thing that we had no corresponding man for he seemed to get a good deal higher wage in Wales than the man in Wales gets where he has a corresponding competitor in the United States, and I could not understand why his wages should shoot up just at the very moment when there was no one corresponding to him in the United States.

Mr. COCKRAN. You have given us, Mr. Williams, in one set of figures, statistics showing the relative cost per ton, and in the next set of figures, which you put under the head of " Tinning department," you have given us day wages?

Mr. WILLIAMS. Yes, sir.

Mr. COCKRAN. Is it the same character of work that is performed by both classes?

Mr. WILLIAMS. No, sir. It is not the same character of work. Of course, it all goes to the production of tin.

Mr. COCKRAN. I understand; but those employees whose wages you have given on the computation of what is paid to them per ton are not the same class that you have mentioned when you gave us the day's wages?

Mr. WILLIAMS. No, sir. In the tinning department, for instance, those are the men that put the coating on the backplates.

Mr. COCKRAN. They are paid by the day?

Mr. WILLIAMS. Yes, sir.

Mr. COCKRAN. The other men are paid by the piece or by the product?

Mr. WILLIAMS. Yes, sir.

Mr. COCKRAN. What do they do?

Mr. WILLIAMS. That is, the rollers?

Mr. COCKRAN. Yes.

Mr. WILLIAMS. They roll the sheet bar and reduce it to the back-plate.

Mr. COCKRAN. They are paid for what they do in the one case, and in the other they are paid by the day?

Mr. WILLIAMS. Yes, sir.

Mr. UNDERWOOD. You stated sometime ago in the estimated difference in cost that the total difference in cost was $5.28 per ton, but that referred merely to those men who are being paid by the ton, or did it refer to the entire difference in labor cost in a ton of tin plate?

Mr. WILLIAMS. It refers to the cost per ton.

Mr. UNDERWOOD. The total differential between the American cost of labor and the Welsh cost of labor, everything included, in a ton of tin plate is $5.28?

Mr. WILLIAMS. Oh, no, sir. I would not presume to stand up here and tell you what it costs to make a ton of tin plate, because I would not be in a position to do it.

Mr. UNDERWOOD. I did not ask you for that. I merely want to find out the difference in labor cost.

Mr. WILLIAMS. This is merely a comparison of the cost between Wales and the United States, and it pertains to men working on the tonnage basis.

Mr. UNDERWOOD. Then the $5.28 which you said was the differential of the total cost did not apply to day wages, but only to the tonnage wages?

Mr. WILLIAMS. Yes, sir; only to the tonnage wages.

Mr. UNDERWOOD. Have you anything there to show the difference per ton in day wages?

Mr. WILLIAMS. No, sir. We did not have sufficient notice to get the statistics up in greater detail, but we did the best we could to get you the information we have now.

Mr. UNDERWOOD. I want to compliment you, Mr. Williams, on the fact that you are the one witness who has appeared before the committee with definite figures and a wage scale. I think most of the other witnesses have been guessing at it.

The CHAIRMAN. I remember some distinctly.

Mr. UNDERWOOD. Now, I want to ask you, Mr. Williams, as to these rollers, as to whom you gave the differential of 87 cents in favor of this country; how many tons do they produce a day?

Mr. WILLIAMS. We have not any limit here now.

Mr. UNDERWOOD. I mean, about.

Mr. WILLIAMS. On the 30-gauge basis, which is a standard gauge, I suppose they turn out from 5,750 to 6,000 pounds a day.

Mr. UNDERWOOD. How much does a man produce per day?

Mr. WILLIAMS. That is the mill.

Mr. UNDERWOOD. I will ask you the question in another way. A roller gets a differential in his favor of 87 cents. How much does he actually make for a day's wage if he works every day?

Mr. WILLIAMS. I would not be positive on the figures, but I would suppose he would make anywhere from $5.50 to $6 a day.

Mr. UNDERWOOD. The reason I want to know this information is because this wage question is a very important one, and the question is whether it is a reasonable wage; and we would like to know what you are getting. Now, as to the doublers, the differential in their favor is 33 cents; but what is the actual amount of wages they receive?

Mr. WILLIAMS. The tonnage varies, and I could not give you the actual amount. While one man in one place would make $4 a day, in another mill he would not make the same output, perhaps.

Mr. UNDERWOOD. Then doublers, you say, would run from $3.50 to $4?

Mr. WILLIAMS. Yes, sir.

Mr. GRIGGS. That depends on efficiency entirely.

Mr. UNDERWOOD. Now, as to the heater, the differential was 43 cents, and you said the day's wage there was about $4?

Mr. WILLIAMS. Yes. That is about what the doubler receives.

Mr. UNDERWOOD. Now, the catcher would receive what?

Mr. WILLIAMS. From $2.75 to $3 a day, I suppose.

Mr. UNDERWOOD. Now, the shearmen; as to them the differential is in favor of Wales. What does the American shearman get per day?

Mr. WILLIAMS. I suppose he would average $3 a day. I want to say that those are approximate figures.

Mr. UNDERWOOD. I understand that. I am familiar with work in mills of that kind, and I know that the figures are always approximate, because the work of the mill and the work of the man may not be continuous. But, then, you know in a general way what a man of that kind will make?

Mr. WILLIAMS. Yes, sir. I am on the safe side in what I am giving you.

Mr. UNDERWOOD. Now, as to the roughers; what is their daily wage?

Mr. WILLIAMS. Their daily wage in tin mills, I think, is about 30 per cent of the rollers' wages.

Mr. UNDERWOOD. What will that make it per day?

Mr. WILLIAMS. You can just figure on what you have there.

Mr. UNDERWOOD. That would be about $2 a day.

Mr. WILLIAMS. Oh, I guess more than that.

Mr. UNDERWOOD. The rollers you gave at $6, and 33 per cent of that would be a third, or $2; but you think it is more than that?

Mr. WILLIAMS. I think it is.

Mr. UNDERWOOD. How much would you say, then?

Mr. WILLIAMS. $2.50 per day.

Mr. UNDERWOOD. Now, as to the helpers.

Mr. WILLIAMS. The helpers would receive $2.40 per day.

Mr. UNDERWOOD. And the heater helpers?

Mr. WILLIAMS. About the same, $2.40.

Mr. UNDERWOOD. And the screw boy?

Mr. WILLIAMS. His wages approximate about the same as the helper's.

Mr. UNDERWOOD. All the balance of the wages you gave work on the daily scale?

Mr. WILLIAMS. Yes, sir.

Mr. UNDERWOOD. In the wages that go into a ton of tin plate—you gave us the amount of wage scale—that is, the total scale—as a differential of $5.28. Will the wage scale of the cost be more or less than that?

Mr. WILLIAMS. It seems to me that it would amount to more.

Mr. UNDERWOOD. How much more do you think?

Mr. WILLIAMS. You can just figure; the differential would be $54.87 on day rates in favor of the United States.

Mr. UNDERWOOD. Per ton?

Mr. WILLIAMS. No; per day on the various jobs enumerated.

Mr. UNDERWOOD. And how much tonnage would that mill have?

Mr. WILLIAMS. The output in Wales is calculated at about 44 boxes per turn.

Mr. UNDERWOOD. And in this country it would be how much?

Mr. WILLIAMS. They would turn out more than that, but I could not give you the exact figures at this time.

Mr. UNDERWOOD. Would it be double as much?

Mr. WILLIAMS. Oh, no—I would rather not pass upon that because I am not in a position to give the exact figures, but I will give you the exact figures in the brief.

Mr. UNDERWOOD. Yes; I wish you would give us the exact figures.

Mr. GRIGGS. In making this differential on tonnage rates, you have to add four men over here in order to do that?

Mr. WILLIAMS. Yes, sir; I suppose we have.

Mr. GRIGGS. That is to say you use four men that are not used in Wales, and add their wages to the wage of the differential in order to make your differential of $5.28. You give the differential of rollers at 87 cents; doublers, 33 cents; heaters, 43 cents; catchers, 59 cents, and shear men, 4 cents, which makes $2.26 differential. Now, you add on the wage of the roughers, the helpers, and the screw boys in order to make your differential of $5.28, and these last four are not employed in the mills in Wales at all?

Mr. WILLIAMS. No.

Mr. GRIGGS. That is, you use more men in order to make a bigger differential?

Mr. WILLIAMS. No; that is on account of the difference of operation in the mills——

Mr. GRIGGS. I am talking about your testimony. I do not care what you do in the mills. You use four new men in order to make a big differential on the tonnage basis here?

Mr. WILLIAMS. The method of operating in Wales is not exactly the method of operating here, but the only difference is that we use more men in the operation in the United States than we do in Wales.

Mr. GRIGGS. Now, is it fair to add these four men that are not used in Wales at all, in order to make a differential?

Mr. WILLIAMS. It is, most assuredly, because the wages of those men enter into the cost.

Mr. GRIGGS. Of course, it enters into the cost, but it does not enter into a question of wage scale, does it?

Mr. WILLIAMS. Yes, sir.

The CHAIRMAN. I want to know right there whether the work done by these four men is done in Wales by the day by any of these men that you have named here?

Mr. WILLIAMS. No, sir.

The CHAIRMAN. No part of it?

Mr. WILLIAMS. No, sir.

Mr. GRIGGS. It is all done there, then, by the men that you quote as paid so much a ton?

Mr. WILLIAMS. Yes, sir.

The CHAIRMAN. And you give the entire number employed here by the ton and there by the ton, and all together they perform similar work in making the tin plates?

Mr. WILLIAMS. Yes, sir.

Mr. RANDELL. Do they perform the same work or just similar work.

Mr. WILLIAMS. Similar work, sir.

Mr. RANDELL. Then you do not mean to say that the same amount of work is done by the men in Wales that is done by the men in the United States?

Mr. WILLIAMS. I will admit that they do turn out a larger output in this country.

Mr. RANDELL. You did not mention that in your summary of expense of computing by the ton.

Mr. WILLIAMS. In my summary I did not give the cost per ton. I stated that I was not in a position to do so.

Mr. RANDELL. But you give the labor by the ton.

Mr. WILLIAMS. I am endeavoring to bring to this committee some information bearing on the relative amount of wages paid in Wales compared with the amount of wages paid in the United States.

Mr. RANDELL. For the committee to understand that, don't you think it is necessary to say that there is a difference in the output?

Mr. WILLIAMS. No, sir.

Mr. RANDELL. If 10 men paid $20 a day would produce a quantity represented by 100, and 10 men paid $15 a day would produce a quantity represented by 50, or one-half of 100, then the wage for the 10 men for the fifteen days would be greater than that for the 10 men paid for twenty days.

Mr. WILLIAMS. I said that I was not in a position to present such figures to this committee; not in a position to know the exact amount turned out in Wales, and therefore I could not make a comparison along that line.

Mr. RANDELL. Why didn't you state that the story was not complete, because you did not know the difference, but that there was a great difference in favor of the output of the American laborer? What is the difference in what the manufacturer, the producer, gets in Wales as compared with what the manufacturer or producer gets in the United States for this same labor?

Mr. WILLIAMS. I say that I am not in a position to give those figures, and I have already stated that when I present my brief I will endeavor to cover that position very clearly and distinctly.

The CHAIRMAN. Yes, you stated that you would do that.

Mr. WILLIAMS. Yes; if the figures are obtainable I will be glad to do it.

Mr. RANDELL. As a matter of fact the tariff at present is practically a prohibitive tariff, is it not, the revenue being very small? I am referring to the importation of these sheets.

Mr. WILLIAMS. I do not know that it is a prohibitive tariff.

Mr. RANDELL. Isn't it a fact that at present they can only bring them in to be used on the Atlantic seaboard, and that the producer in this country has practically a monopoly all over the balance of the United States? Isn't that a fact?

Mr. WILLIAMS. I have some figures covering a period from 1904 to 1907.

Mr. RANDELL. But could you not answer my question "yes" or "no?"

Mr. WILLIAMS. I will answer by giving those figures.

Mr. RANDELL. But can you not answer "yes" or "no?"

Mr. WILLIAMS. I could not, sir.

The CHAIRMAN. I might say, Mr. Randell, that he has not taken up that subject yet, and, I understand, is not through with his statement.

Mr. RANDELL. Oh, I thought the witness was through with his statement.

Mr. WILLIAMS. No; I am not through yet.

The CHAIRMAN. I think you had better complete your statement.

Mr. WILLIAMS. There are fully 17,000 people employed directly in the tin-plate factories of the United States, receiving $12,376.000 a year in wages (year estimated at 260 working days); the number is still larger of those employed in steel works, blast furnaces, ore and coal mines, box factories, acid works, machine shops, and minor industries engaged in furnishing supplies to the tin-plate works, and the employment of all these would be seriously curtailed by a change of duty injurious to the tin-plate industry.

British tin plates in the United States.

For the purpose of showing how the customs drawback system in the United States works out in practice, the British consul in New York supplies figures referring to the tin-plate imports into the United States during the four years 1904–1907. The first column shows the weight of tin plates imported and paying duty and the second column shows the weight of tin plates exported with benefit of drawback.

Year ending June 30—	Imported.	Exported.	Year ending June 30—	Imported.	Exported.
	Pounds.	*Pounds.*		*Pounds.*	*Pounds.*
1904	126,950,000	111,658,352	1906	120,841,000	120,455,345
1905	161,410,000	151,677,870	1907	141,766,000	102,712,630

The CHAIRMAN. How much of that which was imported was reexported and the drawback received on it? Please give the total for the four years.

Mr. WILLIAMS. From the table that I have given it will be seen that in the four years 550,976,000 pounds weight of imported tin plate paid duty and 486,504,197 pounds were reexported, 99 per cent of the duty being refunded. The duty on tin plates under the tariff being 1½ cents per pound, the duty actually paid was only one-hundredth of 1½ cents.

The CHAIRMAN. I wish to call attention to a letter that has been received by the committee referring to you, Mr. Williams, and I want to read it to you, because it will go into the record, and I think it is only fair that you have an opportunity to make whatever statement in regard to it that you may desire to make. The letter purports to come from the United Sons of Vulcan of the United States, 326 Fourth avenue, room 56, Shannon Building, Pittsburg, Pa. [Reads:]

THE UNITED SONS OF VULCAN OF THE UNITED STATES,
ROOM 56 SHANNON BUILDING, 326 FOURTH AVENUE,
Pittsburg, Pa., November 26th, 1908.

TO THE WAYS & MEANS COMMITTEE,
Washington, D. C.

DEAR SIRS: We, the United Sons of Vulcan, the only organized body of mill workers in the Greater Pittsburg (with the exception of 60 financial supporters of the Amalgamated Association) can not allow P. J. McArdle and John Williams, officials of the A. A., to abrogate to themselves the right to *misrepresent* organized mill workers of this great iron center, Pittsburg, before your honorable body, especially in advocacy of the retention of a high protective tariff, a thing that they, only a few weeks ago, endeavored to totally destroy by their undivided support of *Sam. Gompers* in his endeavor to elect *Bryan* to the *Presidency* of the United States, a man whose ambitions were and are to destroy all tariff protection. An official of the A. A. went so far as to make stump speeches in favor of Bryan at Wheeling, W. Va.; then note the inconsistency of his copartners delegating to themselves the authority to represent mill workers before your honorable body with whom they have no connection whatsoever, and if they are not self-appointed they must be in the employ of manufacturers. It is true it still has a standing in some western mills, where the employees are being compelled against their will to support these presumptuous labor leaders.

From your humble servants,

[SEAL.]

JOS. M. MORELAND, *President.*
HENRY MCNALLY, *Vice-Presiden.*
MICHAEL MCCUNE, *Secretary-Treasurer.*
JOHN L. WILLIAMS, *Trustee.*

That will be placed in the record, and in connection with it any statement you may desire to make in regard to it.

Mr. WILLIAMS. I am very much obliged to you, Mr. Chairman, for reading the document, and for giving me an opportunity of defending the Amalgamated Association of Iron, Steel, and Tin Workers.

Mr. COCKRAN. Against what?

Mr. WILLIAMS. Against the charges that were contained in that communication, that we are in the employ of the manufacturers in coming here to represent the interests of the men that are under the jurisdiction of the Amalgamated Association.

I want to say, Mr. Chairman, that the organization referred to is an organization that is being formed, and which has become dissatisfied on account of the fact that the representatives of the Amalgamated Association have endeavored to do their business on a business basis. They are being dissatisfied on account of the fact that we have year after year endeavored to do business with the manufacturers on a conservative basis, and have endeavored, so far as we possibly could, to do the very best, not alone for the men that are working for us, but for the general condition of the iron and steel workers of the country. These men have become dissatisfied on account of the fact that they are not receiving a larger amount of wages than they are receiving to-day, with the result that they have broken away from our organization, and are, in round numbers, not more than 1,000 members on the outside. They control practically nothing. They say they control all the mills in the city of Pittsburg. They have a semblance of organization in some of the mills there, but the outside number of men who belong to that organization, which I want to say is nothing more or less than a rump organization—they do not control more than 1,000 men all told. So far as the iron interests of the country are concerned, the Amalgamated Association controls at least 85 or 90 per cent of the iron mills of the country.

The CHAIRMAN. Not to take up too much time talking about that organization, is it true that you appear at the instance of the manufacturers, or in their interest?

Mr. WILLIAMS. Positively not, sir.

The CHAIRMAN. There is another charge contained in the letter which I will call your attention to, and as some of my friends upon the committee have touched upon that subject which seems to be nearest to them, I will ask if, in the last campaign, you supported Bryan?

Mr. WILLIAMS. To be candid, I want to say that I voted for Bryan.

The CHAIRMAN. Is there anything else in regard to any personal matters in that communication, so far as you are concerned, that you desire to speak of? If so, you may make your explanation. I would not spend too much time on the other organization, as we do not wish to go into the question as to which organization has the greater membership. It is not necessary to do that. I only wished to bring this question to your attention so that you might put in the record any explanation you might wish to make in connection with the letter.

Mr. WILLIAMS. I think it is an unfair position to place me in as a witness, and I want an opportunity to defend my position.

Mr. DALZELL. You have given us statistics with respect to the tin plate that was exported; first imported and then exported, the actual duty paid being only one-hundredth of 1½ cents. If I understood your position it is that if this rebate clause should not exist in the tariff law the American workingman would have the opportunity to make that tin plate that is first imported and then exported and manufactured. Is that your position?

Mr. WILLIAMS. That is my position.

The CHAIRMAN. I want to know in regard to that whether, before that rebate was incorporated into the law, the Standard Oil Company did not buy tin plate and make it up in cans and send it abroad?

Mr. WILLIAMS. I am not in a position to know.

The CHAIRMAN. Did they do that, or do you know?

Mr. WILLIAMS. I think the Standard Oil Company largely uses reexported tin; yes.

The CHAIRMAN. Before this drawback was incorporated into the law, did they not send oil abroad in their own tank vessels, carry it abroad, and use that foreign tin plate?

Mr. WILLIAMS. I think so.

The CHAIRMAN. So that it has not affected your industry in the least, but has given employment to people who make the tin up into tin cans in this country. Is not that correct?

Mr. WILLIAMS. No, sir; it is not correct. It has affected us. We are endeavoring to show that in the past six years the American workingmen have lost over 7,000,000 boxes by not securing that trade.

The CHAIRMAN. How did it affect them when they did not buy it of the American mills before that time? This whole thing was done by the Standard Oil Company, practically. They did not buy any of it from the American tin-plate mills before that time—that is, before there was a rebate?

Mr. WILLIAMS. Taking it for granted that they did not buy it, we consider that, as American workingmen, we are entitled to that business which is done by the foreign manufacturer.

The CHAIRMAN. But suppose they do not buy it here; suppose they buy it abroad?

Mr. WILLIAMS. So far as the Standard Oil Company is concerned, I do not expect them to buy tin plate here if they can get it cheaper elsewhere.

The CHAIRMAN. Of course you do not, so that it would not aid you to get a repeal of the clause, and it would deprive the few workingmen that they employ in making up tin cans in the United States of their jobs.

Mr. WILLIAMS. Of course I can not see it in the same light as you do. I feel that the obligation that this drawback imposes means a good deal to the American workingmen, and I have endeavored to show the number of mills it would run and the number of men it would give employment to for a certain period of time.

The CHAIRMAN. But I think you are stating what you want, and that your wants are not strictly based upon the facts.

Mr. DALZELL. In addition, you have given the different industries that do this importing and exporting business—the oil producers, tobacco manufacturers, the packers of various kinds, and the fruit canners—you have given a list of all of those, have you not?

Mr. WILLIAMS. Yes, sir.

Mr. CLARK. Are you through with your paper?

Mr. WILLIAMS. Yes, sir.

Mr. CLARK. I want to ask you several questions. To begin with, you can not segregate this tin-plate business from everything else. Are you in favor of abolishing this drawback system as to everything in the United States?

Mr. WILLIAMS. Mr. Clark, in answer to that question, I want to say that I am not familiar with the other things that you have in mind, and I want to say that, so far as the tin business is concerned, I am in favor of the abrogation of this drawback.

Mr. CLARK. Of course you are more familiar with the tin business, but isn't it true that if the American manufacturing interests generally shall grow and flourish in the United States, that they must turn their attention more largely to exports than they have been doing?

Mr. WILLIAMS. I think it is impossible, Mr. Clark, under the conditions existing, to export anything. I have endeavored to show that the Amalgamated Association entered into an agreement to give 25 per cent of their wages to get this export trade.

Mr. CLARK. The other question was, If this drawback system, so far as the tariff system is concerned, prevails—and there does not seem to be any imminent danger of its being abolished right away— as long as it prevails, is not the system a great aid to our export trade, not to tin plate especially, but to everything else?

Mr. WILLIAMS. Yes; but I have endeavored to show in my statement, Mr. Clark, that the extra cost in making this plate here would be so small that it would not appreciably affect the export trade?

Mr. CLARK. Well, that is the same thing that turns up all the time. The particular instance is small, but the aggregate is very large.

Can the American tin-plate maker with present facilities make enough tin plate to supply the American market?

Mr. WILLIAMS. We haven't enough domestic plate at present to keep the mills in full operation as it is.

Mr. CLARK. Do you not need the export trade, then, to help you out?

Mr. WILLIAMS. We will get it if the drawback agreement is abrogated; we will make the plate here, estimated at about 1,500,000 boxes per year.

Mr. CLARK. But you would not have any place to sell it; it would not do you any good to make tin plate and then not be able to sell it.

Mr. WILLIAMS. We would have some place to sell it. I do not believe the extra cost would be so much or that it would affect the export trade at all.

Mr. CLARK. Have you ever made any investigation to find out, considering the aggregate number of tin-plate workers that it takes to make a ton of tin plate, whether in Wales they can make a ton of tin plate cheaper than they can in the United States, notwithstanding this differential in wages?

Mr. WILLIAMS. I want to say that as far as cost is concerned that I am not in a position to give figures. I understand that the tin-plate manufacturers intend to file a brief with the committee upon that subject, and they are in a position to get the information.

Mr. CLARK. Do you know whether the cost of living to the laborer or employee of these mills in Wales, living in the same style that the American laborer does, is less than that of the American?

Mr. WILLIAMS. Yes; I think he lives for less.

Mr. CLARK. About how much cheaper, living in the same style? And I would not diminish the style of your living a particle if I could.

Mr. WILLIAMS. I have in my hand a letter from John Hodge, who is a member of Parliament representing one of the districts in the north of England, relative to the cost of living in Great Britain compared to the cost of living in the United States, which I think will answer your question; and with the privilege of the Chair I will read the communication.

Mr. CLARK. I would like to hear it.

Mr. WILLIAMS. He says:

In making comparisons as between the value of earnings in this country and the United States, cost of house rent and living have, of course, to be considered. I might say that we have built a fairly large number of houses for our members, and the rents vary from 5 shillings to 8 shillings 6 pence per week.

And I might say that 5 shillings would be $1.20 of our money, and 8 shillings 6 pence would be about $2.04 of our money.

The houses consist of a kitchen, two sitting rooms, coalhouse, washhouse, and other offices in the basement, and upstairs three bedrooms and a bathroom in the dearer houses, but in the cheaper ones the bath is fixed below in an inclosed place in the kitchen generally. There is a small garden to each house and the differences in the rents is due to some extent to the size of the rooms and also to the difference between the house rents in the localities where the buildings are situated. I think a good indication of the cost of living is to be found in the amount charged to a single workman, and I might say that the amount charged to a skilled single workman in our trade for board and lodgings averages about 14 shillings, or $3.36, per week. I mention these matters so as to give you some little indication in making a comparison between cost of rent and living to an American workingman as against what it costs similar workingmen here.

Mr. CLARK. How much does it cost here?

Mr. WILLIAMS. Why, Mr. Clark, I want to say that in the city of Pittsburg, and in all large industrial establishments, it is absolutely impossible for workingmen to get such a house as is referred to in this communication anywhere at a rent below from $20 to $25 a month.

Mr. CLARK. What I was trying to get at is this: You have stated very elaborately there, and have given the figures, about the higher wages paid in America. I was trying to find out how much would the cheaper living in Wales leave the Welshman who would have small wages even, at the end of the year, than our workingmen?

Mr. WILLIAMS. I will endeavor to give you the information.

Mr. CLARK. You say that it would cost you $25 a month for rent, while it would cost the Welshman but $4.80 a month?

Mr. WILLIAMS. Yes, sir.

Mr. CLARK. Now, do you know anything about whether his table costs as much there as it does here?

Mr. WILLIAMS. This is the only information I have, Mr. Clark, and I do not know anything about that.

Mr. UNDERWOOD. Can you give the price of board for a single man in Pittsburg?

Mr. WILLIAMS. I do not know. I have never boarded, and would not have an opportunity of knowing.

Mr. UNDERWOOD. You have no information along that line?

Mr. WILLIAMS. No, sir.

The CHAIRMAN. Have you ever been in Wales yourself?

Mr. WILLIAMS. Yes; I was born there.

The CHAIRMAN. What is the comparative standard of living between the Welsh workers and the workers of the United States?

Mr. WILLIAMS. I have been in this country a considerable number of years. I was young when I left Wales, but the standard of living I do not suppose is very much different. Of course, I believe that we live higher in the United States than they do there. I think that everything they have in Wales is good and substantial, but they do not get as many delicacies as we have in the United States.

The CHAIRMAN. When was it that you saw the people in the Welsh mines; when did you live there?

Mr. WILLIAMS. I lived there eighteen years ago.

The CHAIRMAN. And you do not know what the standard is now?

Mr. WILLIAMS. No, sir.

The CHAIRMAN. The entire competition in the tin-plate industry is between Wales and the United States, is it not?

Mr. WILLIAMS. I notice by the statistics that there has been some imported from Germany during the past year.

The CHAIRMAN. But practically all of the tin plate in the world is made in the United States and Wales?

Mr. WILLIAMS. Practically so.

The CHAIRMAN. At the time you left there it was practically all made in Wales?

Mr. WILLIAMS. Yes, sir.

The CHAIRMAN. And the tin-plate industry was prospering there at that time?

Mr. WILLIAMS. Yes, sir.

The CHAIRMAN. Isn't it your understanding that they have not prospered since we have been making so much here and taking your market, because they have lost this market?

Mr. WILLIAMS. I want to say that while our mills have been lying idle in the United States during the past year the Welsh mills have been running to their full capacity.

The CHAIRMAN. Please go back to the year before that in making your comparison.

Mr. WILLIAMS. I will say that for the past four years the Welsh mills have been running to their full capacity.

The CHAIRMAN. Then our mills have had no effect upon them at all; the loss of the trade of the United States has had no effect upon them?

Mr. WILLIAMS. No, sir; not any effect at all.

The CHAIRMAN. What proportion of the world's consumption of tin plate is consumed in the United States?

Mr. WILLIAMS. I could not answer that question.

The CHAIRMAN. About three-quarters?

Mr. WILLIAMS. No, sir.

Mr. LONGWORTH. Did I understand you to say that you can rent a 6-room house in Wales for $4.80 per month?

Mr. WILLIAMS. That is what this letter states.

Mr. LONGWORTH. Are those houses owned by the mills?

Mr. WILLIAMS. Not generally, I believe; I think they are owned by private individuals.

Mr. LONGWORTH. What do you suppose a house like that could be built for?

Mr. WILLIAMS. I suppose a house of that kind could be built there very much cheaper than in this country. I think in Wales it could be built for $1,500.

Mr. LONGWORTH. I am trying to get at what return the owner of that house would get on his money. According to your figures he would get $52 a year rent, and the house would cost, say, $1,500. What would the land upon which that house stands cost?

Mr. WILLIAMS. I do not believe that they buy the land outright there, but get it upon leases for ninety-nine years, or something like that.

Mr. LONGWORTH. Would that house be in the city?

Mr. WILLIAMS. Practically so. Of course I do not know very much about it, and I would not be able to give any definite information along that line.

Mr. LONGWORTH. Roughly speaking, you say that the house would cost about $1,500, and the land would probably be worth as much as the house, would it not?

Mr. WILLIAMS. I think it would; yes, sir.

Mr. LONGWORTH. That is $3,000. He would have a return of $52 a year on a $3,000 investment. What percentage would that be after allowing for taxes and repairs?

Mr. WILLIAMS. Not very much.

Mr. LONGWORTH. If you take probably half of that gross rental for taxes and repairs, that would leave you $25 a year, or about that. That would make a return of less than 1 per cent.

The CHAIRMAN. What do you suggest as the rate of duty on tin plate; how much would you reduce it?

Mr. WILLIAMS. I would say in regard to that, that I am not in position to say, but I should say that the rate of duty should be the differential in the cost of production in making tin plate in the foreign countries compared with the cost in the United States.

The CHAIRMAN. You have not worked that out?

Mr. WILLIAMS. No, sir. I am not in a position to work it out on account of the fact that I am not in possession of the information.

The CHAIRMAN. So you do not know whether it ought to be reduced or not?

Mr. WILLIAMS. I merely say that I believe that the duty should be the differential in the cost in making plate abroad compared with the plate in the United States.

The CHAIRMAN. You do not know whether the duty represents the differential between the cost here and abroad, or not?

Mr. WILLIAMS. No, sir. There are manufacturers who will appear before you who will give you that information.

Mr. LONGWORTH. Mr. Williams, will you be so kind as to write to that member of Parliament and ask him to let us know what class of Englishmen are willing to take four-fifths of 1 per cent as their return upon their investments in real estate and buildings? I should like very much to know that. That is the net return on this class of buildings that you referred to..

Mr. RANDELL. And also how much money they have to let out at that rate.

Mr. WILLIAMS. Of course I haven't any definite information. The information I gave you is that which comes in this letter.

Mr. LONGWORTH. But you offer that as evidence as to the cost of living in the place to which you referred?

Mr. CLARK. I want to ask you this question, Mr. Williams: If a tariff is levied ostensibly for the benefit of laboring men, then the laboring men ought to get all of the tariff, ought they not?

Mr. WILLIAMS. Not necessarily.

Mr. CLARK. Why should anybody else on earth get a particle of it if it is levied for the benefit of the laborer?

Mr. WILLIAMS. Everybody would get the benefit of it, Mr. Clark, in the event we got the plate I referred to.

Mr. CLARK. I know; but I am asking you a different question. If a certain tariff is levied in the name of labor, why should not labor get all of that tariff?

Mr. WILLIAMS. There are other people that are affected, Mr. Clark, in getting some of the profit in tin plate.

Mr. CLARK. I know there are, lots of them, but what I am asking you is a plain simple question: If any given tariff is levied in the name of labor—and that is what it is—then the labor ought to get all of that tariff, ought it not?

Mr. WILLIAMS. I don't understand that that tariff is set for labor alone. If I understand a tariff rate, it is for the purpose of protecting the American industries.

Mr. CLARK. I know, but every man who comes in here and testifies testifies that he has got to have a tariff in order to pay wages. I say that if he pays wages out of the tariff that the wage-earner ought to get it.

The CHAIRMAN. Now, Mr. Williams, the protective tariff has enabled you to work in a tin-plate mill, and you would not have had employment there if the mill had not been erected.

Mr. WILLIAMS. No, sir.

The CHAIRMAN. It takes money to erect a mill; it takes capital to own it and to run it, does it not?

Mr. WILLIAMS. Yes, sir.

The CHAIRMAN. If there is a difference in the amount of earnings upon the capital between this country and abroad, people who are capitalists will not put money in tin-plate mills unless they can make up that difference, will they?

Mr. WILLIAMS. I do not know.

The CHAIRMAN. So that in order to give any benefit to labor you must first have the capital invested in the tin-plate mills, is that not so?

Mr. WILLIAMS. It has been invested to such an extent in our country, Mr. Chairman, that the total number of mills erected are larger and more in number than it requires to make the domestic plate of the country.

The CHAIRMAN. Yes; that is correct. You do not expect that the people who own this capital here are so full of philanthropy that they will build mills simply for the profits of the workingmen exclusively, do you?

Mr. WILLIAMS. Most assuredly not.

The CHAIRMAN. So that capital has got to have enough differential duty to pay the cost of capital here and abroad, has it not? Do you not know that? If not, say so.

Mr. WILLIAMS. No; I do not know.

Mr. CLARK. If the statement in the chairman's question is correct, then the tariff is levied to put up the rates of interest in this country to the money lender as well as to pay higher wages. That is the inevitable conclusion to be formed from his question.

Mr. WILLIAMS. I can not answer that question, Mr. Clark.

The CHAIRMAN. The rate of interest in this country is regulated, at least it depends a good deal, upon rates of interest upon farm mortgages in the West, does it not?

Mr. WILLIAMS. Well, I am not going to answer those questions, because I don't know anything about that subject.

Mr. CLARK. Yes; that is getting in to where you do not know.

Mr. WILLIAMS. No, sir; I do not know.

Mr. UNDERWOOD. You stated that you thought that the duty levied on tin plate should be the differential between the cost abroad and the cost here.

Mr. WILLIAMS. Yes, sir.

Mr. UNDERWOOD. That is, as you voted the Democratic ticket, I suppose you indorsed the Democratic platform on these questions?

Mr. WILLIAMS. I did not indorse the Democratic platform in its entirety. [Laughter.]

The CHAIRMAN. Do not ask that same question of Mr. Underwood. [Laughter.]

Mr. UNDERWOOD. I am not testifying.

The CHAIRMAN. And you do not want to be embarrassed.

Mr. UNDERWOOD. What I want to get at, Mr. Williams, is this: If we take the actual cost of production of tin plate in Wales, which is the principal market, and add to that the cost of transporting the product to New York City, which is the cheapest point to bring it into in this country, and then take the cost of manufacturing tin plate in the United States, the actual cost, including all the labor cost that you have given, then, if the cost of the product in the United States is higher than the cost of the product in Wales with the freight added, and deduct one from the other to ascertain the difference of how much the cost product is greater in the United States than the cost product of Wales with the freight added, and fix a tariff at that rate, you say that that is a fair and equitable tariff?

Mr. WILLIAMS. Yes. I said this, that the differential of cost in Wales compared with the differential of cost of making plate in the United States—or, in other words, giving us an opportunity to make the export trade in our own country.

Mr. UNDERWOOD. In other words, to give you equal competition in the American market.

Mr. WILLIAMS. To give us an opportunity of making that plate here.

Mr. UNDERWOOD. You do not ask for more than that?

Mr. WILLIAMS. I do not know what the duty should be.

Mr. UNDERWOOD. I know, but you do not ask for more?

Mr. WILLIAMS. I ask that we be given conditions under which we can make the reexported trade—that which is now being made in Wales—in the American mills by the American workingmen.

Mr. UNDERWOOD. Do you think that the American mills could compete with the mills in Wales on a free-trade basis?

Mr. WILLIAMS. No, sir.

Mr. UNDERWOOD. What effect would that have on the American production of tin?

Mr. WILLIAMS. It would have the effect of putting the American tin-plate manufacturers out of business.

Mr. UNDERWOOD. If we fix the differential in duty on the basis that you state, the difference in cost in Wales and the cost of the American production, do you think that that would enable you to control your business and a large portion of the American market?

Mr. WILLIAMS. In answering that question I desire to say again that what we desire is that we be given an opportunity of working this plate in our own country; and I have stated that I believe the duty would be the differential, and I can not say anything further.

Mr. UNDERWOOD. That is what I wanted. In other words, that is an absolutely prohibitive duty. But you do not stand for that proposition, do you?

[No response.]

Mr. COCKRAN. The figures you have given here, as to the cost of producing this commodity in America as compared with the cost in Wales, would indicate a very decided inferiority in productive capacity of the American laborer.

Mr. WILLIAMS. No, sir; not necessarily so.

Mr. COCKRAN. If it would cost so much more per ton, as you have given here——

Mr. WILLIAMS. Mr. Cockran, I have already stated, in answer to some of the questions that have been asked me relative to the amount of output of the American mills compared with the output of the mills in Wales, that I will endeavor to get that information for you, and when you get that information you will find that the larger number of men employed in the American mills are able to turn out a larger output.

Mr. COCKRAN. That is just what I wanted to get at. The American laborer is capable of a larger output than the foreign laborer?

Mr. WILLIAMS. Yes, sir.

Mr. COCKRAN. So that in making any kind of a comparison or fixing the relative rates of wages the statements are more or less misleading.

Mr. WILLIAMS. I got all the data I could on the matter. I stated that I am not in a position to get the cost. I present these figures in evidence at this time, and if you are in a position to get the cost of production in Wales, then these figures will be invaluable to you in comparison.

Mr. COCKRAN. You can see that if a man producing steel, or any other commodity, could produce twice as much as another, and if he were to pay twice as much wage, there would be more profit accruing to the man that paid the high wages to labor than the man who paid the low wages?

Mr. WILLIAMS. So far as the American workingmen is concerned, they can hold their own with any workingmen in the world. They are as efficient as any in the world.

Mr. COCKRAN. They are more efficient, are they not?

Mr. WILLIAMS. Yes, sir.

Mr. CLARK. Mr. Williams, is there any considerable percentage of men laboring in the American tin mills who are not American citizens—neither naturalized or native?

Mr. WILLIAMS. Why, I believe the largest number of employees in the American tin mills are American citizens. I would be safe in asserting that 85 per cent, possibly, of all men working in the American tin mills, who came from the other side, are American citizens. I think they come here with a desire to become American citizens.

Mr. CLARK. I am talking of your business. Do any of them come here with simply a desire to work a while and then go back? You know that five or six hundred thousand went back recently, and what I was trying to get at was whether any large percentage of that kind of men were employed in the tin mills?

Mr. WILLIAMS. I do not believe one-half of 1 per cent of the men who come over from Wales ever go back. They come here to stay here. They make this country their home, and they become citizens of the country as soon as it is possible for them to do so. I consider that the immigration that has come from Wales is about as intelligent as that from any other country.

Mr. CLARK. I do, too. Most of the workmen in the tin-plate mills of the United States are Welshmen, are they not?

Mr. WILLIAMS. In later years quite a number of Americans are going into the business. When the tin-plate industry first started the workmen were largely composed of men from Wales, but in recent years I do not suppose that one-half of the people employed in the American mills are people of Welsh nationality.

Mr. LONGWORTH. You say that you voted for Bryan this year. Are you going to do it again? [Great laughter.]

Mr. WILLIAMS. Well, no; I think——

Mr. GRIGGS. I would like to come back to this question of efficiency. You say that the American workingman can do anything any workingman in the world can do. Can he compete with any workman in the world?

Mr. WILLIAMS. I think so.

Mr. GRIGGS. Why is it necessary for you to have five extra men per ton over here on your tonnage work?

Mr. WILLIAMS. There is an entirely different method of working, Mr. Griggs, and I have already answered that question in this way, that we turn out a larger output in the American mills, and these figures will be submitted in a brief to the committee.

Mr. GRIGGS. You are going to show that in the brief?

Mr. WILLIAMS. We will endeavor to show that as far as we can.

Mr. GRIGGS. As I understand your position in this matter, you want the drawback done away with?

Mr. WILLIAMS. Yes; the drawback abrogated, and protection for tin-plate industries.

Mr. GRIGGS. What is done with the tin that is imported into this country and then exported?

Mr. WILLIAMS. I have already stated it is used for reexportation in connection with oil, fish, fruit, and other products.

Mr. GRIGGS. It is manufactured over here, is it not, after it has come in here?

Mr. WILLIAMS. No; when it comes into this country it is really a finished product.

Mr. GRIGGS. It comes in as sheet tin?

Mr. WILLIAMS. As tin plate. All they do after it comes in here is to make it into a receptacle to take the American product out.

Mr. GRIGGS. Well, does not that give employment to American labor?

Mr. WILLIAMS. Yes; most assuredly. But what I advocate would not take away the employment of American labor if that was done.

Mr. GRIGGS. Then you simply want to get more employment for more American laborers, is that it?

Mr. WILLIAMS. That is what I want; yes, sir.

Mr. GRIGGS. If I understood your statement correctly, there are about 486,000,000 pounds exported and about 551,000,000 pounds imported. That leaves a very small difference so far as the straight tin is concerned. Does that leave you any control of the American market?

Mr. WILLIAMS. Not absolutely. It is my opinion that the difference in the importations and exportations in that case would simply mean that that amount of tin, if it stayed here, would be practically special orders or a special grade.

Mr. GRIGGS. Supppose the drawback was done away with, that difference between 486,000,000, in round numbers, and 551,000,000 pounds would come in any way, so that the drawback would not affect that part of it.

Mr. WILLIAMS. It is so small.

Mr. GRIGGS. It does not affect that trade at all?

Mr. WILLIAMS. It is very, very small.

Mr. GRIGGS. How does that drawback affect you other than requiring these people who make cans to buy their tin in this country. Is that all?

Mr. WILLIAMS. That is part of it.

Mr. GRIGGS. It is imported to-day and exported to-morrow?

Mr. WILLIAMS. Yes, sir.

Mr. GRIGGS. Do you propose to export tin?

Mr. WILLIAMS. We would export it if we were in a position to do so, most assuredly.

Mr. GRIGGS. Could you export tin at the present prices?

Mr. WILLIAMS. No, sir.

Mr. GRIGGS. Could you export tin at the cost that it is manufactured in this country now?

Mr. WILLIAMS. No, I have endeavored to point out——

Mr. GRIGGS. If the drawback were done away with, how would you be able to export it?

Mr. WILLIAMS. Mr. Griggs, I have endeavored to point out in my statement already made that in order to get a share of this reexporting business, that the association of which I am an official, took off 25 per cent of their wages in order to try to get this business.

Mr. GRIGGS. Do you mean that they accepted wages at 25 per cent less in order to sell to the foreigners rather than the home folks?

Mr. WILLIAMS. Why, no.

Mr. GRIGGS. What do you mean by that 25 per cent less, then?

Mr. WILLIAMS. In order to enable the manufacturer to get this reexport trade, not the foreigner.

Mr. GRIGGS. Isn't that what export means, to go out of the country?

Mr. WILLIAMS. Yes, sir.

Mr. GRIGGS. Do you mean that you are willing to accept 25 per cent less wages on that part of the product?

Mr. WILLIAMS. Yes, sir; in order to compete with the foreign manufacturers.

Mr. GRIGGS. You are willing to accept 25 per cent less in order to be able to sell to a foreigner?

Mr. WILLIAMS. No, sir; I do not want to get confused in the questions.

Mr. DALZELL. I understand his meaning to be that the acceptance of 25 per cent less wages was for the benefit of the American manufacturer, and in no way a benefit to the foreign consumer.

Mr. GRIGGS. That is as I understood it, and that is what I am trying to get at. Did Mr. Dalzell state that correctly?

Mr. WILLIAMS. Yes, sir.

Mr. GRIGGS. Then you are willing to work for 25 per cent less for the foreigner than for the American?

Mr. WILLIAMS. No, sir.

Mr. DALZELL. It is all American in both cases.

Mr. GRIGGS. But the foreigner gets the benefit of the 25 per cent.

Mr. WILLIAMS. No; the American manufacturer gets the benefit of the 25 per cent.

Mr. GRIGGS. The American manufacturer in order to be able to sell goods to a foreigner gets his labor for 25 per cent less for that particular work?

Mr. WILLIAMS. This is the point: When this plate is imported into this country and then sent out again, it is what we call reexported plate. What we desire on the part of the American mills and the American workingmen is this, to make the plate that is now used for reexport purposes. Under the present conditions, in order that we can get even a small part of that trade, it was absolutely necessary that the association of which I am an official should enter into an agreement with the American tin-plate manufacturers, agreeing to a reduction of 25 per cent from the regular schedule of the association in order to stand our part of the share between the cost of the American tin and the Welsh tin.

Mr. GRIGGS. That is exactly what I wanted to get, and that is all.

JOHN WILLIAMS, SECRETARY-TREASURER AMALGAMATED ASSOCIATION OF IRON, STEEL, AND TIN WORKERS OF NORTH AMERICA, FILES STATEMENT RELATIVE TO WALES TIN-PLATE WAGES.

PITTSBURG, PA., *December 1, 1908.*

Hon. SERENO E. PAYNE,
Chairman the Ways and Means Committee,
Washington, D. C.

DEAR SIR: I inclosed under separate cover brief from officials of the Amalgamated Association of Iron, Steel, and Tin Workers, but omitted the inclosure contained herein, which is a scale of prices paid at the present time in the tin-plate mills in Wales. At hearing on November 27 I agreed to turn over same for information of committee.

Yours, truly,

JOHN WILLIAMS,
Secretary-Treasurer.

The Welsh Plate and Sheet Manufacturers' Association list of wages to remain in force until the 30th of June, 1906.

TIN-PLATE MILLS.

[Per dozen boxes.]

	s.	d.
Rollers	3	5
Doublers	2	9
Furnacers	2	7
Behinders	1	5
Shearers	1	1

A box of plates means a basis of 14 by 10 inches, 225 sheets, weighing 110 pounds in mills. Area, 31,500 inches. Allowance for waste to be 2 per cent.

Gains to be paid on all plates above 140 pounds per box in mills and tin house.

Mill furnaces to be relighted by employers after stoppages for repairs or holidays.

Tin-plate sizes are up to and including 54 by 28 inches.

For shearing small squares:

9 inches and under 10 inches	10 per cent extra.
8 inches and under 9 inches	15 per cent extra.
7 inches and under 8 inches	20 per cent extra.
Under 7 inches	25 per cent extra.

A bundler to be provided for each shearer in tin-plate mills.

Openers, 6s. 3d. per 100 boxes, with 9d. extra if outside sheets are thrown out.

Payment to be made on area of 31,500 inches on all tin-plate sizes. In the event of plates being drawn light, due to faulty workmanship, workmen may be penalized by the addition of sheets to make up weight.

That 2 per cent margin be allowed. Gains to be made up weekly. Anything over half a box to be paid for as a box.

The following to be the minimum weights of bars supplied to the mills:

	Tin house weights.	Weight per foot.	Widths.
	Lbs.	*Lbs. oz.*	
C 20 x 14	108	16 0	3
	105	15 8	3
	100	14 12	3
	95	14 0	3
	90	17 6	3
	85	16 8	4
	80	15 8	4
C 19½ x 14	110	15 12	4
C 18¼ x 14	110	15 12	3

Workmen to follow machinery consistent with efficiency of the same, and careful regulation of orders being determined for individual works, and that the men be instructed to utilize the full period of time of each turn and the machinery in use. In case of dispute at any works, a committee of three masters and three men shall visit such works and report to the conciliation board for settlement.

That in the event of breakdown from any cause in the mill, the men employed shall not be expected to remain more than a reasonable time.

Changing rolls.—When broken or damaged during work:

Up to and including 30 inches, 8s. per pair or 4s. per roll.

Up to and including 32 inches, 8s. 6d. per pair or 4s. 3d. per roll.

Up to and including 34 inches, 9s. per pair or 4s. 6d. per roll.

If changed on Saturdays, which means after completion of week's work:

Up to and including 30 inches, 9s. per pair or 4s. 6d. per roll.

Up to and including 32 inches, 9s. 6d. per pair or 4s. 9d. per roll.

Up to and including 34 inches, 10s. per pair or 5s. per roll.

Changing standards.—Rollers, doublers, and furnace men, 6d. per hour; behinders, 4½d. per hour.

Changing leading boxes.—Where there is no intermediate spindle between leading spindle and rolls, 3s.

Changing screw pin, 1s.; changing screw pin and box, 2s. 6d.

Changing carriages or riders, 1s.; top brass, 1s.; bottom brass, 2s. each.

Changing coupling boxes and spindles, 1s.

The above rates for changing rolls, castings, etc., to apply at works of 4 mills and under and where millmen are employed to do the work, and to come into operation on January 1, 1903.

SHEET MILLS

The following rates to be paid for sheets, black plate, and tin plates in sizes exceeding 54 by 28, and wider than 28 inches.

Table No. 1.—Over 54 by 28 up to and including 60 by 30.

Gauge	30	29	28	27/25	24/20	19/14	below
Per ton	21/6	20/6	19/3	18/0	16/0	13/0	12/0
Roller	6/6	6/0	5/10	5/5	4/9	3/10	
Doubler	5/3	5/0	4/8	4/4	3/10	3/1	
Heater	5/0	4/10	4/5	4/2	3/8	2/11	
Behinder	2/8	2/7	2/5	2/4	2/1	1/8	
Shearer	2/1	2/1	1/11	1/9	1/8	1/6	

Table No. 2.—Over 60 by 30 up to and including 96 by 30.

Gauge	30	29	28	27/25	24/20	19/14	below
Per ton	23/0	22/0	21/0	18/0	16/0	13/0.	12/0
Roller	7/0	6/7	6/4	5/5	4/9	3/10	
Doubler	5/7	5/5	5/2	4/4	3/10	3/1	
Heater	5/4	5/2	4/10	4/1	3/8	2/11	
Behinder	2/9	2/9	2/7	2/4	2/1	1/8	
Shearer	2/4	2/1	2/1	1/10	1/8	1/6	

Table No. 3.—From 40 by 31 and wider, up to 36 inches wide.

Gauge	30	29	28	27/25	24/20	19/14	below
Per ton	23/8	22/7	21/6	18/0	16/0	13/0	12/0
Roller	7/2	6/10	6/6	5/5	4/9	3/10	
Doubler	5/10	5/6	5/3	4/4	3/10	3/1	
Heater	5/5	5/3	5/0	4/1	3/8	2/11	
Behinder	3/0	2/10	2/8	2/4	2/1	1/8	
Shearer	2/3	2/2	2/1	1/10	1/8	1/6	

Table No. 4.—Above 36 inches wide.

Gauge	30	29	28	27/25	24/20	19/14	below
Per ton	24/2	23/0	22/0	18/0	16/0	13/0	12/0
Roller	7/4	7/0	6/7	5/5	4/9	3/10	
Doubler	5/10	5/7	5/5	4/4	3/10	3/1	
Heater	5/5	5/4	5/2	4/1	3/8	2/11	
Behinder	3/3	2/9	2/9	2/4	2/1	1/8	
Shearer	2/4	2/4	2/1	1/10	1/8	1/6	

The following sizes, being over 1512 sup. inches, are to be paid the rates of Table No. 1 (whether cut down to smaller size or not) and irrespective of what mills they are worked in:

$54\frac{1}{16}$ x $27\frac{3}{4}$	$58\frac{11}{16}$ x $25\frac{3}{4}$	$63\frac{3}{4}$ x $23\frac{3}{4}$	$69\frac{1}{2}$ x $21\frac{3}{4}$
$55\frac{1}{4}$ x $27\frac{1}{2}$	$59\frac{3}{16}$ x $25\frac{1}{2}$	$64\frac{3}{8}$ x $23\frac{1}{2}$	$70\frac{3}{4}$ x $21\frac{1}{2}$
$55\frac{3}{4}$ x $27\frac{1}{4}$	$59\frac{1}{4}$ x $25\frac{1}{4}$	$65\frac{1}{2}$ x $23\frac{1}{4}$	$71\frac{3}{16}$ x $21\frac{1}{4}$
56 x 27	$60\frac{1}{2}$ x 25	$65\frac{3}{4}$ x 23	72 x 21
$56\frac{9}{16}$ x $26\frac{3}{4}$	$61\frac{1}{4}$ x $24\frac{3}{4}$	$66\frac{1}{4}$ x $22\frac{3}{4}$	73 x $20\frac{3}{4}$
$57\frac{1}{4}$ x $26\frac{1}{4}$	$61\frac{3}{4}$ x $24\frac{1}{2}$	$67\frac{1}{4}$ x $22\frac{1}{2}$	74 x $20\frac{1}{2}$
$57\frac{5}{8}$ x $26\frac{1}{4}$	$62\frac{13}{32}$ x $24\frac{1}{2}$	68 x $22\frac{1}{4}$	$74\frac{1}{4}$ x $20\frac{1}{4}$
$58\frac{3}{16}$ x 26	63 x 24	$68\frac{3}{4}$ x 22	$75\frac{3}{4}$ x 20

Sheets or plates between 29 B. G. and 118 lb. basis are to be paid at 29 B. G. rate, otherwise all other intermediate gauges are to be paid at the lighter gauge rates.

1s. 6d. per ton extra to be paid for 31 G.

2s. 9d. per ton extra to be paid for 32 G.

4s. per ton extra to be paid for 33 G.

$12\frac{1}{2}$ per cent extra to be paid openers on sheets of 60 by 30 and upward.

Helpers to be provided in 42-inch rolls at 5s. per day of eight hours, and also in 36-inch mills on plates above 70 by 30 inches.

Helpers to be provided in 36-inch mills when working orders above 60 by 30.

Defectives 50 per cent less on plates as rolled.

Allowance for waste in mills 2 per cent.

Extras over 8 feet lengths 10 per cent on all gauges.

Extras over 9 feet lengths 15 per cent on all gauges.

Sizes over 26 inches up to 28 inches wide, up to and including 46 inches long, 28–29 W G be paid 15 per cent above tin plate scale.

These exceptions are made owing to the difficulty of working specifications within above limit.

The above rates include roller, doubler, furnaceman, behinder, and shearer.

Rates for changing rolls are left to individual works, as the conditions vary so much.

That in the event of a breakdown from any cause in the mill the men employed shall not be expected to remain more than a reasonable time.

Pickling.—Black and white:

Five shillings nine pence per 100 boxes for 4 mills; 5s. 6d. per 100 boxes for 5 to 8 mills; 5s. 3d. per 100 boxes for 9 to 12 mills.

Or employer's option, day work:

Seven shillings six pence head pickler; 6s. 6d. second pickler; 5s. 10d. third pickler.

In case of any change from piecework to day work, or vice versa, twenty-eight days' notice to be given.

Annealing.—Annealing (black and white):

Coal, 11s. 6d. per 100 boxes; gas, 10s. 6d. per 100 boxes.

Once annealing, 7s. 8d. per 100 boxes; gas, 7s. per 100 boxes.

Payment to be on mill make, and half a week's work to be kept in hand.

Wheeling coal and ashes to be done by employers.

Other work to be carried out as hitherto.

Opening small pots, viz, those used for plates, up to and including 30 by 21, 9d. per pot.

Opening small pots, larger sizes, 1s. per pot.

A payment of 5s. per furnace to be paid for relighting after repairs.

The taking in and taking out of annealing pots to be done as hitherto, except in cases of extraordinary labor.

Annealer's work to begin and end as in the past, except in special cases where the annealing furnaces are inconveniently placed, in which extra labor shall be arranged for by the conciliation board.

In cases where annealing is done by day work the rate to be equal to the above.

		Per day.
		s. d.

Cold rolling:

	s.	d.
Roughers	2	2
Finishers	2	0
Assorters	1	9
Attenders	1	9
Greasers	1	6

As in some districts great difficulties are experienced in getting cold roll labor, such works are allowed to make the best terms they can.

Holidays.—It is mutually agreed that the employers will concede a week's holiday during the months of July or August each year from 1906, details to be agreed upon before the months named

FINISHING DEPARTMENT.

Tinning.—Three pence per box.

Washing.—Three pence per box.

Risers.—First year, 1 pence per box; second year, 1½ pence per box; third year, 1¼ pence per box.

Assorting.—Tin plates, 1 pence per box; black plates, 6 shillings per 100 boxes.

Payment on area crosses and sizes as in mills.

Removing coal and ashes to and from tin house.—This work to be done by employers when water boys do not assist the tinmen. In cases where such boys are engaged, this work to be done by them.

"Make" boards to be put up in tin house, and gains to be made up weekly.

Five pence per hour to be paid the tinman when a breakdown occurs, if he is required to assist.

Six shillings per day of twelve hours to be paid the tinman when working an experimental pot, in the event of his being unable to turn out an ordinary make.

. *Boxing.*—Four shillings per 100 boxes, to include all labor except discharging.

Numbering boxes consecutively, 6 pence per 100 boxes.

Making tin cases—Tin lining.—(Old style), 2 pence per box.

From plates rolled to size and no soldering being required by the employer, except on cover, 3 farthings per box and gains.

Where soldering is required otherwise than on cover, 1 penny per box and gains.

Where plates of the size 20 inches by 10 inches are packed 225 sheets per box, on the basis of 1 pence per box, and where plates are packed 112 per box, on the basis of 3 farthings per box with gains.

Employment to be found, as far as possible, when men are not employed in making tin cases.

Lapping.—To be paid at the rate of 1 farthing per box of 112 plates, with gains, as in the last preceding paragraph mentioned.

Marking top sheets.—Rubber stamp, 3 pence per 100 boxes; iron stamp, 9 pence per 100 boxes.

Such payment shall not include the making or providing the stamp.

Weekly stock-taking, 6 pence per hour if required to be done.

General stock-taking, left to individual works as practice varies so much.

Reopening damaged plates and reboxing, 1 pence per box.

Iron hooping.—Empty boxes (with light steel bands) half-penny per box up to and including 28 inches by 24 inches, 112 sheets. Gains to be paid on 20 by 10 only. Anything over 28 inches by 20 inches, 112 sheets, subject to special arrangements.

All hooping, except as above, be paid for at 1 pence per box.

In all cases the men to cut the iron to lengths.

Crating.—To be paid for at the rate of 1 pence per box, including boxing.

Making Canada cases.—One and one-half pence per single case, and 3 pence per double case.

Corner clipping.—One-half pence per box up to and including 28 inches by 20 inches, 112 sheets. One-half pence per box for 20 by 10, with gains.

Payments on area applies to doubles and Canadas in all departments.

It is recommended that pays should be made fortnightly, with a "sub." alternate weeks.

If any dispute arises in cases of employees not included in the wage agreement, a committee of three masters and three men shall discuss the matter, and failing to agree, the matter shall be reported to the conciliation board for settlement. All disputes shall be settled within a reasonable time.

That any settlement as to wages and conditions arranged for the ensuing year will only be operative from the date upon which an agreement is completed with the other sections of the trade.

In case of dispute at any works, a committee of three masters and three men shall visit such works and report to the conciliation board for settlement.

That the rates paid, and the conditions, must not be more favorable than the foregoing to works outside the employers' association.

E. TRUBSHAW, Esq.,
Chairman.
BEN TILLETT,
General Secretary D. W. R. and G. W. U.
JOHN HODGE,
General Secretary B. S. S. and M. U.
IVOR H. GWYNNE,
General Secretary T. and S. M. U.
WILL. THORNE,
General Secretary G. and G. L. U.

JUNE, 1905.

———

THE MASTER SHEET METAL WORKERS' ASSOCIATION, SYRACUSE, N. Y., WISHES FOR FREE TIN PLATE.

SYRACUSE, N. Y., *December 31, 1908.*

Hon. SERENO E. PAYNE,
  Chairman Ways and Means Committee,
    Washington, D. C.

DEAR SIR: For the past ten years or more the tin-roofing industry of the United States has been declining until now there is hardly a shadow left of a former very prosperous and profitable industry.

Since its organization The National Association of Master Sheet Metal Workers of the United States, composed of local associations from Boston to San Francisco and from New Orleans to Milwaukee, has been trying to discover the reason for the decline of the tin-roofing industry and to restore it to its former prosperous condition.

On or about the 20th day of February, 1906, the board of directors of the National Association of Master Sheet Metal Workers, at their semiannual meeting held in Baltimore, Md., requested the manufacturers, importers, and jobbers of tin plate to meet them in conference to discuss the situation. It was the general opinion of the tin roofers present that the poor quality of the tin plate for roofing purposes was the sole cause, and that if tin plate made of charcoal iron could be obtained as formerly, so that tin roofs would last as long as formerly, the difficulty would be solved and tin roofing would regain its former popularity.

During the past two years several manufacturers, importers, and jobbers have been trying to manufacture or import charcoal iron tin plates for roofing purposes.

It seems that very little charcoal iron tin plate is manufactured in this country, and that, if a good plate is desired, the black sheet before it is tinned is imported from Wales, or the finished plate is imported from there.

The price of a good imported tin plate (20 by 28 inches), including the duty on the same, is from $20 to $25 per box of 112 sheets. This price prohibits the use of good tin for general roofing purposes; some will not, others can not, pay that price, and the result is that in many instances the inflammable tar roof is substituted, which adds greatly to the fire risk in any community; or a cheap, lightly coated steel plate is used, which, when it once begins to rust, goes through very quickly, with the result that tin roofs are indiscriminately condemned and a once very prosperous industry is fast going out of existence.

The members of the Master Sheet Metal Workers' Association of Syracuse, N. Y., as well as many members of the national association, have thought, and so expressed themselves, that if the tariff on tin plates could be removed, so that we could get a good imported charcoal iron plate at a reasonable price, which would reduce the price of tin roofing considerably, more tin roofs would be put on; tin roofs would, as formerly, last from thirty to fifty, and even to sixty and seventy years, and a once prosperous industry would be restored.

I have accordingly been instructed by the Master Sheet Metal Workers' Association of Syracuse, N. Y., to write to you and ask if anything can be done to reduce or remove the tariff on charcoal iron tin plate for roofing purposes.

We see by newspaper reports that such a movement is likely to be considered, and I am very sure that some of our members would like to be heard on that subject.

Respectfully,

OTTO GOEBEL,
Secretary Master Sheet Metal Workers' Association, Syracuse, N. Y., and Secretary of the National Association Master Sheet Metal Workers of the United States.

ROOFING TIN.

[Paragraph 134.]

JOHN H. STEVENS, NEWARK, N. J., CLAIMS THAT THE ROOFING TIN MADE TO-DAY IS OF INFERIOR QUALITY.

NEWARK, N. J., *December 18, 1908.*

COMMITTEE ON WAYS AND MEANS,
Washington, D. C.

GENTLEMEN: As a small property owner and a lifelong Republican protectionist, I call attention to the poor quality of roofing tin which builders have been compelled to use since the American tin manufacturers were freed from foreign competition by a high tariff. Tin roofs put on twenty years ago are intact, but roofs covered with American tin soon rust out and only last from two to ten years, even when kept well painted. The plumbers say that the rust attacks the tin from underneath, a thing unheard of with the former good quality. The loss to property owners throughout the country must be very large. I would respectfully suggest that the duty should be low enough to enable the importation of durable tin whenever our own product is improperly made.

The same is true of galvanized iron used for leaders. Any plumber will tell you that of late years the piping is rapidly attacked by the elements and has to be frequently replaced.

Perhaps this careless indifference to quality by manufacturers who fatten on the liberality of Congress has also affected other iron products—for example, steel rails, which Mr. Schwab testifies are in course of betterment. I think he is wrong, however, in asking us to pay for the cost of the necessary factory changes by maintaining the present tariff, for the foreign manufacturers, in order to meet him in these improvements, will also incur a big expense, and that should balance his burden without making it necessary for consumers to foot the bill.

Very respectfully, yours,

JOHN H. STEVENS.

STEEL BILLETS.

[Paragraph 135.]

THE BUREAU OF CORPORATIONS FURNISHES INFORMATION SHOWING COSTS AND PROFITS ON STEEL BILLETS.

DEPARTMENT OF COMMERCE AND LABOR,
BUREAU OF CORPORATIONS,
Washington, December 17, 1908.

MY DEAR CONGRESSMAN: In accordance with your request, I am sending sheets, showing costs and profits on steel billets, both of the Bessemer and open-hearth basic.

As was pointed out in my letter of December 14, transmitting profits and costs on steel rails, there are two sets of figures here, secured from two totally different sources, and therefore valuable as checks on each other and as showing their general accuracy. The figures in the first table herewith submitted are taken from the profit and loss accounts of the companies examined. The figures in the second table are taken from the cost sheets of those companies. The figures in the first are combined for Bessemer and open-hearth steel, giving a total average cost for five years, for all companies represented, of $20.60 per ton.

The figures for the second set are divided according to Bessemer and open-hearth steel, but if the two are averaged up on a weighted average that average of cost will differ only about 13 cents per ton from the average cost given in the first set. This discrepancy is extremely small when the vastness of the transactions is considered and the enormous number of figures which had to be consulted. It would have been remarkable if there had not been a discrepancy, and the fact that it exists shows the genuineness of the figures, and the fact that it is so small shows that they must be substantially accurate.

While these results are comprised in comparatively few figures, they are the results of a great amount of work—practically 10 or 12 men for nearly a year—and cover all the large companies, practically all the Bessemer ingots produced in the country and more than 75 per cent of the open-hearth ingots for the period used.

Very respectfully,

HERBERT KNOX SMITH,
Commissioner.

Steel billets—Cost of Bessemer and open-hearth steel billets, sold and used at a profit.

	Produced for sale or for use at a profit.			Sold.		
	Tons.	Cost per ton.	Amount.	Tons.	Price per ton.	Profit per ton.
1902	2,565,084	⎰21.73	$55,735,789.47	978,386	$26.33	$4.62
1903	2,119,275	23.01	48,758,554.92	628,070	28.55	5.01
1904	2,697,870	19.34	52,187,831.98	870,829	20.59	1.26
1905	4,365,583	19.19	83,776,622.37	1,414,638	21.95	2.85
1906	4,881,728	20.93	102,153,273.45	1,381,306	25.68	4.48
Total	16,629,540	20.60	342,612,072.19	5,273,319	24.30	3.60

Final commercial cost.	Large Bessemer billets.	Large basic open-hearth billets.
Tons produced	17,908,033	13,422,740
Pig iron and scrap	$14.34	$18.78
Waste	1.95	1.64
Cost of pig iron and scrap in billets	16.29	15.42
Variation in cost ingots	.36	.06
Labor	1.18	1.58
Manganese and fluxes	.37	.59
Fuel	.37	.94
Steam	.49	.87
Molds	.16	.17
Rolls	.03	.04
Materials in repair and maintenance	.27	.47
Supplies and tools	.17	.86
Miscellaneous and general works expense	.29	.89
General expense	.10	.13
Open-hearth rebuilding		.24
Depreciation	.10	.11
Total cost	20.13	20.87

Note.—The difference of $0.33 between the average cost of Bessemer pig iron, $14.01, and that used for Bessemer billet ingots is due to variation in cost of excess tonnage, and to freight on some of the pig iron. This figure, $14.01, here referred to was shown on the cost sheets of rails already transmitted to the committee by my letter of December 14, 1908.

The differences of $0.36 on account of the variation in cost of Bessemer and of $0.06 in cost of O. H. ingots is due chiefly to the fact that only a portion of the ingots made was used for large billets, and the average price at which this portion was used differed by that much from the average cost of all ingots.

The item of labor does not include, for much of the tonnage, the labor in unloading raw materials and in producing steam, which some companies include in the cost of raw materials and in the item "steam."

Only a little more than half of the tonnage of Bessemer and O. H. billets covered by the cost sheets appears in the tonnage of billets sold or used at a profit, the remainder having been used without profit in making other products.

Because of the way in which they are used no report of the total tonnage of steel billets produced in the United States is made, but the cost sheets obtained for Bessemer ingots cover practically all, and of open-hearth ingots more than 75 per cent, of the production of the country for the period.

COMPARATIVE COSTS AND PROFITS.

Costs.

Bessemer billets (any company for any year):

Lowest cost (1905) _____ $17.43

It must be noted, however, that this cost ($17.43) was merely the cost for steel sold. But about nine times as much more steel was made and used by this same company at a cost of $18.26, which is perhaps a fairer and certainly a more significant figure.

Highest cost under normal conditions (1903) _____ 24.95

It should be noted that there were some costs still higher for certain companies, but these were companies apparently just beginning operations and are not fairly representative.

Open-hearth basic billets:

Lowest cost (1905) _____ 18.24

Highest cost (1903) _____ 29.04

Profits.

Bessemer:
Lowest profit (1906) _____ $0. 62
Average profit (1906) _____ 3. 71
Open-hearth basic:
Lowest profit (1906) _____ 4. 90
Average profit (1906) _____ 5. 42

As pointed out in a note above, it has been generally attempted to give figures
that are fairly representative, and not those of companies whose conditions, for
one reason or another, are abnormal, either as dealing in some special product
or having just started, etc. It has been assumed that what the committee desired were figures which would represent different businesses of importance carried on under general conditions.

STEEL BARS AND BILLETS.

[Paragraph 135.]

JOHN O. PEW, YOUNGSTOWN, OHIO, MAKES SUGGESTIONS RELA-
TIVE TO STEEL BARS AND SIMILAR PRODUCTS.

YOUNGSTOWN, OHIO, *December 4, 1908.*
COMMITTEE ON WAYS AND MEANS,
Washington, D. C.

GENTLEMEN: The plant with which I am connected is located at
Youngstown, Ohio, and has an output of about 30,000 tons per
annum. It produces sheet steel from sheet-steel bars or slabs. The
sheet bar or slab mentioned in section 135 is our raw material, and
I am led to make these suggestions by feeling that the committee
might be misled by the fact that the word "bars" in the iron trade
is used in two distinct senses. The merchant "bar" made of steel,
the round and the finished steel product which corresponds with the
bar iron mentioned in section 123, is separate and distinct from the
steel bars in which we take an interest, because they are our raw
material, and we feel that the sheet bar is an unfortunate name for
that form of billet, which is essentially a billet and should not be
called a bar, because it is so distinct and separate and different from
the finished bar iron or bar steel, that to call both things by the
same name may lead to an error in the framing of your bill that
would be exceedingly disastrous to the manufacturers of sheet steel
and tin plate.

The steel bars which we buy and roll down into the finished sheets
would be more properly styled a "billet" than a "bar," but in the
trade they are known as "sheet bars," and should not be carried in
the same schedule as the finished bar steel. The cost of producing
sheet bars of steel is about 30 cents a ton more than the steel billet.
The difference in cost and real value is so slight that the billet and
the sheet bar should, in our judgment, carry the same tariff duty.
We are anxious that no mistake may be made in the adjusting of this
duty.

Briefly, I wish to say that I believe that a careful but not a radical
reduction may be made without serious injury to all the iron schedules. We are paying high wages, and a radical reduction in the protection that we have at present under the Dingley bill would make it
necessary for us to quit business or to reduce wages.

We think that section 135, in its classification, is open to a very serious criticism. The several kinds of steel therein mentioned are classified according to their value in the market. This, it seems to us, ought to be changed to a specific duty that would remain uniform and not go higher if the price of steel should rapidly rise in our market.

It seems that there is no reason why the duty should also be increased by the mere fact that the market value of the steel itself should go from 1 cent a pound to 1.4 cents a pound. The effort in the Dingley bill manifestly was to charge a higher duty for those products upon which a greater amount of labor had been expended, and this was right. The new bill, we think, should do the same thing, but it seems to us that it might be done in a more scientific way. The bloom, the slab, and the sheet bar are all essentially the same thing and can not differ much in cost of production. It is possible, however, that some influence might raise the price of the sheet bar in our market until it would go to $30 per ton, while at the same time the price of billets would remain as they are at practically $24 per ton. Under the classification that exists now in section No. 135 the tariff on the bars would, by a mere change in the quotations of market value, be advanced $4 per ton at a time when, owing to the scarcity of sheet bars in this country, it would be exceedingly disastrous to the sheet-mill industry, making the increasing rise a barrier against relief through importations from abroad at a time when the tariff ought to be lower and not higher; and in the making of the new rates of duty, if it is thought wise by the committee to change this schedule, it is suggested that the prices of these different articles be ascertained as they exist at present, and that as nearly as possible a specific duty be made and omit the ad valorem classification which is now in this section.

THE YOUNGSTOWN IRON AND STEEL ROOFING CO.,
JOHN O. PEW, *Vice-President.*

HON. W. AUBREY THOMAS, M. C., SUBMITS LETTER OF J. WARNER, NILES, OHIO, RELATIVE TO STEEL SHEET BARS AND SLABS.

WASHINGTON, D. C., *January 6, 1909.*

Hon. SERENO E. PAYNE,
Chairman Committee on Ways and Means,
House of Representatives, Washington, D. C.

MY DEAR MR. PAYNE: I inclose herewith a letter addressed to you which accompanied a personal letter that I received from Mr. J. Warner.

I ask that you read Mr. Warner's letter, as I know him to be one of the best-posted men in the iron and steel business, and feel that he is in a position to give your committee valuable information, especially to that part of the business pertaining to sheets and tin plate.

Yours, very truly,   W. AUBREY THOMAS.

NILES, OHIO, *December 19, 1908.*
To the CHAIRMAN WAYS AND MEANS COMMITTEE,
Washington, D. C.

GENTLEMEN: This letter is written to corroborate one sent to the Ways and Means Committee by Mr. John O. Pew, vice-president and general manager of the Youngstown Iron and Steel Roofing Company. Mr. Pew's letter explains the situation clearly, but as an independent manufacturer, dependent upon the large corporations for sheet bars, we wish to add a word to his statement.

What are known as sheets and tin plates are made from what is commercially known as steel sheet bars and slabs. The great labor cost takes place in the making of the sheets from the sheet bars and slabs to the finished product, and is among the best, if not the best, paid of all labor employed in steel mills.

The cost of producing steel billets and steel sheet bars and slabs is practically the same. The steel sheet bar and slab is the billet rolled some thinner, and is made from the initial heat at a cost, as stated by Mr. Pew, of about 30 cents a ton over the billet cost. There is, therefore, no reason why the steel billet and steel sheet bar and slab should not have the same duties.

As explained by Mr. Pew, what is commercially known as " steel bars," is an entirely different product from sheet bars and slabs, and are used for other purposes.

We hope that you will use your efforts to put billets and sheet bars and slabs under the same tariff schedule, as it means much to the independent manufacturers in this country who are dependent practically upon the large concerns for their supply of sheet bars and slabs, and the independent manufacturers are now producing probably 40 per cent of the sheets made in the country.

If what is known as steel sheet bars and slabs are listed under the same tariff schedule as what is known as steel bars, it would be possible, under abnormal conditions, for these corporations to ask a much higher price for steel sheet bars and slabs than is equitable.

Steel sheet bars and slabs are a much cruder material than what is known as steel bars, and constitute the independent sheet and tin plate manufacturers' raw material.

Yours, very respectfully,

THE EMPIRE IRON & STEEL CO.,
By J. WARNER, *President.*

SWEDISH BARS AND BILLETS.

[Paragraph 135.]

JAMES A. COE & CO., IRON AND STEEL MERCHANTS, NEWARK, N. J., ASK FOR REDUCTION OF DUTY ON BARS AND BILLETS.

NEWARK, N. J., *December 1, 1908.*
COMMITTEE ON WAYS AND MEANS,
Washington, D. C.   •

GENTLEMEN: You are no doubt familiar with present high tariff rates on Swedish bars and billets. The quality of the Swedish ores is much superior to any of our native ores for the manufacture of tool steels. The method of manufacture is by a charcoal process; frees the Swedish bar from injurious effects of sulphur coal; the native ore is remarkably free from phosphorus. Swedish bars are used entirely for the manufacture of English tool steels. Our American manufacturers use but a small percentage, if any, of Swedish stock in the manufacture of their different grades of tool steel.

As we have no American substitute for this Swedish stock, I urgently request that you seriously consider the expediency of making a marked reduction in tariff rates. The American tool steels could be improved to a marked per cent if the manufacturers were permitted to use Swedish bars and billets.

With the reduction of cost that would ensue by the use of Swedish stock at lower cost there would be a marked improvement in the quality of American tool steels.

In relation to the tariff on English tool steels, which is now 2 cents per pound on steels valued at not more than 10 cents per pound f. o. b. Liverpool, there should be a corresponding reduction of at least one-half cent per pound on the imported product.

Respectfully submitted.

JAMES A. COE & CO.,
JAMES A. COE, *President.*

STRIP STEEL.

[Paragraph 135.]

BRIEF BY SEARLE & PILLSBURY, REPRESENTING CERTAIN NEW ENGLAND IMPORTERS OF STRIP STEEL, SO CALLED.

BOSTON, MASS., *December 1, 1908.*

COMMITTEE ON WAYS AND MEANS,
Washington, D. C.

GENTLEMEN: After years of litigation, at enormous cost to the importers, and during which time they were obliged to pay the excessively high rate of 45 per cent duty, amounting to many thousands of dollars, it has finally been determined by the United States courts that strip steel is properly dutiable at specific rates under paragraph No. 135, and it is now being imported at from 1.3 to 4.7 cents per pound. Yet under the proposed new schedule published in the Iron Age, November 19, 1908, third new paragraph, following paragraph No. 135, page 1444, a high rate is to be imposed, which will either increase enormously the cost to the consumer or prohibit its further importation. Even now American strip steel practically monopolizes this market and is sold at a much lower price than the imported article can be.

No good, sound reason can be advanced why strip steel should be assessed at the unjust and absurdly high rate proposed, or why it should not remain at the specific rates under paragraph No. 135, where the highest courts have determined it properly belongs. So long as the Government is to depend upon customs duties for a large part of its revenue, there can be no fairer or safer principle than to impose reasonably low and living rates on foreign articles that compete (though to a very limited extent in the case of strip steel) with

American products turned out at a lower cost and selling in the open market at lower prices.

It is the ideal principle, as, while affording to the Government a legitimate and just source of revenue, its effect is to force the American producers, if they wish to secure the entire monopoly of this market, to raise the grade and quality of their products, just as the opposite rule would cut the Government off from a legitimate source of revenue and tend to lower the grade and quality of articles ultimately manufactured from such products.

As the language of the present tariff act has been interpreted by the highest courts in the land, so far as strip steel is concerned, it seems wise to leave it undisturbed, and as the litigation above mentioned, which extended over more than ten years, was enormously expensive both to the Government and to the importers, while the domestic steel interests were enabled, at no expense to themselves whatever and by reason of the absurdly high rates assessed, pending said litigation, which the courts have finally decided were unlawful and unjust, to seize and appropriate to themselves almost the entire strip-steel trade of this country, it seems only fair that in a revision of the tariff, promised and expected to be downward, strip steel should be assessed at least as low a rate as at present, thus leaving to the Government a just source of revenue and to the importers a reasonable amount of business to recoup them for the great expense to which they have been unjustly subjected.

We beg, also, to call the committee's attention to a separate brief which we are filing upon the proposition to impose an additional duty, under paragraph No. 141, for surface finish upon strip steel which has been cold rolled only.

Respectfully submitted.

SEARLE & PILLSBURY,
Attorneys for Edgar T. Ward & Sons.

STEEL BILLETS, BLOOMS AND SLABS.

[Paragraph 135.]

STATEMENT OF W. W. LUKENS, OF PHILADELPHIA, REPRESENTING THE ALAN WOOD IRON AND STEEL CO.

FRIDAY, *December 18, 1908.*

Mr. LUKENS. Mr. Chairman, I am a voluntary witness.

(The witness was here sworn by the chairman.)

Mr. LUKENS. I represent the Alan Wood Iron and Steel Company. Our works are in the Schuylkill Valley. We are independent manufacturers of basic open-hearth steel billets, blooms, and slabs for rerolling and forging, light plates, and sheets. Our markets are the Atlantic seaboard, where we have a small geographical protection against the competition of Pittsburg and other mills to the west of us, and our other market is the Pacific coast, where we are about on an even basis with all other manufacturers because the freight rate from our works to all Pacific coast points is the same as from Pittsburg. It is not necessary for me to tell you, I know, anything about geographical protection, and you must know that we are having more or less of a struggle to keep going. But we are keeping going, and we have been going for a great many years, and the point I want you to consider in what I am going to say is that we are independent, and we are furnishing a good, strenuous, honest competition in the lines that we manufacture, in the territories that we can enter in this country, and of course you can easily see that, situated as we are, with somewhat higher costs on account of our less favorable location with regard to supplies of ore, coke, and coal, unable to enter the enormous consuming territory between the Allegheny Mountains and the Rocky Mountains, on account of rates which are almost prohibitive, and as to the seaboard, we are practically at the seaboard, too great a cut in the tariff is going to hurt us a great deal. You see we would be the first people to be hit by it. And we have been down here listening to the arguments you have been having, and, if you will excuse a small reference to politics, because we voted for tariff revision, we have come to the conclusion that we ought to come down here and tell you how much of a reduction we can stand from the duties that are now in effect and still keep going without the calamity that we sometimes hear will take place if there is any reduction at all, and without cutting the throats of our workmen.

We have tried to figure it out on some logical basis. If we recommend, which I am going to do, a reduction in the duties on the products that we sell, we want some recognition on the raw material question. That is a very serious one with us. The ore question in eastern Pennsylvania is in pretty bad shape. The ore supplies of the country are "pretty well corralled," to use a western expression, and the result is that the eastern merchant pig-iron furnaces, from whom we buy our supply of raw material, so far as pig iron constitutes it, are forced to ask us at times pretty high prices, rather higher prices than we ought to pay. We think, while we are not directly interested in ore, we have reasoned back to ore in order to establish a reduction on our own duties. We think that you ought to give us free ore in eastern Pennsylvania, and I think when I say that that I represent— let me say I do not represent anyone but my own company officially, but I think we are a representative concern. We think you ought to give us free ore.

Now, in round figures, it takes two tons of ore to make one ton of pig iron; therefore it seems logical to us that the duty on pig iron should be reduced $1 a ton, if you give us that free ore, and I do not believe, from the investigations I have made, that there would be more than enough importations of pig iron on that basis to prevent runaway markets, and it seems to me that the condition produced would be a desirable one rather than an undersirable one, so far as the eastern pig-iron market is concerned. I do not want to bear on that too much, because we do not make pig iron. I am only going through this to show how I arrive at my final conclusions.

The other ingredient in a ton of open-hearth steel billets is scrap, and that is one of the things that I want to bring to your attention quite strongly. It is now in the same paragraph with and I think in the same clause with pig iron, at $4 a ton. It seems to me if you want to reduce the tariff, and if you want to work it out on a revenue basis, you have got the best kind of a chance there you could possibly.

have. I have talked with users of scrap, I have talked with producers of scrap, and I have talked with brokers who handle scrap, and I believe those are all the sorts of people who are interested in it, and the only argument I have heard brought up in answer to my recommendation that the duty on scrap be very largely reduced is the fact that it will take the place of pig iron. Now, that might be true in some lines in which we are not interested; for instance, bar iron. I do not know very much about the making of bar iron because we do not make it, but I understand that they do take wrought-iron scrap, with possibly a mixture of pig iron, and make iron bars, so that I am not prepared to say it would not interfere with the pig-iron people to have a heavy reduction on that in some ways, but it certainly would not interfere with anybody, and it would not do anybody, any laborer, or anyone else in this country any harm to put scrap for remelting in open-hearth furnaces on the free list if you want to, and if you want revenue, make the duty 50 cents a ton, and I will guarantee you will get some revenue.

Now, we need that scrap; there is a shortage of it. If there is not a shortage of it the supply can be bought up and laid down on some vacant lot until the man or men who buy it choose to offer it for sale; and the lines of the scrap market are like this, they corner it and it goes skyrocketing up, and it goes up too much, and the market breaks and down it goes with a sickening thud, and we are all topsy-turvy all the time in our cost sheets and the prices we can sell at on account of the raggedness of the market. Scrap is not manufactured. It is a by-product. It is the result of waste and wear. If you find any man who says " I make scrap; I make bars and chop off part of the ends and they are scrap," my answer to that is, probably he is paying some one a good, big salary to keep down the quantity of scrap he makes, so that I do not think it is quite fair for a man of that kind to say that he manufactures scrap. What he is doing is trying not to manufacture it.

I want to call your attention to one more point in connection with that, and then I will hurry on. That is the change in the Bessemer steel situation as compared with the open hearth. That has already been gone into very fully, I think, by Mr. Schwab, who, as the papers said, has sounded the death knell of Bessemer steel. That is quite evident in some figures from the statistics of Mr. Swank, of the American Iron and Steel Association. In the ten years from 1897 to 1907 there was an increase in the production of Bessemer steel in this country of 113 per cent, but the percentage of increase in the production of open-hearth steel was 873 per cent. Now, if you will stop and think that the Bessemer furnaces make scrap, and the open-hearth furnaces use it, you can see that every year, as the Bessemer has lost ground and the open hearth has gained, the proportion of scrap per open-hearth furnace has been steadily going down, and the actual increase in the use of scrap, assuming you use half pig and half scrap, in those ten years was 4,000,000 tons. You see it runs into big figures.

Now, I can not see the slightest objection to reducing the duty to 50 cents a ton.

Mr. UNDERWOOD. If scrap was on the free list, where would it come from in this country?

Mr. LUKENS. That is a pretty difficult question to answer, because we really never tried it. And it is such a queer thing; you can not lay your hand on it. It is not as if you could go and see the plant where it is made. But in a general way we would get it from Cuba and the West Indies. Some of that, or a good deal of it rather, can not be——

The CHAIRMAN. There was 2,000 tons that came in—where does that come form?

Mr. LUKENS. I bought some last year. I do not know of any this year.

Mr. DALZELL. Where do you get your scrap?

Mr. LUKENS. We buy it usually from brokers, and occasionally we buy from, perhaps, customers of ours who have a fairly large output, enough to make it worth while.

Mr. DALZELL. What is the average price of it?

Mr. LUKENS. I do not know, I am sorry to say. It has been this year as low as $13.25 in eastern Pennsylvania, and nobody knows the price of it just now, but it is somewhere between $17 and $18.

Mr. DALZELL. It is along about parallel with the price of pig iron.

Mr. LUKENS. No; it has no relation to the price of pig iron, except as regards its value in the open-hearth furnaces. There it has a value. But you can not compare it with anything, for the simple reason it is not manufactured. You throw away an old saucepan, and nobody knows when the cook is going to burn the bottom out of another one, so you can not estimate the supply. It is more or less visible; people buy it up.

Mr. DALZELL. I suppose you use Cuban ores?

Mr. LUKENS. We are not large users of ore. We buy a little bit, but we have no blast furnace. We buy our pig iron and our scrap and make our steel billets out of that. We are in the same position as a good many other steel makers in eastern Pennsylvania, and one reason we do not rush into the blast-furnace business is the ore question. It is not worth while to build a blast furnace unless you have an ore supply. We have looked into the Cuban ore proposition to some extent, and that has not been worked out, but I think it would help us very much to take the duty off.

Mr. DALZELL. Suppose you take the duty off ore and put the pig iron at $3 per ton, how much can you stand?

Mr. LUKENS. With scrap at 50 cents?

Mr. DALZELL. With scrap at 50 cents.

Mr. LUKENS. Two dollars from billets, because, as I said, it takes half a ton of pig iron to a ton of steel, so that makes 50 cents on billets. If you take $3.50 from the present duty on scrap, I do not think you ought to count more than $1.50 as a corresponding reduction on billets, because we would not get the whole benefit of the reduction of the duty. But I am perfectly willing to concede $1.50.

The CHAIRMAN. How much reduction can you stand if we do not take anything off of ore, pig iron, or scrap?

Mr. LUKENS. Then, I think, in view of our position and the cheerful competition that we are putting up against peculiar conditions, you ought to let us alone.

The CHAIRMAN. There is a question I want to ask you. You manufacture open-hearth steel. The tariff law has contained an item of $12 a ton on charcoal iron made in Sweden and Norway. It has been there a great many years, and there has not been much said about it, but I understand open-hearth steel takes the place of it now. It used to be used largely in the manufacture of scythes and wagon irons and things of that kind, where now they use open-hearth steel. Do you know of any occasion to keep that high duty on charcoal iron?

Mr. LUKENS. No. I think that is another chance to make a little money for the Government and reduce the price of that product.

The CHAIRMAN. There is hardly any of it imported.

Mr. LUKENS. It is no wonder, because it is so high in price no sane American would use it, unless obliged to.

The CHAIRMAN. What do you think would be a fair duty on charcoal iron?

Mr. LUKENS. I had not thought of that until this evening, and I do not know that I would like to say offhand.

The CHAIRMAN. I wish you would look into that and let me know. I have a constituent at home that asks me why they keep that duty on.

Mr. LUKENS. There is not any other place in the world where you can go and get the same iron. It can not be made here, and so far as I can see there is no reason for keeping anything but a nominal duty on it, and I really believe if you make that duty very considerably lower (we have always been in that business, and it has been dying slowly) that we can revive that business.

The CHAIRMAN. Is there any reason why it should be higher in price than open-hearth steel?

Mr. LUKENS. No; not the least reason, because the iron is not produced anywhere else.

Mr. GAINES. What is it used for?

Mr. LUKENS. It is used for any purpose where it is put to severe bending tests, or matters of that kind.

Mr. GAINES. What does it compete with?

Mr. LUKENS. I should say open-hearth steel, in a way, but not entirely. There are a lot of people who would like to buy it to-day, but who can not. They take the next best thing, because it is so very much cheaper. I think if you could give it to them for $10 or $12 a ton less they would buy a good deal more, and we would be glad to make it for them.

The CHAIRMAN. Are there any further questions?

Mr. LUKENS. We make sheets, and we are ready to stand something on sheets if you will give us what we want on raw materials.

Mr. DALZELL. Have you got a schedule made out that you can leave with us?

Mr. LUKENS. I can send it.

Mr. DALZELL. How much reduction can you stand?

Mr. LUKENS. One-tenth of a cent per pound; $2 per ton.

The CHAIRMAN. You are referring to paragraph 133?

Mr. LUKENS. No; paragraph 131.

Mr. CLARK. Do you want to cut all along the line, beginning with yourself, and so on down, or you do not want any change?

Mr. LUKENS. I have tried to make it plain, but that is not it. If you will give us free ore and make the reduction on scrap that we ask for—I have given you almost the full difference that it might make on a ton of steel billets—I have given it all but 25 cents——

Mr. CLARK. I say, your proposition is to begin the cut with you, or to begin at the other end. It does not make any difference where you begin; but if you begin with yourself, go to the bottom, or else let it alone.

Mr. LUKENS. Oh, I think that is fair. Don't you?

Mr. CLARK. I suppose it is, but I am not very expert on making an accumulative tariff.

The CHAIRMAN. Have you come in competition with that Alabama output, when you go over to California?

Mr. LUKENS. Not to a very great extent.

The CHAIRMAN. We have been told about iron pipe that they compete on. Now, they make open-hearth steel, I am told. Do you not have more severe competition from them than from anybody else?

Mr. LUKENS. Do you mean from Alabama?

The CHAIRMAN. From the Alabama product.

Mr. LUKENS. I do not think we do; no. Their freights are so high we are protected there.

———

W. W. LUKENS, OF THE ALAN WOOD IRON AND STEEL COMPANY, PHILADELPHIA, PA., FILES SUPPLEMENTAL STATEMENT RELATIVE TO STEEL BILLETS.

519 ARCH STREET,
Philadelphia, December 29, 1908.

Hon. SERENO E. PAYNE,
Chairman Committee on Ways and Means,
Washington, D. C.

DEAR SIR: In connection with the proposed revision of the Dingley tariff law, we respectfully address you herein in reference to paragraphs Nos. 121, 122, 124, 131, and 135 of the metal schedule.

Our works are at Conshohocken, in the Schuylkill Valley in eastern Pennsylvania, and we manufacture and sell independently in the open market steel billets, blooms, and slabs for forging and rerolling, and light plates and sheets of iron and steel.

Our markets are the Atlantic coast and the Pacific coast. Practically prohibitive freight rates prevent us from entering the vast consuming territory between the Alleghany Mountains and the Rocky Mountains. Situated as we are, therefore, on the Atlantic seaboard, lacking the geographical protection enjoyed by our competitors west of the Alleghany Mountains, unable to enter the great markets of the Central West, and with somewhat higher costs on account of our less favorable location with regard to supplies of ore, coal, and coke, too radical a change in the iron and steel tariffs would much more seriously affect us than manufacturers who are more centrally located with reference to our home markets and the necessary supplies of raw materials.

It is obvious, therefore, that any reduction that would be satisfactory to us should be agreeable to all.

If after due deliberation it is decided to revise the tariff downward in order to fulfill the pledge of the party returned to power, we trust that you may so adjust the revised rates as to prevent too sudden or undue a change in present industrial conditions; and believing that on account of our location our views with reference to the duties on our products may be of value to you, we have given the matter careful consideration. We find that very small reductions only would be possible, and we think that no changes should be made in the duties on our manufactured products, unless we be given at the same time lower rates on certain raw materials. On this basis we respectfully submit the following recommendations to your honorable committee:

1. Iron ore, paragraph 121, present duty 40 cents per ton:

We appeal strongly for free ore. This will conserve our natural resources, which are being depleted too rapidly, and it will help to overcome the disadvantage under which eastern merchant pig-iron furnaces are laboring on account of the practical monopoly of the American ore supply.

2. Pig iron, paragraph 122, present duty $4 per ton:

In round figures it takes 2 tons of ore to make 1 ton of pig iron. It is doubtful whether eastern makers of pig iron would get the entire benefit of the abolition of the duty of 40 cents a ton on iron ore, but assuming that they would, it would make a difference in the cost of pig iron of about $1 per ton. We therefore recommend a reduction of $1 per ton on pig iron, making the new rate $3 per ton, instead of $4 per ton, as at present.

3. Wrought and cast scrap iron and scrap steel, paragraph 122, present duty $4 per ton:

Scrap is not manufactured, but is a by-product, the result of waste and wear. About 50 per cent of it is used in the open-hearth furnace to make one ton of steel, with about an equal quantity of pig iron. Because it is not manufactured, the removal of the duty upon it or a heavy reduction in the rate will not injure anyone, but will have a tendency to reduce the cost of open-hearth steel to the American consumer and will benefit (a) open-hearth steel melters, (b) the laborers engaged in handling the material, (c) and the dealers and brokers who operate in it.

There is a shortage in the supply which has been brought about by the passing of the Bessemer converter and the rise of the open-hearth furnace. The Bessemer steel plant was a maker of scrap, while the open-hearth furnace does not supply itself. In our verbal statement we did not give you certain striking figures. They are as follows:

	Tons.
Production of Bessemer steel in United States in 1907	11,667,549
Production of Bessemer steel in United States in 1897	5,475,315
Increase since 1897	6,192,234

Or increase of over 113 per cent.

Production of basic open-hearth steel in United States in 1907	10,279,315
Production of basic open-hearth steel in United States in 1897	1,056,043
Increase since 1897	9,223,272

Or increase of over 873 per cent.

Production of basic pig iron in United States in 1907	5,375,219
Production of basic pig iron in United States in 1897	556,391
Increase since 1897	4,818,828

Or increase of over 866 per cent.

You will note (a) that in the ten years from 1897 to 1907 the percentage of increase in the production of open-hearth steel was nearly eight times as great as the percentage of increase in the production of Bessemer steel; (b) that during the same period the percentage of increase in the production of basic pig iron (which forms 50 per cent of the charge in an open-hearth furnace) was almost exactly the same as the percentage of increase in the production of open-hearth steel.

In other words, the production of the chief manufactured ingredient of a ton of open-hearth steel has kept pace with the demand, while on the other hand, with manufacturers abandoning their Bessemer converters, we find ourselves facing decreased production and increased consumption, with a consequently steady decline in the available supply of scrap per furnace per annum. This situation has made the scrap market highly speculative, and the cornering of the supply in a given district has become possible. We believe that the removal of the duty on scrap would result in largely increased imports, and if revenue is required for the Government, a nominal duty of not exceeding 50 cents per ton would produce large sums for the Federal Treasury. We therefore recommend a reduction of $3.50 per ton in the duty on scrap, making the new rate 50 cents a ton, instead of $4 as at present.

4. Steel billets, paragraph 135, present duty three-tenths of 1 cent per pound, when valued at 1 cent per pound or less, etc.:

We have stated that approximately one-half a ton of pig iron and one-half a ton of steel scrap are required for the manufacture of 1 ton of open-hearth steel. Our proposed reduction of $1 per ton in the duty on pig iron, therefore, is equivalent to a reduction of 50 cents per ton on steel billets. It would not be possible for manufacturers to realize in their cost sheets the full benefit of our proposed reduction of $3.50 a ton in the duty on scrap iron and steel, but we would be willing to concede $1.50 a ton on steel billets, in view of our proposed reduction on scrap, and this, added to the 50 cents a ton that would logically follow our proposed change in the pig-iron schedule, would make a total reduction in the duty on steel billets of $2 per ton. This is the maximum reduction that could be made on steel billets to-day without seriously affecting every eastern steel manufacturer; and we earnestly request that should you find it necessary to scale down this duty, you will not reduce it more than this. It is likely that importations would begin at once even on this basis. For example, the latest quotation that has come to our notice (November, 1908) on German billets was $26.50 per 2,240 pounds, f. o. b. dock Philadelphia, duty paid. This was based on the present duty of $6.72 per ton. Had the duty been $2 a ton less, as suggested above, the price would have been, presumably, $24.50 per ton, a figure that could not be met with profit by any manufacturer east of the Allegheny Mountains.

5. Sheet steel, paragraph 131, present duty seven-tenths of 1 cent per pound for sheets thinner than No. 10 and not thinner than No. 20, valued at 3 cents a pound or less, etc.:

While it requires 1¼ tons of steel to make 1 ton of sheets, we find by comparing present foreign selling prices that we can stand a ton for ton reduction in the heavier gauges, and therefore suggest the following: Thinner than No. 10, but not thinner than No. 20, wire gauge, one-tenth of 1 cent per pound reduction; thinner than No. 20, but not thinner than No. 25, wire gauge, fifteen one-hundredths of 1 cent per pound reduction; thinner than No. 25, but not thinne-than No. 32, wire gauge, twenty-five one-hundredths of 1 cent per pound reduction; thinner than No. 32 wire gauge, twenty-five oner hundredths of 1 cent per pound reduction; corrugated or crimped, twenty-five one-hundredths of 1 cent per pound reduction.

This would make the new rates as follows: Thinner than No. 10, but not thinner than No. 20, wire gauge, six-tenths of 1 cent per pound; thinner than No. 20, but not thinner than No. 25, wire gauge, sixty-five one-hundredths of 1 cent per pound; thinner than No. 25, but not thinner than No. 32, wire gauge, eighty-five one-hundredths of 1 cent per pound; thinner than No. 32 wire gauge, ninety-five one-hundredths of 1 cent per pound; corrugated or crimped, eighty-five one-hundredths of 1 cent per pound.

6. Charcoal iron bars, blooms, billets, etc., paragraph 124, present duty $12 per ton:

While making our verbal statement before your committee, you asked whether we knew of any reason for keeping this high duty on charcoal iron.

This is made exclusively in Sweden and Norway from the peculiarly fine ores that they mine there, and the pig iron, bars, and blooms are worked throughout with charcoal fires. The result is an iron of such quality as can be reproduced nowhere in the world. Years ago large quantities of it were used in this country, and it is still imported for special purposes, but its high price, plus the high duty, has made the prices of the various products manufactured from it so high as compared with open-hearth steel and other cheaper and poorer forms of so-called charcoal iron that its use has been largely curtailed.

In view of the fact that there is no source of supply for this material in this country, we can see no reason for the retention of so high a duty as $12 a ton. We believe further that a marked reduction will enable us to revive a great deal of the business we have had in the past, and this would be the case with manufacturers of other forms of it, such as wire, bars, skelp, etc.

We should think this duty might at least be cut in half, and do not believe any injury would result to makers of so-called charcoal blooms in this country if it were lower than this. We suggest, however, the advisability of the retention of some of this duty as a source of revenue.

Please bear in mind that we have given you frankly the maximum reductions that we believe could be made to-day without serious disturbance of the industry in this district. We believe that the competition that we and other independent makers of steel are providing for the trade on the Atlantic and Pacific coasts is of value to the country at large, and should be continued. Its value to the consumer and to the small manufacturer who buys our products is unquestionable, and we believe that by just so much as you reduce the duties on the products mentioned above beyond the points that we have recommended by just so much will you force the curtailment of operations east of the Alleghenies and foster a state of monopoly in the steel trade of this country.

If there is any further information that we can give you, or if we can in any way be of service to you in connection with this matter, we shall be most happy to comply with any request that you may make of us.

Yours, very truly,

ALAN WOOD IRON AND STEEL COMPANY,
W. W. LUKENS,
Assistant Secretary and Assistant Treasurer.

Countersigned:

HOWARD WOOD, *President.*
JONATHAN R. JONES, *Secretary and Treasurer.*

STEEL BARS AND PLATES.

[Paragraph 135.]

STATEMENT OF WILLIS L. KING, VICE-PRESIDENT OF THE JONES & LAUGHLIN STEEL COMPANY, OF PITTSBURG, PA.

WEDNESDAY, *November 25, 1908.*

Mr. KING. Mr. Chairman and gentlemen, as I am the first of the iron and steel manufacturers to appear, I would like to say that it was only possible to get a rather full meeting of the steel manufacturers, the different interests connected therewith, in New York yesterday, and it was decided to accept the invitation of the committee to come down here and give them what information we could in the formation of another tariff schedule.

Bearing in mind the request of the committee that a large delegation be not sent, one man was selected from about each of 12 or 15 different branches that will appear here to-day. For myself, I represent the corporation of The Jones & Laughlin Steel Company, of Pittsburg, who manufacture largely steel bars, plates, and structural material, and I would like to talk, with your permission, on those articles.

For some reason which does not appear to me, the tariff of 1897 placed steel bars, a finished product, in the paragraph with blooms and billets and other semifinished products, taking a duty of three-tenths of a cent a pound when valued at 1 cent per pound or less, and four-tenths of a cent per pound when valued above 1 cent and not above $1\frac{4}{10}$ cents per pound.

Mr. COCKRAN. What paragraph is that?

Mr. KING. It is paragraph 135. As I say, steel bars, for some reason—a finished product—was placed in that paragraph with a semifinished product like blooms or billets, while iron bars, in paragraph 123, take a duty of six-tenths of a cent per pound. There is no good or valid reason at present for this difference in a duty between steel and iron bars, and I would ask, on behalf of our company and the other manufacturers whom I have consulted, that the minimum duty on steel bars be advanced to four-tenths of a cent per pound instead of three-tenths of a cent on a minimum of 1 cent value. I would say, however, that I am a little unfortunate in asking for an advance on the first article in the schedule that I am talking about, but I want to assure the committee that I heard the discussion among the other manufacturers in New York yesterday, and they come here prepared to make recommendations for large, and in some cases radical, reductions in the present tariff in their lines, so I do not want you to feel that all the steel manufacturers here ask for increases in duty.

I am advised by recent cabled quotations that steel bars can be purchased, within a few days at least, at 1 cent per pound f. o. b. vessel at Antwerp. The freight is practically 8 shillings, or $2, a ton, which would lay them down at New York at $1\frac{1}{10}$ cents per pound, and adding the duty at present of three-tenths of a cent per pound would make the price of Belgian bars in New York, duty paid, $1\frac{4}{10}$ cents per pound, which is less than the low price of the American or domestic product to-day. That is the reason why I think the duty on bars should be advanced.

Another reason for the advance asked for is the danger of foreign makers dumping this product at prices much less than those of their home market at times when we most need the tonnage to keep our mills running and our labor employed.

Before going on to the plate and structural iron perhaps it would be better for you to ask me any questions that may occur to you, and which I will try to answer.

Mr. DALZELL. This is an improper classification in the present tariff?

Mr. KING. I think so. I think that a finished product ought to be taken out of the unfinished class and put in the finished-product class; in fact, it ought to be in with iron bars, although iron bars, I think, require a larger proportion of labor; and while I do not speak for the manufacturers of iron bars, it may be possible that they think that reducing the duty from six-tenths of a cent, as it is now, to four-tenths of a cent would be too much of a reduction. I think they perhaps would be justified in asking a larger duty on iron bars on account of the larger amount of labor that is spent upon them than upon steel.

The CHAIRMAN. Then there are inequalities in the iron and steel bar schedules?

Mr. KING. At the present time; yes.

The CHAIRMAN. That they are not properly classified; and you suggest that this be classified with what?

Mr. KING. With iron bars; that steel bars should be put in the same paragraph with iron bars, they both being finished articles.

The CHAIRMAN. Would that lower or raise the duty?

Mr. KING. I am asking for four-tenths of a cent on steel bars. If iron bars were put at the same price, that would lower the iron-bar duty two-tenths of a cent, or $4 a ton. But I qualified that statement by saying that I hardly thought it was fair to reduce the iron-bar schedule to that point, because there is more labor expended in the manufacture of iron bars than of steel.

The CHAIRMAN. They should not be classed so as to collect the same duty, in that case?

Mr. KING. No. I did not propose that, but I think they ought to be put into the finished class, and the nearest finished class to a steel bar is an iron bar.

Mr. BOUTELL. Right on that point, the present duty of three-tenths of a cent a pound on steel bars under the Dingley law is the same rate exactly that it was in the preceding law, the Wilson law.

Mr. KING. I did not happen to know that.

Mr. BOUTELL. It is. Therefore the same duty has been in existence now for fourteen years.

Mr. UNDERWOOD. As a matter of fact, therefore, the iron and steel schedule is the same to-day as it was under the Wilson bill, is it not?

Mr. KING. Well, I happen to know of some articles that are in the same schedule, but I really have not compared them all.

Mr. UNDERWOOD. The iron and steel tariffs are the same?

Mr. KING. I think so.

Mr. UNDERWOOD. The great bulk of productions of the iron and steel trade is the same under the Dingley and the Wilson bills, is it not?

Mr. KING. I presume they are.

Mr. BOUTELL. Girders are less and cast-iron pipes are less than under the Wilson bill.

Mr. KING. Under the Dingley law?

Mr. BOUTELL. Yes; double that of beams and cast-iron pipes.

Mr. UNDERWOOD. I want to ask you this question in reference to a comparison with the steel industry: I want to know what is the production of steel bars in the United States.

Mr. KING. It is the largest single article produced in the United States, and I presume that that holds true over the world—that is, that there are more bars made than any other single thing. I would say that the combined product of steel and iron bars would be five and one-half to six million tons. I am speaking now of normal times.

Mr. UNDERWOOD. I will ask you some questions with reference to the year 1907, because, of course, we all recognize that the panic condition prevailing in this country now is not a condition upon which to base an estimate. So I will consider the questions that I ask as relating to the year 1907.

The total production of bars in this country amounts to five and one-half to six million tons. What is the amount of total importations into the country?

Mr. KING. Comparatively small. I have not the exact figures.

Mr. UNDERWOOD. I see here, under this heading that I have before me, that the importations are given, under the total heading, for billets, blooms, and bars, as 41,000,000 pounds, which would only amount to 20,000 tons. That includes billets as well as bars, so that the total importations of billets under the present tariff is very slight, is it not?

Mr. KING. Yes, sir.

Mr. UNDERWOOD. So that the present tariff is practically prohibitive?

Mr. KING. Only at times.

Mr. UNDERWOOD. Of course; but most of the time it is practically prohibitive. When you compare 20,000 tons imported with 5,500,000 tons manufactured here, it is practically prohibitive, is it not?

Mr. KING. It was in that year, of course, because the foreign markets had all they could do to attend to their home markets, just as we had here. They could get better prices there then than by sending to this country.

Mr. UNDERWOOD. As to whether, in theory, this was placed in a tariff for revenue or placed in the tariff for protection, I will ask you: Do the iron and steel interests of this country believe in a prohibitive tariff?

Mr. KING. They believe in a protective tariff.

Mr. UNDERWOOD. Well, I know; but do they believe that a protective tariff is a prohibitive tariff?

Mr. KING. Not necessarily, I think.

Mr. UNDERWOOD. Do they believe it stands on the same basis of true protection at all if it is a prohibitive tariff?

Mr. KING. Yes; I think they do.

Mr. UNDERWOOD. Don't you think that when the tariff question comes up that the question of revenue to the Government should be considered as well as the industry?

Mr. KING. I think that there is something more important than that to consider, the rate of wages we can give to our workingmen here, which is something like 90 per cent—I think it is generally believed and recognized that labor is 90 per cent of everything produced at a profit when the cost of material is taken out.

Mr. UNDERWOOD. Is that so in the production of steel?

Mr. KING. I think so.

Mr. UNDERWOOD. Is not the cost of machinery a very much larger factor in the production of Bessemer steel than wages?

Mr. KING. A very much larger one?

Mr. UNDERWOOD. Yes. When you bring the raw iron from the furnace to the bar in the Bessemer converter, is not the cost of labor a very small item in comparison to the cost of your investment, your capital, and your interest on the investment?

Mr. KING. Very small at that point, but I am taking labor at the mines, transportation, and everything that labor goes into—coal, coke, and everything of that sort.

Mr. UNDERWOOD. You recognize that when you plant a grain of cotton seed that from that time on down to the finished fabric it is all labor. Now, taking our basic material in each industry, and considering the cost of the basic material in each country, and from the raw material or basic material the cost of labor added, what is the difference in the cost of labor between this country and that of the English or Belgium producer, as well as the German producer?

Mr. KING. I am very sorry, sir, that we have not that information, but we expect to give it to you later. But you probably appreciate that that is rather a difficult thing to get accurately, and we haven't got it and haven't had the time to get it since we had the call for this meeting. If you will permit me to say, we expect to get that information and give it to you in writing.

Mr. UNDERWOOD. We would very much like to have it.

Mr. DALZELL. You will file a brief hereafter?

Mr. KING. Yes, sir.

Mr. UNDERWOOD. The committee desires to have the brief and all information it can get; but I wanted to make a comparison with you on these questions. I certainly wish to be correct.

Mr. KING. I will be glad to do what I can in that direction.

Mr. UNDERWOOD. You say that you are entitled to this protection not from the question of revenue, but from the question of labor. Therefore, of course, the cost of labor here and abroad is a material question.

Now, to figure it so that we can carry it easily, what is the cost of a ton of this bar steel, the run of the mill?

Mr. KING. Do you mean in 1907?

Mr. UNDERWOOD. In 1907.

Mr. KING. I would say, roughly, about 1 cent a pound, manufacturing cost.

Mr. UNDERWOOD. Do you count the long or the short ton?

Mr. KING. Well, it makes a little difference, of course. A cent a pound would be $20 a net ton and $22.40 a gross ton. We sell it on the pound price, which means the net ton in this country.

Mr. UNDERWOOD. That would be $20 a ton?

Mr. KING. A net ton of 2,000 pounds; and that would relate to 1907, when we were running full and under the most favorable conditions.

Mr. UNDERWOOD. That is what I was considering. That is the cost price, or the selling price?

Mr. KING. That is as near the cost as I can give.

Mr. UNDERWOOD. Do you know of any of this bar iron being laid down in New York for sale at all, or at any other eastern port, in 1907?

Mr. KING. I think so, but I could not give you instances. During the great demand for materials there was some—I know—structural material (plates) coming into the country, and I believe there was some imported into Boston.

Mr. UNDERWOOD. Do you know what the selling price in Boston was, with the duty added at that time—1907?

Mr. KING. Well, it would probably have been—the English and the German prices were higher then, of course—but I would say it would be a cent and a quarter over there now instead of a cent; $5 a ton more.

Mr. UNDERWOOD. In other words, it would cost, laid down in Boston, $25 a ton.

Mr. KING. Of the foreign material?

Mr. UNDERWOOD. What the foreign material laid down in Boston or New York with the duty added was selling at. That is the real question, in Boston?

Mr. KING. I do not believe I understand whether you want the American selling price or the foreign price laid down at that time.

Mr. UNDERWOOD. You have given me the American cost of production as $20 a ton, and I would like to get the foreign selling prices in Boston or New York, with the duty added.

Mr. KING. Well, as near as I can get to it, I think it would have been $30 a ton in 1907; I think about that.

Mr. UNDERWOOD. Now, how much of that foreign selling price was freight, how much duty, how much profit, and how much labor; or, in other words, how much labor was there in a ton of that foreign selling price, of that $30 a ton.

Mr. KING. The cost of labor?

Mr. UNDERWOOD. Yes.

Mr. KING. I can not give you that; I haven't the figures with me; the figures of foreign labor.

Mr. UNDERWOOD. Well, how much was labor in the $20 ton of home production, at cost; the labor at your factory; and how much in the raw material, or basic material, at your factory?

Mr. KING. You mean just in the operation of making that at the factory, at the mill, without reference to the mines?

Mr. UNDERWOOD. I want to ask you for the price of the raw material, and then the labor at your factory.

Mr. KING. Well, I would like to give this to you subject to correction, because it is only from memory. I would say $5 or $6 a ton, with labor restricted as you have named it.

Mr. UNDERWOOD. Five to six dollars per ton labor. Now, if you added the labor or the raw material that came from the mines, how much additional would that add to it? Upon a ton of pig iron that would mean about a ton and a third of coke and about 2 tons of ore, at the outside—about that. How much would that labor amount to?

Mr. KING. I have a memorandum here of the labor cost on 1 ton of finished material, including the ore and coal and labor, of $8.25.

Mr. UNDERWOOD. That gives the entire labor cost $8.25?

Mr. KING. I want to make my position plain, that this is going into the labor of the mining of the ore, the coal, making the coke, putting through the blast furnace, and the finishing mills; it does not include any loss at all.

Mr. UNDERWOOD. That is all labor up to the point of production, and that includes every bit of it, $8.25?

Mr. KING. Yes.

Mr. UNDERWOOD. Have you any idea in this business as to what is the difference in the cost of labor abroad and at home? You state that you do not know the exact amount, but do you know the percentage of difference?

Mr. KING. Well, you can arrive at that, I think, by the selling prices, to some extent. I would say, generally speaking, that labor on a ton of steel did not amount to more than 60 per cent of ours.

Mr. UNDERWOOD. Their labor was about 60 per cent of ours?

Mr. KING. I would think so.

Mr. UNDERWOOD. That would make their labor about $4.35, then, on a ton, or make a difference of $3.90 in labor between the entire cost of the European product and the American product?

Mr. KING. Yes.

Mr. UNDERWOOD. Now, at the present duty of three-tenths of a cent per pound——

Mr. KING. Yes; $6 a ton.

Mr. UNDERWOOD. The duty on a ton of this is $6. The difference between the cost of American labor and foreign labor is $3.90; therefore it would be $2.10, under the present scale of protective tariff over and above the labor price.

Mr. KING. That seems to be about right.

Mr. UNDERWOOD. And the present tariff is prohibitive, practically prohibitive, because there are only 20,000 tons imported, as compared with five and one-half or six million tons manufactured. Now I want to ask you if, under these circumstances, you think the committee would be justified in increasing this duty?

Mr. KING. I certainly think so. You could not get along on $2 difference in labor; you certainly ought to give us some profit.

Mr. UNDERWOOD. Of course you ought to have some profit, but you wanted the duty based upon the labor cost. You have only 40 per cent of duty in excess of the labor cost, with a very small importation of this bar into this country, 20,000 tons, and which could not seriously affect a market producing five and one-half or six million tons, could it?

Mr. KING. There is a reason for that small—no, I do not think it could. But there is a reason for that small importation. One reason is that it is not very profitable to order abroad, for, in the first place, the buyer must put up his money first; he must take his chances of getting the class of material that he orders, on the sizes being right, and the quality; and if they come here wrong, there is no redress; he has got to take it, for he has paid his money. Then, of course, we must take into consideration the time it takes to get the material to this country, which is an important factor. That, I think, is the principal reason why a great deal more material has not been imported—the trouble in doing it and the risks involved.

Mr. UNDERWOOD. The year that we have been figuring on, 1907, was the year of the highest prices in iron and the year that would most likely invite importation.

Mr. KING. Not when their home market was equally as high.

Mr. UNDERWOOD. The price of iron has greatly dropped since that time?

Mr. KING. It has; yes.

Mr. UNDERWOOD. And the price of iron being so much lower, it would not invite importation as readily as on a high-priced market?

Mr. KING. No; it would not invite it.

Mr. UNDERWOOD. In other words, the principle has always been followed in all trades that when the home market is high the prices for the imported product is high, and the imports are larger than when there are hard times and the home market is dull. That is the universal rule, is it not?

Mr. KING. To some extent, unless there are some other circumstances. The point that I am trying to make plain is that they have practically the same conditions that we have.

Mr. UNDERWOOD. As a matter of fact, there are no importations coming in at all now, are there, of the English bars?

Mr. KING. A few.

Mr. UNDERWOOD. So, as a matter of fact, you practically have no competition from abroad, and you have largely an excess of protection already on your labor cost, and yet you say that the market is dull. I want to ask you if it is not due to the fact that there is overproduction in the United States, in the home market, and not competition.

Mr. KING. Not in normal times. There is this year, certainly.

Mr. UNDERWOOD. That is true in normal times, however. In 1907 you made a fair profit on steel bars, did you not?

Mr. KING. Yes, sir.

Mr. UNDERWOOD. And you could do it again in normal times?

Mr. KING. I think so.

Mr. UNDERWOOD. And you can not do it now because there is overproduction in the home market?

Mr. KING. Yes, sir.

Mr. UNDERWOOD. Then, if you have any reason to give why you, under those conditions, have asked this committee to raise this tariff, I would be glad to hear from you.

Mr. COCKRAN. One moment, please, before coming to that. Your firm, The Jones & Laughlin Steel Company, is practically in the steel combination, the United States Steel Company, is it not?

Mr. KING. Not at all, sir. We are entirely independent.

Mr. COCKRAN. It is a competing company?

Mr. KING. A competing company; yes, sir; entirely.

Mr. COCKRAN. Now, you stated a moment ago that some structural steel came in at Boston during the last year.

Mr. KING. Yes, sir; and more recently two cargoes at San Francisco, within a week.

Mr. COCKRAN. I was about to ask with reference to that. There was a special demand for steel at San Francisco following the fire, was there not?

Mr. KING. Not as much as you would suppose there was.

Mr. COCKRAN. Of course, everything is exaggerated, but there was a large demand, was there not?

Mr. KING. Yes, sir.

Mr. COCKRAN. Did that demand operate to bring in much foreign steel?

Mr. KING. Yes; quite a good deal.

Mr. COCKRAN. How much was brought in?

Mr. KING. I think possibly a third of what was used there—a quarter to a third.

Mr. COCKRAN. How much was that in tons?

Mr. KING. Over what period?

Mr. COCKRAN. At the time of the rebuilding of San Francisco, for the two years following the fire; that is, following 1906, say for the last two years.

Mr. KING. I could not from memory give you the exact figures, but I do happen to know that there are dealers out there who keep a stock of foreign steel, and it is coming in all the time.

Mr. COCKRAN. Can you tell us whether those steel bars imported to meet the San Francisco demand were landed in San Francisco or were they landed in New York and transported by rail to San Francisco?

Mr. KING. They were landed in San Francisco; and that is a point I am glad you mentioned, because we need a great deal more protection in San Francisco, on the Pacific coast, than we do on the eastern coast. There is a very low rate there; they get their product on vessels, and I am informed that they can ship from Antwerp to San Francisco at 35 cents per hundred pounds, which would be, say, $7 a net ton.

Mr. COCKRAN. How much would it cost at New York?

Mr. KING. Our rate out there, from Pittsburg or New York, via rail, would be $15, and that would be $7 foreign rate as against our freight rate of $15; therefore that is a favored place for the importation of steel—the Pacific coast—on account of the great difference in freight rate.

Mr. COCKRAN. Your idea is to balance that favor by a corresponding inflation of the tariff?

Mr. KING. I think we ought to be protected there, just as well as in the eastern part of the country.

Mr. COCKRAN. Your idea is that where there is an inequality in railroad rates in the cost of transportation, it should be balanced by tariff imposition.

Mr. KING. I think so.

Mr. COCKRAN. Now, did you say that you could furnish us with the gross amount that was received at San Francisco during that period?

Mr. KING. I think we can get that; I will try to.

Mr. COCKRAN. And you think it must have been a third of the total consumption?

Mr. KING. A quarter to a third, I would say.

Mr. COCKRAN. We will be glad to know the probable amount of importation; but is there any means of ascertaining what the consumption of domestic steel was in San Francisco immediately following the fire?

Mr. KING. I have no statistics on that.

Mr. COCKRAN. When you say a quarter to a third, you are not basing that upon calculation, but it is purely a guess?

Mr. KING. That is really all.

Mr. DALZELL. You wish to speak on some other subject, do you not?

Mr. COCKRAN. I have some further questions that I wish to ask in a moment.

Mr. POU. Do you export any of your product?

Mr. KING. No, sir; excepting that I may make an exception in some highly finished—one little special cold-roll shafting of which we export a little to England, but with that exception we do nothing in the export line at all.

Mr. HILL. You stated that there was a total production in the United States of about 6,000,000 pounds of iron and steel. What was the proportion of iron to steel?

Mr. KING. I would think that the iron was a million and a quarter to a million and a half, and the steel was the balance.

Mr. HILL. That would make four and three-quarter millions of steel and one and one-quarter millions of iron?

Mr. KING. Yes, sir.

Mr. HILL. And you state that there will be $4 per ton reduction proposed on the iron and $2 a ton increase proposed on the steel?

Mr. KING. No, sir; you misunderstand me. I do not attempt to speak for the manufacturers of iron bars. We do not make them at all at our factory.

Mr. HILL. I understood you to say that you proposed an increase of one-tenth of a cent for steel bars asked for by the iron and the steel representatives who met yesterday, and that you understood that there would be two-tenths of a cent reduction asked for on iron?

Mr. KING. No, sir; you misunderstood me there.

Mr. HILL. What was the statement that you made in regard to the reduction upon iron and increase upon steel?

Mr. KING. I made the statement that the present paragraph covering steel bars was wrong, and that they ought to be in a class with finished material, such as iron bars.

Mr. HILL. Did you not propose to ask for an increase to equalize it with the iron?

Mr. KING. No, sir; I asked for an advance——

Mr. HILL. It would then be unequal, would it not? The iron would still be two-tenths of a cent higher than the steel, would it not?

Mr. KING. But I think it is entitled to a slightly higher duty on account of the greater amount of labor required in making a ton of iron than of steel.

Mr. HILL. The only point I wanted to get at was this, that if you leave iron at six-tenths of a cent a pound, it makes no reduction on the iron, but does make an increase of one-tenth of a cent upon steel; so that really what you come here and ask for is a net increase of one-tenth of a cent upon steel bars?

Mr. KING. Yes, sir.

Mr. HILL. And upon 4,750,000 tons, that would be about $9,000,000 additional to the duty that is now charged on the entire product, which would be an increase of price of about $9,000,000. Is that what you ask for?

Mr. KING. I do not believe that I have made myself plain. In the first place, we do not make iron bars and do not want to speak for those people. The iron manufacturers will be heard later. I am only speaking for an increase on steel bars, because we make those, and we think that the present duty is too low.

Mr. HILL. What you are asking is $2 per ton increase of price on 4,750,000 tons?

Mr. KING. On steel bars alone?

Mr. HILL. Yes.

Mr. LONGWORTH. Is this the only schedule that you propose to raise?

Mr. KING. No, sir; I propose to talk on the structural and plate schedule, of which we are large manufacturers.

Mr. LONGWORTH. I understood you to say at first that it was rather embarrassing to you to advocate——

Mr. KING. Yes; to advocate an advance on the first article that we make.

Mr. LONGWORTH. But you propose to advocate others?

Mr. KING. I do not propose to ask any advance on the balance.

Mr. LONGWORTH. That is all I wanted to know.

Mr. KING. No, sir; no advance.

Mr. CLARK. You say you need more protection on the Pacific coast than on the Atlantic coast?

Mr. KING. Yes, sir; on account of the freight rate.

Mr. CLARK. Do you know of any way of devising a scheme for one tariff on the Pacific coast and another on the Atlantic coast?

Mr. KING. I do not; I think you will have to devise it.

Mr. CLARK. What you really want to do is to bring the Atlantic coast up so that it will make you all right on the Pacific coast. Isn't that what you want?

Mr. KING. No, sir; there is more used in the eastern part of the country than in the western part.

Mr. COCKRAN. You do not really care where it comes from, so long as you get the $9,000,000 do you?

Mr. KING. We do not say that we should get it, but we think our workingmen should get it.

Mr. COCKRAN. I understand; you are speaking now as a philanthropist on behalf of the workingmen, but you do not care who contributes the $9,000,000, so long as it is levied and collected?

Mr. KING. I would rather the foreigners would contribute it than our home people.

Mr. COCKRAN. I have no doubt that you have a philanthrophic preference, but what you are after is the $9,000.000 additional duty?

Mr. KING. Yes, sir; we think we ought to keep that.

Mr. COCKRAN. That is what you want this committee to give you?

Mr. KING. Yes, sir. We are also large manufacturers of structural material and plates in steel, and those carry a duty.

Mr. UNDERWOOD. Please give us the paragraph, Mr. King.

Mr. KING. Paragraph 125, " Beams, girders, joists, and so forth." They carry a duty at present of five-tenths of 1 cent per pound, and I propose to ask the committee, on behalf of our company and the other companies in this same line of business, that that duty be retained as it is, believing as we do that it is no more than an intelligent and proper duty for the protection of the American manufacturers and workingmen.

Mr. UNDERWOOD. Is that all you have to say on that particular schedule?

Mr. KING. Yes, sir.

Mr. UNDERWOOD. I would like to ask you what the production was in this country of beams, girders, and joists in 1907.

Mr. KING. About two million and a quarter tons.

Mr. UNDERWOOD. What did that production cost?

Mr. KING. Well, they cost something more than bars in the straightening; they cost something more on account of some extra work that has to be done on them in the way of straightening them, the extra cost of rolling and waste.

Mr. UNDERWOOD. What would you assume that to be?

Mr. KING. I would say $23 or $24 a net ton, under the most favorable conditions, in 1907.

Mr. UNDERWOOD. How much additional labor cost on this structural material over that of the bars?

Mr. KING. There is an extra labor in handling large and heavy bodies—straightening and shearing.

Mr. UNDERWOOD. You gave the labor cost of the other at $8.25. What do you give the cost of labor upon this?

Mr. KING. That labor cost that I gave of $8.25 was an average labor cost.

Mr. UNDERWOOD. I understood it so.

Mr. KING. Including these as well.

Mr. UNDERWOOD. Yes; the entire product.

Mr. KING. Yes, sir.

Mr. UNDERWOOD. Now, you say the production in this country is two and one-quarter million tons?

Mr. KING. That is, structural iron.

Mr. UNDERWOOD. I notice that there are no importations given here in the statistics that I have.

Mr. DALZELL. Yes, page 541, you will find that there was imported in 1906 98,588,475 pounds, at a value of $1,085,230, and in 1907 there was imported 34,359,271 pounds, at a value of $467,466.

Mr. UNDERWOOD. Thirty-four million pounds were imported in 1907, which would amount to 17,000 tons, so there is a production imported into this country of 17,000 tons against a production of two and one-half million tons in this country?

Mr. KING. The only reason why more was not imported was that they had more at home than they could do at better prices.

Mr. UNDERWOOD. Then that schedule, as is the other schedule, is practically prohibitive, and it gives you over 90 per cent of the business of the country. I notice that in the same year, 1907, you exported $6,954,000 worth, and a large portion of that, so these statistics state, went to Canada?

Mr. KING. Yes, sir.

Mr. UNDERWOOD. Does that conform to your knowledge of the business?

Mr. KING. Yes, sir; I think that is right.

Mr. UNDERWOOD. When you exported this structural material to Canada you had to pay duty to the Canadian government, did you not?

Mr. KING. Yes, sir.

Mr. UNDERWOOD. And you had to compete with the English product that came in at a lesser rate of duty than your product?

Mr. KING. Yes, sir.

Mr. UNDERWOOD. So that you were competing in a foreign market with this product at a higher rate of duty in the most prosperous year that you had had for many years?

Mr. KING. Yes, sir. As I said before, that is all a question of their ability to sell at a better price at home.

Mr. UNDERWOOD. Under those circumstances don't you think, Mr. King, that you can compete with your foreign competitors on your home soil at the present rate of duty when you can compete with him abroad at a higher rate of duty?

Mr. KING. I state that the reason that we didn't export largely was that the duty is not the same as to Canada; but those are all economic questions that are determined by the condition of things in the two countries. It is true that England has a preferential tariff into Canada for their own good.

Mr. UNDERWOOD. How much does that preferential tariff amount to?

Mr. KING. One-third less than the American tariff into Canada.

Mr. UNDERWOOD. If that is the case, and you can compete there with it at a third less, do you not think you can afford to lessen this duty a third, and get some revenue for the Government, considering the fact that the Government is running under a deficit?

Mr. KING. No, sir; I do not think we could consider putting that down a bit, if we are to have what I consider an intelligent and proper protection for American manufactures and labor.

Mr. UNDERWOOD. "Intelligent and proper protection." What do you mean by that? Do you think that a "proper" protection is one that gives you the absolute control of the home market, or one that gives you a fair chance to fight for the home market with your competitors?

Mr. KING. I should say a little more than a fair chance for the home market.

Mr. COCKRAN. A little more than a fair chance is a foul advantage, is it not?

Mr. KING. Not altogether, I think. There is a distinction there. I believe we ought to keep the American market for ourselves.

Mr. UNDERWOOD. In other words, what you believe in is a prohibitive tariff, practically?

Mr. KING. I think that probably is right.

Mr. UNDERWOOD. I would like to ask you whether you, as a business man, want us to amend the Constitution and raise our revenue from an income tax, or from an inheritance tax, or do you believe in raising revenue from tariff taxes?

Mr. KING. I believe that you ought to raise it on luxuries; put more on.

Mr. UNDERWOOD. You believe that we should put a prohibitive duty on iron and steel, and things of that kind, and raise the revenue on coffee and tea?

Mr. KING. They are not luxuries, they are necessities.

Mr. UNDERWOOD. What are luxuries?

Mr. KING. I would say silks, jewelry, diamonds, wines, tobaccos—anything in the line of luxuries that a man could get along without; that he does not need.

Mr. UNDERWOOD. As a matter of fact, of course, on those items that you have named we are receiving practically all of the duty that we can. We can not raise the price on tobacco, but on silks we might raise more revenue by reducing the duty some, but the silk men say that they ought to have a prohibitive tariff there, too. But as a matter of fact it looks as if we had to either lower some of these duties to raise enough revenue to support the Government or else take in some new items like coffee and tea that have never been taxed before. Now, as a business proposition—and you come before this committee to advise us, and we are glad to have your advice—I would like to know whether or not the people in the iron and steel business are not willing under the circumstances, when the Government is needing money, to make a reasonable reduction as long as they have a fair chance to control the market?

Mr. KING. I say that we are able, under an intelligent and protective tariff, to pay our men such wages as I would like to pay them. I do not believe that they would object to a tax on coffee and tea and sugar and what not; that they could afford it.

Mr. BOUTELL. You say: "Intelligent and protective tariff." Those terms are synonymous, are they not?

Mr. KING. With me.

Mr. COCKRAN. Undoubtedly. [Laughter.]

Mr. COCKRAN. You have several other schedules to discuss, have you not?

Mr. KING. Quite a number; yes, sir.

Mr. COCKRAN. Is there any other one, I would like to ask, on which you propose an increase in the existing rate excepting the one on steel bars?

Mr. KING. I think not. I think they are all in line of reductions or else retaining the present tariff.

Mr. COCKRAN. Upon this particular schedule you wish to leave the rates as they are?

Mr. KING. Yes; on beams, girders, and plates.

Mr. COCKRAN. What is called structural steel?

Mr. KING. Yes. There are two schedules, paragraphs 125 and 126, one being for structural materials and the other plates. I have grouped them together, and the duty is the same on both.

Mr. COCKRAN. Are there any others upon which you wish a reduction?

Mr. KING. That is all I desire to talk about.

Mr. COCKRAN. And upon the balance of the schedules, you go into reductions?

Mr. KING. Others are coming to represent them. I am only speaking for the material that we manufacture. There are a great many other lines that we do not go into. Those gentlemen are here and ready to be heard.

Mr. COCKRAN. I thought we were going to get the benefit of your views upon the reductions?

Mr. KING. No; I do not think we ought to speak of that if we do not manufacture them.

Mr. COCKRAN. That is, you do not want any reductions on anything that you produce?

Mr. KING. No, sir. I ask for an advance of one-tenth of a cent on bars, and that the present schedule on plates and structural materials should remain as it is.

Mr. COCKRAN. Oh, I see. When you were talking about your embarrassment at the beginning, you were referring to the order of presentation and not to the subject of presentation.

Mr. KING. I felt embarrassment that I should start off before this committee by asking an advance.

Mr. COCKRAN. Now, as to the condition of this industry. At present you can produce steel as cheap as anywhere in the world?

Mr. KING. At the present time we can?

Mr. COCKRAN. Yes.

Mr. KING. No, sir; that is not a fact.

Mr. COCKRAN. Where can they produce it cheaper than you?

Mr. KING. I would say in England, Belgium, and Germany.

Mr. COCKRAN. What particular articles of steel are there that can be produced cheaper, and what is the difference in the rates?

Mr. KING. I speak more particularly of what we come in competition with—bars, plates, and structural material.

Mr. COCKRAN. Well, take the steel bars. You are selling them at what rate?

Mr. KING. To-day, at the market price, between $1.35 and $1.40 per hundred pounds.

Mr. COCKRAN. How much per ton?

Mr. KING. At $1.40 per hundred would be $28 a net ton, and $1.35 a hundred would be $27 a net ton; that is, $27 and $28.

Mr. COCKRAN. What is their cost of production?

Mr. KING. The way we are running now, I believe it is costing all we get for them, Mr. Cockran.

Mr. COCKRAN. Then it costs $27 to $28 a ton to produce.

Mr. KING. That is what I believe to-day, and running under the conditions that we are.

Mr. COCKRAN. At what rate did you sell this production of yours in Canada?

Mr. KING. At practically the same price.

Mr. COCKRAN. What did it cost you to produce?

Mr. KING. Just as much as the domestic product.

Mr. COCKRAN. How are you able to lay those down in Canada and sell them, and pay duty, when the cost of production at home is $28?

Mr. KING. We do not pay the duty. The consumer over there pays it.

Mr. COCKRAN. At what rate were those sold in Canada?

Mr. KING. They were sold within something like a dollar a ton of the domestic price.

Mr. COCKRAN. And the duty was much higher; the duty was how much, in Canada?

Mr. KING. I really do not know the rate of duty, excepting that we paid more duty than England. I know that England has a preferential duty.

Mr. COCKRAN. What was the return to you for that proportion of your product that you sold in Canada?

Mr. KING. Practically as much as we sold it for in this country.

Mr. COCKRAN. Then, at that rate, it must have sold in Canada for $33 or $34 a ton?

Mr. KING. Certainly; higher there on account of the duty they have to pay.

Mr. COCKRAN. Was English steel selling at that rate also?

Mr. KING. We can not sell unless we sell in competition with them.

Mr. COCKRAN. So that the English steel was selling in Canada at the rate of $34 a ton to compete with you?

Mr. KING. We sell practically at the same price. Unless we meet the conditions over there we can not sell.

Mr. COCKRAN. And you can do that. If you can compete with them in Canada under a disadvantage, why can you not compete with them here, where you have the advantage of transportation, even at less than the present rates of duty?

Mr. KING. Well, they bring that a great distance, and, as I said before, there are some disadvantages in buying abroad on account of the fact of having to pay in advance and taking the risk on quality. They would rather pay us a little more money and have recourse on us if it is not right.

Mr. COCKRAN. But, Mr. King, surely you must see that in selling in Canada you have to pay the cost of transportation to Canada, and you have to pay the duty.

Mr. KING. Understand, we do not have to pay the duty; the buyer pays that.

Mr. COCKRAN. The duty is levied upon that product?

Mr. KING. Yes.

Mr. COCKRAN. And that duty is higher than the duty levied upon a similar product coming from England?

Mr. KING. Yes, sir.

Mr. COCKRAN. It is 33⅓ per cent higher, is it not?

Mr. KING. Yes, sir.

Mr. COCKRAN. And yet, with those disadvantages, you are able to maintain successful competition in Canada?

Mr. KING. Not at all times we can not, Mr. Cockran.

Mr. COCKRAN. Of course there are exceptions, but you can, generally speaking?

Mr. KING. Yes, sir.

Mr. COCKRAN. If you maintain competition with a foreign producer in Canada under those disadvantageous conditions, why can you not maintain competition near at home where you have the advantage in transportation to the market, and where there is no differential duty levied against you as there is in Canada?

Mr. KING. The duty in Canada is about as high as ours in this country—that is, the American duty.

Mr. COCKRAN. I understand that, and that is precisely what gives the point to my questions. You are able to maintain competition in Canada under the disadvantages of a differential tariff, a discriminating tariff that discriminates against you, amounting to one-third of the total amount of tax that is levied there, and I ask why you can not maintain competition in this country where there is no discrimination against you, and where you have the advantage of being relieved from the cost of transportation altogether?

Mr. KING. Well, Mr. Cockran, it is a fact that we do sell cheaper in Canada, and I think all over the world, as a rule, than we do at home, for the purpose of keeping our mills going. There are times when it is an advantage to keep our mills going and our workingmen employed.

Mr. COCKRAN. Did you not say a moment ago that you got exactly the same rates?

Mr. KING. Not exactly, but practically.

Mr. COCKRAN. Yes; the difference is between "practically" and "exactly." Would you just define that? What do you mean by "practically the same" and "exactly the same," if the meaning is not identical?

Mr. KING. I mean that they have in Canada what is called a "dumping clause" to prevent material being sold in there. We can not declare below 5 per cent below the prices current in this country; in other words, they take our domestic price, and we can not declare for a duty there at less than 5 per cent, or else the customer is subject to a large penalty for dumping. That 5 per cent, I think, would represent about the difference—I am trying to get at practically what I told you; that is, as to what I meant by "practical"—that would represent the difference between the Canadian price and ours.

Mr. COCKRAN. That 5 per cent would not even equalize the discrimination in the tariff, would it?

Mr. KING. To that extent, it would.

Mr. COCKRAN. It would only reduce it, it would not extinguish it. Now, to return to my question. In Canada you are able to meet competition successfully under conditions which impose upon you a discriminating tariff. In this country, where you have no such disadvantage, and where you are not required to transport or bring your goods across the sea, why can you not maintain competition equally well, and even better?

Mr. KING. Well, we can not do it.

Mr. COCKRAN. You mean to say that you do not want to do it, do you not?

Mr. KING. We can not do it. I would like to say to the committee that in my opinion it would never be possible in the United States to manufacture as cheaply as those foreign countries do for two reasons, one being the great distance and the great cost of transporting materials to the mill from the largely scattered places that we have to bring it; for instance, we bring our ore 1,100 miles. I do not believe that it would ever be possible for that reason, for the large freight cost in assembling those materials, to compete against the English and the Belgians, who have the material right around them. They have the coal, the ore, and the limestone right within a stone's throw, and they are relieved of that heavy freight. I have gone to the trouble to bring here the cost of freight per ton in Pittsburg on the materials necessary to make a ton of finished material.

Mr. UNDERWOOD. Assembling the raw material?

Mr. KING. Yes.

Mr. UNDERWOOD. How much does it amount to?

Mr. KING. It amounts to $6.65.

Mr. COCKRAN. In spite of all these disadvantages you actually have sold it and do sell it in competition with England and Canada. If you are able to do it there, I ask you why you can not do it here?

Mr. KING. We can not, because the amount sold there is so small.

Mr. COCKRAN. But that would increase the difficulty in selling it over there.

Mr. KING. I do not think it would.

Mr. COCKRAN. Do you mean to tell us that it is easier to dispose of a large amount than a smaller amount?

Mr. KING. I mean if you sell a small volume at a lower price it does not affect you so much as if you had sold a larger volume at a small price.

Mr. COCKRAN. You have stated that you sold practically all at the same price. The difference was simply 5 per cent, and that is your explanation. Surely it is not difficult to see that is your position, unless you can make a further explanation.

Mr. KING. I can not add anything different.

Mr. COCKRAN. Then you can give us no reason beyond that why competition could not be maintained in this country against foreign producers as successfully as it has been in Canada.

Mr. KING. I would not want it to be put down just that way.

Mr. COCKRAN. We do not want it to be put down unless it is the fact. Will you give us an additional explanation?

Mr. KING. I come here after a long experience in the steel business, and I want to state that I believe in a protective duty for America, principally on account of the fact that it increases the wages of the workmen of America. I know that we can not successfully compete with them on account of the handicap of high wages, large freight cost, etc. We can not compete with the world in this home market unless we are protected.

Mr. COCKRAN. You are not testifying as to your experience. You are testifying as to your belief. We are trying to get at the facts on which you base your belief. This act must be framed and passed by Congress, and what the committee wants is the facts and not the belief of a witness.

Mr. KING. Yes, sir.

Mr. COCKRAN. For that reason I ask if you can recall any facts in relation to the production of steel beyond what you have told us to explain why competition can not be maintained by producers in this country of an article which you say you market successfully in Canada under the present tariff.

Mr. KING. We sell very little in Canada.

Mr. COCKRAN. I understand that you say what you have sold was at a profit, and if you have sold that much at a profit you could sell twice as much and also sell it at a profit. So far as your testimony goes you think there is no reason outside of your belief why that is not practicable?

Mr. KING. No.

Mr. COCKRAN. You can give us no reason why competition can not be maintained here against all comers as well as in Canada in the production and sale of this article?

Mr. KING. I do not know that I have anything more to say in addition to what I have already said.

Mr. COCKRAN. You are very frank, Mr. King. Now, I understood you to say that in seeking this increase in steel bars you are seeking to increase the tax on an article in the production of which you are engaged. You have made a profit on the production of steel bars under this tariff?

Mr. KING. Certainly.

Mr. COCKRAN. Then why do you want this additional tax—to make more profit?

Mr. KING. No; but I simply say that it is my belief that if the tariff is not raised that England and Germany, which have heretofore had antiquated facilities, might, if the present duty be allowed to remain—and therefore the present conditions allowed to remain as they are at present—might put in large capital and better facilities, so as to compete with us in this country.

Mr. COCKRAN. I see. Then you want this tariff to quiet your apprehension that you might possibly meet with losses.

Mr. KING. I do not claim that we have made losses in recent years, except the present year on account of the panic.

Mr. COCKRAN. In reference to this industry to which you have testified as being in a state where it is making a profit and in which the conditions are satisfactory, you now ask that we add a taxation which would amount to $9,000,000 on the consumers of this country, and you ask that simply for the purpose of quieting your apprehension. Is that your only reason?

Mr. KING. I make it because I want it to be a certainty that prosperity will be continued in the industry and that we will continue to employ labor.

Mr. COCKRAN. Employ labor? You are employing labor now.

Mr. KING. We want to employ more labor.

Mr. COCKRAN. You testified, as I understood you, that the proportion of labor cost on a ton of finished steel was about 60 per cent. Am I right?

Mr. KING. I testified it was $8.25.

Mr. COCKRAN. Out of the total cost how much would it be?

Mr. KING. Last year it was $31.

Mr. COCKRAN. About 40 per cent?

Mr. KING. That is nearer to it.

Mr. COCKRAN. During the last year you have had a congestion or surplus of stock, as I understand; that is, you have not disposed of all of your stock.

Mr. KING. The steel industry of this country has been running from $33\frac{1}{3}$ per cent to 60 per cent at present, since the panic.

Mr. COCKRAN. Then you have not a surplus stock?

Mr. KING. No, sir.

Mr. COCKRAN. Have you ever tried the policy of reducing prices in order to stimulate consumption?

Mr. KING. Prices have been reduced.

Mr. COCKRAN. How much have they been reduced?

Mr. KING. During the past year?

Mr. COCKRAN. Yes; during the past year, on your product.

Mr. KING. Eight dollars a ton.

Mr. COCKRAN. That is, on your product?

Mr. KING. That is, on the finished steel. It was a little more than $8 a ton, on account of the lack of demand and poor business. The steel business went down from $5 to $6 per ton and the majority of the finished material from $4 to $5 per ton.

Mr. COCKRAN. To continue the inquiry upon your product, steel bars, how much have they been reduced?

Mr. KING. Four or five dollars per ton.

Mr. COCKRAN. It is now selling at $32?

Mr. KING. Yes, sir.

Mr. COCKRAN. When did that reduction occur?

Mr. KING. In the spring or the early part of the year.

Mr. COCKRAN. Did that stimulate production?

Mr. KING. No, sir.

Mr. COCKRAN. What effect did it have on consumption?

Mr. KING. I do not think we are fully over the panic yet, but as we recover gradually from the effects of the panic, I do not know whether the effect of the reduction in price will be to stimulate consumption or to lower the price still further.

Mr. COCKRAN. Did an increase of business follow the reduction in price?

Mr. KING. There was some increase in business.

Mr. COCKRAN. If the increase in business had gone a little further don't you think that production would have been still further stimulated?

Mr. KING. I do not know. I think that the mind of the country was such that they were only buying what they positively had to have. I do not think there was any increase to any great extent.

Mr. COCKRAN. There are two ways in which revenues can be increased from an industry like yours. One would be by increasing prices on a limited production and the other would be by increasing production and getting lower prices. And upon that theory your belief is that an increase of tariff rates will distribute its beneficent results between the workingman and capital. Is that your idea?

Mr. KING. I do not want to intimate that prices ought to be increased materially.

Mr. COCKRAN. Materially? But you want to put on a tariff for the purpose of increasing prices?

Mr. KING. Yes, sir. We want to keep out the foreign article. I do not mean by that to say that home consumption is not affected by the law of supply and demand.

Mr. COCKRAN. You say they are not affected by the law of supply and demand?

Mr. KING. I say they are affected by it substantially.

Mr. COCKRAN. When you say that the operation of the law of supply and demand diminishes the total supply you also say that it would shut out the foreigner.

Mr. KING. Under a reduction he would bring in more than he brings in now.

Mr. COCKRAN. You mean that consumption would equal domestic production, plus the foreign importations?

Mr. KING. Entirely so.

Mr. COCKRAN. To that extent would an increase of tariff taxes shut out the foreign product and diminish the total supply?

Mr. KING. Yes, sir.

Mr. COCKRAN. Then, under those conditions, if the law of supply and demand go into effect, the result must be to put up prices.

Mr. KING. I think that is logical of such an increase as you ask.

Mr. COCKRAN. You are reconciled to the increase of prices by the statement and belief on your part that you distribute the results among capital and laborers?

Mr. KING. About 90 per cent of it goes to labor.

Mr. COCKRAN. Ninety per cent of it goes to labor. And I suppose capital gets the remaining 10 per cent in the nature of compensation for distribution?

Mr. KING. Yes.

Mr. COCKRAN. So that back of all questions among employers and capital and labor as to whether they will be able to levy these exactions, the fact remains that any imposition which is levied must be paid for by the community?

Mr. KING. I think that there must be some imposition some place and I think that is where it ought to be levied. I think the working-man is fully able to take care of himself.

Mr. COCKRAN. You think that the consumer has too much money?

Mr. KING. Well, he is willing to pay.

Mr. CLARK. Is it not a generally accepted opinion that Mr. Andrew Carnegie knows something about the steel business.

Mr. KING. I think so.

Mr. CLARK. Is it true, as he has said, that the mills of this country can make steel cheaper than anybody else on the face of the globe?

Mr. KING. Perhaps so.

Mr. CLARK. Then why do not the steel men of the United States devote themselves to those markets of the world instead of putting up prices to the American consumer of steel?

Mr. KING. I think I would answer that by saying that Mr. Carnegie has been out of the steel business for some eight or nine years.

Mr. COCKRAN. He has taken his money out.

Mr. KING. He is not interested in the business now except in getting interest on his bonds.

Mr. RANDELL. You did not mean to say that he would misrepresent the conditions?

Mr. KING. Well, I want to be charitable. I believe that Mr. Carnegie, having been out of the business eight or nine years, does not fully understand the conditions.

Mr. CLARK. I want to ask you the direct question: Is it true that we make steel cheaper than anybody else in the world?

Mr. KING. It is not.

Mr. CLARK. Then that is the end of the chapter so far as that part of the industry is concerned. Now, is it your idea, that when we ship steel to Canada that the Canadian consumer pays the tariff?

Mr. KING. Yes, sir.

Mr. CLARK. After twenty-five years of wrangling between the high-tariff man and the low-tariff man, the revenue-tariff man and the free trader, they have all gotten together on the proposition that the consumer pays the tariff.

Mr. KING. I think that is true. I am glad that he pays it.

Mr. CLARK. Then that is one question upon which they have all gotten together after a quarter of a century?

Mr. KING. Yes, sir.

Mr. POU. The steel corporation is the largest producer of steel in the world, is it not?

Mr. KING. Yes, sir.

Mr. POU. It has a great deal to do with fixing prices, has it not?

Mr. KING. That is natural, with the large production which they make.

Mr. POU. Is it not a fact that it has such control of all of the different branches of production in steel as to practically fix the price of steel in this country?

Mr. KING. I would not like to put it in that way. I believe that it controls now on an average of 50 per cent of the entire output of all kinds of steel in this country. Since the steel trust controls that much and in a way controls the price, I think it is natural that the people who do the other 50 per cent of the business would try to come as near to that price as they possibly could.

Mr. POU. As a practical proposition the price of steel is largely controlled by the " steel trust," as you call it.

Mr. KING. I think that is a fact.

Mr. POU. I believe you said that you were a competitor of the steel trust.

Mr. KING. Yes, sir.

Mr. POU. Do other manufacturers make the same things which they make?

Mr. KING. Only a small part of them. They manufacture everything in this country made of steel, and that is one of their advantages.

Mr. POU. They make some of the things which you make?

Mr. KING. Yes, sir.

Mr. POU. And therefore you are getting the prices of your product fixed by the trust?

Mr. KING. Well, I do not think that is a fair way to put it; it is rather a bald way to put it. In other words, we get just as much as they do, and we should get as much, because ours is just as good.

Mr. POU. But no better?

Mr. KING. No better.

The CHAIRMAN. I have before me Mr. Carnegie's article in the Century, and I am going to read about a column or so of it on this question, for the benefit of the committee and the gentlemen present, and after that I will ask you some questions in reference to it.

(The chairman read the following:)

The writer has cooperated in making several reductions as steel manufacturers became able to bear reductions. To-day they need no protection, unless perhaps in some new specialties unknown to the writer, because steel is now produced cheaper here than anywhere else, notwithstanding the higher wages paid per man. Not a ton of steel is produced in the world at as small an outlay for labor as in our country. Our coke, coal, and iron cars are much cheaper, because more easily obtained and transported, and our output per man is so much greater, owing chiefly to the large standardized orders obtainable only upon our continent, the specialized rolling mills, machinery kept weeks upon uniform shapes without change of rolls, and several other advantages.

Britain and Germany are the only important steel-manufacturing nations other than ourselves. I am assured by one who has recently examined the matter that he found even in Germany to-day that the cost per ton for labor was greater than with us, unusually high as our wages are at present.

The United States made last year more steel (over 23,000,000 tons) than Germany, Britain, France, and Belgium combined. New steel works are under construction which will produce enough to enable her to make more than the whole world besides. This she will do within five years, probably within three.

The day has passed when any foreign country can seriously affect our steel manufactures, tariff or no tariff. The Republic has become the home of steel, and this is the age of steel. It may probably be found that there exists the small manufacturer of some specialty in steel which still needs a measure of protection. The writer hopes, if such there be, the committee will give patient attention to such cases. It is better to err on the side of giving these too much, rather than too little, support. Every enterprise of this kind should be fostered. The writer speaks only of the ordinary articles and forms of steel as being able to stand without protection. He hopes there are to-day pioneers in several new lines requiring protection which will be generously given temporarily. The committee should welcome such special cases.

The CHAIRMAN. He speaks of other features. I will have the whole article inserted in the record in connection with the correspondence between the chairman of this committee and Mr. Carnegie, in which he was asked to appear here. I wish to ask you some questions in regard to this. He says that he was assured by one who has recently examined the matter that the cost per ton for labor was greater than with us, unusually high as our wages are at present. Have you any information or statistics that will aid this committee in an examination of the question so as to enable us to come to a correct conclusion? I understand that you deny this statement. What we want is evidence upon the subject in order to satisfy the minds of the members of the committee as to whether or not what Mr. Carnegie states is true. Have you any such statistics?

Mr. KING. I have.

The CHAIRMAN. Will you prepare them and give them to the committee?

Mr. KING. I can do so. I do not know what the other gentlemen have.

The CHAIRMAN. The object of this committee is to get the facts in these matters so as to enable it to come to a just conclusion. That is all the people expect of us in reporting this bill. We have endeavored to get people before this committee, people of every kind, who could give us facts and figures or information in regard to the changing of rates, in order that we may come to a just conclusion, but unfortunately up to this time most of the steel men have not been able to come. Only one man in the steel industry, I believe, has indicated his determination to come. The other gentlemen do not seem to have the time nor the disposition to come before the committee. What we want is the facts, and we would like to have you give us the important facts on this subject.

Mr. KING. In regard to that I want to say, as I stated in the beginning of my testimony, that we have not been able to get all the facts on account of the short time which was allowed us. We propose to secure and give you that information at as early a moment as possible.

The CHAIRMAN. I was out when you made that statement and I simply wanted to explain to you that the committee wants the facts.

Mr. KING. Yes, sir.

Mr. RANDELL. In your opinion is this iron and steel industry well established in this country? Is it not one of the best established industries of the country?

Mr. KING. It is.

Mr. RANDELL. You say that you want practically a prohibition?

Mr. KING. Well, I believe in protection.

Mr. RANDELL. You say that prices are at present dictated practically by the terms of the steel trust?

Mr. KING. Yes, sir.

Mr. RANDELL. You also stated, I believe, or claim, that the revenue is not to be considered above protection in the making of this bill?

Mr. KING. Yes, sir.

Mr. RANDELL. Then your idea would be, without going into the question of the constitutionality of it, that to levy a tax for the benefit of this industry is nothing but an excuse for putting on the tariff, while in fact the real object is to keep outside competition from interfering with you on what you desire in your business?

Mr. KING. The experience of the past has demonstrated that the country has always prospered under protection and has languished under a low tariff.

Mr. RANDELL. It is your idea that the business ought to be treated fairly?

Mr. KING. Yes, sir.

Mr. RANDELL. You get protection along with the steel trust?

Mr. KING. We get protection as manufacturers. As a matter of fact, prices have been lower for five years, and, I think, on the average, prices are as cheap as they have ever been in this country.

Mr. RANDELL. You think that we, sitting here as representatives of the people and looking after their interests, ought to fix the tariff to suit the steel trust and let them look after the interests of the people by fixing prices?

Mr. KING. Not at all.

Mr. RANDELL. If there should be a desire to gouge a little bit, where would the people be protected if the trust should conclude to put the tariff too high?

Mr. KING. We could not afford to gouge anybody. It would not be good policy.

Mr. RANDELL. You do not think there would be any gouging done?

Mr. KING. There may be in some instances. I do not think it has been done recently.

Mr. RANDELL. You say that we ought to levy it for the benefit of labor. Is it not a fact, in your opinion, that so far as the great income from this industry is concerned—an income more than is natural to it—that income goes to the manufacturer instead of to the laborer?

Mr. KING. No, sir; I could not agree with you in that statement.

Mr. RANDELL. Does not the manufacturer get more than the laborer? Is it not a fact that the laborer gets the whey or the skimmed milk, while the manufacturer gets the cream?

Mr. KING. I do not know whether that is true or not. The laborer has not been reduced.

Mr. RANDELL. Is not the laborer in a bad condition when he can not get work on full time?

Mr. KING. Certainly.

Mr. RANDELL. But the manufacturers have not been in bad condition at any time.

Mr. KING. They are in a bad condition now. If you should hear some of the manufacturers you would think that they were walking the floor a little.

Mr. RANDELL. Don't you think they could still continue to pay the laborer and still make success of this well-established business?

Mr. KING. I do not understand that you can dictate the pay of labor.

Mr. RANDELL. It has been done.

Mr. KING. They look out for themselves and get their prices.

Mr. GRIGGS. What is the capitalization of your concern?

Mr. KING. Thirty million dollars. Might I make a little explanation of one thing I said this morning?

The CHAIRMAN. Certainly; make it now before any questions are asked you. We would be glad to hear you.

Mr. KING. I would like to say that in response to a question I said the cost of steel bars and other products in the same class under the most favorable conditions in 1907, when we were running full, was about 1 cent per pound. I would like to say that that cost eliminates all profit on that steel from the ground up. That is the actual cost of mining and transporting and putting the coal into coke, and so forth. I also desire to say that that cost was on the most modern, continuous mill, a mill of large products and small labor. I do not want the committee to get the impression that that cost would be the average cost of the ordinary mill; it would be very much higher.

I would also like to·say that the great majority of steel and iron manufacturers for years have taken but little out of their business, but have consistently pursued the policy of putting their profits back into betterments. I would also like to say that in comparing our products with foreign products at seaboard, we have to pay a freight of $3.20 to get it to the seaboard, which ought to be added. It is a charge against us which we can not escape.

Mr. Cockran, you asked me some questions this morning that I could not at the moment answer, about why we could send material into Canada, and I wanted to say to you that our exports into Canada are entirely in the western part of Canada, where we have the advantage of our freight rates, and the foreigner has the disadvantage of paying a heavy freight rate into the interior. We do not import successfully into Canada on the seaboard; we can not do it. I thought it was only proper to make that explanation to you.

Mr. COCKRAN. Yes; but you still have the advantage here in this country over the foreigner, the same advantage that you have up there, have you not?

Mr. KING. I do not see that we have. They have a considerable disadvantage.

Mr. COCKRAN. He has to transport his goods here; does he not pay for the transportation?

Mr. KING. If he goes into the interior, but not on the seaboard. There is quite a large tonnage down on the seaboard that we have to pay.

Mr. COCKRAN. Do I understand you to say, then, that you can maintain competition everywhere except at the seaboard?

Mr. KING. That is practically true.

Mr. COCKRAN. At the seaboard you can not?

Mr. KING. At the seaboard we can not, at the present rate of duty.

Mr. COCKRAN. You can not at the present rate of duty?

Mr. KING. Yes; three-tenths on bars, which I ask advanced to one-tenth for that reason.

Mr. COCKRAN. Did you not say that you had maintained it; that there were only a few thousand tons altogether imported?

Mr. KING. That was entirely owing to this trade. They do not have anything to import in here. They can keep so busy there that they could not send anything in here.

Mr. COCKRAN. You are not speaking from experience. You are merely speculating about importations, because you have not been actually troubled with imports?

Mr. KING. We have not been troubled with imports, that is true, but there is a good reason for it.

Mr. COCKRAN. I repeat, what you said before is absolutely true; you want this tariff to quiet your apprehensions, not to meet any experience you have had?

Mr. KING. I would also like to say that the Canadian government, besides imposing quite a heavy duty on imports, also has a system of bounties that they pay their manufacturers there on all classes of steel material, like pig metal, and so on. I think it imposes on rails manufactured in Canada as much as $8 or $10 a ton. I just wanted to show you that there were other countries that tried to take care of their home manufactures.

Mr. COCKRAN. But you get in there notwithstanding that advantage?

Mr. KING. When we have such advantage with the freight rates that we can.

Mr. COCKRAN. You claim that the freight rate explains it all?

Mr. KING. I think so.

Mr. COCKRAN. But you admit the fact that you do get in there and maintain an active competition against all the foreigners in that market, situated some distance from your place of production?

Mr. KING. Yes; but very much more advantageously fixed for us in regard to the freight rate than for the foreigner.

Mr. COCKRAN. Let us see about the freight rates. If this consumption was entirely in western Canada, you would have to pay freight rates from Pittsburg?

Mr. KING. I know; but they are very much less than the freight rates from Montreal.

Mr. COCKRAN. Then you do not share in the general complaint of freight rates that we heard yesterday, when a great many gentlemen wanted tariff protection to meet what they called "excessive rates" here?

Mr. KING. I do not understand that theory.

Mr. COCKRAN. That you do not understand at all?

Mr. KING. No.

Mr. COCKRAN. In point of fact, you insist that your freight rates from Pittsburg to Canada are lower than the freight rates, say, from——

Mr. KING. From Montreal.

Mr. COCKRAN. To the west of Canada?

Mr. KING. Yes.

Mr. COCKRAN. How much lower?

Mr. KING. I would say from two to three dollars.

Mr. COCKRAN. Two to three dollars a ton——

Mr. KING. Two to three.

Mr. COCKRAN (continuing). Would be the difference?

Mr. KING. I think so.

Mr. COCKRAN. What is the total rate from Pittsburg, for instance? Take from Pittsburg; we will take some definite point, say from Pittsburg to Vancouver?

Mr. KING. I could not tell you that, but I could tell you from Toronto, the nearest point that we would enter Canada. Toronto,

Canada, I could tell you approximately what the freight rate from there would be.

Mr. COCKRAN. If you would send from Pittsburg to Vancouver, you would not send up to Toronto?

Mr. KING. I think we would. I think we would go into Canada there, and go by rail from there. Of course, if they went around by vessel there would be a choice of railroads, whichever would be the cheaper.

Mr. COCKRAN. Could you not transport without breaking bulk by freight from Pittsburg to Vancouver?

Mr. KING. By rail?

Mr. COCKRAN. Yes.

Mr. KING. Yes; I think so.

Mr. COCKRAN. Would that not be cheaper than to ship at Pittsburg and break bulk at the Lakes, transport across on the Lakes, then break bulk again at Toronto?

Mr. KING. You do not break bulk at the Lakes.

Mr. COCKRAN. Do you take the car right on bodily?

Mr. KING. The car goes right straight through at present.

Mr. COCKRAN. You can transport by taking the car from Pittsburg, then to Toronto, and then from Toronto it is sent west by a Canadian road?

Mr. KING. Yes, sir.

Mr. COCKRAN. May I ask what advantage you would have over the Canadian shipper in that way?

Mr. KING. What advantage we would have?

Mr. COCKRAN. Over the Canadian shipper?

Mr. KING. Over the Canadian manufacturer or the foreign manufacturer?

Mr. COCKRAN. Why the Canadian manufacturer?

Mr. KING. Because he would have a higher freight rate to pay to the same point.

Mr. COCKRAN. He could go by water to Toronto probably.

Mr. KING. So could we.

Mr. COCKRAN. To Toronto?

Mr. KING. He could go by water at certain times of the year when the canal is open, but in winter it is frozen up.

Mr. COCKRAN. At least three-fourths of the year?

Mr. KING. Yes.

Mr. COCKRAN. You would have to go by rail from Pittsburg to the lake front?

Mr. KING. Yes.

Mr. COCKRAN. Do you really think there is much difference in the cost of transportation?

Mr. KING. There is a great deal.

Mr. COCKRAN. Give us an idea, because you see, after all, it comes to that. It is only by ascertaining what would be the difference that we can estimate what your net advantage would be in the matter.

Mr. KING. From memory I would say that the rate of freight from Montreal to points where we would naturally reach in Canada in, we will say, the Province of Ontario——

Mr. COCKRAN. I understood you to say the west of Canada; let us say we will take a product now shipped to Vancouver, which is the extreme west of Canada.

Mr. KING. Really, Mr. Cockran, I am not familiar with the rates to Vancouver.

Mr. COCKRAN. You see, that seriously impairs the value of your testimony.

Mr. KING. There is very little that goes to Vancouver. The great bulk goes to the Province of Ontario, tributary to Toronto.

Mr. COCKRAN. That is not very far west in Canada.

Mr. KING. That is in western Canada, as it is called there. It is not in the province of Quebec.

Mr. COCKRAN. Do you base that statement on the difference in rates from Pittsburg to a point west of Ontario?

Mr. KING. Yes.

Mr. COCKRAN. To the west of Ontario?

Mr. KING. All that section through Ontario.

Mr. COCKRAN. To the west of Toronto?

Mr. KING. West of Toronto; yes.

Mr. COCKRAN. You say it would be two to three dollars a ton less to that point?

Mr. KING. My recollection is that the freight rate from Montreal to Toronto and that section on the Canadian road is about 25 cents a hundred pounds. I think we get there from 12 to 14 cents from Pittsburg to Toronto.

Mr. COCKRAN. That would be how much a ton?

Mr. KING. Twenty-five cents would be $5 a net ton.

Mr. COCKRAN. You would get there for about $2.50?

Mr. KING. About the same.

Mr. COCKRAN. So there is an advantage of $2.50.

Mr. KING. Yes, sir.

Mr. COCKRAN. But that advantage in railroad rates would not balance your disadvantage in tariff rates; that advantage in cost of transportation does not equal the disadvantage imposed on you under the differential tariff?

Mr. KING. Yes, sir; it a little more than equals it. The tariff on American goods going into Canada is 35 cents a hundred, or $7 a ton, and the English have a preferential of one-third, which is about $2.

Mr. COCKRAN. Two dollars and fifty cents?

Mr. KING. Seven dollars and fifty cents would be $2.50.

Mr. COCKRAN. It is actually $2.33⅓?

Mr. KING. Yes.

Mr. COCKRAN. The difference in rates is about $2?

Mr. KING. $2.50.

Mr. COCKRAN. So, coming down to the last analysis, your net advantage would be the difference between $2.50 and $2.33⅓, and that only on the product which goes to the west of Ontario.

Mr. KING. Yes, sir.

Mr. POU. What is the largest annual shipment that your mills have ever sent over into Canada in any one year?

Mr. KING. I would say 30,000 to 40,000 tons, perhaps, in a good year.

Mr. POU. How did that compare to the entire annual output of the entire mill?

Mr. KING. We make about 1,000,000 tons.

Mr. POU. You sold that, I believe, about 5 per cent cheaper than the price is in this country?

Mr. KING. I think that would be an average.

Mr. POU. Are you familiar with the export business of the United States Steel Corporation?

Mr. KING. No, sir; I am not. They do export quite largely, I know; we do not.

Mr. POU. Do you know whether they likewise make a less price to foreign countries than they do to this country?

Mr. KING. I think they do.

Mr. POU. Do you know how much less?

Mr. KING. No, sir; I could not tell you. I know they have to meet the conditions in the country in which they sell, of course.

Mr. POU. As a rule all of you do sell a little cheaper outside of this country than you do inside, do you not?

Mr. KING. I think that is true; yes. If you are going to do an export business and need that business to give you full prices and decide that it is policy to do it, you of course must meet the prices that are current in the country that you go to.

Mr. POU. And therefore all large steel manufacturers have an export price and a domestic price?

Mr. KING. Yes.

Mr. POU. The export price is less than the domestic price?

Mr. KING. I think that is true.

Mr. DALZELL. That is so in all countries, is it not?

Mr. KING. So in all countries. In England and Germany it is just as true as it is here.

Mr. GRIGGS. Mr. King, I was asking you this morning, when you went off the stand, what was the capital of your corporation, and you said $30,000,000?

Mr. KING. Yes, sir.

Mr. GRIGGS. What was the original capital of your corporation?

Mr. KING. That goes further back than I go, but it was very small. In other words, I have heard it said that we made 100 tons a day, practically, as against about 4,000 tons a day. It was a few hundred thousand difference. I really believe it was less than $100,000, the original capital.

Mr. GRIGGS. Has your present capital been built up out of that?

Mr. KING. Out of the profits, yes. The profits have been almost entirely put back to build up the business.

Mr. GRIGGS. You have been at the head of the business how long?

Mr. KING. I am not really the president, and I do not like to say that I am at the head of the business, but I have been connected with the business nearly forty years.

Mr. GRIGGS. You are connected with the management of it?

Mr. KING. Yes, sir.

Mr. GRIGGS. And during those forty years from $100,000 you have increased your capital to $30,000,000?

Mr. KING. I want to correct you. The mill goes a good deal further back than I do. It is sixty or sixty-five years' time.

Mr. GRIGGS. Sixty-five years?

Mr. KING. Yes, sir.

Mr. GRIGGS. And have any of you made any fortunes outside by investments of your profits from your steel works?

Mr. KING. To the best of my knowledge and belief there has never been a dividend paid larger than 6 per cent, and very often 4, and a great many years in the past nothing to the stockholders.

Mr. Griggs. Never larger than 6?

Mr. King. Never larger than 6.

Mr. Griggs. Then you have taken from 4 to 6 per cent out of the business?

Mr. King. Not always. In bad times we have not taken anything.

Mr. Griggs. I mean as a general proposition.

Mr. King. I will say in the last eight or ten years we have taken that percentage out.

Mr. Griggs. Do you know how much capital is engaged in the iron and steel industry of the United States?

Mr. King. I could not tell you offhand.

Mr. Griggs. How much at Pittsburg—in what you call the Pittsburg district?

Mr. King. I might get that for you and give it to you before I go away.

Mr. Griggs. I would be very much obliged to you, if you can not give it now.

Mr. King. Yes, sir.

Mr. Griggs. I understood you to say this morning that you thought our expenses ought to be paid by a tax on luxuries entirely. You said coffee and tea were necessities?

Mr. King. Yes.

Mr. Griggs. And that tobacco was a luxury?

Mr. King. Yes.

Mr. Griggs. Did you say that?

Mr. King. I think so.

Mr. Griggs. Don't say that when you go down to Georgia any time, or to North Carolina.

Mr. King. I will be careful.

Mr. Griggs. I just wanted to warn you of that. Now, a gentleman asked you a question this morning which you failed to answer, and with his permission I will repeat it. You did answer it in a way, because you said Mr. Carnegie did not know anything about the business. Now, the question I want you to answer directly is this: Do you think Mr. Carnegie's disinterestedness at present would make him a more or less credible witness?

Mr. King. I think it would make him a less credible witness.

Mr. Griggs. His disinterestedness would make him less credible?

Mr. King. I think so.

Mr. Griggs. That is contrary to all the axioms of law. Of course I know that steel magnates are some of them above law. You said also, if I understood you correctly, that the country was always prosperous under a protective tariff. You remember as far back as 1873, do you not?

Mr. King. Well, yes. I was in business then as a boy.

Mr. Griggs. We were operating then under a protective tariff?

Mr. King. Yes.

Mr. Griggs. They were pretty hard times, were they not?

Mr. King. Very hard; yes, sir.

Mr. Griggs. Then you are mistaken in that?

Mr. King. In that particular case there was a reason for that. It was time for a panic, I guess. Jay Cooke failed, and that precipitated it. I do not think I ought to have said that as a hard and-fast proposition.

Mr. GRIGGS. Sir?

Mr. KING. I should not have made that statement as a hard-and-fast proposition, but I think it is generally true.

Mr. GRIGGS. Generally true?

Mr. KING. Yes, sir.

Mr. GRIGGS. We had a panic in 1890, if you remember.

Mr. KING. 1893, as I recollect.

Mr. GRIGGS. Under President Harrison.

Mr. KING. 1893, as I recollect.

Mr. GRIGGS. No; it began under President Harrison, did it not?

Mr. KING. Well, I guess it did make a start there, maybe.

Mr. GRIGGS. The beginning of the panic is the panic?

Mr. KING. Yes; but it did not get bad until 1893.

Mr. GRIGGS. Of course, but the beginning is the panic. The cause must have been at the beginning, must it not?

Mr. KING. Yes, sir.

Mr. GRIGGS. Then we were operating under a high tariff, were we not; not as high as now, but a high tariff for those days?

Mr. KING. Yes, sir.

Mr. GRIGGS. We have been increasing our tariff as we have gone along. I do not know whether to ask you this next question or not, because you say Mr. Carnegie's disinterestedness would make him a less credible witness. Is the iron and steel trade really divided into three parts, into three spheres in the world, America having one, certain other countries having one, and certain other countries having the other?

Mr. KING. Do you mean any arrangements to control price or regulate price?

Mr. GRIGGS. No; but you trade in one sphere, and they trade in another sphere?

Mr. KING. Yes.

Mr. GRIGGS. Spheres of influence, as it were?

Mr. KING. Yes.

Mr. GRIGGS. Spheres of trade?

Mr. KING. Yes.

Mr. GRIGGS. Is that true?

Mr. KING. That is true; yes. We try to trade in our own country.

Mr. GRIGGS. But you have your sphere of trade which is not interfered with by the manufacturers in the other spheres?

Mr. KING. We will not. If it does not suit them to interfere, it is not interfered with.

Mr. GRIGGS. Is there not an agreement of that sort?

Mr. KING. I think not; not to my knowledge.

Mr. GRIGGS. You do not know anything about it?

Mr. KING. Not a thing.

Mr. GRIGGS. Is there any sort of understanding?

Mr. KING. No understanding of any kind in our business. I never heard of it.

Mr. GRIGGS. I think his statement was that it was divided into three spheres—America controlling one, England another, and Germany, Belgium, and some other country the other.

Mr. KING. I never heard of it.

Mr. GRIGGS. You never heard of it?

Mr. KING. No, sir.

Mr. GRIGGS. Would you not believe it if he said so?

Mr. KING. I do not like you to ask me that question.

Mr. GRIGGS. You need not answer it if you do not want to.

Mr. KING. I prefer not to answer it.

Mr. GRIGGS. I am through.

Mr. POU. Has your stock a market value—the stock of your corporation?

Mr. KING. No, sir. It is a close corporation, owned by a few people, and there has never been a share of stock sold.

WILLIS L. KING, FOR THE JONES & LAUGHLIN STEEL CO., PITTSBURG, PA., FILES SUPPLEMENTAL BRIEF RELATIVE TO STEEL BARS, PLATES, AND STRUCTURAL MATERIAL.

PITTSBURG, PA., *January 20, 1909.*

WAYS AND MEANS COMMITTEE,
Washington, D. C.

GENTLEMEN: The Jones & Laughlin Steel Company, a corporation operating under the laws of the State of Pennsylvania, with a capital of $30,000,000, a product of about 1,000,000 tons yearly, consisting largely of steel bars, plates, and structural material, and employing 15,000 men (including subsidiary companies), herewith begs to submit to you certain facts and statements for the consideration of the Ways and Means Committee in the framing of a new tariff schedule.

The company began as a partnership some sixty years ago with a small capital, has been operating continuously, and has grown to its present importance, we believe, through the beneficent operation of a protective tariff. It has not in any one year taken out dividends larger than 6 per cent, and in many years has not declared any dividends whatever.

Knowing that the committee desires information as to costs here and abroad rather than general statements as to the value of a protective tariff, we beg to submit the following information, which we believe to be correct, namely, that in the more favored districts in Germany and Belgium, steel can be produced to-day at approximately the following figures:

	Per gross ton.
Pig iron	$8.50
Converting same into billets	4.00
Converting billets into finished steel	5.00
Freight on finished material from foreign mills to New York	3.00
Add present duty on steel bars	6.72
Total cost delivered on docks at our seaboard	27.22

or, say, $1.21 per hundred pounds. (The English cost is somewhat higher.)

Compare this with average commercial cost at our works in Pittsburg, viz, at lowest market prices for raw material, during the prosperous year of 1907:

Pig iron	$15.41
Converting same into billets	7.09
Converting billets into finished steel	8.06
	30.56
Add freight to New York	3.58
Total	34.14

or, say, $1.54 per hundred pounds, New York.

This cost to us is divided into the following items:

Transportation, raw materials $8.12; finished to New York $3.58	$11.70
Labor	9.00
Materials, taxes, administration, selling cost, and depreciation	13.44
Total	34.14

To this should be added a reasonable profit, and this question will doubtless receive from your committee the most careful consideration. In it is contained the life of the manufacturer and the comfort and prosperity of his workmen, and as bearing on this question, would call your attention to the fact that the yearly sales of the manufacturer of steel do not exceed, and more often fall below, his actual invested capital. This is because of the very large investment necessary.

The wholesale merchant, on the other hand, selling for cash ten days or thirty days net, may turn over his capital ten to twelve times a year, and a very modest profit of 2 per cent on sales will amount to 20 or 24 per cent on his capital. The profit of the steel maker, however, must be counted on sales equal or less than his capital, and must necessarily be larger if he pays his stockholders 6 per cent, and conserves their interests by keeping the property in that state of modern efficiency only possible by the constant expenditure of large sums in mining, transportation, and manufacturing. No other business in our knowledge requires such a large outlay in these directions.

In comparing costs here and abroad, would call your attention to the large costs for transportation in this country, owing to the widely scattered raw materials, namely, $8.12 to the ton of finished product in the Pittsburg district as against a nominal cost in many of the foreign districts. This item alone will make it impossible for us to successfully compete, if the standard of living and wages for workmen now and for many years current in this country, is to be maintained or ought to be maintained.

We further submit that the lowest cost to the steel manufacturer here was in parts of the years 1898 and 1901, owing to the cheapness of material, freights, and labor, and that this minimum is not again possible, except under similar conditions which, in our opinion, would be deplorable.

We would also ask you to consider the comparison of present prices of foreign and domestic steel in the same finished forms under the present tariff, as per the following table:

	Continental price of material, duty paid, f. o. b. New York.	English price of material, duty paid, f. o. b. New York.	Scotch price of material, duty paid, f. o. b. New York.	American price of material, f. o. b. New York.
	Cents.	Cents.	Cents.	Cents.
Structural	1.63	1.88	1.72	1.76
Plates	1.78	1.93	1.85	1.76
Bars	a 1.81	a 1.64	a 1.52	a 1.56

	Continental price of material, duty paid, f. o. b. Boston.	English price of material, duty paid, f. o. b. Boston.	Scotch price of material, duty paid, f. o. b. Boston.	American price of material, f. o. b. Boston.
	Cents.	Cents.	Cents.	Cents.
Structural	1.63	1.88	1.72	1.78
Plates	1.78	1.93	1.85	1.78
Bars	1.31	1.64	1.524	1.58

a Base.

The above price for foreign material covers an allowance of 2½ cents per hundred pounds to cover custom-house expenses, exchange, etc.

This shows that the foreign maker can successfully compete under the present tariff on the shapes of steel more largely in common use, and the only reason preventing greater imports is that the difference is not sufficient to offset the prepayment for material and consequent risk on quality, size, and weight.

We also submit below a table showing the present foreign rates of freight to our large Atlantic and Pacific seaports, and our domestic rail rates to these same points.

Commodity.	From Antwerp, Liverpool, Hamburg, Newcastle, Bremen, London, Hull, Southampton—			From Pittsburg—
	To—			To—
	San Francisco, San Diego, Seattle, Tacoma.	Portland, East Portland.	Los Angeles (by rail) from San Diego.	San Francisco, Seattle, Tacoma, Los Angeles, Portland, East Portland.
	In carload lots.			In carload lots.
	Cents.	Cents.	Cents.	
Angles	40	55	50	80 cents per 100 pounds, C. L., all rail.
Bars (iron) straight, coiled, or twisted.	40	55	50	71 cents per 100 pounds, C. L., via New York and water, to California points.
Bars (steel) loose, bundled, or eased.	49	64	59	
Iron beams, joints, and girders.	43	58	53	76 cents per 100 pounds, C. L., to Oregon points via New York and water.
Channels	40	55	50	
Columns and base plates.	43	58	53	
Plates	40	55	50	
	In cargo lots.			
	$3.00 to $4.50 per ton of 2,240 pounds.			
To New York	6s. to 7s., or $1.50 to $1.75 per ton of 2,240 pounds.			$3.58 per ton of 2,240 pounds.
Boston				$4.03 per ton of 2,240 pounds.
Philadelphia				$3.36 per ton of 2,240 pounds.
Baltimore				$3.25 per ton of 2,240 pounds.

It is possible to ship from Pittsburg to London, England, and thence to the above Pacific coast points at a less rate than direct from Pittsburg via New York and water, or from Pittsburg all rail.

One of the witnesses appearing before your committee stated that the inland freight from seaboard would always protect the American manufacturer; but we have evidence before us of a shipment of iron bars from Norway to Chicago at 28 cents per hundred pounds, which is only about $2 per ton more than the freight rate from Pittsburg to Chicago, namely, 18 cents per hundred pounds. It is certain, also, that if large imports are made possible by a radical reduction in the tariff, the railroads, in order to get back loads for cars sent to seaboard with export grain, cotton, beef, etc. (which are now largely returned empty), would make such combination rates with the ocean carriers that the foreign material will be distributed from both our Atlantic and Pacific ports to our serious injury practically all over the United States.

At the oral hearing before your committee on November 25, we asked for an increase of one-tenth cent per pound in the duty on steel bars, because we find that in the Dingley tariff steel bars are put in a class with unfinished or semifinished material in paragraph No. 135, which calls for a duty of three-tenths cent per pound when valued at 1 cent per pound or less.

It is our belief that the bars contemplated in this paragraph were meant to cover sheet bars, an unfinished article used in the manufacture of sheets and tin plate. This seems evident because of the duty fixed in paragraph No. 123 on iron bars, namely, six-tenths cent per pound.

We believe the duty of five-tenths cent per pound on beams, girders, angles, channels, etc., paragraph No. 125, is a fair and reasonable one, entailing no hardship on the consumer, but giving just protection to American manufacturers and workmen.   •

We also believe the duty of five-tenths cent per pound on iron and steel plates, paragraph No. 125, should be continued in the new tariff schedule.

There are doubtless many items in the iron and steel schedule of the Dingley tariff which can not be reduced without serious injury to the American people, and a revision of these overprotected items is both desirable and necessary. We think your long and painstaking investigation of conditions and costs will demonstrate that these overprotected articles are generally in the more highly finished forms of steel products, covering comparatively small tonnages, and that the great tonnage of steel in common use in this country in the cheaper forms is not overprotected if the present standard of living and wages in this country is desirable.

Mr. Cochran requested certain information of our Mr. King at the oral hearing on November 25, 1908, which we herewith submit:

First. Subsequent to the fire and earthquake in San Francisco, say from March, 1906, to November, 1908, there were imported into that city approximately 16,000 tons, and, as near as we can determine by a careful investigation, the total consumption of structural material at that point during this time was about 80,000 tons.

We submit below statement in detail of these imports and their value, and would call your attention to the fact that the invoice value of this foreign steel is approximately 98 cents per 100 pounds.

Statistical record of importations of foreign beams to the port of San Francisco, beginning with the quarter ending March 31, 1906, to November 30, 1908.

	Pounds.	Invoice value.
Quarter ending—		
March 31, 1906	7,927,212	$72,301.00
June 30, 1906	5,203,358	53,145.00
September 30, 1906	7,896,547	67,183.00
December 31, 1906	2,317,673	24,799.00
March 31, 1907	4,142,600	46,822.00
June 30, 1907	564,890	6,921.00
September 30, 1907	228,446	2,850.00
December 31, 1907	11,509	245.00
March 31, 1908	1,185,194	15,889.00
June 30, 1908	(a)	(a)
September 30, 1908	426,405	4,489.00
Month of—		
October, 1908	1,058,954	11,342.00
November, 1908	357,750	3,355.00
Total	31,320,038	309,942.00

a Nothing imported.

Second. The capitalization of the firms and corporations manufacturing iron and steel in the Pittsburg district (say a radius of 60 miles from Pittsburg) is about $400,000,000.

Respectfully submitted.

WILLIS L. KING, *Vice-President for*
JONES & LAUGHLIN STEEL COMPANY.
B. F. JONES, Jr., *President.*

BARS OF SPRING STEEL.

[Paragraph 135.]

215 WEST POLK STREET,
Chicago, Ill., January 2, 1908.

COMMITTEE ON WAYS AND MEANS,
Washington, D. C.

DEAR SIRS: We respectfully ask that in the tariff bill which you are preparing, bars of spring steel be put on the free list. Our reason for asking this is as follows:

We are among the largest manufacturers of vehicle springs for automobiles and other vehicles. We have in addition to our domestic business a considerable foreign trade, but competition from foreign countries—France, Germany, England—is such that we have to sell at the very narrowest margin of profit; and, even at that, can in South America sell only one class of springs, which it seems we can produce slightly cheaper than the French. We have found that were it not for the tariff we could buy our raw material cheaper, which would enable us to compete successfully with our foreign competition. We therefore wish the duty to be removed that we may extend our foreign trade.

We are willing that the duty on our product—that is, springs for vehicles—be also removed. We can produce springs in this country as cheaply as anywhere in the world if we are allowed to have access to the markets of the world for our raw material.

Respectfully,

TUTHILL SPRING CO.,
By F. H. TUTHILL, *President.*

STEEL.

HON. WILLIAM S. BENNET, M. C., SUBMITS LETTER RELATIVE TO THE REDUCTION OF THE DUTY ON STEEL.

WASHINGTON, D. C., *December 26, 1908.*

Hon. SERENO E. PAYNE,
House of Representatives, Washington, D. C.

MY DEAR MR. PAYNE: Inclosed please find a very interesting letter from a holder of preferred stock in the United States Steel Corporation.

Very truly, yours,

WILLIAM S. BENNET.

NEW YORK, *December 23, 1908.*

Hon. WILLIAM S. BENNET, M. C.,
House of Representatives, Washington, D. C.

DEAR SIR: Believing that you are interested in the views of your constituents on matters to come before Congress, I wish to respectfully submit my opinions on the tariff question, and particularly in regard to the duty on steel.

I believe that in justice to the people at large the present duty on steel should be largely reduced or removed, the same to be accomplished in a series of reductions, to avoid sudden fluctuations in prices. As the arguments for the reduction have been fully set forth, I shall not attempt to repeat them. I will simply say that with the steel industry so firmly established and so profitable as it is to-day that it seems to me that any enhanced profits that may result from the tariff are a direct subsidy paid to the steel producers without any corresponding public benefit. This overprotection seems to me most unfair and pernicious, once it has been made clearly evident, and I think that the bonus should be transferred to our shipping industry, where it is sorely needed.

In relation to the above I might say that I am holding some preferred stock of the steel corporation, and brokers have quoted one of the directors to me as saying that were the tariff on steel wholly removed the present dividends could be maintained, and it is well known that these are all and more than the original assets of the company justify.

The above opinions are largely shared by my associates here, and I simply tender them for any use that they may be to you.

Respectfully, yours,

RALPH H. STEARNS.

IRON AND STEEL PRODUCTS.

STATEMENT OF JOHN A. TOPPING, OF PITTSBURG, PA., REPRESENTING CERTAIN INDEPENDENT MANUFACTURERS OF IRON AND STEEL PRODUCTS.

WEDNESDAY, *November 25, 1908.*

Mr. TOPPING. Mr. Chairman and gentlemen, I appear before this committee to-day at your invitation as the representative of the Re-

public Iron and Steel Company and some other independent manufacturers of iron and steel, not to advocate any changes at this time
in the existing duty, but to ask for sufficient time to properly investigate the subject. If we find we can make any recommendations
in the way of reductions, we are perfectly willing to do that if it
can be done without abandoning the protective system. We expect
to file a brief at the proper time with your committee, so as to give
you all the information we can obtain on the subject.

While here, however, I am quite willing to give you any general
information you might think proper to ask of me. In other words,
if I can be of any service to you gentlemen in any way, I would be
very glad to assist you, but I have nothing further to say at this
time.

Mr. COCKRAN. You have not made up your mind as to whether
you desire a reduction or an increase?

Mr. TOPPING. Mr. Cockran, I think possibly we will find that there
are some inconsistencies, due to changes in cost and other conditions,
by reason of which we might fairly concede reductions. It may be
that there are some changes that would suggest advances.

Mr. DALZELL. What you want is time to make that examination,
and subsequently to file a brief?

Mr. TOPPING. That is it exactly.

Mr. UNDERWOOD. Will you file with the committee the cost of labor
at your plant, the total cost, and the cost of labor here and the total
cost, and the cost of labor abroad, and state in the brief where your
principal markets are, and also state the cost of shipment from abroad
to those markets and from the plants at home to those markets?

Mr. TOPPING. I will try to secure that for you in that manner, Mr.
Underwood.

Mr. UNDERWOOD. There is another question that I want to ask you:
Do you ship any of your product to the Canadian market?

Mr. TOPPING. No, sir; we do not. I might say, in fuller reply to
that question, that shortly after the first of the year I tried in every
way to find a Canadian market for some of our bars, both iron and
steel; but after an effort on the part of our sales department, who
spent a week or ten days investigating the conditions, they returned
home with reports that were unfavorable to the effort and we abandoned it.

Mr. UNDERWOOD. Will you also state in the brief what your views
are and what information you have as to the exportation? There
was testimony here this morning as to exportations into the Canadian
market. I would like to have your views with respect to exportations to the Canadian market.

Mr. TOPPING. I can not explain the exportation to Canada, except
on the ground that at the point of production, Pittsburg, Cleveland,
or the Mahoning Valley, where we largely operate, or Chicago, with
the advantages of quick service and special considerations of quality,
the necessities of the buyers for quick deliveries might have justified
purchasing on this side at a higher price than they could have bought
on the other side of the water.

Mr. UNDERWOOD. I do not think the testimony this morning was
along that line.

Mr. TOPPING. You asked, as I understood you, as to what explanation I could make, in view of my failure. I can not explain it on

any other ground than that because we failed signally to do anything over there.

Mr. UNDERWOOD. I suppose, then, it is a conceded fact that if the American manufacturer can compete in the Canadian market——

Mr. TOPPING. With whom?

Mr. UNDERWOOD. With the English manufacturer.

Mr. TOPPING. He can not, in my opinion.

Mr. UNDERWOOD. But it is conceded that if he can he is producing on equal terms, because he goes into the Canadian market under a disadvantage.

Mr. TOPPING. If he had the same conditions of duty and the same cost, of course he could; but I think our ability to dispose of the product——

Mr. UNDERWOOD. I think that is a very material question in connection with this subject that you are talking about.

Mr. TOPPING. Yes, sir.

Mr. UNDERWOOD. Because, of course, with the differential in duty against the American manufacturers, if they are competing on equal terms, it is a very important question before this committee, and I want to ask you to address yourself to that question when you file your brief, if you will.

Mr. TOPPING. Yes, sir.

Mr. COCKRAN. Have you exported any steel to any foreign country?

Mr. TOPPING. No, sir; we have not.

Mr. COCKRAN. Have you any idea where the steel that is used in Mexico comes from?

Mr. TOPPING. I think that most of it, or a large part of it, or I will say the greater part of it, comes from continental Europe.

Mr. COCKRAN. A large part of it comes from America, does it not?

Mr. TOPPING. I think that a substantial tonnage comes from America.

Mr. COCKRAN. Mexico gives no advantage to American steel over that coming from abroad, does it?

Mr. TOPPING. No; but oftentimes sales are stimulated by sales of American machinery that call for the construction of a mill or a mine equipment, and that carries with it the suggestion of some steel bars or iron bars, and it saves time in transportation to have them all go in one parcel. For that reason, the saving of time being essential, they will pay, frequently, more for the American product in near-by countries like Mexico and Canada, rather than wait on a ship from England or Germany.

Mr. COCKRAN. Do you know anything about the sale of steel rails in Mexico?

Mr. TOPPING. I do not.

Mr. COCKRAN. You do not know anything about it?

Mr. TOPPING. No, sir.

Mr. HILL. I want to know about this ferromanganese. We collected in duty last year from ferromanganese, $378,000. Mr. Butler, one of the gentlemen who preceded you, said that it was only a question of changing the verbiage of paragraph 122, and that all that was requested was that it be put on the free list, and to leave pig iron and the other products on that list unchanged. What would be the effect of that?

Mr. Topping. The pig iron would not be affected, because the ferro-manganese is used in the manufacture of steel, as an alloy.

Mr. Hill. Would it reduce the cost of tungsten appreciably?

Mr. Topping. It would depend on the character of the steel you were making, as to the degree of carbon that you are trying to secure.

Mr. Hill. I mean on an average.

Mr. Topping. It is pretty hard to express an opinion. What do you mean by an average?

Mr. Hill. Would it reduce it 10 cents a ton?

Mr. Topping. I would not like to make any statement as to the average.

Mr. Hill. Or 25 cents a ton?

Mr. Topping. I say I would not like to make any statement as to that.

Mr. Hill. Oh, I beg your pardon.

Mr. Topping. I would only be able to make a guess, and the guess would not be worth anything to you.

Mr. Hill. It would reduce it somewhat

Mr. Topping. It would have that influence, naturally.

JOHN A. TOPPING, CHAIRMAN OF REPUBLIC IRON AND STEEL COMPANY, FILES SUPPLEMENTAL BRIEF RELATIVE TO IRON AND STEEL PRODUCTS.

115 Broadway,
New York, N. Y., January 1, 1909.

Hon. Sereno E. Payne,
Chairman Committee on Ways and Means,
Washington, D. C.

Dear Sir: On November 25, 1908, I appeared before your committee, in response to their request, to address them on the subject of the iron and steel schedule, relative to tariff revision, but, for reasons stated then, I requested further time to more thoroughly consider the subject, and also the privilege of submitting my views in the form of a brief.

In addressing you now I shall confine myself to the products in which I am directly interested, and concerning which I have direct information, rather than to the exclusive subject of billets and bars, to which I had been invited to confine myself. The products I shall consider are pig iron, steel ingots, billets, slabs, steel bars, bar iron, spikes, bolts, nuts, and polished shafting. These products are covered under the Dingley bill by paragraphs Nos. 122, 123, 130, 135, 141, 145, and 163.

GENERAL STATISTICS.

The magnitude of the iron and steel industry is perhaps common knowledge, but a few statistical figures may be pertinent. The census report for 1905 states that—

The capital invested is _____ $992,774,034
The number of men employed _____ 242,740
The amount of wages paid _____ $141,439,900

These enormous totals, however, in my opinion, do not give the iron and steel interests credit for growth since 1905, or for the large amount of capital invested in mines, steamships, and industrial railways, and must also have excluded such capital as bonds. Taking as a basis for an estimate, the average capital, men employed, and wages paid, from a number of representative companies producing iron and steel, and working out averages and applying the figures to the entire production of the United States, it is estimated that—

Total capital invested is_____ $2, 278, 321, 891. 82
Total number of employees_____ 442, 068
Total wages paid_____ $306, 116, 907. 02
Average per annum per man_____ $691. 62
Average per day (250 days)_____ $2. 76

The United States Steel Corporation alone having invested over $1,400,000,000, with an annual pay roll of over $160,000,000.

By a similar computation of averages, the cash disbursement to capital for 1907 was $70,830,362.86 (5.4 per cent) and to labor for 1907 $306,116,907.02, labor having received over 332 per cent in excess of capital. The company which I represent paid its capital approximately $1,071,000 (5¾ per cent) and its labor $5,832,000, or approximately 444 per cent in excess of its stockholders, which would indicate that the estimates presented have been conservatively calculated. In striking contrast to the estimated average dividend payments of less than 6 per cent paid to the stockholders of American iron and steel manufacturing companies, the Berlin correspondent of the Iron Age (January 14, 1909, issue) states that the average dividends paid to the stockholders of 13 of the largest German manufacturing companies of iron and steel for the year 1907 was 13.66 per cent, and for the year 1908 the average was 11.89 per cent.

MONOPOLY.

There is no monopoly maintained in iron and steel. The tabulations of Mr. J. M. Swank, of the American Iron and Steel Association, of the companies engaged in the business, reports as a total, 190 blast furnace companies and 277 steel works and rolling-mill companies. The total production of the country and the production of the United States Steel Corporation for 1907 is submitted in detail herewith:

Production of iron ore, pig iron, steel works, and finished rolling-mill products, year 1907.

[Gross tons.]

	Total.	United States Steel Corporation.	Independent companies.	Percentage United States steel.
Iron ore...	51,720,619	23,980,558	27,740,061	46.3
Pig iron...	25,781,361	11,422,795	14,358,566	44.3
Ingots, Bessemer open-hearth....................	22,559,477	13,342,992	9,216,485	59.1
Structural shapes................................	1,947,352	1,066,727	873,625	54.9
Wire and wire rods..............................	2,017,583	1,443,191	574,392	71.5
Plates..	2,660,0C0	877,682	1,782,378	33.0
Sheets..	1,588,772			
Tin plate and terneplate........................	514,775	1,070,752	1,080,795	50.0
Bars and similar rolled product.................	5,032,652	1,937,247	3,095,405	38.5
Hoops and bands.................................	616,347	370,000	246,347	60.0
Cotton ties......................................	58,000	30,000	28,000	51.7
Pipe and tubular goods..........................	1,802,627	1,174,629	627,998	65.1
Rails, Bessemer open-hearth, and iron...........	3,633,654	1,879,985	1,753,669	51.7
Total...............................	119,926,279	58,598,558	61,327,721	48.8

Production of iron ore, pig iron, steel works, and finished rolling-mill products year 1907—Continued.

SUMMARY.

[Gross tons.]

	Total.	United States Steel Corporation.	Independent companies.	Percentage United States steel.
Iron ore	51,720,619	23,980,558	27,740,061	46.3
Pig iron	25,781,361	11,422,795	14,358,566	44.8
Crude steel	22,559,447	13,342,992	9,216,485	59.1
Finished product	19,864,822	9,852,213	10,012,609	49.5

NOTE.—This statement is partly compiled from data published by the United States Government Bureau of Statistics and from the American Iron and Steel Association.

From the foregoing table it will be noted that over one-half the production is by independent iron and steel companies, which insures sufficient general competition to influence fair prices. Business generally has prospered under the Dingley bill, this being particularly true of industries dependent upon finished iron and steel as raw material. As an instance of this prosperity, the farm-machinery manufacturers (who are one of the largest consumers of iron and steel) will serve as an illustration, this industry not only supplying our enormous home demand for farm machinery, but at prices which enable them to command the markets of the world. Government reports show a growth of farm-machinery exports from 1897 of $5,302,877 to $25,597,272 in 1907, an increase of approximately 400 per cent in ten years.

IMPORTS AND EXPORTS

Under the present law are rather evenly balanced.

For the year 1907:   Tons.

    Imports _____ 1,891,526

    Exports _____ 1,362,575

The heaviest items of import are iron ore, pig iron, bar steel, billets, and blooms, and these items are among those of smallest export.

At the present level of prices in domestic markets some producers are not realizing a fair profit and some will show losses, but, low as prices are, importations offer some price advantages to consumers at seaboard, this being particularly true of the Pacific and Gulf coasts. If this advantage is increased, government revenue may be increased; but if so, it would be at the expense of home production and at a loss to labor in wages, which would quickly be felt in those markets which supply to labor the necessities of life.

As was previously stated, labor received in wages during the year 1907 approximately $306,000,000, and should there be a revision of the tariff sufficiently radical to force a reduction in the present wage schedule of even one-third it would mean a loss to labor of over $100,-000,000 which now goes to enrich the farmer and others who supply to labor the necessaries of life.

Managing ability and brains can not overcome existing wage differences. We do now and would continue to minimize the amount of labor employed, but geographical advantages abroad, resulting in short inland haulage, with water routes to large markets, and low cost of assembling materials for manufacture, would all combine to force our labor to extreme rates if our markets are exposed to radical tariff reductions. Of the total export tonnage shown by government reports of 1,300,000 tons, over 1,000,000 tons were exported by the United States Steel Corporation; the balance was largely made up of shipments to markets where first cost was not the determining factor.

The export policy of the large companies has tended to steady home markets to secure maximum production, minimum costs, and incidentally to furnish labor fullest employment even though net profits were sacrificed at times. As a general proposition, however, the small manufacturers of iron and steel can not sell abroad without loss, and there are but few companies who could afford to maintain an export business at a loss, as it would require an enormous volume of profitable domestic business to absorb export losses (as do the foreign export pools and syndicates) without too seriously affecting averages and profits.

FOREIGN COMPETITION.

Foreign competition can not be measured by cost of production alone, as under the influence of legalized syndicates or trust agreements the foreign producer follows a policy of extreme aggression, and to this policy governmental railroads and subsidized steamship lines contribute. So destructive has this character of competition become, even to England, that an English writer, Mr. T. Good, in Cassier's Magazine for November, 1908, states: "As an illustration of an incident of losses incurred on exports, that on an operation for six months, a wire-rod syndicate reported domestic profit of £58,000 and loss on exports of £42,000 " (over $203,000).

Further reference to this feature of competition is made in a market report of the Dusseldorf correspondent of the London Iron and Coal Trades Review for March 20, 1908, which states that the home and export prices which prevailed in Germany, in that month, for leading articles of iron and steel were:

Articles.	Home price.	Export price.	Approximate difference, United States equivalent.
	s. d. s.	*s. s.*	
Joists	122 6 to 125	109	$3.84
Blooms	92 6	74	4.44
Billets	100 0	76	5.76
Steel bars	102 6	78 to 79	5.52

The same correspondent writes to the Review for November 27, 1908, as follows: " The wire-rod syndicate, which already pays a bounty of 16s. 6d. ($3.96) per ton to consumers who work for the export market, has just informed them that the payment will be increased by 5s. ($1.20) per ton in order to stimulate the export trade. Converted into drawn wire, the former works out at 18s. 2d. per ton, and the 1s. 6d. paid by the Rhenish-Westphalian Coal Syndicate brings the present total to 19s. 8d., whilst the increased payment now decided upon will raise the bounty to 24s. 8d. per ton " (or $5.99).

The British consul-general at Frankfort (Sir Oppenheimer's report for 1907) also shows a large difference between the export and home consumption price in Germany and Belgium; rates in favor of export sales on coal of 1 mark 50 pfennigs; pig iron, 4 marks 86 pfennigs; billets and semifinished steel, 15 marks; structural material, 20 marks. These differentials increase or decrease as trade conditions suggest. During 1907 German differential on semifinished steel showed a difference of 10 marks (approximately $2.40); in the early part of 1908 this differential was increased to 15 marks (approximately $3.60). It will therefore be seen that the question of policy, in giving employment to German and Belgian labor rather than profit to the operation of producing iron and steel, is a factor of dominant importance, and cost of production is of secondary importance. Under this policy German iron and steel exports have rapidly increased, and now stand at approximately 4,000,000 tons per annum.

FOREIGN AND DOMESTIC COSTS.

Pursuant to the request of your committee, I submit all the data obtainable on foreign costs. Manufacturers generally regard their costs as trade secrets, and guard them closely. This disposition was intensified by newspaper warnings, "Look out for American tariff spies. (New York Times clipping, November 28, 1908, Tageblatt; Berlin.) While official cost sheets are lacking, the table of wages, iron and steel prices, and other general information secured from foreign trade-journal writers, consular reports, and personal representatives abroad, submitted herewith, enables me to present estimated figures of cost which my general experience leads me to believe are approximately correct.

Approximate average labor rates, foreign and domestic, per day.

	Foreign countries.		Respective domestic labor rates.	Domestic rates increase—	
	England.	Belgium.		Over England.	Over Belgium.
BLAST FURNACES.					
Blowing engineers	$1.37	....	$3.00	$1.63	....
Bottom fillers	1.12	....	2.20	1.08	....
Top fillers	1.27	....	2.47	1.20	....
Keepers	1.82	....	2.75	.93	....
Keepers' helpers	.97	....	2.20	1.23	....
Skip engineer	1.18	....	2.60	1.42	....
General labor	.91	....	1.60	.69	....
Per cent of average increase over England, 94.7.					
ROLLING MILLS.					
Roller	7.20	$1.90	13.62	6.42	$11.72
Catcher	1.68	.86	5.56	3.88	4.70
Heater	3.60	1.05	6.16	2.56	5.11
Per cent of average increase over England, 103; over Belgium, 565.					
PUDDLE MILL.					
Boiler	2.16	....	2.90	.74	....
Scrapper	2.16	....	4.10	1.94	....
Per cent of average increase over England, 62.					
GENERAL.					
Engineers	1.44	.86	3.25	1.81	3.39
Pipe fitters	1.27	....	2.45	1.18	....
Mechanics	1.15	....	2.75	1.60	....
Labor	....	.57	1.55	....	.98
Per cent of average increase over England, 118.9; over Belgium, 235.6.					

Authority: United States Daily Consular and Trade Report of November 14, 1908; foreign correspondence reports and British reports of strikes and lockouts of 1891; first report on wages and hours of labor, 1893, and report on changes in rates of wages, etc., 1907; present pay roll rates in effect Mahoning Valley district (Ohio and Pennsylvania).

The lowest cost producing point is generally believed to be for England the Middlesbrough, and for Germany the Lorrain and Luxemburg districts, for the reason that all raw materials are mined locally and assembled at small cost. I am informed that the cost of steel-making pig iron for England, at furnaces well located and equipped, is approximately $9, and Germany approximately $8.50. The general average cost in these countries, however, might be $1 per ton higher. Based on practice in this country, and allowing for labor differences, it is estimated that the pig iron can be converted in England at not to exceed $4.50 and in Germany $4, or average cost for billets in England $14.50, and in Germany $13.50. The total cost of merchant bars, allowing for general practice and difference in labor rates, for England should be approximately 95 cents, and Germany 85 cents per 100 pounds.

To summarize cost results:

	Ohio and Pennsylvania.	Germany (gross tons).	England.
Steel-making pig iron	$15.68	$9.50	$10.00
Steel billets	23.07	13.50	14.50
Merchant steel bars (per 100 pounds)	1.888	.85	.95

OHIO AND PITTSBURG DISTRICT COSTS.

The actual book costs of the company I represent, and a few other large companies who conduct both mining and manufacturing operations, would be somewhat less if capital represented in mining was not credited with any mine profits. It would not be fair, however, to the large tonnage represented by producers of iron and steel, who purchase their coal, coke, limestone, and ore, to base costs otherwise than on market values of these raw materials. In connection with details of domestic costs I also submit tables of direct labor costs, as compared with duty allowed under the Dingley tariff, foreign selling prices, freight rates to seacoast points, with comparative total costs.

Statement showing direct labor cost from mines to finished product.

[Labor, coal, and coke expressed in net tons, but reduced to gross tons.]

Materials used to 1 ton of product.	Labor per ton of materials used.	Total gross ton labor.	Duty on gross ton product.
PIG IRON.			
Iron ore, 1.97 tons	$0.75	$1.48	
Coal in coke, 1.83 tons	$0.72– .96		
Coke, 1.16 tons	.88	1.55	
Limestone, 0.66 ton	.44	.29	
Direct conversion labor	1.06	1.06	
Add labor on steam and water, electric light, laboratory, switching	.12	.12	
Total		4.50	$4.00
LARGE STEEL BILLETS.			
Pig iron, 1.23 tons	4.50	5.54	
Cupola material used, 53 per cent of 1.10 tons =58.3 per cent at 51 cents		.30	
Direct labor		1.38	

Statement showing direct labor cost from mines to finished product—Continued.

Materials used to 1 ton of product.	Labor per ton of materials used.	Total gross ton labor.	Duty on gross ton product.
LARGE STEEL BILLETS—continued.			
Add labor on steam and water, electric light, laboratory, switching..	....	$0.17	....
Total	....	7.39	$6.72
BAR STEEL.			
Billets, 1¼ tons..........................	$7.39	8.31	....
Direct labor	....	4.02	....
Add labor on steam and water, electric light, laboratory, switching	....	.17	....
Total	....	12.50	6.72

NOTE.—Salaries of clerks, managers, and superintendents included, but all labor in transportation, supplies, lubricants, refractories, etc., excluded.

Commercial cost Bessemer pig iron.

[Cost basis current market prices ore, coke, and limestone at Ohio-Pittsburg District.]

Cost items.	Price.	Cost per ton of pig iron.
Net total metallic mixture, 1.97 tons	$4.57	$9.000
Coke, 1.16 tons...	3.36	3.880
Limestone, 0.66 ton	1.09	.720
Labor	....	.938
Steam	....	.088
Materials in repairs and maintenance........................	....	.128
Supplies and tools	....	.080
Miscellaneous and general works expense	....	.378
General administrative charges	....	.2 2
Relinings and renewals.....................................	....	.220
Total...	....	15.634

NOTE.—This cost excludes depreciation and replacement, the charge for which would not be less than 30 cents per ton.

Commercial cost of large Bessemer steel billets.

[Ohio-Pittsburg District.]

Cost items.	Price.	Cost per ton of billets.
Pig iron..	....	$15.643
Scrap, 15 per cent...	$11.03	1.434
Total pig and scrap...................................	....	17.068
Waste...	....	2.031
Cost of pig iron and scrap in billets......................	....	19.099
Labor..	....	1.346
Manganese and fluxes......................................	....	.485
Fuel	....	.419
Steam...	....	.398
Molds...	....	.233
Rolls..	....	.013

Commercial cost of large Bessemer steel billets—Continued.

Cost items.	Price.	Cost per ton of pig iron.
Materials in repairs and maintenance...	....	$0.209
Supplies and tools...	....	.069
Miscellaneous and general works expense	....	.332
General administrative charges	....	.848
Depreciation...	....	.179
Total...	....	23.075

Commercial cost of merchant bar steel.

[Ohio-Pittsburg District.]

Cost items.	Cost per ton steel bars.
Billets	$23.075
Waste	.919
Cost of billets in bar steel	23.994
Labor...	3.986
Fuel..	.841
Steam..	.511
Rolls	.154
Materials in repairs and maintenance	.293
Supplies and tools...	.151
Miscellaneous and general works expense..	.615
General administrative charges..	.624
Depreciation	.435
Total	31.104
Cost per 100 pounds	1.388

NOTE.—Cost embraces all ordinary sizes.

Foreign selling prices compared with domestic costs delivered United States seaboard.

	England.				German.			
	Liverpool.	Freight.	Duty.	Delivered in New York.	Antwerp.	Freight.	Duty.	Delivered in New York.
Pig iron, gross tons..	$12.48	$1.44	$4.00	$17.92				
Billets	21.90	2.16	6.72	30.78	$18.45			$27.09
Blooms..............					18.00	$1.92	$6.72	26.64
Slabs................					17.96			26.60
Bar steel	28.66	2.16	6.72	37.54	22.72	1.92	6.72	31.36
Bar steel, 100 pounds	1.28	.096	.30	1.68	1.01	.085	.30	1.40

	Ohio and Pittsburg district costs.								
	F. O. B. mill.	Freight.	Delivered in New York.	Delivered at San Francisco.		Delivered at New Orleans.		Delivered at Galveston.	
				Freight.	Total.	Freight.	Total.	Freight.	Total.
Pig iron, gross tons..	$15.63	$2.45	$18.08	$14.00	$29.63	$6.72	$22.35	$9.63	$25.26
Blooms..............	23.08	2.60	25.68	13.44	36.52	6.72	29.80	(a)	(a)
Bar steel............	31.10	3.58	84.68	17.92	49.02	6.72	37.82	12.54	48.64
Bar steel, 100 pounds	1.39	.16	1.55	.80	2.19	.30	1.69	.56	1.95

a No rail rate on billets to Galveston.

Foreign selling prices compared with domestic costs delivered United States seaboard—Continued.

	England delivered.				German delivered.			
	Gulf ports.		San Francisco.		Gulf ports.		San Francisco.	
	Freight.	Total.	Freight.	Total.	Freight.	Total.	Freight.	Total.
Pig iron	$1.75	$18.23	$6.25	$22.73	$1.75	....	$6.25	....
Billets	....	....	....	....	....	$26.92	....	$31.42
Blooms	1.75	30.37	6.25	34.87	1.75	28.47	6.25	30.97
Slabs	....	....	....	....	....	26.43	....	30.93
Bars	2.00	37.38	7.50	42.88	2.00	31.44	7.50	36.94
Bars per 100 pounds.	.089	1.66	.335	1.91	.089	1.40	.335	1.65

NOTE.—Foreign market quotations represent gross prices. If subject "Foreign syndicate rebates," would be reduced by $3.84 to $5.52 per ton, and if sold on foreign cost basis the discount would be increased. Freight rates quoted are steamer rates. Tramp vessel rates would be from 50 cents to $1 per ton less, as iron and steel at times is carried as ballast. Present tramp rates to New York: Billets, $1.60; bar steel, $1.75. These figures clearly indicate that present foreign prices are on an export basis and below cost to many producers in the United States.

Authority: Iron and Coal Trades Review, December 4, 1908; The Ironmonger, December 5, 1908.

TARIFF REVISION.

Tariff revision which does not fully equalize the difference in cost between England and Germany's lowest producing points and our highest producing sections, and which does not allow for reasonable profits, will not be protective, but will expose the steel and iron industry and its labor to the disastrous effects of dumping, as practiced by foreign syndicates. It should also be remembered in considering domestic costs that many of the smaller producers of iron and steel suffer the very great disadvantage of being confined to one profit, whereas the larger companies enjoy the cumulative profits from the mines to the mills.

A financial writer for the Wall Street Journal, in the December 22, 1908, issue of that paper, makes the following interesting analysis of the profit showing of a number of industrial companies, in a graphic manner illustrating the advantages enjoyed by the large companies, who are fully self-contained and who produce a diversity of products and whose profits are augmented by profits from by-products, which many of the smaller operators lose or waste, and who further enjoy the advantages of profit on transportation in assembling raw materials and distributing their finished products:

Table showing the net profits after all deductions, excepting dividends, on each ton of steel produced by the United States Steel Corporation, and compared with the net profits of seven independent companies.

Company.	Net profits per ton steel sold.
United States Steel Corporation	$10.20
Independent No. 1	2.70
Independent No. 2	2.50
Independent No. 3	2.97
Independent No. 4	4.50
Independent No. 5	4.60
Independent No. 6	.40
Independent No. 7	3.50

In view of the general facts presented, no horizontal reduction in duty should be made, and I recommend that the present duty be maintained on iron ore, pig iron and scrap, billets and slabs, ferro manganese, ingots, steel bars, and shafting.

The duty on ferromanganese, in my opinion, may be maintained without injury to steel interests for revenue purposes and on the other products for reasons of protection.

The present rate of duty on steel and iron shafting of one-fourth cent per pound ($5 net ton) in excess of the duty on bar steel can not be reduced without loss to labor and capital. The direct labor cost in the manufacture of shafting is approximately $5.30 per ton, and the total cost for polishing or converting a ton of steel bars to shafting would be, approximately, $8.50 per ton for average sizes.

The duty on scrap iron should be retained for the protection of pig iron as a competitive product. Free scrap would also seriously reduce the revenues of all important consumers of finished iron and steel, these consumers producing scrap as a by-product or waste. This loss would particularly affect the railroads and agricultural implement manufacturers.

Reduction may be made, however, on the following items: Bar iron, 10 cents per 100 pounds ($2 net ton); spikes, 25 cents per 100 pounds ($5 net ton). The reduction on bar iron is suggested to correct the present inequality with the steel-bar duty. While bar iron costs more to produce, the reduction proposed will not disturb trade interests. The concession on spikes is suggested because the present rate of duty is more than protective.

On bolts, nuts, and washers I agree with reductions and changes recommended to your committee by Mr. James Lord, president of the American Iron and Steel Manufacturing Company.

Respectfully submitted.

JOHN A. TOPPING,
Chairman of Republic Iron and Steel Company.

I, John A. Topping, of New York City, being duly sworn according to law, do depose and say that the statements made in the foregoing brief, which pertains to the business of manufacturing iron and steel, are true and correct to the best of my knowledge and belief.

JNO. A. TOPPING.

Sworn and subscribed to before me, a notary public, this 15th day of January, 1909.

[SEAL.]   HENRY W. UTTER,
Notary Public, Westchester County.
Certificate filed in New York County.

IRON AND STEEL ABRASIVES.

[Paragraphs 135 and 193.]

THE GLOBE STEEL CO., MANSFIELD, OHIO, WISHES AN ADVANCE OF DUTIES ON METAL ABRASIVES.

MANSFIELD, OHIO, *November 23, 1908.*

Hon. JOHN DALZELL, M. C.:
Ways and Means Committee, Washington, D. C.

DEAR SIR: We are manufacturers of iron abrasives, iron shot, iron grit, and steel shot, and as such we find that we are unable to compete with the 45 per cent duty charged on the same materials brought from Scotland and England. We learn upon investigation that the machinery scrap such as we use costs us from $15 to $17 per ton and costs our competitors from $8 to $10 per ton. Labor there is $1 per day for the ordinary workman and here is from $1.75 to $2. At 45 per cent duty it is simply impossible for us to meet this competition.

We are the only factory of the kind in the United States, and those being the facts we respectfully ask, you being interested in the Pittsburg district, to give us your cooperation when the matter of duty on iron shot, iron abrasives, steel shot, etc., is brought before the Ways and Means Committee for discussion.

If we can be protected in such manner as to make the cost of the foreign goods equal to the cost of our goods, we can unquestionably increase this industry to a point where it would be of profit to the owners and the district in which it is located.

If you can make any suggestions to us that would be of benefit in aiding us in getting this duty advanced on iron abrasives, we shall be very glad to have you do so. If the 45 per cent duty maintains it will simply put us down and out, as it is impossible for us to exist and to meet foreign competition.

Can you suggest to whom it will be best to submit proofs of our inability to meet foreign prices?

Very truly, yours, THE GLOBE STEEL COMPANY.

THE GLOBE STEEL COMPANY, OF MANSFIELD, OHIO, ASKS FOR INCREASE OF DUTIES ON IRON SHOT, STEEL SHOT, IRON GRIT, AND OTHER IRON ABRASIVES.

MANSFIELD, OHIO, *November 27, 1908.*

COMMITTEE ON WAYS AND MEANS,
Washington, D. C.

GENTLEMEN: We desire to place before the Ways and Means Committee this statement of the cost of manufacture of iron shot, steel shot, iron grit, diamond grit, and other abrasives made from iron.

This iron shot is designated as iron shot, steel shot, iron grit, and diamond grit.

The iron is heated to a fluid state in a cupola, then run to a large vat of water where it is sprayed by steam, which causes the metal to be broken up into small spherical drops. These drops solidify immediately upon reaching the water.

As an abrasive this material is used for grinding down rough surfaces of granite, for sawing granite, marble, limestone, and sandstone, for iron-blasting rough surfaces of iron castings, and for any other purposes necessitating an abrasive.

There are in the United States at the present time two plants that make iron abrasives—one at Calais, Me., and the other the Globe Steel Company, at Mansfield, Ohio.

The Globe Steel Company started the manufacture of iron abrasives on June 10, 1908.

Labor	$125.00
Coal	18.00
Coke	19.50
Brick, sand, and limestone	5.00
	167.50
10 per cent for depreciation of plant per week	50.00
6 per cent interest on $25,000 investment per week	10.00
Total	227.50

This 6 per cent interest on $25,000 per week would be $30, but as we melt 30 tons per week it is only $10 per 10 tons.

The cost to produce 1 ton of shot is one-tenth of $227.50, the cost of 10 tons, or $22.75 per ton.

Cost of production as above	$22.75
Burlap sacks	2.00
Crude iron per ton	22.60
Freight to the New England States	5.00
Total	52.35

We find that it will cost about 20 per cent of our cost to market the goods, making the total cost as follows, per ton:

Cost as given above	$52.35
Cost to market goods	10.47
Total	62.82

From the foregoing it is seen that the cost of 1 ton of iron shot for abrasive purposes for a ton containing 2,000 pounds will net us $62.82 cost.

We have ascertained by experiments that it takes $1\frac{1}{3}$ tons of iron, at a valuation of $17 per ton, to produce 1 full ton of iron abrasives, making a cost to us per ton of $22.60 for each ton that is produced and turned out of our factory.

This plant produces 11 sizes of shot. The grading of the sizes depends upon the mesh through which the shot passes when being assorted. We manufacture the following sizes: 1, 2, $2\frac{1}{2}$, 3c, 3, $3\frac{1}{2}$, 4, $4\frac{1}{2}$, 5, $5\frac{1}{2}$, and 6.

Scotch and English shot are graded in the same manner, and the sizes are similar to our grading.

			At $4.85.	Plus 45 per cent duty.	Plus $5 to Boston, ocean freight.
	£	s.	d.			
No. 1	5	12	6	$27.25	$40.23	$45.23
No. 2	5	12	6	27.25	40.23	45.23
No. 2¼	5	12	6	27.25	40.23	45.23
No. 3c	5	12	6	27.25	40.23	45.23
No. 3	6	10	0	31.50	45.67	50.67
No. 3¼	6	10	0	31.50	45.67	50.67
No. 3¾	6	10	0	31.50	45.67	50.67
No. 4	6	10	0	31.50	45.67	50.67
No. 4f	5	12	6	27.25	40.23	45.23
No. 5	5	12	6	27.25	40.23	45.23
No. 5¼	4	0	0	19.40	28.13	33.13
No. 5¾	4	0	0	19.40	28.13	33.13
No. 6	2	15	0	13.30	19.28	24.28
No. 7	2	15	0	13.30	19.28	24.28
No. 8	2	15	0	13.30	19.28	24.28

Importers of foreign shot are offering their material as per schedule undernoted:

Per ton.

No. 1 --- $49.75
No. 2 --- 49.75
No. 2½ -- 54.25
No. 3c -- 54.25
No. 3 --- 57.90
No. 3½ -- 57.90
No. 4 --- 57.90
No. 4½ -- 57.90
No. 5 --- 51.25
No. 5½ -- 38.25
No. 6 --- 29.00

Your committee will see the marked difference between the cost of producing a ton of iron abrasives in America as against the actual cost of a ton imported from Aberdeen. The increased cost of labor, the increased cost of iron, and all others that enter into the production of 1 ton of iron abrasives make it necessary that we urgently request that the output of iron abrasives in this country be protected by a sufficient increase in duty to permit this new industry to grow in strength until such time that it will not need protection.

We therefore urgently request that your committee consider the feasibility of advancing the duty on iron shot, steel shot, iron grit, and other iron abrasives from 45 per cent to 75 per cent duty.

As we have already stated, we are the only factory west of the New England States, and we are positive that if our industry is to grow and become one of the factors of the prosperity of this country and of this particular portion of Ohio, we have to be protected against foreign importations of similar goods.

Respectfully submitted.

THE GLOBE STEEL COMPANY.

———

MANSFIELD, OHIO, *November 30, 1908.*

COMMITTEE ON WAYS AND MEANS,
Washington, D. C.

GENTLEMEN: As a substantial proof to the committee of the price that governs the sale of iron shot or chilled-steel shot, we submit the within communication from the Harrison Supply Company, under date of November 24, 1908, to one of our respective customers, Townsend, Townsend Company, of New York City. In this communication you will observe that they quote a price of $56 per ton on four different sizes of shot. This price is delivered from Boston to New York.

As we have already pointed out to your committee, the actual cost to us to produce and market 1 ton of shot of 2,000 pounds is $62.82. If your committee would like to have us do so, we can produce a letter in which the Harrison Supply Company, who control the entire output of shot from abroad with the exception of one firm, make the claim that their price of $56 per ton is at a profit of 10 per cent to themselves. If this be correct, they could sell their product at $50 per ton, this being apparently the actual cost to them, while it would cost us $62.82.

We trust that your committee will look into this matter carefully and will certainly see that we need protection at the present time. Shall be pleased to have your committee consider the matter.

Very truly, yours,

THE GLOBE STEEL COMPANY,
E. K. BACON, *Manager.*

" BOSTON, MASS., *November 24, 1908.*
" Messrs. TOWNSEND, TOWNSEND & CO.,
" *453 West Twenty-first Street,*
"*New York City, N. Y.*

" GENTLEMEN : Please note, we have an extremely heavy stock of chilled steel shot on hand at the present time. We are sending you, under separate cover to-day, a complete set of samples of our chilled steel shot. All samples are taken from bags ready for shipment. We have ready for immediate shipment about 25 tons of our No. 1F, about 10 tons of No. 2C, 15 tons of No. 2F, possibly 10 tons of No. 3, 5 tons of No. 4C, and a very heavy stock of the finer sizes. We have also about 10 tons of McGregor's shot, No. 2, on hand.

" For your information will state that our chilled steel shot compares in size with McGregor's shot as follows:

" Chilled steel shot No. 1F compares with McGregor's shot No. 2. Chilled steel shot No. 2C compares with McGregor's shot No. 3. Chilled steel shot No. 2F compares with McGregor's shot No. 3½. Chilled steel shot No. 3 compares with McGregor's shot No. 4. Chilled steel shot No. 4C compares with McGregor's shot No. 5.

" If you are ready to purchase from 25 to 50 tons of the sizes named to be shipped at one time, we will name you a special price of $56 per ton, freight paid to New York City; terms strictly spot cash on arrival of goods at New York.

" This offer is made subject to acceptance by return mail.

" Yours, very truly,

" HARRISON SUPPLY COMPANY,
" NATHAN C. HARRISON,
"*Treasurer.*"

HON. CHARLES DICK, SENATOR, FILES LETTER FROM MANSFIELD, OHIO, RELATIVE TO METAL ABRASIVES.

DECEMBER 16, 1908.

Hon. S. E. PAYNE, M. C.,
  Chairman Committee on Ways and Means,
        Washington, D. C.

DEAR MR. PAYNE: The inclosed letter from Capt. Edwin G. Slough, secretary Chamber of Commerce of Mansfield, Ohio, in reference to the duty on iron shot and other iron abrasives, is self-explanatory.

The favor will be appreciated if you will direct that information be furnished Captain Slough as to a hearing before your committee, in order that this matter may be presented in proper form for consideration.

Very truly, yours,   CHARLES DICK.

———

MANSFIELD, OHIO, *December 5, 1908.*

Hon. CHARLES DICK,
  United States Senate, Washington, D. C.

DEAR SIR: I am now writing you as secretary of the chamber of commerce by instruction of the board of directors in relation to securing a proper duty in the proposed new tariff law on iron shot, steel shot, grit, and other iron abrasives.

We have located the only institution of any consequence now in this country (there being one small factory in the East, which is pegging away with little success) which produces this material, which is a granite polisher's grit, or shot, as the case may be, and several of our local people are interested in the enterprise, including a few Scotchmen, who came here from Glasgow to establish a plant.

They find upon actual contact with the trade that the England and Scotland product is underselling them so badly in the market that they can not compete successfully under the duty as it stands, and are asking the duty to be raised from 45 to 75 per cent.

I have gone into the matter quite extensively with our committee of the chamber of commerce, and the evidence which we have taken justifies the statement that an additional duty should be levied to enable this industry to become one of the best institutions of this country, and if this additional duty can be secured it will mean much for the city of Mansfield, as it would result in a great enlargement of the small plant which we are now trying to foster; and of course if this plant progresses others will no doubt be established in other parts of the country.

The secretary of the company is a very frank, truthful gentleman in every way and an honest man, and I have gone into the matter with considerable detail, as I said before, and he tells me they can not make their goods at a profit justifying the investment of capital under the present tariff.

Will you not be good enough to confer with Mr. Payne and some other members of the House committee in relation to this point?

I know you are sufficiently interested in the protective principles to give your personal attention in such an instance, and, at the same

time, you are sufficiently interested in your own State being the bene-
ficiary in the fostering of a new industry in this country.

There is an immense amount of this product used in the United
States, especially in the East.

Respectfully,   EDWIN G. SLOUGH,
        Secretary, Mansfield, Ohio, Chamber of Commerce.

THE CALAIS (ME.) SHOT WORKS ASKS THAT A DUTY OF ONE CENT PER POUND BE PUT ON CHILLED SHOT.

CALAIS, ME., *December 16, 1908.*
COMMITTEE ON WAYS AND MEANS,
        Washington, D. C.

GENTLEMEN: Ten years ago we started at Calais, Me., a plant to
make chilled shot for use in granite mills here and elsewhere. We
have been in competition chiefly with foreign manufacturers, and
feel that in revising the tariff it should be changed from an ad valorem duty of 45 per cent to a specific duty of not less than 1 cent per
pound on all sizes of chilled shot. We have carried on our business
in a most economical manner, and have not in the ten years been
able to get a profit of 6 per cent a year on our investment, leaving
out all allowance for depreciation of plant.

The foreign makers get pig iron for $13.40, which costs us $23. A
reduction in duty on pig iron would not help us, as it would only
be added to the foreign price to us. The foreign freights to New
York are about $3.23, against $5 from Calais.

We do not know the comparative wages in Scotland and here. We
do know, however, that in ten years of hard work we have been constantly facing a foreign competition which has kept our prices down
below a fair business profit, and this has been especially true of small-
sized shot, which has been imported and sold as low as $25 a ton of
2,240 pounds, and this is below cost here.

The duty should apply to all sizes of shot and should be specific
duty, as in the past the valuations have been such that the price has
been forced down to less than the actual cost to us on small sizes.

In 1904 an effort was made by the foreign manufacturers to combine the American makers with them and regulate prices. We declined to do this, and think we ought to have the tariff protection.

Respectfully,
                        THE CALAIS SHOT WORKS,
                        By W. F. BOARDMAN,
                                Treasurer.

THE HARRISON SUPPLY COMPANY, BOSTON, MASS., WISHES IRON SAND PLACED ON THE FREE LIST.

BOSTON, MASS., *December 21, 1908.*
The WAYS AND MEANS COMMITTEE,
        Washington, D. C.

GENTLEMEN: When making a revision of the United States tariff,
we wish you would take into consideration the fact that we are pay-

ing 45 per cent duty on all "iron sand" which comes in under act of July 24, 1897, paragraph 193.

A competitive article is manufactured in the United States to-day and sold for as low as $22 per ton less than we can actually import our material.

We respectfully ask, as representing three of the four iron-sand manufacturers abroad, to have the duty abolished on iron sand.

Yours, very truly,

HARRISON SUPPLY COMPANY,
NATHAN C. HARRISON, *Treasurer.*

THE HARRISON SUPPLY COMPANY, BOSTON, MASS., ASK FOR REDUCTION OF DUTY ON CHILLED SHOT.

34 INDIA WHARF,
Boston, Mass., January 4, 1909.

WAYS AND MEANS COMMITTEE,
Washington, D. C.

GENTLEMEN: We understand that certain individuals or concerns are writing you with a view of having the duty increased on chilled shot or iron sand, which comes in under act of July 24, 1897, paragraph 193. We certainly object to this very strongly indeed. The parties or individuals who are manufacturing shot in this country—and there are only two of them—are each selling their merchandise for less money than we can actually import the material into this country at the present time, and, as stated in previous correspondence, we ask for a considerable reduction on this material or have the duty abolished altogether. Concerns that are manufacturing here to-day can sell their merchandise in competition with any imported article without having any protection in the shape of duty whatever.

Yours, very truly,

HARRISON SUPPLY COMPANY,
NATHAN C. HARRISON, *Treasurer.*

HIGH-SPEED STEEL.

[Paragraph 135.]

STATEMENT OF WILLIAM G. PARK, OF PITTSBURG, PA., CHAIRMAN OF THE CRUCIBLE STEEL COMPANY.

Mr. UNDERWOOD. Mr. Park, will you please give the committee a reference to the paragraph that you desire to address yourself to before you begin?

Mr. PARK. It is under " Iron and steel, steel ingots, cogged ingots, blooms, and slabs."

Mr. DALZELL. It is paragraph 135.

Mr. GRIGGS. May I ask you one question before you begin?

Mr. PARK. Yes, sir.

Mr. GRIGGS. Are you making any money?

Mr. PARK. We are.

Mr. GRIGGS. I am glad to see you.

Mr. PARK. The volume of this business in which I am interested, as covered in this clause, is about three or four hundred thousand tons a year, and it is a class of steel that is higher in price and superior in quality to the ordinary steel, called bar. steel. Most of it is crucible and refined high grade of open-hearth steel. We think that the duty permits of pretty large importations at the time; there is a great deal of it imported, and I do not think we can stand. a very large reduction in the tariff without having the importations increased; but recognizing the fact that a reduction perhaps is in order, we would ask the committee to make it as light as possible. We feel prepared to stand something of a reduction in respect to it. I have talked to several manufacturers in this line of business and they think that about 10 per cent from the present duty would be something that would be acceptable.

Mr. GRIGGS. About 10 per cent below?

Mr. PARK. Ten per cent off of these duties, the duties as they now stand. Then there is a great deal of steel that is made—that has only been made about five years—called high-speed steel for which there is no protection in this Dingley tariff bill. We propose a scale. The highest here is 16-cent steel bearing 4.7 cents a pound duty. We propose 20-cent steel, steel 20 cents a pound and not over 25 cents, 7 cents a pound; 25 cents and not over 30 cents, 10 cents; 30 cents and 36 cents, 15 cents; 36 cents a pound and over, 20 cents. The article that enters into the manufacture of that steel largely is metallic tungsten, which sells for 75 cents a pound, so you can readily see that we have a good reason for asking this.

Mr. DALZELL. You propose to add that to this paragraph, do you?

Mr. PARK. Yes, sir.

Mr. DALZELL. In other words, you extend the description of steel up to a higher figure than is suggested in this paragraph?

Mr. PARK. Yes, sir; on the ground that it is a new article of manufacture.

Mr. DALZELL. Tungsten is something that has been discovered and used since the passage of the Dingley bill, is it not?

Mr. PARK. No, sir; that is an old metal that was discovered many years ago.

Mr. DALZELL. It was not specifically provided for in the McKinley bill though?

Mr. PARK. No; tungsten is provided for in the last bill, the tungsten metal.

Mr. BONYNGE. Where do you get that tungsten from?

Mr. PARK. We get it from a manufacturing concern in York, Pa.

Mr. BONYNGE. Where does the tungsten ore come from?

Mr. PARK. The tungsten ore comes from Spain, Chile, and Germany.

Mr. BONYNGE. Don't you use any from Colorado?

Mr. PARK. From Colorado, yes, sir; I suppose that probably from one-fifth to one-tenth of all that is mined is from Colorado, and some from Spain.

Mr. GRIGGS. How much of this did you manufacture in the last year?

Mr. PARK. I do not suppose the amount manufactured by our company was more than a half million dollars' worth of steel.

Mr. GRIGGS. I notice at the end of the paragraph here—not the paragraph as you have it, but the one we have here—that the importation for last year of blooms, slabs, and bars was valued at $3,032,928. That, of course, does not apply?

Mr. PARK. No, sir.

Mr. GRIGGS. What is the name of the steel?

Mr. PARK. It is tool steel, called high-speed tool steel.

Mr. GRIGGS. Do you know what the importations were last year?

Mr. PARK. I do not know what the importations were, but I think the importation of all of this class of steel that we manufacture is about four or five millions of dollars.

Mr. RANDELL. How much of it was this particular steel?

Mr. PARK. How much of it was high-speed steel?

Mr. GRIGGS. Yes.

Mr. PARK. I suppose a million dollars' worth.

Mr. GRIGGS. That is the particular steel you make?

Mr. PARK. That is this new article of steel; this new article of manufacture.

Mr. GRIGGS. You make other classes of steel, do you?

Mr. PARK. Yes, sir.

Mr. DALZELL. That is a higher class of steel than the crucible steel?

Mr. PARK. Yes, sir; it is crucible steel, but crucible steel of a higher grade.

Mr. GRIGGS. Is that the highest grade of steel that is made?

Mr. PARK. Yes, sir; it is the highest.

Mr. UNDERWOOD. I want to ask you this question: I see that there is considerable importation of ingots, blooms, and slabs and steel bars. I suppose the cheapest point where this can be imported by this country would be New York, because the freight rates are cheaper there from foreign ports.

Mr. PARK. Yes, sir; almost all in New York.

Mr. UNDERWOOD. What is the importing price of blooms after the duty is added, or without the duty, if you can give it to me in that way?

Mr. PARK. What grade of blooms do you mean? If you mean the cheap grade of blooms, such as the steel-rail quality, I suppose it would be about $18 a ton.

Mr. UNDERWOOD. That is without the duty?

Mr. PARK. Without the duty.

Mr. UNDERWOOD. Now, with the duty added, what would that make it in New York?

Mr. PARK. I do not know; I am not familiar with the duty on blooms.

Mr. UNDERWOOD. I understand that it would take sometime to figure it out but I would like to ask you to take your time about it because there is considerable importation given it.

Mr. PARK. Yes, sir.

Mr. UNDERWOOD. Will you please file in your brief the market price of blooms, ingots, and billets at New York without the tariff; then add the tariff so that we will know just exactly what the tariff is and what the New York price of the foreign product is, and then give us the cost of the same things in this country?

Mr. PARK. I am not sure that I can do that because our company does not make these billets.

Mr. UNDERWOOD. Well, as far as you can, please give us the information.

Mr. PARK. Yes, sir.

Mr. BONYNGE. Let me ask you a question for information. Can you get tungsten here from Spain and Chile cheaper than the Colorado tungsten?

Mr. PARK. We have never tried to buy tungsten.

Mr. BONYNGE. Tungsten ore, I mean. Can you get the ore from Spain and Chile cheaper than you can from Colorado here?

Mr. PARK. I think it would be about the same.

Mr. BONYNGE. The same price?

Mr. PARK. The same price, or about the same price, less the duty.

BRIEF SUBMITTED BY SEARLE & PILLSBURY, REPRESENTING NEW ENGLAND IMPORTERS OF HIGH-SPEED STEEL.

BOSTON, MASS., *December 1, 1908.*

COMMITTEE ON WAYS AND MEANS,
Washington, D. C.

GENTLEMEN: The proposed change in paragraph No. 135 of the steel schedule (see Iron Age of November 19, 1908, pp. 1444, 1445) substituting an ad valorem rate on the various kinds of steel covered by said paragraph, valued above 16 cents per pound, instead of the present (excessive) rate of 4.7 cents per pound, is evidently aimed at foreign high-speed steel, which is imported in considerable quantities for the use of American makers of steel tools. The change is no doubt inspired by interested parties, for while the suggestion of a blank ad valorem rate would probably have no special significance to persons not familiar with the steel trade, yet to those in the trade it means an increase in duties beyond the prohibitive point.

Judging from the present ad valorem rates on steel and its manufactures and the ratios which the specific rates bear to the value of the merchandise, any ad valorem rate in paragraph No. 135 on steel valued above 16 cents per pound, which domestic interests would ask for, would mean an increase in the duty on high-speed steel of from 100 per cent to 300 per cent.

Under present conditions American high-speed steel is being sold to manufacturers of steel tools for less than the price of the foreign, without the addition of the duty; which proves conclusively that it can be produced in this country at a less price than the foreign article can be laid down in New York or Boston, even if it were on the free list. Although, as we have said before, high-speed steel is imported in considerable quantities, yet it is a very small item in comparison with the amount of tool steel produced and used in this country, and it could not be imported at all (even at the present rate of duty, which is excessive) but for the fact that the American tool makers find it necessary to use the foreign steel to produce certain tools of a certain quality. But there is a limit to the price that American manufacturers can pay for imported tool steel, and any material increase in duty over the present rate of 4.7 cents per pound would in our opinion exclude the article entirely from this market. If we are right in our judgment, then the bald proposition is simply this, viz, that the United States Government shall forego and surrender the revenue it is now receiving (which amounts, figured upon the statement made to your committee on the 25th day of November, 1908, by the Primos Chemical Company, of Primos, Pa., to about $1,128,000 per annum) from duties on imported high-speed steel, and American mechanics shall be compelled to use inferior tools, for the sole purpose and object of adding to the already enormous profits of the great American steel corporations, who are admittedly the lowest-cost steel producers in the world, or, in other words, to enable the American steel producers to seize and appropriate to themselves the small fraction of the market that foreign high-speed steel has been able to command up to this time by reason of its special and peculiar qualities.

We beg, further, to call the attention of the committee to the fact that the chief argument of the American producers in the past—to wit, that protection was needed because of the duty on tungsten, which enters largely into the manufacture of high-speed steel, and which necessarily had to be imported—no longer avails, for large deposits of tungsten have been found in this country, several of the steel companies having their own tungsten mines, and it can now be obtained in the United States at a lower price than from any foreign country. We again assert that the present rate of 4.7 cents per pound is excessive; that it lays an unnecessary burden upon the American tool maker and the American mechanic; that a lower rate would add, to a certain extent, to the revenue of the Government and would tend to increase the production in this country of superior and high-grade tools; that the American steel producers have no legitimate claim for protection against a foreign article that sells in this market, even without the duty added, at a higher price than their own products.

In an article in the Iron Age, of November 12, 1908, Mr. E. T. Clarage, of Chicago, president of the Columbia Tool Steel Company, characterizes the European manufacturers as being "at the tail end of the procession," and later, in the same article, asserts, "There is no doubt that some exceedingly good steel is manufactured in Europe. This we do not deny, but we have never yet analyzed a piece of European tool steel which could not be duplicated or excelled in this country by any one of half a dozen leading tool-steel makers, and with much more uniformity, in addition to being sold at a lower price."

If this is true, and we know he is correct about prices being lower, why is there any need of protecting the American tool steels unless it be to enrich the makers at the expense of the consumers and to destroy the healthy competition of foreign steels at the expense of the Government's revenues?

In conclusion, we respectfully ask, in the interest of the Government, the consumer, and ourselves, that no ad valorem rate be substituted in paragraph No. 135 for the present specific rate on steel valued above 16 cents per pound, but that the rate be made specific at 3½ cents per pound instead of 4.7 cents per pound, as in the act of July 24, 1897.

Respectfully submitted.

SEARLE & PILLSBURY,

Attorneys for B. M. Jones & Co.,
Houghton & Richards, and Edgar T. Ward & Sons.

STATEMENT OF CHARLES P. SEARLE, OF 50 CONGRESS STREET, BOSTON, MASS., RELATIVE TO HIGH-SPEED STEEL.

THURSDAY, *December 17, 1908.*

(The witness was duly sworn by the chairman.)

Mr. SEARLE. Mr. Chairman and gentlemen, while I am scheduled to speak on the subject of machinery, I find that I haven't sufficient data to proceed on that subject this morning, and I would like until the 15th of next month to file a brief upon that subject. I find, in order to answer certain briefs that have been filed here, that it is necessary for me to send to England for information. I would, however, like to address the committee this morning on the question of high-speed steel.

The CHAIRMAN. I would like to ask two or three questions in regard to the machinery, as I wish to step out for a few minutes. Machinery comes in under the basket clause, does it not?

Mr. SEARLE. Yes, sir.

The CHAIRMAN. That is, 45 per cent.

Mr. SEARLE. Yes.

The CHAIRMAN. Is such a percentage of duty necessary for any machinery coming in?

Mr. SEARLE. It is not. The machinery, as a matter of fact, pays, instead of 45 per cent, from 62 to 65 per cent, because it pays duty upon the packing charges; and I wish to address the committee on that very matter. In order to get accurate information, it is necessary to send to England. I have a lot of statistics upon that subject already, but I do not think they are in such form that I ought to present them. We are asking for a lower rate of duty upon machinery.

The CHAIRMAN. How low?

Mr. SEARLE. Thirty per cent would be ample protection, and we will show it by our figures.

The CHAIRMAN. Upon any class of machinery imported?

Mr. SEARLE. I do not know about that. We especially deal with textile machinery. I appear for Evan Arthur Leigh, 232 Sumner street, Boston, Mass.

The CHAIRMAN. When can you file your brief?

Mr. SEARLE. I would like until the 10th of January, if the committee think that time is not too long.

The CHAIRMAN. Oh, we can not give you until that time, because we will have to have other hearings on the subject if you raise that question of duty.

Mr. SEARLE. Then whatever time you fix as convenient.

The CHAIRMAN. Suppose you go on and make your statement this morning.

Mr. SEARLE. I am not prepared to make a statement on machinery, but I am prepared to make a statement on high-speed steel this morning; but I will submit the brief whenever the committee thinks convenient.

The CHAIRMAN. I would like to have it filed this week.

Mr. SEARLE. I think it would be impossible to do that and do it in an intelligent manner.

The CHAIRMAN. You might file your statistics that you sent to England for later, but on the general subject you can send in your brief earlier than that, can you not?

Mr. SEARLE. I think I could.

The CHAIRMAN. Send the other in as a supplemental brief later.

Mr. SEARLE. I will do that within ten days.

The CHAIRMAN. Very well.

Mr. SEARLE. I desire to address the committee this morning on the question of high-speed steel. The steel which I desire to speak about is covered by paragraph 135 of the tariff act of 1897, and has reference more especially to the classes of steel which pay a duty from 1.2 cents per pound to 4.7 cents per pound.

Mr. DALZELL. Does that cover crucible steel?

Mr. SEARLE. Yes, sir; but I desire to answer a statement filed by Mr. Park, which I think you are familiar with.

In bulletin No. 15 issued by the Department of Commerce and Labor, on page 30, it appears that the importers entered for consumption for the year ending June 30, 1908, steel valued above 16 cents per pound as follows: Pounds, 1,998,255.98; value, $679,771; duties, $93,918.06; rate, 13.82 per cent.

The average value of this steel was 34 cents per pound, and the rate of duty asked for in our brief of 3½ cents per pound is practically a rate of 10 per cent ad valorem. The lowest rate of duty now exacted under paragraph 135 is 11.77 per cent, and the highest rate of duty is 104 per cent.

If any considerable importations of steel are to be made under this section, the rate of duty must be made low in order to encourage importations.

Mr. Claradge in an article in the Iron Age of November 12, 1908, stated as follows: "There is no doubt that some exceedingly good steel is manufactured in Europe; this we do not deny. But we have never yet analyzed a piece of European tool steel which could not be duplicated or excelled in this country by any one of a half dozen tool-steel makers, with much more uniformity, in addition to selling at a lower price." Mr. E. T. Claradge, of Chicago, is president of the Columbia Tool Steel Company, and I would suggest that the committee ask him to come before them and give some figures confirming that statement, with which I do not entirely agree.

Mr. Park, of the Crucible Steel Company, asks that the duty be increased, so that steel which is worth 30 cents a pound shall pay 15 cents per pound and steel worth 35 cents per pound shall pay 20 cents per pound, and Mr. Park stated on page 1937 of the Record that he believed that the importations of this class of steel would be between $4,000,000 and $5,000,000 last year.

When asked how much of it he supposed was high-speed steel, he replied about $1,000,000 worth. This was all crucible steel.

Mr. Park again states, on page 1937 of the Record, that he did not know the amount of the importations of the class of steel which he manufactured, but believed it to be about $4,000,000 or $5,000,000 worth.

Now, as a matter of fact, the value of the steel, other than high-speed steel, such as was manufactured by the Crucible Steel Company, of Pittsburg, of which Mr. Park was president, dutiable at from 1.8 to 2.8 cents per pound, and imported during the year ending June 30, 1908, was only $1,172,446.41, and the duties on the same were $246,977.04.

Of the high-speed steel, the value imported into this country during the same period was $679,771, and the duties were about $93,918, but all of this was not high-speed steel; probably about three-quarters of it, so Mr. Park's figures can not be relied upon in any way.

Of course the business last year generally was poor, but business in high-speed steel was especially active from June to October, 1907, and the importations were very large in the fall of 1907.

The manufacture of high-speed steel in this country and the importations of foreign high-speed steels have been increasing each year. When this steel was first invented it was supposed that it would simply take the place of the old self-hardening steels, which were used for rough work, for heavy planing, turning, etc., but it has since been found that this steel can be used for other purposes, and it is now being put into such tools as milling cutters, twist drills, taps, reamers, etc., and as the American tool makers find new uses for it the production of it is increasing all the time, both at home and abroad.

Mr. Park, in discussing paragraph 135, stated as follows:

The volume of this business in which I am interested, as covered in this clause is about 300,000 or 400,000 tons per year, and it is a class of steel that is higher in price and superior in quality to the ordinary steel called "bar steel." Most of it is crucible and refined high-grade of open-hearth steel.

The amount of the importations of this high class of steel for the year ending June 30, 1908, was only 14,119,249.75 pounds, or less than 7,000 long tons, or about 2 per cent of the total consumption of the country, according to Mr. Park's figures, and yet he has the temerity to come here and ask this committee to increase the duties on high-speed steel 300 to 400 per cent.

Now, I desire to show you that this increase is not needed in any sense of the word. Last September the Navy Department asked for bids for high-speed tool steel, and bids were made. The lowest bid was made by the Carpenter Steel Company, of Reading, Pa. Their bid was 34.7 cents per pound. The Midvale Steel Company, of Philadelphia, was the next bidder, and their bid was 34.8 cents per pound. Mr. Park, of the Crucible Steel Company, was the next bidder, 36.45 cents per pound. The Baldwin Locomotive Company was the fourth bidder, 40½ cents per pound, and the Bethlehem Steel Company was the fifth, at 42 cents per pound. The award was made to the Carpenter Steel Company, of Reading, Pa., at 34.7 per pound. I went yesterday and obtained from the Navy Department a copy of this bid, and I desire to offer it as Exhibit A.

(Following is the exhibit referred to:)

EXHIBIT A.

Schedule 386. Bureau of Ordnance. (High speed steel.) Original, duplicate (indicate which by erasure).

Schedule of supplies for the U. S. Navy (eastern yards, etc.). Bids to be opened at 10 a. m., October 6, 1908.

☞ Bids on this schedule will not be considered unless prepared in accordance with the instructions on the first page of Form A.

Bid of The Carpenter Steel Co., Reading, Pa.

Bidders must enumerate on the line below all classes of this schedule bid on to avoid possibility of bid being overlooked.

Class 181.

EXHIBIT A—Continued.

No. of item.	Articles.	Unit price. Dollars.	Unit price. Cents.	Total. Dollars.	Total. Cents.
	Class 181.—(*Req'n 227, Naval Supply Fund.—Washington, D. C.—Sch. 386.*)				
	To be delivered at the navy yard, Washington, D. C., within 45 days after date of {contract. / bureau order.				
	If unable to make delivery within the time specified, state actual number of days required, bureau reserving right to make award on time stated above.				
	For steel to conform to the specifications strictly as regards the percentages of carbon, silicon, etc., and to be capable of performing in a satisfactory manner work done by the standard tools used at the Naval Gun Factory.				
	For Ord. (turning and boring gun steel and steel castings).				
a	31,650 pounds (about) high speed steel, as specified below .... per pound..	....	84.7	10,982	65
	Square—				
1	2,000 pounds 6¼″.				
2	4,000 pounds 2½″.				
3	1,000 pounds 2¼″.				
4	1,000 pounds 1½″.				
5	1,000 pounds 1¼″.				
6	800 pounds 1″.				
7	300 pounds ⅞″.				
8	200 pounds ¾″.				
9	200 pounds ⅝″.				
10	300 pounds ½″.				
11	250 pounds 5/16″.				
	Flat—				
12	1,500 pounds 5″ x 4″.				
13	1,500 pounds 5″ x 3″.				
14	2,500 pounds 4″ x 3½″.				
15	2,000 pounds 4″ x 3″.				
16	500 pounds 1″ x ⅝″.				
17	1,500 pounds 4″ x 2¼″.				
18	1,500 pounds 3½″ x 3″.				
19	1,000 pounds 3½″ x 2¼″.				
20	1,500 pounds 3″ x 2″.				
21	500 pounds 3″ x 1″.				
22	1,000 pounds 2½″ x 1¾″.				
23	400 pounds 2″ x ⅝″.				
24	350 pounds 2″ x ½″.				
25	300 pounds 2″ x ⅜″.				
26	300 pounds 1¾″ x ½″.				
27	250 pounds 1¾″ x ⅜″.				
28	1,500 pounds 1½″ x ¾″.				
29	300 pounds 1½″ x ½″.				
30	200 pounds 1½″ x ⅜″.				
31	500 pounds 1¼″ x ⅝″.				
32	1,500 pounds 1″ x ½″.				
	The above steel to be crucible high speed steel and of the following general chemical analysis:				
	Carbon not less than .4 per cent or greater than .75 per cent.				
	Silicon not greater than .2 per cent.				
	Phosphorus not greater than .02 per cent.				
	Sulphur not greater than .02 per cent.				
	Manganese not greater than .2 per cent.				
	Chromium not less than 3 per cent or greater than 6 per cent.				
	Tungsten not less than 12 per cent or greater than 19 per cent.				
	Vanadium in such proportions as desired by the manufacturer.				
	To have no other impurities or ingredients except iron, particularly no molybdenum.				
	It shall be of uniform quality throughout, and delivered in bars of commercial length and sizes as called for. It shall be free from cracks, flaws, pipes, and all other mechanical imperfections.				
	Award of contract will be made to the lowest bidder whose steel conforms to the above specifications and is capable of performing the work done by standard tools in use in the Navy Yard, Washington, D. C. Steel to be forged and treated according to the process in vogue at this yard. Any bars found not up to standard at any time shall be replaced at the expense of the contractor.				

It seemed to me, after obtaining this bid, that it was pertinent to know exactly what the cost of this steel would be to the importer; so I telegraphed to my clients, Messrs. Houghton & Richards, of Boston, and asked them what the steel, as furnished the Navy Department under the Carpenter Steel Company bid, would cost the importer, and I received this reply: " Imported steel, Navy Department specifications, would cost the importer about 43 cents per pound."

This high-speed tool steel contains from 15 per cent to 25 per cent of tungsten. The specifications provided by the Navy Department in the bid which I submit calls for tungsten not less than 12 per cent or greater than 19 per cent. The duty of $3\frac{1}{2}$ per cent means a duty of $77 per ton instead of the present duty of about $103.40 per ton, and as stated in our brief, which is printed on page 4146 of the record, it seems to lay an unnecessary burden upon the American tool maker and the American mechanic.

The Midvale Steel Company, of Philadelphia, in a brief which they filed before this committee, stated as follows:

It is always inadvisable to tax materials which enter into the manufacture of special steels, thus increasing their cost to the buyer or restricting their use. If a special rate or any ad valorem rate be placed on these materials, the price of many of which is now exceedingly high by reason of the rarity of the ores from which they are made, it will add greatly to the price of the finished steel, which has now come to be essential for use in the tools of modern machine shops and for other purposes. Such added cost will materially add to the cost of the product of such tools. * * *

It has been suggested that it is advisable to increase the tariff rate on special steels to thereby protect those special steels, which would enable a duty to be placed upon the ferro compounds without affecting the profits on the manufacture of the steel. The objections to this suggestion are many. In the first place, increased duties are contrary to the spirit of the times. In the second place, it is simply an attempt to cure one evil by introducing a greater evil, because it increases the cost to the consumer, not only by the increased price of the raw material entering into the manufacture of the steel, but in addition by reason of the protection given to the finished product. This is repugnant to all idea of progress and the general demand for the lowering of the tariff.

The Midvale Steel Company, who made this statement, made a bid of 34.8 cents per pound in the exhibit covering the bid of the Carpenter Steel Company at the Navy Department; that is, they lost it simply by one-tenth of 1 cent a pound.

Mr. Frank Samuel, in a statement made to this committee, said that the actual cost of labor per ton on billets in this country, due to our improved machinery and methods, would not exceed the average cost of labor per ton in the English mills, and he adds: " Evidence of this fact can be produced before your committee, if you so desire."

The foreign value of ferrotungsten* varies from about $1,000 per ton to $1,900 per ton.

The use of tungsten produces a steel which retains its temper even when red-hot. That is the particular reason why it is so valuable for the film of the incandescent electric light. It has a quality, as I have stated, of enabling the steel to remain hard when heated to a high temperature, thus enabling tools to work even at incandescence.

The high cost of ferrotungsten is not due to the cost of manufacture, but because of the rarity of the ore from which it is made, and the great demand for the same compared with the supply. It has been stated before to your committee that the United States is especially well suited to make ferrotungsten without protection, for one of the chief sources of the supply of tungsten ore in the world is our own State of Colorado, and the water power and the electric facilities enable the manufacturers in this country to produce ferrotungsten readily and cheaply.

The manufacture itself of ferrotungsten from the tungsten ore is by a simple metallurgical process, requiring a little labor, the electric furnace being employed to generate the great heat required to melt this ore, and as to the question of labor or the facilities for manufacture, this country needs no protection in order to enable it to successfully compete with the foreign product. The duty of $3\frac{1}{2}$ cents per pound proposed upon high-speed steel means a duty, as I have stated, of 10 per cent ad valorem. This would mean a protection of from $100 to $190 per ton, according to the value of the tungsten ore.

That, Mr. Chairman, is all the statement I desire to make in regard to high-speed steel.

Mr. DALZELL. Mr. Searle, what do you say as to the duties imposed in section 135 up to 16-cent steel and over?

Mr. SEARLE. I should say that the duties as they now stand are fair, with the exception of the last two provisions, reading as follows: " Valued above 13 cents and not above 16 cents per pound, 2.8 cents per pound; valued above 16 cents per pound "—I think if the duty upon steel valued above 13 cents per pound, but not above 16 cents per pound, were reduced to 2 cents per pound instead of 2.8 cents per pound, and steel valued above 16 cents per pound was reduced from 4.7 cents per pound to $3\frac{1}{2}$ cents per pound, it would be perfectly fair to everybody.

Mr. DALZELL. You think that these duties have a relatively proper adjustment?

Mr. SEARLE. I agree with that.

Mr. DALZELL. Do you think that any of them could be reduced?

Mr. SEARLE. I do.

Mr. DALZELL. Excepting those you have already stated?

Mr. SEARLE. I am stating this because my clients are more especially familiar with this class of steel.

Mr. DALZELL. Mr. Park was willing to have the duties up to 16-cent steel reduced 10 per cent.

Mr. SEARLE. I noticed that in his statement, yes; but he did not seem to state any good reason for having the duty on high-speed steel increased—in fact, he shows in his bid here, which he made to the Navy Department, he underbid us on the present duty about 9 cents a pound. We could not furnish the steel imported for less than 43 cents, and his bid was 36.45 cents.

Mr. DALZELL. You are talking about high-speed steel. That is something that has come into commerce since the passage of the Dingley bill.

Mr. SEARLE. That is very true.

Mr. DALZELL. If it is fair and proper to adjust these duties relatively, according to the price of the steel, why ought you not to continue to increase the duties if the value of this steel increases?

Mr. SEARLE. For the reason that it becomes prohibitive. There is a certain point beyond which one can not import merchandise, and it makes it impossible for us to compete. All of these people are making steel and selling it for 8 or 9 cents per pound less than we can sell it. I read you a statement in regard to that.

Mr. DALZELL. I understand; it is in your brief?

Mr. SEARLE. Yes, sir; from the president of the Columbia Tool Company, who stated that the American tools were superior in every way.

Mr. DALZELL. High-speed steel is above 16 cents?

Mr. SEARLE. Most of it.

Mr. DALZELL. And no provision is made for that now excepting this general clause?

Mr. SEARLE. That is right.

Mr. DALZELL. There is a very wide open competition in the manufacture of this steel, is there not?

Mr. SEARLE. I think there is. I think the manufacture is increasing both abroad and in this country.

I think that is a fair statement. I think 3½ cents a pound would give all the protection necessary.

Mr. DALZELL. Do your figures give the increases in importations?

Mr. SEARLE. They do.

Mr. DALZELL. And also the home production?

Mr. SEARLE. I stated Mr. Park's home production, but I think he is wrong. I think he overstated it, but I gave it exactly as he gave it. I felt that I was obliged to take his figures, but I think he states it in excess of what it actually is.

Mr. DALZELL. More than a half million dollars' worth of steel. He says: " I do not suppose the amount manufactured by our company was more than a half million dollars' worth of steel."

Mr. SEARLE. That is his own company. Then he goes on to state that he thinks that four or five million dollars' worth was made in the whole country.

Mr. DALZELL. You have all of those figures in your brief?

Mr. SEARLE. I think so.

There is another matter that I would like to speak about while I am here. Of course I know that " a little knowledge is a dangerous thing," but for some twenty-five years it has been my business to practice, more or less, with respect to the customs-revenue laws, and my firm, I suppose, has three-quarters of that business in New England.

Mr. CRUMPACKER. Before you leave the high-speed steel subject I would like to ask you two or three questions. Does it cost us any more to produce this class of steel than it costs the foreign producer?

Mr. SEARLE. I think it does.

Mr. CRUMPACKER. And you think that 3½ cents would cover that difference?

Mr. SEARLE. I think a good deal more, because that would be $77 a ton, and I think that is a great deal more than the cost here—the labor cost.

Mr. CRUMPACKER. This steel is specialized; it is produced in the crucible. Do you buy the crude product in the market?

Mr. SEARLE. We—our European principals—buy the ferrotungsten; yes.

The CHAIRMAN. And then, by processes of heating and one thing and another, you bring it up to this high standard of perfection. Is it used in making cutlery largely?

Mr. Searle. Not at all; it is used in making the high-speed tools, where they require great speed, and where you can heat a tool to incandescence and not lose its temper. You have seen the new filaments in electric lights? The tungsten is used there because it will heat to incandescence without destruction of the metal.

Mr. Crumpacker. We can produce as high grade, as good quality, as the foreign manufacturer can?

Mr. Searle. In every way.

Mr. Crumpacker. Can our manufacturer of this kind of steel obtain the material as cheaply as they do abroad, or do they have to pay more for their raw material?

Mr. Searle. On the 29th of last November it was $1,300 a ton, and it varies in America from $1,000 to $1,500 and $1,800 a ton.

Mr. Crumpacker. What is the difference in the cost of labor? What, in your judgment, is the real difference in the cost by the ton of production of this kind of steel here and in England and Germany?

Mr. Searle. I should say that $20 would amply cover the actual cost of producing the steel. I mean the cost of labor alone.

Mr. Crumpacker. That would be a little less than a cent a pound, and a cent a pound by the American ton. And you think that $3\frac{1}{2}$ cents ought to cover reasonable profit, and a cent and a half in addition would be about $30, for good measurement.

Mr. Underwood. Do I understand that you want an increase or a reduction?

Mr. Searle. I want a reduction, Mr. Underwood.

Now, as I stated, I am aware that " a little knowledge is a dangerous thing;" but I have given some attention for a number of years to customs-revenue matters, and it has been my pleasure to appear before your committee several times simply as a spectator. I have read some of the testimony, and I have been amazed at many of the reckless statements which have been made here. And, first, I want to refer to the question of undervaluation.

Coming over on the train from Boston day before yesterday I met one of our leading manufacturers of New England, who believed in practically a prohibitive duty, and he stated to me that the undervaluation was perfectly enormous, not only in his line of business, but in every line of importation. I said, " I think you are mistaken; that the undervaluation won't amount to 2 per cent." He said, " You are wrong." We got a little warm, and he said, " It will amount to more than 10 per cent." I told him that I had appeared in a number of important reappraisement cases in Boston in the course of the year, and that they did not average two a month. " Well," he said, " you don't know anything about it in New York." I said, "I go there occasionally, and I know something about it." He said, " The reappraisements in New York reach up into the thousands, and they amount to more than 10 per cent of the entries." Well, before he got through he called me a big fool. But I was big enough fool to go the next day to the New York custom-house and get some facts, and I thought I would like to make a statement to this committee. These figures were given to me by Mr. Estabrook, the deputy collector in charge of the sixth division. I wanted to get a period of six months. He gave me the books showing the number of advances in valuation from the 10th day of July, 1907, to the 10th day of January, 1908; but inasmuch as it was a little difficult to divide the months, I have taken, for the purpose of my statement before this committee, the months of August, September, October, November, and December—the last five months of 1907. The number of advances in August was 669; in September, 628; in October, 754; in November, 612; and in December, 665; or a total, if my addition is correct, of 3,348. During the same period there were entered at the New York custom-house 164,979 invoices. This would mean that the total number of advances, whether made voluntarily by the importer or made by the appraiser or collector, amounted to about 2 per cent of the total number of invoices. Now, we must bear in mind that many of these advances are for most trivial things—packing charges, and perhaps commission—so it is interesting to go a little further to see how many of them were serious enough to call for reappraisement. During that period I found that there were 1,150 reappraisements. These were asked for covering 164,979 invoices. That means that there were 0.69 of 1 per cent of the invoices in New York during that period that were advanced in value. Now, for the whole country, during the year ended June 30, 1908, there were only 4,959 reappraisements.

The total amount of penal duties on articles undervalued (sec. 32, act of July 24, 1897) was in the whole country only $151,650.08, or much less than one-tenth of 1 per cent of the total duty collected for the year ending June 30, 1908.

I thought this was an interesting statement, showing that here we have, in my opinion, the most efficient board of appraising officials in the world at the port of New York. They are there to detect undervaluations, and have special agents particularly for that purpose. The Treasury Department is working on it all the time by information that they receive, and when people come before this committee and state that reappraisements are general they do not know what they are talking about.

Mr. DALZELL. Does your information show what the character of the goods were and the name on which these advances were made?

Mr. SEARLE. No; but I think I can tell generally what they were, if you want to take my statement as hearsay. I should say it was probably the goods largely coming from Germany and France, more worsted and flannels, and goods of that character.

Mr. UNDERWOOD. This estimate that you made was since the President made the agreement with Germany on appraisements, was it not?

Mr. SEARLE. I do not know; I don't think so.

Mr. UNDERWOOD. Did not that agreement go into effect with Germany on the 1st of July, 1907?

Mr. SEARLE. Possibly it did; I think you are right about that.

Mr. UNDERWOOD. Therefore that would increase the undervaluations rather than otherwise?

Mr. SEARLE. Probably not very much, because it takes some time to get things going; to get the merchandise moving this way.

Now, I would like to make one more statement before the committee. Mr. Wakeman has appeared before this committee for the Protective Tariff League of New York, and if one can believe his statement in regard to protests, one would think they rained all the time—nothing but protests on every question that arises with respect to customs revenue. What is the position of the importer, Mr. Chairman? He pays to the United States Government one-third of all the revenue of the United States to administer this great national domain. Before the passage of the customs administrative bill the importer had some rights. He had a right to bring an action against the collector, and if the collector's action had been illegal, to recover the duties and recover the costs and interest. The customs administrative bill took away the right of the importer to recover his costs and interest. That I do not make any complaint of at the present time. Now, what do they propose to do? They propose to say that the United States Government can take my money illegally, can hold it one to five years, and if at the time that money is taken I open my mouth to enter a protest against it, I have got to pay $5 for it. Now, let us see what the facts are in regard to the protests. One would suppose that the board of appraisers at New York were a very much overworked body of men. I might say here, incidentally, that I have the greatest regard for every one of them, for they are men of great ability, but every one of them is paid more than any circuit judge in New England.

The board of appraisers makes an annual report, and in their annual report for the fiscal year ending June 30, 1908, they state that the number of protests received since the organization of the board in 1890, nineteen years ago, was 550,652, the average protests amounting to about 30,000 a year. For the last nine years the average protests have been 30,345, if my figures are correct. Now, the board say that many of these protests are trivial, and that it consumes a great deal of the time for the board to take care of them, so that it is impossible to do its business. They say here, in their annual report, that they have 35,000 protests on the suspended lists, and they expect that those will be disposed of by January 1, 1909. One case was decided in the United States Supreme Court the other day which disposed of 5,000 protests. One case will perhaps dispose of several thousand more when decided. They say in their report: " Upon the whole, it might be said that all cases which have been submitted for decision before the board, and submission received up to June 30, 1908, were on that date decided; and that the board, with its present organization and force, is keeping perfectly abreast of all current work and is capable of handling all possibilities of such work." Again: " The clerical force of the board at present is fully competent to handle all work before it, and it has proved entirely sufficient for that purpose."

Mr. DALZELL. What do you propose by way of legislation on that subject, Mr. Searle?

Mr. SEARLE. I think the customs-administrative law is very good as it is. If I might be allowed one or two suggestions: Why not let the law stand as it is? It is all right. They have deprived us of our interest and costs, which I say is wrong. Now, Mr. Dalzell, if the Commonwealth of Pennsylvania took your property by the right of eminent domain, and you can not agree with the Commonwealth and the question goes to the jury as to the cost and value of that property, when that is finally decided the Commonwealth of Pennsylvania pays you interest and costs. Now, if the United States Government take my money by so much as 1 mill and keep it for five or ten years, why should they compel me to pay to make protest and ask for its return; why should they not pay interest and costs when returned to me? Burdens on the importer are great, and they should not be increased by placing a fee or tax upon protests. The importer has some rights. Many of them have been taken from him, and I feel that he should be protected in his dealings with the Government.

Mr. UNDERWOOD. I think Mr. Wakeman stated the other day that it was necessary to have this charge for filing protests, that if they did not there would be a great many insincere protests filed.

Mr. SEARLE. I do not think that is so. I have been filing protests a great many years, and we file, in my office, about a thousand a year.

Mr. UNDERWOOD. You stand as an importer. What he said was this: He stated that there were a great many attorneys in this business who represented people, and when goods came in, and they thought there was a case to be made up that they would come in and file a protest for the purpose of holding the case open in order to get the business—not a very professional thing to do; but from his testimony I gather it that it was not an unusual thing to do.

Mr. SEARLE. It can not be done to any great extent, because the number of protests shows that it can not be done; the number was only 30 000 for the last year.

Mr. UNDERWOOD. But it might have been that a large number of that 30.000 was done in that way, and that really they had nothing behind them.

Mr. SEARLE. I do not think that is so. I know, of course, that a large number of protests are filed every day in a serious manner. I never knew an attorney of repute who filed a protest excepting he believed it had merit.

Mr. UNDERWOOD. I do not make any reference here specifically. These statements were merely made before the committee.

Mr. SEARLE. He said that protests were filed over there like April showers, but I think he is wrong about it.

Now, Mr. Dalzell asked a question in regard to the customs administrative act. There is one suggestion that I would like to make, if I may be allowed to do so. It often happens that goods arrive in this country which for some reason or other are under value, and as the law now stands the Secretary of the Treasury has no right to remit any additional duties. I think if the customs administrative act was changed so that if any goods were unintentionally undervalued, and if the Secretary of the Treasury was satisfied that there was no fraud, that the duties should be remitted. Such a change would remove a great deal of ill feeling which now grows out of the question of additional duties.

I am very much obliged to you.

CHARLES P. SEARLE, BOSTON, MASS., REPRESENTING CERTAIN STEEL IMPORTERS, FILES COPIES OF CONTRACTS OF THE CRUCIBLE STEEL COMPANY.

WASHINGTON, D. C., *January 13, 1909.*

Hon. SERENO PAYNE,
    Chairman Ways and Means Committee,
                Washington, D. C.

DEAR SIR: I beg to hand you inclosed copy of a contract dated 7th of November, 1906, of the Crucible Steel Company of America with Riess & Osenberg, of Berlin, for 100,000 marks silver steel;

copy of a contract dated Hamburg, 7th of November, 1906, made by the Crucible Steel Company of America with Riess & Osenberg, of Berlin, for 500,000 kilos of tool steel for twist drills; and original letter of the Crucible Steel Company of America, dated Hamburg, November 8, 1903, to Riess & Osenberg, and also translations of these three papers.

In handing you these papers I beg to draw your attention to the copy of the contract dated Hamburg, 7th of November, 1906, for the delivery of 500,000 kilos of tool steel for twist drills at the price of 66.50 marks per 100 kilos. This would mean a price per American pound of about .0719 per pound. This was subject to a commission of 5 per cent and 2 per cent for cash, and also to a duty of a little more than one-fourth cent per pound, which would bring the net price to about .0649 per pound delivered at Hamburg. This, of course, is not the price which the steel would net the Crucible Steel Company, because it is subject to freights from Pittsburg to New York and from New York to Hamburg. I regard this information as of great value to the committee, demonstrating the fact that during the last few years the Crucible Steel Company of America were abundantly able to export steel to Germany and pay the duty upon it and then undersell the German manufacturers.

If you desire any more information about these lines I shall be very glad to furnish it.

I remain, very respectfully,

CHARLES P. SEARLE,
50 Congress St., Boston, Mass.,
Attorney for Houghton & Richards
and Other Importers of Steel.

EXHIBIT A.

[Translation.]

[The Crucible Steel Company of America, Pittsburg, Pa. General sale for the Continent: Crucible Steel Company of America, G. m. b. H.]

HAMBURG, ALSTERHOF, *November 7, 1906.*

Contract for delivery of 100,000 marks' worth of silver steel.

Between the firm of Riess & Osenberg, Berlin, W. 62, Lutherstr. 28, which in this contract will be called "the firm," and the Crucible Steel Company of America, G. m. b. H., Hamburg, Alsterhof, called "the company," the following contract has been made:

No. 1. The company will sell the firm 100,000 marks' worth of silver steel brand of the Crucible Steel Company of America, Pittsburg, and the firm engages itself to take this quantity for the exclusive use of and delivery to the Wesselmann Bohrer Company, A. G., Zwötzen, by the end of 1908, connecting with the taking of the quantity contracted for on June 23, 1905, part of which is still to be taken.

No. 2. The company will allow the firm the following rebates on the prices of the attached list: 67½ per cent off on polished material; 72½ per cent off on unpolished material.

These prices are understood to include packing, delivered, duty paid, Zwötzen, station of the Prussian State Railroad.

The payment should always be made on the 20th of the month following delivery, with 5 per cent cash discount. The payments should be governed by the dates of the invoices of the company; that is, the date of shipment of the respective lots from Hamburg.

No. 3. The above price is based on the duty of 2.50 marks per 100 kilos. In case a higher duty should be charged, the price will be advanced accordingly. However, should the duty as existing now be advanced by one-half, the firm will have the right to cancel this agreement.

No. 4. The material must be furnished in all the sizes used by the Wesselmann Bohrer Company in the same quality as heretofore. The company is obliged always to furnish uniformly good qualities and to replace inaccurate or defective material.

The material is to be furnished from 0.3 to 0.5 millimeters in foot lengths; from 0.55 to 3.99 millimeters in 1-meter lengths; from 4 millimeters and heavier in 2-meter lengths; and up to 4.99 millimeters inclusive polished, above that unpolished. Deliveries must be made promptly, and as much as possible from stock, but latest for direct shipments from America inside of four months after placing of order. The company agrees to carry a sufficient stock in Hamburg to enable them to make such prompt deliveries.

No. 5. Circumstances beyond our control, as which are also considered the case of war, mobilization, strikes, interruptions in ship and railroad traffic, etc., will free the company according to circumstances entirely or partly of the stated obligations of delivery.

No. 6. The contract dates for both parties from Hamburg.

No. 7. This contract has been made in duplicate and has been signed by mutual agreement by both parties, and one copy of same remains in the possession of each party.

––––––

Exhibit B.

[Translation.]

[Crucible Steel Company of America, Pittsburg, Pa. General sale for the Continent: Crucible Steel Company of America, G. m. b. H.]

HAMBURG, ALSTERHOF, *November 7, 1906.*

Contract for delivery of 500,000 kilos tool steel for twist drills.

Between the firm of Riess & Osenberg, Berlin W. 62, Lutherstr. 28, which in this contract will be called "the firm," and the Crucible Steel Company of America, G. m. b. H., Hamburg, Alsterhof, called "the company," the following contract has been made:

No. 1. The company agrees to deliver 500,000 kilos of annealed crucible tool steel special brand for twist drills of the Crucible Steel Company of America, Pittsburg, and the firm engages itself to gradually take this quantity by the end of 1908 for the exclusive use and delivery to the Wesselmann Bohrer Company, A. G., in Zwötzen, connecting with the fulfillment of the contract made on the 27th of June, 1905.

No. 2. The price agreed upon is 66.50 marks delivered Zwötzen, in shipments of 10,000 kilos, and this price will be valid as soon as the 300,000 kilos of the agreement of the 27th of June, 1905, have been taken and invoiced. On this price the company allows the firm 5 per cent commission and 2 per cent for cash whenever payment is made on the 20th of the month for deliveries of the previous month. The payments should be governed by the date of the invoices of the company; that is, the date of the shipment of the respective lots from Hamburg. In case smaller shipments than 10,000 kilos are made, the additional freight as charged by the railroad will be added; but the commission—that is, the special allowance—will be made only on the price of 10-ton shipments.

No. 3. The price of 66.50 marks is based on the duty of 2.50 marks per 100 kilos. In case a higher duty should be charged, the price will be advanced accordingly. Should, however, the duty as existing now be advanced by one-half the firm will have the right to cancel this agreement.

No. 4. Deliveries have to be made promptly, and orders should be executed not later than six to eight weeks after having been placed. The company agrees to carry sufficient stock in Hamburg in the sizes used by the Wesselmann Bohrer Company to make prompt deliveries, as stated above.

No. 5. Circumstances beyond our control, as which are also considered the case of war, mobilization, strikes, interruption in ship and railroad traffic, etc., will free the company according to circumstances entirely or partly of the stated obligations of delivery.

No. 6. The material is guaranteed to be the same as the samples which were submitted to the Wesselmann Bohrer Company when the contract, which is still in existence, was made. The company is obliged to furnish uniform and good qualities in accordance with the deliveries made heretofore, and to replace material which is unsatisfactory or defective.

No. 7. The contract dates for both parties from Hamburg.

No. 8. This contract has been made in duplicate, and has been signed by mutual agreement by both parties, and one copy of same remains in the possession of each party.

EXHIBIT C.

¡Translation.]

[Crucible Steel Company of America, Pittsburg, Pa.   General agent for Europe, Raphael H. Wolff.]

HAMBURG, HEINTZEHOF, *November 8, 1903.*

Messrs. RIESS & OSENBERG,
  Eisenachstr. 43, Schöneberg, Berlin W.:

I herewith confirm our verbal negotiation in the presence of Director Klemm, of the Wesselmann Bohrer Company, Zwötzen, by which the following agreement was made:

The Wesselmann Bohrer Company agrees to cover their requirements of silver steel for the next two years, amounting to at least 40,000 marks per year, through you exclusively with my company, you being the purchaser.

The contract goes into effect on the day on which I receive the first specification.

As talked over, the shipments from New York should begin three months after receipt of the first specifications, and the deliveries, in about equal quantities, will continue for the two years. The first specification should amount to a complete carload of about 10 to 12 tons, and in connection with this I shall take in stock a corresponding quantity, at least an assorted carload of the current dimensions of silver steel, so as to be able to make prompt deliveries to you or the Wesselmann Bohrer Company. This does not exclude that you may send me further specifications for delivery from America besides the first order which you give me for direct shipment. For the exclusive use of the Wesselmann Bohrer Company, I furnish you silver steel for making spiral drills, unpolished, at 72½ per cent rebate; polished, at 67½ per cent rebate, on the original prices of the silver steel list of my company, duty paid, delivered station Zwötzen, payable on the 15th of the month following the delivery.

As cash discount and commission, I allow you a further rebate of 5 per cent on the net amount of the invoices.

Director Klemm has promised to send me at once a list in which all the dimensions which will be used by this company will be mentioned in millimeters and $\frac{1}{1000}$-inch Stub's and Morse gauge, and I hope that I shall very soon receive this list.

I am desirous of receiving promptly the first specification, because I shall sail next Tuesday, per steamship *Kaiser Wilhelm der Grosse,* for New York, in order to talk over the European business, so that I can personally submit this specification to my company and make the necessary preparation for careful execution.

Awaiting your confirmation, I remain,

  Yours, respectfully,

CRUCIBLE STEEL CO. OF AMERICA,
  R. H. WOLFF, *General Agent.*

CHARLS P. SEARLE, BOSTON, MASS., REPRESENTING STEEL IMPORTERS, SUBMITS ADDITIONAL STATEMENT RELATIVE TO HIGH-SPEED TOOL STEEL.

WASHINGTON, D. C., *January 13, 1909.*

Hon. SERENO PAYNE,
  Chairman Ways and Means Committee,
      Washington, D. C.

DEAR SIR: On the occasion when I had the pleasure of appearing before your committee in behalf of Houghton & Richards, of Boston, on the question of duty upon high-speed steel, I drew your attention to a letter of Mr. Clarage, president of the Columbia Tool Steel Company, which was published in the Iron Age on November 12, 1908, and I beg to append herewith a copy of that letter, and desire specially to draw your attention to the fact that Mr. Clarage claims that the European tool steel can always be duplicated or excelled in this country by any one of the half dozen leading steel-tool makers, and he states in his letter there is more tool steel made in the United States in one day than all Europe produces in a week, and further states that "although tungsten was first experimented with in England, it remained for America to develop the modern high-speed steel with chromium and tungsten combinations, and every one of the European manufacturers has had to take his cue from the Americans. Even recently still further advances have been made in the American manufacture of high-speed steel, of which, as far as we know, the Europeans have not yet learned, and therefore not yet copied."

This statement of Mr. Clarage I hope will receive the careful attention of your committee, for it shows conclusively that no protection whatever is needed by the manufacturers of high-speed steel. We do not ask that the duty be entirely removed, but simply ask that it be reduced to about one-third of the present rates.

I remain, yours, very respectfully,

CHARLES P. SEARLE,
  50 Congress street, Boston,
Attorney for Houghton & Richards and other importers.

[From Iron Age, November 12, 1908.]

TOOL-STEEL MAKING IN EUROPE AND AMERICA.

To the Editor:

It is unfortunate that an article interesting and reasonably correct from a historical standpoint should be perverted by the author in an effort to advertise his own wares. This refers to your article on "Tool-steel making in Styria," published in the issue of November 5. When an American steel maker is asked to address a scientific society, according to American ethics he refrains from taking advantage of the situation to advertise the goods he has for sale. Possibly there may be a different code of ethics in Europe, and from their point of view it may be justifiable to seize upon an opportunity like this to drum up trade.

To anyone who has come in touch with the stolid European workmen the talk of handing down the traditions of the trade from generation to generation is absurd nonsense. One has only to compare the European workmen with the much more intelligent class of men to be found in American steel works. There is more of the disposition in Europe to guard jealously the little secrets of the trade, some of which are at best of questionable value, and the result of this effort is to keep new knowledge out of their works instead of keeping the old knowledge in. There is a law in England imposing a penalty of two years' imprisonment with or without hard labor, or a fine, or both fine and imprisonment, upon any person who improperly discloses trade secrets. In other words, their policy is to fine and imprison anyone who tries to meet with other people in the same occupation and effect an interchange of ideas for the general advancement of the trade. This is characteristic of England and applies equally as well to Austria. This one thing has probably done more than anything else to keep European manufacturers at the tail end of the procession.

EUROPEAN AND AMERICAN CRUCIBLE PRACTICE.

Referring to the article in question, the American tool-steel makers will not agree with many of the statements, particularly in regard to the methods of using crucibles wherein they state a crucible is only used once, and endeavor to furnish a plausible reason. The true reason, without doubt, is that the crucibles are of such poor quality that they will only stand one heat, whereas in America an average of six or seven heats is expected. You may be sure that the European steel maker would get six or seven heats out of his crucible also if he knew how to do it. A new crucible will "throw" more graphite and other elements into the steel than one which has been used several times. The practice of American steel makers is to melt only the lowest grades in the first heat and make their very fine product on the third or fourth heat, in which the character of the steel will not be so much contaminated from the walls of the crucible.

The description of the crucible melting furnace sounds very primitive, particularly the preheating chambers. It is surprising that a concern claiming to be progressive will still stick to what is known as "ladle heats"—that is, the entire content of the furnace is dumped into a ladle in which it does not have time to become thoroughly mixed, and the chances are that each ingot contains as many varieties of steel as there were crucibles used.

Careful research shows that it is impossible to make a large ingot which will show exactly the same analysis at the top, bottom, and center. Why exaggerate this by copying the open-hearth method of teeming, when the peculiar value of crucible steel is in the fact that it is manufactured in small units?

The practice of the American steel manufacturers is to put the product of each crucible into a single ingot, generally 4 inches square, the cooling taking place so quickly that segregation is not possible, and uniformity of material results. Each ingot is cropped and carefully graded according to the carbon percentage, the quality of the steel having previously been determined by the quality of raw material used.

CUSTOMERS' REQUIREMENTS STUDIED HERE.

The American steel maker greatly excels his European competitor in one particular point, and that is, he is not only a steel maker, but he is an engineer of wide and varied experience. He makes it his business not only to understand his own methods of manufacture, but he acquires every detail concerning the requirements of his customer. The result is that he brings to bear on the tool-steel business a rare faculty of judgment in selecting the kind of steel best adapted to each requirement. A tool steel may be of wonderfully good quality, yet if the carbon percentage be too high or too low for the particular kind of tool required, the result will always be disappointing.

The American tool-steel manufacturer is close to his customers and studies their requirements and their practices much more closely than is generally understood. The European manufacturer is so far away from the consumer that it becomes a hit or miss proposition. He can not study the individual requirements.

There is no doubt that some exceedingly good tool steel is manufactured in Europe. This we do not deny, but we have never yet analyzed a piece of European tool steel which could not be duplicated or excelled in this country by any one of half a dozen leading tool-steel makers, and with much more uniformity, in addition to being sold at a lower price.

There is a certain class of people who are always looking for the mysterious. If they could get tool steel made in the moon they would swear by it, even though the quality might be so poor that they really should swear at it.

There is more tool steel made in the United States in one day than all of Europe produces in a week. Our European competitors must remember that William Kelley really was the inventor of the Bessemer process. They must remember, also, that although tungsten was first experimented with in England, it remained for America to develop the modern high-speed steel with chromium and tungsten combinations, and every one of the European manufacturers has had to take his cue from the Americans. Even recently, still further advances have been made in the American manufacture of high-speed steel, of which, as far as we know, the Europeans have not yet learned and therefore not yet copied.

The American steel maker is the greatest student along metallurgical lines in the world. His product is shipped to every corner of the globe, and America may be safely said to take the lead in tool-steel manufacture as well as in modern production of open-hearth and Bessemer products.

E. T. CLARAGE,
President Columbia Tool Steel Company.

CHICAGO, *November 7, 1908.*

CASTINGS FOR ENGINE CYLINDERS.

[Paragraph 135.]

THE CAPITOL FOUNDRY COMPANY, HARTFORD, CONN., THINKS THERE SHOULD BE NEW CLASSIFICATION FOR GASOLINE ENGINE CYLINDER CASTINGS.

HARTFORD, CONN., *December 9, 1908.*

COMMITTEE ON WAYS AND MEANS,
Washington, D. C.

GENTLEMEN: We beg to submit the following statement. As the time is so short we are obliged to make this statement without absolute facts. From our understanding of the present tariff on the class of goods in question, namely, gasoline engine cylinder castings, we understand these goods are admitted on a rough-casting schedule, which we believe to be unjust, as the common castings represent about one-third labor and two-thirds material; and in the case of cylinder castings the labor represented is about 70 per cent of the total cost of the casting. In view of this fact it appears to the writer that the classification under which these goods are admitted should be changed. We believe that the present tariff on the ordinary foundry product is adequate to the protection of the industry, but we can not believe that the same schedule should apply to a product which is so vastly different in its make-up. The labor employed in producing this class of goods must be of the highest possible standard, and the difference in the price paid these workmen is so great that we must produce at least double the amount of work in order to sell our goods at the same margin of profit. Any further information you may desire on this subject will be cheerfully furnished. We remain,

Very truly, yours,

THE CAPITOL FOUNDRY CO.,
F. W. STICKLE, *President.*

COLD-ROLLED STEEL.

[Paragraph 135.]

BRIEF BY SEARLE & PILLSBURY, REPRESENTING CERTAIN NEW ENGLAND IMPORTERS OF STRIP, PLATE, AND SHEET STEEL THAT HAS BEEN COLD ROLLED ONLY.

BOSTON, MASS., *December 1, 1908.*

COMMITTEE ON WAYS AND MEANS,
Washington, D. C.

GENTLEMEN: Paragraph 141 was intended to place an additional duty upon certain forms of steel that had been put through some additional process of tempering, bluing, or polishing to give it an added surface finish, and was undoubtedly for the further protection of American steel producers on account of the labor, manipulation, and cost of such additional processes.

It is now proposed to exact this additional duty upon steel that has been cold rolled only. (See Iron Age of November 19, 1908, p. 1445, par. 141.) It has been decided by the courts of last resort that cold-rolled steel, without any further polishing or brightening process, does not come within the provisions of paragraph 141, largely upon the ground that no apparent reason could be found for such additional duty. This litigation covered especially, if not entirely, cold-rolled strip steel, and the proposed change is no doubt aimed directly at steel in that form.

Strip steel, cold rolled only, is assessed for duty under paragraph 135. The thinner it is desired, the more times it has to be passed through the rolls and the greater its value becomes, and consequently the higher the rate of duty under said paragraph. The rolling necessarily gives it a certain brightness, but that brightness adds in no way to its value. It is not rolled with that purpose in view at all, but simply and solely to get the desired thickness, or rather thinness. The brightening is simply incidental to the process of rolling and can not be avoided, and that it can serve no possible purpose is shown by the fact that in the further processes of manufacturing such steel into the various articles for which it is used it is always and invariably heated, which absolutely destroys any brightness there may be upon its surface.

Bearing in mind that this steel is already assessed under paragraph 135 at rates increasing according to the number of passes through the rolls, because the repeated rolling increases its value, and also incidentally its brightness, and, further, that the domestic interests even now are demanding in this revision of the tariff an entirely absurd and unreasonable increase in the duty on cold-rolled strip steel (see third new paragraph of the new text as published in the Iron Age, above mentioned), what justifiable, or even plausible, reason can possibly be adduced for placing an additional duty upon it on account of a brightness of surface which is not aimed at, is incidental to the process of manufacture, adds nothing to its value, serves no purpose whatever, is destroyed as soon as the steel reaches this country, which is produced without any additional labor and without adding one cent per million tons to the cost of its manufacture?

If among the thousands of demands being made by the domestic interests in this proposed revision of the tariff there is one that is unreasonable and unjustifiable, it is this one.

Respectfully submitted.

SEARLE & PILLSBURY,
Attorneys for Edgar T. Ward & Sons.

WIRE AND WIRE ROPE.

[Paragraph 137.]

JOHN A. ROEBLING'S SONS COMPANY, NEW YORK CITY, SUGGESTS POSSIBLE REDUCTIONS IN THE DUTIES ON WIRE.

NEW YORK CITY, *November 28, 1908.*

Hon. SERENO E. PAYNE,
Chairman Ways and Means Committee,
Washington, D. C.

SIR: On the assumption that the manufacturers of iron and steel wire can fairly be called upon to submit, together with manufacturers of other articles of iron and steel, to reductions in the duties levied under paragraph 137 of the tariff act now in force, and also upon the assumption that reductions in the duty on raw materials used by wire manufacturers will compensate in some degree for the reductions in their own schedule, they beg to suggest a reduction of $\frac{1}{4}$ cent per pound of the specific rates of $1\frac{1}{4}$ cents, $1\frac{1}{2}$ cents, and 2 cents per pound of said paragraph. As this reduction applies to the remaining part of this paragraph it calls for no further change, with the exception in the case of the $\frac{2}{10}$ cent extra for coating wire with other metals. The protection afforded by this item is quite nominal, as the cost of galvanizing small wires runs as high as 3 cents per pound. If this rate of $\frac{2}{10}$ cent was advanced to $\frac{5}{10}$ cent it would be somewhat better, but not much.

Personal investigations during the present year by an expert in the wire trade, confirmed by the printed report of the British Board of Trade publications, disclose the following facts as to wages in the wire district of Germany:

Wire workers' wages of Germany and the United States.

[Basis of a working day of ten hours.]

	At Pittsburg and eastern mills.	At Hagen.	At Mannheim.	At Aachen.
Rod rollers	$5.00 to $7.78	$1.88 to $2.35		$1.05 to $1.21
Furnace men		1.65 to 1.88		
Engineers	2.50 to 3.05			
Mechanics	2.35 to 2.94	.97 to 1.42	$1.21 to $1.42	1.21 to 1.46
Wire drawers	2.80 to 3.87	1.43 to 1.50	1.24 to 1.50	
Laborers	1.46 to 1.90	.75 to .84	.72 to .90	

·Taking the lowest European wages as 100, the above figures show the following:

	Germany.	United States.
	Per cent.	*Per cent.*
Rod rollers	100 to 224	476 to 742
Mechanics	100 to 146	242 to 303
Wire drawers	100 to 121	223 to 312
Laborers	100 to 120	198 to 253

The labor costs are a fair representation of conditions abroad and at home during the past three years. According to the report made by the British Board of Trade and according to conditions in this country, wire workers' wages have advanced moderately during this time, and it is believed they can not be reduced here without labor troubles.

The importation of wire goods during the past fiscal year amounted to $1,332,973, on which a duty of $567,798 was paid, it being equivalent to 42.6 per cent ad valorem. These importations consist almost entirely of the more highly manufactured articles, of which labor is the important item. Any reduction of the ad valorem rates now in effect under paragraph 137 would, under the labor burdens of American manufacturers, bring a serious disaster. An advance to 50 per cent ad valorem would not be inconsistent with duties levied on other articles named in the tariff act upon which much labor is expended.

Respectfully submitted.

JOHN A. ROEBLING'S SONS CO.,
F. W. ROEBLING, *Secretary.*

H. F. LYMAN, CLEVELAND, OHIO, WRITES RELATIVE TO THE ABILITY OF AMERICAN MAKERS OF WIRE ROPE TO UNDERSELL FOREIGN MANUFACTURERS IN FOREIGN MARKETS.

CLEVELAND, OHIO, *November 27, 1908.*
COMMITTEE ON WAYS AND MEANS,
Washington, D. C.

GENTLEMEN: The writer is just in receipt of a telegram from our Mr. J. W. Walton, requesting him to write you the particulars of the writer's conversation with Mr. Roebling in relation to wire rope, which he takes pleasure in doing.

It is impossible to give the date, which was about the year 1900. There had been for a good many years an association among the wire-rope manufacturers which has attempted to regulate the prices made by the manufacturers and also to control through the manufacturers the prices made by jobbers of wire rope, who, as a rule, are agents for some American manufacturer. It was through this association that Mr. Leschen, of the A. Leschen & Sons Rope Company, informed the writer that a fund of about $100,000 had been raised, of which they had contributed their share, to secure proper treatment in the making of the Dingley tariff.

This association held a meeting in New York City at the time the writer refers to, and having been invited, with other jobbers, to meet with the association at different times, the writer finally determined to accept the invitation in this case, and met with them at dinner at the uptown Delmonico restaurant. Our corporation was known as being the principal importer of wire rope, as our sales of wire rope being almost entirely to consumers we were able to make sales based on quality rather than on price. In conversation with Mr. Roebling, who was speaking of the utter lack of necessity of any importations of wire rope on account of the ability of the American makers to take care of us, he made the statement that he was able to sell wire rope in England, underselling the Englishmen, and make money doing so. The writer is perfectly willing to make affidavit as to the correctness of the above statement, but can not place the date with anything like accuracy. There were present at the meeting, beside several of the wire-rope manufacturers, one of the sons of H. Channon, of H. Channon & Co., of Chicago, and the writer believes also a gentleman from St. Louis, but of this is not positive.

The writer was not surprised at the statement, as he had seen prices on wire quoted by the American Steel and Wire Company from their London office to wire-rope manufacturers in England which were nearly 50 per cent less in price than the prices he found existing at the same time on the same grade of wire in this country. This information, however, the writer believes Mr. Walton took with him to Washington.

We do not anticipate that a change in the tariff on wire rope would give us any better margin, but we do feel that a tariff that gives a protection of anywhere from 50 to over 100 per cent on goods that it is acknowledged can be sold at a profit in foreign countries; competing against foreign countries, is a hardship on the user of wire rope which is without excuse.

Yours, respectfully,   H. F. LYMAN.

___

WICKWIRE BROTHERS, CORTLAND, N. Y., URGE RETENTION OF PRESENT DUTIES ON STEEL WIRE AND WOVEN-WIRE GOODS.

CORTLAND, N. Y., *December 18, 1908.*

Hon. SERENO E. PAYNE,
  Chairman Ways and Means Committee,
                              Washington, D. C.

DEAR SIR: Wickwire Bros. (Incorporated), located at Cortland, N. Y., are manufacturers of steel wire and woven-wire goods, carrying their product to such an advanced state of manufacture that labor becomes the important factor. For this reason, we believe that, with the very high wages paid wire workers in the United States, the proviso in paragraph 137, fixing an ad valorem rate of 40 per cent should not be disturbed, except that the 4-cent valuation should be made 5 cents. As the act now stands, the effect is in some cases to place a lower duty on a more highly manufactured article; as an instance, the present rate on wire valued at 4 cents or over at 40 per cent ad valorem is 1.6 cents per pound, while practically the same wire (No. 16 or smaller) valued at 3¾ cents would pay a duty of 2 cents per pound.

We produce a very large quantity of fine galvanized and tinned wire, and for this the extra duty of two-tenths cent per pound is very inadequate, and we believe that the extra duty on "iron and steel wire coated with zinc, tin, or any other metal" could be advanced without injustice.

We notice that another manufacturer in a communication to your committee proposes a reduction of one-fourth cent per pound in the specific rates on wire. We trust this will not be exceeded and believe it to be more than a substantial recognition of the demand for tariff revision.

Respectfully submitted.

WICKWIRE BROTHERS,
T. H. WICKWIRE, *Treasurer.*

JOHN W. WALTON, OF CLEVELAND, OHIO, THINKS THE DUTY ON WIRE ROPE SHOULD BE MODIFIED.

FRIDAY, *November 27, 1908.*

Mr. GRIGGS. Are you a manufacturer?

Mr. WALTON. No, sir; I am a dealer in wire rope and have been for the last thirty-six years. I have been engaged in jobbing, retailing, and also consuming—as a vessel owner. I represent the Upson-Walton Company, of Cleveland, Ohio.

Mr. RANDELL. In reference to what schedule do you appear?

Mr. WALTON. No. 437, wire rope.

Mr. GRIGGS. Do you want the tariff reduced?

Mr. WALTON. Yes; somewhat modified, in the interest of clearness and for the benefit of the consumer. As importers, I suppose we should be interested to maintain this complicated line to avoid the competition which a simpler tariff would give us. I have known a number of instances where competitors were scared by the complication involved in mixed specific and ad valorem duties, and so backed out of importing. Yet in the interests of our own citizens at large, of whom I am proud to be one, I think the duties ought to be simplified.

I have here a large paper giving statistics, which I do not propose to read unless the committee desires it, which gives a list of the comparative wire-rope duties on rods and wire rope, under the McKinley tariff, under the Wilson tariff, and under the present act of 1907.

Mr. UNDERWOOD. Was there any change between the Wilson Act or the Dingley Act and the present act?

Mr. WALTON. Yes, sir.

Mr. UNDERWOOD. Is it given per ton?

Mr. WALTON. It is, but there was no change in wire rope. Under that act the wire rope business was kept intact. The first draft of the Dingley tariff act increased the duty to 45 per cent, on an ad valorem basis, and made 1¼ or 1½ difference between wire and wire rope on the differential.

Mr. UNDERWOOD. The question with us is how it stands under the act that was enacted.

Mr. WALTON. It is the same as it was under the Wilson-Gorman Act.

Mr. UNDERWOOD. How much reduction do you think should be made?

Mr. WALTON. Well, really, I do not know. I can give you from actual, personal knowledge as an importer, three or four samples of the way it is now—actual figures from actual transactions within the last three years. Our importations in the last three years have been something like 1,500,000 pounds. This year it is only about half of what it was during the two preceding years. I will submit to you a table of the difference between British cost of wire and of wire rope, figured at $4.8665 to the pound sterling.

(Following is the table referred to:)

Difference between British cost of wire and of wire rope, figured at $4.8665 to the pound sterling.

	Cost of wire.	Cost of wire rope.	In British coin per hundredweight.	
			Cost of wire.	Cost of wire rope.
			s. d.	*s. d.*
A coil of ¼-inch diameter, 6-strand, 7 wires, bright charcoal	$34	$46	*a* 14 9	*b* 20 0
A coil of ⅜-inch diameter, 6-strand, 19 wires, best agricultural plow steel	428	501	26 9	33 6
A coil of ⅜-inch diameter, 6-strand, 19 wires, best agricultural plow steel	175	199	24 3	29 6
A coil of ¼-inch diameter, 6-strand, 19 wires, best crucible steel	40	50	16 9	21 6
A coil of 7/16-inch diameter, 6-strand, 19 wires, bright charcoal	59	89	15 3	22 0
A coil of 1-inch diameter, 6-strand, 6 by 7 wires, iron tiller rope	100	180	13 3	23 3
A coil of ⅜-inch diameter, 6-strand, 7 wires, best crucible steel	148	183	13 9	18 ⁚

a Less 2¼ per cent.   *b* Less 6 per cent.

If we import a coil of this bright charcoal wire rope, costing in Great Britain $3.29 per hundred, we pay a duty of 3 cents per pound, making, with 25 cents to get it across the water, $6.54 per hundred. Thus we pay a duty on that of 91 per cent.

Mr. UNDERWOOD. That represents the cost in England?

Mr. WALTON. Yes, sir; this particular size of which I have been speaking, which is a 6 by 7 strand of wire, costs $3.29. I have added 25 cents freightage oceanwise, making $6.54.

Mr. UNDERWOOD. Do you mean that you can get it here for that price?

Mr. WALTON. We can land it in New York for that price.

Mr. UNDERWOOD. Six dollars and fifty-four cents.

Mr. WALTON. Yes, sir; that is just the wholesale cost of production of that same article in this country. Not being a manufacturer I can not ascertain the cost of that made in this country.

Mr. DALZELL. You have given the cost landed in New York, duty added?

Mr. WALTON. Yes; $3.29 per hundred pounds, making $6.54, and that is exactly what the American manufacturers charge for it wholesale in large lots.

Mr. UNDERWOOD. They charge that figure for the whole product—that is, the entire amount of the English cost, freight, duty, and everything added?

Mr. WALTON. They could not hit it any closer.

Mr. UNDERWOOD. These cases of the selling price do not give us the information which we need. Can you give us information as to what the relative cost is in the two countries?

Mr. WALTON. No, sir; I do not know what the cost in this country is. I wish I did. I wish that I were interested in a wire-rope mill, for if I were I could demonstrate it to you; but in that case I probably would not be here.

(At this point Mr. Walton opened a package of the several different varieties of wire rope, showed them to the members, and left them as an exhibit.)

Mr. GAINES. What kind of wire rope were you speaking of that cost $6.54 in New York?

Mr. WALTON. That was the cheaper kind of wire rope. This iron rope, the cheaper kind, is used for haulage purposes in England.

Mr. GAINES. What kind of haulage?

Mr. WALTON. Well, I think they are used for both kinds of hauling—that is, the ordinary hauling and in electrically constructed apparatus.

Mr. POU. Is it made of steel?

Mr. WALTON. Yes, sir; this is steel [exhibiting sample].

Mr. GAINES. I will ask you again for what kind of haulage is this wire rope used?

Mr. WALTON. It is used for the transmission of power, and is also used for hauling objects along the ground where abrasion is concerned. It is also used for hauling freight in large quantities. [Exhibiting sample of hoisting rope.] The largest use for this particular kind of rope is in connection with hoists, and also where they use it on small rolls or drums.

Mr. GAINES. Do they use it in mining coal?

Mr. WALTON. Yes, sir; they use it in the coal mines largely. The quality used in coal mines is of good steel.

You have asked about cost. I am not in the secrets of the so-called " Steel trust." I have taken my figures at random from some figures which I have, which are entirely reliable, and they are the actual figures, giving the difference in cost in England in making wire rope. For instance, during the last year or fifteen months the size of material known as ¼-inch 6-strand wire (bright charcoal), cost $34, and it was as high here as $46 for a certain coil.

Mr. LONGWORTH. How much rope in weight or size?

Mr. WALTON. A coil is 5,000 or 6,000 feet. These are the actual figures for five-eighths in diameter, 6-strand, 6 by 19 wire. The best agricultural plow steel costs $428 for the material and the wire rope costs $501. Seven-eighths size of the same material costs for the wire $175 and for the rope $199, which is less difference. The wire which is three-fourths of an inch in diameter, 6 by 19 strand, best crucible steel, costs $40 and the coil costs $50. The seven-sixteenths bright charcoal wire, 6 by 19, costs for the material $59, and the wire-rope cost is $89. When you come to the tiller rope, the coil being 1 inch in diameter, 6 by 7 strand, the cost is $100, and the wire-rope cost is $180.

Mr. GAINES. What is your authority for the figures which you are now quoting?

Mr. WALTON. These are the actual figures. The manufacturers are, under the present tariff law, compelled to state the cost of that wire. That must be done in order to ascertain the rate of duty, as to whether it is ad valorem or specific. If the wire costs as much as 4 cents a pound, it comes under one heading, and if it is more than that, it comes under the other—40 per cent ad valorem—and consequently they have to state in the consular invoice the cost in each case.

Mr. GAINES. That is the importer's declaration.

Mr. WALTON. Yes, sir. I have no doubt that the figures which I give are perfectly accurate. They were given to me by gentlemen in whom I have the greatest confidence. The three-fourths crucible-steel haulage rope used in hoist wire costs $148 and the material costs $183. I can give you this in pounds, shillings, and pence if you prefer it. The last figure in that event would be 13 shillings and 9 pence against 18 shillings per hundred. It would be an average of about 20 per cent between the wire and the wire rope.

Mr. DALZELL. I do not see how we are going to arrive at the proper rate for wire rope on the figures of cost which you give in England if you can not give the cost in this country.

Mr. WALTON. I am not here to tell you that, because I do not know. No manufacturer will tell me what that rate is nor what the profit is.

Mr. DALZELL. Could you figure a duty on that basis?

Mr. LONGWORTH. Even in this case you are not telling the committee what it costs to manufacture it.

Mr. WALTON. I could not tell you the cost of manufacture, but I am willing to give you these figures and papers which I submit and state on my honor that they are absolutely reliable, unless there be some mistake in figuring. I would not agree to have that made public, because that is important in my business and means so much capitalization to me. I will leave that with the committee with the understanding that it is not for publication.

Mr. POU. Is there any combination between the manufacturers of wire rope in this country having the object of keeping up prices?

Mr. WALTON. Generally there is. They have a stipulation that there shall be a fine of $500 entered under agreement; that it shall be inflicted upon anyone who cuts prices. There are times, however, when they have spasms of competition, and we are undergoing one now. Whether that reduction is because of a threatened revision in the tariff, I could not say.

Mr. POU. Generally speaking, you can not buy wire rope cheaper than other people?

Mr. WALTON. All the manufacturers tell me that prices are fixed and they can not vary from them.

Mr. POU. Do you know whether or not there is any agreement or association for that purpose?

Mr. WALTON. Yes, sir; but I do not think it is working now. It is more honored in the breach than in the observance at present.

Mr. DALZELL. How many firms are making it in this country?

Mr. WALTON. There are seven or eight making it now, including those on the Pacific coast. I think there is one on the Pacific coast known as the "Pacific Steel and Wire Company." The American

Steel and Wire Company and John A. Roebling & Son, of Trenton, N. J., are the two leading manufacturers.

Now, as to the cost of making it, I can bring you a gentleman here who can tell you. This not being a court of justice, and not being confined as to hearsay evidence, I can state here that Mr. Roebling told Mr. Lyman personally that he could sell wire rope in England against the English prices and make money.

Mr. DALZELL. Does he sell it there?

Mr. WALTON. I do not think he does.

Mr. WALTON. I will try to be very brief, Mr. Chairman. The example that I gave you this morning, taken at hazard on the first sheet, happened to be of a cheap wire rope, but when you get up into the region of steel the tariff runs somewhat more uniform. I have the leading sizes of bright crucible-steel wire rope, the lowest duty in actual effect being 52 per cent and the highest 71½ per cent. You gentlemen probably are familiar with the tariff tax, as to how it comes to be laid in that way, ad valorem up to a certain point in the wire, and then specific as to lower-priced wires. There is an extra strong crucible or plow steel which runs almost exactly uniformly, 57 to 59 per cent. That is the highest grade made.

The CHAIRMAN. Are you prepared to suggest a specific duty on all forms of wire—all sizes?

Mr. WALTON. I think that would be best, if you take my opinion.

The CHAIRMAN. Can you work out a rate here?

Mr. WALTON. No, sir; I am here to give you facts, believing that you are wiser than I am when it comes to getting at the rate.

The CHAIRMAN. No; we have no technical knowledge of the cost of manufacturing so that we could apportion the rate, specific, to replace the ad valorem, and find out what was the equivalent. If we had a schedule of that kind upon each size of wire, then whatever we might conclude to do about the duty, as to raising or lowering it, we would have something that would make the schedule uniform as to the different sizes.

Mr. WALTON. Yes.

The CHAIRMAN. That is, uniform in its operation. Of course we have not that technical knowledge so that we can do it ourselves.

Mr. WALTON. I am here to give you only the technical knowledge which I myself possess.

The CHAIRMAN. I wish you would work out such a proposition as I have suggested and submit it later.

Mr. WALTON. Let me submit one more brand of wire rope, which is the cheapest used in vessel building and for quarry guys more than any other, except it be in use in buildings. I worked out the duty on some small sizes this morning, seven-sixteenths to five-eights in diameter, and here is a sample of what I am talking about. I will leave with you that sample. It runs the lowest 76 per cent and the highest 94$\frac{4}{10}$ per cent, which seems rather excessive.

(Mr. Walton here exhibited a sample of the rope referred to.)

Of course, there is no importing under that at all. I would like, before I suggest a remedy, to know what the committee want. If you want to raise revenue, you are not doing it at all under this high tariff. There are almost none of us left who are importing. You are charging consumers a very high price for wire rope, and the manufacturers in America are making the profit. The Government is not getting anything out of it at all.

The CHAIRMAN. I can not speak for the committee, but so far as I am concerned I want to get at the facts which will enable me to determine what would be a fair, just, and reasonable protective tariff on this article. There are other articles in the schedule that would come under the class of luxuries, and as to those articles we might want to raise revenue, but as to this, I want a fair protective tariff on the article. That is my idea about it.

Mr. WALTON. I will try and work that out and send it to the committee in writing. I have had no time to do that.

Mr. GRIGGS. My idea is exactly to the contrary.

The CHAIRMAN. I will tell you what I would like to have you do; work out two schedules, one on a just and fair protective basis and the other on a revenue basis. I am putting that up to you, now.

Mr. WALTON. All right, sir; if you will give me a little time.

The CHAIRMAN. Will you file that by the 4th of December?

Mr. WALTON. Yes; I think so. I will have to go home, where I can get more figures than I have here, to do that. Just before recess I was about to present a letter from the American Steel and Wire Company, somewhat old, it is true, dated October 1, 1901, addressed to a manufacturer in Liverpool, in reference to prices which were considerably lower on that side than they were making to anybody on this side of the water. I thought that perhaps that might have some bearing on the case.

The CHAIRMAN. You say you have the prices in the factories on the other side?

Mr. WALTON. I have prices which were actually quoted to a manufacturer in Liverpool from the London house of the American Steel and Wire Company October 1, 1901; no later than that.

The CHAIRMAN. I will be glad if you will file that and have it printed in the hearings.

Mr. WALTON. I will be very glad to put that in the hands of the committee, if you care for it.

The CHAIRMAN. You do not want it printed?

Mr. WALTON. I am willing to have it printed. I do not want these cost sheets printed, but I will be very glad to leave them in the hands of the committee for their information.

The CHAIRMAN. Very well; you will put those things in the hands of the clerk, and he will put them in a sealed envelope and mark it " For the use of the committee, confidentially." We can not do it any other way.

Mr. WALTON. I think you can see that it is a part of our capital in trade, and we can not give away all of our buying methods.

Mr. GRIGGS. What aid will it give to the committee in discussing this matter before the House of Representatives to have it in that way?

Mr. WALTON. You can use the facts which you gather from it, by illustration, as I did this morning; but to have the whole schedule of how we buy our goods and how we pay for them printed would be a material disadvantage to us, and I do not feel authorized to give away all our secrets in that way.

Mr. GRIGGS. No; but I would not testify unless I could.

The CHAIRMAN. I do not mean to say by that that it is to be regarded in strict confidence by everybody that gets hold of it. I do not know how that would be. We would like to get at the facts.

Mr. CLARK. We might do this, like they report things that the President says: We might say that a "person in high authority" says so.

Mr. WALTON. Thank you. [Laughter.] I have no sort of objection, Mr. Chairman, to stating the percentage in each case of duty paid, and I do not see but what that would fill the bill. That is really all you care for.

Mr. GRIGGS. You would not object to that being printed?

Mr. WALTON. No, sir; I am perfectly willing that that should be given, the percentage of the duty on each size.

Mr. GRIGGS. So far as I am concerned I do not want to fool with confidential papers.

The CHAIRMAN. Can you not give us the labor cost in making these different kinds of wire? How do you sell them—by the pound?

Mr. WALTON. Altogether by the foot. We buy by the pound and we sell by the foot.

The CHAIRMAN. Then you can give us the labor cost and the cost of material here, and the labor cost and cost of material abroad, so that we can compare the costs?

Mr. WALTON. I am not an expert in that.

Mr. GAINES. This witness does not propose to do that. Does he not say that he does not know the labor cost abroad?

Mr. DALZELL. No; he says abroad he does, but not here.

The CHAIRMAN. He proposes to give us the labor cost abroad, but not here. We want all this information you can give. We will make up this bill from the information we have. If we have accurate information, we will be more likely to get it accurate, and if we do not have accurate information, we will have to do the best we can. We may or may not do you injustice. You can take your own course.

Mr. WALTON. I told you this morning on five or six sizes the difference between the cost of the wire and the cost of the wire rope in England, of which part is labor and part is profit.

The CHAIRMAN. Is that in the hearings?

Mr. WALTON. That is in evidence. You have that already, and it can be printed.

Mr. GRIGGS. That letter you say you have there from somebody in Liverpool can be printed?

Mr. WALTON. That can be printed. It also has some comments by a Democratic committee here.

Mr. COCKRAN. A Democratic committee or a Democratic committeeman?

Mr. WALTON. It is something about tariffs and trusts. I think that was a part of some campaign document. This document I am perfectly willing to put in evidence. I am perfectly willing to tell the per cent of duty on all kinds of wire rope that were handled, which I can do and swear to it now. I have got the whole column right down here.

Mr. GRIGGS. My suggestion is that you do not put anything in here that you are not willing to make public.

Mr. WALTON. Very well; thank you.

Mr. GRIGGS. And anything that you put in, you arrange so that it can be made public, because I put you on notice that I am going to talk about everything you say here.

Mr. WALTON. I am perfectly willing to give the figures on each size of wire rope and the duty upon it.

I do not know that I have anything further to say, except in regard to the bill. During the time of the Wilson tariff there was an administrative order which interpreted the law in a different way from what it had been before, somewhere along in 1896 or 1897, and if you will be kind enough to look at the sample of wire rope I gave you this morning, you will see the point. They assessed an ad valorem duty as well as a specific duty, as the case might be, not only upon the wires upon which the duty was based, but upon the wire rope completed, which included a hemp core. That hemp core would weigh, roughly speaking, 5 per cent of the weight of the entire rope, the wire costing probably 5 or 6 cents a pound, and the hemp core costing not to exceed 2½ cents a pound; probably 2 cents would be nearer. It hardly seems fair that the law should assess 40 per cent and 1 cent per pound upon a jute or very cheap core, which adds nothing to the strength of the rope, or simply acts as a cushion upon which to form the strands. It is necessary to have a core, but not necessarily a strong one. In point of fact, it is better to have a soft one. But this under the present law is assessed as if it were the wire itself, and that does not seem fair. I think if you gentlemen are touching the law with a view to improving it, there is a point where you can do so without any injustice whatever. It only requires that your attention be called to it, in my judgment, for you to see the justice of that.

I do not wish to take up the time of the committee, and I am very much obliged to you for having heard me, and I see now about what you want, and I will try and put in the hands of the chairman the things spoken of.

Mr. GAINES. I understood you to say this morning that Mr. Roebling, the wire-rope manufacturer of New Jersey, stated to your partner that he could manufacture wire rope in this country and sell it in England in competition with the wire-rope manufacturers there.

Mr. WALTON. Yes.

Mr. GAINES. What is your partner's name?

Mr. WALTON. H. F. Lyman.

Mr. GAINES. When was this conversation had?

Mr. WALTON. I do not know when, but is was several years ago—probably four or five years ago.

Mr. GAINES. Will you find out about that?

Mr. WALTON. Yes.

Mr. GAINES. As soon as you return home, and let the committee know at once?

Mr. WALTON. I can telegraph him and find out this afternoon if you wish.

Mr. GAINES. I wish you would.

Mr. WALTON. If he can fix the time, of course.

EXHIBIT A.

LONDON, E. C., *October 1, 1901.*

Messrs. THE WARRINGTON WIRE ROPE WORKS (Limited),
13 Gorce Piazzas, Liverpool,

GENTLEMEN: In answer to your favor of yesterday's date, we have much pleasure in quoting you the following prices on lots of, say, 40 or 50 tons, our ordinary quality of galvanized plain wire and plain annealed core wire. We give you a full range of extras up to 36 gauge, and would refer you to page 9 of the inclosed catalogue, which gives you the approximate breaking strain up to 20 gauge, although please note that on this cheap quality of wire we do not guarantee any certain breaking strain.

With reference to the galvanized wire, we beg to state that we are sending you under separate cover samples of our ordinary galvanized wire, but would state that we can supply heavier galvanizing, or what we call double galvanized, but require an extra price for same. We believe, however, that our ordinary quality will be sufficient for your requirements, inasmuch as we are supplying this identical material to most of the large manufacturers of rigging wire in the United Kingdom.

Plain annealed core wire, in catchweight coils, no wrapping, c. i. f. Liverpool, Nos. 0 to 8 gauge base, £7 5s. 0d., with the following extras over base for thinner sizes:

Gauge.	Extra.	Gauge.	Extra.	Gauge.	Extra.	Gauge.	Extra.
	s. d.		£. s. d.		£. s. d.		£. s. d.
9	5 0	16	2 2 6	23	6 5 0	30	12 15 0
10	7 6	17	2 10 0	24	7 0 0	31	14 5 0
11	10 0	18	3 0 0	25	7 15 0	32	15 10 0
12	12 6	19	3 10 0	26	8 15 0	33	17 10 0
13	17 6	20	4 0 0	27	9 15 0	34	20 0 0
14	22 0	21	4 15 0	28	10 15 0	35	22 5 0
15	32 6	22	5 10 0	29	11 15 0	36	27 0 0

On our ordinary quality of plain galvanized wire, we quote you a base price from 5 to 8 gauge of £8 5s., catchweight coils, no wrapping, c. i. f. Liverpool, with the following extras for thinner gauges:

Gauge.	Extra.	Gauge.	Extra.	Gauge.	Extra.	Gauge.	Extra.
	£ s. d.		£ s. d.		£ s. d.		£ s. d.
9	0 5 0	16	3 0 0	23	13 10 0	30	25 5 0
10	7 6	17	4 5 0	24	15 10 0	31	27 10 0
11	12 6	18	5 0 0	25	17 0 0	32	28 15 0
12	20 0	19	6 0 0	26	18 15 0	33	30 15 0
13	1 5 0	20	7 10 0	27	20 0 0	34	33 7 6
14	1 10 0	21	9 0 0	28	22 10 0	35	38 10 0
15	2 10 0	22	10 5 0	29	24 0 0	36	45 0 0

Of course, on any sizes thinner than, say, 16-gauge we would recommend same to be packed in paper and canvas, our extra charge for same being 14 shillings per ton, or if wrapped only in paper our extra charge is 5 shillings per ton.

We are in the habit of supplying both these qualities of wire to the decimal of an inch, and we have quite a reputation for supplying this material true to gauge.

Our prices are on standard wire gauges, ¼ gauges to take the price of the next thicker gauge, ½ gauges to take the price of the next thinner gauge.

Terms, 2½ per cent discount, thirty days' sight draft, with documents attached, on a London bank.

We make you these quotations for prompt shipment and subject to your prompt reply, and hope to be favored with your valued order.

Yours, faithfully,

AMERICAN STEEL AND WIRE COMPANY,
THOS. J. FARRELL, *Manager,*
Per H. B. FAGNANI.

EXHIBIT B.

LONDON, E. C., *October 3, 1901.*

Messrs. THE WARRINGTON WIRE ROPE WORKS (Limited),
13 Goree Piazzas, Liverpool.

DEAR SIRS: We beg to acknowledge receipt of your valued favor of yesterday's date, contents of which have our careful attention.

We note you state that you do not believe our ordinary galvanized wire would suit you, but that you would require our extra-heavy galvanized wire.

We beg to state that what we term our extra-heavy galvanized wire, that the amount of spelter on this class of material is exactly the same as what we put on our telegraph wire, and, as you are probably aware, on telegraph wire galvanizing has to stand the immersion test.

For heavy galvanized wire we should require an extra of £1 0s. 0d. per ton, and therefore this would make our base price, 5 to 8 gauge, £9 5s. 0d. per ton, and the extras for finer gauges would be the same as quoted you on the 1st instant.

We would, however, state for your information that we have for some years past supplied our ordinary galvanized wire to a large number of makers in this country who manufacture rigging wire.

Trusting to be favored with your valued order,

We remain, dear sirs, your, faithfully,

AMERICAN STEEL AND WIRE COMPANY,
THOS. J. FARRELL, *Manager,*
Per H. B. FAGNANI.

EXHIBIT C.

Size.	Six strands of seven wires.				Six strands of nineteen wires.			Iron tiller rope, six strands of six strands of seven wires.
	Bright iron.	Bright crucible steel.	Extra strong plow steel.	Galvanized guy wire.	Bright iron.	Bright crucible steel.	Extra strong plow steel.	
	Per cent duty.	Per cent duty.	Per cent duty.	Per cent duty.	Per cent duty.	Per cent duty.	Per cent duty.	Per cent duty.
$\frac{1}{4}$ inch	69$\frac{4}{10}$	52$\frac{8}{10}$	....	....	50$\frac{3}{10}$	45$\frac{5}{10}$	....	28
$\frac{5}{16}$ inch	76$\frac{7}{10}$	57$\frac{1}{10}$	....	76	55$\frac{9}{10}$	48$\frac{3}{10}$	....	46
$\frac{3}{8}$ inch	81$\frac{1}{10}$	63$\frac{4}{10}$	....	84	58$\frac{4}{10}$	53$\frac{2}{10}$	....	50
$\frac{7}{16}$ inch	85$\frac{7}{10}$	73	....	89$\frac{1}{10}$	63$\frac{4}{10}$	55$\frac{3}{10}$	....	....
$\frac{1}{2}$ inch	91$\frac{2}{10}$	76$\frac{7}{10}$	56$\frac{8}{10}$	94$\frac{4}{10}$	69$\frac{4}{10}$	57$\frac{1}{10}$	52$\frac{7}{10}$	53
$\frac{9}{16}$ inch	81$\frac{1}{10}$	66	....	....	73	59$\frac{1}{10}$	....	....
$\frac{5}{8}$ inch	86$\frac{8}{10}$	67	37$\frac{5}{10}$	85	76$\frac{7}{10}$	63$\frac{4}{10}$	50$\frac{4}{10}$	48
$\frac{3}{4}$ inch	93$\frac{8}{10}$	71$\frac{4}{10}$	58	82$\frac{2}{10}$	80$\frac{4}{10}$	71$\frac{1}{10}$	56$\frac{5}{10}$	55
$\frac{7}{8}$ inch	91$\frac{1}{10}$	68$\frac{4}{10}$	59	92	86	76$\frac{7}{10}$	56$\frac{6}{10}$	61
1 inch	99$\frac{5}{10}$	71$\frac{5}{10}$	58$\frac{6}{14}$	....	76	67	57$\frac{5}{10}$	65$\frac{8}{10}$
1$\frac{1}{8}$ inches	....	71$\frac{5}{10}$	....	....	78$\frac{3}{10}$	69$\frac{5}{10}$	57$\frac{7}{10}$	68$\frac{7}{10}$
1$\frac{1}{4}$ inches	....	71$\frac{5}{10}$	....	....	81$\frac{2}{10}$	71$\frac{4}{10}$	58	72
1$\frac{3}{8}$ inches	....	....	....	....	....	71$\frac{4}{10}$	....	....
1$\frac{1}{2}$ inches	....	....	....	....	....	64$\frac{3}{10}$	....	....

Above is based on present British cost of the given sizes and quantities. Example: British cost 14 shillings per hundredweight, at $4.90 exchange, less 6 per cent cash=$2.88 per 100 pounds, on which the duty is $2.50=86$\frac{8}{10}$ per cent of $2.88.

JOHN W. WALTON, CLEVELAND, OHIO, SUBMITS SUPPLEMENTAL STATEMENT RELATIVE TO WIRE ROPE.

CLEVELAND, OHIO, *December 2, 1908.*

Hon. SERENO E. PAYNE,
  Chairman Committee on Ways and Means,
    House of Representatives, Washington, D. C.

SIR: At the time of my appearance before your committee, on the 27th instant, I expected only to lay before you such facts bearing upon the subject of the present tariff on wire rope as an experience of thirty-six years in the trade has taught me.

You have further requested me to formulate a section covering this kind of merchandise, such as I would advise Congress to enact.

After careful consideration I hand you the inclosed, which I believe covers the ground. In my judgment it is high enough to afford not only ample protection but a fair profit to the American manufacturer, and it is low enough to enable the Treasury Department to secure some revenue through importation, while the bulk of the vast amount consumed in this country will continue to be made here.

Wire is made into rope principally by the aid of automatic machinery; common labor enters very little into the cost of its production.

It must not be forgotten that the expenses of freight, insurance, and entry amount to about one-fourth of 1 cent per pound on imported wire rope delivered on the Atlantic seaboard, and more than one-half cent per pound delivered at Pacific ports. This, together with the augmented time consumed in filling orders from abroad, serves to increase the protection. In submitting this proposed section of the statute I have purposely disregarded the question of rates on single wires, preferring to let wire rope and cord stand on a separate basis:

PARAGRAPH —. Wire rope and wire cord, or other cordage, the chief component value of which is drawn wire, twenty-five per centum ad valorem.

I shall be happy to answer any further questions on the part of your committee, and beg to remain,
  Yours, respectfully,   JOHN W. WALTON.

GEO. B. CARPENTER & CO., CHICAGO, ILL., WISH A REDUCTION IN DUTY ON STEEL WIRE.

202–208 SOUTH WATER STREET,
  Chicago, January 7, 1909.

Hon. HENRY S. BOUTELL,
  House of Representatives, Washington, D. C.

DEAR SIR: This house is interested in securing a reduction of the tariff on steel wire, Schedule C, of the Dingley tariff, which provides for a duty of 1¼ to 2 cents per pound, or 40 per cent ad valorem when valued at 4 cents per pound or over.

Our interest in the above item lies in the fact that we are large sellers of wire rope, and especially of a grade of wire rope manufactured from Swedish stock, which stock is not produced in the United States, and it is our opinion that a reduction in the tariff on this item of at least 50 per cent would still leave ample protection for American labor and capital and would result in lower prices for all high-grade steel wire rope, thereby bringing about a direct benefit to the consumers of this important item.

Yours, very truly,

GEO. B. CARPENTER & CO.,
Manufacturers and Jobbers of Twines and Cordage.

THE C. T. PATTERSON COMPANY, NEW ORLEANS, LA., THINKS THE DUTY ON WIRE ROPE UNREASONABLE.

NEW ORLEANS, *December 7, 1908.*

Hon. S. E. PAYNE,
Chairman Ways and Means Committee,
Washington, D. C.

DEAR SIR: As large handlers of wire rope for logging purposes in this territory, we wish to call your attention to the duty on this class of wire.

It amounts to 40 per cent ad valorem and 1 cent per pound, which makes the duty on the rope we have to use 57½ per cent. We consider this absolutely unreasonable, but believe we only have to bring this up with you to have you give it your attention.

The sizes of rope used for logging purposes here are as follows: ½ inch, ⅝ inch, ¾ inch, ⅞ inch, and 1 inch diameter. Rope is made generally with six strands, nineteen wires to the strand, with hemp center.

Yours, truly,   C. T. PATTERSON COMPANY (LIMITED),
C. T. PATTERSON.

STATEMENT OF H. J. BAILEY, REPRESENTING THE BRODERICK & BASCOM WIRE ROPE COMPANY, ST. LOUIS, MO.

WEDNESDAY, *November 25, 1908.*

Mr. GRIGGS. I shall have to make my usual inquiry.

Mr. BAILEY. I do not get quite as much as you do, Mr. Griggs. Are you going to ask how much I am making?

Mr. GRIGGS. Not how much; but are you making any money?

Mr. BAILEY. No, sir.

Mr. GRIGGS. You are not making anything?

Mr. BAILEY. Only a meager salary.

The CHAIRMAN. The manufacturers do not seem to be making any money, and the importers are not making any money.

Mr. BAILEY. That is true, I guess.

Mr. CLARK. They are universally " busted."

Mr. BAILEY. I am here on very brief notice, representing the Broderick & Bascom Wire Rope Company, of St. Louis, Mo., and Seattle, Wash. They are manufacturers of wire rope and strands. They are not drawers of wire, but wire is their principal raw material. Upon brief notice I have prepared a brief, setting forth why, in our opinion, the duty on raw material, which is wire, should be reduced.

Mr. CLARK. Oh, you are all right.

Mr. BAILEY. At this late hour in the evening I do not believe it is necessary for me to take up any further time of the committee, but I will content myself with asking for due consideration for our brief, which no doubt it will receive. I therefore simply wish to file the brief.

The CHAIRMAN. All right; let the brief be filed.

(Mr. Bailey's brief is as follows:)

NOVEMBER 25, 1908.

Hon. SERENO E. PAYNE, M. C.,
Chairman Ways and Means Committee, Washington, D. C.:

In re revision of Dingley tariff, Schedule C, paragraph 137, we respectfully represent to your honorable committee that the present duty on round iron or steel wire is entirely out of proportion to the duty imposed on certain manufactures thereof, more particularly with the duty on wire rope and strand, as will appear more certain from the following figures, quoted from government reports of "Imports entered for consumption, year ending June 30, 1907," and for the year ending June 30, 1908, to wit:

1907.				1908.			
Quantities.		Duty on—		Quantities.		Approximate duty on—	
Wire.	Rope.	Wire.	Rope.	Wire.	Rope.	Wire.	Rope.
Pounds. 16,064,420	*Pounds.* 971,622	*Per cent.* 41.90	*Per cent.* 55.60	*Pounds.* 15,537,042	*Pounds.* 900,747	*Per cent.* 41	*Per cent.* 50

It should be borne in mind that the duty on wire rope is made as above by adding together the duty on the wire and 1 cent per pound additional duty on the rope, and when the duty on the wire is deducted from the above " Duty on rope " it will be seen that the average protection afforded is only approximately as follows:

	1907.	1908.
	Per cent.	*Per cent.*
Average protection on wire	41.90	41
Average net protection on rope	15	14

In order to equalize to some extent this vast difference between the duty on our raw material (wire) and the duty on wire rope, we respectfully submit that Schedule C, paragraph 137, should be amended and revised so as to read as follows, to wit:

"137. Round iron or steel wire, not smaller than No. 13 wire gauge, six-tenths of 1 cent per pound; smaller than No. 13 and not smaller than No. 16 wire gauge, eight-tenths of 1 cent per pound; smaller than No. 16 wire gauge, 1 cent per pound: *Provided,* That all the foregoing valued at more than 6 cents per pound shall pay 30 per cent ad valorem. Iron or steel or other wire not specially provided for in this act, including such as is commonly known as hat wire or bonnet wire, crinoline wire, corset wire, needle wire, piano wire, clock wire, and watch wire, whether flat or otherwise, and corset clasps, corset steels, and dress steels, and sheet steel in strips, twenty-five one-thousandths of an inch thick or thinner, any of the foregoing, whether uncovered or covered with cotton, silk, metal, or other material, valued at more than 4 cents per pound, 45 per cent ad valorem: *Provided,* That articles manufactured from iron, steel, brass, or copper wire shall pay the rate of duty imposed upon the wire used in the manufacture of such articles, and in addition thereto 1¼ cents per pound, except that wire rope and wire strand shall pay the maximum rate of duty which would be imposed upon any wire used in the manufacture thereof, and in addition thereto 1 cent per pound; and on iron or steel wire coated with zinc, tin, or any other metal no additional duty shall be imposed in addition to the rate imposed on the wire from which it is made."

As reasons for the foregoing changes, we submit the following facts, viz:

Wire is the principal raw material entering into the manufacture of wire rope.

We are not manufacturers of wire, but are manufacturers of wire rope exclusively, which is an independent industry of itself, and approximately 40 per cent to 50 per cent of all wire rope made in this country is made by factories that do not manufacture wire.

At the present time we import approximately one-third of the total amount of rope wire brought into the United States, as shown by the United States government statistics.

The rope wire required by us for the manufacture of high-grade steel wire ropes is necessarily drawn from rods of Swedish ore stock not produced in the United States, and must therefore be imported from abroad.

It is generally admitted that wire can be drawn in this country as cheaply as anywhere. The ordinary grades are not imported into the United States at all, and the higher grades could be successfully drawn here from imported rods of Swedish ore stock; still, as independent wire-rope manufacturers, we ought not to be compelled to buy this high-grade wire from American mills, who manufacture wire rope as well as wire, and are therefore competitors of ours.

Furthermore, the schedule of prices of various sizes, as published by the American mills, shows no such variance in prices as is shown by the present tariff for various sizes, and the present tariff is therefore, impliedly at least, too high to meet any requirements for protection to the wire industry in this country. Furthermore, if any further protection is demanded for wire, we believe that the present duty on wire rods could be eliminated altogether, as it is admitted by most manufacturers of wire that no duty is needed on the rods.

Wire-manufacturing industry being among the most prosperous of any industry in the United States, we are quite sure that 20 per cent to 25 per cent protective tariff is more than sufficient to meet all justice and fairness.

Respectfully submitted.

BRODERICK & BASCOM ROPE CO.,
JOHN J. BRODERICK, *President.*

H. J. BAILEY, FOR THE BRODERICK & BASCOMB ROPE CO., ST. LOUIS, FILES SUPPLEMENTAL STATEMENT RELATIVE TO WIRE.

ST. LOUIS, MO., *January 13, 1909.*

Hon. SERENO E. PAYNE,
Chairman, Committee on Ways and Means,
Washington, D. C.

GENTLEMEN: Referring to your communication of December 31, 1908, by Mr. W. K. Payne, clerk, and ours of December 29, 1908, beg to state that, since filing our original brief for revision of Schedule C, Dingley tariff, re steel and iron wire, beg to state that we have endeavored to secure reliable information concerning the cost of production of wire abroad as compared with cost in this country; we have found this no easy task so far as figures for this country are concerned, but we are pleased to submit herewith letters from certain prominent wire manufacturers of England, from which we deduct the following facts, to wit:

Wages in England are based upon piecework, but will average per week of fifty-four hours approximately as follows:

	English.	American.
	Shillings.	
Wire drawers, drawing iron or mile steel wire (which is ordinary "market wire," of which little or none is imported into the United States)	40 to 50	$9.60 to $12.00
Wire drawers, drawing hard-steel wire (such as is imported for wire rope).	55 to 65	13.20 to 14.60
Laborers. who have to prepare the wire for the skilled mechanics, i. e., cleaners, annealers, men who attend patenting furnaces. etc	20 to 30	4.80 to 7.20

The wages paid for similar services in the United States is doubtless considerably more than stated above, but to compensate for this difference in wages it must be borne in mind that in England one man attends to but one thick-wire block; in the United States one man attends to at least four, and often six, thick-wire blocks, while for the finer sizes, say No. 24 to No. 36, there is still a greater difference, and for these sizes in England one man attends to ten to fifteen blocks; in the United States one man (with help of a boy) attends to thirty to fifty blocks.

From the foregoing it will appear that while the individual earnings of the American workman is greater than that of the English workman, still the cost per hundredweight in wages to the American manufacturer is much less than the cost per hundredweight in wages to the English manufacturer, because of the greater amount of work turned out by the American workman, due to the greater number of machines attended to by the American.

Very good raw material is produced in abundance in the United States for the manufacture of mild steel wire, and our American mills are enabled to sell wire at a less price than it can be produced for abroad, as will appear from the inclosed letter from Frederick Smith & Co., in which it is set forth that in busy times they have themselves been compelled to place orders in this country, and have had the wire laid down at their factory in England by American mills at a lower price than they could produce it for themselves.

But the English system of having one man attend to but one block, rigidly enforced by the English labor unions, doubtless insures greater care and exactitude in drawing the higher-grade steel wire, which is essential for the manufacture of strictly high-grade wire rope, and for this reason the English drawn wire is preferable for the very high-grade wire ropes for use where many lives are often at stake and depend upon the quality of the rope.

Still, with the duty on rods abolished, our American mills can doubtless produce this high-grade wire at a lower cost than it can be produced for in England; but the English and Swedish stock is recognized as far superior to anything produced in this country as basic stock for this very high-grade steel wire, and for this reason we believe that free rods is essential to enable our American mills to compete successfully with foreign mills on this high-grade wire.

In accordance with the foregoing schedule of wages in England, we quote from a letter received from Mr. Andrew Rathbone, a prominent manufacturer of wire and wire-drawing machinery, of Warrington, England, the following cost of labor in England:

Annealing, cleaning, patenting, pointing, and drawing the following sizes of wire from No. 5 gauge rod (not including cost of rod), per ton of 2,240 pounds.

No. S. W. G.	Soft.			American.	Mild.			American.	Hard Steel.			American.
	£	s.	d.		£	s.	d.		£	s.	d.	
10	0	11	8	$2.84	2	7	1	$11.45	2	10	10	$12.86
11	0	15	6	3.77	2	11	3	12.47	2	15	6	13.50
12	0	16	10	4.09	2	12	2	12.69	3	1	6	14.96
13	1	1	0	5.10	2	14	2	13.18	3	4	0	15.57
14	1	19	11	9.70	3	5	4	15.89	3	13	8	17.72
15	2	3	9	10.64	3	8	8	16.71	3	16	9	18.67
16	2	4	7	10.84	3	16	2	18.53	4	5	6	20.81
17	2	7	3	11.49	4	2	0	19.95	4	12	7	22.53
18	2	12	8	12.81	4	5	4	20.76	4	16	9	23.54
19	3	2	0	15.08	6	2	7	29.83	6	17	7	33.48
20	3	12	8	17.67	6	10	6	31.75	8	2	2	39.46
21	5	14	2	28.23	8	0	10	39.13	10	1	4	48.99
22	5	19	6	29.07	11	4	8	54.66	12	8	8	60.50
23	6	12	0	32.11	13	3	0	63.99	14	13	0	71.29
24	7	19	2	38.72	15	6	4	74.54	17	2	4	83.30
25	9	11	3	46.53	19	6	4	94.00	22	2	4	107.63
26	11	14	0	56.94	23	6	4	113.47	26	6	4	128.07

The plain roman figures are English pounds, shillings, and pence, and the figures in black are the translations in American dollars and cents.

The above cost does not include common labor, general and incidental expenses, which vary somewhat according to management and system practiced by various manufacturers, and will necessarily be less in a large plant than in a small one; but these figures were compiled by a manufacturer (above named) of long experience in wire drawing and are doubtless as nearly correct as possible.

We feel sure that by comparing above figures with the cost for labor in drawing wire in this country (which can be doubtless obtained from American manufacturers appearing before your committee) you will be enabled to arrive at an equitable schedule of duties for high-grade steel wire, which is really the only kind of wire imported into the United States at present, foreign mills being unable to compete with our American mills on the ordinary market wire referred to above as soft and mild wire, as stated in a preceding paragraph.

With the duty on rods eliminated we are certain that foreign manufacturers can not compete with American mills on the high-grade hard wire, but we do not advocate the entire abolition of all duty on wire for all that. We believe in the principle of protection, but we believe that a revision of present duties on an equitable basis can be arranged by a reduction of, say, 50 per cent of the present duty on wire, which will still leave ample protection to American labor and capital. Our only desire is to assist the committee in arriving at what is, in their opinion, a fair schedule of duties on steel wire and on wire rope.

Re wire rope.—The manufacture of wire rope is an industry complete in itself. There are about eleven or twelve factories in the United States manufacturing wire rope, and of this number approximately one-third manufacture their own wire, which is our raw material, while the remaining two-thirds who operate wire-rope factories exclusively are obliged to depend upon American wire mills for certain grades of wire, and at the same time meet the competition of these wire mills in marketing their product—wire rope; but a certain amount of our raw material—wire—must be imported at present in order to secure the high grades made of Swedish stock, which is not produced in this country; and the present high duty on this steel wire enables the American manufacturer to keep up his price of hard-steel wire, such as plow steel, to an abnormally high figure.

In England there are approximately fifty wire-rope factories, of which number only about eight draw their own wire; and in Europe there are altogether about one hundred rope factories, of which number only about twenty draw their own wire, which seems to verify our assertion that this is an independent industry in itself.

Competition is so keen in Europe on wire rope that a great many factories employ only the cheapest labor, depending much upon the machines to do the work, and using ordinary laborers—boys, and in many cases strong girls to attend the machines. The European manufacturer of wire rope will employ a good foreman at a salary of 40s. to 50s. ($9.60 to $12) per week, and one or two under men at 30s. to 40s. ($7.20 to $9.60) per week, and the majority of other men will receive about 20s. ($4.80) per week, while the boys and girls receive considerably less.

Therefore, the bulk of the labor in a wire-rope factory in Europe will receive approximately $4.80 per week, and only a very few men are employed at higher wages.

In the United States only skilled labor is employed to operate wire-rope machines; no youths under 16 years of age and absolutely no girls are employed. The scale of wages paid in wire-rope factories in this country are approximately as follows: For skilled men, operating wire-rope machines, from $2.50 to $3 per day; for boys, used in spooling wire, etc., from $8 to $10 per week; for foremen, from $80 to $100 per month; for common day laborers, $1.75 to $2 per day.

The present duty on wire rope is 1 cent per pound in addition to the duty on the wire from which it is made; while the minimum duty on wire is $1\frac{1}{4}$ cents per pound, and the maximum 2 cents per pound, or 40 per cent ad valorem. Therefore, for a wire rope imported, which is made of wire taking the minimum duty, the tariff is $1\frac{1}{4}$ cents per pound on the wire, plus 1 cent for the rope, making $2\frac{1}{4}$ cents per pound.

In view of the fact that boys and girls are now employed to make wire rope in Europe, we maintain that the above conditions should be reversed to some extent; and that, with the duty reduced on wire (which is the raw material), there should be a slight advance in the duty on wire rope (which is the finished product of wire).

We believe that a duty of $1\frac{1}{2}$ cents per pound on wire rope will be amply sufficient to protect the industry in this country against the competition of cheap labor abroad.

We recommend to your honorable committee, therefore, that the duty on wire rope be $1\frac{1}{2}$ cents per pound, or not less than $1\frac{1}{4}$ cents per pound, which is now the duty on all other manufactures of wire.

Respectfully submitted.

H. J. BAILEY,
For BRODERICK & BASCOM ROPE CO.

EXHIBIT A.

CALEDONIA WORKS,
Halifax, England, November 23, 1908.

Messrs. BRODERICK & BASCOM ROPE COMPANY,
St. Louis, Mo., U. S. A.

DEAR SIRS: We have just received your letter of November 11, asking us for some information that will be of assistance to you when you appear before the tariff revision committee on all classes of wire, and at the same time you do not object to a reduction on finished ropes, but you want the reduction on the ropes to be in proportion to the duty on the wire.

Now, as far as wire manufacturing is concerned there is no necessity for any duty whatever in order to protect the American wire manufacturer; because wire, in our opinion, can be produced at a less price than it is produced in this country, because of the entirely different system of working prevailing in the States. You will remember that in England one man minds one thick-wire drawing block, but in the States one man minds at least four, and sometimes six, thick-wire blocks; and in the finer sizes, that is, say, No. 24 to 36, there is still a great difference. In England one man attends to ten to fifteen blocks, but in the States one man, with the assistance of a boy, runs thirty to fifty blocks.

The individual earnings of American workmen may be greater than the individual earning of our men, but the cost per hundredweight in wages to the American manufacturer is much less than the cost per hundredweight in wages to the English manufacturer, because of the greater quantity turned out by the American workman, because he minds a larger number of machines. We do not pay our wire-drawers by time, but by piece, but we give you the wages that can be earned in a week of fifty-four hours: Drawing iron or mild steel wire, 40s. to 50s. ($9.60 to $12) per week; drawing hard steel, 55s. to 65s. ($13.20 to $14.60) per week.

These are the wages of skilled workmen. But of course we employ a large number of laborers who have to prepare the wire for the skilled men, i. e., cleaners, annealers, men who tend to patenting furnaces, etc., and the average wages of these men, according to their various duties, runs from 20s. to 30s. ($4.80 to $7.20). Of course we must not forget that the wages are not the only expense in connection with the production of wire; of course there is the power required, which is considerable, and then you must remember the cost of patenting is very heavy because of the great amount of coal consumed; then there is the enormous quantity of acid, and a multitude of other things have to be used in the production of wire. For the ordinary laborers the Americans will pay more than we do, but we think they work longer hours, and there is a great deal more hustling in America than there is with us; therefore, although the weekly wage of your laborers may be more than the weekly wages of our laborers, we are under the impression that the difference is not so great as it appears, because we believe a larger amount of work will be turned out by your men than by ours in the same number of hours.

Now we are under the impression that if the entire duty was taken off mild steel or iron wire the English manufacturers would really have no chance of doing a large business in your country, because you have very good raw material, well suited for mild steel, and your manufacturers are so well installed that they can sell wire if they like at less than it can be produced in this country; in fact, we ourselves in busy times have often bought from the States annealed No. 14 mild steel, delivered at our works in Halifax, at a less price than we could produce it, which we contend is a proof in itself that American manufacturers of this class of wire need no protection whatever. But with respect to high-grade steel wire such as you obtain from us, this is a material that requires greater care in drawing, greater exactitude in size; and our system of one man to one block no doubt gives the workmen a better chance of producing a finer-finished wire than can be produced by a man who has to tend a large number of machines. We fully recognize the fact that this is one of the reasons why we are able to supply this high-grade steel to your country; but the most important reason is that the English and Swedish steels are far better for the production of high-grade wires than any steel that can be produced in America; but we suppose that in the revision of the duty there will be very little or no tariff on English and Swedish steels, and therefore in a short time American wire manufacturers would be able to buy foreign raw material and successfully compete with their English competitors in high-class wire.

Also, it must not be forgotten that living, rent, and clothing are a great deal cheaper in this country than in America; in fact, workmen with £2 a week can support themselves and family better than Americans can with £3 per week, and we may say in this town very good workmen's houses can be obtained, self-contained houses with two living rooms and a wash kitchen on the ground floor and two bedrooms and a bathroom, all in one house, well built of stone, at 6s. to 7s. per week—that is to say, at 1½ to 1¾ dollars per week, all clear of rates. We do not suppose that such a house can be obtained in St. Louis at anything like that price. Of course there are still cheaper houses, with one living room and wash kitchen and two bedrooms, at 4s. per week, but the 6s. a week house is a good modern house.

Now, with respect to galvanized wire, you are quite right in your statement that a large quantity of American spelter is sent from the States to this country, and it is used for many purposes for galvanizing wire; but we wish to be perfectly frank and straightforward, and therefore tell you that we ourselves have not used very much American spelter, because we find the continental brands of spelter to be of superior quality and better suited for our special work; but American spelter is largely used for many other purposes, and when spelter is produced in America and can be sold in foreign countries at the present time it does really seem unfair that when spelter returns to America, forming a cover on wire and other goods, that it should have to pay a duty to enter into the country from which it originally came.

Now, with respect to rope making. As you are aware, we are not rope makers, and it is difficult for us to obtain any really reliable information for you for your guidance. But we do know that in rope making very little skill is required; the machines do the work, and they simply want an intelligent laborer to tend to them. A large rope-making firm will employ a good foreman, pay him 40s. to 50s. per week, and one or two undermen at about 30s. to 40s. per week, but the great bulk of the other men will only get about 20s. per week.

In the north of England it is a very usual custom for big girls to mind stranding machines, but where girls are not employed boys are generally used for the stranding machines and only men employed on the important machines that lay up the big ropes. Altogether the cost of wages in a rope mill is very much less than the cost of wages in a wire mill. The rope makers of this country have got their works so arranged that the cost of production is really very small, because, as you will readily understand, the bulk of the labor is of a very cheap class, and therefore you would be quite right in stating that the bulk of the labor in a rope-making establishment is about 20s. per week and that only a few skilled men are required at a higher rate.

If there is any further information you require we shall be pleased to try and obtain it for you either with respect to the cost of wire manufacturing or to the cost of rope making.

We are, yours, truly,

FREDERICK SMITH & Co.,
Wire Manufacturers, Limited.
GEO. H. SMITH, *Director.*

EXHIBIT B.

CLECKHEATON, *November 23, 1908.*

Messrs. BRODERICK & BASCOM ROPE COMPANY,
805–809 North Main street, St. Louis, U. S. A.

DEAR SIRS: We have yours of the 9th. We note the contents and are pleased to be able to supply you with the information you require, as follows: For patent steel wire we pay 10d. (20 cents) per hour; for plow steel wire, 1s. (24 cents) per hour; for iron wire, 8½d. (17 cents) per hour.

These are the rates of wages for day work, but it is practically universal to pay piece rates, when the wire-drawer comes out quite 2d. to 5d. per hour more than above rates. This is our experience, and our competitors convey the impression that their men are similar. For example, men put on piecework drawing patent wire can earn 1s. per hour—equal to 56s. per week—while on plow wires, such as we supply to you, they can earn 1s. 5d. per hour—equal to 70 to 80 shillings per week. We understand that rope makers make from 5½d. to 8½d. per hour, according to the class of work. You are quite correct in assuming that we use zinc spelter for galvanizing. We hope you will be successful in your appeal and that an increased business in galvanized wires will be the result, and also bright.

Yours, faithfully,

E. & A. SMITH & Co. (LIMITED),
Wire Manufacturers.

EXHIBIT C.

DONCASTER, *November 24, 1908.*

The BRODERICK & BASCOM ROPE COMPANY,
St. Louis, U. S. America.

DEAR SIRS: We are duly in receipt of your letter of the 10th inst., and are pleased to be able to supply you with the information as follows: For patent steel wire, 10d. per hour; for plow steel wire, 1s. per hour; and for iron wire, 8½d. per hour.

The above are the rates of wages for daywork, but it is practically universal to pay piece rates, in which case the wire drawer earns quite 2d. to 5d. per hour more. This is our experience, and our competitors convey the impression that their men are similar.

For example, men put on piecework drawing patent wire can earn 1s. per hour, which is equal to 56s. per week, whilst on plow wire they can earn 1s. 5d. per hour, equal to 70s. or 80s. per week.

We understand that rope makers pay from 5½d. to 8½d. per hour, according to the class of work.

You are quite right in assuming that we use zinc spelter for galvanizing.

We hope you will be successful in your appeal, and that an increased business in galvanized and bright wire will be the result.

Yours, faithfully,
T. S.,
For The Doncaster Wire Company (Limited).

Exhibit D.

Department of Commerce and Labor,
Bureau of Labor,
Washington, December 8, 1908.

Mr. H. J. Bailey,
1228 Alton street, Alton, Ill.

Dear Sir: The chief of the Bureau of Statistics of this department has notified me of your desire for information as to the comparative cost of producing steel wire in this country and England for various sizes per ton.

I regret to inform you, however, that this bureau has no data covering this subject and I am, therefore, unable to comply with your request.

I am, very truly, yours,
G. W. W. Haugh,
Acting Commissioner Bureau of Labor,
Department of Commerce and Labor.

STEEL MUSIC WIRE.

[Paragraph 137.]

JULIUS BRECKWOLDT & CO., OF DOLGEVILLE, N. Y., ASK A REDUCTION OF DUTY ON STEEL MUSIC WIRE.

DOLGEVILLE, N. Y., *December 15, 1908.*

Hon. James S. Sherman, M. C.,
Washington, D. C.

My Dear Sir: As you are undoubtedly aware, I have been interested in the importation of the Rudolf Giese steel music wire, manufactured at Westig, Germany, for the past ten years.

I do not know what measures will be taken by Congress on the tariff question, but generally speaking it looks as if there would be a revision. The American Steel trust has cut a great inroad in the business and are doing their utmost to drive us out of the market. As you will see by the inclosed copy of letter, they are selling spring wire at 22 cents per pound, and it costs us 28 cents to import this wire. You are aware that I am a strong protectionist, out and out, but at the same time I would like to have justice done all around, and believe that the tariff on cast music wire and spring wire should be reduced. The manufacturers in this country can never produce wire of such high standard as that produced by foreigners, as ·it requires the best Swedish steel to make it. Our manufacturers are, so to say, imitators, and it will be a great many years to come before they have the results achieved by the foreign manufacturers.

Furthermore, the extent of the piano business, as well as other lines of manufacturing where these wires are used in this country, is so large and there is so much capital invested that it means a great help to them if they can get the right wire at the right price. It would be detrimental to these industries if they were forced to take inferior goods, which would be largely the case should the American Steel Company drive us out of the market. You can judge from the letter which our agent sends us that they are doing everything in their power to cut into the market. Even if they are not entirely successful in so doing, they compel us to cut the price, and if this state of affairs continues they will discourage us.

Knowing that you have our interests at heart, I wish, if there is cause for it, that you would look after this matter for us and see if you can get the duty reduced. At present we are paying 45 per cent, which is altogether too much protection for the combine; 30 per cent would give us a fighting chance to keep them off. Three or four years ago their influence went so far that we had to add market value to our invoices, notwithstanding the proof of the consul agent in Europe that we entered our goods at the true market value.

Any further information required regarding this matter will be gladly furnished. However, the facts above given are the true state of affairs as they exist to-day, and we think you will agree with us that we are entitled to a redress.

Always to your service, I am,
Yours, very truly,   JULIUS BRECKWOLDT.

———

DAYTON, OHIO, *December 12, 1908.*

Mr. RUDOLF GIESE,
    Dolgeville, N. Y.

DEAR SIR: Inclosed please find order No. 2541 from the Davis Sewing Machine Company. Kindly give this your prompt attention.

In reply to your favor of the 7th, have not answered this sooner owing to the fact that I can not get anything definite from Mr. Gorman, the purchasing agent of the Davis Sewing Machine Company. As I advised you before, they have been fooling around with some domestic wire and have sent back some 650 pounds. He told me this morning that of course the mill asked privilege to replace this, and if they replace wire which is satisfactory, which I doubt, they will keep on sending them the business, as their price is 22 cents per pound.

Mr. Gorman stated that in his own mind he had no doubt they would continue to send us the business, as he felt sure they would be unable to send wire that would be satisfactory, but would not guarantee to take out any stock that you might order for them. Under the existing circumstances do not know what to advise.

Very truly, yours.   CARL LOY.

WIRE STRAINERS.

[Paragraph 137.]

VARIOUS AMERICAN MANUFACTURERS OF WIRE STRAINERS ASK FOR AN INCREASE OF THE DUTY.

WORCESTER, MASS., *November 20, 1908.*

COMMITTEE ON WAYS AND MEANS,
Washington, D. C.

GENTLEMEN: The National Manufacturing Company, the Hamblin & Russell Manufacturing Company, and the Parker Wire Goods Company, all of Worcester, Mass., and the Woods Sherwood Company, of Lowell, Mass., respectfully represent that the importation into the United States of wire strainers, illustrations of which are inclosed, marked "Exhibit A," has wrought and is working great injury to your petitioners, by reason of the low cost of the goods in Germany and the inadequate tariff protection as they are now imported into this country.

Your petitioners estimate that there are nearly one-half million dollars in value of these goods imported annually into the United States, and this importation is increasing so rapidly that the manufacture of the goods in this country has fallen off 50 per cent during the past year, and unless this importation can be made unprofitable by means of tariff legislation the foreign goods will shortly have replaced the goods of American manufacture.

The line of goods in question has been manufactured for many years in this country, giving employment to a large number of operatives, both directly and indirectly, and your petitioners deplore a condition which will deprive these operatives from employment, and for this additional reason relief is asked.

The present rate of duty is 40 per cent ad valorum, plus a specific duty of 1¾ cents, plus two-tenths of 1 per cent per pound.

As these goods are very light in weight, this specific duty adds but very little to the importation cost of the goods.

To afford the American manufacturer any protection whatever, the rate of duty should not be less than 60 per cent ad valorem, plus a specific duty of 20 cents per pound, and to afford adequate protection the specific duty should be as much as 25 cents per pound.

For comparison, the prices which some of the imported goods cost in Germany, also what they cost laid down in American ports, are quoted below. In addition to the above are given the lowest possible prices at which American goods of the same sizes and qualities can be quoted, and even at these prices the goods do not pay the percentage of profit which the investment should warrant.

The sizes quoted are those marked "X" on the illustrated sheet (Exhibit A). Other sizes are in the same proportion as to importation cost and possible selling price.

Number.	Diameter.	Weight per gross.	Cost in Germany.	Imported cost.	Lowest possible selling price.	Present selling price.
	Inches.	*Pounds.*				
0	2½	8	$1.54	$2.31	$3.75	$3.89
1	3	12	1.59	2.46	4.75	5.35
2	3½	15	1.94	3.02	5.50	6.32
3	4	22	2.30	3.63	7.00	8.27

In view of the above, your petitioners would respectfully request that the duty on wire strainers be made as above indicated.

THE NATIONAL MANUFACTURING COMPANY,
F. W. COLLIER, *President.*
THE HAMBLIN & RUSSELL MANUFACTURING COMPANY,
W. V. RUSSELL, *President.*
THE PARKER WIRE GOODS COMPANY,
A. H. PARKER, *President.*
THE WOODS SHERWOOD COMPANY,
I. A. GREEN, *Secretary.*

———

STATEMENT OF F. W. COLLIER, OF WORCESTER, MASS., ASKING AN INCREASE OF DUTY ON WIRE-STRAINERS.

WEDNESDAY, *November 25, 1908.*

Mr. GRIGGS. Are you making any money?

Mr. COLLIER. I am a manufacturer of wire goods.

Mr. GRIGGS. Are you making money?

Mr. COLLIER. In a small way; yes, sir.

Mr. GRIGGS. I congratulate you.

Mr. COLLIER. Thank you. My only excuse for appearing before you and occupying any of your time upon a matter that must seem of small importance to you is that it is a matter of great importance to those whom I represent.

For forty years there has existed in New England particularly, and principally in or near Worcester, Mass., an industry in which are manufactured articles known as wire goods. One of the small New England industries, insignificant in a way, and yet employing from 800 to 1,000 hands. I am representing the National Manufacturing Company, of which I am president; Hamilton & Russell Manufacturing Company; Parker Wire Goods Company, of Worcester; and the Woods Sherwood Company, of Lowell.

The articles manufactured are mostly household utensils. About one-quarter of the product has been of the class of goods known as wire strainers. They are of almost universal use, and still, possibly on account of the small price at which they sell, and possibly on account of lack of alertness on the part of the manufacturers, they have attracted no attention whatever in the previous tariff schedules. They are simply included in that almost infinite classification as goods made of wire " but not otherwise specified," and as such have taken a duty of 40 per cent ad valorem, plus 1¼ cents per pound plus 0.2 of 1 cent per pound. We are asking for 60 per cent ad valorem, plus 2 cents per pound.

Now, while this present duty has proven satisfactory on other lines of our manufacture, on the strainer line it is of no protection whatever, by reason of the low cost to produce abroad, affecting the ad valorem and the light weight of the goods themselves.

They are made of wire cloth of fine mesh and very fine wire, generally No. 30, and bound with a narrow strip of tin plate, so that they weigh, ready for the market, only from 5 to 22 pounds per gross. On most of the other lines of our manufacture the selling price is from 6 to 10 cents per pound, and the specific duty amounts to something, while on the strainers, which are so light and on which labor is the principal item, the selling price has to be from 40 to 50 cents per pound, and the present specific duty amounts to nothing at all. And, of course, this same lightness in weight, together with the fact that they are shipped nested, operates to keep the freight rate so small that it is not a factor.

Now, until recently the normal importation has not been harmful to our normal production, because of the former inferiority of the foreign goods. But in the past two years the Germans have acquired the necessary skill and are now sending over goods that are equally as good as ours, and at about one-half of what we must get, and actually less than our stock and labor. Of course, this has increased their business at our expense, and I would like to say right here that it is this encroachment that we are objecting to, rather than to what I would call a normal importation.

The best estimate that I have been able to make is that this normal importation has been about equal to domestic production, confined, however, to a very few houses, as will later appear. And now, lest anyone should say that this increased importation has no doubt increased our revenue, I must point out that it has not increased it nearly as much as the higher duty asked for would increase it on a normal importation, for we ourselves would not care to have the duty large enough to prohibit this normal importation and we do not ask it. By that I mean that the very large buyers, if they could make any saving at all, would continue to import, while the ordinary jobbing trade who find difficulty in ordering in importing quantities would naturally come back to us from convenience even at a little advance over the importation cost. And I would further say that the advanced duty asked for would not be borne by the consuming public, for the goods are sold uniformly at either 5 or 10 cents, mostly 10 cents. Under the normal importation the principal importers are the 5 and 10 cent syndicates, who could not make a different price if they wanted to, but who are the only ones who would care to order in importing quantities, unless there was a very great saving to be effected, as now.

Now, in asking for this increased rate, we have not followed the plan of asking for a good deal more than we expect or need, in the hope that when the "scaling down" comes we will get what we want; but we have figured it out as best we can so that the industry will be put back on the basis it has been on for the past twenty years, and where the normal importation at slightly less costs then would yield us a profit will yield to the Treasury an even greater revenue than now. And we have done this because we believe that "he is thrice armed who hath his quarrel just."

I might also say that in making our prices we try to make them on a basis of 20 per cent above our total cost. This applies to our entire line, but still we always find at the end of the year that we have made only one-fourth of that percentage on our total sales, from which I believe we are now selling as low as we could possibly sell at a profit.

As to the labor side of the question I would say that there are probably about 200 hands employed in this branch of the industry, all more or less skilled, and the imminent falling off of the business will work hardship to them. On the other hand, the rate that we propose would keep them employed at fair wages. It would easily increase the revenue, and would be borne entirely by a few large importers, who would still be as well off as they were until very recently.

Mr. GRIGGS. How much did you make last year?

Mr. COLLIER. In our entire business?

Mr. GRIGGS. How much did you make last year? You said you were making 5 per cent this year.

Mr. COLLIER. No; I said that every year for the last ten years we had averaged about 5 per cent on our sales.

Mr. GRIGGS. For the last ten years?

Mr. COLLIER. Yes.

Mr. GRIGGS. Is that your dividend?

Mr. COLLIER. No, sir; we pay a dividend on our capital stock. We pay 6 per cent dividends.

Mr. GRIGGS. That is, after paying salaries?

Mr. COLLIER. Yes, sir.

Mr. GRIGGS. You pay a 6 per cent dividend?

Mr. COLLIER. Yes, sir.

Mr. GRIGGS. But you are only making 5 per cent.

Mr. COLLIER. We are making 5 per cent on our sales, but we pay the dividend on the capital stock.

Mr. GRIGGS. Oh, I see. You made 5 per cent on your sales?

Mr. COLLIER. Yes, sir.

Mr. GRIGGS. Then you paid the salaries of the officers besides that, did you not?

Mr. COLLIER. Certainly.

Mr. GRIGGS. I have no more questions.

BRIEF SUBMITTED BY F. W. COLLIER, WORCESTER, MASS., RELATIVE TO INCREASE OF DUTY ON WIRE STRAINERS.

COMMITTEE ON WAYS AND MEANS,
Washington, D. C.

WASHINGTON, D. C., *Nov. 25, 1908.*

GENTLEMEN: The following manufacturers, The National Manufacturing Company, The Hamblin & Russell Manufacturing Company. The Parker Wire Goods Company, all of Worcester, Mass., and the Woods-Sherwood Company, of Lowell, Mass., desire to amend their brief submitted on November 20, on wire strainers, by striking out the third line from the last on the first page of same and substituting therefor the words, " Duty of 2 cents per pound, plus 1¼ cents per pound, plus $\frac{2}{10}$ of 1 per cent per pound." Also by striking out on the last page of the same all of the tables of prices, weights, etc., and substituting therefor as follows:

Diameter.	Weight per gross.	Cost in Germany.	Imported cost.	Our stock and labor.	Our total cost.	Lowest possible selling price.	Present selling price.
	Pounds.	Cents.	Cents.	Cents.	Cents.	Cents.	Cents.
2½ inches	8	1.46	2.31	2.20	3.25	3.75	3.89
3 inches	12	1.47	2.46	2.80	4.25	4.75	5.35
3½ inces....................	15	1.80	3.02	3.30	5.00	5.50	6.32
4 inches	22	2.05	3.63	4.45	6.70	7.00	8.27
Average..............	a 14.25	b 11.9	b 20.1	b 24.1	b 36.2	b 37.00	41.8

a Average weight per gross.
b Average prices per pound of finished product.

The duty asked for would therefore equal 11.9 cents plus 60 per cent, plus 20 cents per pound; or 19.05 cents plus 20 cents; or a total of 39.05 cents per pound.

This slight change has been made necessary by the receipt of later information, the previous statements having been made as the result of information given at the custom-house in our city, but on going more carefully over the schedule itself, we desire to make these changes for the sake of accuracy, although they do not materially affect our case or the changes that we desire to suggest in the schedule.

Labor is paid $9 per week in this country, in Germany $1.50 per week. As our raw material is a highly finished product, this proportion of labor costs applies on all stock and labor costs above original stock cost of about 4 cents per pound.

Signed (for the above manufacturers).

THE NATIONAL MANUFACTURING Co.,
F. W. COLLIER, *President*.

TWIN WIRE HEDDLES.

[Paragraph 137.]

MANUFACTURERS OF TWIN WIRE HEDDLES THINK THAT A DUTY OF SIXTY PER CENT SHOULD BE IMPOSED.

WASHINGTON, D. C., *December 15, 1908.*
Committee on Ways and Means, Washington, D. C.

GENTLEMEN:

First. The merchandise or product involved in twin wire heddles (so called).

Second. This brief is submitted in behalf of F. A. Chase & Co., of Providence, R. I.; Gibbs Loom, Harness and Reed Company, of Clinton, Mass.; Howard Brothers Manufacturing Company, of Worcester, Mass.; and J. H. Williams Company, of Utica, N. Y. These persons and corporations are the only manufacturers of twin wire heddles in the United States.

Third. These persons are interested in paragraph 137, Schedule C (Metals and manufactures of) of the present law.

Fourth. The changed or amended paragraph, as it should be written into the new law, is as follows:

137. Round iron or steel wire, not smaller than number thirteen wire gauge, one and one-fourth cents per pound; smaller than number thirteen and not

smaller than number sixteen wire gauge, one and one-half cents per pound; smaller than number sixteen wire gauge, two cents per pound: *Provided,* That all the foregoing valued at more than four cents per pound shall pay forty per centum ad valorem. Iron or steel or other wire not specially provided for in this act, including such as is commonly known as hat wire, or bonnet wire, crinoline wire, corset wire, needle wire, piano wire, clock wire, and watch wire, whether flat or otherwise, and corset clasps, corset steels and dress steels, and sheet steel in strips, twenty-five one-thousandths of an inch thick or thinner, and of the foregoing, whether uncovered or covered with cotton, silk, metal, or other material, valued at more than four cents per pound, forty-five per centum ad valorem: *Provided,* That articles manufactured from iron, steel, brass, or copper wire shall pay the rate of duty imposed upon the wire used in the manufacture of such articles, and in addition thereto one and one-fourth cents per pound, except that wire rope and wire strand shall pay the maximum rate of duty which would be imposed upon any wire used in the manufacture thereof, and in addition thereto, one cent per pound; and on iron or steel wire coated with zinc, tin, or any other metal, two-tenths of one cent per pound in addition to the rate imposed on the wire from which it is made: *And provided further, That wire heddles made of two strands of wire tinned or soldered together shall pay sixty per centum ad valorem.*

The proposed change in the paragraph consists of the addition of the italicized clause.

Fifth. The reason why the proposed change should be made will appear from a consideration of the facts hereinafter set forth.

A. The twin-wire heddles are made of two strands of tempered-steel wire, tinned or soldered together. They are used in the process of weaving textile fabrics, including those woven of cotton, silk, worsted, and wool. Approximately 100,000,000 heddles of this style are sold in this country annually. This style of heddle originated in Germany about twenty-five years ago; and on that account is commouly called, commercially, "German-style" heddle.

B. The "American-style" heddle (so called) was in general use in this country prior to 1889 or 1890. The "American-style" heddle is made of strands of twisted iron wire.

C. Samples of heddles, duly marked, have been forwarded to the committee, and leave is craved to refer to the same as a part of this brief.

Package marked "Brief of F. A. Chase & Co., Exhibit A," contains samples of the old-style American-pattern heddles made of strands of iron wire.

Package marked "Brief of F. A. Chase & Co., Exhibit B," contains samples of German-style heddles made of parallel strands of tempered-steel wire tinned and soldered together, as put up for sale.

Package marked "Brief of F. A. Chase & Co., Exhibit C," contains samples of German-style heddles strung on a miniature heddle frame to show method of use.

Package marked "Brief of F. A. Chase & Co., Exhibit D," contains samples of German-style heddles with the strands separated to show construction.

D. The "German-style" heddle was first imported into this country in approximately 1889. The use of this style of heddle has been gradually increasing since that year, until at the present time the "German-style" heddle has largely supplanted the "American-style" heddle.

E. The manufacture of the "German-style" heddle was commenced in this country in 1902, and in 1903 the heddles were and since have been produced commercially in this country.

F. Prior to the manufacture of the "German-style" heddle in the United States, this style of heddle was sold at prices much higher than those which now obtain. For example, a 10-inch, No. 28 heddle, which is a usual size, in 1903 was sold at $1.50 per thousand net to the consumer. At the present time, these heddles are sold by importers at a price as low as $1 per thousand.

G. The German manufacturers have manifested and still manifest a determined purpose to reduce prices to a point which will render competition by American manufacturers ruinous to the American. The Germans are represented in America practically by two agents, one located at Boston, Mass., and the other at Leicester, Mass., and through these two agents control the market prices of the imported heddles. The present law is of great assistance to the foreign manufacturer in his efforts to stifle the American attempts to establish and develop this new industry.

The German manufacturers can, and it is believed do, import into this country the heddles manufactured by them at a valuation less than the prices charged by them at home for heddles of the same kind. The factors which enter into the cost of manufacture of twin-wire heddles are labor, raw material, and return on invested capital.

1. Labor is the principal factor. The labor in the manufacture of the foreign heddle is furnished by girls whose weekly wages average from $1.44 to $2.16. The weekly wages paid in this country for like work average from $6 to $8, or practically four times the wages paid in the foreign country.

2. The price of the raw material is established by the present tariff. The only raw material is the tinned wire of which the heddles are constructed and the solder. By paragraph 137, the duty on the wire is 40 per cent ad valorem, and in addition two-tenths of 1 cent per pound on account of the tin coating.

Whether the American manufacturer uses wire of foreign or domestic manufacture, the price to him is substantially the same. It is determined by the duty of 40 per cent ad valorem and two-tenths of 1 per cent per pound. Under the present law, the duty upon the completed heddles is 40 per cent ad valorem on the wire of which the heddle is composed, two-tenths of 1 per cent per pound for the tin coating, and in addition 1¼ cents per pound.

The difference in the duty upon the wire and upon the manufactured article is only 1¼ cents a pound. This is an average difference of 3 cents per thousand on the manufactured article. Assuming an honest valuation of the wire by the importer of heddles, this difference is too little to enable the American manufacturer to pay the American rate of wages and produce the heddles in competition with the foreigner. Much less can he successfully engage in such competition when the imported heddles are regularly and persistently undervalued by importers. It is the question constantly presented in tariff regulation, Shall the wages of American labor be protected and maintained?

3. The return on the capital invested under the present tariff is conspicuous by its absence, and to discuss it is to discuss an abstraction.

Because of the lack of differential between the duty on the wire and the duty on the heddle, it is all that the manufacturer can do to meet the requirements of American wage-earners and the market-demoralizing prices of his foreign competitor. The manufacture of the twin-wire heddle has required the investment of a large amount of capital, at first in experimental manufacture and afterwards and now in the creation and maintenance of plant and costly machinery. Unless there shall be made the change in law requested in this brief, or some other change effectual to prevent the German from under-selling the American at a profit to the German, but preventing profit, and, in many cases, causing positive loss to the American, the American heddle manufacturer will be forced to close his factory and leave the field to his foreign rival. Results: The price will immedi-ately advance to the old rate as it was before an attempt was made to establish this new American industry, no benefit to the American consumer, and loss to and hardship upon the American producer.

Respectfully submitted.

F. A. CHASE & CO.,
GIBBS LOOM, HARNESS AND REED COMPANY,
HOWARD BROTHERS MANUFACTURING COMPANY,
J. H. WILLIAMS COMPANY,
By FREDERIC L. CHASE,
(Of the firm of F. A. Chase & Co.)

STEEL WOOL AND STEEL SHAVINGS.

[Paragraph 137.]

THE AMERICAN STEEL-WOOL MANUFACTURING COMPANY, NEW YORK CITY, ASKS FOR SPECIFIC ENUMERATION OF STEEL WOOL AND STEEL SHAVINGS.

NEW YORK, *December 2, 1908.*

Hon. SERENO E. PAYNE,
Chairman Committee on Ways and Means,
Washington, D. C.

SIR: Steel wool is a highly manufactured article requiring for its manufacture special and expensive machinery and tools and skilled labor. It is used by painters, woodworkers, etc., as an abrasive for the same purposes as sandpaper, emery paper, etc. Steel shavings are the coarser grades.

About ten years ago the Board of United States General Appraisers found that it should be classified under paragraph 135, but this decision was rendered on one-sided testimony, the importers falsely testifying that it was only a by-product and no witnesses were called to controvert this evidence. In 1904 the Treasury Depart-ment directed the collection of duties under paragraph 193, the Secretary drawing attention to the existing anomalous condition, by which some of the grades of this article paid a lower duty than the wire from which they were made. The Board of General Appraisers again found it to be dutiable under paragraph 135, holding that they were constrained to do so "in view of the former decision, but if it had been a new case they would have found for the Govern-ment on the new evidence (under paragraph 193);" a minority decision accompanying this dissented, not approving of the application of stare decisis, and claiming that the board should have found in accordance with the evidence submitted irrespective of any previous decision. The circuit court, on the appeal of both the Government and importer, upheld the board, also in view of stare decisis. The circuit court of appeals decided against the board's decision, as well as against the Government's contention, claiming that paragraph 137 covered the article. It laid stress on the fact that the decision was rendered on the shipment under protest only, as it had been conceded that the goods were made from wire. It held that in the case of each importation the collector would, of course, assess duty on the basis of the highest value of wire which the appearance of the article would warrant, and that if the value were less, or the gauge larger, it would be for the importer to inform the collector of those facts by satisfactory proofs.

As a matter of fact, the identity of the article from which steel wool is made is entirely lost. It is made not only from steel wire, but also from sheet steel, band, and plates (see various patents), so that it is obvious to what confusion and possible fraud the enforcement of the collection of duties under this decision would lead.

Irrespective of all the foregoing, there is positively no question as to the intent of the tariff having been that just such articles as steel wool should come under paragraph 193, which paragraph is really nullified by this decision, for no article made of steel is a more highly manufactured or finished article than steel wool, for the production of which is required expensive and special machinery and tools and the greatest skill, labor forming the greatest part of its cost. This view is also taken by the Treasury Department, where the claim that steel wool rightfully belonged under paragraph 193 has always been maintained.

As steel wool and steel shavings are now recognized staple articles in the trade, we beg to request that the same be enumerated, and to guard against undervaluation, as has been practiced for years, the government having made some confiscations and the Board of General Appraisers raised the values repeatedly (at one time over 200 per cent), we further request that a specific duty be levied. The wages to operators, machinists, and others engaged in the manufacturing of this article in Germany, are approximately one-third of those paid in this country, and labor forms the principal part of the cost of the goods (about 60 per cent); the difference in rent, power, and other expenses, as well as in the material and other necessary articles, is also considerable.

The actual difference in the cost of production between Europe and this country is 9 cents on the coarsest grade and 24 cents on the finest grade of steel wool and about 6 cents on steel shavings. The difference in the cost of production of No. 1 and No. 2 is about 11 cents per pound, and as the sale of these two numbers is greater than of all the others combined (including steel shavings), we request the assessment of duties at the rate of 11 cents per pound on steel wool and steel shavings.

We are impelled to make this suggestion, as we find and are informed by the Government's appraising officer and scientist that it is very difficult, almost impossible, to determine the actual thickness or width of the threads of these articles, so as to distinguish them reliably and draw a line between the coarser grade of steel wool and the finer of steel shavings. To guard against confusion or fraud, it will be to the interest of the Government to let one rate apply on all. The consumption of steel shavings in this country is very small, and the excess of duty which would be collected on steel shavings is more than offset by the benefit which the importers will have on No. 0 and No. 00 steel wool, as the difference in the cost of production on the former is 15 cents and on the latter 24 cents per pound.

We would also beg to suggest that in enumerating the articles these words be added, "or called by any other name," and that the weight of the wrapper be included when imported in pound or other packages.

The freight charges from Europe to this country need not be taken into consideration, being less than 1 cent per pound. To Chicago (which is the principal market for steel wool) the rate from New York is 75 cents per 100 pounds, and only 87½ cents from German and Swiss points.

We are prepared to supply your committee with any additional facts you may require, and beg to add that the price of the goods to the consumer or even the dealer would not be affected by the duty proposed by us. Our object has steadfastly been to market our product with as close a margin as possible, in order to create a general demand for the same by its displacing other abrasives. It has been solely through us that the selling price has been lowered to the present figures—the importers charging vastly higher prices until forced to reduce them.

As the duty proposed by us merely covers the difference in the cost of production, competition between the European and the American manufacturers will continue as it has during the years that the Government has been collecting duty under paragraph 193, in accordance with the Treasury Department's ruling.

While the importers have always been eager for profit, we have documentary evidence to show that their principal object is the output, looking upon the American market as their dumping ground. For this reason we would have been justified in asking for a higher duty, but we only ask for the actual difference in the cost of producing the goods, which is, we believe, also in the spirit of the present and coming administration.

We would add that we can prove that operators whom we pay $7.50 to $8 per week are paid $2.25 to $2.50 in Germany, while machinists are paid $6 to $7 in Germany, against $18 to $30 with us, and the wages paid these people are about 60 per cent of the cost of the goods and over 75 per cent of the manufacturing cost.

In closing our appeal for revision, we respectfully represent to your committee that if a fair and just duty is not imposed on these articles and the paragraph referring to it be not cleared from possible misconstruction by the appraising officers, we may have to abandon our industry, discharge our help (nearly a hundred people), and throw our machinery into the scrap pile, losing all of the capital invested and naught would result from our labors of thirteen years to establish this branch of American manufacture.

Yours, very respectfully,

AMERICAN STEEL WOOL MFG. CO.,
H. WOLF, *Secretary and Treasurer.*

CARD CLOTHING.

[Paragraph 146.]

VARIOUS AMERICAN MANUFACTURERS OF CARD CLOTHING ASK FOR AN INCREASE OF DUTY ON THE MANUFACTURES OR A DECREASE OF DUTY ON RAW MATERIALS.

WASHINGTON, D. C., *November 25, 1908.*

COMMITTEE ON WAYS AND MEANS,
Washington, D. C.

GENTLEMEN: The card-clothing industry is engaged in the production of an article that does not enter into general consumption. The demand for it is consequently limited. But, while the amount of possible production is comparatively small, that industry requires a relatively large amount of capital—probably the largest amount of capital for the value of the goods produced of any industry. In this country, in round numbers, $1,200,000 of capital is employed in the annual production of $1,200,000 worth of goods.

The manufacture of card clothing in the country is an industry that needs increased protection. First, because it pays to its employees wages 150 per cent higher than the wages paid to workmen of the same class in foreign countries. The American manufacturer can not, therefore, under present tariff conditions successfully compete with foreign manufacturers in the labor market; second, because, under the present tariff, in most cases, the duty on the materials entering into the construction of card clothing is greater proportionately than the duty on the manufactured article.

Paragraph 146 provides for card clothing manufactured from tempered steel wire, 45 cents per square foot, all other card clothing 20 cents per square foot.

The two articles entering mostly in the manufacture of card clothing are card cloth and card wire. Card cloth consists either of a certain number of plies of cotton and linen, a certain number of plies of cotton, linen, and rubber, a certain number of plies of cotton, linen, and wool, or a certain number of plies of cotton, linen, wool, and rubber.

The first two items are subject to a duty of 45 per cent ad valorem, while the other two are dutiable at 44 cents a pound and 50 per cent ad valorem, and if valued over 70 cents a pound, 44 cents a pound and 55 per cent ad valorem, which is equivalent to 125 to 160 per cent duty.

The wire is subject to a duty of 40 per cent ad valorem, if same is round (par. 137). Any other 45 per cent, and if tin coated, two-tenths cent per pound additional.

Card clothing is subject to a specific rate, regardless of the materials entering into its construction.

In 1897 there were 1,600 card-setting machines in operation, while in 1906 and 1907, two good business years, there were only 1,039 such machines in operation. Likewise the amount of American-made card clothing used in this country has steadily decreased, while the amount of imported clothing has increased. Statistics show that the total sales of card clothing for the year ending June 30, 1906, were 1,813,685 square feet, of which 422,946 square feet were imported, and for the year ending June 30, 1907, were 1,399,054 square feet, of which 464,716 square feet were imported. It may be noted in this connection that one-third of the total amount sold in this country was imported.

This does not include the card clothing that has been imported with carding machinery since the decision rendered by the general appraisers December 12, 1906 (G. A. 6490, T. D. 27760), which was confirmed by the United States circuit court, district of Massachusetts, December 31, 1907 (T. D. 28688), and was acquiesced in by the Treasury Department February 3, 1908 (T. D. 28732). Since this ruling card clothing imported with carding machinery has paid an ad valorem duty of 45 per cent under paragraph 193, which means that this card clothing only pays a duty of 25 cents per square foot on the lowest-priced card clothing and a duty of 36 cents per square foot on the highest-priced card clothing.

We claim that this was not the intention of the present tariff bill, as it gives a decided advantage to the importer and does not allow the card-clothing manufacturer a chance to compete for this class of work.

The following diagram shows the gradual increase of importations since the Dingley tariff law was enacted:

Year ending June 30—

Year		
1897	203,502.01 square feet tempered steel, at 40 cents per square foot.	
	4,411.77 square feet others, at 20 cents per square foot.	
	13,289.00 square feet tempered steel, at 40 cents per square foot.	
1898	170,662.00 square feet tempered steel, at 45 cents per square foot.	
	5,772.00 square feet others, at 20 cents per square foot.	
1899	319,618.83 square feet tempered steel.	
	3,060.01 square feet others.	
1900	462,192.84 square feet tempered steel.	
	5,031.48 square feet others.	
1901	328,676.94 square feet tempered steel.	
	8,305.00 square feet others.	
1902	267,723.74 square feet tempered steel.	
	3,524.61 square feet others.	
1903	410,307.26 square feet tempered steel.	
	7,105.33 square feet others.	
1904	410,987.67 square feet tempered steel.	
	5,214.33 square feet others.	
1905	408,320.67 square feet tempered steel.	
	4,732.67 square feet others.	
1906	413,244.82 square feet tempered steel.	
	9,702.00 square feet others.	
1907	453,118.23 square feet tempered steel.	
	11,598.17 square feet others.	

These importations were a large increase over the years previous to the enactment of the Dingley law.

Inasmuch as the card-clothing manufacturers of the United States are at so great a disadvantage under the present tariff and are consequently gradually losing their business to the foreign makers, we would respectfully ask that the rate of duty assessed upon card clothing be as follows:

Per square foot.

Card clothing manufactured from round, tempered, steel wire, unless otherwise provided for in this act_____ $0.50

Card clothing made of felt face, wool face of a rubber face cloth containing wool_____ .55

Card clothing manufactured with plated wire, brass wire, bronze wire, double convex wire, angular wire, sectoral wire, and all others not specially provided for in this act_____ .55

Card clothing manufactured of round iron wire_____ .20

Unattached card clothing, imported with machinery, shall be classified as card clothing and pay the rate of duty specified in this act.

Or, in lieu of increasing the present rates on the manufactured product, that such a reduction be made in the present tariff on the materials from which card clothing is made as will enable the domestic manufacturers to compete successfully with their foreign rivals.

With this brief we deposit samples, with tables showing comparative cost price of card clothing made in England and the United States.

Respectfully submitted.

By GEORGE L. HAMILTON,
North Andover, Mass.
For HOWARD BROS. MFG. CO.,
Worcester, Mass.
BECKWITH CARD CO.,
Stafford Springs, Conn.
AMERICAN CARD CLOTHING CO.,
Worcester, Mass.
BENJAMIN BOOTH & CO.,
Philadelphia, Pa.
AMSTERDAM CARD CLOTHING CO.,
Amsterdam, N. Y.
LEICESTER CARD CLOTHING CO.,
Leicester, Mass.
METHUEN NAPPER CO.,
Methuen, Mass.
ASHWORTH BROTHERS,
Fall River, Mass.
DAVIS & FURBER MACHINE CO.,
North Andover, Mass.

GEORGE L. HAMILTON, NORTH ANDOVER, MASS., FOR AMERICAN CARD-CLOTHING MANUFACTURERS, SUBMITS ADDITIONAL INFORMATION RELATIVE TO COST OF MAKING.

WASHINGTON, D. C., *December 1, 1908.*

COMMITTEE ON WAYS AND MEANS,
Washington, D. C.

GENTLEMEN: We beg to submit the following information:

Comparative cost price of 1 square foot of card clothing set with 6-ply, 4-millimeter, felt-faced cloth and No. 34 hardened and tempered steel wire.

England.

1 square foot of cloth	$0.2858	
Add one-fourth margin	.0714	
	$0.3572	
1 pound of wire	.1888	
Manufacturing expenses	.1500	
Cost price in England	.6960	
Duty	.45	
Freight and charges	.03	
		.4800
		1.1760

United States.

1 square foot of cloth		$0. 2858
Duty, freight, and charges		. 4031
		. 6889
Add one-fourth margin		. 1722
		$0. 8611
1 pound of wire		. 1888
Duty, freight, and charges		. 0805
		. 2693
Manufacturing expenses		. 3500
		1. 4804

The duty on the materials to make 1 square foot of this card clothing is—

For card cloth	$0. 5039
For card wire	. 0805
Total	. 5844

The rate on the finished article is $0.4500 per square foot.

Cost of materials.

6-ply 4-millimeter felt face cloth:

Cost in England	10s. 6d. per sq. yd.	
or	$. 2858 per sq. ft.	
Weight of 1 sq. ft	9. 1 ounces	
Cost of 1 lb	. 5025	
Duty one pound	$. 44000	
and 50% ad val	. 25125	
	$. 69125 or per sq. ft	$. 3931
	Fght. & charges	. 0100
	Duty, fght., & charges	$. 4031

No. 34 hardened and tempered steel wire:

Cost in England per stone	9s. 3d.	
or	$. 1888 per lb.	
Duty 40% ad val	$. 0755	
Fght. & charges	. 005	
	Duty, fght., & charges	$. 0805

Comparative cost price of 1 square foot of card clothing set with woolen cloth (1 linen, 1 cotton), natural rubber face, and No. 32 hardened and tempered steel wire:

England.

1 square foot of cloth		$0. 2813
Add ¼ margin		. 0702
		$0. 3515
1 pound of wire		. 1463
Manufacturing expenses		.1500
Cost price in England		. 6478
Duty	$0. 45	
Freight and charges	. 03	
		. 4800
		1. 1278

United States.

1 square foot of cloth_____	$0. 2813
Duty, freight, and charges_____	. 3242
	.6055
Add ¼ margin_____	. 1514
	$0. 7569
1 pound of wire_____	. 1463
Duty, freight, and charges_____	. 0635
	. 2098
Manufacturing expenses_____	. 3500
	1. 3167

The duty on the materials to make 1 square foot of this card clothing is—

For card cloth_____	$0. 4052
For card wire _____	. 0635
Total _____	.4687

The rate on the finished article is $0.4500 per square foot.

Cost of materials.

Woolen cloth (1 linen, 1 cotton) natural rubber face:

Cost in England_____	10s. 4d. per sq. yd.	
or_____	$. 2813 per sq. ft.	
Weight of 1 sq. ft_____	5.8 ounces.	
Cost of 1 lb_____	. 776	
Duty one pound_____	$. 44	
and 55% ad val_____	. 4268	
	$. 8668 or per sq. ft_____	$. 3142
	Freight & charges__	. 0100
	Duty, fght., & charges_____	$. 3242

No. 32 hardened and tempered steel wire:

Cost in England per stone (12 lbs.)_____	7s. 2d.	
or_____	$. 1463 per lb.	
Duty 40% ad val_____	$. 0585	
Freight & charges_____	. 005	
Duty, freight, and charges_____		$. 0635

Comparative cost price of 1 square foot of card clothing set with 7-ply, wool-faced cloth and No. 22/26 double convex hardened and tempered steel wire.

England.

1 square foot of cloth_____	$0. 2950
Add ¼ margin _____	. 0736
	$0. 3686
1½ pounds of wire, at $0.1548_____	. 2322
Manufacturing expenses _____	. 1500
Cost price in England _____	. 7508
Duty_____	. 4500
Freight and charges_____	. 0300
	. 4800
	1. 2308

United States.

```
1 square foot of cloth _____ $0. 2950
Duty, freight, and charges_____   . 4160
                                                             --------
                                                               . 7110
Add ¼ margin_____   . 1776
                                                             --------  $0. 8886
1½ pounds of wire_____   . 2322
Duty, freight, and charges_____   . 1102
                                                             --------
                                                               . 3424
Manufacturing expenses _____   . 3500
                                                             --------
                                                             1. 5810
```

The duty on the materials to make 1 square foot of this card clothing is—

```
For card cloth_____ $0. 5200
For card wire _____   . 1102
                                                             --------
    Total _____   . 6302
```

The rate of the finished article is (per square foot) $0.4500.

Cost of materials.

```
7-ply wool-faced cloth :
    Cost in England _____ 10s. 10d.  per sq. yd.
        or _____     $. 2950 per sq. ft.
    Weight of 1 sq. ft_____              9.4 ounces.
    Cost of 1 lb_____     $. 5021

    Duty one lb _____     $. 44
    and 50% ad val_____      $. 2510 or per sq. ft _____ $. 4060
                                        ----------
                                Freight & charges_____  . 01
                                                                    --------
                                                                    $. 4160
```

```
No. 22/26 double convex hardened and tempered steel wire:
    Cost in England per stone(12 lbs.)_  7s. 7d.
        or _____  $. 1548  per lb.

    Duty 45% ad val_____   . 0696
    Freight & charges_____   . 0050
                                  --------
                    Duty, freight, & charges_____ $. 0746
```

Comparative cost price of 1 square foot of brush clothing set with woolen cloth (1 linen), red rubber face and No. 28 brass wire.

England.

```
1 square foot of cloth_____ $0. 2926
Add ¼ margin_____   . 0734
                                                             --------  $0. 3660
1.8 pounds of wire at $0.2654_____   . 4777
Manufacturing expenses_____   . 1500
                                                             --------
    Cost price in England_____   . 9937
Duty_____  . 20
Freight and charges _____  . 03
                                                             --------
                                                               . 2300
                                                             --------
                                                             1. 2237
```

United States.

```
1 square foot of cloth----------------------------------------- $0. 2926
Duty, freight, and charges------------------------------------   . 3541
                                                                 ───────
                                                                  . 6467
Add ¼ margin --------------------------------------------------   . 1616
                                                                 ───────  $0. 8083
1.8 pounds of wire, at $0.2654--------------------------------   . 4777
Duty, freight, and charges------------------------------------   . 2002
                                                                 ───────
                                                                  . 6779
Manufacturing expenses----------------------------------------   . 3500
                                                                 ───────
                                                                 1. 8362
```

The duty on the materials to make 1 square foot of this card clothing is—

```
For card cloth------------------------------------------------- $0. 4426
For card wire -------------------------------------------------   . 2002
                                                                 ───────
    Total -----------------------------------------------------   . 6428
```

The rate on the finished article is $0.2000 per square foot.

Cost of materials.

Woolen cloth (1 linen) red rubber face:

```
Cost in England----------------10s. 9d. per sq. yd.
    or----------------------- $. 2926 per sq. ft.
Weight of 1 sq. ft-----------  7.2 ounces.
Cost of 1 lb----------------- $. 6502

Duty one pound---------------   . 44
And 50 % ad val-------------   . 3251
                             ───────
                              . 7651 or per sq. ft------ $. 3441
                                     Freight & charges_  . 0100
                                                         ───────
                             Duty, freight & charges___ $. 3541
```

No. 28 brass wire:

```
Cost in England, per lb--------- 1s. 1d.
    or------------------------- $. 2654 per lb.

Duty 40% ad val-------------- $. 1062
Freight & charges-----------   . 0050
                             ───────
                  Duty, frght., & charges___ $. 1112
```

Comparative cost price of 1 square foot of napper clothing set with three-ply vulcanized rubber face and No. 28/32 sectoral phosphor bronze wire:

England.

```
One square foot of cloth--------------------------------------- $0. 2244
Add one-fourth margin-----------------------------------------   . 0560
                                                                 ───────  $0. 2804
One pound of wire---------------------------------------------   . 4500
Manufacturing expenses ---------------------------------------   . 1500
                                                                 ───────
    Cost price in England-------------------------------------   . 8804
Duty -----------------------------------------------------------  . 20
Freight and charges-------------------------------------------   . 03
                                                                 ───────   . 2300
                                                                 ───────
                                                                 1. 1104
```

United States.

```
One square foot of cloth_____ $0. 2244
Duty, freight, and charges_____   .1110
                                                          ————
                                                            .3354
Add one-fourth margin_____    .0838
                                                                    $0. 4192
One pound of wire_____    .4500
Duty, freight, and charges_____   .2075
                                                          ————
                                                            .6575
Manufacturing expenses _____    .3500
                                                                  ————
                                                                  1. 4267
```

The duty on the materials to make 1 square foot of this card clothing is:

```
For card cloth_____ $0. 1387
For card wire_____    .2075
                                                                  ————
    Total _____    .3462
```

The rate on the finished article is $0.2000 per square foot.

Cost of materials.

```
3-ply vulcanized rubber:
    Cost in England_____ 8s. 3d. per sq. yd.
        or _____ $. 2244 per sq. ft.

    Duty 45% ad val.
        Per sq. ft_____ $. 1010
        Freight & charges_____   .01
                                    ————
                        Duty, freight, & charges_____ $. 1110

No. 28/32 sectoral phosphor bronze wire:
    Cost in England, per lb_____ 1s. 10d.
        or _____ $. 4500 per lb.

    Duty 45%_____.  .2025
    Freight & charges_____   .0050
                                      ————
                        Duty, freight, & charges_____ $. 2075
```

EVAN ARTHUR LEIGH, BOSTON, MASS., ASKS FOR AD VALOREM DUTY AND NEW CLASSIFICATION FOR CARD CLOTHING.

30 CONGRESS STREET,
Boston, Mass., December 29, 1908.

COMMITTEE ON WAYS AND MEANS,
Washington, D. C.

GENTLEMEN: In reply to a memorial asking for an increase of duty upon card clothing signed by certain American manufacturers of card clothing we beg to submit the following:

The gentlemen are evidently mistaken when they assert that their industry requires " probably the largest amount of capital for the value of the goods produced of any industry in this country. In round numbers $1,200,000 of capital is employed in the annual production of $1,200,000 worth of goods." If they consult the memorial of certain American manufacturers of textile machinery on page

2711, first print No. 21, they will find that other industries require double the proportionate amount of capital that theirs does, as it appears that three textile machine shops employ, in round numbers, $14,000,000 of capital in the annual production of $7,000,000 worth of goods.

First. Let it be understood that if card clothing were not specially provided for in the tariff it would be dutiable under paragraph No. 193 of the present act as articles or wares in whole or in part of metal, at 45 per cent ad valorem. As card clothing made of round iron wire and dutiable at 20 cents per square foot is not imported to any extent, that feature of the subject may be eliminated, and we shall consider only card clothing dutiable at 45 per cent per square foot, which is the rate paid on all imported clothing, except such as comes in as a part of the carding machine and pays, under the decisions of the courts, 45 per cent ad valorem.

Since 1883 rates of duty on imported card clothing have been as follows, to wit:

1897. 146-card clothing manufactured from tempered steel wire, 45 cents per square foot; all other, 20 cents per square foot.

1894. 132-card clothing manufactured from tempered steel wire, 45 cents per square foot; all other, 20 cents per square foot.

1890. 159-card clothing, manufactured from tempered steel wire, 50 cents per square foot; all other, 25 cents per square foot.

1883. 411-card clothing, 25 cents per square foot; when manufactured from tempered steel wire, 45 cents per square foot.

showing that for more than twenty-five years card clothing has been subjected to a duty higher than that upon other articles or wares manufactured in whole or in part of metal. That such rates are excessive is well known to all persons familiar with textile industries, and yet, after all these years of excessive protection, according to their own statements, fully 33⅓ per cent of all the card clothing used in American mills is imported from England. It is this excessive protection that has enabled the American manufacturers of card clothing, though still using their antiquated methods and machinery, to combine together and maintain their prices just enough below the prices at which foreign clothing can be sold here so as to force an inferior product upon the American mills in all cases where quality is not of first importance. Under the present rates the American manufacturers undersell the importers in all instances, and are continually accepting orders at a large percentage under importers' prices, and importers themselves, in a case where the American article would answer, have bought card clothing from one of the signers of the petition now before you asking for an increase in duty, at more than 10 per cent below the cost of importing the same—allowing for no profit whatever to the importer.

If, with 45 per cent per square foot duty, the American manufacturers can secure two-thirds of the entire card-clothing business in the United States, would it be wise to increase the rate of duty and thereby cut off the importation of such merchandise, in this way reducing the Government's revenue and, at the same time, forcing the American mill owners to a further use of an inferior article?

That the present rate of duty on card clothing is excessive we propose to show from the American manufacturers' own statement.

On page 2040, first print, No. 17, in their remarks about the decisions of the courts, they say: " Since this ruling, card clothing imported with carding machinery has paid an ad valorem rate of duty of 45 per cent under paragraph 193, which means that this card clothing only pays a duty of 25 cents per square foot on the lowest-priced card clothing and a duty of 36 cents per square foot on the highest-priced card clothing."

If this is true, then each 1 cent per square foot means one twenty-fifth of 45 per cent, or $1\frac{8}{10}$ per cent ad valorem, and 45 cents per square foot equals 45 times $1\frac{8}{10}$ per cent, or 81 per cent ad valorem, on the lowest-priced clothing, while each 1 cent per square foot means one thirty-sixth of 45 per cent, or $1\frac{1}{4}$ per cent ad valorem, and 45 cents per square foot equals 45 times $1\frac{1}{4}$ per cent, or $56\frac{1}{4}$ per cent ad valorem on the highest-priced clothing. In other words, instead of being protected to the extent of 45 per cent ad valorem, as other manufacturers of " articles or wares in whole or in part of metal " are, the manufacturers of card clothing are enjoying protection, under the present tariff, to the extent of from $56\frac{1}{4}$ per cent on the highest priced to 81 per cent on the lowest-priced clothing.

Applying these simple calculations to the rates (55 cents per square foot) demanded in the coming revision of the tariff, we find that this infant industry is asking for protection to the extent of from $68\frac{3}{4}$ per cent on the highest-priced to 99 per cent on the lowest-priced clothing.

We note that other domestic interests before your committee have appealed to the promises made in the Republican platform and in the speeches of the President-elect, that in the revision of the tariff there shall be levied "such duties as will equal the difference between the costs of production at home and abroad, together with a reasonable profit to American industries," but that the American manufacturers of card clothing make no such appeal.

We can not account for this unless it be upon the theory that " figures talk " and that a rate of 99 per cent speaks for itself.

There is no need of an extra paragraph or provision for card clothing imported with carding machines, as the question of duty upon such clothing is of no importance whatever to the American manufacturer. English carding machines are invariably sold complete, which means that card clothing for the machine is included in the price, and in no case and under no circumstances would the machines be imported without the clothing, consequently the amount or rate of duty paid can in no way interest the American card-clothing manufacturer, while the difference between 45 per cent per square foot and 45 per cent ad valorem on what card clothing is imported into this country with carding machines is so little that it is of no practical importance to the Government and can be ignored without any appreciable harm to the country's revenue. We can state without fear of contradiction that since the decisions referred to on page 2040 the total value of card clothing imported into this country with carding machines has amounted to less, and considerably less, than $5,000.

The reason for this is that the present rate of 45 per cent on the carding machines themselves is practically prohibitive, so that the foreign manufacturer is almost entirely excluded from this market and the importations of such machines reduced to an insignificant item.

We beg further to call your attention to the fact that the manufacture of card clothing involves, proportionately, less manual labor than almost any known manufacturing industry in the world, and that the duty on card clothing only protects a very small number of laboring people, probably 200 to 300 persons in the whole United States, and, in order to do this, the American cotton spinners have to pay duties so enormous that we have no doubt it would provide a very handsome pension for every working man, woman, or child in the card-clothing trade in the United States. At all events, the number of working people to be affected is too small to warrant an increase in protection, which is already absurdly excessive, and which, to benefit them at all, must either be at the expense of the American cotton manufacturers or else at the expense of the Government's revenue.

For the reasons above set out we ask, in good faith, that in the new tariff the duty on card clothing be made the same rate ad valorem that is imposed upon other articles or wares in whole or in part of metal.

Respectfully submitted.

SEARLE & PILLSBURY.
(For Evan Arthur Leigh, Importer of Card Clothing.)

CAST-IRON PIPE.

[Paragraph 147.]

STATEMENT OF WALTER WOOD, OF 400 CHESTNUT STREET, PHILADELPHIA, PA., RELATIVE TO CAST-IRON PIPE.

TUESDAY, *December 15, 1908.*

(The witness was duly affirmed by the chairman.)

Mr. WOOD. Mr. Chairman, we are manufacturers of cast-iron pipe. The total business of the country is about three-quarters of a million tons. Our product is about 15 per cent of that amount. The trust in our business has a product of about 50 per cent of the total amount. The duty on cast-iron pipe is $8.96 a ton, which is about $5 above the duty on pig iron. It is essential to state it this way to compare it with pig iron, the duty of which is on the gross ton. Pig iron is essentially the largest factor in our manufacture, and whatever you put the pig-iron duty at will be the basis really for estimating the duty on cast-iron pipe. If you reduce pig iron a dollar, that, of course, takes a dollar off the duty on pipe.

The CHAIRMAN. How much pipe would a ton of pig iron make?

Mr. WOOD. There is only about 3 to 5 per cent waste. The waste is a negligible quantity in a broad discussion, but when we come down to our drawbacks we are allowed 5 per cent waste. If there is $2 to come off pig iron, the cast-iron pipe man can stand $2 additional. The duty on pipe being $5 above pig iron, or $9, nearly, is a duty larger than the market really demands, and to that extent is too high; and to that extent also it is detrimental to the comfortable growth of the business.

The CHAIRMAN. What is the labor cost of pipe?

Mr. WOOD. The labor cost in the foundry runs from about $5 to $5.50 per ton, according to the character and weight of the individual pieces of pipe. The material cost, such as coal and other materials which go into the manufacture, will run from $2.50 to $3. The overhead charges of the manufactory will amount to about $1.25—that is, maintenance and sinking fund and various items—and selling expense will be about another dollar, making a total cost, roughly, of about $10 a ton.

The CHAIRMAN. The cost of converting pig iron into pipe is about $10 a ton?

Mr. WOOD. We can roughly put it at $10 a ton.

The CHAIRMAN. And the pig iron is worth, say, $14 to make it, and the pipe would cost $24?

Mr. WOOD. That is a short way of getting at it, sir.

The CHAIRMAN. What is the labor cost in Great Britain?

Mr. WOOD. To answer that question accurately would require a knowledge of their figures. We take it, from what we hear of the general trade abroad, that their costs abroad are, as near as may be, $2 less than ours.

The CHAIRMAN. The total cost of converting pig iron into pipe is $2 less than yours?

Mr. WOOD. Approximately. We take that from what we see of the quotations as bid for contracts.

The CHAIRMAN. Does that correspond with your experience in running in competition with the imported pipe, or is there any imported?

Mr. WOOD. There is practically no pipe imported because the duty is excessive. There has been some imported in the last year. We imported some into California ourselves in the past year.

Mr. DALZELL. There was more last year, 1907, than ever before, according to the statistics.

Mr. WOOD. Roughly, I should say that that is correct.

Mr. DALZELL. One million eight hundred and ninety-eight thousand five hundred and four pounds.

The CHAIRMAN. At what price is that, Mr. Dalzell?

Mr. DALZELL. About 1.3 cents per pound.

Mr. WOOD. That would be roughly correct, sir.

The CHAIRMAN. It is said generally by all concerns that manufacture things that there were lighter imports in 1907 than any other year.

Mr. WOOD. The prices here were high, higher than they really ought to have been, and the importations were possible.

The CHAIRMAN. As to the cost of converting pig iron into pipe, the difference in the cost between this country and abroad is about $2 per ton?

Mr. WOOD. I did not put it in excess of that, sir.

The CHAIRMAN. I would like it if you would give the committee the items of cost—the cost of the pig iron, the coke, and the other materials they may use; and the labor cost per ton of converting the pig iron into pipe.

Mr. WOOD. I think I have given that to you with pretty thorough minuteness, Mr. Chairman, excepting that you might divide your supplies, which I put down at $2.50 to $3—half between coal and half miscellaneous supplies, like wood and tar and pitch and sand, and a large number of little things that every manufacturer has to use. I have given you the labor, the coal, the miscellaneous supplies, the overhead charges, and the selling price all in detail.

The CHAIRMAN. Have you given us the cost of your general force in the office?

Mr. WOOD. I did that in saying a dollar a ton for selling charges.

The CHAIRMAN. You have given us everything excepting the cost of the few incidentals.

Mr. WOOD. I have not got them in my head.

The CHAIRMAN. What would cover that?

Mr. WOOD. About $1.25 to $1.50 ought to cover the supplies, and about $1.25 to $1.50 ought to cover the coal.

The CHAIRMAN. With a differential of $5 is it your idea that the business could then stand and still be on a protected basis?

Mr. WOOD. Our business would be thoroughly protected, sir, if we had a duty of $3 above that of pig iron.

The CHAIRMAN. And only $2 difference in labor. Suppose there is a difference in the cost of supplies——

Mr. WOOD. There is this point to be borne in mind. The computation of $2 which you are alluding to means at the factory in America. Now, the factory in America must have a certain market in order to run, and the freight from Glasgow or Middlesboro to Boston or to Charleston is the same as it would be to Philadelphia and New York; consequently they put their goods at those points at the same price as they would at our home port, while we have to pay about $2 to $3 to reach the different points on the seaboard.

The CHAIRMAN. How much does it cost you for freight to New York?

Mr. WOOD. Freight to New York, I think, is $1.25 a ton, sir; but I am speaking from memory.

Mr. UNDERWOOD. On pig iron or bar?

Mr. WOOD. Cast-iron pipe, sir, is the point I am speaking to.

The CHAIRMAN. What is the freight from Glasgow?

Mr. WOOD. Glasgow to New York—I am speaking of a supposed rate, because there is no published rate. It would roughly be, I should say, from $2 to $3 a ton, according to the contract that they were able to make with the steamship that brought it over.

The CHAIRMAN. Then you do better on freight rates?

Mr. WOOD. At the home port. At Philadelphia our freight would be 50 cents. To Boston or Charleston, $2 to $3; or, to go farther, the California coast, they would get decidedly a better freight rate than we would. The question of protection between what you might call the Atlantic States and the Pacific States is a very serious question.

The CHAIRMAN. What is your freight rate from your point of production to Boston?

Mr. WOOD. $2.70 by rail and about $1.75 by water.

The CHAIRMAN. And to Charleston?

Mr. WOOD. To Charleston it would be about, I should say, $2.50 by water and probably $4 to $5 by rail. I am speaking in a casual way, sir, because I haven't the exact data in mind.

The CHAIRMAN. Do you have a market at Charleston?

Mr. WOOD. No; because that is controlled by the Alabama producers of castings.

The CHAIRMAN. You do not know what it is from the Alabama producing districts to Charleston, I suppose?

Mr. WOOD. I do not accurately know, sir.

The CHAIRMAN. That answers the question.

Mr. BOUTELL. Mr. Wood, how long have you been in business?

Mr. WOOD. Personally, I have been in the business about forty years, sir.

Mr. BOUTELL. The duty on these pipes under the McKinley law was nine-tenths of a cent a pound.

Mr. WOOD. Very possibly, sir; I do not know.

Mr. BOUTELL. And under the Wilson bill six-tenths of a cent a pound and under the present bill four-tenths of a cent a pound.

Mr. WOOD. Very probably, sir.

Mr. BOUTELL. In other words, the present duty is about one-third less than it was under the Wilson bill. What I wanted to ask was whether those changes from nine-tenths of a cent to six-tenths of a cent, and now to four-tenths of a cent, represented pretty fairly the difference in the cost of production at home and abroad at those periods?

Mr. WOOD. I should think that they were always in excess of the cost abroad, sir.

Mr. BOUTELL. So that your suggestion now is that the four-tenths of a cent be lowered?

Mr. WOOD. We can stand a reduction on the four-tenths of a cent and yet control the market.

Mr. BOUTELL. What rate would you suggest, that pig iron remain as it is?

Mr. WOOD. Pig iron remaining as it is, a differential of not over $3 a ton above pig iron—of course that would throw the California——

Mr. BOUTELL. Have you figured out what that would be as expressed in the terms of the tariff, per pound?

Mr. WOOD. It would figure out about one and one-third tenths cent of a cent per pound.

Mr. NEEDHAM. You started to say something about California in your answer just now.

Mr. WOOD. The point is this, sir, that the freight from all of our establishments to California by rail is about $14.50 a ton—gross ton. By water it is about $9 to $10 a ton. The rate from England to the California coast varies according to the character of the shipment from $6 to $15, whether it is by a small shipment in a merchant vessel or whether it is a full cargo by a tramp; so that, as to California, we would either have to have a higher duty on our pipe or California will get the foreign product, or vice versa, she will get the home product and the East would have the lower duty.

Mr. NEEDHAM. This would not be a disadvantage at all to the California consumer?

Mr. WOOD. Not the least, sir.

Mr. HILL. Do you export?

Mr. WOOD. We did at one time; very largely ten years ago.

Mr. HILL. To what countries?

Mr. Wood. I could easier tell you the countries to which we didn't export.

Mr. Hill. But most of the countries of Europe?

Mr. Wood. Abroad; everywhere excepting the Mediterranean and Australia.

Mr. Hill. The Orient, India, and China?

Mr. Wood. Yes; India, not Australia, also to China and Japan, Africa, and England.

Mr. Hill. Did you get drawbacks on that?

Mr. Wood. Not at that time, because we were using domestic iron.

Mr. Hill. If you can compete in China and Japan, why can you not compete at San Francisco with the foreign manufacturers—on equal terms with the foreign manufacturers?

Mr. Wood. Shall I clarify your question a little, sir?

Mr. Hill. Yes; all of my ideas, if you can.

Mr. Wood. If we start on equal values of pig iron, we can not compete in California, as we have a $14.50 freight rate, and England, with tramp steamers under favorable conditions, has from six to seven dollar freight rate.

Mr. Hill. Simply because of the difference in freight?

Mr. Wood. In handling a product like ours freight cuts a very large figure.

Mr. Hill. Does the same difference in freight rate exist so far as China and Japan are concerned, or betwen England and Philadelphia?

Mr. Wood. Sometimes, sir. It varies sometimes so that we have had cheaper rates to China than London has had, while sometimes it is otherwise.

Mr. Hill. Is that the only reason why you can not compete at San Francisco with England, the question of freight rates?

Mr. Wood. Freight rates.

Mr. Hill. You do compete in China and Japan, or you did, on equal terms?

Mr. Wood. When we had equal iron, iron on the same basis, we had a fair chance of competing in Japan and China.

Mr. Hill. What do you mean by "equal iron on the same basis?"

Mr. Wood. Iron at the present time is selling in England on the basis of about $12 a ton. At the present time in this country it is selling on the basis of about $16.50 a ton.

Mr. Hill. The difference between England and this country now is the full difference of the tariff?

Mr. Wood. The difference that exists now; yes, sir.

Mr. Hill. Have you any knowledge as to the cause of that full difference now, and no difference a while ago when the tariff was just the same?

Mr. Wood. It was the difference in the cost of ore, sir, largely, and made up of other things as well.

Mr. Hill. The difference then, now, is the difference in the cost of the ore, not the tariff?

Mr. Wood. That is the largest one item.

The Chairman. Do you happen to remember what you paid for pig iron in 1896?

Mr. Wood. 1896, sir—perhaps the best way for me to answer your question intelligently would be to give you about that time, without any specific or particular year; but about $9.25 to $9.50 was what our pig iron cost us laid down in Philadelphia during the low period following the panic of 1893. Whether that was 1896 or 1897 I do **not** recollect at the moment.

The CHAIRMAN. Do you know what it was in 1897?

Mr. WOOD. As I say, I can not locate the particular year. I have given you the low price that was touched for Philadelphia iron.

The CHAIRMAN. Iron was higher in 1897, wasn't it?

Mr. WOOD. I believe I have covered your question, because I say I do not recollect exactly which year was the lowest.

The CHAIRMAN. As to the domestic pig iron that you bought—I suppose you bought the domestic pig iron as a general rule?

Mr. WOOD. We aim to buy foreign pig iron for our foreign orders.

The CHAIRMAN. And get a drawback?

Mr. WOOD. And get a drawback.

The CHAIRMAN. But for your domestic trade you use domestic iron, do you not?

Mr. WOOD. Excepting when the market runs away and gets so high, then we import.

The CHAIRMAN. It does sometimes happen that you buy foreign instead of domestic on account of the price?

Mr. WOOD. Yes.

The CHAIRMAN. The general domestic price has been considerably less than the foreign, plus the tariff?

Mr. WOOD. Moderately less.

The CHAIRMAN. What do you mean by "moderately" less?

Mr. WOOD. Take it at the present time; it would cost about $18 to import English pig, and the present market for southern pig, delivered at Philadelphia, of the same quality, would be about $17.

Mr. GAINES. Why does not the drawback clause give you equal iron for export? Is it because, on equal iron, you eliminate the question of freights?

Mr. WOOD. The location of the manufacturers abroad is such that there is one large manufacturer who pays practically no freight, and the next largest manufacturer pays about $1.50 freight. We pay $2 freight. When I say the freight, I mean the cost of——

Mr. DALZELL. What is the name of your firm?

Mr. WOOD. R. D. Wood & Co.

Mr. HILL. I understood you to say that the difference in the cost of pig iron was largely the difference in the cost of the ore. Was that correct?

Mr. WOOD. Yes, sir.

Mr. HILL. Have we not the largest ore supply of any country in the world?

Mr. WOOD. I take it that China has. But there is no doubt that the Lake Superior ore——

Mr. HILL. Are not our ore beds more economically worked than in any other country in the world?

Mr. WOOD. That I can not tell you, but there is no doubt but what they are very economically worked.

Mr. HILL. What is the reason why ore costs more here than in England, if we have a larger supply and it is more economically worked?

Mr. WOOD. Well, I can not tell you the real reason.

Mr. HILL. What do you think is the reason?

Mr. WOOD. Because the price is "pegged."

Mr. GAINES. Held up, I suppose.

Mr. UNDERWOOD. Referring to Mr. Hill's question, as to the difference in the price of ore, it is purely a question of difference in freight rate, is it not; the difference in laying the ore down at the furnace? That is where the difference in the cost of ore at the furnace comes, and that is why the cost of iron is greater at Pittsburg than in England. The cost of laying the ore from the Mesabi mines down at Pittsburg is greater than laying the ore down at South Wales, Cumberland, or Lincolnshire, isn't it?

Mr. WOOD. The handling of ore from the ore bodies that you have spoken of is very small, but that is not the difference, sir. I think I explained the difference a moment ago.

Mr. RANDELL. I did not understand just exactly what you said. Did you say that it was a price that had to be paid that made the difference?

Mr. WOOD. I said "pegged."

Mr. UNDERWOOD. I don't understand what you mean by "pegged."

Mr. WOOD. You will have to ask the gentlemen who sell the ore. They can explain that better than I can. I do not know about their business.

Mr. RANDELL. Does that mean that they have the power to charge a certain price and that you have to pay it?

Mr. WOOD. I would rather your committee would find that out. I do not want to be responsible for any testimony excepting what relates to my business.

Mr. RANDELL. If the trouble is the price being "pegged," don't you think it would be better to look after the correction of that rather than make a tariff to suit the pegging price?

Mr. WOOD. That is a question for your committee, sir.

Mr. UNDERWOOD. You testified, I believe, as to the price of pig iron recently, and I would like to ask you, in connection with your comparison with the price of foreign iron, if you are familiar, in the last few years, with the prices of foreign and domestic iron?

Mr. WOOD. What year; 1907?

Mr. UNDERWOOD. I will ask you a specific question as to the German foundry iron in Germany. The price of that in January, 1906, was about $17.50 a ton; is that correct?

Mr. WOOD. I can not tell you whether it is correct or not, but it is very likely correct, because they have the same understandings which we have in this country.

Mr. UNDERWOOD. At the same time the value of the English iron at the furnace was about $14.

Mr. WOOD. In which year; 1906?

Mr. UNDERWOOD. January, 1906.

Mr. WOOD. January, 1906—we were importing iron at that time, and we were paying between $13 and $14 for it.

Mr. UNDERWOOD. In January, 1907, the next year, I will ask you if the German pig, in Germany, was worth about $20 a ton?

Mr. WOOD. I can not tell you what the figures were in Germany, sir.

Mr. UNDERWOOD. The selling price in Germany?

Mr. WOOD. I can not tell you, because the selling price in Germany is an artificial price; it is governed by syndicates.

Mr. UNDERWOOD. I understand; but still it is a selling price there, whether artificially made or not; it is the price on the market.

Mr. WOOD. Our business has never led us to look seriously into the German prices.

Mr. UNDERWOOD. The English price in January, 1907, was about $16, was it not?

Mr. WOOD. No, sir; I think you are a little high on that. I do not think Cleveland warrants have been over 50 to 54 shillings since that time; but I am speaking from memory only.

Mr. UNDERWOOD. I am giving you the top of the market in January, 1907.

Mr. WOOD. I am talking of what is known as ' Cleveland warrants," which is the standard reference for the stock markets on pig iron.

Mr. UNDERWOOD. What price do you fix in January, 1907?

Mr. WOOD. I am not fixing it in January, 1907. I am only saying in a general way that my impression is that the "Cleveland warrants" have run about from 50 to 54 shillings during the past twelve months.

Mr. UNDERWOOD. I do not want the last twelve months, for there is no use in trying those things during a panic, but rather under normal conditions. If you can answer I would like to know what you think the " Scotch warrants" were worth at the furnace about January, 1907.

Mr. WOOD. The trade papers can give you that, but you would be in error in taking " Scotch warrants." You ought to take Middlesboro warrants.

Mr. UNDERWOOD. Why?

Mr. WOOD. The tonnage of Middlesboro stock so overshadows the Scotch stock that it sets the real price.

Mr. UNDERWOOD. The reason I asked was that the quotations from the trade journals gave both.

Mr. WOOD. But what I say is correct as regards the market.

Mr. HILL. You think that the duty is too high on the cast-iron pipe anyhow, even if the pig iron remains as it is?

Mr. WOOD. Any duty that is more than enough is too high, and destructive to manufacturers.

Mr. HILL. If the entire duty were taken off of pig iron, you see no reason why an equivalent amount should not be taken from pipe?

Mr. WOOD. No; it would be a benefit to the business.

Mr. UNDERWOOD. If you take the entire duty off of pig iron, why should not the entire duty be taken off of iron pipe? Why not put both on the same basis?

Mr. WOOD. Because, sir, iron pipe—the conversion from pig iron to iron pipe is a question of labor.

Mr. UNDERWOOD. It is a question of labor from the ore to the furnace?

Mr. WOOD. But let me give you the whole answer, sir. The reason that the price of the conversion of pipe abroad costs a little less than in this country is a question of labor. In the manufacture of iron there is not (excepting in the transportation) very much labor. It is mostly machinery.

Mr. UNDERWOOD. The question of making pig iron?

Mr. WOOD. The question of making pig iron out of Lake Superior ore is a question, leaving out that of transportation——

Mr. UNDERWOOD. Well, now——

Mr. WOOD. Please let me answer your question, sir. The question of making pig iron out of Lake Superior ore, leaving out transportation and the wages of making the coke, is chiefly a question of machinery.

Mr. UNDERWOOD. Very well; now, let us see. Do you know that of your own knowledge, in the making of pig iron, or is that a guess?

Mr. WOOD. I can not give you the exact figures, but as I walk through my friend's large furnaces, mines, and rolling mills, it is very evident.

Mr. UNDERWOOD. What do you say is the cost of making pig iron at Pittsburg?

Mr. WOOD. I do not know, sir.

Mr. UNDERWOOD. Do you know how much it costs to produce the ore from the mines?

Mr. WOOD. I can make a guess, but I do not know.

Mr. UNDERWOOD. Do you know how much it costs to coke a ton of coke?

Mr. WOOD. Simply approximately, sir.

Mr. UNDERWOOD. Do you know how much it costs to lift the ore from the stock house to the bell of the furnace?

Mr. WOOD. The cost of running the skip up the inclined plane.

Mr. UNDERWOOD. Do you know how many men work in the stock house?

Mr. WOOD. I have not pretended to have that knowledge; I do not know.

Mr. UNDERWOOD. Do you know how many men work in the cast house?

Mr. WOOD. I guess it is mostly done by machine pouring, is it not, sir?

Mr. UNDERWOOD. To make cold pig—done by machine pouring?

Mr. WOOD. Largely, sir, but not altogether.

Mr. UNDERWOOD. Somebody has to fix the forms.

Mr. WOOD. That is done by machinery very generally.

Mr. UNDERWOOD. In the average furnace of the United States—I do not think so. Then you do not know what the cost in the cast house is; you do not know what it will cost in the stock house; you do not know the cost of a ton of ore, and you do not know the cost of a ton of coke—as a matter of fact, you really do not know what it costs to make a ton of pig iron—how much labor is in it?

Mr. WOOD. The answer to that is very plain, sir. A man in the pig-iron business knows those things, and a man who is not in the pig-iron business, but in the iron business generally, does not pretend to know exactly what all things cost.

Mr. UNDERWOOD. He does not know.

Mr. WOOD. He hasn't the exact figures.

Mr. UNDERWOOD. What did you pay for your pig in 1906?

Mr. WOOD. Oh, you are asking a fellow to recollect a lot—1906—I really could only give you a rough guess, because I haven't carried those figures in my mind, nor have I brought them with me. The market quotations will show, if you have them there, and perhaps that would be the easiest way to get at it.

Mr. UNDERWOOD. Take the cost of pig at your plant to-day on the present market prices, which are not as satisfactory as they were a year or two ago; what is the cost of pig to-day?

Mr. WOOD. The cost of pig to-day is from $16 to $16.50; that is, the quality that we use.

Mr. UNDERWOOD. Do you make a ton of pipe out of a ton of pig?

Mr. WOOD. Practically, sir, with the waste, as I answered your chairman, of from 3 to 5 per cent.

Mr. UNDERWOOD. How much is the wage that goes into a ton of pipe at your factory?

Mr. WOOD. I think I have given that before, but I will be glad to give it over again. The wage, in rough labor, runs from $5 to $5.50.

Mr. COCKRAN. Per what?

Mr. WOOD. Per ton. Of course, when you are making a very small pipe, a light pipe, it is more, and may run up to $6 or $7, if you take abnormal conditions; but I am taking a fair and square average.

Mr. UNDERWOOD. About $5.50 a ton for wages. What is the wage cost in making this same kind of pipe in England?

Mr. WOOD. I would like to find out, sir. We only have general results to judge those things by.

Mr. UNDERWOOD. And you are not informed then as to the wage scale in England at all?

Mr. WOOD. No more than I am of my competitors 4 miles away from me in America.

Mr. UNDERWOOD. You have no way to discover about the wage scale there?

Mr. WOON. I doubt, if I sat down with my friends on the other side, whether they would tell me. I have intended at various times to ask them that question.

Mr. UNDERWOOD. You sell this cast-iron pipe at your foundry at how much at the present time?

Mr. WOOD. At present we are lucky if we get $24.50, and we will sell you some at $24 if you want it real badly.

Mr. UNDERWOOD. The cost of pig iron is $16.90, the cost of labor is $5.50, that makes it cost you $22.40, and you sell it for $24.50, so that you have about $2 margin to cover everything at the present time.

Mr. WOOD. And are doing a losing business. Because of the high tariff which exists, in the last year or two it has built up domestic competition until it is exasperating.

Mr. UNDERWOOD. You testified a while ago about California and Charleston markets. The California markets naturally belong within the zone of the manufacturers in Colorado, and not to the eastern manufacturers, do they?

Mr. WOOD. No; you are incorrect. The California trade is controlled from the southern foundries by the adjustment of freight rates and the cost of raw material.

Mr. UNDERWOOD. How much does Birmingham supply the California market?

Mr. WOOD. I should say that Birmingham took about 85 per cent of the west coast trade.

Mr. UNDERWOOD. And it also takes the southern trade?

Mr. WOOD. It takes the southern trade.

Mr. UNDERWOOD. So that your real competition, so far as your factories are concerned, is practically at the Atlantic seaboard, is it not?

Mr. WOOD. Our natural market, sir, starts on the Chesapeake, and runs perhaps to Harrisburg, up through Albany, and what is east of those points, so that we are, of all the manufacturers, most seriously subjected to the foreign competition.

Mr. UNDERWOOD. But you have got a short haul, where the differential in freight rate is in your favor, to those markets, as against the English market, on iron pipe—I believe you testified to that effect a while ago?

Mr. WOOD. I did not say that.

Mr. UNDERWOOD. Your figures were that way.

Mr. WOOD. I will run over the figures again. Our water rate to Boston, $1.70, and our rail rate is about $2.70——

Mr. UNDERWOOD. Right there, allow me to interrupt you. Iron pipe is something that does not have to be hurried in shipment. Of course the freight is lower, and it takes the cheapest rate under ordinary circumstances.

Mr. WOOD. Cast-iron pipe takes nearly the cheapest rate.

Mr. UNDERWOOD. Therefore if you have a water rate, that excludes the rail rate entirely, does it not?

Mr. WOOD. No, sir; not at all.

Mr. UNDERWOOD. Why?

Mr. WOOD. Because there are very few parties who have the wharves for the reception of freight, and the majority of our New England shipments, by all odds, are by rail.

Mr. UNDERWOOD. That is merely a question of private wharves in order to land your goods?

Mr. WOOD. And that is the location of the gas works, the pumping stations for the waterworks——

Mr. UNDERWOOD. I am talking of the point of competition, where you come in direct competition with English cast iron; for instance, in Boston, where they lay it down from the ship and you lay it down at your cheapest freight rate. Your cheapest freight is water, isn't it?

Mr. WOOD. Yes.

Mr. UNDERWOOD. That is $1.70?

Mr. WOOD. Yes, sir.

Mr. UNDERWOOD. Now, what is the freight on cast iron from the English ports?

Mr. WOOD. That would be according to the exigencies of the steamer. It might be down to $1.50; but roughly, I should take it, in a general way, at $2.

Mr. UNDERWOOD. I understood you to say a while ago that the freight ranged from $2 to $3 coastwise.

Mr. WOOD. It might be $4 to $6 by rail.

Mr. UNDERWOOD. Will you kindly state, not what the cheapest rate is or what the highest rate is, but, if you have a knowledge of the facts, what the average rate on cast-iron pipe is from English ports to Boston?

Mr. WOOD. I doubt whether there is enough iron pipe brought in to establish a rate, for it has been practically prohibited, so we have to take the going prices of freight.

Mr. UNDERWOOD. There is at least a dollar's difference in the freight rates in your favor if you ship your cast iron to Boston by water and they come to Boston to meet it?

Mr. WOOD. There might in some cases be that. The question of shipping by water is a question that you can not bring down to an exact science, as you can by rail, because it depends upon the desires of the vessel for freight.

Mr. UNDERWOOD. Now, if we put pig iron on the free list, the duty on cast-iron pipe would not only be reduced the difference in cost of pig iron, but it could be reduced very considerably more than that, and yet you would have control of your market?

Mr. WOOD. Yes, sir; you are entirely correct.

Mr. UNDERWOOD. To what extent?

Mr. WOOD. What I said was about $3.

Mr. UNDERWOOD. Three dollars in addition to the differential on pig iron?

Mr. WOOD. That would be ample.

Mr. HILL. I would like to have you clarify one more idea of mine. You said that the high tariff had built up a domestic competition in your line that was exasperating. Why has not that domestic competition lowered the price instead of raising it for the last ten years?

Mr. WOOD. It has so lowered the price this year that our workingmen are without work.

Mr. HILL. I am not speaking of the panic year, but I mean up to 1906. Why did it not lower the price up to that time?

Mr. WOOD. It does lower the price, sir.

Mr. HILL. Has the price been lowered in any respect, excepting to bring it nearer to the cost of pig iron?

Mr. WOOD. That is all. We all have to pay the same price for pig iron.

Mr. HILL. You follow the price of pig iron up?

Mr. WOOD. Yes, sir.

Mr. HILL. It has made your margin of profit lower and lower?

Mr. WOOD. Lower and lower.

Mr. HILL. You have been buying iron for forty years, since you have been in business. In 1888 we made six and one-half million tons. In 1907 twenty-five and one-half million tons. Why didn't we make it cheaper in 1907 than in 1888, considering that we made four times as much? If the increase in competition has had the effect of reducing the price of pipe, why has it not reduced the price of iron?

Mr. WOOD. You have the advantage of having all those tables before you——

Mr. HILL. The increase in the last twenty years has been four times the production of pig iron. Why has not it reduced the price? Why has not the iron fallen in proportion to your price? You say that the effect of competition has been to lower and lower the margin of your profit, and that the increase in price is caused by the increase in the price of iron, which I think is true—and I will say that I am very much gratified at the way you answer these questions, because I want to get information on that subject—but why, in your judgment, has not the same competition lowered the price of iron?

Mr. WOOD. Has it not lowered the price of iron? There have been some years when iron sold at $60. As I have testified, iron can be bought now at between $16 and $17. The exact year when the prices changed could only be known by having the tables before me, you understand. But iron has gone, in my recollection, from $60 and $65——

Mr. HILL. It was $24 last year.

Mr. WOOD. In 1907. The top of the wave was $24. But it would be unfair to say that the business average was $24.

Mr. HILL. Well, it has steadily increased since 1898, has it not?

Mr. WOOD. It has increased, sir, and perhaps steadily.

Mr. HILL. Why? That is what I want to get at. Please tell me why, in your judgment.

Mr. WOOD. Largely the congestion of labor. The cost of everything has gone up in all particulars, and there has been less competition in the sale of iron.

Mr. HILL. Principally the latter?

Mr. WOOD. The figures will show that. I do not wish to speak offhand about that.

Mr. HILL. I was simply asking the question with regard to your judgment. I want to get the information.

Mr. CRUMPACKER. Is your company a member of the agreement that was considered by the court in the Addyston Pipe Company case?

Mr. WOOD. No, sir; the western and southern pipe makers were the ones interested in that.

Mr. CRUMPACKER. That agreement, I understand, is not binding - at all now?

Mr. WOOD. There is none.

Mr. CRUMPACKER. No combination between pipe makers or sellers that you know of?

Mr. WOOD. The only combination is a combination that has been formed by joint ownership of the trust of about ten to thirteen shops.

Mr. CRUMPACKER. How much territory does that cover?

Mr. WOOD. The trust has a shop on the seaboard, a shop at Duluth, a shop at Buffalo, a shop at Birmingham, and served in between— altogether 13 shops.

Mr. CRUMPACKER. How many independent establishments are there?

Mr. WOOD. Ten.

Mr. CRUMPACKER. What percentage of the product does the trust control?

Mr. WOOD. About 50 per cent, sir.

Mr. FORDNEY. Did I understand you to say that you thought it would be beneficial to the trade if the duty on pig iron was removed?

Mr. WOOD. I should say it would be, sir, on the whole.

Mr. FORDNEY. Is it true that the industry of pig iron needs any protection?

Mr. WOOD. It does indeed, sir, if it has to pay high prices for ore.

Mr. FORDNEY. Suppose the man who produced the pig iron owned the iron mine, would he need protection as against the English pig iron or the foreign pig iron?

Mr. WOOD. Ask the man who makes the pig iron.

Mr. FORDNEY. I understood you to say that it could be removed, and you think that it ought to be removed, but that you ought to have protection on your product. Did I understand you correctly?

Mr. WOOD. I will try to boil down what I said to cover the thought that I think was in your mind.

Mr. FORDNEY. Thank you.

Mr. WOOD. As one looking on the trade, knowing it as one casually knows things in everyday life, it would be a benefit to our particular concern to have a lower duty on pig iron, but I do not think that is possible under existing conditions altogether. I should be sorry to see it made too low, because eastern furnaces who have not the Lake Superior ore supply have to buy their ore on the market, and it would be an injustice to our eastern pig-iron furnaces.

Mr. FORDNEY. I certainly misunderstood you. I did not understand you meaning as you now explain it.

Mr. UNDERWOOD. Suppose the ore was free.

Mr. WOOD. You are now asking me to wander in the realms beyond everyday discussion without any figures. If ore was free, it would be difficult to transport in ocean-going vessels quite all the eastern furnaces would require. If ore was free it would reduce the cost of pig iron, I should suppose—and I am only speaking roughly, and you will pardon me for trespassing on somebody else's business which I do not know thoroughly—but it would reduce the cost from 25 to 40 cents a ton.

Mr. FORDNEY. Taking into consideration the cost of your raw material and the amount of protection you have on your finished product, can you afford to stand any reduction of duty on pipe?

Mr. WOOD. This rate between pig iron and pipe now is practically $5. You can reduce it to $3 without doing the business any injury, excepting the California trade, and perhaps Galveston.

Mr. COCKRAN. Tell us just exactly what reduction you think would be feasible on cast-iron pipe, net.

Mr. WOON. The trade would be benefited by the reduction of $2 from the $5, which it is now.

Mr. COCKRAN. How about the reduction on your finished product?

Mr. WOOD. That is what I am answering.

Mr. COCKRAN. Your duty is $5—I thought it was $8.

Mr. WOON. It is $5 above pig iron; it is what we call the " spread."

Mr. COCKRAN. Do I understand that you could stand a réduction of $2, leaving the pig-iron duty where it is?

Mr. WOOD. Yes, sir.

Mr. COCKRAN. How much could you stand it if pig iron were free?

Mr. WOON. Well, it might be one, two, or three.

Mr. FORDNEY. With $5 reduction, you would lose the Pacific coast trade, you think?

Mr. WOOD. The Pacific coast trade would be lost to the eastern manufacturers, unless the shipments went to the interior points to which the railroads charge excessive rates of freight from the seaboard.

Mr. FORDNEY. Do you control most of the Pacific coast trade now?

Mr. WOOD. That goes to Birmingham.

Mr. FORDNEY. But the factories in the United States do?

Mr. WOON. The factories in the United States control the Pacific coast trade, speaking in a general way.

The CHAIRMAN. Would the Birmingham factories lose that trade with the reduction of duty?

Mr. WOOD. I should expect that the Birmingham foundries would lose the trade to the seaports on the Pacific coast?

Mr. COCKRAN. Who would get it?

Mr. WOOD. It would probably go to Germany or England.

Mr. COCKRAN. Did you say that you think the cast-iron pipe could be sent from Germany or England to the Pacific coast cheaper than from Birmingham?

Mr. WOOD. Undoubtedly; one is by rail and the other by water.

Mr. COCKRAN. One is about 2,500 miles and the other something like 8,000 miles, is it not?

Mr. WOOD. I would call it 10,000 miles.

Mr. UNDERWOOD. Do you know the distance from Birmingham to Mobile by water?

Mr. WOOD. I do.

Mr. UNDERWOOD. How far is it?

Mr. WOOD. Approximately it is about 200 to 300 miles.

Mr. UNDERWOOD. Two hundred and eighty-eight miles.

Mr. WOOD. That was a pretty good guess.

Mr. UNDERWOOD. Do you know the freight rate?

Mr. WOOD. I do not know exactly, but I should take it to be about $1.50. I estimate that without speaking from knowledge.

Mr. UNDERWOOD. One dollar to $1.25.

Mr. WOOD. I thought you meant pipe. Pig is lower, of course.

Mr. UNDERWOOD. With that freight rate to the sea, is not the freight rate from the English factories nearly that much to the sea?

Mr. WOOD. There is an output in England of about 10 per cent of our output in this country which is right on the seaboard, and without any freight on their pig iron. There is a capacity at Glasgow of about 15 to 20 per cent of what we make in this country, which has largely to get its iron at a freight of about 5 shillings.

Mr. UNDERWOOD. That 5 shillings would be in the neighborhood of the freight from Birmingham to the sea?

Mr. WOON. Approximately.

Mr. UNDERWOOD. Then, with the freight the same at the point of shipment, is there any reason why the Birmingham manufacturer should not lay the product down as cheaply on the Pacific coast as the English manufacturer, providing he has the ships to do it with?

Mr. WOOD. Your proviso answers that question, sir, entirely; it all depends on the proviso.

Mr. UNDERWOOD. It is a question of ships, and not a question of distance?

Mr. WOOD. Not altogether a question of ships, but also a question of moving lumber from Mobile. Mobile is a point to which people go expecting to get high rates of freight. It is not a question of ships, but of movement of freight.

Mr. UNDERWOOD. I recognize that myself. The English shipper has an advantage in the fact that he has more tramp ships which go around the world. But what I want to lead up to is this, as to whether, in your opinion, when the Panama Canal is finished, the direct communication with the Pacific coast would not put the Alabama manufacturer of pipe and pig iron and rail in a better position to reach the California market than the English manufacturer?

Mr. WOOD. It is a question which is getting to a very narrow point. It is a question really of how much lumber is going from Mobile, and how much coal is going, and whether the steamer is to go there for low freights or not.

Mr. UNDERWOOD. I am assuming that most of the tramp steamers of the world, when the Panama Canal is finished, will go to the Gulf coast to get coal, and that they will take on surplus freight regardless of lumber or anything else. They will not simply go for lumber, but for everything?

Mr. Woon. If you will pardon me for answering that question this way, I will say that it is difficult enough to answer a question as regards the facts, let alone the time when the Panama Canal shall be finished.

Mr. DALZELL. There are no tramp steamers engaged in the coastwise trade of this country?

Mr. UNDERWOOD. We hope some day that the prohibitive coastwise laws may be taken off. That is one of the monopolies that ought to be removed so that we can do business.

The CHAIRMAN. I do not think it would come very soon if the opposition party was in power.

Mr. CLARK. That is a gratuitous prophecy.

The CHAIRMAN. Can you make this pipe cheaper in Birmingham than on the Atlantic coast?

Mr. WOOD. I wish the Trust would tell me, sir. I don't know. But I should rather have white labor than black labor. That is the real analysis of your question.

The CHAIRMAN. I am asking you about the production of cast-iron pipe.

Mr. Woon. As a finished article?

The CHAIRMAN. The cheaper the pig iron the cheaper the production—is that not true?

Mr. WOOD. The differential between pig iron in the East and the pig iron of Birmingham is about $4 a ton, $4 to $4.50 at the present time, in favor of Birmingham.

The CHAIRMAN. If the labor conditions were equal, they could produce the pipe there at $4 to $4.50 a ton cheaper than you can?

Mr. WOOD. You are approximately correct.

WALTER WOOD, PHILADELPHIA, PA., FILES SUPPLEMENTAL BRIEF, IN WHICH HE REFERS TO DRAWBACKS.

PHILADELPHIA, PA., *December 16, 1908.*

COMMITTEE ON WAYS AND MEANS,
Washington, D. C.

GENTLEMEN: Any duty that is more than enough to protect the existence of a business (but not including profits) is too high, and therefore detrimental to a healthy development.

Because with high duties it is impossible to prevent (by admission of small amounts of foreign material) abnormal profits during times of great pressure, thus drawing newcomers into the business and causing those already manufacturing to expand their output on an artificial basis.

The cast-iron pipe industry during the past few years is a marked example of such conditions.

The increase of domestic output has given rise to exasperating competition and caused loss to makers and employees.

Three dollars per ton above the duty on pig iron is ample to protect the cast-iron pipe industry of the United States, although this duty will permit importation to cities near the Pacific coast and perhaps in southern Texas.

Under the present conditions of manufacture of pig iron in the United States it would be unwise for the committee to reduce the tariff more than, at the most, $2 per ton.

Until the price of lake ore is reduced it would be unfair and improper to further reduce the duty.

The influence that the "pegging" of lake ore prices has upon the pig-iron production of the United States (and the impossibility of foreign ores competing effectively) is shown by the table of production and importation of ores in the United States.

Iron ore production by districts.

	Per cent.
Lake region	80. 5
Alabama and Georgia	10. 4
New York	2. 6
Pennsylvania	1. 6
Virginia	1. 6
New Jersey	1. 06
	97. 76
Balance of United States	2. 4

Any considerable reduction in the cost of pig iron must therefore come from the lowering of prices of lake ores.

DRAWBACKS.

In the discussion between those claiming that duties should be entirely removed and those wishing to retain moderate rates, I would strongly urge that the clauses referring to drawbacks should be so adjusted that parties importing material under the reduced rates can still secure practically free-trade privileges by making it possible for them to sell importation certificates to exporters in other parts of the country.

Thus importation certificates could be used for exporting coal into New England, coal from Alabama, wheat into Minneapolis, wheat from California, iron and steel on Pacific coast, and iron and steel from Pennsylvania.

Ores for smelters could be brought into Arizona; metal exported from New York or Baltimore.

A thorough and carefully devised scheme permitting importations of either raw or finished material, if facilitated by drawbacks granted to exportations of similar materials from other parts of the country, will tend to bring into the United States a large amount of trade which it otherwise could not obtain.

Respectfully submitted.

WALTER WOOD.

CHAINS.

[Paragraph 151.]

THE HAND CHAINMAKERS' UNION, PHILADELPHIA, PA., PETITIONS FOR A SUFFICIENTLY PROTECTIVE DUTY ON CHAINS.

PHILADELPHIA, PA., *November 16, 1908.*

MEMBERS OF THE WAYS AND MEANS COMMITTEE.

GENTLEMEN: I, as the president of the Hand Chainmakers' National Union, representing 95 per cent of the chainworkers of the United States, have been requested to address you in the interest of our trade. Knowing that there is likely to be a revision of the tariff laws of our country, I would like to call your attention to the fact that for two years the chain makers of this country have worked about half time, owing to the fact that a large amount of chain has been imported to this country. We, as American mechanics, desire to be protected against foreign competition so that it will be possible for us as American citizens to live and maintain our families.

Hoping that this will meet with your just consideration, gentlemen, I beg leave to remain,

Yours, respectfully,

DAVID CHANCE,
President of the Hand Chainmakers' Union, U. S. A.

STATEMENT OF H. F. MATTERN, OF LEBANON, PA., RELATIVE TO A NEW CLASSIFICATION FOR CHAINS.

FRIDAY, *November 27, 1908.*

Mr. MATTERN. If the chairman please, and gentlemen of the committee——

Mr. GRIGGS. What concern do you represent?

Mr. MATTERN. The Lebanon Chain Works, of Lebanon, Pa.

Mr. GRIGGS. What position do you hold with the company?

Mr. MATTERN. I am vice-president and assistant manager.

Mr. GRIGGS. Are you making any money?

Mr. MATTERN. Not at the present time; no, sir.

Mr. GRIGGS. Did you make some last year?

Mr. MATTERN. We declared a 5 per cent dividend last year.

Mr. GRIGGS. That is a pretty fair dividend. I hope you will do better next year.

The CHAIRMAN. Now, may we have the gentleman proceed?

Mr. GRIGGS. Certainly.

Mr. MATTERN. The chain manufacturers desire to ask the committee to make a revision of the chain schedule by subdividing the schedule into a greater number of classes than at present. The tariff on large sizes of chains we would have reduced and on the small sizes we ask for an advance, so as to equalize and give us an opportunity to compete with foreign manufacturers of chains. The principal thing we want to ask is an opportunity to compete. We do not ask for a prohibitive tariff, but a competing tariff. On small sizes of chains like quarter-inch and five-sixteenths inch there is a great deal more imported than is manufactured in this country, for the reason we are not able to compete with foreign manufacturers under the present duty.

The CHAIRMAN. Now, Mr. Mattern, will you tell us, on chains not less than three-quarters of one inch in diameter, what duty you propose instead of the present duty of one and one-eighth?

Mr. MATTERN. Will you please repeat that question, Mr. Payne?

The CHAIRMAN. I am referring to chains not less than three-quarters of an inch in diameter, on which the duty is now $1\frac{1}{8}$ cents per pound. What do you have to propose as a change?

Mr. MATTERN. We would propose that on sizes 2 inches and larger, which are principally anchor chains, the tariff shall be reduced. I can not make any proposition or suggestion as to what it should be reduced to, because I have been unable to obtain the prices at which that class of chains is sold in foreign markets. I might make an effort to get that information, and I hope to have it inside of a week, and we will then be able to make a few suggestions along the lines of those sizes.

The CHAIRMAN. What is the next size?

Mr. MATTERN. From sizes under 2 inches down to seven-eighths of an inch, inclusive, we would propose that the present tariff be retained.

The CHAIRMAN. That is $1\frac{1}{8}$ cents per pound.

Mr. MATTERN. No, sir; from $1\frac{15}{16}$ to seven-eighths of an inch, inclusive.

The CHAIRMAN. I am talking about the duty. What do you propose to suggest as to the duty on chains from seven-eighths of an inch up to 2 inches?

Mr. MATTERN. The same as at present—not less than $1\frac{1}{8}$ cents and 45 per cent ad valorem.

The CHAIRMAN. What do you propose on the next size?

Mr. MATTERN. In order to enable us to compete with foreign manufacturers on chains of three-quarters of an inch, we would ask 80 per cent, an increase from 45 per cent to 80 per cent. On five-eighths inch, we would ask an increase to 90 per cent, and from nine-sixteenths to a quarter of an inch and less, 100 per cent.

Mr. LONGWORTH. You stated the importations are very small. Do you know what they are?

Mr. MATTERN. The importations of small sizes of chains, like quarter-inch to five-sixteenths, are greater than the amount manufactured in this country. Last year there were about 350 tons of these two sizes imported.

Mr. LONGWORTH. Amounting to how much in value?

Mr. POU. Seventy thousand dollars.

Mr. DALZELL. Three hundred and fifty tons?

Mr. MATTERN. Yes, sir.

Mr. LONGWORTH. The total importations were only $70,000 of all kinds of chains?

Mr. MATTERN. That is very true, but the total importations, if you will notice, are practically all of those small sizes.

Mr. LONGWORTH. What is the total production in this country?

Mr. MATTERN. I can not give you those figures. I have been unable to get them.

Mr. LONGWORTH. In round numbers, what is the value of chains produced in this country?

Mr. MATTERN. I do not have that information either, Mr. Longworth.

The CHAIRMAN. Section 151 specifies that no chains or chain of any description shall bear a lower rate of duty than 45 per cent ad valorem. Do you know anything about what is produced abroad and imported here?

Mr. MATTERN. I have not that information. I have been unable to obtain it. I endeavored to get it.

The CHAIRMAN. We will have it in a few days, when we get our book printed, and we will tell you.

Mr. MATTERN. Thank you.

Mr. UNDERWOOD. On the larger chains, the present duty is absolutely or practically prohibitive, is it not?

Mr. MATTERN. It is; yes, sir.

Mr. UNDERWOOD. And it is only on these smaller chains there is any importation going on at all?

Mr. MATTERN. That is true.

Mr. UNDERWOOD. On these smaller chains, how much does your factory produce?

Mr. MATTERN. You mean our output or as compared with other manufacturers?

Mr. UNDERWOOD. I mean what is your total output?

Mr. MATTERN. We would produce of those smaller chains probably 25 to 30 tons a year.

Mr. UNDERWOOD. And the valuation of that would be how much?

Mr. MATTERN. Three hundred dollars a ton.

Mr. UNDERWOOD. That is about $7,500 to $9,000.

Mr. MATTERN. Yes, sir. I might say that our factory produces principally large chains. The small-chain industry with us is only a small part of our business. It would be larger, of course, if we had a chance to compete with the foreign manufacturers.

Mr. UNDERWOOD. What is the total output of your factory?

Mr. MATTERN. I do not believe I could tell you that exactly.

Mr. LONGWORTH. Can you give it in dollars?

Mr. MATTERN. Yes; I can put it in dollars. The total output is about $300,000 a year, roughly speaking.

Mr. UNDERWOOD. Then this small chain manufacture is a very small proportion of your business?

Mr. MATTERN. It is with us; yes, sir.

Mr. UNDERWOOD. And on the other chains the present duties are prohibitive?

Mr. MATTERN. They are.

Mr. UNDERWOOD. And produce no revenue?

Mr. MATTERN. No, sir.

Mr. UNDERWOOD. That would seem to warrant a very considerable cut on the duty on larger chains?

Mr. MATTERN. Yes, sir; that is, on the larger sizes you have reference to.

Mr. UNDERWOOD. Yes; without seriously interfering with the business in this country.

Mr. MATTERN. If you do not get the tariff lower than the cost to manufacture in this country, and give us a chance to compete, I think the manufacturers will be satisfied.

Mr. UNDERWOOD. I want to ask you if you agree to this proposition: Would you think it a reasonable tariff if we put the tariff here at the difference between the foreign price with freight added, and your cost price?

Mr. MATTERN. No, I do not think it would be. I think it ought to be based on our selling price. We do not get a great deal more than cost out of it anyway, so we do not want it all taken away from us.

Mr. UNDERWOOD. Chains and cables are a pretty heavy commodity for transportation, and the freight must be considerable, across the water?

Mr. MATTERN. It amounts to about 5 per cent of the value.

Mr. UNDERWOOD. If we give you the benefit of the freight rate to this country over and above your cost price, is not that a fair protection for your profit, a fair margin for your profits?

Mr. MATTERN. That is a very small margin in the manufacturing business, because we have fat years and lean years, and wo do not average 5 per cent.

Mr. UNDERWOOD. Are you not just as capable of selling your product as the man abroad is, if you are fighting him on equal terms?

Mr. MATTERN. I do not understand your proposition.

Mr. UNDERWOOD. I ask you if you are not just as capable of selling your product as the man abroad if you meet him upon an equal basis?

Mr. MATTERN. I think we are, and that is the reason we are asking for a reduction in the tariff.

Mr. UNDERWOOD. What is the selling price of 2-inch cable to-day?

Mr. MATTERN. Two-inch cable is about $3.20 a hundred pounds.

Mr. UNDERWOOD. Now, what is the cost price of that?

Mr. MATTERN. About the same.

Mr. UNDERWOOD. About $3.20?

Mr. MATTERN. Yes, sir.

Mr. UNDERWOOD. Where is your principal foreign competition?

Mr. MATTERN. From England.

Mr. UNDERWOOD. What is the selling price of that same cable in England?

Mr. MATTERN. That is information I say I do not have, but which I have been trying to get. On account of the short notice I had to come here, when it was decided I was to come, I found myself unable to get that information, but I hope to have it within a week, and will then advise you fully in that respect.

Mr. UNDERWOOD. As you evidently have not the information we need, I will ask you if you will file your cost price of all these different cable and chain articles, the cost price here at your factory, the price at which it is sold in England, and the freight rate, and at the end of each comparison put the amount of duty opposite the English product. That will give us some information on which we can make some estimates.

Mr. MATTERN. You want the cost price here and the prices sold for in England and the freight rate from England to America?

Mr. UNDERWOOD. Yes; and the duty. That is, give those in separate columns.

Mr. POU. Is your company a corporation?

Mr. MATTERN. Yes, sir.

Mr. POU. What is the capitalization?

Mr. MATTERN. One hundred thousand dollars.

Mr. POU. Did you pay a dividend last year?

Mr. MATTERN. We paid a dividend of 5 per cent.

Mr. UNDERWOOD. Can you state how much in your cost price is labor?

Mr. MATTERN. Yes, sir.

Mr. UNDERWOOD. What is it?

Mr. MATTERN. Do you want that included in the statement?

Mr. UNDERWOOD. Yes; the percentage of your cost prices that covers labor.

Mr. GRIGGS. What is your plant worth now?

Mr. MATTERN. We have a plant worth about $200,000. It has just been recently reconstructed. We built the plant by an issue of bonds and increased the capacity.

Mr. POU. If you get this increase you want in these duties on these smaller chains, will you put up the prices to the consumer?

Mr. MATTERN. No; we could not put up the prices to the consumer, because it would not enable us to get any more money than the German and English makes would sell here for.

Mr. POU. The foreign competition is the only competition you really have, is it not?

Mr. MATTERN. Oh, no. We have American competition.

Mr. POU. I mean practically speaking. You all sell at about the same price, do you not?

Mr. MATTERN. The American manufacturers get very close to the same price; yes, sir. For instance, on quarter-inch chain, the American chain manufacturers receive $8.14 a hundred pounds, whereas the English chain makers receive $4.92 per hundred pounds.

Mr. POU. How many firms are engaged in the business of manufacturing chains that you are putting on the market?

Mr. MATTERN. In the United States?

Mr. POU. Yes, sir.

Mr. MATTERN. About twenty.

Mr. POU. Do you have an association?

Mr. MATTERN. No association; no, sir.

Mr. POU. You have no organization for the purpose of keeping up prices?

Mr. MATTERN. None whatever.

Mr. POU. But you do not cut prices?

Mr. MATTERN. If you went to buy some chains you would find that they do.

Mr. POU. I understood you to say awhile ago the prices made by all American manufacturers were practically the same and that the only real competition you had was from those foreign manufacturers?

Mr. MATTERN. On some small sizes that is the case. I would not like to have that remark considered general, because there is competition in the chain business which is very keen, and some of these small sizes we are obliged to sell practically at cost, because the importers bring the foreign goods in and we can not get any more than what the goods actually cost us and even then we can not compete with them.

Mr. CLARK. You make a large profit on the large chains, do you not?

Mr. MATTERN. We make a small profit on the large chains.

Mr. CLARK. All the chains imported into the United States last year only amounted to $70,894.04.

Mr. MATTERN. Yes, sir.

Mr. CLARK. Do you think that that affected the price of American chains any to the people who use them?

Mr. MATTERN. You will notice that most of the importations, in fact, the bulk of the importation of chains, in that $70,000 are very small sizes.

Mr. CLARK. Yes; $16,828 on less than five-sixteenths of 1 inch in diameter.

Mr. MATTERN. Only $16,000? There are two items in that list.

Mr. CLARK. All on which the specific duty does not amount to 45 per cent, according to the record, amounted in importation to $51,280.04. How much, in your judgment, does the total output or consumption of chains amount to of those less than five-sixteenths of an inch in diameter?

Mr. MATTERN. Compared with what is made in this country?

Mr. CLARK. The whole thing; all of them bought by the American people.

Mr. MATTERN. Oh, it is very small. I should say it would not be more than 3 or 4 or 5 per cent. I do not know exactly. It would not be very much anyway, but that is about it. There is our trouble, that on these small chains we do not have any chance. There is enough business there, so that if we had a chance to compete it would enable us to run a small shop.

Mr. CLARK. What I am trying to get at is this: It seems to me the importation of chains is so small it amounts to nothing in the way of competition to anybody on anything.

Mr. MATTERN. Of course, if you were in the chain business you would look at it in a different light, I suppose, because when we have to compete on chains and our cost compels us to get as much as 16 or 18 cents a pound, and the imported chains are selling in New York at 12 cents a pound, then it is not a pleasant thing to contemplate.

Mr. CLARK. Could you give any reasonable estimate of the money value of all the small chains used in the United States in twelve months? If you do not know, say so, and do not stand off on it.

Mr. MATTERN. No; I do not know.

Mr. CLARK. Very well, then.

The CHAIRMAN. What is the smallest size chain here?

Mr. MATTERN. Less than five-sixteenths.

The CHAIRMAN. Yes; I guess that is right. Now, those are the smallest chains?

Mr. MATTERN. Yes, sir.

The CHAIRMAN. The highest importation in any one year was $20,000, since 1897. On those small-sized chains the specific duty runs over 45 per cent.

Mr. MATTERN. Yes, sir.

The CHAIRMAN. The ad valorem and specific duty is more than 45 per cent. With that specific duty there was only $21,000 worth imported in 1905. Aside from that it runs, say, from $2,000 to $18,000. That is practically prohibitive, is it not?

Mr. MATTERN. Not on those small sizes.

The CHAIRMAN. And an equivalent ad valorem runs all the way from 53 to 64 per cent, and you want that made 90 per cent?

Mr. MATTERN. Yes, sir; and 100 on some of them. We would like to have 100 per cent on most of them.

The CHAIRMAN. What reason do you give for any such doubling of the duty?

Mr. MATTERN. I was just going to explain that. By taking the cost of the chain in England—that is, the selling price, I should say, and the selling price in this country, it can be figured. The quarter-inch-chain selling price in England is $8.68 per hundred pounds. The selling price in New York of the American chain is $18 per hundred pounds. Now, if we get 100 per cent duty on that $8.68 we have still less than $18 per hundred pounds.

Mr. CLARK. How do you manage to keep the English chains out of the market with the duty that you have?

Mr. MATTERN. We do not. That is just the point. They are shipping in more than we make.

The CHAIRMAN. Twenty thousand dollars. Is that one-half of 1 per cent?

Mr. MATTERN. No; it is $50,000.

The CHAIRMAN. No; $20,000 the record shows. It is the 45 per cent duty—that is, $50,000.

Mr. MATTERN. The 45 per cent duty is what the bulk of it is calculated on.

The CHAIRMAN. While there is a specific that does not amount to 45 per cent, the specific duty on this amounts to more than 45 per cent, so it is specific duty and nothing else.

Mr. MATTERN. I do not think this specific duty does amount to more than 45 per cent.

The CHAIRMAN. Yes; but you do not reduce it to 45. You have to keep it above that. This is not under the 45 per cent business at all.

Mr. LONGWORTH. Do you mean to say you can not give us some rough estimate of the production in this country of chains?

Mr. MATTERN. I can not give any information about that.

Mr. LONGWORTH. You produce $300,000 a year yourself?

Mr. MATTERN. Yes, sir.

Mr. LONGWORTH. How many other concerns are there?

Mr. MATTERN. There are about twenty altogether.

Mr. LONGWORTH. Do they produce as much as you do?

Mr. MATTERN. Oh, no; we are one of the largest.

Mr. LONGWORTH. Well, the total production is how much a year? Would you say $5,000,000?

Mr. MATTERN. I should say that would be a fair guess at it.

Mr. LONGWORTH. Considering every form of chain, the total amount imported is $70,000, and you produce $5,000,000, and yet you come and ask for an increased duty?

Mr. MATTERN. The fact of the matter is that the $70,000 applies only to the sizes on which we ask an increased duty. If you want to look at it that way, that is a different proposition.

Mr. CLARK. You can make big chains at a profit, can you?

Mr. MATTERN. We can if we can get a profitable price when the competition is not too keen.

Mr. CLARK. I know; but you did make big chains at a profit?

Mr. MATTERN. Yes, sir.

Mr. CLARK. And you can not make little chains at a profit?

Mr. MATTERN. That is true.

Mr. CLARK. Why do you not quit making little chains and devote yourself to the big chains?

Mr. MATTERN. We have to supply big and little chains to our customers. A man comes along with an order for small chains and big chains, and we have to supply him with them.

Mr. CLARK. I know; but if you can not make them at a profit, why not buy those imported small chains and put them into your stock and sell them so you will make a profit? The trouble about this whole business is that it will set every man in the country trying to do something he can not do.

Mr. MATTERN. If it is the opinion of the committee that we should close down some of our fires and discharge our workmen, and buy imported goods, I suppose that is what we will have to do.

Mr. CLARK. Why could you not make more big chains and keep your furnaces going?

Mr. MATTERN. The same workmen do not make the big chains who make the small ones.

The CHAIRMAN. You do make small chains?

Mr. MATTERN. A few; yes, sir.

The CHAIRMAN. Some one supplies this market. It is not this $20,000 worth that is imported, is it?

Mr. MATTERN. There is more than $50,000 worth there that is imported. That is about the greater bulk of the market.

Mr. DALZELL. Are there chains made in the Pittsburg district?

Mr. MATTERN. Yes, sir.

Mr. DALZELL. Who makes them?

Mr. MATTERN. Very few handmade chains are made there.

Mr. DALZELL. Who makes them?

Mr. MATTERN. The Standard Chain Company and the James Mackay Company. They make mostly machine-made chains, although there are some handmade chains made too.

Mr. POU. If you should get this increase that you ask for, would not that put you in a position so you could eventually reduce the prices somewhat under what they are now?

Mr. MATTERN. Reduce the price of chain?

Mr. POU. Yes, sir.

Mr. MATTERN. I do not see how we could, when we are selling at cost now.

Mr. POU. The higher you put the duty, the cheaper that enables the manufacturer to sell, does it not?

Mr. MATTERN. It does.

Mr. POU. That is what everybody has stated that has been here. Now, what I am asking you is: If you should get this increase, after a while that would enable you to put down prices, would it not?

Mr. MATTERN. That is a manufacturing proposition that I can not see how the raising of the duty would affect one way or the other.

Mr. POU. That has been the past experience of all the manufacturers in this country, has it not, that the higher you put the duty, the more protection you give them, the less price they can sell for?

Mr. MATTERN. I can not see it that way. The selling price depends entirely on the cost of manufacture, regardless of what the tariff or duty may be.

Mr. BOUTELL. Who are your best customers?

Mr. MATTERN. We have sold large quantities of chains to the United States Government. We sell to the large ship-building interests—Cramps, Newport News, Fall River Ship Building Company, New York Ship Building Company, and others. We sell largely to large dredging concerns in New York, like the William H. Taylor Dredging Company, and some dredging concerns in Boston and Philadelphia.

Mr. BOUTELL. Those are large chains?

Mr. MATTERN. Yes, sir.

Mr. BOUTELL. Who are the purchasers of these small chains?

Mr. MATTERN. Oh, the machine shops and large concerns who use cranes. These small chains are used for crane work principally. The Bethlehem Steel Company buys some of that. The Pennsylvania Steel Company buys some.

Mr. DALZELL. Do you represent any person here to-day except your own corporation?

Mr. MATTERN. I represent only our own corporation, except that some of the chain manufacturers made an effort to get together and decide on a suitable proposition to bring before this committee, but they did not respond very freely on account of some of the manufacturers being in Memphis, Tenn., at some convention or other, and the few of us who did meet decided that myself and Mr. Woodhouse, who is also here, should appear before the committee.

———

H. F. MATTERN, LEBANON (PA.) CHAIN WORKS, FILES A SUPPLEMENTAL STATEMENT RELATIVE TO CHAINS.

LEBANON, PA., *January 2, 1909.*

COMMITTEE ON WAYS AND MEANS,
Washington, D. C.

GENTLEMEN: During the tariff hearing held Friday, November 27, the question was asked by one of your honorable committee, Mr. Underwood, that Mr. Mattern file the American cost prices on chains at factories, with freight rate to New York added, compared to the selling prices of English chains f. o. b. Liverpool, plus freight and proposed duty.

In response to this request, we beg leave to submit statement based on prices ruling in England, 1907, compared with the approximate cost in the United States factories for the same period. In both of these instances the prices are figured on the basis of New York delivery.

Comparing notes with other manufacturers, there was necessarily a great variety in the cost of delivery of an article at one given point, but we have endeavored to arrive at what we consider a just and fair average cost, as per schedule hereto attached and marked "Exhibit A."

In arriving at the English selling prices we are not convinced that we have secured the lowest prices that were then being quoted, but have simply submitted prices as named by several leading English manufacturers.

LARGE-SIZE CHAINS.

The chain manufacturers with whom we have conferred, and who represent practically every chain manufacturer in the United States, were hopeful that they could recommend a greater reduction of duty on large-size chains than our schedule represents, but were confronted by the extremely higher labor cost of productive and nonproductive work in this country, to wit:

The wages paid chain makers greatly exceed the wages paid abroad, as shown by the respective tables hereto affixed and marked "Exhibit B."

The nonproductive labor in this country receives from $1.50 to $1.75 per day, whereas the same labor in England consider themselves well paid at $4.50 per week (18 shillings). Would add that nonproductive labor on large-size chains is a very important item in figuring costs, and is work which can not be done by the installation of machinery.

SMALL CHAINS.

On smaller chains, under thirteen-sixteenths of an inch, where an advance is asked, American manufacturers have to compete against chains made by "outworkers" in foreign countries, to whom chain manufacturers abroad supply the material and allow 7 per cent waste. The outworker furnishes his own building or shop, frequently located in the rear of his own home, where male and female labor of 14 years of age and upward are employed. He, the outworker, is therefore a subcontractor, and furnishes, besides his shop, his blast (which is a hand bellows), fuel, and all appliances or tools for the making of chains. Consequently, the manufacturer or factor has merely his labor in receiving and shipping the finished product per 100 pounds, plus his material, to figure his costs.

This permits of chains being sold abroad at prices which can not be met by American manufacturers, whose employees consist of men and boys over 16 years of age, under one roof, supplied with all appliances for chain manufacture, and paid the wage scale hereto attached and marked "Exhibit B," covering only actual prices for welding.

In this connection we respectfully ask a careful study of the wage scales paid our chain makers and the prices paid the outworkers, keeping in view the conditions governing the outworkers.

Referring to the wage scale for handmade chains. Every shop in the United States is a union shop, and which scale manufacturers are compelled to pay, notwithstanding the existing depression, the same scale of wages which were adopted in March of 1907, being 10 per cent advance over the previous scale, while in England the official scale during the year 1907 was the 6-shilling list for out-workers.

We are credibly informed that during the year 1907, notwith-standing the fact that the 6-shilling list was the published list of union wages paid outworkers in England, wages were actually being paid on the basis of the 3-shilling list to outworkers during this time. This disparity between the published union list of wages and the 3-shilling list actually paid is brought about by the fact that while the total number of chain makers in the black district in Eng-land is about 5,000, only about one-fifth of the chain makers were members of the union, thus leaving four-fifths of the chain makers free to accept any price that the chain manufacturer chose to pay, which was an average of 25 to 50 per cent less than the union wages. All of the above facts as to membership of the union, and the number of chain makers employed in the black district in England, were taken from the annual report made by the national secretary, Mr. Sitch, and as published in the Brierley Hill Advertiser (England) in the latter end of November, 1908.

To establish the foregoing statement we submit herewith clipping from the Iron Age, of New York, as published in the issue of Feb-ruary 7, 1907, on the subject of women chain makers in England. In regard to these outworkers, we would respectfully call your atten-tion to the fact that their overhead charges and general expenses can not, in our opinion, exceed 25 per cent of the welding prices, whereas by our factory system all nonproductive labor is paid by the manufacturer in the United States, and represents in the best regulated factories at least 80 per cent of the welding cost, and on the lighter sizes the percentage of the welding cost is from 100 to 125 per cent. By the lighter sizes we refer to the sizes less than one-fourth inch.

WOMEN CHAIN MAKERS OF ENGLAND.

[Iron Age, February 7, 1907.]

J. Sitch, secretary of the Chain Makers and Chain Strikers' Association in Great Britain, has commented quite severely on the condition of the women workers in the chain-making trade of the black country, the district surround-ing Birmingham, England. After a period in which conditions among these workers changed for the better, they are now said to be as bad as at any time. The average wage for a week's work, with long hours, six days in the week, is between 4 and 5 shillings—from $1 to $1.25.

Secretary Sitch, referring to the evils of sweating and of competition for the chance to work, severely reflects on workmen as well as employers. Not a few of the women have husbands who earn good wages. "I was pained to find," he says, "among this class wives of members of the Chain Makers and Chain Strikers' Association who, I know for a fact, earn more in three hours than their wives earn in a week. Some of these men brag about being good trade unionists when they are in a public house, but they are quite content to allow their wives to toil and slave in a chain shop for a mere pittance. Such men are not worthy to be members of a trade union."

In order that your committee may have a clearer view of the chain industry, it may be proper to state that the cost given in " Exhibit A" on stud link BBB, or dredge chain, are all based on handmade chain, in the manufacture of which no machinery can be used, but, rather, all skilled labor.

MACHINE-MADE CHAINS.

Chain made in England to compete with the chain made in the United States known as "machine-made chain" is a very low-grade quality and is known abroad as "hammered chain," in which they use the cheapest grade of iron that can be manufactured, and particularly the smaller sizes of three-sixteenth inch to three-eighth inch, inclusive, which are made by boys and girls and women, who can not earn, under the arbitrary scale of wages paid, more than 6 shillings per week (approximately $1.50), after having paid all of their running expenses, as before referred to.

It is a well-known fact that Parliament recognized that it was a national disgrace to have women working at the forge making chain, and some years ago the British Parliament appointed a committee to investigate employment of women to manufacture chain, with the end in view of passing a law forbidding girls and women working at the forge making chain. This brought about great distress and nearly an uprising in the black district, where the women maintained that they had the right to earn their own living, that they had no other trades, that they and their mothers and grandmothers for generations back have worked at this trade, and they insisted upon the right to labor at their chosen avocation.

Physicians employed by the committee from Parliament reported that no physical injury followed the making of small chains by women and girls, and the committee therefore had no grounds on which to report back to Parliament that a law should be enacted preventing the employment of females in this branch of industry. Comparing the American wages on this class of work, your honorable committee will readily see that the American manufacturer of these small chains is seriously handicapped by the difference in wages paid abroad and here, as chain makers of this class of chain in this country earn from $1.50 to $2.50 per day, according to size of chain. This fact is proven by the selling price of the foreign manufacture, as recently quoted f. o. b. Liverpool.

English prices f. o. b. Liverpool.

Size.	Per 112 pounds.	Per 100 pounds.
₃₁₆ inch	14s. 6d. net	$3.48
¼ inch	13s. 9d. less 10 per cent	2.65
₅₁₆ inch	12s. 9d. less 10 per cent	2.47
⅜ inch	12s. 3d. less 10 per cent	2.33
₇₁₆ inch	12s. 3d. less 10 per cent	2.33
½ inch	11s. 9d. less 10 per cent	2.26
⅝ inch	11s. 3d. less 10 per cent	2.17
¾ inch	10s. 9d. less 10 per cent	2.07
⅞ inch	10s. 6d. less 10 per cent	2.02
1 inch	10s. 6d. less 10 per cent	2.02

In comparison therewith we attach the present average cost prices, Exhibit "A," for this grade of chain. The present production of chain in the United States during 1908 is less than 60 per cent of that of 1907. The industry is sadly depressed, and if undue reduction is made in tariff, so as to allow the free importation of English chain, there are but two courses left to the chain manufacturer in this country, and they are to reduce the price of labor or discontinue the business. The effect of a radical reduction in the tariff would be, in our opinion, first, a reduction in the price paid to laborers; second, a reduction of the number of employees, which would mean that the skilled chain maker, having no work at his trade in which he has spent his life, would be driven down to work as a day laborer and at a day laborer's wages.

CHAINS, IRON OR STEEL.

The following tables are made up by comparing the average of actual English or foreign selling prices f. o. b. Liverpool, as compared with the actual average cost to American manufacturers delivered at New York City in both instances. American costs given do not, however, include any profit whatever. American costs compared with foreign selling prices are in each case figured on the same sizes in each group, and are, as the Ways and Means Committee requested, selling prices ruling on English chain during 1907, and the American costs are the costs for 1907.

Size of chain.	Per 112 pounds.	Per 100 pounds f. o. b. Liverpool.	Average foreign selling price per 100 pounds f. o. b. New York.	Average American cost per 100 pounds f. o. b. New York.
2″ and larger	13s.	$2.80		
Freight, insurance, and wharfage		.18		
Proposed duty ⅞ cent per pound, or 30 per cent ad valorem		.87½	$3.87½	$3.63
Less than 2″, but not less than 13/16″	14s.	3.00		
Freight, insurance, and wharfage		.20		
Proposed duty 1 cent per pound, or 40 per cent ad valorem	40 per cent.	1.20	4.40	4.20
Less than 13/16″, but not less than 13/32″	19s. 5½d.	4.17		
Freight, insurance, and wharfage		.20		
Proposed duty 1½ cents per pound, or 60 per cent ad valorem	60 per cent.	2.50	6.87	7.25
Less than 13/32″ but not less than ¼″	30s. 4d.	6.50		
Freight, insurance, and wharfage		.22		
Proposed duty 2 cents per pound, or 60 per cent ad valorem	60 per cent.	3.90	10.62	11.55

Size of chain.	Per 100 pounds.	F. o. b. foreign point of shipment at seaboard per 100 pounds.	Foreign selling price per 100 pounds.	American cost per 100 pounds.
Less than ¼ inch of any description containing not more than 12 links per foot		$3.48		
Freight, insurance, and wharfage		.18		
Proposed duty, 3 cents		3.00	$6.66	$7.32
Average weight per 100 feet, sizes 2/0 to No. 2: 23 pounds		6.00		
Freight, insurance, and wharfage		.25		
Proposed duty, 3 cents per pound or 60 per cent ad valorem	60 per cent.	3.60	9.85	10.90
Less than ¼ inch of any description containing more than 12 links per foot: Average weight per 100 feet, sizes 2/0 to No. 2—28 pounds		11.00		
Freight, insurance, and wharfage		.25		
Proposed duty, 5 cents per pound or 90 per cent ad valorem	90 per cent.	9.90	21.15	23.50

Foreign selling prices of hammered chain, compared with American common coil chain costs, 1907.

Size of chain.	Per 100 pounds.	English prices per 112 pounds f. o. b. Liverpool.		United States cost f. o. b. New York.
3/16", 12 links per foot	14s. 6d	$3.48		
Freight, insurance, and wharfage		.18		
Proposed duty		3.00		
			$6.66	$7.49
Less than 13/16", but not less than 1/4":				
Average	13s. 3d	2.56		
Freight, insurance, and wharfage		.18		
Proposed duty		2.00		
			4.74	4.91
Less than 13/16", but not less than 19/32":				
Average		2.22		
Freight, insurance, and wharfage		.18		
Proposed duty, 60 per cent		1.33		
			3.73	3.48
Less than 1 1/8", but not less than 13/16":				
Average		2.03		
Freight, insurance, and wharfage		.16		
Proposed duty, 1 cent per pound		1.00		
			3.19	2.97

Comparative wage schedule paid foreign and American union chain makers for the year 1907.

[Chain known in factory as 3/4 inch to 1 1/4 inch, English, "best;" American, "crane." 1 1/4 inch to 1 1/2 inch, English, "special best;" American, "dredge." 2 inch and larger known in both countries as "stud link."]

Size.	Foreign 6s. list.				American, factory or inworkers, 100 pounds.
	Outworkers.		Factory or inworkers.		
	112 pounds.	100 pounds.	112 pounds.	100 pounds.	
1/4 inch, or No. 3	35s. 2d.=$8.44	$7.53	26s. 5d.=$6.35	$5.66	$9.97
9/32 inch, or No. 2	26s. 10d.= 6.45	5.75	20s. 11d.= 5.02	4.48	9.14
5/16 inch	19s. 6d.= 4.68	4.18	14s. 7d.= 3.40	3.03	5.78
3/8 inch	13s. = 3.12	2.78½	9s. 9d.= 2.34	2.09	4.23
7/16 inch	10s. 3d.= 2.46	2.19	7s. 8d.= 1.84	1.64	3.63
1/2 inch	7s. 11d.= 1.90	1.70	5s. 11d.= 1.42	1.27	3.12
5/8 inch	6s. 3d.= 1.50	1.34	4s. 8½d.= 1.13	1.01	2.34
3/4 inch	5s. 5d. = 1.30	1.16	4s. 0½d.= .97	.866	1.94
7/8 inch	4s. 10d. = 1.16	1.03	3s. 7½d.= .87	.747	1.64
1 inch	4s. 3d. = 1.02	.90	3s. 2d.= .76	.68	1.37
1 1/8 inches	3s. 10d. = .92	.82	2s. 10½d.= .69	.61	1.14
1 1/4 inches			3s. 2½d.= .77	.69	1.27
1 3/8 inches			3s. 2½d.= .77	.69	1.14
1 1/2 to 1 15/16 inches			3s. 3½d.= .79	.71	1 14
2 inches			2s. 3d.= .54	.48	.67
2 1/16 inches			2s. 3d.= .54	.48	.67
2 1/8 inches			2s. 4d.= .56	.50	.70
2 3/16 inches			2s. 5d.= .58	.52	.75
2 1/4 inches			2s. 7d.= .62	.53½	.75
2 5/16 inches			2s. 8d.= .64	.57	.84
2 3/8 inches			2s. 9d.= .66	.59	.95
2 1/2 inches			2s. 11d.= .70	.63	1.08

The foregoing arguments and exhibits being actual facts, all of which can be verified, are, we believe, the strongest arguments that can be made for an entirely new schedule on chain to be included in the new tariff schedule which is being prepared, being based on actual costs of manufacture abroad as against the costs of the American manufacturer.

Exhibit A is figured out, as shown thereon, based on foreign selling prices plus the proposed duty to be levied under the new revision. We appeal to your honorable committee that in view of the foregoing you will insert in your proposed revision of tariff to be submitted to the new Congress and urge the passage of the proposed chain schedule as annexed, which schedule is submitted in accordance with the request of your honorable chairman, Mr. S. E. Payne, to the undersigned when appearing before your committee on November 27, 1908.

Signed in behalf of the chain manufacturers of the United States:

LEBANON CHAIN WORKS,
H. F. MATTERN, *Vice-President.*
WOODHOUSE CHAIN WORKS,
Trenton, N. J.,
THOS. T. WOODHOUSE.

PROPOSED SCHEDULE.

Chain or chains, of all kinds, made of iron or steel not less than 2 inches in diameter, seven-eighths cent per pound, but no chain of any description of these sizes shall pay a lower rate of duty than 30 per cent ad valorem.

Chain or chains, of all kinds, made of iron or steel less than 2 inches, but not less than thirteen-sixteenths of an inch diameter, 1 cent per pound, but no chain or chains of any description of these diameters shall pay a lower rate of duty than 40 per cent.

Chain or chains, of all kinds, made of iron or steel less than thirteen-sixteenths of an inch, but not less than thirteen thirty-seconds of an inch in diameter, 1¼ cents per pound, but no chain or chains of any description of these diameters shall pay a lower rate of duty than 60 per cent ad valorem.

Chain or chains, of all kinds, made of iron or steel less than thirteen thirty-seconds of an inch, but not less than one-fourth inch in diameter, 2 cents per pound, but no chain or chains of any description of these diameters shall pay a lower rate of duty than 60 per cent ad valorem.

Chain or chains, of all kinds, made of iron or steel less than one-fourth inch in diameter, containing not more than 12 links per foot, 3 cents per pound, but no chain or chains of any description of these diameters and length of link shall pay a lower rate of duty than 60 per cent ad valorem.

Chain or chains, of all kinds, made of iron or steel less than one-fourth inch in diameter, containing more than 12 links per foot, 5 cents per pound, but no chain or chains of any description of these sizes and length of link shall pay a lower rate of duty than 90 per cent ad valorem.

LEBANON CHAIN WORKS,
H. F. MATTERN,
Secretary and Treasurer.

STATEMENT OF THOS. T. WOODHOUSE, TRENTON, N. J., RELATIVE TO GERMAN PATTERN COIL AND HALTER CHAINS.

FRIDAY, *November 27, 1908.*

The CHAIRMAN. Whom do you represent, Mr. Woodhouse?

Mr. WOODHOUSE. I represent the Woodhouse Chain Works, of Trenton, N. J.

The CHAIRMAN. Very well; you may proceed with your statement.

Mr. WOODHOUSE. Mr. Chairman and gentlemen of the committee, what Mr. Mattern has been talking about principally has been handmade chain, which is a high-grade chain, and in which we are vitally interested as well, but principally I am here to represent what are called German pattern coil and halter chains, of which we make a considerable quantity, or have in the past. Last year we made very little, and I notice by the reports of the Treasury that the importations have increased considerably over 1907—yes, considerably; almost 60 per cent. The chain business is a peculiar one, and you can not consider it as a whole. The total valuation of all the manufacturers of this country is not a fair guide to consult on tariff matters. For instance, our factory is considered almost technically a specialty factory—that is, they make small special chains for all kinds of purposes. We have made in the past, and have educated our workmen up to the making of these small-sized chains, and they can not reverse themselves and go back to the making of heavy chains with profit either to themselves or the factory for which they work. For instance, on less than five-sixteenths-inch chain there was imported during the year 1907-8, on which there was a specific duty levied, a quantity amounting to 186,806 pounds, making a valuation of about $10,000, on which the duties levied were about $5,604. On chain of those sizes, on which there is 45 per cent levied, there was a total of 579,000 pounds imported, of a foreign valuation of $45,000, of a total New York valuation of $65,000—sufficient in that one item to keep a factory of our size working steadily.

Mr. GRIGGS. I happened to be out of the room for a moment when you went on the witness stand. I would like to interrupt you at this point long enough to inquire whether your company is making any money?

Mr. WOODHOUSE. Not this year.

Mr. GRIGGS. How about last year?

Mr. WOODHOUSE. We made some money last year and in 1906.

Mr. GRIGGS. All right, sir; go ahead. I am not astonished.

Mr. WOODHOUSE. No; I do not suppose you are, sir.

I have here, Mr. Chairman and gentlemen, a copy of the English prices, where the f. o. b. Liverpool price is compared with our market prices, which I will submit later in a brief, if the committee so desire. I not only have the copy, but I have the original quotations, some of which I bought a year and a half ago. For instance, on hand-made chain, to which our previous witness referred, on half-inch chain, the American wages are $3.12 a hundred pounds, while the English wages, a copy of which I have, are $1.36 per 100 pounds. But in that cost of wages the English chain maker must include his cost of fuel and factory expense, while the wages we pay are net to the workman. There are no expenses whatever that our workman has to pay out of the $3.12. Now, as a comparison on this same half-inch chain, our prices delivered in New York City to-day are $8.70 per hundred pounds, while I can import it from England and pay the duty and all expenses for $6.18 per hundred pounds, a difference against the American manufacturer of $2.52 per hundred pounds.

Mr. UNDERWOOD. With reference to that imported article, let me ask you where you buy it?

Mr. WOODHOUSE. Where in England?

Mr. UNDERWOOD. Yes.

Mr. WOODHOUSE. I can give a dozen houses, but I will give the two where I made purchases personally. I have quotations from Fellows Brothers, Cradley Heath, England, under date of October 11, 1907——

Mr. UNDERWOOD. That is per hundred pounds?

Mr. WOODHOUSE. I have figured it out on the basis of a hundred pounds.

Mr. UNDERWOOD. What did you pay per hundred pounds at the foreign purchasers in England?

Mr. WOODHOUSE. On half inch?

Mr. UNDERWOOD. Yes; the quotation you have given of $6.18 there?

Mr. WOODHOUSE. The English price f. o. b. Liverpool is $4.12 for 100 pounds, or 19 shillings and 3 pence for 112 pounds, or $4.12 for 100 pounds.

Mr. UNDERWOOD. What is the freight rate to New York?

Mr. WOODHOUSE. The freight rate I could not give as to the specific amount, but it is very small, I presume not over 25 cents a hundred pounds.

Mr. UNDERWOOD. That would make $4.37?

Mr. WOODHOUSE. Yes, sir.

Mr. UNDERWOOD. The difference is the tariff?

Mr. WOODHOUSE. The difference is the tariff. I have found by actual importation that the 45 per cent ad valorem duty, together with the total expenses, is about 50 per cent of the English cost price f. o. b. Liverpool.

Mr. UNDERWOOD. You say the cost price on that same chain in your factory was $8.70?

Mr. WOODHOUSE. No; that is our selling price.

Mr. UNDERWOOD. What is your cost price?

Mr. WOODHOUSE. I do not have that here, but it would not give us over 10 per cent profit.

Mr. UNDERWOOD. We are going to try to ascertain these facts from other sources if you do not have them. We may make mistakes unless you can give them to us accurately.

Mr. WOODHOUSE. If I assert to you we make 10 per cent profit, you can easily get the cost price.

Mr. UNDERWOOD. You make the calculation then and state the cost price.

Mr. WOODHOUSE. The cost price on that class would be $7.83.

Mr. BONYNGE. Is it fair to put their selling price against your cost price?

Mr. WOODHOUSE. You have the selling price in both cases and not the cost price.

Mr. BONYNGE. But in the questions which are being argued, they are putting the selling price with a profit to the foreign manufacturers against the cost price of the American manufacturers, where it should be cost price against cost price, or selling price against selling price, in order to make a fair distinction.

Mr. WOODHOUSE. The result would not be any different. The result would show exactly the same figures whether you took the cost price in each case or the selling price.

Mr. BONYNGE. But not the same if you took the cost price in one case and the selling price in another case.

Mr. WOODHOUSE. I am taking the selling price in both cases.

Mr. UNDERWOOD. I do not agree with you about that, because I think your cost price is going to compete with their selling price in New York, with freight added, and that is where the competition comes in. Above that you get a profit. That is what we are going to try to ascertain—how much profit you ought to get. If we give you a tariff equal to expenses, etc., above the foreign selling price f. o. b. Liverpool and your selling price, will that meet your needs?

Mr. WOODHOUSE. If the committee do just exactly what you intimate, I have no fear about where the tariff will be put.

Mr. UNDERWOOD. You think that will be a satisfactory basis?

Mr. WOODHOUSE. Absolutely so.

Mr. UNDERWOOD. You do not ask a prohibitive tariff?

Mr. WOODHOUSE. No, sir; I do not. I would like to have a protective tariff where we can compete on even terms at least.

Mr. UNDERWOOD. Have you filed any figures showing the selling price abroad, with freight added, and your cost price here?

Mr. WOODHOUSE. I have not the cost price. I have the selling price here of the American and the English chains f. o. b. New York.

Mr. UNDERWOOD. You say that the difference between your cost price and your selling price is about 10 per cent?

Mr. WOODHOUSE. Yes, sir; about 10 per cent.

Mr. UNDERWOOD. We can calculate that safely?

Mr. WOODHOUSE. Yes, sir; very safely. That is the price of handmade chains so far as I have gone.

Mr. UNDERWOOD. What is the percentage of labor cost in that?

Mr. WOODHOUSE. In handmade chains?

Mr. UNDERWOOD. Yes.

Mr. WOODHOUSE. It would be at least 70 per cent—70 to 80 per cent additional on small sizes.

Mr. UNDERWOOD. Seventy or 80 per cent?

Mr. WOODHOUSE. Yes, sir; as the chain makers' wages run. There are other labor costs, nonproductive labor, that would enter into it.

In German-pattern coil and halter chains we are largely interested, because our men are trained to make the small-sized chains and can not with profit to themselves or to the manufacturer change from the small sizes to the large sizes. On these German-pattern coil and halter chains we are asking for a higher tariff on the 2–0 sizes and smaller. On 18 links per foot, 2–0, which is three-sixteenths size wire and weighs 38 pounds to the hundred feet, the American selling price is $5.80 per hundred feet, while the import price, which gives a profit to the importer, is $5.27 per hundred feet, a difference against the American manufacturer on that one size of 53 cents a hundred feet. On the smaller sizes the differences as you go down are greater. On 1–0 the American selling price is $6.18 against the import price of $5.06, and on No. 2, which is nearly one-eighth inch wire, the American selling price is $9.50, while the imported German price is $4.67 per hundred feet.

Mr. UNDERWOOD. What is the amount of importation of chains as compared to the American market?

Mr. WOODHOUSE. On these sizes I have not any absolute facts to rely on, but from judgment and experience I should judge there is about one-third or possibly one-half of this kind of chain that is imported. We are located right close to New York City and feel the direct effect of the importations.

Mr. UNDERWOOD. If your figures are correct as to the American price and the foreign price, with duty added, why is there not more than that that comes in?

Mr. WOODHOUSE. I can not tell you.

Mr. UNDERWOOD. There is a difference of 50 per cent which you gave on the lowest amount.

Mr. WOODHOUSE. That is on the No. 2 size in selling price f. o. b. New York.

Mr. UNDERWOOD. The difference between the American price and the imported price with freight and duty added?

Mr. WOODHOUSE. That is on No. 2.

Mr. UNDERWOOD. Yes; and you said that the difference increased as you went down in sizes.

Mr. WOODHOUSE. Yes, sir; and as the number of links per foot increases.

Mr. UNDERWOOD. Why has not that brought more foreign chains into the American market?

Mr. WOODHOUSE. Possibly because they are not consumed. That may be the only reason; I do not know of any other reason. Another thing, as you go west this country is so great that the farther in you go the greater the expense of transportation from New York to the inland point.

Mr. UNDERWOOD. I thought so; but your factory is located in New Jersey, at the point of landing.

Mr. WOODHOUSE. Yes, sir; but I am speaking of importations.

Mr. UNDERWOOD. I suppose there are western factories that are located nearer the western market that make this same class of chains?

Mr. WOODHOUSE. There are but two in the West, I believe. There are four manufacturers of this line of chains. One is in Kent, Ohio, one is in York, Pa., and our own in Trenton, N. J., and one in Wapakoneta, Ohio.

Mr. CLARK. Do they not make chains in St. Louis?

Mr. WOODHOUSE. Not these sizes. They make what are known as machine-made chains, and there is only one manufacturer in St. Louis of that kind of chains.

Mr. CLARK. You are talking about hand-made chains?

Mr. WOODHOUSE. I am talking about German pattern machine chains and German pattern coil and halter chains just now.

Mr. CLARK. What kind of a duty are you willing to take? What reduction are you willing to accept in the tariff?

Mr. WOODHOUSE. On two-inch and larger.

Mr. CLARK. Do you count the diameter of the link or the diameter of the wire?

Mr. WOODHOUSE. Of the wire; yes, sir.

Mr. HILL. I understand you to say the importations last year were larger than they have been before?

Mr. WOODHOUSE. I do not know as they were much larger than ever before, but in 1907 the total importation in foreign value was $70,108.

Mr. COCKRAN. What chain is that?

Mr. WOODHOUSE. All sizes.

Mr. COCKRAN. Take the smaller sizes.

Mr. WOODHOUSE. I am talking about all the sizes, $70,108.

Mr. HILL. Is that larger or smaller than the importations for year before last?

Mr. WOODHOUSE. I can tell you that, I believe.

Mr. HILL. I think you said the importations were larger last year. I might have misunderstood you.

Mr. WOODHOUSE. I think I was right when I said that. In the fiscal year ending June 30, 1908, the total valuation of those two items was $55,053.

Mr. HILL. What was it for the previous year?

Mr. WOODHOUSE. In 1907 it was $70,000. It is less on those two items, you see, for the previous year. Nineteen hundred and seven was the banner year of importation and of American manufacture.

Mr. COCKRAN. How much was that in that year?

Mr. WOODHOUSE. 1907?

Mr. COCKRAN. Yes.

Mr. WOODHOUSE. On the two smaller sizes?

Mr. COCKRAN. Yes.

Mr. WOODHOUSE. Seventy thousand one hundred and eight dollars.

Mr. HILL. Then on those sizes that is practically all the importation there was?

Mr. WOODHOUSE. Yes, sir; it is nearly all in small sizes.

Mr. HILL. Do you know how much the total American consumption was of those sizes?

Mr. WOODHOUSE. In handmade chains and in German-pattern machine coil and halter chains I would assume from the meager information I have that the consumption is not over three times the importation, so the importation is about one-third of the consumption of this class of chains I am describing and for which I am arguing.

Mr. HILL. Can you confirm that impression and give us the exact information?

Mr. WOODHOUSE. I think I can. I think I can secure that.

Mr. HILL. And will you file it with the committee in a brief?

Mr. WOODHOUSE. Yes, sir.

Mr. COCKRAN. Where do you get those figures?

Mr. WOODHOUSE. From the Bureau of Commerce and Labor.

Mr. CLARK. Have you counted 1908?

Mr. WOODHOUSE. I have 1908 in pen-and-ink figures right from the Bureau of Commerce and Labor.

Mr. COCKRAN. We do not have those figures.

Mr. WOODHOUSE. I got them from the Bureau of Commerce and Labor on Wednesday. In the year 1905 the total importation was $42,000 of those two sizes. In 1906 the importation was $46,700, nearly.

Mr. CLARK. How did they happen to have the high-water mark in 1903 and fall off in 1905 and 1906 and go up again in 1906 and 1907? What made that?

Mr. WOODHOUSE. The general healthy condition of business in the United States, I presume.

The CHAIRMAN. The government reports show the importing price was six-tenths of a cent a pound in 1903, and that the equivalent ad valorem was over 170 per cent.

Mr. WOODHOUSE. They have 1903 and 1904 together here in this record which we have.

The CHAIRMAN. If they put them in at that price, I do not wonder.

Mr. CALDERHEAD. What are the figures you have?

Mr. WOODHOUSE. For the two years, 1903 and 1904.

The CHAIRMAN. That is the only year out of the whole.

Mr. CALDERHEAD. What are the figures?

Mr. WOODHOUSE. The total is $62,677.50 for the two years. I have no other argument to make. I think the figures I have stated are sufficient to any intelligent gentleman to show him that an increase in the tariff duties is necessary to foster and maintain the manufacture of these small chains in the United States.

Mr. COCKRAN. According to your statements, the manufacture of these small chains must be entirely abolished in the United States?

Mr. WOODHOUSE. I beg your pardon?

Mr. COCKRAN. I say according to the statement which you have presented to us here, the manufacture of these small chains must be entirely abolished in the United States.

Mr. WOODHOUSE. It would not be entirely, sir, because necessity knows no law, and will buy a certain number of these chains in this country.

Mr. COCKRAN. Why will they do that, if, as you say, they can be imported at 50 per cent less than you can sell yours for?

Mr. WOODHOUSE. As I said before, necessity knows no law, and if they must have them they must have them, and they will pay our price, and that is our only hope of selling these goods.

Mr. COCKRAN. According to your idea, then, they can be brought in, duty paid, for some 50 per cent less than you can produce them?

Mr. WOODHOUSE. Yes, sir; that is correct.

Mr. COCHRAN. But why should people buy from you if they can buy the imported chains so much cheaper?

Mr. WOODHOUSE. Necessity knows no law, is the only response I make to that.

Mr. COCKRAN. What necessity is there to buy of you?

Mr. WOODHOUSE. If you want an overcoat in a hurry, it does not make any difference what the price of that may be; you must buy it. The same is true of chains. If a man wants a chain and must have it, he will buy it at any price.

Mr. COCKRAN. Do you mean to say that the demand for chains is so pressing that people must buy them right away?

Mr. WOODHOUSE. At times; not always, but at certain times.

Mr. COCKRAN. Are we to infer that no chains are produced in this country except those for which there is an urgent need, so that people buy them rather than wait for the importation of cheaper chains?

Mr. WOODHOUSE. Not entirely; no.

Mr. COCKRAN. Why should they buy at all? Why should anybody buy a domestic chain when he can buy a foreign one for 50 per cent of the cost of the domestic chain?

Mr. WOODHOUSE. Perhaps he is a patriotic American.

Mr. COCKRAN. Even though he is, can he always tell a foreign chain from a domestic chain so as to be sure that in buying it he is giving vent to his patriotism?

Mr. WOODHOUSE. I could; I do not know whether everybody could or not.

Mr. COCKRAN. Your idea is that people buy chains at 100 per cent more than they could buy them for if imported merely to show their patriotism?

Mr. WOODHOUSE. Not necessarily. I say they will sometimes.

Mr. COCKRAN. Do you think that is so?

Mr. WOODHOUSE. Yes, sir; I will any time.

Mr. COCKRAN. You would pay 50 per cent more for an article simply because it was American?

Mr. WOODHOUSE. I would for some things; yes, sir.

Mr. COCKRAN. What things—chains or any old thing that would allow you to express your patriotism?

Mr. WOODHOUSE. Very often I will.

Mr. COCKRAN. Why do you pick out chains as a vehicle for patriotism?

Mr. WOODHOUSE. I did not say so. I said it may be so.

Mr. CLARK. Did you ever go to Europe.

Mr. WOODHOUSE. Yes, sir.

Mr. CLARK. Did you ever buy any clothes when you were there?

Mr. WOODHOUSE. No, sir.

Mr. CLARK. You never did?

Mr. WOODHOUSE. No, sir.

Mr. CLARK. You did not buy anything?

Mr. WOODHOUSE. I bought necessities, of course. When I went over there—I will give you one instance—I had no overcoat and was so cold I had to buy one.

Mr. CLARK. You knew before you went over there it was going to turn cold?

Mr. WOODHOUSE. No; I did not.

Mr. CLARK. Why did you not take your overcoat with you?

Mr. WOODHOUSE. I did not think I would need it. I went over in the summer time.

Mr. CLARK. Are you willing to scale down this tariff on any size of chain?

Mr. WOODHOUSE. On 2-inch and larger; yes, sir.

Mr. CLARK. How much?

Mr. WOODHOUSE. Mr. Mattern will give the necessary data to the committee later on.

Mr. CLARK. How much are you willing to scale the tariff down?

Mr. WOODHOUSE. I could not tell you now.

Mr. CLARK. In the years given here, from 1898 to 1907, the tariff on chains not less than three-quarters of an inch in diameter, as counted by what was actually brought in, ranged all the way from 31.40, the lowest, to 174.84. How much are you willing to scale that down?

Mr. WOODHOUSE. We are basing our argument on the tariff duty as printed. I had no knowledge until I came here on Wednesday as to what the actual importing was. We are basing on the actual letter of the law of the tariff schedule.

Mr. CLARK. Is there any competition among these American chain makers?

Mr. WOODHOUSE. Yes, sir.

Mr. CLARK. Have you not all got together?

Mr. WOODHOUSE. No, sir.

Mr. CLARK. In a combination?

Mr. WOODHOUSE. No, sir; not to my knowledge.

Mr. CLARK. You do not sell at the same prices?

Mr. WOODHOUSE. No, sir.

Mr. CLARK. Except accidentally?

Mr. WOODHOUSE. Except it be by accident.

Mr. CLARK. Oh, accident enters into it?

Mr. WOODHOUSE. Not premeditated accident, either.

Mr. CLARK. How often does that accident occur; 365 days in the year?

Mr. WOODHOUSE. No, sir. It is an absolutely open market in the chain business.

Mr. CLARK. You can make money on the larger sizes of chains?

Mr. WOODHOUSE. On the larger sizes, we make a little.

Mr. CLARK. And you can not make money on the smaller sizes?

Mr. WOODHOUSE. No, sir.

Mr. CLARK. Why do you not quit making the little ones?

Mr. WOODHOUSE. There is not enough consumption in the country to warrant us in doing that. Suppose we all did that?

Mr. CLARK. Somebody could go into some other business.

Mr. LONGWORTH. The witness who preceded you said he made no profit on large chains.

Mr. WOODHOUSE. He can answer for himself.

Mr. LONGWORTH. He said he sold practically at cost.

Mr. WOODHOUSE. That is true at times.

Mr. MATTERN. At the present time.

Mr. WOODHOUSE. All manufacturers at times do sell things at cost.

Mr. CLARK. Is not the explanation for this the fact that some years you are in competition with each other, and some years you all get together?

Mr. WOODHOUSE. Positively no, sir.

Mr. CLARK. That is not so?

Mr. WOODHOUSE. Positively no, sir.

Mr. CLARK. When are you going to tell us how much you are willing to scale this tariff down?

Mr. WOODHOUSE. As soon as the committee would like to have it.

Mr. CLARK. But you are not willing to scale that down unless we are willing to put the other up?

Mr. WOODHOUSE. No, sir. We are willing to give you every data necessary.

Mr. CLARK. What percentage did you make in your factory in 1907?

Mr. WOODHOUSE. Not over 10 per cent.

Mr. CLARK. Did you make 10 per cent?

Mr. WOODHOUSE. Yes, sir.

Mr. CLARK. How much did you make in 1906?

Mr. WOODHOUSE. That I could not tell you. I have not those figures here.

Mr. CLARK. What is the greatest percentage you ever made?

Mr. WOODHOUSE. 1906–7 was the greatest year we ever had.

Mr. COCKRAN. Do you remember what it was that year?

Mr. WOODHOUSE. Not exactly.

Mr. COCKRAN. What is the capital of your company?

Mr. WOODHOUSE. It is about $55,000—a personal affair.

Mr. COCKRAN. Are you an organized corporation?

Mr. WOODHOUSE. No, sir; it is an individual concern.

Mr. GRIGGS. Do you count out the salaries of the officers before counting that per cent?

Mr. WOODHOUSE. That is net and above everything.

Mr. GRIGGS. What do you pay the head of the concern?

Mr. WOODHOUSE. Two thousand five hundred dollars. There is one thing, gentlemen, I omitted to say, and that is, in my figures for the English cost the maximum is given for wages and the minimum for the American cost, which is under the present depression; the prices are lower than they were a year ago.

Then there is another thing about the English manufacturer that possibly many people in the country do not know, and which I do know, because I was born in England, and that is the chain manufacturer in England does not have all his force under one roof, as we do in this country; they are jobbed out and create competition there between one another, so that the actual wages in England sometimes are considerably lower than the record I have here would indicate.

Mr. CLARK. Are you an American citizen now?

Mr. WOODHOUSE. I am an American citizen, and glad to be one.

Mr. CLARK. You spoke of patriotism awhile ago. Congress is charged with the duty of raising more revenue than is coming in now, and the only way we can get more revenue is to cut the rates down. Are you not willing to make a little sacrifice, along with the others, to help Uncle Sam in that matter?

Mr. HILL. Your industry is already a competitor against the chain industry in the United States?

Mr. WOODHOUSE. It is not a competitor.

Mr. HILL. Are you not manufacturing chains now a great deal cheaper than it costs the Government to make them in the navy-yard?

Mr. WOODHOUSE. That follows without argument.

Mr. HILL. Then you have some patriotism, manifested in that way?

Mr. WOODHOUSE. Surely.

Mr. CLARK. If the Government had not gone to making some of its own chains, you would have marked your chains up?

Mr. WOODHOUSE. We do not come in competition with that class of chains. We come in competition with a class of chains that the Government does not handle.

The CHAIRMAN. I want to suggest to you to supply a copy of this schedule in the not far-distant future, with the reductions and the increases where you think they ought to be.

Mr. WOODHOUSE. When can we do that?

The CHAIRMAN. Between this and the 4th of December.
Mr. WOODHOUSE. That is hardly time.
The CHAIRMAN. Well, we will give you until the 15th of December.

THE DIAMOND CHAIN AND MANUFACTURING COMPANY, INDIAN-APOLIS, IND., ASKS MAINTENANCE OF PRESENT TARIFF ON AUTOMOBILE AND BICYCLE CHAINS.

INDIANAPOLIS, IND., *December 15, 1908.*
Hon. SERENO E. PAYNE,
  Chairman Ways and Means Committee,
            Washington, D. C.

DEAR SIR: We, as manufacturers of machine-made sprocket chain, commonly called bicycle chains (roller and block), automobile chains (roller and block), and chains for transmission 'of power, earnestly desire that no reduction be made in the present tariff, 45 per cent ad valorem, on our product. The reasons for our desire are as follows:

Importations of merchandise competing are from Hans Renold, Manchester, England; Brampton Brothers (Limited), Birmingham, England; Coventry Chain Company, Coventry, England; Peugeot Frères, Paris, France; and other makers in England, France, and Germany.

The American industry in block chains for bicycles is about nineteen years old, and was not thoroughly developed at the time the slump came in the manufacture and sale of bicycles, which industry has not revived—the volume is not now of sufficient size to yield a living profit to the present manufacturers of this type of chain.

The manufacture of roller chain is comparatively new; the advent of same came with the automobile, which induced us, along with others, to embark in the business at great investment and expense. With the growth of the automobile industry the automobile trade shifted extensively to gear or shaft drive before we, as makers of chains, could bring our equipment and costs to a point where we could meet foreign competitors.

The steel used by American makers costs approximately 33⅓ per cent more than the same material abroad. American skilled workmen, machinists and operators of screw machines and presses, receive from 17½ cents to 40 cents per hour, and the day is usually limited to eight or nine hours. The same workmen abroad receive from 8 cents to 20 cents per hour, and the day is usually from eight to ten hours.

Taking the American cost represented by 100, the foreign maker can produce the same at approximately 55, and with the present duty, 45 per cent, this product can be offered to the United States trade at 79. Add to this 30 per cent (profit and freight), and these goods can be delivered in New York at approximately 103, depending on the percentage of profit the foreign maker is willing to accept. It is possible and in practice, under the present duty, for the foreign maker to sell his product with profit, delivered in New York, at prices equal to our cost of production, and this condition will continue for many years.

At present we are not able to sell our product in either England, France, or Germany, because our costs will not permit us to compete. For this reason, your records will show that there are actually no exports by the American makers to the above countries. On the other hand there is a considerable quantity of chain imported from the above-named countries into the United States.

A reduction in the duty would be disastrous to us and other chain makers of the United States, while a slight increase would help to develop and increase an industry employing largely skilled labor. We urge a very much closer investigation by the department to prevent undervaluation by the foreign makers, which even at this time seems to be in practice.

We have written the following chain makers in regard to this subject, and inclose herewith their replies for your consideration: Baldwin Chain and Manufacturing Company, Worcester, Mass.; Whitned Manufacturing Company, Hartford, Conn.; Duckworth Chain any Manufacturing Company, Springfield, Mass.; Lefever Arms Company, Syracuse, N. Y.; Link Belt Company, Indianapolis, Ind.

Yours, very truly,

DIAMOND CHAIN MANUFACTURING CO.

EXHIBIT A.

HARTFORD, CONN., *December 18, 1908.*

Mr. L. M. WAINRIGHT,
President Diamond Chain and Manufacturing Company,
Indianapolis, Ind.

DEAR SIR: We have your favor of the 15th instant, inclosing copy of the letter you have dictated to Hon. S. E. Payne, chairman of Ways and Means Committee, in regard to the subject of duty on chains made in foreign countries.

As you have requested us to give you our views on this important subject, we will state that the figures and arguments mentioned in your letter look to us to be sound and correct, and we firmly believe that the American chain makers can not possibly compete with the chain manufacturers in England, France, Germany, etc., unless we can secure materials and competent labor at the lower rates prevailing abroad.

At the present rate of tariff, foreign chains are finding a market in this country at prices as low or lower than our prices on our product notwithstanding the duty, freight, cartage, and commission to agents, and we have certainly spent a large sum for special machinery and apparatus to assist us in making our chains economically. On the bicycle chains we have made no profit for a number of years because of our smaller volume, caused by the change of conditions in the bicycle industry in this country. We have sold a few bicycle chains to Japan at a price also lower than our actual cost with the idea of increasing our volume for the future, but in other foreign countries there seems to be no chance whatever for us to secure orders on account of the still lower prices prevailing in England, France, Germany, etc.

On our automobile chains we are pleased to admit that we have made a reasonable profit, as our chains of this type have been popular in this country, and we have had a sufficient volume to reduce our overhead expense. At the present prices prevailing on automobile chains in this country we feel confident that a small concern could not meet our present quotations without making a loss.

We respectfully urge that no reduction be made in the present tariff on driving chains, believing firmly and sincerely that conditions do not as yet warrant any reduction, and we will appreciate it if you will bring this letter before the proper authorities.

Thanking you in advance, we remain,

Yours, very truly,

THE WHITNEY MFG. COMPANY,
C. E. WHITNEY, *President.*

EXHIBIT B.

WORCESTER, MASS., *December 18, 1908.*

Hon. SERENO E. PAYNE,
Chairman Ways and Means Committee, Washington, D. C.

DEAR SIR: We are manufacturers of drive chains, including bicycle, automobile, and machinery drive chains, of which the automobile department has the largest portion of our business.

The letter written by the Diamond Chain and Manufacturing Company, copy of which was referred to us, is from our point of view an excellent statement of the chain industry and of its relation to imported goods.

If it is true that the object of the tariff is to protect and foster struggling industries in this country for which there is a substantial and growing demand, we believe the drive-chain industry is a typical case.

We understand that the chain industry in England, France, and Germany especially has been very extensively developed for some years, and that they manufacture under the most favorable conditions; that the development of the use of·drive chains in these countries has been developed for some time; hence the manufacturers in these countries are in the most favorable condition to make goods of this character, and are in a position to import them into this country substantially as set forth in said letter.

From our understanding of the situation, from knowledge of the quotations that have been made this season of foreign makers, it is absolutely essential for our existence that the present tariff should not be reduced. On the contrary if we have the protection that we ought to have to enable us to compete, we think it should be raised 50 to 55 per cent.

It is only comparatively recent that the use of chain drive in this country has attracted attention, but it is now steadily growing, both for driving vehicles and machinery.

In view of the history of the industry in this country, the manufacturers of chain drives must of necessity incur considerable extra

expense in the way of experimentation for some time before the manufacturers can develop themselves to sufficient extent to compete with
foreign makers.

Yours, very truly,

BALDWIN CHAIN AND MFG. COMPANY.

EXHIBIT C.

SPRINGFIELD, MASS., *December 18, 1908.*
DIAMOND CHAIN AND MANUFACTURING COMPANY,
Indianapolis, Ind.

GENTLEMEN: Replying to yours of the 15th, we most earnestly hope
there will be no reduction made in the present tariff on cycle and automobile chains.   It would no doubt be the ruination of our business, as
with the present tariff there are a great many chains being imported
and sold in competition with domestic makes, and we have in mind an
English chain that is being delivered in this country at the present
time at a lower price than it would cost us to make.

Respectfully,

DUCKWORTH CHAIN AND MANUFACTURING COMPANY,
GEO. H. EMPSALL, *Secretary and Manager.*

EXHIBIT D.

INDIANAPOLIS, IND., *December 17, 1908.*
Mr. L. M. WAINWRIGHT,
President Diamond Chain and Manufacturing Company, City.

MY DEAR SIR: We beg to acknowledge receipt of copy of your
communication of the 15th instant, addressed to the Hon. Sereno E.
Payne, chairman Ways and Means Committee, upon the subject
of tariff on machine-made chains.   Though we are not largely interested in the particular chains referred to in your communication, we
are largely involved in chains of similar character, which would
probably be subject to the same treatment in considering the tariff
subject.   Having access to the works of some of the foreign manufacturers, and having examined into the methods of their manufacture and into the expenses of their product, we are prepared to say
that any noticeable reduction of the present tariff would operate to
the decided advantage of the foreign manufacturers and to our disadvantage in corresponding degree.   It so happens that to-day we
are being visited by Mr. Charles Renold, of the Hans Renold Company,
of Manchester, England, and in discussing with him methods of manufacture it was developed that they are able to obtain their labor in
nearly all departments at less than one-half the same labor costs us.
We believe that this fact of itself should be sufficient argument
against any reduction that may be proposed.

Yours, very truly,

LINK BELT COMPANY,
GLENN G. HOWE, *Vice-President.*

EXHIBIT E.

SYRACUSE, N. Y., *December 21, 1908.*
COMMITTEE ON WAYS AND MEANS,
　　　　Washington, D. C.

GENTLEMEN: In reference to the hearings now being held before your honorable committee upon the subject of tariff revision, we beg to say:

Some years ago the popularity of the bicycle was such that the manufacture of the wheel in its entirety, or some of the component parts entering into its construction, gave promise of being one of the leading industries of America. Large sums of money were invested for its manufacture, but about the time the plants were equipped for manufacturing the wheel itself was no longer a fashionable fad, and it is now used only in a limited way for strictly commercial uses.

The result is the output of bicycles has been reduced, say, 50 to 75 per cent and the selling price of bicycles reduced 50 to 75 per cent.

In the interval there has been a marked advance in the cost of material, and the increased demand for labor in the metal-working industries has very largely increased the cost of labor.

We are manufacturers of bicycle chains. The industry for the last few years has been scarcely self-sustaining. The manufacturers of chains in foreign countries are able to secure steel at prices 25 to 30 per cent below what we must pay. The manufactured chain is, say, 75 per cent labor. Our labor costs three times that of the same class in foreign countries.

The protection afforded the chain manufacturers under the present schedule has enabled them to partly hold the home market, but we are unable to meet foreign competition in any neutral territory.

Any reduction from the present schedule would admit of the free importation of foreign chains to the exclusion of the American chain. If such conditions existed it would in any event afford only a small added revenue to our Government owing to the limited number of chains that can be marketed.

We unhesitatingly say that the maintenance of the present tariff is absolutely necessary to the existence of this industry.

Respectfully requesting your favorable consideration, we are,
　　　Yours, truly,
　　　　　　　LEFEVER ARMS COMPANY,
　　　　　　　J. F. DURSTON, *President.*

WROUGHT-IRON PIPE.

[Paragraph 152.]

STATEMENT OF J. A. CAMPBELL, REPRESENTING THE YOUNGSTOWN, OHIO, SHEET AND TUBE COMPANY.

WEDNESDAY, *November 25, 1908.*

Mr. CAMPBELL. Mr. Chairman and gentlemen of the committee, I was called to a meeting in New York day before yesterday and was selected to come here and represent the pipe interests, the wrought-iron pipe interests.

Mr. UNDERWOOD. Will you please give us the number on the schedule?

Mr. CAMPBELL. Yes, sir; it is paragraph 152. They did not select me because of any particular fitness——

Mr. GRIGGS. Before you begin I would like to ask you a question. You were selected by some other people to represent them here; you also are in the manufacturing business yourself, are you not?

Mr. CAMPBELL. Yes, sir.

Mr. GRIGGS. I assume that you know as much about their business as they do and ought to be able to inform us so that we can act intelligently with regard to the matter?

Mr. CAMPBELL. I do not represent anybody except our own company. There was nobody in the pipe business there, and that was the reason they selected me. If there had been anybody else they would not have selected me; they would have selected some one else to come here and present their case.

Mr. GRIGGS. You said you were sent here by your own company?

Mr. CAMPBELL. No, sir. I was selected because I was the only pipe man there, by the people at this meeting—the American Iron and Steel Association, and not knowing that I was to give facts or figures except with respect to the knowledge that I have of the business, and I can only speak for our business. We are in the pipe business, making steel and steel billets and sheets.

The CHAIRMAN. What paragraph is that?

Mr. CAMPBELL. It is 152. The schedule calls for 2 cents per pound on " lap welded, butt welded, seamed or jointed iron or steel boiler tubes, pipes, flues, or stays, not thinner than number sixteen wire gauge." That, I would take it, was $40 a ton, and I suppose I will occupy the unique position of being the one fellow who says that this tariff is too high. I am a tariff reformer, I presume, but I am a protectionist.

Mr. GRIGGS. I am glad to see that you are honest with respect to that.

Mr. CAMPBELL. And I have argued to all these people, as a good many others have, that we ought to come here and be honest and say what we think, and that when the tariff is too high that we ought to be willing to accept a reduction, and when it is too low we ought to ask for an advance. I understand there is to be a reduction of the tariff, but there have been a great many inaccuracies that have crept into the tariff because it probably has been a matter of grace. You gentlemen are Congressmen representing different districts, and they all do not think alike, but their districts generally think as they do or as some other district thinks.

The CHAIRMAN. What do you think the duty ought to be on cast iron?

Mr. CAMPBELL. I do not know anything about cast iron prices. This is wrought iron and wrought steel that I represent.

The CHAIRMAN. This says:
" Lap welded, butt welded, seamed, or jointed iron or steel boiler tubes, pipes," etc.

Mr. CAMPBELL. That is wrought iron and wrought steel pipes.

Mr. DALZELL. Two cents a pound?

Mr. CAMPBELL. Yes, sir. It is made from a skelp, and it is turned over and lapped—welded—the butt welded.

The CHAIRMAN. What do you think this duty ought to be, as an honest, square duty?

Mr. CAMPBELL. It ought not to be half what it is in this bill. It says $40 a ton; it ought not to be over $20. That is a cent a pound which would be ample duty to protect us. Now, I can not speak for every other manufacturer.

The CHAIRMAN. How would $10 do in your business?

Mr. CAMPBELL. Well, $10 would not do, ordinarily; but we possibly could get along with a dollar or two less than somebody else; I think our costs are as low as anybody else's costs outside of the United States Steel Corporation.

The CHAIRMAN. What could you get along with?

Mr. CAMPBELL. We could possibly get along with $18 instead of $20 a ton.

Mr. GRIGGS. Let us compromise on $15 now and quit.

Mr. CAMPBELL. No, sir; we want you to remember now, speaking seriously, that you are legislating for a lot of people. I know of a number of mills throughout the East and throughout the Middle West that make pipe and that can not make pipe within four or five dollars a ton as cheap as we can, and if you put this tariff so low you will either force them to put their men to a small wage or put them out of the business. In 1906 two of the largest and best mills in this country went out of business on account of the prices; and we lost money on all the small sizes of pipe which we made during that year.

The CHAIRMAN. What can you lay it down in New York at?

Mr. CAMPBELL. That is a difficult thing, Mr. Chairman.

The CHAIRMAN. What do you deliver it to the factory at?

Mr. CAMPBELL. We make all different sizes, from three-eighths of an inch up to 12 inches—a larger pipe—and each of those sizes costs a little different. Take for instance, the light casing that goes into wheels.

The CHAIRMAN. Can you give the average price per ton at which you could deliver it at your factory?

Mr. CAMPBELL. Yes, sir; I think I could; I think it would be about $45 a ton on steel pipe.

The CHAIRMAN. What can it be laid down for in New York from abroad—that is, the average price?

Mr. CAMPBELL. That I do not know; I have no knowledge on that subject.

The CHAIRMAN. I am trying to get at how you arrive at this duty of $20 a ton.

Mr. CAMPBELL. The way I arrive at that is by comparing it with other commodities. I know nothing about the matter abroad. The labor on pipe is more than any other commodity except two—that is, tin plate and sheets. The labor on tin plates and sheets is higher than on pipes. Pipe is a light commodity; the tonnage is light. The consumption of the country is small as compared with some of the other heavy material, and there is a great deal of labor in threading it and making the coupling and testing it and carrying it on through; a great deal of labor is employed that is not employed in the heavier classes of iron and steel.

The CHAIRMAN. Of course the heavier the pipe the more labor there would be per ton?

Mr. CAMPBELL. Yes, sir.

The CHAIRMAN. And the more expensive it would be per ton?

Mr. CAMPBELL. Yes, sir.

The CHAIRMAN. And the more protection it needs per ton?

Mr. CAMPBELL. Yes, sir; perhaps.

The CHAIRMAN. Now, what is the difference between the large and the small sizes per ton?

Mr. CAMPBELL. That would vary somewhat. Iron and steel pipe is different and the light sizes in casing—that is, what we call casing— oil well supplies, is made in larger sizes, but it is very thin pipe and it costs considerably more than the heavier or extra heavy pipe that we make, and the rims and couplings cost more, and the extra heavy couplings.

The CHAIRMAN. Well, extra large size pipe, what is it worth?

Mr. CAMPBELL. The average small sizes—that is, going down to about ¾ inch, is worth about $45 f. o. b. Pittsburg.

The CHAIRMAN. And the larger or heavier size?

Mr. CAMPBELL. The heavier size would cost a little more. When you get up above 8-inch the cost increases rapidly, and it would probably cost—that is, 8 and 10 inch would probably cost four or five dollars more, and from 12 to 14 inch would cost four or five dollars above that, or $8 above the base, etc.

Mr. BOUTELL. How much of that forty-five came in 1896?

Mr. CAMPBELL. I was not in business in 1896—that is, in the pipe business. Our business is a new business.

Mr. BOUTELL. Do you know what the price of this pipe was in 1896?

Mr. CAMPBELL. Yes, sir; it was about $10 a ton less than it is now.

Mr. BOUTELL. About $35 a ton?

Mr. CAMPBELL. Yes, sir.

Mr. UNDERWOOD. When we get a witness before us who is candid and square, as you are, I think the committee can very well rely upon his judgment. I would like to ask you if you will give the information for the committee, ascertain the cost of this pipe in the competitive markets abroad, what it is selling for there, and ascertain the freight rates to New York City?

Mr. CAMPBELL. I expect to do that in a brief that I will file.

Mr. UNDERWOOD. Will you file that in a brief, together with the cost of production in this country?

Mr. CAMPBELL. Yes, sir.

Mr. UNDERWOOD. That is the information I desire.

Mr. GRIGGS. If you will refer to paragraph 152, you will notice that it says 2 cents a pound on "lap-welded, butt-welded, seamed, or jointed iron or steel boiler tubes, pipes, flues, or stays, not thinner than No. 16 wire gauge, 2 cents per pound; welded cylindrical furnaces, made from plate metal, 2½ cents per pound."

Mr. CAMPBELL. I do not know anything about that; we do not make that, and I can not speak as to it, but I do not think you ought to treat that in the same way that you have treated the pipe, from my general knowledge of it, but I really do not know anything about it— that is, I do not think it would be fair to cut that in two because it was in paragraph 152.

Mr. GRIGGS. But you think we ought to go in for a genuine tariff revision, do you not?

Mr. CAMPBELL. Yes, sir; but bear in mind all the time that this duty ought to be a protective duty, not so high, however, at any time that no material can come into this country, because if you do that it would permit us as manufacturers to get together, if it was legal for us to get together—which it is not—in some way when the demand was greater than the supply, which was true last year, when we could have put the pipe up four, or six, or eight dollars a ton, and the people would have had to pay. It would not have been fair. We could have done that under this tariff, but it would not have been fair. It did not occur, but it might occur at some time, and I do not think that it ought to occur.

Mr. DALZELL. What was the production last year?

Mr. CAMPBELL. I do not know, but I would say in the neighborhood of 2,000,000 tons, about 60 per cent, perhaps, of which the corporation makes, about 40 per cent of which the independents make.

Mr. HILL. About 40 per cent on tubes imported?

Mr. CAMPBELL. That undoubtedly was not the regular practice that we are talking about. That was some specialty or something that happened to come in because this duty is absolutely protective. There is no question about that.

Mr. RANDELL. I would like to ask the witness a question. On this lap welded and other items mentioned in this paragraph, " not thinner than number sixteen wire gauge," which is 2 cents a pound tariff, how much does that cost you f. o. b. at the factory?

Mr. CAMPBELL. About $45 a ton on an average.

Mr. RANDELL. What does it cost you for the labor, not counting anything for the interest on the money invested, nor anything of that kind, but just what does it cost you in expense to produce it?

Mr. CAMPBELL. Well, you would have to specify where we begin, whether we begin at the ore and go through the pig iron and the steel and the skelp and then the pipe.

Mr. RANDELL. Begin with the ore.

Mr. CAMPBELL. I would say, direct and indirect, about $18 to $20 a ton; that means all the transportation and the labor that went into the transportation, the labor that went into the ore and everything that was direct and indirect. I think with regard to tin plate that the direct and indirect labor is in the neighborhood of $30 a ton, as near as it can be figured. I think it is about two-fifths of it.

Mr. RANDELL. This is costing you eighteen or twenty dollars a ton?

Mr. CAMPBELL. Well, that is not direct labor; that is direct and indirect.

Mr. RANDELL. That includes everything.

Mr. CAMPBELL. It includes everything from the ore up, including the transportation and the mining of the coal.

Mr. RANDELL. Excepting interest on your investment?

Mr. CAMPBELL. Everything that enters into it in the way of labor from all sources. Our direct labor on that pipe would not be over——

Mr. RANDELL. I am speaking of all expenses, not only labor but all expenses. You buy your ore, do you not?

Mr. CAMPBELL. If the expense of supplies and everything of that kind entered into it, it would run up above that.

Mr. RANDELL. The expense of buying ore?

Mr. CAMPBELL. Oh, yes, sir; that would go in with this labor that I speak of. It would come in with the mining of the ore and the labor on railroads and boats and the mining of the coal that smelts the ore, makes the coke and transports the coke, and all the different items that go into it, beside the direct labor that we use in making it into pig iron and then into steel and then into skelp and then into pipe, etc., and so on down the line, and loading it on the cars.

There is one other item that I want to speak of, and that is with reference to a subject that another gentleman was billed to speak on, Mr. Robling, on wire. Mr. Robling is not here, and a gentleman from Pittsburg was to take it up.

The CHAIRMAN. Wire and wire products.

Mr. UNDERWOOD. What is the schedule?

Mr. CAMPBELL. It is 137. " Round iron or steel wire, not smaller than number thirteen wire gauge, one and one-fourth cents per pound." I have recently gone into the wire business, that is, the 16th of last March I bought a wire plant, and in talking with Mr. Robling and other people in New York with reference to this, there was a discussion of the matter.

Mr. HILL. Have you examined the proposed revised language under this schedule that you are speaking of now?

Mr. CAMPBELL. No, sir; I have not.

Mr. HILL. That is the one you have just spoken of, paragraph 152, and also this one, paragraph 137?

Mr. CAMPBELL. I did not know there was any proposed revised language.

No. 137 reads: " Round iron or steel wire, not smaller than number thirteen wire gauge, 1¼ cents per pound; smaller than number thirteen and not smaller than number sixteen wire gauge, 1½ cents per pound; smaller than number sixteen wire gauge, 2 cents per pound."

I have not been in the business long enough to know from my own personal knowledge what this tariff ought to be. From our own personal experience in the last few months it does not cut any figure and should have no weight with you. I should say that this tariff was not ample, but when I come to compare it with other things I would say that it was too high. Our business does not show, in the wire end of it, or has not shown a justifiable profit. Our other business has been a profitable business. That is another thing; you have accused everybody of saying that they have not made any money. We have made money for the past four years; our business has been very prosperous, and I believe in talking with these people about this wire that they will be perfectly satisfied if this is reduced the same. Tin plate is three-tenths of a cent a pound, making it from one and a half to one twenty. Now you must remember that in making the tin plate and sheets, that perhaps wire requires about as much labor as any or perhaps more than any other one item, being in about the same class as pipe. Now, with reference to wire nails, wire nails have only one-half a cent a pound, and I know that we can not afford to have that reduced. We are selling wire nails now very cheap, and in looking this matter up on the train coming here yesterday we found that we could lay nails down cheaper in New York than we could make them. That protection, I think, is ample, but I do not think it is too much. I think that you can afford to take off three-tenths of a cent a pound without hurting either labor or capital invested in the wire business, and I believe it would be perfectly satisfactory. But in all these things you want to remember that there are hundreds and hundreds of small concerns that are making sheets and buy their bars and do not produce them as we produce them and as the corporation produces them. There are hundreds of people who are buying this wire and putting it into fences; hundreds of concerns that are buying the rods and putting them into wire, and then into the other forms of production. Some go back farther and buy the billets and have their own rod mill. We produce this stuff from the ore to the finished product, and what might be satisfactory to us and what we might live under, might put them out of business. So that you want to be careful in framing all these bills, in my opinion, and take into consideration the vast number of smaller manufacturers who have the same right to live as the larger ones have. For instance, the corporation could put us out of business if they saw fit at any time because we are not doing a powerful business, while we have a vast advantage over a number of other people because our firm is new and our facilities are first class. We can manufacture the stuff as cheap after we get a start as anybody, we believe, not even excepting the corporation, but we can not bring ours down, we can not mine it and bring it down, because we have no transportation facilities to handle it in that way, nearly as cheap as they can.

The CHAIRMAN. You suggest a reduction, as I understand you, of three-tenths of a cent a pound?

Mr. CAMPBELL. Yes, sir.

The CHAIRMAN. Now, " Round iron or steel wire, not more than thirteen wire gauge, 1¼ cents per pound." You make that ninety-five one-hundredths, do you?

Mr. CAMPBELL. I would make that about a cent a pound and the other about one-twenty.

The CHAIRMAN. " Smaller than number thirteen and not smaller than number sixteen wire gauge, 1½ cents a pound?"

Mr. CAMPBELL. That ought to be about one-twenty.

The CHAIRMAN. " Smaller than number sixteen wire gauge, 2 cents a pound?"

Mr. CAMPBELL. That could be safely three-tenths off; in my opinion that could be reduced that much.

The CHAIRMAN. One and three-tenths you think that ought to be?

Mr. CAMPBELL. Yes, sir; not over that.

The CHAIRMAN. Have you had any question in your business about iron and steel wire covered with cotton and silk or other material?

Mr. CAMPBELL. No, sir; we do not make that.

The CHAIRMAN. You do not know anything about that, then?

Mr. CAMPBELL. No, sir.

The CHAIRMAN. Well, corset and corset steel—you do not make that?

Mr. CAMPBELL. No, sir.

The CHAIRMAN. Not especially provided for in this act shall pay a duty of so much ad valorem, etc. Do you think it necessary to have a bracket like that in addition to the wire schedule?

Mr. CAMPBELL. I am not so much in favor of ad valorem duties myself.

The CHAIRMAN. But there might be some wire that was smaller than thirteen and some larger than thirteen or smaller than sixteen, could there not be?

Mr. CAMPBELL. Yes, sir.

The CHAIRMAN. That is only to catch what does not come under these three brackets?

Mr. CAMPBELL. Yes, sir; I think it might be well to have that in.

The CHAIRMAN. What ad valorem duty would be proper to catch that?

Mr. CAMPBELL. I really could not say; I am not familiar enough with the wire business. I have not been in it long enough.

The CHAIRMAN. I see that they made brass wire three or four years ago and the machinery performed half a dozen operations at once; that is, they drew out a small rod and then the next operation took place; it went two or three times as fast, and they reduced it, etc., until they got very fine wire. There was a continuous motion of that wire from the wire clear out to the machine, the machine going faster for the small concerns and taking it up so there was no catch about it. Do they use that same method in steel wire?

Mr. CAMPBELL. They have tried it, but it has been a failure so far. There is a mill in Buffalo now called the Shenandoah Wire Company that has been doing that for some time, making it a continuous operation, but it has been a failure up to date, and they are out of the business.

The CHAIRMAN. So you do not have a labor-saving device?

Mr. CAMPBELL. No, sir; we have been unable to do it. In fact, we have not tried it.

Mr. RANDELL. I would like to ask one or two questions about the wire. Do you manufacture barbed wire?

Mr. CAMPBELL. We have not made any yet; we will in the next thirty days. We have ordered a number of barbed wire machines.

Mr. RANDELL. In your opinion, does barbed wire need any protection so that you can do business in this country, in order that you may be able to do business?

Mr. CAMPBELL. It absolutely needs protection; yes, sir.

Mr. RANDELL. In order that the business might be carried on?

Mr. CAMPBELL. Yes, sir.

Mr. RANDALL. In other words, the barbed wire business would be discontinued in this country?

Mr. CAMPBELL. Undoubtedly, unless the whole condition in this country changed. If transportation should become cheaper and coal cheaper and coke and ore and all the different things, and labor correspondingly reduced, you might be able to do it, but it would be impracticable at present.

Mr. RANDELL. Is there any barbed wire imported into this country?

Mr. CAMPBELL. I really do not know. I should say not.

Mr. RANDELL. The duty on it is absolutely, is it not?

Mr. CAMPBELL. I presume it is; I have not read it.

Mr. RANDELL. You are well aware that that makes this condition that people who use barbed wire for fences and for other purposes must give whatever price the manufacturers and those who control the product fix. Is that not the situation?

Mr. CAMPBELL. Perhaps they would have to give what they ask, but I do not see that it would have any effect upon wire. Take pipe, for instance; it has been $40 a ton, and some gentleman to-day in the examination said that he would raise $9,000,000, I think, which would increase prices to the people if he put up the price on bars $2 a ton; that is, on four and a half million tons the people would pay

$9,000,000 more for it. Because we have had the $40 on pipe it has not made pipe any cheaper than it would if it had only been $20 a ton.

Mr. RANDELL. The tariff has not made the price any cheaper, you say?

Mr. CAMPBELL. No, sir; the tariff has not made it any higher.

Mr. RANDELL. Then the tariff has not done you any good, as far as raising the price is concerned?

Mr. CAMPBELL. Absolutely; it has kept all of the pipe out of the country and has given us all of our home market. No; it has not done us any good with regard to raising prices, but if we took it off we would have to reduce the price.

Mr. RANDELL. Do you mean to say that on this production, where the price is fixed by those who manufacture and control the products in this country, having a prohibitive tariff, that they have not fixed the price any higher, and that that is the very lowest price that they can afford to take?

Mr. CAMPBELL. No, sir; I do not mean to say that at all.

Mr. RANDELL. It would hardly be human nature, would it?

Mr. CAMPBELL. No, sir; we get all we can—not all we can, really, either; I would not say that, because last year we turned down a lot of business.

Mr. RANDELL. I would like to keep on with this barbed-wire business, if you are not afraid of tiring yourself.

Mr. CAMPBELL. I would like to know what that duty is, first, before I talk about it, if you will give me the paragraph.

Mr. RANDELL. It is under this same paragraph, No. 137.

Mr. CLARK. It is 136, fence wire.

Mr. CAMPBELL. No. 136 is wire rods, but the latter part of No. 137——

Mr. DALZELL. Paragraph 136 covers fence wire. It says: " Rivet, screw, fence, and other iron or steel iron rod, whether round, oval, flat, or square, or in any other shape."

Mr. CAMPBELL. That does not cover wire. That is wire rods.

Mr. UNDERWOOD. I think it comes in under the 25 per cent ad valorem.

Mr. CAMPBELL. In the last clause of paragraph 137 it is stated " that articles manufactured from iron, steel, brass, or copper wire,' That would be wire fence and barbed wire—

Shall pay the rate of duty imposed upon the wire used in the manufacture of such articles, and in addition thereto 1¼ cents per pound, except that wire rope and wire strand shall pay the maximum rate of duty which would be imposed upon any wire used in the manufacture thereof, and in addition thereto 1 cent per pound.

Mr. RANDELL. Now, the tariff on that is 40 per cent ad valorem. You have that now, have you? The tariff is 45 per cent?

Mr. DALZELL. It is 45 per cent ad valorem plus 1¼ cents a pound.

Mr. RANDELL. That would be barbed wire and wire rods?

Mr. GRIGGS. Corset wire is 45 per cent.

Mr. CAMPBELL. That undoubtedly does not apply. That is 4 cents per pound " whether uncovered or covered with cotton, silk, metal, or other material." I think it is the duty on the wire plus the cent and a quarter a pound. That is stated in the last clause of paragraph 137.

Mr. RANDELL. That is 45 per cent and one and a quarter?

Mr. CAMPBELL. No; it would be one and a half, according to gauge. The first part states what each gauge shall pay, or each classification. Then it says that it shall pay that, and in addition one and a quarter cents a pound upon the manufactured product.

Mr. RANDELL. What is the price of the best barbed wire, such as is commonly used for fences in the West?

Mr. CAMPBELL. I do not know, I am sure. We have not manufactured it nor sold it.

Mr. RANDELL. Will anybody be here before the committee, representing those wire people, who will know about that?

Mr. CAMPBELL. There will not be to-day, but in our brief we will give you all of this information.

Mr. RANDELL. But we can not cross-examine a brief, and I desire to get some information from you now because this is a very important matter to our people.

Mr. CAMPBELL. I am very sorry that Mr. Roebling is not here.

Mr. RANDELL. Is it not a fact that without any competition whatever and with a fixed price—a price fixed by the parties having control of the product—the farmers have had to pay the price fixed or do without the wire; is that not really the situation, and has it not been for a number of years?

Mr. CAMPBELL. I do not think so. They are certainly buying wire nails now cheaper——

Mr. RANDELL. I did not ask you about that. I ask you if there is any way on earth to change the price fixed by the parties controlling it?

Mr. CAMPBELL. I do not think they have any way.

Mr. RANDELL. The price is fixed not only for that product but for all the products of iron and steel, practically; they are fixed by the manufacturers and those who control the output of the product, are they not?

Mr. CAMPBELL. Oh, yes, sir.

Mr. RANDELL. Now, where does the farmer or the man who has to buy his wire to make his fence come in; has he any chance to say anything about what the price shall be?

Mr. CAMPBELL. I do not know.

Mr. RANDELL. It is just a question of whether he shall buy or not, is it?

Mr. CAMPBELL. Why should he have anything to say as to what the price shall be?

Mr. RANDELL. Where is there a chance to have any competition?

Mr. CAMPBELL. There are thousands or hundreds of people who make it. He has competition. They do not all sell alike.

Mr. RANDELL. The price of the same grade of wire is the same all over the country, you mean?

Mr. CAMPBELL. You might say that it is practically the same. When we need the business we go out and cut the other fellow 50 cents or a dollar a ton and get it, and he does the same with us.

Mr. RANDELL. You do not know what the cost of wire is to the consumer nor the cost of making it?

Mr. CAMPBELL. No, sir; I know this, that the profit on our wire was less—from what we have already made in the last seven or eight months—than any other commodity we make per ton, and there is as much labor in it, and it is a light product that we turn out, a light tonnage, and we have a big investment for that wire alone, and yet we make a very small amount of money, and if we could not make any more money we would shut the plant down. We are spending a half a million dollars on that part of our plant in order to make it larger.

Mr. RANDELL. Has not the price of barbed wire practically gone up double in the last seven years?

Mr. CAMPBELL. I can not speak with regard to barbed wire in the last seven years.

Mr. RANDELL. Is not barbed wire in this country now in the hands of a trust?

Mr. CAMPBELL. No, sir; it is not, because I know a number of people who make barbed wire outside of the trust.

Mr. RANDELL. What percentage of it is controlled by the trust?

Mr. CAMPBELL. Probably 50 or 60 per cent.

Mr. RANDELL. You say outside of the trust. Your company is outside, is it not?

Mr. CAMPBELL. Yes, sir.

Mr. RANDELL. And you ask the same price practically that the trust ask?

Mr. CAMPBELL. We get all we can.

Mr. RANDELL. You do not put the price down?

Mr. CAMPBELL. We do not if we can sell our products at other prices.

Mr. RANDELL. Now, is it not a fact that if you were to attempt to put the prices down, that you believe, or have reason to believe, or know, that immediately you would come in competition with the trust and would have to fight it; in other words they would endeavor to crush you?

Mr. CAMPBELL. I do not think so; it would cost them too much money to do it. They could do it if they were willing to go to the expense, but for us to make a hundred thousand tons of wire production a year, and for them to undertake, when they make millions of tons a year, to drive us out of the market, they would get awfully tired.

Mr. RANDELL. If the tariff was taken off barbed wire entirely, would that change the price to the consumer in this country?

Mr. CAMPBELL. Yes, sir.

Mr. RANDELL. How much?

Mr. CAMPBELL. Possibly not very much. I think it would change the price.

Mr. RANDELL. About how much?

Mr. CAMPBELL. I do not know; it would probably drive the American out of the business and leave it to the foreigner, and he would put the price up to about where we are selling it now, or perhaps a little less.

Mr. RANDELL. You mean that in your opinion the situation must be such that either the American must make it all or the foreigner must make it all; that they can not both make barbed wire?

Mr. CAMPBELL. No, sir; I said I did not believe that a prohibitive tariff was a good thing, and I do not. I would like to see in ordinary times a little material come in.

Mr. RANDELL. Do you think that the taking off of the tariff on barbed wire would prevent the manufacturers in this country from making barbed wire?

Mr. CAMPBELL. It would depend entirely on the conditions abroad. If they have all the market for their material at home at a better price than they have here, it would not interfere with us. If they have not it would certainly drive us out of the business or drive us to cut the cost of labor and other things that enter into it.

Mr. RANDELL. They have not even touched your business so far, have they?

Mr. CAMPBELL. No, sir; it is a prohibitive tariff.

Mr. RANDELL. And that has been on there ever since the Dingley bill—the prohibitive tariff?

Mr. CAMPBELL. Yes, sir.

Mr. RANDELL. And the effect of that has been to double the price of wire?

Mr. CAMPBELL. Oh, no, sir; absolutely not.

Mr. RANDELL. I thought you said you did not know about that?

Mr. CAMPBELL. I know from general business experience that it has not been enough to double the price of wire.

Mr. RANDELL. I did not ask you whether it had been enough to cause it or whether it would cause the price to be doubled, but I asked you, as a matter of fact, whether it has not been doubled—that is, the price of barbed wire sold in Texas, Oklahoma, and Kansas?

Mr. CAMPBELL. It has not been due to that, but the general advance in all kinds of material and in transportation and labor—if they have advanced, and I think they have—that is all iron and steel products (you have heard the experiences of all these gentlemen here to-day) and I am willing to venture the opinion that that is absolutely true.

Mr. RANDELL. A part of the expenses of your business is transportation, is it not—railroad rates, and things of that sort?

Mr. CAMPBELL. Oh, yes, sir.

Mr. RANDELL. If the tariff was taken off of steel products entirely in this country would that not very much reduce the price of building, building material and railroad building and everything of that sort?

Mr. CAMPBELL. I do not think it would much.

Mr. RANDELL. It would not reduce the price?

Mr. CAMPBELL. It might some.

Mr. RANDELL. If it would not reduce the price you could go ahead and manufacture and sell the same as you are now?

Mr. CAMPBELL. If all those things are going to be on a lower basis they have all got to come together—labor and material and transportation and everything that enters into cost.

Mr. RANDELL. Would that not make the material cheaper?

Mr. CAMPBELL. It might possibly; I think it would have a good effect on the whole country if you did it on all the different things. If you took it off of barbed wire, however, it would not, because there would be enough other things to employ labor and the laborer would say he would not work in the barbed-wire business but would go into some other line of business.

Mr. RANDELL. You think it would be better, then, if the tariff was reduced so as to let the stilted business down on to a natural level?

Mr. CAMPBELL. Yes, sir; everything that is stilted, but I do not want you to understand that I say that it is. There is no instance that I know of where the prices are higher now than they would be if the tariff was reduced, except in this general leveling down of everything that would come if the tariff was taken off.

Mr. R$_{AN}^{DE}_{LL}$. Well, if the taking off of the tariff would not reduce the prices, what difference would it make to you if the tariff was on or not?

Mr. CAMPBELL. It would reduce the prices if you took it off of everything and put all this stuff on the free list, but I say if you took it off of one thing it would not.

Mr. RANDELL. If you took it off of barbed wire it would not reduce the price of barbed wire?

Mr. CAMPBELL. No, sir; it might temporarily, until you put the people out of business and the other people controlled the market and put it back.

Mr. RANDELL. Have you made any calculations on which to base that statement?

Mr. CAMPBELL. No, sir; only from my general business experience.

Mr. RANDELL. You do not even know the cost of barbed wire nor what it brings, do you?

Mr. CAMPBELL. I would like to ask you what you think barbed wire is worth; what you think it ought to bring; you think it is too high.

Mr. RANDELL. I know something about it, but I am not testifying. I have had to use it for fence purposes, but have not used it lately.

Mr. CAMPBELL. I beg your pardon.

Mr. RANDELL. You think if you took the tariff off it would not affect the price; you would get just the same price for your wire?

Mr. CAMPBELL. We would either have to get more than we do now or go out of the business. Our profit last month on wire was $3.48 per ton, a high-class product, and I would not want to sell anything outside of pig iron on such a profit as that.

Mr. RANDELL. Do you not sell barbed wire higher outside of the United States?

Mr. CAMPBELL. We do not sell anything outside of the United States.

Mr. RANDELL. Is there not any barbed wire exported?

Mr. CAMPBELL. I could not say as to that.

Mr. RANDELL. You do not know whether there is or not?

Mr. CAMPBELL. No, sir; I presume there is some.

Mr. RANDELL. There is a large amount, is there not?

Mr. CAMPBELL. I presume so.

Mr. RANDELL. Then, on what basis would you say that the tariff ought to be put on barbed wire so that the farmer can get his barbed wire at a price that would be competitive, so that if you did not furnish him at that he could get it outside of the country?

Mr. CAMPBELL. I do not know; it ought to be on a fair basis, but I am not prepared to say what it should be because I am not posted as to barbed wire. I have never made it and I can not speak with regard to it.

The CHAIRMAN. Farmers do not use so much barbed wire now; they use woven wire, do they not?

Mr. CAMPBELL. Yes, sir; woven wire, for fences.

The CHAIRMAN. It is a great deal better and cheaper, is it not?

Mr. CAMPBELL. Yes, sir.

The CHAIRMAN. The farmers are not complaining about the price of that in my district. Mr. Campbell, I think you ought to look over this schedule with respect to wire and nails, and I think you will come to the conclusion that the tariff on that ought to be reduced also. There are practically no imports under this duty—six or eight or sometimes fifty thousand pounds a year, while we export 89,000,000 pounds in a year. Now, it would look as though that ought to be doctored a little. I wish you would look into it and present a brief on that subject and show what you think ought to be done with respect to it, and why it should be done.

Mr. CAMPBELL. We were only taking the quotations from the market paper that we had from abroad yesterday on the train, and figured it up, and the result of those figures, while we were coming down here on the train, was that the tariff on nails we could not afford to have reduced.

The CHAIRMAN. I think you had better look it over again.

Mr. CAMPBELL. If we find that it can be, I will be very glad to recommend a reduction.

The CHAIRMAN. If they do not do it somebody else may.

Mr. CAMPBELL. That is just what I have preached to all of our people, that we want our friends to revise this tariff, and we want to be fair and give them all the information that they can desire instead of having somebody else take it all off at some future time.

The CHAIRMAN. With respect to this fence wire, there is a cent and a quarter change of duty on that, differential duty of a cent and a quarter, in addition to the duty on the wire. Now, that would look to me to be very large. I wish you gentlemen would look that over, too, and give us the benefit of your experience, together with the figures showing the comparative cost of it abroad and at home, so that we can adjust the duty. I will be obliged if you will remember those two items.

Mr. CAMPBELL. I will be glad to do so. I desire to say with reference to the farmer that my observation has been that the farmer has been pretty prosperous during the last ten years and has paid this outrageous price that the gentleman has spoken of for his wire fence.

The CHAIRMAN. Of course it may be that this feeling with regard to the reduction of the duty on fence wire has grown largely out of political exigencies throughout the country. [Laughter.]

Mr. CAMPBELL. I will look into that matter again carefully and if there ought to be a reduction, and we can afford to have a reduction, we will recommend it.

The CHAIRMAN. There has never been any fence wire imported, as I understand it.

Mr. CAMPBELL. I do not think there ever will be because they can probably import galvanized wire, although I do not believe they can the finer wire.

The CHAIRMAN. I think we had better reduce the duty. If you will give us whatever information you have on that subject we will use your information as discreetly as we can. Otherwise we will go about it and probably act unadvisedly.

Mr. CAMPBELL. We will be glad to do that.

Mr. CLARK. Did you say that you do not know anything about the wire business?

Mr. CAMPBELL. I know very little about it. I have just been in the business since last March.

Mr. CLARK. You and the chairman seem to agree that the use of barbed wire is about played out. That is not true. Where they build a woven-wire fence they put two barbed wires on top of it, and only put three barbed wires, as a rule, before they use the woven-wire fence.

Mr. CAMPBELL. They might do that in Missouri, but they do not do it everywhere.

Mr. CLARK. They do it in Missouri. I have built many miles of woven-wire fence myself, and I know how it is done. The chairman says you build it for chicken fences.

Mr. CAMPBELL. You are both right. They do use it, and use quite a good deal of it; but the woven-wire fence has taken the place of the barbed-wire fence to a very great extent, and they only use it sometimes for bottom strands or top strands, the two strands.

Mr. CLARK. They make woven-wire fences for hog fields and such things as that, but the average pasture of the United States is fenced with barbed wire.

Mr. CAMPBELL. You are very much mistaken. The barbed-wire business is a very small business as compared with the wire fence. You would be surprised if you went over the figures and knew the amount of woven-wire fences that are made throughout this country.

The CHAIRMAN. We have arrived at that advanced state of civilization in New York where no one can build a mile of barbed-wire fence unless his neighbor consents to it; otherwise he would be liable for damages to cattle that may run into that fence.

GODFREY L. CABOT, OF BOSTON, MASS., STATES THAT AMERICAN IRON PIPE IS SOLD FOR LOWER PRICES IN EUROPE THAN IN THIS COUNTRY.

BOSTON, MASS., *December 2, 1908.*

COMMITTEE ON WAYS AND MEANS,
  Washington, D. C.

GENTLEMEN: I write to urge the removal of the duties on iron pipe, rods, bars, and pig iron. I have suffered to the extent of many thousands of dollars a year by reason of these duties, and this loss will increase as my business increases.

Ten years ago I went abroad with the intention of establishing agencies for the sale of American iron pipe in the different countries of Europe. As I had for fifteen years been a buyer of American iron pipe in increasing quantity, and for cash, and had never asked a single maker of pipe to take my note in payment of a bill, I had an excellent credit and was buying American iron pipe of all the different manufacturers at prices that were decidedly favorable as compared with what other buyers in this country were paying. For instance, in the year 1895 I sold a lot of second-hand 2-inch pipe to the Standard Oil Company at precisely the same price that I got by telegram the same day for new pipe from the Oil Well Supply Company, the same size and quality.

Nevertheless, I found in England, France, Switzerland, Italy, Turkey, Russia, Norway, Sweden, and Germany American iron pipe selling at less than I could lay it down for, showing that others were buying American iron pipe for export at a considerably lower price than I could buy it and that I was hopelessly handicapped by the very reason that I was a large buyer for use in this country, which ought to have helped me, and would have under normal conditions.

I respectfully protest against a system which compels American citizens to pay a much higher price for American goods than the same are sold to Europeans. At one time I was buying mercury by the flask at a much higher price than the same goods were sold in China, of American production.

This country has become the greatest manufacturing country in the world. Not only that, but it is doubtful if any two countries in the world manufacture as much as the United States alone. Not only that, it is certain that no two empires in the world, not even the British Empire and the German Empire together, manufacture as much iron and steel as the United States alone. It is, therefore, too late to set up the claim of infant industries needing protection in connection with iron and steel industries in this country, and I earnestly solicit protection for myself and other manufacturers in this country, who ask no favors at the expense of justice to others. We only ask a fair interchange of goods, untrammeled by a protective tariff tax or other artificial restrictions. We only want a fair chance and not to be compelled to pay tribute to others who have been more assiduous in asking favors of the Government.

In conclusion, I beg to say that my interests in this connection are identical with those of other makers of carbon black, and our commodity is the basis of black printing inks throughout this country, and a tax on this industry is, therefore, a tax on the dissemination of knowledge.

Yours, very respectfully,   GODFREY L. CABOT.

HON. IRVING P. WANGER, M. C., WRITES RELATIVE TO NEW CLASSIFICATION OF LAP-WELDED IRON OR STEEL PIPES.

NORRISTOWN, PA., *December 31, 1908.*
COMMITTEE ON WAYS AND MEANS,
House of Representatives.

GENTLEMEN: Referring to the statement of Mr. J. A. Campbell before the committee November 25, 1908, in which he said that the duty on lap-welded, etc., iron or steel pipes, etc., might be reduced from 2 cents per pound, as provided by paragraph 152 of the act of 1897, to 1 cent per pound or even to $18 per ton, Mr. Lewis N. Lukens, president of the Longmead Iron Company, Conshohocken, Pa., informs me that he concurs with Mr. Campbell so far as that statement relates to the sizes of pipe three-eights of an inch and upward to which Mr. Campbell was referring, although when it gets down to three-eighths inch size $18 per ton is scarcely adequate, and when it comes to smaller sizes, to which Mr. Campbell made no reference whatever, then $18 per ton is insufficient.

The Longmead Iron Company manufactures pipe from 3 inches to one-eighth inch in diameter.

From 3 inches down to three-fourths inch the prices (and cost of manufacture) are the same per ton in the several sizes, but getting down to one-half inch, three-eighths inch, one-fourth inch, and one-eighth inch the price of cost advances with each diminishing size; and the occasion for this is evident when it is considered that a small mill with the capacity to produce 80 tons of 3-inch pipe per week will not produce more than from 35 to 40 tons per week of one-fourth inch pipe, nor more than 20 tons per week of one-eighth inch pipe.. Hence it is evident that not only the labor cost per ton, but all of the other expenses, interest upon capital, etc., and other general charges are greatly increased per ton upon the smaller sizes.

Mr. Lukens accordingly asks that paragraph 152 be amended by adding, after the words " not thinner than No. 16 wire gauge," the following: " and of three-eighths inch or larger diameter, 1 cent per pound; of one-fourth inch and less than three-eighths inch in diameter, 1½ cents per pound; of less than one-fourth inch in diameter, 2 cents per pound * * *."

Hoping you have already ascertained the substantial basis for the foregoing distinction in rates and that if not you will investigate the accuracy of this contention and provide accordingly,

Yours, very respectfully,

IRVING P. WANGER,

Member of Congress, Eighth District, Pennsylvania.

———

SUPPLEMENTAL STATEMENT OF J. A. CAMPBELL, YOUNGSTOWN, OHIO, RELATIVE TO WROUGHT-IRON AND STEEL PIPE.

YOUNGSTOWN, OHIO, *January 22, 1909.*

COMMITTEE ON WAYS AND MEANS,

Washington, D. C.

GENTLEMEN: It is our understanding that your committee desired all of the facts and figures based on our operations for 1907, it being a normal year with practically full operations, rather than 1908, when we were only operating at 50 to 60 per cent of our capacity, and, therefore, all figures herewith presented are based on the year 1907.

In computing the cost we have not taken the mill most favorably located, but have used the average cost of five of the leading independent mills in the Pittsburg district, namely: Mark Manufacturing Company, Zanesville, Ohio; the Youngstown Sheet and Tube Company, Youngstown, Ohio; the La Belle Iron Works, Steubenville, Ohio; the Wheeling Steel and Iron Company, Wheeling, W. Va.; Spang, Chalfant & Co. (Incorporated), Pittsburg, Pa.; and as all tubular products are sold based on Pittsburg rate of freight, we have used these rates to seaboard points of delivery. These costs are also based on steel pipe three-quarters of an inch to six inches, which are the sizes most commonly used for steam, water, and gas, and cost less per ton to manufacture than the smaller and larger sizes. We believe, however, that any duty that is applied to these sizes will be satisfactory for the other sizes mentioned, also for iron pipe, casing, and other specials, all of which cost more to produce and bring a correspondingly higher price in the market.

You should bear in mind particularly that the mills represented in this cost are all large and modern plants and we believe are able to manufacture this class of material at the lowest cost of any mills producing similar product in this country, except mills owned by United States Steel Corporation, and that there are many smaller mills which are not so favorably located as to raw material, fuel supply, and transportation, and that their cost of production must necessarily be higher than that submitted herewith.

We have taken as our basis of cost the lowest price of steel skelp (flat steel strips), for the year 1907, from which the pipe is made, and have not gone into the cost of ore, pig iron, and steel, as many of the mills do not produce these commodities but purchase their skelp in the open market.

You will note that it requires 2,576 pounds of steel skelp to make a gross ton (2,240 pounds) of pipe, and this waste is made up of cinder, scale, crop end, and other scrap, the value of which we allow due credit. The fuel, labor, repairs, supplies, etc., are the actual cost per ton, as shown by our books. The item of "general expense" covers insurance, taxes, sales, clerical, and administrative expenses.

The item of labor may look small to you, but we call your attention to the fact that it does not include the cost of labor from the ore in the ground to the finished skelp; besides, the item of "Fuel" includes the labor handling same, and the items "Repairs" and "General expense" are nearly all labor, and the cost of couplings is 65 per cent labor. We have made a careful estimate of the cost of labor to produce a ton of pipe, from the ore in the ground to the finished product, which is about $18, exclusive of transportation labor, and we believe that if we had the actual cost, including everything, it would not be far from $20 per ton. When you stop to consider that this is one of the lightest products, except sheets, tin plate, and wire, and it passes through so many operations from the mining of the ore to the finished product, including the bending, welding, threading, testing, and the making and the threading of the couplings, and that each piece, and each thread and coupling, must be an exact duplicate of the other, and nearly all must be done by skilled workmen in their line, who receive the highest rate of wages, you can readily understand why this labor cost is so high.

In explanation of the item "Depreciation" we find that a mill consisting of two bell-weld and one lap-weld furnaces, equipped with modern machinery and adequate socket and warehouse capacity, including land, railroad tracks, boilers, electric light and power plant, machine shop, foundry, etc., to make a complete plant, will cost about $1,250,000; such a plant would have a capacity of about 54,000 gross tons per year, but on account of stoppages for repairs, and not being a constant demand for the product, our experience is that we could not produce over 40,000 gross tons per year with a plant as above described. We estimate the average life of a plant of this kind would not exceed 20 years, in which period, at the above rate, we would produce 800,000 gross tons, which, divided into the total cost would show that our depreciation should be $1.56 per ton, as shown in our cost; this does not take into consideration the possibility that during this period the entire process of manufacturing may change and we would be obliged to rebuild to conform to improved methods.

We regret to say that we have been unable to secure any detailed costs of producing pipe abroad; we have been able, however, through one of the leading engineers of this country, who spent the year 1907 in Germany, erecting American pipe-mill machinery, to secure the rate of wages paid in that country, and we submit herewith, marked "Exhibit C," our authority for same, and this goes to prove, what we have always understood to be a fact, that the wages that they are obliged to pay are not over 50 per cent of wages paid in this country for similar work. In the case of brick masons you will note that the price which they pay is 10 cents per hour, while we pay 50 to 55 cents per hour.

We wish also to call your attention to the fact that the United Engineering and Foundry Company, who are the leading makers of pipe-mill machinery in this country, have designed and sold a number of mills of the most modern type abroad in the last three years, and are now erecting a large plant in Scotland, which disproves the argument we have heard advanced, that the foreign mills are antiquated, their tonnage small, and consequently their labor per ton higher than our own.

We also know that they are producing abroad pig iron at $8.50 per ton, steel at $13 per ton, and, at this rate, they could produce skelp at not to exceed $18 per gross ton, as compared with our cost of $36.96 per ton. You can readily understand that, beginning with their raw material, or skelp, which is about one-half the cost of ours, they would be able to flood this country with pipe at a time when their home market did not absorb all of their production; and this is especially true in view of the fact that their mills are located a short distance from seaboard, and the Government, who controls the railroads, gives them a concession of 15 to 25 per cent in freight rates on export business; also that their home market selling price is $8 per ton higher than their export prices.

We estimate that the Pittsburg district produces 85 to 90 per cent of the entire tonnage of pipe in this country; the average freight from Pittsburg to the Atlantic seaboard is $3.58 per gross ton; to Tampa, Fla., $11.31; New Orleans, $6.72, and to Galveston and Port Arthur, $11.87 per gross ton; to Pacific coast points it is $14.56 per gross ton, while the freight from foreign mills to our Atlantic seaport cities is, nominally, $3 per net ton; to Gulf ports the same, and to San Francisco, Portland, Seattle, and Tacoma, $7 per gross ton. You should bear in mind, also, that these freights are much lower when vessels are short of cargo or ballast, and that tramp vessels, at times, will take this tonnage at half the nominal rates.

In view of the fact that the Pacific coast furnishes a large market for our product, and that we can have but one rate of duty for the United States, we feel justified in using Pacific coast transportation rates for our comparisons, as we could not rightfully be asked to turn over this large tonnage to our foreign competitors and deprive ourselves, our employees, and the railroads of that proportion of earnings.

We have been unable to secure the selling price of pipe abroad for export during the year 1907, upon which all of our cost figures are based, and in order to give you a fair comparison we give you the present cost of pipe in this country, based on the cost of conversion in

WROUGHT-IRON AND STEEL PIPE—J. A. CAMPBELL. 2141

1907, which is lower than in 1908, because our mills were operating to their full capacity, and the present selling price abroad.

The present price of skelp in the open market is $31.36 per gross ton; figuring this on the same basis of operations as 1907 shows our present cost to be $48.52 per gross ton. We should be allowed $5 a gross ton profit on this class of product, which would make our selling price $53.52 per gross ton f. o. b. mill; with $14.56 added to Pacific coast points would make the present selling price delivered there $68.08. The present selling price of pipe abroad for export, f. o. b. mill, is $38.50 a gross ton; the freight to Pacific coast points is $7, making $45.50 a gross ton, their selling price delivered f. o. b. San Francisco and other Pacific coast ports. This deducted from our selling price of $68.08 (which includes our profit of $5) would show that we should have a duty of $22.58 per gross ton, or 1 cent per pound, in order to put us on an equal basis in this territory.

I wish to impress upon you the fact that the tariff bill you are now framing is likely to cover a period of the next ten years, at least, and that during that time conditions may vary greatly from what they are at present; in other words, the cost of iron and steel products in this country have gradually increased for a number of years and it is not likely that this condition will change during the life of the tariff you now propose to put into effect. This is due largely to the exhaustion of our mineral resources, in increased cost of labor in all of its different ramifications from the mining of ore, coal, and limestone, transportation, and other items heretofore mentioned; and if it should happen that our costs should increase greater than those abroad, we would need more protection than we are asking for at present. Besides, if the conditions abroad should change adversely and they should undertake to keep their factories in operation by dumping the material in this country, as they have done many times in the past, this duty would not cover that condition.

The tonnage of pipe products in this country is approximately two and one-quarter million tons per annum. There is a large amount of capital invested and a large number of men engaged in this work, and to interfere with the continuous employment of these men, or with their wages, would be a serious hardship to the country generally and would affect business of all kinds. If the duty on pipe is made less than we recommend, viz, 1 cent per pound, it will not only reduce the earnings of the stockholders interested in this business, but it must necessarily affect to a greater extent the wages of the men employed, and we do not believe the people in this country will ever submit to a wage rate that will reduce the wage-earner to anything like the conditions of his brother abroad, and the Congress who will do anything to disturb the present prosperity and happiness of this great army of employees can rest assured that they will be held responsible for the result.

Respectfully submitted.

J. A. CAMPBELL,
President the Youngstown Sheet and Tube Company.

Exhibit A.

1907. Cost of three-fourths to 6-inch steel pipe.

2,576 pounds steel skelp at $36.96 per gross ton		$42.50
Less scrap value		1.51
Net material		40.99
Fuel, heating, steam, electric light, and power	$1.12	
Direct labor	5.25	
Repairs: Labor and material	1.03	
Supplies: Oil and grease, shop expense, light and power expense, steam expense, water expense, refractories, balls and bells, threading oil, and rolls	1.04	
General expense: General office expense, sales expense, works expense, insurance, and taxes	2.13	
Couplings, thread protectors, and bundling cord	1.79	
Depreciation	1.56	
		13.92
Total cost, gross ton		54.91

Exhibit B.

Present cost of pipe, three-fourths to 6-inch steel pipe.

2,576 pounds steel skelp, at $31.36 per gross ton		$36.06
Less scrap value		1.46
Net material		34.60
Fuel: Heating, steam, electric light and power	$1.12	
Direct labor	5.25	
Repairs: Labor and material	1.03	
Supplies: Oil and grease, shop expense, light and power expense, steam expense, water expense, refractories, balls and bells, threading oil, and rolls	1.04	
General expense: General office expense, sales expense, works expense, insurance, and taxes	2.13	
Couplings, thread protectors, and bundling cord	1.79	
Depreciation	1.56	
		13.92
Total cost, gross ton		48.52

Exhibit C.

UNITED ENGINEERING AND FOUNDRY COMPANY,
FARMERS' BANK BUILDING,
Pittsburg, Pa., October 26, 1908.

Mr. ANSON MARK,
  (Care of Mark Manufacturing Company),
    Zanesville, Ohio.

DEAR SIR: In answer to your favor of the 23d instant, to Mr. Satler, in reference to wages paid in German pipe mills, would state that welders receive about 10 marks, or $2.50, and laborers from 2.50 marks to 3.50 marks, or about 65 to 90 cents for a day of ten hours. Furnace bricklayers receive 10 cents per hour. The writer has paid a firm of contractors 40 pfennige, or 10 cents, per hour for bricklayers; the contractors paid these men 38 pfennige, or 9.5 cents, per hour. Welders generally receive a bonus if they exceed a given daily production. The bonus is not very large, but is sufficient to encourage them to keep up the output.

Trusting this may give you the information you desire, we are,
  very respectfully,
    UNITED ENGINEERING AND FOUNDRY COMPANY,
    By GEO. D. MUIRHEAD.

WELDED CYLINDRICAL FURNACES.

[Paragraph 152.]

STATEMENT OF F. E. CULLEN, OF OSWEGO, N. Y., REPRESENTING THE FITZGIBBONS BOILER COMPANY.

WEDNESDAY, *November 25, 1908.*

Mr. GRIGGS. I beg your pardon, but are you making any money?

Mr. CULLEN. We ask a reduction of the duty.

Mr. GRIGGS. I am glad to see you. What paragraph is your article in?

Mr. CULLEN. No. 152, covering welded cylindrical furnaces.

Mr. GRIGGS. Just say anything you want to. Go ahead.

Mr. CULLEN. First of all, I represent boiler manufacturers who are compelled to buy the welded cylindrical furnace. It is an English invention. It is manufactured by a single concern in this country. There are German and Belgian and French types which are satisfactory for the same purposes, and in many instances preferable, which, however, can not be obtained in this country because of the duty.

The CHAIRMAN. Is your article patented?

Mr. CULLEN. Well, yes; it is patented, but there are several other types.

The CHAIRMAN. How long does the patent run?

Mr. CULLEN. I am not familiar with that.

The CHAIRMAN. How long has it run?

Mr. CULLEN. I could not tell you that. We are the purchasers of the article, not the manufacturers.

The CHAIRMAN. It is patented, is it?

Mr. CULLEN. Yes, sir. There are two patents, one called the Fox and one the Morrison. The present duty on these furnaces is 2¼ cents per pound. At that price the importations last year as compared with the amount used in this country are very inconsiderable, the amount of importation being 7,100 pounds last year. There are 250 boiler manufacturers in this country called upon to equip their product with the cylindrical welded furnace, which if they purchase at all they must purchase from the Continental Iron Works of Brooklyn. I am informed that the labor cost in the production of this furnace is about 2½ cents per pound. There is, therefore, a 100 per cent protection upon the labor cost. It seems to be perfectly evident from the line of discussion here to-day that the steel plate used in the manufacture of this cylindrical furnace can be purchased at least as cheaply in America as in Europe, and that the only question, therefore, as a basis for a duty is the labor. It seems to the several boiler manufacturers whom I represent here that a tariff of about 80 per cent upon the labor cost of the production would amply protect the American labor, and permit the German and Belgian types of cylindrical furnace to come into America in competition with the single type that is available here to-day, and that absolutely controlled by one concern, and also permit the advantages of this competition to go not only to the manufacturers of boilers but also to the workmen employed, they employing a very much larger number of workmen than the single plant manufacturing the cylindrical furnace. The information is also given me that the men employed in the Continental Iron Works in the manufacture of cylindrical furnaces are imported labor, skilled labor, brought here from the manufacturing centers of Europe where they learned this work; so that the protection is not only prohibitive, 100 per cent on the labor cost of the article, but it is also the protection of British-American labor rather than distinctly American labor. The boiler manufacturers believe that this tariff should be either abolished or so reduced as to equal only the difference between the labor cost in Europe and the labor cost in America, and they believe that this duty at its highest figure would be 1 cent per pound.

There are some facts in connection with the cost of production and transportation which I have not here directly available. I shall be pleased to include those in a brief to be submitted to the committee, and any other information available to us which I have not already submitted.

The CHAIRMAN. We will be very much obliged to you for the information showing the difference between the labor cost abroad and here, as far as you can give it, and if you can show the price at which the foreign article is laid down in the report of New York and the price charged for it in New York, where you say it is manufactured, or in Brooklyn, for the American trade, we will be glad to have that.

Mr. CULLEN. There is so little of it laid down there that its price is going to be very difficult to get.

The CHAIRMAN. There is once in a while an importation?

Mr. CULLEN. Less than four tons were imported last year.

Mr. DALZELL. Can these foreign articles come in without infringing the American patents?

Mr. CULLEN. Yes; I think there is no trouble about that. The patents are all right. The German type in particular has been adopted by the United States Government inspectors and approved, and is used in a very large percentage of the ocean steamships.

The CHAIRMAN. I understood you to say that you represented some American boiler companies.

Mr. CULLEN. All of them.

The CHAIRMAN. How are they interested in it?

Mr. CULLEN. Because they purchase these cylindrical furnaces to put into their boilers. The cylindrical furnace is simply a tube in which is placed the grate and the fire box. It is an internal furnace, as distinct from the external furnace, which is of brick.

The CHAIRMAN. You mean to say it could not be obtained from manufacturers in this country?

Mr. CULLEN. Yes; it could be obtained.

The CHAIRMAN. The tubes are patented, are they not?

Mr. CULLEN. Yes; but there are half a dozen patents. This tube which is now being manufactured in this country is under an English patent, first patented by one named Fox, and subsequently by one named Morrison. Both of these are English patents. There is a German and a Belgian and also, I think, a French type, all of which are equally acceptable, and of which, if this duty were not prohibitive, would come into competition with these two English types.

Mr. GRIGGS. You have done very handsomely as far as you have gone with regard to this cylindrical furnace. What do you think about the tariff on boilers?

Mr. CULLEN. On what?

Mr. GRIGGS. On boilers.

Mr. CULLEN. I am totally unfamiliar with the subject, sir.

Mr. GRIGGS. Do you not represent the boiler people?

Mr. CULLEN. I represent the boiler people, but I am not practical in a boiler line.

Mr. GRIGGS. What is your business?

Mr. BONYNGE. You are not a boiler maker?

Mr. CULLEN. I am a lawyer.

Mr. GRIGGS. Oh! [Laughter.]

BRIEF SUBMITTED BY FRANCIS E. CULLEN, OSWEGO, N. Y., WHO THINKS THE DUTY ON WELDED CYLINDRICAL FURNACES SHOULD BE REDUCED.

OSWEGO, N. Y., *November 25, 1908.*

COMMITTEE ON WAYS AND MEANS,
Washington, D. C.

GENTLEMEN: The tariff of 2½ cents per pound on welded cylindrical furnaces made from plate metal should be reduced or abolished.

The cylindrical welded boiler furnace is an European invention and was used there many years prior to its introduction into the United States.

These furnaces are used principally in making the so-called Scotch boiler, and there are now in the United States about 250 boiler manufacturers who are called upon to equip their product with these cylindrical furnaces.

There is only one plant in the United States making these cylindrical furnaces, and by reason of the crowded condition of that plant at times the manufacturers are unable to obtain within a reasonable time the furnaces required and can not import them by reason of the duty, which works to their embarrassment and also the embarrassment of the consumer, and the manufacturers are unable to import these furnaces by reason of the high duty.

The marine boiler furnace, which is cylindrical welded furnace, is used in nine-tenths of the ocean-going ships. It is an English invention and is manufactured in England only, and while some types of it are better made and preferable in many respects to the American product the manufacturers are unable to import it by reason of the duty.

The Brown furnace, built by John Brown & Co., of England, has been thoroughly tested by experts of this country and is preferable to the American product. It is acceptable to the United States Government, but by reason of the high duty is kept out of the American market.

The skilled labor employed in this country in making these furnaces was imported from the manufacturing centers of Europe, and the present duty is in a measure protecting them.

During the past year thousands of tons of steel plate manufactured here have been exported and the cost of steel plate is proverbially the same price or less abroad than here.

Cents per pound.

Cost of plate here_____ 2
Cost of all labor in manufacturing the cylindrical welded furnace_____ 2½

Total cost_____ 4½

These figures show that the protection provided by this paragraph for British-American imported labor is 100 per cent and is very much larger than is necessary and is working constant embarrassment to American manufacturers and increasing unwarrantedly the cost to American consumers.

The actual cost per pound for manufacturing these furnaces in this country, including skilled labor and all other expenses, is not to exceed 4.3 cents per pound, or $80 per ton, while the duty is 2½ cents per pound, or $50 per ton.

The American furnaces have been sold for 8 cents per pound in competition, and where there is no competition, as is now the fact in this country, at a very much higher price, and the American manufacturers and consumers must pay the cost.

The logical conclusion from the above facts is, that this duty should either be very materially reduced or entirely abolished, as we are simply protecting foreign labor by the duty.

All of which is respectfully submitted.

FRANCIS E. CULLEN.

––––––

CORRUGATED BOILER FURNACES.

[Paragraph 152.]

THE CONTINENTAL IRON WORKS, NEW YORK CITY, THINKS PROVISION OF LAW SHOULD BE REDRAWN.

NEW YORK, *November 18, 1908.*

Hon. SERENO E. PAYNE,
  Chairman Ways and Means Committee,
    House of Representatives, Washington, D. C.

SIR: As the manufacturers of corrugated boiler furnaces for land and marine boilers, we desire to place ourselves on record, first, as protesting against any reduction in the existing tariff on this product; second, to ask for a redrawing of the clause indicated above, for reasons hereinafter set forth.

1. The necessary machinery for the production of corrugated boiler furnaces has been produced at large expense, but the market in this country for this article is exceedingly limited, and during the best of times the demand is not sufficiently great to approximately reach the producing capacity of our manufacturing plant.

The present tariff rate is a specific duty of 2½ cents per pound, and this rate we respectfully suggest be maintained in any revision of the tariff which may be made or contemplated.

At the present rate of duty we are able to just about meet the German and English prices for corrugated furnaces; but should the duty be any less, we would not be able to ward off foreign competition, as the cost of material and labor entering into the construction of corrugated furnaces in Europe is roundly one-third less than what we pay in this country, and therefore we would be obliged to discontinue this portion of our business.

Even at the present rate of duty some corrugated furnaces are brought into this country from abroad, showing that any reduction in the present tariff would open the door to foreign manufacturers and the consequent injury to this company and the workmen in its employ.

2. We respectfully suggest that section 152 of Schedule C—manufactures of iron and steel—be redrawn in any future revision of the tariff schedule, in order to remove the ambiguity which at present exists in it, and prevent any evasion of the payment of a duty of 2½ cents per pound on corrugated boiler furnaces, which is clearly the intention of this clause.

We believe that because of the uncertainty of its language, corrugated boiler furnaces have been brought into this country under the name of tubes or flues, upon the payment of a duty of 2 cents per pound, instead of 2½ cents per pound.

It is true that a corrugated furnace is cylindrical in form, but when the distinctive use to which it is applied in the construction of a steam boiler is considered, there is no process of reasoning which can be applied to bring it under the classification of a tube or flue; hence our request for a redrawing of this particular clause of this schedule. As it stands at present, it is possible to evade the prescribed tariff to the extent of 20 per cent, which is a serious detriment to our business, and one which is not possible for us to successfully meet, should it be allowed to remain in force.

In view of the foregoing, we suggest that paragraph 152 of Schedule C—metals and manufactures of—be altered to read as follows:

Lap welded, butt welded, seamed, or jointed iron or steel boiler tubes, pipes, flues, or stays, not thinner than number sixteen wire gauge, two cents per pound; welded cylindrical furnaces made from rolled plate metal, when corrugated, ribbed, or otherwise reenforced against collapsing pressure, two and one-half cents per pound; all other iron or steel tubes, finished, not specially provided for in this act, thirty-five per centum ad valorem.

Very respectfully,

THE CONTINENTAL IRON WORKS,
THOS. F. ROWLAND, Jr., *Secretary.*

POCKETKNIVES.

[Paragraph 153.]

THE HOLLEY MANUFACTURING COMPANY, LAKEVILLE, CONN., WISHES NO REDUCTION ON POCKET CUTLERY.

LAKEVILLE, CONN., *November 17, 1908.*

Hon. S. E. PAYNE, Member of Congress,
   Chairman of the Ways and Means Committee,
         Washington, D. C.

DEAR SIR: Regarding the contemplated revision of the tariff as affecting the duties on pocketknives, clasp knives, pruning and budding knives, etc., we beg to say that we would be very glad to see the present duties increased. The present situation is sufficiently unfavorable, and in the event of any reduction of the tariff on cutlery, would be disastrous to us.

The manufacture of pocket cutlery in the United States is one of the " infant industries " that has never been sufficiently protected. As a result, there are comparatively few producers in this country, and not above a half dozen of any size. Instead of large fortunes having been made in the business, there have been many failures.

Knives equal in quality to any made abroad are made in this country, and many more and in greater variety would be made if they could be marketed to advantage in competition with foreign goods. Working under patents affects this business very little, as the mechanical principle applying to pocketknives is, in the main, the same as it has been for centuries. The question is chiefly one of placing the product of plentiful, cheap, foreign, skilled labor against the product of scarce, high-priced, skilled labor here. To meet the resultant competition, American manufacturers have had their profits reduced to practically the vanishing point, whereas, if a sufficiently high tariff prevented thousands of dealers from handling foreign-made knives, they would have to be sufficiently patriotic to use domestic goods.

We presume that letters of this general character will have less weight with the revisers of the tariff than exact schedules of comparative costs, etc. These latter will doubtless be supplied by the American Pocket Cutlery Manufacturers' Association, and we trust they will be given full consideration in arranging the details of the revision, but it seems to us that the incontrovertible facts in this case are—

(1) That the pocket cutlery industry in this country is relatively weak, composed of widely scattered units, which it has been impossible, so far, at least, to combine.

(2) That foreign-made knives are imported in great quantities and marketed to advantage to the detriment of American products.

(3) That the only persons affected favorably by the present schedule, and who would be further favorably affected by a reduction of duties, are a number of importers (usually of foreign extraction) in New York City and several other ports of entry.

(4) That there is probably considerable opportunity for undervaluation of imports and other devious methods of evading the duties. We make no specific charges, but such conditions have existed in times past, possibly exist now, and if not properly guarded against will surely exist in the future.

Doubtless this letter will be lost sight of in the mass of your correspondence, but should it happen to assist in fixing in your mind the status of this industry as it will be affected by the action of Congress we shall feel amply repaid.

Respectfully, yours,

HOLLEY MANUFACTURING COMPANY,
MALCOLM D. RUDD,
Treasurer and General Manager.

STATEMENT MADE BY DWIGHT DIVINE, OF ELLENVILLE, N. Y., ADVOCATING THE MAINTENANCE OF PRESENT DUTIES ON POCKETKNIVES.

FRIDAY, *November 27, 1908.*

Mr. GRIGGS. Before you proceed, I would like to know if your concern is making any money?

Mr. DIVINE. Yes, sir.

Mr. GRIGGS. It is?

Mr. DIVINE. Yes, sir.

Mr. GRIGGS. I am glad to hear that. I congratulate you.

The CHAIRMAN. You may proceed with your statement, Mr. Divine.

Mr. DIVINE. Mr. Chairman and gentlemen, our brief was placed before each member of the committee this morning. I do not know whether you have copies there now or not.

Mr. DALZELL. What is your subject?

Mr. DIVINE. Pocket cutlery; pocketknives only.

In the brief now before you we have submitted to your committee as concisely as possible our position in the matter of tariff revision. We will not occupy the time of the committee by reading the same, but content ourselves by stating that we represent an industry in which competition is absolutely unrestrained; which, under the schedules of the Dingley bill, has made moderate progress, both in production and number of operatives employed. It can not be justly charged against the American pocket cutlery industry that profits are exorbitant or unreasonable. We wish to particularly emphasize the fact that never before has the pocketknife value afforded the consumer been so great as under the existing schedule.

We believe that these statements and a consideration by your committee of the facts recited in the brief submitted justify the manufacturers of American pocket cutlery in their attitude that the protection now afforded by the Dingley bill is not greater than is absolutely necessary for the conduct of the industry and the maintenance of present labor conditions.

We do, however, submit that the industry has suffered material damage by the evasion of the intent of the law governing the stamping of the name of the country of origin on pocket cutlery (sec. 8, p. 67). This evasion is accomplished in the following manner: The blades of a knife are regularly stamped with a name of an American city or firm, which in itself implies, and is intended to imply, American manufacture. On the reverse side of the blade tang is placed the name of the country of origin, not, however, stamped in as in the case of the name of the firm, and as all pocketknives are regularly and habitually branded, but instead lightly marked with asphaltum or other substance, all traces of which are easily removed after passing the custom-house.

The result of this " naturalizing " process is the deception of the consumer and inestimable damage to the high standard of quality maintained in the genuine American knife. The present law seems to provide no penalty for violations of this character, and we would respectfully urge upon the committee that in their recommendations as to the administrative features of the new bill they incorporate such provisions as will insure the intended protection of American reputation.

The CHAIRMAN. Are there any questions by any member of the committee?

Mr. UNDERWOOD. You want the present duties continued—or do you want to increase the duty, Mr. Divine?

Mr. DIVINE. We want the present duty continued. We ask that in our brief, which we have filed with the committee; that no change shall be made.

Mr. UNDERWOOD. The percentage of labor that enters into the production is about 40, as I understand?

Mr. DIVINE. About 80 per cent.

Mr. UNDERWOOD. I notice the total value of the manufactured articles in this country was $18,600,000. Is that about correct?

Mr. DIVINE. That is too large. Are you sure you have the right statement?

Mr. UNDERWOOD. This is for 1905. The census of 1905 showed that——

Mr. DIVINE. That includes cutlery in all branches. I am speaking only of pocket cutlery. Pocket cutlery is probably about $3,000,000.

Mr. UNDERWOOD. The production of cutlery in this country is about $3,000,000?

Mr. DIVINE. About that—pocket cutlery. Under the head of cutlery are scissors, razors, and many other edged implements. Table knives come under the head of cutlery.

Mr. UNDERWOOD. And the importations are about $1,000,000?

Mr. DIVINE. Something over $1,000,000—that is, foreign value—and with the duties added would fall but little short of $2,000,000.

Mr. UNDERWOOD. Of course that is the foreign value, leaving out the duty?

Mr. DIVINE. The sale price, of course, is what ours is based on, and to get the relative proportion that would be the proper way.

Mr. UNDERWOOD. The duty is 78 per cent, so the importation of these articles into this country at this time is about one-third?

Mr. DIVINE. About two to three; that is, if you include—which is the only fair way to get at the approximate relative valuation—the proper items. Ours is about $3,000,000 and the importation, with the duty, is about $2,000,000 foreign value.

Mr. UNDERWOOD. What is the difference in wages paid in this country and abroad?

Mr. DIVINE. In Germany it is about as one to three. We pay about three times as much as the Germans. Of course their methods are somewhat different, but as nearly as we can approximate it it is fully that. In England it is about two to one.

Mr. UNDERWOOD. I am inclined to think you have a revenue-producing article here, that produces considerable revenue, more than one-third of which is brought into this country. If there is any difference in wages I do not think you should be changed.

Mr. DIVINE. On our statement the government reports are consolidated for comparison, and it shows the increase.

Mr. GRIGGS. Do you not think if you have caught a Democrat you had better cease your argument? [Laughter.]

Mr. DIVINE. I am not anxious to argue the question, sir. I am glad to answer any questions, however.

BRIEF SUBMITTED BY DWIGHT DIVINE, ELLENVILLE, N. Y., RELATIVE TO DUTIES ON POCKETKNIVES.

WASHINGTON, D. C., *November 27, 1908.*

Ways and Means Committee, Washington, D. C.

GENTLEMEN: In protesting against any changes in the schedules relating to penknives or pocketknives or parts thereof, or erasers or parts thereof, the undersigned committee, representing practically 100 per cent of the manufacturers of American pocket cutlery, respectfully submit the following facts for your consideration:

That the pocket-cutlery industry in the United States is controlled by no "trust," combination, or agreement.

That there are in existence and in operation at the present time about 35 factories (located in New York, Connecticut, Massachusetts, New Jersey, Pennsylvania, and Ohio) engaged in the manufacture of pocket cutlery, each absolutely distinct from all others as to ownership, interest, or control, and in active competition with each other.

That the average proportion of labor to cost of all merchandise imported is about 30 per cent. The actual proportion of labor to cost of American pocket cutlery is 80 per cent.

That it has been proven that cutlery operatives' wages are three times greater in this country than in Germany, and more than double those paid in England.

That the American manufacturers were rapidly losing their business from 1894 until 1897, under the Wilson bill. The shrinkage of sales for the fiscal year ending June 30, 1896, alone figured 25 per cent as compared with the sales of the previous year.

That since the operation of the present schedules the total amount of pocket cutlery produced in the United States has increased from approximately $1,000,000 to $3,000,000; in dozen produced, from 325,000 to approximately 1,000,000.

That more than 4,000 operatives are now employed in the manufacture of pocket cutlery in this country, at wages ranging from $3 to $4.50 per day for skilled workmen.

That despite the advanced rates of duty under the Dingley bill and the increased American production, the importation of foreign pocket cutlery has steadily increased, both in quantity and value, with a corresponding increase in revenue to the Government, while at the same time affording that protection that insures to the American workman a just return for his labor and to the manufacturer a fair margin of profit.

We append herewith a table compiled from the official reports issued by the Department of Commerce and Labor, showing in detail the value of importations, percentage of duty, revenue derived, etc., for a period covering the past twelve years. The years 1895, 1896,

1897, and part of 1898 were under the schedules of the Wilson bill and are included for the purpose of comparison with the results obtained after the Dingley bill became effective in 1898.

Total knife importations, 1895–1907.

Year.	Quantities (dozen).	Value.	Duty.	Unit value.	Ad valorem equivalent.
					Per cent.
1895	1,138,124	$1,130,298	$602,657		ᵃ53½
1896	1,266,882	1,300,762	691,082		ᵃ53½
1897	1,585,014	1,664,359	767,814	$0.076	ᵃ52.40
1898	118,518	111,384	58,248		} ᵇ71.05
1898 (new)	457,564	333,671	257,933		
1899	823,020	604,372	467,133	.061	ᵇ77.25
1900	1,072,995	764,448	588,022	.06	ᵇ76.92
1901	904,323	741,660	592,702	.068	ᵇ79.92
1902	1,014,047	846,538	678,261	.069	ᵇ80.12
1903	1,146,613	818,319	639,864	.059	ᵇ78.19
1904	1,156,273	896,717	695,147	.065	ᵇ77.52
1905	1,091,171	835,599	664,348	.064	ᵇ79.50
1906	958,515	838,129	651,306	.073	ᵇ77.71
1907	1,234,007	1,007,799	788,386	.068	ᵇ78.22

ᵃ Wilson bill.   ᵇ Dingley bill.

(Signed)   DWIGHT DIVINE, *Ellenville, N. Y.,*
              CHARLES F. ROCKWELL, *Meriden, Conn.,*
                     Committee Representing American
                          Pocket Cutlery Manufacturers.

HON. THOMAS W. BRADLEY, M. C., FILES LETTER RELATIVE TO ALLEGED EVASIONS OF SECTION 8, ACT OF 1897, AS APPLIED TO KNIVES AND RAZORS.

WASHINGTON, D. C., *December 19, 1908.*
Hon. SERENO E. PAYNE,
     Chairman Committee on Ways and Means,
          House of Representatives, Washington, D. C.

DEAR MR. CHAIRMAN: In response to your suggestion that a written brief be filed regarding alleged evasions of section 8, tariff law of 1897, in connection with imports of articles named in paragraph 153 of said law, I have the honor to submit the following:

The law providing that all imported goods shall bear the name of the country of origin was first passed in connection with the McKinley tariff, and was based on a copy of the English law submitted to the Ways and Means Committee.

At the time our law was framed and until about 1900 the usual method of stamping the firm name and country of origin on pocketknives and razors was by a steel stamp or die driven deep into the tang of the blade.

It is a matter of record that subsequent to October 9, 1890, imports of German knives were, in some cases, held up until the importer had caused the word "Germany" to be stamped with a steel die on the blade tang of each knife, and this at the appraiser's stores, under the supervision of a customs employee; all this at the importer's expense. I mention this to show that stamping deep with a steel die was the manner in which German and English knives and razors were "usually and ordinarily stamped" as to the name of the country of origin, trade-mark or firm name, and the department enforced the real intent of the law as covered by section 8 of the tariff law of 1897.

For some time past quantities of German knives and razors have passed through the port of New York with the name of country of origin "wash stamped" instead of stamped with steel die, and have also passed with the word "Germany" in "light etching" so shallow as to be easily buffed off. The "wash stamped" name of "Germany" being merely a composition easily wiped off with a cloth moistened with benzine. Even the firm name on front or "mark" side of blade tang is sometimes treated in the same manner, so that both the name of country of origin and firm name may be easily removed.

The proceeding seems to be a scheme for evading the true intent of section 8, and for placing on the American market an inferior grade of German manufacture under the guise of American product. It can readily be understood that a continuance of this practice may steadily depreciate the high standing of reputable American production.

I have no interest in any manufacturing industry; but in my home town of Walden, N. Y., are three manufacturing plants, producing about 50 per cent of the American output of penknives and pocketknives. The people of my town depend on this industry, and I am deeply concerned for the welfare of these pocketknife operatives, whose highly skilled trade may be discredited and probably ruined if evasion of the true intent of section 8 is permitted to continue.

I therefore most earnestly request that section 8 be so amended as to compel stamping by a steel die deep into the tang of pocketknives and razors imported into the United States, and, if practicable, a penalty be fixed for deliberate evasion of this section.

I inclose copy of letter to the Honorable Secretary of the Treasury.

Very respectfully,

THOMAS W. BRADLEY.

————

WASHINGTON, D. C., *December 19, 1908.*

Hon. GEORGE B. CORTELYOU,
　Secretary of the Treasury, Washington, D. C.

MY DEAR Mr. SECRETARY: In connection with outrageous evasion of section 8, tariff law of 1897, I have the honor to file complaint and charges, as follows:

The law providing that all imported goods shall bear the name of the country of origin was first passed in connection with the McKinley tariff, and was based on a copy of the English law submitted by me to the Ways and Means Committee.

At the time our law was framed and until about 1900 the only method of stamping the firm name, trade-mark, and country of origin on pocketknives and razors was by a steel stamp or die driven deep into the tang of the blade.

It is a matter of record that subsequent to October 9, 1890, imports of German knives were, in some cases, held up until the importer had caused the word "Germany" to be stamped with a steel die on the blade tang of each knife, and this at the appraiser's stores, under the supervision of a customs employee; all this at the importer's expense. I mention this to show that stamping deep with a steel die was the manner in which German and English knives and razors were "usually and ordinarily marked," both as to the name of country of origin, trade-mark, and firm name, and that the department enforced the real intent of the law as covered by section 8 of the tariff law of 1897.

For some time, how long I can not state, but for more than a year past, German knives and razors have been passed through the port of New York with the name of the country of origin "wash stamped" instead of stamped with steel die, and have also been passed with the word "Germany" in "light etching" so shallow as to be easily buffed off. The "wash stamped" name of "Germany" being merely a composition easily wiped off with a cloth moistened with benzine. Even the firm name on front or "mark" side of blade tang is treated in same manner, so that both the name of country of origin and firm name may be easily removed and the knives and razors be then steel-die stamped in this country with a name representing the product to be of American manufacture. The entire proceeding is a deliberate and carefully thought-out scheme for evading the true intent of section 8, and of placing on the American market an inferior grade of German manufacture under the guise of a reputable American product.

Five hundred thousand dollars is a low estimate, in my judgment, of the amount of German "wash-stamped" product imported, and evading the intent of section 8, during the year 1908. It can readily be understood that a continuance of this practice will steadily depreciate and eventually ruin the high standing of reputable American production.

Based on information and belief, I submit the following list of importers in New York City that, in my opinion, have been and still are engaged in the practice above clearly explained:

Adolph Kastor & Bros., 109 Duane street; A. L. Silberstein, 476 Broadway; F. A. Clauberg, 27 Park place; Alex Witte, 91 Warren street; Krusius Brothers, 296 Broadway; Westre Brothers, 148 Chambers street; Max Klass, 298 Broadway; Borgfeldt & Co., Washington square.

Both in Newark, N. J., and in New York City are workrooms to which importers send German knives and razors to have the wash-stamped "Germany" buffed off, and, in some cases, to have the wash-stamped name of German maker or importer buffed off and a name similar to that of some reputable American trade-mark steel stamped in lieu thereof. Bleeker and West Eleventh street, New York City, formerly conducted by J. W. Murray, is one place where this work has been and may now be done; 298 Broadway another.

Several importers of German knives and razors have manufacturing plants in this country or close connection with such plants, and also have close connection with manufacturing plants in Germany. The firm of Adolph Kastor & Bros., with a small factory at Camillus, N. Y., and a brother conducting or interested in a large cutlery plant in Solingen, Germany, may be referred to. Hermann Boker & Co., Duane street, New York City, have a knife factory at Newark, N. J., and are closely connected with a large cutlery manufactory in Germany; but this house, with Wiebush and Hilger, of New York City, jealous of the reputation of the goods they import, would be more likely to commend this "wash-stamp" practice than to engage in it.

Several small manufacturers of American knives and razors seek to make profit at the expense of reputation out of this "wash-stamp" practice, and either import direct or through such houses as F. A. Clauberg, 27 Park place, New York City, and Borgfeldt & Co., Washington square, New York City, or others; and removing at their factories the name of the country of origin from foreign product, offer the same, with their own American name or trade-mark stamped thereon, in common with the product of their American factories.

In my judgment, based on information and belief, the following American manufacturers do this or have recently done it:

Schatt & Morgan, Titusville, Pa., and Gowanda, N. Y.

Tidioute Razor Company, Tidioute, Pa.

Case Brothers, Little Valley, N. Y.

Cattaraugus Cutlery Company, or Champlin & Co., Little Valley, N. Y.

Some manufacturers of table cutlery, shears, and other cutlery run side lines of pocketknives and razors, as the Wiss Company, manufacturers of high-grade shears, Newark, N. J., and A. F. Bannister & Co., Newark, N. J., both of whom are familiar with the "wash-stamp" practice. In fact, it is safe to state that the country of origin, wash stamped, or steel-die stamped, is steadily buffed out, or even ground out, as a matter of course, in the Newark factory of A. F. Bannister & Co.

I have not a dollar of interest in any manufacturing industry; but in my home town of Walden, N. Y., are three manufacturing plants, producing about 50 per cent of the American output of pen and pocket knives. The people of my town depend on this industry, and I am deeply concerned for the welfare of these pocketknife operatives, whose highly skilled trade will be discredited and probably ruined if this nefarious evasion of the true intent of section 8 is permitted to continue. I therefore most earnestly request. as follows:

1. That the attention of the appraiser at every United States port of entry be called to this evasion of section 8, tariff law of 1897, and instructed to refuse entry to all imported articles named in paragraph 153 of said law that do not strictly conform to the true intent of said section 8.

2. That appraisers be instructed to rule that the true intent of section 8, "Usually and ordinarily marked, stamped," etc., means stamped by steel die deep into the blade tang, and refers not only to the stamp of the name of the country of origin, but to the name of individual, firm, or corporation or trademark thereon.

3. If a department ruling in relation to section 8, as affecting all articles named in paragraph 153, has not been issued, that such ruling issue as promptly as practicable.

4. That, if the department can consistently do so, I be given a legal opinion as to the erasing of foreign stamps, the restamping with intention to misrepresent and deceive, all as above referred to, and whether there be any federal statute under which persons can be proceeded against. whether amendment to the interstate-commerce law might be made to cover such cases, or whether action under the common law is the only recourse for the consumer or manufacturer injured by the kind of deception herein complained of.

Through the consideration of the Hon. Sereno E. Payne, chairman. I am permitted to submit all points here mentioned to Mr. Thomas J. Doherty, assistant counsel, United States Treasury Department, assigned to the Committee on Ways and Means, with a view of amending section 8, and protecting, so far as practicable, reputable American makers of pen and pocket knives and razors, and have submitted to Mr. Doherty certain exhibits of "wash-stamped" pocketknives. Such exhibits I can submit to the department, if desired.

Very respectfully,

THOS. W. BRADLEY.

———

HON. THOMAS W. BRADLEY, M. C., RECOMMENDS AN AMENDMENT TO PROVISIONS FOR PENKNIVES AND POCKETKNIVES.

WASHINGTON, D. C., *December 20, 1908.*

Hon. SERENO E. PAYNE,
 Chairman Committee on Ways and Means,
  House of Representatives, Washington, D. C.

DEAR MR. CHAIRMAN: Since the year 1900, or thereabouts, penknives and pocketknives have been imported in assembled but unfinished condition. At first the knives were sent in a rough state, but after the invoice value had become accepted more finish was gradually added to subsequent importations until there remained little finishing to be done outside of buffing, edge setting, cleaning, wrapping, and boxing.

As labor of the character required to complete the finishing of these knives in Solingen is not more than two-fifths the rate of wages paid to finishers in the United States, the chief motive may have been to escape payment of full duties to the United States.

Under this system, importers may offer to deliver certain unfinished "wash-stamped" patterns to American manufacturers at about 40 per cent less than factory cost in the United States; and business has been solicited on this basis by an importer with a view of encouraging the American manufacturer to buff off the "wash-stamped" name of country of origin, etc., and stamping in lieu thereof some American name, market the goods as an American product; thus unfairly depriving American workmen.

My expert acquaintance with cutlery manufacture has led certain American manufacturers of pocketknives and their employees to suggest that I request of your committee an amendment to paragraph 153.

I therefore respectfully submit a proposed amendment:

Provided, That blades, handles, or other parts of either or any of the foregoing articles, imported in any other manner than assembled in finished knives or erasers, shall be subject to no less rate of duty than herein provided for penknives, pocketknives, clasp knives, pruning knives, manicure knives, and erasers valued at more than fifty and not more than one dollar and twenty-five cents per dozen: *And provided further,* That all penknives, or pocketknives, clasp knives, pruning knives, budding knives, and erasers or manicure knives of all kinds, assembled or partly assembled but not completely finished, wrapped and boxed, shall be subject to no less rate of duty than herein provided for penknives, pocketknives, clasp knives, pruning knives, manicure knives, and erasers valued at more than one dollar and twenty-five cents and not exceeding three dollars per dozen.

In line 5, word "fifty," as in present law, is amended to read "twenty-five." No other change in existing law until "and provided further," on line 6, which, continued to the end of line 12, is the amendment and addition proposed.

The word "dozen," end of line 12, to precede the word "razors" in paragraph 153.

Very respectfully,   Thos. W. Bradley,
                                                       Twentieth New York.

———

HON. THOMAS W. BRADLEY, M. C., FILES A LETTER IN BEHALF OF THE PENKNIFE AND POCKETKNIFE WORKINGMEN OF THE UNITED STATES.

Washington, D. C., *January 9, 1909.*

Hon. Sereno E. Payne,
        Chairman Committee on Ways and Means,
            House of Representatives, Washington, D. C.

Dear Mr. Chairman: In relation to paragraph 153, present tariff law, I beg the privilege of filing with the Committee on Ways and Means the following statement in behalf of American workingmen engaged in the manufacture of pen and pocket knives:

Theirs is a skilled handicraft. More than four-fifths of these artisans are native born. The percentage paid to them for labor is an average of at least 80 per centum of the full absolute cost of the finished product.

Pen and pocket knives are usually sold by retail merchant to consumer at fixed prices of $0.10, $0.15, $0.25, $0.35, $0.50, $0.75, $1, $1.25, $1.50, $1.75, $2, $2.50, etc., each, according to pattern, finish, and quality.   As a fair instance of the general average plan of selling, a pattern sold by the manufacturer at $3 per dozen is sold by jobber to retailer at $4 and by retail merchant to consumer at $6 per dozen, or 50 cents each knife.

To reduce present duties down to the ad valorem equivalent of the Wilson bill would be sufficient to affect these fixed selling prices to consumers. It would simply reduce the cost of foreign knives, and this would be met by the home manufacturer reducing labor; a proceeding that would add to the profit of the wholesale and retail merchant at the expense of the workingman.

I can find no demand of moment from the trade for reduction in paragraph 153. The goods sold in the United States were never of better average quality than now, prices to the trade and consumer never averaged lower, and at no time did the consumer get better value for his money.

In the interest of the American producer and consumer, and for revenue to the Government, it does seem wise and fair to let the compound duties remain as now fixed on finished pen and pocket knives.

Respectfully,

THOMAS W. BRADLEY.

ALFRED FIELD & CO., NEW YORK CITY, ADVOCATE LOWER DUTIES ON COMMON GRADES OF CUTLERY.

NEW YORK, *December 23, 1908.*

Hon. SERENO E. PAYNE,
Chairman Committee on Ways and Means.

DEAR SIR: We beg to submit herewith a few salient facts in reference to cutlery, covered by paragraph 153, which we hope may not be amiss in helping your committee arrive at a fair and proper rate of duty on these goods.

We have read the statement submitted to your committee by the American manufacturers of cutlery, covering paragraph 155. They state their total sales for 1906 were $3,000,000. It is our opinion this is a very low estimate, but your committee will see that the foreign value of articles imported under this paragraph in the fiscal year 1907 is only $174,835, or, say, 5¾ per cent of the American product according to their statement, and we may be permitted to call the attention of your committee to the fact that a good part of what is imported are goods that bear a very high reputation for quality, like those made by Joseph Rodgers & Sons, George Wostenholm & Sons, John Wilson, etc., and which goods in the main cost considerably more in Sheffield than similar domestic goods are selling for in this market. The enormous duty levied on such goods place them beyond the reach of ordinary people. The statement recommending that the duty on table knives known as "scale tang" be reduced to 25 per cent ad valorem is very amusing to an insider. We very much doubt if there has been as much as $1,000 worth of these knives all told imported in twenty-five years, and these only on account of very high quality, while it is a fact that such knives are exported, and we ourselves have been exporting them for twenty years.

In the tariff discussion of 1890 there was submitted five patterns of these knives made in America and five corresponding patterns made in Sheffield. One gross of each pattern made in America sold for $47.35, and one gross of each pattern made in Sheffield cost in Sheffield $46.82, and we believe the difference against Sheffield is now much greater.

Importations of pocket cutlery, etc., for the last eight years, under paragraph 153, Dingley tariff.

Year ending June 30—	Quantity.	Foreign cost.	Duty.	Average ad valorem rate.	Percentage of trash knives as to the whole.
		Dollars.	*Dollars.*	*Per cent.*	
1901	10,851,937	741,660	592,702	80	
1902	12,168,548	846,538	678,262	80	
1903	13,759,364	818,319	639,864	78	
1904	13,875,282	896,718	695,147	77½	
1905	13,094,058	835,599	664,348	79½	
1906	11,502,188	838,130	651,306	77¾	
1907	14,808,091	1,007,799	788,386	78¼	
1908	10,802,788	845,553	673,127	80	

Paragraph 153 embraces five classifications. The first two classes are trash knives, costing from 2½ to 4 cents each, foreign cost, the importations of which are as follows:

Year ending June 30—	Quantity.	Foreign cost.	Duty.	Average ad valorem rate.	Percentage of trash knives as to the whole.
		Dollars.	*Dollars.*	*Per cent.*	
1901	7,147,711	220,691	115,726	52	65
1902	8,029,386	256,883	136,954	53	66
1903	9,903,301	261,341	133,046	51	72
1904	9,770,017	293,512	151,506	51½	70½
1905	8,881,515	239,953	129,693	54	67¾
1906	7,669,316	265,340	137,071	51¾	66½
1907	10,148,027	319,185	166,045	52	68½
1908	7,808,425	242,741	131,920	54¼	72

It will be seen that these trash knives that are substantially only fit for toys for children and which do not in any important sense come in competition with domestic manufacture, and which on this account were put at the comparatively low rate of a trifle over 50 per cent ad valorem, embrace about 70 per cent in quantity of all importations.

The balance of importations, or, say, 30 per cent of the quantity imported, is as follows:

Year ending June 30—	Quantity.	Foreign value.	Duty.	Average ad valorem rate.
		Dollars.	*Dollars.*	*Per cent.*
1901	3,704,226	520,969	476,976	91½
1902	4,139,162	589,655	541,308	90½
1903	3,856,063	556,978	506,818	91
1904	4,105,265	603,206	543,641	89½
1905	4,212,543	595,646	534,655	89¾
1906	3,832,872	572,790	514,235	89¾
1907	4,660,064	688,614	622,341	90¼
1908	2,994,363	602,812	541,207	90

The average ad valorem duty on the same being over 90 per cent, and the cost of commissions to foreign buyers and transportation expenses bringing the protection to domestic makers close up to 100 per cent, or double the foreign cost.

In 1882 the American product, according to their own statement, which may be found in 1890 tariff hearings, page 72, was $1,320,000. This was under a tariff of 50 per cent ad valorem. On same page will be found their statement claiming their product for 1887 was only $815,000, which was fairly demonstrated at the time was over $1,000,000 short of the real amount, as the following calculation will show:

American product for 1882, as per their table, page 72, 1890 Hearings		$1,320,000
Imports as per government statistics	$1,238,198	
Add duty, 50 per cent	619,099	
		1,857,297
oTtal for 1882		3,177,297
Add for estimated increase of consumption from 1882 to 1887, inclusive, five years, at 2½ per cent per annum, equals 12½ per cent		397,162
Total for 1887		3,574,459

According to manufacturers' table on page 72, 1890 hearings, 1887 figures out as follows:

Importations	$1,419,861	
Deduct estimated razors which are included in government statistics	250,000	
Leaving value of pocketknives	1,169,861	
Add duty, 50 per cent	584,930	
	1,754,791	
American product for 1887, as per their table on page 72	815,000	
		$2,569,791
Amount unaccounted for by American manufacturers		1,004,668

It is pretty clear that the amount unaccounted for must be added to the amount stated as their product for 1887, making that amount $1,819,668 instead of $815,000, and showing that in 1887 the amount of importations, duty paid, was substantially the same as the American product.

We think it quite fair to estimate the increase of consumption at 2½ per cent per annum. We believe this rate is quite under the real truth. On this basis the consumption for the fiscal year ending June 30, 1908, figures as follows:

Total product, foreign and domestic, for 1887		$3,574,459
Add for estimated increase of consumption from 1887 to 1908, inclusive, 20 years, at 2½ per cent per annum, equals 50 per cent		1,787,229
Total for 1908		5,361,688
Importations for fiscal year 1908	$845,554	
Add duties, about 80 per cent	673,127	
	1,518,681	
Add statement of product of American manufacturers, 1908 hearing	3,000,000	
		4,518,681
Amount unaccounted for		843,007

We think any reliable hardware house dealing largely in cutlery will agree that 2½ per cent per annum for increase of consumption is a very low estimate, but in any case the foreign value of knives that come into any sort of competition with the American product amounts to only $602,812 for the fiscal year 1908, and a good proportion of these do not compete with domestic manufacturers because they are sold on reputation, but such knives being primarily high the cost, on account of superior quality, with 90 per cent duty added and transportation expenses in addition, puts them out of the reach of most people. The cost of the better grades of knives is considerably higher in Sheffield than like patterns are selling for by domestic makers, and it does not seem fair to the consumer to put a duty on such grades as substantially prohibits their importation and prevents people that want them from buying them on account of their enormous cost. To illustrate: We have two knives before us now, large two-blade knives, as used by mechanics and farmers, one made in America and the other in Sheffield. These two knives are exactly the same pattern, size, etc., and a novice would as soon select one as the other. The one made in America sells for $4.78 per dozen, and the one made in Sheffield sells in Sheffield for $5.10 per dozen, and the latter, when the present enormous duties are added, with transportation expenses, costs to lay down in America $9.75 per dozen without any profit added for marketing it.

It is our opinion that a very considerable reduction in duties should be made on the grades used by the masses. In this connection we may be permitted to point out that it is our decided opinion that the system of complex duties on cutlery is very unfortunate from the standpoint of honesty. We made a very earnest protest against this system in 1890, saying the tendency would be to drive honest importers out of the business, and this has substantially been our case. To illustrate: Take the third class, or knives paying 40 per cent ad valorem and 60 cents per dozen, embracing a foreign cost of over 50 cents per dozen and not over $1.25 per dozen. A dishonest importer can purchase a knife at, say, $1.31 and invoice it at $1.25. This knife would cost an honest importer to lay down, duty and expenses paid, $3.18, while invoiced at an equivalent of $1.25 would cost only $2.47, the difference being a large profit, and no expert can measure such a difference. It is our full opinion this scheme has been worked very largely. In such a case, with an ad valorem duty of 100 per cent, the Government could only lose in duty 6 cents per dozen, and an honest competitor not suffer much, but in the present case it is seen the Government loses $62\frac{40}{100}$ cents per dozen and the honest importer is knocked out.

Respectfully submitted.

ALFRED FIELD & Co.,
Agents for Joseph Rogers & Sons (Limited).

J. E. B. STUART, COLLECTOR, NEWPORT NEWS, VA., WRITES RELATIVE TO IMPORTED POCKET CUTLERY.

NEWPORT NEWS, VA., *January 11, 1909.*

Hon. SERENO E. PAYNE, M. C.,
The Burlington, Washington, D. C.

SIR: I understand that your committee is now wrestling with the problem of " reduction of tariff on foreign goods."

I came across a little incident to-day, which I would like to file with you.

I visited a retail hardware store in this city and saw two large, heavy carving knives—one made by the John Russell Cutlery Company, Green River Works, Turners Falls, Mass., and the other by George Wostenholm & Son, Sheffield, England.

The American knife had a plain, natural wood handle, was neither oiled, polished, nor stained in any way, and had common steel or iron rivets through it.

The English knife had a handle polished and stained cherry color and was fastened to the blade with little brass screw rivets. The blades were apparently the same. The handles were very different, the English handle being much the more presentable. The price on the American knife is $1.25 at retail, and the price on the English knife is $1 at retail. There is at least 25 cents difference in the appearance of the two knives, which would make a difference of, say, 50 cents in value to the purchaser.

This would not indicate that the tariff is too high on this particular kind of goods. I could see no difference in the blades, and the hardware dealer claimed that one knife was as good as the other.

Respectfully,

J. E. B. STUART, *Collector.*

RAZORS.

[Paragraph 153.]

REPRESENTATIVES OF AMERICAN MANUFACTURERS ASK AN INCREASE OF DUTIES ON RAZORS AND FILE A SUGGESTED SCHEDULE OF RATES.

WASHINGTON, D. C., *December 3, 1908.*

COMMITTEE ON WAYS AND MEANS,
Washington, D. C.

GENTLEMEN: In asking you to increase the tariff on the schedule covering razors, finished and unfinished, the undersigned committee, representing 80 per cent of the product of the manufacturers of American razors, submit the following facts for your consideration:

The razor industry in the United States is not controlled by any trust or combination. This is an industry that had not assumed any proportions at the time of the passage of the Dingley bill. There being only one factory in the United States at that time, no one appeared before the committee to ask for any protection.

Since the enactment of the Dingley bill, however, an effort has been made to manufacture razors in this country. Within the last eight years nine factories for the manufacture of American razors have been started, but owing to the inadequate protection afforded by the present tariff five of them have been forced out of business, or at least to discontinue the manufacture of razors. There are to-day only five manufacturers of American razors, and the reason that these five are now operating is mainly due to the fact that they manufacture principally patented articles, safety razors and specialties.

During the year ending June 30, 1907, the imports of razors amounted to 255,429 dozens, for which the foreign manufacturers received $533,903.88. The duties paid upon these razors amounted to $296,633.20, making the total amount paid by importers

$830,537.08. The price to jobbers of all American-made razors manufactured during the same period did not exceed $150,000.

During the year ending June 30, 1908, the imports of razors amounted to 218,975 dozens, for which the foreign manufacturers received $463,883.79. The duties paid upon these razors amounted to $263,935.11, making the total amount paid by importers $727,768.90. The price to jobbers of all American-made razors manufactured during the same period did not exceed $140,000.

It will thus be seen that of the total amount consumed less than 20 per cent are of American manufacture.

We are advised that the average proportion of labor to cost of all merchandise imported is about 30 per cent. We know that the proportion of labor to cost of American-made razors is actually over 80 per cent.

We submit below table of operatives' wages in Germany as compared with those in the United States.

| | Weekly wages paid. | |
	Germany.	United States.
Forgers	$4.30 to $7.00	$15 to $21
Dry grinders	4.30 to 5.70	12 to 18
Hardeners and temperers	4.30 to 6.00	15 to 21
Concavers	4.30 to 9.00	16 to 24
Polishers	4.30 to 5.70	12 to 21
Razor-handle makers	4.30 to 5.00	12 to 18
Honers	2.50 to 6.00	9 to 15

The tariff schedule attached which we, as American razor manufacturers, ask to be enacted does not protect us to the extent of the full difference in labor costs. As we understand the Republican platform, the proposed tariff revision is to equalize foreign and domestic labor costs. The tariff which we ask for will not be prohibitive, because (1) it will not fully equalize the difference in labor costs, and (2) because the overhead charges of American manufacturers are larger than of their foreign competitors, owing to difference in methods of manufacture. A large proportion of foreign-made razors are made by the workmen in their homes, thus reducing very largely the overhead charges.

In our opinion, the price to the consumer will not be increased because the price of razors, at retail, of the various kinds of grinds and finishes is pretty firmly fixed. There is, on the other hand, an unusual profit between actual cost to the jobber and consumer, amounting in some cases to over 200 per cent.

It will be noticed that while the large proportion of razors consumed in this country are of the $3 classification, the imports under that classification have been relatively small. The reason is that the duties upon the higher classification have been heretofore and are now being evaded by the importation of the higher grade razors in an unfinished condition, to wit, without handles and not in boxes. The blades otherwise complete are imported in this condition at the low tariff and are fitted with handles and boxes in this country. As a matter of fact, many large importers have so-called "naturalization shops," in which foreign-made blades are fitted with American

handles and packed in American boxes. To illustrate: Under the
present tariff a razor costing complete in Germany over $3 per
dozen (which, if correctly classified, would constitute a large part
of the imports) may, by leaving off handles, cases, and boxes, be
imported under the schedule carrying only $1 per dozen specific duty
and 15 per cent ad valorem, whereas it should carry a duty of next
schedule higher, or $1.75 per dozen and 20 per cent ad valorem.

We would call the committee's special attention to the last item
in our proposed schedule, which we hope may not be overlooked,
inasmuch as it will to a large extent eliminate the evasions of the
present tariff, above noted.

Owing to the high standard that has always been maintained by
American manufacturers of razors, the few distributed have made
such a favorable impression on the consumer that he has demanded
them of his dealer and the dealer has been supplying them only under
pressure, from the fact that he could not realize as large a profit as
on German and other imported goods. The importer, in order to
meet this demand, has been stamping the blades on the right side of
tang with American firm name and address, and on opposite side of
tang, etching in a very light manner the word "Germany," which
can be removed at a slight expense by means of acid or a buff wheel.
This work is usually done by the importer, or if the mark is left on
the tang it is very inconspicuous and the razor to all intents and purposes passes as American-made goods.

We therefore request that this imposition on the purchasing public
be eliminated by proper legislation, either in connection with the proposed tariff bill or otherwise. We suggest that the name of the country of origin be required to be plainly stamped into the steel on the
tang of the razor between the handle and blade, and that in case the
name of any person, firm, or corporation appears upon the razor,
the name of the country of origin be plainly stamped into the steel
directly underneath said name.

H. L. HENRY,
(For Geneva Cutlery Co.)
C. W. SILCOX,
(For Robeson Cutlery Co.)
TINT CHAMPLIN,
(For Geo. W. Kern Razor Co.)
Committee.

SUGGESTED SCHEDULE.

On all razors finished or unfinished costing under $1 a dozen, 15
cents per dozen specific and 50 per cent ad valorem.

On all razors costing $1 a dozen and less than $2 per dozen, $1.25
per dozen specific and 50 per cent ad valorem.

On all razors costing $2 per dozen and less than $3, $2 per dozen
specific and 50 per cent ad valorem.

On all razors costing $3 per dozen or more, $2.25 per dozen specific
and 50 per cent ad valorem.

On all finished or unfinished parts of razors, such as blades, handles,
etc., $1.50 per dozen pieces and 50 per cent ad valorem.

STATEMENT OF HON. EDWARD B. VREELAND, A REPRESENTA-
TIVE IN CONGRESS FROM THE STATE OF NEW YORK, RELATIVE
TO THE DUTY ON RAZORS.

FRIDAY, *November 27, 1908.*

Mr. VREELAND. Mr. Chairman and gentlemen, I appear in behalf
of a small industry which hardly at present exists in this country.

Mr. UNDERWOOD. What industry is that?

Mr. VREELAND. I represent Mr. George W. Korn, a manufacturer
of razors living in New York State, in my district.

Mr. GRIGGS. Pardon me for one question right there. Is he making
any money?

Mr. VREELAND. He is not making any money at the present time.

Mr. GRIGGS. Yes.

Mr. VREELAND. He never has made any money since he has been in
the business. That, perhaps, is one of the reasons why he asked me
to appear before this committee.

Mr. GRIGGS. How long has he been in the business?

Mr. VREELAND. Eight years.

Mr. GRIGGS. And he has not made any money?

Mr. VREELAND. Not so far. He has plenty of experience which he
hopes to turn into money in the future.

I want to say that Mr. Korn is ill, and has been for a considerable
time, and is not able to be here. So far as I could, not being technically familiar with the business, I have obtained the facts relating to
it, which I will endeavor to present to the committee, and will furnish later any details as to the technical points that the committee
might want to bring out in a brief.

I assume, Mr. Chairman, that it is the purpose of this committee
in revising the tariff not only to provide adequate protection, but to
maintain the existence of industries which we now have, and if there
is opportunity it will put on duties sufficient to create new industries
in this country as the tin-plate industry was created by the last tariff.
I want to say that in this country when the Dingley bill was adopted
there was practically no manufacturing of razors in this country.
There was only one man trying to make razors. He was making a
specialty and selling it not generally on the market. So no one appeared before the committee asking for protective duties or furnishing information upon which proper schedules could be made up.
Therefore, this is really creating an industry, the industry of making
razors, which I suppose would employ something like 1,000 or 1,200
skilled workmen if they had the right to fill the American market.
Under the existing tariff 10 factories in this country, many of which
made cutlery, have endeavored to make razors. Five of them have
made a failure of it, and discontinued entirely. There are only at
present two firms making razors exclusively in the United States.
One is the factory which I represent, and the other is located in
Geneva, N. Y.

Mr. GRIGGS. Does the Geneva factory make a safety razor?

Mr. VREELAND. I am not referring to specialties; I am speaking of
the old-fashioned Brownsville razor. [Laughter.]

Mr. COCKRAN. Brownsville?

Mr. VREELAND. Mr. Chairman, of the two factories that have been
endeavoring to make razors under the existing tariff, one of them has
been in existence for eight years, the one in my district with which

I am familiar. The other one has been running, I do not know just how many years, but at least equally as long, and I want to say that neither of them has ever paid a dividend, and that both of them are only able to keep running by the manufacture of specialties in their line of business. I know that this factory which I represent manufactures a safety razor which the gentleman from Georgia spoke of. If it was not for the manufacture of that, they would be unable to keep open at all.

Last year the total amount of value, in dollars, of razors made in the United States was very close to $176,000. The value of imported razors was $830,566. That is, we are importing now more than five times the amount in value of razors which we produce in this country. Two hundred and fifty-five thousand dozen were imported from abroad during the past year. Therefore I say that I am asking the committee to put on a tariff duty which will in effect create a new industry which will give employment to a large number of men, and which I do not think will increase the price to the consumer—I mean the actual consumer, the man who buys the razor for his own use.

Mr. GRIGGS. Is there no duty at the present time?

Mr. VREELAND. There is a duty.

Mr. GRIGGS. What is it?

Mr. VREELAND. The average, as shown by importations for the last year, was something over 50 per cent.

Mr. GRIGGS. Fifty per cent?

Mr. VREELAND. Fifty per cent; yes, sir; and if I had time to go into it in detail, which I have not, I think it could be easily shown, as it has been in some other industries that have been represented here, that owing to the method of fixing values, undervaluation, and to the methods of evading the law which prevail—for instance, separating the parts and putting them together after bringing them into this country—while the duty looks large upon the face of it, as a matter of fact it would amount to a very much less sum.

Mr. Chairman and gentlemen, we are willing to stand entirely upon the plank of the Republican platform, which was adopted by the American people in the recent election, as to the method of making the duties upon this article; that is, we are entirely willing to stand upon the amount of labor cost above that in Germany where the most of these razors come from. I might say that almost all of the razors imported come from Germany.

Mr. GRIGGS. Some come from Belgium, do they not?

Mr. VREELAND. Some come from England.

Mr. COCKRAN. From Sheffield?

Mr. VREELAND. From Sheffield; I think very few come from Belgium. The cheaper class of razors all come, I think, from Germany, and some of the higher class of razors come from England. The difference in wages in Germany and the United States perhaps I ought to read for the purpose of having it in the record. These figures I am sure are entirely accurate; they are accurate as to the wages paid in the factories in this country, and I think they are accurate as to the wages obtaining in Germany.

Hence it will appear from these figures that the price paid to the skilled laborer who makes this class of goods in the United States will run fully three times as much as is paid abroad. I will not take the time of the committee in going into some facts about making razors in Germany, except to mention that to quite a large extent they are not made in factories and built up as we have them in this country, but they are made at the homes, made where not only the men of the family, but the women, girls, and boys of the family have little lathes and hand power and finish off these razors and do the work upon them, and take them in, doing it at a price, of course, which is very much below anything we can compete with in this country. I will read the table of duties which we would ask for upon razors:

Less than $1, 15 cents specific, and upon all these 50 per cent ad valorem; from $1 to $2, $1.25 a dozen and 50 per cent ad valorem; from $2 to $3, $2 specific and the same ad valorem. Also, we ask that upon all parts of razors, finished or unfinished, $1.50 per dozen pieces and 50 per cent ad valorem shall be added. The material that goes into a razor does not make a large part of its cost. The lower-priced German razors that come in, razors that are sold in this country at $1.50 a dozen to jobbers, are largely made of Bessemer steel. They will not shave, but they look good and help to fill the market. Invariably in the United States crucible steel, costing from $350 to $400 per ton, is used in the manufacture of these razors. They do not use anything else; and yet that in itself is not a very great item, because a ton of steel makes something over a thousand dozen of five-sixteenths razors, which is the standard razor.

I will file with the committee the details of the labor cost in making up these razors. This shows the razor from the square piece of crucible steel, which is the raw material of the razor maker, which comes to him in long rods of the proper size, so that all he does is to cut it the proper length. This shows the different lines of work which are done upon it before it reaches completion, as well as the work upon the handle. [Exhibiting samples to the committee.]

Mr. GRIGGS. Do you not really think a razor is a luxury? [Laughter.]

Mr. VREELAND. A luxury?

Mr. GRIGGS. Yes.

Mr. VREELAND. Yes; I think a razor is a luxury; and you will notice in the line of duties I have proposed it is treated as a luxury.

Mr. COCKRAN. There is nothing about this committee to suggest it is a luxury, I hope.

Mr. GRIGGS. I hope not. I would not have said it if I thought so.

Mr. CLARK. What is the reason they did not try to manufacture razors in this country a hundred years ago and have not done it since?

Mr. VREELAND. I want to tell the gentleman from Missouri that I am not in the trade and my recollection does not run back a great ways, and I am not familiar with the history of it.

Mr. CLARK. The reason I asked that question is it is rather an astonishing fact that we have not gone into it.

Mr. VREELAND. It is evident that at the present time we could not go into it on account of the difference in the expense of producing them here and in the old country. In the earlier days we did little manufacturing. I will not take the time to read the items making up the cost, following the razor through among the different workmen, but I will file that with the committee. This cost is based upon the razor, a German razor, that pays a duty of $3.

Mr. RANDELL. Three dollars a dozen?

Mr. VREELAND. Three dollars a dozen.

Mr. COCKRAN. You speak of the difference in the rates of wages paid to labor in Germany and in this country. Have you any figures showing the relative productivity of an American and a foreign producer?

Mr. VREELAND. I have no detailed figures on this particular line, but in the two factories that now exist their workmen are made up, quite a percentage of them, of German workmen who came from German factories, and presumably the difference in the amount of work they did before they came over and have done since they arrived here is not very large, although I think that it would be true if we go into the making of razors, as it has been true in all other lines of American manufacture, that the American manufacturer will be able by better organization, or by means of better wages, or through all of those causes, to obtain a greater output.

Mr. COCKRAN. Exactly so. You state here, if I understand you correctly—I understood you to say—that those razors brought in here from Germany are largely made by boys and men in their own homes, without the advantage of effective organization and machinery?

Mr. VREELAND. Yes.

Mr. COCKRAN. And with an organization such as would inevitably arise in this country, the productive power of such workmen would be greatly increased by working in a factory?

Mr. VREELAND. I think it would.

Mr. COCKRAN. Under normal conditions?

Mr. VREELAND. Yes.

Mr. COCKRAN. So that your table of wages, not taking into account these different factors, would hardly be reliable?

Mr. VREELAND. If the gentleman from New York will look at the rates of wages, he will see, for instance, that the grinding and the honing of them, and the different operations on the razors, do not require a factory and do not require much power, and can be done even by hand power at the homes, and it is so done largely in those countries, and we have no means of making them in that cheap method in this country.

Mr. COCKRAN. I suggest that that is the most expensive method of production. If I might express an opinion on it, not knowing any more about it than you, I would say that those articles we see there are articles that essentially have to be polished by machinery.

Mr. VREELAND. They have to be polished by machinery.

Mr. COCKRAN. Yes.

Mr. VREELAND. But what I mean to say is that it does not need a factory to do any one of the pieces of work that are done.

Mr. COCKRAN. Those things could be more effectively done in a factory, I should think.

Mr. VREELAND. I agree with you entirely. The history of all industries demonstrates that if they are once firmly established in this country, American ingenuity and power of organization and the better work that they get by reason of better wages invariably make a larger production per unit than they make abroad. That has been my observation.

Mr. COCKRAN. You represent this gentleman. The object of these increases is not so much to improve his production as it is to levy something on the community, is it not?

Mr. VREELAND. My theory is that if we can make the razors for the American market, employing, say, a thousand skilled men in doing so, it will be in accordance with the trend of protection which at present prevails in this country, and that at least in the end will not result in increasing the price to the last consumer.

Mr. COCKRAN. Surely you do not mean to say that such a very radical increase as you suggest here—for instance, on razors, or some of them, from $1.75 to $3 a dozen, and from 20 per cent ad valorem to 50 per cent—would not have some very serious effect on the price?

Mr. VREELAND. There are two or three razors there, one of which pays a duty of $3, and one of those is made in this country. The gentleman can not tell from the looks of them which is made in this country, because I notice that the requirement of the law which would indicate where it is made is not complied with. That is not indicated on the razor. That brings me to another point, and that is that these razors are marked with very light etching in Germany, and after passing the custom-house that is removed, as it has been doubtless in the case of that one which I exhibited.

Mr. HILL. In giving your wage figures, have you given them by the day or by the unit cost of transferring from one condition to the other?

Mr. VREELAND. We have given the unit cost of a dozen razors.

Mr. HILL. So that the question of day wages does not enter into this exhibit?

Mr. VREELAND. No; it is the unit cost of making a dozen razors from the initial step.

Mr. UNDERWOOD. How many are employed in this industry?

Mr. VREELAND. About 200.

Mr. GRIGGS. That is, in the razor part of it?

Mr. VREELAND. In the one with which I am familiar.

Mr. GRIGGS. They are employed strictly in making razors?

Mr. VREELAND. Yes.

Mr. GRIGGS. You can have them employed in those two factories making other things?

Mr. VREELAND. That includes all that they turn out in the factory.

Mr. GRIGGS. You say they make other specialties? I see on here "The Geneva Cutlery Company."

Mr. VREELAND. Yes; I mean by specialties such things as, for instance, an antirust razor. They turn out an antirust razor which they claim does not rust. I do not know whether it does or not. At least it does not by the time it gets to the retailer. That gives them something on which they can avoid the competition with the German manufacturers, and that gives them something by which they can keep running, where otherwise they could not afford to.

Mr. GRIGGS. You do not catch my point. Does the Geneva Cutlery Company make other cutlery besides razors?

Mr. VREELAND. No; this company makes exclusively razors and razor specialties. That is all that they make. I have stated that, in my opinion—which is not very valuable, because I am not an expert in the business—the man who ultimately buys a razor will not pay any more for it under the schedule which is proposed here than he does now. Take the retail price of razors to-day. There are a lot of German razors running in price—that is, the price upon which they pay a duty—from $1.50 up to $2, which, I think, is the highest.

Mr. Griggs. Is that the Torrey razor which they make?

Mr. Vreeland. Yes.

Mr. Griggs. We do not need any duty to compete on that.

Mr. Vreeland. No.

Mr. Griggs. Anybody will pay anything you want for that razor to get it.

Mr. Vreeland. That, unfortunately, is not true in western New York.

Mr. Cockran. Does Torrey sell his razor in western New York?

Mr. Griggs. I do not know whether he does or not.

Mr. Vreeland. No; they use Korn razors in western New York. I say that this razor would not be any higher to the ultimate consumer than it is now. I state that because, although we are using imported razors, presumably cheaper—they ought to be cheaper—yet the ultimate consumer to-day is paying all that he can afford to pay or all that he could pay for razors. Take a razor that is sold—valued—at $2; that is, that is what they pay a duty on. That sells at present in the retail stores of the country at a dollar. Occasionally they will have a bargain day and they will sell them at 98 cents. The two razors I have exhibited there, one made here and one in Germany, sell at $2, and on those razors a duty of $2 a dozen is paid. Now, mind you, in our opinion the basis of the duty is too low. They undoubtedly are worth more than that, but they are imported on the basis of being worth $2, and the duty is paid upon that. That razor generally sells in the retail stores of this country at $2.

The Chairman. Twenty-four dollars a dozen, $2 apiece?

Mr. Vreeland. We are selling them now by the piece to the man who buys the razor outside of the counter. The jobber probably pays from $4 to $6, and he would sell to the retailer at $7.50 to $9, and the retailer would sell that razor at a dollar [exhibiting razor].

Mr. Griggs. Can you tell us what it costs to make one of these razors?

Mr. Vreeland. Yes, sir; I will file the labor cost and the details of the cost of making that razor with the committee.

Mr. Griggs. Give the entire cost, will you not?

Mr. Vreeland. Yes.

Mr. Griggs. The labor cost and all?

Mr. Vreeland. The labor cost and the cost of material.

Mr. Griggs. What it costs f. o. b. the factory?

Mr. Vreeland. Yes; razors that have fancy handles, and so forth, sell almost invariably for $2.50. Occasionally some man sells them at $2.75. So a three dollar a dozen razor when it gets to the consumer at present is being sold for all that that consumer would pay under this schedule which is here suggested.

Mr. Griggs. Where does all that profit go to?

Mr. Vreeland. It goes to the people who handle the razors.

Mr. Griggs. You mean the wholesaler and the retailer?

Mr. Vreeland. The wholesaler and the retailer.

Mr. Griggs. They, together, get as much profit out of one razor as a dozen razors cost?

Mr. Vreeland. Of course that is not all profit. You take the jobber, and he will sell a dozen razors to a man, and perhaps he will give him a little show case to put in his window, and the expenses are large in all these matters, and we can not assume that that is all profit.

Mr. GRIGGS. That is something put onto the original cost?

Mr. VREELAND. Yes. What I say is that so far as the ultimate consumer is concerned, he is paying to-day for those razors, presumably cheaper, that come in from Germany all that the market will stand for razors. If we commence making these razors in our own factories, it means not an increase to the last man that buys the razor, but it means a smaller price to the middlemen that are handling the razors.

The CHAIRMAN. Could not an ordinary man go to a manufacturer and buy a dozen of these razors and pay for them and keep a couple himself and give the other ten to his friends and make money by the operation, rather than to buy at retail?

Mr. VREELAND. If he could buy them in that way, I should think it would save a good deal of money. He could give the rest away at Christmas and make a very good transaction of it.

I think, gentlemen, that is all the time I desire to take, unless there is some question to be asked with relation to this matter on some point that I have not covered.

Mr. RANDELL. Is not the middleman unnecessarily costly to the public? Can you devise any way that would meet that situation?

Mr. VREELAND. Well, I think as a result of establishing factories in this country that usually one middleman will be done away with; that is, that they will sell directly to the retailers, the storekeepers, through their agents, instead of selling through the jobbers and importers.

Mr. POU. Do you not think that if the increase was made that you suggest here it would be practically prohibitory? Would it not shut out foreign razors almost entirely?

Mr. VREELAND. No; I think they can easily compete. I think that upon this schedule that I have proposed, the figures I give showing the detailed cost of making the $3 razor, will show that the American manufacturer must have good organization in his factory and a large output in order to compete with the Germans at the present prices.

Mr. HILL. This is not the only industry, you know, where the cost of production and distribution is high.

Mr. VREELAND. Yes.

Mr. HILL. That is true of the oil business and of the sewing-machine business in the cost of distribution. It is not all profit to the middleman and the retailer by any manner of means.

Mr. VREELAND. No; it is expensive. There are a great many items to be covered.

Mr. GRIGGS. You never knew 1 gallon of oil to reach the cost of a barrel, did you?

Mr. VREELAND. I do not know that I have.

Mr. HILL. I think it has been true, in the history of the United States, that a barrel of crude oil has been sold for the price at which a single gallon has been distributed to the final consumer.

Mr. GRIGGS. That is crude oil.

Mr. POU. If these men get this profit, I would like to know what Gillette makes at $5 apiece.

Mr. HILL. Well, the business is an open one. It is open for anybody to go into that chooses.

Lightning Source UK Ltd.
Milton Keynes UK
UKHW031824280119
336340UK00011B/1040/P